Production and Operations Management

Strategies and Tactics

Jay Heizer

Jesse H. Jones Professor of Business Administration
Texas Lutheran College

Barry Render

Charles Harwood Professor of Operations Management
Roy E. Crummer Graduate School of Business, Rollins College

Allyn and Bacon

BOSTON   LONDON   TORONTO   SYDNEY   TOKYO   SINGAPORE

Editor-in-Chief, Business and Economics: Rich Wohl
Series Editorial Assistant: Dominique Vachon
Production Administrator: Marjorie Payne
Editorial-Production Service: The Wheetley Co., Inc.
Text Designer: Deborah Schneck
Cover Administrator: Linda Dickinson
Cover Designer: Design Ad Cetera
Composition Buyer: Linda Cox
Manufacturing Buyer: Megan Cochran
Photo Researcher: Photosynthesis/Sarah Evertson

Copyright © 1993, 1991, 1988 by Allyn and Bacon
A Division of Simon & Schuster, Inc.
160 Gould Street
Needham Heights, MA 02194
All rights reserved. No part of the material protected by this copyright
notice may be reproduced or utilized in any form or by any means,
electronic or mechanical, including photocopying, recording, or by any
information storage and retrieval system, without written permission
of the copyright owner.

Many of the designations used by manufacturers and sellers to distinguish
their products are claimed as trademarks. Where those designations appear
in this book, and Allyn and Bacon was aware of a trademark claim, the
designations have been printed in caps or initial caps.

Library of Congress Cataloging-in-Publication Data
Heizer, Jay H.
    Production and operations management: : strategies and tactics/
Jay Heizer, Barry Render. —3rd ed.
        p. cm.
    Includes biographical references and index.
    1. Production management. I. Render, Barry. II. Title.
TS155.H373   1993
658.5—dc20   92-26429
                                                      CIP

ISBN: 0-205-14048-3

Printed in the United States of America

10 9 8 7 6 5 4 3 2   98 97 96 95 94 93

*Photo credits are found on page 871, which should be
considered an extension of the copyright page.*

To Kay Heizer and Reva Shader

About the Authors

Jay Heizer holds the Jesse H. Jones Chair of Business Administration at Texas Lutheran College in Seguin, Texas. He received his B.B.A. and M.B.A. from the University of North Texas and his Ph.D. in Management and Statistics from Arizona State University (1969). He was previously a member of the faculty at Memphis State University, the University of Oklahoma, Virginia Commonwealth University, and the University of Richmond. He has also held visiting positions at Boston University and George Mason University.

Dr. Heizer's industrial experience is extensive. He learned the practical side of Production/Operations Management as a machinist apprentice, production planner for Westinghouse Airbrake, and at General Dynamics, where he worked in engineering administration. Additionally, he has been actively involved in consulting in the P/OM and MIS areas for a variety of organizations including Philip Morris, Firestone, Dixie Container Corporation, Columbia Industries, and Tenneco. He holds the CPIM certification from the American Production and Inventory Control Society.

Professor Heizer has co-authored three books and has published two dozen articles on a variety of management topics. His papers have appeared in the *Acad-*

emy of Management Journal, Journal of Purchasing, Personnel Psychology, and *Engineering Management,* among others. He has taught Production/Operations Management courses in undergraduate, graduate, and executive programs.

Barry Render is the Charles Harwood Distinguished Professor of Operations Management at the Crummer Graduate School of Business at Rollins College, in Winter Park, Florida. He received his M.S. in Operations Research and Ph.D. in Quantitative Analysis at the University of Cincinnati (1975). He previously taught at George Washington University, University of New Orleans, Boston University, and George Mason University, where he held the GM Foundation Professorship in Decision Sciences. Dr. Render has also worked in the aerospace industry for General Electric, McDonnell Douglas, and NASA.

Professor Render has co-authored eight textbooks with Allyn and Bacon, including *Quantitative Analysis for Management, Service Operations Management, Introduction to Management Science,* and *Cases and Readings in Management Science.* His more than one hundred articles on a variety of management topics have appeared in *Decision Sciences, Interfaces, Information and Management, Journal of Management Information Systems, Socio-Economic Planning Sciences,* and *Operations Management Review,* among others.

Dr. Render has also been honored as an AACSB Fellow and named as a Fulbright Scholar. He was twice vice president of the Decision Science Institute Southeast Region and has been Software Review Editor for *Decision Line* since 1989. He is Allyn and Bacon's Series Editor for all Quantitative Methods and Applied Statistics textbooks. Finally, Professor Render has been actively involved in consulting for government agencies and many corporations, including NASA, FBI, U.S. Navy, Fairfax County, Virginia, and C&P Telephone. He teaches Production and Operations Management courses in Rollins College's MBA and Executive MBA programs.

Brief Contents

Contents

Preface

Production and operations management (P/OM) can be one of the most exciting and challenging topics in the business curriculum. This third edition of *Production and Operations Management: Strategies and Tactics* is intended to provide you with a current, complete, and practical introduction to the field. The text is designed for introductory classes at either the undergraduate or MBA level.

We stress the decisions that managers make and the manager's role in increasing productivity in a world economy. We hope that students, after completing the course, will appreciate the role of operations managers in enriching the lives of everyone. The authors are aware that the majority of our readers are not P/OM majors. However, we think that management, marketing, finance, economics, accounting, quantitative methods, and information systems students will find the material both interesting and useful. Adopters of the first two editions seem to have endorsed this premise.

FOCUS OF THE THIRD EDITION

CONTENTS

Strategies and Tactics. As in the previous editions, we balance the coverage of managerial and strategic issues with the tactical perspective found in using specific decision science tools. To provide maximum flexibility, we have a separate part on decision-making techniques as well as chapter supplements located throughout the text. This allows instructors to spend as much or as little time as needed on each component of the course.

International Examples. As productivity and the world economy are so closely linked with our own, we have made a special effort to include international illustrations in our narrative, problems, cases, and *POM in Action* boxes. This emphasis is also tied to our focus on world-class manufacturing, which includes a special table in Chapter 2 that identifies the characteristics of world-class manufacturing. Volvo, British Airways, Nissan, Toyota, and Siemens are just some of the international examples discussed.

State-of-Art Developments. In order to keep up to date, we have added to or expanded our coverage of international quality standards, benchmarking, lean manufacturing, time-based competition, TQM, work cells, animated simulation, and Japanese layout.

Quality Assurance. Due to its increasingly important role throughout the operations process, we have significantly revised and expanded our chapter called Total Quality Management (Chapter 17). We also include a supplement on statistical quality control techniques. With new coverage of European (ISO 9000) and Japanese quality standards, the Baldrige Awards, benchmarking, poka-yoke, and Kaizen, we introduce the latest concepts in the quality discipline.

A Balance of Service and Manufacturing Applications. P/OM has a service as well as a traditional manufacturing aspect. This third edition takes particular note of services. Many chapters include service aspects of operations, while others have special sections that note the distinction between service and manufacturing in P/OM. For instance, in the work measurement sections, we have used service jobs as examples. Similarly, office layouts receive added emphasis, as do service location issues, quality management, and project management applied to services.

PEDAGOGY

Solved Problems. Once again, solved problems are included in this edition. They are provided as models for students as they work unsolved problems on their own.

Data Base Applications. A new feature, "Data Base Applications," has been added to the chapters on linear programming, forecasting, location strategy, layout, aggregate planning, MRP, short-term scheduling, project management, and quality control techniques. These very large problems are intended for analysis by computer. They permit students to spend more time interpreting outputs of realistic problems to supplement problem-solving skills developed with the regular programs.

Three Levels of Problems. The number of end-of-chapter problems has been increased by 20%, and each is identified as one of three levels: introductory (one dot), moderate (two dots), and challenging (three dots). In addition, these problems focus on problem formulation and interpretation as well as calculation. Six new cases have been added to the text as well.

***POM in Action* Boxes.** Articles from a variety of sources such as the *Wall Street Journal, Fortune, Harvard Business Review,* and *Interfaces* are included in chapters and supplements. These boxes bring P/OM to life and help drive home the points made in the chapters. These real P/OM issues can spark the students' interest and enliven class discussion. Eighteen new *POM in Action* boxes appear in this third edition. All boxes retained from the second edition have been rewritten in crisper and shorter versions.

World-Class Profiles. In this edition we have added an exciting new feature as an introduction to the thirteen chapters that deal with strategic and tactical decisions (Chapters 6–18). Full-color tours highlight specific P/OM concepts in 13 world-class firms. All firms were chosen for their leadership in the strategic and tactical decisions of P/OM.

Margin Photos. In addition to the world-class tours, over 50 full-color photos appear for the first time in this edition, along with detailed captions tying them to the contents of their chapters. These photos increase student interest level and add a depth not found in other textbooks.

AB:POM Software. A microcomputer software package, AB:POM (developed by Howard Weiss, Temple University), is again available with the text. This package continues to improve both breadth of functions and user friendliness. The software includes more than a dozen P/OM application programs that range from forecasting to queuing to line balancing to project scheduling to MRP. We think most students appreciate the experience of using a computer to solve problems. However, professors and instructors can structure the course with or without the use of the software. At the end of each problem-oriented chapter, the student will also find an optional explanation of how to use the software for that particular application. In addition, detailed instructions for using the software are located in Appendix F. For most effective learning, the software has been structured to closely match the approach, notation, and terms found in this text.

Other Supplements. Also available with the text are a variety of other supplements. These include: (1) a student *Study Guide* complete with alternate narrative, solved problems, and answered review questions on a chapter-by-chapter basis; (2) *Profiles in Quality,* which contains fifty reviews of how organizations enhance the quality of their products and services; (3) *Profiles of Malcolm Baldrige Award Winners,* which reviews the outstanding performance of companies that have received this award.

Also Available to Instructors. A comprehensive *Annotated Instructor's Edition,* as well as a *Test Bank* and *Instructor's Manual, Transparency Masters,* a *DataDisk* that contains problem data, a complete *Solutions Manual,* and a variety of videos.

Production and Operations Management: Strategies and Tactics, Third Edition, can be ordered for students in one of three ways:

- Text only (without any software)
- With AB:POM (5 1/4″ disks)
- With AB:POM (3 1/2″ disks)

In addition to these features, the text continues to include an updated set of chapter outlines, examples, summaries, key terms, discussion questions, cases, and glossary.

ORGANIZATION OF THE BOOK

We have identified ten decisions that are critical to effective production/operations management. These ten decisions are divided into strategic and tactical decisions, and are presented in a realistic, global, and dynamic environment. We hope this approach presents P/OM decisions in a way that will assist current and future managers in understanding how to manage operations effectively.

Part One is an introduction to P/OM, productivity, and strategy. A brief historical perspective of P/OM is also included.

Part Two introduces some of the quantitative techniques that are often helpful in P/OM. These techniques include decision trees and tables, linear programming, forecasting, queuing, and simulation. Also included as a supplement to Chapter 4 is a brief review of statistics.

Part Three focuses on six strategic management decisions of P/OM. These are product design, process selection, facility location, facility layout, human resources, and procurement/JIT.

Part Four introduces tactical decisions of operations management. These are scheduling, inventory control, total quality management, and maintenance.

We have, for the sake of completeness, included a great deal of material in this text. However, to cover all of the topics in a one-semester course would be unusual. Consequently, we developed the above organization that allows substantial flexibility for the instructor. Instructors may skip over many of the technical chapter supplements (such as linear programming, learning curves, work measurement, statistical quality control). On the other hand, those instructors preferring a quantitative treatment will especially appreciate Part Two, many of the supplements, and the numerous quantitative examples, solved problems, and the software package, AB:POM. We think the result is a text that allows instructors to teach the course in their own way and at their own pace.

ACKNOWLEDGMENTS

We thank the many individuals who were kind enough to assist us in this endeavor. These include the many reviewers who waded through difficult manuscripts and provided us with both help and encouragement. Without the help of these fellow professors, we would never have received the feedback needed to put together a teachable text. The reviewers include Sema Alptekin, University of Missouri-Rolla; Moshen Attaran, Cal State-Bakersfield; John H. Blackstone, University of Georgia; Theodore Boreki, Hofstra University; Jim Goodwin, University of Richmond; James S. Hawkes, University of Charleston; Larry LaForge, Clemson University; Mike Maggard, Northeastern University; Laurie E. MacDonald, Bryant College; David W. Pentico, Duquesne University; Leonard Presby, William Patterson State College of New Jersey; Robert J. Schlesinger, San Diego State University; Vicki L. Smith-Daniels, University of Minnesota-Twin Cities; Stan Stockton, Indiana University; John Swearingen, Bryant College; Bruce M. Woodworth, University of Texas-El Paso; Kambiz Tabibzadeh, Eastern Kentucky University; Damodar Golhar, Western Michigan University; Henry Crouch, Pittsburgh State University; Barbara Flynn, Iowa State University; Joao Neves, Trenton State College; Hugh Leach, Washburn University; M. J. Riley, Kansas State University; Paul Jordan, University of Alaska;

Susan Sherer, Lehigh University; and Marilyn K. Hart, University of Wisconsin-Oshkosh.

In addition, we appreciate the fine people at Allyn and Bacon who provided both help and encouragement during multiyear revision: Rich Wohl, our editor, and Marjorie Payne, who kept the production process moving. The Wheetley Company ushered the manuscript through the day-to-day production tasks. Reva Shader developed a superb index for the text.

We also appreciate the efforts of colleagues who have helped to shape the entire learning package that accompanies this text: Professor Howard Weiss (Temple University) developed AB:POM microcomputer software; John Swearingen and John Harpell (West Virginia University) co-authored the student study guide. Jerry Kinard (Francis Marion College) provided numerous case studies. We have been fortunate to have been able to work with all of these people.

We wish you a pleasant and productive introduction to Production/Operations Management.

J.H.
B.R.

Production and Operations Management

PART ONE

Introduction

Production, production/operations management, and contributors to the discipline are discussed in Chapter 1. The major role of production/operations management in organizations is also discussed, as are career opportunities. Finally, we introduce productivity, its variables, and the production manager's role in enhancing productivity.

Chapter 2 introduces organizational missions and strategies. The major role that P/OM can play in a successful strategy that yields a competitive advantage is discussed. The implementation and dynamics of a P/OM strategy are also presented.

CHAPTER 1

Production/ Operations Management

WHAT IS PRODUCTION/OPERATIONS MANAGEMENT?

Production

Production management and operations management (P/OM)

Production is the creation of goods and services. **Production management and operations management (P/OM)** are activities that relate to the creation of goods and services through the transformation of inputs into outputs. Activities creating goods and services take place in all organizations. In manufacturing firms, the production activities that create goods are usually quite obvious. In them, we can see the creation of a tangible product such as a television set or a Chevy truck. When referring to such activity we tend to use the name *production management*.

In other organizations that do not create physical products, the production function may be less obvious. It may be "hidden" from the public and even from the customer. An example is the transformation that takes place at a bank, airline office, or college. The product that is produced may take some unusual forms such as machine-readable marks on paper, filling an empty seat on an airplane, or education. We call these kinds of companies *service organizations*. The production activity that goes on in these organizations is usually referred to as *operations* or *operations management*. The *POM in Action* box, "Moving Money at 111 Wall Street," provides a brief glimpse of the role of an operations manager at First National City Bank, a large, worldwide bank.

As we progress through the text, we will look at an exciting array of production and operations functions, with examples ranging from General Motors to IBM to McDonald's. We will see how production managers in these firms create the goods and services that enrich our lives. Production/operations managers make the decisions that are necessary to transform resources into goods and services. In this text we will be using the words *production* and *operations,* as well as the combination *production/operations management* (or P/OM), when we discuss this transformation process.

HERITAGE OF OPERATIONS MANAGEMENT

Many of the innovations in operations management were developed by individuals and organizations that appear in Figure 1.1. In the following discussion we note several of these contributions because they provided a foundation that has made other advances possible.

Eli Whitney (1800) is credited for the early popularization of interchangeable parts, which was achieved through standardization and quality control in manufacturing. Through a contract he signed with the U.S. government for 10,000 muskets, he was able to command a premium price because of their interchangeable parts.

Frederick W. Taylor (1881), known as the father of scientific management, contributed to personnel selection, planning and scheduling, motion study, and the now popular field of human factors. An indication of his appreciation of the individual and of human motivation is evident in his work, but his major contribution may have been his belief that management should be much more resourceful and aggressive in the improvement of work methods. Taylor and his colleagues, Henry L. Gantt and Frank and Lillian Gilbreth, were among the first to seek systematically the best way to produce. Another of Taylor's contributions was the distinction between

Frederick W. Taylor's *Principles of Scientific Management* revolutionized manufacturing. A scientific approach to the analysis of daily work and the tools of industry frequently increased productivity 400%. For instance, by 1910, Model T Fords were being assembled with less than two hours of labor.

POM in action

Moving Money at 111 Wall Street

There's a factory on Wall Street in a tall building of concrete and smoky glass that looks identical to the neighboring 24-story structures. However, when workers from the other downtown office buildings complete their day's labors and leave for home, activity at 111 Wall Street continues.

Huge, noisy sorting machines and scurrying robot forklift trucks create an atmosphere of factory-like activity, while trucks carrying raw materials descend on the loading docks. In other large rooms, workers at electric machines produce deafening noise equal to a hundred machine guns.

During one year, $2.5 trillion will be processed in the Operating Group of First National City Bank, where 6,500 laborers perform the physical acts of the otherwise ephemeral business of banking. Accounts are debited and credited. Checks drawn on other banks are put through the clearing houses and sent back to the original writers. First National City Bank's own customers are mailed their canceled checks and bank statements on a monthly basis.

Every 24 hours, approximately 1.5 million checks are delivered by 38 trucks to the loading docks of 111 Wall Street. Hopefully, the last check is put through the mill by 6 A.M. The goal is to send out as many checks as come in.

In the encoding room, dozens of people working feverishly at their keyboards complete an average of 1,200 checks an hour. When they leave the encoding area, the checks are placed into trays and "handed off" to the climate-controlled computer room where 40-foot "Trace" machines sort them for delivery to a multitude of institutions from Chase Manhattan Bank to the Bank of China.

Sources: *The Wall Street Journal*, June 6, 1975; *World of Banking*, **9**, 2 (March–April 1990): 12–18, 30–31.

---

management (for example, those who plan, organize, staff, direct, and control) and labor. He believed that management should assume more responsibility for:

1. assisting employees in selection of the right job, given their capabilities;
2. providing the proper training;
3. providing proper work methods and tools;
4. establishing legitimate incentives for work accomplished.

By 1913, Henry Ford and Charles Sorenson combined what they knew of standardized parts with the quasi-assembly lines of the meat-packing and mail-order industries and added the concept of the coordinated assembly line. During World War II, Sorenson designed the Willow Run assembly line, which eventually produced one B-24 "Liberator" bomber each hour.

Another historically significant contribution is that of quality control. Walter Shewhart (1924) combined his knowledge of statistics with the need for quality control and provided the foundations for statistical sampling and quality control. W. Edwards Deming (1950) believes, as did Frederick Taylor, that management must do more to improve the work environment and processes so that quality can be improved. A summary of significant events in production/operations management is shown in Figure 1.1.

Operations management will continue to progress based on contributions from several other disciplines, including **industrial engineering** and **management sci-**

Industrial engineering
Management science

FIGURE 1.1

Significant Events in Production/Operations Management.

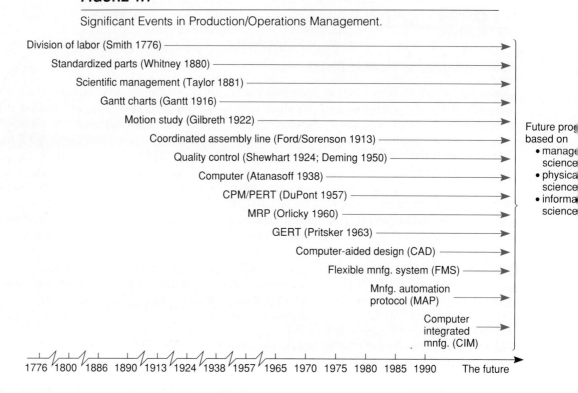

ence. These disciplines have contributed substantially to greater productivity; their significance and power will become apparent as you move through this text. They bring together diverse disciplines such as mathematics, statistics, management, and economics to make possible systematic analysis and improvement of operating systems. Linear programming, queuing theory, simulation, and statistical analysis, as well as a variety of other analytical tools are introduced in other chapters and supplements.

Biological sciences
Physical sciences

Applications from the **biological** and **physical sciences** also have contributed to P/OM in a variety of ways. Innovations from biology, anatomy, chemistry, physics, and the engineering sciences have brought about a variety of new developments. These include new adhesives, chemical processes for printed circuit boards, gamma rays to sanitize food products, and molten tin tables on which to float a higher-quality molten glass as it cools. Chapters 6 and 7 discuss the design of products and processes, which are often dependent upon the biological and physical sciences.

Information sciences

An especially important contribution to P/OM has come from the **information sciences,** which we define as the systematic processing of data to yield information. In a modern business organization, information management implies the use of computers. Information sciences is a discipline that has grown from the contributions of a variety of people, including Charles Babbage and John Vincent Atanasoff. Babbage, in 1832, was the first to design a prototype computer; and Ada, the Countess of Lovelace and daughter of the poet Byron, was the first to design a way to program it. A century later John Atanasoff, while on the faculty of Iowa State, described and built the first digital computer (the ABC computer) in the winter of

1937–38. These and subsequent contributions to computing have provided operations management with a tremendous ability to cope with problems that previously could not have been addressed. Disciplines in which improvements have been made because of information sciences are forecasting, scheduling and shop loading, inventory control, material resource planning, numerical control machinery, computer-aided design (CAD), and, more recently, expert systems and manufacturing automation protocol (MAP). As discussed in the supplement to Chapter 7, the information sciences are contributing in a major way toward improved productivity while at the same time providing society with a greater diversity of goods and services.

Decisions in operations management require individuals who are well versed in *management science,* in *information science,* and often in one of the *biological or physical sciences.* In this chapter we will take a look at the diverse ways a student can prepare for careers in production/operations management. Let us first look, though, at how we organize firms to create goods and services.

ORGANIZING FOR THE CREATION OF GOODS AND SERVICES

To create goods and services all organizations perform three functions. (See Figure 1.2.) These functions are the necessary ingredients not only for production but also for an organization's survival. The functions are listed on page 6.

Lillian M. Gilbreth (1878–1972) and Frank B. Gilbreth (1868–1924) contributed greatly to scientific management principles. Here Frank utilizes a motion study device invented by Lillian. Frank developed time and motion studies, while Lillian devoted herself to industrial psychology. Their contributions led the way to the fields of industrial engineering and ergonomics.

FIGURE 1.2

Three Functions Are Required of All Organizations.

ORGANIZATION	MARKETING	OPERATIONS	FINANCE/ ACCOUNTING
Church	Call on newcomers Proselytize	Conduct weddings Conduct funerals Conduct services Save souls	Count contributions Keep track of pledges Pay the mortgage Pay miscellaneous bills
Fast foods	Advertise on TV Give away promotional materials	Make hamburgers Make french fries Maintain equipment Design new facilities Develop suppliers	Pay suppliers Collect cash Pay employees Pay bank loans
Universities	Mail out catalogues Call on high schools	Research for truth Disseminate truth	Pay faculty Pay support staff Collect tuition
Automobile manufacturer	Advertise on TV, in newspaper, etc. Support auto racing	Design automobiles Manufacture parts Assemble automobiles Develop suppliers	Pay suppliers Pay employees Prepare budgets Pay bank loans Pay dividends Sell stock Borrow funds

1. Marketing, which generates the demand or at least takes the order for a product or service. Nothing happens until there is a sale.
2. Production/operations, which creates the product.
3. Finance/accounting, which tracks how well the organization is doing, pays the bills, and collects the money.

Universities, churches or synagogues, and businesses all perform these functions. (See Figure 1.2.)

An examination of any organized institution, even a volunteer group such as the Boy Scouts of America, will show that it is organized to perform these three basic functions. Charts of how three types of business firms organize themselves to perform these and related functions are shown in Figure 1.3.

WHY STUDY P/OM?

P/OM is one of the three major functions of any organization (as was shown in Figure 1.2), and it is integrally related to all the other business functions. All organizations market (sell), finance (account), and produce (operate), and it is important to know how the P/OM segment of organizations functions. Therefore we study how people organize themselves for productive enterprise. Second, we want to know how goods and services are produced. The production function is the segment of our society that creates the products we consume. Third, we study P/OM because it is such a costly part of an organization. This cost makes it a legitimate focus as societies strive to increase productivity. A discussion of productivity begins in earnest later in this chapter. Table 1.1 shows the large percentage of revenue that is spent in the P/OM function in selected businesses. Indeed, P/OM may provide the best opportunity for an organization to improve its profitability or to enhance its likelihood of survival. For instance, let us consider how a firm might increase its profitability via the production function.

TABLE 1.1 Percentage of Sales Spent on the P/OM Function for Selected Organizations.

	MEAT PACKING INDUSTRY[1]	FURNITURE MANUFAC-TURING[2]	RESTAURANT[3]	HEAVY EQUIPMENT MANUFACTURING[3]
Production/Operations				
Material	79%	40%	38%	42%
Direct labor	8%	15%	20%	12%
Fringes, supervision, supplies	3%	22%	16%	23%
	90%	77%	74%	77%
Selling, Finance, and General and Administrative				
	9%	15%	22%	20%
Interest, Extraordinary Items, Taxes, and Profits				
	1%	8%	4%	3%

Note: All figures are approximate because standardized categories are grouped and rounded.
[1]American Meat Institute, *Meat Facts,* 1984, p. 33.
[2]Adapted from 1980 *Furniture Industries Outlook,* Oct. 1979, Seidman and Seidman, CPA.
[3]Approximate data from various financial statements; prepared by Operations Management, Inc.

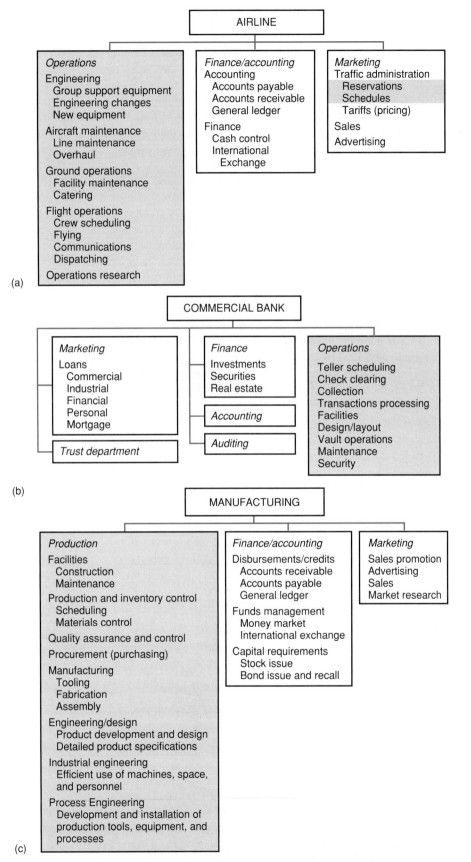

FIGURE 1.3

Organization charts for (a) an Airline, (b) a Bank, and (c) a Manufacturing Organization.

The Hawthorne studies began to determine the impact of lighting on productivity. They recognized the importance of a social system at the workplace. Shown here is part of the relay assembly room at the Hawthorne plant of Western Electric.

Example 1

Landrum Technologies is a small firm that must double its dollar contribution to overhead in order to be profitable enough to purchase the next generation of production equipment. The management has determined that, if the firm fails to increase contribution, its bank will not make the loan and the equipment cannot be purchased. If the firm cannot purchase the equipment, the limitations of the old equipment will preclude Landrum Technologies from remaining in business, and the firm will be unable to provide jobs for its employees or goods and services for its customers. Table 1.2 shows a simple profit and loss statement and three strategic options for the firm. The first strategic option is a *marketing option* where good management may increase sales by 50%. By increasing sales by 50%, contribution will in turn increase 71%, but increasing sales 50% may be more than difficult; it may even be impossible.

Second is a *finance/accounting* option where finance costs are cut in half through good financial management. But elimination of all finance costs is still inadequate for generating the necessary increase in contribution. Contribution is increased by only 21%.

Third is a *P/OM option* where management reduces production costs by 20% and increases contribution by 114%! Given the conditions of our brief example, we now have a bank willing to lend additional funds to Landrum Technology.

TABLE 1.2 Options for Increasing Contribution.

	Current	MARKETING OPTION[1] *Increase Sales Revenue 50%*	FINANCE OPTION[2] *Reduce Finance Costs 50%*	PRODUCTION OPTION[3] *Reduce Production Costs 20%*
Sales	$100,000	$150,000	$100,000	$100,000
Costs of goods	− 80,000	−120,000	− 80,000	− 64,000
Gross margin	20,000	30,000	20,000	36,000
Finance costs	− 6,000	− 6,000	− 3,000	− 6,000
	14,000	24,000	17,000	30,000
Taxes at 25%	− 3,500	− 6,000	− 4,250	− 7,500
Contribution[4]	$ 10,500	$ 18,000	$ 12,750	$ 22,500

[1]Increasing sales 50% increases contribution by $7,500 or 71.0% (7,500/10,500).
[2]Reducing finance costs 50% increases contribution by $2,250 or 21.0% (2,250/10,500).
[3]Reducing production costs 20% increases contribution by $12,000 or 114.0% (12,000/10,500).
[4]Contribution to fixed cost (excluding finance costs) and profit.

The production option taken in Example 1 is the successful strategy recently used by Cummins Engine. Indeed, as you will see from the *POM in Action* box "The Yankee Samurai," this strategy was the only one that made sense. The Cummins case is not unusual. An efficient production function has a high payoff. A goal of the

POM _in action_

The Yankee Samurai

It all began in 1984. First, crated truck engines marked "Komatsu" and "Nissan" appeared on a California dock. Soon after, calls were received from good customers such as Navistar and Freightliner, telling Cummins that they were trying out these Japanese medium-truck engines.

Cummins, a company that held almost 60% of the U.S. heavy-duty diesel-truck engine market, had a lot to lose. After all, if the Japanese were gaining momentum in the medium-engine market, the heavy-engine market could be their next target. To protect themselves, Cummins decided to become more competitive. They cut their prices 10 to 40%. That was the easy part.

Next came cost cutting and simultaneously dealing with inflation. Costs needed to be cut by a minimum of 33% and this was no easy task.

But Cummins decided to learn from the Japanese and studied their production methods. They found that U.S. accounting systems tended to hide certain costs. Cummins also discovered that by using more flexible machinery they could reduce their inventory from 60 days' supply down to 3 or 4 days' supply.

Now it was time to tackle their big item, cutting material costs, which represented 50% of the production budget. Cummins turned to their suppliers for suggestions. Could they help? Yes. It turned out that no one had ever asked before. In three years Cummins was able to lower material costs an impressive 18%. Relationships with suppliers have gone from adversarial to cooperative. In the Cummins' chairman's own words, "We're trying to do everything with our suppliers that we want to do with our customers."

Sources: Forbes, July 14, 1986; _Accountancy,_ 103 (May 1989): 151–153.

production organization, like other segments of an organization, is to operate as efficiently as possible.

The final reason for studying P/OM is to examine the career opportunities in the discipline. Let us examine some aspects of production/operations management careers:

1. What production/operations managers do.
2. Where the P/OM jobs are.
3. How to prepare for a career in P/OM.

WHAT PRODUCTION/OPERATIONS MANAGERS DO

After a brief look at what all managers do we will look more carefully at what P/OM managers do. All good managers perform the basic functions of the management process.[1] The **management process** consists of

Management process

1. _Planning:_ Managers determine objectives and goals for the organization and develop programs, policies, and procedures that will help the organization

---

[1] See Henri Fayol, _General and Industrial Administration_ (London: Sir Isaac Pitman and Sons, 1969); Harold Koontz, _Toward a Unified Theory of Management_ (New York: McGraw-Hill, 1964); and J. G. March and H. Simon, _Organizations_ (New York: John Wiley, 1958).

TABLE 1.3 Activities of Typical Departments in a Manufacturing Firm.

Research and development (R and D)	conducts product research, product development, and product engineering.
Product engineering	fine-tunes product design to enhance production efficiency.
Process engineering	designs, develops, and evaluates production tools, equipment, and processes.
Facilities planning, construction	plans, constructs, maintains, and repairs facilities.
Purchasing	determines the best source for given specification, delivery, and price.
Industrial engineering (IE)	determines most efficient use of machines, space, and personnel.
Methods engineering	directs efforts towards improvement in procedures at the workplace.
Production planning and inventory control (PIC)	schedules the manufacturing processes; manages inventory.
Manufacturing systems	applies the methodology, models, and procedures of mathematics or management information systems to manufacturing operations.
Quality assurance/quality control (QA and QC)	reviews designs, products, and processes to ensure quality objectives are met.
Maintenance	focuses on designing systems and procedures that will create and maintain a reliable system.

attain them. Subordinate plans are also determined for every department, group, and individual in an organization.

2. *Organizing:* Managers develop a structure of individuals, groups, departments, and divisions to achieve objectives.

3. *Staffing:* Managers determine labor requirements and the best way to recruit, train, retain, and terminate the personnel necessary for achieving objectives.

4. *Leading:* Managers lead, supervise, and motivate personnel to achieve objectives.

5. *Controlling:* Managers develop the standards and communication networks necessary to ensure that the organization, staffing, and direction are pursuing appropriate plans and achieving objectives.

Production/operations managers apply this management process to the decisions they make in the P/OM function. In a complex manufacturing organization, managers contribute to production and operations through the activities shown in Table 1.3. Each of these activities can be expected to require planning, organizing, staffing, directing, and controlling.

The activities performed in the departments in Table 1.3 require that operations managers make numerous decisions. Table 1.4 shows some P/OM decisions, the decision area, and the chapters in this text where those decisions are discussed.

TABLE 1.4 Decisions that P/OM Managers Make.

SOME PRODUCTION/OPERATIONS QUESTIONS	DECISION AREA	CHAPTER
How can the P/OM function contribute to organization objectives?	Productivity and strategy	2
What are our criteria for planning? How many units would we expect to sell?	Forecasting	4
What product or service should we offer? How should we design these products and services?	Product selection and design	6
What process will these products require and in what order? What equipment is necessary for these processes?	Process selection and design	7
Where should we put the facility? On what criteria should we base the location decision?	Location	8
How should we arrange the facility? How large must the facility be to meet our plan?	Layout	9
How do we provide a reasonable work environment? How much can we expect our employees to produce?	Human resources	10
Should we make or buy this component? Who are our good suppliers and how many should we have?	Procurement	11
Is subcontracting production a good idea? Are we better off keeping people on the payroll during slowdowns?	Intermediate, short-term, and project scheduling	12,15,16
How much inventory of each item should we have? When do we reorder?	Inventory, MRP	13,14
Who is responsible for quality? How do we define the quality we want in our service or product?	Quality management	17
Who is responsible for reliability and maintenance? How do we build and maintain reliable systems?	Maintenance and reliability	18

These decisions require an understanding of the decision-making process and the impact they have on the operating efficiency and strategy of the firm. In this text we provide an introduction to the proper way to make these decisions. We also note the impact that these decisions may have on the firm's strategy and productivity.

WHERE ARE THE P/OM JOBS?

Figure 1.4 shows the allocation of jobs in the United States. Manufacturing, which has a high portion of P/OM jobs, now constitutes about 18% of all jobs, construction and extractive industries about 6%, and services about 76%. The service sector

FIGURE 1.4

Jobs in the United States.
(*Source:* U.S. Department of Labor, *Monthly Labor Review.*)

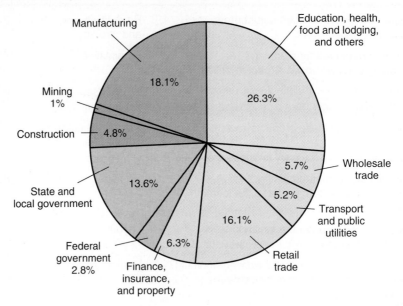

includes government, food and lodging, trade, transportation, finance, insurance, real estate, legal, medical, and repair and maintenance.

Assuming that two-thirds of all jobs in manufacturing and the extractive industries are production/operations jobs and that one-third of all jobs in the service sector are production/operations jobs, then about 40% of *all* jobs are in production and operations. In the United States, which has about 128 million employed, there would be 51 million jobs in the production/operations function. The majority of these are what we would term *blue-collar* or nonprofessional jobs. The remainder are professional and managerial staff, and line jobs in a variety of fields where education, training, and professional qualifications play a significant role. Let us examine some of these P/OM jobs by looking at careers in production/operations management.

PREPARING FOR A CAREER IN P/OM?

How does one get started on a career in the production/operations function of a firm? Let us review the qualifications for individuals seeking entry-level positions in P/OM jobs. The decisions identified in Table 1.4 are made by individuals who work in the disciplines in the shaded areas of Figure 1.3. Competent business students who know their accounting, statistics, finance, and P/OM have an opportunity to enter the entry-level positions in all of these areas. As you read the text, look at the disciplines that can assist you in making these decisions. Then take courses in those areas. The more background a P/OM student has in accounting, statistics, information systems, and mathematics, the more job opportunities that will be available.

In the *production and inventory control* area, entry-level jobs often go to P/OM graduates. A P/OM graduate can enhance his or her qualifications by becoming a certified practitioner in inventory control management (CPIM). This certification is offered by the **American Production and Inventory Control Society (APICS).**[2] Membership in a student or local chapter of APICS is also an excellent way to enhance qualifications for positions in this field.

Manufacturing systems is a term used to describe a wide variety of tasks from operations research to computer-integrated manufacturing. Consequently, the term encompasses a wide variety of opportunities. Most entry-level positions go to majors in mathematics, quantitative management, information systems, management, or P/OM, depending upon the exact nature of the assignment. The **Society of Manufacturing Engineers** is one source of information about careers in manufacturing.[3]

The jobs in *cost analysis, industrial engineering, labor standards, work methods,* and management aspects of *maintenance* often go to business and P/OM graduates, particularly if the student has completed some special course work in these areas. The **Institute of Industrial Engineers** has nationwide chapters, usually with monthly meetings where students are welcome.[4]

Entry-level *purchasing* jobs are often as expeditors or assistant buyers. Business and P/OM graduates have the inside track for such positions. Students can enhance their qualifications by becoming certified purchasing managers (CPM). This is accomplished by successful completion of a series of exams. If the subject matter of Chapter 11 appeals to you, you might contact the **National Association for Purchasing Management** for information about membership and the exam.[5]

Quality control positions, of course, lend themselves to students with a solid background in statistics, whether they be statistics majors or business majors. But these positions also offer opportunities for students in the physical sciences to perform analysis and testing procedures. The **American Society for Quality Control**[6] can provide information about careers in the discipline and their certification exams.

Students with *information science* or *management sciences* backgrounds are important in many ways to the P/OM discipline. They can carve their niche by assisting in developing computerized accounting, ordering, inventory control, forecasting, or personnel systems or in creating mathematical models that help the firm to make better decisions.

In addition to these traditional decision areas, a number of opportunities exist for individuals with other backgrounds. These include the areas discussed earlier in this chapter upon which so much of the future of production/operations management rests: management science, physical science, and information science. All of these fields offer entry-level opportunities. Students in the *physical sciences* can find great opportunity in a wide variety of occupations related to production and operations. These range from protecting the environment to developing new adhesives or steel production processes.

American Production & Inventory Control Society (APICS)

Society of Manufacturing Engineers

Institute of Industrial Engineers

National Association for Purchasing Management

American Society for Quality Control

---

[2] American Production and Inventory Control Society, Certification Department, 500 W. Annandale, Falls Church, VA 22046-4274.

[3] Society of Manufacturing Engineers, One SME Drive, P.O. Box 930, Dearborn, MI 48121.

[4] Institute of Industrial Engineers, 25 Technology Park, Norcross, GA 30092.

[5] National Association for Purchasing Management, P.O. Box 418, Oradell, NJ 07649.

[6] American Society for Quality Control, 230 W. Wells St., Milwaukee, WI 53203.

THE PRODUCTIVITY CHALLENGE

Productivity

Production, as defined earlier, is the creation of goods and services. It is the transformation of resources into products and services. **Productivity** implies the enhancement of the production process. Enhancement of production refers to a favorable comparison of the quantity of resources employed (inputs) to the quantity of goods and services produced (outputs) (see Figure 1.5). A reduction in inputs while output remains constant, or an increase in output while inputs remain constant, represents an improvement in productivity. In an economic sense, inputs are land, labor, capital, and management, which are combined into a production system. Management creates this production system, which provides the conversion of inputs to outputs. Outputs are goods and services, including such diverse items as guns, butter, education, improved judicial systems, and ski resorts.

Measurement of productivity is an excellent way to evaluate a country's ability to provide an improving standard of living for its people. *Only through increases in productivity can the standard of living improve.* Moreover, only through increases in productivity can labor, capital, and management receive additional payments. If returns to labor, capital, or management are increased without increased productivity, prices rise. On the other hand, downward pressure is placed on prices as productivity increases, because more is being produced with the same resources.

Since 1889 the United States has been able to increase productivity at an average rate of nearly 2.5% per year. Such growth doubles our wealth every 30 years. However, we have been unable in recent years to sustain that productivity increase. If U.S. productivity continues to lag, inferiority in the quality of life will soon be upon us. We should determine the reasons for our poor productivity and address them.[7] In this text we examine how to improve productivity by studying the strategic and tactical decisions made by an operations manager.

Productivity Measurement

The measurement of productivity is, in some cases, quite direct, such as when productivity can be measured as labor-hours per ton of a specific type of steel, or as

FIGURE 1.5

The economic system transforms inputs to outputs. An effective feedback loop evaluates process performance against a plan. In this case, it also evaluates customer satisfaction and sends signals to those controlling the inputs and process.

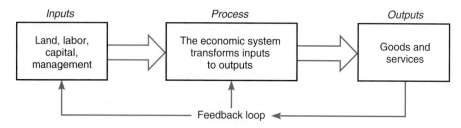

[7] Campbell R. McConnell, "Why Is U.S. Productivity Slowing Down?" *Harvard Business Review* **52** (March–April 1979): 36–60.

the energy necessary to generate a kilowatt of electricity.[8] An example is

$$\text{Productivity} = \frac{\text{Units produced}}{\text{Input used}}$$

$$= \frac{\text{Units produced}}{\text{Labor-hours used}} = \frac{1000}{250} = 4$$

In many instances, however, substantial measurement problems do exist.[9] We will now examine some of these measurement problems:

1. **Quality** may change while the quantity of inputs and outputs remains constant. Compare an automobile of this decade with one of the 1940s. Both are automobiles, but few would deny that the quality has improved. The unit of measure—an automobile—is the same, but the quality has changed.

2. **External elements**[10] may cause an increase or decrease in productivity for which the system under study may not be directly responsible. A more reliable electric power service may greatly improve production, thereby improving the firm's productivity because of this support system rather than because of managerial decisions made within the firm.

3. **Precise units of measures** may be lacking. Not all automobiles require the same inputs—some cars are subcompacts; others are 944 Porsches.

The measurement problems noted above are particularly acute in the service sector. We define the **service sector** as repair and maintenance, government, food and lodging, transportation, insurance, trade, financial, real estate, education, legal, medical, and other professional occupations. Note for instance the measurement problems in a law office where each case is different. Every legal case will vary, altering the accuracy of the measure "cases per labor-hour" or "cases per employee." Because of these measurement problems, productivity within the service sector is difficult to measure accurately. All the same, the operations manager must strive for productivity improvement and the data by which to document progress.

Service sector

Productivity Variables

The United States has had a 2.5% average annual productivity increase for nearly 100 years. This productivity increase consists of three factors,[11] the **productivity variables:**

Productivity variables

1. *labor,* which contributes 0.5% to the increase;
2. *capital,* which contributes 0.4% to the increase;
3. *arts and science of management,* which contributes 1.6%.

---

[8] The quality and time period are assumed to remain constant.

[9] See John W. Henrici, "How Deadly Is the Productivity Disease?" *Harvard Business Review* **59** (November–December 1981): 123–129 for discussion of measurement problems at the national level; and David J. Sumanth, *Productivity Engineering and Management* (New York: McGraw-Hill, 1984) for an excellent discussion at the company level.

[10] These are exogenous variables, that is, variables outside of the system under study that influence it.

[11] See the work of Solomon Fabricant, such as *A Primer on Productivity* (New York: Random House, 1969); Dale W. Jorgensen, *Productivity and U.S. Economic Growth* (Cambridge, MA: Harvard University Press, 1987); and Angus Maddison, "Growth and Slowdown in Advanced Capitalist Economics: Technique of Quantitative Assessment," *Journal of Economic Literature* **25**, 2 (June 1987): 649–698.

FIGURE 1.6

The Contribution of Capital, Labor, and the Arts and Science of Management to the United States' Annual Increase in Productivity.

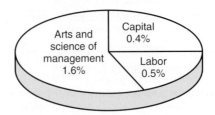

These three factors (Figure 1.6) are critical to productivity improvement. They represent the broad areas in which managers can take action to obtain better productivity.

Labor. Improvement in the contribution of labor to productivity is the result of a healthier, better educated, and better nourished labor force. Some increase may also be attributed to a shorter workweek. Historically, about 20% of the annual improvement in productivity is attributed to improvement in the quality of labor. The three key variables for improved labor productivity have been

1. basic education appropriate for an effective labor force;
2. diet of the labor force;
3. social overhead that makes labor available, such as transportation and sanitation.

Under some conditions, such as a major construction job in an underdeveloped country, the manager may find it difficult to control many of these variables. However, in developed nations, the health of the labor force does not now appear to be the critical variable in increasing productivity.

In developed nations and postindustrialized nations however, a fourth challenge to management is *maintaining and enhancing the skills of labor* in the midst of rapidly expanding technology and knowledge. Recent data suggest that the average U.S. 17-year-old knows half of the mathematics that the average Japanese at the same age knows. More generally, elementary and secondary students in the U.S. fall near the bottom of any comparative international test.[12]

Overcoming shortcomings in the quality of labor while other countries have a better labor force is a major challenge. Perhaps improvements can be found not only through increasing competence of labor, but also via a fifth item, *better utilized labor with a stronger commitment*. Management-by-objective, motivation, flex time, and the human resource strategies of Chapter 10, as well as improved education, may be among the many techniques that will contribute to increased labor productivity. Improvements in labor productivity are possible; however, they can be expected to be increasingly difficult and expensive.

Improving the reading, writing, and arithmetic abilities of workers so that they are capable of handling more difficult jobs in the 1990s is a major concern if productivity is to improve. When the New York Telephone Company recently arranged to have 57,000 applicants take its entry-level examination, which is a simple test measuring basic skills in reading, math, and reasoning, the severity of the problem was clear—less than 4 percent (only 2,100 applicants) passed.

---

[12] Michael L. Dertouzos, Richard K. Lester, and Robert M. Solow, *Made in America: Regaining the Productive Edge* (Cambridge, MA: MIT Commission on Industrial Productivity, MIT Press, 1989); also see "U.S. Science Students Near Root of Class," *Science* **239** (March 1988): 1237; also see Richard M. Wolf, "The NAEP and International Comparisons," *Phi Delta Kappan* (April 1988): 580–581.

Capital. Human beings are tool-using animals. Capital investment provides those tools. Capital investment has increased in the United States every year except for a few very severe recession periods. Annual capital investment in the United States has increased until recent years at the rate of 1.5% of the base investment. This means that the amount of capital invested after allowances for depreciation has grown by 1.5% per year.

As inflation and taxes increase the cost of capital, capital investment becomes increasingly expensive. When the capital invested per employee drops, as it has in recent years, we can expect a drop in productivity. Using labor rather than capital may reduce unemployment in the short run, but it also makes economies less productive and therefore lowers wages in the long run. The trade-off between capital and labor is continually in flux. Additionally, the higher the interest rate, the more projects requiring capital are "squeezed out," that is, are not pursued because the potential return on investment for a given risk has been reduced. Managers adjust their investment plans to changes in capital cost.

Productivity of capital can be increased by making capital work harder. We do this by turning it over more, and operations managers can contribute directly to this increase in capital turnover.

The turnover of capital is sales divided by invested capital as seen below.

$$\text{Turnover of capital} = \frac{\text{Net sales}}{\text{Invested capital}}$$

All other things being equal, the higher the turnover of capital, the higher the productivity of capital. Excellent opportunities for P/OM to enhance productivity through improved capital turnover are described in Procurement and JIT Strategies (Chapter 11), and Scheduling (Chapters 12, 15, and 16).

The Arts and Sciences of Management. Management is a factor of production and an economic resource,[13] and the arts and sciences of management appear to provide the best opportunity for increases in productivity. This category accounts for 60% of the annual increase in productivity (about 1.6% of 2.5% annual increase). Management includes improvements made via the application of technology and the utilization of knowledge.

Improvements to be made via the application of technology and utilization of new knowledge require training and education. Education will remain an important high-cost item in postindustrial societies. Most Western societies are postindustrial societies. They are knowledge societies. A **knowledge society** is one in which much of the labor force has migrated from manual work to work based on knowledge. The research, utilization, and dissemination of knowledge specific to technique and technology may be a current shortcoming of the United States. Although we live in a high technology society, "America invests less in civilian research and development than any of its major industrial competitors."[14] Moreover, Japan seems to be disseminating information faster and more capably than the United States.[15]

Knowledge society

[13] For an excellent discussion of management as an economic resource, see Frederick Harbison and Charles A. Myers, *Management in the Industrial World: International Analysis* (New York: McGraw-Hill, 1959).

[14] "A Time to Dismantle the World Economy," *The Economist* (November 9, 1985): 22.

[15] Robert S. Cuttler, "A Survey of High-Technology Transfer Practices in Japan and in the United States," *Interfaces* **19,** 6 (November–December 1989): 62–77.

POM _in action_

The Challenge Of Producing in Eastern Europe

With the wracking drama befitting a movie, Eastern European countries are facing massive economic and political upheavals. The USSR has become many nations, East Germany is gone, and even xenophobic Albania is opening it doors to Western exchange programs. The big question is how these new and old socialist countries, which all lag behind the U.S., Western Europe, and Asia, will compete in a free market system. Can Western business practices transfer to the East European culture?

Many experts fear that because of work ethic differences they will not. For example, Eastern bloc managers, not used to accountability for profit or loss, have long survived on bribery income. Unmotivated workers may resist having to work hard.

Almost everything produced in Eastern Europe is inferior to what is made in the West. The question is how much that gap will narrow in the 1990s. Poland's own premier called his nation "the kingdom of shoddy goods." In one three-month period, every small Fiat that came off a Polish assembly line was judged unfit for sale. Bulgaria's president stated "even those products that we began to produce under foreign license have been 'Bulgarized'"—that is, they have the imprint of poor production added to them. And a Czechoslavak Institute of Management survey showed that nearly half of all the factory managers consider quality of marginal importance.

Even within Eastern Europe, we should note, there are great differences in culture and work habits. Poles tend to cooperate more, while Romanians are adversarial and highly individualistic. Some older Eastern Europeans have the advantage of remembering work under a free market system some 40 years ago. But Russia's socialist regime is now 70 years old, which means virtually everyone there needs to learn new ways.

One Japanese management expert, Professor M. Maruyama, recommends that Eastern European countries send managers to train in other parts of the world—and carefully examine their own cultures at the same time. Tens of thousands from the socialist countries are already studying business abroad.

As globalization of business continues and management techniques adjust to each country's unique culture, there is no need for Eastern Europeans to be totally pessimistic. After all, it took the Japanese just 20 years to catch up with, and perhaps even pass, Europe and U.S. quality levels.

Sources: "Some Management Considerations in the Economic Reorganization of Eastern Europe," by M. Maruyama, _Academy of Management Executive,_ **2,** 4 (1990): 90–91; "Crash Courses in Capitalism for Ivan the Globe-Trotter." _Business Week_ (May 28, 1990): 42–44.

As we move through the text we will note legal and cultural values that distinguish the U.S. economy from the economy of other nations. We now live in a world economy, and production/operations managers must adjust to both the opportunities and the realities of such an environment. The _P/OM in Action_ box "The Challenge of Producing in Eastern Europe" discusses some of these new opportunities and realities of the world economy.

Because society and commerce are changing, education and training requirements continue to increase. For instance, not only did the introduction of computers require added training, but each generation of new computers requires more training. Each additional management science technique requires education, and new organizational designs require more organizational development. This requirement for more training and education is the inevitable result of the knowledge explosion and the development of a high technology society. The effective operations manager will *ensure that available knowledge and technology are utilized.*

The *more-effective utilization of capital,* as opposed to additional capital, is also important. The manager, as a productivity catalyst, is charged with the task of making improvements in capital productivity within existing constraints.

Recent increases in effectiveness in oil exploration, airline scheduling, inventory management, and feedlot operations are indicative of the strides that can be made through the *utilization of management and management science.* Productivity gains in knowledge societies require managers who are comfortable with technology and management science components of the arts and science of management. In this text we have organized the arts and sciences of management, as they apply to operations management, into ten strategic and tactical decisions. We will discuss these ten decisions in Chapter 2.

The productivity challenge is difficult. A country cannot be a world-class competitor with second-class inputs. Poorly educated labor inputs, inadequate capital inputs, and dated technology are second-class inputs. Low-quality, second-class inputs must be changed to high-quality, first-class inputs. High productivity and high-quality outputs require high-quality inputs.

The Service Sector

Another variable that influences productivity in the United States is the increasing size of the service sector. The service sector is one cause for poor productivity performance in the United States. This is happening because in the service sector work is

1. typically labor intensive;
2. frequently individually processed;
3. often an intellectual task performed by professionals;
4. often difficult to mechanize and automate.

The more intellectual and personal the task, the more difficult it has been to achieve increases in productivity. The low productivity of the service sector is reflected in the fact that although over two-thirds of the U.S. labor force is engaged in service, the service sector contributes only about half of the gross national product. There is hope that further improvements in computer-related technology and expert systems will bring new opportunities for productivity improvement to the service sector.

SUMMARY

Production is one of the three functions basic to all organizations. The production/operations function creates goods and services. Much of the progress of operations management has been made in the twentieth century, but since the beginning of time humankind has been attempting to improve its material well-being. Production/operations management is the primary vehicle for doing so.

The vast majority of productivity improvements (60%) are within the purview of assertive, innovative, entrepreneurial managers functioning in their role as productivity catalysts. Modern technological society consists of complex organizations that cry out for effective management. Though it is a challenging task, managers can improve productivity in this environment. Such improvements in productivity are the responsibility of the professional manager, and professional managers are among the few in our society who *can* make this improvement. The challenge is great, and the rewards to the manager and to society substantial.

KEY TERMS

Production (p. 2)

Production management and operations management (P/OM) (p. 2)

Industrial engineering (p. 3)

Management science (p. 3)

Physical sciences (p. 4)

Information sciences (p. 4)

Management process (p. 9)

American Production and Inventory Control Society (APICS) (p. 13)

Society of Manufacturing Engineers (p. 13)

Institute of Industrial Engineers (p. 13)

National Association for Purchasing Management (p. 13)

American Society for Quality Control (p. 13)

Productivity (p. 14)

Service sector (p. 15)

Productivity variables (p. 15)

Knowledge society (p. 17)

SOLVED PROBLEM

Solved Problem 1.1

Productivity can be measured in a variety of ways, such as labor, capital, energy, material usage, and so on. In this example, Boe Warren, a noted producer of apple pies sold to supermarkets, has been able, with his current equipment, to produce 24 pies per bushel of apples. He currently purchases 100 bushels per day, and each bushel requires three labor-hours to process. He believes that he can hire a professional food broker, who can buy a better-quality apple at the same cost. If this is the case, he can increase his production to 26 pies per bushel. His labor-hours will increase by eight hours per day.

What will be the impact on productivity (pies per labor-hour) if the food broker is hired?

$$\text{Current labor productivity} = \frac{24 \text{ pies} \times 100 \text{ bushels}}{100 \text{ bushels} \times 3 \text{ hours}} = \frac{2400}{300}$$
$$= 8.0 \text{ pies per labor-hour.}$$

$$\text{Labor productivity with food broker} = \frac{26 \text{ pies} \times 100 \text{ bushels}}{(100 \text{ bushels} \times 3 \text{ hrs}) + 8 \text{ hrs}}$$
$$= \frac{2600}{308} = 8.44.$$

Using last year (i.e., 8.0) as a base, the increase is 5.5%: 8.44/8.0 = 1.055 or a 5.5% increase over last year.

DISCUSSION QUESTIONS

1. Define production/operations management in your own words. Will your definition accommodate both manufacturing and service operations?

2. Consider the potential contribution of information sciences to P/OM. Why is the management of information of such great importance in the management of "production"?

3. Figure 1.3 outlines the marketing, operations, and finance/accounting function of three organizations. Prepare a chart similar to Figure 1.3 outlining the same functions for
 a) a large metropolitan newspaper
 b) a local drugstore
 c) a college library
 d) a local service organization (Boy Scouts, Girl Scouts, Rotary International, Lions, Grange, etc.)
 e) a doctor's or dentist's office

 f) a jewelry factory

4. Do the preceding assignment for some other enterprise of your choosing, perhaps an organization where you have worked.

5. What is the difference between production and operations?

6. Identify three disciplines that will contribute in a major way to the future development of P/OM.

7. Can you identify the operation function(s) of a past or current employer? Draw an organization chart for the operations function of that firm.

8. What are the three classic functions of a firm?

9. What departments might you find in the P/OM function of a home appliance manufacturer?

PROBLEMS

· **1.1** Boe and Ann Warren bake apple pies for resale to local supermarkets. They and their three employees invest 50 hours per day making 150 pies.

 a) What is their productivity?

 b) They have discussed reassigning work so the flow through the bakery is smoother. If they are correct and they can do the necessary training, they think they can increase apple pie production to 155 per day. What is their new productivity?

 c) What is their increase in productivity?

· **1.2** Choose a company and identify how changes in the political and economic environment affect the strategy of the P/OM function (all other things remaining the same). For instance, discuss what impact the following factors might have had on P/OM strategy.

 a) major increases in oil prices

 b) water and air quality legislation

 c) fewer young prospective employees entering the labor market in 1985 through 1995

 d) inflation vs. stable prices

: **1.3** Brewerton's Tennessee Sip'n Whiskey is an extraordinary organization established by Frank Brewerton shortly after the Treasury Department began using infrared photography and sniffer planes to find distillers that showed little interest in purchasing revenue stamps. Since Frank's expenses have gone up, he has a new-found interest in efficiency. Frank is interested in determining the productivity of his organization. He has last year's records and good current data. He would like to know if his organization is maintaining the national average of 2.5% annual increase in productivity. He has the data on the following page.

Problem 1.3 continued

	LAST YEAR	NOW
Production	1,000	1,000
Labor (hours)	300	275
Corn mash (bushel)	50	45
Capital invested ($)	10,000	11,000
Energy (Btu)	3,000	2,850

Show the productivity increase for each category and then determine the annual improvement for labor hours, the typical standard for comparison.

BIBLIOGRAPHY

Andrew, C. G., *et al.* "The Critical Importance of Production and Operations Management." *Academy of Management Review* **7** (1982): 143–147.

Babbage, C. *On the Economy of Machinery and Manufacturers,* 4th ed. London: Charles Knight, 1835.

Buffa, E. S. "Research in Operations Management." *Journal of Operations Management* **1** (1980): 1–7.

Burch, E. E., and W. R. Henry. "Production Management Is Alive and Well." *Academy of Management Journal* **17** (1974): 144–149.

Drucker, P. F. *The Concept of the Corporation.* New York: Mentor Executive Library, 1946.

Fabricant, S. *A Primer on Productivity.* New York: Random House, 1969.

George, C. S., Jr. *The History of Management Thought.* Englewood Cliffs, NJ: Prentice-Hall, 1968.

Harbison, F., and C. A. Myers. *Management in the Industrial World.* New York: McGraw-Hill, 1959.

Krugman, P. *The Age of Diminished Expectations.* Cambridge, MA: MIT Press, 1990.

Smith, A. *An Inquiry into the Nature and Causes of the Wealth of Nations.* London: A. Strahan and T. Cadell, 1776.

Taylor, F. W. *The Principles of Scientific Management.* New York: Harper & Bros., 1911.

Taylor, F. W. *Shop Management.* New York: Harper & Bros., 1919.

Tillet, A., T. Kempner, and G. Wills, eds. *Management Thinkers.* Harmondsworth, England: Penguin Books, 1970.

Urwick, L., and E. F. L. Brech. *The Making of Scientific Management,* vol. 1, *The Thirteen Pioneers.* London: Management Publications Trust, 1949.

Wren, Daniel A., *The Evolution of Management Thought.* New York: Ronald Press, 1972.

Developing a P/OM Strategy

INTRODUCTION

In Chapter 1 we discussed production and productivity. We now begin our discussion of the production/operations manager's actions in the firm. The operations manager is responsible for building an effective and efficient transformation system. Operations managers are *effective* when they operate a P/OM function that supports the firm. Operations managers are *efficient* when they support the firm with economical use of resources. In this chapter we discuss the idea of *systems,* the *strategy development process,* and, finally, *developing a P/OM strategy.*

SYSTEMS

Operations managers manage a variety of systems *within the P/OM function.* They do this best if they understand system concepts. P/OM systems are numerous and include inventory and scheduling systems, procurement systems, and maintenance systems. Production/operations managers also respond to a variety of systems *external to the P/OM function.* Some of these are other parts of the firm, such as marketing and finance systems. Others are *external to the firm.* Among those external to the firm are economic systems, a system of world trade, and numerous political systems. Managers who understand both the internal and external systems will be better managers. They will be able to coordinate the linkages of people, material, money, and information that are essential for effective performance.

Viewing the enterprise as a system provides a way of seeing the organization within its environment. This in turn helps develop an effective P/OM mission that contributes to the organization's mission and strategy.

System

The word *system* implies order and arrangement. A **system** is an aggregation of interacting variables. The operations manager designs a system to achieve a particular objective or mission.

One kind of system is a *transformation system* that converts inputs into goods and services. The economy is such a system; the firm is such a system; the production function is such a system. These systems provide the goods and services of our society. The economic system was shown earlier in Chapter 1 (see Figure 1.5). This system has inputs, transformation, and outputs. It also has information flow from consumers. Such an information flow is known as a feedback loop.

The production function and its particular inputs, transformation, and outputs are shown in Figure 2.1. One of the feedback loops is from the firm's clients or customers. This feedback loop lets the inputs and the transformation process know what the customer thinks of its performance.

Subsystems

Complex systems also include smaller systems within them. These subsystems sometimes try to achieve their own relatively narrow objectives. The manager's job is to keep subsystems focused on the goals of the overall system. As an example, a finance department may perceive its goal as holding inventory levels close to zero. The sales department, on the other hand, may be an enthusiastic supporter of large

FIGURE 2.1

The Firm Transforms Inputs to Outputs.

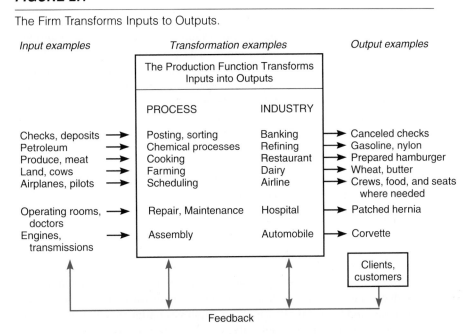

Input examples   *Transformation examples*   *Output examples*

The Production Function Transforms Inputs into Outputs

PROCESS	INDUSTRY

Checks, deposits → Posting, sorting — Banking —→ Canceled checks
Petroleum → Chemical processes — Refining —→ Gasoline, nylon
Produce, meat → Cooking — Restaurant —→ Prepared hamburger
Land, cows → Farming — Dairy —→ Wheat, butter
Airplanes, pilots → Scheduling — Airline —→ Crews, food, and seats where needed

Operating rooms, → Repair, Maintenance — Hospital —→ Patched hernia
doctors
Engines, → Assembly — Automobile —→ Corvette
transmissions

Clients, customers

Feedback

stocks of inventory on the assumption that this will aid in achieving sales goals. When inconsistent objectives such as these occur, the larger system (the firm) may not be operating at its best or optimum level. When the system is not operating at its best level, it is said to be **suboptimized.** By understanding the goals of the subsystem and the linkages between systems, the operations manager has an opportunity to avoid suboptimization. An understanding of the entire system, both internal and external, allows the operations manager to make good decisions that improve the productivity of the operations function.

Suboptimized

STRATEGY DEVELOPMENT PROCESS

In order to develop an effective strategy, organizations first seek to identify opportunities in the economic system. Then we define the organization's mission or purpose in society—what it will contribute to society. This purpose is the organization's (the system's) reason for being, that is, its **mission.** Once an organization's mission has been decided, each functional area within the firm determines its supporting mission. By "functional area" we mean the major disciplines required by the firm, such as marketing, finance/accounting, and production/operations. Missions for each function are developed to support the firm's overall mission.

Mission

We achieve missions via strategies. A **strategy** is a plan designed to achieve a mission. Each functional area has a strategy for achieving its mission and for helping the organization reach the overall mission. In the following section we will describe how missions and strategies are developed.

Strategy

Mission

To ensure a focus on a common purpose, a *mission* is established. A mission should be established in light of the threats and opportunities in the environment and the strengths and weaknesses of the organization. The mission is the concept around which the firm can rally. The mission states the rationale for the organization's existence. Developing a good strategy is difficult, but is easier if the mission has been well defined. The mission can also be thought of as the intent of the strategy—what the strategy is to achieve.

The *mission,* or purpose, of an organization is

- the reason for the firm's existence;
- why society should endorse the allocation of resources to the organization;
- the value created for the customer.

Examples of missions for two firms are:

Telephone and Data Systems, Inc.: "to be the finest in total communications services for our subscribers."[1]

Ford Motor Company: . . . "a worldwide leader in automotive and automotive related products and services as well as in newer industries such as aerospace, communications, and financial services . . . to improve continually our products and services to meet our customers' needs, allowing us to prosper as a business and to provide a reasonable return to our stockholders, the owners of our business."[2]

These brief mission statements provide a rationale and purpose for each firm's existence. Once a mission is established, strategy and its implementation can begin. What an organization does to achieve a mission is its *strategy.*

TOWS Analysis

TOWS

To develop a strategy, we adopt evaluation of the firm via Threats, Opportunities, Weaknesses, and Strengths (TOWS).[3] The **TOWS** concept looks at Threats and Opportunities in the environment and then looks at the Weaknesses and Strengths of the firm itself. The idea is to find an opportunity that matches the strength of the firm—or at least identifies a potential strength that the firm can develop. Similarly, the firm seeks to avoid exposing a weakness.

A two-dimensional strategy matrix with environmental opportunities and threats on one axis and the firm's strengths and weaknesses on the other is shown in Figure 2.2.

An effective way to develop a plan for competitive advantage is to understand the *threats* and *opportunities* in the firm's environment. The threats and opportunities may exist in a number of environmental variables. We define environmental variables to include:

- cultural;
- demographic;
- economic;
- political–legal;
- technological;
- publics.

[1] Annual Report, 1986.

[2] *Quality Progress* (October 1989), 49.

[3] Development of the TOWS concept is generally attributed to the Boston Consulting Group.

FIGURE 2.2

Strategy Matrix. The firm seeks to match its strengths with the opportunities in the environment, while avoiding environmental threats and exposing its own weaknesses.

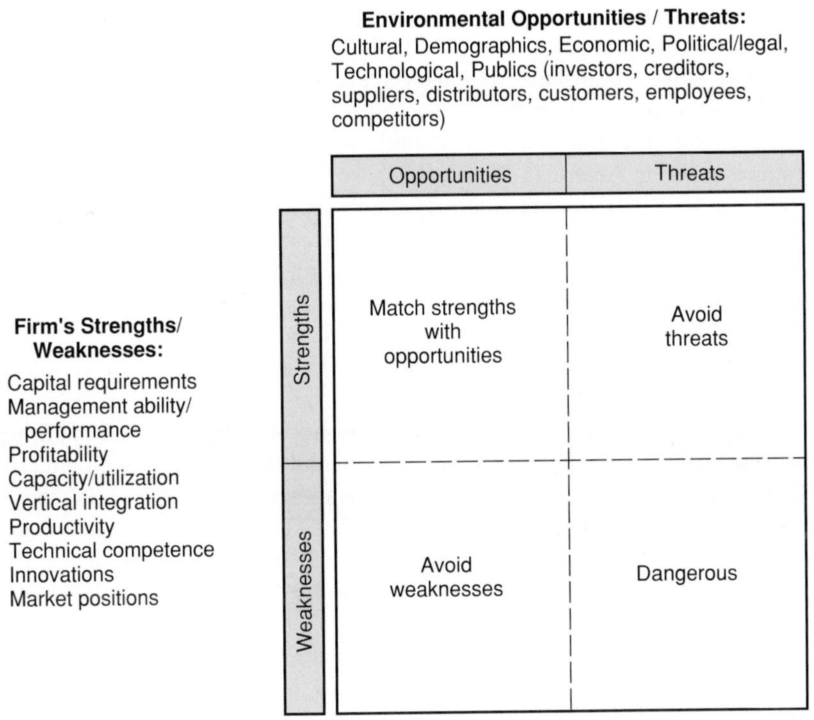

Environmental Opportunities / Threats:
Cultural, Demographics, Economic, Political/legal, Technological, Publics (investors, creditors, suppliers, distributors, customers, employees, competitors)

Firm's Strengths/ Weaknesses:

Capital requirements
Management ability/ performance
Profitability
Capacity/utilization
Vertical integration
Productivity
Technical competence
Innovations
Market positions

	Opportunities	Threats
Strengths	Match strengths with opportunities	Avoid threats
Weaknesses	Avoid weaknesses	Dangerous

The publics of a firm include:

- investors, creditors, and bankers (sources of capital);
- suppliers (sources of raw material and components);
- distributors and customers (those who provide orders);
- employees (those who provide the human resources);
- competitors (those that fight the firm for orders);
- legal system, governments, special-interest groups, and regulators (those that set parameters of acceptable actions).

These environmental variables provide the constraints within which the firm operates. Therefore, firms build intelligence networks that provide the information needed to understand this environment fully. Only then can the firm begin to build a mission and supporting strategy. A brief look at strategic implications of developments in the world economy is presented in Example 1.

Strategy Procedure

As Example 1 suggests, firms evaluate their strengths and weaknesses and the opportunities and threats of the environment. Then the firm positions itself through its strategic and tactical decisions to have a competitive advantage. Firms identify

Example 1

Global Strategy. Postindustrial societies such as those in the European Community (EC) and North America have global as well as local opportunities and threats to consider. Let us take a look at global changes taking place in the economic environment.

First, as we will discuss in Chapter 8, exchange rates, labor rates, productivity, and local attitude and values make a major difference in the location decision. But accepting those constraints, we should notice that most of the products made in America (or anywhere else) are also made elsewhere in the world. Virtually no product is still available from only one national source. Those other places in the world where American products are likely to be produced are places where high-volume, standardized products can be built by productive low-cost labor with few fringe benefits and a burning desire to sell to affluent Western markets. This desire to sell to the Western world is often augmented by national policies such as low taxes, export credits, and subsidies that support such sales.

Second, although the EC is not a low-labor-cost competitor, it is maturing into one huge market. Volume in this market, and therefore the optimum size of facilities in this market, is increasing. This allows surviving firms in the EC to spread their fixed expenses over more units. Therefore these firms could very well be low-cost producers even with high labor costs. And depending upon the trade arrangements that develop with Eastern Europe, low labor cost could be available for the next decade.

Third, communication, travel, and shipments between continents are relatively easy, inexpensive, and rapid. This means that both markets and sources are truly global.

Fourth, the affluent Western world itself is demanding quality, immediate delivery, and options. Affluence allows this market to purchase the latest technology and readily discard the old.

With reference to our TOWS analysis, what are the strengths and weaknesses for Western firms in such an environment? What are the potential competitive advantages for Western firms in this changing world? Perhaps sophisticated, flexible production systems that produce high quality, innovative, option-filled products for a wealthy consumer is reasonable strategy. The products produced would utilize the strengths found in higher skills, technology, and education that are unique to the postindustrialized society. And they would bypass a potential weakness, low labor costs.

Western manufacturing firms that remain in competition with the high-volume, relatively low-technology facilities of the world will be in lean, focused plants (see Chapter 9, Layout), utilizing both a high degree of automation (see Chapter 7, Process Strategy) and worker commitment (see Chapter 10, Human Resources).

the options available that maximize opportunities and minimize threats. The strategy is continually evaluated against the value provided the customer and competitive realities. A procedure that does this is shown in Figure 2.3.

Competitive Situation Analysis

Understand the environment.
Understand expectations of the public.
Identify economic characteristics of the
   industry and environment.
Identify critical factors in the industry.
Evaluate threats of competitors.
Identify competitive positions of
   industry participants.
Evaluate industry opportunities.
Identify future moves of competitors.

Company Situation Analysis

Evaluate present company performance.
Do a TOWS analysis (threats, opportunities,
   weaknesses, and strengths).
Evaluate the company's relative
   competitive strengths.
Identify the strategic issues that the
   company should address.
Identify the weaknesses of the company.
Can the company successfully address
   the weaknesses?

FIGURE 2.3

Implementing Strategy
Via Specific Functional
Decisions: Examples
from Marketing,
Finance/Accounting,
Production/Operations.

Mission Development

The reason for the firm's existence.
Why society should endorse the allocation of resources to the organization.
What value is created for the customer.

Strategy Considerations

Can the company's strengths be matched to the opportunities in the marketplace?
Can the company's weaknesses be overcome?
Can the company anticipate the competitors' moves and respond favorably?
Can the company build a competitive advantage?
Will the company win orders with this strategy in this environment?

Form a Strategy

What strategic steps must be taken to build a competitive advantage?
What steps must be taken to build market share?
What steps must be taken to become world class?
Which strategic decisions are critical for success?
Can the strategy be implemented?

Make and Implement Strategic Decisions in Functional Areas

Marketing	**Finance/Accounting**	**Production/Operations**
Service	Leverage	
Distribution	Cost of capital	
Promotion	Working capital	
Price	Receivables	
Channels of distribution	Payables	
Product positioning	Financial control	
(image, functions)	Lines of credit	

Decisions	Sample Options	Chapter
Product	Customized or standardized	6
Process	Facility size, technology	7
Location	Near supplier or near customer	8
Layout	Work cells or assembly line	9
Human resource	Specialized or enriched jobs	10
Procurement	Single or multiple source suppliers	11
Scheduling	Stable or fluctuating production rate	12,15,16
Inventory	When to reorder; how much to keep on hand	13,14
Quality	How to implement quality; quality standards	17
Reliability and maintenance	Repair as required or preventative maintenance	18

29

The U.S. home appliance market is growing annually at 2% or less, about half of that projected for Europe. Therefore, Whirlpool chairman David Whitwam's strategy is to take Whirlpool global. Whirlpool recently acquired major interest in Ingils Limited of Canada, Vitromatic of Mexico, and a 53% stake in N. V. Philips in Holland. Whirlpool has also moved toward global procurement of 35 strategic materials and components. Appliance giants Maytag, Electrolux, and G.E. have similarly developed and implemented global strategies to enable them to compete internationally and be a part of the new European Community. They are also positioned for the next round of tariff reductions, which should result from the GATT negotiations now concluding.

Mission and strategy development require that the organization find an opportunity in the environment for which it is uniquely qualified. That is, the company identifies its own unique competencies—its own special capabilities that fit an opportunity. The firm seeks its own unique way of utilizing the resources at its command to fill an economic requirement. It does not want to attack the market with exactly the same mission and strategy as a competitor. A direct duplication of another mission and strategy is to be avoided. The smartest strategy in war is the one that wins but avoids the battle. The firm wants to find those voids or requirements in the environment that provide an opportunity for it to mobilize uniquely its resources. The task is to identify and evaluate an opportunity that will allow development of a competitive advantage or enhance an already existing advantage.

DEVELOPING A P/OM STRATEGY

The operations manager is an active participant in the determination of the firm's mission and strategy and how the firm's resources can most effectively be utilized. Only when operations managers understand the organization's overall strategy can they maximize their contribution to developing an effective operations strategy. Moreover, the best utilization of resources requires more than effective marketing and finance. Jazzy ads and new financial leverage schemes do not create better products delivered on time to the customer; only the production function does that.

In this text we discuss how the production function can contribute to competitive advantage. We note specific examples of how firms can address product development, cost, processes and technology, quality management, procurement, human resources, and so forth. If the operations strategy and its implementation do not contribute to the company's strategy, the operations manager has failed.

The significant role that P/OM can play in competitive strategy is evident from a study done by David Aaker. Of 32 broad categories that contribute to sustainable competitive advantage, one-fourth fall into the production (product/process) category.[4] When location and scheduling are added, the total increases to 28%. P/OM has a major role to play in strategy development.

The P/OM function is the third leg of the strategic triad that also includes marketing and finance/accounting. Figure 2.3 provides a brief synopsis of options for marketing, finance, and P/OM. These functions as well as other functions of the firm can make contributions to strategy. Specific contributions to strategy by strategy opportunities for the P/OM function are numerous and include positioning P/OM resources via the strategic decisions introduced in the following section. This text is organized around these ten decisions.

P/OM Strategic and Tactical Decisions

Strategic decisions tend to have implications of long duration (say over one year) and may take over a year to implement. Tactical decisions are those that can be substantially modified in one year or less. Both types of decisions support P/OM and

[4] See David A. Aaker, "Creating a Sustainable Competitive Advantage," *California Management Review* (Winter 1989): 91–106.

company missions. Let us group the P/OM tasks that require strategic and tactical decisions in the following way:

Strategic Decisions of Operations Management

1. **Product strategy.** Product strategy defines much of the transformation process. Production costs, quality, and human resource decisions interact strongly with the design of products. Product decisions often set the lower limits of cost and the upper limits of quality.

2. **Process strategy.** Process options are available for a product. Process decisions commit management to basic approaches to technology, quality, human resource utilization, and maintenance. Various expense and capital commitments are made that will determine much of the firm's basic cost structure.

3. **Location strategy.** Facility location decisions for both manufacturing and service organizations may determine the ultimate success of the operation. Errors made at this juncture may overwhelm other efficiencies.

4. **Layout strategy.** Capacity, use of personnel, procurement, and inventory planning will be influenced by layout. Processes and material must be sensibly located in relation to each other.

5. **Human resource strategy.** Human resources are an integral and expensive part of the total system design. Therefore, the quality of work-life provided, the talent and skills required, and their costs must be determined.

6. **Procurement and just-in-time strategy.** Determination of what is to be made and what is to be purchased with proper emphasis on quality, delivery, and innovation, at a satisfactory price, in an atmosphere of mutual respect between buyer and supplier is necessary for effective procurement.

Tactical Decisions of Operations Management

7. **Inventory and just-in-time tactics.** Inventory decisions can be optimized only when considered in light of customer satisfaction, lead time, production schedules, and human resource planning.

8. **Scheduling tactics.** Feasible and efficient schedules of production must be developed; the demands on human resources and facilities must be determined and controlled.

9. **Quality tactics.** Decisions must be made to determine desired quality; policies and procedures must be established to achieve that quality.

10. **Reliability and maintenance tactics.** Decisions must be made regarding desired levels of reliability and maintenance. Plans for implementation and control of reliability and maintenance are necessary.

Each of the strategic and tactical decisions discussed above and shown in Figure 2.4 on page 32 is presented in one or more chapters in the text.

These ten areas do not, of course, represent all that the operations managers do or should know. For instance, we do not discuss in depth organization theory, accounting, staffing, or human behavior and communication skills, but all are important for the effective operations manager. Moreover, as we shall see in subsequent chapters, these ten P/OM decision areas interact strongly with each other to support the P/OM mission.

FIGURE 2.4

Components of P/OM Mission and Strategy. The P/OM manager uses the strategic and tactical decisions of production/operations when building a P/OM mission and strategy that support the company's mission and strategy.

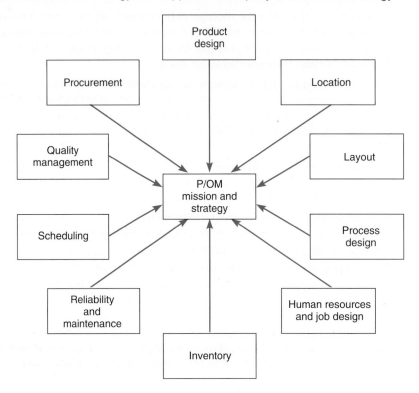

P/OM Strategy Considerations

The operations manager identifies what the P/OM function can and cannot accomplish. A successful P/OM strategy is consistent with:

1. environmental demands (Under what economic and technological conditions is the company attempting to execute its strategy?);
2. competitive demands (What are the strengths and weaknesses of competitors? What are they trying to do?);
3. company strategy (What is the company attempting to do?);
4. product life cycle (Where in the life cycle are the company's offerings?).

Therefore, a P/OM strategy also:

1. identifies and organizes the P/OM tasks (What must this particular P/OM function do, and how should it be organized in relation to other segments of the organization so that it contributes to the firm's mission?);
2. makes the necessary choices within the P/OM function (Since no one does everything exceptionally well, on which particular tasks will P/OM focus?);
3. finds competitive advantage (How will the P/OM function contribute to the unique strength of the organization?).

PIMS Analysis

Additional strategic insight has been provided by the tentative findings of the Strategic Planning Institute.[5] Its **PIMS Program** *(Profit Impact of Market Strategy)* was established in cooperation with the General Electric Corporation. PIMS has collected nearly 100 data items from about 3,000 cooperating organizations. Using the data collected and high *return on investment* (ROI)[6] as a measure of success, PIMS has been able to identify some characteristics of high ROI firms. Among those characteristics that impact strategic P/OM decisions are:

PIMS Program

- high product quality (relative to the competition);
- high capacity utilization;
- high operating effectiveness (the ratio of expected to actual employee productivity);
- low investment intensity (the amount of capital required to produce a dollar of sales);
- low direct cost per unit (relative to the competition).

In the analysis of a firm's relative strengths and weaknesses, these characteristics can be measured and evaluated. They should be considered as an organization develops its strategy.

Strategy Implementation

The production/operations manager develops strategy, groups activities into an organized structure, and staffs with personnel who will get the job done. The manager works with subordinate managers to build plans, budgets, and programs that will successfully implement strategies that achieve missions. Firms tackle this organization of the operations function in a variety of ways. We have identified ten decision areas in the P/OM function. Each firm will make its own choices about how to organize to make these ten decisions. The organization charts shown in Chapter 1 (Figure 1.3) indicate the way that some firms have organized to make these decisions.

The organization of the operations function and its relationship to other parts of the organization varies with the P/OM mission. For example, short-term scheduling in the airline industry is dominated by volatile customer travel patterns. Day-of-week preference, holidays, seasonality, college schedules, and so on, all play a role in changing flight schedules. Consequently, airline scheduling, although a P/OM activity, can be a part of a marketing organization. (Refer back to Figure 1.3a.) Effective scheduling in the trucking industry is reflected in the amount of time trucks travel loaded. However, scheduling of trucks requires information from delivery and pick-up points, drivers, and other parts of the organization. When the organization of the P/OM function results in effective scheduling in the air passenger and commercial trucking industries, a competitive advantage can exist.

By the same token, the importance of, and consequently the emphasis placed on, each of the ten decisions varies with the mission of the operations function. For

Cummins Engine Company manufactures diesel engines for buses, trucks, and heavy-duty equipment for sale worldwide. Cummins is an American organization operating internationally. Since the introduction of its fuel-efficient L10 engine in the United Kingdom, its share of the United Kingdom bus market increased steadily. Cummins prospers by keeping in touch with its suppliers and customers, stressing quality, service, and innovation.

---

[5] R. D. Buzzel and B. T. Gale, *The PIMS Principles* (New York: The Free Press, 1987).

[6] Like other performance measures, *return on investment* has limitations, including sensitivity to the business cycle, depreciation policies and schedules, book value (goodwill), and transfer pricing.

POM *in action*

On a Roll

Michelin is a phenomenon. After World War II, the Michelin family forged rashly and courageously into the development of its controversial new product, the radial tire. Although it experienced great success with that tire, Michelin still ranked only seventh in the worldwide tire industry by the late 1960s. At that point, the company decided that international growth would be its future.

Michelin ran up heavy debts and losses as it proceeded to build new factories at the rate of two a year in the late 1970s. A few years later, the oil shock deflated the tire market, but, fortunately, the company bounced back. Michelin's secret is that it is continuously willing to sacrifice short-term concerns for its two long-term objectives: quality and market share.

Hoping to avoid unions, Michelin prefers to build plants in the southern United States. Eighty percent of production is in numerous countries outside France, and the French represent only a small minority of employees.

Michelin consistently spends 5% of sales on research, which is the same percentage as Japan's Bridgestone. Goodyear attributes its heavy research spending of less than 4% as the reason why it alone of the U.S. majors has avoided a takeover.

Although Michelin concentrates on tires and tire components, it does make maps and restaurant guides for motorists. Goodyear and Bridgestone produce more than 25% of revenue from nontire products, but tires represent more than 90% of Michelin's sales. Almost all materials, including the steel belting and synthetic rubber used in its tires, are produced by Michelin.

Michelin is mainly concerned about its long-term position as exemplified by its purchase of Uniroyal Goodrich. This transaction clearly will push up debt and hold down profits. But for Michelin the aqcuisition is strategic; its cost is secondary.

Sources: Adapted from *Wall Street Journal,* January 5, 1990, pp. 1–8; *Business Week,* October 9, 1989, p. 5.

example, in a factory the important ingredient in the P/OM mission may be on-time shipment to customers (scheduling tactics). In an emergency care center, on the other hand, the focus may be on having the proper personnel present (human resource strategy) and pharmaceuticals available (inventory tactics). Each firm must determine its own way of finding competitive advantage. Michelin, as noted in the *POM in Action* box, "On a Roll," is pursuing competitive advantage by maintaining a focus on quality and market share.

The operations manager provides a means of transforming inputs into outputs. The transformations may be in terms of storage, transportation, manufacturing, dissemination of information, and utility of the product or service. *The operations manager's job is to implement a P/OM strategy that will increase the productivity of the transformation system and provide competitive advantage.*

Define Key Tasks. To assure maximum P/OM contribution to the organization, the operations department needs to focus on those key tasks that are identified as crucial to its success. The operations manager asks, "What activities must be done particularly well for a given operations strategy to be especially successful? Which

---

SAMPLE COMPANY MISSION

To pursue a diversified, growing, and profitable worldwide manufacturing business in electronic components, apparatus, and systems; and to service these products for industry, commerce, agriculture, government, and home.

SAMPLE PRODUCTION/OPERATIONS MANAGEMENT MISSION

To produce products consistent with the company's mission as the worldwide low-cost manufacturer.

SAMPLE P/OM DEPARTMENTAL MISSION

Product Design	To lead in research and engineering competencies in all areas of our primary business, designing and producing products and services with outstanding quality and inherent customer value.
Process Design and Equipment Selection	To determine and design or produce the production process and equipment that will be compatible with low-cost product, high quality, and a good quality of worklife for our employees at economical cost.
Layout	To achieve, through skill, imagination, and resourcefulness in plant layout and work methods, production effectiveness and efficiency while supporting a high quality of worklife for our employees.
Location and Facilities Engineering	To locate, design, and build efficient and economical facilities that will yield high value to the company, its employees, and the community.
Human Resource Management	To provide a good quality of worklife, with well-designed, safe, rewarding jobs, stable employment, and equitable pay, in exchange for outstanding individual contribution from employees at all levels.
Procurement	To cooperate with suppliers and subcontractors to develop stable, effective, and efficient sources of supply for those components that are to be procured from outside sources.
Production Control	To achieve high utilization of manufacturing facilities through effective scheduling.
Inventory Control	To achieve low investment in inventory consistent with high customer service levels and high facility utilization.
Quality Assurance and Control	To attain the exceptional quality that is consistent with our company mission and marketing objectives, by close attention to design, procurement, production, and field service opportunities for enhancing design.
Maintenance	To achieve high utilization of facilities and equipment by effective preventive maintenance and prompt repair of facilities and equipment.

elements contain the highest likelihood of failure, and which will require additional commitment of managerial, monetary, technological, and human resources?"

A sample set of mission statements for the major P/OM decision areas is shown in Figure 2.5.

FIGURE 2.5

Sample Mission for a Company, the Production/Operations Function, and the Major Departments in a Production/Operations Function.

A much stronger yen, the relentless attack by a most worthy competitor, Caterpillar, and the weakening of Komatsu's American position has required Komatsu continually to alter its strategy. In the latest strategy change, Komatsu joined with Dresser Industries to use Dresser's excess capacity in the United States to overcome the strong yen. In addition, the joint venture may help Komatsu gain market share, attain economies of scale, and increase production as markets and exchange rates change.

FIGURE 2.6

Strategy and Issues
During a Product's Life
Cycle.
(*Source:* Various; see for
instance, Michael E.
Porter, *Techniques for
Analyzing Industries and
Competitors,* New York,
The Free Press, 1980,
and Chester R. Watson,
*Dynamic Competitive
Strategy and Product Life
Cycles,* St. Charles, IL,
Challenge Books, 1974.)

	Introduction	Growth	Maturity	Decline
Company Strategy / Issues	Best period to increase market share R&D engineering are critical	Practical to change price or quality image Marketing critical Strengthen niche	Poor time to increase market share Competitive costs become critical Poor time to change price, image, or quality Defend position via fresh promotion and distribution approaches	Cost control critical
			Sales	
P/OM Strategy / Issues	Product design and development critical Frequent product and process design changes Overcapacity Short production runs High skilled-labor content High production costs Limited number of models Utmost attention to quality Quick elimination of market-revealed defects in design	Forecasting critical Product and process reliability Competitive product improvements and options Increase capacity Shift toward product oriented Enhance distribution	Standardization Less rapid product changes—more minor annual model changes Optimum capacity Increasing stability of manufacturing process Lower labor skills Long production runs Attention to product improvement and cost cutting Reexamination of necessity of design compromises	Little product differentiation Cost minimization Overcapacity in the industry Prune line to eliminate items not returning good margin Reduce capacity

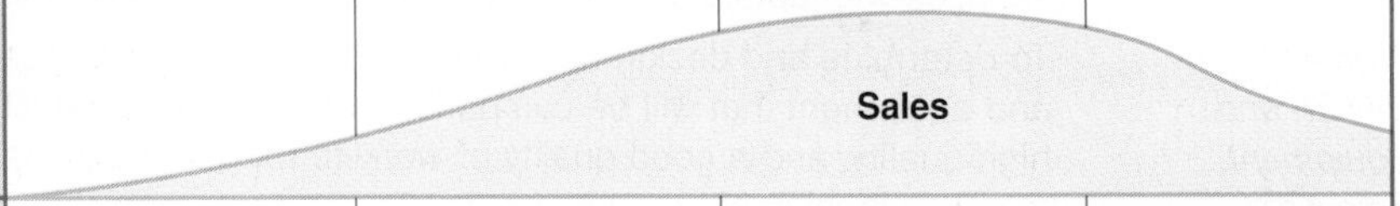

Strategy Dynamics

Changes in the environment and changes in the organization itself require changes
in strategy. *Strategy is dynamic because of changes in the environment.* An example
of how strategy must change as the environment changes is demonstrated by
Komatsu. Komatsu, an international manufacturer of large earth-moving equipment,
has had strategies of quality enhancement, product line growth, and cost reduction

TABLE 2.1 Characteristics of World-Class Production/Operations

WORLD-CLASS PRODUCT STRATEGY

The World-Class Firm:

Focuses on one or only a few products or technologies

Designs products to be quality robust and continually improves product quality

Continually introduces new products, and variations and options for those products

Provides strong communication between customer, product, process, and suppliers

Links product strategy and investment to market share, product life cycles, and breadth of product line

WORLD-CLASS PROCESS STRATEGY

The World-Class Firm:

Designs direct material flows with each operation adding value

Encourages development of special, uniquely efficient proprietary equipment or process

Generates a dollar of sales with low capital requirements relative to the competition

Makes investment decisions on a criterion of winning profitable orders

Uses ROI as only one criterion for investment

WORLD-CLASS LOCATION STRATEGY

The World-Class Firm:

Finds locations that yield an advantage in cost, revenue, customer service, and market penetration

Pursues opportunities internationally

WORLD-CLASS LAYOUT STRATEGY

The World-Class Firm:

Uses work cells and focused facilities

Adds value with each movement of material by streamlining material flow

WORLD-CLASS PROCUREMENT STRATEGY

The World-Class Firm:

Suppliers are evaluated and then developed into world-class performers

Suppliers are integrated into the production system and the requirements of the end customer

Suppliers develop just-in-time techniques

WORLD-CLASS HUMAN RESOURCES STRATEGY

In the World-Class Firm:

A high degree of employee participation and commitment to objectives is present

Few job classifications exist

Employees are cross-trained and can perform a variety of jobs

Open communication is enhanced via few hierarchical levels

Mutual trust and respect are fostered, resulting in a high level of morale

Outstanding staffing via effective recruiting, selection, training, and retention is attained

WORLD-CLASS SCHEDULING TACTICS

In the World-Class Firm:

Capital is effectively used by high utilization

Processes are shut down when demand does not exist

Facility and capital utilization is enhanced via effective scheduling

Stable production schedules (requirements) are developed

Flexibility in production scheduling to meet customer demand is maintained

WORLD-CLASS INVENTORY TACTICS

The World-Class Firm:

Minimizes investment in inventory

Uses JIT techniques to minimize work-in-process inventory and to ensure consistent quality

Uses cycle counting, not annual physical inventories

WORLD-CLASS QUALITY TACTICS

In the World-Class Firm:

Quality is approached via quality management, not quality control

Employee participation in quality enhancement is widespread

Quality is the major determinant of supplier relationships

Continuous quality improvement is seen as a major way to reduce cost as well as win orders

WORLD-CLASS MAINTENANCE TACTICS

In the World-Class Firm:

Preventive maintenance is excellent, reducing variability in throughput

Operating employees are trained to do equipment inspection and minor preventive maintenance within the P/OM function. Komatsu has altered those strategies as the environment has changed.[7]

Second, *strategy is dynamic because of changes within the organization.* All areas of the firm are subject to changes. Changes may be in a variety of areas including procurement, finance, technology, and product life. All may make a difference in an organization's strengths and weaknesses and hence its strategy. Figure 2.6 on page 36 shows possible change in both overall strategy and P/OM strategy during the product's life cycle.

Competitive Advantage

Competitive advantage

When the operations strategy is well integrated with other functional areas of the firm and supports the overall company objectives, competitive advantage can be created. A well-directed operations function increases productivity *and* generates a competitive advantage. **Competitive advantage** implies the creation of a system that has a unique advantage over competitors.

World-class P/OM function

Moreover, firms that compete successfully in the global economy are known as world-class firms. Most such firms, be they manufacturing or service firms, will have P/OM functions that are world class. A **world-class P/OM function** is one that obtains continuous improvement in meeting customer requirements through excellence in the transformation process.

In this text we identify ten strategies and tactics that can make production/operations outstanding. We also introduce the characteristics of world-class firms. These characteristics are addressed as we discuss the various strategic and tactical decisions of P/OM in each chapter. They are summarized in Table 2.1 on page 37.

A world-class P/OM function can contribute to competitive advantage, making the organization successful today and providing products, services, and jobs for tomorrow.

SUMMARY

P/OM is a major function that can contribute in a significant way to the competitiveness of an organization. Organizations realistically identify their strengths and weaknesses. Then they develop effective missions and strategies that account for these strengths and weaknesses and complement the opportunities and threats of the environment. If this is done well, the organization can have competitive advantage and be a world-class performer.

KEY TERMS

System (p. 24)   TOWS (p. 26)
Suboptimize (p. 25)   PIMS (p. 33)
Mission (p. 25)   Competitive advantage (p. 38)
Strategy (p. 25)   World-class P/OM function (p. 38)

[7] Gary Hamel and C. K. Prahalad, "Strategic Intent," *Harvard Business Review* **67,** 3 (May–June 1989): 63–76.

SOLVED PROBLEM

Solved Problem 2.1

How does a company in the very mature and established meat-packing industry win a competitive advantage?[8] Iowa Beef Packers was able to win a strong competitive advantage by restructuring traditional beef processing operations. In beef packing, traditional beef processing operations involved raising cattle on scattered farms and ranches, shipping them live to labor-intensive, unionized slaughtering plants, and then transporting whole sides of beef to grocery retailers whose butcher departments cut them into smaller pieces and packaged them for sale to grocery shoppers.

Solution

Iowa Beef Packers revamped traditional operations with a radically different strategy. Large automated plants employing nonunion labor were built near economically transportable supplies of cattle. Then the meat was partially butchered at the processing plant into smaller high-yield cuts (sometimes sealed in plastic ready for purchase), boxed, and shipped to retailers. Iowa Beef Packers' inbound cattle transportation expenses, traditionally a major-cost item, were cut significantly by avoiding major losses that occurred when live animals were shipped long distances. Additionally, major outbound shipping-cost savings were achieved by not having to ship whole sides of beef with their high waste factor. Iowa Beef's strategy was so successful that it was, by 1985, the largest U.S. meatpacker, surpassing the former industry leaders, Swift, Wilson, and Armour.

DISCUSSION QUESTIONS

1. Describe the registration system at your university. What are its inputs, transformations, and outputs?

2. Would the complex system in which productions/operations managers operate be different with faster feedback loops?

3. What are the similarities and differences in the transformation process between a fast-food restaurant and a computer manufacturer?

4. Identify the ten strategic and tactical decisions of operations management.

5. Identify the transformation that takes place in your automobile repair garage. What are the manifestations of the ten production and operation management (P/OM) decisions at that garage? That is, how is each of the ten decisions accomplished? (Figure 2.3 may be helpful.)

6. Answer question 5 for some other enterprise of your choosing.

7. Based on what you know of the automobile industry, how has the P/OM strategy of General Motors or Ford changed in the last ten years?

8. As a library assignment, identify the mission of a firm and the strategy that supports that mission.

---

[8] Adapted from information in Michael E. Porter, *Competitive Advantage* (New York: Free Press, 1985) p. 109; Arthur A. Thompson, Jr., and A. J. Strickland III, *Strategy Formulation and Implementation* (Homewood, IL: BPI/Irwin, 1989).

CASE STUDY

Minit-Lube, Inc.

In recent years a substantial market has developed for automobile tune-up and lubrication shops. This demand came about because of the change in consumer buying patterns as self-service gas stations proliferated. Consumers acquired the habit of pumping their own gas; this has made a second stop necessary for oil and lubrication. Consequently, Minit-Lube and Jiffy-Lube developed a strategy to accommodate this opportunity.

Minit-Lube stations perform oil changes, lubrication, and interior cleaning in a spotless environment. The buildings are clean, painted white, and surrounded by neatly trimmed landscaping. To facilitate fast service, cars can be driven through three abreast. At Minit-Lube the customer is greeted by service representatives who are graduates of the Minit-Lube school in Salt Lake City. The Minit-Lube school is not unlike McDonald's Hamburger University near Chicago, or Holiday Inn's training school in Memphis, Tennessee. The greeter takes the order, which typically includes fluid checks (oil, water, brake fluid, transmission fluid, differential grease) and the necessary lubrication, as well as filter changes for air and oil. Service personnel in neat uniforms move into action; the standard three-person

team has one person checking fluid levels under the hood; another is assigned interior vacuuming and window cleaning; the third is in the garage pit, removing the oil filter, draining the oil, checking the differential and transmission, and lubricating as necessary. Precise task assignments and good training are designed to put the car in and out of the bay in ten minutes. The idea is to charge no more, and hopefully less, than gas stations, automotive repair chains, and auto dealers, while providing better service.

Discussion Questions

1. What constitutes better service? How does the Minit-Lube operations strategy provide competitive advantage? (*Hint:* Evaluate how Minit-Lube's traditional competitors perform the ten decisions of operations management versus how Minit-Lube performs them.)

2. Is it likely that Minit-Lube or Jiffy-Lube have increased productivity over their more traditional competitors? Why? How would we measure productivity in this industry?

BIBLIOGRAPHY

Buffa, E. S. *Meeting the Competitive Challenge.* Homewood, IL: Dow Jones-Irwin, 1984.

Drucker, P. F. "The Emerging Theory of Manufacturing." *Harvard Business Review* (May–June 1990): 94.

Edmondson, H. E., and S. C. Wheelwright. "Outstanding Manufacturing in the Coming Decade." *California Management Review* **31** (Summer 1989): 70–90.

Fine, C. H., and A. C. Hax. "Manufacturing Strategy: A Methodology and an Illustration." *Interfaces* **15** (November–December 1985): 28–46.

Forrester, J. *Industrial Dynamics.* Cambridge, MA: MIT Press, 1964.

Gale, B. T. "Can More Capital Buy Higher Productivity," *Harvard Business Review* **58,** 4 (July–August 1980): 78–86.

Ginzberg, E. "The Service Sector of the U.S. Economy." *Scientific American* **244** (March 1981): 48–55.

Haas, E. A. "Breakthrough Manufacturing." *Harvard Business Review* **65,** 2 (March–April 1987): 75–81.

Hall, R. W. *Attaining Manufacturing Excellence.* Homewood, IL: Dow Jones-Irwin, 1987.

Hanson, B. P. "Improving Productivity through Systems Management." *Managerial Planning* (May–June 1980): 14.

Harrigan, K. R. *Strategic Flexibility—A Management Guide for Changing Times.* Lexington, Mass.: 1985.

Hayes, R. H., S. Wheelwright, and K. B. Clark. *Dynamic Manufacturing.* New York: The Free Press, 1988.

Hayes, R. H. and S. C. Wheelwright. *Restoring Competitive Edge.* New York: John Wiley, 1984.

Hill, T. *Manufacturing Strategy Text and Cases.* Homewood, IL: Dow Jones-Irwin, 1989.

Hofer, C. W. "Toward a Contingency Theory of Business Strategy." *Academy of Management Journal* **18** (December 1975): 784–810.

Kaplan, R. S. "Yesterday's Accounting Undermines Production." *Harvard Business Review* **62,** 4 (July–August 1984): 95–101.

Karatsu, H. *Tough Words for American Industry.* Cambridge, MA: Productivity Press, 1988.

Kotler, P., L. Fahey, and S. Jatusripitak. *The New Competition.* Englewood Cliffs, NJ: Prentice-Hall, 1985.

Krajewski, L. J., B. E. King, L. P. Ritzman, and D. S. Wong. "A Viable U.S. Manufacturing Strategy: Reshaping the Production Environment." *Operations Management Review* **2** 3 (Spring 1984): 4–10.

Lieberman, M. B., L. J. Lau, and M. D. Williams. "Firm-Level Productivity and Management Influence: A Comparison of U.S. and Japanese Automobile Producers." *Management Science* **36** (October 1990): 1193.

Marucheck, A., R. Pannesi, and C. Anderson. "An Exploratory Study of the Manufacturing Strategy Process in Practice." *Journal of Operations Management* **9** (January 1990): 101.

Mehl, W. "Strategic Management of Operations: A Top Management

Perspective." *Strategic Management of Operations* (September 1983): 1–10.

Ohmae, K. "The Borderless World." *Sloan Management Review* **32** (Winter 1991): 117.

Ohmae, K. "Getting Back to Strategy." *Harvard Business Review* **66** (November–December 1988): 149–156.

Peterson, R. S. "The Critical Issues for Manufacturing Management." *Operations Management Review* **2** (1984): 15–20.

Porter, M. E. *Competitive Strategy.* New York: The Free Press, 1980.

Porter, M. E. *The Competitive Advantage of Nations.* New York: The Free Press, 1990.

Schonberger, R. J. *Japanese Manufacturing Techniques: Nine Hidden Lessons in Simplicity.* Cambridge, MA: Productivity Press, 1982.

Skinner, W. *Manufacturing: The Formidable Competitive Weapon.* New York: John Wiley, 1985.

Skinner, W. "The Productivity Paradox." *Harvard Business Review* **64,** 4 (July–August 1986): 55–59.

Sloan, A. P. *My Years With General Motors.* New York: Doubleday, 1972.

Sumanth, D. J. *Productivity Engineering and Management.* New York: McGraw-Hill, 1984.

Stalk, George, Jr. "Time—The Next Source of Competitive Advantage." *Harvard Business Review* **66** (July–August 1988): 41–51.

Stephanou, S. *The Manufacturing Challenge from Concept to Production.* New York: Van Nostrand Reinhold, 1991.

Steudel, H. J., and P. Desruelle. *Manufacturing in the Nineties: How to Become a Mean, Lean, World-Class Competitor.* New York: Van Nostrand Reinhold, 1991.

Tzu, S. *The Art of War.* Translation by Samuel B. Griffith. London: Oxford University Press, 1971.

Womack, J. P., D. T. Jones, and D. Roos. *The Machine That Changed the World.* New York: Rawson Associates, 1990.

PART TWO

Decision-Making Techniques in P/OM

Techniques for assisting the P/OM in decision making are introduced in Chapter 3. The discussion begins with decision theory, payoff tables, and decision trees. In the Supplement, linear programming is presented.

Forecasting is crucial to determining the demand for products, the size of production facilities, and many other P/OM decisions. A variety of forecasting techniques are presented in Chapter 4. The supplement provides a review of basic statistical concepts and tools.

Finally, in Chapter 5 and its Supplement we introduce waiting line theory and simulation techniques. Both of these techniques are powerful tools to aid P/OM decision makers.

Decision-Making Tools

INTRODUCTION

Operations managers are decision makers. To carry out the goals of their organizations, managers must have an understanding of how decisions are made and know what important decision-making tools are available to them. To a great extent, the success or failure that people and companies experience depends on the quality of their decisions. The manager who insisted on launching the space shuttle *Challenger* (which exploded in 1986) did not rise to power within NASA. The manager who headed the top-selling Mustang's design team eventually became president of Ford.[1]

Model

This chapter and supplement (as well as the next two chapters, which together comprise Part II of the text) use the popular term *model* over and over again. Models lie at the heart of the scientific approach to P/OM decision making. Quite simply, a **model** is a representation of reality. It can be a physical model, such as a scale model of a factory or an airplane for use in a wind tunnel. Or it can be a mathematical model, which is even more common. One simple mathematical model you learned in geometry is the formula Area = Length × Width. But other models can be much more complex and can even represent the operation of a business. Such a business model would have variables to account for production costs, transportation costs, inventory costs, and data-handling costs, as well as a wide variety of other possible inputs and outputs.

Models and the techniques of scientific management can help managers to:

1. gain deeper insight into the nature of business relationships;
2. find better ways to assess values in such relationships;
3. see a way of reducing, or at least understanding, uncertainty that surrounds business plans and actions.

Throughout this book you will be introduced to a broad range of models and tools that help operations managers make better decisions. This chapter first examines the analytic decision-making process, then categorizes the models you will be dealing with, and finally introduces decision theory, which is one of the most popular decision-making tools in use.

THE DECISION PROCESS

What makes the difference between a good decision and a bad decision? A "good" decision, using scientific or analytic decision making, is based on logic, considers all available data and possible alternatives, and follows these six steps:

1. **Define the problem and the factors that influence it.**
   This means stating the problem clearly and concisely, which in many cases is the most important and difficult step.
2. **Establish decision criteria and goals.**
   Managers must develop specific and measurable objectives. Most firms have more than just a goal of maximizing profit.

---

[1] He also later became president of Chrysler Motors. His name, of course, is Lee Iacocca.

3. **Formulate a model or relationship between goals and variables.**
   In other words, we want to develop a representation of the situation—a model. Most models presented in this book contain one or more variables. A variable, as the name implies, is a measurable quantity that may vary or is subject to change.

4. **Identify and evaluate alternatives.**
   This step means generating as many solutions to the problem as possible (and usually quickly). A *range* or set of options is what most managers like to have.

5. **Select the best alternative.**
   This is the solution that best satisfies and is most consistent with the stated goals.

6. **Implement the decision.**
   Carrying out the actions indicated by the alternative that is finally selected is sometimes the most challenging phase of decision making. It involves task assignments and a timetable for implementation.

We should point out that these steps do not always follow one another without some cycling and backtracking. It is not unusual to have to modify one or more steps before the final results are implemented. Still, making "good" decisions in operations problems means performing all six of these steps.

MODELS FOR DECISION MAKING

We have introduced the decision process to aid decision making in operations management. When applied to operations management decisions, this process is closely tied to the use of models and "quantitative" analysis. Since mathematical models are an integral part of this text, in this section we want to give you an overview of their variety and uses.

We also think you should be aware that there are advantages and disadvantages of modeling. We use models to try to represent the reality of a real system by duplicating its important features, appearance, and characteristics. Models are not a panacea: indeed, most models are simplifications of the real world. The emphasis in this book is not on model building per se, but on the use of models to help operations managers make decisions. We think you should know

1. when a model is appropriate and what its assumptions and limitations are;
2. what purpose a model might serve in a particular problem;
3. how to use the model and produce results;
4. how to interpret, in management terms, the results of the model.

Advantages and Disadvantages of Using Models

The mathematical models to be presented in this book are tools that have become widely accepted by managers for several reasons.

1. They are less expensive and disruptive than experimenting with the real-world system.

2. They allow operations managers to ask "what if" types of questions (that is, questions such as "what if" my inventory cost increases 3% next year—how will profits change?).

3. They are built for management problems and encourage management input.

4. They force a consistent and systematic approach to the analysis of problems.

5. They require managers to be specific about constraints and goals relating to a problem.

6. They can help reduce the time needed in decision making.

The main limitations of models are:

1. They may be expensive and time-consuming to develop and test.

2. They are often misused and misunderstood (and feared) because of their mathematical complexity.

3. They tend to downplay the role and value of nonquantifiable information.

4. They often have assumptions that oversimplify the variables of the real world.

Categories of Mathematical Models

The general structure of the problem we face, the amount of information available, and the kind of data we can collect all help determine the appropriateness of a model. Here are *some* of the models you will see in this text.

1. *Algebraic models.* Algebra is a basic mathematical tool that can be used to help solve such common operations problems as break-even analysis and cost-benefit analysis.

2. *Statistical models.* Since many decisions involve uncertainties, the use of probability distributions and statistical theory is very important. Three statistical models are introduced:

    a) Forecasting—the process of making projections into the future of such variables as sales, costs, housing starts, or enrollments.

    b) Quality control—intended to help measure and regulate the degree to which a product or service meets specified standards.

    c) Decision theory—used in decision trees and decision tables to help represent and solve problems requiring decisions made under the condition of risk.

3. *Linear and mathematical programming models.* Linear programming is widely used in product-mix decisions, facility location analysis, production scheduling, labor allocation, and several other areas in operations analysis. The more general term, *mathematical programming,* is also used in this book.

4. *Queuing theory models.* Queuing analysis helps evaluate service systems by determining such factors as queue lengths, waiting time, and utilization rates.

5. *Simulation models.* Computer simulations of real-world systems are valuable tools for analyzing complex service systems, maintenance policies, and investment options.

6. *Inventory models.* Inventory control models are used to help manage a firm's inventory assets by recommending the best quantity and timing of ordering policies.

POM _in action_

Apollo 11 Launch Owes Success to Management Science

Back in 1969, Robert Freitag was head of the NASA team responsible for landing the *Apollo 11* safely on the moon. That mission's success was due to management science concepts and models that allowed thousands of tasks to meet the single objective of getting a man to the moon and home safely again. Here are Freitag's comments about that task:

"I think the feeling most of us in NASA shared was, 'My gosh, now we really have to do it.' It was a pretty awesome event.

"What you do is break it down into pieces: the launch site, the launch vehicles, the spacecraft, the lunar module, and worldwide tracking networks, for example. Then, once these pieces are broken down, you assign them to one organization or another. They, in turn, take those small pieces, like the rocket, and break it down into engines or structures or guidance equipment. And this breakdown, or 'tree,' is the really tough part about managing.

"Three NASA centers, Huntsville (to build the rocket), Houston (to build the spacecraft), and Cape Canaveral (to launch), were the work centers, and they could break their pieces down into about 10 or 20 major industrial contractors who could build the pieces of the rocket. And then each of those industrial contractors would break them down into maybe 20 to 30 or 50 subcontractors—and they, in turn, would break them down into perhaps 300,000 or 400,000 pieces, each of which would end up being the job of one person. But you need to be sure that the pieces come together at the right time, and that they work when put together. Management science helps with that. The total number of people who worked on the *Apollo* was about 400,000 to 500,000, all working toward a single objective."

Source: Introduction to Contemporary Mathematics, New York: W. H. Freeman and Company, 1988, pp. 2–3.

7. *Network models*. Techniques such as program evaluation and review technique (PERT) and critical path method (CPM) assist managers to schedule, control, and monitor large projects such as building a ship or a shopping center.

Let us now proceed with our discussion of modeling by introducing decision theory, one of the most widely used and useful of all decision making tools.

DECISION THEORY

Decision theory is an analytic approach to selecting the best alternative or course of action. It is used in a wide variety of P/OM situations ranging from new product analysis (Chapter 6), to location planning (Chapter 8), to equipment selection (Chapter 7), to scheduling (Chapter 15), to maintenance planning (Chapter 18).

There are typically three classifications in decision theory. They depend upon the degree of certainty of the possible outcomes or consequences facing the decision maker. The three types of decision models are:

1. *Decision making under certainty*—the *decision maker knows with certainty* the consequence or outcome of any alternative or decision choice. For exam-

ple, a decision maker knows with complete certainty that a $100 deposit in a checking account will result in an increase of $100 in the balance of that account.

2. *Decision making under risk*—the *decision maker knows the probability* of occurrence of the outcomes or consequences for each choice. We may not know whether it will rain tomorrow, but we may know that the probability of rain is .3.

3. *Decision making under uncertainty*—the *decision maker does not know the probability* of occurrence of the outcomes for each alternative. For example, the probability that a Democrat will be president twenty years from now is not known.

In decision making under certainty, the decision maker knows the outcome of his or her actions, and he or she will choose the alternative that will maximize his or her well-being or will result in the best outcome. In decision making under risk, the decision maker will attempt to maximize his or her *expected* well-being. The decision approach typically employed is maximization of expected monetary value. The criteria for decision making under uncertainty that we will discuss include *maximax, maximin,* and *equally likely.*

Fundamentals of Decision Theory

Regardless of the complexity of a decision or the sophistication of the technique used to analyze the decision, all decision makers are faced with alternatives and states of nature. The following notation will be used in this chapter:

1. Terms:
   a) *Alternative*—a course of action or a strategy that may be chosen by a decision maker (for example, not carrying an umbrella tomorrow).
   b) *State of nature*—an occurrence or a situation over which the decision maker has little or no control (for example, tomorrow's weather).

2. Symbols used in a decision tree:
   a) □ — a decision node from which one of several alternatives may be selected.
   b) ○ — a state of nature node out of which one state of nature will occur.

To present a manager's decision alternatives, we can develop *decision trees* and *decision tables* using the above symbols.

In constructing a decision tree, we must be sure that all alternatives and states of nature are in their correct and logical places and that we include *all* possible alternatives and states of nature.

Example 1

The Thompson Lumber Company is investigating the possibility of producing and marketing backyard storage sheds. Undertaking this project would require the construction of either a large or a small manufacturing plant. The market for the product produced—storage sheds—could be either favorable or unfavorable. Thompson, of course, has the option of not developing the new product line at all. A decision tree for this situation is presented in Figure 3.1.

FIGURE 3.1

Thompson's decision tree.

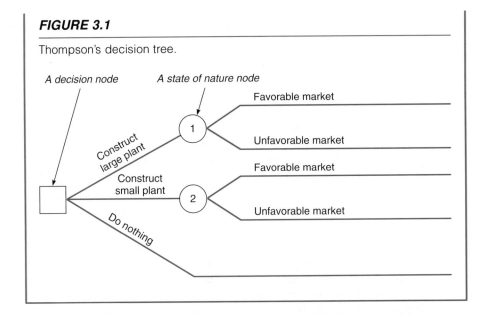

Decision Tables

We may also develop a decision or payoff table to help Thompson Lumber define its alternatives. For any alternative and a particular state of nature, there is a consequence or outcome, which is usually expressed as a monetary value. This is called a conditional value. Note that all of the alternatives in Example 2 are listed down the left side of the table, that states of nature (outcomes) are listed across the top, and that conditional values (payoffs) are in the body of the **decision table.**

Decision table

Example 2

We construct a decision table for Thompson Lumber, including conditional values based on the following information. With a favorable market, a large facility would give Thompson's a net profit of $200,000. If the market is unfavorable, a $180,000 net loss would occur. A small plant would result in a net profit of $100,000 in a favorable market, but a net loss of $20,000 would be encountered if the market was unfavorable.

TABLE 3.1 Decision Table with Conditional Values for Thompson Lumber.

| | STATES OF NATURE | |
ALTERNATIVES	Favorable Market	Unfavorable Market
Construct large plant	$200,000	−$180,000
Construct small plant	$100,000	−$20,000
Do nothing	$0	$0

Decision Making Under Uncertainty. When there is complete uncertainty as to which state of nature in a decision table may occur (that is, we cannot even assess probabilities for each possible outcome), we turn to three criteria for decision making under uncertainty:

Maximax

1. **Maximax**—this criterion finds an alternative that *max*imizes the *max*imum outcome or consequence for every alternative. First, we find the maximum outcome within every alternative, and then we pick the alternative with the maximum number. Since this decision criterion locates the alternative with the *highest* possible *gain,* it has been called an "optimistic" decision criterion.

Maximin

2. **Maximin**—this criterion finds the alternative that *max*imizes the *min*imum outcome or consequence for every alternative. First, we find the minimum outcome within every alternative, and then we pick the alternative with the maximum number. Since this decision criterion locates the alternative that has the *least* possible *loss,* it has been called a "pessimistic" decision criterion.

Equally likely

3. **Equally likely**—this decision criterion finds the alternative with the highest average outcome. We first calculate the average outcome for every alternative, which is the sum of all outcomes divided by the number of outcomes. Then we pick the alternative with the maximum number. The equally likely approach assumes that all probabilities of occurrence for the states of nature are equal and thus each state of nature is equally likely.

Example 3 applies each of these approaches to the Thompson Lumber Company.

Example 3

Given Thompson's decision table of Example 2, determine the maximax, maximin, and equally likely decision criteria.

1. The maximax choice is to construct a large plant. This is the *max*imum of the *max*imum number within each row, or alternative.
2. The maximin choice is to do nothing. This is the *max*imum of the *min*imum number within each row, or alternative.
3. The equally likely choice is to construct a small plant. This is the maximum of the average outcome of each alternative. This approach assumes that all outcomes for any alternative are *equally likely.*

TABLE 3.2

ALTERNATIVES	STATES OF NATURE		Maximum in Row	Minimum in Row	Row Average
	Favorable Market	Unfavorable Market			
Construct large plant	$200,000	−$180,000	$200,000	−$180,000	$10,000
Construct small plant	$100,000	−$20,000	$100,000	−$20,000	$40,000
Do nothing	$0	$0	$0	$0	$0
			Maximax ↑	Maximin ↑	Equally likely ↑

Decision Making under Risk. Decision making under risk, a more common occurrence, is a probabilistic decision situation. Several possible states of nature may occur, each with a given probability. Given a decision table with conditional values and probability assessments for all states of nature, we can determine the **expected monetary value (EMV)** for each alternative. This figure represents the expected value or *average* return for each alternative if we could repeat the decision a large number of times. Picking the alternative that has the maximum EMV is one of the most popular decision criteria.

Expected monetary value (EMV)

The EMV for an alternative is just the sum of possible payoffs of the alternative, each weighted by the probability of that payoff occurring.

EMV (Alternative i) = (Payoff of 1st state of nature) × (Probability of 1st state of nature)
+ (Payoff of 2nd state of nature) × (Probability of 2nd state of nature)
+ · · · + (Payoff of last state of nature) × (Probability of last state of nature)

The following example illustrates the computational procedure typically used to determine the maximum EMV.

Example 4

Thompson Lumber's P/OM manager believes that the probability of a favorable market is exactly the same as that of an unfavorable market; that is, each state of nature has a .50 chance. We can now determine the EMV for each alternative (see Table 3.3).

1. EMV(A_1) = (.5)($200,000) + (.5)(–$180,000) = $10,000
2. EMV(A_2) = (.5)($100,000) + (.5)(–$20,000) = $40,000
3. EMV(A_3) = (.5)($0) + (.5)($0) = $0

The maximum EMV is seen in alternative A_2. Thus, according to the EMV decision criterion, we would build the small facility.

TABLE 3.3

ALTERNATIVES	STATES OF NATURE	
	Favorable Market	Unfavorable Market
Construct large plant (A_1)	$200,000	–$180,000
Construct small plant (A_2)	$100,000	–$20,000
Do nothing (A_3)	$0	$0
Probabilities	.50	.50

Now suppose Thompson Lumber's P/OM manager has been approached by a marketing research firm that proposed to help him make the decision about whether or not to build the plant to produce storage sheds. The marketing researchers claim that their technical analysis will tell Thompson with certainty whether or not the market is favorable for the proposed product. In other words, it will change Thompson's environment from one of decision making under risk to one of decision making under certainty. This information could prevent Thompson Lumber from making a very expensive mistake. The marketing research firm would charge Thompson $65,000 for the information. What would you recommend to Thompson? Should the P/OM manager hire the firm to make the marketing study? Even if the information from the study is perfectly accurate, is it worth $65,000? What would it be worth? Although some of these questions are difficult to answer, determining the value of such *perfect information* can be very useful. It places an upper bound on what you would be willing to spend on information, such as that being sold by a marketing consultant. In the next section, we introduce the concept of the expected value of perfect information.

Expected Value of Perfect Information (EVPI). If a manager was able to determine which state of nature would occur, then he or she would know which decision to make. Once a manager knows which decision to make, the payoff increases because the payoff is now a certainty, not a probability. Since the payoff will increase with knowledge of which state of nature will occur, this knowledge has value. Therefore, we now look at how to determine the value of this information. We call this difference between the payoff under certainty and the payoff under risk the **expected value of perfect information (EVPI).**

Expected value of perfect information (EVPI)

Expected value under certainty

$$\text{EVPI} = \text{Expected value under certainty} - \text{Maximum EMV}$$

To find the EVPI, we must first compute the **expected value under certainty,** which is the expected or average return, if we have perfect information before a decision has to be made. In order to calculate this value, we choose the best alternative for each state of nature and multiply its payoff times the probability of occurrence of that state of nature.

Expected value under certainty = (Best outcome or consequence for 1st state of nature) × (Probability of 1st state of nature) + (Best outcome for 2nd state of nature) × (Probability of 2nd state of nature) + · · · + (Best outcome for last state of nature) × (Probability of last state of nature)

We will use the data and decision table from Example 4 to examine the expected value of perfect information. We do so in Example 5.

Example 5

By referring back to Table 3.3, Thompson Lumber's P/OM manager can calculate the maximum that he would pay for information, that is, the expected value of perfect information, or EVPI. He follows a two-stage process. First of all, the expected value under certainty is computed. Then, using this information, EVPI is calculated. The procedure is outlined as follows.

  1. The best outcome for the state of nature "favorable market" is "build a large facility" with a payoff of $200,000. The best outcome for the state of nature "unfavorable market" is "do nothing" with a payoff of $0. Expected value under certainty = ($200,000)(0.50) + ($0)(0.50) = $100,000. Thus, if we had perfect information, we would expect (on the average) $100,000 if the decision could be repeated many times.

2. The maximum EMV is $40,000, which is the expected outcome without perfect information.

$$EVPI = \text{Expected value under certainty} - \text{Maximum EMV}$$
$$= \$100,000 - \$40,000 = \$60,000$$

Thus the *most* Thompson Lumber should be willing to pay for perfect information is $60,000. This, of course, is again based on the assumption that the probability of each state of nature is 0.50.

Decision Trees

Decisions that lend themselves to display in a decision table also lend themselves to display in a decision tree. We should analyze some decisions, however, using decision trees. It is convenient to use a decision table in problems having one set of decisions and one set of states of nature. Many problems, however, include *sequential* decisions and states of nature. When there are two or more sequential decisions and later decisions are based on the outcome of prior ones, the decision tree approach becomes appropriate. A **decision tree** is a graphic display of the decision process that indicates decision alternatives, states of nature and their respective probabilities, and payoffs for each combination of alternative and state of nature.

Decision tree

Although we may apply all previously discussed decision criteria, expected monetary value (EMV) is the most commonly used and usually the most appropriate criterion for decision tree analysis. One of the first steps in the analysis is to graph the decision tree and to specify the monetary consequences of all contingencies or outcomes for a particular problem.

Analyzing problems with *decision trees* involves five steps:

1. Define the problem.
2. Structure or draw the decision tree.
3. Assign probabilities to the states of nature.
4. Estimate payoffs for each possible combination of alternatives and states of nature.
5. Solve the problem by computing expected monetary values (EMV) for each state of nature node. This is done by working *backward,* that is, starting at the right of the tree and working back to decision nodes on the left.

Example 6

A completed and solved decision tree for Thompson Lumber is presented in Figure 3.2. Note that the payoffs are placed at the right-hand side of each of the tree's branches. The probabilities (first used by Thompson in Example 4) are placed in parentheses next to each state of nature. The expected monetary

A temporary island in the Beaufort Sea off the northern coast of Alaska has been created by sea water projected into the sky. The water freezes immediately into cascading ice crystals and forms a solid mass. For the drilling of a test well, Amoco executives considered several *decision alternatives:* (1) an offshore platform, (2) a drill ship, (3) a gravel island, (4) a concrete island, or (5) the temporary island of ice. Using decision theory, they opted for the ice island, since the cost would be less than half that of the gravel island. In the summer, the ice would melt back to its natural state.

values for each state of nature node are then calculated and placed by their respective nodes. The EMV of the first node is $10,000. This represents the branch from the decision node to construct a large plant. The EMV for node 2, to construct a small plant, is $40,000. Building no plant or doing nothing has, of course, a payoff of $0. The branch leaving the decision node leading to the state of nature node with the highest EMV will be chosen. In Thompson's case, a small plant should be built.

FIGURE 3.2

Completed and solved decision tree for Thompson Lumber.

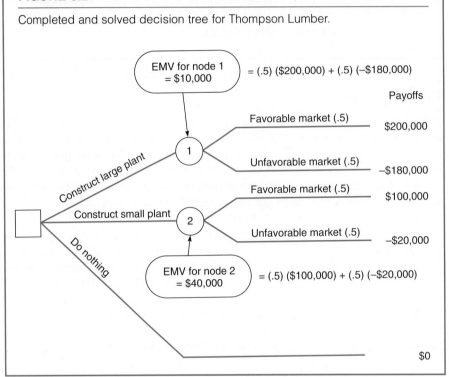

A More Complex Decision Tree. When a *sequence* of decisions must be made, decision trees are much more powerful tools than are decision tables. Let's say that Thompson Lumber has two decisions to make, with the second decision dependent on the outcome of the first. Before deciding about building a new plant, Thompson has the option of conducting its own marketing research survey, at a cost of $10,000. The information from this survey could help it decide whether to build a large plant, a small plant, or not to build at all. Thompson Lumber recognizes that such a market survey will not provide it with *perfect* information, but may *help* quite a bit nevertheless.

Thompson's new decision tree is represented in Figure 3.3 of Example 7. Take a careful look at this more complex tree. Note that *all possible outcomes and alternatives* are included in their logical sequence. This is one of the strengths of using decision trees in making decisions. The manager is forced to examine all possible outcomes, including unfavorable ones. He or she is also forced to make decisions in a logical, sequential manner.

Example 7

Examining the tree in Figure 3.3, we see that Thompson's first decision point is whether to conduct the $10,000 market survey. If it chooses *not* to do the study (the lower part of the tree), it can either build a large plant, a small plant, or no plant. This is Thompson's second decision point. The market will either be favorable (.50 probability) or unfavorable (also .50 probability) if it builds. The payoffs for each of the possible consequences are listed along the right-hand side. As a matter of fact, this lower portion of Thompson's tree is *identical* to the simpler decision tree shown in Figure 3.2.

FIGURE 3.3

Larger decision tree with payoffs and probabilities for Thompson Lumber.

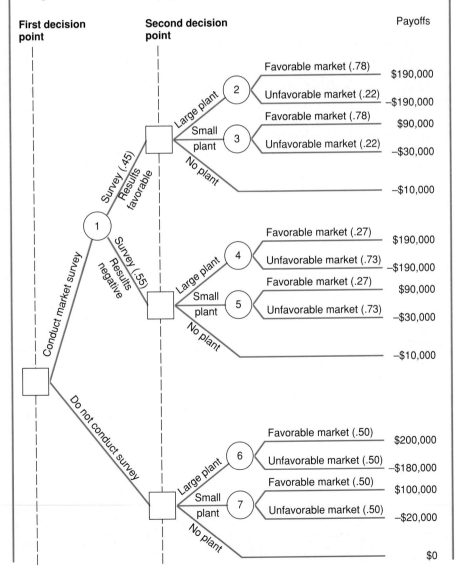

| First decision point | Second decision point | | Payoffs |

Node 2 (Large plant):
- Favorable market (.78) — $190,000
- Unfavorable market (.22) — –$190,000

Node 3 (Small plant):
- Favorable market (.78) — $90,000
- Unfavorable market (.22) — –$30,000

No plant — –$10,000

Survey (.45) Results favorable

Node 1

Survey (.55) Results negative

Node 4 (Large plant):
- Favorable market (.27) — $190,000
- Unfavorable market (.73) — –$190,000

Node 5 (Small plant):
- Favorable market (.27) — $90,000
- Unfavorable market (.73) — –$30,000

No plant — –$10,000

Conduct market survey

Do not conduct survey

Node 6 (Large plant):
- Favorable market (.50) — $200,000
- Unfavorable market (.50) — –$180,000

Node 7 (Small plant):
- Favorable market (.50) — $100,000
- Unfavorable market (.50) — –$20,000

No plant — $0

The upper part of Figure 3.3 reflects the decision to conduct the market survey. State of nature node number 1 has two branches coming out of it. Let us say there is a 45% chance that the survey results will indicate a favorable market for the storage sheds. We also note that the probability is .55 that the survey results will be negative.

The rest of the probabilities shown in parentheses in Figure 3.3 are all *conditional* probabilities. For example, .78 is the probability of a favorable market for the sheds *given* a favorable result from the market survey. Of course, you would expect to find a high probability of a favorable market given that the research indicated that the market was good. Don't forget, though; there is a chance that Thompson's $10,000 market survey didn't result in perfect or even reliable information. Any market research study is subject to error. In this case, there's a 22% chance that the market for sheds will be unfavorable given that the survey results are positive.

Likewise, we note that there is a 27% chance that the market for sheds will be favorable given that Thompson's survey results are negative. The probability is much higher, .73, that the market will actually be unfavorable given that the survey was negative.

Finally, when we look to the payoff column in Figure 3.3, we see that $10,000—the cost of the marketing study—had to be subtracted from each of the top ten tree branches. Thus, a large plant with a favorable market would normally net a $200,000 profit. But because the market study was conducted, this figure is reduced by $10,000. In the unfavorable case, the loss of $180,000 would increase to $190,000. Similarly, conducting the survey and building *no plant* now results in a –$10,000 payoff.

With all probabilities and payoffs specified, we can start calculating the expected monetary value of each of the branches. We begin at the end or right-hand side of the decision tree and work back toward the origin (see Figure 3.4). When we finish, the best decision will be known.

1. Given favorable survey results,

   EMV(node 2) = (.78)($190,000) + (.22)(–$190,000) = $106,400
   EMV(node 3) = (.78)($90,000)+ (.22)(–$30,000) = $63,600

   The EMV of no plant in this case is –$10,000. Thus, if the survey results are favorable, a large plant should be built.

2. Given negative survey results,

   EMV(node 4) = (.27)($190,000) + (.73)(–$190,000) = –$87,400
   EMV(node 5) = (.27)($90,000) + (.73)(–$30,000) = $2,400

   The EMV of no plant is again –$10,000 for this branch. Thus, given a negative survey result, Thompson should build a small plant with an expected value of $2,400.

3. Continuing on the upper part of the tree and moving backward, we compute the expected value of conducting the market survey.

   EMV(node 1) = (.45)($106,400) + (.55)($2,400) = $49,200

4. If the market survey is *not* conducted,

   EMV(node 6) = (.50)($200,000) + (.50)(–$180,000) = $10,000
   EMV(node 7) = (.50)($100,000) + (.50)(–$20,000) = $40,000

The EMV of no plant is $0. Thus, building a small plant is the best choice, given the marketing research is not performed.

5. Since the expected monetary value of conducting the survey is $49,200—versus an EMV of $40,000 for not conducting the study—the best choice is to *seek marketing information*. If the survey results are favorable, Thompson should build the large plant; but if the research is negative, it should build the small plant.

FIGURE 3.4

Thompson's decision tree with EMVs shown. The short parallel lines mean "prune" that branch, as it is less favorable than another available option and may be dropped.

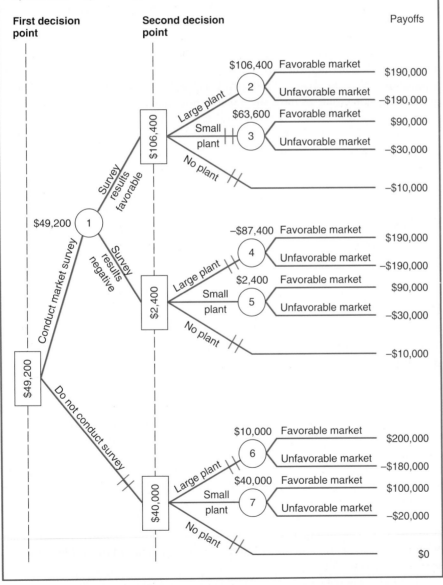

SUMMARY

This chapter examined the decision-making process that operations managers employ to help reach their organizations' goals. We saw that this process involves six steps:

1. defining the problem;
2. setting goals;
3. formulating a model;
4. identifying alternative solutions;
5. selecting the best alternative;
6. implementing the decision.

There are many categories of models that will be introduced in this book—they include schematic, algebraic, forecasting, quality control, decision theory, queuing, simulation, inventory, and network models. One of the most widely used models in operations decisions is decision theory. Decision trees and tables are especially useful for making decisions under risk and uncertainty. Investments in research and development, plant and equipment, and even new buildings and structures can be analyzed with decision theory. Problems in inventory control, aggregate planning, maintenance, scheduling, and production control are just a few other decision theory applications. Another powerful tool that is helpful in operations planning is linear programming, the topic of the supplement to this chapter.

KEY TERMS

Model (p. 44)
Decision table (p. 49)
Maximax (p. 50)
Maximin (p. 50)
Equally likely (p. 50)

Expected monetary value (EMV) (p. 51)
Expected value of perfect information (p. 52)
Expected value under certainty (p. 52)
Decision tree (p. 53)

USING AB:POM

Solving Examples 2 through 5 (Thompson Lumber) with AB:POM

AB:POM, which stands for *Allyn and Bacon Publishing: Production and Operations Management Software,* is a powerful yet user-friendly microcomputer program that accompanies this book. AB:POM can be used in many chapters to solve homework problems and textbook examples. In this section, we would like to introduce you to its use in calculating expected values, maximins, and maximaxes for decision table problems. Homework problems marked throughout the book with a computer symbol can be solved by AB:POM. General use details are provided in Appendix F, at the end of this text.

The general framework for decision tables is given by the number of options available to the decision maker and the number of scenarios that might occur. In our example we will set up a table with three decision options and possible scenarios, as seen in Program 3.1.

The following data are to be entered onto this initial data screen:

PROGRAM 3.1

AB:POM's Decision Table Program with General Screens Shown for a Three-Alternative, Two States-of-Nature Problem

———————————————————— Decision Tables ————————————————————

Number of alternatives (1-10) 3   Number of nature states (1-8) 2
Profits   -maximize profits

———————————————————————— Sample Screen ————————————————————————

Probability->   0.000   0.000
                 state 1 state 2
alternatv 1   0   0
alternatv 2   0   0
alternatv 3   0 .   0

1. *Scenario probabilities.* These occur at the top of the screen after the arrow following "Probability." The maximum probability that may be entered is 1; and the minimum is 0, which also is the default setting at the first screen. The program will issue a warning message if the probabilities do not sum to 1.

2. *Scenario names.* Names for the scenario may be entered. The default names are shown in the sample screen. The maximum length of a name is seven characters.

3. *Option names.* Naming options is possible with length up to 12 characters.

4. *Profits or costs.* The profit (cost) for each combination of options and scenarios is to be entered. The maximum number of digits is seven. This may require some rescaling but the rescaling is very straightforward.

In order to demonstrate the output we use the Thompson Lumber problem data from Examples 2 through 5. The sample problem and output screen appear in Program 3.2. Note that the words and numbers shaded were inputs by the user.

Program 3.2

AB:POM Output for Examples 2–5 (Thompson Lumber)

```
               THOMPSON  LUMBER  EXAMPLES  2-5
Probability ->   0.500      0.500

                FAV MKT   BAD MKT     EMV    Row Min   Row Max
LG. FACILITY    200000   -180000    10000   -180000    200000
SM. FACILITY    100000    -20000    40000    -20000    100000
DO NOTHING           0         0     0.00      0.00      0.00
                column maximum ->   40000      0.00    200000
The maximum expected monetary value is 40000 given by SM. FACILITY
The maximin is      0.00 given by DO NOTHING
The maximax is    200000 given by LG. FACILITY

PERFECT           200000      0.00  100000<-EV under certn
The expected value of perfect information is 60000
```

Optional outputs from AB:POM's Decision Table module include the expected value of perfect information (EVPI) and the expected value under certainty.

SOLVED PROBLEMS

Solved Problem 3.1

Daily demand for cases of Royal Cola soda at Helen's Food Shop has always been five, six, or seven cases. Develop a decision tree that illustrates the decision alternatives as to whether to stock five, six, or seven cases.

Solution
The decision tree is shown in Figure 3.5.

FIGURE 3.5

Demand at Helen's Food Shop.

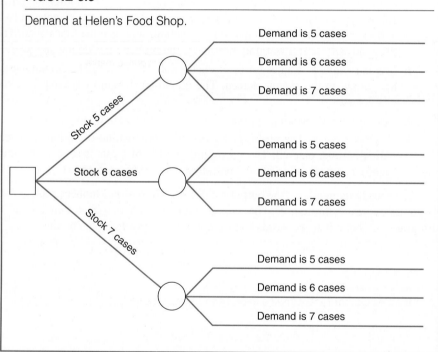

Solved Problem 3.2

A group of medical professionals is considering the construction of a private clinic. If the market is favorable, they could realize a net profit of $100,000. If the market is not favorable, they could lose $40,000. They have also been approached by a marketing research team that will perform a study of the market for an additional $5,000. The results of the study could be either favorable or unfavorable.

They would like to construct a decision tree and indicate its appropriate conditional monetary values. The decision tree is shown in Figure 3.6.

Solution

In determining the conditional monetary value for each branch, we need to subtract $5,000 from those branches of the decision tree that embody research, in other words, the top six terminal branches.

FIGURE 3.6

Decision tree for medical construction.

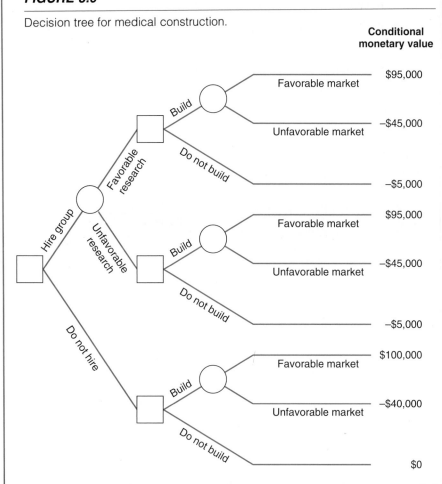

Conditional monetary value

$95,000

Favorable market

−$45,000

Unfavorable market

−$5,000

$95,000

Favorable market

−$45,000

Unfavorable market

−$5,000

$100,000

Favorable market

−$40,000

Unfavorable market

$0

After the conditional values have been determined for each possible outcome, or terminal branch, on the decision tree, the next step is to specify the probabilities of occurrence of each state of nature (see Figure 3.7). Such probabilities can be assessed by the manager/decision maker. Then we can analyze the entire decision tree. Note that all probabilities appear in parentheses next to their appropriate states of nature on the decision tree.

The solution of the decision displayed in Figure 3.7 is to hire the marketing research group. If the research is favorable, the clinic should be built. If the research is not favorable, the clinic should not be built. The decision to hire the marketing research team and make a decision based on their findings has an expected value of $36,140. The expected value of not hiring the marketing research team and building the clinic has an expected value of $30,000. Thus, the best decision is to hire the research team and base the decision on their conclusions.

FIGURE 3.7

Final decision tree reflecting alternatives facing group of medical professionals.

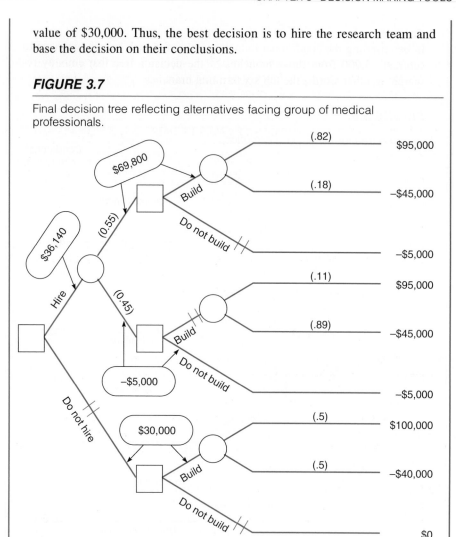

1. Describe each step in the decision process.

2. Why do operations managers build models? What kind are most useful?

3. Give an example of a good decision you made that resulted in a bad outcome. Also give an example of a bad decision you made that had a good outcome. Why was each decision good or bad?

4. What is an alternative? What is a state of nature?

5. Discuss the differences between decision making under certainty, under risk, and under uncertainty.

6. Mary Lillich is trying to decide whether to invest in real estate, stocks, or certificates of deposit. How well she does depends on whether the economy enters a period of recession or inflation. Develop a decision table (excluding the conditional values) to describe this situation.

7. Describe the meaning of EMV and EVPI. Provide an example in which EVPI can help a manager.

8. What techniques are used to solve decision-making problems under uncertainty? Which technique results in an optimistic decision? Which technique results in a pessimistic decision?

PROBLEMS

· **3.1** Kevin Stone is the principal owner of Stone Exploration, Inc. Presently Kevin is considering the possibility of purchasing some more equipment for Stone Exploration. His alternatives are shown in the following table.

EQUIPMENT	FAVORABLE MARKET	UNFAVORABLE MARKET
Drexel D1	$300,000	-$200,000
Oiler J	$250,000	-$100,000
Texan Valve	$75,000	-$18,000

For example, if Kevin purchases a Drexel D1, and there is a favorable market, he will realize a profit of $300,000. On the other hand, if the market is unfavorable, Kevin will suffer a loss of $200,000. But Kevin has always been a very optimistic decision maker.

a) What type of decision is Kevin facing?

b) What decision criterion should he use?

c) What alternative is best?

· **3.2** Julie Walters is considering building a restaurant near the campus. One set of business plans she is considering involves inclusion of a bar for beer sales; the other plan would not provide for beer sales. In either case Julie believes her chance of success to be .6 (and chance of failure to be .4). The proforma statements indicate that including the bar would yield $325,000. The proforma without the bar indicates the net gain would be only $250,000. Failure with the bar would be -$70,000; whereas without the bar failure would be -$20,000. Select the alternative for Julie, using expected monetary value as your decision criterion. Should Julie's business plan include bar sales?

: **3.3** Foto Color is a small supplier of chemicals and equipment used by some photographic stores to process 35-mm film. One product that Foto Color supplies is BC-6. Doug Niles, president of Foto Color, normally stocks 11, 12, or 13 cases of BC-6 each week. For each case that Doug sells, he receives a profit of $35. Because BC-6, like many photographic chemicals, has a very short shelf life, if a case is not sold by the end of the week Doug must discard it. Since each case costs Doug $56, he loses $56 for every case that is not sold by the end of the week. There is a probability of 0.45 of selling 11 cases, a probability of 0.35 of selling 12 cases, and a probability of 0.2 of selling 13 cases.

a) What is your recommended course of action?

b) If Doug is able to develop BC-6 with an ingredient that stabilizes BC-6 so it no longer has to be discarded, how would this change your recommended course of action?

: **3.4** Young Cheese Company is a small manufacturer of several different cheese products. One of the products is a cheese spread that is sold to retail outlets. Peg Young must decide how many cases of cheese spread to manufacture each month. The probability that the demand will be 6 cases is .1, for 7 cases it is .3, for 8 cases it is .5, and for 9 cases it is 1. The cost of every case is $45, and the price Peg gets for each case is $95. Unfortunately, any cases not sold by the end of the month are of no value as a result of spoilage. How many cases of cheese should Peg manufacture each month?

: **3.5** Coleman Moses, chief engineer at Atlantic Chemical, Inc., has to decide whether or not to build a new processing facility, using the latest technology. If the new processing facility works, the company could realize a profit of $200,000. If the processing facility fails, the company could lose $150,000. At this time, Coleman estimates there is a 60% chance that the new process will fail.

The other option is to build a pilot plant and then decide whether or not to build a complete facility. The pilot plant would cost $10,000 to build. Coleman estimates there is a 50/50 chance the pilot plant will work. If the pilot plant works, there is a 90% probability that the complete plant, if it is built, will work. If the pilot plant project does not work, there is only a 20% chance that the complete project (if it is constructed) will work. Coleman faces a dilemma. Should he build the plant? Should he build the pilot project and then make a decision? Help Coleman by analyzing this decision-theory problem.

 : **3.6** Mike Shader, president of WRC Industries, is considering whether or not to build a manufacturing plant in the Ozarks. His decision is summarized in the following table:

ALTERNATIVES	FAVORABLE MARKET	UNFAVORABLE MARKET
Build large plant	$400,000	−$300,000
Build small plant	$80,000	−$10,000
Don't build	$0	$0
Market probabilities	0.4	0.6

a) Construct a decision tree.

b) Determine the best strategy, using expected monetary value (EMV).

c) What is the expected value of perfect information (EVPI)?

· **3.7** Varzandeh Mfg. Corp. buys on-off switches from two suppliers. The quality of the switches from the suppliers is indicated below:

PERCENT DEFECTIVE	PROBABILITY FOR SUPPLIER A	PROBABILITY FOR SUPPLIER B
1	.70	.30
3	.20	.40
5	.10	.30

For example, the probability of getting a batch of switches that are 1% defective from supplier A is .70. Since Varzandeh orders 10,000 switches per order, this would mean that there is a .7 probability of getting 100 defective switches out of the 10,000 switches if supplier A is used to fill the order. A defective switch can be repaired for $0.50. Although the quality of supplier B is lower, it will sell an order of 10,000 switches for $37 less than supplier A.

a) Develop a decision tree.

b) Which supplier should Varzandeh use?

· **3.8** Using the Varzandeh Mfg. Corp. data of Problem 3.7, determine the price reduction required from supplier B for Varzandeh to be indifferent between the two suppliers.

 : **3.9** Even though independent gasoline stations have been having a difficult time, Susan Myers has been thinking about starting her own independent gasoline station. Susan's problem is to decide how large her station should be. The annual returns will depend on both the size of her station and a number of marketing factors related to the oil industry and demand for gasoline. After a careful analysis, Susan developed the following table.

SIZE OF FIRST STATION	GOOD MARKET ($)	FAIR MARKET ($)	POOR MARKET ($)
Small	50,000	20,000	−10,000
Medium	80,000	30,000	−20,000
Large	100,000	30,000	−40,000
Very large	300,000	25,000	−160,000

For example, if Susan constructs a small station and the market is good, she will realize a profit of $50,000.

a) Develop a decision table for this decision.

b) What is the maximax decision?

c) What is the maximin decision?

d) What is the equally likely decision?

: **3.10** Using the data in Problem 3.9, develop a decision tree and determine the best decision based on the highest expected monetary value criteria. Assume each outcome is equally likely.

: **3.11** Carla Davis is hospital administrator for Lowell Hospital. She is trying to determine whether to build a large wing on the existing hospital, a small wing, or no wing at all. If the population of Lowell continues to grow, a large wing could return $150,000 to the hospital each year. If the small wing were built, it would return $60,000 to the hospital each year if the population continues to grow. If the population of Lowell remains the same, the hospital would encounter a loss of $85,000 if the large wing were built. Furthermore, a loss of $45,000 would be realized if the small wing were constructed and the population remains the same. Unfortunately, Carla does not have any information about the future population of Lowell.

a) Construct a decision tree.

b) Construct a decision table.

c) Using the equally likely criterion, determine the best alternative.

d) If the likelihood of growth is .6 and that of remaining the same is .4 and the decision criterion is expected monetary value, what decision should Carla make?

· **3.12** Jim Rice is considering opening a bicycle shop in Oshkosh. Jim enjoys biking, but this is to be a business endeavor from which he expects to make a living. Jim can open a small shop, a large shop, or no shop at all. Because there will be a five-year lease on the building that Jim is thinking about using, he wants to make sure he makes the correct decision. Jim is also thinking about hiring his old marketing professor to conduct a marketing research study to see if there is a market for his services. From the studies conducted, the results could be either favorable or unfavorable. Develop a decision tree for Jim.

: **3.13** Jim Rice (of Problem 3.12) has done some analysis of his bicycle shop decision. If Jim builds a large shop he will earn $60,000 if the market is favorable, but he will lose $40,000 if the market is unfavorable. The small shop will return a $30,000 profit with a favorable market and a $10,000 loss if the market is unfavorable. At the present time he believes there is a 50/50 chance that there will be a favorable market. His old marketing professor will charge him $5,000 for the market research. He has estimated that there is a .6 probability that the market will be favorable. Furthermore there is a .9

probability that the market will be favorable given a favorable outcome of the study. However, the marketing professor has warned Jim that there is a probability of only .12 of a favorable market if the marketing research results are not favorable. Expand the decision tree of Problem 3.12 to help Jim decide what to do.

· **3.14** Dick Holliday is not sure what he should do. He can build either a large video rental section or a small one in his drug store. He can also gather additional information, or simply do nothing. If he gathers additional information, the results could suggest either a favorable or an unfavorable market, but it would cost him $3,000 to gather the information. Dick believes that there is a 50/50 chance that the information will be favorable. If the rental market is favorable, Dick will earn $15,000 with the large section or $5,000 with the small. With an unfavorable video rental market, however, Dick could lose $20,000 with the large section or $10,000 with the small section. Without gathering additional information, Dick estimates that the probability of a favorable rental market is .7. A favorable report from the study would increase the probability of a favorable rental market to .9. Furthermore, an unfavorable report from the additional information would decrease the probability of a favorable rental market to .4. Of course, Dick could forget all of these numbers and do nothing. What is your advice to Dick?

: **3.15** Assume that the research and development department at BRK Labs, Inc., a small pharmaceutical company, has tentatively found an ointment that grows hair. This discovery adds substantial value to BRK Labs. As president of BRK, you must make a recommendation to the investors. You face three choices: first, to sell the discovery to a larger drug company—it is worth $10 million; second, to begin experimental laboratory testing and *then* make a decision; or third, to arrange financing for an all-out, aggressive marketing program, with the hope that testing and development will go well along the way. The real goal of this third option is to move so fast that the competition is left with little chance of catching up.

The experimental laboratory testing program will cost $5 million, and there is a 50/50 chance that favorable results will be found and survive FDA review prior to a larger company preempting BRK Labs. Occasionally, even with unfavorable test results, alternative uses for a drug are found; but this occurs only about once in ten cases, and the value of the formula still drops to only $1 million. On the other hand, if a favorable formulation is found, you estimate the discovery and results are worth $20 million. But because BRK Labs is a small company with limited resources and marketing ability, even with favorable laboratory test results the chance of BRK Labs successfully getting the product approved and on the market is only about 40%. Even with favorable laboratory test results and a decision to market, costs will include not only $5 million in test costs but also an additional $3 million for marketing.

The third choice for BRK Labs is to proceed aggressively on its own and aim for the marketing coup of the decade. As president, you figure there is only about one chance in five of BRK doing this. However, the payoff from BRK successfully doing this is $100 million. (This figure is five times greater than the results mentioned earlier because the $20 million reflects the potential for a competitor to enter the market while BRK is in experimental testing.) Under this third choice marketing costs are $3 million and testing will cost $5 million. Both of these expenses apply for this option whether the product is ultimately successful or not.

a) Draw the decision tree.

b) Determine the expected monetary value (EMV).

c) What do you recommend to the investors? How might this recommendation differ based on the firm's financial status?

d) How sensitive is this solution to changes in probabilities? Does this change your conclusion?

CASE STUDY

Drink-At-Home, Inc.

Drink-At-Home, Inc. (DAH, Inc.), develops, processes, and markets mixes to be used in nonalcoholic cocktails and mixed drinks for home consumption. Ms. Lee, who is in charge of research and development at DAH, Inc., this morning notified Mr. Robert Swan, the president, that exciting developments in the research and development section indicate that a new beverage, an instant piña colada, should be possible because of a new way to process and preserve coconut. Ms. Lee is recommending a major program to develop the piña colada. She estimates that expenditure on the development may be as much as $100,000 and that as much as a year's work may be required. In the discussion with Mr. Swan, she indicated that she thought the possibility of her outstanding people successfully developing such a drink now that she's done all the really important work was in the neighborhood of 90%. She also felt that the likelihood of a competing company developing a similar product in 12 months is .80.

Mr. Swan is strictly a bottom-line guy and is concerned about the sales volume of such a beverage. Consequently, Mr. Swan talked to Mr. Besnette, his market research manager, whose specialty is new product evaluation, and was advised that a market existed for an instant piña colada but was somewhat dependent upon acceptance by both grocery stores and retail liquor stores. Mr. Besnette also indicated that the sales reports show that other firms are considering a line of tropical drinks. If other firms should develop a competing beverage, the market would, of course, be split among them. Mr. Swan pressed Mr. Besnette to make future sales estimates for various possibilities and to indicate the present (discounted value of future profits) value. Mr. Besnette provided the following table:

CONSUMER ACCEPTANCE (SALES POTENTIAL)	PROBABILITY	PRESENT VALUES (DISCOUNTED VALUE OF FUTURE PROFITS)
Substantial	.10	$800,000
Moderate	.60	$600,000
Low	.30	$500,000

Mr. Besnette's figures did not include (1) cost of research and development, (2) cost of new production equipment, or (3) cost of introducing the piña colada. The cost of the new production equipment is expected to be $100,000 because of the special way the coconut needs to be handled, and the cost of introducing the new product is expected to be about $150,000 because of the point-of-purchase displays that would be necessary to introduce the new product.

Ms. Lee has indicated that in addition to (a) doing nothing and (b) orderly development, she does have alternative development proposals, which are:

1. Use a reduced research program to see if someone else comes out with the product first and if not, then proceed with a crash program. The reduced program for the first eight months would cost $10,000 per month. One advantage of this is that if the effort was unsuccessful then development costs would be held to the eight-month figure (8 months × $10,000 = $80,000). The likelihood of success under this approach is the same as the more orderly development, if development proceeds without a competitor entering the field. (The likelihood of a competing company developing a product in 8 months is 0.60). The crash development program would take place in months 9 through 12 and would cost an additional $60,000. It would proceed only if the eight-month study guaranteed a success. The likelihood of Ms. Lee's staff developing the product under this program remains 90%. This became known as the eight-month program.

2. Use a reduced research program and maintain an awareness of industry developments to see if someone else develops a product. If someone else has developed a product at the end of six months, it would cost only an additional $30,000 to analyze their product and duplicate it. The reduced development program would cost $10,000 per month. If the competitive product is not developed, Ms. Lee's staff still has a 90% chance of success but total cost will rise to $120,000. This became known as the six-month program.

Mr. Besnette, being the great marketer that he is, is of course reluctant to be second on the market with a new product. He says that the first product on the market will usually obtain a greater share of the market, and it will be difficult to win those customers back. Consequently, he indicates that only about 50% of the sales that he indicated in the preceding table could be expected if Drink-At-Home waited until competing brands were already on the market. Moreover he suspects that there is only a 50/50 chance that the competitor will be out with a product within the next six months.

Given these options: (1) orderly development of the piña colada, (2) the eight-month modest development effort followed by the crash program, (3) the six-month development effort to see if a competitive product comes on the market, and (4) do nothing, what would you, as a production consultant, recommend based on decision tree analysis, using expected monetary value as your decision criterion?

CASE STUDY

Ruth Jones's Heart Bypass Operation

Ruth Jones, a robust 50-year-old insurance adjuster living in the northern suburbs of Chicago, has been diagnosed by a University of Illinois cardiologist as having a defective heart valve. Although she is otherwise healthy, Jones's heart problem could prove fatal if left untreated.

Firm research data are not yet available to predict the likelihood of survival for a woman of Mrs. Jones's age and condition without surgery. Based on his own experience and recent medical journal articles, the cardiologist tells her that if she elects to avoid surgical treatment of the valve problem, chances of survival would be approximately as follows: only a 50% chance of living one year, a 20% chance of surviving for two years, a 20% rate for five years, and a 10% chance of living to age 58. He places her probability of survival beyond age 58 without a heart bypass to be extremely low.

The bypass operation, however, is a serious surgical procedure. Five percent of the patients succumb during the operation or its recovery stage, with an additional 45% dying during the first year. Twenty percent survive for five years, 13% survive for 10 years, and 8, 5, and 4% survive, respectively, for 15, 20, and 25 years.

Discussion Questions

1. Do you think Mrs. Jones should select the bypass operation?

2. What other factors might be considered?

Source: Written by Barry Render, in B. Render, R. M. Stair, and I. Greenberg, *Cases and Readings in Management Science,* 2nd ed (Boston: Allyn & Bacon, Inc., 1990).

BIBLIOGRAPHY

Bell, D. "Bidding for S. S. Kuniang." *Interfaces* **14** (March–April 1984): 17–23.

Brown, R. "Do Managers Find Decision Theory Useful?" *Harvard Business Review* (May–June 1970): 78–89.

Cohan, D., *et al.* "Using Fire in Forest Management." *Interfaces* **14** (September –October 1984): 8–19.

Hosseini, J. "Decision Analysis and Its Application in the Choice between Two Wildcat Oil Ventures." *Interfaces* **16** (March–April 1986): 75–85.

Huber, G. P. *Managerial Decision Making.* Glenview, IL: Scott Foresman, 1980.

Krzysztofozwizz, R., and D. R. Davis. "Toward Improving Flood Forecast Response System." *Interfaces* **14** (May–June 1984): 1–14.

Pratt, J. W., H. Raiffa, and R. Schlaifer. *Introduction to Statistical Decision Theory.* New York: McGraw-Hill, 1965.

Raiffa, H. *Decision Analysis: Introductory Lectures on Choices Under Certainty.* Reading, MA: Addison-Wesley, 1968.

Render, B., and R. M. Stair, Jr. *Introduction to Management Science.* Boston: Allyn and Bacon, 1992.

Render, B., and R. M. Stair, Jr. *Quantitative Analysis for Management,* 4th ed. Boston: Allyn and Bacon, 1991.

Schlaifer, R. *Analysis of Decisions Under Certainty.* New York: McGraw-Hill, 1969.

Ulvila, J. "Postal Automation Technology: A Decision Analysis." *Interfaces* **17** (March–April 1987): 1–12.

Linear Programming

INTRODUCTION TO LINEAR PROGRAMMING

Many operations management decisions involve trying to make the most effective use of an organization's resources. Resources typically include machinery, labor, money, time, warehouse space, or raw materials. These resources may be used to produce products (such as machinery, furniture, food, or clothing) or services (such as schedules for shipping and production, advertising policies, or investment decisions). **Linear programming (LP)** is a widely used mathematical technique designed to help production and operations managers in planning and decision-making relative to the trade-off necessary to allocate resources.

Linear programming (LP)

A few examples of problems in which LP has been successfully applied in operations management are

1. development of a production schedule that will satisfy future demands for a firm's product and at the same time *minimize* total production and inventory costs;
2. selection of the product mix in a factory to make best use of machine- and labor-hours available while *maximizing* the firm's profit;
3. determination of grades of petroleum products to yield the *maximum* profit;
4. selection of different blends of raw materials in feed mills to produce finished feed combinations at *minimum* cost;
5. determination of a distribution system that will *minimize* total shipping cost from several warehouses to various market locations;
6. scheduling school buses to *minimize* the total number of miles traveled each day in picking up and dropping off students;
7. allocation of police patrol units to high-crime areas to *minimize* response time to 911 emergency calls.

Requirements of a Linear Programming Problem

All LP problems have four properties in common.

1. All problems seek to *maximize* or *minimize* some quantity (usually profit or cost). We refer to this property as the **objective function** of an LP problem. The major objective of a typical firm is to maximize dollar profits in the long run. In the case of a trucking or airline distribution system, the objective might be to minimize shipping costs.

Objective function

2. The presence of restrictions, or **constraints,** limits the degree to which we can pursue our objective. For example, deciding how many units of each product in a firm's product line to manufacture is restricted by available labor and machinery. We want, therefore, to maximize or minimize a quantity (the objective function) subject to limited resources (the constraints).

Constraints

3. There must be *alternative courses of action* to choose from. For example, if a company produces three different products, management may use LP to decide how to allocate among them its limited production resources (of labor, machinery, and so on). If there were no alternatives to select from, we would not need LP.
4. The objective and constraints in linear programming problems must be expressed in terms of *linear equations* or inequalities.

Formulating Linear Programming Problems

One of the most common linear programming applications is the *product mix problem*. Two or more products are usually produced using limited resources. The company would like to determine how many units of each product it should produce so as to maximize overall profit given its limited resources. Let us look at an example.

The Flair Furniture Company. The Flair Furniture Company produces inexpensive tables and chairs. The production process for each is similar in that both require a certain number of hours of carpentry work and a certain number of labor hours in the painting and varnishing department. Each table takes four hours of carpentry and two hours in the painting and varnishing shop. Each chair requires three hours in carpentry and one hour in painting and varnishing. During the current production period, 240 hours of carpentry time are available and 100 hours of painting/varnishing department time are available. Each table sold yields a profit of $7; each chair produced may be sold for a $5 profit.

Flair Furniture's problem is to determine the best possible combination of tables and chairs to manufacture in order to reach the maximum profit. This production mix situation may be formulated as a linear programming problem.

We begin by summarizing the information needed to formulate and solve this problem (see Table S3.1). Further, let us introduce some simple notation for use in the objective function and constraints. Let

$$X_1 = \text{Number of tables to be produced}$$
$$X_2 = \text{Number of chairs to be produced}$$

Now we can create the LP *objective function* in terms of X_1 and X_2:

$$\text{Maximize profit} = \$7X_1 + \$5X_2$$

Our next step is to develop mathematical relationships to describe the two constraints in this problem. One general relationship is that the amount of a resource *used* is to be less than or equal to ($\leq$) the amount of resource *available*.

First Constraint. Carpentry time used is $\leq$ carpentry time available.

$$4X_1 + 3X_2 \leq 240 \text{ (hours of carpentry time)}$$

Second Constraint. Painting/varnishing time used is $\leq$ painting/varnishing time available.

TABLE S3.1 Flair Furniture Company Problem Data.

DEPARTMENT	HOURS REQUIRED TO PRODUCE 1 UNIT		AVAILABLE HOURS THIS WEEK
	(X_1) Tables	(X_2) Chairs	
Carpentry	4	3	240
Painting/varnishing	2	1	100
Profit/unit	$7	$5	

$2X_1 + 1X_2 \leq 100$ (hours of painting/varnishing time)

Both of these constraints represent production capacity restrictions and, of course, affect the total profit. For example, Flair Furniture cannot produce 70 tables during the production period because if $X_1 = 70$, both constraints will be violated. It also cannot make $X_1 = 50$ tables and $X_2 = 10$ chairs. Hence, we note one more important aspect of linear programming. That is, certain interactions will exist between variables. The more units of one product that a firm produces, the less it can make of other products.

GRAPHICAL SOLUTION TO A LINEAR PROGRAMMING PROBLEM

The easiest way to solve a small LP problem such as that of the Flair Furniture Company is the graphical solution approach. The graphical procedure is useful only when there are two decision variables (such as number of tables to produce, X_1, and number of chairs to produce, X_2) in the problem. When there are more than two variables, it is *not* possible to plot the solution on a two-dimensional graph and we must turn to more complex approaches—a topic we treat later in this supplement. But the graphical method is invaluable in providing us with insights into how other approaches work.

Graphical Representation of Constraints.   In order to find the optimal solution to a linear programming problem, we must first identify a set, or region, of feasible solutions. The first step in doing so is to plot the problem's constraints on a graph.

The variable X_1 (tables, in our example) is usually plotted as the horizontal axis of the graph, and the variable X_2 (chairs) is plotted as the vertical axis. The complete problem may be restated as:

$$\text{Maximize profit} = \$7X_1 + \$5X_2$$

Subject to the constraints:

$$4X_1 + 3X_2 \leq 240 \qquad (\textit{carpentry constraint})$$
$$2X_1 + 1X_2 \leq 100 \qquad (\textit{painting/varnishing constraint})$$
$$X_1 \geq 0 \qquad (\textit{Number of tables produced is greater than or equal to 0.})$$
$$X_2 \geq 0 \qquad (\textit{Number of chairs produced is greater than or equal to 0.})$$

We would like to represent graphically the constraints of this problem. The first step is to convert the constraint *inequalities* into *equalities* (or equations); that is,

$$\text{Constraint A: } 4X_1 + 3X_2 = 240$$
$$\text{Constraint B: } 2X_1 + 1X_2 = 100$$

The equation for constraint A is plotted in Figure S3.1 and for constraint B in Figure S3.2.

To plot the line in Figure S3.1, all we need to do is to find the points at which the line $4X_1 + 3X_2 = 240$ intersects the X_1 and X_2 axes. When $X_1 = 0$ (the location where the line touches the X_2 axis), it implies that $3X_2 = 240$ or that $X_2 = 80$. Likewise, when $X_2 = 0$, we see that $4X_1 = 240$ and that $X_1 = 60$. Thus constraint A is

One of the early applications of LP is called the *diet problem*, which was originally used by hospitals to determine the most economical diet for patients. Known in agricultural circles as the *feed mix problem*, the diet problem involves specifying a food or feed ingredient combination that will satisfy nutritional requirements at a minimum cost level. Dairy farmers find that they can use LP to minimize total feed cost, yet still provide a high protein diet that increases the efficiency of milk production in their cows.

FIGURE S3.1

Constraint A

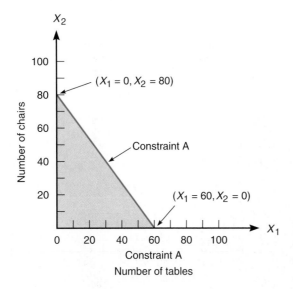

bounded by the line running from $(X_1 = 0, X_2 = 80)$ to $(X_1 = 60, X_2 = 0)$. The shaded area represents all points that satisfy the original *inequality*.

Constraint B is illustrated similarly in Figure S3.2. When $X_1 = 0$, then $X_2 = 100$; and when $X_2 = 0$, then $X_1 = 50$. Constraint B then is bounded by the line between $(X_1 = 0, X_2 = 100)$ and $(X_1 = 50, X_2 = 0)$. The shaded area represents the original inequality.

FIGURE S3.2

Constraint B

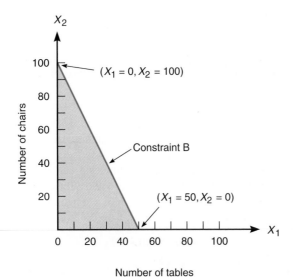

FIGURE S3.3

Feasible Solution Region for the Flair Furniture Company Problem.

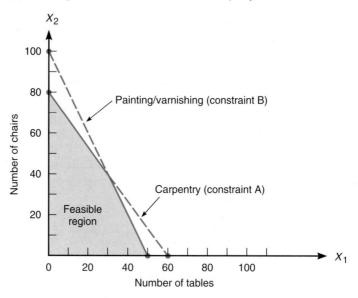

Figure S3.3 shows both constraints together. The shaded region is the part that satisfies both restrictions. The shaded region in Figure S3.3 is called the *area of feasible solutions,* or simply the *feasible region.* This region must satisfy *all* conditions specified by the program's constraints and thus is the region where all constraints overlap. Any point in the region would be a *feasible solution* to the Flair Furniture Company problem. Any point outside the shaded area would represent an *infeasible solution.* Hence, it would be feasible to manufacture 30 tables and 20 chairs ($X_1 = 30$, $X_2 = 20$), but it would violate the constraints to produce 70 tables and 40 chairs. This can be seen by plotting these points on the graph of Figure S3.3.

Iso-Profit Line Solution Method.   Now that the feasible region has been graphed, we may proceed to find the optimal solution to the problem. The optimal solution is the point lying in the feasible region that produces the highest profit.

Once the feasible region has been established graphically, several approaches can be taken in solving for the optimal solution. The speediest one to apply is called the **iso-profit line method**.

Iso-profit line method

We start by letting profits equal some arbitrary, but small, dollar amount. For the Flair Furniture problem we may choose a profit of $210. This is a profit level that can easily be obtained without violating either of the two constraints. The objective function can be written as $\$210 = 7X_1 + 5X_2$.

This expression is just the equation of a line; we call it an *iso-profit line.* It represents all combinations (of X_1, X_2) that would yield a total profit of $210. To plot the profit line, we proceed exactly as we did to plot a constraint line. First, let $X_1 = 0$ and solve for the point at which the line crosses the X_2 axis.

$$\$210 = \$7(0) + \$5X_2$$

$$X_2 = 42 \text{ chairs}$$

FIGURE S3.4

A Profit Line of $210 Plotted for the Flair Furniture Company.

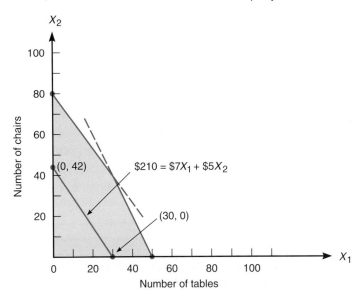

Then let $X_2 = 0$ and solve for X_1.

$$\$210 = \$7X_1 + \$5(0)$$

$$X_1 = 30 \text{ tables}$$

We can now connect these two points with a straight line. This profit line is illustrated in Figure S3.4. All points on the line represent feasible solutions that produce a profit of $210.

Now, obviously, the iso-profit line for $210 does not produce the highest possible profit to the firm. In Figure S3.5, we try graphing two more lines, each yielding a higher profit. The middle equation, $\$280 = \$7X_1 + \$5X_2$, was plotted in the same fashion as the lower line. When $X_1 = 0$,

$$\$280 = \$7(0) + \$5X_2$$

$$X_2 = 56$$

When $X_2 = 0$,

$$\$280 = \$7X_1 + \$5(0)$$

$$X_1 = 40$$

Again, any combination of tables (X_1) and chairs (X_2) on this iso-profit line will produce a total profit of $280.

Note that the third line generates a profit of $350, even more of an improvement. The farther we move from the 0 origin, the higher our profit will be. Another important point to note is that these iso-profit lines are parallel. We now have two clues as to how to find the optimal solution to the original problem. We can draw a series of parallel profit lines (by carefully moving our ruler in a plane parallel to the first profit line). The highest profit line that still touches some point of the feasible

FIGURE S3.5

Four Iso-Profit Lines Plotted for the Flair Furniture Company.

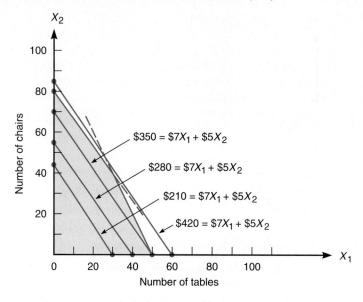

region will pinpoint the optimal solution. Notice that the fourth line ($420) is too high to count.

The highest possible iso-profit line is illustrated in Figure S3.6. It touches the tip of the feasible region at the corner point ($X_1 = 30$, $X_2 = 40$) and yields a profit of $410.

FIGURE S3.6

Optimal Solution for the Flair Furniture Problem.

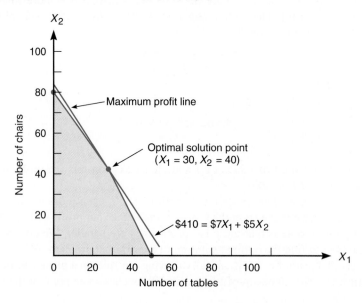

The Corner Point Solution Method. A second approach to solving linear programming problems employs the **corner point method.** This technique is simpler, conceptually, than the iso-profit line approach, but it involves looking at the profit at every corner point of the feasible region.

Corner point method

The mathematical theory behind linear programming states that an optimal solution to any problem (that is, the values of X_1, X_2 that yield the maximum profit) will lie at a *corner point,* or *extreme point,* of the feasible region. Hence, it is necessary to find only the values of the variables at each corner; the maximum profit or optimal solution will lie at one (or more) of them.

Once again we can see (in Figure S3.7) that the feasible region for the Flair Furniture Company problem is a four-sided polygon with four corner, or extreme, points. These points are labeled ①, ②, ③, and ④ on the graph. To find the (X_1, X_2) values producing the maximum profit, we find out what the coordinates of each corner point are and test their profit levels.

Point ①: $(X_1 = 0, X_2 = 0)$ Profit $7(0) + $5(0) = $0

Point ②: $(X_1 = 0, X_2 = 80)$ Profit $7(0) + $5(80) = $400

Point ④: $(X_1 = 50, X_2 = 0)$ Profit $7(50) + $5(0) = $350

We skipped corner point ③ momentarily because in order to *accurately* find its coordinates, we will have to solve for the intersection of the two constraint lines. As you may recall from algebra, we can apply the method of *simultaneous equations* to the two constraint equations.

$$4X_1 + 3X_2 = 240 \quad (carpentry\ line)$$
$$2X_1 + 1X_2 = 100 \quad (painting\ line)$$

FIGURE S3.7

The Four Corner Points of the Feasible Region.

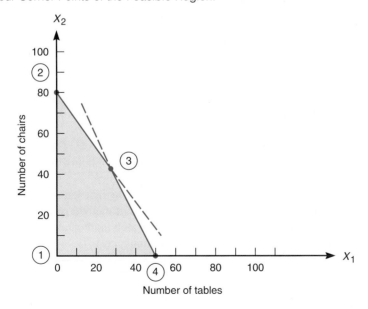

To solve these equations simultaneously, we multiply the second equation by -2:

$$-2(2X_1 + 1X_2 = 100) = -4X_1 - 2X_2 = -200$$

and then add it to the first equation:

$$
\begin{aligned}
+\,4X_1 + 3X_2 &= 240 \\
-\,4X_1 - 2X_2 &= -200 \\
\hline
+\,1X_2 &= 40
\end{aligned}
$$

or

$$X_2 = 40$$

Doing this has enabled us to eliminate one variable, X_1, and to solve for X_2. We can now substitute 40 for X_2 in either of the original equations and solve for X_1. Let us use the first equation. When $X_2 = 40$, then

$$4X_1 + 3(40) = 240$$

$$4X_1 + 120 = 240$$

or

$$4X_1 = 120$$

$$X_1 = 30$$

Thus point ③ has the coordinates ($X_1 = 30$, $X_2 = 40$); we can compute its profit level to complete the analysis.

Point ③: ($X_1 = 30$, $X_2 = 40$)   Profit $= \$7(30) + \$5(40) = \$410$

Because point ③ produces the highest profit of any corner point, the product mix of $X_1 = 30$ tables and $X_2 = 40$ chairs is the optimal solution to Flair Furniture's problem. This solution will yield a profit of $410 per production period, which is the same as we obtained using the iso-profit line method.

Solving Minimization Problems

Many linear programming problems involve *minimizing* an objective such as cost, instead of maximizing a profit function. A restaurant, for example, may wish to develop a work schedule to meet staffing needs while minimizing the total number of employees. A manufacturer may seek to distribute its products from several factories to its many regional warehouses in such a way as to minimize total shipping costs. A hospital may want to provide a daily meal plan for its patients that meets certain nutritional standards while at the same time minimizing food purchase costs.

Iso-cost

Minimization problems can be solved graphically by first setting up the feasible solution region and then using either the corner point method or an **iso-cost** line approach (which is analogous to the iso-profit approach in maximization problems) to find the values of X_1 and X_2 that yield the minimum cost.

Example S1

Wacker Chemicals, Inc., produces two types of photo-developing fluids. The first, a black-and-white picture chemical, costs Wacker $2,500 per ton to produce. The second, a color photo chemical, costs $3,000 per ton.

Based upon an analysis of current inventory levels and outstanding orders, Wacker's production manager has specified that at least 30 tons of the black-and-white chemical and at least 20 tons of the color chemical must be produced during the next month. In addition, the manager notes that an existing inventory of a highly perishable raw material needed in both chemicals must be used within 30 days. In order to avoid wasting the expensive raw material, Wacker must produce a total of at least 60 tons of the photo chemicals in the next month.

We may formulate this information as a minimization LP problem. Let

X_1 = Number of tons of black-and-white picture chemical produced

X_2 = Number of tons of color picture chemical produced

Subject to:

$$X_1 \geq 30 \text{ tons of black-and-white chemical}$$
$$X_2 \geq 20 \text{ tons of color chemical}$$
$$X_1 + X_2 \geq 60 \text{ total tonnage}$$
$$X_1, X_2 \geq 0 \text{ nonnegativity requirements}$$

To solve the Wacker problem graphically, we construct the problem's feasible region, shown in Figure S3.8.

FIGURE S3.8

Wacker Chemical Feasible Region.

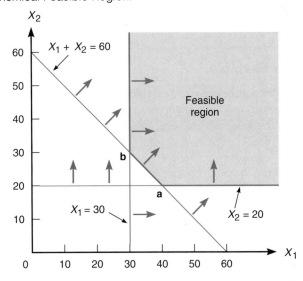

Minimization problems are often unbounded outward (that is, on the right side and on the top), but this characteristic causes no problem in solving them. As long as they are bounded inward (on the left side and the bottom), we can establish corner points. The optimal solution will lie at one of the corners.

In this case, there are only two corner points, **a** and **b** in Figure S3.8. It is easy to determine that at point **a**, $X_1 = 40$ and $X_2 = 20$ and that at point **b**, $X_1 = 30$ and $X_2 = 30$. The optimal solution is found at the point yielding the lowest total cost. Thus

$$\text{Total cost at } \mathbf{a} = 2,500X_1 + 3,000X_2$$
$$= 2,500(40) + 3,000(20)$$
$$= \$160,000$$
$$\text{Total cost at } \mathbf{b} = 2,500X_1 + 3,000X_2$$
$$= 2,500(30) + 3,000(30)$$
$$= \$165,000$$

The lowest cost to Wacker Chemicals, Inc., is at point **a.** Hence the production manager should produce 40 tons of the black-and-white chemical and 20 tons of the color photo chemical.

LINEAR PROGRAMMING APPLICATIONS

The foregoing examples each contained just two variables (X_1 and X_2). Most real-world problems contain many more variables, however. Let us use the principles already developed to formulate a few more-complex problems. The practice you will get by "paraphrasing" the following LP situations should help develop your skills for applying linear programming to other common production and operations situations.

Production Mix Example

Example S2 involves another *production mix* decision. Limited resources must be allocated among various products that a firm produces. The firm's overall objective is to manufacture the selected products in such quantities as to maximize total profits.

Example S2

The Failsafe Electronics Corporation primarily manufactures four highly technical products, which it supplies to aerospace firms that hold NASA contracts. Each of the products must pass through the following departments before they are shipped: wiring, drilling, assembly, and inspection. The time requirements (in hours) for each unit produced and its corresponding profit value are summarized in this table:

POM _in action_

Linear Programming at New England Apple Products

Clothing fashions change every year. And so do food habits. As we shop our supermarket, new products are found and old ones disappear. A decade ago, for example, fruit juices were drunk mostly at breakfast time or when one was sick. Now we drink them anytime. One consequence is that juice companies have created new blends to meet demand.

New England Apple Products, the manufacturer of the _Very Fine_ beverage line, now has sixteen different juice beverages, ranging from apple-cherry to cranapple to grapefruit. There are a large number of combinations of fruit juices possible, but New England Apple has only limited supplies of each juice as ingredients. The firm uses linear programming to decide which combinations to market and how much of each to make. The bottom-line question is: "What product mix will yield the best profit?" Although there are many listed ingredients on the side of each bottle of fruit juice blend, LP is one _hidden_ ingredient.

		DEPARTMENT			
Product	Wiring	Drilling	Assembly	Inspection	Unit Profit
XJ201	.5	3	2	.5	$ 9
XM897	1.5	1	4	1.0	$12
TR29	1.5	2	1	.5	$15
BR788	1.0	3	2	.5	$11

The production time available in each department each month and the minimum monthly production requirement to fulfill contracts are as follows:

DEPARTMENT	CAPACITY (IN HOURS)	PRODUCT	MINIMUM PRODUCTION LEVEL
Wiring	1,500	XJ201	150
Drilling	1,700	XM897	100
Assembly	2,600	TR29	300
Inspection	1,200	BR788	400

The production manager has the responsibility of specifying production levels for each product for the coming month. Let

$$X_1 = \text{Number of units of XJ201 produced}$$
$$X_2 = \text{Number of units of XM897 produced}$$
$$X_3 = \text{Number of units of TR29 produced}$$
$$X_4 = \text{Number of units of BR788 produced}$$

Maximize profit $= 9X_1 + 12X_2 + 15X_3 + 11X_4$

Subject to: $.5X_1 + 1.5X_2 + 1.5X_3 + 1X_4 \leq 1,500$ hours of wiring available

$$3X_1 + 1X_2 + 2X_3 + 3X_4 \leq 1{,}700 \text{ hours of drilling available}$$
$$2X_1 + 4X_2 + 1X_3 + 2X_4 \leq 2{,}600 \text{ hours of assembly available}$$
$$.5X_1 + 1X_2 + .5X_3 + .5X_4 \leq 1{,}200 \text{ hours of inspection}$$
$$X_1 \geq 150 \text{ units of XJ201}$$
$$X_2 \geq 100 \text{ units of XM897}$$
$$X_3 \geq 300 \text{ units of TR29}$$
$$X_4 \geq 400 \text{ units of BR788}$$
$$X_1, X_2, X_3, X_4 \geq 0$$

Production Scheduling Example

One of the most important areas of linear programming application is *production scheduling*. Solving a production scheduling problem allows the production manager to set an efficient, low-cost production schedule for a product over several production periods. Basically, the problem resembles the common product-mix model for each period in the future. Production levels must allow the firm to meet demand for its product within labor and inventory limitations. The objective is either to maximize profit or to minimize the total cost (production plus inventory).

Example S3

The Simone Appliance Company is thinking of manufacturing and selling trash compactors on an experimental basis over the next six months. The manufacturing costs and selling prices of the compactors are projected to vary from month to month. Table S3.2 gives these forecast costs and prices.

TABLE S3.2 Manufacturing Costs and Selling Price.

MONTH	MANUFACTURING COST	SELLING PRICE (DURING MONTH)
July	$60	—
August	$60	$80
September	$50	$60
October	$60	$70
November	$70	$80
December	—	$90

All compactors manufactured during any month are shipped out in one large load at the end of that month. The firm can sell as many units as it produces, but its operation is limited by the size of its warehouse, which holds a maximum of 100 compactors.

Simone's production manager, Tom White, needs to determine the number of compactors to manufacture and sell each month in order to maximize the firm's profit. Simone has no compactors on hand at the beginning of July and wishes to have no compactors on hand at the end of the test period in December.

To formulate this LP problem, Tom White lets

$X_1, X_2, X_3, X_4, X_5, X_6$ = Number of units *manufactured* during July (first month), August (second month), etc.

$Y_1, Y_2, Y_3, Y_4, Y_5, Y_6$ = Number of units *sold* during July, August, etc.

He notes that because the company starts with no compactors (and because it takes one month to gear up and ship out the first batch), it cannot sell any units in July (that is, $Y_1 = 0$). Also, since it wants zero inventory at the end of the year, manufacture during the month of December must be zero (that is, $X_6 = 0$).

Profit for Simone Appliances is sales minus manufacture cost. Hence, Tom White's objective function is

$$\text{Maximize profit} = 80Y_2 + 60Y_3 + 70Y_4 + 80Y_5 + 90Y_6$$
$$-(60X_1 + 60X_2 + 50X_3 + 60X_4 + 70X_5)$$

The first part of this expression is the sales price times the units sold each month. The second part is the manufacture cost, namely, the costs from Table S3.2 times the units manufactured.

To set up the constraints, White needs to introduce a new set of variables: $I_1, I_2, I_3, I_4, I_5, I_6$. These represent the inventory at the end of a month (after all sales have been made and after the amount produced during the month has been stacked in the warehouse). Thus,

Inventory at end of this month	=	Inventory at end of previous month	+	Current month's production	–	This month's sales

For July, this is $I_1 = X_1$, since there is neither previous inventory nor sales. For August,

$$I_2 = I_1 + X_2 - Y_2$$

Constraints for the remaining months are as follows:

$$\text{September:} \quad I_3 = I_2 + X_3 - Y_3$$
$$\text{October:} \quad I_4 = I_3 + X_4 - Y_4$$
$$\text{November:} \quad I_5 = I_4 + X_5 - Y_5$$
$$\text{December:} \quad I_6 = I_5 - Y_6$$

Constraints for the storage capacity are:

$I_1 \leq 100$

$I_2 \leq 100$

$I_3 \leq 100$

$I_4 \leq 100$

$I_5 \leq 100$

$I_6 = 0$ (in order to end up with zero inventory at the end of December)

Labor Scheduling Example

Labor scheduling problems address staffing needs over a specific time period. They are especially useful when managers have some flexibility in assigning workers to jobs that require overlapping or interchangeable talents. Large banks and hospitals frequently use LP to tackle their labor scheduling. Example S4 describes how one bank uses LP to schedule tellers.

Example S4

Arlington Bank of Commerce and Industry is a busy bank that has requirements for between ten and eighteen tellers depending on the time of day. The lunch time, from noon to 2 P.M., is usually heaviest. The table below indicates the workers needed at various hours that the bank is open.

TIME PERIOD	NUMBER OF TELLERS REQUIRED	TIME PERIOD	NUMBER OF TELLERS REQUIRED
9 A.M.–10 A.M.	10	1 P.M.–2 P.M.	18
10 A.M.–11 A.M.	12	2 P.M.–3 P.M.	17
11 A.M.–Noon	14	3 P.M.–4 P.M.	15
Noon–1 P.M.	16	4 P.M.–5 P.M.	10

The bank now employs twelve full-time tellers, but many people are on its roster of available part-time employees. A part-time employee must put in exactly four hours per day, but can start anytime between 9 A.M. and 1 P.M. Part-timers are a fairly inexpensive labor pool, since no retirement or lunch benefits are provided them. Full-timers, on the other hand, work from 9 A.M. to 5 P.M. but are allowed one hour for lunch. (Half the full-timers eat at 11 A.M., the other half at noon.) Full-timers thus provide 35 hours per week of productive labor time.

By corporate policy, the bank limits part-time hours to a maximum of 50% of the day's total requirement.

Part-timers earn $4 per hour (or $16 per day) on average, while full-timers earn $50 per day in salary and benefits on average. The bank would like to set a schedule that would minimize its total labor costs. It will release one or more of its full-time tellers if it is profitable to do so.

We can let

F = Full-time tellers

P_1 = Part-timers starting at 9 A. M. (leaving at 1 P. M.)

P_2 = Part-timers starting at 10 A.M. (leaving at 2 P.M.)

P_3 = Part-timers starting at 11 A.M. (leaving at 3 P.M.)

P_4 = Part-timers starting at noon (leaving at 4 P.M.)

P_5 = Part-timers starting at 1 P.M. (leaving at 5 P.M.)

Objective function:

$$\text{Minimize total daily labor cost} = \$50F + \$16(P_1 + P_2 + P_3 + P_4 + P_5)$$

Constraints: For each hour, the available labor-hours must be at least equal to the required labor-hours.

$$
\begin{array}{lll}
F + P_1 & \geq 10 & \textit{(9 A.M. to 10 A.M. needs)} \\
F + P_1 + P_2 & \geq 12 & \textit{(10 A. M. to 11 A.M. needs)} \\
\tfrac{1}{2}F + P_1 + P_2 + P_3 & \geq 14 & \textit{(11 A.M. to noon needs)} \\
\tfrac{1}{2}F + P_1 + P_2 + P_3 + P_4 & \geq 16 & \textit{(noon to 1 P.M. needs)} \\
F + P_2 + P_3 + P_4 + P_5 & \geq 18 & \textit{(1 P.M. to 2 P.M. needs)} \\
F + P_3 + P_4 + P_5 & \geq 17 & \textit{(2 P.M. to 3 P.M. needs)} \\
F + P_4 + P_5 & \geq 15 & \textit{(3 P.M. to 4 P.M. needs)} \\
F + P_5 & \geq 10 & \textit{(4 P.M. to 5 P.M. needs)}
\end{array}
$$

Only twelve full-time tellers are available, so

$$F \leq 12$$

Part-time worker hours cannot exceed 50 percent of total hours required each day, which is the sum of the tellers needed each hour.

$$4(P_1 + P_2 + P_3 + P_4 + P_5) \leq 0.50(10 + 12 + 14 + 16 + 18 + 17 + 15 + 10)$$

or

$$4P_1 + 4P_2 + 4P_3 + 4P_4 + 4P_5 \leq 0.50(112)$$
$$F, P_1, P_2, P_3, P_4, P_5 \geq 0$$

There are two alternative optimal schedules that Arlington Bank can follow. The first is to employ only ten full-time tellers ($F = 10$) and to start two part-timers at 10 A.M. ($P_2 = 2$), seven part-timers at 11 A.M. ($P_3 = 7$), and five part-timers at noon ($P_4 = 5$). No part-timers would begin at 9 A.M. or 1 P.M.

The second solution also employs ten full-time tellers, but starts six part-timers at 9 A.M. ($P_1 = 6$), one part-timer at 10 A.M. ($P_2 = 1$), two part-timers at 11 A.M. and noon ($P_3 = 2$ and $P_4 = 2$), and three part-timers at 1 P.M. ($P_5 = 3$). The cost of either of these two policies is $724 per day.

THE SIMPLEX METHOD OF LP

Most real-world linear programming problems have more than two variables and thus are too large for graphical solution. A procedure called the **simplex method** may be used to find the optimal solution to multivariable problems. The simplex method is actually an algorithm (or a set of instructions) with which we examine corner points in a methodical fashion until we arrive at the best solution—highest profit or lowest cost. Computer programs exist to solve LP problems with as many as several thousand variables, but understanding the mechanics of the algorithm is useful.

Simplex method

Converting the Constraints to Equations

The first step of the simplex method requires that we convert each inequality constraint in an LP formulation into an equation. Less-than-or-equal-to constraints ($\leq$) can be converted to equations by adding *slack variables*, as illustrated below.

Earlier, we formulated the Flair Furniture Company's product mix problem as follows, using linear programming:

$$\text{Maximize profit} = \$7X_1 + \$5X_2$$

Subject to LP constraints:

$$2X_1 + 1X_2 \leq 100$$
$$4X_1 + 3X_2 \leq 240$$

where X_1 equals the number of tables produced and X_2 equals the number of chairs produced.

To convert these inequality constraints to equalities, we add slack variables S_1 and S_2 to the left side of the inequality. The first constraint becomes

$$2X_1 + 1X_2 + S_1 = 100$$

and the second becomes

$$4X_1 + 3X_2 + S_2 = 240$$

To include all variables in each equation (a requirement of the next simplex step), we add slack variables not appearing in each equation with a coefficient of zero. The equations then appear as

$$2X_1 + 1X_2 + 1S_1 + 0S_2 = 100$$
$$4X_1 + 3X_2 + 0S_1 + 1S_2 = 240$$

Since slack variables represent unused resources (such as time on a machine or labor-hours available), they yield no profit, but we must add them to the objective function with zero profit coefficients. Thus, the objective function becomes

$$\text{Maximize profit} = \$7X_1 + \$5X_2 + \$0S_1 + \$0S_2$$

Setting Up the First Simplex Tableau

To simplify handling the equations and objective function in an LP problem, we place all of the coefficients into a tabular form. We can express the two constraint equations above as:

SOLUTION MIX	X_1	X_2	S_1	S_2	QUANTITY (RHS)
S_1	2	1	1	0	100
S_2	4	3	0	1	240

The numbers (2, 1, 1, 0) and (4, 3, 0, 1) represent the coefficients of the first equation and second equation, respectively.

As in the earlier graphical approach, we begin the solution at the origin, where $X_1 = 0$, $X_2 = 0$, and profit $= 0$. The values of the two other variables, S_1 and S_2, then, must be nonzero. Since $2X_1 + 1X_2 + 1S_1 = 100$, we see that $S_1 = 100$. Likewise, $S_2 = 240$. These two slack variables comprise the initial solution mix—as a matter of fact, their values are found in the quantity column across from each variable.

Since X_1 and X_2 are not in the solution mix, their initial values are automatically equal to zero.

Some production-operations management books call this initial solution a *basic feasible solution* and describe it in vector, or column, form as:

$$\begin{bmatrix} X_1 \\ X_2 \\ S_1 \\ S_2 \end{bmatrix} = \begin{bmatrix} 0 \\ 0 \\ 100 \\ 240 \end{bmatrix}$$

Variables in the solution mix, which is often called the *basis* in LP terminology, are referred to as *basic variables*. In this example, the basic variables are S_1 and S_2. Variables not in the solution mix—or basis—(X_1 and X_2, in this case) are called *nonbasic variables*. Of course, if the optimal solution to this LP problem turned out to be $X_1 = 30$, $X_2 = 40$, $S_1 = 0$, and $S_2 = 0$, or in vector form,

$$\begin{bmatrix} X_1 \\ X_2 \\ S_1 \\ S_2 \end{bmatrix} = \begin{bmatrix} 30 \\ 40 \\ 0 \\ 0 \end{bmatrix}$$

then X_1 and X_2 would be the final basic variables, while S_1 and S_2 would be the nonbasic variables.

Table S3.3 shows the complete initial simplex tableau for Flair Furniture. The terms and rows that you have not seen before are:

C_j: Profit contribution per unit of each variable. C_j applies to both the top row and first column. In the row, it indicates the unit profit for all variables in the LP objective function. In the column, C_j indicates the unit profit for each variable *currently* in the solution mix.

Z_j: In the quantity column, Z_j provides the total contribution (gross profit in this case) of the given solution. In the other columns (under the variables) it represents the gross profit *given up* by adding one unit of this variable into the current solution. The Z_j value for each column is found by multiplying the C_j of the row by the number in that row and jth column and summing.

The calculations for the values of Z_J in Table S3.3 are as follows:

$$Z_j \text{ (for column } X_1) = 0(2) + 0(4) = 0$$
$$Z_j \text{ (for column } X_2) = 0(1) + 0(3) = 0$$

TABLE S3.3 Completed Initial Simplex Tableau.

$C_j \rightarrow$		$7	$5	$0	$0	
$\downarrow$	Solution Mix	X_1	X_2	S_1	S_2	Quantity (RHS)
$0	S_1	2	1	1	0	100
$0	S_2	4	3	0	1	240
	Z_j	$0	$0	$0	$0	$0
	$C_j - Z_j$	$7	$5	$0	$0	(total profit)

$$Z_j \text{ (for column } S_1) = 0(1) + 0(0) = 0$$
$$Z_j \text{ (for column } S_2) = 0(0) + 0(1) = 0$$
$$Z_j \text{ (for total profit)} = 0(100) + 0(240) = 0$$

$C_j - Z_j$: This number represents the net profit (that is, the profit gained minus the profit given up), which will result from introducing one unit of each product (variable) into the solution. It is not calculated for the quantity column. To compute these numbers, we simply subtract the Z_j total from the C_j value at the very top of each variable's column.

The calculations for the net profit per unit $(C_j - Z_j)$ row in this example are:

	COLUMN			
	X_1	X_2	S_1	S_2
C_j for column:	$7	$5	$0	$0
Z_j for column:	0	0	0	0
$C_j - Z_j$ for column:	$7	$5	$0	$0

It was obvious to us when we computed a profit of $0 that this initial solution was not optimal. Examining numbers in the $C_j - Z_j$ row of Table S3.3, we see that total profit can be increased by $7 for each unit of X_1 (tables) and by $5 for each unit of X_2 (chairs) added to the solution mix. A negative number in the $C_j - Z_j$ row would tell us that profits would *decrease* if the corresponding variable were added to the solution mix. An optimal solution is reached in the simplex method when the $C_j - Z_j$ row contains no positive numbers. Such is not the case in our initial tableau.

Simplex Solution Procedures

Once we have completed an initial tableau, we proceed through a series of five steps to compute all of the numbers we need for the next tableau. The calculations are not difficult, but they are sufficiently complex that the smallest arithmetic error can produce a very wrong answer.

We will first list the five steps and then apply them in determining the second and third tableau for the data in the Flair Furniture example.

1. Determine which variable to enter into the solution mix next. Identify the column—hence the variable—with the largest positive number in the $C_j - Z_j$ row of the previous tableau. This step means that we will now be producing some of the product contributing the greatest additional profit per unit.

2. Determine which variable to replace. Since we have just chosen a new variable to enter into the solution mix, we must decide which variable currently in the solution to remove to make room for it. To do so, we divide each amount in the quantity column by the corresponding number in the column selected in step 1. The row with the *smallest nonnegative number* calculated in this fashion will be replaced in the next tableau (this smallest number, by the way, gives the maximum number of units of the variable that we may place in the solution). This row is often referred to as the **pivot row,** and the

Pivot row

column identified in step 1 is called the **pivot column.** The number at the intersection of the pivot row and pivot column is the **pivot number.**

3. Compute new values for the pivot row. To find them, we simply divide every number in the row by the *pivot number.*

4. Compute new values for each remaining row. (In our sample problems there have been only two rows in the LP tableau, but most larger problems have many more rows.) All remaining row(s) are calculated as follows:

$$\begin{pmatrix} \text{New row} \\ \text{numbers} \end{pmatrix} = \begin{pmatrix} \text{Numbers} \\ \text{in old row} \end{pmatrix} - \left[\begin{pmatrix} \text{Number in old row} \\ \text{above or below} \\ \text{pivot number} \end{pmatrix} \times \begin{pmatrix} \text{Corresponding number in} \\ \text{the new row, i.e., the} \\ \text{row replaced in step 3} \end{pmatrix} \right]$$

5. Compute the Z_j and $C_j - Z_j$ rows, as demonstrated in the initial tableau. If all numbers in the $C_j - Z_j$ row are zero or negative, we have found an optimal solution. If this is not the case, we must return to step 1.

All of these computations are best illustrated by way of an example—and best understood by way of several practice problems. The initial simplex tableau computed in Table S3.3 is repeated below. We will follow the five steps just given to reach an optimal solution to the LP problem.

	$C_j \rightarrow$		$7	$5	$0	$0		
		Solution Mix	X_1	X_2	S_1	S_2	Quantity	
$0		S_1	②	1	1	0	100	← pivot row
$0		S_2	4	3	0	1	240	
				pivot number				
	Z_j		$0	$0	$0	$0	$0	
	$C_j - Z_j$		$7	$5	$0	$0	$0	

1st tableau

↑
pivot column
(maximum $C_j - Z_j$ values)

Step 1. Variable X_1 will enter the solution next because it has the highest contribution to profit value, $C_j - Z_j$. Its column becomes the pivot column.

Step 2. Divide each number in the quantity column by the corresponding number in the X_1 column: $100/2 = 50$ for the first row and $240/4 = 60$ for the second row. The smaller of these numbers—50—identifies the pivot row, the pivot number, and the variable to be replaced. The pivot row is identified above by an arrow, and the pivot number is circled. Variable X_1 replaces variable S_1 in the solution mix column, as shown in the second tableau.

Step 3. Replace the pivot row by dividing every number in it by the pivot number ($2/2 = 1$, $1/2 = 1/2$, $1/2 = 1/2$, $0/2 = 0$, $100/2 = 50$). This new version of the entire pivot row appears below.

C_j	SOLUTION MIX	X_1	X_2	S_1	S_2	QUANTITY
$7	X_1	1	1/2	1/2	0	50

Step 4. Calculate the new values for the S_2 row.

$$\begin{pmatrix} \text{Number in} \\ \text{new } S_2 \text{ row} \end{pmatrix} = \begin{pmatrix} \text{Number in} \\ \text{old } S_2 \text{ row} \end{pmatrix} - \left[\begin{pmatrix} \text{Number below} \\ \text{pivot number} \\ \text{in old row} \end{pmatrix} \times \begin{pmatrix} \text{Corresponding} \\ \text{number in the} \\ \text{new } X_1 \text{ row} \end{pmatrix} \right]$$

0	=	4	−	[(4)	×	(1)]
1	=	3	−	[(4)	×	(1/2)]
−2	=	0	−	[(4)	×	(1/2)]
1	=	1	−	[(4)	×	(0)]
40	=	240	−	[(4)	×	(50)]

C_j	SOLUTION MIX	X_1	X_2	S_1	S_2	QUANTITY
$7	X_1	1	1/2	1/2	0	50
0	S_2	0	1	−2	1	40

Step 5: Calculate the Z_j and $C_j - Z_j$ rows.

Z_j (for X_1 column) = $7(1) + 0(0) = $7 $C_j - Z_j = $7 - $7 = 0$

Z_j (for X_2 column) = $7(1/2) + 0(1) = $7/2 $C_j - Z_j = $5 - $7/2 = $3/2$

Z_j (for S_1 column) = $7(1/2) + 0(-2) = $7/2 $C_j - Z_j = 0 - $7/2 = - $7/2$

Z_j (for S_2 column) = $7(0) + 0(1) = 0 $C_j - Z_j = 0 - 0 = 0$

Z_j (for total profit) = $7(50) + 0(40) = $350

	$C_j \rightarrow$ ↓	$7	$5	$0	$0	
	Solution Mix	X_1	X_2	S_1	S_2	Quantity
$7	X_1	1	1/2	1/2	0	50
$0	S_2	0	①	−2	1	40
	Z_j	$7	$7/2	$7/2	$0	$350 (total profit)
	$C_j - Z_j$	$0	$3/2	−$7/2	$0	

2nd tableau

pivot number

← pivot row

↑ pivot column

Since not all numbers in the $C_j - Z_j$ row of this latest tableau are zero or negative, the foregoing solution (that is, $X_1 = 50$, $S_2 = 40$, $X_2 = 0$, $S_1 = 0$; profit = $350) is not optimal, and we proceed to a third tableau and repeat the five steps.

Step 1. Variable X_2 will enter the solution next by virtue of the fact that its $C_j - Z_j = 3/2$ is the largest (and only) positive number in the row. Thus, for every unit of X_2 that we start to produce, the objective function will increase in value by $3/2, or $1.50.

Step 2. The pivot row becomes the S_2 row because the ratio $40/1 = 40$ is smaller than the ratio $50(1/2) = 100$.

Step 3. Replace the pivot row by dividing every number in it by the (circled) pivot number. Since every number is divided by one, there is no change.

Step 4. Compute the new values for the X_1 row.

$$\begin{pmatrix} \text{Number in} \\ \text{new } X_1 \text{ row} \end{pmatrix} = \begin{pmatrix} \text{Number in} \\ \text{old } X_1 \text{ row} \end{pmatrix} - \left[\begin{pmatrix} \text{Number above} \\ \text{pivot number} \end{pmatrix} \times \begin{pmatrix} \text{Corresponding} \\ \text{number in the} \\ \text{new } X_2 \text{ row} \end{pmatrix} \right]$$

1	=	1	−	[(1/2)	×	(0)]
0	=	1/2	−	[(1/2)	×	(1)]
3/2	=	1/2	−	[(1/2)	×	(−2)]
−1/2	=	0	−	[(1/2)	×	(1)]
30	=	50	−	[(1/2)	×	(40)]

Step 5: Calculate the Z_j and $C_j - Z_j$ rows.

Z_j (for X_1 column) = $7(1) + $5(0) = $7 $C_j - Z_j = $7 - 7 = $0

Z_j (for X_2 column) = $7(0) + $5(1) = $5 $C_j - Z_j = $5 - 5 = $0

Z_j (for S_1 column) = $7(3/2) + $5(- 2) = $1/2 $C_j - Z_j = $0 - 1/2 = - $1/2

Z_j (for S_2 column) = $7(- 1/2) + $5(1) = $3/2 $C_j - Z_j = $0 - 3/2 = - $3/2

Z_j (for total profit) = $7(30) + $5(40) = $410

The results for the third tableau are seen in Table S3.4.

Since every number in the third tableau's $C_j - Z_j$ row is zero or negative, we have reached an optimal solution. That solution is: $X_1 = 30$ (tables), and $X_2 = 40$ (chairs), $S_1 = 0$ (slack in first resource), $S_2 = 0$ (slack in second resource), and profit = $410.

TABLE S3.4 Third and Final Tableau.

$C_j \rightarrow$		$7	$5	$0	$0	
↓	Solution Mix	X_1	X_2	S_1	S_2	Quantity
$7	X_1	1	0	3/2	−1/2	30
$5	X_2	0	1	−2	1	40
	Z_j	$7	$5	$1/2	$3/2	$410
	$C_j - Z_j$	$0	$0	−$1/2	−$3/2	

Summary of Simplex Steps for Maximization Problems

The steps involved in using the simplex method to help solve an LP problem in which the objective function is to be maximized can be summarized as follows:

1. Choose the variable with the greatest positive $C_j - Z_j$ to enter the solution.
2. Determine the row to be replaced by selecting the one with the smallest (nonnegative) ratio of quantity to pivot column.
3. Calculate the new values for the pivot row.
4. Calculate the new values for the other row(s).
5. Calculate the C_j and $C_j - Z_j$ values for this tableau. If there are any $C_j - Z_j$ numbers greater than zero, return to step 1.

Shadow Prices

Flair Furniture's final tableau leads us to the subject of shadow prices. Exactly how much should a firm be willing to pay to make additional resources available? Is one more hour of machine time worth $.50 or $1 or $5? Is it worthwhile to pay workers an overtime rate to stay one extra hour each night in order to increase production output? The worth of additional resources is valuable management information.

Fortunately, this information is available to us in the final simplex tableau of an LP problem. An important property of the $C_j - Z_j$ row is that the *negatives of the numbers in its slack variable* (S_j) *columns provide what we call shadow prices.* A **Shadow price**   **shadow price** is the value of one additional unit of a resource in the form of one more hour of machine time or labor time or other scarce resource.

Table S3.4 indicated that the optimal solution to Flair's problem is $X_1 = 30$ tables, $X_2 = 40$ chairs, $S_1 = 0$, $S_2 = 0$, and profit = $410, where S_1 represented slack hours in the carpentry department and S_2 represented slack or unused painting department time.

Suppose Flair is considering adding an extra painter at a salary of $4.00 per hour. Should the firm do so? The answer is *no*—the shadow price of the painting department resource is only 50¢. Thus, the firm will lose $3.50 for every hour the new painter works.

Sensitivity Analysis

Sensitivity analysis   Shadow pricing is actually one form of **sensitivity analysis,** that is, the study of how sensitive the optimal solution would be to errors or changes in inputs to the LP problem. For example, if the manager at Flair Furniture had been off by 100% in setting the net profit per table at $7, would that drastically alter the decision to produce 30 tables and 40 chairs? What would be the impact of 265 carpentry hours being available instead of 240?

Program S3.1 is part of the AB:POM computer-generated output available to help a decision maker know whether or not a solution is relatively insensitive to reasonable changes in one or more of the parameters of the problem. (The complete computer run for these data, including input and full output, is illustrated in Program S3.2 later in this supplement.)

First, let us consider changes to the right-hand side of a constraint. In doing so, in Program S3. 1, we assume changes are made in only one constraint at a time; the other two remain fixed at their original values. *Right-hand side ranging* tells us over

Program S3.1

Sensitivity Analysis for Flair Furniture Using AB:POM

FLAIR FURNITURE EXAMPLE

Solution value = 410

Constraint	Shadow Prices		Original RHS	Lower Limit	Upper Limit
PAINTING	0.50		100.00	80.00	120.00
CARPENTRY	1.50		240.00	200.00	300.00

Variable	Optimal Value	Reduced Cost	Original Coef	Lower Limit	Upper Limit
TABLES	30.00	0.00	7.00	6.666667	10.00
CHAIRS	40.00	0.00	5.00	3.50	5.25

what range of right-hand side values the shadow prices for that constraint will remain valid. In the Flair example, the \$1.50 shadow price for the carpentry constraint will apply even if the current allowance of 240 hours drops as low as 200 or increases as high as 300.

This concept that the right-hand side range limits the shadow price is important in sensitivity analysis. Suppose Flair Furniture could obtain additional carpentry hours at a cost less than the shadow price. The question of how much to obtain is answered by the upper limit in Program S3.1, that is, secure 60 hours more than the current 240 hours.

Now let us look at changes in one of the objective function coefficients. Sensitivity analysis provides, for each decision variable in the solution, the range of profit values over which the answer will be the same. For example, the net profit of \$7 per table (X_1) in the objective function could range from \$6.67 to \$10.00 without the final solution of $X_1 = 30$, $X_2 = 40$ changing. Of course, if a profit coefficient changed at all, the total profit of \$410 would change, even if the optimal quantities of X_1 and X_2 do not.

Artificial and Surplus Variables

Constraints in linear programming problems are seldom all of the "less-than-or-equal-to" ($\leq$) variety seen in the examples thus far in this supplement. Just as common are "greater-than-or-equal-to" ($\geq$) constraints and equalities. To use the simplex method, each of these must be converted to a special form also. If they are not, the simplex technique is unable to set an initial feasible solution in the first tableau.

Example S5

The following constraints were formulated for an LP problem for the Baby Doll Company. We shall convert each for use in the simplex algorithm.

Constraint 1. $25X_1 + 3OX_2 = 900$. To convert an *equality,* we simply add an "artificial" variable (A_1) to the equation:

$$25X_1 + 30X_2 + A_1 = 900$$

An *artificial variable* is a variable that has no physical meaning in terms of a real-world LP problem. It simply allows us to create a basic feasible solution to start the simplex algorithm. An artificial variable is not allowed to appear in the final solution to the problem.

Constraint 2. $5X_1 + 13X_2 + 8X_3 \geq 2,100$. To handle $\geq$ constraints, a "surplus" variable (S_1) is first subtracted and then an artificial variable (A_2) is added to form a new equation:

$$5X_1 + 13X_2 + 8X_3 - S_1 + A_2 = 2,100$$

Surplus variable

A **surplus variable** *does* have a physical meaning—that being the amount over and above a required minimum level set on the right-hand side of a greater-than-or-equal-to constraint.

Whenever an artificial or surplus variable is added to one of the constraints, it must also be included in the other equations and in the problem's objective function, just as was done for slack variables. Each artificial variable is assigned an extremely high cost to ensure that it does not appear in the final solution. Rather than set an actual dollar figure of $10,000 or $1 million, however, we simply use the symbol M to represent a very large number. Surplus variables, like slack variables, carry a zero cost.

Example S6

The Muddy River Chemical Corp. must produce 1,000 lbs of a special mixture of phosphate and potassium for a customer. Phosphate costs $5/lb and potassium costs $6/lb. No more than 300 lbs of phosphate can be used, and at least 150 lbs of potassium must be used.

We wish to formulate this as a linear programming problem and to convert the constraints and objective function into the form needed for the simplex algorithm. Let

$$X_1 = \text{number of pounds of phosphate in the mixture}$$
$$X_2 = \text{number of pounds of potassium in the mixture}$$

Objective function: minimize cost $= \$5X_1 + \$6X_2$.
Objective function in simplex form:

$$\text{Minimize costs} = \$5X_1 + \$6X_2 + \$0S_1 + \$0S_2 + \$MA_1 + \$MA_2$$

REGULAR FORM	SIMPLEX FORM
1st constraint: $1X_1 + 1X_2 = 1,000$	$1X_1 + 1X_2 \qquad\qquad + 1A_1 \qquad\quad = 1,000$
2nd constraint: $1X_1 \qquad\quad \leq 300$	$1X_1 \qquad + 1S_1 \qquad\qquad\qquad = 300$
3rd constraint: $\qquad 1X_2 \geq 150$	$\qquad 1X_2 \quad - 1S_2 \qquad + 1A_2 = 150$

Solving Minimization Problems

Now that we have illustrated a few examples of LP problems with the three different types of constraints, we are ready to solve a minimization problem using the simplex algorithm. Minimization problems are quite similar to the maximization problems tackled earlier in this supplement. The one significant difference involves the $C_j - Z_j$ row. Since our objective is now to minimize costs, the new variable to enter the solution in each tableau (the pivot column) will be the one with the *largest negative* number in the $C_j - Z_j$ row. Thus, we will be choosing the variable that decreases costs the most. In minimization problems, an optimal solution is reached when all numbers in the $C_j - Z_j$ row are *zero* or *positive*—just the opposite from the maximization case. All other simplex steps, as seen below, remain the same.

1. Choose the variable with the largest negative $C_j - Z_j$ to enter the solution.

2. Determine the row to be replaced by selecting the one with the smallest (nonnegative) quantity-to-pivot-column ratio.

3. Calculate new values for the pivot row.

4. Calculate new values for the other rows.

5. Calculate the $C_j - Z_j$ values for this tableau. If there are any $C_j - Z_j$ numbers less than zero, return to step 1.

Example S7

Let us begin to solve Muddy River Chemical's LP formulation of Example S6 using the simplex algorithm.

The initial tableau is set up just as earlier. We note the presence of the $\$M$ costs associated with artificial variables A_1 and A_2, but we treat them as if they were any large number. They have the effect of forcing the artificial variables out of the solution quickly because of their large costs.

$C_j \rightarrow$		$\$5$	$\$6$	$\$0$	$\$0$	$\$M$	$\$M$	
$\downarrow$	Solution Mix	X_1	X_2	S_1	S_2	A_1	A_2	Quantity
$\$M$	A_1	1	1	0	0	1	0	1,000
$\$0$	S_1	1	0	1	0	0	0	300
$\$M$	A_2	0	1	0	-1	0	1	150

As you recall, the numbers in the Z_j row are computed by multiplying the C_j column on the far left of the tableau by the corresponding numbers in each other column.

$$Z_j \text{ (for } X_1 \text{ column)} = (\$M)(1) + (\$0)(1) + (\$M)(0) = \$M$$
$$C_j - Z_j = \$5 - M = -\$M + 5$$
$$Z_j \text{ (for } X_2 \text{ column)} = (\$M)(1) + (\$0)(0) + (\$M)(1) = \$2M$$
$$C_j - Z_j = \$6 - 2M = -\$2M + 6$$
$$Z_j \text{ (for } S_1 \text{ column)} = (\$M)(0) + (\$0)(1) + (\$M)(0) = \$0$$
$$C_j - Z_j = \$0 - 0 = \$0$$

$$Z_j \text{ (for } S_2 \text{ column)} = (\$M)(0) + (\$0)(0) + (\$M)(-1) = -\$M$$
$$C_j - Z_j = \$0 - (-M) = \$M$$

$$Z_j \text{ (for } A_1 \text{ column)} = (\$M)(1) + (\$0)(0) + (\$M)(0) = \$M$$
$$C_j - Z_j = \$M - M = \$0$$

$$Z_j \text{ (for } A_2 \text{ column)} = (\$M)(0) + (\$0)(0) + (\$M)(1) = \$M$$
$$C_j - Z_j = \$M - M = \$0$$

$$Z_j \text{ (for total cost)} = (\$M)(1,000) + (\$0)(300) + (\$M)(150) = \$1,150M$$

1st tableau

$C_j \rightarrow$		$5	$6	$0	$0	$M	$M		
$\downarrow$	Solution Mix	X_1	X_2	S_1	S_2	A_1	A_2	Quantity	
$M	A_1	1	1	0	0	1	0	1,000	
$0	S_1	1	0	1	0	0	0	300	
$M	X_2	0	①	0	−1	0	1	150	← pivot row
	Z_j	$M	$2M	$0	−$M	$M	$M	$1,150M	
	$C_j - Z_j$	−$M + 5	−$2M + 6	$0	$M	$0	$0	(total cost)	

$$\uparrow$$
pivot
column

Variable X_2 will enter the solution next because it has the largest negative $C_j - Z_j$ entry. Variable A_2 will be removed from the solution because the ratio 150/1 is smaller than the ratios of the quantity column numbers to the corresponding X_2 column numbers in the other two rows. That is, 150/1 (the third or A_2 row) is less than 1,000/1 (the first row) and less than 300/0 (the second row). This latter ratio, by the way, involving division by zero, is considered an undefined number—or one that is infinitely large—and hence we may ignore it.

The numbers in the pivot row do not change, in this case, because they are each divided by the (circled) pivot number, that is, 1. The other rows are altered as follows:

A_1 ROW		S_1 ROW	
1 =	1 − (1)(0)	1 =	1 − (0)(0)
0 =	1 − (1)(1)	0 =	0 − (0)(1)
0 =	0 − (1)(0)	1 =	1 − (0)(0)
1 =	0 − (1)(−1)	0 =	0 − (0)(−1)
1 =	1 − (1)(0)	0 =	0 − (0)(0)
−1 =	0 − (1)(1)	0 =	0 − (0)(1)
850 =	1,000 − (1)(150)	300 =	300 − (0)(150)

2nd tableau

$C_j \rightarrow$		$5	$6	$0	$0	$M	$M	
↓	Solution Mix	X_1	X_2	S_1	S_2	A_1	A_2	Quantity
$M	A_1	1	0	0	1	1	−1	850
$0	S_1	1	0	1	1	0	0	300
$6	X_2	0	1	0	−1	0	1	150
	Z_j	$M	$6	$0	$M − 6	$M	−$M + 6	$850M + 900
	$C_j − Z_j$	−$M + 5	$0	$0	−$M + 6	$0	$2M − 6	

The solution at the end of the second tableau is $A_1 = 850$, $S_1 = 300$, $X_2 = 150$, cost = $850M + $900 (not very cheap!). This answer is not optimal because not every number in the $C_j − Z_j$ row is zero or positive. Problem S3.15 allows you to complete the final two tableaus of this example.

KAMARKAR'S ALGORITHM

The biggest change to take place in the field of linear programming solution techniques in four decades was the arrival in 1984 of an alternative to the simplex algorithm. Developed by Narendra Karmarkar, the new method, called Karmarkar's algorithm, often takes significantly less computer time to solve very large-scale LP problems.[1]

As we saw, the simplex algorithm finds a solution by moving from one adjacent corner point to the next, following the outside edges of the feasible region. The major difference is that Karmarkar's method follows a path of points on the *inside* of the feasible region. Its uniqueness is its ability to handle an *extremely* large number of constraints and variables, giving LP users the capability to solve previously unsolvable problems. Although the simplex method will likely continue to be used for many LP problems, a new generation of LP software built around Karmarkar's algorithm is already being used.

SOLVING LP PROBLEMS BY COMPUTER

Large-scale LP problems, which you may be called upon to formulate some day, could, with some long and careful computations, be solved by hand by following the steps of the simplex algorithm. It is, indeed, important to understand how that

Delta Air Lines became the first commercial airline to use the Karmarkar program, called KORBX, developed and sold by AT&T. Delta found that it streamlined the monthly scheduling of 7,000 pilots who fly more than 400 airplanes to 166 cities worldwide. With increased efficiency in allocating limited resources, Delta thinks it will save millions of dollars in crew time and related costs. Another user is the U.S. Military Airlift Command (MAC). Prior to the arrival of KORBX, MAC's LP problem was too big to run on one computer. Even a scaled-down problem that had 36,000 variables and 10,000 constraints took four hours with simplex-based LP software on a mainframe computer. Today, however, models that include the entire, previously unsolvable Pacific Ocean system run in just 20 minutes on KORBX.

[1] For details, see Narendra Karmarkar, "A New Polynomial Time Algorithm for Linear Programming," *Combinatorica,* **4,** 4 (1984): 373–395; or J. N. Hooker, "Karmarkar's Linear Programming Algorithm," *Interfaces,* **16,** 4 (July–August 1986): 75–90.

POM _in action_

Finding Fast Algorithms Means Better Airline Service

Linear-programming techniques have a direct impact on the efficiency and profitability of major airlines. Thomas Cook, president of American Airlines' Decision Technology Group, tells us why optimal solutions are essential in his industry.

"Finding an optimal solution means finding the best solution. Let's say you are trying to minimize a cost function of some kind. For example, we may want to minimize the excess costs related to scheduling crews, hotels, and other costs that are not associated with flight time. So we try to minimize that excess cost, subject to a lot of constraints, such as the amount of time a pilot can fly, how much rest time is needed, and so forth.

"An optimal solution, then, is either a minimum-cost solution or a maximizing solution. For example, we might want to maximize the profit associated with assigning aircraft to the schedule; so we assign large aircraft to high-need segments and small aircraft to low-load segments. Whether it's a minimum or maximum solution depends on what function we are trying to optimize.

"Finding fast solutions to linear-programming problems is also essential. A good example is a major weather disruption. If we get a major disruption at one of the hubs, such as Dallas or Chicago, then a lot of flights may get canceled, which means we have a lot of crews and airplanes in the wrong places. What we need is a way to put that whole operation back together again, so that the crews and airplanes are in the right places. That way, we minimize the cost of the disruption and minimize the passenger inconvenience."

Source: Introduction to Contemporary Mathematics, New York: W. H. Freeman and Company, 1988, pp. 82–83.

algorithm works. The only good way to master the algorithm is to solve several problems by hand. Once you comprehend the mechanics of the simplex technique, however, it should not be necessary to struggle with the manual method again.

Every university and most business and government organizations have access to programs that are capable of solving large linear programming problems. Popular microcomputer software capable of handling large LP problems includes such products as LINDO, STORM, and AB:POM, the package that accompanies this text.

KEY TERMS

Linear programming (LP) (p. 70)

Objective function (p. 70)

Constraints (p. 70)

Iso-profit line method (p. 74)

Corner point method (p. 77)

Iso-cost (p. 78)

Simplex method (p. 85)

Pivot row (p. 88)

Pivot column (p. 89)

Pivot number (p. 89)

Shadow price (p. 92)

Sensitivity analysis (p. 92)

Surplus variable (p. 94)

USING AB:POM

Solving the Flair Furniture Example with AB:POM's LP Module

AB:POM can handle linear programming problems with up to 99 constraints and 99 variables. Data entry and output for the Flair Furniture example used earlier in this chapter are provided in Program S3.2. A nice feature of the program is that it allows

Program S3.2

AB:POM's Computer Analysis of Flair Furniture Data Including Optional Output of Tableau

```
──── Data file: FLAIR ──────────── Linear Programming ──────────────── Solution ────
  Number of constraints (2-99) 2                    Number of variables   (2-99)  2
  maximize
```

FLAIR FURNITURE EXAMPLE

Options ->   Step Cmputr PrtOFF

	TABLES	CHAIRS		RHS	
Objective	7	5			Shadow
CARPENTRY	4	3	≤	240.00	1.50
PAINTING	2	1	≤	100.00	0.50
Values ->	30.00	40.00		$410.00	

Phase 2 Iteration 3   0.38 seconds

```
F1 = Display solution table  F3 = Graph                    F9 = Print   Esc
Press <Esc> key to continue or highlight key or function key for options
```

Iteration 1

	TABLES	CHAIRS	slk 1	slk 2	RHS
maximize	- 7.00	- 5.00	0.00	0.00	0.00
slk 1	2.00	1.00	1.00	0.00	100.00
slk 2	4.00	3.00	0.00	1.00	240.00

Iteration 2

	TABLES	CHAIRS	slk 1	slk 2	RHS
maximize	0.00	- 1.50	3.50	0.00	350.00
TABLES	1.00	0.50	0.50	0.00	50.00
slk 2	0.00	1.00	- 2.00	1.00	40.00

Iteration 3

	TABLES	CHAIRS	slk 1	slk 2	RJS
maximize	0.00	0.00	0.50	1.50	410.00
TABLES	1.00	0.00	1.50	- 0.50	30.00
CHAIRS	0.00	1.00	- 2.00	1.00	40.00

us to give names to the variables (instead of just calling them X_1 and X_2) and to give names to the constraints. Note that information *we* entered at the keyboard is screened.

As output, AB:POM provides optimal values for the variables, optimal cost/profit, shadow prices (duals), and sensitivity analysis. A further option on the LP module is the ability to "step through" the simplex tableaus one at a time. This allows us to observe changes in the solution from one iteration to the next. In addition, AB:POM provides graphical output for problems with only two variables, as shown in Program S3.3. For more technical details on the use of AB:POM, see Appendix F.

Program S3.3

Flair Furniture's Optional Graphic Output

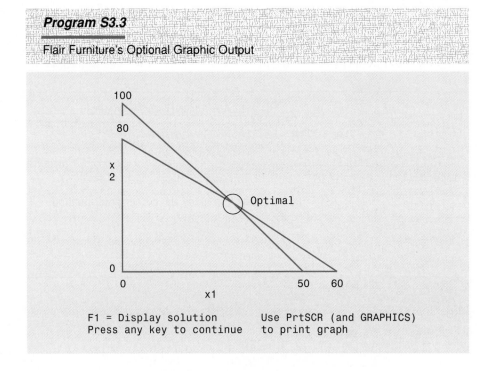

```
F1 = Display solution        Use PrtSCR (and GRAPHICS)
Press any key to continue    to print graph
```

SOLVED PROBLEMS

Solved Problem S3.1

Adolphos, a clothing manufacturer that produces men's shirts and pajamas, has two primary resources available: sewing-machine time (in the sewing department) and cutting-machine time (in the cutting department). Over the next month, Adolphos can schedule up to 280 hours of work on sewing machines and up to 450 hours of work on cutting machines. Each shirt produced requires 1 hour of sewing time and 1.5 hours of cutting time. Outputting each pair of pajamas requires .75 hours of sewing time and 2 hours of cutting time.

To express the LP constraints for this problem mathematically, we let

$$X_1 = \text{Number of shirts produced}$$
$$X_2 = \text{Number of pajamas produced}$$

Solution

First Constraint: $1X_1 + .75X_2 \leq 280$ hours of sewing-machine time available—our first scarce resource

Second Constraint: $1.5X_1 + ②X_2 \leq 450$ hours of cutting-machine time available—our second scarce resource

Note: This means that each pair of pajamas takes 2 hours of the cutting resource.

Adolphos' accounting department analyzes cost and sales figures and states that each shirt produced will yield a $4 contribution to profit and that each pair of pajamas will yield a $3 contribution to profit.

This information can be used to create the LP *objective function* for this problem:

Objective function: Maximize total contribution to profit $= \$4X_1 + \$3X_2$

Solved Problem S3.2

We want to solve the following LP problem using the corner point method.

$$\text{Maximize profit} = \$9X_1 + \$7X_2$$
$$2X_1 + 1X_2 \leq 40$$
$$X_1 + 3X_2 \leq 30$$

Solution

Figure S3.9 illustrates these constraints.

Corner point **a:** $(X_1 = 0, X_2 = 0)$ Profit $= 0$
Corner point **b:** $(X_1 = 0, X_2 = 10)$ Profit $= 9(0) + 7(10) = \$70$
Corner point **d:** $(X_1 = 20, X_2 = 0)$ Profit $= 9(20) + 7(0) = \$180$

Corner point **c** is obtained by solving equations $2X_1 + 1X_2 = 40$ and $X_1 + 3X_1 = 30$ simultaneously. Multiply the second equation by -2 and add it to the first.

$$\begin{array}{r} 2X_1 + 1X_2 = 40 \\ -2X_1 - 6X_2 = -60 \\ \hline -5X_2 = -20 \end{array}$$

Thus $X_2 = 4$.

$$X_1 + 3(X_2 = 4) = 30 \quad \text{or} \quad X_1 + 12 = 30 \quad \text{or} \quad X_1 = 18$$

Corner point **c:** $(X_1 = 18, X_2 = 4)$ Profit $= 9(18) + 7(4) = \$190$

Hence the optimal solution is

$$X_1 = 18, \quad X_2 = 4 \quad \text{Profit} = \$190$$

FIGURE S3.9

Failsafe Electronic Corp's Feasible Region.

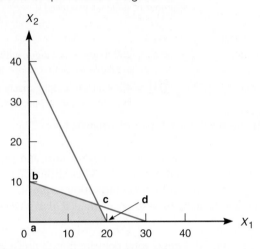

Solved Problem S3.3

The Holiday Meal Turkey Ranch is considering buying two different types of turkey feed. Each feed contains, in varying proportions, some or all of the three nutritional ingredients essential for fattening turkeys. Brand X feed costs the ranch $.02 per pound. Brand Z costs $.03 per pound. The rancher would like to determine the lowest-cost diet that meets the minimum monthly intake requirement for each nutritional ingredient.

The following table contains relevant information about the composition of Brand X and Brand Z feeds, as well as the minimum monthly requirement for each nutritional ingredient per turkey.

COMPOSITION OF EACH POUND OF FEED

Ingredient	Brand X Feed	Brand Z Feed	Minimum Monthly Requirement
A	5 oz.	10 oz.	90 oz.
B	4 oz.	3 oz.	48 oz.
C	.5 oz.	0	1.5 oz
Cost/lb.	$.02	$.03	

Solution

If we let

X_1 = Number of pounds of Brand X feed purchased
X_2 = Number of pounds of Brand Z feed purchased

then we may proceed to formulate this linear programming problem as follows:

$$\text{Minimize cost (in cents)} = 2X_1 + 3X_2$$

subject to these constraints:

$$5X_1 + 10X_2 \geq 90 \text{ ounces} \qquad (\textit{Ingredient A constraint})$$
$$4X_1 + 3X_2 \geq 48 \text{ ounces} \qquad (\textit{Ingredient B constraint})$$
$$1/2X_1 \qquad \geq 1\ 1/2 \text{ ounces} \qquad (\textit{Ingredient C constraint})$$

Figure S3.10 illustrates these constraints.

FIGURE S3.10

Feasible Region for the Holiday Meal Turkey Ranch Problem.

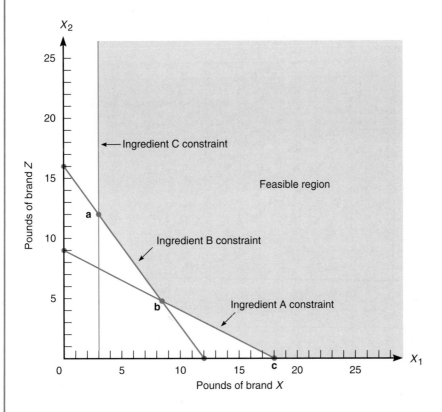

The iso-cost line approach may be used to solve LP minimization problems such as that of the Holiday Meal Turkey Ranch. As with iso-profit lines, we need not compute the cost at each corner point, but instead draw a series of parallel cost lines. The lowest cost line (that is, the one closest in toward the origin) to touch the feasible region provides us with the optimal solution corner.

For example, we start in Figure S3.11 by drawing a 54¢ cost line, namely, $54 = 2X_1 + 3X_2$. Obviously, there are many points in the feasible region that would yield a lower total cost. We proceed to move our iso-cost line toward the lower left, in a plane parallel to the 54¢ solution line. The last point we touch while still in contact with the feasible region is the same as corner point **b** of Figure S3.10. It has the coordinates ($X_1 = 8.4$, $X_2 = 4.8$) and an associated cost of 31.2 cents.

FIGURE S3.11

Graphical Solution to the Holiday Meal Turkey Ranch Problem Using the Iso-Cost Line. Note that the last line parallel to the 54¢ iso-cost line that touches the feasible region indicates the optimal corner point.

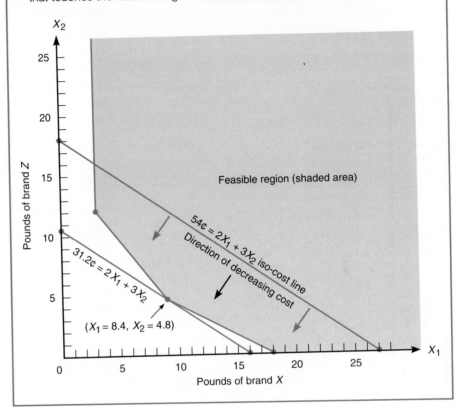

Solved Problem S3.4

Solve the following LP problem.

$$\text{Maximize profit} = \$9X_1 + \$7X_2$$

$$\text{Subject to:} \qquad 2X_1 + 1X_2 \leq 40$$
$$X_1 + 3X_2 \leq 30$$

Solution

We begin by adding slack variables and converting inequalities into equalities.

$$\text{Maximize profit} = 9X_1 + 7X_2 + 0S_1 + 0S_2$$

$$\text{Subject to:} \qquad 2X_1 + 1X_2 + 1S_1 + 0S_2 = 40$$

$$1X_1 + 3X_2 + 0S_1 + 1S_2 = 30$$

The initial tableau is then:

$C_j \rightarrow$		$9	$7	$0	$0	
$\downarrow$ Solution Mix		X_1	X_2	S_1	S_2	Quantity
0	S_1	2	1	1	0	40
0	S_2	1	3	0	1	30
	Z_j	0	0	0	0	0
	$C_j - Z_j$	9	7	0	0	0

The correct second and third tableaus and some of their calculations appear below. The optimal solutions, given in the third tableau, are: $X_1 = 18$, $X_2 = 4$, $S_1 = 0$, $S_2 = 0$, and profit = \$190.

Steps 1 and 2. To go from the first to the second tableau, we note that the pivot column (in the first tableau) is X_1, which has the highest $C_j - Z_j$ value, \$9. The pivot row is S_1 since 40/2 is less than 30/1, and the pivot number is 2.

Step 3. The new X_1 row is found by dividing each number in the old S_1 row by the pivot number, namely, 2/2 = 1, 1/2 = 1/2, 1/2 = 1/2, 0/2 = 0, and 40/2 = 20.

Step 4. The new values for the S_2 row are computed as follows:

$$\begin{pmatrix} \text{Number} \\ \text{in new} \\ S_2 \text{ row} \end{pmatrix} = \begin{pmatrix} \text{Number} \\ \text{in old} \\ S_2 \text{ row} \end{pmatrix} - \left[\begin{pmatrix} \text{Number} \\ \text{below pivot} \\ \text{number} \end{pmatrix} \times \begin{pmatrix} \text{Corresponding} \\ \text{number in the} \\ \text{new } X_1 \text{ row} \end{pmatrix} \right]$$

0	=	1	−	[(1)	× (1)]
5/2	=	3	−	[(1)	× (1/2)]
− 1/2	=	0	−	[(1)	× (1/2)]
1	=	1	−	[(1)	× (0)]
10	=	30	−	[(1)	× (20)]

Step 5. The following new Z_j and $C_j - Z_j$ rows are formed:

Z_j (for X_1) = \$9(1) + 0(0) = \$9 $C_j - Z_j$ = \$9 − \$9 = 0

Z_j (for X_2) = \$9(1/2) + 0(5/2) = \$9/2 $C_j - Z_j$ = \$7 − 9/2 = \$5/2

Z_j (for S_1) = \$9(1/2) + 0(− 1/2) = \$9/2 $C_j - Z_j$ = 0 − 9/2 = − 9/2

Z_j (for S_2) = \$9(0) + 0(1) = \$0 $C_j - Z_j$ = 0 − 0 = 0

Z_j (profit) = \$9(20) + 0(10) = \$180

2nd tableau

$C_j \rightarrow$ $\downarrow$	Solution Mix	$9 X_1	$7 X_2	$0 S_1	$0 S_2	Quantity	
$9	X_1	1	1/2	1/2	0	20	
$0	S_2	0	(5/2)	– 1/2	1	10	← pivot row
	Z_j	$9	$9/2	$9/2	0	$180	
	$C_j - Z_j$	0	$5/2	– $9/2	0		
			↑ pivot column				

The above solution is not optimal, and you must perform steps 1–5 again. The new pivot column is X_2, the new pivot row is S_2, and 5/2 (circled in the second tableau) is the new pivot number.

final tableau

$C_j \rightarrow$ $\downarrow$	Solution Mix	$9 X_1	$7 X_2	$0 S_1	$0 S_2	Quantity
$9	X_1	1	0	3/5	– 1/5	18
$7	X_2	0	1	– 1/5	2/5	4
	Z_j	$9	$7	$4	$1	$190
	$C_j - Z_j$	0	$0	– $4	– $1	

The final solution is $X_1 = 18$, $X_2 = 4$, profit = $190.

Solved Problem S3.5

Convert the following constraints and objective function into the proper form for use in the simplex method.

Objective function: Minimize cost $= 4X_1 + 1X_2$

Subject to the constraints:

$$3X_1 + X_2 = 3$$
$$4X_1 + 3X_2 \geqslant 6$$
$$X_1 + 2X_2 \leqslant 3$$

Solution

Minimize cost $= 4X_1 + 1X_2 + 0S_1 + 0S_2 + MA_1 + MA_2$

Subject to:

$$3X_1 + 1X_2 + 1A_1 = 3$$
$$4X_1 + 3X_2 - 1S_1 + 1A_2 = 6$$
$$1X_1 + 2X_2 + 1S_2 = 3$$

DISCUSSION QUESTIONS

1. Discuss the similarities and differences between minimization and maximization problems, using the graphical solution approaches of linear programming.

2. It has been said that each linear programming problem that has a feasible region has an infinite number of solutions. Explain.

3. The production manager of a large Cincinnati manufacturing firm once made the statement, "I should like to use linear programming, but it's a technique that operates under conditions of certainty. My plant doesn't have that certainty; it's a world of uncertainty. So LP can't be used here." Do you think this statement has any merit? Explain why the manager may have said it.

4. Should people who will be using the results of a new quantitative model such as linear programming become involved in the technical aspects of the problem-solving procedure?

5. C. W. Churchman once said "mathematics . . . tends to lull the unsuspecting into believing that he who thinks elaborately thinks well." Do you think that the best models

are the ones that are the most elaborate and complex mathematically? Why?

6. Explain the purpose and procedures of the simplex method.

7. How do the graphic and simplex methods of solving linear programming problems differ? In what ways are they the same? Under what circumstances would you prefer to use the graphic approach?

8. What are the simplex rules for selecting the pivot column? The pivot row? The pivot number?

9. A particular linear programming problem has the following objective function:

$$\text{Maximize profit} = \$8X_1 + \$6X_2 + \$12X_1 - \$2X_1$$

Which variable should enter at the second simplex tableau? If the objective function was

$$\text{Minimize cost} = \$2.5X_1 + \$2.9X_2 + \$4.0X_3 + \$7.9X_4$$

which variable would be the best candidate to enter the second tableau?

PROBLEMS

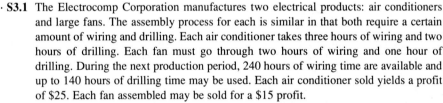 · **S3.1** The Electrocomp Corporation manufactures two electrical products: air conditioners and large fans. The assembly process for each is similar in that both require a certain amount of wiring and drilling. Each air conditioner takes three hours of wiring and two hours of drilling. Each fan must go through two hours of wiring and one hour of drilling. During the next production period, 240 hours of wiring time are available and up to 140 hours of drilling time may be used. Each air conditioner sold yields a profit of $25. Each fan assembled may be sold for a $15 profit.

Formulate and solve this LP production mix situation and find the best combination of air conditioners and fans that yields the highest profit. Use the corner point graphical approach.

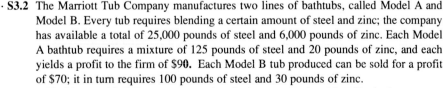 · **S3.2** The Marriott Tub Company manufactures two lines of bathtubs, called Model A and Model B. Every tub requires blending a certain amount of steel and zinc; the company has available a total of 25,000 pounds of steel and 6,000 pounds of zinc. Each Model A bathtub requires a mixture of 125 pounds of steel and 20 pounds of zinc, and each yields a profit to the firm of $90. Each Model B tub produced can be sold for a profit of $70; it in turn requires 100 pounds of steel and 30 pounds of zinc.

Find by graphical linear programming the best production mix of bathtubs.

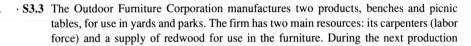 · **S3.3** The Outdoor Furniture Corporation manufactures two products, benches and picnic tables, for use in yards and parks. The firm has two main resources: its carpenters (labor force) and a supply of redwood for use in the furniture. During the next production

cycle, 1,200 hours of labor are available under a union agreement. The firm also has a stock of 3,500 board feet of quality redwood. Each bench that Outdoor Furniture produces requires four labor hours and 10 board feet of redwood; each picnic table takes six labor hours and 35 board feet of redwood. Completed benches will yield a profit of $9 each, and tables will result in a profit of $20 each. How many benches and tables should Outdoor Furniture produce in order to obtain the largest possible profit? Use the graphical linear programming approach.

· **S3.4** MSA Computer Corporation manufactures two models of minicomputers, the Alpha 4 and the Beta 5. The firm employs five technicians, working 160 hours each per month, on its assembly line. Management insists that full employment (that is, *all* 160 hours of time) be maintained for each worker during next month's operations. It requires 20 labor hours to assemble each Alpha 4 computer and 25 labor hours to assemble each Beta 5 model. MSA wants to see at least 10 Alpha 4s and at least 15 Beta 5s produced during the production period. Alpha 4s generate a $1,200 profit per unit, and Beta 5s yield $1,800 each.

Determine the most profitable number of each model of minicomputer to produce during the coming month.

· **S3.5** Solve the following linear programming problem, using the corner point graphical method:

$$\text{Maximize profit} = 4X_1 + 4X_2$$
$$\text{Subject to:} \quad 3X_1 + 5X_2 \leqslant 150$$
$$X_1 - 2X_2 \leqslant 10$$
$$5X_1 + 3X_2 \leqslant 150$$
$$X_1, X_2 \geqslant 0$$

· **S3.6** Consider this linear programming formulation:

$$\text{Minimize cost} = \$1X_1 + \$2X_2$$
$$\text{Subject to:} \quad X_1 + 3X_2 \geqslant 90$$
$$8X_1 - 2X_2 \geqslant 160$$
$$3X_1 + 2X_2 \geqslant 120$$
$$X_2 \leqslant 70$$

a) Graphically illustrate the feasible region and apply the iso-cost line procedure to indicate which corner point produces the optimal solution.

b) What is the cost of this solution?

· **S3.7** Develop your own individual set of constraint equations and inequalities and use them to illustrate graphically each of the following conditions:

a) An "unbounded" problem. That is, a problem that has no constraints forcing profit limitation.

b) An "infeasible" problem. That is, a problem that has no solution, but satisfies all of the constraints.

c) A problem containing redundant constraints. That is, a problem that has one or more constraints that do not affect the solution.

· **S3.8** The mathematical relationships that follow were formulated by an operations research analyst at the Dilts Chemical Company. Which ones are invalid for use in a linear programming problem, and why?

$$\text{Maximize profit} = 4X_1 + 3X_1X_2 + 5X_3$$

$$\begin{aligned}\text{Subject to:} \quad & 2X_1 + X_2 + 2X_3 \leqslant 50 \\ & 8X_1 - 4X_2 \geqslant 6 \\ & 1.5X_1 + 6X_2 + 3X_3 \geqslant 21 \\ & 19X_2 - \tfrac{1}{3}X_3 = 17 \\ & 5X_1 + 4X_2 + 3\sqrt{X_3} \leqslant 80 \\ & -X_1 - X_2 + X_3 = 5 \end{aligned}$$

: **S3.9** Dantzig Corp. makes three products, and has three machines available as resources as given in the following LP problem.

$$\text{Maximize profit} = 4X_1 + 4X_2 + 7X_3$$

$$\begin{aligned}\text{Subject to:} \quad & 1X_1 + 7X_2 + 4X_3 \leqslant 100 \text{ (hours on machine 1)} \\ & 2X_1 + 1X_2 + 7X_3 \leqslant 110 \text{ (hours on machine 2)} \\ & 8X_1 + 4X_2 + 1X_3 \leqslant 100 \text{ (hours on machine 3)} \end{aligned}$$

a) Determine the optimal solution.

b) Is there unused time available on any of the machines with the optimal solution?

: **S3.10** Using the data from Dantzig Corp. in Problem S3.9, determine:

a) What would it be worth to the firm to make an additional hour of time available on the third machine?

b) How much would the firm's profit increase if an extra 10 hours of time were made available on the second machine at no extra cost?

: **S3.11** The Coppins Mfg. Corp. has $250,000 available to invest for 12 months prior to its plant expansion. The money can be placed in treasury notes yielding an 8% return or in municipal bonds at an average rate of 9%. Management requires that at least 50% of the investment be placed in treasury notes. Because of defaults in municipal bonds, it is decided that no more than 40% of the investment be placed in bonds.

How much should be invested in each security to maximize return on investment?

: **S3.12** Gold Furniture manufactures two different types of china cabinets, a French provincial model and a Danish modern model. Each cabinet produced must go through three departments: carpentry, painting, and finishing. The accompanying table contains all relevant information concerning production times per cabinet produced and production capacities for each operation per day, along with net revenue per unit produced. The firm has a contract with an Indiana distributor to produce a minimum of 300 of each cabinet per week (or 60 cabinets per day.) Owner Steve Gold would like to determine a product mix to maximize his daily revenue.

CABINET STYLE	CARPENTRY (HRS./CABINET)	PAINTING (HRS./CABINET)	FINISHING (HRS./CABINET)	NET REVENUE/ CABINET
French provincial	3	1 1/2	3/4	$28
Danish modern	2	1	3/4	$25
Department capacity (hours)	360	200	125	

Formulate this as a linear programming problem.

: **S3.13** The famous E. S. Mann Restaurant is open 24 hours a day. Waiters and busboys report for duty at 3 A.M., 7 A.M., 11 A.M., 3 P.M., 7 P.M., or 11 P.M., and each works an eight-hour shift. The following table shows the minimum number of workers needed during the six periods into which the day is divided.

PERIOD	TIME	NUMBER OF WAITERS AND BUSBOYS REQUIRED
1	3 A.M.– 7 A.M.	3
2	7 A.M.– 11 A.M.	12
3	11 A.M.– 3 P.M.	16
4	3 P.M.– 7 P.M.	9
5	7 P.M.– 11 P.M.	11
6	11 P.M.– 3 A.M.	4

Mann's scheduling problem is to determine how many waiters and busboys should report for work at the start of each time period in order to minimize the total staff required for one day's operation: (*Hint:* Let X_i equal the number of waiters and busboys beginning work in time period i, where $i = 1, 2, 3, 4, 5, 6$.)

 : **S3.14** This is the slack time of year and we would actually like to shut down the plant, but if we laid off our core employees they would probably go to work for our competitor. We could keep our core (full-time year-round) employees busy by making 10,000 round tables per month, or by making 20,000 square tables per month (or some ratio thereof). We do, however, have a contract with a supplier to buy precut table tops for a minimum of 5,000 square tables per month. Handling and storage costs per round table will be $10, while these costs would be $8 per square table.

Draw a graph, algebraically describe the constraint inequalities and the objective function, identify the points bounding the feasible solution area, and find the cost at each point and the optimum solution. Let X_1 equal the thousands of round tables per month and X_2 equal the thousands of square tables per month.

 : **S3.15** Each coffee table produced by Chris Franke Designers nets the firm a profit of $**9**. Each bookcase yields a $12 profit. Franke's firm is small and its resources limited. During any given production period (of one week), 10 gallons of varnish and 12 lengths of high-quality redwood are available. Each coffee table requires approximately one gallon of varnish and one length of redwood. Each bookcase takes one gallon of varnish and two lengths of wood.

Formulate Franke's production mix decision as a linear programming problem, and solve, using the simplex method. How many tables and bookcases should be produced each week? What will the maximum profit be?

 : **S3.16 a)** Set up an initial simplex tableau, given the following two constraints and objective function:

$$1X_1 + 4X_2 \leq 24$$
$$1X_1 + 2X_2 \leq 16$$

$$\text{Maximize profit} = \$3X_1 + \$9X_2$$

You will have to add slack variables.

b) Briefly list the iterative steps necessary to solve the problem in part (a).

c) Determine the next tableau from the one you developed in part (a). Determine whether or not it is an optimum solution.

d) If necessary, develop another tableau and determine whether or not it is an optimum solution. Interpret this tableau.

e) Start with the same initial tableau from part (a) but use X_1 as the first pivot column. Continue to iterate it (a total of twice) until you reach an optimum solution.

: **S3.17** Solve the following linear programming problem graphically. Then set up a simplex tableau and solve the problem, using the simplex method. Indicate the corner points generated at each iteration by the simplex on your graph.

$$\text{Maximize profit} = \$3X_1 + \$5X_2$$

$$\text{Subject to:} \qquad X_2 \leqslant 6$$

$$3X_1 + 2X_2 \leqslant 18$$

$$X_1, X_2 \geqslant 0$$

: **S3.18** Solve the following linear programming problem, first graphically and then by the simplex algorithm.

$$\text{Minimize cost} = 4X_1 + 5X_2$$

$$\text{Subject to: } X_1 + 2X_2 \geqslant 80$$

$$3X_1 + X_2 \geqslant 75$$

$$X_1, X_2 \geqslant 0$$

What are the values of the basic variables at each iteration? Which are the nonbasic variables at each iteration?

: **S3.19** Coleman Distributors packages and distributes industrial supplies. A standard shipment can be packaged in a Class A container, a Class K container, or a Class T container. A single Class A container yields a profit of $8; a Class K container, a profit of $6; and a Class T container, a profit of $14. Each shipment prepared requires a certain amount of packing material and a certain amount of time.

	RESOURCES NEEDED PER STANDARD SHIPMENT	
Class of Container	Packing Material (pounds)	Packing Time (hours)
A	2	2
K	1	6
T	3	4
Total amount of resource available each week	120 pounds	240 hours

John Coleman, head of the firm, must decide the optimal number of each class of container to pack each week. He is bound by the previously mentioned resource restrictions, but also decides that he must keep his six full-time packers employed all 240 hours (6 workers × 40 hours) each week.

Formulate and solve this problem, using the simplex method.

: **S3.20** Complete the job of solving Example S7 by applying the simplex method until an optimal solution is reached. (*Hint:* Two more tableaus are required.)

: **S3.21** New Orleans's Mt. Sinai Hospital is a large, private, 600-bed facility complete with laboratories, operating rooms, and x-ray equipment. In seeking to increase revenues,

Mt. Sinai's administration has decided to make a 90-bed addition on a portion of adjacent land currently used for staff parking. The administrators feel that the labs, operating rooms, and x-ray department are not being fully utilized at present and do not need to be expanded to handle additional patients. The addition of 90 beds, however, involves deciding how many beds should be allocated to the medical staff (for medical patients) and how many to the surgical staff (for surgical patients).

The hospital's accounting and medical records departments have provided the following pertinent information. The average hospital stay for a medical patient is eight days, and the average medical patient generates $2,280 in revenues. The average surgical patient is in the hospital five days and receives a $1,515 bill. The laboratory is capable of handling 15,000 tests per year more than it *was* handling. The average medical patient requires 3.1 lab tests, and the average surgical patient takes 2.6 lab tests. Furthermore, the average medical patient uses one x-ray, while the average surgical patient requires two x-rays. If the hospital were expanded by 90 beds, the x-ray department could handle up to 7,000 x-rays without significant additional cost. Finally, the administration estimates that up to 2,800 additional operations could be performed in existing operating room facilities. Medical patients, of course, require no surgery, while each surgical patient generally has one surgery performed.

Formulate this problem so as to determine how many medical beds and how many surgical beds should be added in order to maximize revenues. Assume that the hospital is open 365 days per year.

· **S3.22** Set up a complete initial tableau for the data (repeated below) that were first presented in Solved Problem S3.5.

$$\text{Minimize cost} = 4X_1 + 1X_2 + 0S_1$$
$$+ 0S_1 + MA_1 + MA_2$$

$$\text{Subject to:} \quad 3X_1 + 1X_2 \qquad\qquad +1A_1 \qquad = 3$$
$$4X_1 + 3X_2 - 1S_2 \qquad\qquad + 1A_2 = 6$$
$$1X_1 + 2X_2 \qquad + 1S_2 \qquad\qquad = 3$$

a) Which variable will enter the solution next?

b) Which variable will leave the solution?

: **S3.23** Solve Problem S3.22 for the optimal solution, using the simplex method.

: **S3.24** Using the data from Problem S3.1 and LP software:

a) Determine the range within which the unit profit contribution of an air conditioner must fall for the current solution to remain optimal.

b) Determine the shadow price for the wiring constraint and range within which that value holds.

: **S3.25** Using the data from Problem S3.2 and LP software:

a) Determine the range within which the unit profit contribution of a Model A tub must fall for the current solution to remain optimal.

b) Determine by how much the unit profit contribution of a Model B tub must increase before it would be desirable to produce any of them.

c) Determine the shadow price for the steel constraint and the range within which that value holds.

d) Determine the shadow price for the zinc constraint and the range within which that value holds.

: **S3.26** Using the data from Problem S3.14 and LP software:

a) Determine the range within which the unit cost of a square table must fall for the current solution to remain optimal.

b) Determine the shadow price for the labor constraint and the range within which that value holds.

c) Determine the shadow price for the contract constraint and the range within which that value holds.

: **S3.27** The advertising director for Diversey Paint and Supply, a chain of four retail stores on Chicago's North Side, is considering two media possibilities. One plan is for a series of half-page ads in the Sunday *Chicago Tribune* newspaper, and the other is for advertising time on Chicago TV. The stores are expanding their lines of do-it-yourself tools, and the advertising director is interested in an exposure level of at least 40% within the city's neighborhoods and 60% in northwest suburban areas.

The TV viewing time under consideration has an exposure rating per spot of 5% in city homes and 3% in the northwest suburbs. The Sunday newspaper has corresponding exposure rates of 4% and 3% per ad. The cost of a half-page *Tribune* advertisement is $925; a television spot costs $2000.

Diversey Paint would like to select the least costly advertising strategy that would meet desired exposure levels. Formulate this, using LP.

: **S3.28** The state of Missouri has three major power-generating companies (A, B, and C). During the months of peak demand, the Missouri Power Authority authorizes these companies to pool their excess supply and to distribute it to smaller independent power companies that do not have generators large enough to handle the demand.

Excess supply is distributed on the basis of cost per kilowatt hour transmitted. The accompanying table shows the demand and supply in millions of kilowatt hours and the costs per kilowatt hour of transmitting electric power to four small companies in cities W, X, Y, and Z.

	TO				
FROM	W	X	Y	Z	EXCESS SUPPLY
A	12¢	4¢	9¢	5¢	55
B	8¢	1¢	6¢	6¢	45
C	1¢	12¢	4¢	7¢	30
Unfilled power demand	40	20	50	20	

a) Formulate an LP model for this problem.

b) Find the least cost distribution system, using an LP computer program.

: **S3.29** The Arden County, Maryland, superintendent of education is responsible for assigning students to the three high schools in his county. He recognizes the need to bus a certain number of students, for several sectors of the county are beyond walking distance to a school. The superintendent partitions the county into five geographic sectors as he attempts to establish a plan that will minimize the total number of student miles traveled by bus. He also recognizes that if a student happens to live in a certain sector and is assigned to the high school in that sector, there is no need to bus him since he can walk from home to school. The three schools are located in sectors B, C, and E.

The table below reflects the number of high-school-age students living in each sector and the distance in miles from each sector to each school.

| | DISTANCE TO SCHOOL | | | |
Sector	School in Sector B	School in Sector C	School in Sector E	No. of Students
A	5	8	6	700
B	0	4	12	500
C	4	0	7	100
D	7	2	5	800
E	12	7	0	400
			Total	2,500

Each high school has a capacity of 900 students.

Set up the objective function and constraints of this problem, using linear programming, so that the total number of student miles traveled by bus is minimized. Then solve the problem, using LP software.

: S3.30   South Central Utilities has just announced the August 1 opening of its second nuclear generator at its Baton Rouge, Louisiana, nuclear power plant. Its personnel department has been directed to determine how many nuclear technicians need to be hired and trained over the remainder of the year.

The plant currently employs 350 fully trained technicians and projects the following labor needs:

MONTH	LABOR NEEDED (IN HOURS)
August	40,000
September	45,000
October	35,000
November	50,000
December	45,000

By Louisiana law, a reactor employee can actually work no more than 130 hours per month. (Slightly over one hour per day is used for check-in and checkout record keeping and for daily radiation health scans.) Policy at South Central Utilities also dictates that layoffs are not acceptable in those months when the nuclear plant is overstaffed. So, if more trained employees are available than are needed in any month, each worker is still fully paid, even though he or she is not required to work the 130 hours. Training new employees is an important and costly procedure. It takes one month of one-on-one classroom instruction before a new technician is permitted to work alone in the reactor facility. Therefore, South Central must hire trainees one month before they are actually needed. Each trainee teams up with a skilled nuclear technician and requires 90 hours of that employee's time, meaning that 90 hours less of the technician's time are available that month for actual reactor work.

Personnel department records indicate a turnover rate of trained technicians at 5% per month. In other words, about 5% of the skilled employees at the start of any month resign by the end of that month.

A trained technician earns an average monthly salary of $2,000 (regardless of the number of hours worked, as noted earlier). Trainees are paid $900 during their one month of instruction.

a) Formulate this staffing problem, using LP.

b) Solve the problem. How many trainees must begin each month?

: **S3.31** Andy's Bicycle Company (ABC) has the hottest new product on the upscale toy market—boys' and girls' bikes in bright fashion colors, with oversized hubs and axles, shell design safety tires, a strong padded frame, chrome-plated chains, brackets, and valves, and a nonslip handlebar. Due to the seller's market for high-quality toys for the newest baby boomers, ABC can sell all the bicycles it manufactures at the following prices: boys' bikes—$220, girls' bikes—$175. This is the price payable to ABC at its Orlando plant.

The firm's accountant has determined that direct labor costs will be 45% of the price ABC receives for the boys' model and 40% of the price received for the girls' model. Production costs other than labor, but excluding painting and packaging, are $44 per boys' bicycle and $30 per girls' bicycle. Painting and packaging are $20 per bike, regardless of model.

The Orlando plant's overall production capacity is 390 bicycles per day. Each boys' bike requires 2.5 labor hours while each girls' model takes 2.4 hours to complete. ABC currently employs 120 workers, who each put in an 8-hour day. The firm has no desire to hire or fire to affect labor availability for it believes its stable work force is one of its biggest assets.

Using a graphical approach, determine the best product mix for ABC.

: **S3.32** Amalgamated Products has just received a contract for frames from Spalding's Landing Gear, Inc. Spalding has strict quality control standards for all of its components including its landing gears frames. Consequently, Spalding has informed Amalgamated that each frame must have the following content:

MATERIAL IN STEEL	MINIMUM PERCENT	MAXIMUM PERCENT
Manganese	2.1	2.3
Silicon	4.3	4.6
Carbon	5.05	5.35

Amalgamated mixes batches of eight different available materials to produce one ton of steel used in the frames. The table that follows details these materials.

MATERIAL AVAILABLE	MANGANESE (%)	SILICON (%)	CARBON (%)	POUNDS AVAILABLE	COST PER POUND
Alloy 1	70.0	15.0	3.0	No limit	$.12
Alloy 2	55.0	30.0	1.0	300	$.13
Alloy 3	12.0	26.0	0	No limit	$.15
Iron 1	1.0	10.0	3.0	No limit	$.09
Iron 2	5.0	2.5	0	No limit	$.07
Carbide 1	0	24.0	18.0	50	$.10
Carbide 2	0	25.0	20.0	200	$.12
Carbide 3	0	23.0	25.0	100	$.09

Formulate (only) the linear programming model that will indicate how much each of the eight materials should be blended into a one-ton load of steel so that Amalgamated meets its requirements while minimizing costs.

: **S3.33**   Modem Corporation of America (MCA) is the world's largest producer of modem communication devices for microcomputers, but the firm is facing several constraints as it prepares its November production plan. First, it has experienced a tremendous demand and has been unable to keep any significant inventory in stock. This situation is not expected to change. Second, the firm is located in a small Iowa town from which additional labor is not readily available. Workers can be shifted from production of one modem to another, however. To produce 9,000 of the 300 Baud Modems in September required 5,000 direct labor hours, and 10,400 of the 1200 Baud Smart Modems absorbed 10,400 direct labor hours. Third, MCA is experiencing a problem affecting the Smart Modems model. Its component supplier is able to guarantee only 8,000 microprocessors for November delivery. Each Smart Modem requires one of these specially made microprocessors. Alternative suppliers are not available on short notice.

MCA INCOME STATEMENT
MONTH ENDED SEPTEMBER 30

	REGULAR MODEMS	SMART MODEMS
Sales	$450,000	$640,000
Less: Discounts	10,000	15,000
Returns	12,000	9,500
Warranty replacements	4,000	2,500
Net Sales	$424,000	$613,000
Sales Costs		
Direct labor	60,000	76,800
Indirect labor	9,000	11,520
Materials cost	90,000	128,000
Depreciation	40,000	50,800
Cost of sales	$199,000	$267,120
Gross Profit	$225,000	$345,880
Selling and General Expenses		
General expenses—variable	30,000	35,000
General expenses—fixed	36,000	40,000
Advertising	28,000	25,000
Sales commissions	31,000	60,000
Total operating cost	$125,000	$160,000
Pre-tax income	$100,000	$185,880
Income taxes (25%)	25,000	46,470
Net income	$ 75,000	$139,410

Ms. Dede Saelens, Director of Manufacturing, wants to plan the optimal mix of the two modem models to produce in November to maximize profits for MCA. The income statement for September is shown above. Costs presented are typical of prior months and are expected to remain at the same levels in the near future.

a) Formulate, using September's data, MCA's problem as a linear program.

b) Solve the problem graphically.

c) Discuss the implications of your recommended solution.

Data Base Application

:S3.34 Mote Enterprises is a Houston manufacturer of tables and accessories for personal computers. The company is caught in a vicious crossfire between rapidly dropping market prices from competitors worldwide for its products and stable domestic costs for its materials. The 15 different products noted below must be scheduled to maximize profits or there will be no jobs and no firm in another three months. Your job as the new P/OM graduate is to address the issues raised this morning by Mr. Warren Mote, the president, in an emergency meeting in his office. Without being told so explicitly, you concluded that if you didn't get the schedule done accurately and in a timely manner you would be history. To your relief the industrial engineers and accountants have provided the data shown below. The issues, as recorded in your notes, are shown in **a** through **f** below.

PRODUCT	STEEL ALLOY REQUIRED (LBS.)	PLASTIC REQUIRED (SQ. FT.)	WOOD REQUIRED (BD.FT.)	ALUMINUM REQUIRED (LBS.)	FORMICA REQUIRED (BD. FT.)	LABOR REQUIRED (HOURS)	MINIMUM MONTHLY DEMAND (UNITS)	CONTRIBUTION TO PROFIT
A158	—	.4	.7	5.8	10.9	3.1	—	$18.79
B179	4	.5	1.8	10.3	2.0	1.0	20	6.31
C023	6	—	1.5	1.1	2.3	1.2	10	8.19
D045	10	.4	2.0	—	—	4.8	10	45.88
E388	12	1.2	1.2	8.1	4.9	5.5	—	63.00
F422	—	1.4	1.5	7.1	10.0	.8	20	4.10
G366	10	1.4	7.0	6.2	11.1	9.1	10	81.15
H600	5	1.0	5.0	7.3	12.4	4.8	20	50.06
I701	1	.4	—	10.0	5.2	1.9	50	12.79
J802	1	.3	—	11.0	6.1	1.4	20	15.88
K900	—	.2	—	12.5	7.7	1.0	20	17.91
L901	2	1.8	1.5	13.1	5.0	5.1	10	49.99
M050	—	2.7	5.0	—	2.1	3.1	20	24.00
N150	10	1.1	5.8	—	—	7.7	10	88.88
P259	10	—	6.2	15.0	1.0	6.6	10	77.01
Availability per month	980	400	600	2,500	1,800	1,000		

a) How many of each of the 15 products should be produced each month?

b) Clearly explain the meaning of each shadow price.

c) A number of workers interested in saving money for the holidays have offered to work overtime next month at a rate of $12.50 per hour. What should the response of management be?

d) Two tons of steel alloy are available from an overstocked supplier at a total cost of $8,000. Should the steel be purchased? All or part of the supply?

e) The accountants have just discovered that an error was made in the contribution to profit for product N150. The correct value is actually $8.88. What are the implications of this error?

f) Management is considering the abandonment of five product lines (those beginning with letters A through E). If no minimum monthly demand is established, what are the implications? Note that there already is no minimum for two of these products. Use the corrected value for N150.

CASE STUDY

Golding Landscaping and Plants, Inc.

Kenneth and Patricia Golding spent a career as a husband and wife real estate investment partnership in Washington, D.C. When they finally retired to a 25-acre farm in northern Virginia's Fairfax County, they became ardent amateur gardeners. Kenneth Golding planted shrubs and fruit trees, while Patricia spent her hours potting all sizes of plants. When the volume of shrubs and plants reached the point where the Goldings began to think of their hobby in a serious vein, they built a greenhouse adjacent to their home and installed heating and watering systems in it.

By 1984, the Goldings realized their retirement from real estate had really only led to a second career—in the plant and shrub business—and they filed for a Virginia business license. Within a matter of months, they asked their attorney to file incorporation documents and formed the firm Golding Landscaping and Plants, Inc.

Early in the new business's existence, Kenneth Golding recognized the need for a high-quality commercial fertilizer that he could blend himself, both for sale and for his own nursery. His goal was to keep his costs to a minimum while producing a top-notch product that was especially suited to the northern Virginia climate.

Working with chemists at Virginia Tech and George Mason Universities, Golding blended "Golding-Grow." It consists of four chemical compounds, C-30, C-92, D-21, and E-11. The cost per pound for each compound is indicated below.

CHEMICAL COMPOUND	COST PER POUND
C-30	$.12
C-92	.09
D-21	.11
E-11	.04

The specifications for Golding-Grow are established as:

a. Chemical E-11 must comprise at least 15% of the blend.

b. C-92 and C-30 must together constitute at least 45% of the blend.

c. D-21 and C-92 can together constitute no more than 30% of the blend.

d. Golding-Grow is packaged and sold in 50-pound bags.

Discussion Questions

1. Formulate an LP problem to determine what blend of the four chemicals will allow Golding to minimize the cost of a 50-pound bag of the fertilizer.

2. Solve to find the best solution.

Source: Barry Render and Ralph Stair, *Introduction to Management Science,* Boston: Allyn and Bacon, 1992.

CASE STUDY

Red Brand Canners

On Monday, September 13, 1990, Mr. Mitchell Gordon, vice president of operations, asked the controller, the sales manager, and the production manager to meet with him to discuss the amount of tomato products to pack that season. The tomato crop, which had been purchased at planting, was beginning to arrive at the cannery, and packing operations would have to be started by the following Monday. Red Brand Canners was a medium-sized company which canned and distributed a variety of fruit and vegetable products under private brands in the western states.

Mr. William Cooper, the controller, and Mr. Charles Myers, the sales manager, were the first to arrive in Mr. Gordon's office. Dan Tucker, the production manager, came in a few minutes later and said that he had picked up

Produce Inspection's latest estimate of the quality of the incoming tomatoes. According to their report, about 20 percent of the crop was Grade A quality and the remaining portion of the 3-million-pound crop was Grade B.

Gordon asked Myers about the demand for tomato products for the coming year. Myers replied that they could sell all of the whole canned tomatoes they could produce. The expected demand for tomato juice and tomato paste, on the other hand, was limited. The sales manager then passed around the latest demand forecast, which is shown in Table S3.5. He reminded the group that the selling prices had been set in light of the long-term marketing strategy of the company and that the potential sales had been forecast at these prices.

CASE STUDY (Continued)

TABLE S3.5 Demand Forecasts

PRODUCT	SELLING PRICE PER CASE	DEMAND FORECAST (CASES)
24—2½ whole tomatoes	$4.00	800,000
24—2½ choice peach halves	5.40	10,000
24—2½ peach nectar	4.60	5,000
24—2½ tomato juice	4.50	50,000
24—2½ cooking apples	4.90	15,000
24—2½ tomato paste	3.80	80,000

Bill Cooper, after looking at Myers' estimates of demand, said that it looked like the company "should do quite well [on the tomato crop] this year." With the new accounting system that had been set up, he had been able to compute the contribution for each product, and according to his analysis the incremental profit on whole tomatoes was greater than the incremental profit on any other tomato product. In May, after Red Brand had signed contracts agreeing to purchase the grower's production at an average delivered price of 6 cents per pound, Cooper had computed the tomato products' contributions (see Table S3.6).

Dan Tucker brought to Cooper's attention that although there was ample production capacity, it was impossible to produce all whole tomatoes since too small a portion of the tomato crop was "A" quality. Red Brand used a numerical scale to record the quality of both raw produce and prepared products. This scale ran from zero to ten, the higher number representing better quality. According to this scale, "A" tomatoes averaged nine points per pound and "B" tomatoes averaged five points per pound. Tucker noted that the minimum average input quality was eight points per pound for canned whole tomatoes and six points per pound for juice. Paste could be made entirely from "B"-grade tomatoes. This meant that whole tomato production was limited to 800,000 pounds.

Gordon stated that this was not a real limitation. He had been recently solicited to purchase 80,000 pounds of Grade A tomatoes at 8 1/2 cents per pound and at that time had turned down the offer. He felt, however, that the tomatoes were still available.

Myers, who had been doing some calculations, said that although he agreed that the company "should do quite well this year," it would not be by canning whole tomatoes. It seemed to him that the tomato cost should be allocated on the basis of quality and quantity rather than by quantity only, as Cooper had done. Therefore, he had recomputed the marginal profit on this basis (see Table S3.7), and from his results had concluded that Red Brand should use 2 million pounds of the "B" tomatoes for paste, and the remaining

TABLE S3.6 Product Item Profitability.

PRODUCT	24—2½ WHOLE TOMATOTES	24—2½ CHOICE PEACH HALVES	24—2½ PEACH NECTAR	24—2½ TOMATO JUICE	24—2½ COOKING APPLES	24—2½ TOMATO PASTE
Sellng price	$4.00	$5.40	$4.60	$4.50	$4.90	$3.80
Variable costs:						
Direct labor	1.18	1.40	1.27	1.32	.70	.54
Variable overhead	.24	.32	.23	.36	.22	.26
Variable selling	.40	.30	.40	.85	.28	.38
Packaging material	.70	.56	.60	.65	.70	.77
Fruit*	1.08	1.80	1.70	1.20	.90	1.50
Total variable costs	3.60	4.38	4.20	4.38	2.80	3.45
Contribution	.40	1.02	.40	.12	1.10	.35
Less allocated overhead	.28	.70	.52	.21	.75	.23
Net Profit	.12	.32	(.12)	(.09)	.35	.12

*Product usage is as given below:

Product	Pounds per Case	Product	Pounds per Case
Whole tomatoes	18	Tomato juice	20
Peach halves	18	Cooking apples	27
Peach nectar	17	Tomato paste	25

CASE STUDY (Continued)

400,000 pounds of "B" tomatoes and all of the "A" tomatoes for juice. If the demand expectations were realized, a contribution of $48,000 would be made on this year's tomato crop.

Discussion Questions

1. Structure this problem verbally, including a written description of the constraints and objective. What are the decision variables?

2. Determine the most profitable mix of products for Red Brand.

Adapted from Stanford Business Cases 1965, 1977 with permission of Stanford University Graduate School of Business, © 1965, 1977 by the Board of Trustees of the Leland Stanford Junior University.

TABLE S3.7 Marginal Analysis of Tomato Products.

PRODUCT	CANNED WHOLE TOMATOES	TOMATO JUICE	TOMATO PASTE
Selling price	$4.00	$4.50	$3.80
Variable cost (excluding tomato cost)	2.52	3.18	1.95
	$1.48	$1.32	$1.85
Tomato cost	1.49	1.24	1.30
Marginal profit	($ .01)	$ .08	$ .55

Z = cost per pound of Grade A tomatoes in cents.
Y = cost per pound of Grade B tomatoes in cents.

$$(600{,}000 \text{ lb} \times Z) + (2{,}400{,}000 \text{ lb} \times Y) = (3{,}000{,}000 \text{ lb} \times 6) \tag{1}$$

$$\frac{Z}{9} = \frac{Y}{5} \tag{2}$$

z = 9.32 cents per pound; Y = 5.18 cents per pound.

BIBLIOGRAPHY

Balbirer, S. D., and D. Shaw. "An Application of Linear Programming to Bank Financial Planning." *Interfaces* **11** (October 1981): 77–82.

Brosch, L. C., R. J. Buck, W. H. Sparrow, and J. R. White. "Boxcars, Linear Programming, and the Sleeping Kitten." *Interfaces* **10** (December 1980): 53–61.

Cabraal, R. A. "Production Planning in a Sri Lanka Coconut Mill Using Parametric Linear Programming." *Interfaces* **11** (June 1981): 16–21.

Ferris, M. C., and A. B. Philpott. "On the Performance of Karmarkar's Algorithm." *Journal of the Operational Research Society* **39** (March 1988): 257–270.

Hilal, S. S., and W. Erikson. "Matching Supplies to Save Lives: Linear Programming the Production of Heart Valves." *Interfaces* **11** (December 1981): 48–56.

Hollorann, T., and J. Byrn. "United Airlines Stationed Manpower Planning System." *Interfaces* **16** (January–February 1986): 39–50.

Jackson, B. L., and J. M. Brown. "Using LP for Crude Oil Sales at Elk Hills." *Interfaces* **10** (June 1980): 65–70.

Leff, H. S., M. Dada, and S. C. Graves. "An LP Planning Model for a Mental Health Community Support System." *Management Science* **32** (February 1986): 139–155.

Marsten, R. E., and M. R. Muller. "A Mixed Integer Programming Approach to Air Cargo Fleet Planning." *Management Science* **26** (November 1980): 1096–1107.

Nauss, R. M., and B. R. Keeler. "Minimizing Net Interest Cost in Municipal Bond Bidding." *Management Science* **27** (April 1981): 365–376.

Oliff, M., and E. Burch. "Multiproduct Production Scheduling at Owens-Corning Fiberglass." *Interfaces* **15** (September–October 1985): 25–34.

Render, B., and R. M. Stair. *Quantitative Analysis for Management,* 4th ed. Boston: Allyn and Bacon, 1991.

Render, B., and R. M. Stair. *Introduction to Management Science.* Boston: Allyn and Bacon, 1992.

Roy, A., E. E. Defalomir, and L. Lasdon. "An Optimization-Based Decision Support System for a Product Mix Problem." *Interfaces* **12** (April 1982): 26–33.

Sullivan, R., and S. Secrest. "A Simple Optimization DSS for Production Planning at Dairyman's Cooperative Creamery." *Interfaces* **15** (September–October 1985): 46–53.

Wild, W. G. "The Startling Discovery Bell Labs Kept in the Shadows." *Business Week* (Sept. 21, 1987): 69+.

Williams, P. W. "A Linear Programming Approach to Production Scheduling." *Production and Inventory Management* **11** (Third Quarter, 1970).

Forecasting

INTRODUCTION

Every day managers make decisions without knowing what will happen in the future. Inventory is ordered without certainty as to what sales will be; new equipment is purchased despite uncertainty about demand for products; and investments are made without knowing what profits will be. Managers are always trying to make better estimates of what will happen in the future in the face of uncertainty. Making good estimates is the main purpose of forecasting.

In this chapter we examine different types of forecasts, and we present a variety of forecasting models with such names as moving averages, exponential smoothing, and linear regression. The purpose is to show that there are many ways for managers to forecast the future. We also provide an overview of the subject of business sales forecasting and describe how to prepare, monitor, and judge the accuracy of a forecast. Good forecasts are an *essential* part of efficient service and manufacturing operations; they are also an important modeling tool in both strategic and tactical decision making.

WHAT IS FORECASTING?

Forecasting

Forecasting is the art and science of predicting future events. It may involve taking historical data and projecting them into the future with some sort of mathematical model. It may be a subjective or intuitive prediction of the future. Or it may involve a combination of these, that is, a mathematical model adjusted by a manager's good judgment.

As we introduce different forecasting techniques in this chapter, you will realize that there is seldom one single superior method. What works best in one firm under one set of conditions may be a complete disaster in another organization, or even in a different department of the same firm. In addition, you will realize that there are limits as to what can be expected from forecasts. They are seldom, if ever, perfect; they are also costly and time-consuming to prepare and monitor.

Few businesses, however, can afford to avoid the process of forecasting by just waiting to see what happens and then taking their chances. Effective planning in both the short and long run depends on a forecast of demand for the company's products.

Forecasting Time Horizons

Forecasts are usually classified by the future time horizon that they describe.[1] The three categories, all of which are useful to operations managers, are:

1. *Short-range forecast.* This has a time span of up to one year but is generally less than three months. It is used for planning purchasing, job scheduling, work force levels, job assignments, and production levels.

---

[1] For details, see J. F. Magee and D. M. Boodman, *Production Planning and Inventory Control,* 2nd ed. (New York: McGraw-Hill, 1967).

2. *Medium-range forecast.* A medium-range, or intermediate, forecast generally spans from three months up to three years. It is useful in sales planning, production planning and budgeting, cash budgeting, and analyzing various operating plans.

3. *Long-range forecast.* Generally three years or more in time span, long-range forecasts are used in planning for new products, capital expenditures, facility location or expansion, and research and development.

Intermediate and long-run forecasts have three features that differentiate them from short-range forecasts. First, intermediate and long-run forecasts deal with more comprehensive issues and support management decisions regarding planning and products, plants, and processes. Implementing some facility decisions, such as opening a new Saturn auto manufacturing plant, can take five to eight years from inception to completion. Second, short-term forecasting usually employs different methodologies than do longer-term ones. Mathematical techniques such as moving averages, exponential smoothing, and trend extrapolation (all of which we shall examine shortly) are common to short-run projections. Broader, *less* quantitative methods are useful in predicting such issues as whether a new product, like the optical disk recorder, should be introduced in a company's product line. And third, as you would expect, short-range forecasts tend to be more accurate than longer-range forecasts. Factors that influence demand change every day; so as the time horizon lengthens, it is likely that one's forecast accuracy will diminish. It almost goes without saying, then, that sales forecasts need to be updated regularly in order to maintain their value and integrity. After each sales period, the forecast should be reviewed and revised.

The Influence of Product Life Cycle

Another factor to consider when developing sales forecasts, especially longer ones, is the product's life cycle. Products, and even services, do not sell at a constant level throughout their lives. Most successful products pass through four stages: (1) introduction, (2) growth, (3) maturity, and (4) decline.

Products in the first two stages of their life cycle need longer forecasts than those in the maturity and decline stages. Forecasts are useful in projecting different staffing levels, inventory levels, and factory capacity as the product passes from the first to the last stage. The subject of introducing new products, and their life cycles, is treated in more detail in Chapter 6.

To get a grasp on future trends in the world of medical research, Bristol-Myers Squibb Company questioned 220 well-known research scientists. These leaders made a *jury of executive opinion* suggesting that the treatment of disease will concentrate on the disease's cause. In other words, rather than treat diseases like cancer through symptom elimination, medical treatment will focus on attacking individual cells of the disease itself. As a result of this qualitative forecasting, Bristol-Myers created the fluorescence-activated cell sorter, which targets antibodies of tumor cells through the use of lasers and computers.

TYPES OF FORECASTS

Organizations use three major types of forecasts in planning the future of their operations. The first two, economic and technological forecasting, are specialized techniques that may be outside the role of the operations manager; they are described briefly here. The emphasis in this book will be on the third, demand forecasts.

1. Economic forecasts address the business cycle by predicting inflation rates, money supplies, housing starts, and other planning indicators.

Economic forecasts

Technological forecasts

2. **Technological forecasts** are concerned with rates of technological progress, which can result in the birth of exciting new products, requiring new plants and equipment.

Demand forecasts

3. **Demand forecasts** are projections of demand for a company's products or services. These forecasts, also called sales forecasts, drive a company's production, capacity, and scheduling systems and serve as inputs to financial, marketing, and personnel planning.

FORECASTING APPROACHES

There are two general approaches to forecasting, just as there are two ways to tackle all decision modeling. One is quantitative analysis; the other is a qualitative approach. **Quantitative forecasts** employ a variety of mathematical models that use historical data and/or causal variables to forecast demand. Subjective or **qualitative forecasts** incorporate important factors such as the decision maker's intuition, emotions, personal experiences, and value system in reaching a forecast. Some firms use one approach; some use the other; but in practice a combination or blending of the two styles is usually most effective.

Quantitative forecasts

Qualitative forecasts

Overview of Qualitative Methods

In this section we consider four different *qualitative* forecasting techniques.

Jury of executive opinion

1. **Jury of Executive Opinion.** This method takes the opinions of a small group of high-level managers, often in combination with statistical models, and results in a group estimate of demand.

Sales force composite

2. **Sales Force Composite.** In this approach, each salesperson estimates what sales will be in his or her region; these forecasts are then reviewed to ensure they are realistic, then combined at the district and national levels to reach an overall forecast.

Delphi method

3. **Delphi Method.** This iterative group process allows experts, who may be located in different places, to make forecasts. There are three different types of participants in the Delphi process: decision makers, staff personnel, and respondents. The decision makers usually consist of a group of five to ten experts who will be making the actual forecast. The staff personnel assist the decision makers by preparing, distributing, collecting, and summarizing a series of questionnaires and survey results. The respondents are a group of people whose judgments are valued and are being sought. This group provides inputs to the decision makers before the forecast is made. An application of this technique is presented in the *POM in Action* box, "A Delphi Forecast for Alaska."

Consumer market survey

4. **Consumer Market Survey.** This method solicits input from customers or potential customers regarding their future purchasing plans. It can help not only in preparing a forecast but also in improving product design and planning for new products.

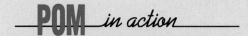

A Delphi Forecast for Alaska

Alaska's economy is dominated by oil. An amazing 90% of the state's budget is derived from 1.5 million barrels of oil pumped daily at Prudhoe Bay. That means short-term volatile oil prices, intermediate-term price trends and reservoir depletion, and long-term ability for Alaska to diversify all influence that state's economy.

Building a broader resource and economy based on income from one industry, oil, is a major developmental challenge. Therefore, forecasting became necessary for any long-range plan.

Statistical forecasting does not usually help in long-range planning in a developing economy because it is hard to rely on historical data and trends. Instead, the Delphi method is typically used to pre-dict events. It became the heart of long-range forecasting in Alaska.

To achieve real credibility, the Delphi forecast had to appear objective and speak with the authority of highly visible leaders and of panelists with expert credentials. The panel had to represent all groups and opinions in the state and all geographic areas. This meant a large panel—but it would work because Delphi panelists do not meet in person.

Delphi was the perfect forecasting tool because panelist travel could be avoided. It also meant leading Alaskans could participate because their schedules were not impacted by meetings and distances.

Sources: Interfaces, **15,** 6 (November–December 1985): 100–109; and *Group and Organization Studies,* **15,** 1 (March 1990): 5–19.

Overview of Quantitative Methods

Five quantitative forecasting methods are addressed in this chapter. They are:

1. Naive approach
2. Moving averages   } time series models
3. Exponential smoothing
4. Trend projection
5. Linear regression causal model   } causal model

Time Series Models. The first four of these are called **time series** models. They predict on the basis of the assumption that the future is a function of the past. In other words, they look at what has happened over a period of time and use a series of past data to make a forecast. If we are predicting weekly sales of lawn mowers, we use the past weekly sales for lawn mowers in making the forecast.

Time series

Causal Models. Linear regression, a causal model, incorporates into the model the variables or factors that might influence the quantity being forecast. A causal model for lawn mower sales might include factors such as new housing starts, advertising budget, and competitors' prices.

Eight Steps to a Forecasting System

Regardless of the method used to forecast, the same eight steps are followed:

1. Determine the use of the forecast—what objectives are we trying to obtain?
2. Select the items that are to be forecasted.
3. Determine the time horizon of the forecast—is it short-, medium-, or long-term?
4. Select the forecasting model(s).
5. Gather the data needed to make the forecast.
6. Validate the forecasting model.
7. Make the forecast.
8. Implement the results.

These steps present a systematic way of initiating, designing, and implementing a forecasting system. When the system is to be used to generate forecasts regularly over time, data must be routinely collected, and the actual computations used to make the forecast can be done automatically, usually by computer.

TIME SERIES FORECASTING

A time series is based on a sequence of evenly spaced (weekly, monthly, quarterly, and so on) data points. Examples include weekly sales of IBM PS/2s, quarterly earnings reports of AT&T stock, daily shipments of Eveready batteries, and annual U.S. consumer price indices. Forecasting time series data implies that future values are predicted *only* from past values and that other variables, no matter how potentially valuable, are ignored.

Decomposition of a Time Series

Analyzing time series means breaking down past data into components and then projecting them forward. A time series typically has four components: trend, seasonality, cycles, and random variation.

1. *Trend (T)* is the gradual upward or downward movement of the data over time.
2. *Seasonality (S)* is a data pattern that repeats itself after a period of days, weeks, months, or quarters (the latter being from where the term *seasonality* arose, i.e., the seasons, fall, winter, spring, and summer). There are six common seasonality patterns:

PERIOD OF PATTERN	LENGTH	NUMBER OF SEASONS IN PATTERN
Week	Day	7
Month	Week	4–4$\frac{1}{2}$
Month	Day	28–31
Year	Quarter	4
Year	Month	12
Year	Week	52

3. *Cycles (C)* are patterns in the data that occur every several years.[2] They are usually tied into the business cycle and are of major importance in short-term business analysis and planning.

4. *Random variations (R)* are "blips" in the data caused by chance and unusual situations; they follow no discernible pattern.

Figure 4.1 shows a time series and its components.

There are two general forms of time series models in statistics. The most widely used is a multiplicative model, which assumes that demand is the product of the four components:

$$\text{Demand} = T \times S \times C \times R$$

An additive model provides an estimate by adding the components together. It is stated as:

$$\text{Demand} = T + S + C + R$$

In most real-world models, forecasters assume that the random variations are averaged out over time. They then concentrate on only the seasonal component and a component that is a combination of trend and cyclical factors.

Quantitative forecasting techniques are used by the Carnation Co. to manage the manufacturing process. The Carnation Data Center (shown here) first makes a historical review to determine the quantity each product sold in the past. Marketing and promotion plans are incorporated and sales offices give additional estimates. The forecast is a major tool used to determine the buying and scheduling of two million tons of material annually for the 24 manufacturing plants owned by Carnation.

FIGURE 4.1

Product Demand Charted Over Four Years with Trend and Seasonality Indicated.

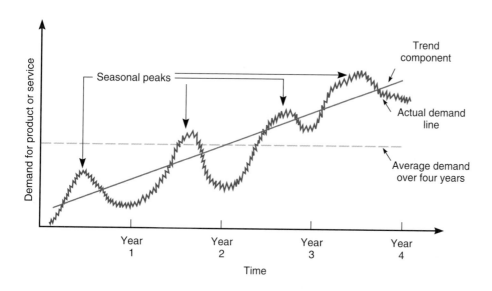

[2] According to Arthur F. Burns and Wesley C. Mitchell *(Measuring Business Cycles,* New York: National Bureau of Economic Research, 1946, p. 3) "Business cycles are a type of fluctuation found in the aggregate economic activity of nations that organize their work mainly in business enterprises: A cycle consists of expansions occurring at about the same time in many economic activities, followed by similarly general recessions, contractions, and revivals which merge into the expansion phase of the next cycle; this sequence of changes is recurrent but not periodic; in duration business cycles vary from more than one year to ten or twelve years."

Naive Approach

Naive approach

The simplest way to forecast is to assume that demand in the next period is just equal to demand in the most recent period. In other words, if sales of a product, say cellular phones, were 68 units in January, we can forecast that February's sales will also be 68 phones. Does this make any sense? It turns out that for some product lines, selecting this **naive approach** is the most cost-effective and efficient objective forecasting model. It at least provides a starting point against which the more sophisticated models that follow can be compared. (See Table 4.1, at the end of this chapter for a broader overview of this and other models discussed in Chapter 4.)

Moving Averages

Moving averages

Moving averages are useful if we can assume that market demands will stay fairly steady over time. A four-month moving average is found by simply summing the demand during the past four months and dividing by 4. With each passing month, the most recent month's data are added to the sum of the previous three months' data, and the earliest month is dropped. This tends to smooth out short-term irregularities in the data series.

Mathematically, the simple moving average (which serves as an estimate of the next period's demand) is expressed as:

$$\text{Moving average} = \frac{\Sigma \text{ Demand in previous } n \text{ periods}}{n} \tag{4.1}$$

where n is the number of periods in the moving average—for example, four, five, or six months, respectively, for a four-, five-, or six-period moving average.

Example 1

Storage shed sales at Donna's Garden Supply are shown in the middle column of the following table. A three-month moving average appears on the right.

MONTH	ACTUAL SHED SALES	THREE-MONTH MOVING AVERAGE
January	10	
February	12	
March	13	
April	16	(10 + 12 + 13)/3 = 11 2/3
May	19	(12 + 13 + 16)/3 = 13 2/3
June	23	(13 + 16 + 19)/3 = 16
July	26	(16 + 19 + 23)/3 = 19 1/3
August	30	(19 + 23 + 26)/3 = 22 2/3
September	28	(23 + 26 + 30)/3 = 26 1/3
October	18	(26 + 30 + 28)/3 = 28
November	16	(30 + 28 + 18)/3 = 25 1/3
December	14	(28 + 18 + 16)/3 = 20 2/3

Weighted Moving Averages

When there is a trend or pattern, weights can be used to place more emphasis on recent values. This makes the techniques more responsive to changes since more recent periods may be more heavily weighted. Deciding which weights to use requires some experience and a bit of luck. Choice of weights is somewhat arbitrary since there is no set formula to determine them. If the latest month or period is weighted too heavily, the forecast might reflect a large unusual change in the demand or sales pattern too quickly.

A weighted moving average may be expressed mathematically as:

$$\frac{\text{Weighted}}{\text{moving average}} = \frac{\Sigma\,(\text{Weight for period } n)(\text{Demand in period } n)}{\Sigma\,\text{Weights}} \tag{4.2}$$

Example 2

Donna's Garden Supply (See Example 1) decides to forecast storage shed sales by weighting the past three months as follows:

WEIGHTS APPLIED	PERIOD
③	Last month
②	Two months ago
①	Three months ago
6	Sum of weights

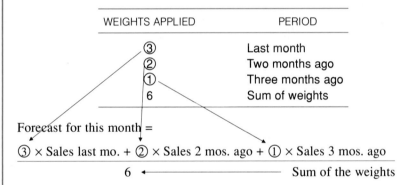

Forecast for this month =

$$\frac{③ \times \text{Sales last mo.} + ② \times \text{Sales 2 mos. ago} + ① \times \text{Sales 3 mos. ago}}{6 \longleftarrow \text{Sum of the weights}}$$

The results of this weighted average forecast are shown in the following table.

MONTH	ACTUAL SHED SALES	THREE-MONTH WEIGHTED MOVING AVERAGE
January	10	
February	12	
March	13	
April	16	[(3 × 13) + (2 + 12) + (10)]/6 = 12 1/6
May	19	[(3 × 16) + (2 + 13) + (12)]/6 = 14 1/3
June	23	[(3 × 19) + (2 + 16) + (13)]/6 = 17
July	26	[(3 × 23) + (2 + 19) + (16)]/6 = 20 1/2
August	30	[(3 × 26) + (2 + 23) + (19)]/6 = 23 5/6
September	28	[(3 × 30) + (2 + 26) + (23)]/6 = 27 1/2
October	18	[(3 × 28) + (2 + 30) + (26)]/6 = 28 1/3
November	16	[(3 × 18) + (2 + 28) + (30)]/6 = 23 1/3
December	14	[(3 × 16) + (2 + 18) + (28)]/6 = 18 2/3

In this particular forecasting situation, you can see that weighting the latest month more heavily provides a much more accurate projection.

FIGURE 4.2

Actual Demand vs. Moving Average and Weighted Moving Average Methods for Donna's Garden Supply.

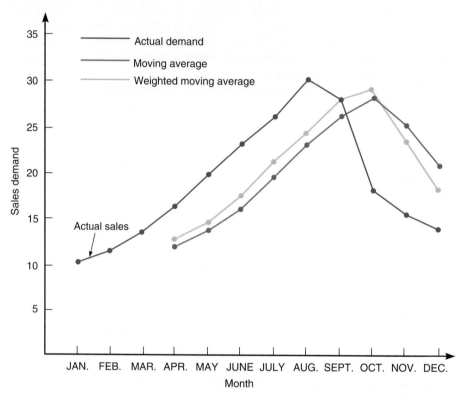

Both simple and weighted moving averages are effective in smoothing out sudden fluctuations in the demand pattern in order to provide stable estimates. Moving averages do, however, have three problems. First, increasing the size of *n* (the number of periods averaged) does smooth out fluctuations better, but it makes the method less sensitive to *real* changes in the data. Second, moving averages cannot pick up trends very well. Since they are averages, they will always stay within past levels and will not predict a change to either a higher or lower level. Finally, moving averages require extensive records of past data.

Figure 4.2, a plot of the data in Examples 1 and 2, illustrates the lag effect of the moving average models.

Exponential Smoothing

Exponential smoothing

Exponential smoothing is a forecasting method that is easy to use and efficiently handled by computers. Although it is a type of moving average technique, it involves very *little* record keeping of past data. The basic exponential smoothing formula can be shown as follows:

$$\text{New forecast} = \text{Last period's forecast}$$
$$+ \alpha \text{ (Last period's actual demand − last period's forecast)} \quad (4.3)$$

Smoothing constant

where α is a weight, or **smoothing constant,** that has a value between 0 and 1, inclusive. Equation (4.3) can also be written mathematically as:

$$F_t = F_{t-1} + \alpha(A_{t-1} - F_{t-1}) \tag{4.4}$$

where

$$F_t = \text{the new forecast}$$
$$F_{t-1} = \text{the previous forecast}$$
$$\alpha = \text{smoothing constant } (0 \leq \alpha \leq 1)$$
$$A_{t-1} = \text{previous period's actual demand}$$

The concept is not complex. The latest estimate of demand is equal to our old estimate adjusted by a fraction of the difference between the last period's actual demand and the old estimate.

Example 3

In January, a car dealer predicted a February demand for 142 Ford Tauruses. Actual February demand was 153 autos. Using a smoothing constant of $\alpha = .20$, we can forecast the March demand using the exponential smoothing model. Substituting into the formula, we obtain:

$$\text{New forecast (for March demand)} = 142 + .2(153 - 142)$$
$$= 144.2$$

Thus the demand forecast for Ford Tauruses in March is rounded to 144.

The *smoothing constant,* α, can be changed to give more weight to recent data (when α is high) or more weight to past data (when α is low). To demonstrate this weighting concept, Equation 4.4 can be rewritten algebraically in the form:

$$F_t = \alpha A_{t-1} + \alpha(1-\alpha)A_{t-2} + \alpha(1-\alpha)^2 A_{t-3} + \alpha(1-\alpha)^3 A_{t-4} + \cdots + \alpha(1-\alpha)^n A_{t-n} \tag{4.5}$$

where the weights add up to 1. Even though this time series goes back n periods (where n can be a very long time), the importance of older past periods declines quickly as α is increased. When α reaches the extreme of 1.0, then in Equation 4.5, $F_t = 1.0 A_{t-1}$. All the older values drop out, and the forecast becomes identical to the naive model mentioned earlier in this chapter. That is, the forecast for the next period is just the same as this period's demand.

The following table helps illustrate this concept. For example, when $\alpha = .5$, we can see that the new forecast is based almost entirely on demand in the last three or four periods. When $\alpha = .1$, the forecast places little weight on recent demand and takes *many* periods (about 19) of historic values into account.

	WEIGHT ASSIGNED TO				
Smoothing Constant	Most Recent Period (α)	2nd Most Recent Period $\alpha(1-\alpha)$	3rd Most Recent Period $\alpha(1-\alpha)^2$	4th Most Recent Period $\alpha(1-\alpha)^3$	5th Most Recent Period $\alpha(1-\alpha)^4$
$\alpha = .1$	.1	.09	.081	.073	.066
$\alpha = .5$	.5	.25	.125	.063	.031

Selecting the Smoothing Constant. The exponential smoothing approach is easy to use, and it has been successfully applied by banks, manufacturing companies, wholesalers, and other organizations. The appropriate value of the smoothing constant, α, however, can make the difference between an accurate forecast and an inaccurate forecast. In picking a value for the smoothing constant, the objective is to obtain the most accurate forecast. The overall accuracy of a forecasting model can be determined by comparing the forecasted values with the actual or observed values.

The forecast error is defined as:

$$\text{Forecast error} = \text{Demand} - \text{Forecast}$$

Mean absolute deviation (MAD)

One measure of the overall forecast error for a model is the **mean absolute deviation (MAD).** This is computed by taking the sum of the absolute values of the individual forecast errors and dividing by the number of periods of data (n):

$$\text{MAD} = \frac{\Sigma \ |\text{Forecast errors}|}{n} \tag{4.6}$$

Let us apply this concept with a trial-and-error testing of two values of α in Example 4.

Example 4

The port of Baltimore has unloaded large quantities of grain from ships during the past eight quarters. The port's operations manager wants to test the use of exponential smoothing to see how well the technique works in predicting tonnage unloaded. He assumes that the forecast of grain unloaded in the first quarter was 175 tons. Two values of α are examined, α = .10 and α = .50. The following table shows the *detailed* calculations for α = .10 only:

QUARTER	ACTUAL TONNAGE UNLOADED	ROUNDED FORECAST USING α = .10*	ROUNDED FORECAST USING α = .50*
1	180	175	175
2	168	176 = 175.00 + .10(180 − 175)	178
3	159	175 = 175.50 + .10(168 − 175.50)	173
4	175	173 = 174.75 + .10(159 − 174.75)	166
5	190	173 = 173.18 + .10(175 − 173.18)	170
6	205	175 = 173.36 + .10(190 − 173.36)	180
7	180	178 = 175.02 + .10(205 − 175.02)	193
8	182	178 = 178.02 + .10(180 − 178.02)	186
9	?	179 = 178.22 + .10(182 − 178.22)	184

* Forecasts rounded to the nearest ton.

To evaluate the accuracy of each smoothing constant we can compute the absolute deviations and MADs.

QUARTER	ACTUAL TONNAGE UNLOADED	ROUNDED FORECAST WITH $\alpha = .10$	ABSOLUTE DEVIATION FOR $\alpha = .10$	ROUNDED FORECAST WITH $\alpha = .50$	ABSOLUTE DEVIATION FOR $\alpha = .50$
1	180	175	5	175	5
2	168	176	8	178	10
3	159	175	16	173	14
4	175	173	2	166	9
5	190	173	17	170	20
6	205	175	30	180	25
7	180	178	2	193	13
8	182	178	4	186	4
	Sum of absolute deviations		84		100
	$MAD = \dfrac{\Sigma \text{ deviations}}{n}$		10.50		12.50

On the basis of this analysis, a smoothing constant of $\alpha = .10$ is preferred to $\alpha = .50$ because its MAD is smaller.

Besides the mean absolute deviations (MAD), two other measures of the accuracy of historical errors in forecasting are sometimes used. **Mean squared error (MSE)** is the average of the squared differences between the forecasted and observed values. **Mean absolute percent error (MAPE)** is the absolute difference between the forecasted and observed values expressed as a percentage of the observed values.

Mean squared error (MSE)

Mean absolute percent error (MAPE)

Exponential Smoothing with Trend Adjustment

As with any moving average technique, simple exponential smoothing fails to respond to trends. To illustrate a more complex exponential smoothing model, let us consider one that adjusts for trend. The idea is to compute a simple exponential smoothing forecast as above and then adjust for positive or negative lag in trend. The formula is:

Forecast including trend (FIT_t) = New forecast (F_t) + Trend correction (T_t)

To smooth out the trend, the equation for the trend correction uses a smoothing constant, β, in the same way the simple exponential model uses α. T_t is computed by:

$$T_t = (1 - \beta)T_{t-1} + \beta(F_t - F_{t-1}) \tag{4.7}$$

where

T_t = smoothed trend for period t

T_{t-1} = smoothed trend for previous period

β = trend smoothing constant that we select

F_t = simple exponential smoothed forecast for period t

F_{t-1} = forecast for previous period

There are three steps to compute a trend-adjusted forecast.

Step 1. Compute a simple exponential forecast for time period t (F_t).

Step 2. Compute the trend by using the equation

$$T_t = (1 - \beta)T_{t-1} + \beta(F_t - F_{t-1})$$

To start step 2 for the first time, an initial trend value must be inserted (either by a good guess or by observed past data). After that, trend is computed.

Step 3. Calculate the trend adjusted exponential smoothing forecast (FIT_t) by the formula

$$FIT_t = F_t + T_t$$

Example 5

A large Portland manufacturer uses exponential smoothing to forecast demand for a pollution control equipment product. It appears that a trend is present.

MONTH	DEMAND	MONTH	DEMAND
1	12	6	26
2	17	7	31
3	20	8	32
4	19	9	36
5	24		

Smoothing constants are assigned the values of $\alpha = .2$ and $\beta = .4$. Assume the initial forecast for month 1 was 11 units.

Step 1. Forecast for month 2 (F_2) = Forecast for month 1 (F_1) + α (Month 1 demand – Forecast for month 1):

$$F_2 = 11 + .2(12 - 11)$$
$$= 11.0 + .2 = 11.2 \text{ units}$$

Step 2. Compute the trend present. Assume an initial trend adjustment of zero, that is, $T_1 = 0$.

$$T_2 = (1 - \beta)T_1 + \beta(F_2 - F_1)$$
$$= 0 + .4(11.2 - 11.0)$$
$$= .08$$

Step 3. Compute the forecast including trend (FIT):

$$FIT_2 = F_2 + T_2$$
$$= 11.2 + .08$$
$$= 11.28 \text{ units}$$

We will do the same calculations for the third month also.

Step 1. $F_3 = F_2 + \alpha$ (Demand in month $2 - F_2$)
$= 11.2 + .2(17 - 11.2) = 12.36$

Step 2. $T_3 = (1 - \beta)T_2 + \beta(F_3 - F_2)$
$= (1 - .4).08 + .4(12.36 - 11.2) = .51$

Step 3. $FIT_3 = F_3 + T_3$
$= 12.36 + .51 = 12.87$

So the simple exponential forecast (without trend) for month 2 was 11.2 units, and the trend-adjusted forecast was 11.28 units. In month 3, the simple forecast (without trend) was 12.36 units, and the trend-adjusted forecast was 12.87 units. Naturally, different values of T_1 and β can produce even better estimates.

The following table completes the forecasts for the nine-month period. Figure 4.3 compares actual demand, forecast without trend (F_t) and forecast with trend (FIT_t).

MONTH	ACTUAL DEMAND	FORECAST, F_t (WITHOUT TREND)	TREND	ADJUSTED FIT_t
1	12	11.00	0	—
2	17	11.20	.08	11.28
3	20	12.36	.51	12.87
4	19	13.89	.92	14.81
5	24	14.91	.96	15.87
6	26	16.73	1.30	18.03
7	31	18.58	1.52	20.10
8	32	21.07	1.91	22.98
9	36	23.25	2.02	25.27

FIGURE 4.3

Actual Compared to Forecasts.

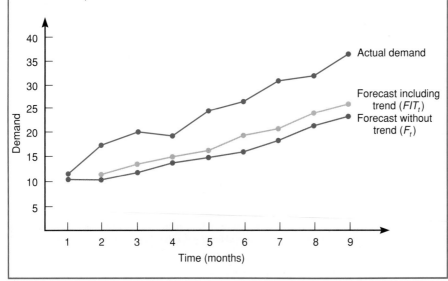

The value of the trend smoothing constant, β, resembles the α constant in that a high β is more responsive to recent changes in trend. A low β gives less weight to the most recent trends and tends to smooth out the trend present. Values of β can be found by the trial-and-error approach, with the MAD used as a measure of comparison.

Simple exponential smoothing is often referred to as first-order smoothing, and trend-adjusted smoothing is called second-order, or double, smoothing. Other advanced exponential smoothing models are also in use, including seasonal-adjusted and triple smoothing, but these are beyond the scope of this book.[3]

Trend Projections

Trend projection

The last time series forecasting method we will discuss is **trend projection.** This technique fits a trend line to a series of historical data points and then projects the line into the future for medium-to-long-range forecasts. Several mathematical trend equations can be developed (for example, exponential and quadratic), but in this section we will look at *linear* (straight line) trends only.

If we decide to develop a linear trend line by a precise statistical method, we can apply the *least squares method.* This approach results in a straight line that minimizes the sum of the squares of the vertical differences from the line to each of the actual observations. Figure 4.4 illustrates the least squares approach.

FIGURE 4.4

The Least Squares Method for Finding the Best Fitting Straight Line, Where the Asterisks Are the Locations of the Seven Actual Observations or Data Points.

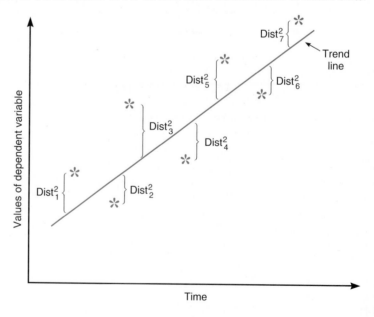

[3] For more details, see E. S. Gardner, "Exponential Smoothing: The State of the Art," *Journal of Forecasting,* **4,** 1 (March 1985), or R. Brown, *Smoothing, Forecasting and Prediction* (Englewood Cliffs, NJ: Prentice-Hall, 1973).

A least squares line is described in terms of its y-intercept (the height at which it intercepts the y-axis) and its slope (the angle of the line). If we can compute the y-intercept and slope, we can express the line with the following equation:

$$\hat{y} = a + bx \qquad (4.8)$$

where

$\hat{y}$ (called "y hat") = computed value of the variable to be predicted (called the dependent variable)

$a = y$-axis intercept

b = slope of the regression line (or the rate of change in y for given changes in x)

x = the independent variable (which is *time* in this case)

Statisticians have developed equations that we can use to find the values of a and b for any regression line. The slope b is found by

$$b = \frac{\Sigma xy - n\bar{x}\bar{y}}{\Sigma x^2 - n\bar{x}^2} \qquad (4.9)$$

where

b = slope of the regression line

Σ = summation sign

x = values of the independent variable

y = values of the dependent variable

$\bar{x}$ = the average of the value of the x's

$\bar{y}$ = the average of the values of the y's

n = the number of data points or observations

We can compute the y-intercept a as follows:

$$a = \bar{y} - b\bar{x} \qquad (4.10)$$

Example 6 shows how to apply these concepts.

Example 6

Shown below are data on the demand for electrical generators from a midwestern manufacturer over the period 1986–92. Let us fit a straight-line trend to these data and forecast 1993 demand.

YEAR	ELECTRICAL GENERATORS SOLD	YEAR	ELECTRICAL GENERATORS SOLD
1986	74	1990	105
1987	79	1991	142
1988	80	1992	122
1989	90		

With a series of data over time, we can minimize the computations by transforming the values of x (time) to simpler numbers. Thus, in this case, we can designate 1986 as year 1, 1987 as year 2, and so on.

YEAR	TIME PERIOD	GENERATOR DEMAND	x^2	xy
1986	1	74	1	74
1987	2	79	4	158
1988	3	80	9	240
1989	4	90	16	360
1990	5	105	25	525
1991	6	142	36	852
1992	7	122	49	854
	$\Sigma x = 28$	$\Sigma y = 692$	$\Sigma x^2 = 140$	$\Sigma xy = 3{,}063$

$$\bar{x} = \frac{\Sigma x}{n} = \frac{28}{7} = 4 \qquad \bar{y} = \frac{\Sigma y}{n} = \frac{692}{7} = 98.86$$

$$b = \frac{\Sigma xy - n\bar{x}\bar{y}}{\Sigma x^2 - n\bar{x}^2} = \frac{3{,}063 - (7)(4)(98.86)}{140 - (7)(4^2)} = \frac{295}{28} = 10.54$$

$$a = \bar{y} - b\bar{x} = 98.86 - 10.54(4) = 56.70$$

Hence, the least squares trend equation is $\hat{y} = 56.70 + 10.54x$. To project demand in 1993, we first denote the year 1993 in our new coding system as $x = 8$:

$$\text{(Sales in 1993)} = 56.70 + 10.54(8)$$
$$= 141.02, \text{ or } 141 \text{ generators}$$

We can estimate demand for 1994 by inserting $x = 9$ in the same equation:

$$\text{(Sales in 1994)} = 56.70 + 10.54(9)$$
$$= 151.56, \text{ or } 152 \text{ generators}$$

To check the validity of the model, we plot historical demand and the trend line in Figure 4.5. In this case, we may wish to be cautious and try to understand the 1991–1992 swings in demand.

SEASONAL VARIATIONS IN DATA

Time series forecasting such as that in Example 6 involves looking at the *trend* of data over a series of time observations. Sometimes, however, recurring variations at certain seasons of the year make a *seasonal* adjustment in the trend line forecast necessary. Demand for coal and fuel oil, for example, usually peaks during cold winter months. Demand for golf clubs or suntan lotion may be highest in summer. Analyzing data in monthly or quarterly terms usually makes it easy for a statistician to spot seasonal patterns. Seasonal indices can then be developed by several common methods. Example 7 illustrates one way to compute seasonal factors from historical data.

FIGURE 4.5

Electrical Generators and the Computed Trend Line.

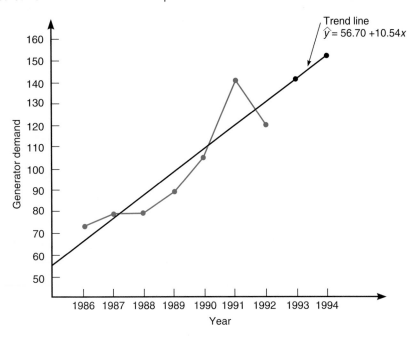

Example 7

Monthly sales of one brand of telephone answering machine at Wurst Supplies are shown below for 1991–1992.

MONTH	SALES DEMAND 1991	SALES DEMAND 1992	AVERAGE 1991–92 DEMAND	AVERAGE MONTHLY DEMAND*	SEASONAL INDEX†
Jan.	80	100	90	94	.957
Feb.	75	85	80	94	.851
Mar.	80	90	85	94	.905
Apr.	90	110	100	94	1.064
May	115	131	123	94	1.309
June	110	120	115	94	1.223
July	100	110	105	94	1.117
Aug.	90	110	100	94	1.064
Sept.	85	95	90	94	.957
Oct.	75	85	80	94	.851
Nov.	75	85	80	94	.851
Dec.	80	80	80	94	.851
			Total average demand = 1,128		

* Average monthly demand = $\dfrac{1,128}{12 \text{ months}}$ = 94

† Seasonal index = $\dfrac{\text{Average 1991–92 demand}}{\text{Average monthly demand}}$

Using these seasonal indices, if we expected the 1993 annual demand for answering machines to be 1,200 units, we would forecast the monthly demand as follows:

MONTH	DEMAND	MONTH	DEMAND
Jan.	$\frac{1,200}{12} \times .957 = 96$	July	$\frac{1,200}{12} \times 1.117 = 112$
Feb.	$\frac{1,200}{12} \times .851 = 85$	Aug.	$\frac{1,200}{12} \times 1.064 = 106$
Mar.	$\frac{1,200}{12} \times .904 = 90$	Sept.	$\frac{1,200}{12} \times .957 = 96$
Apr.	$\frac{1,200}{12} \times 1.064 = 106$	Oct.	$\frac{1,200}{12} \times .851 = 85$
May	$\frac{1,200}{12} \times 1.309 = 131$	Nov.	$\frac{1,200}{12} \times .851 = 85$
June	$\frac{1,200}{12} \times 1.223 = 122$	Dec.	$\frac{1,200}{12} \times .851 = 85$

For simplicity, trend calculations were ignored and only two periods were used for each monthly index in the above example. Example 8 illustrates how indices that have already been prepared can be applied to adjust trend line forecasts.

Example 8

Management of Davis's Department Store has used time series regression to forecast retail sales for the next four quarters. The sales estimates are $100,000, $120,000, $140,000, and $160,000 for the respective quarters. Seasonal indices for the four quarters have been found to be 1.30, .90, .70, and 1.15, respectively.

To compute a seasonalized or adjusted sales forecast, we just multiply each seasonal index by the appropriate trend forecast:

$$\hat{y}_{\text{seasonal}} = \text{Index} \times \hat{y}_{\text{trend forecast}}$$

Hence for

Quarter I:	$\hat{y}_{\text{I}} = (1.30)(\$100,000) = \$130,000$
Quarter II:	$\hat{y}_{\text{II}} = (.90)(\$120,000) = \$108,000$
Quarter III:	$\hat{y}_{\text{III}} = (.70)(\$140,000) = \$98,000$
Quarter IV:	$\hat{y}_{\text{IV}} = (1.15)(\$160,000) = \$184,000$

Example 9 provides a third illustration of seasonalized data.

Example 9

As another example of an estimated trend line and seasonality adjustments, we borrow data from a San Diego hospital that used 66 months of adult inpatient hospital days to reach the following equation:[4]

$$\hat{y} = 8091 + 21.5x$$

where

$$\hat{y} = \text{patient days}$$
$$x = \text{time, in months}$$

On the basis of this model, the hospital forecasts patient days for the next month (period 67) to be:

$$\text{Patient days} = 8091 + 21.5(67) = 9530 \qquad \text{(trend only)}$$

As well as this model recognized the slight upward trend line in the demand for inpatient services, it ignored the seasonality that the administration knew to be present. The table below provides actual seasonal indices based on the same 66 months. Such seasonal data, by the way, were found to be typical of hospitals nationwide. Note that January, March, July, and August seem to exhibit significantly higher patient days on average; and February, September, November, and December reveal lower patient days.

MONTH	SEASONALITY INDEX	MONTH	SEASONALITY INDEX
January	1.0436	July	1.0302
February	.9669	August	1.0405
March	1.0203	September	.9653
April	1.0087	October	1.0048
May	.9935	November	.9598
June	.9906	December	.9805

To correct the time-series extrapolation for seasonality, the hospital multiplied the monthly forecast by the appropriate seasonality index. Thus, for period 67, which was a January,

$$\text{Patient days} = (9530)(1.0436) = 9946 \qquad \text{(trend and seasonal)}$$

Using this method, patient days were forecasted for January through June (periods 67 through 72) as 9946, 9236, 9768, 9678, 9554, and 9547. This study led to better patient-day forecasts, as well as more accurate forecast budgets.

---

[4] *Source:* W. E. Sterk and E. G. Shryock, "Modern Methods Improve Hospital Forecasting," *Healthcare Financial Management,* **41,** 3 (March 1987): 96–98.

CAUSAL FORECASTING METHODS: REGRESSION AND CORRELATION ANALYSIS

Causal forecasting models usually consider several variables that are related to the variable being predicted. Once these related variables have been found, a statistical model is built and used to forecast the variable of interest. This approach is more powerful than the time series methods that use only the historic values for the forecasted variable.

Many factors can be considered in a causal analysis. For example, the sales of a product might be related to the firm's advertising budget, the price charged, competitors' prices and promotional strategies, or even the economy and unemployment rates. In this case, sales would be called the *dependent variable* and the other variables would be called *independent variables*. The manager's job is to develop the best statistical relationship between sales and the independent variables. The most common quantitative causal forecasting model is **linear regression analysis.**

Linear regression analysis

Using Regression Analysis to Forecast

We can use the same mathematical model we employed in the least squares method of trend projection to perform a linear regression analysis. The dependent variables that we want to forecast will still be $\hat{y}$. But now the independent variable, x, need no longer be time.

$$\hat{y} = a + bx$$

where

$\hat{y}$ = value of the dependent variable, sales here

a = y-axis intercept

b = slope of the regression line

x = the independent variable

Example 10

Tongren Construction Company renovates old homes in Orono, Maine. Over time, the company has found that their dollar volume of renovation work is dependent on the Orono area payroll. The following table lists Tongren's revenues and the amount of money earned by wage earners in Orono during the years 1987–1992.

TONGREN'S SALES ($000,000), y	LOCAL PAYROLL ($000,000,000), x
2.0	1
3.0	3
2.5	4
2.0	2
2.0	1
3.5	7

Tongren's management wants to establish a mathematical relationship that will help it predict sales. First, they need to determine whether there is a straight-line (linear) relationship between area payroll and sales, so they plot the known data on a scatter diagram.

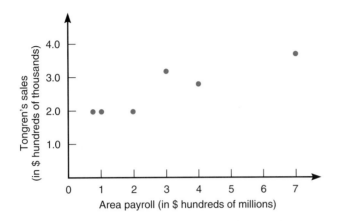

It appears from the six data points that there is a slight positive relationship between the independent variable, payroll, and the dependent variable, sales. As payroll increases, Tongren's sales tend to be higher.

We can find a mathematical equation by using the least squares regression approach.

SALES, y	PAYROLL, x	x^2	xy
2.0	1	1	2.0
3.0	3	9	9.0
2.5	4	16	10.9
2.0	2	4	4.0
2.0	1	1	2.0
3.5	7	49	24.5
$\Sigma y = 15.0$	$\Sigma x = 18$	$\Sigma x^2 = 80$	$\Sigma xy = 51.5$

$$\bar{x} = \frac{\Sigma x}{6} = \frac{18}{6} = 3$$

$$\bar{y} = \frac{\Sigma y}{6} = \frac{15}{6} = 2.5$$

$$b = \frac{\Sigma xy - n\bar{x}\bar{y}}{\Sigma x^2 - n\bar{x}^2} = \frac{51.5 - (6)(3)(2.5)}{80 - (6)(3^2)} = .25$$

$$a = \bar{y} - b\bar{x} = 2.5 - (.25)(3) = 1.75$$

The estimated regression equation, therefore, is:

$$\hat{y} = 1.75 + .25x$$

or

$$\text{Sales} = 1.75 + .25 \text{ payroll}$$

Glidden Paints assembly lines fill thousands of cans per hour. To predict demand for its products, the firm uses causal forecasting methods such as linear regression, with independent variables such as disposable personal income and GNP. Although housing starts would be a natural variable, Glidden found it correlated poorly with past sales. It turns out that most Glidden paint is sold through retailers to customers who already own homes or businesses.

> If the local chamber of commerce predicts that the Orono area payroll will be $6 hundred million next year, we can estimate sales for Tongren with the regression equation:
>
> $$\text{Sales (in hundred thousands)} = 1.75 + .25(6)$$
> $$= 1.75 + 1.50 = 3.25$$
>
> or
>
> $$\text{Sales} = \$325,000$$

The final part of Example 10 illustrates a central weakness of causal forecasting methods like regression. Even when we have computed a regression equation, it is necessary to provide a forecast of the independent variable x—in this case, payroll—before estimating the dependent variable y for the next time period. Although this is not a problem for all forecasts, you can imagine the difficulty of determining future values of *some* common independent variables (such as unemployment rates, gross national product, price indices, and so on).

Standard Error of the Estimate

The forecast of $325,000 for Tongren's sales in Example 10 is called a *point estimate* of y. The point estimate is really the mean, or expected value, of a distribution of possible values of sales. Figure 4.6 illustrates this concept.

FIGURE 4.6

Distribution About the Point Estimate of $6 Hundred Million Payroll.

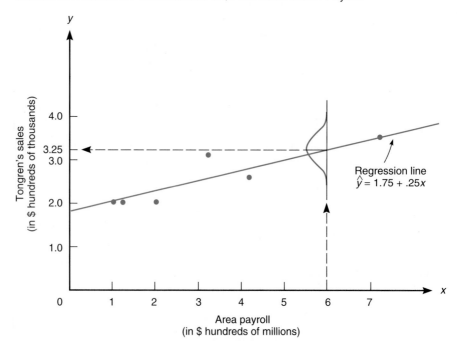

To measure the accuracy of the regression estimates we need to compute the **standard error of the estimate,** $S_{y,x}$. This is called the *standard deviation of the regression*. Equation 4.11 is the same expression found in most statistics books for computing the standard deviation of an arithmetic mean:

Standard error of the estimate

$$S_{y,x} = \sqrt{\frac{\Sigma(y - y_c)^2}{n - 2}} \qquad (4.11)$$

where

$$y = \text{the } y\text{-value of each data point}$$

$$y_c = \text{the computed value of the dependent}$$
$$\text{variable, from the regression equation}$$

$$n = \text{the number of data points}$$

Equation 4.12 may look more complex, but it is actually an easier-to-use version of Equation 4.11. Either formula provides the same answer and can be used in setting up prediction intervals around the point estimate.[5]

$$S_{y,x} = \sqrt{\frac{\Sigma y^2 - a\Sigma y - b\Sigma xy}{n - 2}} \qquad (4.12)$$

Example 11

Let us compute the standard error of the estimate for Tongren's data in Example 10. The only number we will need that is not available to solve for $S_{y,x}$ is Σy^2. Some quick addition reveals $\Sigma y^2 = 39.5$. Therefore,

$$S_{y,x} = \sqrt{\frac{\Sigma y^2 - a\Sigma y - b\Sigma xy}{n - 2}}$$

$$= \sqrt{\frac{39.5 - 1.75(15.0) - .25(51.5)}{6 - 2}}$$

$$= \sqrt{.09375} = .306 \text{ (in \$ hundred thousands)}$$

The standard error of the estimate is then \$30,600 in sales.

Correlation Coefficients for Regression Lines

The regression equation is one way of expressing the nature of the relationship between two variables.[6] The equation shows how one variable relates to the value and changes in another variable.

---

[5] When the sample size is large ($n > 30$), the prediction interval for an individual value of y can be computed using normal tables. When the number of observations is small, the t-distribution is appropriate. See Neter, Wasserman, and Whitmore's *Applied Statistics,* 3rd ed. (Newton, MA: Allyn & Bacon, 1991).

[6] Regression lines are not "cause and effect" relationships. They describe only the relationship between variables.

FIGURE 4.7

Four Values of the Correlation Coefficient.

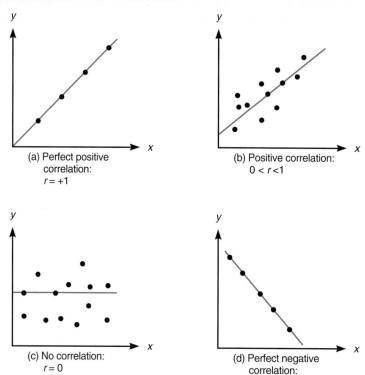

(a) Perfect positive correlation: $r = +1$

(b) Positive correlation: $0 < r < 1$

(c) No correlation: $r = 0$

(d) Perfect negative correlation: $r = -1$

Coefficient of correlation

Another way to evaluate the relationship between two variables is to compute the **coefficient of correlation.** This measure expresses the degree or strength of the linear relationship. Usually identified as r, the coefficient of correlation can be any number between +1 and -1. Figure 4.7 illustrates what different values of r might look like.

To compute r we use much of the same data needed earlier to calculate a and b for the regression line. The rather lengthy equation for r is:

$$r = \frac{n\Sigma xy - \Sigma x\Sigma y}{\sqrt{[n\Sigma x^2 - (\Sigma x)^2]\,[n\Sigma y^2 - (\Sigma y)^2]}} \tag{4.13}$$

Example 12

In Example 10 we looked at the relationship between Tongren Construction Company's renovation sales and payroll in Orono. To compute the coefficient of correlation for the data shown, we need only add one more column of calculations (for y^2) and then apply the equation for r.

y	x	x^2	xy	y^2	
2.0	1	1	2.0	4.0	
3.0	3	9	9.0	9.0	
2.5	4	16	10.0	6.25	New
2.0	2	4	4.0	4.0	column
2.0	1	1	2.0	4.0	
3.5	7	49	24.5	12.25	
$\Sigma y = 15.0$	$\Sigma x = 18$	$\Sigma x^2 = 80$	$\Sigma xy = 51.5$	$\Sigma y^2 = 39.5$	

$$r = \frac{(6)(51.5) - (18)(15.0)}{\sqrt{[(6)(80) - (18)^2][(6)(39.5) - (15.0)^2]}}$$

$$= \frac{309 - 270}{\sqrt{(156)(12)}} = \frac{39}{\sqrt{1872}}$$

$$= \frac{39}{43.3} = .901$$

This r of .901 appears to be a significant correlation and helps to confirm the closeness of the relationship between the two variables.

Although the coefficient of correlation is the measure most commonly used to describe the relationship between two variables, another measure does exist. It is called the *coefficient of determination*. This is simply the square of the coefficient of correlation, namely, r^2. The value of r^2 will always be a positive number in the range of $0 \leq r^2 \leq 1$. The coefficient of determination is the percent of variation in the dependent variable (y) that is explained by the regression equation. In Tongren's case, the value of r^2 is .81, indicating that 81% of the total variation is explained by the regression equation.

Multiple Regression Analysis

Multiple regression is a practical extension of the model we just observed. It allows us to build a model with several independent variables. For example, if Tongren Construction wanted to include average annual interest rates in its model to forecast renovation sales, the proper equation would be:

Multiple regression

$$\hat{y} = a + b_1 x_1 + b_2 x_2 \tag{4.14}$$

where

$$\hat{y} = \text{the dependent variable, sales}$$

$$a = y\text{-intercept}$$

$$x_1 \text{ and } x_2 = \text{values of the two independent variables,}$$
$$\text{area payroll and interest rates, respectively}$$

The mathematics of multiple regression becomes quite complex (and is usually tackled by computer), so we leave the formulas for a, b_1, and b_2 to statistics textbooks.

Example 13

The new multiple regression line for Tongren Construction, calculated by computer software, is:

$$\hat{y} = 1.80 + .30x_1 - 5.0x_2$$

We also find that the new coefficient of correlation is .96, implying the inclusion of the variable x_2, interest rates, adds even more strength to the linear relationship.

We can now estimate Tongren's sales if we substitute values for next year's payroll and interest rate. If Orono's payroll will be $600 million and the interest rate will be .12 (12%), sales will be forecast as:

$$\text{Sales (\$ hundred thousands)} = 1.80 + .30(6) - 5.0(.12)$$
$$= 1.8 + 1.8 - .6$$
$$= 3.00$$

or

$$\text{Sales} = \$300,000$$

MONITORING AND CONTROLLING FORECASTS

Once a forecast has been completed, it is important that it not be forgotten. No manager wants to be reminded when his or her forecast is horribly inaccurate, but a firm needs to determine why the actual demand (or whatever variable is being examined) differed significantly from that projected.[7]

Tracking signal

One way to monitor forecasts to ensure they are performing well is to employ a tracking signal. A **tracking signal** is a measurement of how well the forecast is predicting actual values. As forecasts are updated every week, month, or quarter, the newly available demand data are compared to the forecast values.

The tracking signal is computed as the *running sum of the forecast errors* (RSFE) divided by the *mean absolute deviation* (MAD):

$$\frac{\text{Tracking}}{\text{signal}} = \frac{\text{RSFE}}{\text{MAD}}$$

$$= \frac{\Sigma(\text{Actual demand in period} - \text{Forecast demand in period } i)}{\text{MAD}} \qquad (4.15)$$

where

$$\text{MAD} = \frac{\Sigma|\text{Forecast errors}|}{n}$$

as seen earlier in Equation 4.6.

---

[7] If the forecaster *is* accurate, that individual usually makes sure that everyone is aware of his or her talents. Very seldom does one read articles in *Fortune, Forbes,* or *The Wall Street Journal,* however, about money managers who are consistently off by 25% in their stock market forecasts.

POM *in action*

Wrong When It Hurts Most

Some of the best brains in the United States are concentrated in the field of short-term macroeconomic forecasting. Stephen McNees of the Federal Reserve Bank of Boston has been analyzing the track records of the best-known forecasters for the past two decades. Although they were successful over half the time, McNees observed four periods over which their errors were large. For example, in the summer of 1981, the median one-year-ahead forecast of five prominent forecasters had predicted 2.1% growth in U.S. GNP for 1982. Instead, the economy plunged into a deep recession, with a GNP decline of 1.8%. As journalist Warren Brooks commented, "This is like forecasting partly cloudy and getting a ten-inch snowstorm instead. After all, in economics as in meterology, it's the ability to predict stormy change that makes forecasting useful."

Sources: "The Track Record of Macroeconomic Forecasts," *New England Economic Review,* November–December 1983; and "Scenarios: Uncharted Water Ahead," *Harvard Business Review,* September–October 1985.

Positive tracking signals indicate that demand is greater than forecast. Negative signals mean that demand is less than forecast. A good tracking signal, that is, one with a low RSFE, has about as much positive error as it has negative error. In other words, small deviations are okay, but the positive and negative ones should balance one another so the tracking signal centers closely around zero.

Once tracking signals are calculated, they are compared to predetermined control limits. When a tracking signal exceeds an upper or lower limit, a flag is tripped. This means there is a problem with the forecasting method, and management may want to reevaluate the way it forecasts demand. Figure 4.8 shows the graph of a

FIGURE 4.8

A Plot of Tracking Signals.

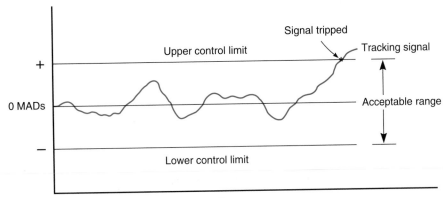

tracking signal that is exceeding the range of acceptable variation. If the model being used is exponential smoothing, perhaps the smoothing constant needs to be readjusted.

How do firms decide what the upper and lower tracking limits should be? There is no single answer, but they try to find reasonable values—in other words, limits not so low as to be triggered with every small forecast error, and not so high as to allow bad forecasts to be regularly overlooked. George Plossl and Oliver Wight, two inventory control experts, suggested using maximums of ±4 MADs (for high-volume stock items) and ±8 MADs (for lower-volume items).[8] Other forecasters suggest slightly lower ranges. One MAD is equivalent to approximately .8 standard deviations, so that ±2 MADs = ±1.6 standard deviations, ±3 MADs = ±2.4 standard deviations, and ±4 MADs = ±3.2 standard deviations. This suggests that for a forecast to be "in control," 89% of the errors are expected to fall within ±2 MADs, 98% within ±3 MADs, or 99.9% within ±4 MADs.[9]

Example 14 shows how the tracking signal and RSFE can be computed.

Example 14

Kimball Bakery's quarterly sales of croissants (in thousands), as well as forecast demand and error computations, are shown below. The objective is to compute the tracking signal and determine whether forecasts are performing adequately.

QUARTER	FORECAST DEMAND	ACTUAL DEMAND	ERROR	RSFE	FORECAST ERROR	CUMULATIVE ERROR	MAD	TRACKING SIGNAL
1	100	90	−10	−10	10	10	10.0	−1
2	100	95	− 5	−15	5	15	7.5	−2
3	100	115	+15	0	15	30	10.0	0
4	110	100	−10	−10	10	40	10.0	−1
5	110	125	+15	+5	15	55	11.0	+ .5
6	110	140	+30	+35	30	85	14.2	+2.5

$$MAD = \frac{\Sigma \, \text{Forecast errors}}{n} = \frac{85}{6} = 14.2$$

$$\text{Tracking signal} = \frac{\text{RSFE}}{\text{MAD}} = \frac{35}{14.2} = 2.5 \text{ MADs}$$

This tracking signal is within acceptable limits. We see that it drifted from − 2.0 MADs to + 2.5 MADs.

---

[8] See G. W. Plossl and O. W. Wight, *Production and Inventory Control* (Englewood Cliffs, NJ: Prentice-Hall, 1967).

[9] To prove these three percentages to yourself, just set up a normal curve for ±1.6 standard deviations (*z* values). Using the normal table in Appendix A you find that the area under the curve is .89. This represents ± 2 MADs. Likewise, ± 3 MADs = ± 2.4 standard deviations encompasses 98% of the area, and so on for ± 4 MADs.

Adaptive Smoothing

A lot of research has been published on the subject of adaptive forecasting. Adaptive forecasting refers to computer monitoring of tracking signals and self-adjustment if a signal passes its preset limit. For example, when applied to exponential smoothing, the α and β coefficients are first selected on the basis of values that minimize error forecasts, and then adjusted accordingly whenever the computer notes an errant tracking signal. This is called **adaptive smoothing.**

Adaptive smoothing

THE COMPUTER'S ROLE IN FORECASTING

Forecast calculations are seldom performed by hand in this day of computers. Many academic and commercial packaged programs are readily available to handle time series and causal projections.

Popular mainframe oriented packages include General Electric's *Time Series Forecasting,* and IBM's IMPACT (Inventory Management Program and Control Technique). Popular university packages are SAS, SPSS, BIOMED, SYSTAB, AB:POM, and Minitab. These, and a wide selection of others, are also available for microcomputer use.

SUMMARY

Forecasts are a critical part of the operations manager's function. Demand forecasts drive the production, capacity, and scheduling systems in a firm and affect the financial, marketing, and personnel planning functions.

In this chapter we introduced a variety of qualitative and quantitative forecasting techniques. Qualitative approaches employ judgment, experience, intuition, and a host of other factors that are difficult to quantify. Quantitative forecasting uses historical data and causal relations to project future demands. Table 4.1 on page 152 compares ten of the approaches mentioned on a variety of scales, including time span, sophistication, computer needs, costs, inputs, and accuracy. It is excerpted from one of several excellent articles on forecasting in the *Harvard Business Review* that we recommend you read.[10]

No forecasting method, as you can see in Table 4.1 and as we learned in this chapter, is perfect under all conditions. And even once management has found a satisfactory approach, it must still monitor and control its forecasts to make sure errors do not get out of hand. Forecasting can often be a very challenging, but rewarding, part of managing.

---

[10] The articles are by J. C. Chambers, *et al.,* "How to Choose the Right Forecasting Technique," *Harvard Business Review,* **49,** 4 (July–August 1971): 45–74; and D. M. Georgoff and R. G. Murdick, "Manager's Guide to Forecasting," *Harvard Business Review,* **64,** 1 (January–February 1986): 110–120.

TABLE 4.1 Overview of Ten Forecasting Approaches.

	NAIVE EXTRAPOLATION	SALES-FORCE COMPOSITE	JURY OF EXECUTIVE OPINION	DELPHI TECHNIQUE	CONSUMER MARKET SURVEY	MOVING AVERAGES	EXPONENTIAL SMOOTHING	TIME SERIES EXTRAPOLATION	REGRESSION MODELS	ECONOMETRIC MODELS
Time Span, Urgency, Frequency										
Span: Is the forecast period a present need, or short-, medium-, or long-term projection?										
	Present need to medium	Short or medium	Short or medium	Medium or long	Medium	Short, medium, or long	Present need to short or medium	Short, medium, or long	Short, medium, or long	Short, medium, or long
Urgency: Is the forecast needed immediately?										
	Rapid results are a strong advantage of this technique. Dev short Ex short	Forecast can be assembled, combined, and adjusted relatively quickly. Dev short Ex moderate	In-house group forecasts are quicker than outside experts. Dev short Ex short to moderate	Urgency seriously compromises quality. Dev moderate Ex moderate to long	Method of gathering data may cause a substantial time lag. Dev moderate Ex long to extended	Rapid results are a strong advantage of this technique. Dev short Ex short	→	Computation is quick if data are available: data gathering can cause delays. Dev short to moderate Exec short	Model formulation takes time, but forecast computation is quick. Dev moderate to long Exec short to moderate	Model building is lengthy, but producing forecast is quick. Dev long to extended Exec short to moderate
Frequency: Are frequent forecast updates needed?										
	Can easily accommodate frequent updates.	Forecast can be quickly compiled, but data collection restricts rapidity.	Can accomplish quickly.	Usually used for one-time forecasts, but they can be revised as new information becomes available.	Depending on methodology, frequent updates are possible, but updates are generally provided at extended intervals.	Forecast can be systematically updated easily.	→	→	→	Forecast can be updated quickly if data are available.
Resource Requirements										
Mathematical sophistication: Are quantitative skills limited?										
	Minimal quantitative capabilities are required.	→	→	→	Technical competencies are generally needed.	Minimal quantitative capabilities are required.	→	→	A fundamental compentency level is required.	A high level of understanding is required.
Computer: Are computer capabilities limited?										
	Computer capabilities are not essential.	Nominal processing does not require a computer.	→	→	A computer is generally needed for data analysis.	A computer is helpful for repetitive updating.	→	→	A computer is essential for most cases.	A computer is essential for all cases.
Financial: Are only limited financial resources available?										
	Very inexpensive to implement and maintain.	Inexpensive to implement and maintain.	Financial requirements are nominal for executive groups; they may be higher for outside experts.	Expense depends on makeup and affiliation of participants.	Generally expensive for good controls.	If data are readily available, out-of-pocket costs are minimal.	→	→	If data are on hand, development costs are moderate.	Development costs are substantial; operating costs are moderate.
Input										
Antecedent: Are only limited past data available?										
	Some past data are required, but extended history is not essential.	Past data are helpful but not always essential.	→	→	Past data are useful but not essential.	Past history is essential.	Only recent forecasts and current data are required once α is determined.	→	Past history is essential with detail required.	Extended history is helpful in initial development.
Output										
Accuracy: Is a high level of accuracy critical?										
	Often provides a limited practical level of accuracy.	Can be very accurate or subject to substantial bias.	May be most accurate under dynamic conditions.	Not particularly accurate, but usually most accurate when horizons are extended and conditions are dynamic.	Has limited predictability with durables, somewhat better with nondurables.	Accurate under stable conditions.	Generally rates high in accuracy for short-term forecasts.	Normally accurate for trends and stationary series.	Can be accurate if variable relationships are stable and the proportion of explained variance is high.	Give spotty performances in dynamic environments.

Source: Harvard Business Review, **64,** 1, January–February 1986, pp. 110–120.

KEY TERMS

Forecasting (p. 122)
Economic forecasts (p. 123)
Technological forecasts (p. 124)
Demand forecasts (p. 124)
Quantitative forecasts (p. 124)
Qualitative forecasts (p. 124)
Jury of executive opinion (p. 124)
Sales force composite (p. 124)
Delphi method (p. 124)
Consumer market survey (p. 124)
Time series (p. 125)
Naive approach (p. 128)
Moving averages (p. 128)

Exponential smoothing (p. 130)
Smoothing constant (p. 130)
Mean absolute deviation (MAD) (p. 132)
Mean squared error (MSE) (p. 133)
Mean absolute percent error (MAPE) (p. 133)
Trend projection (p. 136)
Linear regression analysis (p. 142)
Standard error of the estimate (p. 145)
Coefficient of correlation (p. 146)
Multiple regression (p. 147)
Tracking signal (p. 148)
Adaptive smoothing (p. 151)

USING AB:POM

AB:POM's forecasting program handles both time series models (such as moving averages, exponential smoothing, and least squares trend analysis) and causal models (such as simple and multiple regression). The initial forecasting menu is shown in Program 4. la. If the time series option is selected, you may then select one of the five models shown in Program 4.1b.

Program 4.1 a&b

AB:POM Forecasting Screens: Second Screen (b) Available if Times Series Analysis Option Is Chosen in First Screen (a)

```
                              ─────────── Options ───────────────────────

4.1(a)    Time Series Analysis


          Least Squares-Simple and Multiple Regression

           Select menu option by highlighted letter
          or point with arrow keys and then press
          RETURN key
```

```
                    Toggle Menu

4.1(b)    Moving averages (Unweighted)
          Weighted moving averages
          Exponential smoothing
          Exponential smoothing with trend
          Least squares trend
```

Solving Examples 1, 4, and 10 with AB:POM

To illustrate the use of the first time series model, the data from Donna's Garden Supply, seen in Example 1, is run in Program 4.2. Note that the information we entered is shaded. Program outputs include the next period's forecast, standard error, Bias, MAD, and MSE.

Program 4.2

AB:POM's Moving Averages Forecasting Program Using Example 1 Data

———————————————————— Forecasting ———————————————————— Solution ——

Number of past data periods (2–99) 12

———————————————— DONNA'S GARDEN SUPPLY, EXAMPLE 1 ————————————————

Method ->   Moving averages (Unweighted)

n pds ->   3

	Period (x)	Demand (y)	Forecast	Error	|Error|	Error^2
Jan	1	10.00				
Feb	2	12.00				
Mar	3	13.00				
Apr	4	16.00	11.6667	4.33333	4.33333	18.7778
May	5	19.00	13.6667	5.33333	5.33333	28.4444
Jun	6	23.00	16.00	7.00	7.00	49.00
Jul	7	26.00	19.3333	6.66667	6.66667	44.4444
Aug	8	30.00	22.6667	7.33333	7.33333	53.7778
Sep	9	28.00	26.3333	1.66667	1.66667	2.77778
Oct	10	18.00	28.00	-10.00	10.00	100.0000
Nov	11	16.00	25.3333	-9.3333	9.33333	87.11
Dec	12	14.00	20.6667	-6.6667	6.66667	44.4445
TOTALS	78.00	225.00		6.33333	58.3333	428.778
AVERAGE	6.50	.541667		.703704	6.48148	47.6420
				(Bias)	(MAD)	(MSE)

              Next period's forecast   16.00   Standard error = 7.826491

Program 4.3 demonstrates the input/output for exponential smoothing, using Example 4's data. We entered: (1) the number of data periods, (2) the model desired, (3) alpha, (4) the eight demands, (5) the initial forecast of 175, and (6) the titles for each period (i.e., QTR1, QTR2, and so on). Output is similar to that of the moving average model in Program 4.2.

Finally, to illustrate a causal regression model, we use the Tongren Construction data of Example 10. There is only one independent variable, so this is also called simple regression. Outputs of Program 4.4 include the regression line, correlation coefficient, and standard error.

In all cases, the data points can also be graphed by pressing the F3 function key.

Program 4.3

AB:POM's Exponential Smoothing Program Using Example 4 Data

———————————————————————— Forecasting ———————————————————— Solution ——
Number of past data periods (2–99)   8

————————————————————— PORT OF BALTIMORE, EXAMPLE 4 —————————————————

Method -> Exponential Smoothing

alpha (α)   0.100

	Period (x)	Demand (y)	Forecast	Error	|Error|	Error^2
QTR 1	1	180.00	175.00			
QTR 2	2	168.00	175.50	-7.50	7.50	56.25
QTR 3	3	159.00	174.75	-15.75	15.75	248.063
QTR 4	4	175.00	173.175	1.82500	1.82500	3.33061
QTR 5	5	190.00	173.357	16.6425	16.6425	276.97
QTR 6	6	205.00	175.022	29.9783	29.9783	898.70
QTR 7	7	180.00	178.020	1.98042	1.98042	3.92208
QTR 8	8	182.00	178.218	3.78	3.78	14.31
TOTALS	36.00	1439.00		30.9586	77.4586	1501.54
AVERAGE	4.50	0.5625		4.42265	11.0655	214.506
				(Bias)	(MAD)	(MSE)

              Next period's forecast   178.60   Standard error = 17.3294

F1 = Summary Table F3 = Graph   F9 = Print   Esc
Press <Esc> key to continue or highlighted key or function key for options

Program 4.4

AB:POM's Linear Regression Program Using Example 10 Data

—— Data file:Tongren2 ——————————— Forecasting ——————— Solution ——

Number of past data periods (2-99)   6   Number of independ. variables (1-6)   1

TONGREN

Method >   Least Squares-Simple and Multiple Regression

	B 0	B 1				
Coef ->	1.75	0.25				
	SALES	PAYROLL	Forecast	Error	|Error|	Error^2
1987	2.00	1.00	2.00	0.00	0.00	0.00
1988	3.00	3.00	2.50	0.50	0.50	0.25
1989	2.50	4.00	2.75	-0.25	0.25	0.0625
1990	2.00	2.00	2.25	-0.25	0.25	0.0625
1991	2.00	1.00	2.00	0.00	0.00	0.00
1992	3.50	7.00	3.50	0.00	0.00	0.00
TOTALS				0.00	1.00	0.375
AVERAGE				0.00	.166667	0.0625
				(Bias)	(MAD)	(MSE)

Regression line = SALES = 1.75   +0.25*PAYROLL
Correlation coefficient = 0.9013878 Standard error = .3061862

F1 = Summary Table   F9 = Print   Esc
Press <Esc> key to continue or highlight key or function key for options

SOLVED PROBLEMS

Solved Problem 4.1

Sales of Cool-Man air conditioners have grown steadily during the past five years (see table). The sales manager had predicted in 1987 that 1988 sales would be 410 air conditioners. Using exponential smoothing with a weight of $\alpha = .30$, develop forecasts for 1989 through 1993.

YEAR	SALES	FORECAST
1988	450	410
1989	495	
1990	518	
1991	563	
1992	584	
1993	?	

Solution

YEAR	FORECAST
1988	410.0
1989	422.0 = 410 + .3 (450 − 410)
1990	443.9 = 422 + .3 (495 − 422)
1991	466.1 = 443.9 + .3 (518 − 443.9)
1992	495.2 = 466.1 + .3 (563 − 466.1)
1993	521.8 = 495.2 + .3 (584 − 495.2)

Solved Problem 4.2

Room registrations in the Toronto Towers Plaza Hotel have been recorded for the past nine years. Management would like to determine the mathematical trend of guest registration in order to project future occupancy. This estimate would help the hotel determine whether a future expansion will be needed. Given the following time series data, develop a regression equation relating registrations to time. Then forecast 1994 registrations. Room registrations are in the thousands:

1984: 17   1985: 16   1986: 16   1987: 21   1988: 20
1989: 20   1990: 23   1991: 25   1992: 24

Solution

YEAR	TRANSFORMED YEAR, x	REGISTRANTS, y (IN THOUSANDS)	x^2	xy
1984	1	17	1	17
1985	2	16	4	32
1986	3	16	9	48
1987	4	21	16	84
1988	5	20	25	100
1989	6	20	36	120
1990	7	23	49	161
1991	8	25	64	200
1992	9	24	81	216
	$\Sigma x = 45$	$\Sigma y = 182$	$\Sigma x^2 = 285$	$\Sigma xy = 978$

$$\bar{x} = \frac{45}{9} = 5, \qquad \bar{y} = \frac{182}{9} = 20.22$$

$$b = \frac{\Sigma xy - n\bar{x}\bar{y}}{\Sigma x^2 - n\bar{x}^2} = \frac{978 - (9)(5)(20.22)}{285 - (9)(25)} = \frac{978 - 909.9}{285 - 225} = \frac{68.1}{60} = 1.135$$

$$a = \bar{y} - b\bar{x} = 20.22 - (1.135)(5) = 20.22 - 5.675 = 14.545$$

$$\hat{y} \text{ (registrations)} = 14.545 + 1.135x$$

The projection of registrations in 1994 (which is $x = 11$ in the coding system used) is:

$$\hat{y} = 14.545 + (1.135)(11) = 27.03$$

or 27,030 guests in 1994.

Solved Problem 4.3

Quarterly demand for Jaguar XJ6's at a New York auto dealer is forecast with the equation

$$\hat{y} = 10 + 3x$$

where x = quarters, and

$$
\begin{aligned}
&\text{Quarter I of } 1991 = 0 \\
&\text{Quarter II of } 1991 = 1 \\
&\text{Quarter III of } 1991 = 2 \\
&\text{Quarter IV of } 1991 = 3 \\
&\text{Quarter I of } 1992 = 4 \\
&\text{and so on}
\end{aligned}
$$

and

$$\hat{y} = \text{quarterly demand}$$

The demand for sports sedans is seasonal, and the indices for Quarters I, II, III, and IV are .80, 1.00, 1.30, and .90, respectively. Forecast demand for each quarter of 1993. Then seasonalize each forecast to adjust for quarterly variations.

Solution

Quarter II of 1992 is coded $x = 5$; Quarter III of 1992, $x = 6$; and Quarter IV of 1992, $x = 7$. Hence, Quarter I of 1993 is coded $x = 8$; Quarter II, $x = 9$; and so on.

$\hat{y}(1993 \text{ Quarter I}) = 10 + 3(8) = 34$ Adjusted forecast $= (.80)(34) = 27.2$

$\hat{y}(1993 \text{ Quarter II}) = 10 + 3(9) = 37$ Adjusted forecast $= (1.00)(37) = 37$

$\hat{y}(1993 \text{ Quarter III}) = 10 + 3(10) = 40$ Adjusted forecast $= (1.30)(40) = 52$

$\hat{y}(1993 \text{ Quarter IV}) = 10 + 3(11) = 43$ Adjusted forecast $= (.90)(43) = 38.7$

DISCUSSION QUESTIONS

1. Briefly describe the steps that are used to develop a forecasting system.

2. What is a time-series forecasting model?

3. What is the difference between a causal model and a time-series model?

4. What is a judgmental forecasting model, and when is it appropriate?

5. What is the meaning of least squares in a regression model?

6. What are some of the problems and drawbacks of the moving average forecasting model?

7. What effect does the value of the smoothing constant have on the weight given to the past forecast and the past observed value?

8. Briefly describe the Delphi technique.

9. What is MAD, and why is it important in the selection and use of forecasting models?

PROBLEMS

· **4.1** Laurie Lombard has developed the following forecasting model:

$$\hat{y} = 36 + 4.3x$$

where

$\hat{y}$ = demand for K10 air conditioners and
x = the outside temperature (°F).

a) Forecast demand for K10 when the temperature is 70°F.

b) What is demand for a temperature of 80°F?

c) What is demand for a temperature of 90°F?

· **4.2** Data collected on the yearly demand for 50-lb. bags of fertilizer at Donna's Garden Supply are shown in the following table. Develop a three-year moving average to forecast sales. Then estimate demand again with a weighted moving average in which sales in the most recent year are given a weight of 2 and sales in the other two years are each given a weight of 1. Which method do you think is best?

YEAR	DEMAND FOR FERTILIZER (THOUSANDS OF BAGS)
1	4
2	6
3	4
4	5
5	10
6	8
7	7
8	9
9	12
10	14
11	15

· **4.3** Develop a two- and a four-year moving average for the demand for fertilizer in Problem 4.2.

· **4.4** In Problems 4.2 and 4.3, four different forecasts were developed for the demand for fertilizer. These four forecasts are a two-year moving average, a three-year moving average, a weighted moving average, and a four-year moving average. Which one would you use? Explain your answer.

: **4.5** Use exponential smoothing with a smoothing constant of .3 to forecast the demand for fertilizer given in Problem 4.2. Assume that last period's forecast for year 1 is 5,000 bags to begin the procedure. Would you prefer to use the exponential smoothing model or the weighted average model developed in Problem 4.2? Explain your answer.

· **4.6** Using smoothing constants of .6 and .9, develop a forecast for the sales of Cool-Man air conditioners. See Solved Problem 4.1.

· **4.7** What effect did the smoothing constant have on the forecast for Cool-Man air conditioners? See Solved Problem 4.1 and Problem 4.6. Which smoothing constant gives the most accurate forecast?

· **4.8** Use a three-month moving average forecasting model to forecast the sales of Cool-Man air conditioners. See Solved Problem 4.1.

· **4.9** Using the trend projection method, develop a forecasting model for the sales of Cool-Man air conditioners. See Solved Problem 4.1.

: **4.10** Would you use exponential smoothing with a smoothing constant of .3, a three-month moving average, or trend to predict the sales of Cool-Man air conditioners? Refer to Solved Problem 4.1 and Problems 4.8 and 4.9.

: **4.11** Demand for heart transplant surgery at Washington General Hospital has increased steadily in the past few years, as seen in the following table.

YEAR	HEART TRANSPLANT SURGERIES PERFORMED
1	45
2	50
3	52
4	56
5	58
6	?

The director of medical services predicted six years ago that demand in year 1 would be for 41 surgeries.

a) Use exponential smoothing, first with a smoothing constant of .6 and then with one of .9, to develop forecasts for years 2 through 6.

b) Use a three-year moving average to forecast demand in years 4, 5, and 6.

c) Use the trend projection method to forecast demand in years 1 through 6.

d) With MAD as the criterion, which of the above four forecasting approaches is best?

: **4.12** Consulting income at Liz Xarhakos Associates for the period February–July has been as follows:

MONTH	INCOME (IN THOUSANDS)
February	70.0
March	68.5
April	64.8
May	71.7
June	71.3
July	72.8

Use trend-adjusted exponential smoothing to forecast August's income. Assume that the initial forecast for February is $65,000 and the initial trend adjustment is 0. The smoothing constants selected are $\alpha = .1$ and $\beta = .2$.

: **4.13** Resolve Problem 4.12 with $\alpha = .1$ and $\beta = .8$. Using MAD, which smoothing constants provide a better forecast?

: **4.14** Sales of industrial vacuum cleaners at Jack Peters Supply Co. over the past 13 months are shown below.

SALES (IN THOUSANDS)	MONTH
11	January
14	February
16	March
10	April
15	May
17	June
11	July
14	August
17	September
12	October
14	November
16	December
11	January

a) Using a moving average with three periods, determine the demand for vacuum cleaners for next February.

b) Using a weighted moving average with three periods, determine the demand for vacuum cleaners for February. Use 3, 2, and 1 for the weights of the most recent, second most recent, and third most recent periods, respectively. For example, if you were forecasting the demand for February, November would have a weight of 1, December would have a weight of 2, and January would have a weight of 3.

c) Evaluate the accuracy of each of these methods.

d) What other factors might Peters consider in forecasting sales?

: **4.15** The operations manager of a musical instrument distributor feels that demand for bass drums may be related to the number of television appearances by the popular rock group Green Shades during the previous month. The manager has collected the data shown in the following table.

DEMAND FOR BASS DRUMS	GREEN SHADES TV APPEARANCES
3	3
6	4
7	7
5	6
10	8
8	5

a) Graph these data to see whether a linear equation might describe the relationship between the group's television shows and bass drum sales.

b) Use the least squares regression method to derive a forecasting equation.

c) What is your estimate for bass drum sales if the Green Shades performed on TV nine times last month?

· **4.16** A study to determine the correlation between bank deposits and consumer price indices in Birmingham, Alabama, revealed the following (which was based on $n = 5$ years of data):

$$\Sigma x = 15$$
$$\Sigma x^2 = 55$$
$$\Sigma xy = 70$$
$$\Sigma y = 20$$
$$\Sigma y^2 = 130$$

a) Find the coefficient of correlation. What does it imply to you?

b) What is the standard error of the estimate?

 : **4.17** The accountant at Leslie Wardrop Coal Distributors, Inc., notes that the demand for coal seems to be tied to an index of weather severity developed by the U.S. Weather Bureau. That is, when weather was extremely cold in the United States over the past five years (and hence the index was high), coal sales were high. The accountant proposes that one good forecast of next year's coal demand could be made by developing a regression equation and then consulting the *Farmer's Almanac* to see how severe next year's winter will be. For the data in the following table, derive a least squares regression and compute the coefficient of correlation of the data. Also compute the standard error of the estimate.

COAL SALES, y (IN MILLIONS OF TONS)	WEATHER INDEX, x
4	2
1	1
4	4
6	5
5	3

: **4.18** Thirteen students entered the P/OM program at Mason University two years ago. The following table indicates what their grade point averages (GPAs) were after being in the program for two years and what each student scored on the SAT exam when he or she was in high school. Is there a meaningful relationship between grades and SAT scores? If a student scores a 350 on the SAT, what do you think his or her GPA will be? What about a student who scores 800?

STUDENT	SAT SCORE	GPA
A	421	2.90
B	377	2.93
C	585	3.00
D	690	3.45
E	608	3.66
F	390	2.88
G	415	2.15
H	481	2.53

STUDENT	SAT SCORE	GPA
I	729	3.22
J	501	1.99
K	613	2.75
L	709	3.90
M	366	1.60

· **4.19** Dr. Jerilyn Ross, a New York City psychologist, specializes in treating patients who are phobic and afraid to leave their homes. The following table indicates how many patients Dr. Ross has seen each year for the past ten years. It also indicates what the robbery rate was in New York City during the same year.

YEAR	NUMBER OF PATIENTS	CRIME RATE (ROBBERIES PER 1,000 POPULATION)
1	36	58.3
2	33	61.1
3	40	73.4
4	41	75.7
5	40	81.1
6	55	89.0
7	60	101.1
8	54	94.8
9	58	103.3
10	61	116.2

Using trend analysis, how many patients do you think Dr. Ross will see in years 11, 12, and 13? How well does the model fit the data?

: **4.20** Using the data in Problem 4.19, apply linear regression to study the relationship between the crime rate and Dr. Ross's patient load. If the robbery rate increases to 131.2 in year 11, how many phobic patients will Dr. Ross treat? If the crime rate drops to 90.6, what is the patient projection?

· **4.21** Accountants at the firm Gets and Farnsworth believed that several traveling executives submit unusually high travel vouchers when they return from business trips. The accountants took a sample of 200 vouchers submitted from the past year; they then developed the following multiple regression equation relating expected travel cost ($\hat{y}$) to number of days on the road (x_1) and distance traveled (x_2) in miles:

$$\hat{y} = \$90.00 + \$48.50x_1 + .40x_2$$

The coefficient of correlation computed was .68.

a) If Bill Tomlinson returns from a 300-mile trip that took him out of town for five days, what is the expected amount he should claim as expenses?

b) Tomlinson submitted a reimbursement request for $685. What should the accountant do?

c) Should any other variables be included? Which ones? Why?

· **4.22** In the past, Laura Gustafson's tire dealership sold an average of 1,000 radials each year. In the past two years 200 and 250, respectively, were sold in fall, 300 and 350 in winter, 150 and 165 in spring, and 300 and 285 in summer. With a major expansion planned,

Mrs. Gustafson projects sales next year to increase to 1,200 radials. What will the demand be each season?

: **4.23** Passenger miles flown on Northeast Airlines, a commuter firm serving the Boston hub, are shown below for the past 12 weeks.

WEEK	ACTUAL PASSENGER MILES (IN THOUSANDS)
1	17
2	21
3	19
4	23
5	18
6	16
7	20
8	18
9	22
10	20
11	15
12	22

a) Assuming an initial forecast for week 1 of 17,000 miles, use exponential smoothing to compute miles for weeks 2 through 12. Use $\alpha = .2$.

b) What is the MAD for this model?

c) Compute the RSFE and tracking signals. Are they within acceptable limits?

: **4.24** Bus and subway ridership in Washington, D.C., during the summer months are believed to be heavily tied to the number of tourists visiting that city. During the past 12 years, the following data have been obtained:

YEAR	NUMBER OF TOURISTS (MILLIONS)	RIDERSHIP (MILLIONS)	YEAR	NUMBER OF TOURISTS (MILLIONS)	RIDERSHIP (MILLIONS)
1	7	1.5	7	16	2.4
2	2	1.0	8	12	2.0
3	6	1.3	9	14	2.7
4	4	1.5	10	20	4.4
5	14	2.5	11	15	3.4
6	15	2.7	12	7	1.7

a) Plot these data and decide if a linear model is reasonable.

b) Develop a regression relationship.

c) What is expected ridership if ten million tourists visit the city in a year?

d) Explain the predicted ridership if there are no tourists at all.

e) What is the standard error of the estimate?

f) What is the model's correlation coefficient and coefficient of determination?

:**4.25** Emergency calls to the 911 system of Winter Park, Florida, for the past 24 weeks are shown below.

WEEK	CALLS	WEEK	CALLS	WEEK	CALLS
1	50	9	35	17	55
2	35	10	20	18	40
3	25	11	15	19	35
4	40	12	40	20	60
5	45	13	55	21	75
6	35	14	35	22	50
7	20	15	25	23	40
8	30	16	55	24	65

a) Compute the exponentially smoothed forecast of calls for each week. Assume an initial forecast of 50 calls in the first week, and use $\alpha = .1$. What is the forecast for the 25th week?

b) Reforecast each period using $\alpha = .6$.

c) Actual calls during the 25th week were 85. Which smoothing constant provides a superior forecast? Explain and justify the measure of error used.

:**4.26** Using the 911 call data in Problem 4.25, forecast calls for weeks 2 through 25 with a trend-adjusted exponential smoothing model. Assume an initial forecast for 50 calls for week 1 and an initial trend of zero. Use smoothing constants of $\alpha = .3$ and $\beta = .1$. Is this mode better than that of Problem 4.25? What adjustment might be useful for further improvement? (Again, assume actual calls in week 25 were 85.)

:**4.27** Orlando Power and Light has been collecting data on demand for electric power in its UCF subregion for only the past two years. Those data are shown below:

MONTH	DEMAND IN MEGAWATTS		MONTH	DEMAND IN MEGAWATTS	
	Last Year	This Year		Last Year	This year
Jan.	5	17	July	23	44
Feb.	6	14	Aug.	26	41
Mar.	10	20	Sept.	21	33
Apr.	13	23	Oct.	15	23
May	18	30	Nov.	12	26
June	15	38	Dec.	14	17

The utility needs to be able to forecast demand for each month next year in order to plan for expansion and to arrange to borrow power from neighboring utilities during peak periods. Yet the standard forecasting models discussed in this chapter will not fit the data observed for the two years.

a) What are the weaknesses of the standard forecasting techniques as applied to this set of data?

b) Since known models are not really appropriate here, propose your own approach to forecasting. Although there is no perfect solution to tackling data such as these (in other words, there are no 100% right or wrong answers), justify your model.

c) Forecast demand for each month next year, using the model you propose.

: **4.28** Attendance at Orlando's newest Disney-like attraction, Vacation World, has been as follows:

YEAR	QUARTER	GUESTS (IN THOUSANDS)
1990	Winter	73
	Spring	104
	Summer	168
	Fall	74
1991	Winter	65
	Spring	82
	Summer	124
	Fall	52
1992	Winter	89
	Spring	146
	Summer	205
	Fall	98

Compute seasonal indices, using all of the above data.

· **4.29** Samantha Shane, manager of Shane's Department Store, has used time series extrapolation to forecast retail sales for the next four quarters. The sales estimates are $120,000, $140,000, $160,000, and $180,000 for the respective quarters. Seasonal indices for the four quarters have been found to be 1.25, .90, .75, and 1.15, respectively. Compute a seasonalized or adjusted sales forecast.

Data Base Application

: **4.30** Gardner Savings and Loan is proud of its long tradition in Tampa, Florida. Begun by Cathy Gardner four years after World War II, the S&L has bucked the trend of financial and liquidity problems that have plagued the industry since 1985. Deposits have increased slowly but surely over the years, despite recessions in 1956, 1979, 1983, and 1992. Ms. Gardner believes it necessary to have a long-range strategic plan for her firm, including a five-year forecast of deposits. She examines the past deposit data and also peruses Florida's Gross State Product (GSP) over the same 44 years. (GSP is analagous to Gross National Product, GNP, but on the state level.)

a) Using exponential smoothing, with $\alpha = .6$, then trend analysis, and finally linear regression, discuss which forecasting model fits best for Gardner's strategic plan. Justify why one model should be selected over another.

b) Carefully examine the data. Can you make a case for excluding a portion of the information? Why? Would that change your choice of model?

YEAR	DEPOSITS[1]	GSP[2]	YEAR	DEPOSITS[1]	GSP2	YEAR	DEPOSITS[1]	GSP[2]
1949	.25	.4	1964	2.3	1.6	1979	24.1	3.9
1950	.24	.4	1965	2.8	1.5	1980	25.6	3.8
1951	.24	.5	1966	2.8	1.6	1981	30.3	3.8
1952	.26	.7	1967	2.7	1.7	1982	36.0	3.7
1953	.25	.9	1968	3.9	1.9	1983	31.1	4.1
1954	.30	1.0	1969	4.9	1.9	1984	31.7	4.1
1955	.31	1.4	1970	5.3	2.3	1985	38.5	4.0
1956	.32	1.7	1971	6.2	2.5	1986	47.9	4.5
1957	.24	1.3	1972	4.1	2.8	1987	49.1	4.6
1958	.26	1.2	1973	4.5	2.9	1988	55.8	4.5
1959	.25	1.1	1974	6.1	3.4	1989	70.1	4.6
1960	.33	.9	1975	7.7	3.8	1990	70.9	4.6
1961	.50	1.2	1976	10.1	4.1	1991	79.1	4.7
1962	.95	1.2	1977	15.2	4.0	1992	94.0	5.0
1963	1.7	1.2	1978	18.1	4.0			

[1] In $ millions.
[2] In $ billions.

CASE STUDY

The North-South Airline

In 1988, Northern Airlines[11] merged with Southeast Airlines to create the fourth largest U.S. carrier. The new North-South Airline inherited both an aging fleet of Boeing 727-200 aircraft and Stephen Ruth. Ruth was a tough former Secretary of the Navy who stepped in as new President and Chairman of the Board.

Ruth's first concern in creating a financially solid company was maintenance costs. It was commonly surmised in the airline industry that maintenance costs rise with the age of the aircraft. He quickly noticed that historically there has been a significant difference in the reported B727-200 maintenance costs (from ATA Form 41s) both in the airframe and engine areas between Northern Airlines and Southeast Airlines, with Southeast having the newer fleet.

On November 12, 1988, Peg Young, Vice President for Operations and Maintenance, was called into Ruth's office and asked to study the issue. Specifically, Ruth wanted to know (1) whether the average fleet age was correlated to direct airframe maintenance costs, and (2) whether there

[11] Dates and names of airlines and individuals have been changed in this case to maintain confidentiality. The data and issues described here are actual.

was a relationship between average fleet age and direct engine maintenance costs. Young was to report back with the answer, along with quantitative and graphical descriptions of the relationship, by November 26.

Young's first step was to have her staff construct the average age of Northern and Southeast B727-200 fleets, by quarter, since the introduction of that aircraft to service by each airline in late 1979 and early 1980. The average age of each fleet was calculated by first multiplying the total number of calendar days each aircraft had been in service at the pertinent point in time by the average daily utilization of the respective fleet to total fleet hours flown. The total fleet hours flown was then divided by the number of aircraft in service at that time, giving the age of the "average" aircraft in the fleet.

The average utilization was found by taking the actual total fleet hours flown at September 30, 1987, from Northern and Southeast data, and dividing by total days in service for all aircraft at that time. The average utilization for Southeast was 8.3 hours per day, and the average utilization for Northern was 8.7 hours per day. Since the available cost data were calculated for each yearly period ending at the end of the first quarter, average fleet age was calculated at the same points in time.

CASE STUDY (Continued)

The fleet data are shown in Table 4.2. Airframe cost data and engine cost data are both shown paired with fleet average age in that table.

1. Prepare Peg Young's response to Stephen Ruth.

TABLE 4.2 North-South Airline Data for Boeing 727-200 Jets.

	NORTHERN AIRLINE DATA			SOUTHEAST AIRLINE DATA		
Year	Airframe Cost per Aircraft	Engine Cost per Aircraft	Average Age (Hours)	Airframe Cost per Aircraft	Engine Cost per Aircraft	Average Age (Hours)
1981	$51.80	$43.49	6,512	$13.29	$18.86	5,107
1982	54.92	38.58	8,404	25.15	31.55	8,145
1983	69.70	51.48	11,077	32.18	40.43	7,360
1984	68.90	58.72	11,717	31.78	22.10	5,773
1985	63.72	45.47	13,275	25.34	19.69	7,150
1986	84.73	50.26	15,215	32.78	32.58	9,364
1987	78.74	79.60	18,390	35.56	38.07	8,259

CASE STUDY

Kwik Lube

Dick Johnson, a successful textbook author and English professor at the University of Washington, retired from teaching in 1972, at age 40. His net worth was approximately a half-million dollars.

In 1979, during a trip to Los Angeles, he came across a very interesting type of new business. It was a very small gas station that specialized only in oil changes and lubrication jobs. The old gas station had been remodeled, the gas pumps had been removed, and the large sign above the small building read "OIL AND LUBE—$10 and 10 MINUTES." For two hours, Dick observed the converted gas station from a restaurant across the street.

During the next month, Dick made three trips to Los Angeles to talk to the owner, George, about how he got into the business and how the business worked. Dick paid George $1,000 for his advice and information and promised never to compete directly with George or ever to open or operate a similar type of business in the Los Angeles area.

After talking to his lawyer and accountant, Dick started to organize a new business—Kwik Lube. In March 1980, Dick had built his first Kwik Lube, and by the end of 1980, he had completed two additional Kwik Lubes in the Seattle

area. The total gross revenues in 1980 from all three stations was $260,000.

Between 1980 and 1984, business picked up rapidly. Total gross sales in 1981 and 1982 were $680,000 and $750,000 respectively. In 1983, total gross sales for the three Kwik Lube stations was $750,000, and in 1984, total gross sales was $780,000. Dick was convinced that this sales increase was due to his not significantly increasing the price of his basic service, which was to change the oil, change the filter, and do a lube job. In 1980, the total price was $9.95. In 1983, the total price per job was $10.95, and by 1984, the total price was only $12.95.

In addition to running his three Kwik Lube stations in Seattle, Dick desired to franchise his idea in other cities in Washington and in other states such as Oregon, Idaho, and Montana. During the last three years, Dick had acquired considerable knowledge about this type of business. He was able to obtain the best possible prices for oil, lubricants, and filters. If he franchised Kwik Lube, he would even be able to make a profit from selling oil, filters, and lubricants.

Dick invested over $20,000 in lawyers' fees and another $2,000 in talking to other companies in the franchise business. He decided to set his franchise fee at $18,000, plus 6%

CASE STUDY (Continued)

of the gross sales of the stations. In addition, each new Kwik Lube station had to conform to exacting standards for the building and all of the equipment. Depending on the location, Dick could build and equip a Kwik Lube station for under $200,000. Like his own Kwik Lube stations, these new stations would have two car or vehicle bays. In 1985, Dick sold his first franchise to T. A. Williams and another franchise to an investor in Eugene, Oregon. By 1988, Dick had sold a total of 11 franchises in Spokane, Washington; Eugene, Oregon; Portland, Oregon; Butte, Montana; and Boise, Idaho. In addition, Dick experienced a substantial growth rate for total gross sales for his three Kwik Lube stations in Seattle. In 1985, total gross sales were $990,000. In 1986, total gross sales were $1,040,000; in 1987, $1,200,000; and in 1988, $1,330,000.

Dick knew that it would only be a matter of time before someone else would start to compete directly with his Kwik Lube stations, but he never believed that the first competition would be in Seattle. Construction on the first two Speedy Lube stations started in 1988, and both stations were in operation in early 1989. The two stores were almost identical to the Kwik Lube stations, but Speedy Lube was priced two dollars less than Kwik Lube's current price, which was now $19.95. Dick never dreamed that this new competition would cut so deeply into his total gross sales. Total gross sales for the three Kwik Lube stations in Seattle dropped to $1,110,000 for 1989, and the situation did not look any better for 1990. (Indeed, when 1990 figures became available, sales were again only $1,110,000.)

Soon after the total gross sales figures came in for 1989, Dick got some startling information from one of his friends in Spokane. Over 50% of the stock in Speedy Lube, Inc. was owned by Richland, Inc., a holding company owned by T. A. Williams. Dick was outraged that one of the people who purchased a franchise from him was directly competing with his Kwik Lube stores and in direct violation of the franchise contract, which contained a noncompetition clause.

Dick had only two goals for the coming year: (1) to shut down the two Speedy Lube stations, and (2) to regain his lost sales for the two years from T. A. Williams. Both objectives were to be accomplished with a lawsuit.

Dick Johnson's lawyer strongly suggested that Dick employ an expert witness to testify on his behalf against Speedy Lube. While there seemed to be no question about who would win the case, Dick's lawyer believed that an expert witness could more accurately determine the damages. In addition, most juries place more importance on expert testimony. As a result, Dick decided to employ the services of Dr. Warren Gunn.

Dr. Gunn was a professor of marketing at Eastern Washington University, which was very close to Spokane. He had more than ten years' experience as an expert witness, and his specialty was determining damages for antitrust and franchise cases. His basic strategy was to find data about the same industry or a similar one in a location resembling the area in which the original problem occurred. In this case, Dr. Gunn needed data about the fast oil and lubrication business in a location similar to Seattle. Because Dick originally obtained his idea from a small station in Los Angeles and because Los Angeles had hundreds of these types of businesses by 1989, Dr. Gunn decided to collect data in the Los Angeles area. This would require the development and pilot testing of a questionnaire that could determine the total gross number of cars serviced for fast oil and lubrication businesses in the Los Angeles area between 1980 and 1990.

Although the questionnaire study would cost $20,000 to perform, Dr. Gunn and Dick both believed that it was the best approach. The data were collected in two weeks, and are summarized in Table 4.3. Both Dr. Gunn and Dick knew that if the results of the questionnaire were not favorable, they would not use it during the case.

TABLE 4.3 Analysis of Average Fast Oil and Lubrication. Total Gross Sales for Cars Serviced at Los Angeles Stations (Using Two Bays as a Basis for Comparison).

YEAR	AVERAGE TOTAL SALES	YEAR	AVERAGE TOTAL SALES
1980	$190,000	1986	$350,000
1981	220,000	1987	390,000
1982	250,000	1988	440,000
1983	240,000	1989	470,000
1984	260,000	1990	520,000
1985	330,000		

Discussion Questions

1. Using the data in Table 4.3, compute the loss for Kwik Lube stations during the last two years using regression.

2. How accurate can the results claim to be?

3. Was it worth $20,000 to perform the marketing research?

4. What other factors might be introduced into the lawsuit?

Source: Adapted from B. Render, R. M. Stair, and I. Greenberg, *Cases and Readings in Management Science,* 2nd ed. Boston: Allyn & Bacon, 1990.

BIBLIOGRAPHY

Ashley, R., and J. Guerard. "Applications of Time Series Analysis to Texas Financial Forecasting." *Interfaces* **13** (August 1983): 46–55.

Ashton, A. H., and R. H. Ashton. "Aggregating Subjective Forecasts." *Management Science* **31** (December 1985): 1499–1508.

Becker, B. C., and A. Sapienza. "Forecasting Hospital Reimbursement." *Hospital and Health Services Administration* **32** (November 1987): 521–530.

Box, G. E. P., and G. Jenkins. *Time Series Analysis: Forecasting and Control.* San Francisco: Holden Day, 1970.

Brown, R. G. *Statistical Forecasting for Inventory Control.* New York: McGraw-Hill, 1959.

Brozovich, J. P., and D. Loftus. "Physician-Administrator Decision Making for High-Technology Purchases." *Health Care Management Review* **6** (Summer 1981): 63–73.

Bunn, D. W., and J. P. Seigal. "Forecasting the Effects of Television Programming upon Electricity Loads." *Journal of the Operational Research Society* **34** (January 1983): 17–25.

Chambers, J. C., C. Satinder, S. K. Mullick, and D. D. Smith. "How to Choose the Right Forecasting Techniques." *Harvard Business Review* **49** (July–August 1971): 45–74.

Claycombe, W. W., and W. G. Sullivan. "Current Forecasting Techniques." *Journal of System Management* (September 1978): 18–20.

Gardner, E. S. "Exponential Smoothing: The State of the Art." *Journal of Forecasting* **4** (March 1985).

Georgoff, D. M., and R. G. Murdick. "Managers Guide to Forecasting." *Harvard Business Review* **64** (January–February 1986): 110–120.

Gips, J., and B. Sullivan. "Sales Forecasting—Replacing Magic with Logic." *Production and Inventory Management Review* **2** (February 1982).

Lane, D., *et al.* "Forecasting Demand for Long Term Care Services." *Health Services Research* **20** (October 1985): 435–459.

Lee, D. R. "A Forecast of Lodging Supply and Demand." *The Cornell HRA Quarterly* **25** (August 1984): 27–40.

Mabert, V. A., and R. L. Stocco. "Managing and Monitoring a Forecasting System: The Chemical Bank Experience." *Journal of Bank Research* **13** (Autumn 1982): 195–201.

Mahmoud, E. "Accuracy in Forecasting: A Summary." *Journal of Forecasting* (April–June 1984).

Makridakis, S., S. C. Wheelright, and V. E. McGee. *Forecasting: Methods and Applications,* 2nd ed. New York: John Wiley and Sons, 1983.

Murdick, R., B. Render, and R. Russell. *Service Operations Management.* Boston: Allyn and Bacon, 1990.

Parker, G. C., and E. L. Segura. "How to Get a Better Forecast." *Harvard Business Review* **49** (March–April 1971): 99–109.

Plossl, G. W., and O. W. Wight. *Production and Inventory Control.* Englewood Cliffs, NJ: Prentice-Hall, 1967.

Render, B., and R. M. Stair. *Cases and Readings in Quantitative Analysis for Management.* Boston: Allyn and Bacon, 1982.

Render, B., and R. M. Stair. *Introduction to Management Science.* Boston: Allyn & Bacon, 1992.

Render, B., and R. M. Stair. *Quantitative Analysis for Management,* 4th ed. Boston: Allyn and Bacon, 1991.

Schnaars, S. P., and R. J. Bavuso. "Extrapolation Models on Very Short-Term Forecasts." *Journal of Business Research* **14** (1986): 27–36.

Van Dyke, D. T. "Why Economists Make Mistakes." *The Bankers Magazine* (May–June 1986): 69–75.

Young, M. A. "Sources of Competitive Data for the Management Strategist." *Strategic Management Journal* **10** (July–August 1989): 285–293.

Statistical Tools for Managers

INTRODUCTION

The purpose of this supplement is to provide you with a review of several important statistical tools that you will find useful in many chapters of the text. Applications of statistics permeate the subject of operations management because so much of decision making depends on probabilities due to limited or uncertain information. An understanding of the concepts of probability distributions, expected values, and variances are needed in the study of decision trees (Chapters 3, 6, and 7), forecasting (Chapter 4), queuing models and simulation (Chapter 5), work measurement (Chapter 10), learning curves (Chapter 11), inventory (Chapter 13), project management (Chapter 16), quality control (Chapter 17), and maintenance (Chapter 18).

DISCRETE PROBABILITY DISTRIBUTIONS

Discrete probability distribution

In this section we explore the properties of **discrete probability distributions.** When we deal with discrete variables, there is a probability value assigned to each event. These values must be between 0 and 1, and they must sum to 1. Let us consider an example that relates to a sampling of student grades.

Example S1

The Dean at East Florida University, Nancy Birdsong, is concerned about the undergraduate statistics training of new MBA students. In a sampling of 100 applicants for next year's MBA class, she asked each student to supply his or her final grade in the course in statistics taken as a sophomore or junior. To translate from letter grades to a numeric score, the Dean used the following system:

| **5.** A | **4.** B | **3.** C | **2.** D | **1.** F |

The responses to this query of the 100 potential students are summarized in Table S4. 1. Also shown is the probability for each possible grade outcome. This discrete probability distribution is computed using the relative frequency approach. Probability values are also often shown in graph form as in Figure S4.1.

TABLE S4.1 Probability Distribution for Grades.

GRADE LETTER OUTCOME	SCORE VARIABLE (x)	NUMBER OF STUDENTS RESPONDING	PROBABILITY, $P(x)$
A	5	10	.1 = 10/100
B	4	20	.2 = 20/100
C	3	30	.3 = 30/100
D	2	30	.3 = 30/100
F	1	10	.1 = 10/100
		Total = 100	1.0 = 100/100

FIGURE S4.1

Probability Function for Grades.

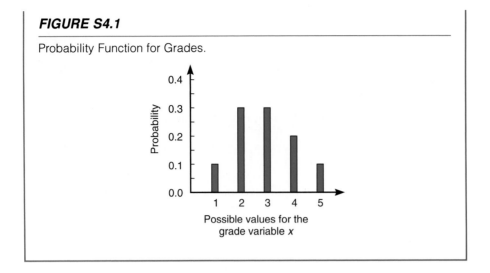

This distribution follows the three rules required of all probability distributions:

1. the events are mutually exclusive and collectively exhaustive;
2. the individual probability values are between 0 and 1 inclusive;
3. the total of the probability values sum to 1.

The graph of the probability distribution in Example Sl gives us a picture of its shape. It helps us identify the central tendency of the distribution (called the expected value) and the amount of variability or spread of the distribution (called the variance).

Expected Value of a Discrete Probability Distribution

Once we have established a probability distribution, the first characteristic that is usually of interest is the "central tendency" or average of the distribution.[1] The **expected value,** a measure of central tendency, is computed as a weighted average of the values of the variable:

Expected value

$$\mathrm{E}(x) = \sum_{i=1}^{n} x_i P(x_i) = x_1 P(x_1) + x_2 P(x_2) + \cdots + x_n P(x_n) \qquad (S4.1)$$

where

$$x_i = \text{the variable's possible values}$$
$$P(x_i) = \text{the probability of each of the variable's possible values}$$

The expected value of any discrete probability distribution can be computed by multiplying each possible value of the variable x_i by the probability $P(x_i)$ that outcome will occur, and summing the results, indicated by the summation sign, Σ.

---

[1] If the data we are dealing with has not been grouped into a probability distribution, the measure of central tendency is called the arithmetic mean, or simply, the average. Here is the mean of the following seven numbers: 10, 12, 18, 6, 4, 5, 15.

$$\text{Arithmetic mean } \overline{X} = \frac{\Sigma X}{n} = \frac{10 + 12 + 18 + 6 + 4 + 5 + 15}{7} = 10$$

Example S2

Here is how the expected grade value can be computed for the question in Example S1.

$$E(x) = \sum_{i=1}^{5} x_i P(x_i) = x_1 P(x_1) + x_2 P(x_2) + x_3 P(x_3) + x_4 P(x_4) + x_5 P(x_5)$$

$$= (5)(.1) + (4)(.2) + (3)(.3) + (2)(.3) + (1)(.1)$$

$$= 2.9$$

The expected grade of 2.9 implies that the mean statistics grade is between D (2) and C (3), and that the average response is closer to a C, which is 3. Looking at Figure S4.1, we see that this is consistent with the shape of the probability function.

Variance of a Discrete Probability Distribution

Variance

In addition to the central tendency of a probability distribution, most decision makers are interested in the variability or the spread of the distribution. The **variance** of a probability distribution is a number that reveals the overall spread or dispersion of the distribution.[2] For a discrete probability distribution, it can be computed using the following equation:

$$\text{Variance} = \sum_{i=1}^{n} (x_i - E(x))^2 P(x_i) \tag{S4.2}$$

where

$$x_i = \text{the variable's possible values}$$
$$E(x) = \text{the expected value of the variable}$$
$$P(x_i) = \text{probability of each possible value of the variable}$$

To compute the variance above, the expected value is subtracted from each value of the variable squared, and multiplied by the probability of occurrence of that value. The results are then summed to obtain the variance.

---

[2] Just as the variance of a probability distribution shows the dispersion of the data, so does the variance of ungrouped data, that is, data not formed into a probability distribution. The formula is: Variance $= \Sigma(X - \overline{X})^2 / n$. Using the numbers 10, 12, 18, 6, 4, 5, and 15, we find that $\overline{X} = 10$. Here are the variance computations:

$$\text{Variance} = \frac{(10 - 10)^2 + (12 - 10)^2 + (18 - 10)^2 + (6 - 10)^2 + (4 - 10)^2 + (5 - 10)^2 + (15 - 10)^2}{7}$$

$$= \frac{0 + 4 + 64 + 16 + 36 + 25 + 25}{7}$$

$$= \frac{170}{7} = 24.28$$

We should also note that when the data we're looking at represents a *sample* of a whole set of data, we use the term $n - 1$ in the denominator, instead of n, in the variance formula.

A related measure of dispersion or spread is the **standard deviation.** This quantity is also used in many computations involved with probability distributions. The standard deviation, σ, is just the square root of the variance:

$$\sigma = \sqrt{\text{Variance}} \qquad\qquad \text{(S4.3)}$$

Standard deviation

Example S3

Here is how this procedure is done for the statistics grade survey question:

$$\text{Variance} = \sum_{i=1}^{5} (x_i - E(x))^2 \, P(x_i)$$

$$= (5 - 2.9)^2(.1) + (4 - 2.9)^2(.2) + (3 - 2.9)^2(.3)$$
$$+ (2 - 2.9)^2(.3) + (1 - 2.9)^2(.1)$$

$$= (2.1)^2(.1) + (1.1)^2(.2) + (.1)^2(.3) + (-.9)^2(.3) + (-1.9)^2(.1)$$

$$= .441 + .242 + .003 + .243 + .361$$

$$= 1.29$$

The standard deviation for the grade question is

$$\sigma = \sqrt{\text{Variance}}$$
$$= \sqrt{1.29} = 1.14$$

CONTINUOUS PROBABILITY DISTRIBUTIONS

There are many examples of continuous variables. The time it takes to finish a project, the number of ounces in a barrel of butter, the high temperature during a given day, the exact length of a given type of lumber, and the weight of a railroad car of coal are all examples of continuous variables. Since variables can take on an infinite number of values, the fundamental probability rules must be modified for continuous variables.

As with discrete probability distributions, the sum of the probability values must equal 1. Because there are an infinite number of values of the variables, however, the probability of *each value* of the variable *must be 0.* If the probability values for the variable values were greater than 0, then the sum would be infinitely large.

The Normal Distribution

One of the most popular and useful continuous probability distributions is the **normal distribution,** which is characterized by a bell-shaped curve. The normal distribution is completely specified when values for the mean, μ, and the standard deviation, σ, are known.

Normal distribution

The Area Under the Normal Curve. Because the normal distribution is symmetrical, its midpoint (and highest point) is at the mean. Values of the x-axis are then measured in terms of how many standard deviations they are from the mean.

FIGURE S4.2

Three Common Areas Under Normal Curves.

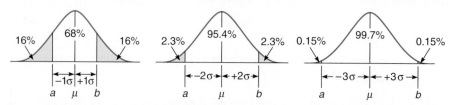

The area under the curve (in a continuous distribution) describes the probability that a variable has a value in the specified interval. The normal distribution requires complex mathematical calculations, but tables that provide areas or probabilities are readily available. For example, Figure S4.2 illustrates three commonly used relationships that have been derived from standard normal tables (a procedure we will discuss in a moment). The area from point *a* to point *b* in the first drawing represents the probability, 68%, that the variable will be within one standard deviation of the mean. In the middle graph, we see that about 95.4% of the area lies within plus or minus 2 standard deviations of the mean. The third figure shows that 99.7% lies between ±3σ.

Translated into an application, Figure S4.2 implies that if the expected lifetime of a computer chip is μ = 100 days, and if the standard deviation is σ = 15 days, we can make the following statements:

1. 68% of the population of computer chips studied have lives between 85 and 115 days (namely, ±1σ).

2. 95.4% of the chips have lives between 70 and 130 days (±2σ).

3. 99.7% of the computer chips have lives in the range from 55 to 145 days (±3σ).

4. Only 16% of the chips have lives greater than 115 days (from first graph, the area to the right of + 1σ).

Using the Standard Normal Table. To use a table to find normal probability values, we follow two steps.

Step 1. Convert the normal distribution to what we call a *standard normal distribution.* A standard normal distribution is one that has a mean of 0 and a standard deviation of 1. All normal tables are designed to handle variables with μ = 0 and σ = 1. Without a standard normal distribution, a different table would be needed for each pair of μ and σ values. We call the new standard variable *z*. The value of *z* for any normal distribution is computed from the equation:

$$z = \frac{x - \mu}{\sigma} \tag{S4.4}$$

where

x = the value of the variable we want to measure

μ = the mean of the distribution

σ = the standard deviation of the distribution

z = the number of standard deviations from x to the mean, μ

FIGURE S4.3

Normal Distribution Showing the Relationship Between z Values and x Values.

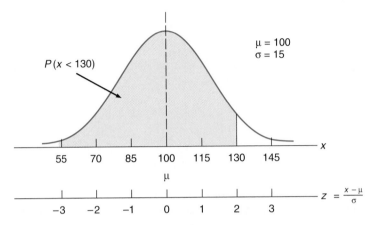

For example, if $\mu = 100$, $\sigma = 15$, and we are interested in finding the probability that the variable x is less than 130, then we want $P(x < 130)$.

$$z = \frac{x - \mu}{\sigma} = \frac{130 - 100}{15} = \frac{30}{15} = 2 \text{ standard deviations}$$

This means that the point x is 2.0 standard deviations to the right of the mean. This is shown in Figure S4.3.

Step 2. Look up the probability from a table of normal curve areas. Appendix A is such a table of areas for the standard normal distribution. It is set up to provide the area under the curve to the left of any specified value of z.

Let us see how Appendix A can be used. The column on the left lists values of z, with the second decimal place of z appearing in the top row. For example, for a value of $z = 2.00$ as just computed, find 2.0 in the left-hand column and .00 in the top row. In the body of the table, we find that the area sought is .97725, or 97.7%. Thus,

$$P(x < 130) = P(z < 2.00) = 97.7\%$$

This suggests that if the mean lifetime of a computer chip is 100 days with a standard deviation of 15 days, the probability that the life of a randomly selected chip is less than 130 is 97.7%. By referring back to Figure S4.2, we see that this probability could also have been derived from the middle graph. (Note that $1.0 - .977 = .023 = 2.3\%$, which is the area in the right-hand tail of the curve.)

Example S4 illustrates the use of the normal distribution further.

Example S4

Holden Construction Co. builds primarily three- and four-unit apartment buildings (called triplexes and quadraplexes) for investors, and it is believed that the total construction time in days follows a normal distribution. The mean time to construct a triplex is 100 days, and the standard deviation is 20 days. If the firm finishes this triplex in 75 days or less, it will be awarded a bonus payment of $5,000. What is the probability Holden will receive the bonus?

FIGURE S4.4

Probability Holden Will Receive the Bonus by Finishing in 75 Days.

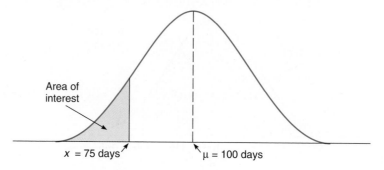

Figure S4.4 illustrates the probability we are looking for in the shaded area. The first step is to compute the z value:

$$z = \frac{x - \mu}{\sigma} = \frac{75 - 100}{20} = \frac{-25}{20} = -1.25$$

This z value indicates that 75 days is -1.25 standard deviations to the left of the mean. But the standard normal table is structured to handle only positive z values. To solve this problem, we observe that the curve is symmetric. The probability Holden will finish in *less than 75 days is equivalent* to the probability it will finish in *more than 125 days.* We first find the probability Holden will finish in less than 125 days. That value was .89435. So the probability it will take more than 125 days is

$$P(x > 125) = 1.0 - P(x < 125) = 1.0 - .89435 = .10565$$

Thus, the probability of completing the triplex in 75 days is .10565, or about 10%.

A second example: What is the probability the triplex will take between 110 and 125 days? We see in Figure S4.5 that

$$P(110 < x < 125) = P(x < 125) - P(x < 110)$$

FIGURE S4.5

Probability of Holden Completion Between 110 and 125 Days.

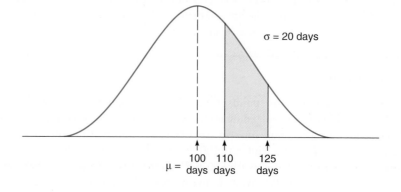

That is, the shaded area in the graph can be computed by finding the probability of completing the building in 125 days or less *minus* the probability of completing it in 110 days or less.

Recall that $P(x < 125 \text{ days})$ is equal to .89435. To find $P(x < 110 \text{ days})$, we follow the two steps developed earlier.

1. $z = \dfrac{x - \mu}{\sigma} = \dfrac{110 - 100}{20} = \dfrac{10}{20} = .50$ standard deviations

2. From Appendix A, we see that the area for $z = .50$ is .69146. So the probability the triplex can be completed in less than 125 days is .69146. Finally,

$$P(110 < x < 125) = .89435 - .69146 = .20289$$

The probability that it will take between 110 and 125 days is about 20%.

SUMMARY

The purpose of this supplement was to assist readers in tackling decision-making issues that involve probabilistic (uncertain) information. A background in statistical tools is quite useful in studying operations management. Two types of probability distributions, discrete and continuous, were examined. Discrete distributions assign a probability to each specific event. Continuous distributions, such as the normal, describe variables that can take on an infinite number of values. The normal, or bell-shaped, distribution is very widely used in business decision analysis and is referred to throughout this book.

KEY TERMS

Discrete probability distribution (p. 172)
Expected value (p. 173)
Variance (p. 174)

Standard deviation (p. 175)
Normal distribution (p. 175)

DISCUSSION QUESTIONS

1. What is the difference between a discrete probability distribution and a continuous probability distribution? Give your own example of each.

2. What is the expected value and what does it measure? How is it computed for a discrete probability distribution?

3. What is the variance and what does it measure? How is it computed for a discrete probability distribution?

4. Name three business processes that can be described by the normal distribution.

PROBLEMS

· **S4.1** Iris Thompson Health Food stocks five loaves of Vita-Bread. The probability distribution for the sales of Vita-Bread is listed in the following table. How many loaves will Iris sell on the average?

NUMBER OF LOAVES SOLD	PROBABILITY
0	.05
1	.15
2	.20
3	.25
4	.20
5	.15

: **S4.2** What is the expected value and variance of the following probability distribution?

VARIABLE, x	PROBABILITY
1	.05
2	.05
3	.10
4	.10
5	.15
6	.15
7	.25
8	.15

· **S4.3** Sales for Hobi-seat, a 17-foot catamaran sailboat, have averaged 250 boats per month over the last five years with a standard deviation of 25 boats. Assuming that the demand is about the same as past years and follows a normal curve, what is the probability sales will be less than 280 boats?

: **S4.4** Refer to Problem S4.3. What is the probability that sales will be over 265 boats during the next month? What is the probability that sales will be under 250 boats next month?

: **S4.5** Precision Parts is a job shop that specializes in producing electric motor shafts. The average shaft size for the E300 electric motor is .55 inches, with a standard deviation of .10 inches. It is normally distributed. What is the probability that a shaft selected at random will be between .55 and .65 inches?

: **S4.6** Refer to Problem S4.5. What is the probability that a shaft size will be greater than .65 inches? What is the probability that a shaft size will be between .53 and .59 inches? What is the probability that a shaft size will be under .45 inches?

: **S4.7** An industrial oven used to cure sand cores for a factory manufacturing engine blocks for small cars is able to maintain fairly constant temperatures. The temperature range of the oven follows a normal distribution with a mean of 450°F and a standard deviation of 25°F. Alan Steinharter, president of the factory, is concerned about the large number of defective cores that have been produced in the last several months. If the oven gets hotter than 475°F, the core is defective. What is the probability that the oven will cause a core to be defective? What is the probability that the temperature of the oven will range from 460 to 470°F?

: **S4.8** Suzan Nassoiy, production foreman for the Virginia Fruit company, estimates that the average sales of oranges is 4,700 and the standard deviation is 500 oranges. Sales follow a normal distribution.

a) What is the probability that sales will be greater than 5,500 oranges?

b) What is the probability that sales will be greater than 4,500 oranges?

c) What is the probability that sales will be less than 4,900 oranges?

d) What is the probability that sales will be less than 4,300 oranges?

: **S4.9** Susan Smith has been the production manager of Medical Suppliers, Inc., for the last seventeen years. Medical Suppliers, Inc., is a producer of bandages and arm slings. During the last five years, the demand for the No-Stick bandage has been fairly constant. On the average, sales have been about 87,000 packages of No-Stick. Susan has reason to believe that the distribution of No-Stick follows a normal curve, with a standard deviation of 4,000 packages. What is the probability sales will be less than 81,000 packages?

BIBLIOGRAPHY

Breiman, L. *Probability.* Reading, MA: Addison-Wesley, 1968.

Campbell, S. *Flaws and Fallacies in Statistical Thinking.* Englewood Cliffs, NJ: Prentice-Hall, 1974.

Feller, W. *An Introduction to Probability Theory and Its Applications.* Vols. 1 and 2. New York: John Wiley & Sons, 1957 and 1968.

Goldberg, S. *Probability—An Introduction.* Englewood Cliffs, NJ: Prentice-Hall, 1960.

Huff, D. *How to Lie with Statistics.* New York: Norton, 1954.

Render, B., and R. M. Stair. *Quantitative Analysis for Management.* 4th ed. Boston: Allyn & Bacon, 1991.

Tsokos, C. *Probability Distributions: An Introduction to Probability Theory with Applications.* North Scituate, MA: Duxbury Press, 1972.

Waiting Line Models

INTRODUCTION

The body of knowledge about waiting lines, often called **queuing theory,** is an important part of P/OM and a valuable tool for the operations manager. **Waiting lines** are a common situation—they may, for example, take the form of cars waiting for repair at an auto service center, printing jobs waiting to be completed at a print shop, or students waiting for a consultation with their professor. Table 5.1 lists just a few P/OM uses of waiting line models.

Just as decision trees (Chapter 3), linear programming (Chapter 3 Supplement), and forecasting (Chapter 4) are models employed in a wide variety of operations decisions throughout this book, waiting line models are useful in both manufacturing and service areas. Analysis of queues in terms of waiting line length, average waiting time, and other factors helps us to understand service systems (such as bank teller stations), maintenance activities (that might repair broken machinery), and shop floor control activities. As a matter of fact, patients waiting in a doctor's office and broken drill presses waiting in a repair facility have a lot in common from a P/OM perspective. Both use human resources and equipment resources to restore valuable production assets (people and machines) to good condition.

Operations managers recognize the trade-off that must take place between the cost of providing good service and the cost of customer or machine waiting time. Managers want queues that are short enough so that customers don't become unhappy and either leave without buying or buy but never return. However, managers are willing to allow some waiting if the waiting is balanced by a significant savings in service costs.

One means of evaluating a service facility is to look at total expected cost, a concept illustrated in Figure 5.1. Total cost is the sum of expected service costs plus expected waiting costs.

Service costs are seen to increase as a firm attempts to raise its level of service. Managers in *some* service centers can vary their capacity by having standby personnel and machines that can be assigned to specific service stations to prevent or shorten excessively long lines. In grocery stores, managers and stock clerks can operate extra checkout counters when needed. In banks and airport check-in points, part-time workers may be called in to help. As service improves (that is, speeds up), however, the cost of time spent waiting in lines decreases. Waiting cost may reflect lost productivity of workers while their tools or machines are awaiting repairs or

TABLE 5.1 Common Queuing Situations.

SITUATION	ARRIVALS IN QUEUE	SERVICE PROCESS
Supermarket	Grocery shoppers	Checkout clerks at cash register
Highway toll booth	Automobiles	Collection of toll at booth
Doctor's office	Patients	Treatment by doctors and nurses
Computer system	Programs to be run	Computer processes jobs
Telephone company	Callers	Switching equipment to forward calls
Bank	Customers	Transactions handled by teller
Machine maintenance	Broken machines	Repairpeople fix machines
Harbor	Ships and barges	Dockworkers load and unload

FIGURE 5.1

The Tradeoff Between Waiting Costs and Service Costs.

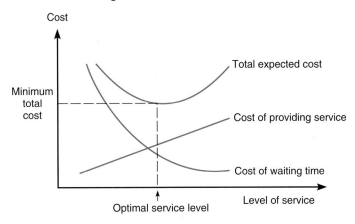

may simply be an estimate of the cost of customers lost because of poor service and long queues. In some service systems (for example, emergency ambulance service), the cost of long waiting lines may be intolerably high.

CHARACTERISTICS OF A WAITING LINE SYSTEM

In this section, we take a look at the three parts of a waiting line, or queuing, system:

1. arrivals or inputs to the system;
2. queue discipline, or the waiting line itself;
3. service facility.

These three components have certain characteristics that must be examined before mathematical queuing models can be developed.

Arrival Characteristics

The input source that generates arrivals or customers for the service system has three major characteristics. These three important characteristics are the size of the *arrival population,* the *pattern* of arrivals at the queuing system, and the *behavior* of the arrivals.

Size of the Source Population. Population sizes are considered to be either unlimited (essentially infinite) or limited (finite). When the number of customers or arrivals on hand at any given moment is just a small portion of potential arrivals, the arrival population is considered **unlimited,** or **infinite.** For practical purposes, examples of unlimited populations include cars arriving at a highway toll booth, shoppers arriving at a supermarket, and students arriving to register for classes at a large university. Most queuing models assume such an infinite arrival population. An example of a **limited,** or **finite,** population is a copying shop with only eight copying machines, which might break down and require service.

Unlimited, or infinite, population

Limited, or finite, population

Pattern of Arrivals at the System. Customers either arrive at a service facility according to some known schedule (for example, one patient every fifteen minutes or one student for advising every half-hour) or else they arrive *randomly*. Arrivals are considered random when they are independent of one another and their occurrence cannot be predicted exactly. Frequently in queuing problems, the number of arrivals per unit of time can be estimated by a probability distribution known as the **Poisson distribution**. For any given arrival rate (such as two customers per hour, or four trucks per minute), a discrete Poisson distribution can be established by using the formula:

Poisson distribution

$$P(x) = \frac{e^{-\lambda}\lambda^x}{x!} \text{ for } x = 0, 1, 2, 3, 4, \ldots \tag{5.1}$$

where

$P(x)$ = probability of x arrivals

x = number of arrivals per unit of time

λ = average arrival rate

e = 2.7183 (which is the base of the natural logarithms)

With the help of the table in Appendix D, these values are easy to compute. Figure 5.2 illustrates the Poisson distribution for $\lambda = 2$ and $\lambda = 4$. This means that if the average arrival rate is $\lambda = 2$ customers per hour, the probability of 0 customers arriving in any random hour is about 13%, probability of 1 customer is about 27%, 2 customers about 27%, 3 customers about 18%, 4 customers about 9%, and so on. The chances that 9 or more will arrive are virtually nil. Arrivals, of course, are not always Poisson (they may follow some other distribution) and should be examined to make certain that they are well approximated by Poisson before that distribution is applied.

A P_3 of .0625 means the chance of having more than three customers in an airport check-in line at a certain time of day is one chance in sixteen. If American Airlines can live with four or more passengers in line about 6% of the time, one service agent will suffice. If not, more check-in positions and staff will have to be added.

FIGURE 5.2

Two Examples of the Poisson Distribution for Arrival Times.

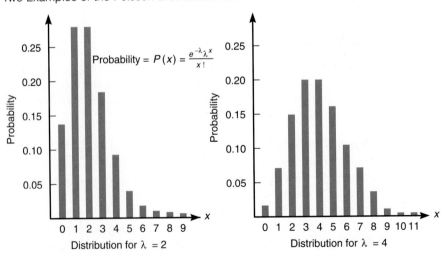

Behavior of the Arrivals. Most queuing models assume that an arriving customer is a patient customer. Patient customers are people or machines that wait in the queue until they are served and do not switch between lines. Unfortunately, life is complicated by the fact that people have been known to balk or to renege. Customers who *balk* refuse to join the waiting line because it is too long to suit their needs or interests. *Reneging* customers are those who enter the queue but then become impatient and leave without completing their transaction. Actually, both of these situations just serve to accentuate the need for queuing theory and waiting line analysis.

Waiting Line Characteristics

The waiting line itself is the second component of a queuing system. The length of a line can be either limited or unlimited. A queue is *limited* when it cannot, by law or physical restrictions, increase to an infinite length. This may be the case in a small barbershop that has only a limited number of waiting chairs. Analytic queuing models are treated in this chapter under an assumption of *unlimited* queue length. A queue is *unlimited* when its size is unrestricted, as in the case of the toll booth serving arriving automobiles.

A second waiting line characteristic deals with *queue discipline*. This refers to the rule by which customers in the line are to receive service. Most systems use a queue discipline known as the **first-in, first-out rule (FIFO).** In a hospital emergency room or an express checkout line at a supermarket, however, various assigned priorities may preempt FIFO. Patients who are critically injured will move ahead in treatment priority over patients with broken fingers or noses. Shoppers with fewer than ten items may be allowed to enter the express checkout queue (but are *then* treated as first-come, first-served). Computer programming runs are another example of queuing systems that operate under priority scheduling. In most large companies, when computer-produced paychecks are due out on a specific date, the payroll program has highest priority over other runs.[1]

First-in, first-out rule (FIFO)

Service Facility Characteristics

The third part of any queuing system is the service facility. Two basic properties are important: (1) the configuration of the service system and (2) the pattern of service times.

Basic Queuing System Configurations. Service systems are usually classified in terms of their number of channels (for example, number of servers) and number of phases (for example, number of service stops that must be made). A **single-channel queuing system,** with one server, is typified by the drive-in bank that has only one open teller, or by a drive-through fast-food restaurant. If, on the other hand, the bank had several tellers on duty, and each customer waited in one common line for the first available teller, then we would have a **multiple-channel queuing system** at work. Most banks today are multichannel service systems, as are

Single-channel queuing system

Multiple-channel queuing system

---

[1] The term *FIFS* (first in, first served) is often used in place of FIFO. Another discipline, LIFS (last in, first served), is common when material is stacked or piled and the items on top are used first.

Single-phase system

most large barber shops, airline ticket counters, and post offices.

A **single-phase system** is one in which the customer receives service from only one station and then exits the system. A fast-food restaurant in which the person who takes your order also brings you the food and takes your money is a single-phase system. So is a driver's license agency in which the person taking your application also grades your test and collects the license fee. But if the restaurant requires you

FIGURE 5.3

Basic Queuing System Configurations.

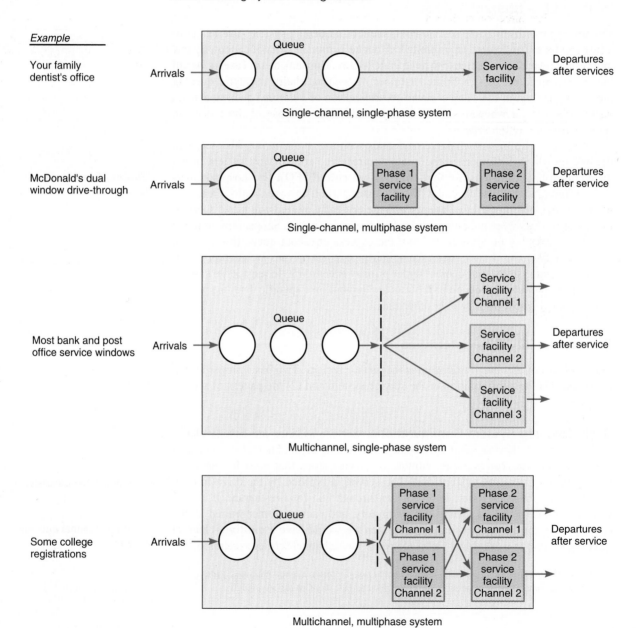

to place your order at one station, pay at a second, and pick up the food at a third service stop, it becomes a **multiphase system.** Likewise, if the driver's license agency is large or busy, you will probably have to wait in a line to complete the application (the first service stop), then queue again to have the test graded (the second service stop), and finally go to a third service counter to pay the fee. To help you relate the concepts of channels and phases, Figure 5.3 presents four possible configurations.

Multiphase system

Service Time Distribution. Service patterns are like arrival patterns in that they may be either constant or random. If service time is constant, it takes the same amount of time to take care of each customer. This is the case in a machine-performed service operation such as an automatic car-wash. More often, service times are randomly distributed. In many cases, we can assume that random service times are described by the **negative exponential probability distribution.** This is a mathematically convenient assumption if *arrival rates* are Poisson distributed.

Negative exponential probability distribution

Figure 5.4 illustrates that if *service times* follow an exponential distribution, the probability of any very long service time is low. For example, when an average service time is 20 minutes, seldom if ever will a customer require more than 90 minutes in the service facility. If the mean service time is one hour, the probability of spending more than 180 minutes in service is virtually zero.

Measuring the Queue's Performance

Queuing models help managers make decisions that balance desirable service costs with waiting line costs. Some of the many measures of a waiting line system's

FIGURE 5.4

Two Examples of the Negative Exponential Distribution for Service Times.

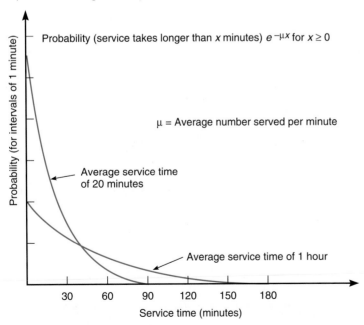

Probability (service takes longer than x minutes) $e^{-\mu x}$ for $x \geq 0$

μ = Average number served per minute

Average service time of 20 minutes

Average service time of 1 hour

Probability (for intervals of 1 minute)

Service time (minutes)

performance that are commonly obtained in a queuing analysis are as follows:

1. the average time each customer or object spends in the queue;
2. the average queue length;
3. the average time each customer spends in the system (waiting time plus service time);
4. the average number of customers in the system;
5. the probability that the service facility will be idle;
6. the utilization factor for the system;
7. the probability of a specific number of customers in the system.

THE VARIETY OF QUEUING MODELS

A wide variety of queuing models may be applied in operations management. However, rather than go into detail about all of them, we will introduce you to four of the most widely used models. These four are outlined in Table 5.2, and examples of each follow in the next few sections. More complex models are described in queuing theory textbooks[2] or can be developed through the use of simulation, which is noted in the supplement to this chapter. Note that all four queuing models listed in Table 5.2—the simple system, the multichannel, the constant service, and the

TABLE 5.2 Queuing Models Described in This Chapter.

MODEL	NAME (WITH TECHNICAL NAME IN PARENTHESES)	EXAMPLE	NUMBER OF CHANNELS	NUMBER OF PHASES	ARRIVAL RATE PATTERN	SERVICE TIME PATTERN	POPULATION SIZE	QUEUE DISCIPLINE
A	Simple system (M/M/1)	Information counter at department store	Single	Single	Poisson	Exponential	Unlimited	FIFO
B	Multichannel (M/M/S)	Airline ticket counter	Multi-channel	Single	Poisson	Exponential	Unlimited	FIFO
C	Constant service (M/D/1)	Automated car wash	Single	Single	Poisson	Constant	Unlimited	FIFO
D	Limited population (finite population)	Shop with only a dozen machines that might break	Single	Single	Poisson	Exponential	Limited	FIFO

[2] See, for example, W. Griffin, *Queuing: Basic Theory and Applications* (Columbus: Grid Publishing, 1978); or R. B. Cooper, *Introduction to Queuing Theory,* 2nd ed. (New York: Elsevier-North Holland, 1980).

POM _in action_

Conquering Those Killer Queues

Queues and ideas on how to shorten them are important to store managers who want to be faster than their competitors in taking their customers' money. One major discount chain had, for years, set a policy that another checkout register should open if there were more than three people in any line.

The airlines have also learned a few things about queues after listening to their customers howl when their baggage took forever to retrieve. Los Angeles International Airport (LAX), for example, is built so that passengers have a long distance to walk to the claim area. But by the time they arrive, their bags are usually waiting. Even though LAX passengers spend more total time retrieving bags than do travelers at other major airports, airlines have found that they don't complain as much.

One way banks find to ease the pain of queues is to entertain customers. For the past 30 years, Manhattan Savings Bank has provided live entertainment during the busy lunch hours. Pianists perform, organ players play, new boats shine in boat shows, cats meow in cat shows, and purebred dogs preen. In office buildings and hotels, mirrors next to elevators seem to make people happier to wait. People comb their hair; they check their clothes. One study showed that guests in hotels with mirrors thought elevators were faster in arriving than customers in hotels where there were no mirrors near the elevators. The _reality_ was that elevator delays were exactly the same—the only difference was _perception_.

If there is any organization that is sensitive to waiting, it's Disney World, where a line for a hot ride like Space Mountain can run to almost 2,000 people. Telling people how long they have to wait is important feedback. And like the Manhattan Bank, Disney provides entertainment for people who are waiting. It also posts signs giving the estimated time from that point to the ride or exhibit. That way parents can decide which ride is more important. Queuing experts say there is nothing worse than blind waiting.

Sources: New York Times, September 25, 1988, pp. 1,11; _Journal of the Operational Research Society,_ **40,** 8 (August 1989): 741–750; and _Operations Research,_ **35,** 6 (November–December 1987): 895–905.

limited population—have three characteristics in common. They all assume:

1. Poisson distribution arrivals;
2. FIFO discipline;
3. a single service phase.

In addition, they describe service systems that operate under steady, ongoing conditions. This means that arrival and service rates remain stable during the analysis.

Model A: Single-Channel Queuing Model with Poisson Arrivals and Exponential Service Times

The most common case of queuing problems involves the _single-channel,_ or single-server, waiting line. In this situation, arrivals form a single line to be serviced by a single station (Figure 5.3). We assume that the following conditions exist in this type of system:

1. Arrivals are served on a first-come, first-served (FIFO) basis, and every arrival waits to be served, regardless of the length of the line or queue.

TABLE 5.3 Queuing Formulas for Model A—Simple System, also called M/M/1

λ = Mean number of arrivals per time period

μ = Mean number of people or items served per time period

L_s = Average number of units (customers) in the system

$$= \frac{\lambda}{\mu - \lambda}$$

W_s = Average time a unit spends in the system (waiting time plus service time)

$$= \frac{1}{\mu - \lambda}$$

L_q = Average number of units in the queue   *EXPECTED VALUE*

$$= \frac{\lambda^2}{\mu(\mu - \lambda)}$$

W_q = Average time a unit spends waiting in the queue

$$= \frac{\lambda}{\mu(\mu - \lambda)}$$

ρ = Utilization factor for the system · *(the service part of the system)*

$$= \frac{\lambda}{\mu}$$

P_0 = Probability of 0 units in the system (that is, the service unit is idle)

$$= 1 - \frac{\lambda}{\mu} \; \simeq \; 1 - utilization$$

$P_{n > k}$ = Probability of more than k units in the system, where n is the number of units in the system

$$= \left(\frac{\lambda}{\mu}\right)^{k+1}$$

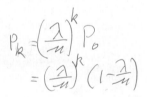

$$P_k = \left(\frac{\lambda}{\mu}\right)^k P_0$$

$$= \left(\frac{\lambda}{\mu}\right)^k \left(1 - \frac{\lambda}{\mu}\right)$$

2. Arrivals are independent of preceding arrivals, but the average number of arrivals (arrival rate) does not change over time.

3. Arrivals are described by a Poisson probability distribution and come from an infinite (or very, very large) population.

4. Service times vary from one customer to the next and are independent of one another, but their average rate is known.

5. Service times occur according to the negative exponential probability distribution.

6. The service rate is faster than the arrival rate.

When these conditions are met, the series of equations shown in Table 5.3 can be developed. Examples 1 and 2 illustrate how Model A (which in technical journals is known as the M/M/1 model) may be used.

Example 1

Jones, the mechanic at Golden Muffler Shop, is able to install new mufflers at an average rate of three per hour (or about one every 20 minutes), according to a negative exponential distribution. Customers seeking this service arrive at the shop on the average of two per hour, following a Poisson distribution. The customers are served on a first-in, first-out basis and come from a very large (almost infinite) population of possible buyers.

From this description, we are able to obtain the operating characteristics of Golden Muffler's queuing system:

$$\lambda = 2 \text{ cars arriving per hour}$$

$$\mu = 3 \text{ cars serviced per hour}$$

$$L_s = \frac{\lambda}{\mu - \lambda} = \frac{2}{3-2} = \frac{2}{1}$$
$$= 2 \text{ cars in the system, on average}$$

$$W_s = \frac{1}{\mu - \lambda} = \frac{1}{3-2} = 1$$
$$= 1 \text{ hour average waiting time in the system}$$

$$L_q = \frac{\lambda^2}{\mu(\mu - \lambda)} = \frac{2^2}{3(3-2)} = \frac{4}{3(1)} = \frac{4}{3}$$
$$= 1.33 \text{ cars waiting in line, on average}$$

$$W_q = \frac{\lambda}{\mu(\mu - \lambda)} = \frac{2}{3(3-2)} = \frac{2}{3} \text{ hr.}$$
$$= 40 \text{ min. average waiting time per car}$$

$$\rho = \frac{\lambda}{\mu} = \frac{2}{3}$$
$$= 66.6\% \text{ of time mechanic is busy}$$

$$P_0 = 1 - \frac{\lambda}{\mu} = 1 - \frac{2}{3}$$
$$= 0.33 \text{ probability there are 0 cars in the system}$$

Probability of More than k Cars in the System.

k	$P_{n > k} = (2/3)^{k + 1}$
0	.667 ← Note that this is equal to $1 - P_0 = 1 - .33 = .667$.
1	.444
2	.296
3	.198 ← Implies that there is a 19.8% chance that more than three cars are in the system.
4	.132
5	.088
6	.058
7	.039

Once we have computed the operating characteristics of a queuing system, it is often important to do an economic analysis of their impact. The waiting line model described above is valuable in predicting potential waiting times, queue lengths, idle times, and so on, but it does not identify optimal decisions or consider cost factors. As stated earlier, the solution to a queuing problem may require management to make a trade-off between the increased cost of providing better service and the decreased waiting costs derived from providing that service. Let us consider the costs involved in Example 1.

The Epcot Center and Disney World in Orlando, Disneyland in California, EuroDisney near Paris, and Disney Japan near Tokyo all have one feature in common—long lines and seemingly endless waits. But Disney is one of the world's leading companies in the scientific analysis of queuing theory. It analyzes queuing behaviors and can predict which rides will draw what length crowds. To keep visitors happy, Disney does three things: (1) it makes lines appear to be constantly moving forward; (2) it entertains people while they wait; and (3) it posts signs telling visitors how many minutes in line they are away from each ride. That way parents can decide whether a 20-minute wait for Small World is worth more than a 30-minute wait for Mr. Frog's Wild Ride.

Example 2

The owner of the Golden Muffler Shop estimates that the cost of customer waiting time, in terms of customer dissatisfaction and lost goodwill, is $10 per hour of time spent *waiting* in the line. Since the average car has a 2/3-hour wait (W_q) and there are approximately sixteen cars serviced per day (two per hour times eight working hours per day), the total number of hours that customers spend waiting for mufflers to be installed each day is

$$\frac{2}{3}(16) = \frac{32}{3} = 10\frac{2}{3} \text{ hr.}$$

Hence, in this case,

$$\text{Customer waiting-time cost} = \$10\left(10\frac{2}{3}\right) = \$107 \text{ per day}$$

The only other major cost that Golden's owner can identify in the queuing situation is the salary of Jones, the mechanic, who earns $7 per hour, or $56 per day. Thus

$$\text{Total expected costs} = \$107 + \$56$$
$$= \$163 \text{ per day}$$

This approach will be useful in Solved Problem 5.2.

TABLE 5.4 Queuing Formulas for Model B—Multichannel System, also Called M/M/S.

M = The number of channels open
λ = Average arrival rate
μ = Average service rate at each channel

The probability that there are zero people or units in the system is

$$P_0 = \frac{1}{\left[\displaystyle\sum_{n=0}^{M-1} \frac{1}{n!}\left(\frac{\lambda}{\mu}\right)^n\right] + \frac{1}{M!}\left(\frac{\lambda}{\mu}\right)^M \frac{M\mu}{M\mu - \lambda}} \quad \text{for } M\mu > \lambda$$

The average number of people or units in the system is

$$L_s = \frac{\lambda\mu(\lambda/\mu)^M}{(M-1)!(M\mu - \lambda)^2}\, P_0 + \frac{\lambda}{\mu}$$

The average time a unit spends in the waiting line or being serviced (namely, in the system) is

$$W_s = \frac{\mu(\lambda/\mu)^M}{(M-1)!(M\mu - \lambda)^2}\, P_0 + \frac{1}{\mu} = \frac{L_s}{\lambda}$$

The average number of people or units in line waiting for service is

$$L_q = L_s - \frac{\lambda}{\mu}$$

The average time a person or unit spends in the queue waiting for service is

$$W_q = W_s - \frac{1}{\mu} = \frac{L_q}{\lambda}$$

Model B: Multiple-Channel Queuing Model

The next logical step is to look at a multiple-channel queuing system, in which two or more servers or channels are available to handle arriving customers. Let us still assume that customers awaiting service form one single line and then proceed to the first available server. An example of such a multichannel, single-phase waiting line is found in many banks today. A common line is formed, and the customer at the head of the line proceeds to the first free teller. (Refer back to Figure 5.3 for a typical multichannel configuration.)

The multiple-channel system presented here again assumes that arrivals follow a Poisson probability distribution and that service times are exponentially distributed. Service is first-come, first-served, and all servers are assumed to perform at the same rate. Other assumptions listed earlier for the single-channel model apply as well.

The queuing equations for Model B (which also has the technical name of M/M/S) are shown in Table 5.4 on page 194. These equations are obviously more complex than the ones used in the single-channel model; yet they are used in exactly the same fashion and provide the same type of information as the simpler model. The AB:POM microcomputer software described later in this chapter proves very useful in solving multiple-channel, as well as other, queuing problems.

Example 3

The Golden Muffler Shop has decided to open a second garage bay and to hire a second mechanic to handle muffler installations. Customers, who arrive at the rate of about $\lambda = 2$ per hour, will wait in a single line until one of the two mechanics is free. Each mechanic installs mufflers at the rate of about $\mu = 3$ per hour.

To find out how this system compares to the old single-channel waiting line system, we will compute several operating characteristics for the $M = 2$ channel system and compare the results with those found in Example 1.

$$P_0 = \frac{1}{\left[\sum_{n=0}^{1} \frac{1}{n!}\left(\frac{2}{3}\right)^n\right] + \frac{1}{2!}\left(\frac{2}{3}\right)^2 \frac{2(3)}{2(3)-2}}$$

$$= \frac{1}{1 + \frac{2}{3} + \frac{1}{2}\left(\frac{4}{9}\right)\left(\frac{6}{6-2}\right)} = \frac{1}{1 + \frac{2}{3} + \frac{1}{3}} = \frac{1}{2}$$

$= .5$ probability of zero cars in the system.

Then,

$$L_s = \frac{(2)(3)(2/3)^2}{1![2(3)-2]^2}\left(\frac{1}{2}\right) + \frac{2}{3} = \frac{8/3}{16}\left(\frac{1}{2}\right) + \frac{2}{3} = \frac{3}{4}$$

$= .75$ average number of cars in the system

$$W_s = \frac{L_s}{\lambda} = \frac{3/4}{2} = \frac{3}{8} \text{ hr.}$$

$= 22.5$ min. average time a car spends in the system

$$L_q = L_s - \frac{\lambda}{\mu} = \frac{3}{4} - \frac{2}{3} = \frac{1}{12}$$

= .083 average number of cars in the queue

$$W_q = \frac{L_q}{\lambda} = \frac{.083}{2} = .0415 \text{ hr.}$$

= 2.5 min. average time a car spends in the queue

We can summarize these characteristics and compare them to those of the single-channel model as follows:

	SINGLE CHANNEL	TWO CHANNELS
P_0	.33	.5
L_s	2 cars	.75 car
W_s	60 min.	22.5 min.
L_q	1.33 cars	.083 car
W_q	40 min.	2.5 min.

The increased service has a dramatic effect on almost all characteristics. In particular, time spent waiting in line drops from 40 minutes to only 2.5 minutes.

Model C: Constant Service Time Model

Some service systems have constant service times instead of exponentially distributed times. When customers or equipment are processed according to a fixed cycle, as in the case of an automatic car wash or an amusement park ride, constant service times are appropriate. Because constant rates are certain, the values for L_q, W_q, L_s, and W_s are always less than they would be in Model A, which has variable service rates. As a matter of fact, both the average queue length and the average waiting time in the queue are halved with Model C. Constant service model formulas are given in Table 5.5. Model C also has the technical name of M/D/1 in the literature of queuing theory.

TABLE 5.5 Queuing Formulas for Model C—Constant Service, also Called the M/D/1 Model.

Average length of queue: $L_q = \dfrac{\lambda^2}{2\mu(\mu - \lambda)}$

Average waiting time in queue: $W_q = \dfrac{\lambda}{2\mu(\mu - \lambda)}$

Average number of customers in system: $L_s = L_q + \dfrac{\lambda}{\mu}$

Average waiting time in system: $W_s = W_q + \dfrac{1}{\mu}$

Example 4

Garcia-Golding Recycling, Inc., collects and compacts aluminum cans and glass bottles in New York City. Their truck drivers, who arrive to unload these materials for recycling, currently wait an average of 15 minutes before emptying their loads. The cost of the driver and truck time while in queue is valued at $60 per hour. A new automated compactor can be purchased that will process truck-loads at a constant rate of 12 trucks per hour (that is, 5 minutes per truck). Trucks arrive according to a Poisson distribution at an average rate of 8 per hour. If the new compactor is put in use, its cost will be amortized at a rate of $3 per truck unloaded. The firm hires a summer college intern, who conducts the following analysis to evaluate the costs vs. benefits of the purchase:

Current waiting cost/trip = (1/4 hr. waiting now) ($60/hr. cost) = $15/trip

New system: $\lambda = 8$ trucks/hr. arriving $\mu = 12$ trucks/hr. served

Average waiting time in queue = $W_q = \dfrac{\lambda}{2\mu(\mu - \lambda)} = \dfrac{8}{2(12)(12 - 8)} = \dfrac{1}{12}$ hr.

Waiting cost/trip with new compactor = (1/12 hr. wait) ($60/hr. cost) = $ 5/trip

Savings with new equipment = $15(current system) – $5(new system) = $10/trip

Cost of new equipment amortized   = $ 3/trip

Net savings $ 7/trip

Model D: Limited Population Model

When there is a limited population of potential customers for a service facility, we need to consider a different queuing model. This model would be used, for example, if you were considering equipment repairs in a factory that has five machines, if you were in charge of maintenance for a fleet of 10 commuter airplanes, or if you ran a hospital ward that has 20 beds. The limited population model permits any number of repair people (servers) to be considered.

The reason this model differs from the three earlier queuing models is that there is now a *dependent* relationship between the length of the queue and the arrival rate. To illustrate the extreme situation, if your factory had five machines and all were broken and awaiting repair, the arrival rate would drop to zero. In general, as the waiting line becomes longer in the limited population model, the arrival rate of customers or machines drops lower.

Table 5.6 on page 198 displays the queuing formulas for the limited population model. Note that they employ a different notation than seen in Models A, B, and C. To simplify what can become very time-consuming calculations, finite queuing tables have been developed that determine D and F. D represents the probability a machine needing repair will have to wait in line. F is a waiting time efficiency factor. D and F are needed to compute most of the other finite model formulas.

TABLE 5.6 Queuing Formulas and Notation for Model D—Limited Population.

FORMULAS

Service factor	$X = \dfrac{T}{T + U}$
Average number waiting	$L = N(1 - F)$
Average waiting time	$W = \dfrac{L(T + U)}{N - L} = \dfrac{T(1 - F)}{XF}$
Average number running	$J = NF(1 - X)$
Average number being serviced	$H = FNX$
Number of population	$N = J + L + H$

NOTATION

D = Probability that a unit will have to wait in queue

F = Efficiency factor

H = Average number of units being served

J = Average number of units not in queue or in service bay

L = Average number of units waiting for service

M = Number of service channels

N = Number of potential customers

T = Average service time

U = Average time between unit service requirements

W = Average time a unit waits in line

X = Service factor

Source: L. G. Peck and R. N. Hazelwood, *Finite Queuing Tables,* New York: John Wiley & Sons, 1958.

A small part of the published finite queuing tables is illustrated in this section. Table 5.7 provides for a population of $N = 5$.[3]

To use Table 5.7, we follow four steps:

1. Compute X (the service factor, where $X = T/(T + U)$.
2. Find the value of X in the table, then find the line for M (where M is the number of service channels).
3. Note the corresponding values for D and F.
4. Compute $L, W, J, H,$ or whichever are needed to measure the service system's performance.

---

[3] Limited, or finite, queuing tables are available to handle arrival populations of up to 250. Although there is no definite number that we can use to divide limited from unlimited populations, the general rule of thumb is this: if the number in the queue is a significant proportion of the arrival population, use a limited population queuing model. For a complete set of N values, see *Finite Queuing Tables,* by Peck and Hazelwood (John Wiley & Sons, 1958).

TABLE 5.7 Finite Queuing Tables for a Population of $n = 5$.

X	M	D	F	X	M	D	F	X	M	D	F	X	M	D	F	X	M	D	F
				.100	1	.386	.950	.200	2	.194	.976	.330	4	.012	.999	.520	2	.779	.728
				.105	2	.059	.997		1	.689	.801		3	.112	.986		1	.988	.384
.012	1	.048	.999		1	.404	.945	.210	3	.032	.998		2	.442	.904	.540	4	.085	.989
.019	1	.076	.998	.110	2	.065	.996		2	.211	.973		1	.902	.583		3	.392	.917
.025	1	.100	.997		1	.421	.939		1	.713	.783	.340	4	.013	.999		2	.806	.708
.030	1	.120	.996	.115	2	.071	.995	.220	3	.036	.997		3	.121	.985		1	.991	.370
.034	1	.135	.995		1	.439	.933		2	.229	.969		2	.462	.896	.560	4	.098	.986
.036	1	.143	.994	.120	2	.076	.995		1	.735	.765		1	.911	.569		3	.426	.906
.040	1	.159	.993		1	.456	.927	.230	3	.041	.997	.360	4	.017	.998		2	.831	.689
.042	1	.167	.992	.125	2	.082	.994		2	.247	.965		3	.141	.981		1	.993	.357
.044	1	.175	.991		1	.473	.920		1	.756	.747		2	.501	.880	.580	4	.113	.984
.046	1	.183	.990	.130	2	.089	.993	.240	3	.046	.996		1	.927	.542		3	.461	.895
.050	1	.198	.989		1	.489	.914		2	.265	.960	.380	4	.021	.998		2	.854	.670
.052	1	.206	.988	.135	2	.095	.993		1	.775	.730		3	.163	.976		1	.994	.345
.054	1	.214	.987		1	.505	.907	.250	3	.052	.995		2	.540	.863	.600	4	.130	.981
.056	2	.018	.999	.140	2	.102	.992		2	.284	.955		1	.941	.516		3	.497	.883
	1	.222	.985		1	.521	.900		1	.794	.712	.400	4	.026	.997		2	.875	.652
.058	2	.019	.999	.145	3	.011	.999	.260	3	.058	.994		3	.186	.972		1	.996	.333
	1	.229	.984		2	.109	.991		2	.303	.950		2	.579	.845	.650	4	.179	.972
.060	2	.020	.999		1	.537	.892		1	.811	.695		1	.952	.493		3	.588	.850
	1	.237	.983	.150	3	.012	.999	.270	3	.064	.994	.420	4	.031	.997		2	.918	.608
.062	2	.022	.999		2	.115	.990		2	.323	.944		3	.211	.966		1	.998	.308
	1	.245	.982		1	.553	.885		1	.827	.677		2	.616	.826	.700	4	.240	.960
.064	2	.023	.999	.155	3	.013	.999	.280	3	.071	.993		1	.961	.471		3	.678	.815
	1	.253	.981		2	.123	.989		2	.342	.938	.440	4	.037	.996		2	.950	.568
.066	2	.024	.999		1	.568	.877		1	.842	.661		3	.238	.960		1	.999	.286
	1	.260	.979	.160	3	.015	.999	.290	4	.007	.999		2	.652	.807	.750	4	.316	.944
.068	2	.026	.999		2	.130	.988		3	.079	.992		1	.969	.451		3	.763	.777
	1	.268	.978		1	.582	.869		2	.362	.932	.460	4	.045	.995		2	.972	.532
.070	2	.027	.999	.165	3	.016	.999		1	.856	.644		3	.266	.953	.800	4	.410	.924
	1	.275	.977		2	.137	.987	.300	4	.008	.999		2	.686	.787		3	.841	.739
.075	2	.031	.999		1	.597	.861		3	.086	.990		1	.975	.432		2	.987	.500
	1	.294	.973	.170	3	.017	.999		2	.382	.926	.480	4	.053	.994	.850	4	.522	.900
.080	2	.035	.998		2	.145	.985		1	.869	.628		3	.296	.945		3	.907	.702
	1	.313	.969		1	.611	.853	.310	4	.009	.999		2	.719	.767		2	.995	.470
.085	2	.040	.998	.180	3	.021	.999		3	.094	.989		1	.980	.415	.900	4	.656	.871
	1	.332	.965		2	.161	.983		2	.402	.919	.500	4	.063	.992		3	.957	.666
.090	2	.044	.998		1	.638	.836		1	.881	.613		3	.327	.936		2	.998	.444
	1	.350	.960	.190	3	.024	.998	.320	4	.010	.999		2	.750	.748	.950	4	.815	.838
.095	2	.049	.997		2	.170	.980		3	.103	.988		1	.985	.399		3	.989	.631
	1	.368	.955		1	.665	.819		2	.422	.912	.520	4	.073	.991				
.100	2	.054	.997	.200	3	.028	.998		1	.892	.597		3	.359	.927				

Source: From L. G. Peck and R. N. Hazelwood, *Finite Queuing Tables,* New York: John Wiley & Sons, 1958, p. 4 © 1985, John Wiley & Sons, Inc.

Example 5

Past records indicate that each of the five laser computer printers at the U.S. Department of Energy, in Washington, D.C., needs repair after about 20 hours of use. Breakdowns have been determined to be Poisson distributed. The one technician on duty can service a printer in an average of two hours, following an exponential distribution. Printer downtime costs $120 per hour. Technicians are paid $25 per hour. Should the DOE hire a second technician?

Assuming the second technician can repair a printer in an average of two hours, we can use Table 5.7 (since there are $n = 5$ machines in this limited population) to compare the costs of one vs. two technicians.

1. First, we note that $T = 2$ hours and $U = 20$ hours.
2. Then, $X = \dfrac{T}{T+U} = \dfrac{2}{2+20} = \dfrac{2}{22} = .091$ (close to .090).
3. For $M = 1$ server, $D = .350$ and $F = .960$.
4. For $M = 2$ servers, $D = .044$ and $F = .998$.
5. The average number of printers *working* is $J = NF(1 - X)$.
   For $M = 1$, this is $J = (5)(.960)(1 - .091) = 4.36$.
   For $M = 2$, it is $J = (5)(.998)(1 - .091) = 4.54$.
6. The cost analysis follows:

NUMBER OF TECHNICIANS	AVERAGE NUMBER PRINTERS DOWN ($N - J$)	AVERAGE COST/HR. FOR DOWNTIME ($N - J$)($120/HR.)	COST/HR. FOR TECHNICIANS (AT $25/HR.)	TOTAL COST/HR.
1	.64	$76.80	$25.00	$101.80
2	.46	$55.20	$50.00	$105.20

This analysis suggests that having only one technician on duty will save a few dollars per hour ($105.20 − 101.80 = $3.40).

MORE COMPLEX QUEUING MODELS AND THE USE OF SIMULATION

Many practical waiting line problems that occur in production and operations service systems have characteristics like the four mathematical models described above. Often, however, *variations* of this specific case are present in an analysis. Service times in an automobile repair shop, for example, tend to follow the normal probability distribution instead of the exponential. A college registration system in which seniors have first choice of courses and hours over all other students is an example of a first-come, first-served model with a preemptive priority queue discipline. A physical examination for military recruits is an example of a multiphase system, one that differs from the single-phase models discussed in this chapter. A recruit first lines up to have blood drawn at one station, then waits to take an eye exam at the next station, talks to a psychiatrist at the third, and is examined by a doctor for medical problems at the fourth. At each phase, the recruit must enter another queue and wait his or her turn.

Models to handle these cases have been developed by operations researchers. The computations for the resulting mathematical formulations are somewhat more complex than the ones covered in this chapter, though.[4] And many real-world

[4] Often the *qualitative* results of queuing models are as useful as the quantitative results. Results show that it is inherently more efficient to pool resources, use central dispatching, and provide single multiple-server systems rather than multiple single-server systems.

queuing applications are too complex to be modeled analytically at all. Such problems are said to be mathematically intractable. When this happens, analysts usually turn to *computer simulation,* the topic of the supplement to this chapter.

SUMMARY

Queues are an important part of the world of operations management. In this chapter we described several common queuing systems and presented mathematical models for analyzing them.

The models illustrated were Model A, the basic single-channel, single-phase system with Poisson arrivals and exponential service times; Model B, the multi-channel equivalent of Model A; Model C, a constant service rate model; and Model D, a limited population system. All four of these allowed for Poisson arrivals, first-in, first-out service, and a single-service phase. Typical operating characteristics examined included average time spent waiting in queue and in the system, average number of customers in the queue and system, idle time, and utilization rate.

We emphasized that a variety of queuing models exist for which all of the assumptions of the traditional models need not be met. In these cases, we use more complex mathematical models or turn to a technique called Monte Carlo simulation. The application of simulation to problems of queuing systems and inventory control follows in the supplement.

KEY TERMS

Queuing theory (p. 184)
Waiting line (p. 184)
Unlimited, or infinite, population (p. 185)
Limited, or finite, population (p. 185)
Poisson distribution (p. 186)
First-in, first-out rule (FIFO) (p. 187)

Single-channel queuing system (p. 187)
Multiple-channel queuing system (p. 187)
Single-phase system (p. 188)
Multiphase system (p. 189)
Negative exponential probability distribution (p. 189)

USING AB:POM

SOLVING EXAMPLE 3 WITH AB:POM'S QUEUING MODULE

As in this chapter, there are four AB:POM queuing models from which to select, each with or without cost analysis (see Program 5.1):

1. Simple system with Poisson arrivals, exponential service times, 1 server (also called M/M/1);
2. Multi-channel system with Poisson arrivals, exponential service times, more than one server (also called M/M/S);
3. Constant service time model with Poisson arrivals, constant service time, 1 server (also called M/D/1);
4. Finite (limited) population model.

These four programs can compute waiting costs charged against either the time a customer spends in the system or the time spent waiting in the queue.

Program 5.1

AB:POM's Queuing Options

———— Waiting Line Models ————————— Data Screen ————

```
——————————————————————— Model ———————————
              Single Channel
              Multiple Channel
              Constant Service Time
              Limited Population


   Select menu option by highlighted letter or point
 with arrow keys and then press RETURN key
```

Data entry is quite simple after the model has been selected. All that's required is the arrival rate (λ), the service rate (μ), the number of servers, and, in the case of the finite population model only, the population size.

Program 5.2

AB:POM's Queuing Program Using Example 3's Data With Optional Conversion of Times into Minutes and Optimal Probability Output

———————————— Waiting Line Models ————————— Solution ————

Multiple Channel

———————— GOLDEN MUFFLER SHOP, EXAMPLE 3 ————————

arrival rate (lambda)	2.00	Average server utilization	.3333333
service rate (mu)	3.00	Average number in the queue (Lq)	0.083333
number of servers	2	Average number in the system (Ls)	0.7500
		Average time in the queue (Wq)	0.041667
		Answer * 60	2.50
		Average time in the system (Ws)	0.3750
		Answer * 60	22.50

```
F1 = Multiply wait and sys times by 60 F2 = Display Probabilities  F9 = Print  Esc
Press <Esc> key to continue or highlighted key or function key for options
```

```
                          GOLDEN MUFFLER SHOP, EXAMPLE 3
                          Number in    Probability   Cumulative   Decum
                          system, k    P (n=k)       P (n<k)      P (n>k)
arrival rate (lambda)   2.00      0       .5000       0.5000      0.5000
                                  1       .3333       0.8333      0.1667
service rate (mu)       3.00      2       .1111       0.9444      0.0556
                                  3       .0370       0.9815      0.0185
number of servers          2      4       .0123       0.9938      0.0062
                                  5       .0041       0.9979      0.0021
                                  6       .0014       0.9993      0.0007
                                  7       .0005       0.9998      0.0002
                                  8       .0002       0.9999      0.0001
                                  9       .0001       1.0000      0.0000
```

The left-hand side of Program 5.2 shows the input data for Example 3, the Golden Muffler Shop with two mechanics. The right-hand side illustrates the program's outputs. As options, we requested (by pressing the Fl function key) that average times be converted to minutes, and (by pressing F2) that probabilities be printed.

SOLVED PROBLEMS

Solved Problem 5.1

Sid Das and Sons Brick Distributors currently employ one worker whose job is to load bricks on outgoing company trucks. An average of 24 trucks per day, or 3 per hour, arrive at the loading gate, according to a Poisson distribution. The worker loads them at a rate of 4 per hour, following approximately the exponential distribution in his service times.

Das believes that adding a second brick loader will substantially improve the firm's productivity. He estimates that a two-person crew at the loading gate will double the loading rate from four trucks per hour to eight trucks per hour. Analyze the effect on the queue of such a change and compare the results to those found with one worker. What is the probability that there will be more than three trucks either being loaded or waiting?

Solution

	NUMBER OF BRICK LOADERS	
	1	2
Truck arrival rate (λ)	3/hr.	3/hr.
Loading rate (μ)	4/hr.	8/hr.
Average number in system (L_s)	3 trucks	.6 trucks
Average time in system (W_s)	1 hr.	.2 hr.
Average number in queue (L_q)	2.25 trucks	.225 truck
Average time in queue (W_q)	3/4 hr.	.075 hr.
Utilization rate (ρ)	.75	.375
Probability system empty (P_0)	.25	.625

Probability of More Than *k* Trucks in System

	PROBABILITY $n > k$	
k	*One Loader*	*Two Loaders*
0	.75	.375
1	.56	.141
2	.42	.053
3	.32	.020

These results indicate that when only one loader is employed, the average truck must wait three-quarters of an hour before it is loaded. Furthermore, there are an average of 2.25 trucks waiting in line to be loaded. This situation may be unacceptable to management. Note the decline in queue size after the addition of a second loader.

Solved Problem 5.2

Truck drivers working for Sid Das and Sons (see Solved Problem 5.1) earn $10 per hour on the average. Brick loaders receive about $6 per hour. Truck drivers waiting *in the queue or at the loading gate* are drawing a salary but are productively idle and unable to generate revenue during that time. What would be the *hourly* cost savings to the firm associated with employing two loaders instead of one?

Referring to the data in Solved Problem 5. 1, we note that the average number of trucks *in the system* is 3 when there is only one loader and .6 when there are two loaders.

Solution

	NUMBER OF LOADERS	
	1	*2*
Truck driver idle time costs [(Average number of trucks) × (hourly rate)] = (3)($10) =	$30	$ 6 = (.6)($10)
Loading costs	6	12 = (2)($6)
Total expected cost per hour	$36	$18

The firm will save $18 per hour by adding the second loader.

Solved Problem 5.3

Sid Das and Sons Brick Distributors are considering building a second platform or gate to speed the process of loading their brick trucks. This system, they think, will be even more efficient than simply hiring another loader to help out on the first platform (as in Solved Problem 5.1).

Assume that workers at each platform will be able to load four trucks per hour each and that trucks will continue to arrive at the rate of three per hour. Then apply the appropriate equations to find the waiting line's new operating conditions. Is this new approach indeed more speedy than the other two considered?

Solution

$$P_0 = \cfrac{1}{\left[\displaystyle\sum_{n=0}^{1} \frac{1}{n!}\left(\frac{3}{4}\right)^n\right] + \frac{1}{2!}\left(\frac{3}{4}\right)^2 \frac{2(4)}{2(4)-3}}$$

$$= \cfrac{1}{1 + \frac{3}{4} + \frac{1}{2}\left(\frac{3}{4}\right)^2 \left(\frac{8}{8-3}\right)} = .454$$

$$L_s = \frac{3(4)(3/4)^2}{(1)!(8-3)^2}(.4545) + \frac{3}{4} = .873$$

$$W_s = \frac{.873}{3} = .291 \text{ hr.}$$

$$L_q = .873 - 3/4 = .123$$

$$W_q = \frac{.123}{3} = .041 \text{ hr.}$$

Looking back at Solved Problem 5.1, we see that although length of the *queue* and average time in the queue are lowest when a second platform is open, the average number of trucks in the *system* and average time spent waiting in the system are smallest when two workers are employed loading at a *single* platform. Hence, we would probably recommend not building a second gate.

Solved Problem 5.4

Beth Israel Hospital's Cardiac Care Unit (CCU) has five beds, which are virtually always occupied by patients who have just undergone major heart surgery. Two registered nurses are on duty in the CCU in each of the three eight-hour shifts. About every two hours (following a Poisson distribution) one of the patients requires a nurse's attention. The nurse will then spend an average of 30 minutes (exponentially distributed) assisting the patient and updating medical records regarding the problem and care provided.

Since immediate service is critical to the five patients, two important questions are: What is the average number of patients being attended by the nurses, and what is the average time a patient spends waiting for one of the nurses to arrive at bedside?

Solution

$$N = 5 \text{ patients}$$
$$M = 2 \text{ nurses}$$
$$T = 30 \text{ minutes}$$
$$U = 120 \text{ minutes}$$
$$X = \frac{T}{T+U} = \frac{30}{30+120} = 0.20$$

From Table 5.7, with $X = .20$ and $M = 2$, we see that

$$F = .976$$

$$H = \text{Average number being attended to} = FNX$$

$$= (.976)(5)(.20) = .98 \approx \text{one patient at any given time}$$

$$W = \text{Average waiting time for a nurse} = \frac{T(1-F)}{XF}$$

$$= \frac{30(1-.976)}{(.20)(.976)} = 3.69 \text{ minutes}$$

DISCUSSION QUESTIONS

1. What is the waiting line problem? What are the components in a waiting line system?

2. What are the assumptions underlying the queuing models described in this chapter?

3. Describe the important operating characteristics of a queuing system.

4. Why must the service rate be greater than the arrival rate in a single-channel queuing system?

5. Briefly describe three situations in which the first-in, first-out (FIFO) discipline rule is not applicable in queuing analysis.

6. Provide examples of four situations in which there is a limited, or finite, waiting line.

7. What are the components of the following queuing systems? Draw and explain the configuration of each.

a) Barber shop
b) Car wash
c) Laundromat
d) Small grocery store

8. Do doctors' offices generally have random arrival rates for patients? Are service times random? Under what circumstances might service times be constant?

9. Do you think the Poisson distribution, which assumes independent arrivals, is a good estimation of arrival rates in the following queuing systems? Defend your position in each case.

a) Cafeteria in your school
b) Barber shop
c) Hardware store
d) Dentist's office
e) College class
f) Movie theater

PROBLEMS

· **5.1** The R. Dillman Electronics Corporation retains a service crew to repair machine breakdowns that occur on an average of $\lambda = 3$ per day (approximately Poisson in nature). The crew can service an average of $\mu = 8$ machines per day, with a repair time distribution that resembles the exponential distribution.

a) What is the utilization rate of this service system?

b) What is the average down time for a machine that is broken?

c) How many machines are waiting to be serviced at any given time?

d) What is the probability that more than one machine is in the system? Probability that more than two are broken and waiting to be repaired or being serviced? More than three? More than four?

: **5.2** Barry's Car Wash is open six days a week, but its heaviest day of business is always Saturday. From historical data, Barry estimates that dirty cars arrive at the rate of 20 per hour all day Saturday. With a full crew working the hand wash line, he figures that cars can be cleaned at the rate of one every two minutes. One car at a time is cleaned in this example of a single-channel waiting line.

Assuming Poisson arrivals and exponential service times, find the:

a) average number of cars in line

b) average time a car waits before it is washed

c) average time a car spends in the service system

d) utilization rate of the car wash

e) probability no cars are in the system

f) Barry is thinking of switching to an all-automated car wash that uses no crew. The equipment under study washes one car every minute at a constant rate. How will your answers to **(a)** and **(b)** change with the new system?

: **5.3** Jenine Duffey manages a large Montgomery, Alabama, movie theater complex called Cinema I, II, III, and IV. Each of the four auditoriums plays a different film; the schedule is set so that starting times are staggered to avoid the large crowds that would occur if all four movies started at the same time. The theater has a single ticket booth and a cashier who can maintain an average service rate of 280 movie patrons per hour. Service times are assumed to follow an exponential distribution. Arrivals on a normally active day are Poisson distributed and average 210 per hour.

In order to determine the efficiency of the current ticket operation, Jenine wishes to examine several queue operating characteristics.

a) Find the average number of moviegoers waiting in line to purchase a ticket.

b) What percentage of the time is the cashier busy?

c) What is the average time a customer spends in the system?

d) What is the average time spent waiting in line to get to the ticket window?

e) What is the probability that there are more than two people in the system? More than three people? More than four?

: **5.4** A university cafeteria line in the student center is a self-serve facility in which students select the food items they want, then form a single line to pay the cashier. Students arrive at a rate of about four per minute according to a Poisson distribution. The single cashier takes about 12 seconds per customer, following an exponential distribution.

a) What is the probability there are more than two students in the system? More than three students? More than four?

b) What is the probability that the system is empty?

c) How long will the average student have to wait before reaching the cashier?

d) What is the expected number of students in the queue?

e) What is the average number in the system?

f) If a second cashier is added (who works at the same pace), how will the operating characteristics computed in **(b)**, **(c)**, **(d)**, and **(e)** change? Assume customers wait in a single line and go to the first available cashier.

: **5.5** The wheat harvesting season in the American Midwest is short, and farmers deliver their truckloads of wheat to a giant central storage bin within a two-week span. Because of this, wheat-filled trucks waiting to unload and return to the fields have been known to back up for a block at the receiving bin. The central bin is owned cooperatively, and it is to every farmer's benefit to make the unloading/storage process as efficient as possible. The cost of grain deterioration caused by unloading delays and the cost of truck rental and idle driver time are significant concerns to the cooperative members. Although farmers have difficulty quantifying crop damage, it is easy to assign a waiting and unloading cost for truck and driver of $18 per hour. The storage bin is open and operated 16 hours per day and seven days per week during the two-week harvest season and is capable of unloading 35 trucks per hour according to an exponential distribution. Full trucks arrive all day long (during the hours the bin is open) at a rate of about 30 per hour, following a Poisson pattern.

To help the cooperative get a handle on the problem of lost time while trucks are waiting in line or unloading at the bin, find the:

a) average number of trucks in the unloading system

b) average time per truck in the system

c) utilization rate for the bin area

d) probability that there are more than three trucks in the system at any given time

e) total daily cost to the farmers of having their trucks tied up in the unloading process

f) The cooperative, as mentioned, uses the storage bin heavily only two weeks per year. Farmers estimate that enlarging the bin would cut unloading costs by 50% next year. It will cost $9,000 to do so during the off-season. Would it be worth the cooperative's while to enlarge the storage area?

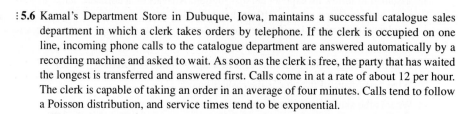 **: 5.6** Kamal's Department Store in Dubuque, Iowa, maintains a successful catalogue sales department in which a clerk takes orders by telephone. If the clerk is occupied on one line, incoming phone calls to the catalogue department are answered automatically by a recording machine and asked to wait. As soon as the clerk is free, the party that has waited the longest is transferred and answered first. Calls come in at a rate of about 12 per hour. The clerk is capable of taking an order in an average of four minutes. Calls tend to follow a Poisson distribution, and service times tend to be exponential.

The clerk is paid $5 per hour, but because of lost goodwill and sales, Kamal's loses about $25 per hour of customer time spent waiting for the clerk to take an order.

a) What is the average time that catalogue customers must wait before their calls are transferred to the order clerk?

b) What is the average number of callers waiting to place an order?

c) Kamal's is considering adding a second clerk to take calls. The store would pay that person the same $5 per hour. Should it hire another clerk? Explain.

· 5.7 Customers arrive at an automated coffee-vending machine at a rate of four per minute, following a Poisson distribution. The coffee machine dispenses a cup of coffee at a constant rate of 10 seconds.

a) What is the average number of people waiting in line?

b) What is the average number in the system?

c) How long does the average person wait in line before receiving service?

: 5.8 Jack McCanna's Barber Shop is a popular haircutting and styling salon near the campus of the University of New Haven. Four barbers work full-time and spend an average of 15 minutes on each customer. Customers arrive all day long at an average rate of 12 per hour. Arrivals tend to follow the Poisson distribution, and service times are exponentially distributed. The software described in this chapter may be used to answer these questions.

a) What is the probability that the shop is empty?

b) What is the average number of customers in the barber shop?

c) What is the average time spent in the shop?

d) What is the average time that a customer waits to be called to the barber chair?

e) What is the average number waiting to be served?

f) What is the shop's utilization factor?

g) Jack is thinking of adding a fifth barber. How will this affect the utilization rate?

: **5.9** The administrator at a large hospital emergency room faces a problem of providing treatment for patients who arrive at different rates during the day. There are four doctors available to treat patients when needed. If not needed, they can be assigned to other responsibilities (for example, lab tests, reports, x-ray diagnoses) or else rescheduled to work at other hours.

It is important to provide quick and responsive treatment, and the administrator feels that, on the average, patients should not have to sit in the waiting area for more than five minutes before being seen by a doctor. Patients are treated on a first-come, first-served basis and see the first available doctor after waiting in the queue. The arrival pattern for a typical day is:

TIME	ARRIVAL RATE
9 A.M.–3 P.M.	6 patients/hour
3 P.M.–8 P.M.	4 patients/hour
8 P.M.–midnight	12 patients/hours

These arrivals follow a Poisson distribution, and treatment times, 12 minutes on the average, follow the exponential pattern.

How many doctors should be on duty during each period in order to maintain the level of patient care expected? *Suggestion:* Use the microcomputer software described in this chapter.

: **5.10** One mechanic services five drilling machines for a steel plate manufacturer. Machines break down on an average of once every six working days, and breakdowns tend to follow a Poisson distribution. The mechanic can handle an average of one repair job per day. Repairs follow an exponential distribution.

a) How many machines are waiting for service, on the average?

b) How many drills are in running order, on the average?

c) How much would the waiting time be reduced if a second mechanic were hired?

: **5.11** Two technicians monitor a group of five computers that run an automated manufacturing facility. It takes an average of 15 minutes (exponentially distributed) to adjust a computer that develops a problem. The computers run for an average of 85 minutes (Poisson distributed) without requiring adjustments. What is the:

a) average number of computers waiting for adjustment?

b) average number being adjusted?

c) average number of computers not in working order?

: **5.12** The Kahn Department Store has approximately 300 customers shopping in its store between 9 A.M. and 5 P.M. on Saturdays. In deciding how many cash registers to keep open each Saturday, Renee Kahn, the owner, considers two factors: customer waiting time (and the associated waiting cost) and the service costs of employing additional checkout clerks. Checkout clerks are paid an average of $4 per hour. When only one is on duty, the waiting time per customer is about 10 minutes (or 1/6 of an hour); when two clerks are on duty, the average checkout time is 6 minutes per person; 4 minutes when three clerks are working; and 3 minutes when four clerks are on duty.

Ms. Kahn has conducted customer satisfaction surveys and has been able to estimate that the store suffers approximately $5 in lost sales and goodwill for every *hour* of customer time spent waiting in checkout lines. Using the information provided, determine the optimal number of clerks to have on duty each Saturday in order to minimize the store's total expected cost.

CASE STUDY

New England Castings

For over 75 years, New England Castings, Inc., has manufactured wood stoves for home use. In recent years, with increasing energy prices, George Mathison, president of New England Castings, has seen sales triple. This dramatic increase in sales has made it difficult for George to maintain quality in all of the wood stoves and related products.

Unlike other companies manufacturing wood stoves, New England Castings is *only* in the business of making stoves and stove-related products. Their major products are the Warmglo I, the Warmglo II, the Warmglo III, and the Warmglo IV. The Warmglo I is the smallest wood stove, with a heat output of 30,000 BTUS, while the Warmglo IV is the largest, with a heat output of 60,000 BTUs.

The Warmglo III outsold all of the other stoves by a wide margin. The heat output and available accessories were ideal for the typical home. The Warmglo also had a number of outstanding features that made it one of the most attractive and heat-efficient stoves on the market. These features, along with the accessories, resulted in expanding sales and prompted George to build a new factory to manufacture Warmglo III stoves. An overview diagram of the factory is shown in Figure 5.5.

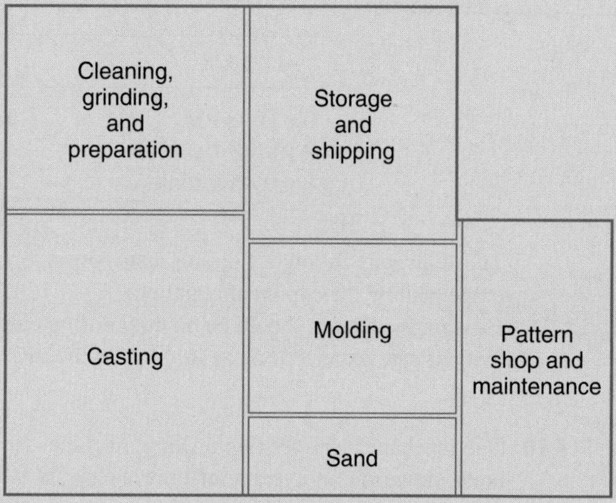

The new foundry used the latest equipment, including a new Disamatic that helped in manufacturing stove parts. Regardless of new equipment or procedures, casting operations have remained basically unchanged for hundreds of years. To begin with, a wooden pattern is made for every cast-iron piece in the stove. The wooden pattern is an exact duplication of the cast-iron piece that is to be manufactured. New England Castings has all of its patterns made by Precision Patterns, Inc., and these patterns are stored in the pattern shop and maintenance room. Then, a specially formulated sand is molded around the wooden pattern. There can be two or more sand molds for each pattern. Mixing the sand and making the molds is done in the molding room. When the wooden pattern is removed, the resulting sand molds form a negative image of the desired casting. Next, the molds are transported to the casting room, where molten iron is poured into the molds and allowed to cool. When the iron has solidified, the molds are moved into the cleaning, grinding, and preparation room. The molds are dumped into large vibrators that shake most of the sand from the casting. The rough castings are then subjected to both sandblasting

FIGURE 5.5

Overview of Factory.

to remove the rest of the sand and grinding to finish some of the surfaces of the castings. The castings are then painted with a special heat-resistant paint, assembled into workable stoves, and inspected for manufacturing defects that may have gone undetected thus far. Finally, the finished stoves are moved to storage and shipping, where they are packaged and shipped to the appropriate locations.

At present, the pattern shop and the maintenance department are located in the same room. One large counter is used both by maintenance personnel to get tools and parts, and by sand molders who need various patterns for the molding operation. Pete Nawler and Bob Dillman, who work behind the counter, are able to service a total of ten people per hour (about five per hour each). On the average, four people from maintenance and three people from the molding department arrive at the counter per hour. People from the molding department and from maintenance arrive randomly, and to be served they form a single line.

Pete and Bob have always had a policy of first come, first served. Because of the location of the pattern shop and maintenance department, it takes about three minutes for an individual from the maintenance department to walk to the

CASE STUDY (Continued)

pattern and maintenance room, and it takes about one minute for an individual to walk from the molding department to the pattern and maintenance room.

After observing the operation of the pattern shop and maintenance room for several weeks, George decided to make some changes to the layout of the factory. An overview of these changes appears in Figure 5.6.

Separating the maintenance shop from the pattern shop had a number of advantages. It would take people from the maintenance department only one minute instead of three to get to the new maintenance department. Using motion and time studies, George was also able to determine that improving the layout of the maintenance department would allow Bob to serve six people from the maintenance department per hour, and improving the layout of the pattern department would allow Pete to serve seven people from the molding shop per hour.

Discussion Questions

1. How much time would the new layout save?

2. If maintenance personnel were paid $9.50 per hour and molding personnel were paid $11.75 per hour, how much could be saved per hour with the new factory layout?

FIGURE 5.6

Overview of Factory after Changes.

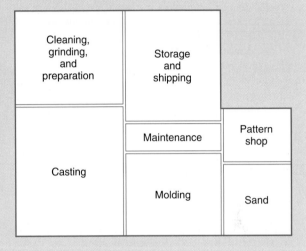

Source: B. Render, R. M. Stair, and I. Greenberg, *Cases and Readings in Management Science,* 2nd ed., Boston: Allyn & Bacon,

CASE STUDY

The Winter Park Hotel

Background: Queuing Theory at Hotels

Queues form because people arrive more rapidly than they can be served. Since the arrival of hotel and restaurant guests is essentially random, lines are inevitable.

Queues provide the service operation with a capacity buffer. Productivity at the hotel front desk is largely dependent on the flow of customers. The desk is at its greatest efficiency when it has a steady flow of guests at all stations. Weighing against the hotel's desire for efficiency, however, is the guest's desire for prompt service. Adding employees to speed up service will ultimately decrease efficiency, because some clerks will inevitably be idle from time to time. And when all waiting guests have been served, employee productivity drops to nothing. Management's task, with the help of queuing analysis, is to schedule enough employees so that customers are served promptly enough, but not so many employees that some stand idle.

For the customer with a confirmed reservation at a hotel, there is little alternative to waiting in the queue, since hotel policy is generally to charge the customer for the room whether it is used or not. Even if the guest is not liable for room charges, he or she might be slow to balk or renege, given the likelihood that the next inn might be full or that the lines would be as long. That the guest remains in the line, however, does not indicate great satisfaction.

Some hotels have established a form of dedicated channel, known as concierge or executive check-in, for frequent-guest program participants, but few hotels have applied queuing theory to the extent that other service industries have. No queuing system predominates at hotel front desks.

The Winter Park Hotel

Donna Shader, the manager of the Winter Park Hotel, is considering how to restructure the front desk to reach an optimum level of staff efficiency and guest service. At present, the hotel has five clerks on duty, each with a separate

CASE STUDY (Continued)

waiting line, during peak check-in time of 3:00 P.M. to 5:00 P.M. Observation of arrivals during this time shows that an average of 90 guests arrive each hour (although there is no upward limit on the number that could arrive at any given time). It takes an average of three minutes for the front-desk clerk to register each guest.

Ms. Shader is considering three plans for improving guest service by reducing the length of time guests spend waiting in line. The first proposal would designate one employee as a quick-service clerk for guests registering under corporate accounts, a market segment that fills about 30% of all occupied rooms. Since corporate guests are pre-registered, their registration takes just two minutes. With these guests separated from the rest of the clientele, the average time for registering a typical guest would climb to 3.7 minutes. Under plan one, noncorporate guests would choose any of the remaining four lines.

The second plan is to implement a single-line system. All guests could form a single waiting line to be served by whichever of five clerks became available. This option would require sufficient lobby space for what could be a substantial queue.

The use of an automatic "teller" machine (ATM) for check-in is the basis of the third proposal. Given that initial use of this new technology might be minimal, Shader estimated that 20% of customers, primarily frequent guests, would be willing to use the machines. (This might be a conservative estimate if the guests perceive direct benefits from using the ATM, as bank customers do. Citibank reports that some 80% of its Manhattan customers use its ATMs.) Ms. Shader would set up a single queue for customers who prefer human check-in clerks. This would be served by the five clerks, although Shader is hopeful that the machine will allow a reduction to four.

Discussion Question

1. Determine the average amount of time that a guest spends checking in. How would this change under each of the stated options?

Source: Adapted from B. Render, R. M. Stair, and I. Greenberg, *Cases and Readings in Management Science,* 2nd ed. Boston: Allyn & Bacon, 1990.

BIBLIOGRAPHY

Byrd, J. "The Value of Queuing Theory." *Interfaces* **8,** 3 (May 1978): 22–26.

Cooper, R. B. *Introduction to Queuing Theory.* New York: Macmillan Co., 1972.

Corkindale, D. R. "Queuing Theory in the Solution of a Transport Evaluation Problem." *Operational Research Quarterly* **26,** 2: 259.

Cox, D. R., and W. L. Smith. *Queues.* New York: John Wiley & Sons, 1965.

Davis, M. M. "A Study of the Relationship between Customer Satisfaction and Waiting Time." *Proceedings of the Northeast Decision Sciences Institute Meeting* (March 1986).

Edmond, E. D., and R. P. Maggs. "How Useful Are Queue Models in Port Investment Decisions for Container Berths?" *Journal of the Operations Research Society* **29,** 8.

Erikson, W. "Management Science and the Gas Shortage." *Interfaces* **4,** 4 (August 1974): 47–51.

Eschcoli, Z., and I. Adiri. "Single-Lane Budget Serving Two-Lane Traffic." *Naval Research Logistics Quarterly* **24** (March 1977): 113–125.

Foote, B. L. "Queuing Case Study of Drive-In Banking." *Interfaces* **6,** 4 (August 1976): 31.

Gostl, J., and I. Greenberg. "An Application of Queuing Theory to the Design of a Message-Switching Computer System." *Communications of the ACM* **28,** 5 (May 1985): 500–505.

Graff, G. "Simple Queuing Theory Saves Unnecessary Equipment." *Industrial Engineering* **3** (February 1971): 15–18.

Grassmann, W. K. "Finding the Right Number of Servers in Real-World Queuing Systems." *Interfaces* **18,** 2 (March–April 1988): 94–104.

Green, L., and P. Kolesar. "The Feasibility of One-Officer Patrol in New York City." *Management Science* **30,** 8 (August 1984): 964–981.

Morse, P. M. *Queues, Inventories and Maintenance.* New York: John Wiley & Sons, 1958.

Panico, J. A. *Queuing Theory: A Study of Waiting Lines for Business, Economics and Sciences.* Englewood Cliffs, NJ: Prentice-Hall, 1969.

Paul, R. J., and R. E. Stevens. "Staffing Service Activities with Waiting Line Models." *Decision Sciences* **2** (April 1971): 206–218.

Render, B., and R. M. Stair. *Introduction to Management Science.* Boston: Allyn & Bacon, 1992.

Render, B., and R. M. Stair. *Quantitative Analysis for Management.* 4th ed. Boston: Allyn & Bacon, 1991.

Sze, D. Y. "A Queuing Model for Telephone Operator Staffing." *Operations Research* **32,** 2 (March–April 1984): 229–249.

Worthington, D. J. "Queuing Models for Hospital Waiting Lists." *Journal of the Operational Research Society* **38,** 5 (May 1987): 413–422.

SUPPLEMENT

CHAPTER 5

INTRODUCTION

Simulation models abound in our world. Boeing Aircraft uses them to test the aerodynamics of proposed jets; the U.S. Army simulates war games on computers; business students use management gaming to simulate realistic business competition; and thousands of organizations develop simulation models to help make operations decisions.

Simulation models are estimated to be in use in over half of the large manufacturing companies in the United States. Table S5.1 lists just a few areas in which simulation is now being applied.

SIMULATION DEFINED

Simulation

Simulation is the attempt to duplicate the features, appearance, and characteristics of a real system. In this supplement, we will show how to simulate part of an operations management system by building a mathematical model that comes as close as possible to representing the reality of the system. The model will then be used to estimate the effects of various actions. The idea behind simulation is (1) to imitate a real-world situation mathematically, (2) then to study its properties and operating characteristics, and (3) finally to draw conclusions and make action decisions based on the results of the simulation. In this way, the real-life system is not touched until the advantages and disadvantages of what may be a major policy decision are first measured on the system's model.

To use simulation, a P/OM manager should:

1. define the problem;
2. introduce the important variables associated with the problem;
3. construct a numerical model;
4. set up possible courses of action for testing;
5. run the experiment;
6. consider the results (possibly modify the model or change data inputs);
7. decide what course of action to take.

TABLE S5.1 Some Applications of Simulation.

Ambulance location and dispatching	Bus scheduling
Assembly-line balancing	Design of library operations
Parking lot and harbor design	Taxi, truck, and railroad dispatching
Distribution system design	Production facility scheduling
Scheduling aircraft	Plant layout
Labor-hiring decisions	Capital investments
Personnel scheduling	Production scheduling
Traffic-light timing	Sales forecasting
Voting pattern predicting	Inventory planning and control

FIGURE S5.1

The Process of Simulation.

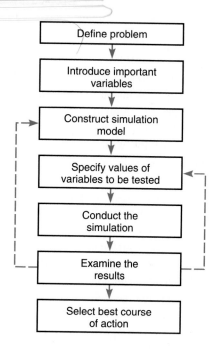

These steps are illustrated in Figure S5.1

The problems tackled by simulation may range from very simple to extremely complex, from bank teller lines to an analysis of the U.S. economy. Although very small simulations may be conducted by hand, effective use of this technique requires some automated means of calculation, namely, a computer. Even large-scale models, simulating perhaps years of business decisions, can be handled in a reasonable amount of time by computer. Though simulation is one of the older operations management tools, it was not until the introduction of computers in the mid-1940s and early 1950s that it became a practical means of solving large-scale management and military problems.

In this supplement, we examine the basic principles of simulation and then tackle some problems in the areas of waiting line analysis (from Chapter 5) and inventory control (to be treated in Chapter 13). Why do we use simulation in these areas when mathematical models described in other chapters can solve the problems? The answer is that simulation provides an alternative approach. It can handle, for example, queuing problems in which arrivals at a facility are not Poisson distributed, service times are not exponentially distributed or constant, or the FIFO priority system is inappropriate. (Recall that these were all basic assumptions of queuing in Chapter 5). In Chapter 18, we will use the tools learned in this supplement to simulate a firm's maintenance policy.

ADVANTAGES AND DISADVANTAGES OF SIMULATION

Simulation is a tool that has become widely accepted by managers for several reasons. The main *advantages* of simulation are:

1. Simulation is relatively straightforward and flexible.
2. Simulation can be used to analyze large and complex real-world situations that cannot be solved by conventional operations management models.
3. Simulation allows for the inclusion of real-world complications that most P/OM models cannot permit. Simulation can use *any* probability distribution that the user defines; it does not require standard distributions.
4. "Time compression" is possible with simulation. The effects of P/OM policies over many months or years can be obtained by computer simulation in a short time.
5. Simulation allows "what-if" types of questions. Managers like to know in advance what options will be most attractive. With a computerized model, a manager can try out several policy decisions within a matter of minutes.
6. Simulations do not interfere with the real-world system. It may be too disruptive, for example, actually to experiment with new policies or ideas in a hospital, school, or manufacturing plant.
7. Simulation allows us to study the interactive effect of individual components or variables in order to determine which ones are important.

The main *disadvantages* of simulation are:

1. Good simulation models can be very expensive; they may take years to develop.
2. Simulation does not generate optimal solutions to problems as does linear programming. It is a trial-and-error approach that may produce different solutions in repeated runs.
3. Managers must generate all of the conditions and constraints for solutions that they want to examine. The simulation model does not produce answers by itself.
4. Each simulation model is unique. Its solutions and inferences are not usually transferable to other problems.

MONTE CARLO SIMULATION

Monte Carlo method

When a system contains elements that exhibit chance in their behavior, the **Monte Carlo method** of simulation may be applied. The basis of Monte Carlo simulation is experimentation on the chance (or *probabilistic*) elements through random sampling.

The technique breaks down into five simple steps:

1. Setting up a probability distribution for important variables;
2. Building a cumulative probability distribution for each variable;
3. Establishing an interval of random numbers for each variable;

POM _in action_

Simulation Modeling at Burger King

Burger King executives realized quickly that corporate productivity had to be a top priority in light of the ever changing fast-food hamburger restaurant business. A series of computer simulation models were developed to address a wide variety of issues. Several of these issues are outlined below.

- In determining the ideal distance between the drive-thru order station and the pick-up window, simulation models were developed. It was determined that a longer distance reduced waiting time, and consequently 12 to 13 additional customers could be served per hour. This translated into an annual benefit of over $10,000 per restaurant and provides an additional $15 million in annual system-wide sales capacity.

- Hoping to expand the sales capacity of the drive-thru during peak hours, a second drive-thru window was suggested. This second window was to be placed in series to the first, rather than in a two-lane configuration. The simulation model assessing this approach predicted a sales increase of 15% during the busiest lunch hours. Predicated on the average drive-thru percentages and the average restaurant sales during the lunch hour, the second window increased sales more than $13,000 per year per restaurant.

- Computer simulation indicated a delay of an average 8 seconds per customer if new small special sandwiches were to be introduced to the menu. This would represent a $13,000 loss in sales for an average restaurant annually. Consequently, it was recommended not to introduce these sandwiches. This prevented a possible $39 million loss in capacity to the whole Burger King system.

Sources: Interfaces, December 1981, pp. 35–41; and _Business Week,_ October 22, 1990, pp. 60–61.

4. Generating random numbers;
5. Actually simulating a series of trials.

In this section we examine each of these steps in turn.

Step 1. Establishing Probability Distributions. The basic idea in Monte Carlo simulation is to generate values for the variables making up the model being studied. There are a lot of variables in real-world systems that are probabilistic in nature and that we might want to simulate. To name just a few:

1. inventory demand on a daily or weekly basis;
2. lead time for inventory orders to arrive;
3. times between machine breakdowns;
4. times between arrivals at a service facility;
5. service times;
6. times to complete project activities;
7. number of employees absent from work each day.

One common way to establish a _probability distribution_ for a given variable is to examine historical outcomes. The probability, or relative frequency, for each possible outcome of a variable is found by dividing the frequency of observation by the total number of observations. Let us consider an example.

TABLE S5.2 Demand for Barry's Auto Tire.

(1) Demand for Tires	(2) Frequency	(3) Probability of Occurrence	(4) Cumulative Probability
0	10	$^{10}/_{200}$ = .05	.05
1	20	$^{20}/_{200}$ = .10	.15
2	40	$^{40}/_{200}$ = .20	.35
3	60	$^{60}/_{200}$ = .30	.65
4	40	$^{40}/_{200}$ = .20	.85
5	30	$^{30}/_{200}$ = .15	1.00
	200 days	$^{200}/_{200}$ = 1.00	

The daily demand for radial tires at Barry's Auto Tire over the past 200 days is shown in columns 1 and 2 of Table S5.2. We can convert this demand to a probability distribution (if we assume that past arrival rates will hold in the future) by dividing each demand frequency by the total demand, 200; the result is shown in column 3.

Step 2. Building a Cumulative Probability Distribution for Each Variable. The conversion from a regular probability distribution, such as in column 3 of Table S5.2, to a **cumulative probability distribution** is an easy job. In column 4, we see that the cumulative probability for each level of demand is the sum of the number in the probability column (column 3) added to the previous cumulative probability.

Cumulative probability distribution

Step 3. Setting Random Number Intervals. Once we have established a cumulative probability distribution for each variable included in the simulation, we must assign a set of numbers to represent each possible value or outcome. These are referred to as **random number intervals.** Basically, a **random number** is a series of digits (say two digits from 01, 02, . . . , 98, 99, 00) that have been selected by a totally random process.

Random number intervals
Random number

If there is a 5% chance that demand for a product (such as Barry's radial tires) will be 0 units per day, then we will want 5% of the random numbers available to correspond to a demand of 0 units. If a total of 100 two-digit numbers is used in the simulation, we could assign a demand of 0 units to the first five random numbers: 01, 02, 03, 04, and 05.[1] Then a simulated demand for 0 units would be created every time one of the numbers 0İ to 05 was drawn. If there is also a 10% chance that demand for the same product will be one unit per day, we could let the next ten random numbers (06, 07, 08, 09, 10, 11, 12, 13, 14, and 15) represent that demand—and so on for other demand levels.

Similarly, we can see in Table S5.3 that the length of each interval on the right corresponds to the probability of one of each of the possible daily demands. Hence, in assigning random numbers to the daily demand for three radial tires, the range of the random number interval (36 to 65) corresponds *exactly* to the probability (or proportion) of that outcome. A daily demand for three radial tires occurs 30% of the

---

[1] Alternatively, we could have assigned the random numbers 00, 01, 02, 03, 04 to represent a demand of 0 units. The two digits 00 can be thought of as either 0 or 100. As long as five numbers out of one hundred are assigned to the 0 demand, it doesn't make any difference which five they are.

TABLE S5.3 The Assignment of Random Number Intervals for Barry's Auto Tire.

DAILY DEMAND	PROBABILITY	CUMULATIVE PROBABILITY	INTERVAL OF RANDOM NUMBERS
0	.05	.05	01 through 05
1	.10	.15	06 through 15
2	.20	.35	16 through 35
3	.30	.65	36 through 65
4	.20	.85	66 through 85
5	.15	1.00	86 through 00

time. Any of the 30 random numbers greater than 35 up to and including 65 are assigned to that event.

Step 4. Generating Random Numbers. Random numbers, that is, numbers drawn in such a way that each digit (0 through 9) has an equal chance of being drawn, may be generated for simulation problems in two ways. If the problem is very large and the process being studied involves thousands of simulation trials, computer programs are available to generate the random numbers needed. If the simulation is being done by hand, the numbers may be selected from a table of random digits.

TABLE S5.4 Table of Random Numbers.

52	06	50	88	53	30	10	47	99	37	66	91	35	32	00	84	57	07
37	63	28	02	74	35	24	03	29	60	74	85	90	73	59	55	17	60
82	57	68	28	05	94	03	11	27	79	90	87	92	41	09	25	36	77
69	02	36	49	71	99	32	10	75	21	95	90	94	38	97	71	72	49
98	94	90	36	06	78	23	67	89	85	29	21	25	73	69	34	85	76
96	52	62	87	49	56	59	23	78	71	72	90	57	01	98	57	31	95
33	69	27	21	11	60	95	89	68	48	17	89	34	09	93	50	44	51
50	33	50	95	13	44	34	62	64	39	55	29	30	64	49	44	30	16
88	32	18	50	62	57	34	56	62	31	15	40	90	34	51	95	26	14
90	30	36	24	69	82	51	74	30	35	36	85	01	55	92	64	09	85
50	48	61	18	85	23	08	54	17	12	80	69	24	84	92	16	49	59
27	88	21	62	69	64	48	31	12	73	02	68	00	16	16	46	13	85
45	14	46	32	13	49	66	62	74	41	86	98	92	98	84	54	33	40
81	02	01	78	82	74	97	37	45	31	94	99	42	49	27	64	89	42
66	83	14	74	27	76	03	33	11	97	59	81	72	00	64	61	13	52
74	05	81	82	93	09	96	33	52	78	13	06	28	30	94	23	37	39
30	34	87	01	74	11	46	82	59	94	25	34	32	23	17	01	58	73
59	55	72	33	62	13	74	68	22	44	42	09	32	46	71	79	45	89
67	09	80	98	99	25	77	50	03	32	36	63	65	75	94	19	95	88
60	77	46	63	71	69	44	22	03	85	14	48	69	13	30	50	33	24
60	08	19	29	36	72	30	27	50	64	85	72	75	29	87	05	75	01
80	45	86	99	02	34	87	08	86	84	49	76	24	08	01	86	29	11
53	84	49	63	26	65	72	84	85	63	26	02	75	26	92	62	40	67
69	84	12	94	51	36	17	02	15	29	16	52	56	43	26	22	08	62
37	77	13	10	02	18	31	19	32	85	31	94	81	43	31	58	33	51

Source: Reprinted from *A Million Random Digits with 100,000 Normal Deviates,* Rand (New York: The Free Press, 1995). Used by permission.

Step 5.   Simulating the Experiment. We may simulate outcomes of an experiment by simply selecting random numbers from Table S5.4. Beginning anywhere in the table, we note the interval in Table S5.3 into which each number falls. For example, if the random number chosen is 81 and the interval 65 to 85 represents a daily demand for four tires, then we select a demand of four tires.

Example S1

Let us illustrate the concept further by simulating 10 days of demand for radial tires at Barry's Auto Tire (see Table S5.3). We select the random numbers needed from Table S5.4, starting in the upper left-hand corner and continuing down the first column.

DAY NUMBER	RANDOM NUMBER	SIMULATED DAILY DEMAND
1	52	3
2	37	3
3	82	4
4	69	4
5	98	5
6	96	5
7	33	2
8	50	3
9	88	5
10	90	5
		39 Total 10-day demand

39/10 = 3.9 = Tires average daily demand

It is interesting to note that the average demand of 3.9 tires in this 10-day simulation differs significantly from the *expected* daily demand, which we may calculate from the data in Table S5.3:

$$\text{Expected demand} = \sum_{i=1}^{5} (\text{probability of } i \text{ units}) \times (\text{demand of } i \text{ units})$$

$$= (.05)(0) + (.10)(1) + (.20)(2) + (.30)(3) + (.20)(4) + (.15)(5)$$

$$= 0 + .1 + .4 + .9 + .8 + .75$$

$$= 2.95 \text{ tires}$$

However, if this simulation were repeated hundreds or thousands of times, the average *simulated* demand would be nearly the same as the *expected* demand.

In the past, most simulations were done by mathematical experts, who developed long, complex computer printouts. But with graphic displays, simulation can be played out on the screen, step-by-step, for users to watch. "Animation gives managers confidence in the results," says simulation pioneer and creator of SLAM, Alan B. Pritsker. Such software can make a major contribution to productivity, with the U.S. being a world leader in developing user-friendly programs in all phases of manufacturing operation.

Naturally, it would be risky to draw any hard and fast conclusions regarding the operation of a firm from only a short simulation. It is also unlikely that anyone would actually want to go to the effort of simulating such a simple model containing only one variable. Simulating by hand does, however, demonstrate the important principles involved and may be useful in small-scale studies. As you might expect, the computer can be a very helpful tool in carrying out the tedious work in larger simulation undertakings.

SIMULATION OF A QUEUING PROBLEM

An important area of simulation application has been in the analysis of waiting line problems. As mentioned in Chapter 5, the assumptions required for solving queuing problems analytically are quite restrictive. For most realistic queuing systems, simulation may actually be the only approach available.

This section illustrates the simulation at a large unloading dock and its associated queue. Arrivals of barges at the dock are not Poisson distributed, and unloading rates (service times) are not exponential or constant. As such, the mathematical waiting line models of Chapter 5 cannot be used.

Example S2

Fully loaded barges arrive at night in New Orleans following their long trips down the Mississippi River from industrial midwestern cities. The number of barges docking on any given night ranges from 0 to 5. The probability of 0, 1, 2, 3, 4, and 5 arrivals is displayed in Table S5.5. In the same table, we establish cumulative probabilities and corresponding random number intervals for each possible value.

TABLE S5.5 Overnight Barge Arrival Rates and Random Number of Intervals.

NUMBER OF ARRIVALS	PROBABILITY	CUMULATIVE PROBABILITY	RANDOM NUMBER INTERVAL
0	.13	.13	01 through 13
1	.17	.30	14 through 30
2	.15	.45	31 through 45
3	.25	.70	46 through 70
4	.20	.90	71 through 90
5	.10	1.00	91 through 00
	1.00		

A study by the dock superintendent reveals that because of the nature of their cargo, the number of barges unloaded also tends to vary from day to day. The superintendent provides information from which we can create a probability distribution for the variable *daily unloading rate* (see Table S5.6). As we just did for the arrival variable, we can set up an interval of random numbers for the unloading rates.

Barges are unloaded on a first-in, first-out basis. Any barges that are not unloaded the day of arrival must wait until the following day. Tying up a barge in dock is an expensive proposition, and the superintendent cannot ignore the angry phone calls from barge line owners reminding him that "time is money!"

TABLE S5.6 Unloading Rates and Random Number Intervals.

DAILY UNLOADING RATES	PROBABILITY	CUMULATIVE PROBABILITY	RANDOM NUMBER INTERVAL
1	.05	.05	01 through 05
2	.15	.20	06 through 20
3	.50	.70	21 through 70
4	.20	.90	71 through 90
5	.10	1.00	91 through 00
	1.00		

He decides that, before going to the Port of New Orleans's controller to request additional unloading crews, a simulation study of arrivals, unloadings, and delays should be conducted. A 100-day simulation would be ideal, but for purposes of illustration, the superintendent begins with a shorter 15-day analysis. Random numbers are drawn from the top row of Table S5.4 to generate daily arrival rates. They are drawn from the second row of Table S5.4 to create daily unloading rates. Table S5.7 shows the day-to-day port simulation.

TABLE S5.7 Queuing Simulation of Port of New Orleans Barge Unloadings.

(1) Day	(2) Number Delayed from Previous Day	(3) Random Number	(4) Number of Nightly Arrivals	(5) Total to Be Unloaded	(6) Random Number	(7) Number Unloaded
1	—[1]	52	3	3	37	3
2	0	06	0	0	63	0[2]
3	0	50	3	3	28	3
4	0	88	4	4	02	1
5	3	53	3	6	74	4
6	2	30	1	3	35	3
7	0	10	0	0	24	0[3]
8	0	47	3	3	03	1
9	2	99	5	7	29	3
10	4	37	2	6	60	3
11	3	66	3	6	74	4
12	2	91	5	7	85	4
13	3	35	2	5	90	4
14	1	32	2	3	73	3[4]
15	0	00	5	5	59	3
	20 Total delays		41 Total arrivals			39 Total unloadings

1. We can begin with no delays from the previous day. In a long simulation, even if we started with five overnight delays, that initial condition would be averaged out.
2. Three barges *could* have been unloaded on day 2. But because there were no arrivals and no backlog existed, zero unloadings took place.
3. The same situation as noted in footnote 2 takes place.
4. This time four barges could have been unloaded, but since only three were in queue, the number unloaded is recorded as 3.

The superintendent will likely be interested in at least three useful and important pieces of information:

$$\text{Average number of barges delayed to the next day} = \frac{20 \text{ delays}}{15 \text{ days}}$$

$$= 1.33 \text{ barges delayed per day}$$

$$\text{Average number of nightly arrivals} = \frac{41 \text{ arrivals}}{15 \text{ days}}$$

$$= 2.73 \text{ arrivals per night}$$

$$\text{Average number of barges unloaded each day} = \frac{39 \text{ unloadings}}{15 \text{ days}}$$

$$= 2.60 \text{ unloadings per day}$$

When the above data are analyzed in the context of delay costs, idle labor costs, and the cost of hiring extra unloading crew, it will be possible for the dock superintendent and port controller to make a better staffing decision. They may even elect to resimulate the process assuming different unloading rates that would correspond to increased crew sizes. Although simulation is a tool that cannot guarantee an optimal solution to problems such as this, it can be helpful in recreating a process and identifying good decision alternatives.

SIMULATION AND INVENTORY ANALYSIS

In Chapter 13 we will introduce the subject of deterministic inventory models. These commonly used models are based on the assumption that both product demand and reorder lead time are known, constant values. In most real-world inventory situations, though, demand and lead time are variables, and accurate analysis becomes extremely difficult to handle by any means other than simulation.

In this section we will present an inventory problem with two decision variables and two probabilistic components. The owner of the hardware store we are about to describe would like to establish *order quantity* and *reorder point* decisions for a particular product that has probabilistic (uncertain) daily demand and reorder lead time. He wants to make a series of simulation runs, trying out various order quantities and reorder points, in order to minimize his total inventory cost for the item. Inventory costs in this case will include an ordering, holding, and stockout cost.

Example S3

Simkin's Hardware sells the Ace model electric drill. Daily demand for the drill is relatively low but subject to some variability. Over the past 300 days, Simkin has observed the sales shown in column 2 of Table S5.8. He converts this historical frequency into a probability distribution for the variable daily demand (column 3). A cumulative probability distribution is formed in column 4 of Table S5.8. Finally, Simkin establishes an interval of random numbers to represent each possible daily demand (column 5).

TABLE S5.8 Probabilities and Random Number Intervals for Daily Ace Drill Demand.

(1) Demand for Ace Drill	(2) Frequency	(3) Probability	(4) Cumulative Probability	(5) Interval of Random Numbers
0	15	.05	.05	01 through 05
1	30	.10	.15	06 through 15
2	60	.20	.35	16 through 35
3	120	.40	.75	36 through 75
4	45	.15	.90	76 through 90
5	30	.10	1.00	91 through 00
	300 days	1.00		

When Simkin places an order to replenish his inventory of Ace electric drills, there is a delivery lag of from one to three days. This means that lead time may also be considered a probabilistic variable. The number of days it took to receive the past 50 orders is presented in Table S5.9. In a fashion similar to that for the demand variable, Simkin establishes a probability distribution for the lead time variable (column 3 of Table S5.9), computes the cumulative distribution (column 4), and assigns random number intervals for each possible time (column 5).

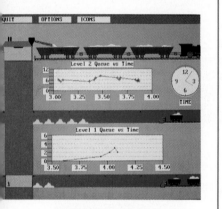

SIMSCRIPT, one of the most widely used special-purpose simulation languages, has graphic capabilities that include animation of the system being simulated. The software permits specialized simulations of such diverse applications as telecommunications systems, factories, and weather movement.

TABLE S5.9 Probabilities and Random Number Intervals for Reorder Lead Time.

(1) Lead Time (days)	(2) Frequency	(3) Probability	(4) Cumulative Probability	(5) Interval of Random Numbers
1	10	.20	.20	01 through 20
2	25	.50	.70	21 through 70
3	15	.30	1.00	71 through 00
	50 orders	1.00		

The first inventory policy that Simkin's Hardware wants to simulate is an order quantity of 10 with a reorder point of 5. That is, every time the on-hand inventory level at the end of the day is five or less, Simkin will call his supplier and place an order for ten more drills. If the lead time is one day, by the way, the order will not arrive the next morning, but rather at the beginning of the following working day.

The logic of the simulation process is presented in Figure S5.2. Such a *flow diagram* or *flowchart* is useful in the logical coding procedures for programming this simulation process. The entire process is simulated below for a 10-day period. We assume that beginning inventory is 10 units on day 1. We took the random numbers from column 2 of Table S5.4.

FIGURE S5.2

Flow Diagram for Simkin's Inventory Example.

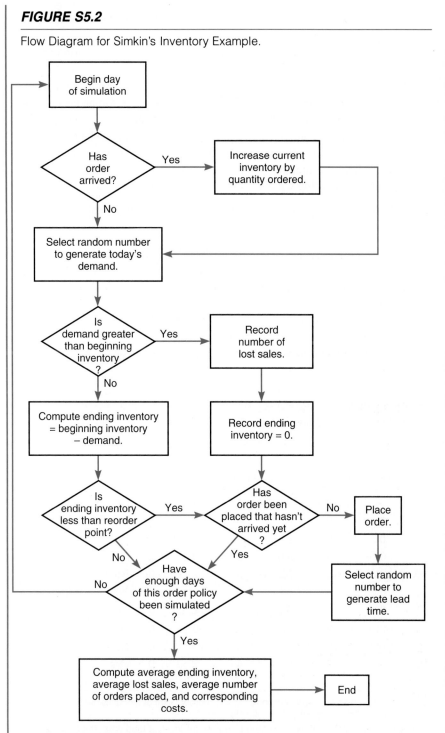

Table S5.10 was filled in by proceeding one day (or line) at a time, working from left to right. It was a four-step process:

1. Begin each simulated day by checking whether any ordered inventory has just arrived. If it has, increase the current inventory by the quantity ordered (10 units, in this case).

2. Generate a daily demand from the demand probability distribution by selecting a random number.

3. Compute ending inventory = beginning inventory minus demand. If on-hand inventory is insufficient to meet the day's demand, satisfy as much as possible and note the number of lost sales.

4. Determine whether the day's ending inventory has reached the reorder point (five units). If it has, and if there are no outstanding orders, place an order. Lead time for a new order is simulated by choosing a random number and using the distribution in Table S5.9.

Simkin's first inventory simulation yields some interesting results. The average daily ending inventory is:

$$\text{Average ending inventory} = \frac{41 \text{ total units}}{10 \text{ days}} = 4.1 \text{ units/day}$$

We also note the average lost sales and number of orders placed per day:

$$\text{Average lost sales} = \frac{2 \text{ sales lost}}{10 \text{ days}} = 0.2 \text{ units/day}$$

$$\text{Average number of orders placed} = \frac{3 \text{ orders}}{10 \text{ days}} = 0.3 \text{ orders/day}$$

TABLE S5.10 Simkin Hardware's First Inventory Simulation.
Order Quantity = 10 Units; Reorder Point = 5 Units.

(1) Day	(2) Units Received	(3) Beginning Inventory	(4) Random Number	(5) Demand	(6) Ending Inventory	(7) Lost Sales	(8) Order?	(9) Random Number	(10) Lead Time
1		10	06	1	9	0	No		
2	0	9	63	3	6	0	No		
3	0	6	57	3	(3)[1]	0	Yes	(02)[2]	1
4	0	3	(94)[3]	5	0	2	No[4]		
5	(10)[5]	10	52	3	7	0	No		
6	0	7.	69	3	4	0	Yes	33	2
7	0	4	32	2	2	0	No		
8	0	2	30	2	0	0	No		
9	(10)[6]	10	48	3	7	0	No		
10	0	7	88	4	3	0	Yes	14	1
				Totals:	41	2			

1. This is the first time inventory dropped to the reorder point of five drills. Since no prior order was outstanding, an order is placed.

2. The random number 02 is generated to represent the first lead time. It was drawn from column 2 of Table S5.4 as the next number in the list being used. A separate column could have been used from which to draw lead time random numbers if we had wanted to do so, but in this example we did not do so.

3. Again, notice that the random digits 02 were used for lead time (see footnote 2). So the next number in the column is 94.

4. No order is placed on day 4 because there is one outstanding from the previous day that has not yet arrived.
5. The lead time for the first order placed is one day, but as noted in the text, an order does not arrive the next morning, but rather the beginning of the following day. Thus, the first order arrives at the start of day 5.
6. This is the arrival of the order placed at the close of business on day 6. Fortunately for Simkin, no lost sales occurred during the two-day lead time until the order arrived.

These data are useful in studying the inventory costs of the policy being simulated.

Example S4

Simkin estimates that the cost of placing each order for Ace drills is $10, the holding cost per drill held at the end of each day is $0.50, and the cost of each lost sale is $8. This information enables us to compute the total daily inventory cost for the simulated policy in Example S3. Let us examine the three cost components:

$$\text{Daily order cost} = (\text{Cost of placing one order})$$
$$\times (\text{Number of orders placed per day})$$
$$= \$10 \text{ per order} \times .3 \text{ orders per day} = \$3$$

$$\text{Daily holding cost} = (\text{Cost of holding one unit for one day})$$
$$\times (\text{Average ending inventory})$$
$$= 50¢ \text{ per unit per day} \times 4.1 \text{ units per day} = \$2.05$$

$$\text{Daily stockout cost} = (\text{Cost per lost sale})$$
$$\times (\text{Average number of lost sales per day})$$
$$= \$8 \text{ per lost sale} \times .2 \text{ lost sales per day} = \$1.60$$

$$\text{Total daily inventory cost} = \text{Daily order cost} + \text{Daily holding cost}$$
$$+ \text{Daily stockout cost} = \$6.65$$

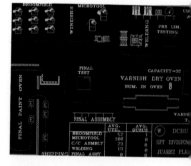

CINEMA simulation software, designed by Systems Modeling Corp., is a graphical system that allows users to model and analyze a variety of problems with minimal programming knowledge. CINEMA can handle complex problems ranging from scheduling food processing lines to designing an assembly facility, all with animation software. Functions are selected through a menu system with the touch of one key.

Now once again we want to emphasize something very important. This simulation should be extended many more days before we draw any conclusions as to the cost of the order policy being tested. If a hand simulation is being conducted, 100 days would provide a better representation. If a computer is doing the calculations, 1,000 days would be helpful in reaching accurate cost estimates.[2]

Let's say that Simkin *does* complete a 1,000-day simulation of the above policy (order quantity = 10 drills, reorder point = 5 drills). Does this complete his analysis? The answer is no—this is just the beginning! Simkin must now compare *this* potential strategy to other possibilities. For example, what about order quantity = 10, reorder point = 4; or order quantity = 12, reorder point = 6; or order quantity = 14, reorder point = 5? Perhaps every combination of values of order quantity from 6 to 20 drills and reorder point from 3 to 10 should be simulated. After simulating all reasonable combinations of order quantities and reorder points, Simkin would likely select the pair yielding the lowest total inventory cost. Problem S5.4 gives you a chance to help Simkin begin this series of comparisons.

[2] Moreover, even with a 1,000-day simulation, the generated distribution should be compared with the desired distribution to ensure valid results.

THE ROLE OF COMPUTERS IN SIMULATION

Computers are critical in simulating complex tasks. They can generate random numbers, simulate thousands of time periods in a matter of seconds or minutes, and provide management with reports that make decision making easier. As a matter of fact, a computer approach is almost a necessity in order for us to draw valid conclusions from a simulation. Since we require a very large number of simulations, it would be a real burden to rely on pencil and paper alone.

Two types of computer programming languages are available to help this simulation process. The first, *general purpose languages,* includes FORTRAN, BASIC, COBOL, PL/1, and PASCAL. If you have taken an introductory computer course, you undoubtedly have been exposed to one or more of these.

Let us look now at the second type of programming languages available: *special purpose simulation languages.* These have been specially developed to handle simulation problems and have three advantages: (1) they require less programming time for large simulations, (2) they are usually more efficient and easier to check for errors, and (3) they have random number generators already built in as subroutines. The major special purpose languages are GPSS (*G*eneral *P*urpose *S*ystem *S*imulator, developed by IBM), SIMSCRIPT (created by the Rand Corporation), DYNAMO (developed at MIT), and GASP (*G*eneral *A*ctivity *S*imulation *P*ackage, also by IBM).

A sample of a microcomputer-based GPSS program is provided in Figure S5.3. It represents a queuing simulation in which customers arrive at a bank according to a known arrival pattern. If a teller is free, the deposit is made; if the teller is busy, the customer enters a queue. When the transaction is completed, the customer "gives up" the teller, and departs the simulation. Quite similar GPSS programs can be written to handle such diverse queuing analyses as waiting at a barber shop, buying a ticket at a theater, or receiving service at a repair facility.

Commercial, easy-to-use prewritten simulation programs are also available. Some are generalized to handle a wide variety of situations ranging from queuing

FIGURE S5.3

GPSS Language Sample Simulation for a Bank.
(*Source:* Minuteman Software, P.O. Box 171, Stowe, MA 01775.)

```
20      GENERATE        300,100,,,300       ;Create next customer.
30      QUEUE           TELLER              ;Begin queue time.
40      SEIZE           TELLER              ;Own or wait for teller.
50      DEPART          TELLER              ;End queue time.
60      ADVANCE         400,200             ;Bank deposit takes a few minutes.
65      TABULATE        LINETABLE           ;Record waiting line in histogram.
70      RELEASE         TELLER              ;Deposit done. Give up the teller.
80      TERMINATE       1                   ;Customer leaves the simulation.
90      START           50,,,1              ;
```

:**S5.8** Julia Walters owns and operates one of the largest Mercedes-Benz auto dealerships in Washington, D.C. In the past 36 months her sales of this luxury car have ranged from a low of 6 new cars to a high of 12 new cars, as reflected in the following table:

SALES OF NEW CARS/MONTH	FREQUENCY
6	3
7	4
8	6
9	12
10	9
11	1
12	1
	36 months

She believes that sales will continue during the next 24 months at about the same historical rates, and that delivery times will also continue to follow this pace (stated in probability form):

DELIVERY TIME (IN MONTHS)	PROBABILITY
1	.44
2	.33
3	.16
4	.07
	1.00

Walter's current policy is to order 14 cars at a time (two full truckloads, with 7 autos on each truck), and to place a new order whenever the stock on hand reaches 12 autos. What are the results of this policy when simulated over the next two years?

:**S5.9** Refer to Problem S5.8. Julia Walters establishes the following relevant costs: (1) the carrying cost per Mercedes per month is $600; (2) the cost of a lost sale averages $4,350; and (3) the cost of placing an order is $570. What is the total inventory cost of the policy simulated in Problem S5.8?

:**S5.10** Julia Walters (see Problems S5.8 and S5.9) wishes to try a new simulated policy, ordering 21 cars per order, with a reorder point of 10 autos. Which policy is better, this one or the one formulated in Problems S5.8 and S5.9?

:**S5.11** The Eichler Corporation is the nation's largest manufacturer of industrial-size washing machines. A main ingredient in the production process is 8-by10-foot sheets of stainless steel. The steel is used for both interior washer drums and outer casings.

Steel is purchased weekly on a contractual basis from the RTT Foundry, which, because of limited availability and lot sizing, can ship either 8,000 or 11,000 square feet of stainless steel each week. When Eichler's weekly order is placed, there is a 45% chance that 8,000 square feet will arrive and a 55% chance of receiving the larger-size order.

Eichler uses the stainless steel on a stochastic (nonconstant) basis. The probabilities of demand each week are:

STEEL NEEDED PER WEEK (SQ. FT.)	PROBABILITY
6,000	.05
7,000	.15
8,000	.20
9,000	.30
10,000	.20
11,000	.10

Eichler has a capacity to store no more than 25,000 square feet of steel at any time. Because of the contract, orders *must* be placed each week regardless of the on-hand supply.

a) Simulate stainless steel order arrivals and use for 20 weeks. (Begin the first week with a starting inventory of 0 stainless steel.) If an end-of-week inventory is ever negative, assume that "back orders" are permitted and fill the demand from the next arriving order.

b) Should Eichler add more storage area? If so, how much? If not, comment on the system.

: **S5.12** Dr. Elaine Ross practices dentistry in Orlando, Florida. Ross tries hard to schedule appointments so that patients do not have to wait beyond their appointed time. Her October 20 schedule is shown in the accompanying table.

SCHEDULED APPOINTMENT AND TIME		EXPECTED TIME NEEDED
Adams	9:30 A.M.	15
Brown	9:45 A.M.	20
Crawford	10:15 A.M.	15
Dannon	10:30 A.M.	10
Erving	10:45 A.M.	30
Fink	11:15 A.M.	15
Graham	11:30 A.M.	20
Hinkel	11:45 A.M.	15

Unfortunately, not every patient arrives exactly on schedule, and expected times to examine patients are just that, *expected*. Some examinations take longer than expected, while some take less time.

Ross's experience dictates the following:

a) 20% of the patients will be 20 minutes early;

b) 10% of the patients will be 10 minutes early;

c) 40% of the patients will be on time;

d) 25% of the patients will be 10 minutes late;

e) 5% of the patients will be 20 minutes late.

She further estimates that:

a) 15% of the time she will finish in 20% less time than expected;

b) 50% of the time she will finish in the expected time;

c) 25% of the time she will finish in 20% more time than expected;

d) 10% of the time she will finish in 40% more time than expected.

Dr. Ross has to leave at 12:15 P.M. on October 20 in order to catch a flight to a dental convention in New York. Assuming she is ready to start her workday at 9:30 A.M., and that patients are treated in order of their scheduled exam (even if one patient arrives after an early one), will she be able to make the flight? Comment on this simulation.

: **S5.13** Blacksburg, Virginia's General Hospital has an emergency room that is divided into six departments: (1) the initial exam station to treat minor problems or make diagnoses; (2) an x-ray department; (3) an operating room; (4) a cast-fitting room; (5) an observation room (for recovery and general observation before final diagnoses or release); and (6) an out-processing department (where clerks check patients out and arrange for payment or insurance forms).

The probabilities that a patient will go from one department to another are presented in the accompanying table.

a) Simulate the trail followed by 10 emergency room patients. Proceed, one patient at a time, from each one's entry at the initial exam station until he or she leaves through out-processing. You should be aware that a patient can enter the same department more than once.

b) Using your simulation data, what are the chances that a patient enters the x-ray department twice?

FROM	TO	PROBABILITY
Initial exam at	X-ray department	.45
emergency	Operating room	.15
room entrance	Observation room	.10
	Out-processing clerk	.30
X-ray department	Operating room	.10
	Cast-fitting room	.25
	Observation room	.35
	Out-processing clerk	.30
Operating room	Cast-fitting room	.25
	Observation room	.70
	Out-processing clerk	.05
Cast-fitting room	Observation room	.55
	X-ray department	.05
	Out-processing clerk	.40
Observation room	Operating room	.15
	X-ray department	.15
	Out-processing clerk	.70

: **S5.14** Management of the First Syracuse Bank is concerned over a loss of customers at its main office downtown. One solution that has been proposed is to add one or more "drive-through" teller stations to make it easier for customers in cars to obtain quick service without parking. Greg Bell, the bank president, thinks the bank should risk only the cost of installing one drive-through. He is informed by his staff that the cost (amortized over a 20-year period) of building a drive-through is $12,000 per year. It also costs $16,000 per year in wages and benefits to staff each new teller window.

The director of Management Analysis, Pat Walters, believes that the following two factors encourage the immediate construction of two drive-through stations, however. According to a recent article in *Banking Research* magazine, customers who wait in long lines for drive-through teller service will cost banks an average of $1.00 per minute, in loss of goodwill. Also, adding a second drive-through will cost an additional $16,000 in staffing, but amortized construction costs can be cut to a total of $20,000 per year if two drive-throughs are installed together, instead of one at a time. To complete her analysis, Mrs. Walters collected one month's worth of arrival and service rates at a competing downtown bank's drive-through stations. These data are shown below.

Interarrival Times for 1,000 Observations		Customer Service Time for 1,000 Customers	
TIME BETWEEN ARRIVALS (IN MINUTES)	NUMBER OF OCCURRENCES	SERVICE TIME (IN MINUTES)	NUMBER OF OCCURRENCES
1	200	1	100
2	250	2	150
3	300	3	350
4	150	4	150
5	100	5	150
		6	100

a) Simulate a one-hour time period, from 1 to 2 P.M., for a single-teller drive-through.

b) Simulate a one-hour time period, from 1 to 2 P.M., for a two-teller system.

c) Conduct a cost analysis of the two options. Assume the bank is open 7 hours per day and 200 days per year.

CASE STUDY

Biales Waste Disposal, GmbH

Biales Waste Disposal, GmbH, headquartered in the industrial city of Dusseldorf, Germany, operates seven specially constructed semitrailers and cabs for commercial long-distance hauling of radioactive waste materials. Each truck averages one completed load per week, picking up the radioactive containers from chemical companies and other manufacturers in central Europe. The loads are carefully driven to a government dump site near Dresden, which until the reunification was a manufacturing center in East Germany. Currently, pickups are made in eight countries: Italy, Germany, Austria, France, Belgium, Netherlands, Denmark, and Poland.

Biales maintains an office in the capital of each country that it serves. Staffing not only includes a manager and a secretary at each national office, but a part-time lobbyist/attorney to assist in the many political, cross-cultural, border, and legal issues that arise in the nuclear waste disposal industry.

Sybil Biales, owner of the firm, is seriously considering dropping Italy as a source of business. Last year, only 25 truckloads of wastes were handled there. Since textile manufacturers in northern Italy are the primary source of trucking for Biales, the size and revenues from their shipments will determine if it is profitable to retain an office and do business in that country.

To analyze the Italian market, Biales gathers data on last year's shipments and revenues. Each of the 25 trucks that were loaded in Italy last year carried between 26 and 50 barrels of waste. The income generated per barrel differed significantly (ranging from 50 to 80 German marks, or Dmarks) based on the type of radioactive material being loaded and the weight of the barrels to be shipped. (See the accompanying table for details.)

Biales decided that if she were to simulate 25 truckloads out of Italy she could determine if it would be profitable to continue to operate there next year. She estimates that each

CASE STUDY (Continued)

shipment to the Dresden dump site costs 900 Dmarks, including driver, gasoline, and truck expenses; other cargo and loading and unloading costs average 120 Dmarks per shipment. In addition, it costs 41,000 Dmarks per year to operate the Italian office. This includes salaries and indirect overhead costs that are allocated from the home office in Dusseldorf.

Discussion Question

1. Will the shipments in Italy next year generate enough revenues to cover Biales' costs there?

Biales' Italian Data

NUMBER OF BARRELS OF WASTE LOADED	NUMBER OF TIMES TRUCK CARRIED THIS SIZE LOAD LAST YEAR	REVENUE PER BARREL (Dmarks)	NUMBER OF TRIPS AT THIS REVENUE
26–30	3	50	5
31–35	4	60	11
36–40	6	70	7
41–45	9	80	2
46–50	3		
	25		25

CASE STUDY

Abjar Transport Company

In 1988, Samir Khaldoun, after receiving an MBA degree from a leading university in the United States, returned to Jeddah, Saudi Arabia, where his family has extensive business holdings. Samir's first assignment was to stabilize and develop a newly formed, family-owned transport company—Abjar Transport.

An immediate problem facing Samir was the determination of the number of trucks needed to handle the forecasted freight volume. Heretofore, trucks were added to the fleet on an "as needed" basis without comprehensive capacity planning. This approach created problems of driver recruitment, truck service and maintenance, and excessive demurrage because of delays at unloading docks and retention of cargo containers.

Demurrage penalties are quite high for the Jeddah Islamic port. The following is a demurrage schedule for unloaded freight:

1. A ten-day "free period" is allowed to clear the dock of freight.

2. After the "free period," a penalty of one riyal[1] will be levied per cargo ton for the first 24 hours. A penalty of two riyals per cargo ton will be assessed for the second 24 hours; a penalty of three riyals per cargo ton will be levied for the third 24 hours; and so forth.

[1]Approximately three riyals equal one U.S. dollar.

As one can see from this schedule, high demurrage penalties will be assessed if freight is unduly delayed at the Jeddah dock.

Samir forecasts that Abjar's freight volume should average 160,000 tons per month with a standard deviation of 30,000 tons. Freight is unloaded on a uniform basis throughout the month. Based on past experience, the amount handled per month is assumed to be normally distributed.

After extensive investigation, Samir concluded that the fleet should be standardized to 40-foot Mercedes 2624 2 × 4 tractor-trailer rigs, which are suitable for carrying two 20-foot containers, one 30-foot container, or one 40-foot container. Cargo capacity is approximately 60 tons per rig. Each tractor-trailer unit is estimated to cost 240,000 riyals. Moreover, they must meet Saudi Arabian specifications—double cooling fans, oversized radiators, and special high-temperature tires. Historical evidence suggests that these Mercedes rigs will operate 96 percent of the time.

Approximately 25 percent of the freight handled by these tractor-trailer rigs is containerized in container lengths of 20, 30, and 40 feet. (The balance of the freight—75 percent—is not containerized.) The 20-foot containers hold approximately 20 tons of cargo; the 30-foot containers hold 45 tons; and the 40-foot containers hold 60 tons of freight. Approximately 60 percent of the containerized freight is shipped in 40-foot units; 20 percent is shipped in 30-foot

CASE STUDY   (Continued)

units; and 20 percent is transported in 20-foot units. The demurrage schedule for containers is as follows:

1. A five-day "free period" is allowed to return containers to the port.

2. After the "free period" a penalty of 1,000 riyals is levied per container for the first 24 hours. A penalty of 2,000 riyals is assessed per container for the second 24 hours. A penalty of 3,000 riyals per container is assessed for the third 24 hours, and so forth.

Abjar Transport picks up freight at the dock and delivers it directly to customers, or warehouses it for later delivery. Based on his study of truck routing and scheduling patterns, Samir concluded that each rig should pick up freight at the dock three times each day.

An analysis of financial statements reveals that the profit and overhead contribution of each ton of freight handled is 2.25 riyals. The Khaldoun family has estimated that its opportunity cost for investment capital is 20 percent.

Discussion Question

1. How many tractor-trailer rigs should make up the Abjar Transport fleet?

Source: Cases and Readings in Management Service by B. Render, R. Stair and I. Greenberg, Allyn & Bacon, Boston, 1988.

BIBLIOGRAPHY

Chung, K. H. "Computer Simulation of a Queuing System." *Production and Inventory Management,* **10,** 1 (1969): 75–82.

Cooper, K. G. "Naval Ship Production: A Claim Settled and a Framework Built." *Interfaces,* **10,** 6 (December 1980): 20–30.

Ernshoff, J. R., and R. L. Sisson. *Computer Simulation Models.* New York: Macmillan Co., 1970.

Fillmer, J. L., and J. Mellichamp. "Simulation: An Operational Planning Device for the Bell System." *Interfaces,* **12,** 3 (June 1982): 54–59.

Flowers, A. D., and J. R. Cole. "An Application of Computer Simulation to Quality Control in Manufacturing." *IIE Transactions,* **17,** 3 (September 1985): 277–283.

Ginter, P. M., and A. C. Ricks. "Strategic Models and Simulations: An Emerging Decision-Making Aid." *Journal of Systems Management,* **35** (June 1984): 12–16.

Gordon, G. *System Simulation.* Englewood Cliffs, NJ: Prentice-Hall, 1969.

Halder, S. W., and J. Banks. "Simulation Software Products for Analyzing Manufacturing Systems." *Industrial Engineering* (July 1986): 98–103.

Hannan, E. L., and L. A. Smith. "A Simulation of the Effects of Alternative Rule System for Jai Alai." *Decision Sciences,* **12** (1981): 75–84.

Heizer, J. H., and A. P. de la Garza. "Using Simulation to Evaluate Airplane Dealership Operations." *Airport Services Management,* **16,** 6 (June 1976): 30–32.

Johnson, A. P., and V. M. Fernandes. "Simulation of the Number of Spare Engines Required for an Aircraft Fleet." *Journal of the Operational Research Society,* **29,** 1 (1978): 33–36.

Kaplan, A., and S. Frazza. "Empirical Inventory Simulation: A Case Study." *Decision Sciences,* **14** (January 1983): 62–75.

Kelton, W. D. "Statistical Analysis Methods Enhance Usefulness, Reliability of Simulation Models." *Industrial Engineering* (September 1986): 74–84.

Lambo, E. "The Use of Simulation Models to Improve Health Institutions in Nigeria." *Interfaces,* **13,** 3 (June 1983): 29–35.

Law, A. M. "Introduction to Simulation." *Industrial Engineering* (May 1986): 46–63.

Law, A. M., and M. G. McComas. "How Simulation Pays Off." *Manufacturing Engineering* (February 1988): 37–39.

Matta, K. F. "A Simulation Model for Repairable Items/ Spare Parts Inventory Systems." *Computers and Operations Research,* **12,** 4 (1985): 395–409.

Mize, J. H., and J. G. Cox. *Essentials of Simulation.* Englewood Cliffs, NJ: Prentice-Hall, 1968.

Morrow, J. "Simulation Helps C&P." *Interfaces,* **12** (June 1982): 58–61.

Naylor, T. H., J. L. Balintfy, D. S. Burdick, and K. Chu. *Computer Simulation Techniques.* New York: John Wiley & Sons, 1966.

Render, B., R. M. Stair, and I. Greenberg. *Cases and Readings in Management Science,* 2nd ed. Boston: Allyn & Bacon, Inc., 1990.

Render, B., and R. M. Stair. *Introduction to Management Science.* Boston: Allyn & Bacon, 1992.

Render, B., and R. M. Stair. *Quantitative Analysis for Management,* 4th ed. Boston: Allyn & Bacon, 1991.

Russell, R. A., and R. Hickle. "Simulation of a CD Portfolio." *Interfaces,* **16,** 3 (May–June 1986): 49–54.

Ruth, R. J., L. Wyszewianski, and G. Herline. "Kidney Transplantation: A Simulation Model for Examining Demand and Supply." *Management Science,* **31,** 5 (May 1985): 515–525.

Shannon, R. E. *Systems Simulation: The Art and Science.* Englewood Cliffs, NJ: Prentice-Hall, 1975.

Solomon, S. L. *Simulation of Waiting Lines.* Englewood Cliffs, NJ: Prentice-Hall, 1983.

Stein, K. J. "Simulation Techniques Converging to Meet Military, Commercial Needs." *Aviation Week & Space Technology* (March 18, 1985): 239.

Trunk, C. "Simulation for Success in the Automated Factory." *Material Handling Engineering* (May 1989): 64–76.

Wagner, T. "Discrete Simulation Modeling for Corporate Manpower Planning." *Omega* (May–June 1985): 201–210.

Watson, H. J. *Computer Simulation in Business.* New York: John Wiley & Sons, 1981.

Welch, N., and J. Gussow. "Expansion of Canadian National Railway's Line Capacity." *Interfaces,* **16,** 1 (January–February 1986): 51–64.

Yuang, P. Y., P. Philipoom, and L. P. Rees. "Q-Gert vs. GPSS." *Journal of Systems Management* (August 1983): 36–41.

PART THREE

Strategic Decisions in P/OM

Strategic decisions are major decisions that are fundamental to the performance of an organization. They are also expensive and not easily modified; consequently these decisions have long-term implications for an organization's competitive position. The six strategic decisions identified in this text are product, process, location, layout, human resources, and procurement and JIT.

Product Strategy

Product Design Provides Competitive Advantage at Maytag

The Maytag image is built on quality. *Consumer Reports* has rated Maytag tops in dependability for the past 26 years, far outdistancing its competitors. Maytag has turned its reputation for reliability into profits, including a 27% average return on equity over the past five years. Consumers typically pay a premium of as much as 20% over the competition for a Maytag washing machine. The Maytag Company has fed the profits from their reliable washing machines to the parent company, Maytag Corporation, where they have been invested in refrigerators, dishwashers,

The new washer transmission designed by Maytag can switch from slow reciprocal motion of the agitator shaft during the wash cycle to fast rotary motion of the wash tub during the wring cycle. During the wring cycle, a clutch locks the gears so the entire transmission spins. Here, Maytag's V.P. of Research John Mellinger displays the transmission.

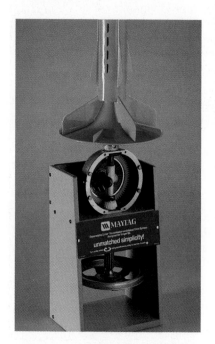

The new design using only 40 pieces is more reliable. The reduction in parts means a substantial reduction in cost with fewer designs and purchases, as well as less inventory and manufacturing expense.

and microwave ovens. These brands now include Magic Chef, Admiral, and Norge.

Most people never see a washing machine transmission, but the transmission is its heart; it is the transmission that turns the agitator (that cone-shaped piece of hard plastic that sits inside the tub). The transmission is a major part of the reason for Maytag's quality reputation. What made the old transmission so reliable was its simplicity. It had three gears and a handful of pulleys, arms, and pinion assemblies—a total of about 65 parts, radically fewer than its predecessors or competitors.

Maytag has introduced a new transmission, which is down to a single gear reduction instead of three—a total of about 40 parts. Inside the gear case, a Y-shaped yoke converts the rotary motion of a single gear into back-and-forth motion of the agitator.

Transmission redesign also required redesign of the agitator, necessary because the new agitator swishes to-and-fro at 153 strokes a minute instead of the old 64 strokes a minute. The added speed increased the chance the clothes will snag and tear, so the product design group downsized the agitator to protect fabrics.

Since the new transmission uses fewer parts, Maytag's manufacturing costs are reduced. In addition, the new machine can be assembled in an automated factory. The old transmission was assembled by hand.

The assembly line, which took two years to design and build, includes automated vision systems to check to see that seals are applied properly and that oil is correctly dispensed.

The new transmission went through the wringer, undergoing Maytag's simulated 20-year test. Test machines filled with heavy towels were run for over 1,800 hours. The design was then test-marketed in Chicago on 25,000 machines; of those only 40 failed. None of the failures were from a design flaw in the new transmission.

After each housing is cast, the transmission passes through the Gardner grinder, which smooths any rough edges; it is not touched again by human hands until the transmission reaches the automatic assembly line for installation into the washing machine. The assembly line consists

After-sale service and reliability are part of the design team's task. The new Maytag transmission comes with a ten-year warranty, which is twice as long as the warranty on previous machines, but on-site service, when it is necessary, will be easier. Instead of taking the entire machine apart from the top, the Maytag repairman now removes the machine's front panel and unscrews the gear-case cover to diagnose the problem.

Product design provides competitive advantage at Maytag.

Adapted from:
"Wake Up, Maytag Man!" *Forbes* (Nov. 13, 1989): 308–310.

A vision system located at one of the final assembly points is used to ensure that the sealant, a liquid gasket material, is a continuous bead on the housing and at the correct width.

INTRODUCTION

In Chapter 2 we identified six strategic or long-run decisions of operations management. They are:

1. product strategy;
2. process strategy;
3. location strategy;
4. layout strategy;
5. human resource strategy;
6. procurement and just-in-time strategies.

In this chapter we will discuss the first of these, product strategy.

Product strategy

Product strategy is the selection, definition, and design of products. Products and services are as diverse as a manufactured GE toaster, an appendectomy, a Colonel Sanders' chicken nugget dish, or a bank's IRA account service. The objective of a *product strategy* is to ensure a competitive advantage for the product.

Product success and a competitive advantage are more likely with the use of a product development team. And the production function itself should have available the necessary:

1. managerial ability;
2. technological skills;
3. financial resources;
4. human resources.

When these abilities, skills, and resources do not support a product with a competitive advantage, the product should probably not be produced or offered. Product selection and design decisions should involve the entire organization, because they affect the entire organization.

Changing a strategic product commitment can be a lengthy and expensive process. In this chapter we look at efficiently performing product selection, development, and documentation. Moving a product from idea to market can be critical to organizational success.

PRODUCT SELECTION

Product Options

Management has options in the selection, definition, and design of products. Product selection is choosing the product or service to provide customers or clients. For instance, hospitals specialize in various types of patients and various types of medical procedures. They select their product when they decide what kind of hospital to be. A hospital's management may decide to operate a general purpose hospital, a maternity hospital, or, as in the case of Shouldice, a hospital specializing in hernias (see the *POM in Action* box, "A Canadian Hospital Does Brisk Business in Rupture Repairs"). Numerous other options exist for hospitals, just as they exist for McDonald's or General Motors.

POM _in action_

A Canadian Hospital Does Brisk Business in Rupture Repairs

Taking off a weekend to undergo major surgical repair of a hernia, Arthur J. Remillard, Jr., of Thornhill, Ontario, strolled in and walked gently out of the operating room. He later that day joined some fellow patients in a game of billiards. The following Monday morning, he was back to his job.

The above scenario is characteristic of the 6,000 hernias repaired yearly at Shouldice Hospital. Shouldice, an 88-bed institution with a staff of eight surgeons, is probably the only hospital in the world that treats exclusively hernias.

Undoubtedly, Shouldice has become the best service expert of the hospital business because of the techniques developed in its unusual specialty. Other hospitals may require a seven-day stay for hernia repair, but Shouldice discharges its patients only 72 hours after surgery. As one would expect, the cost at Shouldice is less than a third of the cost at a large Toronto hospital.

Using a local anesthetic shortens recovery time and reduces the risks of postoperative complications. It also enables patients to enter and leave the operating room under their own power.

Because of the hospital's policy of "early ambulation," patients get back on their feet and out of the hospital as soon as possible. In contrast, large hospitals wheel patients in and out of the operating arenas and confine them to bed for several days.

At Shouldice, the accomodations are functional, motel-like rooms that are without telephones and television sets. All meals are served in a communal dining hall. The incision is not jeopardized because the Shouldice surgeons repair the hernia by overlapping the three layers of muscle in the abdominal wall with continuous stitches of stainless steel wire.

Shouldice proudly claims their annual rate of hernia recurrence is a mere 1% as compared to the average recurrence rate for the condition of 10%.

Sources: Health Industry Total, **55,** 1, January 1992; and _The Wall Street Journal_, February 7, 1978.

Product decisions are fundamental and have implications for all of the other P/OM decisions. The strategy implications are substantial and pervasive. The example below indicates the implications of a rather minor part substitution.

An appliance maker found that it could extend the life of a product and save $1.75 per unit in warranty costs by substituting a newly designed part. Against expectation, it turned out that the new part would add more than $2 to the cost of each unit—hardly an attractive proposition, operationally speaking. But on strategic grounds the move still made excellent sense. By sparing the end user cost and inconvenience over the product's lifetime, it would strengthen the company's sales message and increase the product's value in the customer's eye. Management's decision to go ahead has since been rewarded by a hefty gain in market share.[1]

---

[1] Reprinted by permission of the _Harvard Business Review._ Excerpts from "Breakthrough Manufacturing," by Elizabeth A. Hass (March/April 1987). Copyright © 1987 by the President and Fellows of Harvard College; all rights reserved.

Generation of New Product Opportunities

Product selection, definition, and design take place on a continuing basis because so many new product opportunities exist.[2] Five factors influencing market opportunities are:

1. *Economic change,* which brings increasing levels of affluence in the long run but causes economic cycles and price changes in the short run. For instance, in the long run, more and more people can afford an automobile, but in the short run a change in fuel prices may alter the demand for automobiles.

2. *Sociological and demographic change,* which may appear in such factors as decreasing family size. This alters the size preference for homes, apartments, and automobiles.

3. *Technological change,* which makes possible everything from home computers to mobile phones to artificial hearts.

4. *Political change,* which brings about new trade agreements, tariffs, and government contract requirements.

5. Other changes, which may be brought about through *market practice, professional standards, suppliers,* and *distributors.*

Operations managers must be aware of these factors and be able to anticipate changes in products, product volume, and product mix.

Product Life

Products are born; they live, and they die. They are cast aside by a changing society. It may be helpful to think of a product's life as divided into four phases as we did in Chapters 2 and 4. Those phases were introduction, growth, maturity, and decline.

FIGURE 6.1

Product Life Cycle.

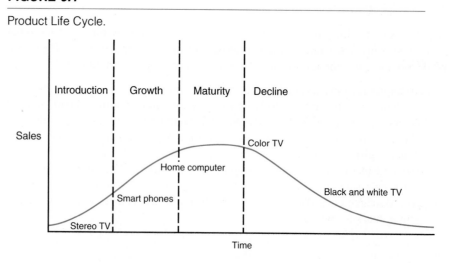

---

[2] See for instance an interesting article by Tom Peters, "All Markets Are Now Immature," *Industry Week* (July 3, 1989): 14–16.

FIGURE 6.2

Estimated World Sales of Dynamic Random Access Memory.

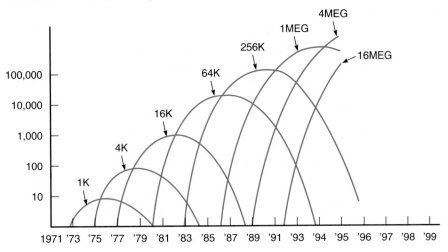

The general phases of product life cycle are depicted in Figure 6.1. That figure also reveals the relative positions of five products: stereo TVs, "smart" phones, home computers, color TVs, and black-and-white TVs. A specific case that shows the growth, maturity, and decline of shipments of dynamic random access memory, known as DRAM chips, is shown in Figure 6.2.

The relationship of product sales, related cost, and profit over the life cycle of a product are shown in Figure 6.3. Note that typically a firm has a negative cash flow while it develops a product. When the product is successful, those losses may be recovered. Eventually the successful product may yield a profit prior to its decline. However, the profit is fleeting.

FIGURE 6.3

Product Life Cycle, Sales, Cost, and Profit.

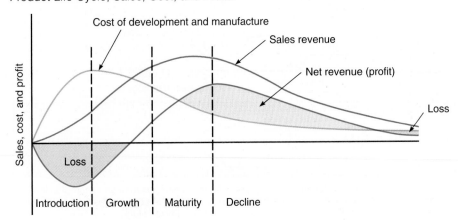

Product life cycles may be a matter of a few hours (a newspaper), months (seasonal fashions), years (Betamax video recorders), or decades (Volkswagen Beetle). Regardless of the length of the cycle, the task for the operations manager is the same: to design a system that helps introduce new products successfully. If the operations function cannot perform effectively at this stage, the firm may be saddled with losers—products that cannot be produced efficiently and perhaps not at all.

An organization cannot survive without introducing new products. Older products are maturing and others in periods of decline must be replaced. This requires a constant successful introduction of new products and active participation by the operations manager. Successful firms have learned how to turn opportunities into successful products.

Figure 6.4 shows product ideas going through seven stages, starting with ideas and ending with the introduction of a new product. How well this process is managed may well determine not only product success but also the firm's future. Product development emphasis can be external (market driven) or internal (technology and innovation driven) or a combination. Outstanding organizations find the best combination.

In spite of efforts to introduce new products, many do not succeed. Consequently, product selection, definition, and design occur frequently. It is estimated that only one out of twenty-five products introduced actually succeeds! However, many more products go through product development, final production design, and preliminary stages of production, but are not introduced. This means that the number

FIGURE 6.4

Product Development Stages.

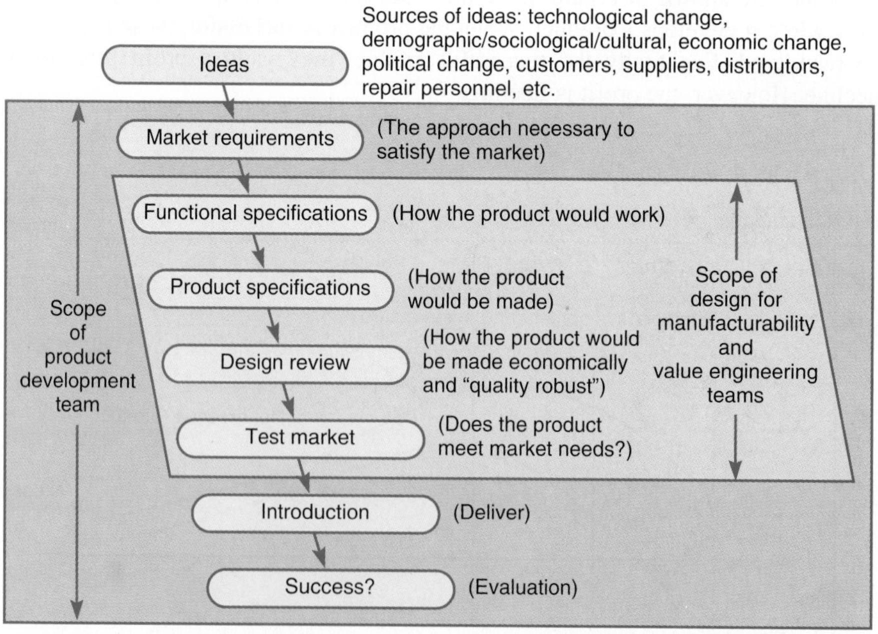

Product concepts are developed from a variety of sources, both external and internal to the firm. Concepts that survive the product idea stage progress through various stages with nearly constant review in a highly participative environment to minimize failure.

FIGURE 6.5

Product Development Yields Few Successes.

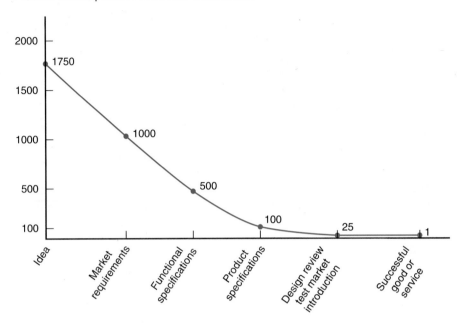

of products that must be reviewed for production and, in some cases, actually produced can be substantial, perhaps as many as 500 for each financially successful product. The relative number of products surviving a given development state is shown in Figure 6.5. Production managers and their organizations must be able to accommodate this volume of new product ideas while maintaining activities to which they are already committed.[3]

Time-Based Competition

Product life cycles are becoming shorter. This increases the importance of product development. Therefore, faster developers of new products continually gain on slower developers[4] and obtain a competitive advantage. This concept is called **time-based competition.**

Recent work done by Kim Clark has indicated that Japanese auto manufacturers are designing and introducing cars at about twice the rate of American manufacturers.[5] This gives the faster developer a number of advantages. Those who can

Time-based competition

[3] See a discussion of this issue in Rosabeth Moss Kanter, "Swimming in New Streams: Mastering Innovation Dilemmas," *California Management Review,* **31,** 4 (Summer 1989): 45–69.

[4] See related discussion in George Stalk, Jr., "Time—The Next Source of Competitive Advantage," *Harvard Business Review* (July–August 1988): 41–51; Joseph Blackburn, *Time-Based Competition: The Next Battleground in American Manufacturing* (Homewood, IL: Irwin/Business One, 1990); "Manufacturing: About Time," *Economist* (April 11, 1990): 72.

[5] Kim Clark, as reported in James P. Womack, Daniel T. Jones, and Daniel Roos, *The Machine That Changed the World* (New York: Rawson Associates, 1990), p. 111.

POM *in action*

Developing a Successful New Printer at Hewlett-Packard

Hewlett-Packard needed a blockbuster product in the mid-1980s. Research had shown that personal computer users wanted a new printer on the market. It could be relatively slow, but it had to print as clearly as a laser model and sell for under $1,000, less than half the going price for a laser. A team of researchers, engineers, and marketing experts met in late 1985 to study the possibilities.

In its first step, the team defined exactly what customers needed and examined the shortcomings of existing low-cost printers. Still in the conceptualizing phase, product engineers were brought in to confirm that Hewlett-Packard could produce the printer and print head. The team then, as a second step, submitted a plan of action. Management quickly stamped its approval.

Now the team had to design a prototype that could be tested: it had to meet performance, reliability, cost, and manufacturability goals. Hewlett-Packard started with an assembly of components, handwired to printed circuit boards, to represent the technical core of the printer. As soon as the prototype proved feasible and on-target for market needs, the project team was enlarged. Specialists in mechanical design, control software, and parts sourcing were added to help produce several working prototypes. These models were assembled complete with cabinets, software, panel, and paper-handlers, and handed to consumers to try out. Based on this trial, print quality still had to be improved, but the DeskJet was ready for production.

Just 26 months after Hewlett-Packard first explored the idea, the DeskJet printer was launched. It was an immediate success.

Sources: Harvard Business Review, May–June 1990, p. 156; and *Info World,* **10,** 26, June 27, 1988, pp. 58–59.

---

introduce products faster can use more recent technology. Additionally, those who introduce products faster gain experience in the numerous issues inherent in design, test, manufacture, and introduction of new products. Those who develop products faster are learning faster. Faster product introduction has a cumulative and positive effect not only in the marketplace but also on innovative design, quality improvements, and cost reduction. As an example, see the *POM in Action* box describing Hewlett-Packard's new printer introduction.

PRODUCT DEVELOPMENT

The best product development approach seems to be a formal team approach. Such teams are known variously as Product Development Teams, Design for Manufacturability Teams, and Value Engineering Teams. The Japanese bypass the team issue by not subdividing their organization into research and development, engineering, production, and so forth. Consistent with the Japanese style of group effort and teamwork, these activities are all in one organization. The Japanese culture and management style is more collegial and the organization less structured than in most Western countries. Therefore, they find it unnecessary to have "teams" provide the necessary communication and coordination. However, the typical West-

TABLE 6.1 Product Development Performance by Regional Auto Industries.

	JAPANESE PRODUCERS	EUROPEAN VOLUME PRODUCERS	AMERICAN PRODUCERS
Average Engineering Hours per New Car (millions)	1.7	2.9	3.1
Average Development Time per New Car (in months)	46.2	57.3	60.4
Number of Employees in Project Team	485.0	904.0	903.0
Number of Body Types per New Car	2.3	2.7	1.7
Average Ratio of Shared Parts	18%	28%	38%
Ratio of Delayed Products	1 in 6	1 in 3	1 in 2
Time from Production Start to First Sale (months)	1.0	2.0	4.0
Return to Normal Productivity After New Model (months)	4.0	12.0	5.0
Return to Normal Quality After New Model (months)	1.4	12.0	11.0

Source: Adapted from James P. Womack, Daniel T. Jones, and Daniel Roos, *The Machine That Changed the World,* Maxwell Macmillan International, New York, 1990, p. 118. Data is representative of performance in the mid-1980s. Hopefully, the world auto industry is becoming more competitive.

ern style and the conventional wisdom is to use teams. Successful product development teams typically have:

1. support of top management;
2. qualified, experienced leadership with decision-making authority;
3. formal organization of the group or team;
4. training programs to teach the skills and techniques of product development;
5. a diverse, cooperative team;
6. adequate staffing, funding, and vendor assistance.

Just how much difference *management* makes in product development is shown in Table 6.1.

Product Development Teams

Product development teams are charged with the responsibility of moving from market requirements for a product to achieving a product success. (Refer back to Figure 6.4.) Such teams often include marketing, manufacturing, purchasing, quality assurance, and field service personnel. Many teams also include representatives from vendors. Regardless of the formal nature of the product development effort, research suggests that success is more likely to occur in an open, highly participative environment where those with potential contributions are allowed to make them.

At 3M, one of the leaders in product innovation, employees from various disciplines work together in teams to design new products. Here employees are developing a new respirator.

Product development teams

**Design for
manufacturability and
value engineering teams**

Design for Manufacturability and Value Engineering Teams

The objective of a product development team is to make the product or service a success. This includes marketability, manufacturability, and serviceability. **Design for manufacturability and value engineering teams,** on the other hand, have a somewhat narrower charge. They are charged with improvement of designs and specifications at the research, development, design, and production stages of product development.

Advantages. In addition to immediate, obvious cost reduction, design for manufacturability and value engineering may produce other benefits. These include:

1. reduced complexity of the product;
2. additional standardization of components;
3. improvement of functional aspects of the products;
4. improved job design;
5. improved job safety;
6. improved maintainability (serviceability) of the product;
7. quality robust design.

Quality robust design means that the product is designed so that small variations in production or assembly do not adversely affect the product. For instance, AT&T recently developed an integrated circuit that could be used in many products to amplify voice signals. As originally designed, the circuit had to be manufactured very precisely to avoid variations in the strength of the signal. Such a circuit would have been costly to make because of stringent quality controls needed during the manufacturing process. But AT&T's engineers, after testing and analyzing the design, realized that if the resistance of the circuit were reduced—a minor change with

FIGURE 6.6
_____

Cost Reduction Is Possible via Value Engineering and Value Analysis.

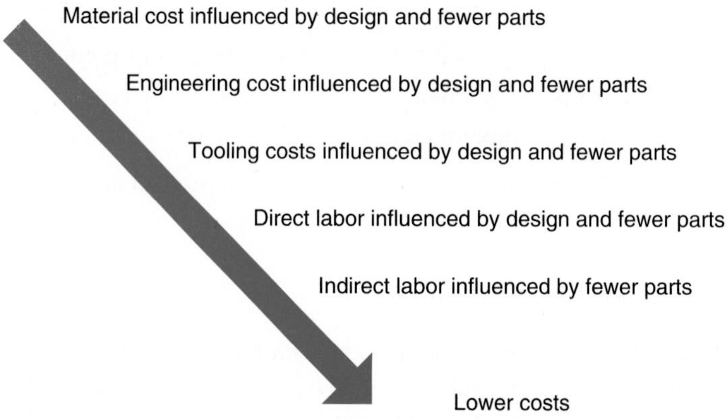

Material cost influenced by design and fewer parts

Engineering cost influenced by design and fewer parts

Tooling costs influenced by design and fewer parts

Direct labor influenced by design and fewer parts

Indirect labor influenced by fewer parts

Lower costs

Value engineering and value analysis reduce the resources needed for a given output; value engineering and value analysis enhance productivity

FIGURE 6.7

Cost Reduction of a Bracket via Value Engineering and Value Analysis.
(*Source:* Robert Goodell Brown, *Management Decisions for Production Operations,* Hinsdale, IL: The Dryden Press, Inc., 1971, p. 353.)

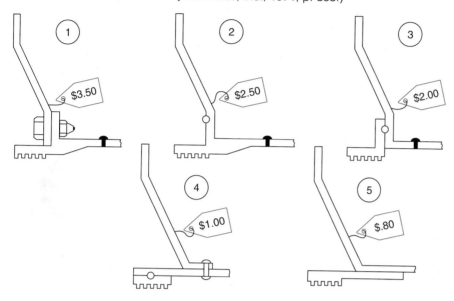

no associated costs—the circuit would be far less sensitive to manufacturing variations. The result was a 40% improvement in quality.[6]

Product development teams, design for manufacturability teams, and value engineering teams may be the best cost-avoidance technique available to operations management. They yield value improvement by defining the essential function(s) of the item and by achieving that function without lowering quality. Value engineering programs, when effectively managed, typically reduce cost between 15% and 70% without reducing quality. Some studies have indicated that for every dollar spent on value engineering, $10 to $25 in savings can be realized!

The impact that product design has on virtually all aspects of operating expense is illustrated in Figure 6.6. Figure 6.6 is a vivid representation of the need for comprehensive, thorough evaluation of the product's design prior to a commitment to produce. The cost reduction achieved for a specific bracket via value engineering is shown in Figure 6.7.

The success of the team approach at NCR corporation is indicated in their new 2760 electronic cash register. The cash register goes together with no screws or bolts. The entire terminal consists of just fifteen vendor produced components. The number of parts has been reduced by 85%, the number of suppliers by 65%, and the time to assemble by 25%.

Value Analysis

Value engineering takes place when the product is selected and designed. The corollary technique, **value analysis,** however, takes place during the production process when it is clear that a new product is a success. Improvement leads to either a better product or a product made more economically. The techniques and advantages for value analysis are the same as for value engineering, although minor

Value analysis

[6] John Mayo, "Process Design as Important as Product Design," *Wall Street Journal* (October 29, 1984): 32.

changes in implementation may be necessary because analysis is taking place while the product is being produced.

Potential Problems. When those originally charged with design of the product think they are being second-guessed by the value analysis team (who may be operating without the original pressures that existed at the time of the original design), resentment may develop. This problem can be overcome by including those people who designed the product as a part of the value analysis team and by developing an attitude that "all products can be improved." A second problem may be that insufficient time is available to incorporate the changes into the product or process because of continuing pressure to produce the product.

A manufacturer may spend millions of dollars on research and development to get a new product to market. With many products, the first company into production may have its product adopted for use in a variety of applications that will generate sales for years. It may become the "standard." Consequently, there is often more concern with getting the product to market than with product design or process efficiency. Rapid introduction to the market may be good management because until competition begins to introduce copies or improved versions, the product can sometimes be priced high enough to earn a return even using somewhat inefficient production design and methods. This emphasis on rapid introduction of a product does put pressure on the product development effort but is not, in the final analysis, an excuse for performing the task poorly.

Operations Strategy Influenced by Product Life Cycle

Just as operations managers must be prepared to develop new products, they must also be prepared to strengthen the existing product line. Products should be periodically examined to see where they are in the product life cycle and to see if they need enhancement or modification. A successful product strategy requires deciding the action to take with regard to each product. *Different strategies are appropriate as the product's position in its life cycle changes.* A firm, therefore, identifies products or families of products and their position in the life cycle. The manager may be able to determine the stage in the product life cycle by plotting revenues or units and noting the slope of the curve.

First, let us consider those products that are in an *introductory phase* of their life cycle; they may warrant unusual expenditures for (1) research, (2) product development, (3) process modification and enhancement,[7] and (4) supplier development. A product in the introductory stage may require such effort because it is still being "fine-tuned" for the market, as are the techniques (process) by which it is produced. For example, when video cassette recorders (VCRs) were first introduced, the features desired by the public were still being determined. By the same token production managers were still groping for the best manufacturing techniques.

The second phase of the life cycle is the *growth phase.* Here product design begins to stabilize. In this phase, effective forecasting of required capacity is necessary. Procurement of additional capacity or enhancement of existing capacity to accommodate the increase in product demand may be necessary.

The third phase is one of *product maturity.* By the third phase, competitors have

---

[7] See the discussion of process selection in Chapter 7.

entered the market, so high-volume production with reduced innovation may be appropriate. Improved cost control, reduction in options, and a paring down of the product line may be effective or necessary to profitability and market share.

The final phase is one of *product decline*. Here management may need to be ruthless in identifying those products whose life cycle is at an end. Unless dying products make some unique contribution to the firm or its product line or can be sold with an unusually high contribution to the firm's profit, their production should be terminated.[8] Dying products are typically poor products in which to invest resources and managerial talent.

Altering product strategies as the product moves through the product life cycle was also discussed in Chapter 2 (see particularly Figure 2.6).

Product-by-Value

The effective operations manager directs efforts toward reducing costs and improving contributions to those items that show the greatest promise. This is the Pareto principle applied to product mix. Resources are invested in the critical few and not the trivial many. **Product-by-value analysis** lists products in descending order of their individual dollar contribution to the firm. Product-by-value analysis also lists the *total annual* dollar contribution of the product. Low contribution on a per unit basis by a particular product may look substantially different if it represents a large portion of the company's sales.

Product-by-value analysis

A product-by-value report allows management to evaluate possible strategies for each product. These might include increasing cash flow (for example, increasing contribution by raising selling price or lowering cost), increasing market penetration (for example, improving quality and/or reducing cost or price), or reducing costs (for example, improving the production process). The report may also tell management which product offerings should be eliminated and which fail to justify further investment in research and development or capital equipment. The report focuses management's attention on strategic opportunities for each product.

DEFINING AND DOCUMENTING THE PRODUCT

Once new products or services are selected for introduction, they must be defined. First, a product or service is defined in terms of its functions, that is, what it is to do. The product is then designed; that is, it is determined how the functions are to be achieved. Management typically has a variety of options as to how a product is to achieve its functional purpose. For instance, when producing an alarm clock, aspects of design such as the color, size, or location of buttons may make substantial differences in ease of manufacture, quality, and market acceptance.

Rigorous specifications of a product are necessary to assure efficient production. Equipment, layout, and human resources cannot be decided upon until the product is defined, designed, and documented. Therefore every organization needs documents to define its products. This is true of everything from meat patties, to cheese, to computers, to a medical procedure. In the case of cheese a written specification is typical. Indeed, written specifications or standard grades typically

---

[8] Contribution is defined as the difference between direct cost and selling price. Direct costs are labor and material that go into the product.

POM _in action_

A French-Fry Diary: From Idaho Furrow to Golden Arches

McDonald's, one of the giants in the fast-food industry, approaches their french fry preparation with an obsession—and lavishes great attention on this popular side order. A strip of potato must meet at least 60 specifications before its approval for consumption. Interstate 47 is the name of their very special blend of frying oil.

The russet Burbank, more commonly known as the Idaho, is the potato of choice at McDonald's. Bill Atchley, an executive of McDonald's, explains that all potatoes are not alike and the russet Burbank potato has a distinctive taste and a higher ratio of solids to water, which makes for crispier fries.

The J. R. Simplot potato factory in Caldwell, Idaho, is responsible for processing a good portion of the billion potatoes McDonald's uses each year, as well as preparing potatoes for other companies. Workers on the assembly line scrupulously inspect the potatoes and carefully pluck out any that are undesirable. Like the others, those going to McDonald's are chopped, prefried, and frozen.

However, for McDonald's, preparation is different. While other fries are quick-scalded in water, McDonald's steams their potatoes because McDonald's believes the water removes nutrients and flavor. The fries are then prefried and dried. The time and heat elements are covered by patent.

In lieu of dipping in sugar as other fries are, Mac fries are sprayed. This process causes the fries to brown evenly and appear more natural.

The length of the fry is also given careful consideration. McDonald's relentlessly insists upon 40% of all fries being between two and three inches long; another 40% must be over three inches. A few stubby ones constitute the final 20%.

Sources: Marketing and Media Decisions, March 1989, pp. 47–49; _The Wall Street Journal,_ February 8, 1982; and _Packaging,_ April 1989, pp. 52–57.

---

exist and provide the definition for many products. For instance, Monterey Jack cheese has a written description that specifies the characteristics necessary for each Department of Agriculture grade. A portion of the Department of Agriculture grade for Monterey Jack Grade AA is shown in Figure 6.8. Similarly, McDonald's Corp. has 60 specifications for potatoes that are to be made into McDonald's french fries (see the _POM in Action_ box).

Engineering drawing

In the case of an airplane, as in most manufactured items, a component is typically defined by a drawing, usually referred to as an engineering drawing. An **engineering drawing** shows the dimensions, tolerances, materials, and finishes of a component. The engineering drawing will be an item on a bill-of-material. An engineering drawing is shown in Figure 6.9 and a bill-of-material for a manufactured item is shown in Figure 6.10(a). The **bill-of-material** lists the components, their description, and the quantity of each required to make one unit of a product. A bill-of-material is often referred to as a B-O-M. An engineering drawing shows how to make one item on the bill-of-material. A correction or modification of an engineering drawing is known as an **engineering change notice (ECN).**

Bill-of-material (BOM)

Engineering change notice (ECN)

In the food service industry bills-of-material manifest themselves in portion control standards. The portion control standard for a "Juicy Burger" is shown in Figure 6.10(b). In a more complex product, a bill-of-material is referenced on other bills-of-material of which they are a part. In this manner subunits (subassemblies)

FIGURE 6.8

Monterey Jack.

§ 58.2469 Specifications for U.S. grades of Monterey (Monterey Jack) cheese

A portion of the general requirements for the U.S. grades of Monterey cheese are as follows:

(a) *U.S. grade AA*. U.S. grade AA Monterey cheese shall conform to the following requirements:

(1) *Flavor.* Is fine and highly pleasing, free from undesirable flavors and odors. May possess a characteristic Monterey cheese flavor or may be lacking in flavor development. May possess a very slight acid or feed flavor, but shall be free from any undesirable flavors and odors.

(2) *Body and texture.* A plug drawn from the cheese shall be reasonably firm. It shall have numerous small mechanical openings evenly distributed throughout the plug. It shall not possess sweet holes, yeast holes, or other gas holes. The texture may be definitely curdy or may be partially broken down if more than 3 weeks old.

(3) *Color.* Shall have a natural, uniform, bright attractive appearance.

(4) *Finish and appearance*—(i) *Bandaged and paraffin-dipped.* The rind shall be sound, firm, and smooth providing a good protection to the cheese.

(ii) *Paraffin-dipped.* The rind shall be sound, firm, and smooth providing a good protection to the cheese.

(iii) *Rindless.* The wrapper or covering shall be practically smooth, properly sealed with adequate overlapping at the seams or sealed by any other satisfactory type of closure.

Code of Federal Regulation, Parts 53 to 109, Revised as of Jan 1, 1985; Published by Office of the Federal Register National Archives & Records Service, General Service Administration

FIGURE 6.9

Engineering Drawing.

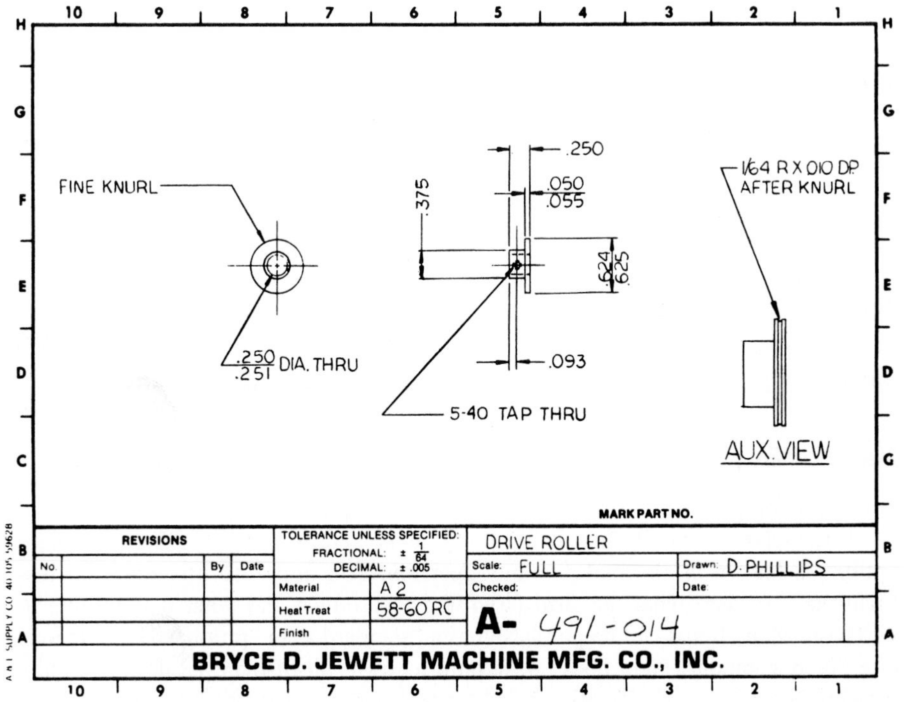

FIGURE 6.10

Bills-of-Material Take Different Forms in a Manufacturing Plant (a) and a Fast-Food Restaurant (b), but in Both Cases the Product Must Be Defined.

Bill of Material
for a Panel Weldment

NUMBER	DESCRIPTION	QTY
A 60-71	PANEL WELDM'T	1
A 60-7	LOWER ROLLER ASSM.	1
R 60-17	ROLLER	1
R 60-428	PIN	1
P 60-97	BRASS WASHER	1
O1-97-1150	WASHER	1
P 60-2	LOCKNUT	1
A 60-72	GUIDE ASSM. REAR	1
R 60-57-1	SUPPORT ANGLE	1
A 60-4	ROLLER ASSM.	1
P 60-53	SLEEVE	1
P 60-99	WEAR PLATE	1
02-50-1150	BOLT	1
02-50-0020	LOCK NUT	1
02-75-1550	BOLT	1
02-75-0020	LOCK NUT	1
A 60-73	GUIDE ASSM. FR.	1
A 60-74	SUPPORT WELDM'T	1
R 60-99	WEAR PLATE	1
02-50-1150	BOLT	1
02-50-0020	LOCK NUT	1
11-65-3	BUMPER BLOCK	1
11-60-63	WIPER RING	1

(a)

Portion Control Standard
for a Hamburger

PRODUCT: Juicy Burger

DESCRIPTION	QTY
Buns	1
Cheese	1 slice
Meat patties	2
Pickle slice	2
Dehydrated onions	1/250 pkg.
Sauce	1/137.5
Lettuce	1/26 head

(b)

are part of the next higher unit (their parent bill-of-material), which ultimately make a final product. Products, in addition to being defined by a written specification, a portion control document, or bill-of-material, can be defined in other ways. For example, products such as chemicals, paints, or petroleums may be defined by formulas or proportions that describe how they are to be made.

Make or Buy

Make or buy decision

For many components of products, firms have the option of producing the component themselves or purchasing it from an outside source. Choosing between these options is known as the make or buy decision. The **make or buy decision** distinguishes between what the firm is willing to produce and what it is willing to purchase. Many items can be purchased as a "standard item" produced by someone else. Such a standard item does not require its own bill-of-material or engineering drawing because its specification as a standard item is adequate. Examples are the standard nuts and bolts listed on the bill-of-material shown in Figure 6.10(a), for which there will be SAE (Society of Automotive Engineers) specifications. Therefore, there typically is no need for the firm to duplicate this specification in another document. Making what is known as the make or buy decision is discussed in more detail in Chapter 11.

Group Technology

Modern engineering drawings will also include codes to facilitate what is known as group technology. **Group technology** requires that components be identified by a coding scheme that specifies the type of processing (such as drilling) and the parameters of the processing (such as size). An example of how families of parts may be grouped is shown in Figures 6.11(a) and (b). Machines can then process families of parts as a group, minimizing setups, routings, and material handling. Successful implementation of group technology leads to:

Group technology

1. improved design;
2. reduced raw material and purchases;
3. simplified production planning and control;
4. improved routing and machine loading;
5. reduced tooling setup time, and work-in-process and production time.

FIGURE 6.11

(a) Manufactured Components (Not Grouped);
(b) Manufactured Components (Grouped)
Source: Joseph Tulkoff, Lockheed Aeronautical Systems Company—Georgia Division.

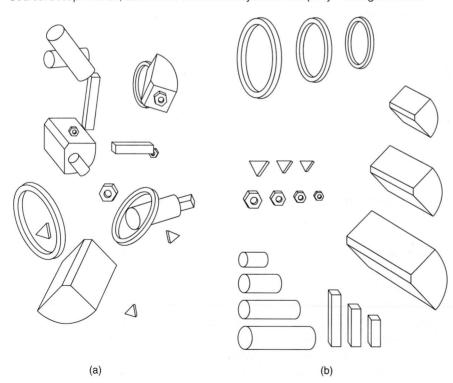

(a)   (b)

Another advantage of group technology is that personnel charged with the responsibility of design have a systematic way to review, via group technology codes, a family of components to see if an existing component might not suffice on a new project. Use of an existing component has the advantage of completely eliminating all the costs connected with the design and development of the new part. That is potentially a major cost reduction. The application of group technology helps the entire organization, as many costs are reduced.

Computer-Aided Design and Computer-Aided Manufacture

Computer-aided design (CAD)

Product design is greatly enhanced through the use of **computer-aided design (CAD).** Where CAD is used, a design engineer starts by developing a rough sketch or, conceivably, just an idea. The designer then utilizes a graphic display as a drafting board to construct the geometry of a design. As a geometric definition is completed, a sophisticated CAD system will allow the designer to determine various kinds of engineering data, such as strength or heat transfer. CAD will also allow the designer to ensure that parts fit together so there will be no interferences when parts are subsequently assembled. Thus, if the designer is sketching the fender for an automobile, the brackets and related panels are changed as the fender is changed. Analysis of existing, as well as new, designs can be done expediently and economically. (These advances in CAD systems are discussed further in the supplement to Chapter 7.)

Once the designer is satisfied with the design, it becomes part of a drawing database on electronic media. The CAD system, through a library of symbols and details, also helps to ensure adherence to the drafting standards.

Computer-aided manufacture (CAM)

The field of computer-aided design is merging with the field of **computer-aided manufacture (CAM).** Current CAD technology has branched out to provide tooling departments with data and to produce code for numerically controlled machines. Thus we have the integration of computer-aided design (CAD) and computer-aided manufacturing (CAM), resulting in CAD/CAM. In this manner the initial programming generated at the design stage can be used to create code that will be used not only by drafting departments, but also in tooling and manufacturing departments. Because the CAD data are available for subsequent use by others, tool design personnel and programmers of numerically controlled machines are aided. They can now proceed to design tooling and programs with confidence that they have the latest accurate engineering data and engineering drawings.

Benefits of CAD/CAM

There are several benefits to the CAD/CAM approach:

1. *Product quality.* CAD provides an opportunity for the designer to investigate more alternatives, potential problems, and dangers.
2. *Shorter design time.* Since time is money, the shorter the design phase, the lower the cost.
3. *Production cost reductions.* Lower inventory cost, more efficient use of personnel through improved scheduling, and faster implementation of design changes lower costs. Group technology as a part of CAD/CAM further reduces costs by grouping families of parts for manufacture.

4. *Database availability.* Consolidating current accurate product data so everyone is operating from the same information results in dramatic cost reductions. This is particularly true in tooling departments and preparation of numerical control tape.

5. *New range of capabilities.* For instance, the ability to rotate and depict objects in three-dimensional form, to check clearances, to relate parts and attachments, to improve use of numerically controlled machine tools—all provide new capability for manufacturing. CAD/CAM removes substantial detail work, allowing designers to concentrate on the conceptual and imaginative aspects of their task. This is a major benefit of CAD/CAM.

PRODUCTION DOCUMENTS

Once a product is selected and designed, its production is assisted by a variety of documents. We will briefly review some of these.

An **assembly drawing** simply shows an exploded view of the product. An assembly drawing is usually a three-dimensional drawing, known as an isometric drawing; the relative locations of the components are shown in relation to each other to show how to assemble the unit (see Figure 6.12(a)).

Assembly drawing

The **assembly chart** shows in schematic form how a product is assembled. Manufactured components, purchased components, or a combination of both may be shown on an assembly chart. The assembly chart identifies the point of produc-

Assembly chart

FIGURE 6.12

Assembly Drawing and Assembly Chart.

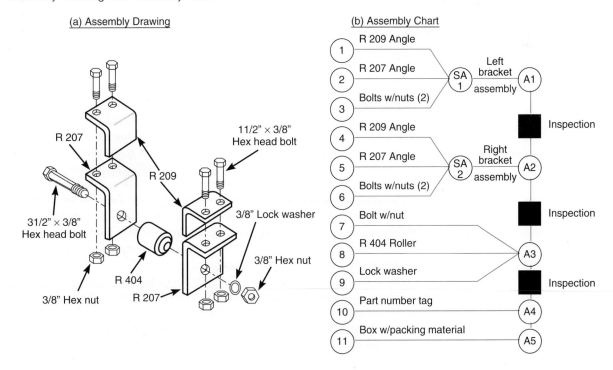

(a) Assembly Drawing

(b) Assembly Chart

tion where components flow into subassemblies and ultimately into a final product. An example of an assembly chart is shown in Figure 6.12(b).

Route sheet

The **route sheet** lists the operations (including assembly and inspection) necessary to produce the component with the material specified in the bill-of-material. The route sheet for an item will have one entry for each operation to be performed on the item. When route sheets include specific methods of operation and labor standards, they are often known as *process sheets*. In a manufacturing environment the route sheets may reference the bill-of-material, engineering drawings, and assembly drawings.

Job instructions

Organizations also often find it necessary to develop **job instructions,** which provide detailed instructions about how to perform the task. Where there are a large variety of jobs, job instructions change often. Instruction manuals are used where the jobs seldom change. Quality control test procedures or manuals are also used to specify how to evaluate the product and its components to ensure that they meet design specifications. Various **standards manuals** provide standard times for setup

Standards manuals

and information about speed, capacity, and tolerances, and perhaps other pertinent data for each operation in a process. They also provide data about the cost of using each alternative. Standards manuals are found not only in manufacturing environments but also in most operating areas, such as a well-organized institutional kitchen or a computer center.

Work order

The **work order** is an instruction to make a given quantity of a particular item, usually to a given schedule. The ticket that a waiter writes in your favorite restaurant is a work order. In a hospital or factory the work order is a more formal order that provides authorization to draw various pharmaceuticals or items from inventory, to perform various functions, and to assign personnel to perform those functions. In many applications the work order and the route sheet include quantity and schedule information.

Configuration Management

Engineering change notices (ECNs) change some aspect of the product's definition or documentation, such as an engineering drawing or a bill-of-material. For a complex product that has a long manufacturing cycle, such as a Boeing 747, the changes may be so numerous that no two 747s are built exactly alike—which is indeed the case. Such dynamic design change has fostered the development of a discipline known as configuration management, which is concerned with product

Configuration management

identification, control, and documentation. **Configuration management** is the system by which a product's planned and changing configurations are accurately identified and for which control and accountability of change are maintained.

In a product where technology is in ferment or where safety is an important issue, ECNs are incorporated immediately. This is typical of the aircraft industry. In more traditional manufacturing, ECNs may be grouped and implemented at one time, perhaps semiannually. Grouping ECNs for implementation aids quality control, standardization, and production efficiency.

A related technique also exists in the pharmaceuticals industry where *lots* (a small batch) of drugs are tracked to facilitate an audit trail. Each lot is given a lot number, which can be tracked through its specific processing steps. This is necessary because possible variations in the formulation, processing, packaging, and shipment of the drug may affect its purity or intended usefulness.

SOME OBSERVATIONS ON SERVICES

Our discussion so far has focused on what we can call tangible products, that is, goods. On the other side of the product coin are, of course, services. Service industries include intangibles such as banking, finance, insurance, transportation, and communications.[9] They also include those medical procedures that leave only the tiniest scar after an appendectomy, as well as the shampoo and cut at a hair salon.

Thus the first thing that is different about service is that it is *usually intangible* (your purchase of a ride in an empty airline seat between two cities) as opposed to a tangible product.

The second thing is that services are often *produced and consumed simultaneously;* there is no stored inventory. For instance, the beauty salon produces a haircut that is consumed simultaneously, or the doctor produces an operation that is consumed as it is produced. We have not yet figured out how to inventory haircuts or appendectomies.

The third item that makes services different is that although many goods are standardized or have standardized components, *many services are unique.* Your mix of financial coverage, which manifests itself in investments and insurance policies, may not be the same as anyone else's, just as the medical procedure or a haircut produced for you is not exactly like anyone else's.

The fourth thing that makes the service product unique is *high customer interaction.* It's often difficult to standardize, automate, and be as efficient as we would like because customer interaction demands a uniqueness. This uniqueness in many cases is what the customer is paying for; therefore, the operations manager must ensure that the product is designed so that it can be delivered in the required unique manner.

The fifth item that makes service unique is *inconsistent product definition.* Product definition may be rigorous, as in the case of an insurance policy, or casual, as in the case of a haircut. Moreover, the haircut definition not only varies with each customer, but often with each haircut, even for the same customer. Similarly, the insurance policy, although rigorously defined, varies with regard to customer, type of coverage, and amount of coverage.

In spite of these differences between products and services, there is still an operations function to be performed. This occurs when the insurance company defines the product (say an insurance policy), processes the purchase transaction, issues premium statements, and processes those premiums. The same would be the case for a stock transaction where the "back room," which is the operations center, handles the transaction. The same is true of a transaction at your local bank: the operations center processes the transaction. (In Chapter 1, the *POM in Action* box, "Moving Money at 111 Wall Street" described the check clearing operations of a large bank.) In the case of an airline, the operations function schedules the planes, crews, and meals, and usually manages the maintenance function. So, although service products are often unique, the operations function continues to perform a transformation function as was shown in the organization charts of Chapter 1.

Many firms currently use CAD/CAM technology as shown here to design new products. The rule of thumb is that a state-of-the-art CAD work station not only speeds up product development, but can enhance engineering productivity 400%. In this photo, a new ski is being designed.

---

[9] The *Statistical Abstract of the United States* considers services as: wholesale and retail trade, finance, insurance, real estate, and government. Most definitions also include education, health care, and the legal and lodging industries.

APPLICATION OF DECISION TREES TO PRODUCT DESIGN

Decision trees, introduced in Chapter 3, are a technique of use for new product decisions as well as for a wide variety of other management problems. They are particularly helpful when there are a series of decisions and various outcomes that lead to *subsequent* decisions, followed by other outcomes. You may recall from Chapter 3 that to form a decision tree we follow the procedure outlined below:

1. Be sure that all possible alternatives and states-of-nature are included in the tree. This includes an alternative of "doing nothing."
2. Payoffs are entered at the end of the appropriate branch. This is the place to develop the payoff of achieving this branch.
3. The objective is to determine the expected value of each course of action. We accomplish this by starting at the end of the tree (the right-hand side) and working toward the beginning of the tree (the left), calculating values at each step and "pruning" alternatives that are not as good as others from the same node.

The example of Silicon, Inc., which follows, demonstrates the use of a decision tree applied to product design.

Example 1

Silicon, Inc., a semiconductor manufacturer, is investigating the possibility of producing and marketing a microprocessor. Undertaking this project will require either purchasing a sophisticated CAD/CAM system or hiring and training several additional engineers. The market for the product could be either favorable or unfavorable. Silicon, Inc., of course, has the option of not developing the new product at all.

With favorable acceptance by the market, sales would be 25,000 processors selling for $100 each, and with unfavorable acceptance, sales would be only 8,000 processors selling for $100 each. The cost of the CAD/CAM equipment is $500,000, but that of hiring and training three new engineers is only $375,000. However, manufacturing cost should drop from $50 each when manufacturing without CAD/CAM to $40 each when manufacturing with CAD/CAM.

The probability of favorable acceptance of the new microprocessor is 0.40; the probability of unfavorable acceptance is .60. See Figure 6.13.

The expected monetary values (EMVs) have been circled at each step of the decision tree. For the top branch:

$$\text{EMV (Purchase CAD/CAM system)} = (.4)(\$1,000,000) + (.6)(\$-20,000)$$
$$= \$388,000$$

This represents the results that will occur if Silicon, Inc., purchases CAD/CAM.

The expected value of hiring and training engineers is the second series of branches:

$$\text{EMV (Hire/train engineers)} = (.4)(\$875,000) + (.6)(\$25,000)$$
$$= \$365,000$$

The EMV of doing nothing is $0.

Since the top branch has the highest expected monetary value (an EMV of $388,000 vs. $365,000 vs. $0) it represents the best decision. Management should purchase the CAD/CAM system.

FIGURE 6.13

Decision Tree for Development of a New Product.

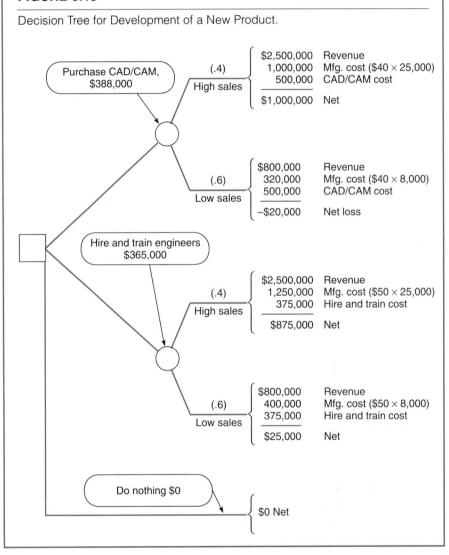

Decision trees are a powerful technique because they can also depict sequential decisions. That is, a manager can make a decision, analyze the states-of-nature that may occur, and then determine the available alternatives given each of those states-of-nature. We present a two-stage decision tree in Solved Problem 6.2.

TRANSITION TO PRODUCTION

Eventually, our product has been selected, designed, and defined. The product has progressed from an idea, to a functional definition, and then to a prototype. Now, management must make a decision as to further development, production, or termination of the product idea. One of the arts of modern management is knowing when to move a product from development to production; this movement is known as *transition to production*. The research and development (R & D) staff and engineering personnel are always interested in making improvements in the product. Because this staff tends to see product development as evolutionary, they may never have a completed product. Management must know when the product meets the functional definition, even though it is not perfect. And they must know when it is producible so the product can be moved from development to production. A number of high technology companies have addressed this issue by being somewhat ruthless in recognizing that their technology is so much in ferment that the development groups never will have what they view as a completed project. Therefore management says, "You are finished, and we will proceed with production." As noted in our earlier discussion, the cost of late product introduction is high.

Once this decision is made there is usually a period of trial production to ensure that the design is indeed producible. This is the manufacturability test. This also gives the production staff the opportunity to develop proper tooling, quality control procedures, and training of personnel to ensure that production can be initiated successfully. Finally, when the product is deemed both marketable and producible, line management will assume responsibility.

Some companies appoint a project manager or use an ongoing product development team to ensure that the transition from the development phase to production is successful. This is often necessary because of the wide range of resources and talents that must be brought to bear to ensure satisfactory production of a product that is still in flux. Other firms find that integration of the product development and manufacturing organizations is advantageous. This allows for easy shifting of resources between the two organizations as needs change. The production manager's job is to make the transition from R & D to production smooth and without gaps.

SUMMARY

Selecting, designing, and defining a product has implications for all subsequent operations decisions. The operations manager must be imaginative and resourceful in the product development process. Products are defined by written specification, bills-of-material, and engineering drawings. Group technology, computer-aided design, and value engineering are helpful product design techniques. Assembly drawings, assembly charts, route sheets, job instruction, work orders, and standards manuals assist the manager in defining a product for production.

Once a product is in production, value analysis is appropriate for quality and production review. Configuration management allows the manager to track and document the product that has been produced.

How products move through their life cycle of introduction, growth, maturity, and decline influences the strategy the operations manager should pursue. And decision trees, because of their ability to deal with the sequential series of probabil-

ities and decisions, are particularly useful techniques in many management decisions, including those related to product strategies.

KEY TERMS

Product strategy (p. 246)
Time-based competition (p. 251)
Product development teams (p. 253)
Design for manufacturability and value
engineering teams (p. 254)
Quality robust design (p. 254)
Value analysis (p. 255)
Product-by-value analysis (p. 257)
Engineering drawing (p. 258)
Bill-of-material (BOM) (p. 258)
Engineering change notice (ECN) (p. 258)
Make or buy decision (p. 260)

Group technology (p. 261)
Computer-aided design (CAD) (p. 262)
Computer-aided manufacture (CAM)
(p. 262)
Assembly drawing (p. 263)
Assembly chart (p. 263)
Route sheet (p. 264)
Job instructions (p. 264)
Standards manuals (p. 264)
Work order (p. 264)
Configuration management (p. 264)

SOLVED PROBLEMS

Solved Problem 6.1

B. King, president of King Electronics, Inc., has two design options for her
new line of high-resolution cathode ray tubes (CRTs) for computer-aided
design workstations. The life cycle sales forecast for the CRT is 100,000
units.

Design option A has a .90 probability of yielding 59 good CRTs per 100
and a 0.10 probability of yielding 64 good CRTs per 100. This design will
cost $1,000,000.

Design option B has a .80 probability of yielding 64 good units per 100
and a 0.20 probability of yielding 59 good units per 100. This design will
cost $1,350,000.

Good or bad, each CRT will cost $75. Each good CRT will sell for $150.
Bad CRTs, believe it or not, are destroyed and have no salvage value. There
is little disposal cost as they break up when thrown in the trash. Therefore
we ignore any disposal costs in this problem.

Solution

We draw the decision tree to reflect the two decisions and the probabilities
associated with each decision. We then determine the payoff associated with
each branch. This is shown in Figure 6.14.

For design A,

$$\text{EMV (Design A)} = (.9)(\$350,000) + (.1)(\$1,100,000)$$
$$= \$425,000$$

For design B,

$$\text{EMV (Design B)} = (.8)(\$750,000) + (.2)(\$0)$$
$$= \$600,000$$

The highest payoff is design option B at $600,000.

FIGURE 6.14

Decision Tree for Solved Problem 6.1.

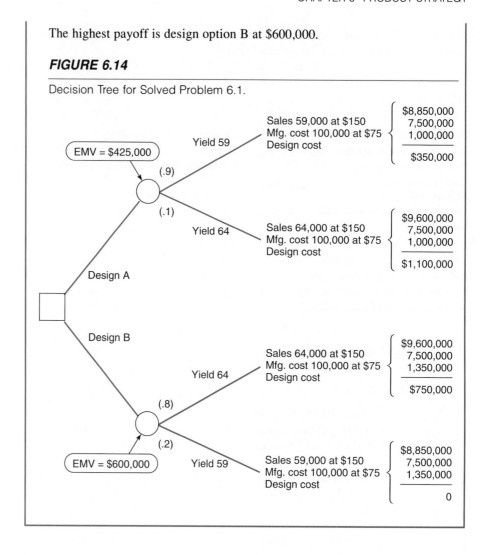

Solved Problem 6.2

Using the data in Solved Problem 6.1, let us examine what happens to the decision if Ms. King can increase the yield when the yield is 59 out of each 100. If the yield is 59 per 100, a special expensive phosphorous for the screen can be used at an added cost of $50.00 per CRT. This procedure will be good for only 5 units per 100 (that is, this procedure can bring the yield up to only 64 per 100).

Solution

The modified decision tree and the new payoffs are shown in Figure 6.15.

We have made a second decision on those branches where the yield was only 59 per 100 and have modified the payoffs by adding the revenue and costs associated with the correction of 5 units per 100. We then pruned those branches with the lowest payoff (which, in both cases, was the branch labeled "Do not correct"). Here are the EMV calculations:

$$\text{EMV (Design A)} = (.9)(\$850,000) + (.1)(\$1,100,000)$$
$$= \$875,000$$

$$\text{EMV (Design B)} = (.8)(\$750,000) + (.2)(\$500,000)$$
$$= \$700,000$$

Using the high payoff branches, we conclude that the expected monetary values are $875,000 from design A and $700,000 from design B. Therefore, the decision when King Electronics has the option of correcting 5 units per 100 is to correct them and use Design A.

FIGURE 6.15

Decision Tree for Solved Problem 6.2.

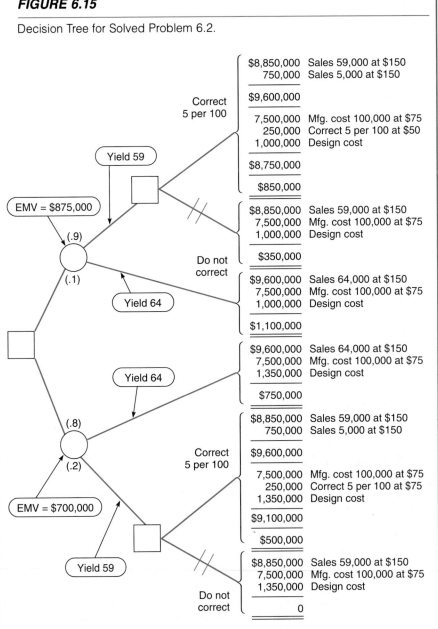

$8,850,000	Sales 59,000 at $150
750,000	Sales 5,000 at $150
$9,600,000	
7,500,000	Mfg. cost 100,000 at $75
250,000	Correct 5 per 100 at $50
1,000,000	Design cost
$8,750,000	
$850,000	

$8,850,000	Sales 59,000 at $150
7,500,000	Mfg. cost 100,000 at $75
1,000,000	Design cost
$350,000	

$9,600,000	Sales 64,000 at $150
7,500,000	Mfg. cost 100,000 at $75
1,000,000	Design cost
$1,100,000	

$9,600,000	Sales 64,000 at $150
7,500,000	Mfg. cost 100,000 at $75
1,350,000	Design cost
$750,000	

$8,850,000	Sales 59,000 at $150
750,000	Sales 5,000 at $150
$9,600,000	
7,500,000	Mfg. cost 100,000 at $75
250,000	Correct 5 per 100 at $75
1,350,000	Design cost
$9,100,000	
$500,000	

$8,850,000	Sales 59,000 at $150
7,500,000	Mfg. cost 100,000 at $75
1,350,000	Design cost
0	

EMV = $875,000

Yield 59

Correct 5 per 100

Do not correct

(.9)

(.1)

Yield 64

Yield 64

(.8)

(.2)

Correct 5 per 100

Do not correct

EMV = $700,000

Yield 59

DISCUSSION QUESTIONS

1. What management techniques may prove helpful in making the transition from R & D to production?

2. Why is it necessary to document a product explicitly?

3. What techniques do we use to document a product?

4. Configuration management has proved particularly useful in what industries? Why?

5. How does computer-aided design help other departments?

6. What is group technology and why is it proving helpful in our quest for productivity improvement?

7. What savings can be expected by computer-aided design?

8. How does computer-aided design help computer-aided manufacture?

9. What are the four phases of the product life cycle?

10. How does product selection (and design) affect quality?

PROBLEMS

· **6.1** Prepare a bill-of-material for a ballpoint pen.

· **6.2** Draw an assembly chart for a ballpoint pen.

· **6.3** Prepare a bill-of-material for a simple table lamp. Identify the items that you, as manufacturer of the body and related components, are likely to make and that you are likely to purchase. Justify your decision for each.

· **6.4** Prepare an assembly chart for the table lamp in Problem 6.3.

· **6.5** As a library project, find a series of group technology codes.

: **6.6** Given the contribution made on each of the three products below and their position in the life cycle, identify a reasonable operations strategy for each.

Table for Problem 6.6

PRODUCT	PRODUCT CONTRIBUTION (PERCENT OF SELLING PRICE)	COMPANY CONTRIBUTION (PERCENT OF TOTAL ANNUAL CONTRIBUTION DIVIDED BY TOTAL ANNUAL SALES)	POSITION IN LIFE CYCLE
Portable computer	30%	40%	Growth
Laptop computer	30%	50%	Introduction
Hand calculator	50%	10%	Decline

 : **6.7** The product planning group of Hawkes Electric Supplies, Inc., has determined that they need to design a new series of switches. They must decide upon one of three design strategies. The market forecast is for 200,000 units. The better and more sophisticated the design strategy and the more time spent on value engineering, the less will be the variable cost. The chief of engineering design, Dr. Lorraine Harris, has decided that the following costs are a good estimate of the initial and variable costs connected with each approach. These are:

a) Low-tech: a low-technology, low-cost process consisting of hiring several new junior engineers. This has a cost of $45,000 and variable cost probabilities of .2 for $.55 each, .5 for $.50, and .3 for $.45.

b) Subcontract: a medium-cost approach utilizing a good outside design staff. This approach would have an initial cost of $65,000 and variable cost probabilities of .7 of $.45, .2 of $.40, and .1 of $.35.

c) High-tech: a high-technology approach utilizing the very best of the inside staff and the latest computer-aided design technology. This approach has a fixed cost of $75,000 and variable cost probabilities of .9 of $.40 and .1 of $.35.

What is the best decision based on an expected monetary value (EMV) criterion? (*Note:* We want the lowest EMV as we are dealing with costs in this problem.)

: **6.8** Faber Manufacturing, Inc., of St. Paul, Minn., has the option of (a) proceeding immediately with production of a new top-of-the-line stereo TV, which has just completed prototype testing or (b) having the value analysis team complete a study. If Warren Fisher, VP for Operations, proceeds with the existing prototype (option A), the firm can expect sales to be 100,000 units at $550 each with a probability of .6, and a .4 probability of 75,000 at $550. If, however, he uses the value analysis team (option B), the firm expects sales of 75,000 units at $750 with a probability of .7, and a .3 probability of 70,000 units at $750. Cost of the value analysis is $100,000. Which option has the highest expected monetary value (EMV)?

: **6.9** Ritz Products' materials manager, Larry Mann, must make a determination to make or buy a new semiconductor for the wrist TV they are about to produce. One million of the product are expected to be produced over the life cycle. If the product is made, the start-up and production cost of the make decision is $ 1,000,000, with a probability of .4 that the product will be satisfactory and .6 probability that it will not. If the product is not satisfactory, the firm will have to reevaluate the decision. If the decision is reevaluated, the choice will be to spend another $1,000,000 to redesign the semiconductor or to purchase. Likelihood of success the second time the make decision is made is .9. If the second make decision also fails, the firm must purchase. Regardless of when the purchase takes place, the best judgment Larry Mann has of cost is that Ritz Products will pay $.50 for each purchased semiconductor plus $1,000,000 in vendor development cost.

a) Assuming that Ritz Products must have the semiconductor (stopping or doing without is not a viable option), what is their best decision?

b) What criteria did you use to make this decision?

c) What is the worst that can happen to Ritz Products on this particular decision? What is the best that can happen?

CASE STUDY

Modern Optical, Inc.

Based on their extensive knowledge of the optical machine marketplace, George Spalding and June Hicks decided to form Modern Optical, Inc. Modern Optical was to design a low-priced, low-maintenance machine, the ClearLens, to be used in the manufacture of plastic and polycarbonate lenses. The target market for the ClearLens is the small laboratory and the growing number of one-hour eye facilities, or super stores, as they are known in the trade.

These super stores typically have a small laboratory in the store to process the customer's prescription on the premises rather than sending it to a traditional optical lab for processing. The stores accentuate the need for low-maintenance equipment because their small staffs typically do not include maintenance personnel or even personnel trained in mechanical maintenance. The ClearLens will provide a low-cost, effective alternative to the higher priced machines now on the market, and its design will focus on the plastic and polycarbonate market, which now dominates over 70%

CASE STUDY (Continued)

of total prescriptions. The successful production of a moderately priced machine will also allow Modern Optical, Inc., to participate in the market to equip traditional labs. Once established in this market, the opportunity either to produce or to manufacture other equipment and supplies should exist. The customers in this market are receptive to a mix of auxiliary equipment.

The concept of the ClearLens is the culmination of six years of development by June and George and represents the first significant advance in refining and polishing of eyeglass lenses since the early 1950s. The design criteria for the ClearLens include the following:

1. The machine would incorporate an advanced polishing motion and would therefore provide superior optics. (The motion of the ClearLens is covered by a United States patent and is a method type patent. Method type patents protect basic processes and are more difficult to overcome and are therefore more defensible than apparatus type patents.)

2. The machine would be designed for durability and low maintenance and would reduce, if not eliminate, many of the production problems caused by machine downtime and machine rebuilding time now common in optical laboratories.

3. The machine would be of a modular construction and would therefore allow for easy replacement of modules and, as necessary, maintenance of the modules away from the laboratory environment.

Discussion Questions

1. Modern Optical, Inc., no doubt has a great idea, but how are June and George going to proceed with manufacture? Can you outline a procedure for them to follow?

2. What problems can they expect?

3. Where will they be on the product life cycle versus the life cycle of the established machines and how will this affect their operations strategy?

Note: Names of the firm and principals have been changed but the situation and issues described are actual.

BIBLIOGRAPHY

Berliner, C., and J. A. Brimson. *Cost Management for Today's Advanced Manufacturing.* Boston: Harvard Business School Press, 1988.

Bootroyd, G. "Design for Assembly—The Key to Design for Manufacturing." *International Journal of Advanced Manufacturing Technology* (1987).

Budnik, A. S. "Value Engineering, a Form of Industrial Engineering." *Journal of Industrial Engineering* **4** (July–August 1964): 184–187.

Burt, D. N., and W. R. Soukup. "Purchasing's Role in New Product Development." *Harvard Business Review* **63** (September–October 1985): 90–97.

Canton, I. D. "Learning to Love the Service Economy." *Harvard Business Review* **62** (May–June 1984): 89–97.

Choi, M., and W. E. Riggs. "GT coding and Classification Systems for Manufacturing Cell Design." *Production and Inventory Management Journal* **32** (First Quarter 1991): 28.

"Design Teams Include Vendor." *Purchasing* **24** (September 1981).

Eppen, G. D., W. A. Hanson, and R. K. Martin. "Bundling—New Products, New Markets, Low Risk." *Sloan Management Review* **32** (Summer 1991): 7.

Finkin, E. F. "Developing and Managing New Products." *Journal of Business Strategy* **3** (Spring 1983): 41.

Gallagher, C. C., and W. A. Knight. *Group Technology Production Methods in Manufacturing.* New York: Halsted Press (John Wiley & Sons), 1987.

Meyer, M. H., and E. B. Roberts. "New Product Strategy in Small Technology-Based Firms: A Pilot Study." *Management Science* **32** (July 1986): 806–821.

Miles, L. *Techniques of Value Analysis and Engineering.* New York: McGraw-Hill, 1961.

Mosier, C. T., and R. E. Janaro. "Toward a Universal Classification and Coding System for Assemblies." *Journal of Operations Management* **9** (January 1990): 44.

Samoras, T. T., and F. L. Czerwinski. *Fundamentals of Configuration Management.* New York: John Wiley & Sons, 1971.

Smith, P. G., and D. G. Reinertsen. *Developing Products in Half the Time.* New York: Van Nostrand Reinhold, 1991.

Souder, W. E. *Managing New Product Innovations.* Lexington, MA: Lexington Books, 1987.

Takeuchi, H., and I. Nonaka. "The New New Product Development Game." *Harvard Business Review* **64** (January–February 1986): 137–146.

Thietart, R. A., and R. Vivas. "An Empirical Investigation of Success Strategies for Businesses along the Product Life Cycle." *Management Science* **30** (December 1984): 1405–1423.

Value Engineering in Manufacturing. Englewood Cliffs, NJ: Prentice-Hall, 1967.

Walleigh, R. "Product Design for Low-Cost Manufacturing." *Journal of Business Strategy* (July–August 1989).

Wheelwright, S. C., and W. E. Sasser, Jr. "The New Product Development Map." *Harvard Business Review* **67** (May–June 1989): 112–125.

Zirger, B. J., and M. A. Maidique. "A Model of New Product Development: An Empirical Test." *Management Science* **36** (July 1990): 867.

Zurn, J. T. "Problem Discovery Function: A Useful Tool for Assessing New Product Introduction." *IEEE Transactions on Engineering Management* **38** (May 1991): 116–119.

Process Strategies

Process Selection Yields a Competitive Advantage at Nucor

In Crawfordsville, Indiana, Nucor produces sheet steel in a nearly *continuous process* with small variety. But with modest changes in the steel mix, alloys, and in size and finish of the steel, a wide variety of market requirements are met. This nearly continuous process is toward the right on our process continuum (see Figure 7.1).

Nucor builds and operates a type of steel mill known as the "mini mill." Mini mills are smaller, cheaper, and less complex, and have proven more efficient than integrated mills. Mini mills typically make steel from scrap rather than from ore. About half of the steel consumed in the U.S. is produced this way.

Steel is produced in two phases. The first phase is preparation of steel of the proper mix, that is, with the proper alloys. In the second phase, steel is formed into the desired shapes and finishes for the market.

In the first phase, raw material in the form of scrap is loaded into two 125-ton electric arc furnaces. A massive electric charge with a thunderous roar melts the scrap. At this point an analysis is made of the alloy and a variety of additional ingredients added, depending upon the nature of the scrap and the product desired. The melted steel, at about 3000 degrees, is called a *heat;* it is poured into a ladle and carried by an overhead crane to a casting machine. Once in the casting machine,

This AC electric-arc furnace holds 125 tons. Electrodes lowered into cold scrap steel in the furnace produce arc heat to melt the scrap.

The ladle, equipped with magnetic stirring and vacuum degassing features, is opened, and steel exits into the continuous caster. Steel pours from the ladle via a ceramic nozzle into a metering vessel called a *tundish,* and then to a special mold that can adjust the slab's dimensions.

the liquid steel is solidified as a continuous red-hot 2-inch-thick ribbon of steel and is cut into lengths as it cools. This ribbon of steel can be cast in widths up to 52 inches wide. They are called *slabs* and weigh about twenty-five tons.

Steel slab entering the rolling mill.

Here the shaped steel exits the caster mold as a two-inch thick by fifty-two-inch wide slab, and enters the hot tunnel furnace, where its temperature is uniformly raised to the level needed for rolling. A higher-quality sheet can be produced if slab temperature is uniform.

The coiling of rolled sheet steel. Each roll is about twenty-five tons.

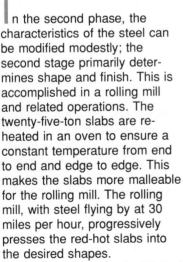

In the second phase, the characteristics of the steel can be modified modestly; the second stage primarily determines shape and finish. This is accomplished in a rolling mill and related operations. The twenty-five-ton slabs are re-heated in an oven to ensure a constant temperature from end to end and edge to edge. This makes the slabs more malleable for the rolling mill. The rolling mill, with steel flying by at 30 miles per hour, progressively presses the red-hot slabs into the desired shapes.

The Crawfordsville facility typically makes sheet steel, which is rolled into coils. Subsequent finishing operations such as pickling, annealing, and tempering can modify the characteristics of the sheet steel depending on customer desires and market.

Nucor operates twenty-four hours a day, six days a week, with the seventh day reserved for scheduled maintenance.

At Nucor, process selection provides a competitive advantage in several ways.

First, Nucor casts steel close to the final shape of the product, eliminating unnecessary capital equipment and personnel.

Second, the continuous process eliminates a substantial amount of reheating prior to rolling. This yields major savings in energy cost.

Third, an efficient process combined with an effective incentive system yields the highest productivity found in any steel mill in the world. Nucor's labor hours per ton of steel may be half that of competitors.

Fourth, the process technology used at Crawfordsville results in high productivity *and* high quality. The process results in excellent control of steel characteristics, and reduced labor, energy, and work-in-process, as well as a net savings in capital investment.

How does Nucor maintain a competitive advantage? Through excellent operations management, including the right process strategy.

INTRODUCTION

In Chapter 6 we examined the need for the selection, definition, and design of products. We now turn to the production of these products. A major decision for the operations manager is finding the best way to produce. This chapter looks at ways to help managers develop what is called a process strategy.

Process strategy

A **process** (or transformation) **strategy** is the approach that an organization takes to transform resources into goods and services. We use both terms, *process* and *transformation,* to describe this strategy. The *objective of a process strategy* is to find a way to produce goods that meet customer requirements and product specifications within cost and other managerial constraints.

The process selected will have a long-run effect on efficiency and production, as well as the flexibility, cost, and quality of the goods produced. Therefore, much of a firm's strategy is determined at the time of the process decision. The payoff from effective process selection prior to initial production is much more fruitful than the same effort expended later trying to improve the wrong process.

THREE TYPES OF PROCESSES

Process Focus

Perhaps as much as 75% of U.S. production is accomplished in a setting of very small volume or batches of different products—in places called "job shops." Low-volume products may be as diverse as oceangoing tugboats, gourmet French meals, heart transplants, or a special set of ornate hinges for the front door of a house of worship. These low-volume, high-variety processes are also known as **intermittent processes.** The facilities are organized around *process;* they have a **process focus.** The layout and supervision have a process focus.

Intermittent processes
Process focus

Product focus

Product Focus

High-volume, low-variety processes are **product focused.** The facilities are organized around *products.* They are also called **continuous processes.** They have very long, continuous production runs, hence the name. Such products as glass, paper, tin sheets, light bulbs, and nuts and bolts are made via a continuous process. Some products, such as light bulbs, are discrete; others, such as rolls of paper, are nondiscrete. It is only with standardization (as popularized by Eli Whitney) and statistical quality control (as introduced by Walter Shewhart) that firms have been able to use a continuous process. An organization producing the same light bulb or hot dog bun day after day can organize around a product. Such an organization has an inherent ability to set standards and maintain a given quality, as opposed to an organization that is producing unique products every day.

Continuous processes

Repetitive Focus

Production need not be at either of the above extremes of the process continuum but may be a repetitive process that falls somewhere in between. **Repetitive processes** use modules. **Modules** are parts or components previously prepared, often in a continuous process.

Repetitive processes
Modules

TABLE 7.1 Comparision of a Low-Volume, High-Variety Process, a Repetitive Process, and a High-Volume, Low-Variety Process

CHARACTERISTICS OF A LOW-VOLUME, HIGH-VARIETY PROCESS (PROCESS FOCUS)	CHARACTERISTICS OF A MODULAR PROCESS (REPETITIVE FOCUS)	CHARACTERISTICS OF A HIGH-VOLUME, LOW-VARIETY PROCESS (PRODUCT FOCUS)
1. Small quantity and large variety of products are produced.	1. Long runs, usually a standardized product with options, are produced from modules.	1. Large quantity and small variety of products are produced.
2. Equipment used is general purpose rather than special purpose.	2. Some special equipment and fixtures to aid in use of an assembly line.	2. Equipment used is special purpose rather than general purpose.
3. Operators must be more broadly skilled.	3. Employees are modestly trained.	3. Operators are less broadly skilled.
4. There are many job instructions because each job changes.	4. Repetitive operations reduce training and changes in job instructions.	4. Work orders and job instructions are few, because they are standardized.
5. Raw material inventories are high relative to the value of the product.	5. Just-in-time procurement techniques are used.	5. Raw materials inventories are low relative to the value of the product.
6. Work-in-process is high compared to output.	6. Just-in-time inventory techniques are used.	6. Inventory of work-in-process is low compared to output.
7. Slow movement of units through the plant.	7. Movement is measured in hours and days.	7. Swift movement of units through the facility is typical.
8. Materials are moved via small flexible equipment.	8. Materials are moved by conveyor, transfer machines, programmable AGVs, etc.	8. Materials are moved by connected pipes, material guides, webbing feeds, etc.
9. Wide aisles and ample storage are typical.	9. Medium or narrow aisles, little storage space.	9. The facility is built around equipment, machinery, and product flows.
10. Finished goods are usually made to order and not stored.	10. Finished goods are made to frequent forecasts.	10. Finished goods are usually made to a forecast and stored.
11. Order-oriented scheduling is complex and primarily concerned with the trade-off between inventory availability, capacity, and customer service.	11. Period-oriented scheduling often overlaps operations and is designed to build various models and options from a variety of modules to forecasts.	11. Period-oriented scheduling is relatively simple and primarily concerned with establishing a rate of output sufficient to meet sales forecasts.
12. Fixed costs tend to be low and variable costs high.	12. Fixed costs are dependent on flexibility of the facility.	12. Fixed costs tend to be high and variable costs low.
13. Costing, often done by the job, is estimated prior to doing the job, but known only after the job.	13. Costs are usually known, because of extensive prior experience.	13. Because fixed costs are high, costs are highly dependent on utilization of capacity.

The repetitive process line is the classic assembly line. The repetitive process is widely used, including the assembly of virtually all automobile and household appliances. The repetitive strategy has more structure and consequently less flexibility than a job shop.

Fast-food firms are an example of a repetitive process using modules. This type of production allows more customizing than a continuous process; so modules (for example, meat, cheese, sauce, tomatoes, onions) are assembled to get a quasi-custom product, a cheeseburger. In this manner the firm obtains both the economic advantages of the continuous model (where many of the modules are prepared) and the custom advantage of the low-volume, high-variety model.

Table 7.1 compares the major characteristics of low-volume, high-variety, repetitive, and high-volume, low variety processes.

Moving toward World-Class Performance with Lean Production

Lean producers

The attributes of *world-class* producers were discussed in Chapter 1. Here we note the characteristics of *lean* producers. **Lean producers**[1] is the term used to describe repetitive producers[2] who are world-class. The lean producer's mission is to achieve perfection. Lean production also means reducing staff positions so that those responsible are doing the entire job, from housekeeping chores, to execution, to planning. Lean production calls for continuous learning, creativity, and teamwork. It requires the full commitment and application of everyone's capabilities.

Lean producers understand what the customer wants and they rapidly design quality products to meet those requirements. Product *development* is faster, cheaper, and higher-quality in a lean environment (see Table 6.1 in Chapter 6). Table 7.2 shows that lean *production* also has a high payoff. The advantages held by lean producers are spectacular. The documented attributes of lean producers include the following:

- They remove waste by focusing on inventory reduction. They eliminate virtually all inventory. This means, as we shall see in our inventory chapters, that a bad unit being moved from one process to another *is* allowed to stop the entire system. The removal of inventory removes the safety nets that allow a poor product to make its way through the product process.

- They use just-in-time techniques to reduce inventory and the waste caused by inventory. They drive down the time and cost of switching production from one product to another. We discuss these techniques in Chapters 13 and 14.

- They build systems that help employees produce a perfect part every time. Lean production expects no less.

- They reduce space requirements. The technique is to minimize the distance a part travels. We discuss the design of efficient layouts in Chapter 9.

- They develop close relationships with suppliers; suppliers understand their needs and their customers' needs.

- They educate suppliers to accept responsibility for helping meet customer needs. Chapter 11 discusses evaluating suppliers and developing good supplier relationships.

- They strive for continually declining costs by eliminating all but value-added activities. They eliminate material handling, inspection, inventory, and re-

---

[1] John Krafcik is given credit for coining the term *lean production*.

[2] *Synchronous manufacturing* is another term currently in vogue to describe efficient repetitive processes. General Motors has gone so far as to add the title Synchronous Manufacturing Manager to its lexicon.

TABLE 7.2 Summary of Automotive Assembly Plant Performance

| | LEAN PRODUCERS | OTHERS | | |
	(Japanese in Japan)	(Japanese in North America)	(American in North America)	(All Europe)
Inventories (days for 8 sample parts)	.2	1.6	2.9	2.0
Quality (assembly defects/100 vehicles)	60.0	65.0	82.3	97.0
Space (sq. ft./vehicle/year)	5.7	9.1	7.8	7.8
Supplier Share of Engineering	51%	14%	37%	32%
Work Force:				
Productivity (hours/veh.)	16.8	21.2	25.1	36.2
% of Work Force in Teams	69.3	71.3	17.3	.6
Number of Job Classes	11.9	8.7	67.1	14.8
Training of New Production Workers (hours)	380.3	370.0	46.4	173.3
Suggestions/Employee	61.6	1.4	.4	.4
Absenteeism	5.0	4.8	11.7	12.1

Source: Adapted from: James P. Womack, Daniel T. Jones, and Daniel Roos, *The Machine That Changed the World* (New York: Macmillan, 1990), pp. 92, 118.

work jobs because they do not add value to the product. They retain only those activities that add value. Waste is eliminated.

- They develop the work force. They constantly improve job design, training, employee participation and commitment, and work teams. We discuss these issues in Chapter 10.
- They make jobs more challenging, pushing responsibility to the lowest level possible. They reduce the number of job classes.

Viewed in this context, we see that traditional production techniques have set *limited* goals. For instance, traditionally, managers have accepted the production of a limited number of defective parts and have accepted safety stock as a limit on inventory reduction. Lean producers, on the other hand, set their sights on perfection; no bad parts and no inventory. The results are continually declining costs that are obtained via quality workmanship, zero inventory, a focus on teamwork and communications, and continuous self-improvement as employees broaden their skills. Lean producers are constantly building a better production system. A better system allows ever more challenging work for the employee and more rapid response to the market.

Lean production requires a commitment to remove continuously those activities that do not add value to the product. Lean production is a waste-reduction philosophy. Lean producers enter a never ending battle to reduce idle time, change-over time, inventory, poor quality, poor suppliers, poor product design, and poor performance. Only when this is done is the organization lean and world-class.

Two lean producers are noted in the *POM in Action* box, "World-Class Lean Producers."

Comparison of Process Strategies

Figure 7.1 further compares the three process strategies we have just described and summarizes their relationships. On the left vertical axis of the figure the volume and variety of products are indicated. On the diagonal we have identified the type of operations that exist within each process strategy. A firm must operate on the shaded diagonal, or it will be in one of the poor strategy areas. Looking at the continuum in Figure 7.1 from the point of view of a restaurant, on the upper left we could have a restaurant preparing gourmet meals; farther down the diagonal we would find limited-menu restaurants, where more specialized equipment and standardized methods are used. The continuous process example for food preparation would be the production of french fries—peeled, cut, sized, and packaged in a continuous oriented environment. These are then shipped to restaurants and need only be cooked prior to serving.

Advantages exist at both ends of the continuum. Unit costs will be less in the continuous process case if high volume exists. While the theoretical cost per unit may be less, we do not always use the continuous processes (that is, specialized equipment and specialized facility). That is too expensive for low volumes. A low-volume, unique service or product is more economical when produced under process focus. The bottom row of Figure 7.1 indicates that equipment utilization in

At General Mills' Red Lobster, like most large restaurant chains, the restaurant is simply the end of a long production line. At the beginning of the line, raw material goes in . . . at Red Lobster that means 60 million pounds of seafood a year. The seafood is purchased from all over the world. The shrimp arrives in frozen boxes from Ecuador and Thailand at a General Mills processing plant in St. Petersburg, Florida. There the shrimp is loaded onto a conveyor belt to be peeled, deveined, cooked, quick frozen (above), sorted (below), and repacked for ultimate delivery to individual restaurants.

FIGURE 7.1

Process Strategy Orientation.

Volume and Variety of Products	Process Focus; Low-Volume, High-Variety Process (Intermittent)	Repetitive Process (Modular)	Product Focus; High-Volume, Low-Variety Process (Continuous)
One or very few units per lot	Projects		**Poor strategy** (Fixed cost and cost of changing to other products are high.)
Very small runs, high variety		Job shops	
Modest runs, modest variety			Disconnected repetitive
Long runs, modest variations			Connected repetitive
Very long runs, changes in attributes (such as grade, quality, size, thickness, etc.)	**Poor strategy** (Variable costs are high.)		Continuous
Equipment utilization	5%–25%	20%–75%	70%–80%

POM _in action_

World-Class Lean Producers

Nucor, discussed in the photo essay at the beginning of this chapter, is a lean producer. When world leaders of the steel industry meet, one of the questions often asked is, "What is Nucor doing now?" Nucor sets the standards in the steel industry. It is innovative in satisfying customer demands, it is participative, it is profitable, and it produces steel at a fraction of the cost of most competitors. Nucor operates factories with a future.

Mars, a leader in the candy industry, is also a lean producer. Mars follows the customer so closely that it has a huge market share. Mars also has high profitability and such high productivity that the firm operates with 30% fewer employees than its closest competitor. One of the reasons for high productivity

is that equipment is valued at replacement cost so there is a built-in bias toward having the latest equipment. At Mars, quality is an obsession, but you look for someone with _quality_ in their title and you find no one. However, if you look for people concerned about quality you find everyone. At Mars, communication takes a front seat, manifesting itself in a unique office layout where managers are engaged in effective communication at all levels. The typical Mars office layout puts the boss in the center of a large room with no walls, but surrounded by subordinates. Frills, like private offices, are rare.

Sources: "Quality Control from Mars," _Wall Street Journal_ (January 27, 1992): A10; and _Fortune_ (September 26, 1988): 98–104.

---

processes is often in the range of 5% to 25%. Utilization above 15% suggests moving to the right on the process strategy continuum. Machine utilization provides a good measure of efficiency. Utilization is good data to study because there is often high correlation between capital cost (capital utilization), labor costs, and labor utilization with machine utilization.[3] The move from process focused to repetitive or product focused can yield significant increases in capital utilization. Material cost, floor space utilization, and assembly cost also tend to favor continuous-oriented production. The _POM in Action_ box, "Burgers! Shakes!" relates how McDonald's started a whole new industry by moving from the left toward the right of the continuum.

However, changing a production system from the process-focused model to the product-focused model is usually expensive. In some cases, this switch may necessitate starting over. Consequently, choosing where to operate on the process strategy continuum may determine the transformation strategy for an extended period.

The idea is to move to the right as far as possible to increase utilization without fixed costs becoming intolerable or the necessary product variety being destroyed. Movement to the right on the continuum is desirable if the:

1. _cash flows_ to pay the fixed cost are adequate, and
2. risk of _lower demand_ is insignificant, and
3. necessary _product variety_ can be maintained.

---

[3] Donald D. Deming, "When to Shift to Straight-Line Production," _Harvard Business Review,_ **37,** 6 (November–December 1959): 53–59.

POM _in action_

Burgers! Shakes!

In 1947, between 35% and 40% of gross income was being paid out as wages by restaurants. In December of 1948, Richard and Mac McDonald, wearied of contending with "drunken fry cooks and dishwashers," wanted a new approach. They switched their drive-in to a limited and rigidly standardized menu and disbanded carhop service.

In just a few months, with the drive-in's swift service, low prices, and elimination of tipping, a sizable following developed. Workers, teenagers, and families looking for fast and inexpensive eating were forming lines at windows where fifteen-cent hamburgers, ten-cent french fries, and twenty-cent milk shakes were available.

The new McDonald's system was based on meticulous attention to detail. The McDonald brothers developed dispensers that put an exact amount of catsup or mustard on every bun. A bank of infrared lamps was installed to maintain the french fries' heat.

Glassware and china were replaced by disposable paper goods. Shakes and malts were made directly in cups by shortening the spindles on the multi-mixers. Consequently, there would be no metal mixing containers to wash, no wasted ingredients, no wasted motion, and no wasted time. Microphones were installed to amplify the customer's voice and clarify orders.

By 1952, it took twenty seconds for the McDonalds to serve a customer a hamburger, a drink, french fries, and ice cream. Reports of this efficiency spread through the restaurant industry. In May of 1952, _American Restaurant_ magazine told of this compact, self-service, drive-in capable of selling 30,000 orders of french fries a month. McDonald's had axed labor costs to less than 17% of gross income.

Sources: The Atlantic Monthly (December 1985); and _Personnel Journal_ (November 1989).

Machinery, Equipment, and Technology

The choice of machinery and equipment for the transformation process also requires consideration of quality, capacity, and flexibility. Operations personnel develop documentation that indicates the capacity and size of each option, the tolerance it maintains, and its maintenance requirements. Any one of these attributes may be the deciding factor regarding the use of a process.

Alternative methods of production are present in virtually all operations functions, be they hospitals, restaurants, or manufacturing facilities. Therefore, operations managers have to be:

1. _effective leaders_ so they can bring new processes to their organizations;
2. _current with state-of-the-art technology_ in order to know when new processes ought to be considered;
3. _versed in analytical procedures_ to evaluate options objectively.

Picking the best transformation strategy for a firm means understanding its specific industry, established processes, and technology. Although the study of specific industries and their technology is outside the scope of the book, an example of the impact of technology on productivity is provided in the _POM in Action_ box,

POM *in action*

Smooth Flying

Jet engine parts of all sizes and complexities are cast at Precision Castparts Corp. out of exotic alloys such as titanium and nickel. Using a technique called investment casting, Precision surrounds a wax replica of the part by a ceramic shell (the investment) to make a mold. When the mold is heated, the wax melts away, and molten alloy is poured in. Precision's process is so refined that its products rival the strength of parts that are forged and then machined.

Some of the firm's parts, like the fan for a GE jet engine, can be extremely complex. The CF6-80C engine, power plant to the giant Boeing 747 jet, used to have a frame made up of hundreds of small stainless steel parts welded together. Precision replaced the frame with a large single piece of cast titanium. With this investment casting process, engine manufacturers end up with a lighter-weight product at a cost savings approaching 50%.

Sources: Aviation Week & Space Technology (May 22, 1991): 72–73; and *Forbes* (September 18, 1989): 94–95.

"Smooth Flying." As the reading suggests, those firms not using the *investment casting* process for high-stress engine components will operate at a distinct disadvantage. Selection of an approach, such as investment casting, for the transformation process can provide a unique advantage. The selection of machinery and equipment can also provide competitive advantage. Many firms, for instance, develop a unique machine or technique within the established processes that provides an advantage. This advantage may result in added flexibility in meeting customer requirements, lower cost, or higher quality. Modification might also allow for a more stable production process that takes less adjustment, maintenance, and training of operators. In any case, a competitive advantage for winning orders has been developed.

SERVICE PROCESS STRATEGY

The process strategy continuum in Figure 7.1 can be applied to services as well as manufacturing. For instance, empirical evidence suggests that much of the service industry is producing in very small lots. This is probably true for legal services, medical services, dental services, and restaurants. They are often producing in lot sizes as small as one. Such organizations would be in the upper left of Figure 7. 1.

Service Sector Considerations

As Figure 7.1 indicates, in process-focused facilities, equipment utilization is extremely low—perhaps as low as 5%. This is true not only for manufacturing but also for services. An x-ray machine in a dentist's office and much of the equipment in a fine dining restaurant have low utilization. Hospitals, too, can be expected to be in that range, which would suggest why their costs are considered high. Why such low utilization? In part because excess capacity for peak loads is desirable. Hospital administrators, as well as managers of other service facilities and their patients and customers, expect equipment to be available as needed. Another reason utilization is low is poor scheduling (although substantial efforts have been made to forecast demand in the service industry) and the resulting imbalance in the use of facilities.

The service industry moves to the right of Figure 7.1 by establishing fast-food restaurants, legal clinics, auto lubrication shops, auto tune-up shops, etc. Notice how McDonald's moved to the right on our process continuum, as indicated in the *POM in Action* box earlier in this chapter. As the variety of services is reduced, we would expect per-unit cost to drop also. This is typically what happens.

Customer Contact and Process Strategy

Customer contact is an important variable in a transformation system. In a process that directly interfaces with the customer, one expects the customer to affect process performance adversely. Activities in the service sector are a good example. In a restaurant, a medical facility, a law office, or a retail store, too much interaction between the customer and the process keeps the process from operating as smoothly as it otherwise might. Individual attention and customizing of the product or service for the customer can play havoc with a process. The more the process can be insulated from the customer's unique requirements, the lower will be the cost. This separation can be accomplished in a variety of ways, as shown in Table 7.3.

In the remainder of this chapter we deal with three perspectives to help managers make the process decision. The first of these perspectives is the *capacity issue*. We use forecasting techniques and decision trees as aids in reaching good capacity decisions. Second, we introduce *break-even analysis* for the single and multiple product case and apply it to process selection. Third, we address the *investment* side of process strategy by introducing strategy considerations, net present value techniques, variable cost, and cash flow. These three perspectives provide substantial insight for a successful process strategy.

TABLE 7.3 Customer Contact and Process Strategy. These Techniques Are Used to Improve Productivity in Production/Operations in the Service Sector.

TECHNIQUE	EXAMPLE
Restricting the offerings	Limited-menu restaurant
Customizing at delivery	Customizing vans at delivery rather than at production
Structuring service so customers must go where the service is offered	A bank where customers go to a service representative to open a new account, to loan officers for loans, or to tellers for deposits and withdrawals
Self-service so customers examine, compare, and evaluate at their own pace	A supermarket or department store
Separate services that may lend themselves to some type of automation	Automatic teller machines

FIGURE 7.2

By Combining Products That Have Complementary Seasonal Patterns,
Capacity Can Be Better Utilized. A smoother demand for sales also
contributes to improved scheduling and better human resource strategies.

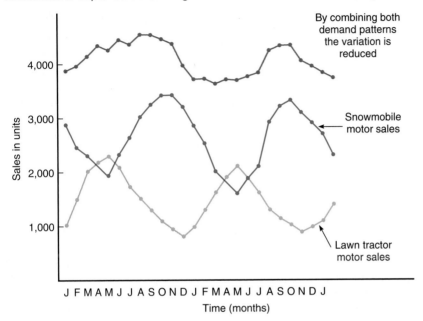

CAPACITY

Because determining the size of a facility is critical to a firm's success, we now
investigate the concepts and techniques of capacity planning. First, we note how a
firm can manage its demand, given that a certain capacity exists. We then examine
techniques that can help us evaluate capacity requirements. These techniques include forecasting and decision-tree analysis, which were introduced in Chapters 4
and 3, respectively.

Demand Management

A manager may have the ability to alter demand. In the case where *demand exceeds
capacity,* the firm may be able to curtail demand simply by raising prices, scheduling long lead times (which may be inevitable), and discouraging marginally profitable business. In the case where *capacity exceeds demand,* the firm may want to
stimulate demand through price reductions or aggressive marketing, or accommodate the market in a better way through product changes.

Unused facilities (that is, excess capacity) mean excess fixed costs; inadequate
facilities reduce revenue below what is possible. Therefore, various tactics for
matching capacity to demand exist. Internal changes include adjusting the process
to a given volume through:

1. staffing changes;

2. adjusting equipment and processes, which might include purchasing additional machinery or selling or leasing existing equipment;

3. improving methods to increase throughput; and/or

4. redesigning the product to facilitate more throughput.

Another capacity issue with which management may be confronted is a seasonal or cyclical pattern of demand. In such cases management may find it helpful to find products with complementing demand patterns, that is, products for which the demand is the opposite. For example, in Figure 7.2 the firm is adding a line of snowmobile engines to its line of lawn mower engines to smooth demand. With appropriate complementing products, perhaps the utilization of facility, equipment, and personnel can be smoothed.

The foregoing tactics can be used to adjust demand to existing facilities. The strategic issue is, of course, how to have a facility of the correct size. We will, therefore, now address how to determine capacity and decide upon the size of a facility.

Capacity Management

Capacity

Capacity is the maximum output of a system in a given period. Capacity is normally expressed as a rate, such as the number of tons of steel that can be produced per week, per month, or per year. For many companies, measuring capacity can be straightforward. It is the maximum number of units that can be produced in a specific time. However, for some organizations, determining capacity can be more difficult. Capacity can be measured in terms of beds (a hospital), active members (a church), or the number of counselors (a drug abuse program). Other organizations use total work time available as a measure of overall capacity.

Designed capacity

The **designed capacity** of a facility is the maximum capacity that can be achieved under ideal conditions. Most organizations operate their facilities at a rate less than the designed capacity. They do so because they have found that they can operate more efficiently when their resources are not stretched to the limit. The expected capacity might be 92% of the designed capacity. This concept is called effective capacity or utilization.

Effective capacity or utilization

Effective capacity or utilization is simply the percent of design capacity actually expected. It can be computed from the following formula:

$$\text{Effective capacity or utilization} = \frac{\text{Expected capacity}}{\text{Design capacity}}$$

Effective capacity or utilization is the maximum capacity a firm can expect to achieve given its product mix, methods of scheduling, maintenance, and standards of quality.

Another consideration is efficiency. Depending on how facilities are used and managed, it may be difficult or impossible to reach 100% efficiency. Typically, **efficiency** is expressed as a percentage of the effective capacity. Efficiency is a measure of actual output over effective capacity:

Efficiency

$$\text{Efficiency} = \frac{\text{Actual output}}{\text{Effective capacity}}$$

The **rated capacity** is a measure of the maximum usable capacity of a particular facility. Rated capacity will always be less than or equal to the design capacity. The equation used to compute rated capacity is given below:

Rated capacity

$$\text{Rated capacity} = (\text{Designed capacity})(\text{Utilization})(\text{Efficiency})$$

We determine rated capacity in the following example.

Example 1

The Sara James Bakery has a plant for processing breakfast rolls. The facility has an efficiency of 90%, and the utilization is 80%. Three process lines are used to produce the rolls. The lines operate seven days a week and three eight-hour shifts per day. Each line was designed to process 120 standard (that is, plain) rolls per hour. What is the rated capacity?

In order to compute the rated capacity, we multiply the design capacity (which is equal to the number of lines times the number of hours times the number of rolls per hour) times the utilization times the efficiency. Each facility is used seven days a week, three shifts a day. Therefore, each process line is utilized for 168 hours per week ($168 = 7$ days $\times$ 3 shifts per day $\times$ 8 hours per shift). With this information, the rated capacity can be determined. This is done below.

$$\begin{aligned}
\text{Rated capacity} &= (\text{Designed capacity})(\text{Utilization})(\text{Efficiency}) \\
&= [(120)(3)(168)]\,(.8)(.9) = 43{,}546 \text{ rolls/week}
\end{aligned}$$

Forecasting Capacity Requirements

Determining future capacity requirements can be a complicated procedure, one based in large part on future demand. When demand for goods and services can be forecasted with a reasonable degree of precision, determining capacity requirements can be straightforward. It normally requires two phases. During the first phase, future demand is forecasted with traditional methods. During the second phase, this forecast is used to determine capacity requirements.

Using regression analysis as a forecasting tool (described in detail in Chapter 4), let us look at an example.

Example 2

During the last several years, demand for rolls from Sara James Bakery has been steady and predictable. Furthermore, there has been a direct relationship between rolls produced and rated capacity expressed in hours per week. This has allowed the executives of Sara James Bakery to forecast rated capacity with a fair degree of accuracy, using a simple regression line. Sara James Bakery has compiled the following data that it would like to use to forecast future demand for rated capacity.

MONTH	RATED CAPACITY (IN HOURS/WEEK)
January	500
February	510
March	514
April	520
May	524
June	529

With the above data, it is possible to forecast rated capacity requirements. We now do so, using the least squares technique presented in Chapter 4:

$$\text{Slope} = b = \frac{\Sigma xy - n\,\overline{x}\,\overline{y}}{\Sigma x^2 - n\overline{x}^2}$$

$$y \text{ intercept} = a = \overline{y} - b\overline{x}$$

and

$$\hat{y} = a + bx$$

TIME PERIOD	x	y	x^2	xy
January	1	500	1	500
February	2	510	4	1,020
March	3	514	9	1,542
April	4	520	16	2,080
May	5	524	25	2,620
June	6	529	36	3,174
	$\Sigma x = 21$	$\Sigma y = 3097$	$\Sigma x^2 = 91$	10,936

$$\overline{x} = \frac{\Sigma x}{n} = \frac{21}{6} = 3.5 \qquad \overline{y} = \frac{\Sigma y}{n} = \frac{3{,}097}{6} = 516.16$$

$$b = \frac{(10{,}936) - (6)(3.5)(516.16)}{(91) - (6)(12.25)} = \frac{10{,}936 - 10{,}839.31}{91 - 73.50} = \frac{96.69}{17.50} = 5.5$$

$$a = 516.16 - (5.5)(3.5) = 516.16 - 19.32 = 496.84$$

Therefore capacity needs in August (month $x = 8$) will be:

$$\hat{y}_8 = a + bx = 496.84 + 5.5x$$

$$= 496.84 + 5.5(8)$$

$$= 496.84 + 44.0$$

$$= 540.84 \approx 541 \text{ hours/week}$$

Once the rated capacity has been forecasted, the next step is to determine the incremental size of each addition to capacity. At this point the assumption is made that management knows the technology and the *type* of facilities to be employed to satisfy these future demand requirements.

Figure 7.3 reveals how new capacity can be planned for future demand growth.

FIGURE 7.3

Adding Capacity.

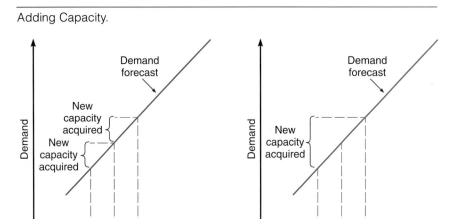

(a)

(b)

As seen in Figure 7.3(a), new capacity is acquired at the beginning of year one. This capacity will be sufficient to handle increased demand until the beginning of year two. At the beginning of year two, new capacity is again acquired, which will allow the organization to meet demand until the beginning of year three. This process can be continued indefinitely into the future.

The capacity plan shown in Figure 7.3(a) is only one of an almost limitless number of plans to satisfy future demand. In this figure, new capacity was acquired at the beginning of year one and at the beginning of year two. In Figure 7.3(b), a large increase in capacity is acquired at the beginning of year one, which will satisfy future demand until the beginning of year three.

Figures 7.3(a) and 7.3(b) reveal only two possible alternatives. In some cases, deciding between alternatives can be relatively easy. The total cost of each alternative can be computed, and the alternative with the least total cost can be selected. In other cases, determining the capacity of future facilities can be much more complicated. Some companies use break-even analysis and net-present value analysis, both of which are discussed later in this chapter. In most cases, numerous subjective factors are difficult to quantify and measure. These factors include technological options; actions by competitors; building restrictions; cost of capital; human resource options; and local, state, and federal laws and regulations.

When future demand for goods and services and rated capacity are subject to substantial fluctuation, the procedures suggested above may not be adequate. In these cases, "probabilistic" models to solve capacity requirements problems may be more appropriate. Typically, the decision will be what size facility to build to meet future demand. In some cases, no new facilities should be acquired. The major variable deals with demand factors and the market acceptance for the goods and services being produced. In some cases, the levels of future market acceptance can be categorized. (See, for instance, Example 3, where we have categorized market acceptance as favorable or unfavorable.) One technique that has been used successfully in making capacity planning decisions with an uncertain future is decision theory. Decision theory includes the use of both decision tables and decision trees.

Decision Trees Applied to Capacity Decisions

Decision trees were discussed in Chapter 3 and again in Chapter 6. Decision trees require specifying alternatives and various states-of-nature. For capacity planning situations, the state-of-nature usually is future demand or market favorability. By assigning probability values to the various states-of-nature, it is possible to make decisions that maximize the expected value of the alternatives. This is done in the following example using a decision tree.

Example 3

Southern Hospital Supplies, a company that makes hospital gowns, is considering capacity expansion. Its major alternatives are to do nothing, build a small plant, build a medium plant, or build a large plant. The new facility would produce a new type of gown, and currently the potential or marketability for this product is unknown. If a large plant is constructed and a favorable market exists, a profit of $100,000 could be realized. On the other hand, a large plant would result in a $90,000 loss with an unfavorable market. If a medium plant were to be constructed, a $60,000 profit would be realized with a favorable market. A $10,000 loss would result from an unfavorable market. A small plant, on the other hand, would return $40,000 with favorable market conditions. If the market conditions were unfavorable, the hospital supply company would lose only $5,000. Of course, there is always the option of doing nothing.

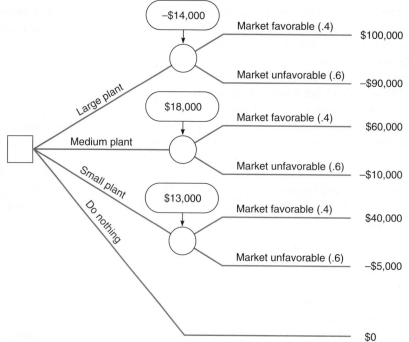

Recent market research indicates that there is a .4 probability of a favorable market, which means that there is also a .6 probability of an unfavorable market. With this information, the alternative that will result in the highest expected monetary value (*EMV*) can be selected:

$$\text{EMV (large plant)} = (.4)(\$100{,}000) + (.6)(-\$90{,}000) = -\$14{,}000$$
$$\text{EMV (medium plant)} = (.4)(\$60{,}000) + (.6)(-\$10{,}000) = +\$18{,}000$$
$$\text{EMV (small plant)} = (.4)(\$40{,}000) + (.6)(-\$5{,}000) = +\$13{,}000$$
$$\text{EMV (do nothing)} = \$0$$

Based on an EMV criteria Southern should build a medium plant.

BREAK-EVEN ANALYSIS

The objective of **break-even analysis** is to find the point, in dollars and units, at which costs equal revenues. This point is the break-even point. Break-even analysis requires an estimation of fixed cost, variable cost, and revenue. We will proceed by first defining the fixed and variable costs and then the revenue function.

Break-even analysis

  Fixed costs are costs that continue even if no units are produced. Examples include depreciation, taxes, debt, and mortgage payments. **Variable costs** are those that vary with the volume of units produced. The major components of variable costs are labor and materials. However, other costs, such as the portion of the utilities that varies with volume, are also variable costs.

Fixed costs
Variable costs

  Another element in break-even analysis is the **revenue function.** It begins at the origin and proceeds upward to the right, increasing by the selling price of each unit. This revenue line is shown in Figure 7.4. Where the revenue function crosses the total cost line is the break-even point, with a profit corridor to the right and a loss corridor to the left. The profit and loss corridors are also shown in Figure 7.4.

Revenue function

FIGURE 7.4

Basic Break-even Point

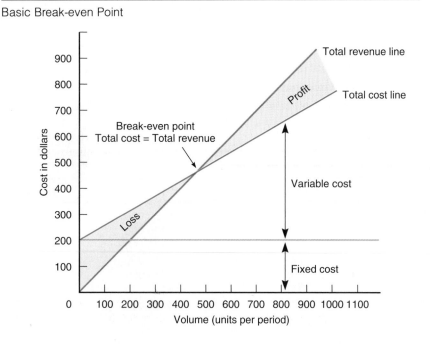

A number of assumptions underlie this basic model. Notably, costs and revenue are shown as straight lines. They are shown to increase linearly, that is, in direct proportion to the volume of units being produced. However, neither fixed costs nor variable costs (nor, for that matter, the revenue function) need be a straight line. For example, fixed costs change as more capital equipment or warehouse space is used; labor costs change with overtime or as marginally skilled workers are employed; and the revenue function may change with such factors as volume discounts.

There are two graphic approaches to break-even analysis. The first is to define those costs that are fixed and sum them. The variable costs are then estimated by an analysis of labor, materials, and other costs connected with the production of each unit. The fixed costs are drawn as a horizontal line beginning at that dollar amount on the vertical axis. The variable costs are then shown as an incrementally increasing cost, originating at the intersection of the fixed cost on the vertical axis and increasing with each change in volume as we move to the right on the volume (or horizontal) axis. Both fixed and variable cost information is usually available from a firm's cost accounting department, although an industrial engineering department may also maintain cost information.

The second way to approach break-even analysis is to determine total costs for a few accounting periods and then to plot these costs above the respective volume. Some sample data are provided in Table 7.4 below. When plotted, these data provide a line that represents the total of both fixed and variable costs. Do not expect the points to fall exactly on a straight line, as they probably will not. However, a regression line (or a straight line approximating one) can be drawn to show the total costs. This has been done in Figure 7.5. Where the total cost line intersects the vertical axis is a reasonable approximation of fixed cost. This is point A in Figure 7.5 (on p. 295).

The respective formulas for the break-even point in units and dollars are shown below. Let:

BEP (x) = Break-even point in units

BEP ($\$$) = Break-even point in dollars

P = Price per unit (dollars received per unit after all discounts)

x = The number of units produced

TR = Total revenue = Px

F = Fixed costs

V = Variable costs per unit

TC = Total costs = $F + Vx$

TABLE 7.4 Volume, Cost, and Revenue.

	VOLUME (UNITS)	COST	REVENUE
January	300	$120,000	$130,000
February	350	$125,000	$150,000
March	500	$135,000	$200,000
April	550	$140,000	$220,000
May	250	$110,000	$100,000
June	200	$100,000	$ 85,000
July	400	$120,000	$175,000

FIGURE 7.5

Plot of Data from Table 7.3.

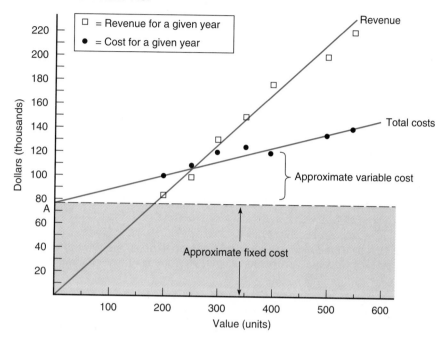

Setting total revenue equal to total costs, we get

$$TR = TC$$

or

$$Px = F + Vx$$

Solving for x, we get

$$BEP(x) = \frac{F}{P - V}$$

and

$$BEP(\$) = BEP(x)P$$

$$= \frac{F}{P - V} P = \frac{F}{(P - V)/P}$$

$$= \frac{F}{1 - V/P}$$

$$\text{Profit} = TR - TC$$

$$= Px - (F + Vx)$$

$$= Px - F - Vx$$

$$= (P - V)x - F$$

Using these equations, we can solve directly for break-even point and general

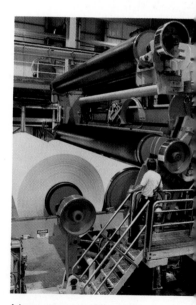

A large paper machine such as this one owned by Georgia Pacific Corporation requires a major capital expenditure. But, while fixed costs are high, variable costs are low. And maintaining a high volume of output above the break-even point is critical to profitability.

profitability. The two formulas that are of particular interest are:

$$\text{Break-even in units} = \frac{\text{Total fixed cost}}{\text{Price} - \text{Variable cost}} \tag{7.1}$$

$$\text{Break-even in dollars} = \frac{\text{Total fixed cost}}{1 - \dfrac{\text{Variable cost}}{\text{Selling price}}} \tag{7.2}$$

The object of break-even analysis is to aid process selection by identifying the processes with the lowest total cost for the volume expected. Such a point will, of course, also indicate the largest profit corridor. We are, therefore, able to address two issues: the low-cost process and the absolute amount of profit. Only by directly addressing both issues can the process decision be successful. Figure 7.6 shows three alternative processes compared on a single chart. Such a chart is sometimes called a **crossover chart.**

Crossover chart

FIGURE 7.6

Crossover Charts. Three different processes can be expected to have three different costs. However, at any given volume, only one will have the lowest cost.

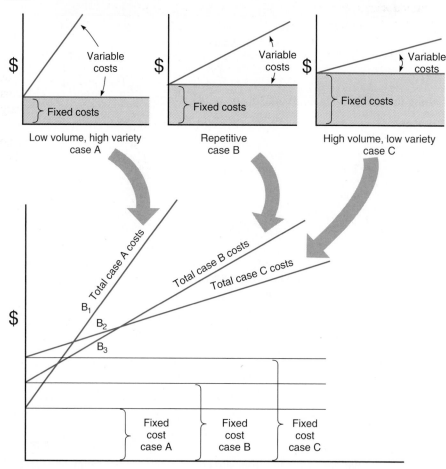

Single-Product Case

Let us determine in Example 4 the break-even point in dollars and units for one product.

Example 4

Smith, Inc., has fixed costs of $10,000 this period. Direct labor is $1.50 per unit, and material is $.75 per unit. The selling price is $4.00 per unit.

The break-even point in dollars is computed as follows:

$$BEP(\$) = \frac{F}{(1 - V/P)} = \frac{\$10,000}{1 - [(1.50 + .75)/(4.00)]} = \frac{\$10,000}{.4375} = \$22,857.14$$

and the break-even point in units is:

$$BEP(x) = \frac{F}{P - V} = \frac{\$10,000}{4.00 - (1.50 + .75)} = 5714$$

Note that, in this example, we must use the *total* variable costs (that is, both labor and material).

Multiproduct Case

The break-even analysis for the single-product case has one major failing. It does not address the typical firm's variety of offerings. Most firms, from manufacturers to restaurants (even fast-food restaurants) have a variety of offerings. Each offering may have a different selling price and variable cost. Utilizing break-even analysis, we modify Equation 7.2 to reflect the proportion of sales for each product. We do this by "weighting" each product's contribution by its proportion of sales. The formula is then

$$BEP(\$) = \frac{F}{\sum\left[\left(1 - \frac{V_i}{P_i}\right) \times \left(W_i\right)\right]} \tag{7.3}$$

where:

V = Variable cost per unit

P = Price per unit

F = Fixed cost

W = The percent each product is of total dollar sales

i = each product

Example 5

The costs from Le Bistro, a French-style deli, are shown below. Fixed costs are $3,500 per month.

ITEM	PRICE	COST	FORECASTED UNIT SALES
Sandwich	$2.95	$1.25	7,000
Soft drink	.80	.30	7,000
Homemade chips	.59	.18	1,000
Baked potato w/topping	1.55	.47	5,000
Tea	.75	.25	5,000
Breakfast menu	2.95	1.20	2,000
Crepe	1.75	.55	2,500
Milkshake	1.75	.80	2,000
Salad bar	2.85	1.00	3,000

With a variety of offerings, we proceed with break-even analysis just as in a single-product case, except that we weight each of the products by its proportion of total sales here.

Multiproduct Break-even—Determining Contribution

1	2	3	4	5	6	7	8
Item (i)	Selling Price (P)	Variable Cost (V)	(V/P)	1 − (V/P)	Forecasted Sales	% of Sales	Weighted Contribution (= Col. 5 × Col. 7)
Sandwich	$2.95	$1.25	.42	.58	$20,650	.340	.197
Soft drink	.80	.30	.38	.62	5,600	.092	.057
Homemade chips	.59	.18	.31	.69	590	.010	.007
Baked potato w/topping	1.55	.47	.30	.70	7,750	.128	.090
Tea	.75	.25	.33	.67	3,750	.062	.042
Breakfast menu	2.95	1.20	.41	.59	5,900	.097	.057
Crepe	1.75	.55	.31	.69	4,375	.072	.050
Milkshake	1.75	.80	.46	.54	3,500	.058	.031
Salad bar	2.85	1.00	.35	.65	8,550	.141	.091
					$60,665	1.000	.622

For instance, revenue for sandwiches is $20,650, which is 34.0% of the total revenue of $60,665. Therefore, the contribution for sandwiches is "weighted" by .340. The weighted contribution is .340 × .58 = .197. In this manner, its relative contribution would be properly reflected.

Using this approach for each product, we find that the total weighted contribution is .622 for each dollar sales, and the break-even point in dollars is $67,524:

$$BEP(\$) = \frac{F}{\sum \left[\left(1 - \frac{V_i}{P_i} \right) \times \left(W_i \right) \right]}$$

$$= \frac{\$3,500 \times 12}{.622} = \frac{\$42,000}{.622}$$

$$= \$67,524$$

The information given in this example implies total daily sales (52 weeks at six days each) of

$$\frac{\$67,524}{312 \text{ days}} = \$216.42$$

Break-even figures by product provide the manager with added insight as to the realism of his or her sales forecast. They indicate exactly what must be sold each day. Once break-even analysis of this type has been prepared, analyzed, and judged to be reasonable, decisions can be made about the types of equipment needed. Indeed, a better judgment of the likelihood of success of the enterprise can now be made.

Break-even Analysis Applied to Capacity Decisions

The impact of capacity decisions can be shown through the use of break-even analysis. This is shown in Figure 7.6. If the forecast volume is lower than actual volume, the firm may have chosen the wrong process. Then higher per-unit cost will result because the firm is operating with the wrong process, say Point B1, rather than a Point B2 or B3. A capacity decided upon at the time the process was selected is difficult to change.

Additionally, the farther to the right of the continuum (referring back to Figure 7.1), the more likely it is that equipment and process units will be in large and costly chunks. If demand fluctuates or is uncertain, then process flexibility may be particularly important. Altering the size of a continuous oriented strategy often means a major redesign and substantial expense. There is more flexibility on the left of the continuum, where modest changes are possible.

STRATEGY DRIVEN INVESTMENTS

Increasingly, managers realize that sustained profits come from building competitive advantage, not from a good financial return on a specific process.[4] A good financial return is only one criterion for a new investment. Improving competitive position in the long run is the primary criterion. A short-term focus on financial return is usually self-defeating. Proposals to invest in processes that increase production flexibility, product quality, or breadth of the product line may be difficult to support if the focus is solely on return on investment. We recommend that the traditional approach to investment analysis (just looking at financial returns) be enhanced by strategic considerations. Specifically, the strategic considerations we suggest are:

1. that investments be made as *part of a coordinated strategic plan*. Where are these investments taking the organization? Investments should not be made as isolated expenditures, but as part of a coordinated strategic plan that will place the firm in an advantageous position. The question to be asked is, "Will these investments eventually win customers?"

[4] For an excellent discussion on investments that support competitive advantage, see Terry Hill, *Manufacturing Strategy: Text and Cases* (Homewood, IL: Irwin, 1989). Also see "Selling Rockwell on Automation," *Business Week* (June 6, 1988): 104.

2. that investments *yield a competitive advantage* (flexibility of process, speed of delivery, quality, etc.).

3. that investments *consider product life cycles.*

4. that a *variety of operating factors be included in the financial return analysis,* for instance, as we show in the following discussion, reductions in scrap, rework, floor space, and inventory increase returns. Other factors, such as maintenance requirements, training of personnel, increases in inventory, installation expense, and scrap values may also be part of the analysis.

5. that investments be *tested in light of several revenue projections* to ensure that up-side potential and down-side risk are considered.

Once the strategy implications of potential investments have been considered, traditional investment analysis is appropriate. We introduce the investment aspects of process selection next. Additionally, in the supplement to this chapter we discuss some of the technological advances making their way into both the manufacturing and service sectors.

Investment, Variable Cost, and Cash Flow

Because process alternatives exist, so do options with regard to capital investment and variable cost. Managers must choose from among different financial options as well as process alternatives. The number of initial alternatives may be large, but analysis of six major factors (cost, volume, human resource constraints, technology, quality, and reliability) typically reduces the number of alternatives to a few. Analysis should show the capital investment, variable cost, and cash flows for each alternative.

Table 7.5 illustrates three process options. Each process has a different fixed and variable cost. Current variable costs, the potential cost reduction, the new variable cost, and the additional fixed cost are shown. Note that part of the increase in fixed cost is required now, and some is required at the end of the first year. The data also provide the information needed for the cash requirements analysis presented in Table 7.6, which indicates that the firm must have $5,000 now and $25,000 in the first period for investment in Process A. However, less cash will be required in subsequent periods because variable costs are reduced by $6 per unit. The impact of these cash flows, as well as the absolute investment, may influence process selection. Table 7.7 is a detailed analysis of the cash flows of one of the alternatives—Process A.

TABLE 7.5 Investment and Variable Cost for Processes A, B, and C.

	Current Variable Cost	COST REDUCTION				New Variable Cost	Additional Capital Cost in First Year	Additional Capital Cost Now
		Labor	Scrap and Rework	Floor Space	Inventory			
Process A	$20.00	$3.00	$2.00	$.50	$.50	$14.00	$25,000.00	$5,000.00
Process B	20.00	1.25	1.75	.00	.50	16.50	15,000.00	5,000.00
Current process C	20.00	—	—	—	—	20.00	—	—

TABLE 7.6 Change in Cash Flows for Processes A, B, and C.

	NOW (DEPOSIT)	FIRST YEAR	SECOND YEAR THROUGH FIFTH YEAR
Process A	($5,000.00)[1]	($25,000.00)[2]	$6.00 times no. of units sold[3]
Process B	(5,000.00)[1]	(15,000.00)[2]	$3.50 times no. of units sold[3]
Current process C	.00	.00	.00

[1] Cash outflow if process purchased; that is, ( ) means negative cash flows.
[2] Cash outflow in first year if process purchased.
[3] Cash increase in second year through fifth year as result of cost reduction.

TABLE 7.7 Cash Flow Analysis for Process A.

	NOW (DEPOSIT)	FIRST YEAR	SECOND YEAR	THIRD YEAR	FOURTH YEAR	FIFTH YEAR
Capital investment	($5,000)	($25,000)				
New mfg. cost at $14 (1,000 units for 1 year) (500 units for 2 years) (100 units for 1 year)			$14,000	$ 7,000	$ 7,000	$1,400
Current cost at $20			20,000	10,000	10,000	2,000
Net savings			6,000	3,000	3,000	600
Salvage value (cash inflow)			—	—	—	5,000
Depreciation (1/10 per year)		3,000	3,000	3,000	3,000	3,000
Tax adjustment*			—	—	—	—
Cash flow	(5,000)	(22,000)	9,000	6,000	6,000	8,600

* Taxes are not considered in this example; however, if they were, the adjustment to cash flow would be made here.

Net Present Value

In addition to capital, variable cost, and cash flow considerations, management should consider evaluating investments via the net present value payback approach or internal rate of return.

Determining the discount value of a series of future cash receipts is known as the **net present value** technique. By way of introduction, let us consider the time value of money. Say you invest $100.00 in a bank at 5% for one year. Your investment will be worth $100.00 + $100.00 (0.05) = $105.00. If you invest the $105.00 for a second year it will be worth $105.00 + $105.00 (.05) = $110.25 at the end of the second year. Of course, we could calculate the future value of $100.00 at 5% for as many years as we wanted by simply extending this analysis. But there is an easier way to express this relationship mathematically. For the first year:

$$\$105 = \$100(1 + .05)$$

Net present value

For the second year:

$$\$110.25 = \$105(1 + .05) = \$100(1 + .05)^2$$

In general,

$$F = P(1 + i)^N \tag{7.4}$$

where:

F = the future value (such as \$110.25 or \$105)

P = the present value (such as \$100.00)

i = the interest rate (such as .05)

N = the number of years (such as 1 year or 2 years).

In most investment decisions, however, we are interested in calculating the present value of a series of future cash receipts. Solving for P, we get

$$P = \frac{F}{(1 + i)^N} \tag{7.5}$$

When the number of years is not too large, the above equation is effective. When the number of years, N, is large, the formula is cumbersome. For 20 years you would have to compute $(1 + i)^{20}$. Without a sophisticated calculator, this computation would be difficult indeed. Interest-rate tables, such as Table 7.8, alleviate this situation. First, let us rearrange the present value equation:

$$P = \frac{F}{(1 + i)^N} = FX \text{ (a factor)} \tag{7.6}$$

TABLE 7.8 Present Value of $1.

YEAR	5%	6%	7%	8%	9%	10%	11%	12%	13%	14%
1	.952	.943	.935	.926	.917	.909	.901	.893	.885	.877
2	.907	.890	.873	.857	.842	.826	.812	.797	.783	.769
3	.864	.840	.816	.794	.772	.751	.731	.712	.693	.675
4	.823	.792	.763	.735	.708	.683	.659	.636	.613	.592
5	.784	.747	.713	.681	.650	.621	.593	.567	.543	.519
6	.746	.705	.666	.630	.596	.564	.535	.507	.480	.456
7	.711	.665	.623	.583	.547	.513	.482	.452	.425	.400
8	.677	.627	.582	.540	.502	.467	.434	.404	.376	.351
9	.645	.592	.544	.500	.460	.424	.391	.361	.333	.308
10	.614	.558	.508	.463	.422	.386	.352	.322	.295	.270
11	.585	.527	.475	.429	.388	.350	.317	.287	.261	.237
12	.557	.497	.444	.397	.356	.319	.286	.257	.231	.208
13	.530	.469	.415	.368	.326	.290	.258	.229	.204	.182
14	.505	.442	.388	.340	.299	.263	.232	.205	.181	.160
15	.481	.417	.362	.315	.275	.239	.209	.183	.160	.140
16	.458	.394	.339	.292	.252	.218	.188	.163	.141	.123
17	.436	.371	.317	.270	.231	.198	.170	.146	.125	.108
18	.416	.350	.296	.250	.212	.180	.153	.130	.111	.095
19	.396	.331	.277	.232	.194	.164	.138	.116	.098	.083
20	.377	.312	.258	.215	.178	.149	.124	.104	.087	.073

where

$$X = 1/(1 + i)^N$$

and

$$F = \text{Future value}$$

Thus all we have to do is find the factor and multiply it by F to calculate the present value P. The factors, of course, are a function of the interest rate i and the number of years N. Table 7.8 lists some of these factors.

Let us consider an example.

Example 6

An investment will produce $1,000 two years from now. What is this amount worth today (that is, what is the present value) if the interest rate is 6%?

To solve this problem, we simply look in Table 7.8 for an interest rate of 6% and two years. The factor is .890, and thus the present value is $1,000(0.890) = $890.00.

Equations 7.4, 7.5 and 7.6 are used to determine the present value of one future cash amount, but there are situations in which an investment generates a series of uniform and equal cash amounts. This type of investment is called an *annuity*. For example, an investment might yield $300 per year for three years. Of course, you could use the above formula three times, for one, two, and three years, but there is a shorter method. Although there is a formula that can be used to solve for the present value of an annual series of uniform and equal cash flows (an annuity), an easy-to-use table has been developed for this purpose. Like the customary present value computations, this calculation involves a factor. The factors for annuities are in Table 7.9 (on p. 304). The basic relationship is:

$$S = RX$$

where

X = a factor from Table 7.8

S = the present value of a series of uniform annual receipts, and

R = the receipts that are received every year for the life of the investment (the annuity).

The present value of a uniform annual series of amounts is an extension of the present value of a single amount, and thus Table 7.9 can be directly developed from Table 7.8. The factors for any given interest rate in Table 7.9 are nothing more than the cumulative sum of the values in Table 7.8. In Table 7.8 for example, .952, .907, and .864 are the factors for years one, two, and three when the interest rate is 5%. The cumulative sum of these factors is 2.723 = .952 + .907 + .864. Now find in Table 7.9 where the interest rate is 5% and the number of years is three. The factor for the present value of an annuity is 2.723, as you would expect. Table 7.9 can be very helpful in reducing the computations necessary to make financial decisions.

TABLE 7.9 Present Value of an Annuity of $1.

YEAR	5%	6%	7%	8%	9%	10%	12%	14%	16%	18%
1	.952	.943	.935	.926	.917	.90	.893	.877	.862	.847
2	1.859	1.833	1.808	1.783	1.759	1.73	1.690	1.647	1.605	1.566
3	2.723	2.673	2.624	2.577	2.531	2.48	2.402	2.322	2.246	2.174
4	3.546	3.465	3.387	3.312	3.240	3.17	3.037	2.914	2.798	2.690
5	4.329	4.212	4.100	3.993	3.890	3.79	3.605	3.433	3.274	3.127
6	5.076	4.917	4.766	4.623	4.486	4.35	4.111	3.889	3.685	3.498
7	5.786	5.582	5.389	5.206	5.033	4.86	4.564	4.288	4.039	3.812
8	6.463	6.210	6.971	5.747	5.535	5.33	4.968	4.639	4.344	4.078
9	7.108	6.802	6.515	6.247	5.985	5.75	5.328	4.946	4.607	4.303
10	7.722	7.360	7.024	6.710	6.418	6.14	5.650	5.216	4.833	4.494
11	8.306	7.887	7.499	7.139	6.805	6.49	5.988	5.453	5.029	4.656
12	8.863	8.384	7.943	7.536	7.161	6.81	6.194	5.660	5.197	4.793
13	9.394	8.853	8.358	7.904	7.487	7.10	6.424	5.842	5.342	4.910
14	9.899	9.295	8.745	8.244	7.786	7.36	6.628	6.002	5.468	5.008
15	10.380	9.712	9.108	8.559	8.060	7.60	6.811	6.142	5.575	5.092
16	10.838	10.106	9.447	8.851	8.312	7.82	6.974	6.265	5.669	5.162
17	11.274	10.477	9.763	9.122	8.544	8.02	7.120	6.373	5.749	5.222
18	11.690	10.828	10.059	9.372	8.756	8.20	7.250	6.467	5.818	5.273
19	12.085	11.158	10.336	9.604	8.950	8.36	7.366	6.550	5.877	5.316
20	12.462	11.470	10.594	9.818	9.128	8.51	7.469	6.623	5.929	5.353
25	14.094	12.783	11.654	10.675	9.823	9.07	7.843	6.873	6.097	5.467
30	15.373	13.765	12.409	11.258	10.274	9.42	8.055	7.003	6.177	5.517

Let us look at an example using the annuity table.

Example 7

River Road Medical Clinic is thinking of investing in a sophisticated new piece of medical equipment. It will generate $7,000 per year in receipts for five years. What is the present value of this cash flow? Assume an interest rate of 6%.

$$S = RX = \$7,000(4.212) = \$29,484$$

The factor from Table 7.9 (4.212) was obtained by finding that value when the interest rate is 6% and the number of years is five. There is another way of looking at this example. If you went to a bank and took a loan for $29,484 today, your payments would be $7,000 per year for five years if the bank used an interest rate of 6% compounded yearly. Thus $29,484 is the *true* present value of the investment.

The net present value method is considered to be one of the best methods of ranking investment alternatives. The procedure is straightforward; you simply compute the present value of all cash flows for each investment alternative. When deciding among investment alternatives, you pick the investment that has the highest net present value. Similarly, when making several investments, those with higher net present values are preferable to investments with lower net present values.

Example 8

Quality Plastics, Inc., is considering two different investment alternatives. Investment A has an initial cost of $35,000, and investment B has an initial cost of $30,000. Both investments have a useful life of six years. The cash flows for these investments are given below. The cost of capital or the interest rate (i) is 8%.

INVESTMENT A CASH FLOW	INVESTMENT B CASH FLOW	YEAR	PRESENT VALUE FACTOR AT 8%
$10,000	$9,000	1	.926
10,000	9,000	2	.857
11,000	9,000	3	.794
12,000	9,000	4	.735
11,000	9,000	5	.681
5,000	9,000	6	.630

To find the present value of the cash flows for each investment, we multiply the present value factor by the cash flow for each investment for each year. The sum of these present value calculations minus the initial investment is the net present value of each investment. The computations appear in the following table.

YEAR	INVESTMENT A PRESENT VALUES	INVESTMENT B PRESENT VALUES
1	$ 9,260 = (.926)($10,000)	$ 8,334 = (.926)($9,000)
2	8,570 = (.857)($10,000)	7,713 = (.857)($9,000)
3	8,734 = (.794)($11,000)	7,146 = (.794)($9,000)
4	8,820 = (.735)($12,000)	6,615 = (.735)($9,000)
5	7,491 = (.681)($11,000)	6,129 = (.681)($9,000)
6	3,150 = (.630)($5,000)	5,670 = (.630)($9,000)
Totals:	$46,025	$41,607
Minus initial investment	–35,000	–30,000
Net present value	$11,025	$11,607

The net present value criterion shows investment B to be more attractive than investment A because it has a higher present value.

In Example 8, it was not necessary to make all of those present value computations for investment B. Because the cash flows are uniform, Table 7.9, the annuity table, gives the present value factor. Of course, we would expect to get the same answer. As you recall, Table 7.9 gives factors for the present value of an annuity. In this example, for payments of $9,000, cost of capital is 8% and the number of years is six. Looking in Table 7.9 under 8% and six years, we find a factor of 4.623. Thus the present value of this annuity is (4.623)($9,000) = $41,607. Look at the table in Example 8. Indeed, we get the same value, as expected.

Although net present value is one of the best approaches to evaluating investment alternatives, it does have its faults. Limitations of the net present value
approach include:

1. Investments with the same present value may have significantly different
   project lives and different salvage values.
2. Investments with the same net present value may have different cash flows.
   Different cash flows may make substantial differences in the company's
   ability to pay its bills.
3. The assumption that we know future interest rates, which we do not.
4. The assumption that payments are always made at the end of the period
   (week, month, or year), which is not usually the case.

SUMMARY

The processes that operations managers use to perform transformations can be as
important as the products themselves. Transformation processes determine much of
the fixed and variable cost, as well as quantity and quality of the product. The
process decision can result in selection of a transformation technology that is
process focused or product focused or someplace in between. However, it must be
of a capacity and technology that will provide a competitive advantage.

Good forecasting, break-even analysis, crossover charts, decision trees, cash
flow, and net present value (NPV) techniques are particularly useful to operations
managers when making the process decision.

KEY TERMS

Process strategy (p. 278)

Intermittent process (p. 278)

Process focus (p. 278)

Product focus (p. 278)

Continuous process (p. 278)

Repetitive process (p. 278)

Modules (p. 278)

Lean producers (p. 280)

Capacity (p. 288)

Designed capacity (p. 288)

Effective capacity or utilization (p. 288)

Efficiency (p. 288)

Rated capacity (p. 289)

Break-even analysis (p. 293)

Fixed costs (p. 293)

Variable costs (p. 293)

Revenue function (p. 293)

Crossover chart (p. 296)

Net present value (p. 301)

SOLVED PROBLEMS

Solved Problem 7.1

Joe Biggs works part-time making canoe paddles in Wisconsin. His annual
fixed cost is $10,000, direct labor is $3.50 per paddle, and material is $4.50

per paddle. The selling price will be $12.50 per paddle. What is break-even in dollars? What is break-even in units?

Solution

$$BEP(\$) = \frac{F}{1 - V/P} = \frac{\$10,000}{1 - (\$8.00/\$12.50)} = \frac{\$10,000}{.36} = \$27,777$$

$$BEP(x) = \frac{F}{P - V} = \frac{\$10,000}{\$12.50 - \$8.00} = \frac{\$10,000}{\$4.50} = 2,222 \text{ units}$$

Solved Problem 7.2

Your boss, Mr. La Forge, has told you to evaluate two machines. After some questioning, you are assured that they have the following costs. Assume:

a) the life of each machine is five years, and

b) the company thinks it knows how to make 14% on investments no riskier than this one.

	MACHINE A	MACHINE B
Original cost	$10,000	$20,000
Labor cost per year	2,000	3,000
Floor space per year	500	600
Energy (electricity) per year	1,000	900
Maintenance per year	2,500	500
Total annual cost	$ 6,000	$ 5,000
Salvage value	$ 2,000	$ 7,000

Determine via the present value method which machine to tell Mr. La Forge to purchase if money is worth 14% to the company.

Solution

		MACHINE A		
	Column 1		Column 2	Column 3
Now	1.000	Expense	$10,000	$10,000
1 yr.	.877	Expense	6,000	5,262
2 yr.	.769	Expense	6,000	4,614
3 yr.	.675	Expense	6,000	4,050
4 yr.	.592	Expense	6,000	3,552
5 yr.	.519	Expense	6,000	3,114
				$30,592
5 yr.	.519	Salvage Revenue	$ 2,000	− 1,038
				$29,554

		MACHINE B		
	Column 4		Column 5	Column 6
Now	1.000	Expense	$20,000	$20,000
1 yr.	.877	Expense	5,000	4,385
2 yr.	.769	Expense	5,000	3,845
3 yr.	.675	Expense	5,000	3,375
4 yr.	.592	Expense	5,000	2,960
5 yr.	.519	Expense	5,000	2,592
				$37,157
5 yr.	.519	Salvage Revenue	$ 7,000	− 3,633
				$33,524

We obtain the present value figures in columns 1 and 4 from Table 7.8. We use 1.0 for payments with no discount applied against them (that is, when payments are made now, there is no need for a discount). The other values in columns 1 and 4 are from the 14% column and the respective year (for example, the intersection of 14% and 1 year is .877, etc.). Columns 3 and 6 are the products of the present value figures times the combined cost of labor and maintenance. This computation is made for each year ($2,000 + $500 + $1,000 + $2,500) × .877 = $5,262. The same computation is made for salvage value. The salvage value of the product is subtracted from the summed costs, because it is a receipt of cash. Since the sum of the net costs for Machine B is larger than the sum of the net costs for Machine A, Machine A is the low-cost purchase, and your boss should be so informed.

Solved Problem 7.3

Sara James Bakery, described earlier in Examples 1 and 2, has decided to increase its facilities by adding one additional process line. The firm will have four process lines, each working seven days a week, three shifts per day, eight hours per shift. Utilization is 90%. This addition, however, will reduce their overall system efficiency to 85%. Compute the new rated capacity with this change in facilities.

Solution

$$\text{Rated capacity} = \text{Design capacity} \times \text{Utilization} \times \text{Efficiency}$$
$$= [(120)(4 \times 7 \times 3 \times 8)] \times (.9) \times (.85)$$
$$= (80,640) \times (.9) \times (.85)$$
$$= 61,689.6 \text{ per week}$$
$$\text{or}$$
$$= 120 \times 4 \times .9 \times .85$$
$$= 367.2 \text{ per hour.}$$

DISCUSSION QUESTIONS

1. What are the advantages of standardization? How do we obtain variety while maintaining standardization?

2. What type of process is used for each of the following?
  a) beer
  b) business cards
  c) automobiles
  d) telephone
  e) "Big Macs"
  f) custom homes

3. In an affluent society, how do we produce a wide number of options for products at low cost?

4. What products would you expect to have made by a repetitive process?

5. Where does the manager obtain data for break-even analysis?

6. What keeps plotted variable and fixed-cost data from falling on a straight line?

7. What keeps plotted revenue data from falling on a straight line?

8. What are the assumptions of break-even analysis?

9. How might we isolate the production/operations process from the customer?

10. What are assumptions of the net present value technique?

11. Identify two services located at the intermittent side of the process strategy continuum (Figure 7.1).

PROBLEMS

· **7.1** An investment will produce $1,000 two years from now. What is the amount worth today? That is, what is the present value if the interest rate is 9%?

· **7.2** What is the present value of $5,600 when the interest rate is 8% and the return of $5,600 will not be received for 12 years?

· **7.3** River Road Medical Clinic is contemplating an investment in a new x-ray machine that would require an initial investment of $7,000. The salvage value is $0. This investment will generate $8,600 per year in receipts. The life of the investment is four years. What is the present value of this investment? Use an interest rate of 11%.

: **7.4** Mr. Kulonda, vice president for operations at McClain Manufacturing, has to make a decision between two investment alternatives. Investment A has an initial cost of $61,000, and investment B has an initial cost of $74,000. The useful life of investment A is six years; the useful life of investment B is seven years. Given a cost of capital of 9% and the following cash flows for each alternative, determine the most desirable investment alternative according to the net present value criterion.

INVESTMENT A CASH FLOW	INVESTMENT B CASH FLOW	YEAR
$19,000	$19,000	1
19,000	20,000	2
19,000	21,000	3
19,000	22,000	4
19,000	21,000	5
19,000	20,000	6
19,000	11,000	7

: **7.5** An electronics firm is currently manufacturing an item that has a variable cost of $0.50 per unit and a selling price of $1.00 per unit. Fixed costs are $14,000. Current volume is 30,000 units. The firm can substantially improve the product quality by adding a new piece of equipment at an additional fixed cost of $6,000. Variable cost would increase to $0.60, but volume should jump to 50,000 units due to a higher-quality product. Should the company buy the new equipment?

: **7.6** The electronics firm in Problem 7.5 is now considering the new equipment with a price increase to $1.10 per unit. With the higher-quality product, the new volume is expected to be 45,000 units. Under these circumstances, should the company purchase the new equipment and increase the selling price?

· **7.7** Given the following data, calculate BEP(x), BEP($), and the profit at 100,000 units:
$$P = \$8/\text{unit} \quad V = \$4/\text{unit} \quad F = \$50,000$$

: **7.8** Betty Huntsman has been asked to evaluate two machines. After some investigation, she determines that they have the following costs. She is told to assume that:

a) the life of each machine is three years

b) the company thinks it knows how to make 12% on investments no more risky than this one.

	MACHINE A	MACHINE B
Original cost	$10,000	$20,000
Labor per year	2,000	4,000
Maintenance per year	4,000	1,000
Salvage value	2,000	7,000

Determine, via the present value method, which machine Betty should recommend.

: **7.9** Your boss has told you to evaluate two warming ovens for Tink-the-Tinkers, a gourmet sandwich shop. After some questioning of vendors and receipt of specifications you are assured the ovens have the following attributes and costs. The following two assumptions are appropriate:

1. the life of each machine is five years

2. the company thinks it knows how to make 14% on investments no more risky than this one.

	THREE SMALL WARMING OVENS AT $1,250 EACH	TWO LARGE HIGH-QUALITY WARMING OVENS AT $2,500 EACH
Original cost	$3,750	$5,000
Estimated labor per year in excess of larger models with transfer bottom	$750 (total)	
Cleaning and maintenance	$750 ($250 ea.)	$400 ($200 ea.)
Salvage value	$750 ($250 ea.)	$1,000 ($500 ea.)

a) Determine via the present value method which machine to tell your boss to purchase.

b) What assumption are you making about the ovens?

c) What assumption are you making in your methodology?

: **7.10** Tom Miller and Jeff Vollman have opened a copy service on Commonwealth Avenue. They estimate their fixed cost at $12,000 and their variable cost of each copy sold at $.01. They expect their selling price to average $.05.

a) What is their break-even point in dollars?

b) What is their break-even point in units?

: **7.11** Dr. Roth, a prolific author, is considering starting her own publishing company. She will call it DSI Publishing, Inc. DSI's estimated costs are:

Fixed	$250,000.00
Variable cost per book	$20.00
Selling price per book	$30.00

How many books must DSI sell to break even?

: **7.12** In addition to the costs in Problem 7.11, Dr. Roth wants to pay herself a salary of $50,000 per year.

a) Now what is her break-even point in units?

b) What is her break-even point in dollars?

: **7.13** As a prospective owner of a club known as the Red Rose, you are interested in determining the volume of sales dollars necessary for the coming year to reach the break-even point. You have decided to break down the sales for the club into four categories, the first category being liquor and beer. Your estimate of the beer sales is that 30,000 drinks will be served. The selling price for each unit will average $1.50; the cost is $.75. The second major category is meals, which you expect to be 10,000 units with an average price of $10.00 and a cost of $5.00. The third major category is desserts and wine, of which you also expect to sell 10,000 units, but with an average price of $2.50 per unit sold and a cost of $1.00 per unit. The final category is lunches and inexpensive sandwiches, which you expect to total 20,000 units at an average price of $6.25 with a food cost of $3.25. Your fixed cost (that is, rent, utilities, etc.) is $1,800 per month plus $2,000 per month for entertainment.

a) What is your break-even point in dollars?

b) What is the expected number of meals each day if you are open 360 days a year?

: **7.14** Using the data in Problem 7.13, make the problem more realistic by adding labor cost at one-third of meals and sandwiches cost. Also add variable expenses (kitchen supplies, tablecloths, napkins, etc.) at 10% of cost for all categories.

a) What is your break-even point?

b) If you expect to make a profit of $35,000 (before taxes) for your 12-hour days, what must your total sales be?

: **7.15** As operations manager of Baby Furniture, Inc., you must make a decision about expanding your line of nursery furniture (that is, cribs, toy chests, dressers, etc.). In discussing the possibilities with your sales manager, Mrs. Lockard, you decide that there definitely will be a market and that your firm should enter that market. However, because nursery furniture is often painted rather than stained, you decide you need another process line. There is no doubt in your mind about the decision, and you are sure that you should have a second process. But you do question how large to make it. A large process line is going to cost $300,000; a small process line will cost $200,000. The question, therefore, is the demand for nursery furniture. After extensive discussion with Mrs. Lockard and Mr. Utecht of Utecht Market Research, Inc., you determine that the best estimate you can make is that there is a two-out-of-three chance of profit from sales as large as $600,000 and a one-out-of-three chance as low as $300,000.

With a large process line, you could handle the high figure of $600,000. However, with a small process line you could not and would be forced to expand (at a cost of $150,000), after which time your profit from sales would be $500,000 rather than the $600,000 because of the lost time in expanding the process. If you do not expand the small process, your profit from sales would be held to $400,000. If you build a small process and the demand is low, you can handle all of the demand.

Should you open a large or small process line?

: **7.16** You are the new manager of the university basketball concession booths. You have been told in no uncertain terms that concession sales will support themselves. The following table provides the information you have been able to put together thus far.

ITEM	SELLING PRICE	VARIABLE COST	% OF REVENUE
Soft drink			
Large	$1.10	$ .65	10%
Medium	.75	.45	10%
Small	.60	.40	20%
Hot dog	.75	.45	10%
Coffee	.50	.25	20%
Miscellaneous snacks	.40	.30	30%

Last year's manager, Terry Roundball, has advised you to be sure to add 10% of variable cost as a waste allowance for all categories.

You estimate labor cost to be (five booths with three people each) $250.00. Even if nothing is sold, your cost will be $250.00, so you decide to consider this a fixed cost. Booth rental, which is a contractual cost at $50 *each* per game, is also a fixed cost.

a) What is break-even volume for all booths per game?

b) How many hot dogs would you expect to sell at break-even?

: **7.17** Rank the following investments according to net present value. Each alternative requires an initial investment of $20,000. Assume a 10% cost of capital.

YEAR	CASH FLOWS FROM INVESTMENT 1	CASH FLOWS FROM INVESTMENT 2	CASH FLOWS FROM INVESTMENT 3
1	$ 1,000	$ 7,000	$10,000
2	1,000	6,000	5,000
3	3,000	5,000	3,000
4	15,000	4,000	2,000
5	3,000	4,000	1,000
6	1,000	4,000	1,000
7	—	4,000	1,000
8	1,000	2,000	—
9	—	—	1,000

: **7.18** What is the net present value of an investment that costs $123,545, and has a salvage value of $44,560? The annual profit from the investment is $14,667 each year for 5 years. The cost of capital at this risk level is 12%.

· **7.19** The initial cost of an investment is $65,000 and the cost of capital is 10%. The return is $16,000 per year for eight years. What is the net present value?

CASE STUDY

Herrmann Enterprises

Herrmann Enterprises was considering moving some of their production from traditional numerically controlled machines to a flexible machining system (FMS). Their traditional numerical control machines have been operating in a high-variety, low-volume, intermittent manner. Their machine utilization, as near as they can figure it, is hovering around 10%. The machine tool sales people and a consulting firm want to put the machines together in an FMS. They believe that a $3,000,000 expenditure on machinery and the transfer machines will handle about 30% of Herrmann's work. The firm has not yet entered all its parts into a comprehensive group technology system, but believes that the 30% is a good estimate. This 30% fits very nicely into a "family." A reduction, because of higher utilization, should take place in the number of pieces of machinery. The firm should be able to go from fifteen to about four machines and personnel should go from fifteen to perhaps as low as three. Similarly, floor space reduction will go from 20,000 feet to about 6,000. Throughput of orders should also improve with this family of parts being processed in one to two days

rather than seven to ten. Inventory reduction is estimated to yield a one-time $750,000 savings, and annual labor savings should be in the neighborhood of $300,000.

While the projections all look very positive, an analysis of the project's return-on-investment showed it to be between 10% and 15% per year. The company has traditionally had an expectation that projects should yield well over 15% and have payback periods of substantially less than five years.

Discussion Questions

1. As a production manager for Herrmann Enterprises, what do you recommend? Why?

2. Prepare a case by a conservative plant manager for maintaining the status quo until the returns are more obvious.

3. Prepare the case for an optimistic sales manager that you should move ahead with the FMS now.

BIBLIOGRAPHY

Buzacott, J. A., and David D. Yao. "Flexible Manufacturing Systems: A Review of Analytical Models." *Management Science* **32** (July 1986).

Dawson, B. L. *A Computerized Robot Joins the Ranks of Advanced Manufacturing Technology.* Publication 8240. Cincinnati, OH: Cincinnati Milacron.

Ferguson, J. T., and J. H. Heizer. *Real Estate Investment Analysis.* Boston: Allyn & Bacon, 1990.

Froelich, L. "Robots to the Rescue." *Datamation* **28** (January 1981): 85–96.

"Future Flexibility Designed into New Hart Beverage Plant." *Beverage Industry* (November 4, 1977): 88.

Groover, M. P., and E. W. Zimmers, Jr. *CAD/CAM Computer-Aided Design and Manufacturing.* Englewood Cliffs, NJ: Prentice-Hall, 1980.

Hayes, R. H., and W. J. Abernathy. "Managing Our Way to Economic Decline." *Harvard Business Review* **58** (July–August 1980):

67–77.

Heizer, J. H. "Manufacturing Productivity: Japanese Techniques Not Enough." *Industrial Management* (September–October 1986): 21–23.

Hounshell, D. A. *From the American System to Mass Production, 1800–1932.* Baltimore: Johns Hopkins University Press, 1984.

Jaikumar, R. "Postindustrial Manufacturing." *Harvard Business Review* **64** (November–December 1986): 69–76.

Leonard-Barton, D., and W. A. Kraus. "Implementing New Technology." *Harvard Business Review* **63** (November–December 1985): 102–110.

Malpas, R. "The Plant After Next." *Harvard Business Review* **61** (July-August 1983): 122–130.

Morris, J. S., and R. J. Tersine. "A Simulation Analysis of Factors Influencing the Attractiveness of Group Technology Cellular Layout." *Management Science* **36** (December 1990).

Parsaei, H. R., and A. Mital. *Economic Aspects of Advanced Produc-tion and Manufacturing Systems.* New York: Van Nostrand Reinhold, 1991.

Primrose, P. *Investment in Manufacturing Technology.* New York: Van Nostrand Reinhold, 1991.

Rolan, T. H. "Process." *Industry Week* (May 30, 1983): 67.

Russell, R. S., P. Y. Huang, and Y. Leu. "A Study of Labor Allocation Strategies in Cellular Manufacturing." *Decision Sciences* **22** (July–August 1991): 594.

Schonberger, R. J. "Frugal Manufacturing." *Harvard Business Re-view* **65** (September–October 1987): 95–100.

Teresko, J. "Group Technology: Shortening the Manufacturing Cir-cuit." *Industry Week* (July 19, 1978).

"Where DuPont Thinks Its New Process Will Score." *Business Week* (September 19, 1983): 45.

Whitney, D. E. "Real Robots Do Need Jigs." *Harvard Business Review* **64** (May–June 1986): 110–116.

Information Technology in P/OM

INTRODUCTION

In this supplement we introduce the issue of information technology in P/OM. Technology can be a powerful tool in developing a competitive advantage,[1] via both product and process strategy.[2] The firms that achieve the most success at using technology as competitive advantage appear to be organizations that:

- plan for a more distant time horizon;
- have a narrow product line; they "stick to their knitting" and know their product and customer exceedingly well;
- have strong internal technical capabilities that are tied to their strategic analysis;
- have consistent and stable strategic management; they seem to be better at implementing the changes necessary for effective use of technology.

Because information technology is so pervasive, most of this supplement focuses on its application to P/OM.

INFORMATION TECHNOLOGY IN MANUFACTURING

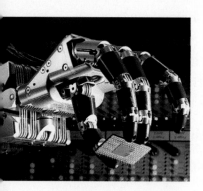

One of the great advantages of robots is that they can be reprogrammed for different movements by merely changing the electronic signals that control them. However, one of the limitations of robots has been their inability to "sense" their strength or position or the pressure that is being exerted when they "grab" or "bump" something. Consequently, substantial effort has been made in recent years in this area. This picture indicates the tremendous strides being made in this area as robotic "fingers" pick up and hold a semiconductor chip.

Information sciences are having a major impact on both manufacturing and services. Among the tools provided by the information sciences are computer-aided design (CAD), computer-aided manufacturing (CAM), flexible manufacturing systems (FMS), and computer-integrated manufacturing (CIM). The electronic flow of data that ultimately becomes information provides the communication that ties ever improving equipment together. This electronic flow of information is also able to control information and allow the replacement of manual operations with automatic operations. The impact of information runs across the entire manufacturing spectrum shown in Figure S7.1.

Information technology in manufacturing will expand the flexible manufacturing and computer integrated manufacturing block shown in Figure S7.1. Flexible Manufacturing Systems (FMS) and Computer-Integrated Manufacturing (CIM) will include a huge range of volumes without losing the ability to deal with variety. At the left are the general-purpose machines, traditionally requiring substantial manual intervention; but information technology will allow the rapid economical flow of control data to computerized machines that will replace even some of this relatively low-cost, highly flexible manual equipment. In the middle are various versions of automated equipment, including direct numerical control (DNC) machines linked together in automated sequences to perform processing. At the other extreme are continuous processes such as paper making and textile spinning.

---

[1] See, for example, W. J. Abernathy and K. B. Clark, "Innovation: Mapping the Winds of Creative Destruction," *Research Policy,* **14** (1985): 3; M. E. Porter, "The Technological Dimension of Competitive Strategy," in R. S. Rosenbloom, ed., *Research on Technology Innovation, Management and Policy* (Greenwich, CT: JAI Press), p. 3; A. L. Frohman, "Putting Technology into Strategic Planning," *California Management Review,* **27,** 2 (Winter 1985): 48; and A. C. Cooper and D. Schendl, "Strategic Responses to Technology Threats," in M. L. Tuchman and W. L. Moore, eds., *Readings in the Management of Innovation,* 2nd ed. (Cambridge, MA: Ballinger, 1988), p. 249.

[2] For an excellent discussion of the strategic uses of technology in product innovation see Joseph Morone, "Strategic Use of Technology." *California Management Review* (Summer 1989): 81–110.

FIGURE S7.1

Process Options: Information science is increasing the overlap between process options.

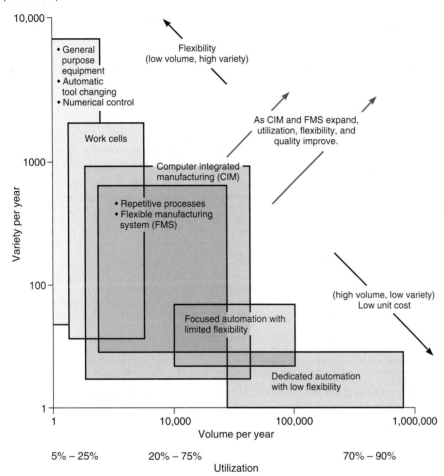

Computer-Aided Design (CAD)

Computer-aided design, introduced in Chapter 6, is also expanding. Designers save time and money with CAD, which shortens development cycles for automobiles, electronics, and other products. Using CAD, designers can create and modify models with three-dimensional perspective. The speed and ease with which sophisticated designs can be manipulated and modified make review of numerous options possible before final commitments are made.

Numerical Control

Recent microprocessor developments allow increased flexibility of equipment, particularly when manufacturing discrete items. This is a result of the ease with which the machines can now be reprogrammed because of information technology. The

Numerical control (NC)
Computer numerical control (CNC)

transition from manual and mechanical controls to electronic control has allowed this flexibility. Machines without computer memory but that are controlled by paper or magnetic tape are called **numerical control (NC)** machines. Machines with their own memory are called **computer numerical control (CNC)** machinery. Electronic control is accomplished by writing computer programs to control a machine. The machine output is then the product. The computer program is written much as one might write a BASIC or COBOL program to produce a paycheck. The languages used include **APT** (Automatically Programmed Tool) and **Compact II**.[3]

APT
Compact II

Process Control

Process control

Process control is the use of information technology to control a physical process. These processes usually meet our definition of a *continuous process*. For instance, process control is used to measure the moisture content and thickness of paper as it travels over a paper machine at a thousand feet per minute. Process control is also used to determine temperatures, pressures, and quantities in petroleum refineries, petrochemical processes, cement plants, steel mills, nuclear reactors, and other continuous processes.

Process control systems operate in a number of ways, but the following is typical:

- They have sensors—often analog devices collecting data.
- The analog devices read data on some periodic basis, perhaps once a minute, or once every two seconds.
- The measurements are translated into digital signals, which are transmitted to a digital computer.
- Computer programs read the file (the digital data) and analyze the data.
- The resulting output may take numerous forms. These include a message on a computer console or printer, a signal to a motor to change a valve setting, a warning light or horn, or a statistical process control chart.

Robots are used not only for labor savings, but more importantly, for those jobs that are dangerous, or monotonous, or require consistency, as in the even spraying of paint on an automobile.

Robot

Robots

Where a machine is flexible and has the ability to hold, move, and perhaps "grab" items, we tend to use the word **robot**. However, in spite of movies, cartoons, and stories about robots, they are not mechanical people. They are mechanical devices that may have a few electronic impulses stored on a semiconductor chip that will activate motors or switches. When robots are part of a transformation system, they usually provide the movement of material between machines. They may also be used effectively to perform tasks that are especially monotonous, or dangerous, or where the task can be improved by the substitution of mechanical for human effort. This would be the case where consistency, accuracy, speed, or the necessary strength or power can be enhanced by the substitution of machines for people.

Robots and programmable machines are now cost competitive for a wide range of applications from small batch jobs through long continuous jobs. Less flexible and, consequently, less expensive robots may substitute for specialized equipment even in continuous processes. Robot control and instructions are similar to those

---

[3] Compact II is a registered trademark of Manufacturing Data Systems, Inc., Ann Arbor, Michigan.

used for numerically controlled machine tools. These instructions provide complete task control providing position, orientation, velocity, and acceleration. Communication between the operator and the robot is typically provided by a computer terminal, although robots can also be instructed via a "lead-through" method. Once instructions are entered, they are stored in computer memory and modified or edited as changes are made in the product or processing.

Automated Guided Vehicles (AGVs)

Automated material handling can take the form of monorails, conveyers, robots, or automated guided vehicles (AGVs). **Automated guided vehicles (AGVs)** are electronically guided and controlled carts used in manufacturing to move parts and equipment. They are also used in offices to move mail and in hospitals and in jails to deliver meals.

Automated guided vehicles (AGVs)

Flexible Manufacturing System (FMS)

In the sophisticated case, material handling equipment is used to complement direct numerical control (DNC) machines. The material handling equipment can be robots,

FIGURE S7.2

Computer-Integrated Manufacturing (CIM). Computer-aided design (CAD), Computer-aided manufacturing (CAM), flexible manufacturing systems (FMS), brought together.
(*Source:* Adapted from March 6, 1986 issue of *Business Week* by special permission, copyright © 1986 by McGraw-Hill, Inc.)

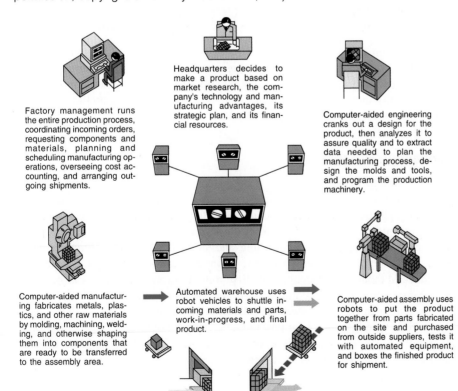

Factory management runs the entire production process, coordinating incoming orders, requesting components and materials, planning and scheduling manufacturing operations, overseeing cost accounting, and arranging outgoing shipments.

Headquarters decides to make a product based on market research, the company's technology and manufacturing advantages, its strategic plan, and its financial resources.

Computer-aided engineering cranks out a design for the product, then analyzes it to assure quality and to extract data needed to plan the manufacturing process, design the molds and tools, and program the production machinery.

Computer-aided manufacturing fabricates metals, plastics, and other raw materials by molding, machining, welding, and otherwise shaping them into components that are ready to be transferred to the assembly area.

Automated warehouse uses robot vehicles to shuttle incoming materials and parts, work-in-progress, and final product.

Computer-aided assembly uses robots to put the product together from parts fabricated on the site and purchased from outside suppliers, tests it with automated equipment, and boxes the finished product for shipment.

transfer machines, or automated guided vehicles; it moves materials from one workstation to another. The material handling equipment and the workstation may be connected to a common centralized computer facility, which provides the instructions for routing jobs to the appropriate workstation and the instructions for each workstation. Such an arrangement is an automated work cell or, as it is more commonly known, a **flexible manufacturing system (FMS).**

Flexible manufacturing system (FMS)

While technological problems still exist, computer-aided scheduling and the improved utilization possible with FMS are making this technology ever more popular.

Computer-Integrated Manufacture (CIM)

A flexible manufacturing system can be extended backward electronically into the engineering (computer-aided design), production, and inventory control departments. In this way, computer-aided drafting can ultimately generate the necessary electronic code (instructions) to control a **direct numerically controlled (DNC)** machine. If this machine is connected to others and to material handling equipment as a part of a flexible manufacturing system, then the entire system would be **computer-integrated manufacturing (CIM)** (Figure S7.2).

Direct numerical control (DNC)

Computer-integrated manufacturing (CIM)

In a computer-integrated manufacturing environment, a design change initiated at a computer-aided design (CAD) terminal can result in that change being made in the part produced in a matter of minutes.

INFORMATION SCIENCES IN OPERATIONS SUPPORT

The information sciences are making a major impact in three additional areas that have applications in operations. These areas are transaction processing, management information systems, and decision support systems. The type of information that is typically included in discussions of transaction processing and management information systems is shown in Figure S7.3.

Transaction Processing

Transaction processing system

A **transaction processing system** is a system that addresses the multitude of transactions that occur within and between firms. These transactions have traditionally been paper transactions and include payroll, order entry, invoicing, receipt of checks, inventory, personnel, etc. When these transactions are moved from paper transactions to computerized processing and storage, we have a computer-based transaction system. The paperwork transactions at General Motors were so horrendous that GM thought it prudent to buy Electronic Data Systems, Inc. (EDS), so that these transactions could be computerized and the cost reduced. To the extent that such systems can be automated beyond those of the competitors, a competitive advantage in speed, accuracy, or cost reduction may be obtained. If General Motors has a billion paper transactions a year and is able to reduce the cost of each transaction by $5, the savings is tremendous.

FIGURE S7.3

DSS, MIS, and Transaction Processing in Production/Operations Management.
(*Source:* Adapted from Andersen Consulting, *Foundations of Business Systems*, Hinsdale, IL: Dryden Press, 1989, pp. 124–125.)

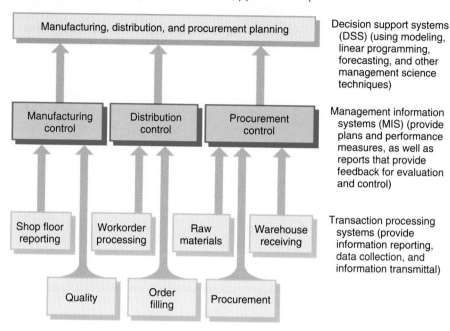

Management Information System (MIS)

The second form of information system is the **management information system (MIS).** MIS systems are dedicated to obtaining, formatting, manipulating, and presenting data in the form of information to managers when needed. Information systems make their presence known in P/OM in a variety of ways, from scheduling to material requirements planning (MRP).

In the service industry new applications include such things as authorizing payment of your bill from your hotel room via a channel on the room's television set. The labor savings at the registration desk plus enhanced service for the customer is currently providing a competitive advantage to Sheraton Hotels. Management information systems are used in the lodging industry in a variety of ways, as shown in the *POM in Action* box, "Working Smart."

Management information system (MIS)

Decision Support System (DSS)

Another area where information science is helping operations in service as well as in manufacturing is through the use of a decision support system. A **decision support system (DSS)** is a logical extension of MIS that aids managers in *modeling* and decision making. Rather than simply providing information, a DSS allows a manager to perform "what if" analysis given certain financial or operating parameters. A DSS also can incorporate such analytic tools as forecasting models (Chapter

Decision support system (DSS)

POM *in action*

Working Smart: Service Firms Struggle to Raise Productivity

Information technology is making a difference in the hotel industry. Hotel owners can now precisely track a maid's time through the use of a security system. When a maid enters a room, a card is inserted that notifies the front desk computer as to the maid's location. "We can show her a printout of how long she takes to do the room," says a major investor in a Salisbury franchise.

The security system also enables guests to use their own credit cards as keys to unlock their door. And there are other uses for the system. The com-

puter can bar a guest's access to the room after checkout time and automatically controls the air conditioning or heat, turning it on at check-in and off at check-out.

A 92-room hotel with the system opened with the equivalent of only 11 full-time employees—a general manager, 4.5 desk clerks, five housekeepers, and a part-time maintenance person.

Sources: Lodging Hospitality, June 1991, p. 50, and December 1991, p. 110; and *The Wall Street Journal,* June 1, 1989, p. A8.

4), decision trees (Chapter 3), PERT/CPM (Chapter 16), and many other ways of examining the data in the information system. Graphical outputs are a common part of the power of a DSS.

Expert Systems (ES)

Expert systems (ES)

Expert systems (ES) are computer programs that mimic human logic and "solve" problems much as a human expert would. The idea behind the use of an expert system is to capture in a computer program the knowledge and skills of a person who is an expert in a given field. Indeed, five advantages of the ES are that they:

1. make decisions faster than the expert;
2. derive the benefits of having an expert at its disposal without having the expert present;
3. equal and surpass, at least in terms of consistency, the human expert;
4. free the human expert for other work;
5. can be disseminated to numerous nonexperts for education and training.

Although the idea is quite simple, the mechanics of making an expert system work are difficult. To make the system function there must be a knowledge base that is supplied by an expert. Every step of the process must be programmed meticulously, including any and all options to decisions made throughout the process. This computerized knowledge base is designed to be updated periodically to include new rules and facts. An electronic representation of the expert's thought process is called the "inference engine"—this fuels the knowledge base. Figure S7.4 shows an example of how an expert system for scheduling jobs in a plant works.

Although the use of expert systems is widespread and rapidly expanding, limitations do exist. Among these are determining the relevance of data and recognizing the lack of data—these abilities have yet to be incorporated into expert systems.

Motorola, located in Boynton Beach, Florida, uses a flexible manufacturing system to make "pagers." This system builds to custom order pagers in 90 minutes instead of days. About 50 employees track production and 42 computers and robots assemble "pagers" that are custom programmed with one of 29 million unique codes. Motorola recently received the Malcolm Baldrige National Quality Award.

POM in action

Credit Authorization at American Express

The American Express Company has no set charging limits. To help the company decide whether to approve a specific charge, an expert system is used to sort through as many as 13 data bases. This feature has value for competitive reasons, but more importantly, it has eased the stiff administrative challenge of determining a customer's credit level. A merchant calls AMEX to authorize a charge whenever a customer makes a large purchase. Before the expert system was in place, the AMEX employee had to use his or her own discretion. If a specific purchase was outside a customer's normal buying pattern, the AMEX employee had to search through other data bases to gather more information. Now, the Authorizer's Assistant ES conducts the search and makes recommendations to the person who authorizes the approval decision. The whole process takes place in seconds, while the merchant is still on the phone.

Sources: "Putting Expert Systems to Work," *Harvard Business Review,* **66,** 2, March–April 1988, p. 92; and "The Expert Back Office," *Institutional Investor,* **22,** 14, December 1988, pp. 7–9.

FIGURE S7.4

How an Expert Scheduling System Works.

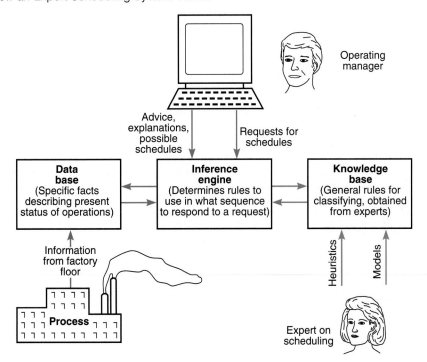

TABLE S7.1 Expert systems in P/OM.

NAME	USE	EXPLANATION
XCON (eXpert CONfigurer), Digital Equipment Corp.	Configuration	Checks sales orders and then specifies the components needed to configure the computer system
Authorizer's Assistant, American Express	Credit	Helps determine the appropriate level of credit, based on a variety of criteria
CONSULTANT, IBM	Bids	Helps field service representatives prepare bids by analyzing elements in the request for quotation
PROPLAN	Scheduling	Schedules machine parts based on facilities available, machine capability, and geometric features of the parts
SPC (Statistical Process Control), Automatix, Inc.	Process control	Data are statistically analyzed to guide modifications to the manufacturing process to anticipate malfunctions
DELTA (Diesel Electric Locomotive Trouble-shooting), General Electric	Maintenance	Assists maintenance personnel in isolating and repairing various faults in diesel electric locomotives
FADES (Facilities Design Expert System)	Layout	Develops a good facility design in situations where quantitative tools and human judgment can be combined

Adapted from H. Raghav Rao and B. P. Lingaraj, "Expert Systems in Production and Operations Management: Classification and Prospects," *Interfaces,* **18** (November–December 1988): 80–91; and Dorothy Leonard-Barton and John J. Sviokla, "Putting Expert Systems to Work," *Harvard Business Review,* **66** (March–April 1988): 92.

Table S7.1 provides an indication of the areas where expert systems have been developed. Their names and a brief explanation are also included. An ES at American Express Company is discussed in the *POM in Action* box, "Credit Authorization at American Express." A number of expert systems are discussed in more detail in the appropriate chapters of this text.

SUMMARY

Innovations in information technology are strongly contributing to improvements in P/OM. These advances are being made in a number of areas, but particularly in information sciences. Information sciences are improving management information systems, transaction processing systems, and decision support systems. Information technology is also enhancing machine controls from numerical controls to computer integrated manufacturing. These advances will, with proper management, allow improved flexibility in meeting customer requirements, higher quality, and greater utilization of resources.

KEY TERMS

Numerical control (NC) (p. 318)
Computer numerical control (CNC) (p. 318)
APT (p. 318)
Compact II (p. 318)
Process control (p. 318)
Robot (p. 318)
Automated guided vehicle (AGV) (p. 319)
Flexible manufacturing system (FMS) (p. 320)

Direct numerical control (DNC) (p. 320)
Computer-integrated manufacturing (CIM) (p. 320)
Transaction processing system (p. 320)
Management information system (MIS) (p. 321)
Decision support system (DSS) (p. 321)
Expert systems (ES) (p. 322)

DISCUSSION QUESTIONS

1. What are the components of an expert system?

2. In what kind of situations are expert systems being used?

3. What is the difference between a management information system (MIS) and a decision support system (DSS)?

4. Give some recent examples of information technology successfully applied to new products and new processes in (a) manufacturing and (b) services.

5. Distinguish between flexible manufacturing systems (FMS) and computer-integrated manufacturing (CIM).

6. What kinds of enhancements are being made to computer-aided design (CAD) systems?

CASE STUDY

Dare We Diversify?

A technology company comfortably ensconced in a niche wonders how to branch out.

In 1984 Glenn Wienkoop took his boss, David Bossen, to lunch and outlined a proposition for diversifying their factory-controls company, Measurex Corp. Measurex (1989 sales, $284 million) had made a real success of itself by sticking to its primary business, computer-controlled manufacturing systems for process industries, with most of the business coming from the paper industry.

The time seemed right to broaden the customer base. But there was reason for caution: Wienkoop wanted to take Measurex's software know-how and apply it to factory controls for so-called discrete manufacturing (repetitive manufacturing), where objects like autos, aerospace parts, or

circuit boards go down an assembly line. Measurex, though, was known for process controls, where the manufactured goods come out in a continuous stream, like paper. If it made the leap, there was the danger that resources would be diverted away from paper industry customers, who accounted for well over 70% of the company's sales.

Bossen's answer was to create a new company, with Wienkoop at its head, to take Measurex's controls software and develop solutions for other industries.

In 1986 Wienkoop moved into a separate building across the railroad tracks from Measurex's Cupertino, Calif., headquarters and set to work building Measurex Automation Systems.

Wienkoop had his work cut out. Controls for discrete

CASE STUDY (Continued)

manufacturing are more complex than process controls and, not surprisingly, have attracted the attention of big computer companies like IBM, Digital Equipment, and Hewlett-Packard. The guts of a process control system are microwave, x-ray, infrared, and ultraviolet sensors. For discrete manufacturing, though, the software is likely to be more important than the hardware.

Discussion Questions

1. How does Measurex's strategy fit with the strategies discussed in this chapter for technological companies?

2. What are the changes in information technology being sold by the parent company, Measurex Corp., and the new company, Measurex Automation Systems?

Source: Adapted by permission of FORBES magazine. © Forbes, Inc., 1991.

BIBLIOGRAPHY

Bahrami, H., and Evans, S. "Strategy Making in High Technology Firms: The Empiricist Mode." *CMR* **31** (Winter 1989): 107–128.

Bestor, J. "Using Expert Systems to Improve Lenders' Performance During Mergers and Acquisitions." *The Journal of Commercial Bank Lending* (September–October 1987): 89–94.

Brown, R. "Knowledge Based Scheduling and Resource Allocation in the CAMPS Architecture." *Proceedings of the International Conference on Expert Systems and the Leading Edge in Production Planning and Control* (1987).

Fisher, E. L. "An AI Based Methodology for Factory Design." *AI Magazine* **3** (Fall 1986): 72–85.

Frohman, A. "Technology as a Competitive Weapon." *Harvard Business Review* **60** (January–February 1982): 97–104.

Grant, R. M., R. Krishnan, A. B. Shani, and R. Baer. "Appropriate Manufacturing Technology: A Strategic Approach." *Sloan Management Reveiew* **33** (Fall 1991): 43.

Johnston, D. A., and D. M. McCutcheon. "Planning the Implementation of New Technology." *Operations Management Review* **6** (Fall 1987; Winter 1988): 1–7.

Jovic, F. *Process Control Systems.* New York: Van Nostrand Reinhold, 1991.

Leonard-Barton, D., and J. Sviokla. "Putting Expert Systems to Work." *Harvard Business Review* **66** (March–April 1988): 91–98.

Marsh, C. A. "MARS—An Expert System Using the Automated Reasoning Tool to Schedule Resources." *Robotics and Expert Systems—Proceedings of Robex's 85—Instrument Society of America:* 123–125.

Matsushima, K., N. Okada, and T. Sata. "The Integration of CAD and CAM by Application of AI Techniques." *Annals of CIRP* **31** (1982): 329–332.

Mertens, P., and Kanet, J. J. "Expert Systems in Production Management: An Assessment." *Journal of Operations Management* **6** (August 1986): 393–404.

Meyer, M. H., and K. F. Curley. "Putting Expert Systems Technology to Work." *Sloan Management Review* **32** (Winter 1991): 21.

National Research Council. *Management of Technology: The Hidden Competitive Advantage.* Washington, DC: National Academy Press, 1987.

Nelson, C. W., and R. Balachandra. "Choosing the Right Expert System Building Approach." *Decision Sciences* **22** (Spring 1991): 354.

Oliff, M. D. *Expert Systems and Intelligent Manufacturing.* New York: Elsevier Science Publishing, 1988.

Orciuch, E., and Frost, J. "ISA: Intelligent Scheduling Assistant." *IEEE Conference on AI Applications* (1984): 314–320.

Quinn, J. B., J. J. Baruch, and P. C. Paquette. "Technology in Services." *Scientific American* **257** (December 1987): 50–58.

Roberts, H. "Expert Systems and the Personnel Department." *Personnel Management* (June 1988): 52–55.

Roth, A. V., C. Gaimon, and L. Krajewski. "Optimal Acquisition of FMS Technology Subject to Technological Progress." *Decision Sciences* **22** (Spring 1991): 308.

Shortlife, E. H., B. G. Buchanan, and E. A. Feigenbaum. "Knowledge Engineering for Medical Decision Making: A Review of Computer Based Clinical Decision Aids." *Proceedings of IEEE G7* (1979): 1207–1224.

Silverman, B. G. (ed.) *Expert Systems for Business.* Reading, MA: Addison-Wesley, 1987.

Stefik, M., J. Aikins, R. Balzer, J. Benoit, L. Birnbaum, F. Hayes-Roth, and E. Sacerdoti. "The Organization of Expert Systems: A Tutorial." *Artificial Intelligence* **13** (March 1986): 135–173.

Turban, E. *Decision Support and Expert Systems: Managerial Perspectives.* New York: Macmillan, 1988.

Wiegner, K. K. "Dare We Diversify?" *Forbes* (February 5, 1990): 160.

Wu, B. *Fundamentals of Manufacturing Systems Design and Analysis.* New York: Van Nostrand Reinhold, 1991.

Yellowlees, R. A. "White Collar Productivity: The Technology Challenge." *Industrial Management* (March–April 1986): 14–17.

Location Strategies

*Location Provides
Competitive Advantage
at Federal Express*

In the 1960s Delta Airlines initiated the "hub" concept at the Atlanta Airport. The hub concept allowed them to bring passengers from throughout their network to a central hub where passengers change planes—hopefully to another Delta plane. Planes were scheduled so Delta would have a critical number of arrivals and departures periodically during the day.

At the Federal Express hub in Memphis, Tennessee, approximately 100 Federal Express aircraft converge each night with more than 700,000 documents and packages.

Fred Smith, founder and president of Federal Express, received a C on a college paper in which he proposed basically the same idea, but for small packages. Since then, he has proven that the hub concept provides a radial distribution system that is unique and effective. He selected Memphis, Tennessee, as the central hub.

Each night, except Sunday, Federal Express brings to Memphis packages from throughout the world that are going to cities for which Federal Express does not have direct flights. The central hub permits service to a far greater number of points with fewer aircraft than the traditional linear system (directly from city A to city B). The central hub system also allows Federal Express an opportunity to match aircraft flights with package loads each night and to reroute flights when load volume requires it. This ability to match flights with demand and the resulting flexibility afford

At the preliminary sort area, packages and documents are sorted and sent to a secondary sorting area. The Memphis facility covers 1,500,000 square feet; it is big enough to hold 33 football fields.

considerable savings in operating costs. Federal Express also believes that the central hub system helps reduce mishandling and delay in transit because there is total control over the packages from pick-up point through delivery.

Federal Express manages a very complex network with over 432 planes worldwide. The U.S. aircraft leave cities throughout the nation on schedules that allow them to arrive about midnight at Memphis, where packages are sorted and exchanged until about 4:00 A.M. Then the planes depart, typically returning to their city of origin.

Memphis provides Federal Express with an uncongested airport, centrally located in the United States, with very few hours of closure because of weather. Competing carriers fly out of airports with substantially more weather problems and often with a less desirable location relative to their customers. Location, although unquantifiable in regard to safety, may be a contributor to the Federal Express safety record. In its nearly 20 years of existence, Federal Express has never had an aircraft crash.

Containers carrying documents and packages are loaded onto a Federal Express aircraft. A series of rollers moves the containers into position on the aircraft; a system of locking mechanisms secures the containers in place on the floor.

At a Federal Express station, employees are picking those items for a particular route and are loading them into a Federal Express van for delivery to their final destination.

At the outbound slide/load area the packages and documents that have already gone through the primary and secondary sorts are checked by city, state, and zip code and then placed in containers that will be loaded onto aircraft for delivery to their final destinations in 170 countries.

References: Various sources supplied by Federal Express; Robert A. Sigafoos and Roger Easson, *Absolutely, Positively Overnight! The Unofficial History of Federal Express* (Memphis, TN: St. Luke's Press, a division of Plaintree Publishing, Ltd., 1988); Christopher H. Loveloc, "Developing and Managing the Customer-Service Function in the Service Sector," in John Grepiel, Michael Solomon, and Carol Suprenant (eds.), *The Service Encounter* (Lexington, MA: Lexington Books, D. C. Heath & Co., 1985).

INTRODUCTION

One of the most important long-term cost and revenue decisions a company makes is where to locate its operation. Location is a critical element in determining fixed and variable costs for both industrial and service firms. Depending on the product and type of production or service taking place, transportation costs alone can total as much as 25% of the product's selling price. That is, one-fourth of the total revenue of a firm may be needed just to cover freight expenses of the raw materials coming in and the finished product going out.[1] Other costs that may be influenced by location include taxes, wages, and raw material costs. The choice of locations can alter total production and distribution costs by as much as 10%. Lowering costs by 10% of total production costs through optimum location selection may be the easiest 10% savings management ever makes.

Once an operations manager has committed an organization to a specific location, many costs are firmly in place and difficult to reduce. For instance, if a new factory location is in a region with high energy costs, even good management with an outstanding energy strategy is starting at a disadvantage. The same is true of a good human resource strategy if labor in the selected location is expensive, ill trained, or has a poor work ethic. Consequently, hard work to determine an optimal facility location is a good investment.

This chapter first examines the variables of location analysis and then explores techniques that may prove helpful in determining location. We will look at approaches for service facilities as well as for industrial plants and warehouses.

The Objective of Location Strategy

The development of a location strategy depends upon the type of firm being considered. Industrial location analysis decisions focus on minimizing costs; retail and professional service organizations typically have a focus of maximizing revenue. Warehouse location, on the other hand, may be determined by a combination of cost and speed of delivery. The *objective of location strategy* is to maximize the benefit of location to the firm.

METHODS OF LOCATION STRATEGY

There are four major methods for solving location problems:

1. *Weighted methods*—methods that
   a) assign weight and points to various factors,
   b) determine tangible costs, such as taxes, land, and labor,
   c) investigate intangible costs, such as community attitude or quality of the state government, and
   d) look at both the short- and long-run costs.
2. *Locational break-even methods*—a special case of break-even analysis and crossover charts that were introduced in Chapter 7.

---

[1] David Anderson, "Your Company's Logistics Management: An Asset or a Liability in the 1980s?" *Transportation Review,* Data Resources, Inc. (Winter 1983): 119.

3. *Center of gravity method*—a mathematical technique used for finding a location for a single warehouse that services a number of retail stores.

4. *Transportation method*—a linear programming method based on the techniques introduced in the supplement to Chapter 3.

Before discussing these, we will look at some location considerations.

LOCATION CONSIDERATIONS

A number of factors keep location decisions from being analyzed objectively and based solely on cost. Among these factors are labor productivity, foreign exchange, and changing attitudes toward the industry, unions, employment, zoning, pollution, taxes, and so forth.

Labor Productivity

The appeal of low wage rates often provides an enticement to particular locations, domestic or foreign; but an analysis that focuses on wage rates is inadequate if it does not also reflect labor productivity. As discussed in Chapter 1, differences exist in productivity in various countries. What management is really interested in is the combination of productivity and the wage rate. For example, a firm paying $12.00

FIGURE 8.1

Manufacturing Labor Costs of Twenty Nations, 1990
For most firms the cost of labor includes much more than merely wages. Non-wage costs—pension plans, social security taxes, free meals, extra holidays, and a host of other perks—can be hefty. Of the 20 countries in the chart, only in Italy do manufacturing firms' non-wage expenses exceed wage costs, accounting for 51% of total labor costs in 1990. Germany has the steepest overall costs, with non-wage items making up 46% of its total. The cheapest labor is to be found in Portugal, where overall costs are only a fifth of Germany's. (*Source:* Copyright 1991, *The Economist, Ltd.* Reprinted with permission from The New York Times Special Features.)

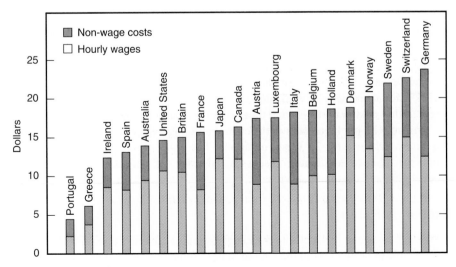

POM _in action_

U.S. Semiconductor Makers Automate, Cut Chip Production in Southeast Asia

For over 10 years, American semiconductor makers have segregated production into onshore and off-shore operations. Highly skilled chores had been accomplished in the domestic plants. Final work, which required a great deal of labor but less skill, had been handled in overseas facilities, where wages were low.

Because of automation this scenario is changing. Machines now have the capacity to mount circuits onto metal frames, wire the circuits into place, and even test the finished product for flaws. They do all this, and at a quicker rate than humans.

While a Southeast Asian worker can wire 120 integrated circuits to his frame in an hour, using manual equipment, an automated machine in the U.S. can wire 640 circuits in an hour. One worker is capable of monitoring eight machines at a time, and thus the output per person is an overwhelming 5,120

circuits an hour.

Clearly, labor becomes a smaller portion of the entire manufacturing cost. Considering inventory and transportation costs, it becomes wise to assemble chips in a U.S. facility in preference to an Asian one, even if the Asian plant is equally automated, according to some analysts.

For countries such as Malaysia, the Philippines, and Singapore, which have been heavily involved in electronics for jobs and exports, these developments have significant implications. While Southeast Asian governments are anxiously observing the trend toward onshore manufacture, Singapore and Malaysia are considering generous tax incentives and low-interest loans to entice U.S. semiconductor makers.

Sources: The Wall Street Journal, August 21, 1985, p. 28; _Business Week,_ October 25, 1991, pp. 76–79; _Far Eastern Economic Review,_ December 12, 1991, pp. 72–73.

per hour with 1.25 units produced per hour will spend less on labor than one paying $10.00 per hour with productivity of 1.0 units per hour.

$$\frac{\text{Labor cost per hour}}{\text{Productivity (that is, units per hour)}} = \text{Cost per Unit}$$

Case 1: $\dfrac{\$12 \text{ Wages per hour}}{1.25 \text{ Units produced per hour}} = \dfrac{\$12}{1.25} = \$9.60$

Case 2: $\dfrac{\$10 \text{ Wages per hour}}{1.00 \text{ Units produced per hour}} = \dfrac{\$10}{1.00} = \$10.00$

Employees with poor training, poor education, or poor work habits may not be a good buy even at low wages. By the same token, employees who cannot or will not always reach their place of work are not much good to the organization even at low wages. Labor cost per unit is sometimes called the labor content of the product.

Productivity per labor-hour is the crucial unit. Figure 8.1 on page 331 shows the wage rates per hour for 20 Western nations. The _POM in Action_ box, "U.S. Semiconductor Makers Automate," discusses the trade-off between low labor costs, productivity, and customer service.

Exchange Rates

Both wage rates and productivity may suggest that production in a foreign location is preferable to production in the United States. Sometimes exchange rates allow for

POM _in action_

Orlando Woos United with Bevy of Incentives

Orlando's proposal to win United Airlines' aircraft maintenance center features financial incentives of $154 million. A key part of the proposal would require local government entities to contribute a total of $70 million over five years. Orlando is competing with 10 other cities, including Denver, Indianapolis, Louisville, and Oklahoma City, for the prized $1 billion aircraft repair base, where United expects to employ 7,000 people by 1998.

Some packages are double the value of what Orlando would like to offer. Denver's tax breaks, bond financing, and other benefits, for example, total nearly $335 million. A United spokeswoman declined to comment on Orlando's proposal or compare it with those of other cities.

The consortium envisioned by the Orlando Airport Authority would be composed of local government entities pledging United a combined $14 million a year for five years. Of the $70 million total, $60 million would reduce United's leasing costs for five years. The authority has suggested building the hangar complex and leasing it to the airline—a

means of reducing United's initial investment. The remaining $10 million to be raised by local governments would give the airline training and job creation programs. In addition to money, the county would pay for road improvements and new water and sewer lines. Each community in the consortium would have to weigh how much economic benefit it would derive from new jobs.

Although Louisville is a finalist, Kentucky's Governor Wallace Wilkinson has just rescinded the state's offer to provide United with $300 million in benefits. An angry Wilkinson likened United's bidding war to squeezing "every drop of blood out of a turnip."

Logistically, Orlando and Dulles Airport (outside Washington, D.C.) make the most sense, say airline analysts, because they represent growth centers for United on the East Coast. But United is obviously going after the dollars.

Source: The Orlando Sentinel, July 27, 1991, pp. A1, A7; and October 19, 1991, pp. A1, A6.

exporting from one country to another country where the unit of exchange is less dear. However, management needs to question the stability of such exchange rates. For example, the value of the Japanese yen increased by about 40% in relation to the U.S. dollar in just 1 1/2 years in the mid-1980s. In that same time period, the Mexican peso decreased by 206% in relation to the U.S. dollar. Changes could well make what was a good location in 1992 a disastrous one in 1997.

Costs

We can divide location costs into two categories, tangible and intangible. **Tangible costs** are defined as readily identifiable costs that can be measured with some precision. Tangible costs include utilities, labor, material, taxes, depreciation, and other costs the accounting department and management can identify. These costs, as well as such costs as transportation of raw materials, transportation of finished goods, and site construction, are necessary ingredients for location cost analysis.

Tangible costs

Intangible costs and future costs, which are less easily quantified, can be addressed through weighting techniques we will describe shortly. These costs include quality of education, public transportation facilities, community attitudes

Intangible costs

POM _in action_

"Multinational," as We Know It, Is Obsolete

Business, according to Peter Drucker, must not organize by country lines, but internationally along product lines. Drucker cites the hypothetical example of a German subsidiary of a typical U.S. multinational.

Presume its management has been completely German for 70 years and it is accepted as a German company. "Let's say it's Procter & Gamble GmbH," states Drucker. "It has all the Procter & Gamble brands, and it basically sells in the German market. But now comes the demand of global strategy that says we should concentrate on making all of our intermediate chemicals in Bangladesh or Brazil or Thailand. The Germans will fight tooth and nail against this interference with their autonomy. The union will fight you and you will be attacked by the German newspapers. You will be the ugly American."

Drucker maintains that even substantial local subsidiaries are in small markets. "The market in India or Brazil or Mexico or Malaysia is not yet big enough to support a major company," cites Drucker, "and yet you have to move in and invest heavily because the market tomorrow is going to be 100 million people. The Japanese put a robotized plant into India. And you may say, robotization in India, where labor is so cheap? Isn't that insane? No, say the Japanese, because we don't want to commit ourselves to employing 10,000 people in India, because you cannot get rid of them. And yet we have to have the bases in India to reach a massive market."

Sources: Forbes, August 26, 1985, pp. 30–32; and _Across the Board,_ June 1990, pp. 48–52.

---

toward the industry and the company, and quality and attitude of prospective employees, as well as such variables as climate, recreational facilities, professional sports, and other quality-of-life variables that may influence the recruitment of personnel. It appears that United Airlines' recent location decision (see the _POM in Action_ box on page 333) was heavily weighted by _tangible_ costs.

Attitudes

Attitudes of national, state, and local governments toward private property, zoning, pollution, and employment stability are all in flux. Governmental attitudes at the time a location decision is made may not be lasting ones. Moreover, management may find that these attitudes can be influenced by leadership. The importance of recognizing the globalization of business and the impact of local values is presented in the _POM in Action_ box, " 'Multinational,' as We Know It, Is Obsolete."

WEIGHTED APPROACH TO EVALUATION

Grant Thornton, a consulting firm headquartered in Chicago, surveyed state manufacturing associations to help develop a set of typical location factors and their relative weights (see Table 8.1). Identifying such factors and their weights is a necessary step in the weighted approach to location evaluation. The **weighted approach technique** (also called the factor weighting method) is a good way to instill objectivity into the process of identifying hard-to-evaluate costs that are related to location. Moreover, the weighted method is popular because a wide variety of *qualitative* factors can be included. Managers can also consider the results of more *quantitative* approaches (such as crossover charts and the linear programming transportation method) when making a final decision.

Weighted approach technique

TABLE 8.1 Locational Factors and Weights.

The following 21 factors have been identified as important to manufacturing firms:

FACTOR	WEIGHT
Labor costs	
Wages	8.29%
Unionization	5.99%
Changes in wages	5.44%
Changes in unionization	4.81%
	23.95%
Availability and productivity of resources	
Available workforce	6.66%
Energy costs	4.93%
Value added	4.70%
Labor-hours lost	4.09%
	20.38%
State and local government fiscal policies	
Expenditure vs. personal income growth	4.65%
Tax effort	4.50%
Changes in taxes	4.09%
State business incentives	4.03%
Debt growth vs. personal income growth	3.59%
	20.86%
State regulated employment costs	
Workers' compensation insurance levels	5.73%
Unemployment compensation benefits	4.75%
Average workers' compensated insurance cost per case	5.16%
Unemployment compensation trust fund net worth	4.16%
	19.80%
Selected quality of life issues	
Education	4.86%
Cost of living	3.56%
Transportation	3.21%
Health care	3.38%
	15.01%

Source: 10th Annual Grant Thornton Manufacturing Climates Study © 1989. The factors were developed in discussion with state manufacturing associations, state economic development directors, and state Chambers of Commerce by Grant Thornton, Chicago, 1989.

Assembly plants operating along the Mexican side of the border, from Texas to California, are called *maquiladoras.* Some 1,400 firms, and industrial giants such as General Motors, Zenith, Hitachi, and GE operate these plants, which were designed to help both sides of the impoverished border region. After the 1982 devaluation of the peso, the number of *maquiladoras* nearly tripled and it is believed that by the year 2000 as many as three million workers will be employed in these cross-border plants. Mexican wages are low and at current exchange rates, companies don't look to the Far East as they once did.

By enhancing tangible cost data with productivity, exchange rates, and intangible factors such as quality of education, recreation facilities, and labor skills needed, management can begin to develop an objective view of the relative advantages of various locations. The six steps in the weighting methods are:

1. Develop a list of relevant factors (such as those in Table 8.1).
2. Assign a weight to each factor to reflect its relative importance in the company's objectives.
3. Develop a scale for each factor (for example, 1–10 or 1–100 points).
4. Have management score each location for each factor, using the scale in step 3.
5. Multiply the score by the weights for each factor, and total the score for each location.
6. Make a recommendation based on the maximum point score, considering the results of quantitative approaches as well.

Example 1

Mademoiselle Linda Cosmetics of New Hampshire has decided to expand its production of Musk Cologne by opening a new factory location. The expansion is due to limited capacity at its existing plant. The rating sheet in Table 8.2 provides a list of not-easily-quantifiable factors that management has decided are important; their weightings and their rating for two possible sites—St. Cloud, Minnesota, and Billings, Montana are shown.

TABLE 8.2 Weights, Scores, and Solution.

FACTOR	WEIGHT	SCORES (OUT OF 100) St. Cloud	Billings	WEIGHTED SCORES St. Cloud	Billings
Labor costs and attitude	.25	70	60	(.25)(70) = 17.5	(.25)(60) = 15.0
Transportation system	.05	50	60	(.05)(50) = 2.5	(.05)(60) = 3.0
Education and health	.10	85	80	(.10)(85) = 8.5	(.10)(80) = 8.0
Tax structure	.39	75	70	(.39)(75) = 29.3	(.39)(70) = 27.3
Resources and productivity	.21	60	70	(.21)(60) = 12.6	(.21)(70) = 14.7
Totals	1.00			70.4	68.0

Table 8.2 also indicates use of weights to evaluate alternative site locations. Given the option of 100 points assigned to each factor, the St. Cloud location is preferable. By changing the points or weights slightly for those factors about which there is some doubt, we can analyze the sensitivity of the decision. For instance, we can see that changing the scores for labor costs and attitudes by 10 points can change the decision.

For instances where a decision is sensitive to minor changes, further analysis of either the weighting or the points assigned may be appropriate. Alternatively, management may conclude that these intangible factors are not the proper criteria on which to base a location decision and therefore place primary weight on the more quantitative aspects of the decision.

LOCATIONAL BREAK-EVEN ANALYSIS

Locational break-even analysis is the use of cost-volume analysis to make an economic comparison of location alternatives. By identifying fixed and variable costs and graphing them for each location, we can determine which one provides the lowest cost. Locational break-even analysis can be done mathematically or graphically. The graphic approach has the advantage of providing the range of volume over which each location is preferable.

The three steps to locational break-even analysis are:

Locational break-even analysis

1. Determine the fixed and variable cost for each location.
2. Plot the costs for each location, with costs on the vertical axis of the graph and annual volume on the horizontal axis.
3. Select the location that has the lowest total cost for the expected production volume.

Example 2

A manufacturer of automobile carburetors is considering three locations— Akron, Bowling Green, and Chicago—for a new plant. Cost studies indicate that fixed costs per year at the sites are $30,000, $60,000, and $110,000, respectively; and variable costs are $75 per unit, $45 per unit, and $25 per unit, respectively. The expected selling price of the carburetors produced is $120. The company wishes to find the most economical location for an expected volume of 2,000 units per year.

For each of the three, we can plot the fixed costs (those at a volume of zero units) and the total cost (fixed costs + variable costs) at the expected volume of output. These lines have been plotted in Figure 8.2.

For Akron,

$$\text{Total cost} = \$30,000 + \$75(2,000) = \$180,000$$

For Bowling Green,

$$\text{Total cost} = \$60,000 + \$45(2,000) = \$150,000$$

For Chicago,

$$\text{Total cost} = \$110,000 + \$25(2,000) = \$160,000$$

With an expected volume of 2,000 units per year, Bowling Green provides the lowest cost location. The expected profit is:

$$\text{Total revenue} - \text{Total cost} = \$120(2,000) - \$150,000 = \$90,000/\text{yr.}$$

FIGURE 8.2

Crossover Chart for Locational Break-even Analysis.

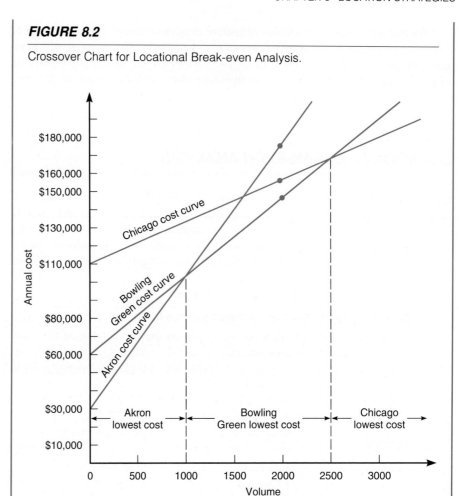

The chart also tells us that for a volume of less than 1,000, Akron would be preferred, and for a volume greater than 2,500 Chicago would yield the greatest profit. The crossover points are 1,000 and 2,500.

CENTER OF GRAVITY METHOD

Center of gravity method

The **center of gravity method** is a mathematical technique used for finding a location for a single warehouse that services a number of retail stores. The method takes into account the location of markets, the volume of goods shipped to those markets, and shipping costs in finding a best location for a central warehouse.

The first step in the center of gravity method is to place the locations on a coordinate system. This will be illustrated in Example 3. The origin of the coordinate system and the scale used are arbitrary, just as long as the relative distances are correctly represented. This can be done easily by placing a grid over an ordinary map. The center of gravity is determined by Equations 8.1 and 8.2:

$$C_x = \frac{\sum_i d_{ix} W_i}{\sum_i W_i} \tag{8.1}$$

$$C_y = \frac{\sum_i d_{iy} W_i}{\sum_i W_i} \tag{8.2}$$

where

$C_x = x$ coordinate of the center of gravity

$C_y = y$ coordinate of the center of gravity

$d_{ix} = x$ coordinate of location i

$d_{iy} = y$ coordinate of location i

$W_i = $ volume of goods moved to or from location i

Note that Equations 8.1 and 8.2 include the term W_i, the volume of supplies transferred to or from location i.

Since the number of containers shipped each month affects cost, distance alone should not be the principal criterion. The center of gravity method assumes that cost is directly proportional to both distance and volume shipped. The ideal location is that which minimizes the weighted distance between the warehouse and its retail outlets, where the distance is weighted by the number of containers shipped.

Example 3

Consider the case of Jeanne's Garden Shop, a chain of six upscale retail gift shops.[2] The firm's store locations are in Cincinnati, Knoxville, Chicago, Pittsburgh, New York, and Atlanta; they are currently being supplied out of an old and inadequate warehouse in Cincinnati, the site of the chain's first store. Data on demand rates at each outlet are shown in Table 8.3.

TABLE 8.3 Demand for Jeanne's Garden Stores.

RETAIL STORE LOCATION	NUMBER OF CONTAINERS SHIPPED PER MONTH
Cincinnati	400
Knoxville	300
Chicago	200
Pittsburgh	100
New York	300
Atlanta	100

[2] Modified from an example given by James R. Evans, *et al., Applied Production and Operations Management,* 2nd ed. (St. Paul, MN: West, 1987), pp. 159–162.

Even with reduced tax benefits and a saturated hotel market, opportunities for making good money still exist when hotel/motel locations are right. Good sites include those near hospitals and medical centers. As medical complexes in metropolitan areas continue to increase, so does the need for hotels to house patients' families. Additionally, medical services such as outpatient care, shorter hospital stays, and more diagnostic tests increase the need for hotels near hospitals.

The firm has decided to find some "central" location in which to build a new warehouse. Its current store locations are shown in Figure 8.3. For example, location 1 is Cincinnati, and from Table 8.3 and Figure 8.3, we have:

$$d_{1x} = 60$$
$$d_{1y} = 95$$
$$W_1 = 400$$

Using the data in Table 8.3 and Figure 8.3 for each of the other cities, in Equations 8.1 and 8.2 we find:

$$C_x = \frac{(60)(400) + (80)(300) + (30)(200) + (90)(100) + (127)(300) + (65)(100)}{400 + 300 + 200 + 100 + 300 + 100}$$
$$= 76.9$$

$$C_y = \frac{(95)(400) + (75)(300) + (120)(200) + (110)(100) + (130)(300) + (40)(100)}{400 + 300 + 200 + 100 + 300 + 100}$$
$$= 98.9$$

This location (76.9, 98.9) is shown by the crosshair in Figure 8.3. By overlaying a U.S. map on this exhibit, we find that this location is near the border of southern Ohio and West Virginia. The firm may well wish to consider Huntington, West Virginia, or a nearby city as an appropriate location.

FIGURE 8.3

Coordinate Locations of Six Jeanne's Garden Stores.

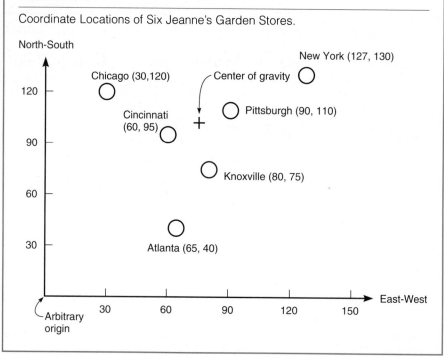

SERVICE/RETAIL/PROFESSIONAL SECTOR

While the focus in industrial sector location analysis is on minimizing cost, the focus in the service sector is on maximizing revenue. This is because manufacturing costs tend to vary substantially between locations, but in service firms costs vary little within a market area. Therefore, for the service firm, a specific location

TABLE 8.4 Location Strategies—Service vs. Industrial Organizations.

SERVICE/RETAIL/PROFESSIONAL	INDUSTRIAL LOCATION
Revenue Focus	*Cost Focus*
Volume/revenue	**Tangible costs**
Drawing area	Transportation cost of raw material
Purchasing power	Shipment cost of finished goods
Competition	Energy cost per BTU
Advertising/promotion/pricing	Utility costs
	Labor
Physical quality	Raw material
Parking/access	Taxes, etc.
Security/lighting	
Appearance/image	**Intangible and future costs**
Associated business	Attitude toward union
	Quality of life
Cost determinants	Education expenditures by state
Management caliber	Quality of state and local government
Operation policies	
Techniques	*Techniques*
Correlation analysis to determine importance of above factors for a particular type of operation	Linear programming (transportation method)
Traffic counts	Weighted approach to intangibles
Demographic analysis of drawing area	Break-even analysis
Purchasing power analysis of drawing area	Crossover charts
Assumptions	*Assumptions*
Location is a major determinant of revenue	Location is a major determinant of cost
Issues manifesting from high customer contact dominate	Most major costs can be identified explicitly for each site
Costs are relatively constant for a given area; therefore, the revenue function is critical	Low customer contact allows focus on the identifiable costs
	Intangible costs can be objectively evaluated

Facility location is a top priority to McDonald's executives. Restaurant sites on tollways have been one profitable choice. Higher construction costs for tollway locations were more than offset by increased sales. The above tollway restaurant in Illinois experienced sales increases from two to ten times higher than those of former restaurants on the identical sites. McDonalds has earmarked more nonconventional sites, such as hospitals, airports, and tollways, for future use.

influences revenue more than it does cost. This means that the location focus for service firms should be on determining the volume of business and revenue. There are eight major components of volume and revenue for the service firm. These are:

1. purchasing power of the customer drawing area;
2. service and image compatibility with demographics of the customer drawing area;
3. competition in the area;
4. quality of the competition;
5. uniqueness of the firm's and competitive locations;
6. physical qualities of facilities and neighboring businesses;
7. operating policies of the firm;
8. quality of management.

Realistic analysis of these factors can provide a reasonable picture of the revenue expected. Table 8.4 on page 341 provides a summary of location strategies for both service and industrial organizations.

THE TRANSPORTATION TECHNIQUE

Transportation technique

The objective of the **transportation technique** is to determine the best pattern of shipments from several points of supply (sources) to several points of demand (destinations) so as to minimize total production and transportation costs. Usually, there is a given production capacity of goods at each source and a given requirement for the goods at each destination. Every firm with a network of supply and demand points faces such a problem. The complex Volkswagen supply network (shown in Figure 8.4) provides one such illustration.

FIGURE 8.4

Worldwide Distribution of Volkswagens and Parts.
(*Source:* Copyright 1985, *The Economist, Ltd.* Reprinted with permission from The New York Times Special Features.)

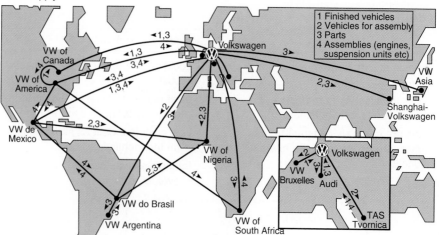

Although the linear programming (LP) technique introduced in Chapter 3 can be used to solve this type of problem, more efficient, special purpose algorithms have been developed for the transportation application. As in the LP approach, the transportation technique finds an initial feasible solution and then makes step-by-step improvement until an optimal solution is reached. Unlike the LP simplex method, the transportation method is fairly simple to compute.

To begin the analysis of a transportation problem, management must determine the capacity at each factory, requirements at each warehouse, and cost of shipping from each source to each destination. Data for Hot Tubs Corporation, a manufacturer of hot tubs, are presented in Figures 8.5 and 8.6.

The next step is to set up a transportation matrix. Its purpose is to summarize conveniently and concisely all relevant data and to keep track of algorithm computations. Using the information from the Hot Tubs Corporation displayed in Figures 8.5 and 8.6, we can construct a transportation matrix as shown in Figure 8.7.

FIGURE 8.5

Transportation Problem.

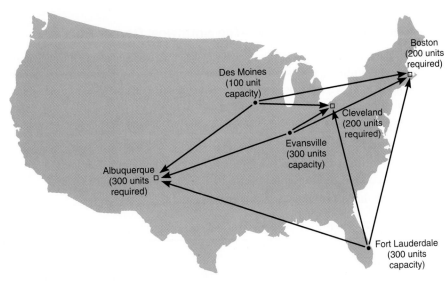

FIGURE 8.6

Transportation Costs Per Hot Tub for Hot Tubs Corporation.

From \ To	Albuquerque	Boston	Cleveland
Des Moines	$5	$4	$3
Evansville	$8	$4	$3
Fort Lauderdale	$9	$7	$5

FIGURE 8.7

Transportation Matrix for Hot Tubs Corporation.

From \ To	Albuquerque	Boston	Cleveland	Factory capacity
Des Moines	$5	$4	$3	100
Evansville	$8	$4	$3	300
Fort Lauderdale	$9	$7	$5	300
Warehouse requirements	300	200	200	700

Des Moines capacity constraint → (points to 100)

Cell representing a possible source-to-destination shipping assignment (Evansville to Cleveland) → (points to $3 in Evansville–Cleveland)

Cost of shipping 1 unit from Fort Lauderdale factory to Boston warehouse → (points to $7)

Cleveland warehouse demand → (points to 200)

Total demand and total supply → (points to 700)

Developing an Initial Solution—The Northwest Corner Rule

Northwest corner rule

Once the data are arranged in tabular form, we must establish an initial feasible solution to the problem. One systematic procedure, known as the **northwest corner rule,** requires that we start in the upper left-hand cell (or northwest corner of the table) and allocate units to shipping routes as follows:

1. Exhaust the supply (factory capacity) of each row before moving down to the next row.
2. Exhaust the (warehouse) requirements of each column before moving to the next column on the right.
3. Check that all supplies and demands are met.

Example 4

In Figure 8.8 we use the northwest corner rule to find an initial feasible solution to the Hot Tubs Corporation problem. Five steps are required in this example to make the initial shipping assignments:

1. Assign 100 tubs from Des Moines to Albuquerque (exhausting Des Moines' supply).
2. Assign 200 tubs from Evansville to Albuquerque (exhausting Albuquerque's demand).
3. Assign 100 tubs from Evansville to Boston (exhausting Evansville's supply).
4. Assign 100 tubs from Fort Lauderdale to Boston (exhausting Boston's demand).
5. Assign 200 tubs from Fort Lauderdale to Cleveland (exhausting Cleveland's demand and Fort Lauderdale's supply).

FIGURE 8.8

Northwest Corner Solution to Hot Tubs Corporation Problem.

From \ To	(A) Albuquerque	(B) Boston	(C) Cleveland	Factory capacity
(D) Des Moines	$5 100	$4	$3	100
(E) Evansville	$8 200	$4 100	$3	300
(F) Fort Lauderdale	$9	$7 (100)	$5 200	300
Warehouse requirements	300	200	200	700

Means that the firm is shipping 100 hot tubs from Fort Lauderdale to Boston

We can easily compute the total cost of this shipping assignment as $4,200 (see Table 8.5).

TABLE 8.5 Computed Shipping Cost.

ROUTE		HOT TUBS SHIPPED	COST PER UNIT	TOTAL COST
From	To			
D	A	100	$5	$ 500
E	A	200	8	1,600
E	B	100	4	400
F	B	100	7	700
F	C	200	5	1,000
				Total: $4,200

The solution given in Example 4 is feasible since it satisfies all demand and supply constraints. We would be very lucky if this solution yielded the minimum transportation cost for the problem. However, it is more likely that we shall have to employ an additional procedure to reach an optimal solution.

The Stepping-Stone Method

The **stepping-stone method** is an iterative technique for moving from an initial feasible solution to an optimal solution. It is used to evaluate the cost effectiveness of shipping goods via transportation routes not currently in the solution. We test each unused cell, or square, in the transportation table by asking the following question: "What would happen to total shipping costs if one unit of the product (for example, one hot tub) were tentatively shipped on an unused route?" We conduct the test as follows:

Stepping-stone method

1. Select any unused square to evaluate.

2. Beginning at this square, trace a closed path back to the original square via squares that are currently being used (only horizontal and vertical moves are permissible). You may, however, step over either an empty or an occupied square.

3. Beginning with a plus (+) sign at the unused square, place alternate minus signs and plus signs on each corner square of the closed path just traced.

4. Calculate an improvement index by adding the unit cost figures found in each square containing a plus sign and then by subtracting the unit costs in each square containing a minus sign.

5. Repeat steps 1 through 4 until you have calculated an improvement index for all unused squares. If all indices computed are greater than or equal to zero, you have reached an optimal solution. If not, it is possible to improve the current solution and decrease total shipping costs.

Example 5

We can apply the stepping-stone method to the Hot Tubs Corporation data in Figure 8.8 to evaluate unused shipping routes. The four currently unassigned routes are: Des Moines to Boston, Des Moines to Cleveland, Evansville to Cleveland, and Fort Lauderdale to Albuquerque.

Steps 1 and 2. Beginning with the Des Moines to Boston route, first trace a closed path using only currently occupied squares (see Figure 8.9) and then place alternate plus signs and minus signs in the corners of this path. Note that we can use only squares currently used for shipping to turn the corners of the route we are tracing. Hence, the path Des Moines–Boston to Des Moines–Albuquerque to Fort Lauderdale–Albuquerque to Fort Lauderdale–Boston to Des Moines–Boston would not be acceptable since the Fort Lauderdale–Albuquerque square is empty. It turns out that *only one closed route exists for each empty square.* Once this one closed path is identified, we can begin assigning plus and minus signs to these squares in the path.

Step 3. How do we decide which squares get plus signs and which squares get minus signs? The answer is simple. Since we are testing the cost effectiveness of the Des Moines to Boston shipping route, we pretend we are shipping one hot tub from Des Moines to Boston. This is one more unit than we *were* sending between the two cities, so we place a plus sign in the box. But if we ship one more unit than before from Des Moines to Boston, we end up sending 101 hot tubs out of the Des Moines factory. Because the Des Moines factory's capacity is only 100 units, we must ship one hot tub less from Des Moines to Albuquerque. This change prevents us from violating the limit constraint. To indicate that we have reduced the Des Moines to Albuquerque shipment, we place a minus sign in its box. Continuing along the closed path, we notice that we are no longer meeting the warehouse requirement for 300 units. In fact, if we reduce the Des Moines to Albuquerque shipment to 99 units, we must increase the Evansville to Albuquerque load by one unit, to 201 hot tubs. Therefore, we place a plus sign in that box to indicate the increase. You may also observe that those squares where we turn (and only those squares) will have plus or minus signs. Finally, note that if we assign 201 hot tubs to the Evansville to Albuquerque route, then we must reduce the Evans-

FIGURE 8.9

Stepping-Stone Evaluation of Alternative Routes for Hot Tubs Corporation.

Evaluation of Des Moines to Boston square

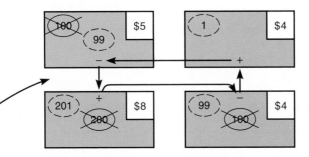

Result of proposed shift in allocation = 1 × $4 − 1 × $5 + 1 × $8 − 1 × $4 = +$3

To From	(A) Albuquerque	(B) Boston	(C) Cleveland	Factory capacity
(D) Des Moines	$5 100	Start $4	$3	100
(E) Evansville	$8 200	$4 100	$3	300
(F) Fort Lauderdale	$9	$7 100	$5 200	300
Warehouse requirements	300	200	200	700

ville to Boston route by one unit, to 99 hot tubs, in order to maintain the Evansville factory's capacity constraint of 300 units. Thus we insert a minus sign in the Evansville to Boston box. As a result, we have balanced supply limitations among all four routes on the closed path.

Step 4. We compute an improvement index for the Des Moines to Boston route by adding unit costs in squares with plus signs and subtracting costs in squares with minus signs. Hence we have:

Des Moines to Boston index = $4 − $5 + $8 − $4 = + $3

This means that for every hot tub shipped via the Des Moines to Boston route, total transportation costs will increase by $3 over their current level.

Let us now examine the Des Moines to Cleveland unused route, one slightly more difficult to trace with a closed path. Again, you will notice that we turn each corner along the path only at squares on the existing route. The path can go through the Evansville to Cleveland box but cannot turn a corner, and we cannot place a plus or minus sign there. We may use only an occupied square as a stepping stone (see Figure 8.10 on p. 348):

Des Moines to Cleveland index = $3 − $5 + $8 − $4 + $7 − $5 = + $4

Thus, opening this route will also not lower total shipping costs.

The other two routes may be evaluated in a similar fashion:

$$\text{Evansville to Cleveland index} = \$3 - \$4 + \$7 - \$5 = +\$1$$
$$(\text{closed path} = EC - EB + FB - FC)$$

$$\text{Fort Lauderdale to Albuquerque index} = \$9 - \$7 + \$4 - \$8 = -\$2$$
$$(\text{closed path} = FA - FB + EB - EA)$$

Because this last index is negative, a cost savings can be attained by making use of the (currently unused) Fort Lauderdale to Albuquerque route.

FIGURE 8.10

Testing Des Moines to Cleveland.

From \ To	(A) Albuquerque	(B) Boston	(C) Cleveland	Factory
(D) Des Moines	$5 100 −	$4	Start $3 +	100
(E) Evansville	$8 200+ → −	$4 100	$3	300
(F) Fort Lauderdale	$9	$7 + 100 → −	$5 200	300
Warehouse requirements	300	200	200	700

In Example 5 we saw that a better solution is possible due to the presence of a negative improvement index on one of the unused routes. Each negative index represents the amount by which total transportation costs could be decreased if one unit or product were shipped by the source-destination combination. The next step, then, is to choose that route (unused square) with the largest negative improvement index. We can then ship the maximum allowable number of units on that route and reduce the total cost accordingly. What is the maximum quantity that can be shipped on the new money-saving route? That quantity is found by referring to the closed path of plus signs and minus signs drawn for the route and selecting the smallest number found in the squares containing minus signs.

To obtain a new solution, we add that number to all squares on the closed path with plus signs and subtract it from all squares on the path assigned minus signs.

One iteration of the stepping-stone method is now complete. Again, we must test to see if it is optimal or whether we can make any further improvements. This is done by evaluating each unused square as described above.

Example 6

To improve Hot Tubs' solution, we can use the improvement indices calculated in Example 5. The largest (and only) negative index is the Fort Lauderdale to Albuquerque route as shown in Figure 8.11.

FIGURE 8.11

Transportation Table: Route FA.

From \ To	(A) Albuquerque	(B) Boston	(C) Cleveland	Factory
(D) Des Moines	$5 100	$4	$3	100
(E) Evansville	$8 200	$4 100	$3	300
(F) Fort Lauderdale	$9	$7 100	$5 200	300
Warehouse	300	200	200	700

The maximum quantity that may be shipped on the newly opened route (FA) is the smallest number found in squares containing minus signs—in this case, 100 units. Why 100 units? Since the total cost decreases by $2 per unit shipped, we know we would like to ship the maximum possible number of units. Previous stepping-stone calculations indicate that each unit shipped over the FA route results in an increase of one unit shipped from E to B and a decrease of one unit in both amounts shipped from F to B (now 100 units) and from E to A (now 200 units). Hence, the maximum we can ship over the FA route is 100 units. This solution results in zero units being shipped from F to B. Now we add 100 units (to the zero now being shipped) on route FA; then proceed to subtract 100 from route FB, leaving zero in that square (but still balancing the row total for F); then add 100 to route EB, yielding 200; and finally, subtract 100 from route EA, leaving 100 units shipped. Note that the new numbers still produce the correct row and column totals as required. The new solution is shown in Figure 8.12.

Total shipping cost has been reduced by (100 units) × ($2 saved per unit) = $200 and is now $4,000. This cost figure, of course, can also be derived by

FIGURE 8.12

Solution at Next Iteration (Still Not Optimal).

From \ To	(A) Albuquerque	(B) Boston	(C) Cleveland	Factory
(D) Des Moines	$5 100	$4	$3	100
(E) Evansville	$8 100	$4 200	$3	300
(F) Fort Lauderdale	$9 100	$7	$5 200	300
Warehouse	300	200	200	700

multiplying each unit shipping cost by the number of units transported on its route, namely:

$$100(\$5) + 100(\$8) + 200(\$4) + 100(\$9) + 200(\$5) = \$4,000$$

Looking carefully at Figure 8.12, you should be able to see that it, too, is not yet optimal. Route EC (Evansville–Cleveland) has a negative cost improvement index. Can you find the final solution on your own?

Demand Not Equal to Supply

Dummy sources
Dummy destinations

A common situation in real-world problems is the case where total demand is not equal to total supply. We can handle these "unbalanced" problems easily with the solution procedures discussed above if we first introduce **dummy sources** or **dummy destinations.** In the event that total supply is greater than total demand, we create a dummy destination, so the demand exactly equals the surplus. If total demand is greater than total supply, we introduce a dummy source (factory) with a supply equal to the excess of demand over supply. In each case we assign cost coefficients of zero to each square on the dummy location because in fact these units will not be shipped. Hence, the cost is zero.

Example 7

Hot Tubs Corporation increases the rate of production of hot tubs in its Des Moines factory to 250. To reformulate this unbalanced problem, we refer back to the data presented in Example 3 and present the new matrix in Figure 8.13. We use the northwest corner rule to find the initial feasible solution. Once the problem is balanced, solution can proceed in the normal way.

FIGURE 8.13

Northwest Corner Rule with Dummy.

From \ To	(A) Albuquerque	(B) Boston	(C) Cleveland	Dummy	Factory capacity
(D) Des Moines	$5 250	$4	$3	0	250
(E) Evansville	$8 50	$4 200	$3 50	0	300
(F) Fort Lauderdale	$9	$7	$5 150	0 150	300
Warehouse requirements	300	200	200	150	850

New Des Moines capacity

Total cost = 250($5) + 50($8) + 200($4) + 50($3) + 150($5) + 150(0) = $3,350

Degeneracy

In order to apply the stepping-stone method to a transportation problem, we must observe a rule pertaining to the number of shipping routes being used. That rule may be stated as follows: *The number of occupied squares in any solution (initial or later) must be equal to the number of rows in the table plus the number of columns minus 1.* Solutions that do not meet this rule are called degenerate.

Degeneracy occurs when there are too few squares or shipping routes being used. As a result, it becomes impossible to trace a closed path for one or more unused squares. You might observe that no problem discussed in this chapter thus far has been degenerate. The original Hot Tubs problem, for example, had five assigned routes (three rows or factories + 3 columns or warehouses – 1). Example 7, employing a dummy warehouse, had six assigned routes (3 rows + 4 columns – 1) and was not degenerate either.

To handle degenerate problems, we artifically create an occupied cell; that is, we place a zero or *very* small amount (representing a fake shipment) in one of the unused squares and *then treat that square as if it were occupied.* The square chosen, it should be noted, must be in such a position as to allow all stepping-stone paths to be closed or traced.

Example 8

Martin Shipping Company has three warehouses from which it supplies its three major retail customers in San Jose. Martin's shipping costs, warehouse supplies, and customer demands are presented in the transportation table below. To make the initial shipping assignments in the table we apply the northwest corner rule (see Figure 8.14).

The initial solution is degenerate because it violates the rule that the number of used squares must equal the number of rows plus the number of columns minus one. To correct the problem, we may place a zero in the unused square that represents the shipping route from warehouse 2 to customer 1. Now we can close all stepping-stone paths and compute improvement indices.

FIGURE 8.14

Martin's Northwest Corner Rule.

From \ To	Customer 1	Customer 2	Customer 3	Warehouse supply
Warehouse 1	100 $8	$2	$6	100
Warehouse 2	0 $10	100 $9	20 $9	120
Warehouse 3	$7	$10	80 $7	80
Customer demand	100	100	100	300

The MODI Method

**Modified distribution
(MODI) method**

The **MODI (modified distribution) method** allows us to compute improvement indices for each unused square without drawing all of the closed paths. Thus, it can often provide considerable time savings over the stepping-stone method for solving transportation problems.

In applying the MODI method, we begin with an initial solution obtained by using the northwest corner rule. We must compute a value for each row (call the values R_1, R_2, R_3, if there are three rows) and for each column (K_1, K_2, K_3, if there are three columns) in the transportation table. In general, we let:

R_i = value assigned to row i

K_j = value assigned to column j

C_{ij} = Cost in square ij (cost of shipping from source i to destination j)

The MODI method consists of five steps:

1. To compute the values for each row and column, set $R_i + K_j = C_{ij}$ but only for those squares that are currently used or occupied. For example, if the square at the intersection of row 2 and column 1 is occupied, we set $R_2 + K_1 = C_{21}$.
2. After you have written all equations, set $R_1 = 0$.
3. Solve the system of equations for all R and K values.
4. Compute the improvement index for each unused square by the formula

$$\text{Index} = C_{ij} - R_i - K_j$$

5. Select the largest negative index and proceed to solve the problem as you did using the stepping-stone method.

Example 9

Given the initial solution to the Hot Tubs problem (Example 4), we can use the MODI method to calculate an improvement index for each unused square. The initial transportation table is repeated in Figure 8.15.

We first set up an equation for each occupied square:

1. $R_1 + K_1 = 5$
2. $R_2 + K_1 = 8$
3. $R_2 + K_2 = 4$
4. $R_3 + K_2 = 7$
5. $R_3 + K_3 = 5$

Letting $R_1 = 0$, we can easily solve, step by step, for K_1, R_2, K_2, R_3, and K_3.

1. $0 + K_1 = 5 \Rightarrow K_1 = 5$
2. $R_2 + 5 = 8 \Rightarrow R_2 = 3$
3. $3 + K_2 = 4 \Rightarrow K_2 = 1$
4. $R_3 + 1 = 7 \Rightarrow R_3 = 6$
5. $6 + K_3 = 5 \Rightarrow K_3 = -1$

The improvement index for each unused cell is $C_{ij} - R_i - K_j$:

$$\text{Des Moines to Boston} = C_{12} - R_1 - K_2 = 4 - 0 - 1 = \$3$$
$$\text{Des Moines to Cleveland} = C_{13} - R_1 - K_3 = 3 - 0 - (-1) = \$4$$
$$\text{Evansville to Cleveland} = C_{23} - R_2 - K_3 = 3 - 3 - (-1) = \$1$$
$$\text{Fort Lauderdale to Albuquerque} = C_{31} - R_3 - K_1 = 9 - 6 - 5 = -\$2$$

Note that these indices are exactly the same as the ones calculated in Example 5. Now only one closed path, from Fort Lauderdale to Albuquerque, is necessary in order to proceed with the stepping-stone solution procedures.

FIGURE 8.15

Transportation Table.

R_i / From	K_j To	K_1 Albuquerque	K_2 Boston	K_3 Cleveland	Factory capacity
R_1	Des Moines	$5 / 100	$4	$3	100
R_2	Evansville	$8 / 200	$4 / 100	$3	300
R_3	Fort Lauderdale	$9	$7 / 100	$5 / 200	300
	Warehouse requirements	300	200	200	700

At the end of this chapter, we provide instructions for using AB: POM's transportation software module. Most linear programming problems, including this special class of problems known as transportation problems, are, in practice, solved not by hand but via a computer. You may find solving the problems in this chapter, using the software provided, a helpful exercise.

Facility Location Analysis

As noted earlier, the location of a new factory or warehouse is an issue of major financial importance to a firm. Ordinarily, several alternative locations must be considered and evaluated. Even though a wide variety of subjective factors must be considered, rational decisions are needed to minimize costs.

The transportation methods just studied prove useful when considering alternative facility locations within the framework of one overall production-distribution system. Each new potential plant or warehouse will produce a different allocation of shipments, depending on its own production and shipping costs and the costs of each existing facility. The choice of a new location depends on which will yield the minimum cost for the entire system. This concept is illustrated in Example 10.

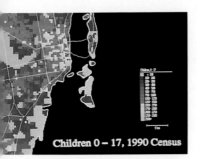

Children 0 – 17, 1990 Census

Retail store location is aided by analysis of demographics. Here the concentration of children between 0 and 17 is shown in various colors. If you were going to open a children's clothing store or locate a city park, what areas would you investigate?

Example 10

Williams Auto Top Carriers currently maintains plants in Atlanta and Tulsa to supply major distribution centers in Los Angeles and New York. Because of an expanding demand, Williams has decided to open a third plant and has narrowed the choice to one of two cities—New Orleans and Houston. Table 8.6 gives the pertinent production and distribution costs as well as the plant capacities and distribution demands.

TABLE 8.6 Production Costs, Distribution Costs, Plant Capacities, and Market Demands for Williams Auto Top Carriers.

| | FROM PLANTS | TO DISTRIBUTION CENTERS | | NORMAL PRODUCTION | UNIT PRODUCTION COST |
		Los Angeles	New York		
Existing plants	Atlanta	$8	$5	600	$6
	Tulsa	$4	$7	900	$5
Proposed locations	New Orleans	$5	$6	500	$4 (anticipated)
	Houston	$4	$6*	500	$3 (anticipated)
Forecast demand		800	1,200	2,000	

* Indicates distribution cost (shipping, handling, storage) will be $6 per carrier between Houston and New York.

The important question that Williams faces is: "Which of the new locations will yield a lower cost for the firm in combination with the existing plants and distribution centers?" To determine the answer, we need to solve two transportation problems, one for each possible combination. The location that shows a lower total cost of distribution and production to the existing system will be recommended.

We begin by setting up a transportation table that represents the opening of a third plant in New Orleans (see Figure 8.16). We use the northwest corner method to find an initial solution. The total cost of this first solution is seen to be $23,600. Note that the cost of each individual "plant to distribution center" route is found by adding the distribution costs (in the body of Table 8.6) to the respective unit production costs (in the right-hand column of Table 8.6). Thus, the total production-plus-shipping cost of one auto top carrier from Atlanta to Los Angeles is $14 ($8 for shipping plus $6 for production).

$$\text{Total cost} = (600 \text{ units} \times \$14) + (200 \text{ units} \times \$9)$$
$$+ (700 \text{ units} \times \$12) + (500 \text{ units} \times \$10)$$
$$= \$8,400 + \$1,800 + \$8,400 + \$5,000$$
$$= \$23,600$$

Is this initial solution optimal? The stepping-stone method can be employed to test it and to compute improvement indices for unused routes.

FIGURE 8.16

Williams Transportation Table for New Orleans Plant.

From \ To	Los Angeles	New York	Production capacity
Atlanta	$14 / 600	$11	600
Tulsa	$9 / 200	$12 / 700	900
New Orleans	$9	$10 / 500	500
Demand	800	1,200	2,000

Improvement index for Atlanta to New York route = + $11 (Atlanta to N.Y.) – $14 (Atlanta to L.A.) + $9 (Tulsa to L.A.) – $12 (Tulsa to N.Y.)

= – $6

Improvement index for New Orleans to Los Angeles route = + $9 (New Orleans to L.A.) – $10 (New Orleans to N.Y.) + $12 (Tulsa to N.Y.) – $9 (Tulsa to L.A.)

= $2

Since the firm can save $6 for every unit it ships from Atlanta to New York, it will want to improve the initial solution and send as many as possible (600, in this case) on this currently unused route (see Figure 8.17).

You may want to confirm that the total cost is now $20,000, a saving of $3,600 over the initial solution.

Now, we must test the two unused routes to see if their improvement indices are negative numbers.

FIGURE 8.17

Improved Transportation Table for Williams.

From \ To	Los Angeles	New York	Production capacity
Atlanta	$14	$11 / 600	600
Tulsa	$9 / 800	$12 / 100	900
New Orleans	$9	$10 / 500	500
Demand	800	1,200	2,000

> Index for Atlanta to Los Angeles = $14 − $11 + $12 − $9 = $6
> Index for New Orleans to Los Angeles = $9 − $10 + $12 − $9 = $2
>
> Since both indices are greater than zero, we have reached an optimal solution using the New Orleans plant. If Williams elects to open the New Orleans plant, the firm's total production and distribution cost will be $20,000.

Example 10, however, provides only half the answer to Williams's problem. The same procedure would be followed to determine the minimum cost with the new plant in Houston. Determining this cost is left as an exercise; you can help provide complete information and recommend a solution by solving Problem 8.4.

SUMMARY

Location may determine up to 10% of the total cost of an industrial firm. Location is also a critical element in determining revenue for the service/retail/professional firm. Industrial firms need to consider both tangible and intangible costs. We typically address industrial location problems via a weighted approach, locational break-even analysis, and the transportation method of linear programming.

For service/retail/professional organizations, analysis is typically made of a variety of variables including purchasing power of a drawing area, competition, advertising and promotion, physical qualities of the location, and operating policies of the organization.

KEY TERMS

Tangible costs (p. 333)
Intangible costs (p. 333)
Weighted approach technique (p. 335)
Locational break-even analysis (p. 337)
Center of gravity method (p. 338)
Transportation technique (p. 342)
Northwest corner rule (p. 344)

Stepping-stone method (p. 345)
Dummy sources (p. 350)
Dummy destinations (p. 350)
Degeneracy (p. 351)
Modified distribution (MODI)
method (p. 352)

USING AB:POM

Solving Examples 1 and 3, With AB:POM's Facility Location Module

The facility location module in AB:POM includes two different models. The first, the Qualitative Weighting Model (also known as the factor rating method) is used to solve Example 1. The second, Two-Dimensional Siting, is applied to the center-of-gravity problem described in Example 3.

In running the Qualitative Weighting Model, we first tell AB:POM how many factors (up to 16) and locations (up to 6) to consider. In Example 1's Table 8.2 we rated two cities over five factors. Program 8.1 illustrates the simplicity of this model. Its particular strength is in demonstrating the sensitivity of one or more weights or scores on the final selection.

Program 8.1

AB:POM's Qualitative Weighting Model Applied to Example 1.

	Plant location			Solution
Number of factors (1–12) 5			Number of locations (1–6) 2	

COSMETIC COMPANY, EXAMPLE 1

FACTORS	Weight	city 1	city 2
LABOR	0.25	70.00	60.00
TRANSPORT	0.05	50.00	60.00
EDUCATION	0.10	85.00	80.00
TAXES	0.39	75.00	70.00
POWER	0.21	60.00	70.00
Weighted score		70.35	68.00

The location with the best (highest) score is city 1

F9 = Print   Esc
Press <Esc> key to continue or highlight key or function key for options

The second module, Two-Dimensional Siting, is illustrated in Program 8.2 on page 358. This screen shows both the input and output for Example 3, Jeanne's Garden Shop. The mean location at the bottom of the screen is the computed center of gravity for the X and Y coordinates. In this program, we enter:

1. *Site names* (if desired)
2. *Weight/trips.* This is the weight, number of trips, or number of units shipped to or from each site.
3. *X (or East-West) coordinates.*
4. *Y (or North-South) coordinates.*

The optimal location, based on the mean, is $X = 76.9$, $y = 98.9$, exactly as we computed in Example 3.

Program 8.2

AB:POM's Facility Location Module, Two-Dimensional Site Analysis of Example 3

─────────────── Plant location ─────────────── Solution ───────

Number of sites (1–12)   6

─────────────── JEANNE'S GARDEN SHOPS, EXAMPLE 3 ───────────────

				Weighted Coordinates	
SITES	Weight/trips	x coord	y coord	X-coord	Y-coord
CINCINNATI	400.00	60.00	95.00	24000.0	38000.0
KNOXVILLE	300.00	80.00	75.00	24000.0	22500.0
CHICAGO	200.00	30.00	120.00	6000.00	24000.0
PITTSBURGH	100.00	90.00	110.00	9000.00	11000.0
NEW YORK	300.00	127.00	130.00	38100.0	39000.0
ATLANTA	100.00	65.00	40.00	6500.00	4000.00
TOTAL	1400.00	452.00	570.00	107600	138500
AVERAGE		75.3333	95.00	76.8571	98.9286

The unweighted center of gravity is x = 75.33334   y = 95
The   weighted center of gravity is x = 76.85714   y = 98.92857

                                                      F9 = Print   Esc
Press <Esc> key to continue or highlight key or function key for options

Solving Examples 4, 5, and 6 with AB:POM's Transportation Model Module

In this transportation computer analysis, we use the data from the Hot Tubs Corporation, seen earlier in Examples 4, 5, and 6. After entering the number of origins and destinations, we are prompted, in Program 8.3, to provide appropriate demand data, supply data, and unit shipping costs.

AB:POM does *not* require that we add dummy rows or columns—it will handle that issue automatically. The program can handle up to 99 rows or columns. We *do* need to instruct AB:POM as to whether we wish to maximize or minimize the objective. (*Most* transportation problems are minimized.) Origin and destination names may be entered as an option.

Program 8.4a displays the solutions screen to the Hot Tubs problem. As an option, (see Program 8.4b) marginal costs (cost indexes) may be displayed. Another powerful feature allows users to "step through" the problem by pointing to the cell routing desired.

For problems that are larger than 7 by 16, both the input and output screen are slightly different than just seen.

Program 8.3

Data Entry Screen for Transportation Problem in Examples 4, 5, 6

```
―――――――――――――――――――― Transportation ―――――――――――――――――― Data  Screen ――――

Number of sources (1—99)   3                    Number of destinations (1—99)   3
minimize
―――――――――――――――――――――――――――――――――――――――――――――――――――――――――――――――――――――――――――

―――――――――――――――――― HOT TUBS CORP., EXAMPLES 4-6 ――――――――――――――

Options -> NO steps Comptr PrntOFF

                        ALBUQ       BOSTON     CLEVELD      Supply

DES MOINE                 5           4          3          100
EVANSVILL                 8           4          3          300
FT. LAUD                  9           7          5          300

Demand                   300         200        200

―――――――――――――――――――――――――――――――――――――――――――――――――――――――――――――――――――――――――――
                                                                            Esc
```

Program 8.4

AB:POM Solution to Transportation Problem in Examples 4, 5, 6

(a)   HOT TUBS CORP., EXAMPLES 4—6

SHIPMENTS	ALBUQ	BOSTON	CLEVELD	Supply
DES MOINE	100			100
EVANSVILL		200	100	300
FT. LAUD	200		100	300
Demand	300	200	200	

The minimum total cost = $3,900

(b)   HOT TUBS CORP., EXAMPLES 4—6

IMPROV IND	ALBUQ	BOSTON	CLEVELD	Supply
DES MOINE		+2	+2	100
EVANSVILL	+1			300
FT. LAUD		+1		300
Demand	300	200	200	

The minimum total cost = $3,900

SOLVED PROBLEMS

Solved Problem 8. 1 [3]

Just as cities and communities can be compared for location selection by the weighted approach model, as we saw earlier in this chapter, so can actual site decisions within those cities be helped. Table 8.7 illustrates four factors of importance to Washington, D.C., health officials charged with opening that city's first public AIDS clinic. Of primary concern (and given a weight of 5) was location of the clinic so it would be as accessible as possible to the largest number of patients. The annual lease cost also was of some concern due to a tight budget. A suite in the new City Hall, at 14th and U Streets, was highly rated because its rent would be free. An old office building near the downtown bus station received a much lower rating because of its cost. Equally important as lease cost was the need for confidentiality of patients and, therefore, for a relatively inconspicuous clinic. Finally, because so many of the staff at the AIDS clinic would be donating their time, the safety, parking, and accessibility of each site were of concern as well.

Solution

From the three right-most columns in Table 8.7, the weighted scores are summed. It appears that the bus terminal area can be excluded from further consideration, but that the other two sites are virtually identical in total score. The city may now consider other factors, including political ones, in selecting between the two remaining sites.

TABLE 8.7 Potential AIDS Clinic Sites in Washington, D.C.

FACTOR	Importance Weight	POTENTIAL LOCATIONS* Homeless Shelter (2nd and D, SE)	City Hall (14th and U, NW)	Bus Terminal Area (7th and H, NW)	WEIGHTED SCORES Homeless Shelter	City Hall	Bus Terminal Area
Accessibility for infectives	5	9	7	7	45	35	35
Annual lease cost	3	6	10	3	18	30	9
Inconspicuous	3	5	2	7	15	6	21
Accessibility for health staff	2	3	6	2	6	12	4
				Total scores:	84	83	69

* All sites are rated on a 1 to 10 basis, with 10 as the highest score and 1 as the lowest.

[3] Source: R. Murdick, B. Render, and R. Russell, *Service Operations Management* (Boston: Allyn & Bacon, 1990), pp. 147–149.

Solved Problem 8.2

Chuck Bimmerle is considering opening a new foundry in Denton, Texas, Edwardsville, Illinois, or Fayetteville, Arkansas, to produce high-quality rifle sights. He has assembled the following fixed- and variable-cost data:

| | | PER UNIT COSTS | | |
LOCATION	FIXED COST PER YEAR	Material	Labor	Variable Overhead
Denton	$200,000	$ .20	$ .40	$ .40
Edwardsville	$180,000	$ .25	$ .75	$ .75
Fayetteville	$170,000	$1.00	$1.00	$1.00

a) Graph the total cost lines.

b) Over what range of annual volume is each facility going to have a competitive advantage?

c) What is the point volume at the intersection of Edwardsville and Fayetteville?

Solution

FIGURE 8.18

Graph of Total Cost Lines for Solved Problem 8.2.

a) A graph of the total cost lines is shown in Figure 8.18.

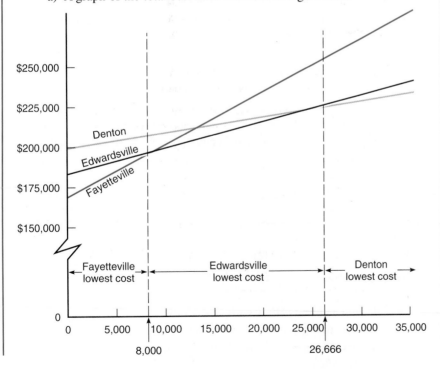

b) Below 8,000 units, the Fayetteville facility will have a competitive advantage (lowest cost); between 8,000 units and 26,666 units, Edwardsville has an advantage; and above 26,666, Denton has the advantage. (We have made the assumption in this problem that other costs, that is, delivery, and intangible factors are constant regardless of the decision.)

c) From the chart we can see that the cost line for Fayetteville and the cost line for Edwardsville cross at about 8,000. We can, with a little algebra, also determine this point:

$$\$180,000 + 1.75Q = \$170,000 + 3.00Q$$
$$\$10,000 = 1.25Q$$
$$8,000 = Q$$

Solved Problem 8.3

Don Yale, president of Hardrock Concrete Company, has plants in three locations and is currently working on three major construction projects, located at different sites. The shipping cost per truckload of concrete, plant capacities, and project requirements are provided below:

a) Formulate an initial feasible solution to Hardrock's transportation problem, using the northwest corner rule.

b) Then evaluate each unused shipping route (each empty cell) by applying the stepping-stone method and computing all improvement indices. Remember to

1. check that supply and demand are equal
2. load the table via the northwest corner method
3. check that there are the proper number of occupied cells for a "normal" solution, namely number of rows + number of columns − 1 = number of occupied cells

	TO			
FROM	Project A	Project B	Project C	PLANT CAPACITY
Plant 1	$10	$4	$11	70
Plant 2	$12	$5	$ 8	50
Plant 3	$ 9	$7	$ 6	30
Project requirements	40	50	60	150

4. find a closed path to each empty cell
5. determine the index for each unused cell
6. move as many units as possible to the cell that provides the most improvement (if there is one)
7. repeat steps 3 through 6 until no further improvement can be found

Solution

a) Northwest corner solution

Initial cost = 40($10) + 30($4) + 20($5) + 30($8) + 30($6) = $1,040.

From \ To	Project A	Project B	Project C	Plant capacities
Plant 1	$10 40	$4 30	$11	70
Plant 2	$12	$5 20	$8 30	50
Plant 3	$9	$7	$6 30	30
Project requirements	40	50	60	150

b) Using the stepping-stone method, the following improvement indices are computed:

Path: plant 1 to project C = $11 − $4 + $5 − $8 = + $4

(Closed path = 1C to 1B to 2B to 2C)

From \ To	Project A	Project B	Project C	Plant capacities
Plant 1	10	4 − ---→ +	11	70
Plant 2	12	5 + ←--- −	8	50
Plant 3	9	7	6	30
Project requirements	40	50	60	150

Path: plant 1 to project C

Path: plant 2 to project A = $12 − $5 + $4 − $10 = + $1

(Closed path = 2A to 2B to 1B to 1A)

From \ To	Project A	Project B	Project C	Plant capacities
Plant 1	10 − ---→ +	4	11	70
Plant 2	12 + ←--- −	5	8	50
Plant 3	9	7	6	30
Project requirements	40	50	60	150

Path: plant 2 to project A

Path: plant 3 to project A = \$9 − \$6 + \$8 − \$5 + \$4 − \$10 = \$0
(Closed path = 3A to 3C to 2C to 2B to 1B to 1A)

From \ To	Project A	Project B	Project C	Plant capacity
Plant 1	10	4	11	70
Plant 2	12	5	8	50
Plant 3	9	7	6	30
Project requirements	40	50	60	150

Path: plant 3 to project A

Path: plant 3 to project B = \$7 − \$6 + \$8 − \$5 = \$4
(Closed path = 3B to 3C to 2C to 2B)

From \ To	Project A	Project B	Project C	Plant capacity
Plant 1	10	4	11	70
Plant 2	12	5	8	50
Plant 3	9	7	6	30
Project requirements	40	50	60	150

Path: plant 3 to project B

Since all indices are greater than or equal to zero (all are positive or zero), this initial solution provides the optimal transportation schedule, namely, 40 units from 1 to A, 30 units from 1 to B, 20 units from 2 to B, 30 units from 2 to C, and 30 units from 3 to C.

Had we found a path that allowed improvement, we would move all units possible to that cell and then check every empty cell again.

DISCUSSION QUESTIONS

1. In terms of the strategic objective, how do industrial and service location decisions differ?

2. In recent years the federal government has increased the latitude that railroads have in setting rates and deregulated much of the rate-setting structure of trucks and airlines. What will be the long-range impact of this deregulation on location strategies?

3. The Grant Thornton study generated the factor weights shown in Table 8. 1. Would all companies rate these factor weights of equal importance? If so, why? If not, why not?

4. When, in solving a transportation problem:
   a) is a northwest corner solution optimal?
   b) is a MODI method optimal?

5. Urban Jones, city manager of a large Eastern city, responding to a group of manufacturers who were complaining about the impact of increased taxes, said that taxes levied by a city were not an important consideration to new businesses contemplating moving to that city. If you were president of the local Chamber of Commerce, how would you respond? If you are a person who is concerned about the unemployment rate in the inner city, how would you respond?

6. The transportation method is, as the name implies, a technique that primarily addresses transportation costs. How can you also address production costs with the transportation method?

7. Explain the assumptions behind the center of gravity method. How can the model be used in a service facility location?

8. How do service facility location decisions differ from industrial location decisions?

PROBLEMS

· **8.1** Consolidated Refineries, headquartered in Houston, must decide among three sites for the construction of a new oil processing center. The firm has selected the six factors listed below as a basis for evaluation and has assigned rating weights from one to five on each factor.

FACTOR NO.	FACTOR NAME	RATING WEIGHT
1	Proximity to port facilities	5
2	Power source availability and cost	3
3	Work force attitude and cost	4
4	Distance from Houston	2
5	Community desirability	2
6	Equipment suppliers in area	3

Management has rated each location for each factor on a 1 to 100 point basis.

FACTOR NO.	LOCATION A	LOCATION B	LOCATION C
1	100	80	80
2	80	70	100
3	30	60	70
4	10	80	60
5	90	60	80
6	50	60	90

What site will be recommended?

· **8.2** The fixed and variable costs for four potential plant sites for a ski equipment manufacturer are shown below.

SITE	FIXED COST PER YEAR	VARIABLE COST PER UNIT
Atlanta	$125,000	$ 6
Burlington	75,000	5
Cleveland	100,000	4
Denver	50,000	12

a) Graph the total cost lines for the four potential sites.

b) Over what range of annual volume is each location the preferable one (that with lowest expected cost)?

c) If expected volume of the ski equipment is 5,000 units, which location would you recommend?

: **8.3** Determine whether the new solution table presented in Example 6 contains the optimal transportation allocation for Hot Tubs Corporation. If not, compute an improved solution and test it for optimality.

: **8.4** In Example 10, Williams Auto Top Carrier proposed opening a new plant in either New Orleans or Houston. The firm's management found that the total system cost (of production plus distribution) would be $20,000 if they chose the New Orleans site.

What would be the total cost if Williams opened a plant in Houston? At which of the two proposed locations (New Orleans or Houston) should Williams open the new facility?

· **8.5** After one iteration of the stepping-stone method, Jack Wilson Paint Company produced the transportation table below.

Complete the analysis, determining an optimal shipping solution for Jack Wilson.

Jack Wilson Paint Company

From \ To	Warehouse 1	Warehouse 2	Warehouse 3	Factory capacity
Factory A	$8 120	$5	$6	120
Factory B	$15	$10 80	$14	80
Factory C	$3 30	$9	$10 50	80
Warehouse requirements	150	80	50	280

Cost = $2350

: **8.6** The initial solution for the Hardrock Concrete Company's shipping problem, derived by using the northwest corner rule, is presented below. Apply the MODI method in order to determine whether this allocation is optimal.

Hardrock Concrete Company

From \ To	Project A	Project B	Project C	Plant capacity
Plant 1	$10 40	$4 30	$11	70
Plant 2	$12	$5 20	$8 30	50
Plant 3	$9	$7	$6 30	30
Project requirements	40	50	60	150

:**8.7** The JC Clothing Group owns factories in three towns (W, Y, and Z), which distribute to three JC retail dress shops in three other cities (in A, B, and C). The table below summarizes factory availabilities, projected store demands, and unit shipping costs.

a) Complete the analysis, determining the optimal solution for shipping at the JC Clothing Group.

b) How do you know if it is optimal or not?

JC Clothing Group

From \ To	Dress shop A	Dress shop B	Dress shop C	Factory availability
Factory W	$4	$3	$3	35
Factory Y	$6	$7	$6	50
Factory Z	$8	$2	$5	50
Store demand	30	65	40	135

:**8.8** Sound Track Stereos assembles its high-fidelity stereophonic systems at three plants and distributes systems from three regional warehouses. The production capacities at each plant, demand at each warehouse, and unit shipping costs are presented below.

a) Set up this transportation problem by adding a dummy plant. Then use the northwest corner rule to find an initial basic feasible solution.

b) What is the optimal solution?

Sound Track Stereos

From \ To	Warehouse A	Warehouse B	Warehouse C	Plant supply
Plant W	$6	$4	$9	200
Plant X	$10	$5	$8	175
Plant Y	$12	$7	$6	75
Warehouse demand	250	100	150	500 / 450

:**8.9** Whybark Mill Works (WMW) ships French doors to three building supply houses from its mills in Mountpelier, Nixon, and Oak Ridge. Determine the best shipment schedule for WMW from the data provided by Joe Sawyer, the traffic manager at WMW. Use the northwest corner starting procedure and the stepping-stone method. Refer to table on page 368.

:**8.10** Using the data in Problem 8.8, resolve via the MODI method.

:**8.11** Using the data in Problem 8.9, resolve, using the MODI method.

Whybark Mill Works

From \ To	Supply house 1	Supply house 2	Supply house 3	Mill capacity (in tons)
Mountpelier	$3	$3	$2	25
Nixon	$4	$2	$3	40
Oak Ridge	$3	$2	$3	30
Supply house demand (in tons)	30	30	35	95

 : **8.12** The B. Hall Real Estate Investment Corporation has identified four small apartment buildings in which it would like to invest. Mrs. Hall has approached three savings and loan companies regarding financing. Because Mrs. Hall has been a good client in the past and has maintained a high credit rating in the community, each savings and loan company is willing to consider providing all or part of the mortgage loan needed on each property. Each loan officer has set differing interest rates on each property (rates are affected by the neighborhood of the apartment building, condition of the property, and desire by the individual savings and loan to finance various size buildings), and each loan company has placed a maximum credit ceiling on how much it will lend Mrs. Hall in total. This information is summarized in the table below.

SAVINGS AND LOAN COMPANY	PROPERTY (%)				MAXIMUM CREDIT LINE
	Hill St.	Banks St.	Park Ave.	Drury Lane	
First Homestead	8	8	10	11	$80,000
Commonwealth	9	10	12	10	$100,000
Washington Federal	9	11	10	9	$120,000
Loan required to purchase building	$60,000	$40,000	$130,000	$70,000	

Each apartment building is equally attractive as an investment to Mrs. Hall, so she has decided to purchase all buildings possible at the lowest total payment of interest. From which savings and loan companies should she borrow to purchase which buildings? More than one savings and loan can finance the same property.

: **8.13** Bruce Hearns, vice president for operations of HHN, Inc., a manufacturer of cabinets for telephone switches, is constrained from meeting the five-year forecast by limited capacity at the existing three plants. These three plants are Waterloo, Pusan, and Bogota. You, as his able assistant, have been told that because of existing capacity constraints and the expanding world market for HHN cabinets, a new plant is to be added to the existing three plants. The real estate department has advised Mr. Hearns that two sites seem particularly good because of a stable political situation and tolerable exchange rate. These two acceptable locations are Dublin, Ireland, and Fontainebleau, France. Mr. Hearns suggests that you should be able to take the data on page 369 and determine where the fourth plant should be located on the basis of production costs and transportation costs. *Note:* This problem is degenerate with the data for both locations. Refer to table on page 369.

MARKET AREA	PLANT LOCATION				
	Waterloo	Pusan	Bogota	Fontainebleau	Dublin
Canada					
Demand 4,000					
Production cost	50	30	40	50	45
Transportation cost	10	25	20	25	25
South America					
Demand 5,000					
Production cost	50	30	40	50	45
Transportation cost	20	25	10	30	30
Pacific Rim					
Demand 10,000					
Production cost	50	30	40	50	45
Transportation cost	25	10	25	40	40
Europe					
Demand 5,000					
Production cost	50	30	40	50	45
Transportation cost	25	40	30	10	20
Capacity	8000	2000	5000	9000	9000

: **8.14** Spalding Manufacturing Company has hired you to evaluate their shipping costs. The table below shows their present demand, capacity, and freight costs between each factory and each warehouse. Find the shipping pattern with the lowest cost.

From \ To	Warehouse 1	Warehouse 2	Warehouse 3	Warehouse 4	Plant capacity
Factory 1	4	7	10	12	2000
Factory 2	7	5	8	11	2500
Factory 3	9	8	6	9	2200
Warehouse demand	1000	2000	2000	1200	

: **8.15** Cerveny Corporation is considering adding an additional plant to their three existing facilities in Decatur, Minneapolis, and Carbondale. Both St. Louis and East St. Louis are being considered. Evaluating only the transportation costs per unit as shown in the table, which site is best?

TO	FROM EXISTING PLANTS			
	Decatur	Minneapolis	Carbondale	Demand
Blue Earth	$20	$17	$21	250
Ciro	25	27	20	200
Des Moines	22	25	22	350
Capacity	300	200	150	

	FROM PROPOSED PLANTS	
TO	*East St. Louis*	*St. Louis*
Blue Earth	$29	$27
Ciro	30	28
Des Moines	30	31
Capacity	150	150

: **8.16** Using the data from Problem 8.15 plus the unit production costs shown below, which locations yield the lowest cost?

LOCATION	PRODUCTION COSTS
Decatur	$50
Minneapolis	60
Carbondale	70
East St. Louis	40
St. Louis	50

: **8.17** A Detroit seafood restaurant is considering opening a second facility in the suburb of West Bloomfield. The table below shows its ratings of five factors at each of four potential sites. Which site should be selected?

		SITE			
FACTOR	WEIGHT	1	2	3	4
Affluence of local population	10	70	60	85	90
Construction and land cost	10	85	90	80	60
Traffic flow	25	70	60	85	90
Parking availability	20	80	90	90	80
Growth potential	15	90	80	90	75

· **8.18** In placing a new medical clinic, county health offices wish to consider three sites. The pertinent data are given in the table below. Which is the best site?

		SCORES		
LOCATION FACTOR	WEIGHT	*Downtown*	*Suburb A*	*Suburb B*
Facility utilization	9	9	7	6
Average time per emergency trip	8	6	6	8
Employee preferences	5	2	5	6
Accessibility to major roadways	5	8	4	5
Land costs	4	2	9	6

: **8.19** The main post office in Tampa, Florida, is due to be replaced with a much larger, more modern facility that can handle the tremendous flow of mail that has followed that city's growth since 1970. Since all mail, incoming or outgoing, travels from the seven regional post offices in Tampa through the main post office, its site selection can mean a big difference in overall delivery and movement efficiency. Using the data in the following table, calculate the center of gravity for the proposed new facility.

REGIONAL POST OFFICE	X, Y MAP COORDINATES	TRUCK ROUND-TRIPS PER DAY
Ybor City	(10, 5)	3
Davis Island	(3, 8)	3
Dale-Marbry	(4, 7)	2
Palma Ceia	(15, 10)	6
Bayshore	(13, 3)	5
Temple Terrace	(1, 12)	3
Hyde Park	(5, 5)	10

· **8.20** Jeanne's Garden Shop, whose warehouse decision was documented in Example 3 with Table 8.3 and Figure 8.3, has decided its retail outlets are too far-flung geographically. To alleviate the situation, it intends to close the New York store and open a new store in Milwaukee. It is hoped that the demand in Milwaukee, which has coordinates of (31, 140), will equal that of the New York store. Where should the warehouse be relocated?

· **8.21** Laurie Shader is proprietress of two exclusive women's clothing stores in Miami. In her plan to expand to a third location, she has narrowed her decision down to three sites—one in a downtown office building, one in a shopping mall, and one in an old Victorian house in the suburban area of Coral Cables. She feels that rent is absolutely the most important factor to be considered, while walk-in traffic is 90% as important as rent. Further, the more distant the new store is from her two existing stores the better, she thinks. She weights this factor to be 80% as important as walk-in traffic. Laurie developed the table below, where she graded each site on the same system used in her MBA program in college. Which site is preferable?

	DOWNTOWN	SHOPPING MALL	CORAL GABLES HOUSE
Rent	D	C	A
Walk-in traffic	B	A	D
Distance from existing stores	B	A	C

Data Base Applications

: **8.22.** The unification of Europe has brought about changes in airline regulation that dramatically affect major European carriers such as British International Air, SAS, KLM, Air France, Alitalia, and Sabena. With ambitious expansion plans, British International Air (BIA) has decided it needs a second service hub on the continent, to complement its large Heathrow (London) repair facility. The location selection is critical, and with the potential for 4,000 new skilled blue-collar jobs on the line, virtually every city in Western Europe is actively bidding for BIA's business.

After initial investigations by Harry Zipper, head of the Operations Department, BIA has narrowed the list to 16 cities. Each is then rated on 12 factors, with the table on page 372 resulting.

Table for Data Base Application 8.22

| | | LOCATION | | | | | | | | | | | | | | |
| | | ITALY | | | FRANCE | | | GERMANY | | | SPAIN | SWITZERLAND | | HOLLAND | | DENMARK | PORTUGAL |
Factor	Importance Weight	Milan	Rome	Genoa	Paris	Lyon	Nice	Munich	Bonn	Berlin	Madrid	Bern	Zurich	Amsterdam	The Hague	Copenhagen	Lisbon
Financial incentives	85	8	8	8	7	7	7	7	7	7	9	8	8	9	9	8	10
Skilled labor pool	80	4	6	5	9	9	7	10	8	9	4	9	10	9	8	7	3
Existing facility	70	5	3	2	9	6	5	9	9	2	5	7	8	8	2	8	6
Wage rates	70	9	8	9	4	6	6	4	5	5	10	3	3	5	9	5	10
Competition for jobs	70	7	3	8	2	8	7	4	8	9	6	5	4	3	7	6	6
Ease of air traffic access	65	5	4	6	2	8	8	4	8	9	5	5	5	3	9	4	6
Real estate cost	40	6	4	7	4	6	6	3	4	5	8	2	1	3	5	4	7
Communication links	25	6	7	6	9	9	9	10	9	8	2	8	8	8	6	9	2
Attractiveness to relocating executives	15	4	8	3	9	6	6	2	3	3	4	9	8	9	6	7	3
Political considerations	10	6	6	6	8	8	8	8	8	8	5	9	9	8	8	8	2
Expansion possibilities	10	10	2	8	1	5	4	4	5	6	5	3	2	3	8	4	6
Union strength	10	1	1	1	5	5	5	6	6	6	9	8	8	7	7	5	9

a) Help Zipper rank the top three cities that BIA should consider as its new site for servicing aircraft.

b) After further investigation, Harry Zipper decides that an existing set of hangar facilities for repairs is not nearly as important as earlier thought. In lowering the weight of that factor to a 30, does the ranking change?

c) After Zipper makes the change above (in part b), Germany announces it has reconsidered its offer of financial incentives, with an additional 200 million German mark package to entice BIA. Accordingly, BIA has raised Germany's rating to a 10 on that factor. Is there any change in top rankings in part **b**?

8.23. Cramer Pharmaceuticals holds a dominant position in the southeast United States, with over 800 discount retail outlets. These stores are served with twice-weekly deliveries from Cramer's 13 warehouses, which in turn are supplied daily by 7 factories that manufacture about 70% of all of the chain's products.

It is clear to Marcia Cramer, the VP-Operations, that an additional warehouse is desperately needed to handle growth and backlogs. Three cities, Mobile, Tampa, and Huntsville, are under final consideration. The table on page 373 illustrates the current and proposed factory/warehouse capacities/demands and shipping costs per average box of supplies.

a) Based on shipping costs only, which city should be selected for the new warehouse?

b) Ocala's capacity, a study shows, can increase to 500 boxes per day. Would this affect your decision in part **a**?

c) Because of a new intrastate shipping agreement, rates for shipping from each factory in Florida to each warehouse in Florida drop by $1 per carton. How does this affect your answer to questions **a** and **b**?

TABLE FOR DATA BASE APPLICATION 8.23

Factory \ Warehouse	Atlanta GA	New Orleans LA	Jackson MS	Birmingham AL	Montgomery AL	Raleigh NC	Ashville NC	Columbia SC	Orlando FL	Miami FL	Jacksonville FL	Wilmington NC	Charlotte NC	Mobile AL	Tampa FL	Huntsville AL	Capacity (cartons per day)
Valdosta, GA	$3	$5	$4	$3	$4	$6	$8	$8	$9	$10	$8	$8	$11	$4	$6	$3	500
Ocala, FL	4	6	5	5	6	7	6	7	2	3	2	6	7	5	2	5	300
Augusta, GA	1	4	3	2	2	6	7	8	7	9	6	8	9	3	5	2	400
Stuart, FL	3	5	2	6	6	5	5	6	2	2	3	5	5	6	3	5	200
Biloxi, MS	4	1	4	3	3	8	9	10	7	13	9	8	8	2	6	3	600
Starkville, MS	3	3	1	2	2	6	5	6	6	8	7	7	8	3	6	2	400
Durham, NC	4	8	8	7	7	2	2	2	6	8	5	1	2	8	7	8	500
Requirements (cartons/day)	150	250	50	150	100	200	150	300	250	300	300	100	150	300	300	300	

CASE STUDY

Southern Recreational Vehicle Company

In October 1989, top management of Southern Recreational Vehicle Company of St. Louis, Missouri, announced its plans to relocate its manufacturing and assembly operations by constructing a new plant in Ridgecrest, Mississippi. The firm, a major producer of pickup campers and camper trailers, had experienced five consecutive years of declining profits as a result of spiraling production costs. The costs of labor and raw materials had increased alarmingly; utility costs had gone up sharply; and taxes and transportation expenses had climbed upward steadily. In spite of increased sales, the company suffered its first net loss since operations were begun in 1977.

When management initially considered relocation, they closely scrutinized several geographic areas. Of primary importance to the relocation decision were the availability of adequate transportation facilities, state and municipal tax structures, an adequate labor supply, positive community attitudes, reasonable site costs, and financial inducements. Although several communities offered essentially the same incentives, the management of Southern Recreational Vehicle Company was favorably impressed by the efforts of the Mississippi Power and Light company to attract "clean, labor-intensified" industry and the enthusiasm exhibited by state and local officials who actively sought to bolster the state's economy by enticing manufacturing firms to locate within its boundaries.

Two weeks prior to the announcement, management of Southern Recreational Vehicle Company finalized its relocation plans. An existing building in Ridgecrest's industrial park was selected (the physical facility had previously housed a mobile home manufacturer that had gone bankrupt due to inadequate financing and poor management); initial recruiting was begun through the State Employment Office; and efforts to lease or sell the St. Louis property were initiated. Among the inducements offered Southern Recreational Vehicle Company to locate in Ridgecrest were:

1. Exemption from county and municipal taxes for five years,

2. Free water and sewage services,

3. Construction of a second loading dock—free of cost—at the industrial site,

4. An agreement to issue $500,000 in industrial bonds for future expansion,

5. Public-financed training of workers in a local industrial trade school.

In addition to these inducements, other factors weighed heavily in the decision to locate in the small Mississippi town. Labor costs would be significantly less than those incurred in St. Louis; organized labor was not expected to be as powerful (Mississippi is a right-to-work state); and utility costs and taxes would be moderate. All in all, management of Southern Recreational Vehicle Company felt that its decision was sound.

On October 15, the following announcement was attached to each employee's paycheck:

To: Employees of Southern Recreational Vehicle Company

From: Gerald O'Brian, President

CASE STUDY (Continued)

The Management of Southern Recreational Vehicle Company regretfully announces its plans to cease all manufacturing operations in St. Louis on December 31. Because of increased operating costs and the unreasonable demands forced upon the company by the union, it has become impossible to operate profitably. I sincerely appreciate the fine service that each of you has rendered to the company during the past few years. If I can be of assistance in helping you find suitable employment with another firm, please let me know. Thank you again, for your cooperation and past service.

Source: Written by Professor Jerry Kinard (Francis Marion College) and Joe C. Iverstine.

Discussion Questions

1. Evaluate the inducements offered Southern Recreational Vehicle Company by community leaders in Ridgecrest, Mississippi.

2. What problems would a company experience in relocating its executives from a heavily populated industrialized area to a small rural town?

3. Evaluate the reasons cited by Mr. O'Brian for relocation. Are they justifiable?

4. What responsibilities does a firm have to its employees when a decision to cease operations is made?

CASE STUDY

Custom Vans, Inc.

Custom Vans, Inc., specializes in converting standard vans into campers. Depending on the amount of work and customizing to be done, the customizing could cost less than $1,000 to over $5,000. In less than four years, Tony Rizzo was able to expand his small operation in Gary, Indiana, to other major outlets in Chicago, Milwaukee, Minneapolis, and Detroit.

Innovation was the major factor in Tony's success in converting a small van shop into one of the largest and most profitable custom van operations in the Midwest. Tony seemed to have a special ability to design and develop unique features and devices that were always in high demand by van owners. An example was Shower-Rific, which was developed by Tony only six months after Custom Vans, Inc., was started. These small showers were completely self-contained, and they could be placed in almost any type of van and in a number of different locations within a van. Shower-Rific was made of fiberglass, and contained towel racks, built-in soap and shampoo holders, and a unique plastic door. Each Shower-Rific took 2 gallons of fiberglass and 3 hours of labor to manufacture.

Most of the Shower-Rifics were manufactured in Gary in the same warehouse where Custom Vans, Inc., was founded. The manufacturing plant in Gary could produce 300 Shower-Rifics in a month, but this capacity never seemed to be enough. Custom Van shops in all locations were complaining about not getting enough Shower-Rifics, and because Minneapolis was farther away from Gary than the other locations, Tony was always inclined to ship

Shower-Rifics to the other locations before Minneapolis. This infuriated the manager of Custom Vans at Minneapolis, and after many heated discussions, Tony decided to start another manufacturing plant for Shower-Rifics at Fort Wayne, Indiana. The manufacturing plant at Fort Wayne could produce 150 Shower-Rifics per month.

The manufacturing plant at Fort Wayne was still not able to meet current demand for Shower-Rifics, and Tony knew that the demand for his unique camper shower would grow rapidly in the next year. After consulting with his lawyer and banker, Tony concluded that he should open two new manufacturing plants as soon as possible. Each plant would have the same capacity as the Fort Wayne manufacturing plant. An initial investigation into possible manufacturing locations was made, and Tony decided that the two new plants should be located in Detroit, Michigan; Rockford, Illinois; or Madison, Wisconsin. Tony knew that selecting the best location for the two new manufacturing plants would be difficult. Transportation costs and demands for the various locations should be important considerations.

The Chicago shop was managed by Bill Burch. This Custom Van shop was one of the first established by Tony, and it continued to outperform the other locations. The manufacturing plant at Gary was supplying 200 Shower-Rifics each month, although Bill knew that the demand for the showers in Chicago was 300 units. The transportation cost per unit from Gary was $10, and although the transportation cost from Fort Wayne was double that amount, Bill was always pleading with Tony to get an additional 50 units

CASE STUDY (Continued)

from the Fort Wayne manufacturer. The two additional manufacturing plants would certainly be able to supply Bill with the additional 100 showers he needed. The transportation costs would, of course, vary, depending on which two locations Tony picked. The transportation cost per shower would be $30 from Detroit, $5 from Rockford, and $10 from Madison.

Wilma Jackson, manager of the Custom Van shop in Milwaukee, was the most upset about not getting an adequate supply of showers. She had a demand for 100 units, and at the present time, she was only getting half of this demand from the Fort Wayne manufacturing plant. She could not understand why Tony didn't ship her all 100 units from Gary. The transportation cost per unit from Gary was only $20, while the transportation cost from Fort Wayne was $30. Wilma was hoping that Tony would select Madison for one of the manufacturing locations. She would be able to get all of the showers needed, and the transportation cost per unit would be only $5. If not Madison, a new plant in Rockford would be able to supply her total needs, but the transportation cost per unit would be twice as much as it would be from Madison. Because the transportation cost per unit from Detroit would be $40, Wilma speculated that even if Detroit became one of the new plants, she would not be getting any units from Detroit.

Custom Vans, Inc., of Minneapolis was managed by Tom Poanski. He was getting 100 showers from the Gary plant. Demand was 150 units. Tom faced the highest transportation costs of all locations. The transportation cost from Gary was $40 per unit. It would cost $10 more if showers were sent from the Fort Wayne location. Tom was hoping that Detroit would not be one of the new plants, as the transportation cost would be $60 per unit. Rockford and Madison would have a cost of $30 and $25, respectively, to ship one shower to Minneapolis.

The Detroit shop's position was similar to Milwaukee's—only getting half of the demand each month. The 100 units that Detroit did receive came directly from the Fort Wayne plant. The transportation cost was only $15 per unit from Fort Wayne, while it was $25 from Gary. Dick Lopez, manager of Custom Vans, Inc., of Detroit, placed the probability of having one of the new plants in Detroit fairly high. The factory would be located across town, and the transportation cost would be only $2 per unit. He could get 150 showers from the new plant in Detroit and the other 50 showers from Fort Wayne. Even if Detroit were not selected, the other two locations were not intolerable. Rockford had a transportation cost per unit of $35, and Madison had a transportation cost of $40.

Tony pondered the dilemma of locating the two new plants for several weeks before deciding to call a meeting of all the managers of the van shops. The decision was complicated, but the objective was clear—to minimize total costs. The meeting was held in Gary, and everyone was present except Wilma.

Tony: Thank you for coming. As you know, I have decided to open up two new plants at Rockford, Madison, or Detroit. The two locations, of course, will change our shipping practices, and I sincerely hope that they will supply you with the Shower-Rifics that you have been wanting. I know you could have sold more units, and I want you to know that I am sorry for this situation.

Dick: Tony, I have given this situation a lot of consideration, and I feel strongly that at least one of the new plants should be located in Detroit. As you know, I am now getting only half of the showers that I need. My brother, Leon, is very interested in running the plant, and I know he would do a good job.

Tom: Dick, I am sure that Leon could do a good job, and I know how difficult it has been since the recent layoffs by the auto industry. Nevertheless, we should be considering total costs and not personalities. I believe that the new plants should be located in Madison and Rockford. I am farther away from the other plants than any other shop, and these locations would significantly reduce transportation costs.

Dick: That may be true, but there are other factors. Detroit has one of the largest suppliers of fiberglass, and I have checked prices. A new plant in Detroit would be able to purchase fiberglass for $2 less than any of the other existing or proposed plants.

Tom: At Madison, we have an excellent labor force. This is primarily due to the large number of students attending the University of Madison. These students are hard workers, and they will work for $1 less per hour than the other locations that we are considering.

Bill: Calm down, you two. It is obvious that we will not be able to satisfy everyone in locating the new plants. Therefore, I would like to suggest that we vote on the two best locations.

Tony: I don't think that voting would be a good idea. Wilma was not able to attend, and we should be looking at all of these factors together in some type of logical fashion.

Discussion Question

1. Where would you locate the two new plants and why?

Source: Written by R. M. Stair, Jr., in Barry Render and Ralph M. Stair, *Quantitative Analysis for Management,* 4th ed., Boston: Allyn & Bacon, 1991.

BIBLIOGRAPHY

Ashton, J. E., and F. X. Cook, Jr. "Time to Reform Job Shop Manufacturing." *Harvard Business Review* **67** (March–April 1989): 106–111.

Cerveny, R. P. "An Application of Warehouse Location Technique to Bloodmobile Operations." *Interfaces* **10** (December 1980): 89–93.

Craig, C. S., *et al.* "Models of the Retail Location Process." *Journal of Retailing* **60** (April 1984): 5–36.

Davis, S. G., *et al.* "Strategic Planning for Bank Operations with Multiple Check-Processing Locations." *Interfaces* **16** (November–December 1986): 1–12.

DeSanta, R. "All That Glitters Is Not Upscale." *Progressive Grocer* (April 1987): 112–117.

Domich, P. D., K. L. Hoffman, R. H. F. Jackson, and M. A. McClain. "Locating Tax Facilities: A Graphics-Based Microcomputer Optimization Model." *Management Science* **37** (August 1991): 960.

Fitzsimmons, J. A. "A Warehouse Location Model Helps Texas Comptroller Select Out-of-State Audit Officers." *Interfaces* **13** (October 1983): 40–45.

Ghosh, A., and C. S. Craig. "Formulating Retail Location Strategy in a Changing Environment." *Journal of Marketing* **47** (Summer 1983): 56–58.

Goodchild, M. F. "ILACS: A Location Allocation Model for Retail Site Selection." *Journal of Retailing* **60** (April 1984): 84–100.

Keating, J. W. "Facility Planning in a Decentralized Structure: Three Key Areas of Responsibility." *Industrial Development* (July–August 1986).

Kimes, S. E., and J. A. Fitzsimmons. "Selecting Profitable Hotel Sites at La Quinta Motor Inns." *Interfaces* **20** (March–April 1990): 12.

Lord, D. J., and C. D. Lynds. "The Use of Regression Models in Store Location Research." *Akron Business and Economic Review* (Summer 1981): 13–14.

Maas, M. "In Offices of the Future: The Productivity Value of Environment." *Management Review* (March 1983).

Mahajan, V., S. Sharma, and D. Srinivas. "An Application of Portfolio Analysis for Identifying Attractive Retail Locations." *Journal of Retailing* **61** (Winter 1985): 19–34.

Merredew, C. "A Model Facility Delivery Process." *Industrial Development* (July–August 1986).

Miller, D. "The Components of a Facility Review." *Industrial Development* (March–April 1986).

Min, H. "A Multiobjective Retail Service Location Model for Fast Food Restaurants." *Omega* **15** (1987): 429–441.

Molinero, C. M. "Schools in Southampton: A Quantitative Approach to School Location, Closure, and Staffing." *Journal of Operational Research Society* **39** (1988): 339–350.

Murdick, R., B. Render, and R. Russell. *Service Operations Management.* Boston: Allyn and Bacon, 1990.

Pacione, M. (ed.) *Progress in Industrial Geography.* London: Croom Helm, 1985.

Price, W. L., and M. Turcotte. "Locating a Blood Bank." *Interfaces* **16** (September–October 1986): 17–26.

Render, B., and R. M. Stair. *Introduction to Management Science.* Boston: Allyn & Bacon, 1992.

Render, B., and R. M. Stair. *Quantitative Analysis for Management,* 4th ed. Boston: Allyn & Bacon, 1991.

Rudd, H. F., Jr., J. W. Viger, and R. M. Davis. "The LMMD Model: Choosing the Optimal Location for a Small Retail Business." *Journal of Small Business Management* **21** (April 1983): 46.

Shapiro, R. D., and R. E. Bohn, "Implications of Cost Service Trade-offs on Industry Logistics Structures." *Interfaces* **15** (November–December 1985): 47–59.

Spohrev, G. A., and T. R. Kmak, "Qualitative Analysis Used in Evaluating Alternative Plant Location Scenarios." *Journal of Industrial Engineering* (August 1984): 52–56.

Teodorovic, D., *et al.* "Optimal Locations of Emergency Service Depots for Private Cars in Urban Areas: Case Study of Belgrade." *Transportation Planning and Technology* **11** (1986): 177–188.

"The Checklist of Site Selection Factors." In *Site Selection Handbook.* Atlanta, GA: Conway, 1978.

Von Hohenbalken, B., and D. S. West. "Predation Among Supermarkets: An Algorithmic Locational Analysis." *Journal of Urban Economics* **15** (1984): 244–257.

Zarrillo, M. J. "Strategies for Selecting a Mixed-Use Corporate Site." *Industrial Development* (March–April 1986).

Operations Layout Strategy

Siemens Finds Competitive Advantage with Effective Layout

Siemens, the $46-billion-dollar-a-year electronics giant, is Germany's largest corporation and is second in size worldwide to only one company, General Motors. This world-class manufacturer is a leader in computers, building systems, industrial automation, consumer appliances, power generation, semiconductors, medical engineering, and communications systems. Siemens' 1989 hostile takeover of Britain's Plessey Company brought it into the U.S. manufacturing arena as the number three producer of telephone switching systems (behind AT&T and Northern Telecom).

Switching systems allow phone callers to communicate through central switchboards. Siemens' vast array of telephone switching systems can accommodate the phone company in a town of a few hundred people up to one in a city of over a million.

Siemens manufactures over 700 types of switching boards and has 15 different testing systems. It creates switching systems through both high volume production *and* a job shop approach. When Siemens inherited the 363,000-square-foot manufacturing plant in Lake Mary, Florida, there was much to be done. The facility had been owned by a succession of three conglomerates and little investment in the latest manufacturing equipment had been made by any of them.

This semi-automated assembly line presents one circuit board at a time to an operator. A light shines on the board to show the operator where to do the next assembly task (such as inserting an electronic component). This hybrid of semi-automated assembly requires less tooling and is more flexible than a fixed line or one driven totally by robots. It is slower than a fixed assembly line, but yields higher quality while minimizing human variability. All work on one board is done at one workstation, so this is not a traditional assembly line.

As the 20,000 different parts needed in production enter the stockroom from the unloading docks, most go to Siemens' automated storage and retrieval system. This $3 million state-of-the-art blend of computers, robotics, and mechanics transports components from receiving to testing to stocking and picking workstations. Watching it in action is like standing inside a huge vending machine as the whirring and humming machinery retrieves the selected item and presents it. The automated stockroom system: (1) frees 30,000 square feet of stockroom space, (2) reduces time to receive materials by 50%, and (3) maintains accurate inventory.

To bring the Lake Mary plant up to world-class standards, Siemens invested millions of dollars in a new layout—and another $3 million in an automated stockroom system for parts control. In an amazing feat, Siemens revamped the layout of the whole factory without shutting down or losing one day's production. To do so it turned the flow of production from north-south to a U-shaped east-west layout that begins with receiving at one dock and ends with shipping at another. The new layout contributes to reduced work-in-process as well as to Siemens' just-in-time philosophy.

The implementation of a new layout has become a case study in management excellence. The new look involved not only sophisticated new equipment and a new production flow, but a new "feel" and "culture" as well. Dirty old flooring was replaced with light "anti-static" tile (at a cost of $6 per square foot). Three-quarters of a mile of walls were removed to open up the work area. All lighting was changed from dull fluorescent to a new extremely bright light. Ceilings were painted white. And smoking, dirt, and posters at work stations were banned. A "new look" team of eight employees became ambassadors of change to encourage their coworkers to buy in to some of the draconian measures. This meshes with the ideas of Ron Lowery, Director of Operations, who states: "In most companies that can lay claims to world-class operations, one of

Thirty-two of Siemens' switching system circuit boards are assembled in this fully automated Computer Integrated Manufacturing (CIM) line. Nearly 700 other products are processed in the computer-controlled semi-automated line.

Circuit boards pass through a wave-soldering machine, which uses the latest technology and "nonreactive flux" to solder component leads so that chemical "cleaning" is no longer required. This change eliminates undesirable pollutants from the process and improves quality.

the first things you'll notice when you walk into their operations is that they're absolutely sparkling."

The challenge to layout designers is to make the best use of every inch of space. Any new system must allow the production flow to be quick, systematic, and logical—from raw materials in one door to finished product out the other. According to Lowery, "the objective for the new layout is to drive work-in-process inventory levels down drastically since materials are the largest component of product cost." Indeed, Siemens has done so. Work-in-process has been reduced considerably, with a corresponding reduction in capital investment.

Siemens once again proves why it is world class; the firm has obtained competitive advantage via an effective layout.

In the telecommunications business, only two hours of downtime are permitted in a 40-year product lifetime. Therefore stringent testing procedures are established. Key elements of the telephone systems built by Siemens are totally redundant, meaning each component has an identical backup, which is automatically activated in case of failure. Here switching systems are lined up for final testing—they have yet to be installed in cabinet boxes.

INTRODUCTION

Layout is one of the six strategic areas that will determine the long-run efficiency of operations. The *objective of the layout strategy* is to develop an economic layout that will meet the requirements of:

1. product design and volume (product strategy);
2. process equipment and capacity (process strategy);
3. quality of work life (human resource strategy);
4. building and site constraints (location strategy).

A layout specifies the arrangement of processes (such as welding, milling, and painting), the related equipment, and work areas, including customer service and storage areas. An effective layout also facilitates the flow of materials and people within and between areas. Management's goal is to arrange (lay out) the system so that it operates at peak effectiveness and efficiency. Layout decisions include the best placement of machines (in a production setting), offices and desks (in an office setting), or service centers (in settings such as hospitals or department stores). To achieve these layout objectives, a variety of strategies have been developed. Among them are six that we will discuss in this chapter:

Fixed-position layout

1. **Fixed-position layout**—addresses the layout requirements of large, bulky projects such as ships and buildings.

Process-oriented layout

2. **Process-oriented layout**—deals with low-volume, high-variety production (also called "job shop" or intermittent production).

Office layout

3. **Office layout**—positions workers, their equipment, and spaces/offices to provide for movement of information.

Retail/service layout

4. **Retail/service layout**—allocates shelf space and responds to customer behavior.

Warehouse layout

5. **Warehouse layout**—addresses trade-offs between space and material handling.

Product-oriented layout

6. **Product-oriented layout**—seeks the best personnel and machine utilization in repetitive or continuous production.

Examples for each of these classes of layout problems are noted in Table 9.1.

Of these six layout strategies, only a few have undergone extensive mathematical analysis. The layout and design of physical facilities is still as much an art as it is a science. We introduce in this chapter some of the art as well as some of the science for effective and efficient layouts.

A good layout requires determining:

1. *Capacity and space requirements.* Capacity decisions are a prerequisite to a good layout. Only when we know the personnel, machines, and equipment required can we proceed with the layout and provide space for each component. In the case of office work, operations managers must make judgments about the space requirements for each employee. It may be a 6×6-foot cubicle plus allowance for hallways, aisles, rest rooms, cafeterias, stairwells, elevators, and so forth; or it may be spacious executive offices and conference rooms. Management must also consider allowances for safety requirements that address noise, dust, fumes, temperature, and space around equipment and machines.

TABLE 9.1 Layout Strategies.

PROJECT (FIXED-POSITION)	JOB SHOP (PROCESS-ORIENTED)	OFFICE	RETAIL (SERVICE/RETAIL)	WAREHOUSE (STORAGE)	REPETITIVE/CONTINUOUS (PRODUCT-ORIENTED)
Example:					
Shipbuilding	Most hospitals	Insurance company	Grocery store	Distributors	TV assembly line
Construction	Kitchen	Software house	Drug store	Warehousing	Meat packer
Road building	Machine shop		Department store	Aging facilities	Auto manufacturer
Problem:					
Move material to the limited storage areas around the site.	Material flow varies with each product.	Locate workers requiring frequent contact close to one another.	Expose customer to high-margin items.	Low-cost storage with low-cost material handling.	Balancing product flow from one workstation to the next.

2. *Material handling equipment.* Decisions are also required about equipment to be used, including conveyors, cranes, and automatic carts to deliver material or the mail.

3. *Environment and aesthetics.* Decisions may be required about windows, planters, and height of partitions to facilitate air flow, to reduce noise, to provide privacy, and so forth.

4. *Flows of information.* Judgments about the best way to facilitate communications must also be made. This may require decisions about proximity as well as open spaces versus half-height dividers versus private offices.

5. *Cost of moving between the various work areas.* There may be unique considerations related to the difficulty of movements or the importance of certain areas being adjacent to each other. For example, the movement of molten steel is more difficult than the movement of cold steel.

FIXED-POSITION LAYOUT

A *fixed-position layout* is one in which the project remains stationary and requires workers and equipment to come to the one work area. Examples of this type of project are a ship, a highway, a bridge, a house, and a burning oil well.

The techniques for addressing the fixed-position layout are not well developed. Construction sites and shipbuilding sites address this issue on an *ad hoc* basis. The construction industry usually has a "meeting of the trades" to assign space for various time periods. As you would suspect, this often yields less than an optimum solution, as the discussion may be more political than analytical. Shipyards, on the other hand, have loading areas called "platens" adjacent to the ship, which are loaded by a scheduling department.

The fixed-position layout is complicated by three factors.

1. There is limited space at virtually all sites.

2. At different stages in the construction process different materials are needed;

therefore, different items become critical as the project develops. This adds the dynamics of scheduling to the layout problem.

3. The volume of materials needed is dynamic. For example, the rate of use of steel panels for the hull of a ship changes as the project progresses.

Because the fixed-position layout is so difficult to solve well at the site, an alternative strategy is to complete as much of the project as possible off site. This approach is used in the shipbuilding industry when standard units, say pipe-holding brackets, are assembled in a nearby assembly line process (a product-oriented facility). Ingall Ship Building Corporation has built similar sections of a ship (modules) or the same section of several similar ships in a product-oriented line. This is their strategy to bring added efficiency to shipbuilding.[1] Similarly, other shipbuilding firms are experimenting with group technology (see Chapter 6) to produce components.[2]

PROCESS-ORIENTED LAYOUT

The *process-oriented layout* can simultaneously handle a wide variety of products or services. In fact, it is most efficient when making products that have different requirements or when handling customers who have different needs. A process-oriented layout is typically the low-volume, high-variety strategy discussed in Chapter 7. In this job shop environment, each product or each small group of products has a different sequence of operations. A product or small order is produced by moving it from one department to another in the sequence required for that product. Figure 9.1 illustrates this process for two products, A and B. A good example of the process-oriented layout is a hospital or clinic. A continuous inflow of patients, each with his or her own request, requires routing through records areas, admissions, laboratories, operating rooms, intensive care areas, pharmacies, nursing stations, and so on.64

A big advantage of process-oriented layout is its flexibility in equipment and labor assignments. The breakdown of one machine, for example, need not halt an entire process; work can be transferred to other machines in the department. Process-oriented layout is also especially good for handling the manufacture of parts in small batches, or **job lots,** and for the production of a wide variety of parts in different sizes or forms.

The disadvantages of process-oriented layout come from the general-purpose use of the equipment. Orders take more time and money to move through the system because of difficult scheduling, setups, and material handling. In addition, labor skill requirements and work-in-process inventories are higher because of larger imbalances in the production process. High labor skill needs increase the required

Job lots

[1] "Ingall's 130 Million Dollar Ship Factory," *Shipbuilding and Shipping Record*, **115,** 22 (London: Transport and Technical Publications Ltd.): 25–26.

[2] Naboru Yamamoto, Kiyohi Terai, and Tatsumi Kurioka, "The Continuous Flow Production System Which Has Applied to Hull Works in Shipbuilding Industry," *Selected Journal of the Society of Naval Architects of Japan,* No. 35, Society of Naval Architects of Japan, Shiba-Kotohiracho, Minato-Ku, Tokyo, Japan, **5,** 70, pp. 153–174.

FIGURE 9.1

A Process Layout Showing the Routing of Two Families of Parts.

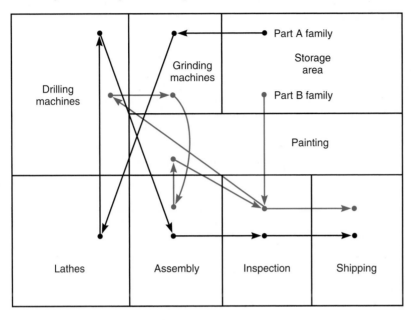

level of training and experience; high work-in-process increases capital investment.[3]

In process layout planning, the most common tactic is to arrange departments or work centers in the most economical locations. In many facilities, optimal placement in the most economical location means minimizing material handling costs. Process layout planning entails placing departments with large interdepartmental flows of parts or people next to one another. Material handling cost in this approach depends upon: (1) the number of loads (or people) to be moved during some period of time between two departments (*i* and *j*) and (2) the distance-related costs between departments. Cost can be a function of distance between departments. The *objective can be expressed as follows:*

$$\text{Minimize cost} = \sum_{i=1}^{n} \sum_{j=1}^{n} X_{ij} C_{ij}$$

where

n = Total number of work centers or departments

i, j = Individual departments

X_{ij} = Number of loads moved from department i to department j

C_{ij} = Cost to move a load between department i and department j

Process-oriented facilities (and fixed-position layouts as well) try to minimize the loads or trips times distance-related costs. The term C_{ij} combines the distance and a weighting factor into one factor. This assumes not only that the difficulty of

---

[3] The differences between process-oriented (low-volume, high-variety) and product-oriented (high-volume, low-variety) approaches were shown in Chapter 7.

movement is equal but also that the pickup and set-down costs are constant. This is not always the case, but for the moment we will summarize these data (that is, cost, difficulty, and pickup and set-down cost) into this one variable. The best way to understand the steps of process layout is to look at an example.

Example 1

The Walters Company's management wants to arrange the six departments of its factory in a way that will minimize interdepartmental material handling costs. They make an initial assumption (to simplify the problem) that each department is 20 × 20 feet and that the building is 60 feet long and 40 feet wide. The process layout procedure that they follow involves six steps.

Step 1. *Construct a "from-to matrix"* showing the flow of parts or materials from department to department (Figure 9.2) on page 385.

Step 2. *Determine the space requirements* for each department. Figure 9.3 on page 386 shows the available plant space.

Step 3. *Develop an initial schematic diagram* showing the sequence of departments through which parts will have to move. Try to place departments with a heavy flow of materials or parts next to one another. (See Figure 9.4 on page 386).

Step 4. *Determine the cost* of this layout by using the material-handling cost equation shown earlier; that is,

$$\text{Cost} = \sum_{i}^{n} \sum_{j}^{n} X_{ij} C_{ij}$$

For this problem, the Walters Company assumes that a forklift carries all interdepartmental loads. The cost of moving one load between adjacent departments is estimated to be $1. Moving a load between nonadjacent departments costs $2. Hence, the handling cost between departments 1 and 2 is $50 ($1 × 50 loads), $200 between departments 1 and 3 ($2 × 100 loads), $40 between departments 1 and 6 ($2 × 20 loads), and so on. The total cost for the layout shown in Figure 9.4 then, is

$$
\begin{aligned}
\text{Cost} = \ & \$50 \ + \ \$200 \ + \ \$40 \ + \ \$30 \ + \ \$50 \\
& \text{(1 and 2)} \ \text{(1 and 3)} \ \text{(1 and 6)} \ \text{(2 and 3)} \ \text{(2 and 4)} \\
& + \ \$10 \ + \ \$40 \ + \ \$100 \ + \ \$50 \\
& \quad \text{(2 and 5)} \ \text{(3 and 4)} \ \text{(3 and 6)} \ \text{(4 and 5)} \\
& = \$570
\end{aligned}
$$

Step 5. By trial and error (or by a more sophisticated computer program approach that we will discuss shortly), *try to improve this layout* to establish a reasonably good arrangement of departments.

Looking at both the flow graph and the cost calculations, it appears desirable to place departments 1 and 3 closer together. They currently are nonadjacent, and the high volume of flow between them causes a large handling expense. Looking the situation over, we need to check the effect of shifting departments and possibly raising, instead of lowering, overall costs.

FIGURE 9.2

(a) Interdepartmental Flow of Parts. (b) A Relationship Chart Is an Alternative Way to Present the Flows Between Departments. For example, the high flows between 1 and 3, and 3 and 6 are immediately apparent. Departments 1, 3, and 6, therefore, should be close together.

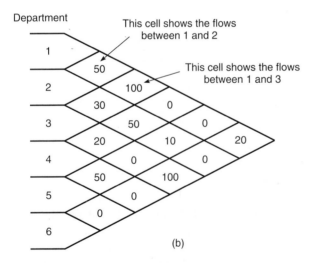

Number of loads per week

Department	1	2	3	4	5	6
1		50	100	0	0	20
2			30	50	10	0
3				20	0	100
4					50	0
5						0
6						

(a)

Department

This cell shows the flows between 1 and 2

This cell shows the flows between 1 and 3

1

50

2

100

30

0

3

50

0

20

10

20

4

0

0

50

100

5

0

0

6

(b)

One possibility is to switch departments 1 and 2. This exchange produces the second departmental flow graph (Figure 9.5 on page 387), which shows that it is possible to reduce the cost to $480, a saving in material handling of $90.

$$\text{Cost} = \underset{(1 \text{ and } 2)}{\$50} + \underset{(1 \text{ and } 3)}{\$100} + \underset{(1 \text{ and } 6)}{\$20} + \underset{(2 \text{ and } 3)}{\$60} + \underset{(2 \text{ and } 4)}{\$50}$$

$$+ \underset{(2 \text{ and } 5)}{\$10} + \underset{(3 \text{ and } 4)}{\$40} + \underset{(3 \text{ and } 6)}{\$100} + \underset{(4 \text{ and } 5)}{\$50}$$

$$= \$480$$

FIGURE 9.3

Building Dimensions and a Possible Department Layout.

Room 1	Room 2	Room 3
Department 1	Department 2	Department 3
Department 4	Department 5	Department 6

Room 4 — Room 5 — Room 6

← 60' →

40'

FIGURE 9.4

Interdepartmental Flow Graph Showing Number of Weekly Loads.

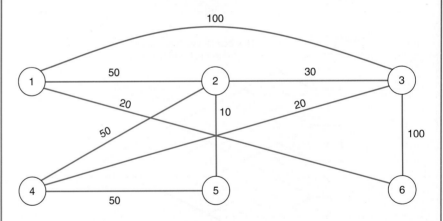

This, of course, is only one of a large number of possible changes. For a six-department problem there are actually 720 (or 6! = 6 × 5 × 4 × 3 × 2 × 1) potential arrangements! In layout problems, we seldom reach an optimal solution and may have to be satisfied with a "reasonable" one reached after a few trials. Suppose the Walters Company is satisfied with the cost figure of $480 and the flow graph of Figure 9. 5. The problem may not be solved yet. Often a sixth step is necessary.

Step 6. *Prepare a detailed plan* considering space or size requirements of each department; that is, arrange the departments to fit the shape of the building and its nonmovable areas (such as the loading dock, washrooms, and stairways). Often this step involves making certain that the final plan can be accommodated by the electrical system, floor loads, aesthetics, and other factors.

FIGURE 9.5

Second Interdepartmental Flow Graph.

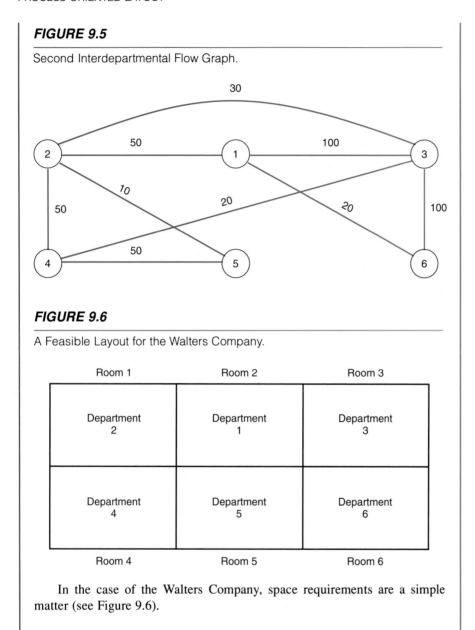

FIGURE 9.6

A Feasible Layout for the Walters Company.

Room 1	Room 2	Room 3
Department 2	Department 1	Department 3
Department 4	Department 5	Department 6
Room 4	Room 5	Room 6

In the case of the Walters Company, space requirements are a simple matter (see Figure 9.6).

The graphic approach we have been discussing is adequate for small problems. A schematic of this procedure is shown in Figure 9.7.[4] However, this method does not suffice for larger problems. When 20 departments are involved in a layout problem, over 600 *trillion* different department configurations are possible. Fortunately, computer programs have been written to handle layouts of up to 40 departments. The best-known of these is **CRAFT** (Computerized Relative Allocation of

CRAFT

[4] Also see Richard Muther, *Systematic Layout Planning,* 2nd ed. (Boston: Cahners, 1976) for a similar approach to what the author calls simplified layout planning.

FIGURE 9.7

Summary of the Process-Layout Procedure.

1. Determine number of trips
   between each department
   and construct a "from-to matrix."

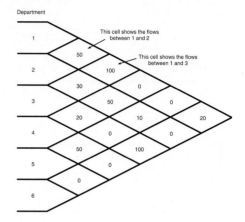

2. Determine space requirements
   and distance between
   each department.

3. Develop an initial schematic diagram.

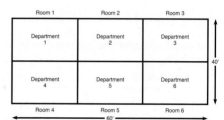

4. Determine the cost of this
   layout (multiply the trips
   by the distance).

$$\sum_{i=1}^{n} \sum_{j=1}^{n} x_{ij} c_{ij}$$

5. By trial and error,
   try to improve the layout.

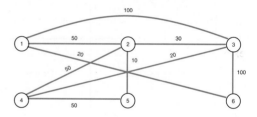

6. Prepare a detailed plan
   that evaluates other factors.

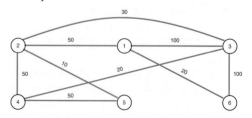

FIGURE 9.8

In This Six-Department Example, CRAFT Has Rearranged the Initial Layout (a) with a Cost of $201.00, to the New Layout with a Lower Cost of $143.90 as Shown in (b).

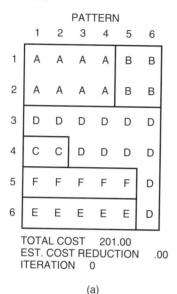

PATTERN
1 2 3 4 5 6

	1	2	3	4	5	6
1	A	A	A	A	B	B
2	A	A	A	A	B	B
3	D	D	D	D	D	D
4	C	C	D	D	D	D
5	F	F	F	F	F	D
6	E	E	E	E	E	D

TOTAL COST   201.00
EST. COST REDUCTION   .00
ITERATION   0

(a)

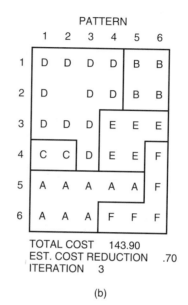

PATTERN
1 2 3 4 5 6

	1	2	3	4	5	6
1	D	D	D	D	B	B
2	D		D	D	B	B
3	D	D	D	E	E	E
4	C	C	D	E	E	F
5	A	A	A	A	A	F
6	A	A	A	F	F	F

TOTAL COST   143.90
EST. COST REDUCTION   .70
ITERATION   3

(b)

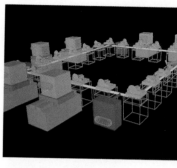

Historically, 3-dimensional physical models were often built to address the layout problem. We now use 3-dimensional computer models to achieve the same purpose but at greatly reduced cost. Here a transmission assembly line using AutoMod II is shown.

Facilities Technique),[5] a program that produces "good," but not always "optimal" solutions. CRAFT is a search technique that systematically examines alternative departmental rearrangements to reduce the total material handling cost (see Figure 9.8). CRAFT has the added advantage of allowing not only load and distance to be examined, but also of introducing a third factor, a difficulty rating.

Computerized techniques have been developed for both the two-dimensional and three-dimensional cases—the two-dimensional case is a one-story facility successfully addressed by CRAFT. The three-dimensional case is a multistory facility and is addressed by **SPACECRAFT**.[6] And, as we have discussed, manual as well as computer techniques exist.

SPACECRAFT

Expert Systems in Layout

CRAFT and SPACECRAFT are just two of the computerized techniques to aid in the design and layout of facilities. But even the other popular programs, such as CORELAP, ALDEP, and COFAD, do not consider expert knowledge in ranking alternative plans. They do not have built-in rules to consider the creative aspects that a human designer would.

FADES (Facilities Design Expert System) is an *expert system* that combines

[5] E. S. Buffa, G. S. Armor, and T. E. Vollman, "Allocating Facilities with CRAFT," *Harvard Business Review,* **42,** 2 (March–April 1964): 136–159.

[6] R. V. Johnson, "SPACECRAFT for Multi-Floor Layout Planning," *Management Science,* **28,** 4 (1982): 407–417. A discussion of CRAFT, COFAD, PLANET, CORELAP, and AIDED is available in James M. Moore and James A. Tompkins, *Computer Aided Layout: A User's Guide,* Publication Number 1 in the monograph series, *Facilities Planning and Design Division,* American Institute of Industrial Engineers, Inc., 77–1.

judgmental rules of human experts with the mathematical tools we have introduced earlier in this section.[7] It develops good facility designs for unstructured situations. FADES reflects the new breed of artificial intelligence decision-making aids described in detail in the supplement to Chapter 7.

Work Cells

A special case of process-oriented layout is the work cell. Although the idea of work cells was first presented by R. E. Flanders in 1925,[8] it is only with the increasing use of group technology (see Chapter 6) that the technique has reasserted itself. Cellular work arrangements are used where volume warrants a special arrangement of machinery and equipment. In a manufacturing environment, group technology identifies products that have similar characteristics and allows not just a particular batch (for example, several units of the same product), but a family of batches, to **Work cell** be processed in a particular work cell.[9] The **work cell** idea is to take machines that would ordinarily be dispersed in various process departments and arrange them in a small group so that the advantages of product-oriented systems can be brought to bear on a particular batch or family of batches (Figure 9.9). The work cell is built around the product. The advantages of work cells are:[10,11]

1. *Reduced work-in-process inventory* because the work cell is set up to provide a balanced flow from machine to machine.

2. *Less floor space* required because less space is needed between the machines to accommodate the work-in-process inventory.

3. *Reduced raw material and finished goods inventories* because less work in process allows more rapid movement of materials through the work cell.

4. *Reduced direct labor cost* because of better flow of material and improved scheduling. The time to move from one piece to another and from one batch within the family to another is substantially reduced.

5. *Heightened sense of employee participation* in the organization and the product because employees accept more responsibility for quality, since quality problems are readily identified with the work cell and the employee.

6. *Increased utilization of equipment and machinery* because of better scheduling and faster material flow.

7. *Reduced investment in machinery and equipment* because good facility utilization reduces the number of machines and the amount of equipment and tooling.

In conflict with advantages 6 and 7 above, Greene and Sadowski have reported an increase in capital investment and lower machine utilization when work cells are

---

[7] See E. L. Fisher, "An AI Based Methodology for Factory Design," *AI Magazine*, **3,** 4 (Fall 1986): 72–85 and E. L. Fisher and S. F. Nof, "FADES," *Proceedings of the Annual IIE Meeting* (1984): 74–82.

[8] R. E. Flanders, "Design Manufacture and Production Control of a Standard Machine," *Transactions of ASME*, **46** (1925).

[9] Small batches in a process-oriented facility (e.g., a job shop) are called *job lots.*

[10] Burton I. Zisk, "Flexibility Is Key to Automated Material Transport System for Manufacturing Cells," *Industrial Engineering* (November 1983): 58–64.

[11] Williams J. Dumoliem and William P. Santen, "Cellular Manufacturing Becomes Philosophy of Management at Components Facility," *Industrial Engineering* (November 1983): 72–76.

FIGURE 9.9

Improving Layouts by Moving to the Work Cell Concept.

Note in both (a) and (b) that U-shaped work cells
can reduce material and employee movement.
The U shape may also reduce space requirements

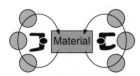

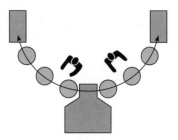

(a) Current layout—workers in
small closed areas.
Cannot increase output
without a third worker.

Improved layout—workers can
assist each other. May be able
to add a third worker.

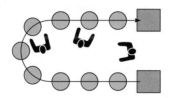

(b) Current layout—straight
lines are hard to balance.

Improved layout—in U shape,
workers have better access.
Four workers were reduced
to three.

utilized.[12] Perhaps different firms achieve different utilization depending upon their ability to switch cell configuration and move personnel, as well as upon the initial cost of their particular machinery and equipment.

The requirements of cellular production include:

1. group technology codes or their equivalent;
2. a high level of training and flexibility on the part of employees;
3. either staff support or flexible, imaginative employees to establish the work cells initially.

Various forms of work cells are described in Table 9.2.

Focused Work Center and the Focused Factory

When a firm has *identified a large family of like products and the forecast is stable and of adequate volume,* a focused work center may be organized. A **focused work center** moves production from a general-purpose, process-oriented facility to a large work cell. The large work cell may be a part of the present plant, in which case it

Focused work center

[12] Timothy J. Greene and Randall P. Sadowski, "A Review of Cellular Manufacturing Assumptions, Advantages and Design Techniques," *Journal of Operations Management* **4,** 2 (February 1984): 85–97.

TABLE 9.2 Work Cells, Focused Work Centers, and the Focused Factory.

WORK CELL	FOCUSED WORK CENTER	FOCUSED FACTORY
A work cell is a temporary product-oriented arrangement of machines and personnel in what is ordinarily a process-oriented facility.	A focused work center is a permanent product-oriented arrangement of machines and personnel in what is ordinarily a process-oriented facility.	A focused factory is a permanent facility to produce a product or component in a product-oriented facility. Many of the focused factories currently being built in America were originally part of a process-oriented facility.
Example: A job shop with machinery and personnel rearranged to produce 30 unique control panels.	*Example:* Pipe bracket manufacturing at a shipyard.	*Example:* A plant to produce window mechanisms for automobiles.

Focused factory

may be called a focused work center. Or it may be separated and called a **focused factory.** A fast-food restaurant is a focused factory. Burger King, for example, changes the number of personnel and task assignments rather than moving machines and equipment. In this manner, they balance the assembly line to meet changing production demands. In effect, the "layout" changes numerous times each day.

The term *focused factories* may also refer to facilities that are focused in ways other than by product line or layout. For instance, a facility may be focused in regard to meeting quality, new product introduction, or flexibility requirements.[13]

Focused facilities in manufacturing and in services appear to be better able to stay in tune with their customers, to produce quality products, and to operate at higher margins. This is true whether they are steel mills such as SMI, Nucor, or Chaparral, or restaurants such as McDonald's and Burger King.

OFFICE LAYOUT

The criteria for a rational approach to office layouts in terms of work flow are the same as those for manufacturing tangible goods. That is, we can organize around either processes or products. In most organizations, however, there is some middle ground where, for example, the accounts receivable department handles receivables, the order department handles incoming orders, and the accounts payable department handles results of purchases and other bills. This middle ground can be thought of as cellular organizations arranged and rearranged as work procedures and volumes change. The frequent rearrangement of offices is witness to the flexibility of this cellular relationship.

Office environments also have other considerations. In a manufacturing environment, the concern may be with the flow of parts and material, but office workers are concerned with the movement of information. Movement of information is carried out by:

---

[13] See, for example, Wickham Skinner, "The Focused Factory," *Harvard Business Review* **52**, 3 (May–June 1974):113–121.

- individuals in face-to-face conversations;
- individuals conversing by phone and by computers (simultaneous);
- mail, hard documents;
- electronic mail;
- group discussions or meetings;
- intercom speakers.

If *all* work were carried out by phone and telecommunications, the layout problem would be greatly simplified, but it is the movement of people and hard documents that largely dictates the nature of office facility layouts.

Figure 9.10 shows another relationship chart (you saw one earlier in Figure 9.2b). This one is an extremely effective way 'to plan office activities. This chart, prepared for an office of consulting engineers, indicates that Mr. Shader must be (1) near the engineers' area, (2) near the phones to a lesser extent, (3) still less near the secretary and central files, and (4) not at all near the photocopy or storage room. When charting relationships, including phone or window availability is usually unrealistic. However, they are included in Figure 9.10, mostly to illustrate the degree of detail to which an office planner can go if necessary.

General office area guidelines indicate an average of about 100 square feet per person (including corridors). A major executive is allotted about 400 square feet, and a conference room area is based on 25 square feet per person, up to 30 people. In contrast, restaurants provide from 16 to 50 square feet per customer (total kitchen and dining area divided by capacity). By making effective use of the vertical

FIGURE 9.10

Office Relationship Chart.
(*Source:* Richard Muther, *Systematic Layout Planning,* 2nd ed. Boston: Cahners Publishing Co., 1976. Used with permission.)

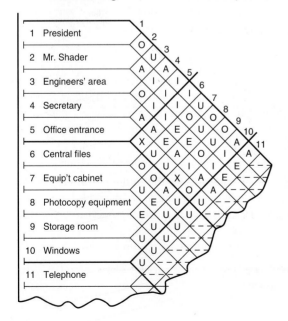

Value	CLOSENESS
A	Absolutely necessary
E	Especially important
I	Important
O	Ordinary closeness OK
U	Unimportant
X	Not desirable

dimension in a workstation, some office designers expand upward instead of out-ward. This keeps each workstation unit (what designers call the "footprint") as small as possible.

In closing this discussion of office layout, we should point out that there are additional layout considerations (some of which apply to a factory as well as to an office). These are considerations that have to do with teamwork, authority, and status. Should all or only part of the work area be air conditioned? Should all employees use the same entrance, rest rooms, lockers, and cafeteria? As mentioned earlier, layout decisions are part art and part science. The science part, flow of paper in an office, can be analyzed in the same manner as the flow of parts in a process layout.

RETAIL STORE LAYOUT

A hypothesis that has been widely accepted for the retail case is that sales vary directly with customer exposure to products. Consequently, a requirement for good profitability is to expose customers to as many products as possible. Studies do show that the greater the rate of exposure, the greater the sales; hence, the higher return on investment. The operations manager has two distinct variables to manipulate. They are:

1. the overall arrangement or flow pattern for the store;
2. the allocation of space within that arrangement to various products.

Although the *POM in Action* box, "Rethinking the Supermarket" suggests that there is no longer any set pattern for store layouts, we can still note five ideas that are helpful for determining the overall arrangement of many stores.

1. Locate the high-draw items around the periphery of the store. Thus, we tend to find dairy products on one side of a supermarket and bread and bakery products on another. An example of this is shown in Figure 9.11.
2. Use prominent locations for high-impulse and high-margin items such as housewares, beauty aids, and shampoos.
3. Distribute what are known in the trade as "power items"—items that may dominate a purchasing trip—to both sides of an aisle, and disperse them to increase the viewing of other items. This results in a "bounce" pattern of shopping that increases exposure and hence sales of those items located adjacent to the power items.
4. Use end aisle locations because they have a very high exposure rate.
5. Convey the image of the store by careful selection in the positioning of the lead-off department. Produce remains a popular choice in stores, but manag-ers who want to convey a low-price message may want to start off with a wall of values. Others will position the bakery and deli up front to appeal to convenience-oriented customers who want prepared foods.

With these five ideas in mind, we move to the second phase of retail store layout, which is to allocate space to various products.[14]

---

[14] "Computers Revolutionize Shelf Allocation," *Chain Store Age/Supermarkets* (November 1980): 66.

POM *in action*

Rethinking the Supermarket

One reason supermarkets have looked pretty similar for most of the last 40 years is that they have been using the same layout. However, demographics and shopping patterns are changing. Increasingly, food is purchased in restaurants, from fine dining to fast-food and carry-out. The supermarket has to fight sundry restaurants and snack foods for the consumer's dollar. This is partly the result of more families where both parents work, but also because Western society has become more of a "grazing" society. In the "grazing" society, consumers nibble frequently during the day. The result is the family meal prepared at home and the related purchase of groceries become less frequent. Consequently, supermarkets are rethinking their layouts.

The contemporary supermarket may now include a fast-food restaurant, a deli, a photo lab, a video store, and a place to do your banking and pay your bills. The high-draw items, such as meats, dairy, bakery, and produce items may still be at the far end of the store, but the high-margin items like the deli, gourmet foods, the pharmacy, beer and wine, and cosmetics are positioned for maximum exposure. And a variety of other services have been added to draw customers.

Sources: See John H. Taylor, "Mr. Smith Goes to Riverside," *Forbes* (February 17, 1992): 58–63; "Nice Guys Can Finish Last," *Progressive Grocer,* **70,** 2 (February 1991): 94–99; and "Finding a Better Angle," *Supermarket Business,* **45,** 5 (May 1990): 111–114.

The *objective of retail layout is to maximize profitability per square foot of shelf space*. The criteria may be modified to the needs of the product line by using linear

FIGURE 9.11

Store Layout with Dairy and Bread, High-Draw Items, in Different Corners of the Store.

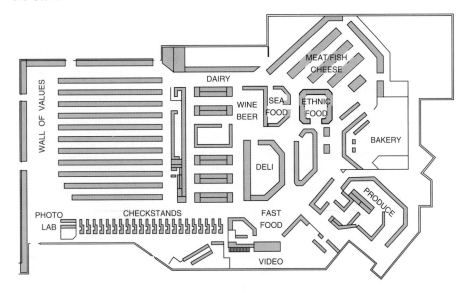

Federal-Mogul, a large manufacturer of auto engine parts, took a radical approach to the layout of its state-of-the-art distribution center in Alabama. With over 50,000 different stock items that must be stored, retrieved, picked, packed, and shipped, a nonautomated system simply wouldn't work. The solution was a 70-foot-high, 7-mile automated storage and retrieval system, a 26-aisle, 24-foot-high rail guided picking vehicle system, and a generous dose of computer control.

foot of shelf space in lieu of square foot of shelf space. Big-ticket, or expensive, items may yield greater dollar sales, but the profit per square foot may be lower. Additionally, determining actual cost per item means determining spoilage, pilferage, breakage, and returns, as well as the necessary labor to stock and sell. There are, of course, other issues, such as having a full line of merchandise regardless of margin. A drug store selling only high-margin shampoo would have met the criteria, but it would have a different set of problems.

Rapid manipulation of data via computers, accurate reports, and the capture of sales data through point-of-sale terminals allows retail store managers an opportunity to find optimum allocation of space. A number of computerized programs exist that can assist managers in evaluating the profitability of various merchandise.

One such program is SLIM (Store Labor and Inventory Management), which can assist store managers in determining when shelf space is adequate to accommodate another full case. Sales and restocking information can be collected directly from a point-of-sale terminal, combined with a program such as SLIM, and the profitability established per product. This is a strong management tool for retail store layout.

Another software package is COSMOS (Computerized Optimization and Simulation Modeling for Operating Supermarkets). COSMOS matches shelf space with delivery schedules, allocating sufficient space to minimize out-of-stock between loads. A disadvantage of COSMOS is that analysis traditionally has been based on warehouse withdrawal figures rather than actual store sales. This means a good bit of the product could still be in the store. Once again, point-of-sale terminals providing prompt information can provide comprehensive and current data to aid retail store layout.[15]

WAREHOUSING AND STORAGE LAYOUTS

The objective of *warehouse layout* is to find the optimum trade-off between handling cost and warehouse space. Consequently, management is to maximize the utilization of the total "cube" of the warehouse—that is, utilize its full volume while maintaining low material handling costs. We define material handling costs as all the costs related to the incoming transport, storage, and outgoing transport of the material. These costs include equipment, people, material, supervision, insurance, and depreciation. Effective warehouse layout must, of course, also minimize the damage and spoilage of material within the warehouse. Management minimizes the sum of the resources spent on finding and moving material plus the deterioration and damage to the material itself. The variety of items stored and the number of items "picked" has direct bearing on the optimum layout. A warehouse storing a few items lends itself to higher density more than a warehouse storing a variety of items. Modern warehouse management is, in many instances, an automated procedure utilizing automatic stacking cranes, conveyors, and sophisticated controls that manage the flow of materials.

[15] See "There Are Two Kinds of Supermarkets: The Quick and the Dead," *Business Week* (August 11, 1986): 62–63; and "At Today's Supermarket, the Computer Is Doing It All," *Business Week* (August 11, 1986): 64–65.

PRODUCT-ORIENTED LAYOUT

Product-oriented layouts are organized around a product or a family of similar high-volume, low-variety products. The assumptions are:

1. Volume is adequate for high equipment utilization.
2. Product demand is stable enough to justify high investment in specialized equipment.
3. Product is standardized or approaching a phase of its life cycle that justifies investment in specialized equipment.
4. Supplies of raw material and components are adequate and of uniform quality (adequately standardized) to ensure they will work with the specialized equipment.

Repetitive production and continuous production, discussed in Chapter 7, utilize product layouts.

One version of a product-oriented layout is a fabrication line; another is an assembly line. The **fabrication line** builds components, such as automobile tires or metal parts for a refrigerator, on a series of machines. An **assembly line** puts the fabricated parts together at a series of workstations. Both are the repetitive processes discussed in Chapter 7, and in both cases the line must be balanced. That is, the work performed on one machine must balance with the work performed on the next machine in the fabrication line, just as the work done at one workstation by an employee on an assembly line must balance with the work done at the next workstation by the next employee. Fabrication lines tend to be machine paced and require mechanical and engineering changes to facilitate balancing. Assembly lines, on the other hand, tend to be paced by work tasks assigned to individuals or to workstations. Assembly lines, therefore, can be balanced by moving tasks from one individual to another. In this manner, the amount of *time* required by each individual or station is equalized. Figure 9.12 shows that the final assembly of even some huge

Fabrication line
Assembly line

FIGURE 9.12

Even Large Jetliners Benefit from Assembly Lines.
(*Source: The Washington Post,* Sunday, February 19, 1989.)

After the wings, tail, fuselage, and nose sections are moved to the staging area and joined together, a tractor tows the aircraft to the next position.

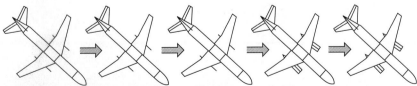

Position 5
Hydraulic lines, electrical cables, and wiring are strung through the airplane. Plumbing, pneumatic tubing, and all air-conditioning ducts are installed.

Position 4
Refinements are made on items installed at position 5. Cables and wiring are hooked up to wing flaps, slats, doors, and landing gear.

Position 3
"Interiors" are installed: Galleys, lavatories, video systems, and the safety slides attached to exit doors.

Position 2
Interior work is finished, including installation of seats, overhead bins, and partitions. Jet engines are attached and partially connected. Installation of cockpit avionics begins.

Position 1
Interiors and engine connections are completed. The aircraft undergoes shakedown tests. It then moves to another building for painting, a three-day process.

products, such as a Boeing 757 airplane, is done in a product layout.

The central problem in product-oriented layout planning is to balance the output at each workstation on the production line so that it is nearly the same, while obtaining the desired amount of output. Management's goal is to create a smooth, continuous flow along the assembly line with a minimum of idle time at each person's workstation. A well-balanced assembly line has the advantage of high personnel and facility utilization *and* equity between employees' work loads. Some union contracts include a requirement that work loads must be nearly equal among those on the same assembly line. The term most often used to describe this process is **assembly line balancing.** Indeed the *objective of the product-oriented layout is to minimize imbalance in the fabrication or assembly line.*

Assembly line balancing

The main advantage of product-oriented layout is the low variable cost per unit usually associated with high-volume, standardized products. The product-oriented layout also keeps material handling costs low, reduces work-in-process inventories, and makes training and supervision easier. These advantages often outweigh the disadvantages of product layout, namely:

1. High volume is required because of the large investment needed to set up the process.
2. Work stoppage at any one point ties up the whole operation.
3. There is a lack of flexibility in handling a variety of products or production rates.

Since the problems of fabrication lines and assembly lines are similar, we will phrase our discussion in terms of an assembly line. On an assembly line, the product typically moves via automated means, such as a conveyor, through a series of workstations until completed (Figure 9.13). This is the way automobiles are assembled, television sets and ovens are produced, and fast-food hamburgers are made. Product-oriented layout uses more automated and specially designed equipment than is found in a process layout.

Boeing, Seattle's largest employer and the world's largest manufacturer of commercial jetliners, employs a modular construction to assemble its "parts." These "parts" of tail, aft body section, center body section, wings, front body, and nose are joined in a fixed position layout. Workers inch the body sections together, measuring and leveling them for a perfect fit. Landing gear is installed and the airplane is ready for the first of its final assembly line operations, which are illustrated in Figure 9.12.

FIGURE 9.13

An Assembly-Line Layout.

Assembly Line Balancing

Line-balancing is usually undertaken to minimize imbalance between machines or personnel while meeting a required output from the line. In order to produce at a specified rate, management must know the tools, equipment, and work methods used. Then the time requirements for each assembly task (such as drilling a hole, tightening a nut, or spray-painting a part) must be determined. Management also needs to know the precedence relationship among the activities, that is, the sequence in which various tasks need to be performed. Let us construct a precedence chart for the task data presented in Example 2.

Example 2

We want to develop a precedence diagram for an electrostatic copier that requires a total assembly time of 66 minutes. Table 9.3 and Figure 9.14 give the tasks, assembly times, and sequence requirements for the copier.

TABLE 9.3 Precedence Data.

TASK	PERFORMANCE TIME (MINUTES)	TASK MUST FOLLOW TASK LISTED BELOW	
A	10	—	
B	11	A	This means that
C	5	B	tasks B and E
D	4	B	cannot be done
E	12	A	until task A has
F	3	C,D	been completed.
G	7	F	
H	11	E	
I	3	G,H	
Total time	66		

FIGURE 9.14

Precedence Diagram.

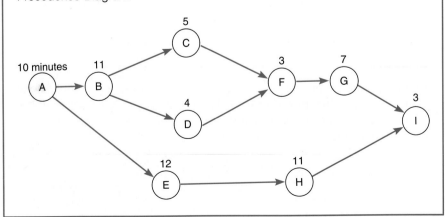

Once we have constructed a precedence chart summarizing the sequences and performance times, we turn to the job of grouping tasks into job stations to meet the specified production rate. This process involves three steps:

Cycle time

1. Take the demand (or production rate) per day and divide it into the productive time available per day (in minutes or seconds). This operation gives us what is called the **cycle time,** namely, the time the product is available at each workstation:

$$\text{Cycle time} = \frac{\text{Production time available per day}}{\text{Demand per day or production rate per day}}$$

2. Calculate the theoretical minimum number of workstations. This is the total task-duration time divided by the cycle time. Fractions are rounded to the next higher whole number:

$$\text{Minimum number of work stations} = \frac{\sum_{i=1}^{m} \text{Time for task } i}{\text{Cycle time}}$$

where m is the number of assembly tasks.

3. Perform the line balance by assigning specific assembly tasks to each workstation. An efficient balance is one that will complete the required assembly, follow the specified sequence, and keep the idle time at each workstation to a minimum. A formal procedure for doing this is:

   a) Identify a master list of work elements and separate the available work elements from the unavailable work elements.
   b) Eliminate those work elements that have been assigned.
   c) Eliminate those work elements whose precedence relationship has not been satisfied.
   d) Eliminate those elements for which there is inadequate time available at the workstation.
   e) Identify a unit of work that can be assigned, such as the first unit of work in the list, the last unit of work in the list, the unit of work with the shortest time, the unit of work with the longest time, a randomly selected unit of work, or some other criterion.
   f) Switch the work elements to find the best balance available.

Example 3 illustrates a simple line-balancing procedure.

Example 3

On the basis of the precedence diagram and activity times given in Example 2, the firm determines that there are 480 productive minutes of work available per day. Furthermore, the production schedule requires that 40 units be completed as output from the assembly line each day. Hence,

$$\text{Cycle time (in minutes)} = \frac{480 \text{ minutes}}{40 \text{ units}}$$

$$= 12 \text{ minutes/unit}$$

$$\text{Minimum number of workstations} = \frac{\text{total task time}}{\text{cycle time}} = \frac{66}{12}$$

$$= 5.5 \text{ or } 6 \text{ stations}$$

FIGURE 9.15

A Six-Station Solution to the Line-Balancing Problem.

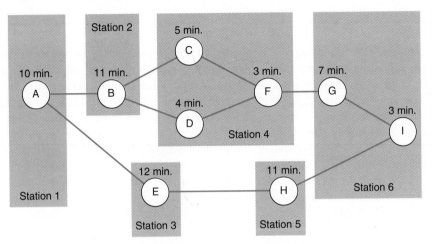

In the case of slaughtering operations, the assembly line is actually a disassembly line. The line balancing procedures described in this chapter are the same as for an assembly line. The chicken processing plant shown here must balance the work of several hundred employees. Division of labor produces efficiency. Because one's skills develop with repetition, there is less time lost in changing tools, and specialized tools are developed. The total labor content in each of the chickens processed is a few minutes. How long would it take you to process a chicken by yourself?

Figure 9.15 shows one solution that does not violate the sequence requirements and in which the tasks are grouped into six stations. To obtain it, appropriate activities were moved into workstations that use as much of the available cycle time of 12 minutes as possible. The first workstation consumes 10 minutes and has an idle time of 2 minutes.

The second workstation uses 11 minutes, and the third consumes the full 12 minutes. The fourth workstation groups three small tasks and balances perfectly at 12 minutes. The fifth has 1 minute of idle time; the sixth (consisting of tasks G and I) has 2 minutes of idle time per cycle. Total idle time for this solution is 6 minutes per cycle.

We can compute the efficiency of a line balance by dividing the total task time by the product of the number of workstations times the assigned cycle time:

$$\text{Efficiency} = \frac{\sum \text{task times}}{(\text{Number of workstations}) \times (\text{Assigned cycle time})}$$

Management often compares different levels of efficiency for various numbers of workstations. In this way, the firm can determine the sensitivity of the line to changes in the production rate and workstation assignments.

Example 4

We can calculate the balance efficiency for Example 3 as follows:

$$\text{Efficiency} = \frac{66 \text{ minutes}}{(6 \text{ stations}) \times (12 \text{ minutes})} = \frac{66}{72} = 91.7\%$$

Opening a seventh workstation, for whatever reason, would decrease the efficiency of the balance to 78.6%:

$$\text{Efficiency} = \frac{66 \text{ minutes}}{(7 \text{ stations}) \times (12 \text{ minutes})} = 78.6\%$$

Large-scale line-balancing problems, like large process layout problems, are often solved by computers. Several different computer programs are available to handle the assignment of workstations on assembly lines with 100 (or more) individual work activities. Both the computer routine called COMSOAL (Computer Method for Sequencing Operations for Assembly Lines)[16] and ASYBL (General Electric's Assembly Line Configuration program) are widely used in larger problems to evaluate the thousands or millions of possible workstation combinations much more efficiently than could ever be done by hand.

The AB:POM microcomputer software described at the end of this chapter also handles a variety of smaller problems and illustrates the problem described in Examples 2, 3, and 4. It offers five different heuristics (or "rules of thumb") for balancing the line.

A Japanese Perspective on Layout

Before closing this chapter, we want to point out the impact that Japan has had on the rethinking of facility layout. Their ideas about continuous improvement and work simplification have affected not only the *physical* layout, but behavioral considerations such as employee involvement as well.

For example, in the traditional facility, when equipment failure caused an assembly line to halt, workers waited for supervisors, repairmen, or managers to fix things. More and more, though, employees follow the Japanese model that when a line stops, *everyone* acts to help solve the problem. The Japanese culture encourages such teamwork. And supervisors tend to develop skills at coordinating groups of workers.

The Japanese also tend to favor U-shaped assembly lines over the straight ones. This helps in five ways: (1) tasks can be grouped so inspection is immediate; (2) fewer workers are needed; (3) workers can reach more linear feet of the line; (4) the line can be more efficiently balanced; and (5) communication is enhanced. The concept of a U-shaped line was presented earlier in Figure 9.9.

SUMMARY

Good layout strategies make a substantial difference in operating efficiency. The six classic layout situations are: (1) fixed position, (2) process-oriented, (3) office, (4) retail, (5) warehouse, and (6) product-oriented. A variety of techniques have

---

[16] A. L. Arcus, "COMSOAL: A Computer Method of Sequencing Operations for Assembly Line," *International Journal of Production Research,* **4,** 4 (1966).

been developed in attempts to solve these layout problems. Industrial firms focus on reducing material movement and assembly line balancing. Retail firms focus on product exposure. Storage layouts focus on the optimum trade-off between storage costs and material handling costs.

Often the variables in the layout problem are so wide-ranging and numerous as to preclude finding an optimal solution. For this reason, layout decisions, while having received substantial research effort, remain something of an art.

KEY TERMS

Fixed-position layout (p. 380)

Process-oriented layout (p. 380)

Office layout (p. 380)

Retail/service layout (p. 380)

Warehouse layout (p. 380)

Product-oriented layout (p. 380)

Job lot (p. 382)

CRAFT (p. 387)

SPACECRAFT (p. 389)

Work cell (p. 390)

Focused work center (p. 391)

Focused factory (p. 392)

Fabrication line (p. 397)

Assembly line (p. 397)

Assembly line balancing (p. 398)

Cycle time (p. 400)

USING AB:POM

Solving Example 1 Using AB:POM's Facility Layout Module

AB:POM's facility layout module can be used to place up to 8 departments in 8 rooms in order to minimize the total distance traveled as a function of the distances between the rooms and the flow between departments. The program performs pairwise comparisons, exchanging departments until no exchange will reduce the total amount of movement.

After the number of departments is entered (which is 6 in the case of Example 1), then the data screen will be generated and appear as in Program 9.1. The data essentially consist of two tables of numbers—one for the flows and one for the distances:

1. *Department names.* The department names appear in both the column and the row of the top matrix. While the names appear in both places, it is only possible to change the names in the column. When you do this, the name at the row will automatically change.

2. *Room names.* The room (or area) names behave in an identical fashion to the department names. Only the column names can be changed but the row name will automatically follow.

3. *Interdepartmental flows.* The number of trips from one department to another is indicated in the top matrix termed the flow matrix.

4. *Distance Matrix.* The distance between rooms is entered in this table. Typically the distance matrix will be symmetric, but all entries must still be made.

The solution to Example 1 appears on the right side of Program 9.1. Here's how to interpret the results. Department 1 started in Room 1 in the initial layout of

Program 9.1

AB:POM's Facility Layout Program Applied to Walters Company Data

Data file: WALTERS ———————— Operations Layout ———————— Solution ——

Number of departments (1–6) 6

WALTERS COMPANY, EXAMPLE 1

Flow matrix

	Dept 1	Dept 2	Dept 3	Dept 4	Dept 5	Dept 6	Department in Room
Dept 1	0	50	100	0	0	20	Dept 1 in Room 5
Dept 2	0	0	30	50	10	0	Dept 2 in Room 3
Dept 3	0	30	0	20	0	100	Dept 3 in Room 1
Dept 4	0	0	0	0	50	0	Dept 4 in Room 4
Dept 5	0	0	0	0	0	0	Dept 5 in Room 2
Dept 6	20	0	0	0	0	0	Dept 6 in Room 6

Distance Matrix

	Room 1	Room 2	Room 3	Room 4	Room 5	Room 6
Room 1	0	1	2	1	1	2
Room 2	1	0	1	1	1	1
Room 3	2	1	0	2	1	1
Room 4	1	1	2	0	1	2
Room 5	1	1	1	1	0	1
Room 6	2	1	1	2	1	0

The total movement is 480

F9 = Print   Esc

Press <Esc> key to continue or highlighted key or function key for options

Example 1; it's now in Room 5. Department 2 started in Room 2; it's now in Room 3. Department 3 began in Room 3; it's now in Room 1, and so on.

The sum of the products of the number of trips times the distance is listed at the bottom of Program 9.1. This is what we are trying to minimize.

Solving Examples 2, 3 and 4 Using AB:POM's Assembly Line Balancing Module

AB:POM's module for line balancing can handle a line with up to 99 tasks, each with up to 6 immediate predecessors. The cycle time can be given directly, or can be computed if the production rate is input.

We first enter the number of tasks and then are prompted for:

1. *Task Names* (which can be up to 8 characters long). This is optional input.
2. *Time Units* (either seconds or minutes or hours)
3. *Task Times*
4, 5, 6, and 7. *Cycle time.* The cycle time can be entered in one of two ways. The easiest way to enter the cycle time is directly on the right of "cycle time." While this is the easiest method, it is also common to determine the cycle time

from the demand rate. This is entered as three parts. Positions 5, 6, and 7 in the row labeled "demand" are used to give the rate. Positions 5 and 6 are numerical while position 7 can be changed from seconds to minutes to hours. The program assumes 60 seconds per minute and 60 minutes per hour.

You are not permitted to have entries for both position 4 and positions 5, 6, and 7. Either the cycle time must be set to 0 or the demand rate must be 0. If not, an error message will occur, asking you to correct the screen.

8. *Heuristic rule.* There are five different "rules" which can be used in balancing the line. They are:

> longest operation time
> most following tasks
> ranked positional weight
> shortest operation time and
> least number of following tasks.

The default rule is longest operation time, but others can be tried by toggling. Note that no heuristic guarantees an "optimal" solution. Each is simply a rule-of-thumb approach for trying to find a good solution.

Assembly line balancing is one of the programs that erases the input on the screen in order to provide the output. Therefore, it is generally useful to print both the filled-in data screen and the solution screen. In Program 9.2 we show the filled-in data screen for the data in Examples 2, 3, and 4.

Program 9.2

AB:POM's Assembly Line Balancing Program Data Entry Screen

──────── Balancing, Assembly line ──────── Data Screen ────────

Number of tasks (1-99)   9

───

──────── ASSEMBLY LINE BALANCING, EXAMPLES 2-4 ────────

Rule   Longest operation time

Demand rate   40 units per   480.00 minutes

Cycle Time   0.00

Task	minutes	Predecessors										
a	10.00	- -		- -	- -	- -	- -	- -
b	11.00	A		- -	- -	- -	- -	- -
c	5.00	B		- -	- -	- -	- -	- -
d	4.00	B		- -	- -	- -	- -	- -
e	12.00	A		- -	- -	- -	- -	- -
f	3.00	C	D	- -	- -	- -	- -
g	7.00	F		- -	- -	- -	- -	- -
h	11.00	E		- -	- -	- -	- -	- -
i	3.00	G	H	- -	- -	- -	- -

Program 9.3

AB:POM's Assembly Line Balancing Output for Examples 2–4

```
──────────────── ASSEMBLY LINE BALANCING, EXAMPLES 2–4 ────────────
Longest operation time              Cycle time = 12 minutes
Station      Task    Time    Time left ready tasks
                                          a
   1          a      10.00      2.00  b,e
   2          e      12.00      0.00  b,h
   3          b      11.00      1.00  h,c,d
   4          h      11.00      1.00  c,d
   5          c       5.00      7.00  d
              d       4.00      3.00  f
              f       3.00      0.00  g
   6          g       7.00      5.00  i
              i       3.00      2.00
Time allocated (cyc*sta) =    72.00; Min (theoretical) # of stations = 6
Time needed    (sum task) =   66.00; EFFICIENCY = 91.67%;
Idle time (alloc-needed) =     6.00  minutes per cycle
```

Program 9.3 contains the results of this run. The output should be clear. Note that a ready task is any task that has had its precedence met.

SOLVED PROBLEMS

Solved Problem 9.1

The Snow-Bird Hospital is a small emergency-oriented facility located in a popular ski resort area in northern Michigan. Its new administrator, Mary Lord, decides to reorganize the hospital, using the process-layout method she studied in business school. The current layout of Snow-Bird's eight emergency departments is shown in Figure 9.16.

FIGURE 9.16

Snow-Bird Hospital Layout.

Snow-Bird Hospital Layout

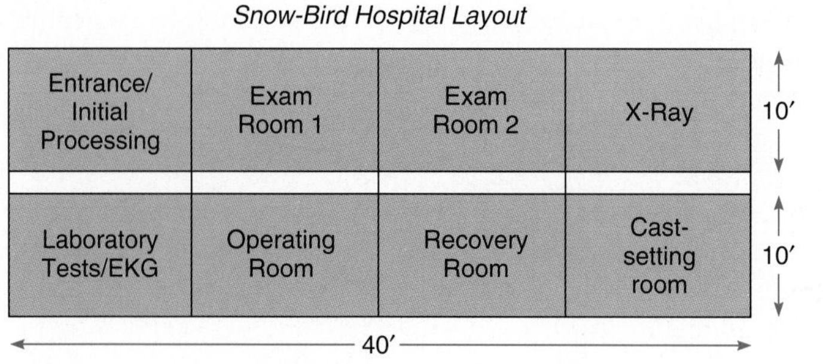

FIGURE 9.17

Number of Patients Moving Between Departments in One Month.

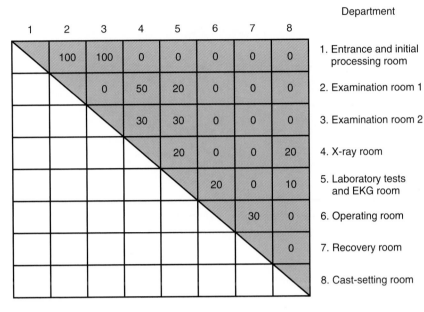

	1	2	3	4	5	6	7	8	Department
1		100	100	0	0	0	0	0	1. Entrance and initial processing room
2			0	50	20	0	0	0	2. Examination room 1
3				30	30	0	0	0	3. Examination room 2
4					20	0	0	20	4. X-ray room
5						20	0	10	5. Laboratory tests and EKG room
6							30	0	6. Operating room
7								0	7. Recovery room
8									8. Cast-setting room

The only physical restriction perceived by Ms. Lord is the need to keep the entrance and initial processing room in its current location. All other departments or rooms (each 10 feet square) can be moved if the layout analysis indicates it would be beneficial.

Mary's first step is to analyze records in order to determine the number of trips made by patients between departments in an average month. The data are shown in Figure 9.17. The objective, Ms. Lord decides, is to lay out the rooms so as to minimize the total distance walked by patients who enter for treatment. She writes her objective as:

$$\text{Minimize patient movement} = \sum_{i=1}^{8} \sum_{j=1}^{8} X_{ij} C_{ij}$$

where

X_{ij} = Number of patients per month (loads or trips) moving from department i to department j

C_{ij} = Distance in feet between departments i and j (which, in this case, is the equivalent of cost per load to move between departments)

Note that this is only a slight modification of the cost objective equation shown earlier in the chapter.

Departments next to one another, such as entrance and examination room 1, are assumed to carry a walking distance of 10 feet. Diagonal departments are also considered adjacent and assigned a distance of 10 feet. Nonadjacent departments such as entrance and examination room 2 or entrance and recovery room are 20 feet apart, while nonadjacent rooms such as entrance and x-ray are 30 feet apart. (Hence, 10 feet is considered 10 units of cost, 20 feet is 20 units of cost, and 30 feet is 30 units of cost.)

FIGURE 9.18

Current Snow-Bird Patient Flow.

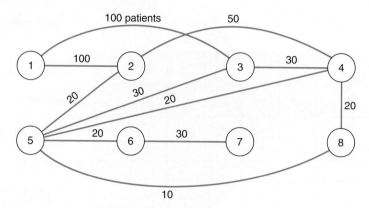

Given the above information, redo the layout of Snow-Bird Hospital to improve its efficiency in terms of patient flow.

Solution

First, establish Snow-Bird's current layout, as shown in Figure 9.18. Using Snow-Bird's current layout, the patient movement may be computed.

$$\text{Total movement} = (100 \times 10') + (100 \times 20') + (50 \times 20') + (20 \times 10')$$
$$\phantom{\text{Total movement} = }\text{1 to 2}\text{1 to 3}\text{2 to 4}\text{2 to 5}$$
$$+ (30 \times 10') + (30 \times 20') + (20 \times 30') + (20 \times 10')$$
$$\text{3 to 4}\text{3 to 5}\text{4 to 5}\text{4 to 8}$$
$$+ (20 \times 10') + (10 \times 30') + (30 \times 10')$$
$$\text{5 to 6}\text{5 to 8}\text{6 to 7}$$
$$= 1{,}000 + 2{,}000 + 1{,}000 + 200 + 300 + 600 + 600$$
$$+\, 200 + 200 + 300 + 300$$
$$= 6{,}700 \text{ feet}$$

FIGURE 9.19

Improved Layout.

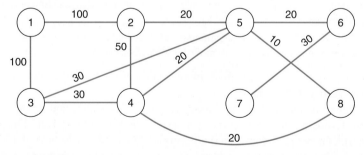

It is not possible to prove a mathematically "optimal" solution, but you should be able to propose a new layout that will reduce the current figure of

6,700 feet. Two useful changes, for example, are to switch rooms 3 and 5 and to interchange rooms 4 and 6. This change would result in the schematic shown in Figure 9.19.

$$
\begin{aligned}
\text{Total movement} = \; & \underset{1 \text{ to } 2}{(100 \times 10')} + \underset{1 \text{ to } 3}{(100 \times 10')} + \underset{2 \text{ to } 4}{(50 \times 10')} + \underset{2 \text{ to } 5}{(20 \times 10')} \\
& + \underset{3 \text{ to } 4}{(30 \times 10')} + \underset{3 \text{ to } 5}{(30 \times 20')} + \underset{4 \text{ to } 5}{(20 \times 10')} + \underset{4 \text{ to } 8}{(20 \times 20')} \\
& + \underset{5 \text{ to } 6}{(20 \times 10')} + \underset{5 \text{ to } 8}{(10 \times 10')} + \underset{6 \text{ to } 7}{(30 \times 10')} \\
= \; & 1{,}000 + 1{,}000 + 500 + 200 + 300 + 600 + 200 \\
& + 400 + 200 + 100 + 300 \\
= \; & 4{,}800 \text{ feet}
\end{aligned}
$$

Do you see any room for further improvement? (See Problem 9.1.)

Solved Problem 9.2

An assembly line, whose activities are shown in Figure 9.20 on page 410, has an eight-minute cycle time. Draw the precedence graph and find the minimum possible number of workstations. Then arrange the work activities into workstations so as to balance the line. What is the efficiency of this line balance?

TASK	PERFORMANCE TIME (MINUTES)	TASK MUST FOLLOW THIS TASK
A	5	—
B	3	A
C	4	B
D	3	B
E	6	C
F	1	C
G	4	D,E,F
H	$\underline{2}$	G
	28	

Solution

The theoretical minimum number of workstations is:

$$
\frac{\sum t_i}{\text{Cycle time}} = \frac{28 \text{ minutes}}{8 \text{ minutes}} = 3.5 \text{ or } 4 \text{ stations}
$$

The precedence graph and one good layout are shown in Figure 9.20.

$$
\text{Efficiency} = \frac{\text{Total task time}}{(\text{Number of workstations}) \times (\text{Cycle time})} = \frac{28}{(4)(8)} = 87.5\%
$$

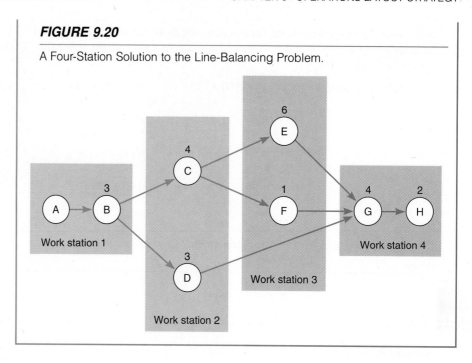

FIGURE 9.20

A Four-Station Solution to the Line-Balancing Problem.

DISCUSSION QUESTIONS

1. What is the layout strategy of your local print shop?

2. How would you go about collecting data to help a small business, like a print shop, improve its layout?

3. What are the five layout strategies presented in this chapter?

4. What are the advantages and disadvantages of product layout?

5. What are the advantages and disadvantages of process layout?

6. What are the advantages and disadvantages of work cells?

7. What layout innovations have you noticed recently in retail establishments?

8. What techniques can be used to overcome the inherent problems of fixed-position layout?

9. What layout variables might you want to consider as particularly important in an office layout where computer programs are written?

PROBLEMS

: 9.1 In Solved Problem 9.1 we improved Snow-Bird's layout to 4,800 feet of movement. Is an improved layout possible? What is it?

: 9.2 Registration period at Southeastern University has always been a time of emotion, commotion, and lines. Students must move among four stations to complete the trying semiannual process. Last semester's registration, held in the fieldhouse, is described in Figure 9.21. You can see, for example, that 450 students moved from the paperwork station (A) to advising (B), while 550 went directly from A to picking up their class cards

FIGURE 9.21

Registration Flow of Students.

Interstation Activity Mix

	Pickup paperwork and forms	Advising station	Pickup class cards	Verification of status and payment
	(A)	(B)	(C)	(D)
Paperwork/forms (A)	---	450	550	50
Advising (B)	200	---	200	0
Class cards (C)	0	0	---	750
Verification/payment (D)	0	0	0	---

Existing Layout

(C). Graduate students, who for the most part had preregistered, proceeded directly from A to the station where the registration was verified and payment collected (D). The layout used last semester is also shown in Figure 9.21. The registrar is preparing to set up this semester's stations and is anticipating similar numbers.

a) What is the "load × distance," or cost, of the layout shown?

b) Provide an improved layout and compute its cost.

: **9.3** You have just been hired as the Director of Operations for Bellas Chocolates, in Blacksburg, Virginia, a purveyor of exceptionally fine chocolates. Bellas Chocolates has four kitchen layouts under consideration for its recipe making and testing department. The strategy is to provide the best kitchen layout possible so the food scientists can devote their time and energy toward product improvement, not wasted effort in the kitchen. You have been asked to evaluate these four kitchen layouts and prepare a recommendation for your boss, Mr. Bellas, so that he can proceed with placing the contract for building the testing kitchens. (See Figure 9.22.)

: **9.4** Using the kitchen layouts in Problem 9.3, collect load data (the number of trips between workstations) from an operating kitchen of your choosing, perhaps at home, and determine which is the best layout.

: **9.5** Georgetown Phone Directory prints and distributes a yellow-page phone book for the northwest area of Washington, D.C. Its white-collar staff of clerical and managerial employees currently occupies the first floor of a U-shaped office building in Washington that is configured as shown in Figure 9.23 on page 413. (The firm's warehouse and production facilities are next door.) This organization loses time and money because of unnecessary personnel, information, and materials movements. Without moving the production or shipping departments, see if you can reorganize the facility and create shorter communications distances.

FIGURE 9.22

Layout Options.

Number of trips between work centers:

From: \ To:		Refrigerator 1	Counter 2	Sink 3	Storage 4	Stove 5
Refrig.	1	0	8	13	0	0
Counter	2	5	0	3	3	8
Sink	3	3	12	0	4	0
Storage	4	3	0	0	0	5
Stove	5	0	8	4	10	0

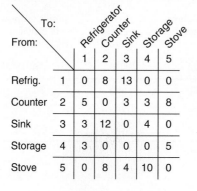

Kitchen layout #1

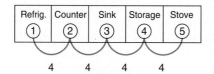

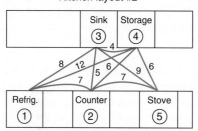

Kitchen layout #2

Kitchen layout #3

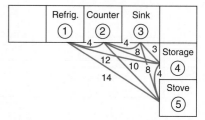

Kitchen layout #4

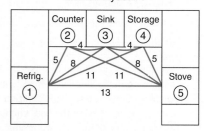

: **9.6** The preinduction physical examination given by the U.S. Army involves the following seven activities:

ACTIVITY	AVERAGE TIME (MINUTES)
Medical history	10
Blood tests	8
Eye examination	5
Measurements (i.e., weight, height, blood pressure)	7
Medical examination	16
Psychological interview	12
Exit medical evaluation	10

These activities can be performed in any order, with two exceptions: The medical history must be taken first and the exit medical evaluation is the final step. At present there are three paramedics and two physicians on duty during each shift. Only a physician can perform the exit evaluation or conduct the psychological interview. Other activities can be carried out by either physicians or paramedics.

a) Develop a layout and balance the line. How many people can be processed per hour?

b) What activity is the current bottleneck?

c) If one more physician and one more paramedic can be placed on duty, how would you redraw the layout? What is the new throughput?

 : **9.7** A final assembly plant for Dictatape, a popular dictation company, produces the DT, a hand-held dictation unit. There are 400 minutes available in the final assembly plant for the DT, and the average demand is 80 units per day. The final assembly requires six separate tasks. Information concerning these tasks is given in the following table. What tasks should be assigned to various workstations, and what is the overall efficiency of the assembly line?

TASK	PERFORMANCE TIME (MINUTES)	TASK MUST FOLLOW TASK LISTED BELOW
1	1	—
2	1	1
3	4	1,2
4	1	2,3
5	2	4
6	4	5

: **9.8** SCFI, South Carolina Furniture, Incorporated, produces all types of office furniture. The Executive Secretary is a chair that has been designed using ergonomics to provide comfort during long work hours. The chair sells for $130. There are 480 minutes available during the day, and the average daily demand has been 50 chairs. There are eight tasks. Given the information on page 414, solve this assembly line balancing problem.

FIGURE 9.23

Layout for Georgetown Phone.

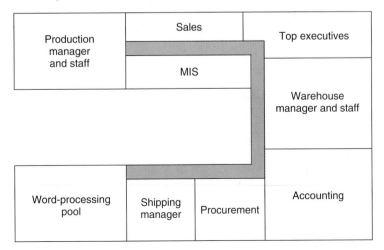

TASK	PERFORMANCE TIME (MINUTES)	TASK MUST FOLLOW TASK LISTED BELOW
1	4	—
2	7	1
3	6	1,2
4	5	2,3
5	6	4
6	7	5
7	8	5
8	6	6,7

: **9.9** Tailwind, Inc., produces high-quality but expensive training shoes for runners. The Tailwind shoe, which sells for $110, contains both gas- and liquid-filled compartments to provide more stability and better protection against knee, foot, and back injuries. Manufacturing the shoes requires 10 separate tasks. How should these tasks be grouped into workstations? There are 400 minutes available for manufacturing the shoe in the plant each day. Daily demand is 60. The information for the tasks is as follows:

TASK	PERFORMANCE TIME (MINUTES)	TASK MUST FOLLOW TASK LISTED BELOW
1	1	—
2	3	1
3	2	2
4	4	2
5	1	3,4
6	3	1
7	2	6
8	5	7
9	1	5,8
10	3	9

: **9.10** Mach 10 is a one-person sailboat designed to be used in the ocean. Manufactured by Creative Leisure, Mach 10 can handle 40-mph winds and over 10-foot seas. The final assembly plant for Creative Leisure is in Cupertino, California. At this time, 200 minutes are available each day to manufacture Mach 10. The daily demand is 60 boats. Given the following information, how many workstations would you recommend?

TASK	PERFORMANCE TIME (MINUTES)	TASK MUST FOLLOW TASK LISTED BELOW
1	1	—
2	1	1
3	2	1
4	1	3
5	3	3
6	1	3
7	1	4,5,6
8	2	2
9	1	7,8

⌨ **:9.11** Because of the expected high demand for Mach 10, Creative Leisure has decided to increase the manufacturing time available to produce the Mach 10 (see Problem 9.10). What impact would 300 available minutes per day have on the assembly line? What impact would 400 minutes have?

⌨ **:9.12** Nearbeer Products, Inc., manufactures drinks that taste the same as a good draft beer but do not contain any alcohol. With changes in drinking laws and demographics, there has been an increased interest in Nearbeer Lite. Nearbeer Lite has fewer calories than the regular beer, is less filling, and tastes great. The final packing operation for Nearbeer Lite requires 13 tasks. Nearbeer bottles Nearbeer Lite five hours a day, five days a week. Each week there is a demand for 3,000 bottles of Nearbeer Lite. Given the following information, solve this assembly line balancing problem.

DATA FOR PROBLEMS
9.12 AND 9.13

Task	Performance Time (minutes)	Task Must Follow Task Listed Below
1	0.1	—
2	0.1	1
3	0.1	2
4	0.2	2
5	0.1	2
6	0.2	3,4,5
7	0.1	1
8	0.1	7
9	0.2	7,8
10	0.1	9
11	0.2	6
12	0.2	10,11
13	0.1	12

⌨ **:9.13** Nearbeer's president, John Kosek, believes that weekly demand for Nearbeer Lite could explode (see Problem 9.12). What would happen if demand doubled?

⌨ **:9.14** Suppose production requirements in Solved Problem 9.2 increase and necessitate a reduction in cycle time from eight minutes to seven minutes. Balance the line once again using the new cycle time. Note that it is not possible to combine task times so as to group tasks into the minimum number of workstations. This condition occurs in actual balancing problems fairly often.

⌨ **:9.15** Dr. Wu, operations manager at Nesa Electronics, prides herself on excellent assembly line balancing. She has been told that the firm needs 1,400 electronic relays completed per day. There are 420 minutes of productive time in each working day (which is equivalent to 25,200 seconds). Group the assembly line activities on page 416 into appropriate workstations and calculate the efficiency of the balance.

TASK	TIME (SECONDS)	MUST FOLLOW TASK	TASK	TIME (SECONDS)	MUST FOLLOW TASK
A	13	—	G	5	E
B	4	A	H	6	F,G
C	10	B	I	7	H
D	10	—	J	5	H
E	6	D	K	4	I,J
F	12	E	L	15	C,K

DATA BASE APPLICATION

 : **9.16** As the Hunnewell Bicycle Co., in Omaha, completes plans for its new assembly line, it identifies 25 different tasks in the production process. Neil Hunnewell, the VP-operations, now faces the job of balancing the line. He lists precedences and provides time estimates for each step based on work sampling techniques. Hunnewell's goal is to produce 1,000 bicycles per standard 40-hour work week.

TASK	TIME (in seconds)	PREDECESSOR TASKS
K3	60	—
K4	24	K3
K9	27	K3
J1	66	K3
J2	22	K3
J3	3	—
G4	79	K4,K9
G5	29	K9,J1
F3	32	J2
F4	92	J2
F7	21	J3
F9	126	G4
E2	18	G5,F3
E3	109	F3
D6	53	F4
D7	72	F9,E2,E3
D8	78	E3,D6
D9	37	D6
C1	78	F7
B3	72	D7,D8,D9,C1
B5	108	C1
B7	18	B3
A1	52	B5
A2	72	B5
A3	114	B7,A1,A2

a) Balance this operation, using various "heuristics." Which is best?

b) What happens if the firm can change to a 41-hour work week?

CASE STUDY

State Automobile License Renewals

Henry Coupe, the manager of a metropolitan branch office of the state Department of Motor Vehicles, attempted to perform an analysis of the driver's license renewal operations. Several steps were to be performed in the process. After examining the license renewal process, he identified the steps and associated times required to perform each step, as shown in the following table:

State Automobile License Renewals Process Times.

STEP	AVERAGE TIME TO PERFORM (SECONDS)
1. Review renewal application for correctness	15
2. Process and record payment	30
3. Check file for violations and restrictions	60
4. Conduct eye test	40
5. Photograph applicant	20
6. Issue temporary license	30

Coupe found that each step was assigned to a different person. Each application was a separate process in the sequence shown above. Coupe determined that his office should be prepared to accommodate the maximum demand of processing 120 renewal applicants per hour.

He observed that the work was unevenly divided among the clerks, and the clerk who was responsible for checking violations tended to shortcut her task to keep up with the other clerks. Long lines built up during the maximum demand periods.

Coupe also found that jobs 1, 2, 3, and 4 were handled by general clerks who were each paid $6.00 per hour. Job 5 was performed by a photographer paid $8 per hour. Job 6, the issuing of a temporary license, was required by state policy to be handled by a uniformed motor vehicle officer. Officers were paid $9.00 per hour, but they could be assigned to any job except photography.

A review of the jobs indicated that job 1, reviewing the application for correctness, had to be performed before any other step could be taken. Similarly, job 6, issuing the temporary license, could not be performed until all the other steps were completed.

The branch offices were charged $5 per hour for each camera to perform photography.

Henry Coupe was under severe pressure to increase productivity and reduce costs, but he was also told by the regional director of the Department of Motor Vehicles that he had better accommodate the demand for renewals. Otherwise, "heads would roll."

Discussion Questions

1. What is the maximum number of applications per hour that can be handled by the present configuration of the process?

2. How many applications can be processed per hour if a second clerk is added to check for violations?

3. Assuming the addition of one more clerk, what is the maximum number of applications the process can handle?

4. How would you suggest modifying the process in order to accommodate 120 applications per hour?

Source: Sasser, W. Earl, Paul R. Olson, and D. Daryl Wyckoff, *Management of Services Operations: Text, Cases, and Readings,* Boston: Allyn & Bacon, Inc., 1978.

CASE STUDY

The Palm Beach Institute of Sports Medicine

Introduction

Many orthopedic M.D.s, cardiologists, and sports medicine physicians have recognized the need for implementing diagnoses through physical therapy and fitness programs. Many more people are participating in sports and exercise such as tennis and jogging that may result in some type of injury. As a result, some physicians are forming close connections with quality sports medicine centers or are investing in limited partnerships to develop their own.

CASE STUDY (Continued)

The medical profession is the portal provider of many sports medicine center services. Therefore, a referral network is essential among physicians and sports medicine centers (SMC). The SMC is differentiated from health or fitness clubs because of this connection and the number of certified employees per member in the center.

Background

Dana Van Pelt opened a physical therapy practice in Pompano Beach, Florida, in 1980. As a registered physical therapist (RPT) and a certified athletic trainer (ATC), Mr. Van Pelt had a deep interest in conditioning and reconditioning of the body. In 1984 he therefore opened a sports medicine and physical therapy center in Boca Raton, north of Pompano Beach. This was so successful that it soon outgrew its quarters. In 1986, Van Pelt had the good fortune to locate about 7,600 square feet of floor space in Boca Raton, consisting of the entire fourth floor of the Galen Building. This location was within two blocks of the Community Hospital and in the center of a complex of medical buildings surrounding the area.

The organization of the now-named Palm Beach Institute of Sports Medicine (PBISM) consisted of Dana Van Pelt, President; Larry Carlino, Physical Therapist (PT) and Executive Director of Physical Therapy; three other physical therapists; three athletic trainers; one health/fitness instructor; four supporting physical therapy aides; three receptionists; and two business specialists. A number of nearby medical and paramedical specialists were also closely associated with PBISM by virtue of consulting arrangements.

Dana paid particular attention to the business aspects, long-range plans, and physical therapy advances and equipment. Larry Carlino was concerned with the management of day-to-day operations of the physical therapy aspects. Ron DeAngelo, one of the athletic trainers, managed the fitness operations. Duties were not highly specified, and the three worked as an informal team for the principal goals of the center.

Philosophy

The philosophy of PBISM is to promote a quality lifestyle for all participating members as well as those utilizing the institute's conditioning and rehabilitation programs.

Layout: A Continuing Challenge

When Dana was planning his move to the Galen building, the fourth floor was cleared to appear as shown in Figure 9.24. This area was to contain three offices, a conference room, examination rooms, treatment areas (partitioned with curtains), a large wet room with underwater treadmill, business office, men's and women's locker rooms, waiting room, reception area opposite the elevator, glass-paneled office overlooking the major equipment areas, and three equipment areas. The equipment areas were planned to be a back treatment area, a large conditioning equipment and stretching area, and an isokinetic equipment area. The items of equipment are listed in Table 9.4. Two or three duplicates of some items of equipment were contemplated because of general heavy usage.

TABLE 9.4 Equipment

1. Treadmill
2. Airdyne bike
3. Life cycle
4. Bodyguard bike
5. Versa climber
6. Nordic Trak
7. Precor skier
8. Precor rower
9. (a) Keiser (lower body)
   (b) Keiser (upper body)
10. (a) Eagle back extension
    (b) Eagle abdominal flexion
11. Orthotron
12. Cybex back extension
13. Cybex back rotation
14. Stair master
15. Underwater treadmill
16. Quinton 3000 stress test unit
17. Abdominal slant board
18. Bench
19. Dumbbell rack

CASE STUDY (Continued)

FIGURE 9.24

Floor Layout of Gutted Building Area.
(*Source:* R. Murdick, B. Render, and R. Russell, *Service Operations Management,* Boston: Allyn & Bacon, 1990, p. 204.)

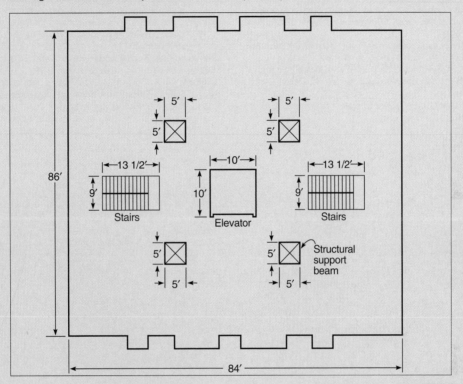

The general pattern for members to follow was to:

1. pick up their exercise plan sheet and clipboard;
2. warm up on one of the bikes;
3. stretch;
4. work out on upper body equipment;
5. work out on lower body equipment;
6. work out on abdomen and back machines.

In some cases, members would spend 30 to 45 minutes, or more, on aerobic devices such as bikes, treadmills, the Versa Climber, the Nordic (ski) Trak, or the rower. The equipment layout would have to be modified at a later date, Dana knew, based on the accumulated operating experience with the new SMC.

Discussion Questions

1. Draw an organization chart for PBISM.
2. Prepare a layout of the floor plan of the Institute. Get advice and comments from other students or a health club manager.
3. Lay out the arrangement of equipment within the floor plan.

Source: Adapted from Robert G. Murdick, Barry Render, and Roberta Russell, *Service Operations Management,* Boston: Allyn & Bacon, 1990, pp. 202–205.

BIBLIOGRAPHY

Ackerman, K. B., and B. J. La Londe. "Making Warehousing More Efficient." *Harvard Business Review* **58** (March–April 1980): 94–102.

Arcus, A. L. "COMSOAL: A Computer Method for Sequencing Operations for Assembly Line." *International Journal of Production Research* **4** (1966).

Baybars, I. "A Survey of Exact Algorithms for the Simple Assembly Line Balancing Problem." *Management Science* **32** (August 1986): 909–932.

Beer, I. B. "Efficiency and Productivity Profit." *Restaurant Business* (November 1, 1987): 147–161.

Buffa, E. S., G. S. Armor, and T. E. Vollman. "Allocating Facilities with CRAFT." *Harvard Business Review* **42** (March–April 1984): 136–159.

DeSanta, R. "All That Glitters Is Not Upscale." *Progressive Grocer* (April 1987): 112–117.

Dietrich, R. "The Rethinking of the Supermarket." *Progressive Grocer* (December 1982): 49–67.

Heller, W. "Tracking Shoppers through the Combination Store." *Progressive Grocer* (November 1988): 47–54.

Huang, P. Y., and B. L. W. Houck. "Cellular Manufacturing: An Overview and Bibiliography." *Production and Inventory Management* **26** (Fourth Quarter 1985): 83–92.

May, W., and R. Horne. "Considerations for Developing Standards in Long Cycle Assembly." *Industrial Engineering* (March 1990): 38–43.

Murdick, R., B. Render, and B. Russell. *Service Operations Management.* Boston: Allyn & Bacon, 1990.

Oldham, G. R. "Effects of Changes in Workspace Partitions and Spacial Density on Employee Reactions: A Quasi-Experiment." *Journal of Applied Psychology* (1988): 253–258.

Human Resource Strategy

Alaska Airlines Develops a Competitive Advantage Via Human Factors

Ergonomics and human factors provide an opportunity to improve human performance. Such opportunities exist in a variety of applications, from typewriter keyboards to aircraft controls. Two recent advances in aircraft controls are currently being introduced in commercial aircraft.

The new generation of aircraft cockpit displays utilizes our knowledge of human factors to make planes safer and easier to fly. The new displays are designed to reduce the chance of human error, which is estimated to be a factor in about two-thirds of commercial air accidents. Fractions of a second in the cockpit can literally mean the difference between life and death.

One approach to improved cockpit displays is to simplify the instrument panel. Designers have simplified the instrument panel by dispensing with the array of traditional round analog dials and gauges found in older planes.

This newer contemporary "glass cockpit" displays information in more concise form than a row of round dials by using cathode ray tubes (CRTs). CRTs allow the pilots to determine more rapidly a variety of control variables including air speed, altitude, and rate of climb.

In spite of such advances, the human requirements for a fighter jet are still tremendous. Many military aircraft require the use of lit-

Traditional round analog dials and gauges can present a lot of difficult-to-interpret information.

A glass cockpit with less clutter because of fewer dials and gauges can net a faster pilot-response time.

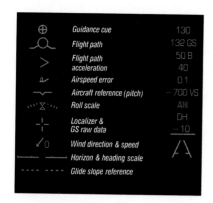

⊕	Guidance cue	130
Ω	Flight path	132 GS
>	Flight path acceleration	50 B / 40
⋏	Airspeed error	0.1
‿	Aircraft reference (pitch)	− 700 VS
⋅⋅ Σ ⋅⋅	Roll scale	AIII
╌┼╌	Localizer & GS raw data	DH / − 10
⁄0	Wind direction & speed	⋀
──	Horizon & heading scale	
┄┄	Glide slope reference	

The symbols in the "heads-up" display (shown in the photos to the right) are interpreted above.

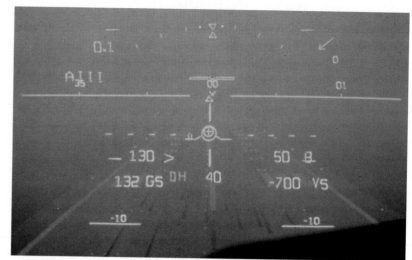

erally hundreds of acronyms and symbols. For instance, a fighter jet, such as McDonald Douglas F/A-18, has 675 acronyms and 177 symbols that can be displayed in four different sizes on three different CRTs. In addition, there are 73 warning indicators, 10 throttle switches, and 20 controls around the three CRTs.

These demands on the human system have led to a second innovation, which uses our knowledge of human factors to present 19 critical controls directly on a "heads-up" display. A "heads-up" display allows the pilot to look through the data that appear on the visor of a helmet, a fold-down screen, or a windshield. This technology, which is already being used in military aircraft, is now being introduced in commercial aircraft. And Alaska Airlines is leading the way.

With fleet operations in Seattle, Washington, an area often hit with fog and low visibility conditions, Alaska Airlines expects installation of the new heads-up displays to improve operating capabilities. This improvement in human factors should reduce

Alaska Airlines has begun using heads-up displays. Displays such as the one shown in the top photo allow images and critical flight information to be projected on a fold-down screen, as shown in the bottom photo, so the pilot can fly "heads-up."

pilot error *and* improve pilot response. Hopefully, this will yield safer flights and ultimately a competitive advantage at Alaska Airlines.

References: Flight Dynamics, Inc., P.O. Box 230690, Portland, OR 97223; *Scientific American*, July 1991; and *Aviation Week and Space Technology*, November 4, 1991.

INTRODUCTION

At 9 A.M. the assembly line has been moving for only one hour, but already the day is dragging. In position five on line four, Annette Fullbright catches the next circuit board crawling down the line. At the current pace, one board passes her workstation every minute and a half. Forty down, 280 left to go today. Over in quality control, Ismael Hernandez puts his soldering gun back in its holster, fidgets with his left shirt sleeve and steals a quick glance at his watch. Thirty more minutes before coffee break. Two and a half hours to lunch. Seven and a half more until quitting time.[1]

Scenes such as these are repeated a thousand times over every day all over the world. Why are Annette's and Ismael's jobs like this? Is it a good human resource strategy for firms to have such jobs? In this chapter we will examine these and related questions.

Human performance is crucial to an organization's performance. An organization does not function without people; it does not function well without competent people; it does not excel without competent, motivated people. How the operations manager formulates a human resource strategy determines the talents available to operations. Human resources are expensive. In many organizations a third of total cost is in wages and salaries, and within the operations function these costs range from 8% to 80%. Because of the importance of personnel and their cost, early consideration of human resource strategy options is necessary.

Objective of the Human Resource Strategy

The *objective of a human resource strategy* is to manage labor and design jobs so human resources:

1. are efficiently utilized within the constraints of other strategic operations management decisions;
2. have a reasonable quality of work life in an atmosphere of mutual commitment and trust.

Quality of work life

Mutual commitment
Mutual trust

By reasonable **quality of work life** we mean a job that not only is reasonably safe and for which the pay is equitable, but also that achieves an appropriate level of both physical and psychological requirements. By **mutual commitment** we mean both management and employee strive to meet common objectives. By **mutual trust** we mean reasonable, documented employment policies that are honestly and equitably implemented to the satisfaction of both management and employee.[2] When management has a genuine respect for its employees and their contribution to the firm, establishing a reasonable quality of work life and mutual trust is not particularly difficult.

This chapter is devoted to how the operations manager can achieve this objective.

---

[1] Roger Thurow, "Life On The Job," *Wall Street Journal* (June 1, 1981): 1.

[2] With increasing frequency we find companies calling their employees *associates, individual contributors,* or members of a particular *team.*

Human Resource Strategy Constraints

Many decisions that are made about human resources are constrained by other strategic decisions, previously discussed. First, the product mix may determine seasonality and stability of employment. Second, technology, equipment, and processes may have implications for safety and job content. Third, the location decision may have an impact on the ambient environment in which the employees work. Finally, decisions regarding layout may dictate, in large part, job content.

The technology decision imposes substantial constraints. For instance, some of the jobs in steel mills are dirty, noisy, and dangerous, as we see in the following quote.

> The temperature in Alfred Hardy's work area approaches 140 degrees. Flames shoot up from furnaces all around, and sparks the size of firecrackers spray into the air. Mr. Hardy must keep constant watch to dodge moving containers of molten iron that roll past his work area. With every breath, he inhales burnt resins and furnace smoke. He is surrounded by the constant staccato of air hammers, the roar of furnaces, and the whining and clatter of various machines. Once he finishes with one furnace, Mr. Hardy, bathed in sweat, covered with grime, scarred with the burn marks of 20 years, climbs out and starts shoveling the molten slag from beneath the next furnace.[3]

Similarly, as the next paragraph about Mr. Decena's job demonstrates, some of the jobs in slaughterhouses may also have job designs of limited appeal.

> Mr. Decena, a 33-year-old Mexican-American, works at one of the nastiest and most gruesome of manual jobs. Each morning by the time the sun has begun to rise across San Antonio, Mr. Decena has shaved the hair and sliced the fat from over 100 butchered hogs. He is a cog in an assembly line process of 38 men who kill, butcher, gut, and pass on for processing the hogs and cattle slaughtered at a Cudahy meat-packing plant. For 45 hours a week, his senses are bombarded by the screams of animals that sense impending death and the stomach-crunching stench of their corpses after they are butchered. He processes one hog every 45 seconds.

We are not going to change jobs like Hardy's and Decena's without making changes in our other strategic decisions. Knowledge of the technology available, combined with location and layout decisions, and the proper capital investment decisions may yield efficiency and a tolerable, if not an ideal, quality of work life. The trade-offs are difficult.

Much of our fifth strategic decision, the human resource strategy, is a result of other operation design decisions (Figure 10.1). Consequently, it behooves a prudent manager to ensure that such decisions are considered simultaneously. The manager blends ingredients so that the result is an effective, efficient system where individuals have optimum job design.

The Three Dimensions of Human Resource Strategy

Acknowledging the constraints imposed on human resource strategy, we now look at three distinct decision areas of human resource strategy. These are:

---

[3] From "The Dirty Work," *Wall Street Journal* (July 16, 1981): 1, 8.

FIGURE 10.1

Constraints on Human Resource Strategy. The effective operations manager understands how decisions blend together to constrain the human resource strategy.

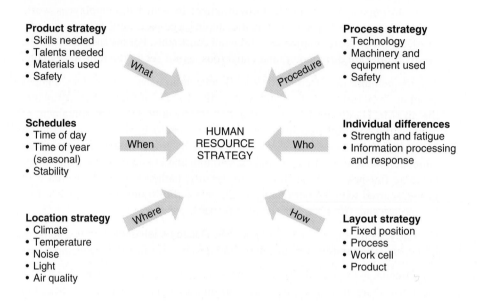

Labor planning

1. *Labor planning.* **Labor planning** is determining staffing policies that deal with
   a) employment stability, and
   b) work schedules.

Job design

2. *Job design.* **Job design** is specifying the tasks that constitute a job for an individual or a group. A job consists of a variety of tasks; a task consists of a number of elements; and an element consists of micromotions. We will examine job design from the perspective of four components. They are
   a) job specialization and enrichment,
   b) psychological components,
   c) ergonomics and work methods, and
   d) motivation and incentive systems.

Labor standards

3. *Labor standards.* **Labor standards** help us specify the labor required for given levels of production once jobs have been defined. We establish labor standards via
   a) historical data,
   b) work sampling,
   c) method time measurement, and
   d) stopwatch standards.

The supplement to this chapter discusses labor standards and work measurement in some detail.

LABOR PLANNING

Employment Stability Policies

Let us look at two labor planning strategies. They are:

1. *Follow demand exactly.* This is line A in Figure 10.2. Following demands exactly has the advantage of keeping direct labor costs tied closely to production but incurs other costs.

    These other costs include (a) hiring and termination costs, (b) unemployment insurance, and (c) perhaps a labor wage premium to entice personnel to accept unstable employment. Such a policy tends to treat labor as a variable cost.

2. *Hold employment constant.* This is line B in Figure 10.2. Holding employment constant has the advantage of maintaining a trained work force and keeping the hiring, termination, and unemployment costs to a minimum. The disadvantage is that employees may not be utilized fully when demand is low, and the firm may find meeting demand difficult when demand is high. Such a policy tends to treat labor as a fixed cost. We will discuss further implications of these strategies in Chapter 12, Aggregate Planning Tactics.

Maintaining a stable work force may yield a wage rate lower than that paid by firms that do not. This may provide a competitive advantage. However, managers who choose a strategy resulting in a fluctuating work force may also be choosing the most efficient option available to them. Such a firm may have highly seasonal work and few options for managing demand. For example, a salmon canner on the Columbia River processes when the salmon are running. Conceivably however, the firm can find complementary labor demands in other products or operations, such as making the cans and labels or repairing and maintaining facilities.

Firms must make a decision as to employment stability. The above strategies and others can be efficient *and* provide a reasonable quality of work life.

FIGURE 10.2

Work Force Strategies.

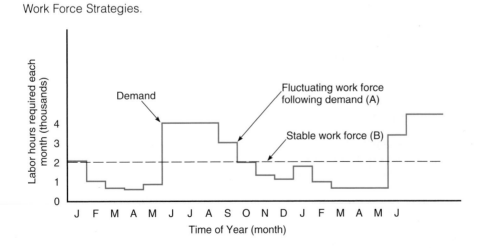

Work Schedules

Standard work schedule

Flextime

Although the **standard work schedule** in America is five eight-hour days, variations do exist. A currently popular variation is a work schedule called flextime. **Flextime** allows employees, within limits, to determine their own schedules. A flextime policy might allow an employee (with proper notification) to be at work at 8 A.M. plus or minus two hours. This allows more autonomy and independence on the part of the employee. Some firms have found flextime a low-cost fringe benefit that enhances job satisfaction. The problem from the P/OM perspective is that much production work requires full staffing for efficient operations. A machine that requires three people cannot run at all if only two show up. Having a waiter show up to serve lunch at 1:30 P.M. rather than 11:30 A.M. is not much help either.

Some industries find that their process strategy has severely constrained their human resource scheduling option. For instance, paper manufacturing, petroleum refining, and power stations must be staffed around the clock except for maintenance and repair shutdown. Firms in these industries are severely constrained when implementing variable-time policies.

Flexible work week

Another work schedule is a **flexible work week.** This often manifests itself in four 10-hour days. This works in many operations functions, provided suppliers and customers can be accommodated. Firms that have high process start-up times (say to get a boiler up to operating temperature or a plastic molding machine running properly) find longer workday options particularly appealing.

Part-time status

Another option is to have shorter days rather than longer days. This often moves employees to **part-time status.** Such an option is particularly attractive in service industries, where staffing for peak loads is necessary. Banks and restaurants are frequent practitioners of this technique. Additionally, many firms are able to reduce labor costs by reducing fringe benefits for part-time employees.

Job Classifications and Work Rules

Who can do what, when they can do it, and under what conditions are determined by job classifications and work rules. Part of an operations manager's task is to manage the unexpected. The more flexibility a firm has when staffing and establishing work schedules, the more efficient it can be. Building morale and meeting staffing requirements is easier if managers have fewer job classifications and work-rule constraints.

JOB DESIGN

Specialization

Labor specialization

Job design's importance as a management variable is credited to Adam Smith.[4] Smith suggested that a division of labor, also known as **labor specialization,** would assist in reducing labor costs in several ways:

    1. *development of dexterity* and faster learning by the employee because of repetition,

[4] Adam Smith, *On the Creation of the Wealth of Nations,* 1876.

2. *less loss of time* because the employee would not be changing jobs or tools,
3. *development of specialized tools* and the reduction of investment because each employee has only a few tools needed for a particular task.

Charles Babbage determined that a fourth consideration was important for labor efficiency.[5] Since pay tends to follow skill with a rather high correlation, Babbage suggested *paying exactly the wage needed for the particular skill required.* If the entire job consists of only one skill, then we would pay for only that skill; otherwise, we would tend to pay for the highest skill contributed by the employee. These four advantages of labor specialization are still valid today.

A classic example of labor specialization is the assembly line, as described in the opening paragraph of this chapter. Such systems are often very efficient, although they may require employees to do repetitive, mind-numbing jobs. The wage rate for many of these jobs, however, is very good. Given the relatively high wage rate for the modest skills required in many of these jobs, there is often a large pool of employees from which to choose. This is not an incidental consideration for the manager with responsibility for staffing the operations function. It is estimated that 2% to 3% of the work force in industrialized nations perform highly specialized, repetitive assembly line jobs. The traditional way of developing and maintaining worker commitment under labor specialization has been good selection (matching people to the job), good wages, and incentive systems.

Job Enlargement/Job Enrichment

In recent years there has been an effort to improve the quality of work life by moving from the structure suggested by Adam Smith and Charles Babbage toward a more enriched job design. We do this by **job enlargement** and **job enrichment.** An enlarged job is one in which we group a variety of tasks of about the same skill. As one wag put it, enlarged jobs allow the employee to do a number of boring things instead of just one. **Job rotation** is a version of job enlargement, where the job *per se* is not enlarged, but rather the employee is allowed to move from one specialized job to another. An enriched job is one that includes some of the planning and control necessary for job accomplishment. An enriched job is sometimes called *vertical enlargement,* as opposed to job enlargement, which may be termed *horizontal enlargement* (Figure 10.3).

Job enlargement
Job enrichment

Job rotation

Enriched jobs allow the employee to accept more responsibility. For employees who accept this responsibility, we may well expect some enhancement in productivity and product quality. Among the positive aspects of job enrichment are:

1. reduced turnover;
2. reduced tardiness and absenteeism;
3. improved quality;
4. improved productivity.

Managers who enrich jobs and build communication systems that elicit suggestions from employees have an added efficiency potential.

[5] Charles Babbage, *On the Economy of Machinery and Manufacturers* (London, 1832), Chapter 18.

FIGURE 10.3

Horizontal and Vertical Enlargement.

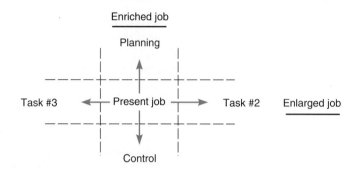

Job Enrichment at Volvo.[6]   Volvo has made a valiant effort to dispense with the assembly line altogether at its Swedish Kalmar Plant. Assembly groups are of 15 to 20 people each. All the employees, it is hoped, have the impression of working in individual workshops in which they are allowed to vary the speed of their automobile body carrier from 3 meters a minute to 30 meters a minute. Production at the Kalmar plant is split into three primary areas: body, chassis, and final assembly. Assembly personnel are given the opportunity to work as a team on one of these sections. The teams are allowed to rotate jobs among themselves and to establish, within limits, their own work pace. They are allowed some flexibility in work pace because they have storage areas in which they temporarily store partially completed cars. These buffer stocks are built between work areas. Figure 10.4 shows the layout of the Kalmar Plant.

Work groups also attempt to have each team do a major job so that they perceive the completion of a meaningful unit of work. For instance, a team may be in charge of installing all the electrical wiring and equipment. Instead of work cycles being one to two minutes, as they are in many automobile plants, they are 20 to 30 minutes. However, the Kalmar plant is reported to have had a capital expenditure of 11% more than the same type of facility built in a more traditional manner. And the factory layout at Kalmar took almost twice as much floor space as a more traditional automobile assembly facility. It is not clear that the reduced turnover, absenteeism, and increased productivity has yielded a net economic gain at Volvo. Similar issues exist at Volvo's new plant at Uddevalla; see the *POM in Action* box, "Edges Fray on Volvo's Brave New Humanistic World."

Job Enrichment at Buick City.   General Motors, at Buick City, has also introduced assembly teams in automobile assembly and engine outfitting areas. As is the case with Volvo, units are mounted on automated guide vehicles, which allows for a flexible path, flexibility in storage, and modest changes in the production rate. The jobs are enlarged and modestly enriched, as employees are expected to perform a variety of tasks and some scheduling. Engines are outfitted for particular vehicles. For instance, for four different types of V-8 and V-6 engines, assembly teams install

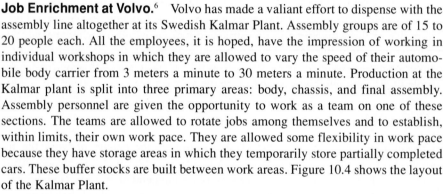

Disasters at nuclear power plants in the U.S. (Three Mile Island) and in the Ukraine (Chernobyl) have frightened federal and local regulators into increasingly stricter maintenance and reliability standards. There is even a question as to whether some nuclear plants under construction in the U.S. will ever be completed. Some experts believe that there is still insufficient attention given to the human side of reactor control systems. Designers, they believe, don't appreciate the fact that plants are man-machine systems.

---

[6] Peter J. Mullins, "Volvo's Kalmar Plant—Ten Years On," *Automotive Industries* (August 1984); Pehr G. Gyllanhammer, "How Volvo Adapts Work to People," *Harvard Business Review,* **55,** 4 (July–August 1977): 102–113.

air-conditioning compressors, alternators, hoses, wiring harnesses, and so on. The operators can change the speed of the line from 49 engines per hour to 60 engines per hour. Engines are not released until the operators are satisfied that the work is properly completed.

Job enlargement and job enrichment are just two of many changes General Motors has introduced at Buick City that affect efficiency. However, there are indications that quality has improved, that employees are accepting more responsibilities, and that absenteeism has been reduced because of these two concepts.

Limitations to Job Enlargement/Job Enrichment. If job enlargement and enrichment is so good, why is it not universally used? Let us identify some of its limitations:

1. *Higher capital cost.* Job enlargement and job enrichment require facilities that cost more than a conventional layout. This extra expenditure must be generated through savings (greater efficiency) or through higher prices.

2. *Many individuals prefer simple jobs.* Some studies indicate that many employees, a majority in some cases, opt for the less complex jobs.[7] In a discussion about improving the quality of work life, it seems appropriate that we not forget the importance of individual differences. These differences provide latitude for the resourceful operations manager when designing jobs.

FIGURE 10.4

Keeping Volvo's Workers Calm at Kalmer.
(*Source:* Copyright 1976, *The Economist, Ltd.* Reprinted with permission from The New York Times Special Features.)

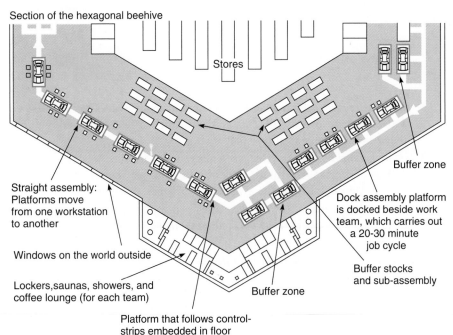

Section of the hexagonal beehive

Stores

Buffer zone

Straight assembly:
Platforms move
from one workstation
to another

Dock assembly platform
is docked beside work
team, which carries out
a 20-30 minute
job cycle

Windows on the world outside

Buffer stocks
and sub-assembly

Lockers, saunas, showers, and
coffee lounge (for each team)

Buffer zone

Platform that follows control-
strips embedded in floor

[7] Michell Fein, "Job Enrichment Does Not Work," *Atlanta Economic Review* (November–December 1975): 50–54.

POM in action

Edges Fray on Volvo's Brave New Humanistic World

Since 1988, when Volvo opened its car-assembly factory in Uddevalla, Sweden, it has claimed leadership in one of the boldest experiments in what is known as humanistic manufacturing. But this noble gamble is looking more and more like a noble failure, with productivity far from the exacting standards of world competition.

At Uddevalla, Volvo became the first large-scale carmaker to turn its back on a system that has prevailed in the industry since the days of Henry Ford: the assembly line. Volvo's chairman wanted to prove that the craftsman approach of having a small team of highly skilled workers build an entire car, when linked with advanced materials handling, could compete after all.

The Uddevalla approach of cutting out layers of management and removing all foremen aimed to give workers more control over their jobs, reduce the tedium of the assembly line, and encourage workers to broaden their skills. In doing so, Volvo hoped also to tackle the special Swedish problem of absenteeism and turnover, which are among the highest in the developed world.

But as the chart shows, it takes 50 hours of labor to assemble a car at Uddevalla, compared to 37 hours at Volvo's 17-year-old plant at Kalmar, and 25 hours at its conventional assembly line in Ghent, Belgium. Volvo is ready to concede that it has little faith in the plant's ability to achieve world-class productivity levels.

Company	Location	Hours	Regional Averages	
Volvo	Ghent, Belgium	25	Japan—domestic	17
Volvo	Kalmar, Sweden	37	Japan—U.S.	22
Volvo	Uddevalla, Sweden	50	U.S.—domestic	25
			Europe	36

Sources: The New York Times, July 7, 1991, p. F5; *Modern Materials Handling,* November 1990, pp. 52–55; and *Business Week,* August 28, 1989, pp. 92–93.

3. *Higher wage rates are required.* People often receive wages for their highest skills, not their lowest.[8] So, enlarged and enriched jobs may well require a higher average wage than jobs that are not.

4. *Smaller labor pool exists.* Because enlarged and enriched jobs require more skill and acceptance of more responsibility, the job requirements have increased. Depending upon the availability of labor, this may be a constraint.

5. *Increased accident rates may occur.* Enlarged and enriched jobs may contribute to a higher accident rate.[9] This indirectly increases wages, insurance costs, and workmen's compensation.

6. *Current technology may not lend itself to job enlargement and enrichment.* The disassembly jobs at the slaughterhouse, the computer assembly jobs at the modern office park, and the toll-booth operator jobs are that way because the alternative technologies (if any) are thought to be unacceptable.

[8] Charles Babbage, *On the Economy of Machinery and Manufacturers* (London, 1832), Chapter 18.

[9] J. Tsaari and J. Lahtella, "Job Enrichment: Cause of Increased Accidents?" *Industrial Engineering* (October 1978): 41–45.

These six points provide the constraints on job enlargement and job enrichment. The practices increase costs. Therefore, for the firm to have a competitive advantage, its savings must be greater than its cost. It is not always obvious that such is the case. There is no guarantee that productivity or quality will improve with the installation of job enrichment or job enlargement. The strategic decision is not an easy one.

Psychological Components of Job Design

An effective human resources strategy also requires consideration of the psychological components of job design. Psychological components of job design focus on how to improve the quality of work life, job satisfaction, and motivation by designing jobs that meet some minimum psychological requirements. Let us now identify these psychological parameters of good job design.

Performance during a pit stop makes a difference between winning and losing a race. Activity charts are used to orchestrate the movement of members of a pit crew, an operating room staff, or machine operators in a factory. Solved Problem 10.1 shows an activity chart applied to a pit crew.

Hawthorne Studies. The Hawthorne studies were conducted in the late 1920s at the General Electric Hawthorne Plant near Chicago. Publication of the findings in 1939[10] demonstrated conclusively that there is a dynamic social system at the workplace. Ironically, these studies were initiated to determine the impact of lighting on productivity. Instead they found the social system and distinct roles played by employees to be more important than the intensity of the lighting. They also found that individual differences may be dominant in what an employee expects from the job and what the employee thinks her or his contribution to the job should be. The Hawthorne studies introduced psychology to the workplace.

Maslow's Hierarchy of Needs. Maslow's hierarchy of needs (Figure 10.5) suggests that well-designed jobs should allow employees to address both physiological and psychological needs.[11] Furthermore, Maslow's hierarchy suggests that once employees have satisfied lower-level needs, they seek to satisfy those needs at the next higher level. Ideally then, jobs should contain ingredients that allow people to satisfy needs at all levels. Job design then has the potential of providing both satisfaction and motivation as the employee seeks to satisfy higher-level needs.

Herzberg Motivation/Hygiene Factors.[12] Frederick Herzberg, in his **dual-factor theory,** suggests jobs can contain hygiene elements (these are dissatisfiers if not fulfilled) and motivators (these can motivate and excite people about their job). His dual-factor theory is shown in Figure 10.5.

Dual-factor theory

If we make the assumption that virtually any job in the Western world can and should provide for Maslow's lower needs and Herzberg's hygiene elements, then *good* job design will also include Maslow's higher needs and Herzberg's motivators. Per H. Engelstad addresses these psychological components of job design when he offers the six following guidelines:[13]

[10] F. J. Roethlisberger and William J. Dickinson, *Management and the Workers*, Science Editions (New York: John Wiley, 1964, copyright 1939, by the President & Fellows of Harvard College).

[11] Abraham H. Maslow, "A Theory of Human Motivation," *Psychological Review,* **50** (1943): 370–396.

[12] Frederick Herzberg, B. Mausner, and B. B. Snyderman, *The Motivation to Work* (New York: John Wiley, 1965).

[13] Per H. Engelstad, "Sociotechnical Approach to Problems of Process Control," in *Design of Jobs,* Louis E. Davis and James C. Taylor, eds. (Santa Monica, CA: Goodyear Publishing Co., 1979), pp. 184–205.

FIGURE 10.5

Maslow's Hierarchy of Needs and Herzberg's Dual-Factor Theory Compared.

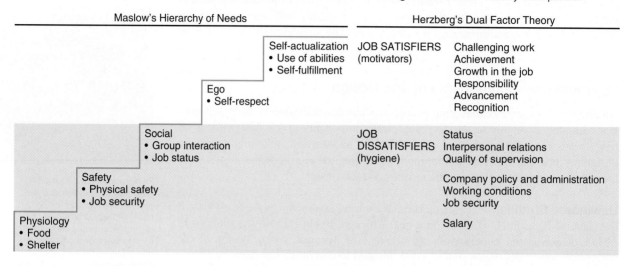

1. The need for the content of a job to be *reasonably demanding* for the individual in terms other than sheer endurance, and yet provide some variety (not necessarily novelty);
2. The need for an *opportunity to learn* on the job and to go on learning;
3. The need for some minimal *area of decision-making* that the individual can call his or her own;
4. The need for some minimal degree of *social support and recognition* at the workplace;
5. The need to be able to *relate what individuals do and what they produce to their social life*;
6. The need to feel that the *job leads to some sort of desirable future.*

The idea is to use the psychological components of job design not only to improve the quality of work life and job satisfaction but also to motivate employees. Employees should be as committed as management to meeting organizational objectives. World-class firms build environments that motivate employees to contribute, and motivation often includes employee involvement. Employee involvement includes participation fostered by supervisory action, teams, committees, and job design. The rather frightening result for those firms that do not utilize the contributions of employees in the quest for production/operations excellence is depicted in the *POM in Action* box, "Why the West Will Lose."

Ergonomics and Work Methods

Scientific Management. You may recall from the discussion of scientific management in Chapter 1 that, in the late 1880s, Frederick W. Taylor began the era of scientific management.[14] He and his contemporaries began to examine personnel

---

[14] Frederick W. Taylor, *Scientific Management* (New York: Harper & Row, 1911), p. 204.

POM _in action_

Why the West Will Lose

**Extract from remarks made by Mr. Konosuke Matsushita of the Matsushita Electric Industrial Company, Japan, to a group of Western managers.**

We are going to win and the industrial West is going to lose. Your firms are built on the Taylor model; even worse, so are your heads. With your bosses doing the thinking while the workers wield the screwdrivers, you are convinced deep down that this is the right way to run a business.

For you, the essence of management is getting the ideas out of the heads of the bosses into the hands of labor.

We are beyond the Taylor model: business, we know, is now so complex and difficult, the survival of firms so hazardous in an environment increasingly unpredictable, competitive, and fraught with danger, that their continued existence depends on the day-to-day mobilization of every ounce of intelligence.

For us, the core of management is precisely this art of mobilizing and pulling together the intellectual resources of all employees in the service of the firm. Because we have measured better than you the scope of the new technological and economic challenges, we know that the intelligence of a handful of technocrats, however brilliant and smart they may be, is no longer enough for a real chance of success.

Only by drawing on the combined brain power of all its employees can a firm face up to the turbulence and constraints of today's environment.

This is why our large companies give their employees three to four times more training than yours; this is why they foster within the firm such intensive exchange and communication; this is why they seek constantly everybody's suggestions and why they demand from the educational system increasing numbers of bright and well-educated graduates, because these people are the lifeblood of industry.

Source: Industrial Participation, Spring 1985, p. 8.

selection, work methods, work standards, and motivation. They examined the role of management and employees at the workplace and were concerned with:

1. matching employees to the task (individual differences);
2. work methods (improving task performance);
3. work standards (so both employee and employer would know what was to be done and what constituted a fair day's work).

With the foundation provided by Taylor and his contemporaries, we have developed a body of knowledge about people's capabilities and limitations. This knowledge is necessary because humans are a hand/eye animal possessing exceptional capabilities and some limitations. Because managers must design jobs that can be done, we are now going to introduce briefly a few of the issues related to people's capabilities and limitations.

The operations manager is interested in building a good interface between human and machine. Studies of this interface are known as **ergonomics.** Ergonomics means "the study of work." (_Ergo_ is from the Greek word for _work._) In America the term _human factors_ is often substituted for the word _ergonomics._

Ergonomics

Male and female adults come in limited configurations. Therefore, design of the workplace depends on biomechanics and anthropometric data. Biomechanical and

POM _in action_

Ergonomics at Ford

The friendliest place for a human to work has never been an auto plant. More often than not, employees have to adapt to equipment, not vice versa. This translates into unnecessary bending and stretching, which has negative effects on health and also decreases productivity. The cure does not necessarily dictate major changes of the assembly line, however. Sometimes, small adjustments of just one or two inches will do the job.

Slightly changing work surface heights, moving handles to more accessible spots, or even leaning a parts bin in a particular way can lower worker strain.

These discoveries are the result of a four-year, $2.5 million project sponsored by Ford Motor Co. and the University of Michigan's Center for Ergonomics. Based on early findings, Ford claims both quality and productivity are up at factories where ergonomic suggestions were implemented. Workers are also feeling better on the job, says a United Auto Workers spokesman. The program, he added, is "an everybody-wins situation."

Sources: Business Week, May 12, 1986, p. 67; Manufacturing Systems, March 1988, pp. 18–20; and Automation, March 1988, pp. 24–26.

anthropometric data provide the basic strength and measurement data needed to design tools and the workplace. The design of tools and the workplace can make jobs easy or impossible. We now have the ability, through the use of computer modeling, to put what we know of anthropometric and biomechanical data to use analyzing human motions and efforts.

FIGURE 10.6

Levels of Illumination Recommended for Various Task Conditions.
(_Source:_ C. T. Morgan, J. S. Cook III, A. Chapanis, and M. W. Lund (eds.) _Human Engineering Guide to Equipment Design_ (New York: McGraw-Hill, 1963) as presented in Alphonse Chapanis, _Man-Machine Engineering_ (Belmont, CA: Wadsworth Publishing Company, Inc.), p. 57.)

TASK CONDITION	TYPE OF TASK OR AREA	ILLUMINATION LEVEL (FT-C)	TYPE OF ILLUMINATION
Small detail, low brightness contrast, prolonged periods, high speed, extreme accuracy	Sewing, inspecting dark materials, etc.	100	General plus supplementary (e.g., desk lamp)
Normal detail, prolonged periods	Reading, parts assembly, general office and laboratory work	20–50	General (e.g., overhead ceiling fixture)
Good contrast, fairly large objects	Recreational facilities	5–10	General
Large objects	Restaurants, stairways, bulk-supply warehouses	2–5	General

FIGURE 10.7

Decible Levels (dB) and Sound-Power Ratios for Various Sounds. Decible levels are *A*-weighted sound levels measured with a sound-level meter. (*Source:* A. P. G. Peterson and E. E. Gross, Jr., *Handbook of Noise Measurement,* 7th ed. New Concord, Mass., General Radio Co., as presented in Ernest J. McCormick, *Human Factors in Engineering and Design* (New York: McGraw-Hill, 1976) p. 116.)

Sound-Power Ratio	Decibels	Environment Noises	Specific Noise Sources	Decibels
1,000,000,000,000	120		Jet takeoff (200 ft)	120
100,000,000,000	110	Casting shakeout area	Riveting machine*	110
10,000,000,000	100	Electric furnace area	Cutoff saw* Pneumatic peen hammer*	100
1,000,000,000	90	Boiler room Printing press plant	Textile weaving plant* Subway train (20 ft)	90
100,000,000	80	Tabulating room Inside sports car (50 mph)	Pneumatic drill (50 ft)	80
10,000,000	70		Freight train (100 ft) Vacuum cleaner (10 ft) Speech (1 ft)	70
1,000,000	60	Near freeway (auto traffic) Large store Accounting office		60
100,000	50	Private business office Light traffic (100 ft) Average residence	Large transformer (200 ft)	50
10,000	40	Minimum levels, residential areas in Chicago at night		40
1,000	30	Studio (speech)	Soft whisper (5 ft)	30

*At operator's position

Package weight is 54 lbs.

Let us look briefly at one instance of anthropometric data used in the work area. A writing desk has an optimum height depending on the size of the individual and the task to be performed. The common height for a writing desk is 29 inches. For typing or data entry at a CRT, the surface should be lower. The preferred chair and desk height should result in a very slight angle between the body and arm when the individual is viewed from the front and when the back is straight.[15] This is the critical measurement; it can be achieved via adjustment in either table or chair height.

Do the desks you use yield such an angle? Can you adjust your desk or chair height? The *POM in Action* box, "Ergonomics at Ford," discusses a current Ford Motor Company project.

The Work Environment. The physical environment in which employees work affects their performance, safety, and quality of work life. Illumination, noise and vibration, temperature, humidity, and air quality are work environment factors under the control of the organization and the operations manager. The manager must approach them as controllable.

Illumination is necessary, but the proper level depends upon the work being

How Simulation Works: The computerized mannequin ADAM shows the strain put on Lockheed human factors engineer Rick Davids' back as he installs an electronics box in a section of the Trident II D-5 Fleet Ballistic Missile.

[15] Edwin R. Tichauer, "Biomechanics Sustains Occupational Safety and Health," *Industrial Engineering* (February 1976): 46–55.

POM *in action*

Redesigning Tools Reduces Carpal Tunnel Syndrome

Carpal tunnel syndrome is a wrist disorder that afflicts 23,000 workers annually and costs employers and insurers an average of $30,000 per affected worker. Government statistics reveal that most of the hand and wrist disorders occur among the tool-using population. Comparison of groups of trainees in electronic assembly has shown that it is better to bend pliers than to bend the wrist. With bent pliers and wrists straight, no cases of carpal tunnel syndrome were reported (see (a) below). A majority of the workers with the pliers on the right (see (b) below) reported some type of problem after twelve weeks of training.

Therefore it is not shocking that the new trend among toolmakers is to redesign tools with carpal tunnel syndrome in mind. Several firms have jumped on the bandwagon. Cooper Industries has redesigned the handle and trigger on its power drill line so that the tools better fit the hand. The new handles come in different sizes and replace the standard one-size-fits-all models. Triggers are easier to use and placed so they may be controlled by either middle or index fingers. Ingersoll-Rand plans to introduce a new line of tools that will automatically make adjustments to the individual user's physique. As one executive said: "Ergonomics is the future."

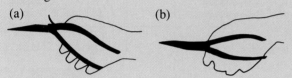

(a)   (b)

Sources: "Tooling Out Carpal Tunnel Syndrome," *The Wall Street Journal,* March 11, 1991, and Tichauer, E. R. "Biomechanics Sustain Occupational Safety and Health," *Industrial Engineering,* Feb. 1976, p. 47.

performed. Figure 10.6 provides some guidelines. However, other factors of lighting are important. These other factors include reflective ability, contrast of the work surface with surroundings, glare, and shadows.

Noise of some form is usually present in the work area, and many employees seem to adjust well. However, high levels of sound will damage hearing. Figure 10.7 (on p. 437) provides indications of the sound generated by various activities. (Note that decibel scales are log scales, not linear ones.) Extended periods of exposure to decibel levels above 90dB have been judged to be permanently damaging to hearing. The Occupational Safety and Health Administration (OSHA) requires ear protection above this level if exposure equals or exceeds eight hours. Even at low levels, noise and vibration can be distracting. Therefore most managers make substantial effort to reduce noise and vibration through good machine design, enclosures, or segregation of sources of noise and vibration.

Temperature and humidity parameters have been well established. Managers with activities operating outside of the established comfort zone should expect some adverse effect on performance.

Controlling (Adjusting and Providing Input to the Machine). Any operator response to a machine, be it via hand tools, pedals, levers, or buttons, needs to be evaluated. Does the operator have the strength, reflexes, perception, and mental capacity to provide the necessary control? The *POM in Action* box, "Redesigning Tools Reduces Carpal Tunnel Syndrome," represents examples of hand tool design to be considered when designing jobs.

FIGURE 10.8

(a) Flow Diagram of an Office Procedure—Proposed Method. Requisition is written in triplicate by supervisor and approved by purchasing agent.
(b) Process Chart of an Office Procedure—Proposed Method for the Flow Diagram.
(*Source:* R. M. Barnes, *Motion and Time Study* (New York: John Wiley, 1968), pp. 78–79. Copyright © 1968, by John Wiley & Sons. Reprinted by permission.)

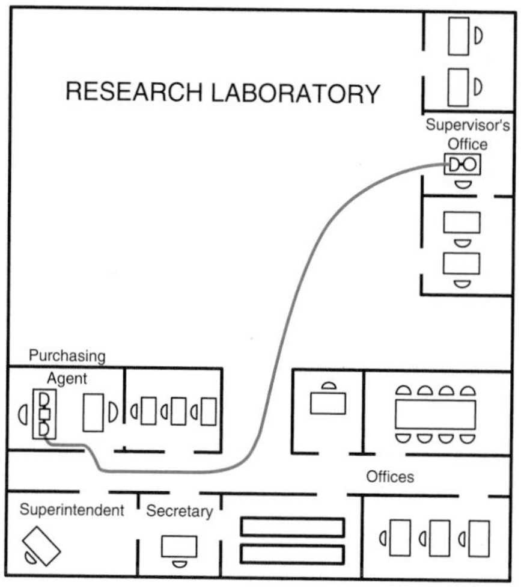

(a)

Present Method ☐	PROCESS CHART		
Proposed Method ☒			

SUBJECT CHARTED ___Requisition for small tools___   DATE _____
Chart begins at supervisor's desk and ends at   CHART BY ___J.C.H.___
purchasing agent's desk   CHART NO. ___R 149___
DEPARTMENT ___Research laboratory___   SHEET NO. _1_ OF _1_

DIST. IN FEET	TIME IN MINS.	CHART SYMBOLS	PROCESS DESCRIPTION
		●⇨☐D▽	Purchase order written in triplicate by supervisor
		○⇨☐D▽	On supervisor's desk (awaiting messenger)
75		○⇨☐D▽	By messenger to purchasing agent
		○⇨☐D▽	On purchasing agent's desk (awaiting approval)
		○⇨■D▽	Examined and approved by purchasing agent
		○⇨☐D▽	On purchasing agent's desk (awaiting transfer to main office)
		○⇨☐D▽	
75		1 1 1 3	Total

(b)

Feedback (Providing Information to the Operator). Feedback to operators is provided by *sight, sound,* and *feel.* Selection of feedback to operators should not be left to chance. Research regarding the proper displays for use under various conditions is available to the operations manager.[16] The second case at the end of the chapter discusses the problems of communicating to operators at the Three Mile Island nuclear facility. The case provides a perspective on just how important the proper design of dials and gauges to provide feedback to operators can be.

Methods Analysis. Methods analysis focuses on *how* a task is accomplished. Whether controlling a machine or making or assembling components, how a task is done makes a difference in performance, safety, and quality. Using knowledge from ergonomics and methods analysis, methods engineers are charged with ensuring that quality and quantity standards are achieved efficiently and safely. Methods analysis and related techniques are useful in office environments as well as in the factory. Methods techniques are used to analyze:

1. Movement of individuals or material. The analysis is performed using *flow diagrams* and *flow process charts* with varying amounts of detail.
2. Activity of human and machine and crew activity. This analysis is performed using *activity charts* (also known as man–machine charts and crew charts).
3. Body movement (primarily arms and hands). This analysis is performed using *micro-motion charts.*

Flow diagrams are schematics (drawings) used to investigate movement of

Flow diagrams

[16] Henry Dreyfuss, *The Measure of Man* (New York: Whitney Library of Design, 1960).

Process charts

people or material. They provide a systematic procedure for looking at long-cycle repetitive tasks (Figure 10.8a). **Process charts** use symbols [17] (Figure 10.8b) to help us understand the movement of people or material. In this way, movement and delays can be reduced and operations made more efficient. Figure 10.8b shows a process chart used to supplement the flow diagram shown in Figure 10.8a.

Activity charts

Activity charts are used to study and improve utilization of an operator and a machine or some combination of operators (a "crew") and machines. Through observation, the analyst records the present method and then on a second chart the proposed improvement. (See Figure 10.9.)

Operations chart

Body movement is analyzed by an **operations chart.** It is designed to show economy of motion by pointing out wasted motion and idle time (delay). The operations chart (also known as right-hand, left-hand chart) is shown in Figure 10.10 on page 441.

Motivation and Incentive Systems

Our discussion earlier in this chapter of Maslow's need structure and Herzberg's dual-factor theory provides insight into the psychological factors that may contrib-

FIGURE 10.9

Activity Chart.
(*Source:* Adapted from L. S. Aft, *Productivity Measurement and Improvement,* © 1983, p. 67. Reprinted by permission of Prentice-Hall, Inc., Englewood Cliffs, NJ.)

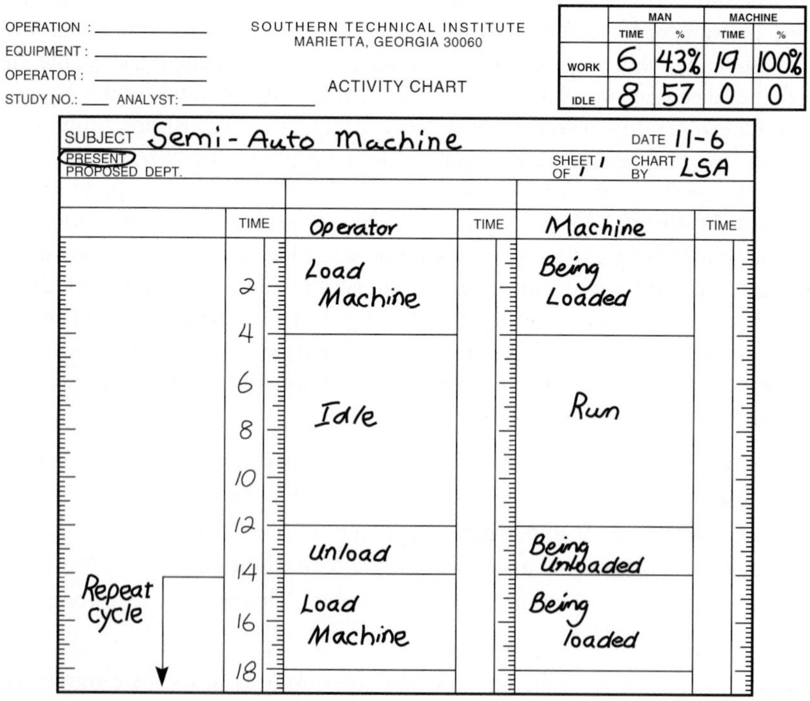

[17] The standard American Society of Mechanical Engineers (ASME) process symbols are ○ = operation; ⟁ = transportation, □ = inspection; D = delay; ▽ = storage.

FIGURE 10.10

Operation Chart (Left-Hand/Right-Hand Chart) for Bolt—Washer Assembly.
(*Source:* Adapted from L. S. Aft, *Productivity Measurement and Improvement*,
1983, p. 75. Reprinted by permission of Prentice-Hall, Inc., Englewood Cliffs, NJ.)

LEFT-HAND / RIGHT-HAND CHART
SOUTHERN TECHNICAL INSTITUTE
MARIETTA, GEORGIA 30060

PROCESS Bolt Washer Assembly
STUDY NO.
OPERATOR SRA
ANALYST
DATE 11/ 6 / 82   SHEET NO. 1 of 1
METHOD (PRESENT) PROPOSED)
REMARKS

SYMBOLS	PRESENT		PROPOSED		DIFFERENCE	
	LH	RH	LH	RH	LH	RH
○ OPERATIONS	5	10				
⇨ TRANSPORTATIONS						
☐ INSPECTIONS						
D DELAYS	10	5				
▽ STORAGES						
TOTALS	15	15				

LEFT-HAND ACTIVITY Present METHOD	DIST.	SYMBOLS	SYMBOLS	DIST.	RIGHT-HAND ACTIVITY Present METHOD
1 Reach for Bolt		●⇨☐D▽	○⇨☐■▽		Idle
2 Grasp Bolt		●⇨☐D▽	○⇨☐■▽		Idle
3 Move Bolt to Work		●⇨☐D▽	○⇨☐■▽		Idle
Area		○⇨☐D▽	○⇨☐D▽		
4 Hold Bolt		○⇨☐■▽	●⇨☐D▽		Reach for Washer
5 Hold Bolt		○⇨☐■▽	●⇨☐D▽		Grasp Washer
6 Hold Bolt		○⇨☐■▽	●⇨☐D▽		Move Washer to Bolt
7 Hold Bolt		○⇨☐■▽	●⇨☐D▽		Assemble Washer on
		○⇨☐D▽	○⇨☐D▽		Bolt

ute to job satisfaction and motivation. In addition to these psychological factors, there are monetary factors. Money often serves as a psychological as well as a financial motivator. Monetary rewards take the form of bonuses, gain sharing, and incentive systems.

Bonuses, typically in cash or stock options, are often used at executive levels to reward management. **Gain sharing** techniques reward employees for improvements made in an organization's performance. The most popular of these is the Scanlon plan, where any reduction in the cost of labor is shared between management and labor.[18] **Incentive systems** based on individual or group productivity are used in close to half of the manufacturing firms in America. These systems are often based on the employee or crew achieving production above a predetermined standard. The standard can be based on a standard time per task or number of pieces made. Standard time systems are sometimes called **measured daywork**, where employees are paid based on the amount of standard time accomplished. A **piece rate** system assigns a standard time for each piece, and the employee is paid based on the number of pieces made. Both systems typically guarantee the employee at least a base rate for the shift.

Bonus
Gain sharing

Incentive system

Measured daywork
Piece rate

WORLD-CLASS LEAN PRODUCTION

When human resource strategy has been properly implemented with good job design and effective manpower planning in an environment of mutual commitment and

---

[18] Fred G. Lesieur, and Elbridge S. Puckett, "The Scanlon Plan Has Proved Itself," *Harvard Business Review,* **47,** 5 (September–October 1969): 109–118.

Lean production   mutual trust, the result can be *lean production*. Under **lean production,** highly trained employees are committed to removing waste and doing only those activities where value is added. Employees analyze every detail of serving the customer and are increasingly successful in squeezing out waste. The concept of lean production varies substantially from a more traditional effort to make jobs ever more simple and require ever less training. Indeed, when effectively implemented, lean production utilizes the employee's *mental* as well as physical attributes to continually improve the production system. Because of a reasonable quality of work life and mutual trust, the employee buys into mutual commitment. In this way the production process is constantly improving and ever higher levels of efficiency are achieved. Under lean production the employee is not a robot; he or she is a full-fledged member of the organization who uses both mental and physical abilities to help serve the customer through ever higher levels of productivity.

LABOR STANDARDS

Labor plans require knowledge of the human resources required. Therefore, labor standards are established. *Labor standards* are the amount of time required to perform a job or part of a job. Every firm has labor standards, although they may vary from those established via informal methods to those established by professionals. Only when accurate labor standards exist can management know what its labor requirements are, what its costs should be, and what constitutes a fair day's work. Techniques for setting labor standards are presented in the supplement to this chapter.

SUMMARY

How well a firm manages its human resource strategy ultimately determines its success. The P/OM activity usually has a large role to play in achieving human resource objectives. The first objective is to achieve efficient use of human resources within the operations function. This is often a major goal of a firm because operations is usually the function with the highest labor cost, and labor is often a large part of the total cost of the product. The second objective is the design of jobs that are effective, safe, and provide a reasonable quality of work life for the employee in an atmosphere of mutual respect.

KEY TERMS

Quality of work life (p. 424)   Labor standards (p. 426)
Mutual commitment (p. 424)   Standard work schedule (p. 428)
Mutual trust (p. 424)   Flextime (p. 428)
Labor planning (p. 426)   Flexible work week (p. 428)
Job design (p. 426)   Part-time status (p. 428)

SOLVED PROBLEM

Solved Problem 10.1

As pit crew manager for *Prototype Sports Car,* you have just been given the pit stop rules for next season. You will be allowed only six people over the pit wall at any one time and one of these must be a designated *fire extinguisher/safety* crewman. This crewman must carry a fire extinguisher and may not service the car. However, the fire extinguisher/safety crewman may also signal the driver where to stop the car in the pit lane and when to leave the pit.

You expect to have air jacks on this year's car. These built-in jacks require the use of only an air hose to make them work. Fuel will also be supplied via a hose, with a second hose used for venting air from the fuel cells. The rate of flow for the fuel hose will be 1 gallon per second. The tank will hold 25 gallons. You expect to have to change all four tires on most pit stops. The length of the races will vary this year, but you expect that the longer races will also require the changing of drivers. Recent stop-watch

FIGURE 10.11

Position of Car and Six Crewmen.

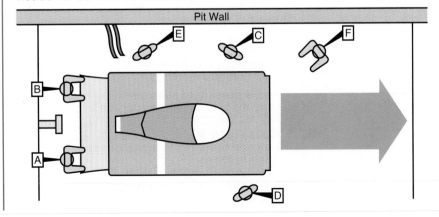

MULTIPLE ACTIVITY CHART

Chart No.:	Sheet No.:	Of:	S U M M A R Y		
PRODUCT:				PRESENT (min.)	PROPOSED	SAVING

	PRESENT (min.)	PROPOSED	SAVING
CYCLE TIME			
Man			
Machine			
WORKING			
Man			
Machine			
IDLE			
Man			
Machine			
UTILIZATION			
Man			
Machine			

PROCESS: Pit stop for GTO cars

MACHINE(S):

OPERATIVE: CLOCK NO.:

CHARTED BY: DATE:

CREW / NOTES

TIME (min.)

CREW — A, B, C, D, E, F

TIME (min.)	A	B	C	D	E	F
0.025	Remove tire	Install air hose / Remove tire	Remove tire	Remove tire	Move to car /hoses / Gas flows	Move to car /hoses
0.050						S
0.075						A
0.100		Remove tire				F
0.125						E
0.150	Mount new tire		Mount new tire	Mount new tire		T
0.175						Y
0.200						
0.225						C
0.250						R
0.275	Move to air jack hose	Mount new tire	Help driver	Wipe wind-shield		E
0.300						W
0.325						M
0.350		Move to rear			24.5 gal of gas	A
0.375						N
0.400	Idle	Idle			24.5 seconds	
0.425						
0.450			Idle	Idle		
0.475	Push	Push			Idle	Idle

NOTES

Fire Extinguisher/ Safety crewman F, goes over the pit wall to signal the driver where to stop the car.

Crewmen A, C, D, move to the car with tires.
B places the air jack hose in the connection at the rear of the car.
B then returns to pit wall for the fourth tire.
E moves to the car with two hoses (one for fuel & one to remove air).

F is ready with the fire extinguisher.
If the driver is to change, the first driver is out in the first five seconds.

If there is a driver change, the new driver enters the car.

A, C, D, have their tires mounted.
D wipes the windshield with towels from belt.
C helps the driver as necessary with seat belt & ice to cool suit.
A removes the air jack hose.

B has tire mounted.

B moves to the rear of the car.
A removes the air jack hose when B, C, and D signal their tires are mounted.

A and B prepare to push car.
E (fuel man) disconnects fuel lines.
F signals completion of fuel loading.

F moves to front of car on the pit side and prepares to signal driver when to leave.
A, B, C, and D, signal F when they are ready.

F signals driver when all is ready.
A and B push car out of pits.

studies have verified the following times for your experienced crew. These times are:

Activity	Time in Minutes
Install air hose	.075
Remove tire	.125
Mount new tire	.125
Move to air jack hose	.050
Move to rear of car	.050
Help driver	.175
Wipe windshield	.175
Load fuel (per gallon)	.016

Your job is to develop the initial plan for the best way to utilize your six-person pit crew. The six crewman are identified with letters, as shown in Figure 10.11 on page 443. You decide to use an activity chart similar to the one shown in Figure 10.9 to aid you.

Solution
Your activity chart showing each member of the crew what they are to do during each second of the pit stop is shown in the chart on page 444.

DISCUSSION QUESTIONS

1. What are some of the worst jobs you know about? Why are they bad jobs? Why do people want these jobs?

2. What factor would you add to, or delete from, Per Engelstad's six psychological factors given in the chapter?

3. If you were redesigning the job described in Question 1, what changes would you make? Are your changes realistic? Would they improve productivity (not just production, but productivity)?

4. How would you define a good "quality of work life"?

5. What is the difference between job enrichment, job enlargement, job rotation, and job specialization?

6. Do you know of any jobs that push the man-machine interface to the limits of human capabilities?

7. Why prepare flow diagrams and process charts for tasks that are poorly done?

8. What do Maslow's hierarchy of needs and Herzberg's dual-factor theory tell us about job design?

9. What are the major characteristics of a good job design?

PROBLEMS

· **10.1** Make a flow process chart for going from the living room to the kitchen for a glass, to the refrigerator for milk, and to a kitchen cabinet for cookies. Use a layout of your choosing. How can you make the task more efficient (that is, less time or fewer steps)?

· **10.2** Draw an activity chart for a machine operator with the following operation. The relevant times are:

Prepare mill for loading (cleaning, oiling, and so on)	.50 min.
Load mill	1.75 min.
Mill operating (cutting material)	2.25 min.
Unload mill	.75 min.

: **10.3** Draw an activity chart (a multiactivity chart) for a concert (for example, Phil Collins, Neil Diamond, Grateful Dead, Bruce Springsteen) and determine how to put the concert together so the star has reasonable breaks. For instance, at what point is there an instrumental number, a visual effect, a duet, a dance moment, that allows the star to pause and rest physically or at least rest his or her voice? Do other members of the show have moments of pause or rest?

· **10.4** Make an operations chart of one of the following:

    a) putting a new eraser in (or on) a pencil,

    b) putting a paper clip on two pieces of paper,

    c) putting paper in a typewriter.

· **10.5** Having made the operations chart in Problem 10.4 and now being told that you were going to do the task 10,000 times, how would you improve the procedure? Prepare an operations chart of the improved task. What motion, time, and effort have you saved over the life of the task by redesigning it?

· **10.6** For a job you have had, rate each of Englestad's psychological components on a scale from 1 to 10. What is your total score? What about the job could have been changed so you would be inclined to give it a higher score?

: **10.7** Using the data provided in Solved Problem 10.1, prepare an activity chart (a crew chart) similar to the one in the solved problem, but based on having a total of only five crew members.

: **10.8** Using the data provided in Solved Problem 10.1, prepare an activity chart similar to the one in the solved problem. However, fuel will now be delivered at the rate of $1\frac{1}{2}$ gallons per second.

CASE STUDY

The Fleet that Wanders

Bill Southard runs Southard Truck Lines. He recently purchased 10 new tractors for his operation from ARC Trucks. His relations with his drivers have historically been excellent, but they do not like the new tractors. The complaint is that the new tractors are hard to control on the highway; they "wander." When the drivers have a choice, they choose the older tractors. Mr. Southard, after numerous discussions with the drivers, concludes that the new tractors do indeed have a problem. They get much better gas mileage, should have lower maintenance costs, and have the latest antilock-

ing brakes. Since each tractor costs almost $50,000, Mr. Southard has a total investment of nearly $500,000 in the new fleet. He is trying to improve his fleet performance by reducing maintenance and fuel costs. This has not happened. Additionally, he wants to keep his drivers happy. This has not happened either. Consequently, he has a rather serious talk with the manufacturer of the trucks.

The manufacturer, ARC Trucks of Canyon, Texas, redesigned the front suspension for this model of tractor. The firm tells him the new front end is great. Bill Southard finds

CASE STUDY (Continued)

out, however, that there have been minor changes in some front suspension parts on the model since he purchased his trucks.

ARC Trucks refuses to make any changes in the tractors Mr. Southard purchased. No one has suggested there is a safety problem, but the drivers are adamant that they have to work harder to keep the new tractors on the road. Mr. Southard has new tractors that spend much of their time sitting in the yard while drivers use the old tractors. His costs, therefore, are higher than they should be. He is con-

sidering court action, but legal counsel suggests that he document his case.

Discussion Questions

1. What suggestions do you have for Mr. Southard?

2. Having been exposed to introductory material about ergonomics, can you imagine an analytical approach to documenting the problems reported by the drivers?

CASE STUDY

Human Factors at Three Mile Island

Prior to the mishap at Three Mile Island's Unit 2 (TMI-2), Lockheed Space and Missiles Corp. conducted a survey that found that very little human engineering was applied to existing control boards. The survey quotes the following comment from one designer as typical: "I have no pride of authorship in the layout of these boards. The client has to live with them. Nobody here cares that much. The Nuclear Regulatory Commission (NCR) is only interested in knowing whether or not there is a certain function covered on the boards—either in front or in back."

At TMI's Unit 2 the reactor drain tank indicators, which could have told the operators that the electromatic relief valve was leaking, were behind the control panel, and their significance was not recognized. The most repetitive phrase heard by the survey investigators during their interviews with panel designers was "client preference," a polite way of saying that the utilities got exactly what they ordered.

Lawrence Kanous of Detroit Edison had similar comments. "There is," he said, "little gut-level appreciation of the fact that plants are indeed man-machine systems. Insufficient attention is given," he asserted, "to the human side of such systems, since most designers are hardware-oriented."

One industry study divided the control panel problems into those that can be altered without changing the boards and those that will require completely new control boards.

The following improvements, the study indicated, can be made without physically changing the control boards:

1. Eliminate hunt-and-peck among a lot of controls by the use of clearly defined summary labels and taped lines of

demarcation.

2. Color-code the boards or use control handles of different shapes.

3. Attach color bands for different limit conditions to each meter and replace poorly marked meter scales.

4. Add additional chart recorders where those currently in use are overloaded and largely illegible.

5. Replace maintenance tags with lucite panels or magnetic markers, so they don't obscure controls.

Remaining Problems

Some flaws, the study said, cannot be changed without ripping out the old control boards. Since at the present time the industry has no plans to retrofit new boards, these problems will remain:

1. Nonfunctional grouping of controls and instruments.

2. Reversed-image duplications of control boards. This was apparently done to save costs in cutting different lengths of cable, but it violates a basic principle of human engineering to have two identical control boards mirror images of one another.

3. Inaccessible instruments. An operator sometimes has to stand on a chair to read a meter.

4. Inaccessible controls. To handle some emergency operations, an operator must run back and forth across the control room.

5. Unnecessarily large controls that increase panel size.

CASE STUDY (Continued)

6. Hundreds of confusing annunciator warnings during an accident. Warning lights went off at TMI-2 but it was impossible for the operators to tell which light belonged to which indicating instrument. This cannot be remedied without major rebuilding of the present control boards.

The exact sequence of events at Three Mile Island may never be repeated if only because pressurized water reactor operators by now have received simulator training for that precise sequence. But other accident scenarios are possible.

Discussion Questions

1. What might the designers of the control panel at Three Mile Island have done differently to improve feedback to the operators?

2. Who was responsible for the control panel design at Three Mile Island?

Source: Excerpted from Robert Sugarman, "Nuclear Power and the Public Risk," *IEEE Spectrum,* November 1979, pp. 63–66.

BIBLIOGRAPHY

Barnes, R. M. *Motion and Time Study, Design and Measurement of Work.* New York: John Wiley & Sons, 1968.

Chapman, A. *Man-Machine Engineering.* Belmont, CA: Wadsworth Publishing Co., 1965.

Corlett, N., J. Wilson, F. Manencia, eds. *Ergonomics of Working Posture.* New York: Taylor and Francis, 1986.

Davis, L. E., and J. C. Taylor, eds. *Design of Jobs.* Santa Monica, CA: Goodyear Publishing Co., 1979.

Dreyfuss, H. *The Measure of Man.* New York: Whitney Library of Design, 1970.

Gershoni, H. "Allowances for Heat Stress." Technion-Israel, Institute of Technology, Haifa, Israel, *Industrial Engineering* (September 1979): 20–24.

Hackman, J. R. "Work Redesign and Motivation." *Current Issues in Personnel Management.* Boston: Allyn & Bacon, 1986.

Konz, S. *Work Design.* Columbia, OH: Grid, Inc., 1979.

McCormick, E. J. *Human Factors in Engineering and Design,* 4th ed. New York: McGraw-Hill, 1976.

Nadler, G. *Work Design: The Systems Concept.* Homewood, IL: Richard D. Irwin, Inc., 1970.

Work Measurement

LABOR STANDARDS

Effective management of the labor resource requires knowledge of labor standards. Labor standards are necessary to determine the:

1. labor content of items produced (the labor cost);
2. staffing needs of organizations (how many people it will take to make the required production);
3. cost and time estimates prior to production (to assist in a variety of decisions from developing cost estimates for customers, to the make-or-buy decision);
4. crew size and work balance (who does what on a group activity or assembly line);
5. production expected (both manager and worker should know what constitutes a fair day's work);
6. basis of wage-incentive plans (what provides a reasonable incentive);
7. efficiency of employees and supervision (a standard is necessary against which to determine efficiency).

Properly set labor standards represent the amount of time it should take an average employee to perform specific job activities under normal working conditions. The *POM in Action* box, "Lincoln Electric's Incentive Pay System," indicates an incentive system application of effective labor standards.

How are labor, or production, standards set? Labor standards are set four ways:

1. historical experience;
2. time studies;
3. predetermined time standards;
4. work sampling.

This supplement covers each of these techniques.

HISTORICAL EXPERIENCE

Historical experience

Labor standards can be estimated based on **historical experience,** that is, how many labor-hours were required to do a task the last time it was performed. Historical standards have the distinct advantage of being relatively easy and inexpensive to obtain. They are usually available from employee time cards or production records. But they are not objective. And we do not know their accuracy. Do they represent a reasonable work pace or a poor work pace? Are unusual occurrences included? Because these variables are unknown, their use is not recommended. Instead, we will stress the three work-measurement methods that are preferred to set production standards.

TIME STUDIES

Time study

The classical stopwatch study, or time study, originally proposed by Frederick W. Taylor in 1881, is still the most widely used time-study method. A **time-study** procedure involves timing a sample of a worker's performance and using it to set a

POM *in action*

Lincoln Electric's Incentive Pay System

Lincoln Electric was founded by John C. Lincoln in 1895 to make an electric motor he had developed. When his brother James joined the organization in 1907, they began emphasizing employee motivation, and since that time, the company has endorsed the message that the business must prosper if employees are to benefit.

The company has encouraged workers to own a stake in its property by allowing employees to buy stock at book value. (The employees are required to sell the stock at book value when they leave.) Approximately 70% of the employees own stock, and together they hold nearly 50% of the outstanding shares. Most of the remaining stock in the maker of motors and welding equipment is held by members of the Lincoln family who are not involved in company operations.

The company calls "the low cost of high wages" its incentive-pay system. Each employee inspects his or her own parts and must correct any imperfect work on personal time. Each is responsible for the quality of his or her own work. Records are maintained reflecting who worked on each piece of equipment. Should inferior work slip by and be discovered by Lincoln's quality control people or by customers, the worker's merit rating, bonus, and pay are lowered.

However, some employees feel the system can cause some unfriendly competition as well. Since a certain number of merit points is allotted to each department, an exceptionally high rating for one person may mean a lower rating for another.

Lincoln is now one of the leading makers of arc-welding equipment and its success has encouraged several major companies to leave the industry, while others have sought more specialized market niches. Customers are delighted with the company's quality. One purchasing agent who buys $1.8 million of Lincoln's welding equipment a year says, "I don't ever remember having one problem with quality from Lincoln."

Sources: The Wall Street Journal, August 12, 1983, p. 23; and *HR Magazine,* November 1990, pp. 73–76.

standard. A trained and experienced person can establish a standard by following these eight steps:

1. Define the task to be studied (after methods analysis has been conducted).
2. Break down the task into precise elements (parts of a task that often take no more than a few seconds).
3. Decide how many times to measure the task (the number of cycles or samples needed).
4. Time and record the elemental times and ratings of performance.
5. Compute the average actual cycle time. The **average actual cycle time** is the arithmetic mean of the times for *each* element measured, adjusted for unusual influences for each element:

$$\text{Average actual cycle time} = \frac{\text{Sum of the times recorded to perform each element}}{\text{Number of cycles observed}} \qquad \text{(S10.1)}$$

Average actual cycle time

6. Compute the **normal time** for each element. This measure is a "performance rating" for the particular worker pace observed:

$$\text{Normal time} = (\text{Average actual cycle time}) \times (\text{Rating factor}) \qquad \text{(S10.2)}$$

Normal time

The performance rating adjusts the observed time to what a normal worker could expect to accomplish. For example, a normal worker should be able to walk three miles per hour. He or she should also be able to deal a deck of 52 cards into four equal piles in 30 seconds. There are numerous films specifying work pace on which professionals agree; and activity bench marks have been established by the Society for the Advancement of Management. However, performance rating is still something of an art.

7. Sum the normal times for each element to develop a total normal time for the task.

Standard time

8. Compute the **standard time.** This adjustment to the total normal time provides for allowances such as *personal* needs, unavoidable work *delays,* and worker *fatigue:*

$$\text{Standard time} = \frac{\text{Total normal time}}{1 - \text{Allowance factor}} \qquad (S10.3)$$

Personal time allowances are often established in the range of 4% to 7% of total time, depending upon nearness to restrooms, water fountains, and other facilities. Delay standards are often set as a result of the actual studies of the delay that occurs. Fatigue standards are based on our growing knowledge of human energy expendi-

FIGURE S10.1

Rest Allowances (in percentage) for Various Classes of Work.
(*Source:* Excerpted from B. W. Niebel, *Motion and Time Study,* 7th ed. (Homewood, IL: Richard D. Irwin, 1982) p. 393. Copyright © 1982 by Richard D. Irwin, Inc.)

1. Constant allowances:

   a) Personal allowance 5
   b) Basic fatigue allowance 4

2. Variable allowances:

  A) Standing allowance 2

  B) Abnormal position allowance:

    a) Slightly awkward 0
    b) Awkward (bending) 2
    c) Very awkward (lying, stretching) 7

  C) Use of force, or muscular energy in lifting, pulling, pushing
    Weight lifted (pounds):

    10 1
    20 3
    30 5
    40 9
    50 13
    60 17

  D) Bad light:
    a) Slightly below recommended 0
    b) Well below 2
    c) Quite inadequate 5

  E) Atmospheric conditions (heat and humidity):
    Variable 0–10

  F) Close attention:
    a) Fairly fine work 0
    b) Fine or exacting 2
    c) Very fine or very exacting 5

  G) Noise level:
    a) Continuous 0
    b) Intermittent—loud 2
    c) Intermittent—very loud or high-pitched . 5

  H) Mental strain:
    a) Fairly complex process 1
    b) Complex or wide span of attention . . . 4
    c) Very complex 8

  I) Tediousness:
    a) Rather tedious 0
    b) Tedious 2
    c) Very tedious 5

ture[1] under various physical and environmental conditions. A sample set of personal and fatigue allowances is shown in Figure S10.1 on page 452.

Example S1

The time study of a work operation yielded an average actual cycle time of 4.0 minutes. The analyst rated the observed worker at 85%. This means the worker performed at 85% of normal when the study was made. The firm uses a 13% allowance factor. We want to compute the standard time.

$$\text{Average actual time} = 4.0 \text{ min.}$$

$$\text{Normal time} = (\text{Average actual cycle time}) \times (\text{Rating factor})$$

$$= (4.0)(.85)$$

$$= 3.4 \text{ min.}$$

$$\text{Standard time} = \frac{\text{Normal time}}{1 - \text{Allowance factor}} = \frac{3.4}{1 - .13} = \frac{3.4}{.87}$$

$$= 3.9 \text{ min.}$$

Let us now look at an example in which we are given a series of actual stopwatch times for each element.

Example S2

Management Science Associates promotes its management development seminars by mailing thousands of individually typed letters to various firms. A time study has been done on the task of preparing letters for mailing. On the basis of the observations below, Management Science Associates wants to develop a time standard for the task. The firm's personal, delay, and fatigue allowance factor is 15%.

The procedure after the data have been collected is as follows:

JOB ELEMENT	CYCLE OBSERVED (IN MINUTES)					PERFORMANCE RATING
	1	*2*	*3*	*4*	*5*	
(A) Type letter	8	10	9	21*	11	120%
(B) Type envelope address	2	3	2	1	3	105%
(C) Stuff, stamp, seal, and sort envelopes	2	1	5*	2	1	110%

1. Delete all unusual or nonrecurring observations such as those marked with an asterisk (*). (They might be due to an unscheduled business interruption, a conference with the boss, or a mistake of an unusual nature; these are not part of the job.)

---

[1] Ernest J. McCormick, *Human Factors in Engineering and Design* (New York: McGraw-Hill, 1976), pp. 171–178. Also see: Haim Gershoni, "Allowances for Heat Stress," *Industrial Engineering* (September 1979): 20–24.

Sleep Inn is showing the world that big gains in productivity can be made not only by manufacturers, but in the service industry as well. Designed with labor efficiency in mind, Sleep Inn is staffed with 13% fewer employees than similar budget hotels. Its features include a laundry room that is almost completely automated, round shower stalls that eliminate dirty corners, and closets that have no doors for maids to open and shut.

2. Compute the average cycle time for each job element:

$$\text{Average time for A} = \frac{8 + 10 + 9 + 11}{4}$$
$$= 9.5 \text{ min.}$$

$$\text{Average time for B} = \frac{2 + 3 + 2 + 1 + 3}{5}$$
$$= 2.2 \text{ min.}$$

$$\text{Average time for C} = \frac{2 + 1 + 2 + 1}{4}$$
$$= 1.5 \text{ min.}$$

3. Compute the normal time for each job element:

$$\text{Normal time for A} = (\text{Average actual time}) \times (\text{Rating})$$
$$= (9.5)(1.2)$$
$$= 11.4 \text{ min.}$$
$$\text{Normal time for B} = (2.2)(1.05)$$
$$= 2.31 \text{ min.}$$
$$\text{Normal time for C} = (1.5)(1.10)$$
$$= 1.65 \text{ min.}$$

Normal times are computed for each element because the rating factor may vary for each element, which it did in this case.

4. Add the normal times for each element to find the total normal time (the normal time for the whole job):

$$\text{Total normal time} = 11.40 + 2.31 + 1.65$$
$$= 15.36 \text{ min.}$$

5. Compute the standard time for the job:

$$\text{Standard time} = \frac{\text{Total normal time}}{1 - \text{allowance factor}} = \frac{15.36}{1 - .15}$$
$$= 18.07 \text{ min.}$$

Thus, 18.07 minutes is the time standard for this job.

Time study is a sampling process, and the question of sampling error in the average actual cycle time naturally arises. Error, according to statistics, varies inversely with sample size. In order to determine just how many cycles should be timed, consideration of the variability of each element in the study is necessary.

The easiest means of finding the necessary sample size is to use standard charts such as the one in Figure S10.2 on page 455. Such charts help estimate sample sizes that offer the user 95% or 99% confidence that the sample average cycle time will be within 5% of the true average. To use the chart, we follow four steps:

1. Compute the average cycle time, $\overline{X}$.

2. Find the standard deviation, s, based on the sample data:

$$s = \sqrt{\frac{\Sigma \, (\text{Each sample observation} - \overline{X})^2}{\text{Number in sample} - 1}} \tag{S10.4}$$

FIGURE S10.2

Chart for Estimating Sample Size with ±5% Accuracy for Given Coefficient of Variation Values.
(*Source:* A. Abruzzi, *Work Measurement* (New York: Columbia University Press, 1952), p. 161. Copyright © 1952 by Columbia University Press. Used by permission of the publisher.)

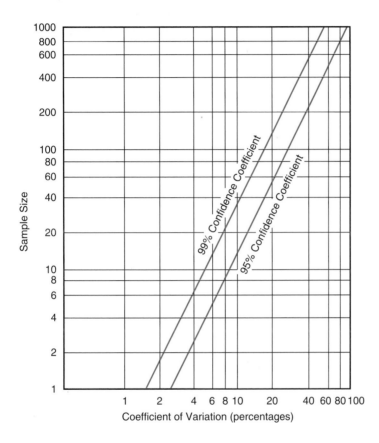

3. Compute the coefficient of variation, which is just the standard deviation divided by the mean, that is,

$$\text{Coefficient of variation} = \frac{s}{\overline{X}} \qquad (S10.5)$$

4. Find the appropriate coefficient of variation on the horizontal axis in Figure S10.2, proceed up to the curve that gives the desired confidence coefficient, and then read the sample size on the left-hand scale.

Example S3

A sample of 12 cycles taken in a study resulted in an average cycle time of 2.80 minutes with a standard deviation of .56 minute. In order to be 95% confident that the resultant standard time is within 5% of the true average, we need to know whether this sample size of 12 observations is large enough. To find the answer we compute the coefficient of variation:

$$\frac{s}{\overline{X}} = \frac{.56}{2.80}$$

$$= .20$$

Turning to Figure S10.2 for a coefficient of variation of 20%, we see that the required sample size is about 60 cycles. Thus, the sample of 12 cycles is not large enough, and the observation process should continue.

Time studies provide accuracy in setting labor standards, but they have two disadvantages. First, they require a trained staff of analysts. Second, labor standards cannot be set before the task is actually performed. This leads us to two alternative work measurement techniques.

PREDETERMINED TIME STANDARDS

Predetermined time standards

A third way to set production standards is to use predetermined time standards. **Predetermined time standards** divide manual work into small basic elements that have established times (based on very large samples of workers). To estimate the time for a particular task, the time factors for each basic element of that task are added together. For any given firm to develop a comprehensive system of predetermined time standards would be prohibitively expensive. Consequently, a number of systems are commercially available. Among these are MTM and CSD. The most common predetermined time standard is *methods time measurement* (MTM), which is a product of the MTM Association.[2] CSD (computerized standard data) is a product of Rath and Strong, a management consulting firm. Predetermined time standards are an outgrowth of basic motions called therbligs. The term *therblig* was coined by Frank Gilbreth (*Gilbreth* spelled backwards with the *t* and *h* reversed). Therbligs include activities such as select, grasp, position, assemble, reach, hold, rest, and inspect. These activities are stated in terms of time measurement units (TMUs), which are each equal to only .00001 hour or .0006 minute. MTM values for various therbligs are specified in very detailed tables. Figure S10.3 on page 457 provides, as an example, the set of time standards for the motion REACH. Note that reaching 4 inches for a part will have a very different TMU from reaching 12 inches.

[2] MTM is really a family of products available from the Methods Time Measure Association. The products include MTM-1, MTM-2, and MTM-3. Each of these provides varying degrees of precision. MTM-1 is typically recommended for cycle times up to one minute, MTM-2 for cycle times between one and four minutes, and MTM-3 for cycle times over four minutes. Also available is 4M, a computer-based system for creating and maintaining labor standards based on MTM-1 data. All MTM systems are based on original research, and many of these serve specific groups of activities. For example, MTM-HC deals with the health care industry, MTM-C handles clerical activities, MTM-M involves microscope activities, MTM-V deals with machine shop tasks, and so on. There are MTM Associations in the United States and in twelve other countries. MTM-UAS, used in setting laboratory standards, was developed by the German MTM Association.

FIGURE S10.3

Methods Time Measurement Data for REACH Motion.

DISTANCE MOVED INCHES	TIME TMU				HAND IN MOTION	
	A	B	C or D	E	A	B
¾ or less	2.0	2.0	2.0	2.0	1.6	1.6
1	2.5	2.5	3.6	2.4	2.3	2.3
2	4.0	4.0	5.9	3.8	3.5	2.7
3	5.3	5.3	7.3	5.3	4.5	3.6
4	6.1	6.4	8.4	6.8	4.9	4.3
5	6.5	7.8	9.4	7.4	5.3	5.0
6	7.0	8.6	10.1	8.0	5.7	5.7
7	7.4	9.3	10.8	8.7	6.1	6.5
8	7.9	10.1	11.5	9.3	6.5	7.2
9	8.3	10.8	12.2	9.9	6.9	7.9
10	8.7	11.5	12.9	10.5	7.3	8.6
12	9.6	12.9	14.2	11.8	8.1	10.1
14	10.5	14.4	15.6	13.0	8.9	11.5
16	11.4	15.8	17.0	14.2	9.7	12.9
18	12.3	17.2	18.4	15.5	10.5	14.4
20	13.1	18.6	19.8	16.7	11.3	15.8

Case and Description
A Reach to object in fixed location, or to object in other hand or on which other hand rests.
B Reach to single object in location that may vary slightly from cycle to cycle.
C Reach to object jumbled with other objects in a group so that search and select occur.
D Reach to a very small object or where accurate grasp is required.
E Reach to indefinite location to get hand in position for body balance or next motion or out of way.

Source: Copyrighted by the MTM Association for Standards and Research. No reprint permission without written consent from the MTM Association, 16–01 Broadway, Fair Lawn, NJ, 07410.

Example S4

Riveting a transistor board in an assembly process is assigned an MTM value of 70.0 TMU, based on industry data standards. Before riveting, a worker must reach 16 inches for a small part (17.0 TMU), grasp the part (9.1 TMU), move the part to the assembly (27.0 TMU), and position the transistor (32.3 TMU).

This very small task, which consists of five elements, takes a total of 155.4 TMU (17.0 + 9.1 + 27.0 + 32.3 + 70.0). Translating into minutes involves multiplying 155.4 TMU × .0006 minute = .0932 minute = 5.6 seconds.

Predetermined time standards have several advantages relative to direct time studies. First, they may be established in a laboratory environment, which will not upset production activities (which time studies tend to do). Second, the standard can be set before a task is done and can be used for planning. In addition, no performance ratings are necessary—and the method is widely accepted by unions as a fair means of setting standards. Predetermined time standards are particularly effective in firms that do substantial numbers of studies where the tasks are similar. Some firms use both time studies and predetermined time standards to ensure accurate labor standards.

Examples from the Service Sector

MTM's health care and clerical (MTM-HC and MTM-C) standards have extended the use of predetermined time standards to help set *service* labor standards. Figure S10.4 provides the set of time standards for the motion GET and PLACE. To use GET and PLACE (which is the most complex in the MTM system), one needs to know what is "gotten," its approximate weight, and where and how far it is placed. Two service sector illustrations will help clarify this concept.

Example S5

Pouring a tube specimen in a hospital lab is a repetitive task for which the MTM data in Figure S10.4 may be used to develop standard times. The sample tube is in a rack, and the centrifuge tubes are in a nearby box. A technician removes the sample tube from the rack, uncaps it, gets the centrifuge tube, pours, and places both tubes in the rack.

The first work element involves getting the tube from the rack. Suppose the conditions for GETTING the tube and PLACING it in front of the technician are

- weight (less than 2 pounds)
- conditions of GET (easy)
- place accuracy (approximate)
- distance range (8 to 20 inches)

Then the MTM element for this activity is AA2 (as seen from Figure S10.4). The rest of Table S10.1 is developed from similar MTM tables.

TABLE S10.1 MTM-HC Analysis: Pouring Tube Specimen.

ELEMENT DESCRIPTION	ELEMENT	TIME	FREQUENCY	TOTAL
Get tube from rack	AA2	35	1	35
Get stopper, place on counter	AA2	35	1	35
Get centrifuge tube, place at sample tube	AD2	45	1	45
Pour (3 seconds)	PT	1	83	83
Place tubes in rack (simo)	PC2	40	1	40
			Total TMU	238

.0006 × 238 = Total Standard minutes = .14

Source: A. S. Helms, B. W. Shaw, and C. A. Lindner, "The Development of Laboratory Workload Standards through Computer-Based Work Measurement Technique, Part I," *Journal of Methods-Time Measurement,* **12,** p. 43. Used with permission of MTM Association for Standards and Research.

FIGURE S10.4

Sample MTM Table for GET and PLACE Motions.
(*Source:* Copyrighted by the MTM Association for Standards and Research.
No reprint permission without consent from the MTM Association, 16-01
Broadway, Fair Lawn, N.J., 07410.)

MTM® ASSOCIATION	UNIVERSAL ANALYZING SYSTEM	UAS

JANUARY 1984	IF TRAINING IN MTM AND UAS IS LACKING, USAGE OF THIS TABLE LEADS TO WRONG RESULTS	TIME UNITS			
		TMU	SEC	MIN	HRS
		1	0.036	0.0006	0.00001

TIME VALUES IN TMU

GET AND PLACE			DISTANCE RANGE IN IN.	<8	>8 <20	>20 <32
WEIGHT	CONDITIONS OF GET	PLACE ACCURACY	CODE	1	2	3
<2 LBS	EASY	APPROXIMATE	AA	20	35	50
		LOOSE	AB	30	45	60
		TIGHT	AC	40	55	70
	DIFFICULT	APPROXIMATE	AD	20	45	60
		LOOSE	AE	30	55	70
		TIGHT	AF	40	65	80
	HANDFUL	APPROXIMATE	AG	40	65	80
>2 LBS <18 LBS		APPROXIMATE	AH	25	45	55
		LOOSE	AJ	40	65	75
		TIGHT	AK	50	75	85˙
>18 LBS <45 LBS		APPROXIMATE	AL	90	106	115
		LOOSE	AM	95	120	130
		TIGHT	AN	120	145	160

PLACE	CODE	1	2	3
APPROXIMATE	PA	10	20	25
LOOSE	PB	20	30	35
TIGHT	PC	30	40	45

© MTM ASSOCIATION COPYRIGHT 1984

Most MTM calculations, by the way, are computerized, so the user need only key in the appropriate MTM codes, such as AA2 in Example S5.

WORK SAMPLING

Work sampling

The fourth method of developing labor or production standards, work sampling, was developed by an Englishman, L. Tippet, in the 1930s. **Work sampling** estimates the percent of the time that a worker spends working on various tasks. The method involves random observations to record the activity that the worker is performing.

Work sampling is used in:

1. *Ratio delay studies.* These estimate the percentage of time employees spend in unavoidable delays. The results are used to investigate work methods, to estimate activity costs, and to set allowances in labor standards.
2. *Setting labor standards.* For setting standard task times, the observer must be experienced enough to rate the worker's performance.
3. *Measuring worker performance.* Sampling can develop a performance index for workers for periodic evaluations.

The work-sampling procedure can be summarized in seven steps:

1. Take a preliminary sample to obtain an estimate of the parameter value (such as percent of time a worker is busy).
2. Compute the sample size required.
3. Prepare a schedule for observing the worker at appropriate times. The concept of random numbers (discussed in the supplement to Chapter 5) is used to provide for random observation.
4. Observe and record worker activities; rate the worker's performance.
5. Record the number of units produced during the applicable portion of the study.
6. Compute the normal time per part.
7. Compute the standard time per part.

To determine the number of observations required, management must make a statement about the desired confidence level and accuracy. But first the work analyst must select a preliminary value of the parameter under study (step 1 above). The choice is usually based on a small sample of perhaps 50 observations. The following formula then gives the sample size for a desired confidence and accuracy:

$$n = \frac{Z^2 \, p(1-p)}{h^2} \qquad \text{(S10.6)}$$

where

n = Required sample size

Z = Standard normal deviate for the desired confidence level ($Z = 1$ for 68% confidence, $Z = 2$ for 95.45% confidence, and $Z = 3$ for 99.7% confidence—these values are obtained from the normal table in Appendix A)

p = Estimated value of sample proportion (of time worker is observed busy or idle)

h = Accuracy level desired, in percent

POM *in action*

Computer Monitoring at AT&T, Giant Foods, and Northwest Orient

Taylor's stopwatch approach gave management the capacity to assess each worker's productivity. But today's computerized time-and-motion studies have far surpassed Taylor in allowing minute analysis of an individual's output.

Although opposed by unions, the use of computer monitoring has spread quickly in the past few years, as indicated by the applications below:

- A huge computer system is utilized at AT&T Communications to monitor each telephone operator's "average work time" or AWT. AWT is the time consumed on each call and has been set at 30 seconds. Should an operator continually take longer than most co-workers, discipline or dismissal is a possibility.
- Optical scanners at Giant Food Stores are used to read the codes on each item at the checkout counters. This procedure provides inventory control, quicker checkout, and also monitors the cashier's speed. The food items and dollar rung by each cashier and the number of customers served is recorded on the printout, which Giant posts in the workplace.
- At Northwest Orient Airlines, data entry workers are expected to type between 9,000 and 16,000 keystrokes per hour as they feed payroll and ticketing information into company computers. The computer keeps track of speed, and while slower typists can be penalized by losing pay, fast workers are rewarded with flexibility in arranging their schedules. A speed at least 75% as fast as the three fastest workers must be maintained by all workers, or they can be dismissed.

Sources: The Washington Post, September 2, 1984, p. A-18; and Computerworld, January 6, 1992, p. 21.

Example S6

The head of a large typing pool estimates that the typists are idle 25% of the time. The supervisor would like to take a work sample that would be accurate within 3% and wants to have 95.45% confidence in the results.

In order to determine how many observations should be taken, the supervisor applies the equation:

$$n = \frac{Z^2 \, p(1-p)}{h^2}$$

where

n = Sample size required

Z = 2 for 95.45% confidence level

p = Estimate of idle proportion = 25% = .25

h = Accuracy desired of 3% = .03

It is found that:

$$n = \frac{(2)^2(.25)(.75)}{(.03)^2} = 833 \text{ observations}$$

Thus, 833 observations should be taken. If the percent idle time noted is not close to 25% as the study progresses, then the number of observations may have to be recalculated and increased or decreased as appropriate.

Work sampling is used to set labor standards in a fashion similar to that used in time studies. The analyst, however, simply records whether a worker is busy or idle during the observation. After all the observations have been recorded, the worker rated, and the units produced counted (steps 4 and 5), we can determine the normal time by the formula:

$$\text{Normal time} = \frac{\left(\begin{array}{c}\text{Total study}\\\text{time}\end{array}\right) \times \left(\begin{array}{c}\text{Percent of time employee}\\\text{observed working}\end{array}\right) \times \left(\begin{array}{c}\text{Performance}\\\text{rating factor}\end{array}\right)}{\text{Number of pieces produced}}$$

The standard time is the normal time adjusted by the allowance factor, computed as:

$$\text{Standard time} = \frac{\text{Normal time}}{1 - \text{Allowance factor}}$$

Example S7

A work-sample study conducted over the 80 hours (or 4,800 minutes) of a two-week period yielded the following data. The number of parts produced was 225 by an operator who was performance-rated at 100%. The operator's idle time was 20%, and the total allowance given by the company for this task is 25%.

$$\text{Normal time} = \frac{\left(\begin{array}{c}\text{Total}\\\text{time}\end{array}\right) \times \left(\begin{array}{c}\text{Percent of time}\\\text{working}\end{array}\right) \times \left(\begin{array}{c}\text{Rating}\\\text{factor}\end{array}\right)}{\text{Number of units completed}}$$

$$= \frac{(4,800 \text{ min.})(.80)(1.00)}{225} = 17.07 \text{ min./part}$$

$$\text{Standard time} = \frac{\text{Normal time}}{1 - \text{Allowance factor}}$$

$$= \frac{17.07}{1 - .25} = 22.76 \text{ min./part}$$

Work sampling offers several advantages over time study methods. First, it is less expensive, since a single observer can observe several workers simultaneously. Second, observers usually don't require much training, and no timing devices are needed. Third, the study can be delayed temporarily at any time with little impact on the results. And fourth, because work sampling uses instantaneous observations over a long period, the worker has little chance of affecting the study's outcome.

The disadvantages of work sampling are: (1) it does not break down work elements as completely as time studies, (2) it can yield biased or incorrect results if the observer does not follow random routes of travel and observation, and (3) it is less effective than time studies when cycle times are short.

SUMMARY

Labor standards are required for an efficient operations system. They are needed for production planning, labor planning, costing, and evaluating performance. They can also be used as a basis for incentive systems. They are used in both the factory and the office. Standards may be established via historical data, time studies, predetermined time standards, and work sampling.

KEY TERMS

Historical experience (p. 450)   Standard time (p. 452)
Time study (p. 450)   Predetermined time standards (p. 456)
Average actual cycle time (p. 451)   Work sampling (p. 460)
Normal time (p. 451)

SOLVED PROBLEMS

Solved Problem S10.1

A work operation consisting of three elements has been subjected to a stopwatch time study. The observations recorded are shown below. By union contract, the allowance time for the operation is personal time 5%, delay 5%, and fatigue 10%. Determine the standard time for the work operation.

JOB ELEMENT	CYCLE OBSERVATION5 (IN MINUTES)						PERFORMANCE RATING
	1	2	3	4	5	6	
A	.1	.3	.2	.9	.2	.1	90%
B	.8	.6	.8	.5	3.2	.7	110%
C	.5	.5	.4	.5	.6	.5	80%

Solution

First, delete the two observations that appear to be very unusual (.9 minutes for job element A and 3.2 minutes for job element B). Then,

$$\text{A's average cycle time} = \frac{.1 + .3 + .2 + .2 + .1}{5} = .18 \text{ min.}$$

$$\text{B's average cycle time} = \frac{.8 + .6 + .8 + .5 + .7}{5} = .68 \text{ min.}$$

$$\text{C's average cycle time} = \frac{.5 + .5 + .4 + .5 + .6 + .5}{6} = .50 \text{ min.}$$

A's normal time = (.18)(.90)   = .16 min

B's normal time = (.68)(1.10)   = .75 min

C's normal time = (.50)(.80)   = .40 min

Normal time for job = .16 + .75 + .40 = 1.31 min.

$$\text{Standard time} = \frac{1.31}{1 - .20} = 1.64 \text{ min.}$$

Solved Problem S10.2

A preliminary work sample of an operation indicates the following:

Number of times operator working	60
Number of times operator idle	40
Total number of preliminary observations	100

What is the required sample size for a 99.7% confidence level with ±4% precision?

Solution

$$n = \frac{Z^2 p(1-p)}{h^2} = \frac{(3)^2(.6)(.4)}{(.04)^2} = 1{,}350 \text{ sample size}$$

Solved Problem S10.3

Each printed circuit board at Maggard Micro Manufacturing, Inc. (3M), has a semiconductor pressed into predrilled slots. The elemental motions for normal time used by 3M are:

Reach 6 inches for semiconductor	10.5 TMU
Grasp the semiconductor	8.0 TMU
Move semiconductor to printed circuit board	9.5 TMU
Position semiconductor	20.1 TMU
Press semiconductor into slots	20.3 TMU
Move board aside	15.8 TMU

(Each time measurement unit is equal to .0006 min.) Determine the normal time for this operation in minutes and in seconds.

Solution

Add the time measurement units together:

$$10.5 + 8.0 + 9.5 + 20.1 + 20.3 + 15.8 = 84.2$$

Time in minutes = (84.2)(.0006 min.) = .05052 min.

Time in seconds = (.05052)(60 sec.) = 3.0312 sec.

Solved Problem S10.4

To obtain the random sample needed for work sampling, a manager divides a typical workday into 480 minutes. Using a random-number table to decide what time to go to an area to sample work occurrences, the manager records observations on a tally sheet such as the one that follows.

STATUS	TALLY	FREQUENCY
Productively working	⦀⦀ ⦀⦀ ⦀⦀ |	16
Idle	||||	4

Solution

In this case, the supervisor made 20 observations and found that employees were working 80% of the time. So, out of 480 minutes in an office workday, 20%, or 96 minutes, was idle time, and 356 minutes was productive. Note that this procedure describes what a worker *is* doing, not necessarily what he or she *should* be doing.

DISCUSSION QUESTIONS

1. Why do operations managers require labor standards?

2. How do we establish a fair day's work?

3. Is a "normal" pace the same thing as a 100% pace?

4. What is the difference between "normal" and "standard" time?

5. What kind of work pace would you expect from an employee during a time study? Why?

6. As a new time study engineer in your plant, you are engaged in studying an employee operating a drill press. Somewhat to your surprise, one of the first things you notice is that the drill press operator is doing a lot of operations besides just drilling holes. Your problem is what to include in your time study. From the following examples, indicate how, as the individual responsible for labor standards in your plant, you would handle them.

  a) Every so often, perhaps every 50th unit or so, the drill press operator takes an extra-long look at the piece, which apparently is misshaped, and then typically throws it in the scrap barrel.

  b) Approximately 1 out of 100 units has a rough edge and will not fit in the jig properly; therefore, the drill press operator picks up the piece, hits the lower right-hand edge with a file a few times, puts the file down, and returns to normal operation.

  c) About every hour or so, the drill press operator stops to change the drill in the machine, even if he is in the middle of a job. (We can assume that the drill has become dull.)

  d) Between every job and sometimes in the middle of jobs, the drill press operator turns off the machine and goes for stock.

  e) The drill press operator is idle for a few minutes at the beginning of every job waiting for the setup man to complete the setup. Some of the setup time is used in going for stock, but the drill press operator typically returns with stock before the setup man is finished with the setup.

  f) The operator stops to talk to you.

  g) The operator lights up a cigarette.

  h) The operator opens his lunch pail (it is not lunch time), removes an apple, and takes an occasional bite.

  i) The operator drops a part, and you pick it up and hand it to him. Does this make any difference in the time study? How?

PROBLEMS

· **S10.1** An analyst clocked the cycle time for welding a part onto truck doors at 5.3 minutes. The performance rating of the worker timed was estimated at 105%. Find the normal time for this operation.

According to a local union contract, each welder is allowed three minutes of personal time per hour and two minutes of fatigue time per hour. Further, it is estimated that there should be an average delay allowance of one minute per hour. Compute the allowance factor, and then find the standard time for this welding activity.

: **S10.2** A time study of a factory worker revealed an average cycle time of 3.20 minutes, with a standard deviation of 1.28 minutes. These figures were based on a sample of 45 cycles observed.

Is this sample adequate in size for the firm to be 99% confident that the standard time is within 5% of the true value? If not, what should the proper number of observations be? (Refer to Figure S10.2).

: **S10.3** The data in the following table represent time-study observations for a metalworking process. On the basis of these observations, find the standard time for the process, assuming a 25% allowance factor.

ELEMENT	PERFORMANCE RATING	OBSERVATIONS (MINUTES PER CYCLE)						
		1	2	3	4	5	6	7
1	90%	1.80	1.70	1.66	1.91	1.85	1.77	1.60
2	100%	6.9	7.3	6.8	7.1	15.3*	7.0	6.4
3	115%	3.0	9.0*	9.5*	3.8	2.9	3.1	3.2
4	90%	10.1	11.1	12.3	9.9	12.0	11.9	12.0

* Disregard—unusual observation.

: **S10.4** Based on a careful work study in the Smith and Johnson Company, the results shown in the table below are observed:

ELEMENT	CYCLE (IN MINUTES					PERFORMANCE RATING
	1	2	3	4	5	
Prepare daily reports	35	40	33	42	39	120%
Photocopy results	12	10	36*	15	13	110%
Label and package reports	3	3	5	5	4	90%
Distribute reports	15	18	21	17	45†	85%

* Photocopying machine broken.
† Power outage.

a) Compute the normal time for each work element.

b) If the allowance for this type of work is 15%, what is the standard time?

c) How many observations are needed for a 95% confidence level within 5% accuracy? (*Hint:* Calculate the standard deviation of each element, its coefficient of variation, and apply Figure S10.2.)

: **S10.5** The Division of Continuing Education at Virginia College promotes a wide variety of executive training courses for its audience of firms in the Arlington, Virginia, region.

The division's director believes that individually typed letters add a personal touch to marketing. To prepare letters for mailing, she conducts a time study of her secretaries. On the basis of the observations shown in the table below, she wishes to develop a time standard for the whole job.

The college has an allowance factor of 12%. The director decides to delete all unusual observations from the time study.

	CYCLE OBSERVED (IN MINUTES)						PERFORMANCE
ELEMENT	1	2	3	4	5	6	RATING
Typing letter	2.5	3.5	2.8	2.1	2.6	3.3	85%
Typing envelope	.8	.8	.6	.8	3.1	.7	100%
Stuffing envelope	.4	.5	1.9	.3	.6	.5	95%
Sealing, sorting	1.0	2.9	.9	1.0	4.4	.9	125%

: **S10.6** A time study at the phone company observed a job that contained three elements. The times and ratings for 10 cycles are shown in the table below.

	PERFORMANCE	OBSERVATIONS (MINUTES PER CYCLE)									
ELEMENT	RATING	1	2	3	4	5	6	7	8	9	10
1	85%	.40	.45	.39	.48	.41	.50	.45	.39	.50	.40
2	88%	1.5	1.7	1.9	1.7	1.8	1.6	1.8	1.8	2.0	2.1
3	90%	3.8	3.4	3.0	4.8	4.0	4.2	3.5	3.6	3.7	4.3

a) Find the average cycle time for each element.

b) Find the normal time for each element.

c) Assuming an allowance factor for 20% of job time, determine the standard time for this job.

d) How many cycles are needed to provide an 80% confidence level (within 5% accuracy)?

: **S10.7** The Dubuque Cement company packs 80-pound bags of concrete mix. Time study data for the filling activity are shown in the table below.

The company's policy is a 20% allowance for workers. Compute the standard time for this work task. How many cycles are necessary for 99% confidence, within 5% accuracy?

	CYCLE TIME (SECONDS PER CYCLE)					PERFORMANCE
ELEMENT	1	2	3	4	5	RATING
Grasp and place bag	8	9	8	11	7	110%
Fill bag	36	41	39	35	112*	85%
Seal bag	15	17	13	20	18	105%
Place bag on conveyor	8	6	9	30†	35†	90%

* Bag breaks open.
†Conveyor jams.

: **S10.8** An office worker is clocked performing three work elements, with the results shown in the table on page 468. The allowance for tasks such as this is 15%.

	MINUTES FOR CYCLE						PERFORMANCE RATING
ELEMENT	1	2	3	4	5	6	
1	13	11	14	16	51	15	100%
2	68	21	25	73	26	23	110%
3	3.0	3.3	3.1	2.9	3.4	2.8	100%

a) Find the normal time per cycle.

b) Find the standard time per cycle.

: **S10.9** Installing mufflers at the Ross Garage in Queens, New York, involves five work elements. Richard Ross times workers performing these tasks seven times with the results shown in the table below.

JOB ELEMENT	CYCLE OBSERVATIONS (MINUTES)							PERFORMANCE RATING
	1	2	3	4	5	6	7	
1. Select correct mufflers	4	5	4	6	4	15	4	110%
2. Remove old muffler	6	8	7	6	7	6	7	90%
3. Weld/install new muffler	15	14	14	12	15	16	13	105%
4. Check/inspect work	3	4	24	5	4	3	18	100%
5. Complete paperwork	5	6	8	—	7	6	7	130%

By agreement with his workers, Ross allows a 10% fatigue factor and a 10% personal-time factor. To compute standard time for the work operation, Ross excludes all observations that appear to be unusual or nonrecurring.

a) What is the standard time for the task?

b) How many cycles are needed to assure a 95% confidence level?

: **S10.10** Sample observations of an assembly-line worker made over a 40-hour work week revealed that the worker produced a total of 320 completed parts. The performance rating was 125%. The sample also showed that the worker was busy assembling the parts 80% of the time. Allowances for work on the assembly line total 10%. Find the normal time and standard for this task.

· **S10.11** A bank wants to determine the percent of time its tellers are working and idle. It decides to use work sampling, and its initial estimate is that the tellers are idle 30% of the time. How many observations should be taken to be 95.45% confident that the results will not be more than 5% away from the true result?

: **S10.12** A work sample taken over a 160-hour work month produced the following results. What is the standard time for the job?

Units manufactured	220
Idle time	20%
Performance rating	90%
Allowance time	10%

· **S10.13** Sharpening your pencil is an operation that may be broken down into eight small elemental motions. In MTM terms, each element may be assigned a certain number of TMUs, as shown on page 469.

Reach four inches for the pencil	6 TMU
Grasp the pencil	2 TMU
Move the pencil six inches	10 TMU
Position the pencil	20 TMU
Insert the pencil into the sharpener	4 TMU
Sharpen the pencil	120 TMU
Disengage the pencil	10 TMU
Move the pencil six inches	10 TMU

What is the total normal time for sharpening one pencil? Convert this time to minutes and seconds.

CASE STUDY

International Garment Factory

When International Garment began operations in Laredo, Texas, in 1986, all workers were employed under an hourly wage system. In the company's infancy, management chose to implement a wage plan based on time worked rather than on the basis of goods produced (incentive system) because adequate work procedures had not been analyzed and work measurement techniques had not been conducted. In 1990, the firm adopted a profit-sharing plan in which all production workers participated. Profit sharing was initially begun to create a proprietary interest on the part of the employees. The share of net profits to be distributed to employees varied from year to year (depending upon the economic status of the firm); each person's share was based upon annual earnings and length of service.

Today, management of International Garment is contemplating a wage incentive plan in lieu of profit sharing. Three consecutive years of high costs and low profits caused employees to become disenchanted with the profit-sharing plan. As a result, they began bargaining for higher wages to offset inflation and poor profit-sharing earnings, which had significantly cut into their purchasing power.

An incentive wage plan seemed appropriate, since the sewing operations satisfied the following conditions:

1. The work was standardized; that is, the work methods, materials, and operations were uniform from one unit to the next.

2. There existed a positive relationship between the amount of skill and effort exerted by the worker and the physical output.

3. Units of production could be counted and credited to the proper person.

4. Increased productivity would result in lower unit cost.

5. Employees who produced the greatest number of acceptable units would receive the highest compensation.

Management seriously considered two different incentive pay plans—"straight piecework" and "piecework with a guaranteed minimum wage." Before a decision was made, the company's industrial engineer conducted methods analysis of each operation and applied appropriate work measurement techniques (motion-and-time study) in determining production standards. To compute the per unit pay for the plans, the industrial engineer set a time standard for each unit. Then the number of units per hour was calculated. Finally, the number of units per hour was divided into the base wage rates (as determined by job evaluation), thereby giving the per unit rate.[3]

Under a "straight piecework" plan, the direct labor cost per unit remains constant at 12¢ per unit produced.

After plotting on the graph the relationship between direct labor cost and output, the industrial engineer noticed that the relationship differed from that of the company's time-based pay system whereby direct labor cost per unit was curvilinear as productivity increased.

Under the "piecework with a guaranteed minimum wage" plan, direct labor cost per unit decreases up to a point as productivity increases and remains constant thereafter. The relationships among earnings, output, and unit labor cost are shown in Figure S10.5 on page 470.

For the job of sewing on pockets, the standard is $0.12 per unit. For an output of 40 units or less, the employee would earn $4.80 per hour, the base rate of pay. For produc-

---

[3] For example, a standard time of .025 hours per unit was set for sewing on a shirt pocket (40 per hour). By dividing the base rate of pay ($4.80/hr.) by 40, the rate per unit, $.12, was established.

CASE STUDY (Continued)

tivity over 40 units, the worker would earn an additional $0.12 per unit.

    The management of International Garment felt that the "piecework with a guaranteed minimum wage" plan was somewhat superior to its existing plan, but it, too, failed to discriminate among workers who produced "at average" and those who produced "below average." Yet, management also recognized serious shortcomings of the "straight piecework" plan.

Discussion Questions

1. Which plan would you recommend for International Garment Factory? Why?

2. List specific drawbacks of each incentive pay plan.

3. Can you design another wage incentive plan that would be better for International Garment Factory? Explain why you favor your plan.

Source: Dean Jerry Kinard (Francis Marion College).

Figure S10.5

Earnings, Outputs, and Unit Labor Costs.

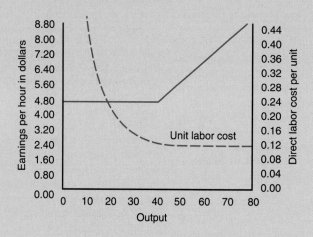

BIBLIOGRAPHY

Aft, L. S. *Productivity Measurement and Improvement.* Reston, VA: Reston Publishing, 1983.

Anthony, G. M. "I.E.'s Measure Work, Write Standards for White Collar Workers at Financial Institutions." *Industrial Engineering* **18** (January 1984): 77–81.

Barnes, R. M. *Motion and Time Study.* New York: John Wiley & Sons, 1980.

Denton, D. K. "Work Sampling: Increasing Service and White Collar Productivity." *Management Solutions* (March 1987): 36–41.

Helms, A. S., *et al.* "The Development of Laboratory Workload Standards through Computer-Based Work Measurement Techniques: Part III." *Journal of Methods-Time Measurement* **12**: 51–54.

Karger, D. W. *Advanced Work Measurement.* New York: Industrial Press, 1982.

Konz, S. *Work Design.* Columbia, OH: Grid, Inc., 1975.

Lindner, C. A. "The Application of Computer-Based Work Measurement in a Community Hospital." Working Paper, University Community Hospital, Tampa, Florida, March 10, 1986.

Nadler, G. *Work Design: A Systems Concept.* Homewood, IL: Irwin, 1976.

Neibel, B. W. *Motion and Time Study.* Homewood, IL: Irwin, 1976.

Procurement and Just-In-Time Strategies

AT&T Assures Vendor Quality and a Competitive Advantage

AT&T is in the process of reducing its supplier base and involving the remaining suppliers in quality-improvement activities. These activities are the responsibility of commodity teams, which have representatives from Quality Assurance, Purchasing, and Engineering. The teams receive assistance from a number of quality assurance functions and use a four-phase process to select suppliers. These four phases are:

    I: Identify potential suppliers
    II: Assess supplier capabilities
    III: Identify approved suppliers
    IV: Identify preferred suppliers

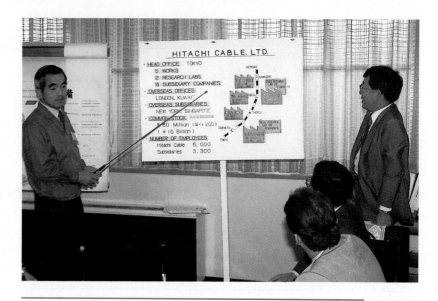

As part of the AT&T vendor quality assessment program, vendors provide company profile and capability information, often in formal presentations, to the commodity teams.

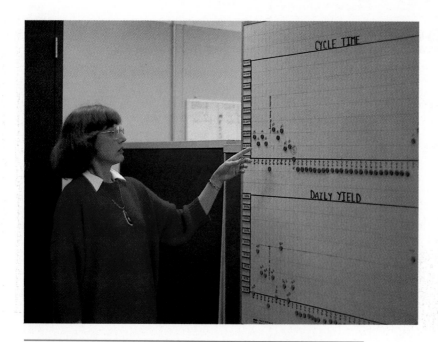

As part of AT&T's vendor quality improvement program, key supplier variables, such as order cycle time and quality yield, are tracked to determine effectiveness of the program.

Once the potential suppliers have been identified, these AT&T teams use a three-step approach. The three steps are:

Vendor Quality Assessment, the first step, focuses on determining approved and preferred suppliers and includes a thorough evaluation of each vendor's qualifications and potential capability. Consistent with this assessment, engineering strength for specific technologies and products is reviewed. Then a comprehensive evaluation of the supplier's quality system comes under scrutiny. Ultimately, product approval, which includes evaluation of the product to meet technical specifications, may be granted. At that point the supplier gains "approved" or "preferred" status.

Acceptance testing of vendor quality is an integral part of vendor evaluation. Such testing often takes place at the vendor's plant prior to first piece delivery.

Successful vendor performance in meeting AT&T's JIT schedule results in less inventory and reduction of required space. The combination of 100% good quality and JIT delivery results in reduced costs and a competitive advantage.

The second step, **Vendor Quality Information,** focuses on maximizing the advantage to the vendor and AT&T. Once vendors are approved, the commodity team seeks information from suppliers to see if these outstanding vendors have other products that meet AT&T's needs.

The third step, **Vendor Quality Improvement,** focuses on feedback and continuous improvement. Commodity teams work closely with suppliers in a continuing effort to improve quality. AT&T has structured vendor feedback meetings where quality concerns, engineering concerns, product information, purchasing information, and forecasting information are shared. The AT&T teams work with suppliers so that the relationship is viewed as a cooperative effort.

This process of identifying, assessing, selecting, and developing suppliers enhances the procurement process at AT&T. AT&T's ability to exchange information with suppliers improves quality to their mutual advantage. The result is that AT&T has a competitive advantage because of procurement.

Source: Adapted from *Quality Excellence Achieved,* BBP, Professional Information Group of Simon & Schuster, p. 127.

Vendors now deliver on AT&T's JIT schedule directly to the production line.

INTRODUCTION

Procurement

No organization finds it economical to make all the material it uses. The advantages of specialization are too pervasive. Consequently, some items are procured from others. This leads to the creation of a procurement function and the role of a purchasing agent. **Procurement** is the acquisition of goods and services. The *objectives of the procurement function* are to:

1. help identify the products and services that can best be obtained externally;
2. develop, evaluate, and determine the best supplier, price, and delivery for those products and services.

Production Environment

Purchasing agent

In the production environment, the purchasing function is usually managed by a **purchasing agent** who has legal authority to execute contracts on behalf of the firm. In a large firm, the purchasing agent may also have a staff that includes buyers and expediters. Buyers represent the company, performing all activities of the purchasing department except the signing of contracts. Expediters assist buyers in following up on purchases to ensure timely delivery. In *manufacturing* firms, the procurement function is supported by product engineering drawings and specifications, quality control documents, and testing activities that evaluate the purchased items.

Service Environments

In many *service* environments purchasing's role is diminished because the primary product is an intellectual one. In legal and medical organizations, for example, the main items to be procured are office facilities, furniture and equipment, autos, and supplies. However, in services such as transportation and restaurants, the purchasing function is critical. An airline that purchases planes that are not efficient for its route structure or a steak house that does not know how to buy steak is in trouble. Resources must be expended and training provided to ensure that, in such situations, purchasing is competently addressed.

In the wholesale and retail segment of services, purchasing is performed by a buyer who has responsibility for the sale and profit margins on the purchased merchandise that will be resold. Buyers in this nonmanufacturing environment may have little support other than historical customer behavior and standard grades. For instance, a USDA grade (such as AA eggs, or U.S. choice meat), a textile standard or blend, or standard sizes may take the place of engineering drawings and quality control documents found in manufacturing environments.

Make or Buy

Make-or-buy decision

A wholesaler or retailer buys everything that he or she sells; a manufacturing operation hardly ever does. Manufacturers, restaurants, and assemblers of products buy components and subassemblies that go into final products. As we discussed in Chapter 6, choosing products and services that can be advantageously obtained externally as opposed to produced internally is known as the **make-or-buy decision.** The purchasing department's role is to evaluate alternative suppliers and provide current, accurate, complete data that are relevant to the buy alternative. Table 11.1

TABLE 11.1 Considerations for the Make-or-Buy Decision.

REASONS FOR MAKING:	REASONS FOR BUYING:
1. Lower production cost	1. Lower acquisition cost
2. Unsuitable suppliers	2. Preserve supplier commitment
3. Assure adequate supply (quantity or delivery)	3. Obtain technical or management ability
4. Utilize surplus labor facilities and make a marginal contribution	4. Inadequate capacity
5. Obtain desired quality	5. Reduce inventory costs
6. Remove supplier collusion	6. Ensure flexibility and alternative sources of supply
7. Obtain unique item that would entail a prohibitive commitment for a supplier	7. Product improvements may be difficult because it is a sideline; additional design or process resources required for R&D
8. Maintain organizational talents and protect personnel from a layoff	8. Reciprocity
9. Protect proprietary design or quality	9. Item is protected by a patent or trade secret
10. Increase or maintain size of the company (management preference)	10. Services (janitorial, security, and so on) contracting eliminates a support activity and frees management to deal with its primary business

lists a wide variety of considerations in the make-or-buy decision.

Regardless of the decision, it should be reviewed periodically. Vendor competence and costs change, as do production capabilities and costs within the firm.

THE PROCUREMENT OPPORTUNITY

The cost of purchases for both manufacturing and service firms as a percent of the value of shipments is shown in Table 11.2. The range varies from a high of 83% for petroleum and coal products to a low of 27% for tobacco. These numbers indicate

TABLE 11.2 Percent of Sales Spent on Purchases.

INDUSTRY GROUP	PERCENT MATERIALS (MATERIAL DIVIDED BY SALES)	INDUSTRY GROUP	PERCENT MATERIALS (MATERIAL DIVIDED BY SALES)
All industries, total	54%	Printing and publishing	35%
Food and kindred products	63%	Chemicals, allied products	48%
Tobacco products	27%	Petroleum and coal products	83%
Apparel, other textile products	49%	Stone, clay, glass products	46%
Lumber and wood products	60%	Machinery, except electric	48%
Furniture and fixtures	48%	Electric, electronic equipment	45%
Paper and allied products	54%	Transportation equipment	60%

Source: Derived from U.S. Bureau of the Census, Annual Survey of Manufacturers, 1989, Industry Statistics, Section 1, p. 10

a significant opportunity to reduce costs.

The amount of leverage available to the operations manager via an effective procurement function is evident in Table 11.3.

Firms spending 50% of their sales dollar on purchases and having a net profit of 7% would require $3.51 worth of sales in order to equal the savings that accrues the company from a one dollar savings in procurement. These numbers indicate the strong role that procurement can play in profitability. This is true in both manufacturing and service organizations.

Example 1

The Goodwin Company spends 50% of its sales dollar on purchased goods. The firm has a net profit of 5%. Of the remaining 45%, 22.5% is fixed and the remaining 22.5% is variable. From Table 11.3 we see that the dollar value of sales needed to generate the same profit as results from one dollar of purchase savings would be $3.64.

VERTICAL INTEGRATION

Vertical integration

Procurement can be modified to take the form of vertical integration. By **vertical integration** we mean developing the ability to produce goods or services previously

---

TABLE 11.3 Dollars of Additional Sales Needed to Equal One Dollar Saved Through Purchasing.*

NET PROFIT OF FIRM	PERCENT OF SALES SPENT FOR PURCHASES							
	20%	30%	40%	50%	60%	70%	80%	90%
2%	$2.44	$2.78	$3.23	$3.85	$4.76	$6.25	$9.09	$16.67
3%	$2.41	$2.74	$3.17	$3.77	$4.65	$6.06	$8.70	$15.38
4%	$2.38	$2.70	$3.13	$3.70	$4.55	$5.88	$8.33	$14.29
5%	$2.35	$2.67	$3.08	$3.64	$4.44	$5.71	$8.00	$13.33
6%	$2.33	$2.63	$3.03	$3.57	$4.35	$5.56	$7.69	$12.50
7%	$2.30	$2.60	$2.99	$3.51	$4.26	$5.41	$7.41	$11.76
8%	$2.27	$2.56	$2.94	$3.45	$4.17	$5.26	$7.14	$11.11
9%	$2.25	$2.53	$2.90	$3.39	$4.08	$5.13	$6.90	$10.53
10%	$2.22	$2.50	$2.86	$3.33	$4.00	$5.00	$6.67	$10.00

* The required increase in sales assumes that 50% of the costs other than purchases are variable and that 1/2 of the remaining (less profit) are fixed. Therefore, at sales of $100 (50% purchases and 2% margin), $50 are purchases, $24 are other variable costs, $24 are fixed costs, and $2 profit. Increasing sales by $3.85 yields the following:

Purchases at 50%	$51.93
Other Variable Cost	24.92
Fixed Cost	24.00
Profit	3.00
	$103.85

Through $3.85 of additional sales, we have increased the profit by $1, from $2 to $3. The same increase in margin could have been obtained by reducing purchasing costs by $1.

purchased, or actually buying a supplier or a distributor. Vertical integration can take the form of forward or backward integration as shown in Figure 11.1. Vertical integration can offer a strategic opportunity for the operations manager. For firms whose internal analysis suggests that they have the necessary capital, managerial talent, and required demand, vertical integration may provide substantial opportunities for cost reduction. Other advantages in inventory reduction and scheduling can accrue to the company that effectively manages vertical integration or close, mutually beneficial relationships with suppliers.

Because purchased items represent such a large part of the costs of sales, it is obvious why so many organizations find interest in vertical integration. A classic example of vertical integration in modern American industry is Ford Motor Company. Henry Ford, Sr., understood the advantages of controlling his supply. Control of supply aided him in cost reduction, quality determination, and timely delivery. Consequently, by 1920 Ford Motor Company had integrated backward, producing not only cars but also its own glass and steel at the River Rouge plant. For some components, Ford was also able to integrate forward, from mining to delivery. It has been estimated that ore was transformed into steel, fabricated into components, assembled into cars, painted, and driven off the assembly line within 48 hours. Vertical integration appears particularly advantageous when the organization has large market share or has the management talent to operate the acquired vendor successfully.[1] However, backward integration may be particularly dangerous for firms in industries undergoing technological change if management is unable to keep abreast of those changes or invest the financial resources necessary for the next technological evolution.[2]

Sanford Corporation is one of America's largest producers of highlighters and markers. Sanford is vertically integrated, making its own inks, which gives it a research, development, quality, and product flexibility advantage.

FIGURE 11.1

Vertical Integration Can Take a Variety of Forms.

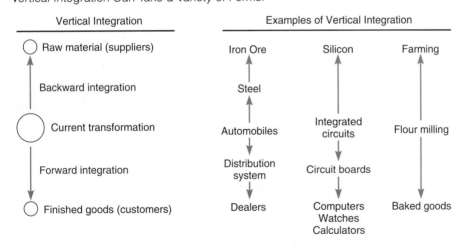

[1] Robert D. Buzzell, "Is Vertical Integration Profitable?" *Harvard Business Review,* **61,** 1 (January–February 1983): 92–102.

[2] See for instance Robert H. Hayes and William J. Abernathy, "Managing Our Way to Economic Decline," *Harvard Business Review,* **58,** 4 (July–August 1980): 72–73.

PROCUREMENT MANAGEMENT

The Procurement Focus

A firm that decides to buy materials rather than make them or vertically integrate must manage a procurement function. We will now discuss some important aspects of procurement management.

Purchasing management

The purchasing department's focus depends upon the cost of inventory, cost of transportation, availability of supply, and quality of suppliers. A firm may have to have some competence in all areas of **purchasing management,** but exceptional competence may be required in only a few areas, such as source management, supply management, and materials management.

Source management

One focus of procurement is **source management.** A sourcing thrust suggests that management is concerned about developing new reliable suppliers. The product may be a high-technology, custom-made, or specialty item for which there are few, if any, suppliers. Management must be able to seek out likely suppliers, develop their ability to produce, and negotiate acceptable relationships.

Supply management

Alternatively, procurement may focus on **supply management.**[3] A supply management focus suggests a concern with long-term availability of high-dollar or critical purchases; future reliable supplies are critical to success of the enterprise. An example is General Motors' development of palladium and platinum suppliers and working with those suppliers so it would have reliable and reasonably priced raw materials for catalytic converters. The evaluation was global, and development of the supplier was expensive. A supply management focus is also necessary if the dollar value of the purchases or fluctuations in cost are substantial. The extreme of this focus is for the firm to pursue backward integration to assure future supplies.

Materials management

Another system that is sometimes useful in operations management is a **materials management** system. Procurement may be combined with various warehousing and inventory activities to form such a system. The purpose of materials management is to obtain efficiency of operations through the integration of all material acquisition, movement, and storage activities in the firm. When transportation and inventory costs are substantial and exist on both the input and output side of the production process, an emphasis of materials management may be appropriate. The potential for competitive advantage is found via both reduced costs and improved customer service. Approximately half of 206 manufacturing companies surveyed by Jeff Miller and Peter Gilman had moved to some form of material management structure.[4]

Vendor Relations

The competitive advantage available through procurement is available only with effective vendor relations. Viewing the supplier as an adversary is counterproductive. Long-term, close relationships with a few suppliers is a better way (see the

---

[3] Peter Kraljic, "Purchasing Must Become Supply Management," *Harvard Business Review,* **61,** 5 (September–October 1983): 109–117.

[4] Jeffrey G. Miller and Peter Gilman, "Materials Managers: Who Needs Them?" *Harvard Business Review,* **57,** 4 (July–August 1979): 143.

POM _in action_

Firms Slash Vendor Rolls

Corporate America's drive for quality is squeezing thousands of suppliers.

Suppliers are struggling—and spending fortunes—to meet escalating standards that companies are setting for suppliers. Those that fail find themselves out in the cold as companies slash weak sisters from their supplier rolls.

The pressure on suppliers results from American industry's struggle to slim down and tone up to meet global competition. Companies around the country are cutting back the number of suppliers they use by as much as 90%. They are demanding higher levels of service and product quality from the survivors. And they are willing to pay a premium on the theory that getting things right initially is cheaper in the long run.

"A revolution is going on in the relationships between suppliers and customers," says J. M. Juran, chairman emeritus of the Juran Institute, a Wilton, Conn., industrial consulting firm.

In the change, many suppliers will eventually "fade away," says Richard Buetow, senior vice president of Motorola, Inc. In the current climate of world-wide competition, he adds, no one can "accept just sweat; you have to show results." Over the past several years, Motorola has cut its 10,000-company supplier base by 70% and is still slashing.

Sources: Wall Street Journal, August 16, 1991, p. B1; _Production & Inventory Management Journal,_ Third Quarter, 1991, pp. 22–25.

DATA TABLE Diminishing Suppliers. Many companies are cutting back the number of suppliers they use and demanding higher quality from those they keep.

	NUMBER OF SUPPLIERS[1]		
	Current	_Previous_[2]	_% Change_
Xerox	500	5,000	−90%
Motorola	3,000	10,000	−70
Digital Equipment	3,000	9,000	−67
General Motors	5,500	10,000	−45
Ford Motor	1,000	1,800	−44
Texas Instruments	14,000	22,000	−36

[1] Companies have different ways of counting their supplier base. For example, some count only direct manufacturing suppliers, while others count service and support suppliers.
[2] Number of suppliers firm had prior to starting reduction programs.

POM in Action box, "Firms Slash Vendor Rolls"). A healthy vendor relationship is one in which the supplier is committed to helping the purchaser improve its product and increase its sales. Suppliers can also be a source of ideas about new technology, materials, and processes. Good procurement functions are a vehicle for conveying such information to the proper personnel in the organization. The purchaser builds relationships that interest the supplier in such a commitment to the purchaser, its products, and its customers. Likewise, healthy relationships also include those in which the purchaser is committed to keeping the supplier informed of possible changes in product and production schedule. The purchasing function and suppliers must develop mutually advantageous relationships. Because an outstanding operations function requires excellent vendor relations, purchasing conducts a three-stage process.

Vendor Evaluation. The first stage, *vendor evaluation,* involves finding potential vendors and determining the likelihood of their becoming good suppliers. This phase requires the development of evaluation criteria. The standards noted in Figure

FIGURE 11.2

Vendor Rating Form Used by J. M. Huber Corporation. Evaluation categories are weighted according to importance (for example, "Product" category is weighted 1.25; "Service" is next at 0.69). Individual factors (for example, quality, delivery, and so on) have descending values, from four points for excellent to one point for poor. Total of points in each category is multiplied by the weight for that category.
(*Source:* Stuart F. Heinrite and Paul V. Farrel, *Purchasing: Principles and Applications* (Englewood Cliffs, NJ: Prentice-Hall, 1981) p. 239.)

VENDOR RATING REPORT   J.M. HUBER CORPORATION

COMPANY — TOTAL RATING

Company:	Excellent (4)	Good (3)	Fair (2)	Poor (1)	Products:	Excellent (4)	Good (3)	Fair (2)	Poor (1)
Size and/or Capacity	4				Quality	4			
Financial Strength		3			Price		3		
Operational Profit		3			Packaging	4			
Manufacturing Range	4				Uniformity		3		
Research Facilities			2		Warranty	4			
Technical Service		3			Total 18	12	6		
Geographical Locations	4				1.25 x Total = 22.50				
Management		3			*Sales Personnel*				
Labor Relations		3			1. Knowledge				
Trade Relations		3			His company		3		
Total 32	12	18	2		His product	4			
.63 x Total = 20.16					Our industry		3		
Service					Our Company		3		
Deliveries on Time	4				2. Sales Calls				
Condition on Arrival		3			Properly Spaced	4			
Follow Instructions		3			By Appointment		3		
Number of Rejections	4				Planned and Prepared		3		
Handling of Complaints		3			Mutually Productive	4			
Technical Assistance			2		3. Sales-Service				
Emergency Aid		3			Obtain Information		3		
Supply Up to Date Catalogues, Etc.			2	1	Furnish Quotations Promptly	4			
Supply Price Changes Promptly	4				Follow Orders		3		
Total 27	12	12	2	1	Expedite Delivery		3		
.69 x Total = 18.63					Handle Complaints		3		
					Total 43	16	27		
					.48 x Total = 20.64				

11.2 represent such criteria. Both the criteria and the weights are dependent upon the needs of the organization. The selection of competent suppliers is critical. If good suppliers are not selected, then all other purchasing efforts are wasted. As firms move toward fewer longer-term suppliers, the issues of financial strength, quality, management, research, and technical ability play an increasingly important role. These attributes should be noted in the evaluation process.

Vendor Development. The second stage is *vendor development*. Assuming a firm wants to proceed with a particular vendor, how does it integrate this supplier into its system? Purchasing makes sure the vendor has an appreciation of quality requirements, engineering changes, schedules and delivery, the payment system, and procurement policies. Vendor development may include everything from training, to engineering and production help, to formats for electronic information transfer. Procurement policies might include issues such as percent of business done with any one supplier or with minority businesses.

Negotiations. The third stage is *negotiations*.[5] **Negotiation strategies** are of three classic types. First is the *cost-based price model*. This model requires that the supplier open its books to the purchaser. The contract price is then based on time and materials or on a fixed cost with an escalation clause to accommodate changes in the vendor's labor and materials cost. Second is the *market-based price model*. In this model, price is based on a published price or index. Paperboard prices, for instance, are published weekly in the "yellow sheet,"[6] and nonferrous metal prices in *Metals Week*.[7] Third, one can derive a price based on *competitive bidding*. In many cases where suppliers are not willing to discuss costs or where near-perfect markets do not exist, competitive bidding is often appropriate. Competitive bidding is the typical policy in many firms for the majority of their purchases. The policy usually requires that the purchasing agent have several potential suppliers of the product (or its equivalent) and quotations from each. The major disadvantage is that the development of long-term relations between the buyer and seller are hindered. Competitive bidding may effectively determine cost. But it may also make difficult the communication and performance that is vital for engineering changes, quality, and delivery. Competitive bidding also hinders the just-in-time techniques we will be discussing shortly.

A fourth negotiation technique may be some *combination* of the above three approaches. The supplier and purchaser may agree on review of certain cost data, or accept some form of market data for raw material costs, or agree that the supplier will "remain competitive."

The net result of a good supplier relationship must be one where both partners have established a degree of mutual trust and a belief in the competence of each other. (See the *POM in Action* box, "Suppliers for Lean Production.")

Both Levi Strauss as the purchaser and Milliken as the supplier have found advantages in a closer relationship. Milliken developed a *partners for profit* program so its customers could concentrate on their business rather than on the management of raw materials inventory. Shown here is a Levi Strauss factory that is benefiting from this program.

[5] E. Raymond Cory, *Procurement Management: Strategy, Organization, and Decision-Making* (Boston: CBI Publishing Co., 1978).

[6] "The yellow sheet" is the commonly used name of the *Official Board Markets,* published by Magazines for Industry, Chicago, IL. It contains announced paperboard prices for containerboard and boxboard.

[7] *Metals Week,* A. Patrick Ryan, ed. and publisher, New York, N.Y.

**POM** _in action_

Suppliers for Lean Production

Mutual suspicion and distrust traditionally hover over the relationship between auto manufacturers and parts suppliers. In their attempt to conceal their profits, suppliers maintain a cloak of secrecy about their operations. And even after an automaker has selected a supplier, other suppliers are routinely lined up so they can be played against each other in the future.

Suppliers maintain large and expensive inventories to ensure enough parts are on hand should there be sudden changes in demand. Since the supplier and assembler deal at arm-length with one another, there is little cooperation to reduce the number of defective parts.

Toyota turned the mass-production supply system upside down in its efforts to counteract these problems. First, the company divided its suppliers into individual tiers with diverse responsibilities. A major component, such as car seats or the electrical system, was assigned to first-tier suppliers; a second-tier company would then be called by the first-tier supplier to provide individual parts or subsystem com-

ponents. Often, a third level of suppliers was developed by the second-tier firms.

After the decision to develop a new model is made, Toyota immediately selects the first-tier companies and deals exclusively with them. As an integral part of the product-development team, these suppliers are given performance specifications, not engineering specifications, as in the mass-production system.

While the top Japanese "lean" producers work directly with fewer than 300 first-tier suppliers on a development project, other "fat" plants have up to 2,500 suppliers. The secrecy built into the mass-production system doesn't exist with the lean manufacturers, who are privy to complete information about their suppliers' operations, including costs and quality levels. _Cooperation_ is the word describing the relationship between manufacturer and supplier, since all desire a long-term stable relationship.

Sources: The Business World, September 23, 1990; _California Management Review,_ Summer 1990, pp. 71–85.

Procurement Techniques

Blanket Orders. Blanket orders are unfilled orders with a vendor.[8] A blanket order is a contract to purchase certain items from the vendor. It is not an authorization to ship anything. Shipment is made only upon receipt of an agreed-upon document, perhaps a shipping requisition or shipment release.

Invoiceless Purchasing. Invoiceless purchasing is an extension of good purchaser–supplier relations. In an invoiceless purchasing environment, there is typically one supplier for all units of a particular product. If the supplier provides all four wheels for each lawn mower produced, then management knows how many wheels it purchased. It just multiplies the quantity of lawn mowers produced times four and issues a check to the supplier for that amount.

Electronic Ordering and Funds Transfer. Electronic ordering and funds transfer reduce paper transactions. Paper transactions consist of a purchase order, a

---

[8] Unfilled orders are also referred to as "open" orders or "incomplete" orders.

purchase release, a receiving document, authorization to pay an invoice (which is matched with the approved receiving report), and finally the issuance of a check. Purchasing departments can reduce this barrage of paperwork by electronic ordering, acceptance of all parts as 100% good, and electronic funds transfer to pay for units received. General Motors is expected to save billions of dollars over the next few years through exactly this kind of electronic transfer.[9]

Transactions between firms are increasingly done via electronic data interchange. **Electronic data interchange (EDI)** is a standardized data transmittal format for computerized communications between organizations. EDI provides data transfer for virtually any business application, including purchasing. Data are transmitted directly from electronic media of the sender via a third party (usually the phone company) to electronic media of the receiver. The standardized format allows both the sender and receiver to know what information is to be located where in the format. For instance, under EDI, data for a purchase order such as order date, due date, quantity, part number, purchase order number, address, etc., is fitted into the standard EDI format. The data are then sent, usually from one computer to another, by phone line. The receiving organization knows where the data are on the specified format; a computer program is used to read those data into the receiving company's files. Not only can electronic ordering reduce paperwork, but it also speeds up the traditionally long procurement cycle.

Electronic data interchange (EDI)

Stockless Purchasing. The term *stockless purchasing* has come to mean that the supplier maintains the inventory for the purchaser. If the supplier can maintain the stock of inventory for a variety of customers who use the same product or whose differences are very minor, say perhaps at the packaging stage, then there may be a net savings. Consignment inventories, discussed shortly, are a related option.

Standardization. The purchasing department should make special efforts toward increased levels of standardization. That is, rather than obtaining a variety of very similar components with labeling, coloring, packaging, or perhaps even slightly different engineering specifications, the purchasing agent should endeavor to have those components standardized.

JUST-IN-TIME PURCHASING (JIT)

In the traditional flow of material through the transformation process, incoming material is delayed at receiving and incoming inspection; work-in-process is delayed at numerous workstations; and finished goods is delayed at finished goods inventory. **Just-in-time purchasing** (JIT) is directed toward the reduction of waste that is present at receiving and incoming inspection; it also reduces excess inventory, poor quality, and delay. This waste is present in virtually all production processes—and procurement is a critical function in removing the waste and making JIT work. Every moment material is held should add value. And every movement of material should add value.

Just-in-time purchasing

[9] See Jeffrey G. Miller and Thomas E. Vollmann, "The Hidden Factory," *Harvard Business Review,* **63,** 5 (September–October 1985): 142–150.

Table 11.4 shows the characteristics of JIT purchasing, and the *POM in Action* box discusses Harley Davidson's drive toward JIT.

Goals of Just-in-Time Purchasing

The goals of JIT purchasing are:

1. *Elimination of unnecessary activities.* For instance, receiving activity and incoming inspection activity are unnecessary under just-in-time. If purchasing personnel have been effective in selecting and developing vendors, the purchased items can be received without formal counting, inspection, and testing procedures. To do its job well, the purchasing staff requires support from other sections of the operations function. Production can contribute by

TABLE 11.4 Characteristics of JIT Purchasing.

SUPPLIERS

Few suppliers
Nearby suppliers
Repeat business with same suppliers
Active use of analysis to enable desirable suppliers to become/stay price competitive
Clusters of remote suppliers
Competitive bidding mostly limited to new part numbers
Buyer plant resists vertical integration and subsequent wipeout of supplier business
Suppliers encouraged to extend JIT buying to *their* suppliers

QUANTITIES

Steady output rate (a desirable prerequisite)
Frequent deliveries in small lot quantities
Long-term contract agreements
Minimal release paperwork
Delivery quantities variable from release to release but fixed for whole contract term
Little or no permissible overage or underage of receipts
Suppliers encouraged to package in exact quantities
Suppliers encouraged to reduce their production lot sizes (or store unreleased material)

QUALITY

Minimal product specifications imposed on supplier
Help suppliers to meet quality requirements
Close relationships between buyers' and suppliers' quality assurance people
Suppliers encouraged to use process control charts instead of lot sampling inspection

SHIPPING

Scheduling of inbound freight
Gain control by use of company-owned or contract shipping, contract warehousing, and trailers for freight consolidation/storage where possible—instead of using common carriers

Source: Richard J. Schonberger and James P. Gilbert, "Just-in-Time Purchasing: A Challenge for U.S. Industry." Copyright 1983 by The Regents of the University of California. Reprinted from the *California Management Review,* Vol. 26, No. 1. By permission of The Regents.

Automobile seats made two hours earlier are being delivered to Chrysler's Sterling Heights, Michigan, factory. The seats are then quickly transferred in proper sequence to the assembly line for JIT installation.

POM *in action*

Harley's Drive Toward Just-in-Time

Harley Davidson's motorcycle business was on the ropes when it seriously began to look at just-in-time manufacturing.

In its initial efforts, Harley erred by taking a legalistic approach in trying to sign up suppliers for a just-in-time system. Contracts of 35 pages devoted to spelling out suppliers' obligations to Harley were used. Harley turned to more informal arrangements (with two-page contracts) when months passed and only a few companies signed up. As Harley realized it needed to take steps to enhance supplier relationships, groups of its buyers and engineers fanned out to visit suppliers. They began refining and simplifying designs, and assisted suppliers in reducing stepup time between jobs by modifying equipment to allow for speedy die changes. Courses in statistics to teach workers how to chart small changes in the performance of their equipment were given to suppliers by Harley. This system provided early warnings when machines were drifting out of tolerance.

For Harley and its suppliers results have been excellent—Harley is profitable once again. Because of the refinement in the quality of its motorcycles, as well as greatly updated manufacturing techniques, Harley's bill for warranty repairs, scrap, and reworking of parts has been reduced 60%.

Harley's program improved what might be called the infrastructure of the system. While it shifted business to suppliers closer to its plants, it also diminished the number of suppliers. For example, about three-quarters of the suppliers to its Milwaukee engine plant are now located within a 175-mile radius of the city's suburbs. The company has reduced the need for safety stocks—inventories kept as insurance against breakdowns in transportation—merely by reducing the distances from its suppliers.

Sources: Fortune, June 9, 1986, p. 64; *Management Accounting,* September 1990, pp. 61–62; and *Purchasing,* October 13, 1988, pp. 50–54.

providing accurate, stable schedules, adequate lead time for engineering changes to be implemented, and time to develop ethical suppliers.

2. *Elimination of in-plant inventory.* Virtually no raw material inventory is necessary if materials that meet quality standards are delivered where and when they are needed. Raw material inventory is necessary only if there is reason to believe that supplies are undependable. Likewise, parts or components for processing at some intermediate stage should be delivered in small lots directly to the using department as needed. Reduction or elimination of inventory allows problems with other aspects of the production process to be observed and corrected. Inventory tends to hide problems.

3. *Elimination of in-transit inventory.* General Motors has estimated that at any given time, over one-half of its inventory is in transit.[10] Modern purchasing departments address in-transit inventory reduction by encouraging suppliers and prospective suppliers to locate near the plant. The shorter the flow of material and money in the resource "pipeline," the less inventory (see Figure 11.3). Another way to reduce in-transit inventory is to have inventory on **consignment.** Under a consignment arrangement, the supplier maintains title to the inventory. For instance, an assembly plant may find a hardware supplier

Consignment

[10] "Auto Makers Have Trouble with 'Kanban'," *Wall Street Journal* (April 7, 1982), p. 1.

that is willing to locate its warehouse where the user currently has its stock-room. In this manner, when hardware is needed, it is no farther than the stockroom. And the supplier can ship to other, perhaps smaller, purchasers from the "stockroom." The supplier bills the user on the basis of the signed pick-up receipt or number of units shipped.

4. *Quality and reliability improvement.* This is best done by reducing the number of suppliers and increasing long-term commitments to suppliers. To obtain improved quality and reliability, vendors and purchasers must have mutual understanding and trust. To achieve deliveries only when needed, in the exact quantities needed, also requires perfect quality—or as it is also known, zero defects. And, of course, both the supplier and the delivery system must be excellent.

FIGURE 11.3

Shorter Processing Time Lowers Costs.

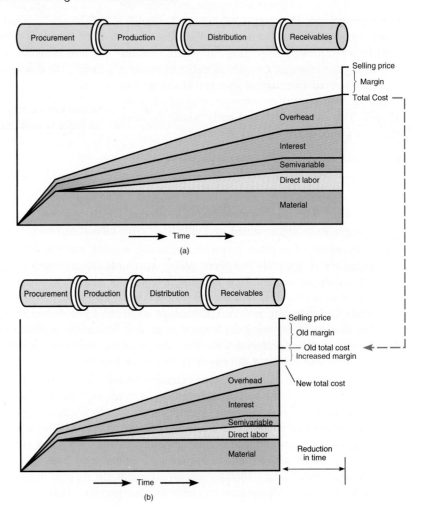

Supplier Concerns

Procurement works with production personnel and suppliers to build an organization that supports JIT and overcomes concerns that suppliers may have about JIT. A successful implementation of JIT purchasing requires that these concerns be overcome. These supplier concerns include:[11]

1. *Desire for diversification.* Many suppliers do not want to tie themselves to long-term contracts with one customer. The suppliers' perception is that their risk is reduced if they have a variety of customers.

2. *Poor customer scheduling.* Many suppliers have little faith in the purchaser's ability to reduce orders to a smooth, coordinated schedule.

3. *Engineering changes.* Frequent engineering changes with inadequate lead time for suppliers to implement tooling and process changes play havoc with JIT. Purchasing personnel must find ways to insulate their prospective JIT suppliers from these changes.

4. *Quality assurance.* Production with "zero defects" is not considered realistic by many suppliers.

5. *Small lot sizes.* Suppliers often have processes that are designed for large lot sizes, and they see frequent delivery to the customer in small lots as a way to transfer holding costs to the supplier.

6. *Proximity.* Depending upon the customer's location, frequent supplier delivery of small lots may be seen as economically prohibitive.

Purchasing may have to enlist the help of its own production personnel to assist suppliers in overcoming many of the above objections, but there is no doubt that those firms that do not develop JIT suppliers will soon be at a distinct disadvantage both domestically and internationally. For those who remain skeptical of the use of JIT, we would point out that virtually every restaurant in the world practices JIT, and with minimal staff support.

BREAK-EVEN ANALYSIS APPLIED TO PURCHASING

When a purchaser understands the cost structure of suppliers, more intelligent negotiations and purchase can take place. Cost data may be obtained from the supplier itself, from financial statements, or from analysis of the supplier's sales or purchases, labor, and overhead costs. The objective is to determine both the fixed and variable portions of the supplier's cost. Once this is done, the purchaser is in a much better position to work with the supplier. If we know the approximate cost structure and related break-even of the supplier, then we know the impact of our purchases on the supplier. Under some conditions, an astute buyer can purchase more during the next buying cycle (say a year) at lower cost and leave the supplier better off financially. Let us look at Example 2 to see how this is done.

---

[11] This summary is based on a study by Tom Schmitt and Mary Connors, "A Survey of Suppliers' Attitudes Toward the Establishment of JIT," *Operations Management Review,* **3,** 4 (Summer 1985): 36.

Example 2

Using the data in Figure 11.4, Willmington Auto Repair Stations (WARS) knows that Tarleton Tires makes a combination of units for various customers that moves them out on the (horizontal) percent capacity axis to point A. WARS also knows that it purchases about half of the tires made by Tarleton. Analysis in the WARS purchasing department suggests that Tarleton is not operating at capacity, but at about 70% of capacity. Tarleton's realistic capacity and top efficiency is point B on the capacity axis (about 85%). WARS can move some purchases from another supplier (with whom it has had quality problems) to Tarleton. It is therefore very interested in the impact of such a move on Tarleton. If Tarleton maintains its existing sales and adds 15% from WARS to its volume, Tarleton's profit corridor increases (the vertical distance *X* is larger than the vertical distance *Y*) even if the slope of the revenue line is slightly less. (With WARS paying less per tire, the revenue line drops to the proposed level.) But because volume has increased with an attendant increase in the profit corridor, Tarleton has more profit and WARS pays less for its tires.

FIGURE 11.4

Purchasing Break-even Analysis. WARS reduces costs while Tarleton Tire increases profit.

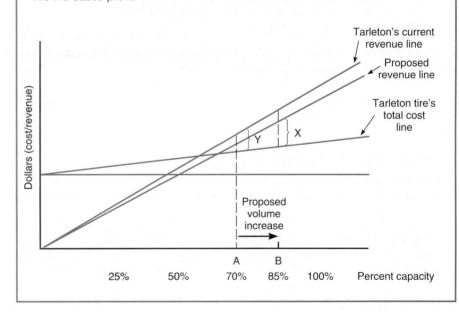

Example 2 shows one avenue a resourceful purchasing department can pursue to reduce costs *and* to improve the strength of a supplier. There are, of course, some issues that the supplier, Tarleton Tires, must address. Among these issues is the concern that Tarleton may have if it devotes 50% of its capacity to one customer. Such a move may limit its flexibility in the marketplace. Second, if Tarleton thinks it can sell that capacity at a higher price, then the WARS offer may not be of interest.

SUMMARY

Procurement is responsible for a substantial portion of the cost of many firms, including most manufacturing, restaurant, wholesale, and retail firms. Consequently, procurement provides a great opportunity for such firms to develop a competitive advantage. The procurement function may focus on traditional purchasing activities, source development, supply management, or materials management; but at some time procurement may have to engage in all of these activities regardless of the focus. Developing close, long-term relationships with suppliers of integrity is, for many organizations, a prerequisite to efficient operations. For many firms, just-in-time purchasing is another contribution that procurement can make to competitive advantage.

Among the quantitative techniques of particular help to procurement is break-even analysis. Break-even analysis has implications for procurement and purchasing as well as for company strategy.

KEY TERMS

Procurement (p. 474)

Purchasing agent (p. 474)

Make-or-buy decision (p. 474)

Vertical integration (p. 476)

Purchasing management (p. 478)

Source management (p. 478)

Supply management (p. 478)

Materials management (p. 478)

Negotiation strategies (p. 481)

Electronic data interchange (EDI) (p. 483)

Just-in-time purchasing (p. 483)

Consignment (p. 485)

SOLVED PROBLEM

Solved Problem 11.1

Super Discount knows that Plastics, Inc., of San Diego, Calif., makes a great plastic cabinet for small items for home and shop. Through its research, Super Discount suspects that Plastics is operating at only 75% of capacity. Super Discount wants to do a major promotion of the plastic cabinet and would like all of Plastics' remaining capacity. Super Discount judges that the maximum effective capacity of Plastics is 88%. (See the horizontal axis of Figure 11.5 on page 490.)

Super Discount is interested in the impact of such a move on Plastics and thinks Plastics' profit corridor will increase. Super Discount's purchasing agent explains to the management of Plastics that the profit corridor (Z) is larger even if the slope of the Plastics, Inc., revenue line is slightly less. (The Plastics' revenue line moves from Plastics(a) to Plastics(b).) This means Super Discount is paying less per cabinet, but because volume has increased, with an attendant increase in the profit corridor (that is, Z is greater than X), Plastics has more profit and Super Discount pays less for its cabinets.

FIGURE 11.5

Purchasing Break-even Analysis

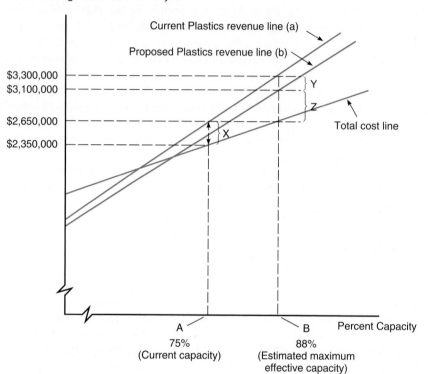

How much less can Super Discount expect to pay for cabinets? What is Plastics' increase in profit?

Solution

The dollar value of X is $300,000 ($2,650,000 − $2,350,000). This is Plastics' current profit. The dollar value of Y is $200,000 ($3,300,000 − $3,100,000), and this represents the savings to Super Discount. The dollar value of Z minus X is the increase in profit to Plastics if it accepts the contract, approximately $150,000 (Z − X = $450,000 − $300,000 = $150,000).

DISCUSSION QUESTIONS

1. Under what conditions might a firm decide to organize its procurement function as a materials management function? As a supply management function? As a source management function?

2. What can the procurement function do to implement just-in-time techniques with suppliers?

3. What information does purchasing receive from other functional areas of the firm?

4. How does a traditional adversarial relationship with suppliers change when a firm makes a decision to move to just-in-time deliveries?

5. What are the three basic approaches to negotiations?

6. What are the characteristics of JIT purchasing?

7. What reservations do suppliers have about JIT purchasing?

PROBLEMS

· **11.1** Using Tables 11.2 and 11.3, determine how much a food firm with a net profit of 8% has to increase its sales to equal one dollar of procurement savings.

· **11.2** Using the data in Example 2, what is the impact on WARS' costs if WARS wants Tarleton Tires, Inc., to have additional funds for research?

· **11.3** Using the data in Solved Problem 11. 1, what is the impact on Plastics if Super Discount wants Plastics to increase its engineering budget by $200,000 for a new plastic cabinet design?

· **11.4** As purchasing agent for Woolsey Enterprises in Golden, Colorado, you ask your buyer to provide you with a ranking of "excellent," "good," "fair," or "poor" for a variety of characteristics for two potential vendors. You suggest that the rankings be consistent with the vendor evaluation form shown in Figure 11.2. The buyer has returned the ranking shown on page 492.

How do you rank these potential vendors? (Hint: Figure 11.2 provides an excellent approach.)

· **11.5** As purchasing manager of the consolidated purchasing department of Hahn and Pinto, you have decided to use decision tree techniques to evaluate the cost of (1) a blanket contract from the home office, (2) individual large contracts from the home office, or (3) orders placed directly by the three company plants. Regardless of how the orders are placed, you expect the total quantity purchased to be 100,000 lineal feet of multi-strand wire. You estimate the cost and related probability for each of the three alternatives as follows:

	PROBABILITY	COST
Individual orders placed by the home office	.50	.71
	.25	.68
	.25	.74
Individual orders placed by each plant	.40	.82
	.50	.65
	.10	.70
Blanket order	1.0	.70

a) Use a decision tree to analyze the alternatives, using highest expected monetary value as a decision criteria. (Hint: Review Chapter 3 and Chapter 6 for examples and explanations of decision trees.)

b) As purchasing agent, what is your recommendation for the purchase?

c) What will be the expected total cost to the firm next year if your recommendation is followed?

Problem 11.4's Vendor Evaluation

Company	VENDOR RATING FOR:							
	DONNA INC.				KAY CORP.			
	Excellent (4)	Good (3)	Fair (2)	Poor (1)	Excellent (4)	Good (3)	Fair (2)	Poor (1)
Size and/or Capacity			✔			✔		
Financial Strength				✔			✔	
Operational Profit				✔			✔	
Manufacturing Range			✔				✔	
Research Facilities			✔		✔			
Technical Service			✔			✔		
Geographical Locations			✔			✔		
Management			✔			✔		
Labor Relations				✔			✔	
Trade Relations			✔				✔	
Service								
Deliveries on Time		✔				✔		
Condition on Arrival		✔				✔		
Follow Instructions			✔					✔
Number of Rejections				✔				✔
Handling of Complaints		✔				✔		
Technical Assistance			✔			✔		
Emergency Aid				✔				✔
Supply Up-to-Date Catalogues, Etc.				✔				✔
Supply Price Changes Promptly				✔				✔
Products								
Quality	✔				✔			
Price			✔				✔	
Packaging			✔				✔	
Uniformity			✔				✔	
Warranty			✔				✔	
Sales Personnel								
1. Knowledge								
His Company			✔					✔
His Products				✔			✔	
Our Industry			✔				✔	
Our Company				✔			✔	
2. Sales Calls								
Properly Spaced			✔					✔
By Appointment				✔				✔
Planned and Prepared				✔			✔	
Mutually Productive				✔			✔	
3. Sales-Service								
Obtain Information			✔					✔
Furnish Quotations Promptly				✔		✔		
Follow Orders			✔					✔
Expedite Delivery				✔			✔	
Handle Complaints		✔				✔		

492

CASE STUDY

Blue & Gray, Inc.

Blue & Gray, Inc., manufactures a line of power and hand tools for industrial and home use that is marketed under its own name. In addition, the company produces parts and accessories for power tools that are marketed by a large retail chain under the chain's name. Blue & Gray, Inc., must meet the quality requirements and delivery schedules as established by the chain.

During 1992, sales of parts and accessories to the chain exceeded $5,000,000. Management of Blue & Gray believed that sales to the chain contributed significantly to overhead and profit as well as to stable employment. However, during peak periods of sales, the company purchased parts and accessories from smaller firms for use in its own product line as well as to complete orders for the chain.

In March 1992, the treasurer, production manager, and purchasing agent met to decide whether to produce or purchase from an outside supplier 2,000 reduction gears, which were part of an order for the retail chain.

The Blue & Gray cost accounting system recorded actual material costs. However, product costing of direct labor was at a standard rate per hour. The treasurer recognized that this use of a standard rate per hour for all operations resulted in some error in costing individual parts. He believed, however, that the standard labor rate was accurate enough for practical purposes, since actual labor rates did not vary widely and, in most instances, parts passed through similar machining operations.

Both fixed and variable overhead were charged to products at the standard rate per direct labor hour. The current labor rates and the overhead accounts, as they were grouped by the company according to their fixed or variable characteristics, are shown below.

The production manager, Duncan Gray, stated that Blue & Gray could make the gears in a continous production run at 200 per hour. Furthermore, there was sufficient free ma-

Direct labor	$15.00
Variable overhead	7.00
Plant supervision (above basic budget)	
Plant indirect labor (material handling)	
Supplies	
Engineering	
Cost accounting of labor	
Heat, light, and power	
Workman's comp. taxes	
Health insurance	
Employer's Social Security contribution	
Fixed overhead	6.00
Administrative expense	
Selling expense	
Taxes and insurance—general	
Factory superintendent	
Plant supervision—basic budget	
Repairs and depreciation—building	
Equipment depreciation and obsolescence	
Total per hour	$28.00

chine time that other production would not be influenced unfavorably by the addition of this order. The material for the gears, he reported, would cost $1,000.

The purchasing agent, Elwood Blue, observed that a smaller company would sell the gears to Blue & Gray at a price of $0.6322 per gear. Vendor evaluation personnel have given the firm a high rating. The final decision on what to do is up to Elwood, the purchasing agent.

Discussion Questions

1. What should Elwood recommend: make or buy?

2. How should he justify his decision?

BIBLIOGRAPHY

Ammer, D. S. *Material Management and Purchasing.* Homewood, IL: Richard D. Irwin, 1980.

Ansarl, A., and B. Modarress. "Just-in-Time Purchasing: Problems and Solutions." *Journal of Purchasing and Materials* **22** (Summer 1986): 11–15.

Blumenfeld, D. E., L. D. Burns, C. F. Daganzo, M. C. Frick, and R. W. Hall. "Reducing Logistics Costs at General Motors." *Interfaces* **17** (January–February 1987): 26–47.

Burt, D. N., and W. R. Soukup. "Purchasing's Role in New Product Development." *Harvard Business Review* **63** (September–October 1985): 90–97.

Chapman, S. N., and P. L. Carter. "Supplier/Customer Inventory Relationships under JIT." *Journal of the Decision Sciences Institute* (Winter 1990).

Chatterjee, S. "Gains in Vertical Acquisitions and Market Power: Theory and Evidence." *The Academy of Management Journal*

34 (June 1991): 36.

Eccles, R. G. "Control with Fairness in Transfer Pricing." *Harvard Business Review* **61** (November–December 1983): 149–160.

Freeland, J. R. "A Survey of Just-in-Time Purchasing Practices in the United States." *Production and Inventory Management Journal* **32** (Second Quarter 1991): 43.

Helper, S. "How Much Has Really Changed Between U.S. Automakers and Their Suppliers?" *Sloan Management Review* **32** (Summer 1991): 15.

Schneider, L. M. "New Era in Transportation Strategy." *Harvard Business Review* **63** (March–April 1985): 118–126.

Schorr, J. E., and T. F. Wallace. *High Performance Purchasing.* Williston, VT: Oliver Wight Limited Publications, Inc., 1986.

Shapiro, Roy D. "Get Leverage from Logistics." *Harvard Business Review* **62** (May–June 1984): 119–126.

Tersine, R. J., and J. H. Campbell. *Modern Materials Management.* New York: North-Holland, 1977.

Walleigh, R. C. "Getting Things Done: What's Your Excuse for Not Using JIT?" *Harvard Business Review* **64** (March–April 1986): 39–54.

Learning Curves

INTRODUCTION

Learning curves

Log-log graph

In 1936, T. P. Wright of Curtis-Wright Corporation published the first report of **learning curves** applied to industry.[1] Learning curves, or as they are sometimes called, experience curves, are based on the premise that organizations, like people, get better at their tasks as the tasks are repeated. A graph of labor-hours per unit versus the number of units produced normally has the negative exponential distribution shape illustrated in Figure S11.1(a). When plotted as a **log-log graph,** a learning curve appears as shown in Figure S11.1(b). Figures S11.1(a) and (b) show the ability of the Ford Motor Company to reduce costs for the Model T. When the *rate* of change is constant, a log-log graph yields a straight line. For many analytical purposes this is helpful, as it is easier to use and extrapolate.

By convention, the learning curve is based on a doubling of productivity. That is, when production doubles, the decrease in time per unit is the rate of the learning curve. So, if the learning curve is an 80% rate, the second unit takes 80% of the time of the first unit, the fourth unit takes 80% of the time of the second unit, the eighth unit takes 80% of the time of the fourth unit, and so forth. This is shown as:

$$Y \times L^n = \text{Time required for } N\text{th unit} \qquad \text{(S11.1)}$$

FIGURE S11.1

(a) Price of Model T, 1909–1923 (average list price in 1958 dollars plotted as an arithmetic graph). (b) Price of Model T, 1909–1923 (average list price in 1958 dollars plotted as a log-log graph).
(*Source:* Adapted from William J. Abernathy and Kenneth Wayne, "Limits of the Learning Curve," *Harvard Business Review,* **52,** 5 (September–October 1974): 109–119.)

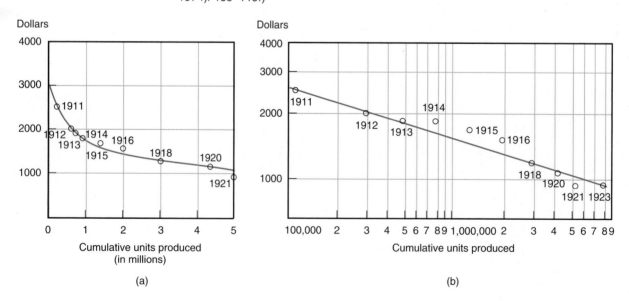

[1] T. P. Wright, "Factors Affecting the Cost of Airplanes," *Journal of the Aeronautical Sciences* (February 1936).

where

$$Y = \text{Unit cost or unit time}$$
$$L = \text{Learning curve rate}$$
$$n = \text{Number of times } Y \text{ is doubled}$$

So if the first unit of a particular product took 10 labor hours, and if a 70% learning curve is present, the hours the fourth unit will take require doubling twice—from 1 to 2 to 4. Therefore the formula is:

$$\text{Hours required for unit } 4 = 10 \times 0.7^2 = 4.9 \text{ hours}$$

Different organizations and different products have different learning curves. The rate of learning varies depending upon the quality of management and the potential of the process and product. *Any change in process, product, or personnel disrupts the learning curve.* Caution should be exercised in assuming that a learning curve is continuing and permanent. See, for instance, what happened to Ford when it began changing models in 1928 (Figure S11.2).[2] Cunningham found industry variations from 60% to 94%, as shown in Table S11.1.[3] The lower the number, such as 60% compared to 90%, the steeper the slope and the faster the drop in costs. Stable, standardized, labor-intensive products and processes tend to have costs that decline more steeply than others. Between 1929 and 1955, the steel industry was able to reduce labor-hours per unit to 79% each time cumulative production doubled, and the labor-hours per barrel of petroleum declined to 84% each time total production doubled.

FIGURE S11.2

The Ford Experience Curve (in 1958 Constant Dollars).
(*Source:* Adapted from William J. Abernathy and Kenneth Wayne, "Limits of the Learning Curve," *Harvard Business Review,* **52,** 5 (September–October 1974): 109–119.)

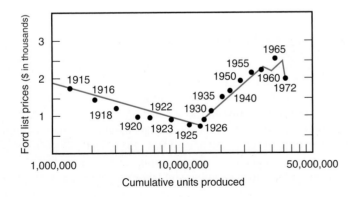

[2] See also Winfred B. Hirshmann, "Profit from the Learning Curve," *Harvard Business Review,* **42,** 1 (January–February 1964): 125–139.

[3] James A. Cunningham, "Using the Learning Curve as a Management Tool," *IEEE Spectrum* (June 1980): 46.

TABLE S11.1 Examples of Learning Curve Effects in U.S. Industry.

EXAMPLE	IMPROVING PARAMETER	CUMULATIVE PARAMETER	LEARNING CURVE SLOPE, PERCENT	TIME FRAME
1. Model T Ford production	Price	Units produced	86	1910–1926
2. Aircraft assembly	Direct labor-hours per unit	Units produced	80	1925–1957
3. Equipment maintenance at GE	Average time to replace a group of parts	Number of replacements	76	Around 1957
4. Labor-hours per barrel	Average direct labor-hours per barrel refined	Millions of barrels refined in the U.S.	84	1860–1962
5. Electric power generation	Mils per kW-hour	Millions of kW-hours	95*	1910–1955
6. Steel production	Production worker labor-hours per unit produced	Units produced	79	1920–1955
7. Integrated circuits	Average price per unit	Units produced	72*	1964–1972
8. Hand-held calculator	Average factory selling price	Units produced	74	1975–1978
9. Disk memory drives	Average price per bit	Number of bits	76	1975–1978

* Constant dollars.

Source: James A. Cunningham, "Using the Learning Curve as a Management Tool," *IEEE Spectrum,* June 1980, p. 45. © 1980 IEEE.

Learning curves are useful for a variety of applications. These include:

1. internal labor forecasting, production scheduling, establishing costs and budgets;
2. external purchasing and subcontracting of items (see the SMT case at the end of this supplement);
3. strategic evaluation of company and industry performance.

APPLYING THE LEARNING CURVE

Expressing the time it takes to produce a certain unit versus the number of units produced in the form of a mathematical relationship enables us to determine how long it will take to produce any unit as a function of how many units have been produced before it. Although this procedure helps in determining how long it takes to produce a given unit, the consequences of this type of analysis are more far-reaching. Costs are dropping and efficiency is going up for individual firms and the industry. Severe problems in scheduling and labor planning can occur if operations are not adjusted for implications of the learning curve. Learning curve improvement may result in labor and productive facilities being idle a portion of the time, increasing costs unnecessarily. Furthermore, firms may refuse other projects or work because they do not consider the effect of learning. The foregoing are only a few of the ramifications of not considering the effect of learning. Learning curve effects occur in marketing and financial planning. From a purchasing perspective our interest is in judging what a supplier's cost should be for further production.

If you know the learning factor and the time it takes to produce the first unit, you can determine, with use of logs, how long it will take to produce any subsequent unit with the following formula:

$$Y_N = Y_1 N^x \qquad\qquad (S11.2)$$

where

Y_N = Number of labor-hours required to produce the Nth unit

Y_1 = Number of labor-hours required to produce the first unit

N = Unit number (N is 4 for the fourth unit, 5 for the fifth unit, and so on)

$X = \dfrac{\log L}{\log 2}$, and

L = Learning factor

Example S1

The learning factor for Southern Telecom's new telephone switching system (called a PBX) is 80%. It took 56,000 hours to complete the first switching system. How long will it take to complete the eighth?

$$Y_N = Y_1 N^x$$
$$Y_8 = (56{,}000 \text{ hours})(8)^{\log 0.8/\log 2}$$
$$= (56{,}000 \text{ hours})(8^{-.3219})$$
$$= \frac{56{,}000 \text{ hours}}{8^{0.3219}} = \frac{56{,}000 \text{ hours}}{1.95}$$
$$= 28{,}718 \text{ hours}$$

How many labor-hours should the production manager schedule for the ninth system? How long will it take to complete the 10th system?

$$Y_9 = (56{,}000 \text{ hours})(9)^{\log 0.8/\log 2}$$
$$= (56{,}000 \text{ hours})(9)^{-.3219}$$
$$= \frac{56{,}000 \text{ hours}}{9^{0.3219}} = \frac{56{,}000 \text{ hours}}{2.03}$$
$$= 27{,}586 \text{ hours}$$

$$Y_{10} = (56{,}000 \text{ hours})(10)^{\log 0.8/\log 2}$$
$$= \frac{56{,}000 \text{ hours}}{10^{.3219}} = \frac{56{,}000 \text{ hours}}{2.098}$$
$$= 26{,}686 \text{ hours}$$

From the results in Example S1 we can see that *it takes less time to complete each additional system.* It took 28,718 hours to complete the eighth PBX system; it took 27,586 hours to complete the ninth system; and it took 26,686 hours to complete the tenth system. Second, we note that *the time saving decreased for each additional unit.* It takes (28,718 − 27,586) = 1,132 hours less time to produce unit 9 versus unit 8. It takes (27,586 − 26,686) = 900 hours less time to produce unit 10 versus unit 9. Thus, the amount of time saved in completing each unit decreases with each additional unit. These two points are major implications of the learning-curve effect. The mathematical model for the learning curve is consistent with these assumptions.

TABLE S11.2 Learning-curve Coefficients.

% BASE	70%	80%	82%	84%	86%	88%	90%
2	7.4860	3.5230	3.0650	2.6750	2.3430	2.0580	1.8120
5	4.6720	2.6230	2.3580	2.1250	1.9190	1.7380	1.5770
10	3.2700	2.0980	1.9330	1.7850	1.6510	1.5290	1.4190
20	2.2900	1.6740	1.5850	1.4990	1.4200	1.3460	1.2770
30	1.8580	1.4730	1.4120	1.3540	1.3000	1.2490	1.2010
40	1.6020	1.3430	1.3000	1.2590	1.2210	1.1840	1.1490
50	1.4290	1.2500	1.2200	1.1900	1.1630	1.1360	1.1110
60	1.3000	1.1780	1.1580	1.1370	1.1180	1.0990	1.0810
70	1.2010	1.1210	1.1080	1.0940	1.0810	1.0880	1.0560
80	1.1220	1.0740	1.0660	1.0580	1.0500	1.0420	1.0340
90	1.0560	1.0340	1.0310	1.0270	1.0230	1.0200	1.0160
100	1.0000	1.0000	1.0000	1.0000	1.0000	1.0000	1.0000
110	.9521	.9696	.9731	.9764	.9796	.9827	.9855
120	.9105	.9428	.9492	.9551	.9610	.9670	.9726
125	.8915	.9307	.9381	.9454	.9526	.9552	.9667
130	.8737	.9200	.9279	.9359	.9447	.9528	.9609
140	.8410	.8974	.9084	.9188	.9294	.9399	.9501
150	.8117	.8776	.8905	.9029	.9156	.9280	.9402
160	.7852	.8595	.8744	.8885	.9028	.9170	.9309
170	.7611	.8428	.8591	.8752	.8910	.9067	.9225
175	.7498	.8352	.8520	.8687	.8854	.9020	.9185
180	.7390	.8274	.8452	.8624	.8798	.8974	.9144
190	.7187	.8133	.8322	.8510	.8698	.8885	.9070
200	.7000	.8000	.8200	.8400	.8600	.8800	.9000
220	.6665	.7759	.7981	.8201	.8423	.8646	.8870
240	.6373	.7543	.7783	.8022	.8265	.8508	.8754
260	.6116	.7349	.7607	.7863	.8123	.8384	.8649
280	.5887	.7177	.7447	.7717	.7992	.8270	.8550
300	.5682	.7019	.7301	.7586	.7875	.8161	.8492
400	.4900	.6400	.6724	.7056	.7396	.7744	.8100
500	.4368	.5956	.6308	.6671	.7045	.7432	.7830
600	.3977	.5617	.5987	.6372	.6771	.7187	.7616
700	.3674	.5345	.5729	.6129	.6548	.6985	.7440
800	.3430	.5120	.5514	.5927	.6361	.6815	.7290
900	.3228	.4929	.5331	.5754	.6200	.6668	.7161
1000	.3058	.4765	.5172	.5604	.6059	.6540	.7047

Source: R. W. Conway and Andrew Schultz, Jr., "The Manufacturing Progress Function," *Journal of Industrial Engineering,* **10,** 1, January–February 1959, pp. 39–54, © Institute of Industrial Engineers, 25 Technology Park/Atlanta, Norcross, Georgia, 30092; and Thomas E. Vollman, *Operations Management,* Reading, Mass.: Addision-Wesley Publishing Co., 1973, pp. 381–384. Reproduced by permission of the AIIE and Addison-Wesley.

The use of logs can be cumbersome, but there is a simple method that makes the learning-curve technique usable and practical. This technique is embodied in Table S11.2 and the following equation:

$$Y_N = Y_B C \qquad\qquad (S11.3)$$

where

Y_N = Number of labor-hours required to produce the Nth unit

Y_B = Number of labor-hours required to produce the base (B) unit

C = A learning-curve coefficient

The learning-curve coefficient, C, is a function of the percent of the Nth unit divided by the base unit. You will need to know the learning factor, L, in order to use the technique.

The following example uses the above equation and Table S11.2 to calculate learning-curve effects.

Example S2

It took 125,000 hours to produce the first of several tugboats you expect to purchase for your shipping company, Great Lakes Services, Inc. Boats two and three have been produced with a learning factor of 86%. At $40 per hour, what should you, as purchasing agent, expect to pay for the fourth unit?

First, compute the ratio of the desired unit to base percent:

$$\% \text{ base} = \frac{\text{Unit 4}}{\text{Unit 1}} = 400\%$$

Next, search Table S11.2 for a percent base of 400% and a learning factor of 86%. The learning-curve coefficient, C, is 0.7396. To produce the fourth unit, then, takes:

$$Y_N = Y_B C$$
$$Y_4 = (125,000 \text{ hours})(.7396)$$
$$= 92,450 \text{ hours}$$

To find cost, multiply by $40:

$$92,450 \text{ hours} \times \$40/\text{hour} = \$3,698,000$$

STRATEGIC IMPLICATIONS OF LEARNING CURVES

So far we have shown two examples of learning-curve use. The first illustrated how operations personnel can forecast labor-hour requirements for a product. In the second, we saw how purchasing personnel can determine a supplier's cost, which can assist the purchaser during price negotiations. The third and final application of learning curves applies to strategic planning.

POM *in action*

Building Strategy on the Learning Curve at Texas Instruments

Learning curve strategies are especially appropriate when products, such as handheld calculators or PCs, are very sensitive to price changes. Texas Instruments found that cutting prices could lead to huge demand jumps. Extra demand in turn sped Texas Instruments' progress down the learning curve by allowing quick increases in output. Lower costs then provided the flexibility for more price cuts and for another cycle of this process.

In the case of the hand calculator, advances in C-MOS (a type of semiconductor) technology and a large price-sensitive demand provided chances for huge growth. When Texas Instruments entered the fray in 1972 with a learning-curve strategy, costs per unit plunged from thousands of dollars to under $10 in less than 10 years. Sales skyrocketed, and Texas Instruments reaped the benefits of being a leader instead of a follower.

The PC market provides an ironic illustration of the same lesson. Home computers, also demand price-sensitive, have a steep learning curve. But Texas Instruments allowed Commodore to lead in the cost-reduction and price-cutting game. It paid the price for its mistake.

It is critical to understand competitors before embarking on a learning-curve strategy. A competitor is weak if it is undercapitalized, stuck with high costs, or burdened with a corporate parent that does not understand the logic of learning curves.

Strong and dangerous competitors control their costs, have solid financial positions for the large investments needed, and a track record of using an aggressive learning-curve strategy. Taking on such a competitor in a price war may help only the consumer.

Sources: Harvard Business Review, **63,** 2, March–April 1985, p. 148; and *Industry Week,* February 6, 1984, p. 57.

FIGURE S11.3

Industry Learning Curve for Price Compared with Company Learning Curve for Cost.

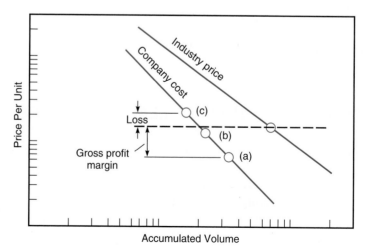

The *POM in Action* box, "Building Strategy on the Learning Curve at Texas Instruments," suggests segments of the semiconductor industry actively pursue a steep learning curve. An example of a steep semiconductor industry price line is so labeled in Figure S11.3. If a particular company believes its cost line to be the "company cost" line and the industry price is indicated by the dashed horizontal line, then the company must have costs at the points below the dotted line (for example, point a or b) or else operate at a loss (point c). When a firm's strategy is to pursue the company curve, a curve steeper than the industry average, it does this by:

1. following an aggressive pricing policy;
2. focusing on continuing cost reduction and productivity improvement;
3. building on shared experience;
4. keeping capacity growing ahead of demand.

Costs may drop as a firm pursues the learning curve, but volume must increase for the learning curve to exist. For instance, Figure S11.4 shows the units that have to be produced per year for a reduction of 25% when operating with a 60% or 80% learning curve. In recent years much of the computer industry has operated at a 25% cost reduction. The volumes and cost reductions implied by learning curves and as demonstrated by the data of Table S11.1 and Figure S11.4 suggest the difficulty of achieving such an objective.

FIGURE S11.4

The 80% and 60% Curves Show the Number of Units That Must Be Produced to Reduce Costs 25% Annually if the Firm Is Operating on One of Those Curves.
(*Source:* James A. Cunningham, "Using the Learning Curve as a Management Tool," *IEEE Spectrum* (June 1980): 47. © 1980 IEEE.)

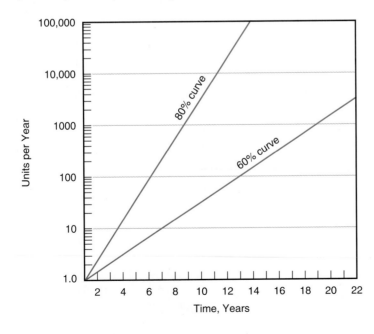

Developing a competitive strategy via the learning curve is not, as Example S3 suggests, a solution for everyone.

Example S3

Seymore Computers, Inc., just completed production of the first Seymore Mark II Computer, a supercomputer that has established a world standard. The firm expects the industry to continue to reduce costs by 25% annually with an 80% learning curve. By the sixth year, how many computers will Seymore have to produce each year to keep up with the industry curve?

From Figure S11.4, we find the intersection of year six and the 80% curve. They intersect at 100. Therefore, Seymore has to establish marketing and production plans for production of 100 units per year by the sixth year.

Since the total world-wide demand for supercomputers is less than 20 per year, it seems unlikely that this is a reasonable strategy. Perhaps maintaining low levels of production with state-of-the-art technology is preferable to a standardized product for Seymore.

Learning-curve graphs can also provide rapid information about cost and volume. While Figure S11.4 shows the volumes necessary for a 25% cost reduction on an 80% and 60% curve, Figure S11.5 shows the expected cost reduction when operating on the 60%, 70%, 80%, and 90% learning curves.

FIGURE S11.5

Volume Required to Stay on the Standard Learning Curve.
(*Source:* James A. Cunningham, "Using the Learning Curve as a Management Tool," *IEEE Spectrum* (June 1980): 47. © 1980 IEEE.)

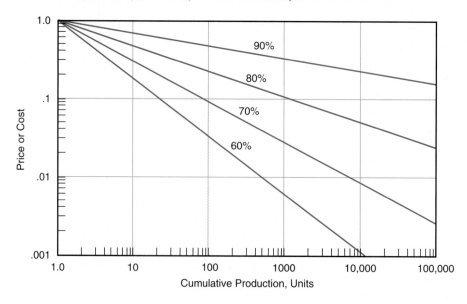

Example S4

Chip Makers Extraordinair, Inc., of San Jose, just made its first 512K RAM chip at a production cost of $1,000. If the industry is on a 70% curve, at what cost should the firm be producing the 1,000th unit?

From Figure S11.5, the 70% curve intersects 1,000 units between .02 and .03, say about 0.028. Therefore,

$$.028 \times \$1,000 = \$28.00$$

The 1,000th unit should have a cost of about $28.

If Chip Makers believes that the 70% curve for the industry is accurate, then it must structure the organization and costs to produce at this $28 level.

SUMMARY

The learning curve is a powerful tool for the operations manager. This tool can assist operations managers in determining future cost standards for items produced as well as purchased. Additionally, the learning curve can provide understanding about company and industry performance.

KEY TERMS

Learning curves (p. 496)   Log-log graph (p. 496)

USING AB:POM

Solving Example S1 Using the Learning Curve Module

AB:POM's learning curve module is used to develop learning curves based on two different sets of assumptions. In the first model the length of time that future units will take to produce is determined by a given learning coefficient. In the second model the learning coefficient is determined by the amounts of time for a first and last unit. In either case the output is displayed in tabular form and can also be displayed as a graph.

The inputs are as follows:

1. *Model selection.* Two models are available. In the first model (which is the default), it is assumed that the learning coefficient is known. In the second model, it is assumed that the production time for the Nth unit is known and the learning curve coefficient is found. In either case the program will display the production times for units from 1 to n and the cumulative production time for these units.

2. *Time for unit 1.* This is the length of time that it takes to manufacture the first unit.

3. *Number of the last unit.* This is the item number for the last unit that will be displayed and/or used for computations. If the number is above 20 then the production time will not be displayed for every unit but will be displayed over intervals so that all of the output will fit on one screen.

4. *Learning curve coefficient.* This is a number between 0 and 1. The learning curve coefficient is only entered for the first model. The second model will determine the learning curve coefficient based on the next data input item.

5. *Time to make last unit.* The last piece of information for the second model is the time it takes to produce the last unit rather than the learning curve coefficient. Based on this piece of information the learning curve coefficient will be determined.

As a sample problem, we use the data from Example S1. This appears in Program S11.1. The input data on the left indicate that the first unit takes 56,000 hours to manufacture; the last unit is unit number 10 and the learning coefficient is 80%. That is, the decrease in time is such that with the doubling of the unit number, the time is 80% of the previous time.

The output on the right consists of two columns that run from 1 to the last unit, 10. Note that production times do not exactly match Example S1, since the log functions were rounded.

As an optional output a graph can be plotted by pressing the [F1] function key.

Program S11.1

AB:POM's Learning Curve Module Applied to Example S1

———————————————— Experience (learning) Curves ———————————————— Solution ————

————————————————————— SOUTHERN TELECOM, EXAMPLE S1 —————————————

	Unit Number	Production Time	Cumulative Time
	1	56000.000	56000.000
	2	44800.000	100800.00
	3	39317.809	140117.81
Labor time for first unit, Y1 56000.00	4	35840.000	175957.81
	5	33355.691	209313.50
Unit number of last unit, N 10	6	31454.246	240767.75
	7	29931.414	270699.16
Learning coefficient 0.800	8	28672.000	299371.16
	9	27605.180	326976.34
	10	26684.553	353660.91

F1 = Display graph F2 = Other graph   F9 = Print   Esc
Press <Esc> key to continue or highlighted key or function key for options

SOLVED PROBLEMS

Solved Problem S11.1

a) How long does it take Southern Telecom (described in Example S1) to manufacture the eleventh telephone branching system when the tenth one took 26,686 hours?

b) As purchasing agent for a Fortune 1000 company, you expect to purchase units 10 through 12 of the new switching system. What would be your expected cost for the units if the manufacturer charges $30 for each labor-hour?

Solution

(a)
$$\% \text{ base} = \frac{PBX_{11}}{PBX_{10}} = \frac{11}{10} = 110\%$$

We find C from Table S11.2 at the intersection of % base (110) and learning factor (80%):

$$Y_n = Y_B C$$
$$Y_{11} = (26,686 \text{ hours})(.9696) = 25,874 \text{ hours}$$

(b)
$$Y_{10} = 26,686 \text{ hours}_{10} \text{ [from part (a) above]}$$
$$Y_{11} = 25,874 \text{ hours}_{11} \text{ [from part (a) above]}$$

For Y_{12},

$$\% \text{ base} = \frac{12}{10} = 120\%$$

Then from Table S11.2 (intersection of 80% and 120), we have $C = .9428$. Thus,

$$Y_{12} = (26,686)(.9428) = 25,160$$
$$\text{Total hours for all units} = 26,686 + 25,874 + 25,160 = 77,720$$
$$\text{Total cost} = \text{hours} \times \text{dollars}$$
$$= 77,720 \times \$30 = \$2,331,600$$

Solved Problem S11.2

If the first time you perform a job takes 60 minutes, how long will the eighth time take if you are on an 80% learning curve?

Solution

Three doublings from 1 to 2 to 4 to 8 implies 8^3. Therefore we have

$$60 \times .8^3 = 60 \times .512 = 30.72 \text{ minutes}$$

or, using Table S11.2, we have 8/1 = 800%. The intersection of 800 and 80% is .5120. Therefore:

$$60 \times .512 = 30.72 \text{ minutes}$$

DISCUSSION QUESTIONS

1. What are some of the limitations to the use of learning curves?

2. What techniques can a firm use to move to a steeper learning curve?

3. What are the approaches to solving learning curve problems?

4. What are the implications for Great Lakes Services, Inc., of Example S2 if the engineering department wants to change the engine in the third and subsequent tugboats Great Lakes Services purchases?

5. What is the advantage of a log-log graph?

6. Under what conditions should a firm avoid "pricing on the learning curve"?

PROBLEMS

: S11.1 As the purchasing agent for Boating Services, Inc., you are interested in determining what you can expect to pay for tugboat number four if the third boat took 20,000 hours to produce. What would you expect to pay for tugboat number five? Number six? Use an 86% L.C. and a $40/hr. labor charge.

: S11.2 Using the data from Problem S11.1 and Example S2, how long will it take to complete the 12th boat? How long will it take to complete the 15th boat? How long will it take to complete boats 12 through 15 inclusive? At $40 per hour, what can you, as purchasing agent, expect to pay for the four boats?

: S11.3 Dynamic RAM Corporation produces semiconductors and has a learning curve of .7. The price per bit is 100 millcents when the volume is $.7 \times 10^{12}$ bits. What is the expected price at 1.4×10^{12} bits? What is the expected price at 89.6×10^{12} bits?

· S11.4 If it takes 80,000 hours to produce the first jet engine at T.R.'s aerospace division and the learning factor is 90%, how long does it take to produce the eighth engine?

: S11.5 It takes 28,718 hours to produce the eighth locomotive at a large French manufacturing firm. If the learning factor is 80%, how long does it take to produce the tenth locomotive?

: S11.6 If the first unit of a production run takes one hour and the firm is on an 80% learning curve, what will unit 100 take? (Hint: Apply the coefficient in Table S11.2 twice).

: S11.7 As the estimator for Umble Enterprises, your job is to prepare an estimate for a potential service contract from a customer. The potential contract is for the service of diesel locomotive cylinder heads. The shop has done some of these in the past on a sporadic basis. The time for each cylinder head has been exactly four hours and similar work has been accomplished at an 86% learning curve. The customer wants you to quote in batches of twelve and twenty.

    a) Prepare the quote.

    b) After preparing the quote, you find a labor ticket for this customer for five locomotive cylinder heads. From the sundry notations on the labor ticket you conclude that the fifth unit took 2.5 hours. What do you conclude about the learning curve and your quote?

: S11.8 Using the log-log chart on page 509, answer the following questions.

    a) What are the implications for management that has forecast its cost on the optimum line?

b) What could be causing the fluctuations above the optimum line?

c) If management forecasted the tenth unit on the optimum line, what was that forecast in hours?

d) If management built the tenth unit as indicated by the actual line, how many hours did it take?

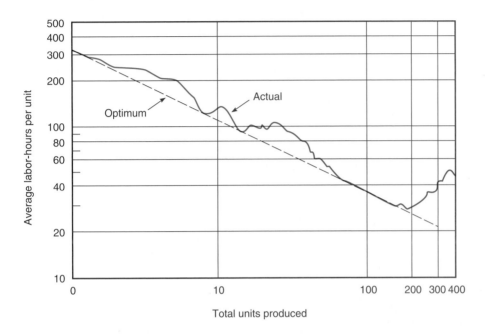

CASE STUDY

Learning Curves Applied to SMT

SMT and one other, much larger company were asked by IBM to bid on 85 more units of a particular computer product. The RFQ requested that the overall bid be broken down to show the hourly rate, the parts and materials component in the price, and any charges for subcontracted services. SMT quoted $1.62 million and supplied the cost breakdown as requested. The second company submitted only one total figure, $5.0 million, with no cost breakdown. The decision was made to negotiate with SMT.

The IBM negotiating team included two purchasing managers and two cost engineers. One cost engineer had developed manufacturing cost estimates for every component, working from engineering drawings and cost-data books that he had built up from previous experience and that contained time factors, both setup and run times, for a large variety of operations. He estimated materials costs by working both from data supplied by the IBM Corporate Purchasing Staff and from purchasing journals. He visited SMT facilities to see the tooling available so that he would

know what processes were being used. He assumed that there would be perfect conditions and trained operators, and he developed cost estimates for the 158th unit (previous orders were for 25, 15, and 38 units). He added 5%, for scrap-and-flow loss; 2%, to allow for the use of temporary tools, jigs, and fixtures; 5% for quality control; and 9% for purchasing burden. Then, using an 85% learning curve, he backed up his costs to get an estimate for the first unit. He next checked the data on hours and materials for the 25, 15, and 38 units already made and found that his estimate for the first unit was within 4% of actual cost. His check, however, had indicated a 90% learning-curve effect on hours per unit.

In the negotiations, SMT was represented by one of the two owners of the business, two engineers, and one cost estimator. The sessions opened with a discussion of learning curves. The IBM cost estimator demonstrated that SMT had in fact been operating on a 90% learning curve. But, he argued, it should be possible to move to an 85% curve,

CASE STUDY (Continued)

given the longer runs, reduced setup time, and increased continuity of workers on the job that would be possible with an order for 80 units. The owner agreed with this analysis and was willing to reduce his price by 4%.

However, as each operation in the manufacturing process was discussed, it became clear that some IBM cost estimates were too low because certain crating and shipping expenses had been overlooked. These oversights were minor, however, and in the following discussions the two parties arrived at a common understanding of specifications and reached agreements on the costs of each manufacturing operation.

At this point, SMT representatives expressed great concern about the possibility of inflation in materials costs. The IBM negotiators volunteered to include a form of price escalation in the contract, as previously agreed among themselves. IBM representatives suggested that if overall materials costs changed by more than 10%, the price could be adjusted accordingly. However, if one party took the initiative to have the price revised, the other could require an analysis of *all* parts and materials invoices in arriving at the new price.

Another concern of the SMT representatives was that a large amount of overtime and subcontracting would be required to meet IBM's specified delivery schedule. IBM negotiators thought that a relaxation in the delivery schedule might be possible if a price concession could be obtained. In response the SMT team offered a 5% discount,

and this was accepted. As a result of these negotiations the SMT price was reduced almost 20% below its original bid price.

In a subsequent meeting called to negotiate the prices of certain pipes to be used in the system, it became apparent to an IBM cost estimator that SMT representatives had seriously underestimated their costs. He pointed out this apparent error because he could not understand why SMT had quoted such a low figure. He wanted to be sure that SMT was using the correct manufacturing process. In any case, if SMT estimators had made a mistake it should be noted. It was IBM's policy to seek a fair price both for itself and for its suppliers. IBM procurement managers believed that if a vendor was losing money on a job, there would be a tendency to cut corners. In addition, the IBM negotiator felt that by pointing out the error, he generated some goodwill that would help in future sessions.

Discussion Questions

1. What are the advantages and disadvantages to IBM and SMT from this approach?

2. How does SMT's proposed learning rate compare with that of other companies?

Source: Adapted from E. Raymond Corey, *Procurement Management: Strategy, Organization, and Decision Making,* Boston, MA: CBI Publishing Co., 1977, pp. 4–6.

BIBLIOGRAPHY

Abernathy, W. J., and K. Wayne. "Limits of the Learning Curve." *Harvard Business Review* **52** (September–October 1974): 109–119.

Bitran, G. R., and D. Tirupati. "Approximation for Networks of Queues with Overtime." *Management Science* **37** (March 1991): 282.

Boren, W. H. "Some Applications of the Learning Curve to Government Contracts." *N.A.A. Bulletin* (October 1964): 21.

Bowers, W. B. "Who's Afraid of the Learning Curve." *Purchasing* (March 24, 1966): 77.

Camm, J. "A Note on Learning Curve Parameters." *Decision Sciences* (Summer 1985): 325–327.

Chen, J. "Modeling Learning Curve and Learning Complementarity for Resource Allocation and Production Scheduling." *Decision Sciences* (April 1983): 170–184.

Dutton, J., A. Thomas, and J. Butler. "The History of Progress Functions as a Material Technology." *Business History Review* (Summer 1984): 204–233.

Hall, G., and S. Howell. "The Experience Curve from the Economist's Perspective." *Strategic Management Journal* (July–September 1985): 197–210.

Hart, C. W., G. Spizizen, and D. D. Wyckoff. "Scale Economies and the Experience Curve." *The Cornell H.R.A. Quarterly* **25** (May 1984): 91–103.

Taylor, M. L. "The Learning Curve—A Basic Cost Projection Tool." *N.A.A. Bulletin* (February 1961): 21–26.

Womer, N. "Estimating Learning Curves from Aggregate Monthly Data." *Management Science* (August 1984): 982–991.

Yelle, L. E. "Adding Life Cycles to Learning Curves." *Long Range Planners* (December 1983): 82–87.

PART FOUR

Tactical Decisions in P/OM

Tactical decisions are those decisions about which something can be done in the short run. They are the operating and controlling decisions as opposed to the strategic and long-range planning decisions discussed in Part 3. Tactical decisions, however, like the long-run decisions, can contribute significantly to an organization's competitive advantage. The four tactical decisions are scheduling, inventory, quality, and maintenance and reliability.

Aggregate Planning Tactics

Aggregate Scheduling Yields High Utilization of Facilities and a Competitive Advantage at Anheuser-Busch

Beer is produced in a product-focused facility, one that produces high volume and low variety. Product-focused production processes usually require high fixed cost, but typically have the benefit of low variable costs. Maintaining high use of such facilities is critical because high capital costs require high use to be competitive. Performance above the break-even point requires high use and downtime is disastrous.

Anheuser-Busch is a major beer producer, producing close to 40% of the beer consumed in the U.S. Anheuser-Busch achieves efficiency at such volume by doing an excellent job of

In the starting cellar control room, information technology in the form of process control uses programmable logic controllers (PLCs) and computer software to monitor the starting cellar process, where wort is in its final stage of preparation before being fermented into beer.

Shown here are brew kettles where wort, later to become beer, is boiled and hops are added for the flavor and bitter character they impart.

matching capacity to demand. Demand must be matched to capacity in the long, intermediate, and short runs.

- In the long run, Anheuser-Busch matches total demand to total plant capacity.

- Intermediate planning is, in many respects, the aggregate planning problem. Anheuser-Busch matches fluctuating demand by brand to specific plant, labor, and inventory capacity. Meticulous cleaning between batches, effective maintenance, and efficient aggregate scheduling contribute to high facility utilization, a major factor in all high capital investment facilities.

- The short run requires planning and scheduling for some 300 different products, packages, and labels.

Beer production can be divided into four stages. The first stage is the selection and assurance of raw material delivery and quality. The second stage is the actual brewing process from milling to aging. The third stage is packaging into the wide variety of containers desired by the market. The final and fourth stage is distribution, which includes temperature controlled delivery and storage. Each stage has its resource limitations. Developing the aggregate plan to make it all work is demanding.

Additionally, the Anheuser-Busch production function adds uniqueness to the production process. Unique aspects of their production process include a second natural carbonation step, rather than artificially adding carbon dioxide, and the addition of beechwood chips during aging to promote a more effective fermentation. These features within the production function contribute to demand.

Finally, Anheuser-Busch builds competitive advantage in the beer industry by attention to quality—from farm inspections, to distribution and storage standards, to coding cans to ensure traceability.

Effective aggregate scheduling is a major ingredient in competitive advantage at Anheuser-Busch.

Automated guided vehicles are used to transfer full kegs to storage prior to shipping.

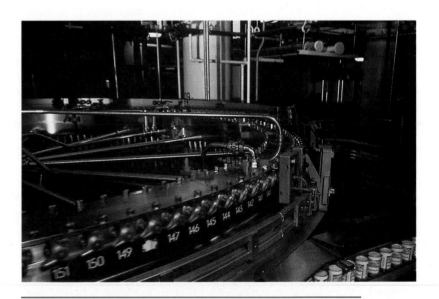

The canning line imprints on each can a code that identifies the day, year, and 15-minute period of production; the plant at which the product was brewed and packaged; and the production line used. This allows any quality control problems to be tracked and corrected.

INTRODUCTION

Aggregate planning

Planning is one of the main functions of a manager. **Aggregate planning** is concerned with determining the quantity and timing of production for the intermediate future, often from three to eighteen months ahead. Operations managers try to determine the best way to meet forecasted demand by adjusting production rates, labor levels, inventory levels, overtime work, subcontracting rates, and other controllable variables. The *objective of the process usually is to minimize costs over the planning period.* Other objectives may be to minimize fluctuations in the work force or inventory levels, or to obtain a certain standard of service performance.

The purpose of this chapter is to describe the nature of the aggregate planning decision, to show how the aggregate plan fits into the overall planning process, and to describe several techniques that managers use in developing a plan. Stress is given to both manufacturing and service sector firms.

THE PLANNING PROCESS

In Chapter 4, we saw that demand forecasting can address short-, medium-, and long-range problems. Long-range forecasts help managers deal with capacity and strategic issues and are the responsibility of top management. Management formulates policy-related questions, such as facility location and expansion, new product development, research funding, and investment over a period of several years.

Tactical scheduling decisions

Medium-range planning begins once long-term capacity decisions are made. This is the job of the operations manager, who makes tactical decisions. **Tactical scheduling decisions** include making monthly or quarterly plans, which address the problem of fluctuating demands. All of these plans need to be consistent with top management's long-range strategy and work within the resources allocated by earlier strategic decisions. The heart of the medium- (or "intermediate-") range plan is the aggregate production plan.

Short-range planning extends up to a year but is usually less than three months. This plan is also the responsibility of operations personnel, who work with supervisors and foremen, to "disaggregate" the intermediate plan into weekly, daily, and hourly schedules. Tactics for dealing with short-term planning involving loading, sequencing, expediting and dispatching, and other issues are discussed in Chapter 15.

Figure 12.1 illustrates the time horizons and features for short-, intermediate-, and long-range planning.

THE NATURE OF AGGREGATE PLANNING

As the term *aggregate* implies, an aggregate plan means combining the appropriate resources into general, or overall, terms. Given the demand forecast, the facility capacity, overall inventory levels, the size of the work force, and related inputs, the planner has to select the rate of output for the facility over the next three to eighteen months. The plan can be for manufacturing firms, for hospitals, for colleges, or for the company that printed and bound this textbook.

FIGURE 12.1

Planning Horizons.

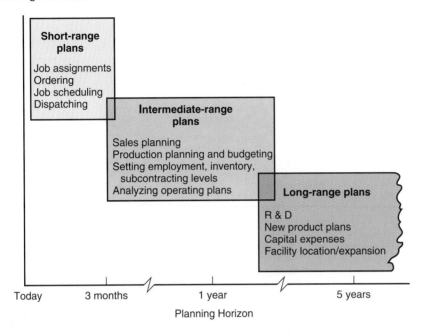

Take, for example, a company that produces four different models of microcomputers as its main business. There are: (1) laptops, (2) desktops, (3) advanced technology machines with high-speed chips, and (4) home/game-oriented PCs. The aggregate plan for this company might have the following output (in units of production) for this family of microcomputers each month in the upcoming three quarters:

QUARTER 1			QUARTER 2			QUARTER 3		
Jan.	Feb.	Mar.	April	May	June	July	Aug.	Sept.
1,500	1,200	1,100	1,000	1,300	1,500	1,800	1,500	1,400

A *service-oriented* company that contracts to provide microcomputer training for managers provides a second example. The firm offers courses on Lotus, dBase, Harvard Graphics, WordPerfect, and a wide variety of other subjects and employs several instructors to meet the demand from business and government for its services. Demand for training tends to be very low near holiday seasons and during summer, when many people take their vacations. To meet the fluctuating needs for courses, the company can perhaps hire and lay off instructors, advertise to increase demand in slow seasons, or subcontract its work to other training agencies during peak periods. However, subcontracting can open the door to competition and the risk of losing a client.

Notice that in both of the preceding companies the operations planner makes decisions about intermediate-range capacity without getting into details of specific products, parts, or people.

FIGURE 12.2

Relationships of the Aggregate Plan.

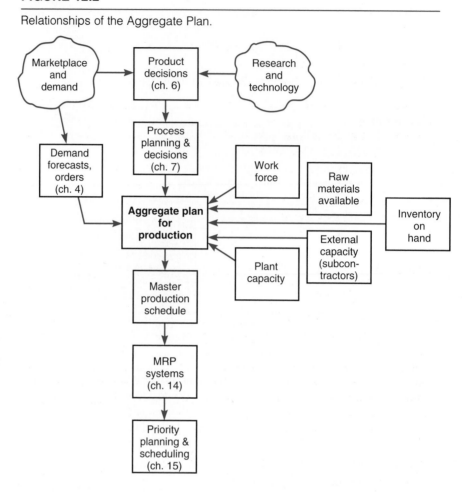

Aggregate planning is part of a larger production planning system; therefore understanding the interfaces between the plan and several internal and external factors is useful. Figure 12.2 shows that not only does the operations manager receive input from the marketing department's demand forecast, but he or she has to deal with financial data, personnel, capacity, and availability of raw materials as well. In a manufacturing environment the resulting master production schedule provides input to material requirements planning (MRP) systems, which address the procurement or production of parts or components needed to make the final product. Detailed work schedules for people and priority scheduling for products result as the final step of the production planning system.

AGGREGATE PLANNING STRATEGIES

There are several questions the operations manager must answer when generating an aggregate plan:

1. Should inventories be used to absorb changes in demand during the planning period?

2. Should changes be accommodated by varying the size of the work force?

3. Should part-timers be used, or should overtime and idle time absorb fluctuations?

4. Should subcontractors be used on fluctuating orders so that a stable work force can be maintained?

5. Should prices or other factors be changed to influence demand?

All of these are legitimate planning strategies available to management. They involve the manipulation of inventory, production rates, labor levels, capacity, and other controllable variables. When only one variable at a time is changed, we are using what is called a **pure strategy.** Generally, a *mixture* of strategies is used to arrive at a feasible production plan. Let us examine each of eight pure strategies in more detail. The first five listed below are called **passive strategies** because they do not try to change demand but attempt to absorb the fluctuations in it. The last three are **active strategies** through which firms try to influence the demand pattern to smooth out its changes over the planning period.

Pure strategy

Passive strategy

Active strategy

Pure Strategies

The eight pure strategies are:

1. *Changing inventory levels.* Managers can increase inventory during periods of low demand to meet high demand in future periods. If we select this pure strategy, costs associated with storage, insurance, handling, obsolescence, pilferage, and capital invested will increase. (These costs typically range from 5% to 50% of the value of an item annually.) On the other hand, when the firm enters a period of increasing demand, shortages can result in lost sales due to potentially longer lead times and poorer customer service.

2. *Varying work force size by hiring or layoffs.* One way to meet demand is to hire or lay off production workers to match production rates. But often new employees need to be trained and the average productivity drops temporarily as they are absorbed into the firm. Layoffs or firings, of course, lower the morale of all workers and can lead to lower overall productivity.

3. *Varying production rates through overtime or idle time.* It is sometimes possible to keep a constant work force, but to vary working hours. When demand is on a large upswing, though, there is a limit on how much overtime is realistic. Overtime pay costs more money, and too much overtime can wear workers down to the point that their overall productivity drops off. Overtime usually also implies increased overhead associated with keeping the facility open and heated or cooled the extra hours. On the other hand, when there is a period of decreased demand, the company must somehow absorb workers' idle time—usually a difficult process.

4. *Subcontracting.* A firm can also acquire temporary capacity by subcontracting some work during peak demand periods. Subcontracting, however, has several pitfalls. First, it is costly; second, it risks opening the door of your client to a competitor; and third, it is often hard to find the perfect subcontract supplier, one who always delivers the quality product on time.

5. *Using part-time workers.* Especially in the service sector, part-time workers can fill in for unskilled labor needs. This is evidenced in fast-food restaurants, retail stores, and supermarkets.

Federal Express' huge aircraft fleet is used to near capacity for nighttime delivery of packages but is 100% idle during the daytime. In an attempt to better utilize their capacity (and leverage their assets), Federal considered two services with opposite or countercyclical demand patterns to their nighttime service—commuter passenger service and passenger charter service. However, after a thorough analysis of these new services, the 12% to 13% return on investment was judged insufficient for the risks involved.

POM *in action*

Using Incentives to Match Production with Demand at John Deere

Moline, Illinois—John Deere and Company, the granddaddy of farm equipment manufacturers, has seen plenty of booms and busts before. Like most people these days, farmers are guarding their money instead of stocking up on expensive new equipment. In recent decades, dozens of firms in farm equipment have folded. But Deere is the perennial survivor. It succeeds by paying fanatical attention to costs and by manufacturing excellent machinery.

Deere's CEO explains that his firm uses incentives to try to match production to the seasonal farm economy's demand. During the fall and winter off-seasons, sales are helped with incentives and price cuts. Whereas in the early 1980s only 25% of Deere's big machines were ordered in advance of seasonal use, today about 70% are. This is double the rest of the industry's early-order rate.

Short-term margins are hurt, with incentives and bargaining lopping 15% off list price, but Deere keeps its market share. It also helps control costs, since Deere can produce more steadily all year long.

Sources: Forbes, May 27, 1991, pp. 46–47; and *Manufacturing Systems,* November 1987, pp. 34–39.

6. *Influencing demand.* When demand is low, a company can try to increase demand through advertising, promotion, increased personal selling, and price cuts. Airlines and hotels have long offered weekend discounts and off-season rates; telephone companies charge less at night; some colleges give discounts to senior citizens to fill classes; and air conditioners are least expensive in winter. Special advertising, promotions, selling, and pricing are not always able, however, to balance the demand with the production capacity. The *POM in Action* box describes how John Deere uses this strategy.

7. *Back ordering during high demand periods.* Back orders are orders for goods or services that a firm accepts but is unable (either on purpose or by chance) to fill at the moment. If customers are willing to wait without loss of their goodwill or order, back ordering is a possible strategy. Many auto dealers purposely back order, but the approach is often unacceptable in the sale of many consumer goods.

8. *Counterseasonal product mixing.* A widely used active smoothing strategy among manufacturers is to develop a product mix of counterseasonal items. Examples include companies that make both furnaces and air conditioners or lawn mowers and snowblowers. Service companies (and manufacturers also, for that matter) who follow this strategy, however, may find themselves involved in services or products beyond their area of expertise or beyond their target market.[1]

These eight strategies, along with their advantages and disadvantages, are summarized in Table 12.1.

---

[1] A good discussion of this subject in general is given by W. E. Sasser, "Match Supply and Demand in Service Industries," *Harvard Business Review,* **54,** 6 (November–December 1976): 133–140, and by R. C. Vergin, "Production Scheduling under Seasonal Demand," *Journal of Industrial Engineering,* **17,** 5 (May 1966).

TABLE 12.1 Aggregate Planning Strategies: Advantages and Disadvantages.

STRATEGY	ADVANTAGES	DISADVANTAGES	COMMENTS
1. Changing inventory level. (Produce inventory in some periods for later demand.)	Changes in required human resources are gradual or none; no abrupt changes in production are needed.	Inventory holding costs. Shortages, resulting in lost sales, may occur if demand increases.	This applies mainly to production, not service, settings.
2. Varying work force size by hiring or layoffs to track demand.	Avoids the costs of other alternatives.	Hiring and layoff costs may be significant; training costs may be incurred.	Used where many unskilled people desire only supplementary income.
3. Varying production rates through overtime or idle time.	Allows matching of seasonal fluctuations without hiring/training costs.	Overtime premiums; lower productivity; tired workers; may not meet demand.	Allows flexibility within the aggregate plan.
4. Subcontracting	Permits flexibility and smoothing of the firm's output.	Loss of quality control; reduced profits; loss of future business.	Applies mainly in production settings.
5. Using part-time workers.	Less costly and more flexible than full-time workers	High turnover and training costs; quality may suffer; scheduling difficult.	Good for unskilled jobs in areas with large temporary labor pools.
6. Influencing demand through ads, price cuts, etc.	Tries to use excess capacity. Discounts draw new customers.	Uncertainty in demand. Hard to exactly match demand to supply.	Creates marketing ideas. Overbooking used in some businesses.
7. Back ordering during high demand periods.	May avoid overtime; keeps capacity constant.	Customer may go elsewhere or may stay, but goodwill is lost.	Many companies backlog, and customers are willing to wait.
8. Counterseasonal product and service mixing.	Fully utilizes resources; allows stable work force.	May require skills or equipment outside firm's areas of expertise.	Risky finding products or services with opposite demand patterns.

Mixed Strategies

Although each of the eight pure strategies described above might produce a cost-effective aggregate plan, a combination of them (called a **mixed strategy**) often works best. Mixed strategies involve the combination of two or more controllable variables to set a feasible production plan. For example, a firm might use a combination of overtime, subcontracting, and inventory leveling as its strategy. Since there can be a huge combination of different possible mixed strategies, managers find that aggregate planning can be a fairly challenging task. Finding the one "optimal" aggregate plan is not always possible.

The mix of strategy options will be different for service firms, for they may not stock inventory. Subcontracting, as noted earlier, is dangerous because it may allow the subcontractor to "steal" the client. Consequently, service firms usually address aggregate scheduling via changes in personnel. They do this by cross-training and job rotation of staff, by changing labor schedules, and by using part-timers.

Mixed strategy

POM in action

Aggregate Scheduling at a European Manufacturer

An innovative human resource policy helped one European consumer goods manufacturer not only to cut costs but to improve responsiveness to customers as well. A highly seasonal business, the company had to ship about 80% of its products in two summer months. Management traditionally relied on overtime, temporary workers, and inventory buildup to deal with the huge increase in demand. Problems with this approach were not unusual. For one thing, when the firm built inventory many months in advance, it was unable to meet changing customer demands. For another, during the two busy months, numerous problems—customer complaints, urgent needs for parts, schedule changes, outages—plagued management.

The solution to regaining a competitive position was to persuade workers to accept an innovative contract. Throughout the year, employees would receive their regular 40-hour-per-week pay. But scheduling would change from March through mid-July to 50-hour production weeks. Then when the peak period ended, a 30-hour week schedule through November began. During this slack time, components common to several models were produced.

This flexible use of workers helped the firm reduce its working capital needs by 40% and double its peak season capacity. Keeping a quality advantage, the firm is once again competitive in price.

Sources: Academy of Management Review, January 1990, pp. 103–112; and *Harvard Business Review,* **65,** 2, March–April 1987, p. 78.

Level Scheduling

Level scheduling

Level scheduling, or level capacity planning, is a strategy popularized by the Japanese and their desire for "lifetime employment." **Level scheduling** involves aggregate plans in which daily capacities from month to month are uniform. In effect, firms like Toyota and Nissan keep production systems at uniform levels and may let the finished goods inventory of autos go up or down to buffer the difference between monthly demand and production level or find alternative work for production employees. Their philosophy is that stable employment leads to better-quality autos, less turnover, less absenteeism, and more employee commitment to corporate goals.

Level scheduling usually results in lower production costs than other strategies. Workers tend to be more experienced, so supervision is easier, costs of hiring/ firing and overtime are minimized, and the operation is smoother with less dramatic startups and shutdowns. The *POM in Action* box, "Aggregate Scheduling at a European Manufacturer," discusses another approach to level scheduling.

METHODS FOR AGGREGATE PLANNING

In the rest of this chapter we will describe several techniques managers use in aggregate planning. They range from what we call an "intuitive" method, to the widely used charting (or graphical) method, to a series of more formal mathematical approaches, including the transportation method of linear programming. The techniques will be addressed in this order:

1. intuitive approach
2. graphical or charting method
3. mathematical approaches
   a) linear programming
   b) linear decision rules
   c) management coefficient model
   d) simulation
   e) search decision rules

Intuitive Approach

Let us begin with perhaps the least desirable method, a nonquantitative, intuitive approach to planning. Conflicts among departments in large organizations are not unusual. For instance, marketing managers want to have broad product lines to sell from and plenty of inventory in stock to meet their customers' demands. Financial managers prefer to minimize inventory to reduce carrying costs. The jobs of manufacturing managers are easier when there are few products to produce. Because of conflicts such as these, planning and policy may boil down to the strongest individual rather than the best plan.

In other companies that have not formalized the aggregate planning process, management sometimes uses the same plan from year to year and adjusts it up or down just enough to meet the new demand. If the old plan was not close to optimal, the firm has locked itself into a series of wasteful decisions.

Graphical and Charting Methods

Graphical and charting techniques are popular because they are easy to understand and use. Basically, these plans work with a few variables at a time to allow planners to compare projected demand with existing capacity. They are trial-and-error approaches that do not guarantee an optimal production plan, but they require only limited computations and can be performed by clerical staff.

Graphical and charting techniques

In general, five steps are followed in the graphical method:

1. Determine the demand in each period.
2. Determine what the capacity is for regular time, overtime, and subcontracting each period.
3. Find the labor costs, hiring and layoff costs, and inventory holding costs.
4. Consider company policy that may apply to the workers or to stock levels.
5. Develop alternative plans and examine their total costs.

These steps are illustrated in Examples 1 to 4.

Example 1

A Charlotte manufacturer of roofing supplies has developed monthly forecasts for an important product and presented the period January–June in Table 12.2. The demand per day is computed by simply dividing the expected demand by the number of working days each month.

TABLE 12.2

MONTH	EXPECTED DEMAND	PRODUCTION DAYS	DEMAND PER DAY (COMPUTED)
January	900	22	41
February	700	18	39
March	800	21	38
April	1,200	21	57
May	1,500	22	68
June	1,100	20	55
	6,200	124	

To illustrate the nature of the aggregate planning problem, the firm also draws a histogram (Figure 12.3) that charts the daily demand each month. The dotted line across the chart represents the production rate required to meet average demand. It is computed by:

$$\text{Average requirement} = \frac{\text{Total expected demand}}{\text{Number of production days}} = \frac{6,200}{124} = 50 \text{ units/day}$$

FIGURE 12.3

Graph of Forecast and Average Forecast Demand.

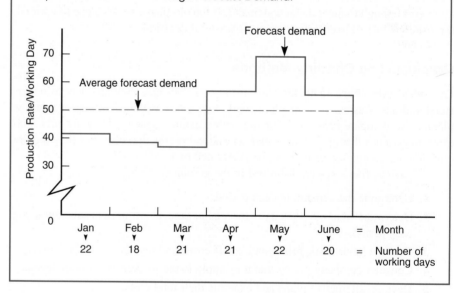

The histogram in Figure 12.3 illustrates how the forecast differs from the average demand. Some strategies for meeting the forecast were listed earlier. The firm, for example, might staff to yield a production rate that meets the average demand (as indicated by the dashed line). Or it might produce a steady rate of, say, 30 units and then subcontract excess demand to other roofing suppliers. A third plan might be to combine overtime work with some subcontracting to absorb demand. Examples 2–4 illustrate three possible strategies.

Example 2

One possible strategy (call it plan 1) for the manufacturer described in Example 1 is to maintain a constant work force throughout the six-month period. A second (plan 2) is to maintain a constant work force at a level necessary for the lowest demand month (March) and to meet all demand above this level by subcontracting. Yet a third plan is to hire and lay off workers as needed to produce to exact monthly requirements. Table 12.3 provides cost information necessary for the analysis.

TABLE 12.3 Cost Information.

Inventory carrying cost	$5/unit/month
Subcontracting cost (marginal cost per unit above in-house manufacturing cost)	$10/unit
Average pay rate	$5/hour ($40/day)
Overtime pay rate	$7/hour (above 8 hours)
Labor-hours to produce a unit	1.6 hours/unit
Cost of increasing production rate (training and hiring)	$10/unit
Cost of decreasing production rate (layoffs)	$15/unit

Analysis of Plan 1. In analyzing this approach, which assumes that 50 units are produced per day, we have a constant work force, no overtime or idle time, use no safety stock, and use no subcontractors. The firm accumulates inventory during the slack period of demand, which is January through March, and depletes it during the higher-demand warm season, April through June. We assume beginning inventory = 0, and planned ending inventory = 0.

MONTH	PRODUCTION AT 50 UNITS/DAY	DEMAND FORECAST	MONTHLY INVENTORY CHANGE	ENDING INVENTORY
January	1,100	900	+ 200	200
February	900	700	+ 200	400
March	1,050	800	+ 250	650
April	1,050	1,200	− 150	500
May	1,100	1,500	− 400	100
June	1,000	1,100	− 100	0
				1,850

$$\frac{\text{Total units of inventory carried over}}{\text{from one month to the next month}} = 1,850 \text{ units}$$

Work force required to produce 50 units/day = 10 workers

(Since each unit requires 1.6 labor-hours to produce, each worker can make 5 units in an eight-hour day. Hence to produce 50 units, 10 workers are needed.)

Plan 1's costs are computed as follows:

COSTS	CALCULATIONS
Inventory carrying	$ 9,250 (= 1,850 units carried × $5/unit)
Regular time labor	49,600 (= 10 workers × $40/day × 124 days)
Other costs (overtime, hiring, layoffs, subcontracting)	0
Total cost	$58,850

The histogram for Example 2 was shown in Figure 12.3. Some planners prefer a cumulative graph to display visually how the forecast deviates from the average requirements. Such a graph is provided in Figure 12.4.

FIGURE 12.4

Cumulative Graph for Plan 1.

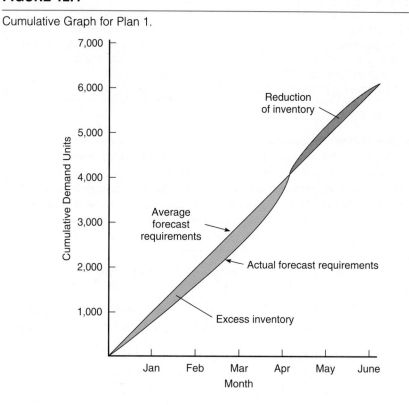

Example 3

A constant work force is also maintained in plan 2, but set low enough to meet demand in March, the lowest month. To produce 38 units/day in-house, 7.6 workers are needed. (You can think of this as 7 full-time workers and 1 part-timer.) All other demand is met by subcontracting. Subcontracting is thus required in every month. No inventory holding costs are incurred in plan 2.

Since 6,200 units are required during the aggregate plan period, we must compute how many can be made by the firm and how many subcontracted for:

In-house production = 38 units/day × 124 production days

= 4,712 units

Subcontract units = 6,200 − 4,712 = 1,488 units

Plan 2's costs are:

COSTS	CALCULATIONS
Regular time labor	$37,696 (= 7.6 workers × $40/day × 124 days)
Subcontracting	14,880 (= 1,488 units × $10/unit)
Total cost	$52,576

Example 4

The final strategy, plan 3, involves varying the work force size by hiring and firing as necessary. The production rate will equal the demand. Table 12.4 shows the calculations and the total cost of plan 3. Recall that it costs $15 per unit produced to reduce production from the previous month's level and $10 per unit change to increase production through hirings.

The final step in the graphical method is to compare the costs of each proposed plan and to select the approach with the least total cost. A summary analysis is provided in Table 12.5.

Of course, many other feasible strategies can be considered in a problem like this, including combinations that use some overtime. Although charting and graphing is a popular management tool, its help is in evaluating strategies, not generating them. A systematic approach that considers all costs and produces an effective solution is needed. Linear programming is one such approach.

TABLE 12.4 Cost Computations for Plan 3.

MONTH	FORECAST (UNITS)	BASIC PRODUCTION COST (DEMAND × 1.6 HRS/UNIT × $5/HR.)	EXTRA COST OF INCREASING PRODUCTION (HIRING COST)	EXTRA COST OF DECREASING PRODUCTION (LAYOFF COST)	TOTAL COST
January	900	$ 7,200	—	—	$ 7,200
February	700	5,600	—	$3,000 (= 200 × $15)	8,600
March	800	6,400	$1,000 (= 100 × $10)	—	7,400
April	1,200	9,600	4,000 (= 400 × $10)	—	13,600
May	1,500	12,000	3,000 (= 300 × $10)	—	15,000
June	1,100	8,800	—	$6,000 (= 400 × $15)	14,800
		$49,600	$8,000	$9,000	$66,600

TABLE 12.5 Comparison of the Three Plans.

COST	PLAN 1 (CONSTANT WORK FORCE OF 10 WORKERS)	PLAN 2 (WORK FORCE OF 7.6 WORKERS PLUS SUBCONTRACT)	PLAN 3 (HIRING AND LAYOFFS TO MEET DEMAND)
Inventory carrying	$ 9,250	$ 0	$ 0
Regular labor	49,600	37,696	49,600
Overtime labor	0	0	0
Hiring	0	0	8,000
Layoffs	0	0	9,000
Subcontracting	0	14,880	0
Total cost	$58,850	$52,576	$66,600

Mathematical Techniques for Planning

This section briefly describes some of the mathematical approaches to aggregate planning that have been developed over the past 30 years.

The Transportation Method of Linear Programming. When an aggregate planning problem is viewed as one of allocating operating capacity to meet the forecasted demand, it can be formulated in a linear programming format. The **transportation method of LP** (discussed in Chapter 8) is not a trial-and-error approach like charting but produces an optimal plan for minimizing costs. It is also flexible in that it can specify the regular and overtime production in each time period, the number of units to be subcontracted, extra shifts, and the inventory carryover from period to period.

In Example 5, the supply consists of on-hand inventory and units produced by regular time, overtime, and subcontracting. Costs, in the upper right-hand corner of each cell of the matrix, relate to units produced in a given period or units carried in inventory from an earlier period.

Transportation method of LP

Example 5

Harpell Radial Tire Company developed data that relate to production, demand, capacity, and costs at its West Virginia plant, as shown on page 529. Table 12.6 illustrates the structure of the transportation table and an initial feasible solution.

You should note the following:

1. Carrying costs are $2 per tire per month. Thus tires produced in one period and held one month will have a $2 higher cost. Since holding cost is linear, two months holdover costs $4.

2. Transportation problems require that supply equal demand. Hence, a dummy column called "unused capacity" has been added. Costs of not using capacity are zero.

3. The quantities in each column are the levels of inventory needed to meet demand requirements. We see that demand of 800 tires in March is met by using 100 tires from beginning inventory and 700 tires from regular time.

	SALES PERIOD		
	March	April	May
Demand	800	1,000	750
Capacity:			
Regular	700	700	700
Overtime	50	50	50
Subcontracting	150	150	130
Beginning inventory	100 tires		

	COSTS
Regular time	$40/tire
Overtime	$50/tire
Subcontract	$70/tire
Carrying cost	$2/tire/month

TABLE 12.6

SUPPLY FROM		DEMAND FOR				TOTAL CAPACITY AVAILABLE (SUPPLY)
		Period 1 (March)	Period 2 (April)	Period 3 (May)	Unused Capacity (Dummy)	
Beginning inventory		0 / 100	2	4	0	100
Period 1	Regular time	40 / 700	42	44	0	700
	Overtime	50	52 / 50	54	0	50
	Subcontract	70	72 / 150	74	0	150
Period 2	Regular time		40 / 700	42	0	700
	Overtime		50 / 50	52	0	50
	Subcontract		70 / 50	72	0 / 100	150
Period 3	Regular time			40 / 700	0	700
	Overtime			50 / 50	0	50
	Subcontract			70	0 / 130	130
TOTAL DEMAND		800	1,000	750	230	2,780

The optimal solution to this problem can be easily found using our AB:POM microcomputer software package described at the end of this chapter.

The transportation LP problem described here was originally formulated by E. H. Bowman in 1956.[2] Although it works well in analyzing the effects of holding inventories, using overtime, and subcontracting, it does not work when more factors are introduced. So, when hiring and layoffs are introduced, the more general method of simplex linear programming, seen in the Supplement to Chapter 3, must be used.

When the Bowman model *is* appropriate, computer software is available to solve aggregate planning problems easily.

Linear decision rule

Linear Decision Rule.[3] The **linear decision rule** (LDR) is an aggregate planning model that attempts to specify an optimum production rate and work force level over a specific period. It minimizes the total costs of payroll, hiring, layoffs, overtime, and inventory through a series of quadratic cost curves.

Management Coefficients Model. A *heuristics decision rule* is a method that a manager applies based on his or her experiences in tackling a problem. Many decisions in the world of production and operations management are subject to "rules of thumb" that decision makers apply.

Management coefficient model

A classic heuristics application is E. H. Bowman's **management coefficient model.**[4] This unique approach builds a formal decision model around a manager's experience and performance. The theory is that the manager's past performance is pretty good, so it can be used as a basis for future decisions. The technique uses a regression analysis of past production decisions made by managers. The regression line provides the relationship between variables (say, demand and labor) for future decisions. According to Bowman, managers' deficiencies were mostly inconsistencies in decision making.

Scheduling by simulation

Simulation. A computer model called **scheduling by simulation** was developed in 1966 in R. C. Vergin.[5] This simulation approach used a search procedure to look for the minimum-cost combination of values for the size of the work force and the production rate.

Search decision rule

Search Decision Rule. The **search decision rule,** developed by W. H. Taubert, is a pattern search algorithm that tries to find the minimum-cost combination of various work force and production levels.[6] A computer is needed to make the thousands of systematic searches for points that produce a cost reduction. Search rules such as this do not yield optimal solutions but are flexible enough to be used on any type of cost function.

[2] See E. H. Bowman, "Production Planning by the Transportation Method of Linear Programming," *Operations Research,* **4,** 1 (February 1956): 100–103.

[3] Because LDR was developed by Charles C. Holt, Franco Modigliani, John F. Muth, and Nobel Prize-winner Herbert Simon, it is popularly known as the HMMS rule. For details, see C. C. Holt, *et al., Production Planning, Inventories, and Work Force* (Englewood Cliffs, NJ: Prentice-Hall, 1960).

[4] E. H. Bowman, "Consistency and Optimality in Managerial Decision Making," *Management Science,* **9,** 2 (January 1963): 310–321.

[5] R. C. Vergin, "Production Scheduling under Seasonal Demand," *Journal of Industrial Engineering,* **17,** 5 (May 1966): 260–266.

[6] W. H. Taubert, "A Search Decision Rule for the Aggregate Scheduling Problem," Management Science, **14,** 6 (February 1968): 343–359.

Comparison of Aggregate Planning Methods

Although the search decision rule and other mathematical models have been found in research to work well under certain conditions[7] and linear programming has found some acceptance in industry,[8] the fact is that most sophisticated planning models are not widely used. Why is this the case? Perhaps it reflects the average manager's attitude about what he or she views as overly complex models. Planners, like all of us, like to understand how and why the models on which they are basing important decisions work. This may explain why the simpler charting and graphical approach is more generally accepted.

Table 12.7 highlights some of the main features of the planning methods we discussed in this chapter.

DISAGGREGATION

The output of the aggregate planning process is usually a production schedule for family groupings of products. It tells an auto manufacturer how many cars to make, but not how many should be two-doors versus four-doors or red versus green. It tells a steel manufacturer how many tons of steel to produce, but does not differentiate rolled steel from sheet steel.

TABLE 12.7 Summary of Aggregate Planning Methods.

TECHNIQUE	SOLUTION APPROACHES	IMPORTANT ASPECTS
Graphical methods	Trial and error	Simple to understand and easy to use. Many solutions; one chosen may not be optimal.
Linear Programming	Optimization	LP software available; permits sensitivity analysis and new constraints; linear functions may not be realistic.
Linear Decision Rule	Optimization	Model takes 1 to 3 months to develop; complex cost functions not always valid; does not always produce a feasible solution.
Management Coefficient Model	Heuristic	Simple, easy to implement; tries to mimic manager's decision process; uses regression; subjective selection of rule.
Simulation	Trial and error	Able to test many relationships among variables; can be costly; computerized; can handle any cost function.
Search Decision Rules	Heuristic	Widely used; permits any cost functions; can test alternative decisions and do sensitivity analysis; 3 to 6 months to develop; expensive search cycle.

[7] W. B. Lee and B. M. Khumwala, "Simulation Testing of Aggregate Production Planning Models in an Implementation Methodology," *Management Science,* **20,** 6 (February 1974): 903–911.

[8] W. N. Ledbetter and J. F. Cox, "Operations Research in Production Management," *Production and Inventory Management* (Third Quarter 1977): 84–91.

As we saw, the details and parameters resulting from the plan include staffing, subcontracting, inventory stocking, and weekly or monthly production levels. But even though all this is important information, the firm needs more to operate smoothly. What it needs is a plan dealing with specific products: What quantities should each one be produced in, and by what date? The process of breaking the aggregate plan down into greater detail is called **disaggregation.**

Disaggregation
Master production schedule

Disaggregation results in a **master production schedule** (MPS). The MPS, described in more detail in Chapter 14, Material Requirements Planning, specifies:

1. the sizing and timing of specific item production quantities;
2. the sizing and timing of manufactured or purchased components;
3. the sequencing of individual orders or jobs;
4. the short-term allocation of resources to individual operations.

AGGREGATE PLANNING IN SERVICES

Some service organizations conduct aggregate planning in exactly the same way as we did in examples 1 through 5 in this chapter. Most services pursue a number of the eight *pure* strategies listed earlier in Table 12.1 in combination, resulting in a *mixed* aggregate planning strategy for meeting demand. In actuality, in some firms, such as banking, trucking, and fast foods, aggregate planning may be even easier than in manufacturing.

Approaches to aggregate planning differ by the type of service provided. Here are four service scenarios.[9]

Restaurant Example

Aggregate planning in the case of a high-volume product output business such as a restaurant is directed toward (1) smoothing the production rate, (2) finding the size of the work force to be employed, and (3) attempting to manage demand to keep equipment and employees working. The general approach usually requires building inventory during slack periods and depleting inventory during peak periods.

Since this is very similar to manufacturing, traditional aggregate planning methods may be applied to high-volume tangible services as well. One difference that should be noted is that in services, inventory may be perishable. In addition, the relevant units of time may be much smaller than in manufacturing. For example, in fast-food restaurants, peak and slack periods may be measured in hours and the "product" may be inventoried for only as long as 10 minutes.

Miscellaneous Services Example

Most "miscellaneous" services, many financial services, hospitality services, transportation services, and many communication and recreation services provide a high-volume, but intangible output. Aggregate planning for these services rests principally on planning for human resource requirements and managing demand.

Part-time workers are a proven planning resource tactic, especially in restaurants and supermarkets. McDonald's, for example, has found that hiring retired workers for part-time jobs pays off. Older workers are effective and loyal employees whose absentee rates are typically much lower than those of their teenage co-workers.

---

[9] These four scenarios and their discussion are excerpted from R. Murdick, B. Render, and R. Russell, *Service Operations Management* (Boston: Allyn & Bacon, 1990), pp. 219–221.

The goal is to level the demand peak and to design methods for fully utilizing labor resources during forecasted low-demand periods.

National Chains Example

With the advent of national chains of small service businesses such as funeral homes, fast-food outlets, photocopy/printing centers, and computer centers, the question of aggregate planning versus independent planning at each business establishment becomes an issue. One component of aggregate planning for a service chain is centralized purchasing, which has many advantages. Output also may be centrally planned when demand can be influenced through special promotions. This approach is advantageous because it reduces advertising costs and helps regulate cash flow at the independent sites.

Airline Example

A final service example may be found in the airline industry. Consider an airline that has its headquarters in New York, two hub sites in cities such as Atlanta and Dallas, and 150 offices in airports throughout the country. Aggregate planning consists of tables or schedules of:

- number of flights in and out of each hub;
- number of flights on all routes;
- number of passengers to be serviced in all flights;
- number of air personnel and ground personnel required at each hub and airport.

This is considerably more complex than aggregate planning for a single site or a number of independent sites. Additional capacity decisions are focused on determining the percentage of seats to be allocated to various fare classes in order to maximize profit or yield. This type of capacity allocation problem is called **yield management.**

Yield management

HIERARCHICAL PLANNING SYSTEMS

Before we leave this chapter, it is important to convey the reality that aggregate planning and disaggregation are quite complex decision problems. Mathematical and heuristic models that try to include all aspects of these problems tend to be too difficult for managers to use.

Hierarchical planning systems are an approach to breaking decisions down into more manageable terms by partitioning them in a traditional managerial hierarchy. Figure 12.5 suggests that top-level managers should make strategic decisions, such as how many car tires to produce at each of their company's several plants. They should not decide which sizes and what quantities of each tire should be made at each plant. That is a tactical decision best left to the midlevel plant manager. The plant manager can also decide how much to produce and stock each period (season) and how many workers to hire or fire. Operational decision making is done at the supervisory level, by shop managers who determine details of scheduling and production. This hierarchical approach, which should include a feedback loop, may

Hierarchical planning systems

FIGURE 12.5

Hierarchical Planning Process.
(*Source:* Harlan C. Meal, "Putting Production Decisions Where They Belong,"
Harvard Business Review, **62**, 2 (March–April 1984): 102–111.)

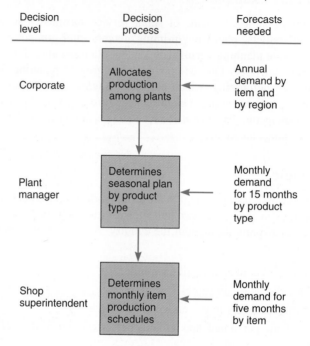

not result in an "optimal" solution, but it yields better and more timely results than attempts to optimize a very dynamic system.[10]

SUMMARY

The aggregate plan sets levels of inventory, production, subcontracting, and employment over an intermediate time range, usually 3 to 18 months. This chapter describes several aggregate planning techniques, ranging from the popular charting approach to a variety of mathematical and computer-oriented models such as linear programming.

The aggregate plan is an important tactical responsibility of an operations manager and a key to smooth production. Output from the aggregate plan leads to a more detailed master production schedule, which is the basis for disaggregation, job scheduling, and MRP systems.

Although the discussion in the early part of this chapter dealt mostly with the manufacturing environment, we just saw that aggregate plans for service systems are similar. Banks, restaurants, airlines, and auto repair facilities are all service systems that can employ the concepts developed here. Regardless of the industry or

---

[10] For more details, see G. R. Bitran and A. C. Hax, "On the Design of Hierarchical Production Planning Systems," *Decision Sciences,* **8,** 1 (January 1977): 28–55.

planning method, though, the most important issue is the implementation of the plan. Managers appear to be more comfortable with less complex and less mathematical approaches to planning, often because they are untrained in using quantitative methods. Several of the computerized techniques, including expert systems,[11] hold promise for the future improvement of the planning process and may find gradual acceptance.

KEY TERMS

Aggregate planning (p. 516)
Tactical scheduling decisions (p. 516)
Pure strategy (p. 519)
Passive strategy (p. 519)
Active strategy (p. 519)
Mixed strategy (p. 521)
Level scheduling (p. 522)
Graphical and charting techniques (p. 523)
Transportation method of LP (p. 528)

Linear decision rule (p. 530)
Management coefficient model (p. 530)
Scheduling by simulation (p. 530)
Search decision rule (p. 530)
Disaggregation (p. 532)
Master production schedule (p. 532)
Yield management (p. 533)
Hierarchical planning system (p. 533)

USING AB:POM

Solving Example 2 With AB:POM's Aggregate Planning Module

AB:POM's Aggregate Planning module performs aggregate or production planning for up to 12 time periods. Given a set of demands for future periods, you can try various plans to determine a least cost plan based on holding, shortage, production, and changeover costs. The initial input is the number of periods in the planning horizon.

When the data screen is initialized, you will be asked to choose the method to be used. Four methods are available. More help is available on each of these methods AFTER you choose the method. The methods are: *smooth production, produce to demand, produce a minimum amount,* and *user defined.*

In addition to the method, there is a *toggle* on the second row that lets you indicate whether excess demands should first be handled by overtime or by subcontracting. That is, if your *production amount* is larger than *regular time* capacity—which option should be used next.

The table has two different sides. On the left side capacities can be given while on the right side the costs can be given. Furthermore, the costs may be the same in each period or may vary from period to period. If they are the same, then the easiest way to enter the column is to go to the top of the column and place the cost.

Initial inventory is set at the top of the demand column.

In Programs 12.1 and 12.2 we will illustrate the use of AB:POM for analyzing Plan 1 (the first strategy) for Example 2. That "user defined" plan kept a constant

---

[11] See H. R. Rao and B. P. Lingaraj, "Expert Systems in Production and Operations Management," *Interfaces,* **18,** 6 (November–December 1988): 80–91.

Program 12.1

AB:POM's Aggregate Planning Program, with Options Menu and Data Entry Screen for Plan 1 of Example 2

```
                        ──────── Toggle  Menu ────────
                        Smooth production (let inventory vary)
                        Produce to demand (let work force vary)
                        Constant Reg time, then OT and sub
                        User defined
```

```
── Data file: PLAN1 ──────── Aggregate Planning ──────── Data Screen ──
   Number of time periods (1–99) 6
```

```
──────────── ANALYSIS OF PLAN1 OF EXAMPLE 2 ────────────
METHOD —>  User defined
PRIORITY  Overtime precedes subcontracting
All Pds ->        0       0       0   $8.00  $11.20   $10.   $5.0   $0.0   $0.0   0.00
                SCHEDULE                        C O S T S
      Pd Demnd  Regtm  Ovrtm  Subcn Regtim Ovrtim Subcon Holdng Shortg Incres Decres
Init       0       0      0      0
Pd1      900    1100      0      0   8.00  11.20  10.00   5.00   0.00   0.00   0.00
Pd2      700     900      0      0   8.00  11.20  10.00   5.00   0.00   0.00   0.00
Pd3      800    1050      0      0   8.00  11.20  10.00   5.00   0.00   0.00   0.00
Pd4     1200    1050      0      0   8.00  11.20  10.00   5.00   0.00   0.00   0.00
Pd5     1500    1100      0      0   8.00  11.20  10.00   5.00   0.00   0.00   0.00
Pd6     1100    1000      0      0   8.00  11.20  10.00   5.00   0.00   0.00   0.00
```

Program 12.2

Output of AB:POM's Aggregate Planning Analysis of Plan 1

```
──────────── ANALYSIS OF PLAN1 OF EXAMPLE 2 ────────────
METHOD —>   User defined
PRIORITY  Overtime precedes subcontracting
All Pds —>       0       0       0   8.00  11.20  10.00   5.00   0.00   0.00   0.00
                SCHEDULE                        U N I T S
      Pd Demnd  Regtm  Ovrtm  Subcn Regtim Ovrtim Subcon Holdng Shortg Incres Decres
Init       0       0      0      0
Pd1      900    1100      0      0   1100      0      0    200      0   1100      0
Pd2      700     900      0      0    900      0      0    400      0      0    200
Pd3      800    1050      0      0   1050      0      0    650      0    150      0
Pd4     1200    1050      0      0   1050      0      0    500      0      0      0
Pd5     1500    1100      0      0   1100      0      0    100      0     50      0
Pd6     1100    1000      0      0   1000      0      0      0      0      0    100
TOTL    6200    6200      0      0   6200      0      0   1850      0   1300    300
            SUBTOTAL COSTS —>        49600      0      0   9250      0      0      0
            TOTAL COST = 58850
```

work force throughout the 6-month planning period.

Program 12.1 contains a sample input screen. Program 12.2 provides the corresponding output screen.

Solving Aggregate Planning Problems With AB:POM's Transportation LP Module

AB:POM's Transportation Model module was first introduced as a tool for facility location in Chapter 8. In using the transportation linear programming program, we can also view the "origins" as supply sources and the "destinations" as periods, usually months or quarters. The program may then be used to solve Example 6 (Harpell Radial Tire Company) and other problems. Origin and destination names should be edited to reflect the aggregate plan. Cells that are clearly not feasible for the plan (namely, those that require backordering) should be given *very* high costs. This will force the computer to avoid producing in those sources. For details as to the use of this approach, refer back to Programs 8.3 and 8.4.

SOLVED PROBLEMS

Solved Problem 12.1

The roofing manufacturer described in Examples 1 to 4 wishes to consider yet a fourth planning strategy (plan 4). This one maintains a constant work force of eight people and uses overtime whenever necessary to meet demand. Cost information in Table 12.2 is to be used. Again, assume beginning and ending inventories are equal to zero.

Solution
Employ 8 workers and use overtime when necessary. Carrying costs will be encountered now.

MONTH	PRODUCTION AT 40 UNITS/DAY	BEGINNING OF MONTH INVENTORY	FORECAST DEMAND THIS MONTH	OVERTIME PRODUCTION NEEDED	ENDING INVENTORY
Jan.	880	—	900	20	0
Feb.	720	0	700	0	20
Mar.	840	20	800	0	60
Apr.	840	60	1,200	300	0
May	880	0	1,500	620	0
June	800	0	1,100	300	0
				1240 units	80 units

Carrying cost totals = 80 units × $5/unit/month = $400

To produce 1,240 units at overtime rate (of $7/hour) requires 1,984 hours.

Overtime pay = $7/hour × 1,984 hours = $13,888

Regular pay: 8 workers × $40/day × 124 days = $39,680

COST	PLAN 4 (WORK FORCE OF 8 PLUS OVERTIME)
Carrying cost	$ 400 (80 units carried × $5/unit)
Regular labor	39,680 (8 workers × $40/day × 124 days)
Overtime	13,888 (1,984 hours × $7/hour)
Hiring or firing	0
Subcontracting	0
Total costs	$53,968

Solved Problem 12.2

A Dover, Delaware, plant has developed the accompanying supply, demand, cost, and inventory data. The firm has a constant work force and meets all of its demand. Allocate the production capacity to satisfy demand at a minimum cost. What is the cost of this plan? (See solution on page 539.)

SUPPLY CAPACITY AVAILABLE (IN UNITS)

Period	Regular Time	Overtime	Subcontract
1	300	50	200
2	400	50	200
3	450	50	200

DEMAND FORECAST

Period	Demand (Units)
1	450
2	550
3	750

OTHER DATA

Initial inventory   50 units

Regular time cost per unit $50
Overtime cost per unit $65
Subcontract cost per unit $80
Carrying cost per unit per period $1

Solution to Solved Problem 12.2

SUPPLY FROM		DEMAND FOR				TOTAL CAPACITY AVAILABLE (SUPPLY)
		Period 1	Period 2	Period 3	Unused Capacity (Dummy)	
Beginning inventory		0 — 50	1	2	0	50
Period 1	Regular time	50 — 300	51	52	0	300
	Overtime	65 — 50	66	67	0	50
	Subcontract	80 — 50	81	82	0 — 150	200
Period 2	Regular time		50 — 400	51	0	400
	Overtime		65 — 50	66	0	50
	Subcontract		80 — 100	81 — 50	0 — 50	200
Period 3	Regular time			50 — 450	0	450
	Overtime			65 — 50	0	50
	Subcontract			80 — 200	0	200
Total	DEMAND	450	550	750	200	1,950

Cost of Plan

Period 1: 50($0) + 300($50) + 50($65) + 50($80) = $22,250

Period 2: 400($50) + 50($65) + 100($80)   = $31,250

Period 3: 50($81) + 450($50) + 50($65) + 200($80) = $45,800

Total cost $99,300

DISCUSSION QUESTIONS

1. What is the purpose of aggregate planning? Describe some active and passive strategies for implementing plans.

2. What is the difference between pure and mixed production planning strategies? Name four pure strategies.

3. Why are mathematical models not more widely used in aggregate planning?

4. What are the advantages and disadvantages of varying the size of the work force to meet demand requirements each period?

5. Why would some firms have longer planning horizons than others?

6. What is the relationship between the aggregate plan and the MPS?

7. Explain the concept of disaggregation.

8. Briefly describe four mathematical approaches to aggregate planning.

9. How does the aggregate planning differ for services versus manufacturing?

PROBLEMS

: 12.1 Develop two more plans for the roofing manufacturer described in Examples 1 to 4 and Solved Problem 1. For plan 5, the firm wishes to maintain a constant work force of six and to pay overtime to meet demand. In plan 6, a constant work force of seven is selected, and the remainder of demand is filled by subcontracting work. Which of the six plans should the firm select? Why?

 : 12.2 The president of SEA Enterprises, Soozi Eichler, projects the firm's aggregate demand requirements over the next eight months as follows:

Jan.	1,400	May	2,200
Feb.	1,600	June	2,200
Mar.	1,800	July	1,800
Apr.	1,800	Aug.	1,400

Her operations manager is considering three plans, all of which begin in January with 200 units on hand. Stockout cost of lost sales is $100 per unit. Inventory holding cost is $20 per unit per month. Ignore any idle time costs.

Plan A—Vary the work force level to meet exactly the demand requirements. The December rate of production is 1,600 units per month. The cost of hiring additional workers is $5,000 per 100 units. The cost of laying off workers is $7,500 per 100 units.

Plan B—Produce at a constant rate of 1,400 units per month (which will meet the minimum demands). Then subcontract additional units at a premium price of $75 per unit.

Plan C—Keep a stable work force by maintaining a constant production rate equal to the average requirements and by varying inventory levels. Plot the demand with a histogram that also shows average requirements.

Which plan should the operations manager recommend to Ms. Eichler?

: 12.3 SEA's operations manager (see Problem 12.2) is also considering these two mixed strategies:

Plan D—Keep the current work force stable at 1,600 units per month. Permit a maximum of 20% overtime at an additional cost of $50 per unit. A warehouse now constrains the maximum allowable inventory on hand to 400 units or less.

Plan E—Keep the current work force, which is producing 1,600 units per month, and subcontract to meet the rest of the demand.

: 12.4 Certo and Herbert is a VCR manufacturer in need of an aggregate plan for July–December. The company has gathered the data on page 541:

	COSTS
Holding cost	$8/VCR/month
Subcontracting	$80/VCR
Regular time labor	$10/hour
Overtime labor	$16/hour above 8 hours/worker/day
Hiring cost	$40/worker
Layoff cost	$80/worker

DEMAND	
July	400
August	500
September	550
October	700
November	800
December	700

OTHER DATA	
Current work force	8 people
Labor hours/VCR	4 hours
Workdays/month	20 days
Beginning inventory	150 VCRs

What will the two following strategies cost?

a) Vary the work force to have exact production to meet the forecast demand. Begin with eight workers on board at the end of June.

b) Vary overtime only, and use a constant work force of eight.

: **12.5** Develop your own aggregate plan for Certo and Herbert (see Problem 12.4). Justify your approach.

: **12.6** Carla Kimball, the operations manager at Kimball and Kimball Furniture, has received the following estimates of demand requirements.

APR.	MAY	JUNE	JULY	AUG.	SEPT.
1,000	1,200	1,400	1,800	1,800	1,600

Assuming stockout costs for lost sales are $100 and inventory carrying costs are $25/unit/month, evaluate these two plans on an *incremental* cost basis.

Plan A—Produce at a steady rate (equal to minimum requirements) of 1,000 units per month and subcontract the additional units at a $60 per unit premium cost.

Plan B—Vary the work force, which is at a current production level of 1,300 units per month. The cost of hiring additional workers is $3,000 per 100 units produced. The cost of layoffs is $6,000 per 100 units cut back.

: **12.7** Carla Kimball (see Problem 12.6) is considering two more mixed strategies. Using the data above, compare plans C and D with the earlier ones and make a recommendation.

Plan C—Keep the current work force steady at a level producing 1,300 units per month. Subcontract the remainder to meet demand. Assume 300 units remain from March that are available in April.

Plan D—Keep the current work force at a level capable of producing 1,300 units per month. Permit a maximum of 20% overtime at a premium of $40 per unit. Assume warehouse limitations permit no more than 180 units carryover from month to month. This means that any time inventories reach 180, the plant is kept idle. Idle time per unit is $60. Any additional needs are subcontracted at a cost of $60 per incremental unit.

· **12.8** Consider the following aggregate planning problem for one quarter.

	REGULAR TIME	OVERTIME	SUBCONTRACTING
Production capacity/month	1,000	200	150
Production cost/unit	$5	$7	$8

Assume there is no initial inventory and a forecasted demand of 1,250 units in each of the three months. Carrying cost is $1 per unit per month. Solve this aggregate planning problem.

: **12.9** A firm had developed the accompanying supply, demand, cost, and inventory data. Allocate the production capacity to meet demand at a minimum cost. What is the cost?

	SUPPLY AVAILABLE			
PERIOD	REGULAR TIME	OVERTIME	SUBCONTRACT	DEMAND FORECAST
1	30	10	5	40
2	35	12	5	50
3	30	10	5	40

Initial inventory	20 units
Regular-time cost per unit	$100
Overtime cost per unit	$150
Subcontract cost per unit	$200
Carrying cost per unit per month	$4

: **12.10** The production planning period of 512K RAM boards for CDM personal computers is four months. Cost data are as follows:

Regular-time cost per board	$70
Overtime cost per board	$110
Subcontract cost per board	$120
Carrying cost per board per month	$4

Capacity and demand for RAM boards for each of the next four months are:

	PERIOD			
	Month 1	Month 2	Month 3*	Month 4
Demand	2,000	2,500	1,500	2,100
Capacity				
Regular time	1,500	1,600	750	1,600
Overtime	400	400	200	400
Subcontract	600	600	600	600

* Factory closes for two weeks of vacation.

CDM expects to enter the planning period with 500 RAM boards in stock. Back-ordering is not permitted (meaning, for example, that boards produced in the second month cannot be used in the first month). Set a production plan that minimizes costs.

: **12.11** Haifa Instruments, an Israeli producer of portable kidney dialysis units and other medical products, develops a four-month aggregate plan. Demand and capacity (in units) are forecast as follows:

CAPACITY SOURCE	MONTH 1	MONTH 2	MONTH 3	MONTH 4
Labor				
Regular time	235	255	290	300
Overtime	20	24	26	24
Subcontract	12	15	15	17
Demand	255	294	321	301

The cost of producing each dialysis unit is $985 on regular time, $1,310 on overtime, and $1,500 on a subcontract. Inventory carrying cost is $100 per unit per month. There is to be no beginning or ending inventory in stock. Set up a production plan that minimizes cost.

: **12.12** A Birmingham, Alabama, foundry produces cast iron ingots according to a three-month capacity plan. The cost of labor averages $100 per regular shift hour and $140 per overtime (O.T.) hour. Inventory carrying cost is thought to be $4 per labor-hour of inventory carried. There are 50 direct labor-hours of inventory left over from March. For the next three months, demand and capacity (in labor-hours) are as follows:

	CAPACITY		
MONTH	Regular Labor-Hours	O.T. Labor-Hours	DEMAND
April	2,880	355	3,000
May	2,780	315	2,750
June	2,760	305	2,950

Develop an aggregate plan for the three-month period.

: **12.13** A large Omaha feedmill prepares its six-month aggregate plan by forecasting demand for 50-pound bags of cattle feed as follows: January, 1,000 bags; February, 1,200; March, 1,250; April, 1,450; May, 1,400; and June, 1,400. The feedmill plans to begin the new year with no inventory left over from the previous year. It projects that capacity (during regular hours) for producing bags of feed will remain constant at 800 until the end of April, and then increase to 1,100 bags per month when a planned expansion is completed on May 1. Overtime capacity is set at 300 bags per month until the expansion, at which time it will increase to 400 bags per month. A friendly competitor in Sioux City, Iowa, is also available as a backup source to meet demand—but it insists on a firm contract and can provide only 500 bags total during the six-month period.

Cost data are as follows:

Regular-time cost per bag (until April 30)	$12
Regular-time cost per bag (after May 1)	$11
Overtime cost per bag (during entire period)	$16
Cost of outside purchase per bag	$18.50
Carrying cost per bag per month	$1

Develop a six-month production plan for the feedmill.

: **12.14** The Kelly Chemical Supply Company manufactures and packages expensive vials of mercury. Given the accompanying demand, supply, cost, and inventory data, allocate production capacity to meet demand at minimum cost. A constant work force is expected, and no back orders are permitted.

	SUPPLY CAPACITY (IN UNITS)			DEMAND
PERIOD	Regular Time	Overtime	Subcontract	(IN UNITS)
1	25	5	6	32
2	28	4	6	32
3	30	8	6	40
4	29	6	7	40

OTHER DATA

Initial inventory	4 units
Ending inventory desired	3 units
Regular-time cost per unit	$2,000
Overtime cost per unit	$2,475
Subcontract cost per unit	$3,200
Carrying cost per unit per period	$200

: **12.15** Given the following information, solve for the minimum cost plan:

	PERIOD					
	1	2	3	4	5	Subcontracting:
Demand	150	160	130	200	210	100 units available over the five
Capacity						month period
Regular	150	150	150	150	150	Beginning inventory: 0 units
Overtime	20	20	10	10	10	Ending inventory required: 20 units

	COST
Regular-time cost per unit	$100
Overtime cost per unit	$125
Subcontract cost per unit	$135
Inventory cost per unit per period	$3

Assume that back orders are not permitted.

Data Base Application

:**12.16** Beth Chortkoff, owner of a dry cleaning equipment manufacturer, develops an eight-month aggregate plan. Demand and capacity (in units) are forecast as follows:

CAPACITY SOURCE	JAN.	FEB.	MAR.	APR.	MAY	JUNE	JULY	AUG.
Labor								
Regular time	235	255	290	300	300	290	300	290
Overtime	20	24	26	24	30	28	30	30
Subcontract	12	16	15	17	17	19	19	20
Demand	255	294	321	301	330	320	345	340

The cost of producing each dry cleaning unit is $1,000 on regular time, $1,300 on overtime, and $1,500 on a subcontract. Inventory carrying cost is $100 per unit per month. There is no beginning or ending inventory in stock and no backorders are permitted from period to period.

a) Set up a production plan that minimizes cost by producing exactly what the demand is each month and letting the work force vary. What is this plan's cost?

b) Through better planning, regular time production can be set at exactly the same value, 275, per month. Does this alter the solution?

c) If overtime costs rise from $1,300 to $1,400, will your answer to part **a** change? What if they fall to $1,200?

CASE STUDY

Campus Police at Southeast Florida State University

The campus police chief at Southeast Florida State University is attempting to develop a two-year plan for the department that involves a request for additional resources. Recently, the university administration has suggested that the department change its image and operating strategy from that of "policing" to a more comprehensive "public safety" approach.

The department currently has 26 sworn officers. The size of the force has not changed over the past 15 years. Al-though the size of the student population also has remained stable, several changes have occurred in the university environment that have prompted the campus police chief to review his operations and request additional resources. These changes include:

The university has expanded geographically. More buildings and other facilities have been added, some in outlying areas miles away from the main campus.

CASE STUDY (Continued)

Traffic and parking problems have increased because more students bring their cars to campus.

More portable, expensive equipment with high theft potential is dispersed across the campus (e.g., there are over 10,000 personal computers on campus).

Alcohol and drug problems have increased.

The size of the athletic program and its facilities have increased dramatically.

The size of the surrounding community has doubled.

The police need to spend more time on education and prevention programs in an attempt to become more fully integrated into the university community.

The university is located in a small town, 35 miles from an urban center. During the summer months, the student population is around 5,000. This number swells to 30,000 during fall and spring semesters. Thus demand for police and other services is significantly lower during the summer months. Demand for police services also varies by

—time of the day (peak time between 10 P.M. and 2 A.M.)

—day of the week (weekends are the busiest)

—weekend of the year (on football weekends, 50,000 extra people come to campus)

—special events (check-in, check-out, Founder's Day, commencement, and so on)

Football weekends are especially difficult to staff. Extra police services are typically needed from 8:00 A.M. to 5:00 P.M. on five football Saturdays. All 26 officers are called in to work double shifts. Over 40 law enforcement officers from surrounding locations are paid to come in on their own time, and a dozen state police lend a hand free of charge (when they are available). Twenty-five students and local residents are paid to work traffic and parking. During the last academic year (a nine-month period), overtime payments to campus police officers totalled over $30,000.

Other relevant data include the following:

The average starting salary for a police officer is $18,000.

Work-study, part-time students, and local residents who help with traffic and parking are paid $4.50 an hour.

Overtime is paid to police officers who work over 40 hours a week at the rate of $13.00 an hour. Extra officers who are hired part-time from outside agencies also earn $13.00 an hour.

There seems to be an unlimited supply of officers who will work for the university when needed for special events.

With days off, vacations, and average sick leave considered, it takes five persons to cover *one* 24-hour, 7-day-a-week position.

The schedule of officers during fall and spring semesters is typically (refer to table):

	WEEKDAYS	WEEKEND
First shift (7 A.M.–3 P.M.)	5	4
Second shift (3 P.M.–11 P.M.)	5	6
Third shift (11 P.M.–7 A.M.)	6	8

Staffing for football weekends and special events is *in addition to* the preceding schedule. Summer staffing is, on average, half that shown above.

The police chief feels that his present staff is stretched to the limit. Fatigued officers are potential problems for the department and the community. In addition, neither time nor personnel have been set aside for crime prevention, safety, or health programs. Interactions of police officers with students, faculty, and staff are minimal and usually negative in nature. In light of these problems, the chief would like to request funding for four additional officers, two assigned to new programs and two to alleviate the overload on his current staff. He would also like to begin limiting overtime to 10 hours per week for each officer.

Discussion Questions

1. Which variations in demand for police services should be considered in an aggregate plan for resources? Which variations can be with short-term scheduling adjustments?

2. In what terms would you define capacity for the department? What additional information do you need to determine capacity requirements?

3. Evaluate the current staffing plan. What does it cost? Are 26 officers sufficient to handle the normal workload?

4. What would be the additional cost of the chief's proposal? How would you suggest that the chief justify his request?

5. How much does it currently cost the university to provide police services for football games? What would be the pros and cons of subcontracting this work completely to outside law enforcement agencies?

6. Can you propose any other alternatives? What suggestions do you have for duties of police officers in nonpeak periods?

Source: R. Murdick, Barry Render, and R. Russell, *Service Operations Management*, Boston: Allyn & Bacon, 1990, pp. 236–237.

BIBLIOGRAPHY

Coker, J. L. "Analyzing Production Switching Heuristics for Aggregate Planning Models Via an Application." *Production and Inventory Management* (Fourth Quarter 1985): 1–13.

Eilon, S. "Five Approaches to Aggregate Production Planning." *AIIE Transactions* **7** (June 1975): 118–131.

Fisk, J. C., and J. P. Seagle. "Integration of Aggregate Planning with Resource Requirements Planning." *Production and Inventory Management* (Third Quarter 1978): 87.

Johnson, R. E., and L. B. Schwarz. "An Appraisal of the Empirical Performance of the Linear Decision Rule for Aggregate Planning." *Management Science* **24** (April 1978): 844–849.

Krajewski, L. J., and L. B. Ritzman. "Disaggregation in Manufacturing and Service Organizations." *Decision Sciences* **8** (January 1977): 1–18.

Levitt, T. "Production Line Approach to Service." *Harvard Business Review* **50** (September–October 1972): 41–52.

Lovelock, C. H. *Services Marketing*. Englewood Cliffs, NJ: Prentice-Hall, 1984.

McLeavey, D. W., and S. L. Narasimham. *Production Planning and Inventory Control*. Boston: Allyn & Bacon, 1985.

Murdick, R., B. Render, and R. Russell, *Service Operations Management*. Boston: Allyn & Bacon, 1990.

Northcraft, G. B., and R. B. Chase. "Managing Service Demand at the Point of Delivery." *Academy of Management Review* **10** (January 1985): 66–75.

Pessemier, E. A. *New-Product Decisions*. New York: McGraw-Hill, 1986.

Rothstein, M. "Hotel Overbooking as a Markovian Sequential Decision Process." *Decision Sciences* **5** (1974): 389–394.

Rothstein, M. "Operations Research and the Airline Overbooking Problem." *Operations Research* **33** (1985): 237–248.

Sasser, W. E., R. P. Olsen, and D. D. Wycoff. *Management of Service Operations: Text, Cases and Readings*. Boston: Allyn & Bacon, 1978.

Sasser, W. E. "Match Supply and Demand in Service Industries." *Harvard Business Review* **54** (November–December 1976): 133–140.

Vollman, T. E., W. L. Berry, and D. C. Whybark. *Manufacturing Planning and Control Systems*. Homewood, IL.: R. D. Irwin Co., 1984.

Wight, O. W. *Production and Inventory Management in a Computer Age*. Boston: Cahners Books, 1974.

Inventory Management and Just-In-Time Tactics

JIT Brings a Competitive Advantage to Harley-Davidson

Harley-Davidson is a repetitive manufacturer. This means that they assemble modules. Like most repetitive manufacturers, Harley produces on an assembly line and the end product takes a variety of forms depending on the mix of modules. In Harley's case, the modules are motorcycle components in the form of two engine types in three displacement sizes for twenty street bike models, which are available in thirteen colors and two wheel options. This adds up to ninety-five combinations. In addition Harley produces four police, two Shrine, and nineteen custom paint options. This requires that no fewer that 20,000 different pieces be assembled on one product line.

The Harley-Davidson engines are produced in Milwaukee and shipped to York, Pennsylvania. At the production facilities in York, both suppliers and the production departments deliver to the assembly line on a just-in-time basis. Harley, of course, groups parts that require similar processes together into families. The result is work cells. Work cells perform in one location all the operations necessary for production of specific modules.

Harley-Davidson was founded in Milwaukee in 1903. Since that time it has competed with hundreds of manufacturers, foreign and domestic. The competition has been tough. One of those competitive battles was

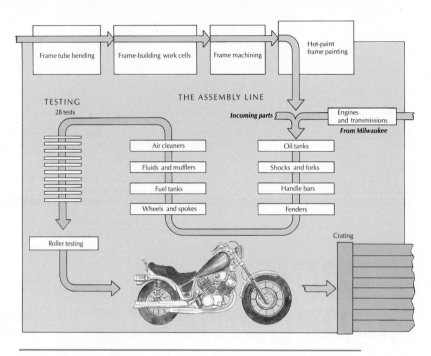

This is a flowchart of Harley's York, Pennsylvania, assembly plant.

with the Japanese. Indeed, after almost nine decades Harley is the only motorcycle company still producing in the United States.

The Japanese motorcycle invasion of the 1970s caught Harley in the crossfire between Honda and Yamaha. The competition was so intense that Honda introduced 81 new models and Yamaha 34 in only eighteen months. To meet the challenge, Harley-Davidson management emphasized quality improvement. An emphasis on quality is a marvelous tonic for any management and Just-in-Time (JIT) tactics force operations managers to address improvements in virtually every area. At Harley-Davidson this meant product and

process improvement, JIT inventory, and a host of other modern manufacturing methods. But mostly it meant a total quality control program driven by JIT.

Engines, having arrived just-in-time from the Milwaukee engine plant in their own protective shipping containers, are placed on an overhead conveyor for movement to the assembly line.

It all comes together on "the line." It takes about four hours for a Harley to get from the start to the end. Every 2.3 minutes, another Harley rolls. Each worker has specific responsibilities, and any worker who spots a problem has authority to stop the line until the problem has been corrected.

Most containers are specially made for individual parts, and many feature padding to protect the finish. Containers serve an important role in inventory reduction: the containers are the only place inventory is stored on the assembly line, so they serve as a signal to supply new parts to the line. After all the pieces have been removed, the container is returned to its originating cell, to signal the worker there to build more.

Harley purchased computer-aided design software to redesign its engines, new tube-bending equipment and a climate-controlled room for operating it, and a variety of other process upgrades from a chrome-plating line to a new painting process. Harley also organized the production process into work cells. However, Harley soon realized that to be world-class producers of quality motorcycles, they also had to change some basic ways they did business. These actions included:

Management Commitment Management gave full support to programs of continuous improvement, employee participation, supplier commitment, JIT, and statistical process control; and Harley provided the training and the organizational environment where these concepts could and would work.

Continuous Improvement Management decided that establishing tight manufacturing specifications would not be enough. Harley would continuously fight for ever higher standards of quality and process improvement. They would focus on target specifications, not tolerances.

Just-in-Time Inventory (JIT) Large parts inventories with their inherent problems and high costs were eliminated. Now, management insists on delivery of small quantities of parts with no defects to the assembly line. The concept applies to suppliers as well as workers within Harley-Davidson. Indeed, Harley is so good at supplier development, they now do consulting in this area.

Statistical Process Control (SPC) Employees received the statistical training and responsibility for determining the quality of their own output.

Completed Harleys coming from the assembly line in preparation for a series of 28 tests and inspections.

INTRODUCTION

Inventory is one of the most expensive assets of many companies, representing as much as 40% of total invested capital. Operations managers have long recognized that good inventory control is crucial. On one hand, a firm can try to reduce costs by reducing on-hand inventory levels. On the other hand, customers become dissatisfied when frequent inventory outages (called stockouts) occur. Thus, companies must strike a balance between inventory investment and customer service levels. As you would expect, cost minimization is a major factor in obtaining this delicate balance.

Inventory is any stored resource that is used to satisfy a current or future need. Raw materials, work-in-process, and finished goods are examples of inventory.

All organizations have some type of inventory planning and control system. A bank has methods to control its inventory of cash. A hospital has methods used to control blood supplies and pharmaceuticals. Government agencies, schools, and, of course, virtually every manufacturing and production organization are concerned with inventory planning and control.

In cases of physical products, the organization must determine whether or not to produce goods or to purchase them. Once this has been determined, the next step is to forecast demand as discussed in Chapter 4. Then operations managers determine the inventory necessary to service that demand. In *this* chapter we discuss inventory management. Two basic questions we need to answer are *how much to order* and *when to order*.

FUNCTIONS OF INVENTORY

Inventory can serve several important functions that add flexibility to the operation of a firm. Three uses of inventory are (1) the decoupling function, (2) a hedge against price changes and inflation, and (3) quantity discounts.

The Decoupling Function

The major function of inventory is to *decouple* production and distribution processes. When the supply or demand for an inventory item is irregular, maintaining inventory may be a good decision. For example, if product demand is high only during the summer, the firm may want to make sure that inventory is adequate to meet this high demand. This might require production in the winter, in which case the inventory level would build up during the winter to be used during the summer. This decouples production from demand and avoids the cost of shortages and stockouts. Similarly, if a firm's supplies fluctuate, raw material inventories may be necessary for decoupling input from the transformation process. Production processes may also fluctuate within the firm. When two related processes are not synchronized, inventory can separate (decouple) the two processes, allowing each to operate at its own pace.

A Hedge Against Inflation

Inventory can be a hedge against price changes and inflation. Placing cash reserves in the bank might enable the firm to obtain a good return. On the other hand, the value of inventory may increase even more. Thus, inventory may be a better investment. Of course, the cost and the risk of holding or carrying inventory must be considered. As a matter of policy, most firms do not allow operations personnel to speculate in this manner.

Quantity Discounts

Another use of inventory is to take advantage of quantity discounts. Many suppliers offer discounts for large orders. Purchasing in larger quantities can substantially reduce the cost of products. There are, however, disadvantages of buying in larger quantities. Higher costs due to storage, spoilage, damaged stock, theft, and insurance will be incurred. By investing in more inventory, less cash will be available to invest elsewhere.

INVENTORY MANAGEMENT

Operations managers establish systems for managing inventory. In this section we briefly examine two ingredients of such systems: (1) how inventory items can be classified (called ABC analysis) and (2) how accurate inventory records can be maintained.

ABC Analysis

ABC analysis divides on-hand inventory into three classifications on the basis of annual dollar volume.[1] ABC analysis is an inventory application of what is known as the Pareto principle. The Pareto principle states that there are a critical few and trivial many.[2] The idea is to focus resources on the critical few and not the trivial many.

    To determine annual dollar volume for ABC analysis, we measure the *annual demand* of each inventory item times the *cost per unit*. Class A items are those on which the annual dollar volume is high. Such items may represent only about 15% of the total inventory items, but they represent 70% to 80% of the total inventory cost. Class B items are those inventory items of medium annual dollar volume. These items may represent about 30% of the items and 15% to 25% of the value. Those with low annual dollar volume are class C, which may represent only 5% of the annual dollar volume but about 55% of the total items.

    Graphically, the inventory of many organizations would appear as presented in Figure 13.1 (on p. 554). An example of the use of ABC analysis is shown in Example 1.

ABC analysis

---

[1] H. Ford Dickie, *Modern Manufacturing* (formerly *Factory Management and Maintenance*) (July 1951).

[2] Vilfredo Pareto, nineteenth-century Italian economist.

FIGURE 13.1

Graphic Representation of ABC Analysis.

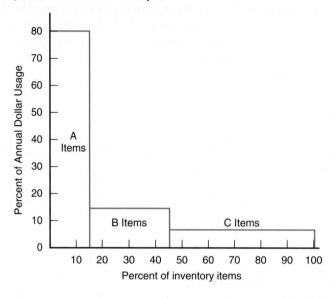

Example 1

Silicon Chips, Inc., maker of super-fast 1-meg chips, has organized its 10 inventory items on an annual dollar volume basis. Shown below are the items, their annual demand, unit cost, annual dollar volume, and the percent each item represents of the total. To the right of the table below, we show these items grouped into ABC classifications.

ABC CALCULATION

Item Stock Number	Percent of Number of Items Stocked	Annual Volume (Units)	Unit Cost	Annual Dollar Volume	Percent of Annual Dollar Volume		Class
#10286	20%	1,000	$ 90.00	$ 90,000	38.8%	72%	A
#11526		500	154.00	77,000	33.2%		A
#12760		1,550	17.00	26,350	11.4%		B
#10867	30%	350	42.86	15,001	6.5%	23%	B
#10500		1,000	12.50	12,500	5.4%		B
#12572		600	$ 14.17	8,502	3.7%		C
#14075		2,000	.60	1,200	.5%		C
#01036	50%	100	8.50	850	.4%	5%	C
#01307		1,200	.42	504	.2%		C
#10572		250	.60	150	.1%		C
		8,550		$232,057	100.0%		

Criteria other than annual dollar volume can determine item classification. For instance, anticipated engineering changes, delivery problems, quality problems, or high unit cost may dictate upgrading items to a higher classification. The advantage of dividing inventory items into classes allows policies and controls to be established for each class.

Policies that may be based on ABC analysis include the following:

1. The purchasing resources expended on supplier development should be much higher for individual A items than for individual C items.
2. A items, as opposed to B and C items, should have tighter physical inventory control; perhaps they belong in a more secure area, and perhaps the accuracy of inventory records for A items should be verified more frequently.
3. Forecasting A items may warrant more care than forecasting other items.

Better forecasting, physical control, supplier reliability, and an ultimate reduction in safety stock can all result from inventory management techniques such as ABC analysis.

Record Accuracy

Good inventory policies are meaningless if management does not know what inventory is on hand. Accuracy of records is a critical ingredient in production and inventory systems. Record accuracy allows organizations to move away from being sure "some of everything" is in inventory to focusing on only those items that are needed. Only when an organization can determine accurately what it has on hand can it make precise decisions about ordering, scheduling, and shipping.

To ensure accuracy, incoming and outgoing record keeping must be good, as must be stockroom security. A well-organized stockroom will have limited access, good housekeeping, and storage areas that hold fixed amounts of inventory. Bins, shelf space, and parts will be labeled accurately.

Cycle Counting

Even though an organization may have gone to substantial efforts to record inventory accurately, these records must be verified through a continuing audit. Such audits are known as **cycle counting.** Historically, many firms take annual physical inventories. This often means shutting down the facility and having inexperienced people counting parts and material. Inventory records should instead be verified via cycle counting. Cycle counting uses inventory classifications developed through ABC analysis. With cycle counting procedures, items are counted, records are verified, and inaccuracies are periodically documented. The cause of inaccuracies is then traced and appropriate remedial action taken in accordance with the classification of the item. A items will be counted frequently, perhaps once a month; B items will be counted less frequently, perhaps once a quarter; and C items will be counted perhaps once every six months. Example 2 illustrates how many items of each classification to count.

Cycle counting

Example 2

Cole's Trucks, Inc., a builder of high-quality refuse trucks, has about 5,000 items in its inventory. After hiring Matt Clark, a bright young P/OM student, for the summer, the firm determined that it has 500 A items, 1,750 B items, and 2,750 C items. The policy is to count A items every month (every 20 working days), B items every quarter (every 60 working days), and C items every six months (every 120 working days). How many items should be counted each day?

ITEM CLASS	QUANTITY	CYCLE COUNTING POLICY	NUMBER OF ITEMS COUNTED PER DAY
A	500	Each month (20 working days)	500/20 = 25/day
B	1,750	Each quarter (60 working days)	1,750/60 = 29/day
C	2,750	Every six months (120 working days)	2,750/120 = 23/day
			77/day

77 items are counted each day.

Cycle counting also has the advantage of:

1. eliminating the shutdown and interruption of production necessary for annual physical inventories;
2. eliminating annual inventory adjustments;
3. providing professional personnel to audit the accuracy of inventory;
4. allowing the cause of the errors to be identified and remedial action to be taken;
5. maintaining accurate inventory records.

JUST-IN-TIME INVENTORY

Just-in-time inventory

Inventories in production and distribution systems often exist "just in case" something goes wrong, that is, just in case some variation from the production plan occurs. In such a concept, inventory exists between all segments of production and distribution. We suggest that good inventory tactics require not "just-in-case," but "just-in-time" (JIT) inventory. **Just-in-time inventory** is the minimum inventory necessary to keep a perfect system running. With just-in-time inventory, the exact amount of good items arrive at the moment they are needed, not a minute before or a minute after the units are required. Let us examine this idea.

To achieve just-in-time inventory, managers *reduce variability caused by both internal and external factors.* If inventory exists because of variability in the process, then managers eliminate the variability. Inventory hides variability—a polite word for problems. If managers can get rid of the variability, they need very little inventory. What causes variability?

Most variability is caused by tolerating waste or by poor management. (See the

POM

The Revolution Against Waste

Just-in-time (JIT) implies a sweeping reorganization of work and society. The JIT factory attacks four types of waste: inventories, changeovers, defects, and human resources. The war against waste begins and ends with factory layout. The long production lines and huge "economic lots" of the Industrial Revolution, with goods passing through monumental, single-operation machines, are gone. Now each work cell, arranged in a U-shape, contains several small machines performing different operations. The cells produce goods a unit at a time, and produce them only after a customer buys them.

Inventory is waste. It wastes space because it takes up storage room. It wastes money because it has to be financed. It wastes time because it has to be transported. Nothing is wasted that can be sold; so produce nothing that cannot be sold.

"Time is money!" said Benjamin Franklin. "Bolts are our enemies!" Japan's Shigeo Shingo tells us. Motion that does not add value to a product is waste. Single clamps replace most bolts, and the remaining ones tighten with one turn. Workers can easily rearrange production cells to accommodate product improvements or even new designs. Almost nothing in such a factory is bolted down. Everything is on casters.

Defects are waste. When workers produce units one at a time, they can test each product or component at each production stage. Machines in work cells with "human-touch" functions sense defects and stop automatically when they occur. An entire production line can stop when someone finds a defect. Before JIT, defective products were replaced from inventory. In a JIT factory there are no such buffers. Getting it right the first time is all-important. Waste removal thus has a by-product: quality.

Sources: Manufacturing Engineering, January 1990, p. 104; and *Manufacturing Systems,* May 1989, pp. 26–30.

POM in Action box, "The Revolution Against Waste.") Some of the reasons variability occurs are:

1. employees, machines, and suppliers produce units that do not conform to standards, are late, or are not the proper quantity; or
2. engineering drawings or specifications are inaccurate; or
3. production personnel try to produce before drawings or specifications are complete; or
4. customer demands are unknown.

The variability described above may require that a firm maintain various types of inventories. These include raw material inventory, work-in-process inventory, maintenance/repair/operating supply (**MRO**) inventory, and finished goods inventory.

MRO

Raw material inventories can be used to decouple suppliers from the production process. However, the preferred approach is to eliminate supplier variability in quality, quantity, or delivery time. Some *work-in-process inventory* may exist because of the time it takes for a product to be made (called cycle time) as shown in Figure 13.2. Reducing the cycle time reduces inventory. Often this is not difficult. As Figure 13.2 shows, most of the time a product is "being made," it is in fact sitting

FIGURE 13.2

The Material Flow Cycle.

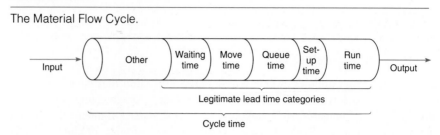

idle. Actual work time or "run" time is a small portion of the material flow time, perhaps as low as 5%.

MRO inventories exist because need and timing for some maintenance and repair of equipment is unknown. While the demand for some MRO inventories (as we will see in Chapter 18) is a function of maintenance schedules, other MRO demands must be forecasted. Similarly, *finished goods* may be inventoried because customer demands for a given time period may not be known.

For the above reasons, inventory exists. The just-in-case approach to inventory management deals with variability by "decoupling" the various stages of the process. Decoupling is accomplished by increasing inventory until inventory is adequate to allow for all of the variability. If variability is large, management ends up with huge amounts of inventory.

Another and better idea is to get rid of variability and problems. Figure 13.3 shows a stream full of rocks. The water in the stream represents inventory flow, and the rocks represent problems such as late deliveries, machine breakdown, and poor employee performance. The water level in the stream hides variability and problems. Because problems are hidden by inventory, they are sometimes hard to find.

Therefore, to achieve just-in-time inventory, management must begin by reducing inventory. Reducing inventory uncovers the rocks that represent the variability and problems currently being tolerated. With reduced inventory, management chips away at the exposed problems until the stream is clear, and then makes additional cuts in inventory, chipping away at the next level of exposed problems. Ultimately there will be virtually no inventory and no problems (variability).

Perhaps the manager who said "Inventory is the root of operations management evil" was not far from the truth. If inventory is not evil, it tends to hide the evil at great cost.

Just-in-Time Production

Just-in-time production has come to mean elimination of waste, synchronized manufacture, and little inventory. The key to JIT is producing small lot sizes to standards. Reducing the size of batches can be a major help in reducing inventory and inventory costs. When inventory usage is constant, the average inventory level is the sum of the maximum inventory plus the minimum inventory divided by two. Expressing the average inventory level algebraically, we have:

$$\text{Average inventory level} = \frac{\text{Maximum inventory} + \text{Minimum inventory}}{2}$$

The average inventory drops as the inventory reorder quantity drops because

FIGURE 13.3

Inventory Hides Problems, Just as Water in a Stream Hides the Rocks (a).
Reduce inventory so the problems can be found; solve those problems, then
reduce inventory again. Eventually the material should flow smoothly (b).

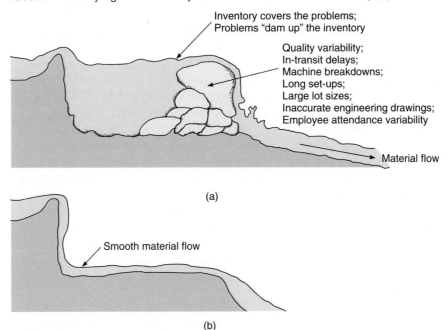

Inventory covers the problems;
Problems "dam up" the inventory

Quality variability;
In-transit delays;
Machine breakdowns;
Long set-ups;
Large lot sizes;
Inaccurate engineering drawings;
Employee attendance variability

Material flow

(a)

Smooth material flow

(b)

the maximum inventory level drops. Moreover, as noted earlier, the smaller the lot
size (batch), the fewer problems are hidden. Only when problems are identified can
they be solved and the organization become more efficient. We therefore want to
decrease total inventory and attendant lot sizes. One of the ways to achieve small
lot sizes is to move inventory through the shop only as needed rather than pushing
it on to the next workstation, whether they are ready for it or not. When inventory
is moved only as needed, it is referred to as a *pull* system and the ideal lot size is
one. The Japanese call this system *Kanban.*

Kanban

Kanban is a Japanese word for "card." In their effort to reduce inventory, the
Japanese use systems that "pull" inventory through the shop. Often a card is used to
signal the need for more material, hence the name Kanban. The need for the next
batch of material may signal the need for movement of existing inventory from one
workstation to the next or the need to produce parts, subassemblies, or assemblies.
The card is the authorization for the next batch. The system has been modified in
many facilities so that, even though it is called a Kanban, the card does not exist. In
some cases, an empty position on the floor is indication that the next lot is needed
(Figure 13.4). In other cases, some sort of signal, such as a flag or rag (Figure 13.5)
is used to signify that it is time for the next batch.

    The batches are typically very small, usually a matter of a few hours' worth of
production. Such a system requires tight schedules and frequent setups of machines.
Small quantities of everything must be produced several times a day. Such a system
must run smoothly because any shortage has an almost immediate impact on the

Kanban

POM *in action*

Blue Bell Trims Its Inventory

Blue Bell Company, the maker of Wrangler jeans and other clothes, is one of the world's largest apparel manufacturers. With annual sales totaling over $1 billion, it employs over 27,000 people worldwide. Using 37 plants to manufacture and stock basic styles of men's jeans (each called a "stock keeping unit," or SKU), Wrangler makes 35 million pairs of jeans a year.

Blue Bell faced a challenge in finding a better balance of the cost of carrying inventory against the risk of shortages. Records indicated that inventory had not been well balanced; some SKU's reported months of supply, while others were out of stock.

The economic and competitive pressures that Blue Bell faced were severe. Not only were SKU inventories out of balance, but the high cost of carrying inventory had become critical. Financing inven-

tory had dramatically forced up Blue Bell's costs of doing business.

The EOQ model was implemented by management to take quick action to reverse the situation. By designing, testing, and providing a new production planning process, inventories were reduced more than 31% (from $371 million to $256 million) without a decrease in sales or customer service. The new process also resulted in lowered manufacturing costs by roughly $1 million. A major factor in this achievement was the strong support of top management. Their support was conveyed down the line so that employees at all levels became enthusiastically involved.

Sources: Forbes, **143,** 3, February 6, 1989, pp. 41–42; *Forbes,* **141,** 1, May 16, 1988; and *Interfaces,* **15,** 1, January–February 1985, pp. 34–52.

FIGURE 13.4

Diagram of Stockpoint Lanes at Tachikawa Spring Co. Press Shop. From the status shown in the diagram, the lane has just been filled with part G82; they may be working on part H31 and getting ready for part G30, but that depends on the pull signals.
(*Source:* Robert W. Hall, *Zero Inventories,* Homewood, IL: Dow-Jones-Irwin, 1983, p. 51.)

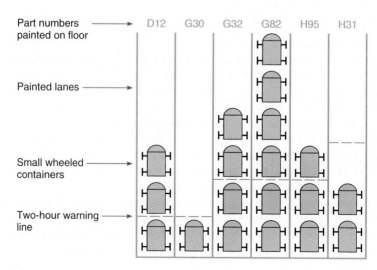

FIGURE 13.5

Diagram of Outbound Stockpoint with Warning Signal Marker.
(*Source:* Robert W. Hall, *Zero Inventories,* Homewood, IL: Dow-Jones-Irwin, 1983, p. 51.)

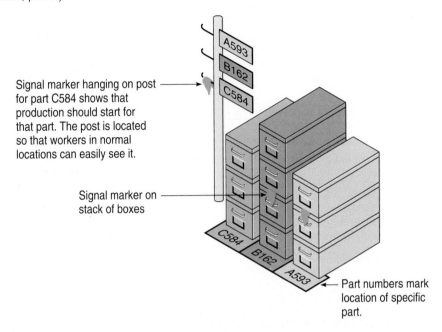

Signal marker hanging on post for part C584 shows that production should start for that part. The post is located so that workers in normal locations can easily see it.

Signal marker on stack of boxes

Part numbers mark location of specific part.

entire system. Kanban places added emphasis on meeting schedules and reducing the time and cost required by setups.

Whether it is called Kanban or not, the advantages of small inventory are significant. For instance, small batches allow a very limited amount of faulty material. Numerous aspects of inventory are bad, and only one aspect, availability, is good. Among the bad aspects are poor quality, obsolescence, damage, occupied space, committed assets, increased insurance, increased material handling, and increased accidents. These costs are called holding costs or carrying costs.

Holding, Ordering, and Setup Costs

Holding costs are the costs associated with holding or "carrying" inventory over time. Therefore holding costs also include costs related to storage, such as insurance, extra staffing, interest, and so on. Table 13.1 shows the kinds of costs that need to be evaluated to determine holding costs. Many firms find it difficult to evaluate inventory holding costs realistically. Consequently, inventory holding costs are typically understated.[3]

Holding costs

Small order quantity requires, as we shall see shortly, a low ordering cost for each order. **Ordering cost** includes costs of supplies, forms, order processing, clerical support, and so forth. When orders are being manufactured, ordering costs also exist, but they are known as setup costs.

Ordering cost

Setup cost is the cost to prepare a machine or process for manufacturing an order. The operations manager, prior to determining when to order or how much to

Setup cost

[3] Jack G. Wacker, "Can Holding Costs Be Overstated for 'Just-in-Time' Manufacturing System?" *Production and Inventory Management,* **27** (Third Quarter, 1986): 11–14.

TABLE 13.1 Determining Inventory Holding Costs.*

CATEGORY	COST AS A PERCENT OF INVENTORY VALUE

Housing costs
    Building rent or depreciation
    Building operating cost
    Taxes on building
    Insurance on building
	6%
	(3 to 10%)

Material handling costs
    Equipment, lease, or depreciation
    Power
    Equipment operating cost
	3%
	(1 to 3.5%)

Labor cost from extra handling and supervision	3% (3 to 5%)

Investment costs
    Borrowing costs
    Taxes on inventory
    Insurance on inventory
	11%
	(6 to 24 %)

Pilferage, scrap, and obsolescence	3% (2 to 5%)
Overall carrying cost	26%

* All figures are approximate, as they vary substantially depending on the nature of the business, location, and current interest rates. Any inventory cost of less than 20% is suspect, but annual inventory costs often approach 40% of the value of inventory.

order, should endeavor to reduce ordering costs. This may be done by efficient procedures such as electronic ordering and payment (as discussed in Chapter 11) and by reducing setup costs. In many environments setup cost is highly correlated with **setup time.** Whatever the setup time, it is probably longer than innovative managers should accept. Setups usually require a substantial amount of work prior to an operation actually being accomplished at the work center. Much of the preparation required by a setup can be done prior to shutting down the machine or process. Setup times can be reduced substantially as shown in Figure 13.6.

Setup time

Machines and processes that traditionally have taken hours to set up are now being set up in less than a minute by the more imaginative world-class manufacturers. Reducing setup times is an excellent way to contribute to a reduction in inventory investment and to improve productivity.

INVENTORY MODELS

Independent versus Dependent Demand

Inventory control models assume that demand for an item is either independent of or dependent on the demand for other items. For example, the demand for refrigerators is usually independent of the demand for toaster ovens. Many inventory

FIGURE 13.6

Setup Times Can Be Reduced. Doing so improves capital utilization, increases capacity, and allows economic order quantities to be lower. Reduced setup time is a major component of moving toward just-in-time production.

Setup time
90 minutes

Separate setup into preparation, and actual setup, doing as much as possible while the machine/process is operating
30 minutes

Move material closer and improve material handling
20 minutes

Standardize and improve tooling
15 minutes

Use one-touch system (hydraulic, air, magnetic, and so on) to eliminate adjustments
10 minutes

Training operators and standardizing work procedures
2 minutes

Sub minute average setup

problems, however, are interrelated; the demand for one item is dependent on the demand for another item. Consider a manufacturer of small power lawn mowers. The demand for lawn mower wheels and spark plugs is dependent on the demand for lawn mowers. Four wheels and one spark plug are needed for each finished lawn mower. Usually when the demand for different items is dependent, the relationship between the items is known and consistent. Thus, management schedules production based on the demand for the final products and computes the requirements for components. This chapter focuses on managing *independent* demand items. Chapter 14 presents the topic of *dependent* demand.

Types of Inventory Models

In this section we introduce inventory models that assist in answering two important questions that apply to each item in stock:

1. when to place an order for an item;
2. how much of an item to order.

We will consider four independent demand models:

1. economic order quantity (EOQ) model;
2. production order quantity model;
3. back order inventory model;
4. quantity discount model.

Here a Harley-Davidson employee is laser-trimming fenders at a fixture setup. Harley workers have standardized die and fixture setups and located them near the machine where they will be used. An operator simply rolls up the next fixture or die and sets up for the next job in an average of 12 minutes, saving an average of 30 minutes over Harley's earlier processes. With over 500 operations requiring such setups, the saving is substantial enough to give Harley a competitive edge.

The Basic Economic Order Quantity (EOQ) Model

The economic order quantity (EOQ) is one of the oldest and most commonly known inventory control techniques. Research on its use dates back to a 1915 publication by Ford W. Harris. EOQ is still used by a large number of organizations today. This technique is relatively easy to use, but it does make a number of assumptions. The more important assumptions are:

1. Demand is known and constant.
2. Lead time, that is, the time between the placement of the order and the receipt of the order, is known and constant.
3. Receipt of inventory is instantaneous. In other words, the inventory from an order arrives in one batch, at one time.
4. Quantity discounts are not possible.
5. The only variable costs are the cost of setting up or placing an order (setup cost) and the cost of holding or storing inventory over time (holding or carrying cost). These costs were discussed in the previous section.
6. Stockouts (shortages) can be completely avoided, if orders are placed at the right time.

With these assumptions, the graph of inventory usage over time has a sawtooth shape as in Figure 13.7. In Figure 13.7, Q represents the amount that is ordered. If this amount is 500 dresses, all 500 dresses arrive at one time when an order is received. Thus, the inventory level jumps from 0 to 500 dresses. In general, an inventory level increases from 0 to Q units when an order arrives.

Because demand is constant over time, inventory drops at a uniform rate over time. (Refer to the sloped line in Figure 13.7.) When the inventory level reaches 0, the new order is placed and received, and the inventory level again jumps to Q units (represented by the vertical lines). This process continues indefinitely over time.

FIGURE 13.7

Inventory Usage Over Time.

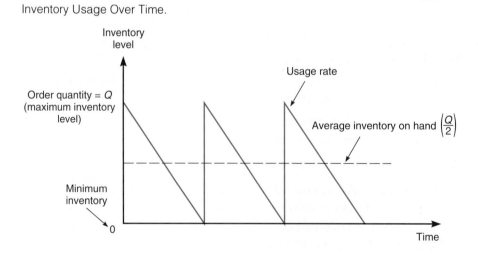

FIGURE 13.8

Total Cost as a Function of Order Quantity.

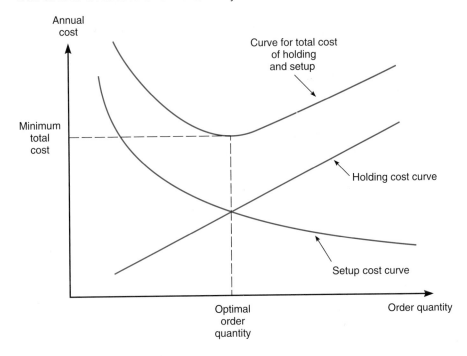

Inventory Costs. The objective of most inventory models is to minimize the total costs. With the assumptions just given, the significant costs are the setup (or ordering) cost and the holding (or carrying) cost. All other costs, such as the cost of the inventory itself, are constant. Thus, if we minimize the sum of the setup and holding costs, we will also be minimizing the total costs. To help you visualize this, in Figure 13.8 we graph total costs as a function of the order quantity, Q. The optimal order size, $Q^\star$, will be the quantity that minimizes the total costs. As the quantity ordered increases, the total number of orders placed per year will decrease. Thus, as the quantity ordered increases, the annual setup or ordering cost will decrease. But as the order quantity increases, the holding cost will increase due to larger average inventories that are maintained.

You should note that in Figure 13.8 the optimal order quantity occurred at the point where the ordering cost curve and the carrying cost curve intersected. This was not by chance. With the EOQ model the optimal order quantity will occur at a point where the total setup cost is equal to the total holding cost.[4] We use this fact to

---

[4] This is the case where holding costs are linear and begin at the origin—that is, when inventory costs do not decline (or increase) as inventory volume increases and all holding costs are in small increments. Additionally, there is probably some learning each time a setup (or order) is executed, which lowers subsequent setup costs. Consequently, the EOQ model is probably a special case. However, we abide by the conventional wisdom that this model is a reasonable approximation.

develop equations that solve directly for $Q^\star$. The necessary steps are:

1. Develop an expression for setup or ordering cost.
2. Develop an expression for holding cost.
3. Set setup cost equal to holding cost.
4. Solve the equation for the best order quantity.

Using the following variables we can determine setup and holding costs and solve for $Q^\star$:

$$Q = \text{Number of pieces per order}$$
$$Q^\star = \text{Optimum number of pieces per order (EOQ)}$$
$$D = \text{Annual demand in units for the inventory item}$$
$$S = \text{Setup or ordering cost for each order}$$
$$H = \text{Holding or carrying cost per unit per year}$$

1. Annual setup cost = (No. of orders placed/yr.)(Setup or order cost/order)

$$= \left(\frac{\text{Annual demand}}{\text{No. units in each order}} \right) (\text{Setup or order cost/order})$$

$$= \left(\frac{D}{Q} \right) (S)$$

$$= \frac{D}{Q} S$$

2. Annual holding cost = (Average inventory level)(Holding cost/unit/year)

$$= \left(\frac{\text{Order quantity}}{2} \right) (\text{Holding cost/unit/year})$$

$$= \left(\frac{Q}{2} \right) (H)$$

$$= \frac{Q}{2} H$$

3. Optimal order quantity is found when annual setup cost = annual holding cost, namely,

$$\frac{D}{Q} S = \frac{Q}{2} H$$

4. To solve for $Q^\star$, simply cross-multiply terms and isolate Q on the left of the equals sign.

$$2DS = Q^2 H$$

$$Q^2 = \frac{2DS}{H}$$

$$Q^\star = \sqrt{\frac{2DS}{H}} \tag{13.1}$$

Now that we have derived equations for the optimal order quantity, $Q^\star$, it is possible to solve inventory problems directly, as is done in Example 3.

Example 3

Squirt, Inc., a company that markets painless hypodermic needles to hospitals, would like to reduce its inventory cost by determining the optimal number of hypodermic needles to obtain per order. The annual demand is 1,000 units; the setup or ordering cost is $10 per order; and the holding cost per unit per year is $.50. Using these figures, we can calculate the optimal number of units per order:

1. $Q^\star = \sqrt{\dfrac{2DS}{H}}$ 3. $Q^\star = \sqrt{4,000}$

           4. $Q^\star = 200$ units

2. $Q^\star = \sqrt{\dfrac{2(1,000)(10)}{0.50}}$

We can also determine the expected number of orders placed during the year (N) and the expected time between orders (T) as follows:

$$\text{Expected number of orders} = N = \frac{\text{Demand}}{\text{Order quantity}} = \frac{D}{Q^\star} \tag{13.2}$$

$$\text{Expected time between orders} = T = \frac{\text{Number of working days in a year}}{N} \tag{13.3}$$

Example 4

Using the data from Squirt, Inc., in Example 3, and a 250-day working year, we find the number of orders (N) and the expected time between orders (T) as:

$$N = \frac{\text{Demand}}{\text{Order quantity}}$$

$$= \frac{1,000}{200} = 5 \text{ orders per year}$$

$$T = \frac{\text{Number of working days/year}}{\text{Expected number of orders}}$$

$$= \frac{250 \text{ working days/year}}{5 \text{ orders}} = 50 \text{ days between orders}$$

As mentioned earlier in this section, the total annual inventory cost is the sum of the setup and holding costs:

$$\text{Total annual cost} = \text{Setup cost} + \text{Holding cost} \tag{13.4}$$

In terms of the variables in the model, we can express the total cost TC as:

$$TC = \frac{D}{Q}S + \frac{Q}{2}H \tag{13.5}$$

Example 5

Again using the Squirt, Inc., data (Examples 3 and 4), we determine that the total annual inventory costs are:

$$TC = \frac{D}{Q}S + \frac{Q}{2}H$$

$$= \frac{1,000}{200}(\$10) + \frac{200}{2}(\$.50)$$

$$= (5)(\$10) + (100)(\$.50)$$

$$= \$50 + \$50 = \$100$$

Often the total inventory cost expression is written to include the actual cost of the material purchased. If we assume that the annual demand and the price per hypodermic are known values (for example, 1,000 hypodermics per year at $P = \$10$), total annual cost should include purchase cost. Material cost does not depend on the particular order policy found to be optimal, since regardless of how many units are ordered each year, we still incur an annual material cost of $D \times P = (1,000)(\$10) = \$10,000$. (Shortly, we will discuss the case in which this may not be true, namely, when a quantity discount is available to the customer who orders a certain amount each time.)

Robust
 The EOQ model has another major distinction: it is robust. By **robust** we mean that it gives satisfactory answers even with substantial variation in the parameters. As we have observed, determining accurate ordering costs and holding costs for inventory is often difficult. Consequently, a robust model is advantageous. Total cost of the EOQ changes little in the neighborhood of the minimum. The curve is very shallow. This means that variations in setup costs, holding costs, demand, or even EOQ make relatively modest differences in total cost.

Example 6

To illustrate, we use the data from Example 5. If management underestimated total annual demand by 50% (say it is actually 1,500 units rather than 1,000 units) while using the same Q, the annual inventory cost increases only $25.00 ($100 versus $125) or 25%, as shown in Example 6. Similarly, if management cuts its order size by 50% from 200 to 100, cost increases by $25 ($100 versus $125) or 25%.

a) If demand in Example 5 is actually 1,500 rather than 1,000, but management uses an EOQ of $Q = 200$ (when it should be $Q = 244.9$ based on $D = 1,500$), total costs increase 25%:

$$\text{Annual cost} = \frac{D}{Q}S + \frac{Q}{2}H$$

$$= \frac{1,500}{200}(\$10) + \frac{200}{2}(\$.50)$$

$$= \$75.00 + \$50.00 = \$125.00$$

b) If the order size is reduced from 200 to 100, but other parameters remain the same, cost also increases 25%:

$$\text{Annual Cost} = \frac{1{,}000}{100}\,(10) + \frac{100}{2}\,(\$.50)$$

$$= \$100.00 + \$25.00 = \$125.00$$

Reorder Points

Now that we have decided how much to order, we shall look at the second inventory question, when to order. Simple inventory models assume that receipt of an order is instantaneous. In other words, they assume that a firm will wait until its inventory level for a particular item reaches zero before placing an order, and that it will receive the items immediately. However, the time between the placement and receipt of an order, called the **lead time** or delivery time, can be as short as a few hours to as long as months. Thus, the when-to-order decision is usually expressed in terms of a reorder point, the inventory level at which an order should be placed. See Figure 13.9.

Lead time

The **reorder point (ROP)** is given as:

$$\text{ROP} = (\text{Demand per day})(\text{Lead time for a new order in days}) \qquad (13.6)$$
$$= d \times L$$

Reorder point (ROP)

This equation for ROP *assumes that demand is uniform and constant.* When this is

FIGURE 13.9

The Reorder Point (ROP) Curve.

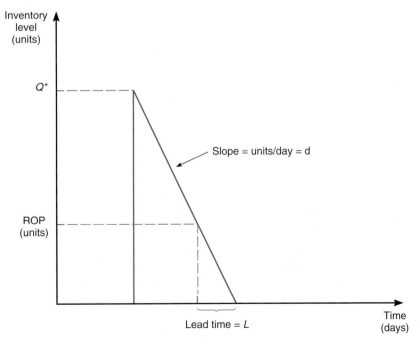

Safety stock

not the case, extra stock, often called **safety stock,** should be added.

The demand per day, d, is found by dividing the annual demand, D, by the number of working days in a year:

$$d = \frac{D}{\text{Number of working days in a year}}$$

Computing the reorder point is demonstrated in Example 7.

Example 7

Electronic Assembler, Inc., has a demand for TX512 semiconductors of 8,000 per year. The firm operates a 200-day working year. On the average, delivery of an order takes three working days. We calculate the reorder point as follows:

$$d = \text{Daily demand} = \frac{D}{\text{Number of working days}} = \frac{8,000}{200}$$

$$= 40$$

$$\text{ROP} = \text{Reorder point} = d \times L = 40 \text{ units/day} \times 3 \text{ days}$$

$$= 120 \text{ units}$$

Hence, when the inventory stock drops to 120, an order should be placed. The order will arrive three days later, just as the firm's stock is depleted.

Production Order Quantity Model

In the previous inventory model, we assumed that the entire inventory order was received at one time. There are times, however, when the firm may receive its inventory over a period of time. Such cases require a different model, one that does not require the instantaneous receipt assumption. This model is applicable when

FIGURE 13.10

Change in Inventory Levels Over Time for the Production Model.

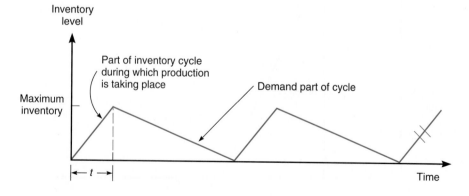

inventory continuously flows or builds up over a period of time after an order has been placed or when units are produced and sold simultaneously. Under these circumstances, we take into account the daily production (or inventory flow) rate and the daily demand rate. Figure 13.10 shows inventory levels as a function of time.

Because this model is especially suitable for the production environment, it is commonly called the **production order quantity model.** It is useful when inventory continuously builds up over time and the traditional economic order quantity assumptions are valid. We derive this model by setting ordering or setup costs equal to holding costs and solving for $Q^\star$. Using the following symbols, we can determine the expression for annual inventory holding cost for the production run model:

Production order quantity model

$$Q = \text{Number of pieces per order}$$

$$H = \text{Holding cost per unit per year}$$

$$p = \text{Daily production rate}$$

$$d = \text{Daily demand rate, or usage rate}$$

$$t = \text{Length of the production run in days}$$

1. $\begin{pmatrix} \text{Annual inventory} \\ \text{holding cost} \end{pmatrix} = (\text{Average inventory level}) \times \begin{pmatrix} \text{Holding cost} \\ \text{per unit per year} \end{pmatrix}$

$$= (\text{Average inventory level}) \times H$$

2. $\begin{pmatrix} \text{Average inventory} \\ \text{level} \end{pmatrix} = (\text{Maximum inventory level})/2$

3. $\begin{pmatrix} \text{Maximum} \\ \text{inventory level} \end{pmatrix} = \begin{pmatrix} \text{Total produced during} \\ \text{the production run} \end{pmatrix} - \begin{pmatrix} \text{Total used during} \\ \text{the production run} \end{pmatrix}$

$$= pt - dt$$

But $Q = \text{total produced} = pt$, and thus $t = Q/p$. Therefore,

$$\text{maximum inventory level} = p\left(\frac{Q}{p}\right) - d\left(\frac{Q}{p}\right)$$

$$= Q - \frac{d}{p}Q$$

$$= Q\left(1 - \frac{d}{p}\right)$$

4. Annual inventory holding cost (or simply holding cost)

$$= \frac{\text{Maximum inventory level}}{2}(H) = \frac{Q}{2}\left[1 - \left(\frac{d}{p}\right)\right]H$$

Using the expression for holding cost above and the expression for setup cost developed in the basic EOQ model, we solve for the optimal number of pieces per order by equating setup cost and holding cost:

$$\text{Setup cost} = (D/Q)S$$

$$\text{Holding cost} = \frac{1}{2}HQ\left[1 - (d/p)\right]$$

If an order of size 30-32 Levis takes four weeks to arrive and the store sells ten pairs each week, then the re-order point must occur when there are forty pair remaining. Refer to the Western Ranchman Outfitters case in this chapter for a further view of this issue.

Set ordering cost equal to holding cost to obtain $Q^\star$:

$$\frac{D}{Q}S = \tfrac{1}{2}\,HQ\,[1 - (d/p)]$$

$$Q^2 = \frac{2DS}{H\,[1 - (d/p)]}$$

$$Q_p^\star = \sqrt{\frac{2DS}{H\,[1 - (d/p)]}} \tag{13.7}$$

We can use the above equation, $Q_p^\star$, to solve for the optimum order or production quantity when inventory is consumed as it is produced.

Example 8

Given the following values, solve for the optimum number of units per order.

Annual demand $= D = 1{,}000$ units

Setup cost $= S = \$10$

Holding cost $= H = \$.50$ per unit per year

Daily production rate $= p = 8$ units daily

Daily demand rate $= d = 6$ units daily

1.
$$Q_p^\star = \sqrt{\frac{2DS}{H\,[1 - (d/p)]}}$$

2.
$$Q_p^\star = \sqrt{\frac{2(1000)(10)}{.50\,[1 - (6/8)]}}$$

$$= \sqrt{\frac{20{,}000}{.50(1/4)}} = \sqrt{160{,}000}$$

$$= 400 \text{ units}$$

You may want to compare this solution with the answer in Example 3. Eliminating the instantaneous receipt assumption, where $p = 8$ and $d = 6$, has resulted in an increase in $Q^\star$ from 200 in Example 3 to 400. Also note that:

$$d = \frac{D}{\text{Number of days the plant is in operation}}$$

We can also calculate $Q_p^\star$ when annual data are available. When annual data are used, we can express $Q_p^\star$ as:

$$Q_p^\star = \sqrt{\frac{2DS}{H\,[1 - (D/P)]}} \tag{13.8}$$

where

$D =$ Annual demand rate

$P =$ Annual production rate

FIGURE 13.11

Change in Inventory Over Time with Back Orders.

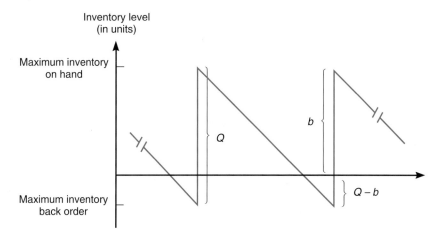

Back-Order Inventory Model

In other inventory models we have not allowed inventory shortages, that is, insufficient stock to meet current demand. There are many situations in which planned shortages or stockouts may be advisable. This is the case especially for expensive items that have high holding costs. Car dealerships and appliance stores rarely stock every model for this reason.

In this section, we will assume that stockouts and back-ordering are allowable. The model is called the **back-order inventory model** or planned shortages inventory model. The basic assumptions for this model are the same as for previous models. In addition, however, we will assume that sales will not be lost due to a stockout. We will use the same variables, with the addition of B, the cost of back-ordering one unit for one year. Thus,

Back-order inventory model

$$Q = \text{Number of pieces per order}$$
$$D = \text{Annual demand in units}$$
$$H = \text{Holding cost per unit per year}$$
$$S = \text{Setup cost for each order}$$
$$B = \text{Back-ordering cost per unit per year}$$
$$b = \text{Remaining units after the back order is satisfied}$$
$$Q - b = \text{Amount back-ordered}.$$

Figure 13.11 shows the inventory level as a function of time.

The total cost must include the cost of being out of stock (back-ordering cost):

$$T_c = \text{Setup cost} + \text{Holding cost} + \text{Back-ordering cost}.$$

We can use calculus to solve for $Q^\star$ and $S^\star$ once the total cost is expressed using the above variables. The results are as follows:

$$Q^\star = \text{Optimum order size in units}$$

$$= \sqrt{\left(\frac{2SD}{H}\right)\left(\frac{H+B}{B}\right)} \tag{13.9}$$

$b^\star$ = Optimum remaining units after back-ordering

$$= \sqrt{\left(\frac{2SD}{H}\right)\left(\frac{B}{B+H}\right)}$$

or

$$b^\star = Q^\star\left(\frac{B}{B+H}\right) \tag{13.10}$$

and

$Q^\star - b^\star$ = Optimum amount back-ordered in units

$$= Q^\star - Q^\star\left(\frac{B}{B+H}\right)$$

or

$$Q^\star - b^\star = Q^\star\left(1 - \frac{B}{B+H}\right) \tag{13.11}$$

Example 9

Richmond Tool and Die Company is a wholesaler of high-speed electric drill bits. Data for one model that the firm handles, the G-28 titanium bit, are given below. We wish to find the optimum order size for the G-28 bit and optimum number of bits to be back-ordered.

$$D = 20{,}000 \text{ drill bits per year}$$
$$H = \$2$$
$$S = \$15$$
$$B = \$10$$

1. $$Q^\star = \sqrt{\left(\frac{2SD}{H}\right)\left(\frac{H+B}{B}\right)}$$

2. $$Q^\star = \sqrt{\left(\frac{2(15)(20{,}000)}{2}\right)\left(\frac{2+10}{10}\right)}$$

$$= \sqrt{300{,}000\left(\frac{12}{10}\right)} = \sqrt{360{,}000}$$

3. $$Q^\star = 600 \text{ units per order}$$

4. $$Q^\star - b^\star = Q^\star\left(1 - \frac{B}{B+H}\right)$$

5. $$Q^\star - b^\star = 600\left(1 - \frac{10}{10+2}\right)$$

$$= 100 \text{ units back-ordered each inventory cycle}$$

Quantity Discount Models

Quantity discount

To increase sales, many companies offer quantity discounts to their customers. A **quantity discount** is simply a reduced price (P) for the item when it is purchased in larger quantities. It is not uncommon to have a discount schedule with several

TABLE 13.2 A Quantity Discount Schedule.

DISCOUNT NUMBER	DISCOUNT QUANTITY	DISCOUNT (%)	DISCOUNT PRICE (P)
1	0 to 999	0	$5.00
2	1,000 to 1,999	4	$4.80
3	2,000 and over	5	$4.75

discounts for large orders. A typical quantity discount schedule appears in Table 13.2.

As can be seen in the table, the normal price of the item is $5. When 1,000 to 1,999 units are ordered at one time, then the price per unit drops to $4.80; and when the quantity ordered at one time is 2,000 units or more, the price is $4.75 per unit. As always, management must decide when and how much to order. But with quantity discounts, how does the operations manager make these decisions?

As with other inventory models discussed so far, the overall objective will be to minimize the total cost. Since the unit cost for the third discount in Table 13.2 is the lowest, you might be tempted to order 2,000 units or more to take advantage of the lower product cost. Placing an order for that quantity with the greatest discount price, however, might not minimize the total inventory cost. As the discount quantity goes up, the product cost goes down, but the holding cost increases because the orders are large. Thus, the major trade-off when considering quantity discounts is between the reduced product cost and the increased holding cost. When we include the cost of the product, the equation for the total annual inventory cost becomes:

Total cost = Setup cost + Holding cost + Product cost

or

$$T_c = \frac{D}{Q}S + \frac{QH}{2} + PD \qquad (13.12)$$

where

D = Annual demand in units

S = Ordering or setup cost per order or per setup

P = Price per unit

H = Holding cost per unit per year.

Now, we have to determine the quantity that will minimize the total annual inventory cost. Because there are several discounts, this process involves four steps:

1. For each discount, calculate a value for $Q^\star$, using the following equation:

$$Q^\star = \sqrt{\frac{2DS}{IP}} \qquad (13.13)$$

You should note that the holding cost is IP instead of H. Because the price of the item is a factor in annual holding cost, we cannot assume that the holding cost is a constant when the price per unit changes for each quantity discount. Thus, it is common to express the holding cost (I) as a percentage of unit price (P) instead of as a constant cost per unit per year, H.

FIGURE 13.12

Total Cost Curve for the Quantity Discount Model.

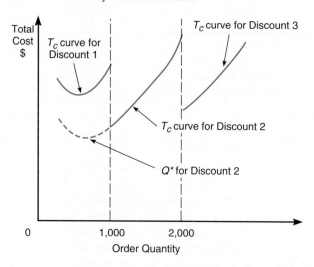

2. For any discount, if the order quantity is too low to qualify for the discount, adjust the order quantity upward to the lowest quantity that will qualify for the discount. For example, if $Q^{\star}$ for discount 2 in Table 13.2 were 500 units, you would adjust this value up to 1,000 units. Look at the second discount in Table 13.2. Order quantities between 1,000 and 1,999 will qualify for the 4% discount. Thus, we will adjust the order quantity up to be 1,000 units if $Q^{\star}$ is below 1,000 units.

   The reasoning for step 2 may not be obvious. If the order quantity is below the quantity range that will qualify for a discount, a quantity within this range may still result in the lowest total cost.

   As shown in Figure 13.12, the total cost curve is broken into three different total cost curves. There is a total cost curve for the first ($0 \leqslant Q \leqslant 999$), second ($1,000 \leqslant Q \leqslant 1,999$), and third ($2,000 \leqslant Q$) discount. Look at the total cost (T_c) curve for discount 2. $Q^{\star}$ for discount 2 is less than the allowable discount range, which is from 1,000 to 1,999 units. As the figure shows, the lowest allowable quantity in this range, which is 1,000 units, is the quantity that minimizes the total cost. Thus, the second step is needed to ensure that we do not discard an order quantity that may indeed produce the minimum cost. Note that an order quantity computed in step 1 that is greater than the range that would qualify it for a discount may be discarded.

3. Using the total cost equation above, compute a total cost for every $Q^{\star}$ determined in steps 1 and 2. If you had to adjust $Q^{\star}$ upward because it was below the allowable quantity range, make sure to use the adjusted value for $Q^{\star}$.

4. Select that $Q^{\star}$ that has the lowest total cost as computed in step 3. It will be the quantity that will minimize the total inventory cost.

Let us see how this procedure can be applied with an example.

Example 10

Jamie's Discount Store stocks toy race cars. Recently, they have been given a quantity discount schedule for the cars. This quantity schedule was shown in Table 13.2. Thus, the normal cost for the toy race cars is $5. For orders between 1,000 and 1,999 units, the unit cost is $4.80; and for orders of 2,000 or more units, the unit cost is $4.75. Furthermore, the ordering cost is $49 per order, the annual demand is 5,000 race cars, and the inventory carrying charge as a percentage of cost, I, is 20% or .2. What order quantity will minimize the total inventory cost?

The first step is to compute $Q^\star$ for every discount in Table 13.2. This is done as follows:

$$Q_1^\star = \sqrt{\frac{2(5,000)(49)}{(.2)(5.00)}} = 700 \text{ cars/order}$$

$$Q_2^\star = \sqrt{\frac{2(5,000)(49)}{(.2)(4.80)}} = 714 \text{ cars/order}$$

$$Q_3^\star = \sqrt{\frac{2(5,000)(49)}{(.2)(4.75)}} = 718 \text{ cars/order}$$

The second step is to adjust upward those values of $Q^\star$ that are below the allowable discount range. Since $Q_1^\star$ is between 0 and 999, it does not have to be adjusted. $Q_2^\star$ is below the allowable range of 1,000 to 1,999, and therefore, it must be adjusted to 1,000 units. The same is true for $Q_3^\star$. It must be adjusted to 2,000 units. After this step, the following order quantities must be tested in the total cost equation:

$$Q_1^\star = 700$$

$$Q_2^\star = 1,000 - \text{adjusted}$$

$$Q_3^\star = 2,000 - \text{adjusted}$$

The third step is to use the total cost equation and compute a total cost for each of the order quantities. This is accomplished with the aid of Table 13.3.

TABLE 13.3 Total Cost Computations for Jamie's Discount Store.

DISCOUNT NUMBER	UNIT PRICE	ORDER QUANTITY	ANNUAL PRODUCT COST	ANNUAL ORDERING COST	ANNUAL HOLDING COST	TOTAL
1	$5.00	700	$25,000	$350	$350	$25,700
2	$4.80	1,000	$24,000	$245	$480	$24,725
3	$4.75	2,000	$23,750	$122.5	$950	$24,822.5

The fourth step is to select that order quantity with the lowest total cost. Looking at Table 13.3, you can see that an order quantity of 1,000 toy race cars will minimize the total cost. It should be recognized, however, that the total cost for ordering 2,000 cars is only slightly greater than the total cost for ordering 1,000 cars. Thus, if the third discount cost is lowered to $4.65, for example, then this order quantity might be the one that minimizes the total inventory cost.

PROBABILISTIC MODELS WITH CONSTANT LEAD TIME

All of the inventory models we have discussed so far make the assumption that the demand for a product is constant and uniform. We now relax this assumption. The following inventory models apply when product demand is not known but can be specified by means of a probability distribution. These types of models are called **probabilistic models.**

Probabilistic models

An important concern of management is maintaining an adequate service level in the face of uncertain demand. The service level is the complement of the probability of a stockout. For instance, if the probability of a stockout is 0.05, then the service level is .95. Uncertain demand raises the possibility of a stockout. One method of reducing stockouts is to hold extra units in inventory to avoid this possibility. Such inventory is usually referred to as safety stock. It involves adding a number of units of safety stock as a buffer to the reorder point. As you recall from our previous discussion:

$$\text{Reorder point} = \text{ROP} = d \times L$$

$$d = \text{Daily demand}$$

$$L = \text{Order lead time, or number of working days}$$
$$\text{it takes to deliver an order}$$

The inclusion of safety stock (ss) changes the expression to:

$$\text{ROP} = d \times L + ss \tag{13.14}$$

The amount of safety stock depends on the cost of incurring a stockout and the cost of holding the extra inventory. Example 11 shows how this is done for AMP, Inc.

Example 11

AMP, Inc., has determined that its reorder point is $50(d \times L)$ units. Its carrying cost per unit per year is $5, and stockout cost is $40 per unit. AMP has experienced the following probability distribution for inventory demand during the reorder period. The optimum number of orders per year is six.

	NUMBER OF UNITS	PROBABILITY
	30	.2
	40	.2
ROP →	50	.3
	60	.2
	70	.1
		1.0

How much safety stock should AMP keep on hand?

The objective is to find the safety stock that minimizes the total additional inventory holding costs and stockout costs on an annual basis. The annual holding cost is simply the holding cost multiplied by the units added to the ROP. For example, a safety stock of 20 units, which implies that the new ROP, with safety stock, is 70(= 50 + 20) raises the annual carrying cost by $5(20) = $100.

The stockout cost is more difficult to compute. For any level of safety stock, the stockout cost is the expected cost of stocking out. We can compute it by multiplying the number of units short by the probability by the stockout cost by the number of times per year the stockout can occur (or the number of orders per year). Then we add stockout costs for each possible stockout level for a given ROP. For zero safety stock, a shortage of 10 units will occur if demand is 60, and a shortage of 20 units will occur if the demand is 70. Thus the stockout costs for zero safety stock are:

(10 units short)(.2)($40/stockout)(6 possible stockouts per year)
$$+ \ (20 \text{ units short})(.1)(\$40)(6) = \$960$$

The following table summarizes the total costs for each alternative.

SAFETY STOCK	ADDITIONAL HOLDING COST	STOCKOUT COST		TOTAL COST
20	(20)($5) = $100	$0		$100
10	(10)($5) = $50	(10)(.1)($40)(6)	= $240	$290
0	0	(10)(.2)($40)(6) + (20)(.1)($40)(6)	= $960	$960

The safety stock with the lowest total cost is 20 units. This safety stock changes the reorder point to 50 + 20 = 70 units.

When it is difficult or impossible to determine the cost of being out of stock, a manager may decide to follow a policy of keeping enough safety stock on hand to meet a prescribed customer service level. For instance, Figure 13.13 on page 581 shows the use of safety stock when demand is probabilistic. We see that the safety stock, ss, in Figure 13.13 is 16.5, and the reorder point is also increased by 16.5.

The manager may want to define the service level as meeting 95% of the demand (or conversely having stockouts only 5% of the time). Assuming that demand during lead time (the reorder period) follows a normal curve, only the mean and standard deviation are needed to define the inventory requirements for any given service level. Sales data are usually adequate for computing the mean and standard deviation. In the following example we use a normal curve with a known mean (μ) and standard deviation (σ) to determine the safety stock necessary for a 95% service level.

Example 12

The Schaefer Company carries an inventory item that has a normally distributed demand during the reorder period. The mean (average) demand during the reorder period is 350 units, and the standard deviation is 10. Schaefer wants to follow a policy that results in stockouts occurring 5% of the time. How much safety stock should the firm maintain? The following figure may help you visualize the example:

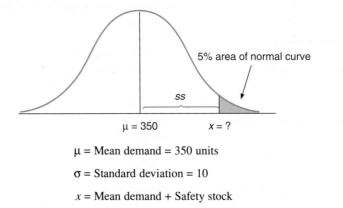

μ = Mean demand = 350 units

σ = Standard deviation = 10

x = Mean demand + Safety stock

ss = Safety stock = $x - \mu$

$$Z = \frac{x - \mu}{\sigma} \qquad (13.15)$$

We use the properties of a standardized normal curve to get a Z value for an area under the normal curve of .95 (or $1 - .05$). Using a normal table (see Appendix A), we find a Z value of 1.65. Also:

$$Z = \frac{x - \mu}{\sigma} = \frac{ss}{\sigma}$$

$$= 1.65 = \frac{ss}{\sigma}$$

Solving for safety stock gives:

$$ss = 1.65(10) = 16.5 \text{ units}$$

This was the situation illustrated in Figure 13.13.

FIXED-PERIOD SYSTEMS

The inventory models we have considered so far in this chapter all fall into a class called *fixed-quantity systems*. That is to say, the same fixed amount is added to inventory every time an order for an item is placed. We saw that orders are event triggered with the event triggering a reorder point occurring any time.

Fixed-period system   In a **fixed-period system,** on the other hand, the inventory level is checked on a uniform time frequency. It is time-triggered, with the replenishment of inventory occurring by the passage of a given amount of time. Therefore, there is no tally of the on-hand balance of an item when a withdrawal takes place. The stock on hand is counted only when the ordering date occurs. The quantity ordered is the amount necessary to bring the inventory level up to a prespecified target level. Figure 13.14 illustrates this concept.

FIGURE 13.13

Probabilistic Demand.

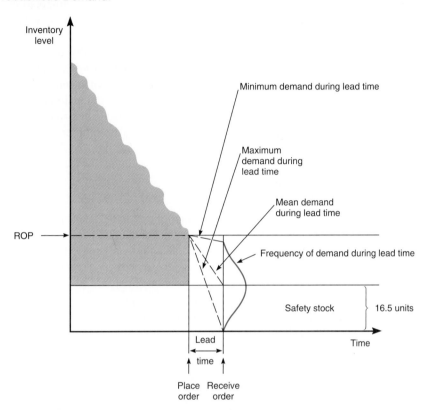

The advantage of the fixed-period system is that there is no physical count of inventory items after an item is withdrawn—this occurs only when the time for the next review comes up. This procedure is also convenient administratively, especially if inventory control is one of several duties of an employee.

FIGURE 13.14

Inventory Level in a Fixed-Period System.

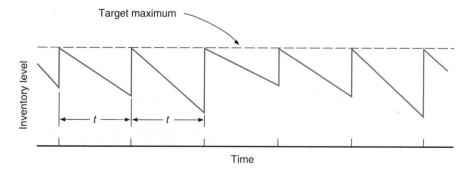

This type of inventory control system and the placement of orders on a periodic basis are appropriate when vendors make routine (i.e., at a fixed time interval) visits to customers to take fresh orders or when purchasers want to combine orders to save ordering and transportation costs (therefore, they will have the same review period for similar inventory items).

The disadvantage of this system is that since there is no tally of inventory during the review period, there is the possibility of a stockout during this time. This scenario is possible if a large order draws the inventory level down to zero right after an order is placed. Therefore, a higher level of safety stock (as compared to a fixed quantity system) needs to be maintained to provide protection against stockout both during the review period and during the time required for a fresh order to come in.

MARGINAL ANALYSIS

Marginal analysis

For many inventory models, the optimal stocking policy can be determined through **marginal analysis,** which takes into account marginal profit (MP) and marginal loss (ML). Given any inventory level, we would add an additional unit to the inventory level only if its expected marginal profit equals or exceeds its expected marginal loss. This relationship is expressed symbolically below. First, we let:

$$\hat{p} = \text{Probability that demand will be greater than or equal}$$
$$\text{to a given supply (or the probability of selling at } least$$
$$\text{one additional unit)}$$

$$1 - \hat{p} = \text{Probability that demand will be less than supply}$$

The expected marginal profit is then found by multiplying the probability that a given unit will be sold by the marginal profit, $\hat{p}(\text{MP})$. Likewise, the expected marginal loss is the probability of not selling the unit multiplied by the marginal loss, or $(1 - \hat{p})(\text{ML})$. The decision rule is:

$$\hat{p}(\text{MP}) \geq (1 - \hat{p})(\text{ML})$$

With some basic mathematical manipulations, we can determine the level of p that will help solve inventory problems:

$$\hat{p}(\text{MP}) \geq \text{ML} - \hat{p}(\text{ML})$$

or

$$\hat{p}(\text{MP}) + \hat{p}(\text{ML}) \geq \text{ML}$$

or

$$\hat{p}(\text{MP} + \text{ML}) \geq \text{ML}$$

or

$$\hat{p} \geq \frac{\text{ML}}{\text{MP} + \text{ML}} \tag{13.16}$$

We can use this relationship to solve inventory problems directly. This type of analysis is especially good for one-time inventory decisions when reordering and back-ordering are not possible. We present the use of marginal analysis in Example 13. Note that we have added three possible demands (five, six, and seven units, with probabilities of .2, .3, and .5, respectively). As long as the cumulative probability exceeds p, we keep stocking additional units.

Example 13

Cases of a tissue paper product sell for $6 each. The cost per case is $3, and unsold cases may be returned to the supplier, who will refund the cost for each case returned minus $1 per case for handling and storage. The probability distribution of demand is as follows:

DEMAND	PROBABILITY THAT DEMAND WILL BE AT THIS LEVEL
5	.2
6	.3
7	.5

1. From the previously developed relationship (Equation 13.16), we know that:

$$\hat{p} \geq \frac{ML}{MP + ML} \tag{13.16}$$

2. The next step is to determine $\hat{p}$. As you recall, $\hat{p}$ is the probability that demand will be at this level or greater. We can compute this *cumulative* probability as follows:

DEMAND	PROBABILITY THAT DEMAND WILL BE AT THIS LEVEL	PROBABILITY THAT DEMAND WILL BE AT THIS LEVEL OR GREATER
5	.2	$1.0 \geq 0.25$
6	.3	$.8 \geq 0.25$
7	.5	$.5 \geq 0.25$

$$ML = \text{Marginal loss} = \$1$$
$$MP = \text{Marginal profit} = \$6 - \$3 = \$3$$

Thus

$$\hat{p} \geq \frac{1}{3 + 1} \geq .25$$

3. We keep adding additional cases as long as the $\hat{p} \geq ML/(MP + ML)$ relationship holds. If we stock seven cases, our marginal profit will be greater than our marginal loss:

$$\hat{p} \text{ at 7 cases} \geq \frac{ML}{MP + ML}$$

Thus the optimal policy is to stock seven cases of tissue paper.

TABLE 13.4 Statistical Models for Independent Demand Summarized.

Q = Number of pieces per order	T_c = Total cost = Ordering cost +
EOQ = Optimal order quantity	Carrying cost + Product cost
ROP = Reorder point	P = Price
D = Annual demand in units	I = Annual inventory carrying cost
S = Setup or ordering cost for each order	as a percentage of price
H = Holding or carrying cost per unit per year	$\hat{p}$ = Probability
in dollars	MP = Marginal profit
B = Back-ordering cost per unit per year	ML = Marginal loss
b = Remaining units after back order is satisfied	μ = Mean demand
$b^\star$ = Optimum units remaining after back order	σ = Standard deviation
p = Daily production rate	x = Mean demand + Safety stock
d = Daily demand rate	ss = Safety stock
t = Length of production run in days	Z = Standardized value under the normal curve

EOQ

$$Q^\star = \sqrt{\frac{2DS}{H}} \tag{13.1}$$

EOQ production run model

$$Q^\star = \sqrt{\frac{2DS}{H\,[1-(d/p)]}} \tag{13.7}$$

EOQ with back-ordering cost

$$Q^\star = \sqrt{\left(\frac{2SD}{H}\right)\left(\frac{H+B}{B}\right)} \tag{13.9}$$

Optimum remaining units after back-ordering

$$b^\star = \sqrt{\left(\frac{2SD}{H}\right)\left(\frac{B}{B+H}\right)} = Q^\star\left(\frac{B}{B+H}\right) \tag{13.10}$$

Optimum amount back-ordered in units

$$Q^\star - b^\star = Q^\star\left(1 - \frac{B}{B+H}\right) \tag{13.11}$$

Total cost

$$T_c = \text{Total cost} = \text{Setup cost} + \text{Holding cost} + \text{Product cost} = \frac{D}{Q}S + \frac{QH}{2} + PD \tag{13.12}$$

Quantity discount EOQ model

$$Q^\star = \sqrt{\frac{2DS}{IP}} \tag{13.13}$$

Probability model

$$Z = \frac{x-\mu}{\sigma} = \frac{ss}{\sigma} \tag{13.15}$$

Marginal analysis

$$\hat{p} \geq \frac{ML}{MP+ML} \tag{13.16}$$

SUMMARY

Inventory represents a major investment for most firms. This investment is often larger than it should be because firms find it easier to have "just-in-case" inventory rather than "just-in-time" inventory. Inventories are of four types:

1. raw material and purchased components;
2. work-in-process;
3. maintenance, repair, and operating (MRO);
4. finished goods.

In this chapter we discussed independent inventory, ABC analysis, record accuracy, and inventory models used to control independent inventories. The EOQ model, production run model, quantity discount model, and back-order model can all be solved using the microcomputer software supplied with this text and described shortly. A summary of the inventory models presented in this chapter is shown in Table 13.4.

KEY TERMS

ABC analysis (p. 553)
Cycle counting (p. 555)
Just-in-time inventory (p. 556)
MRO (p. 557)
Kanban (p. 559)
Holding cost (p. 561)
Ordering cost (p. 561)
Setup cost (p. 561)
Setup time (p. 562)
Robust (p. 568)

Lead time (p. 569)
Reorder point (ROP) (p. 569)
Safety stock (p. 570)
Production order quantity model
(p. 571)
Back-order inventory model (p. 573)
Quantity discount (p. 574)
Probabilistic models (p. 578)
Fixed-period system (p. 580)
Marginal analysis (p. 582)

USING AB:POM

Solving Example 8 (Production Run Model) with the Inventory Module

All four of the EOQ family of models presented in this chapter can be solved by AB:POM. We illustrate the production run model, using the data from Example 8. Program 13.1 on page 586 shows the data we entered on the left-hand side, and the computed output on the right. We should note that:

Holding cost (H) may be entered in dollars (by simply typing the value) or as a percentage of the price of the item (by typing the percentage with the % sign). *Holding cost* (H) and *demand rate* (D) must both be in the same time unit, that is, either daily, annual, etc.

Days per year will vary depending upon the *daily demand rate* (d). If the *production rate* (p) and *daily demand rate* (d) are entered, then the *days per year* entry will be

Program 13.1

AB:POM's Production Run Module

```
                          Example 8
Model                 Production order quantity model
Demand Rate (D)           1000.00  Optimal order quantity (Q*)      400.00
Setup costs (S)             10.00  Maximum inventory level (Imax)   100.00
Holding costs (H)            0.50
Production Rate (p)          8.00  Inventory $$ (Hold, Setup, Short)    $50.00
Days per year            166.6667  Unit costs (pD)                 $1,000.00
   or
Daily demand rate (d)        6.00  Total cost                      $1,050.00
Unit cost                    1.00
```

automatically computed and default to the appropriate value. If the *production rate* (p) is in days, but the *demand rate* (D) entry is annual, *days per year* must be entered.

Solving Example 10 (Quantity Discount Model) With AB:POM

As a second inventory illustration, Program 13.2 uses the quantity discount data for Jamie's Discount Store from Example 10. Starting and ending values for each price range must be input. The input is shown on the left of Program 13.2 and the answers on the right.

Program 13.2

AB:POM's Quality Discount Module

```
                         Jamie's Discount Store
Model                   EOQ with quantity discount
Demand Rate (D)     5000.00  Optimal order quantity (Q*)      1000.00
Setup cost (S)        49.00  Maximum inventory level (Imax)   1000.00
Holding cost (H)     20.00%
Price Ranges                 Inventory $$ (Hold, Setup, Short)    $725.00
   From      To     Price  Unit costs (PD)                  $24,000.00
      1     999      5.00  Total Cost                       $24,725.00
   1000    1999      4.80
   2000  999999      4.75
```

SOLVED PROBLEMS

Solved Problem 13.1

The Taylor Computer Corporation purchases 8,000 transistors each year for use in the minicomputers it manufactures. The unit cost of each transistor is $10, and the cost of carrying one transistor in inventory for a year is $3. Ordering cost is $30 per order.

What are the optimal order quantity, the expected number of orders placed each year, and the expected time between orders? Assume that Taylor operates a 200-day working year.

Solution

$$Q^\star = \sqrt{\frac{2DS}{H}} = \sqrt{\frac{2(8,000)(30)}{3}} = 400 \text{ units}$$

$$N = \frac{D}{Q^\star} = \frac{8000}{400} = 20 \text{ orders}$$

$$\text{Time between orders} = T = \frac{\text{No. working days}}{N} = \frac{200}{20} = 10 \text{ working days}$$

Hence, an order for 400 transistors is placed every 10 days. Presumably, then, 20 orders are placed each year.

Solved Problem 13.2

Annual demand for the notebook binders at Eck's Stationery Shop is 10,000 units. Mary Eck operates her business 300 days per year and finds that deliveries from her supplier generally take 5 working days. Calculate the reorder point for the notebook binders that she stocks.

Solution

$$d = \frac{10,000}{300} = 33.3 \text{ units/day}$$

$$\text{ROP} = d \times L = (33.3 \text{ units/day})(5 \text{ days}) = 166.7 \text{ units}$$

Thus, Mary should reorder when her stock of notebook binders reaches 167.

Solved Problem 13.3

Freeman, Inc., has an annual demand rate of 1,000 units but can produce at an average annual production rate of 2,000 units. Setup cost is $10, and carrying cost is $1.00. What is the optimal number of units to be produced each time?

Solution

$$Q^\star = \sqrt{\frac{2DS}{H\left[1 - (D/P)\right]}}$$

$$= \sqrt{\frac{2(1,000)(10)}{1[1 - (1,000/2,000)]}} = \sqrt{\frac{20,000}{1/2}} = \sqrt{40,000}$$

$$= 200 \text{ units}$$

Solved Problem 13.4

Kanet's Home Center allows back-ordering on most of its major appliances, including dishwashers. The annual demand for one type of dishwasher is 100. It costs approximately $10 to place an order, and the annual carrying cost is $4 per year per unit. Back-ordering cost is approximately $5. What is the optimal order quantity and what is the optimal number of remaining units after the back order has been satisfied?

Solution

$$Q^\star = \sqrt{\left(\frac{2DS}{H}\right)\left(\frac{H+B}{B}\right)}$$

$$= \sqrt{\frac{2(10)(100)}{4}\left(\frac{4+5}{5}\right)} = \sqrt{500\left(\frac{9}{5}\right)} = \sqrt{900}$$

$$Q^\star = 30 \text{ dishwashers}$$

$$b^\star = Q^\star\left(\frac{B}{B+H}\right) = 30\left(\frac{5}{4+5}\right)$$

$$b^\star = 17 \text{ dishwashers}$$

Solved Problem 13.5

What safety stock should Orkin Corporation maintain if mean sales are 80 during the reorder period, the standard deviation is 7, and Orkin can tolerate stockouts 10% of the time?

Solution

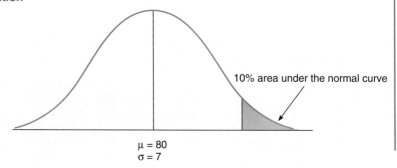

10% area under the normal curve

$\mu = 80$
$\sigma = 7$

From Appendix A, Z at an area of .9 (or $1 - .10$) = 1.28

$$Z = 1.28 = \frac{x - \mu}{\sigma} = \frac{ss}{\sigma}$$

$$ss = 1.28\sigma$$
$$= 1.28(7) = 8.96 \text{ units, or } 9 \text{ units}$$

DISCUSSION QUESTIONS

1. With the advent of low-cost computing, do you see alternatives to the popular ABC classifications?

2. What is the difference between the standard EOQ model and the production inventory model?

3. What are the main reasons that an organization has inventory?

4. Describe the costs that are associated with ordering and maintaining inventory.

5. What are the assumptions of the EOQ model?

6. How sensitive is EOQ to variations in demand or costs?

7. Does the production model or the standard EOQ model yield a higher EOQ if setup costs and holding costs are the same? Why?

8. When is a good time for cycle counting personnel to proceed with auditing a particular item?

9. What impact does a decrease in setup time have on EOQ?

10. What is meant by service level?

11. How would a firm go about determining a service level?

12. What happens to total inventory costs (and EOQ) if inventory holding costs per unit increase as inventory increases (that is, increase at an increasing rate)?

13. What happens to total inventory costs (and EOQ) if there is a fixed cost associated with inventory holding costs (for example, leasing the warehouse)?

14. Describe the difference between a fixed-quantity and a fixed-period inventory system.

PROBLEMS

· **13.1** Baker Enterprise has 10 items in inventory. Ken Baker asks you, the recent P/OM graduate, to divide these items into ABC classifications. What do you report back to Mr. Baker?

ITEM	ANNUAL DEMAND	COST/UNIT
A2	3000	$ 50
B8	4000	12
C7	1500	45
D1	6000	10
E9	1000	20
F3	500	500
G2	300	1,500
H2	600	20
I5	1750	10
J8	2500	5

· **13.2** Sarita Uribe opened a new beauty products retail store. There are numerous items in inventory, and Sarita knows that there are costs associated with inventory. However, her time is limited so she cannot carefully evaluate the inventory policy for all products.

Sarita wants to classify the items according to the dollars invested in them. The following table provides information about the 10 items that she carries:

ITEM NUMBER	UNIT COST	DEMAND (UNITS)
E102	$4.00	800
D23	8.00	1200
D27	3.00	700
R02	2.00	1000
R19	8.00	200
S107	6.00	500
S123	1.00	1200
U11	7.00	800
U23	1.00	1500
V75	4.00	1500

Use ABC analysis to classify these items into categories A, B, and C.

· **13.3** It takes approximately two weeks (14 days) for an order of steel bolts to arrive once the order has been placed.

   The demand for the bolts is fairly constant; on the average, the manager has observed that the hardware store sells 500 of these bolts each day. Since the demand is fairly constant, she believes she can avoid stockouts completely if she orders the bolts at the correct time. What is the reorder point?

: **13.4** Barbara Brown is the purchasing agent for Central Valve Company, which sells industrial valves and fluid-control devices. One of their most popular valves is the Western, which has an annual demand of 4,000 units. The cost of each valve is $90.00, and the inventory carrying cost is estimated to be 10% of the cost of each valve. Barbara has made a study of the costs involved in placing an order for any of the valves that Central Valve stocks, and she has concluded that the average ordering cost is $25.00 per order. Furthermore, it takes about 8 days for an order to arrive from the supplier. During this time, the demand per week for Central valves is approximately 80.

   a) What is the economic order quantity?

   b) What is the reorder point?

   c) What is the total annual inventory cost (carrying cost + ordering cost)?

   d) What is the optimal number of orders per year?

   e) What is the optimal number of days between any two orders assuming there are 200 working days per year?

: **13.5** Happy Pet, Inc., is a large pet store located in Long Beach Mall. Although the store specializes in dogs, it also sells fish, turtle, and bird supplies. Everlast Leader, a leather lead for dogs, costs Happy Pet $7.00 each. There is an annual demand for 6,000 Everlast Leaders. The manager of Happy Pet has determined that the ordering cost is $20 per order, and the carrying cost as a percentage of the unit cost is 15%. Happy Pet is now considering a new supplier of Everlast Leaders. Each lead would cost only $6.65; but in order to get this discount, Happy Pet would have to buy shipments of 3,000 Everlast Leaders at a time. Should Happy Pet use the new supplier and take this discount for quantity buying?

· **13.6** Doug Brauer uses 1,500 per year of a certain subassembly that has an annual holding cost of $45 per unit. Each order placed costs Doug $150. Doug operates 300 days per year and has found that an order must be placed with his supplier six working days before he can expect to receive that order. For this subassembly, find:

a) the economic order quantity

b) the annual holding cost

c) the annual ordering cost

d) the reorder point

: **13.7** Annie Engstrom, of Engstrom Plumbing, uses 1,200 of a certain spare part that costs $25 for each order and $24 annual holding cost. Calculate the total cost for order sizes of 25, 40, 50, 60, and 100. Identify the economic order quantity and consider the implications for making an error in calculating the economic order quantity.

· **13.8** Judy Shaw's Dream Store sells water beds and assorted supplies. The best-selling bed in the store has an annual demand of 400 units. The ordering cost is $40; the holding cost is $5 per unit per year. There are 250 working days per year, and the lead time is 6 days.

a) To minimize the total cost, how many units should be ordered each time an order is placed?

b) If the holding cost per unit were $6 instead of $5, what would the optimal order quantity be?

: **13.9** Norris Harrell's Computer Store in Houston sells a printer for $200. Demand for this is constant during the year, and annual demand is forecasted to be 600 units. The holding cost is $20 per unit per year, while the cost of ordering is $60 per order. Currently, the company is ordering 12 times per year (50 units each time). There are 250 working days per year and the lead time is 10 days.

a) Given the current policy of ordering 50 units at a time, what is the total of the annual ordering cost and the annual holding cost?

b) If the company used the absolute best inventory policy, what would the total of the ordering and holding costs be?

c) What is the reorder point?

: **13.10** Jan Kottas is the owner of a small company that produces electric knives used to cut fabric. The annual demand is for 8,000 knives, and Jan produces the knives in batches. On average, Jan can produce 150 knives per day; during the production process, demand for knives has been about 40 knives per day. The cost to set up the production process is $100.00, and it costs Jan $0.80 to carry a knife for one year. How many knives should Jan produce in each batch?

: **13.11** Don Williams, inventory control manager for Cal-Tex, receives wheel bearings from Wheel-Rite, a small producer of metal parts. Wheel-Rite can produce only 500 wheel bearings per day. Cal-Tex receives 10,000 wheel bearings from Wheel-Rite each year. Since Cal-Tex operates 200 working days each year, the average daily demand of wheel bearings by Cal-Tex is 50. The ordering cost for Cal-Tex is $40 per order, and the carrying cost is $0.60 per wheel bearing per year. How many wheel bearings should Cal-Tex order from Wheel-Rite at one time? Wheel-Rite has agreed to ship the maximum number of wheel bearings that it produces each day to Cal-Tex once an order has been received.

: **13.12** Although Mary Carlton never wants to be out of stock, it is simply impossible for her to keep a supply of every kitchen appliance from every manufacturer. Mary has an annual demand for Good Point, a popular toaster, of approximately 3,000 units. The ordering cost is $25, and the carrying cost is $4 per unit per year. Because Good Point is such a popular toaster, when customers ask for it and Mary is out of stock, the customers always place a back order. Although Mary does not like disappointing customers, she knows she will not lose sales when she does not have any Good Point toasters in stock. Mary estimates that the total cost of back-ordering is $75 per unit. How many Good Point toasters should Mary order at one time? How many toasters will be back-ordered?

:**13.13** Rob Schware cannot believe the number of health food products available on the market. Rob's store, Do It Natural, is known for stocking many healthful food products. Rob's customers are also very loyal; if Rob doesn't have a particular health food product, they will place an order and be content to wait until a new shipment arrives. Vitayum is not one of Rob's most popular food supplements, but Rob does order Vitayum on a regular basis. The annual demand for Vitayum is 500 bottles. The ordering cost is $4.00 per order, and the carrying cost is $0.50 per bottle per year. Rob believes that the cost of placing a back order for Vitayum is $10.00 per bottle per year.

a) How many bottles of Vitayum should Rob order if he doesn't allow back-ordering?

b) How many bottles of Vitayum should he order with back-ordering?

c) If the lead time is 10 days and the daily demand is three bottles per day, what is the reorder point when back-ordering is allowed?

d) What is the amount back-ordered?

:**13.14** McLeavey Manufacturing has a demand for 1,000 pumps each year. The cost of a pump is $50. It costs McLeavey Manufacturing $40 to place an order, and the carrying cost is 25% of the unit cost. If pumps are ordered in quantities of 200, McLeavey Manufacturing can get a 3% discount on the cost of the pumps. Should McLeavey Manufacturing order 200 pumps at a time and take the 3% discount?

:**13.15** Flagstaff Products offers the following discount schedule for its $4' \times 8'$ sheets of quality plywood.

ORDER	UNIT COST
9 sheets or less	$18.00
10 to 50 sheets	$17.50
More than 50 sheets	$17.25

Home Sweet Home Company orders plywood from Flagstaff Products. Home Sweet Home has an ordering cost of $45. The carrying cost is 20%, and the annual demand is 100 sheets. What do you recommend?

:**13.16** Should the quantity discount be taken, given the following data on a hardware item stocked by the Niles Brothers Paint Store?

$$D = 2,000 \text{ units}$$
$$S = \$10$$
$$H = \$1$$
$$P = \$1$$
$$\text{Discount price} = \$.75$$
$$\left(\begin{array}{l}\text{Quantity needed to} \\ \text{qualify for discount}\end{array}\right) = 2,000 \text{ units}$$

: **13.17** The regular price of a tape deck component is $20. On orders of 75 units or more, the price is discounted to $18.50. On orders of 100 units or more, the discount price is $15.75. At present, Sound Business, Inc., a manufacturer of stereo components, has an inventory carrying cost of 5% per unit per year, and its ordering cost is $10. Annual demand is 45 components. What should Sound Business, Inc., do?

: **13.18** The demand for barbecue grills has been fairly large in the last several years, and Knell Supplies, Inc., usually orders new barbecue grills five times a year. It is estimated that the ordering cost is $60 per order. The carrying cost is $10 per grill per year. Furthermore, Knell Supplies, Inc., has estimated that the stockout cost is $50 per unit. The reorder point is 650 units. Although the demand each year is high, it varies considerably. The demand during the lead time appears in the following table.

DEMAND DURING LEAD TIME	PROBABILITY	DEMAND DURING LEAD TIME	PROBABILITY
600	.3	900	.05
650	.2	950	.05
700	.1	1000	.03
750	.1	1050	.03
800	.05	1100	.02
850	.05		1.00

The lead time is 12 working days. How much safety stock should Knell Supplies, Inc., maintain?

: **13.19** A product is ordered once each year, and the reorder point without safety stock (dL) is 100 units. Inventory carrying cost is $10 per unit per year, and the cost of a stockout is $50 per unit per year. Given the following demand probabilities during the reorder period, how much safety stock should be carried?

DEMAND DURING REORDER PERIOD	PROBABILITY
0	.1
50	.2
ROP → 100	.4
150	.2
200	.1
	1.0

: **13.20** For a given product, ML = $4 and MP = $1. What stocking policy would you recommend in regard to the following demand distribution?

DEMAND (IN UNITS)	PROBABILITY THAT DEMAND WILL BE AT THIS LEVEL	DEMAND (IN UNITS)	PROBABILITY THAT DEMAND WILL BE AT THIS LEVEL
0	.05	7	.10
1	.05	8	.05
2	.05	9	.05
3	.1	10	.03
4	.15	11	.02
5	.15		1.00
6	.20		

: **13.21** Dara Dean, Inc., an organization that sells children's art sets, has an ordering cost of $40 for the BB-1 set. The carrying cost for BB-1 is $5 per set per year. In order to meet demand, Dara Dean orders large quantities of BB-1 seven times a year. The stockout cost for BB-1 is estimated to be $50 per set. Over the last several years, Dara Dean has observed the following demand during the lead time for BB-1.

DEMAND DURING LEAD TIME	PROBABILITY
40	.1
50	.2
60	.2
70	.2
80	.2
90	.1
	1.0

The reorder point for BB-1 is 60 units. What level of safety stock should be maintained for BB-1?

CASE STUDY

Sturdivant Sound Systems

Sturdivant Sound Systems manufactures and sells stereo and quadraphonic sound systems in both console and component styles. All parts of the sound systems, with the exception of turntables, are produced in the Rochester, New York, plant. Turntables used in the assembly of Sturdivant's systems are purchased from Morris Electronics of Concord, New Hampshire.

Cathy Gardner, purchasing agent for Sturdivant Sound Systems, submits a purchase requisition for the multispeed turntables once every four weeks. The company's annual requirements total 5,000 units (20 per working day), and the cost per unit is $60. (Sturdivant does not purchase in greater quantities because Morris Electronics, the supplier, does not offer quantity discounts.) Rarely does a shortage of turntables occur because Morris promises delivery within one week following receipt of a purchase requisition. (Total time between date of order and date of receipt is 10 days.)

Associated with the purchase of each shipment are procurement costs. These costs, which amount to $20 per order, include the costs of preparing the requisition, inspecting and storing the delivered goods, updating inventory records, and issuing a voucher and a check for payment. In addition to procurement costs, Sturdivant Sound Systems incurs inventory carrying costs that include insurance, storage, handling, taxes, and so forth. These costs equal $6 per unit per year.

Beginning in August of this year, management of Sturdivant Sound Systems will embark on a company-wide cost control program in an attempt to improve its profits. One of the areas to be closely scrutinized for possible cost savings is inventory procurement.

Discussion Questions

1. Compute the optimal order quantity.

2. Determine the appropriate reorder point (in units).

3. Compute the cost savings that the company will realize if it implements the optimal inventory procurement decision.

4. Should procurement costs be considered a linear function of the number of orders?

Source: Professors Jerry Kinard (Francis Marion College) and Joe Iverstine.

CASE STUDY

Western Ranchman Outfitters

Western Ranchman Outfitters (WRO) is a family-owned and operated mail order and retail store business in Cheyenne, Wyoming. It bills itself as "The Nation's Finest Western Store" and carries high-quality western apparel and riding supplies. Its catalog is mailed all over the world; the store and its president, John Veta, have appeared in a short article in *Fortune* magazine; and clothes from WRO were featured in *Mademoiselle*.

One of WRO's staple items is the button-front, shrink-to-fit blue jean made by Levi Strauss (model no. 501). This is the original riveted denim pant that cowboys shrank by sitting in a tub of hot water. It is the epitome of durability and fit and is still a popular jean. When Mr. Veta was asked his stockout philosophy for this item, he answered, "Would you expect a drugstore to have aspirin?" Further, Mr. Veta has had a pleasant relationship with Levi Strauss for all the years of his business career.

Don Randell, director of merchandising, takes a physical inventory of this item once a month. His records show annual usage, amount on hand, quantity ordered, and quantity received (which has been averaging 185 pairs per month, except in January–March when it averages 150 pairs per month), all dated by the month. The store attempts to keep a safety stock adequate for 60 days for two reasons: production problems of the supplier and a hedge against unusually large orders.

Mr. Randell described the problems of ordering. "The rag business," as it is known, "is made up of the most disorganized group of people I've ever had the opportunity to be associated with," according to Randell. The problems he cited include not specifying a delivery date, unexplained late deliveries, a general lack of productivity, and lead times of up to six months.

Randell contrasted this situation with his experience in the flexible packaging industry, where reliability was a hallmark, and a delay of a single day warranted notification to the customer.

The most recent eight-month period is used to illustrate WRO's ordering difficulties. While the sample figures in Table 13.5 may seem peculiar, they reflect WRO's philosophy of offering a full range of sizes and Mr. Randell's attempts to predict Levi Strauss' delivery pattern so that the store is close to obtaining the stock it needs. For example, in the last eight months, no one bought a pair sized 27 × 36. Nevertheless six were ordered and received so that should such a customer appear, he would be able to satisfy his needs. For size 27 × 34, 33 were ordered, but only 21 were received, which is very close to the 18 sold in the eight months of the previous year. The 27-inch and 28-inch waist

TABLE 13.5 Usage and Ordering of the Levi 501 for Selected Sizes.

SIZE (IN INCHES) WAIST × LENGTH	USAGE	NUMBER ORDERED	NUMBER RECEIVED
27 × 28	11	—	—
27 × 29	1	—	—
27 × 30	6	—	—
27 × 31	—	—	—
27 × 32	4	—	—
27 × 33	—	—	—
27 × 34	18	33	21
27 × 36	—	6	6
28 × 28	—	—	—
28 × 29	—	—	—
28 × 30	—	—	—
28 × 31	—	3	3
28 × 32	4	—	—
28 × 33	7	—	—
28 × 34	8	21	12
28 × 36	27	30	18
	86	93	60*

* Approximately 64% of the number ordered were received.

sizes shown in the exhibit are but two of the many available waist sizes, of course—waist sizes up to 60 inches are produced and sold.

Randell places an order for Levi blue jeans every month, doing his best to ensure an adequate supply for the business. Normally, WRO customers are not disappointed when requesting the Levi 501. However, in the past two months, the Wyoming Game and Fish Department has been requiring extra pairs of this jean, and WRO has not always had this exact jean in stock. Since there are at least four styles that satisfy the state requirements, the problem is usually overcome with other styles or brands.

Annual demand at WRO for the Levi 501 is 2,000 pairs. The cost of placing an order is about $10, the carrying cost is 12%, and the cost of the Levi to WRO is $10.05 per pair.

Discussion Question

1. Evaluate Randell's ordering policy. How does it compare with formal mathematical approaches?

Source: From Barry Render, R. M. Stair and I. Greenberg, *Cases and Readings in Management Science,* 2nd ed., Boston: Allyn & Bacon, 1990. Used with permission.

CASE STUDY

LaPlace Power and Light

The Southeastern Division of LaPlace Power and Light Company is responsible for providing dependable electric service to customers in and around the area of Metairie, Kenner, Destrehan, LaPlace, Lutcher, Hammond, Pontchatoula, Amite, and Bogalusa, Louisiana. One material used extensively to provide this service is the 1/0 AWG aluminum triplex cable, which delivers the electricity from the distribution pole to the meter loop on the house.

The Southeastern Division Storeroom purchases the cable that this division will use. For the coming year, this division will need 499,500 feet of this service cable. Since this cable is only used on routine service work, practically all of it is installed during the five normal workdays. The current cost of this cable is 41.4 cents per foot. Under the present arrangement with the supplier, the Southeastern Storeroom must take one-twelfth of its annual need every month. This agreement was reached in order to reduce lead time by assuring LaPlace a regular spot on the supplier's production schedule. Without this agreement, the lead time would be about twelve weeks. No quantity discounts are offered on this cable; however, the supplier requires that a minimum of 15,000 feet be on an order. The Southeastern Storeroom has the space to store a maximum of 300,000 feet of 1/0 AWG aluminum service cable.

Associated with each cable shipment are ordering costs of $50, which include all the costs from making the purchase requisitions to issuing a check for payment. In addition, inventory carrying costs (including taxes) on all items in stores are considered to be 10% of the purchase price per unit per year.

Because the company is a government-regulated, investor-owned utility, both the Louisiana Public Service Commission and its stockholders watch closely how effectively the company, including inventory management, is managed.

Discussion Question

1. Evaluate the effectiveness of the current ordering system. Can it be improved?

BIBLIOGRAPHY

Austin, L. M. "Project EOQ: A Success Story in Implementing Academic Research." *Interfaces* **7** (August 1977): 1–12.

Brown, R. G. *Decision Rules for Inventory Management.* New York: Holt, Rinehart & Winston, 1967.

Fordyce, J. M., and F. M. Webster. "The Wagner-Whitin Algorithm Made Simple." *Production and Inventory Management* (Second Quarter 1986): 21–30.

Freeland, J. R., J. P. Leschke, and E. N. Weiss. "Guidelines for Setup-Cost Reduction Programs to Achieve Zero Inventory." *Journal of Operations Management* **9** (January 1990):85.

Hall, R. *Zero Inventories.* Homewood, IL: Dow Jones-Irwin, 1983.

Hirano, H. *JIT Factory Revolution.* Cambridge, MA: Productivity Press, 1989.

Jinchiro, N., and R. Hall. "Management Specs for Stockless Production." *Harvard Business Review* **63** (May–June 1983): 89–91.

Mondon, Y. "Adaptive Kanban System Helps Toyota Maintain Just-in-Time Production." *Journal of Industrial Engineering* (May 1981): 28.

Shingo, S. *A Revolution in Manufacturing: The SMED System.* Cambridge, MA: Productivity Press, 1986.

Showalter, M. J., M. S. Froseth, and M. J. Maxwell. "Production-Inventory Systems Design for Hospital Food Service Operations." *Production and Inventory Management* (Second Quarter 1984): 67–81.

Vollmann, T. E., W. L. Berry, and D. C. Whybark. *Manufacturing Planning and Control Systems.* Homewood, IL: Irwin, 1988.

Wagner, H. J., and T. M. Whitin, "Dynamic Version of the Economic Lot Size Model." *Management Science* (October 1958).

Wantuck, K. "Calculating Optimum Inventories." APICS, *International Conference Proceeding* (1978).

Wight, O. W. *Production and Inventory Management in the Computer Age.* Boston: Cahmers, 1974.

Material Requirements Planning (MRP)

MRP Provides a Competitive Advantage for Collins Industries

Collins Industries, headquarted in Hutchinson, Kansas, is the largest manufacturer of ambulances in the world. The $150 million firm is an international competitor that sells more than 20% of its vehicles to markets outside the United States. It competes with some very tough rivals, both domestically and worldwide, but remains a world leader. In its largest ambulance plant, located in Winter Park, Florida, vehicles are produced on assembly lines (i.e., a repetitive process). There are 12 major ambulance designs assem-

On the six parallel assembly lines, ambulances move forward each day to the next workstation. The MRP system makes certain that just the materials needed at each station arrive overnight for assembly the next day.

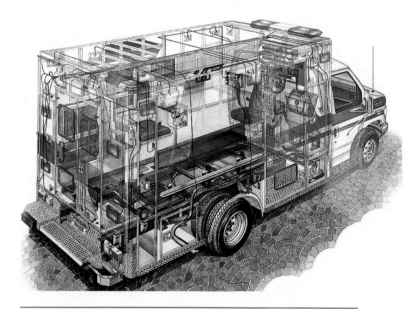

This cutaway of one ambulance interior indicates the complexity of the product, which for some rural locations may be the equivalent of a hospital emergency room in miniature. To complicate production, virtually every ambulance is custom-ordered, with 7,000 different options available. This necessitates precise orders and good bills-of-materials.

bled at the Florida plant, and they use 18,000 different inventory items, including 6,000 manufactured parts and 12,000 purchased parts.

This variety of products and the nature of the process demand good material requirements planning. The system at Collins Industries is a net change system with daily updates. The firm uses the MAPICS DB software on an IBM AS400 minicomputer. Effective use of MAPICS forces Collins to maintain accurate bills-of-material and inven-

This photo shows a worker wiring an electronic board. Ambulance wiring is so complex that there are an average of 15 miles of wire in a Collins vehicle. Compare this to the 16 miles in a sophisticated F-16 fighter jet.

The company uses a job shop environment to feed assembly line needs. It maintains a complete carpentry shop (to provide interior cabinetry), a metal fabrication shop (to construct the shell of the ambulance), a paint shop (to prepare, paint, and detail each vehicle), an electrical shop (to provide for the complex electronics in a modern ambulance), and as shown here, an upholstery shop (to make interior seats and benches).

tory records. The system has reduced inventory by over 30% in just the past two years.

There are four key activities that Collins insists must be done properly. They are:

1. *Maintaining a sound material plan.* The material plan must meet both the requirements of the master schedule and the capabilities of the production facility.

2. *Executing the plan.* The best method to control material is to make sure that the plan is executed as designed. This is a particularly important issue at Collins and may be a major contributor to their excellent results.

3. *Reducing inventory.* By effecting "time-phased" material deliveries, negotiating consignment of vendor inventory, and constantly reviewing procurement methods, Collins reduces inventory investment.

4. *Maintaining record integrity.* At Collins, record accuracy is recognized as a fundamental ingredient of the successful MRP program. Their cycle counters are charged with material audits that not only correct errors but also investigate the source of such errors and initiate corrective action.

Collins Industries has used MRP as the catalyst for low inventory, quality, production to schedule, and accurate records. Collins has found competitive advantage via MRP.

INTRODUCTION

The inventory models discussed in Chapter 13 assumed that the demand for one item was independent of the demand for another item. For example, the demand for refrigerators may be *independent* of the demand for dishwashers. Moreover, the demand today may have little, if anything, to do with the demand tomorrow.

However, demand for many items may be dependent. By *dependent,* we mean the demand for one item is related to the demand for another item. Consider an auto manufacturer. The carmaker's demand for auto tires and radiators depends on the production of autos. Four tires and one radiator go into each finished car. Demand for items is *dependent* when the relationship between the items can be determined. Therefore, once management can make a forecast of the demand for the final product, quantities required for all components can be computed, because all components are *dependent* items. The Boeing Aircraft operations manager scheduling production of one plane per week, for example, knows the requirements down to the last rivet. For any product, all components of that product are *dependent* demand items. *More generally, for any item where a schedule can be established, dependent techniques should be used.*

Dependent techniques, when they can be used, are preferable to the models of Chapter 13. This is true for all component parts, subassemblies, and supplies when a schedule is known. It is true not only for manufacturers and distributors, but also for a wide variety of firms from restaurants[1] to hospitals.[2] When dependent techniques are used in a production environment, they are called **material requirements planning (MRP).** When dependent techniques are used in distribution environments, they are called **distribution resource planning (DRP).**

Material requirements planning (MRP)

Distribution resource planning (DRP)

DEPENDENT INVENTORY MODEL REQUIREMENTS

In this chapter we examine the requirements of dependent inventory models for both production and distribution. Then we look at how to use these models. Effective use of dependent inventory models requires that the operations manager know the:

1. master production schedule (what is to be made and when);
2. specifications or bill-of-material (how to make the product);
3. inventory availability (what is in stock);
4. purchase orders outstanding (what is on order);
5. lead times (how long it takes to get various components).

In this chapter each of these requirements is discussed in the context of material requirements planning (MRP); we then introduce distribution resource planning (DRP).

---

[1] John G. Wacker, "Effective Plannning and Cost Control for Restaurants: Making Resource Requirements Planning Work," *Production and Inventory Management,* **26** (First Quarter 1985): 55–70.

[2] David W. Pentico, "Material Requirements Planning: A New Tool for Controlling Hospital Inventories," *Hospital Topics,* **57** (May–June 1979): 40–43.

FIGURE 14.1

The Planning Process.

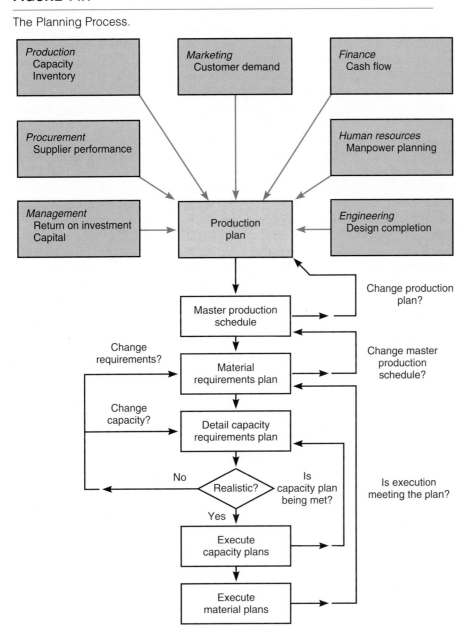

Master Production Schedule

A **master production schedule** specifies what is to be made and when. The schedule must be in accordance with a production plan. The production plan sets the overall level of output in broad terms (for example, product families, standard hours, or dollar volume). The production plan is derived from the aggregate planning techniques of Chapter 12. Such plans include a variety of inputs, including financial plans, customer demand, engineering capabilities, labor availability, inventory fluc-

**Master production
schedule**

tuations, supplier performance, and other considerations. Each contributes in its own way to the production plan, as shown in Figure 14.1, which shows the planning process from the production plan to execution. Each of the lower-level plans must be feasible. When it is not, feedback to the next higher level is used to make the necessary adjustment. One of the major strengths of MRP is its ability to determine precisely the feasibility of a schedule within capacity constraints. This planning process can yield excellent results. The production plan sets the upper and lower bounds on the master production schedule. From this production planning process the master production schedule is developed.

The master production schedule tells us what is required to satisfy demand and meet the production plan. This schedule establishes what items to make and when. Managers must adhere to the plan for a reasonable length of time (usually a major portion of the production cycle). Many organizations establish a master production schedule and then "fix" the near-term portion of the plan. The fixed portion of the schedule is then referred to as the "fixed," "firm," or "frozen" schedule. Only changes beyond the fixed schedule are permitted. The schedule then becomes a rolling production schedule. For example, a fixed seven-week plan has an additional week added to it as each week is completed, so there is always a seven-week fixed schedule. Note that the master production schedule is a statement of production, not a forecast of demand. It shows the units that are to be produced. The master schedule can be expressed in terms of

1. an end item in a continuous (make-to-stock) company;
2. a customer order in a job shop (make-to-order) company;
3. modules in a repetitive (assemble-to-stock) company.

A master production schedule for two products, A and S, might look like Table 14.1.

Specifications or Bills-of-Material

As simple as determining how to make a product may sound, it is difficult in practice. As we saw in Chapter 6, there is usually a rush to get a new product to market. Therefore the drawings and specifications may be incomplete. Moreover, the drawings and specifications that are complete often contain errors; dimensions are wrong; quantities are not specified; two drawings have been issued for the same

---

TABLE 14.1 Master production schedule for products A and S.

GROSS REQUIREMENTS FOR PRODUCT A									
Week	6	7	8	9	10	11	12	13	14	and so on
Amount	50		100	47	60		110	75	

GROSS REQUIREMENTS FOR PRODUCT S									
Week	7	8	9	10	11	12	13	14	15	16	and so on
Amount	100	200	150			60	75		100	

component or subassembly; or, on occasion, no drawing exists. For these reasons **engineering change notices (ECNs)** are created, further complicating the process.

Units to be produced are often specified via a bill-of-material, which we introduced in Chapter 6. A **bill-of-material (BOM)** is a list of quantities of components, ingredients, and materials required to make a product. A home kitchen recipe specifying ingredients and quantities and a full set of drawings for an airplane are both bills-of-material (although they do vary somewhat in scope). A drawing and bill-of-material exists for an entire product such as a pencil, a truck, or a Boeing 757. Other drawings and bills-of-material are created for each of the major components and subassemblies. For each component and subassembly there is a drawing that specifies its components. In turn, its components or subassemblies are specified in a similar fashion until every nut, bolt, ounce of paint, instruction booklet, etc., is specified. A bill-of-material for item A in Example 1 consists of items B and C. The individual drawings describe not only physical dimensions, but also any special processing as well as the raw material from which each part is made. Items above any level are called *parents;* items below any level are called *components* or *children.*

A bill-of-material provides the product structure. The following example shows how to develop the product structure and "explode" it to reveal the requirements for each component.[3]

Engineering change notice (ECN)

Bill-of-material (BOM)

Example 1

Fun Lawn's demand for product A is 50 units. Each unit of A requires two units of B and three units of C. Each unit of B requires two units of D and three units of E. Furthermore, each unit of C requires one unit of E and two units of F. And each F requires one unit of G and two units of D. Thus the demand for B, C, D, E, F, and G is completely dependent on the demand for A. Given this information, we can construct a product structure for the related inventory items:

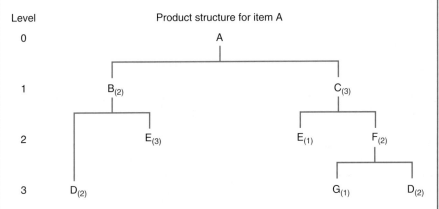

The structure has four levels: 0, 1, 2, and 3. There are four parents: A, B, C, and F. Each parent item has at least one level below it. Items B, C, D, E, F,

---

[3] This problem was described and a matrix algebra solution presented by A. Vaszonyi, "The Use of Mathematics in Production and Inventory Control," *Management Science,* **1** (October 1954): 70–85.

and G are components because each item has at least one level above it. In this structure, B, C, and F are parents and components. The number in parentheses indicates how many units of that particular item are needed to make the item immediately above it. Thus $B_{(2)}$ means that it takes two units of B for every unit of A, and $F_{(2)}$ means that it takes two units of F for every unit of C.

Once we have developed the product structure, we can determine the number of units of each item required to satisfy demand. This information is displayed in the following table:

Part B:	$2 \times$ number of As =	(2)(50) =	100
Part C:	$3 \times$ number of As =	(3)(50) =	150
Part D:	$2 \times$ number of Bs + $2 \times$ number of Fs =	(2)(100) + (2)(300) =	800
Part E:	$3 \times$ number of Bs + $1 \times$ number of Cs =	(3)(100) + (1)(150) =	450
Part F:	$2 \times$ number of Cs =	(2)(150) =	300
Part G:	$1 \times$ number of Fs =	(1)(300) =	300

Thus for 50 units of A, we will need 100 units of B, 150 units of C, 800 units of D, 450 units of E, 300 units of F, and 300 units of G.

For manufacturers like Harley-Davidson who produce a large number of end products from a relatively small number of options, modular bills-of-material provide an effective solution.

Bills-of-material not only specify requirements, but are also useful for costing, and they can serve as a list of items to be issued to production or assembly personnel. When bills-of-material (BOM) are used in this way, they are usually called *pick lists*.

Modular bills

Modular Bills. Bills-of-material may be organized around product modules (see Chapter 6). Modules are not final products to be sold but are components that can be produced and assembled into units. They may be major components of the final product or product options. The bills-of-material for these modules are called **modular bills.** Bills-of-material are sometimes organized as modules (rather than as part of a final product) because production scheduling and production are often facilitated by organizing around relatively few modules rather than a multitude of final assemblies. For instance, a firm may make 138,000 different final products but have only 40 modules that are mixed and matched to produce the 138,000 final products.[4] The firm forecasts, prepares its master production schedule, and builds to the 40 modules, not the 138,000 configurations of the final product. The 40 modules can be assembled for specific orders at final assembly.

Planning bills

Planning Bills and Phantom Bills. Other special kinds of bills-of-material exist. These include planning bills and phantom bills. **Planning bills** are created in order to assign an artificial parent to the bill-of-material. This is advantageous under two conditions: (1) where we want to group subassemblies together to reduce the number of items to be scheduled, and (2) where we want to issue "kits" to the production department. For instance, it may not be efficient to issue cotter pins with each of numerous subassemblies, so we call this a *kit* and generate a planning bill.

[4] Dave Garwood, "Stop Before You Use the Bill Processor . . . ," *American Production and Inventory Control Society* (Second Quarter 1970): 73–75.

The planning bill specifies the *kit* to be issued. A planning bill may also be known as **pseudo bill** or **kit number. Phantom bills-of-material** are bills-of-material for components, usually subassemblies that exist only temporarily. They go directly into another assembly. Therefore they are coded to receive special treatment; lead times are zero, and they are handled as an integral part of their parent item. They are never inventoried.

Pseudo bills
Kit number
Phantom bills-of-material

Low-Level Coding. Low-level coding of an item in a BOM is necessary when identical items exist at various levels in the BOM. **Low-level coding** means the item is coded at the lowest level at which it occurs. For example, item D in Example 1 is coded at the lowest level at which it is used. Item D could be coded as part of B and occur at level 2. But since D is also part of F, and F is level 2, item D becomes a level 3 item. Low-level coding allows easy computing of the requirements of an item. When the BOM has thousands of items and when requirements are frequently recomputed, the ease and speed of computation becomes a major concern.

Low-level coding

Accurate Inventory Records

Knowledge of what is in stock is the result of good inventory management, as discussed in Chapter 13. Good inventory management is an absolute necessity for an MRP system to work. If the firm has not yet achieved at least 99% record accuracy, then material requirements planning will not work.

Purchase Orders Outstanding

Knowledge of outstanding orders should exist as a by-product of well-managed purchasing and inventory control departments. When purchase orders are executed, records of those orders and their scheduled delivery date must be available to production personnel. Only with good purchasing data can managers prepare good production plans and effectively execute an MRP system.

Lead Times for Each Component

Management must determine when products are needed. Only then can it be determined when to purchase, produce, or assemble. This means operations personnel determine wait, move, queue, setup, and run times for each component. When grouped together, these times are called **lead times.** When the bill-of-material for

Lead times

TABLE 14.2 Lead Times for Product A.

COMPONENT	LEAD TIME
A	1 week
B	2 weeks
C	1 week
D	1 week
E	2 weeks
F	3 weeks
G	2 weeks

FIGURE 14.2

Time-Phased Product Structure.

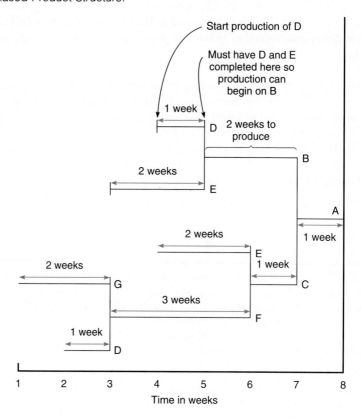

item A (Example 1) is turned on its side and lead times (see Table 14.2 on page 605) are added to each component (time on the horizontal axis), then we have a time-phased product structure. This is shown in Figure 14.2.

BENEFITS OF MRP

In the inventory models of Chapter 13, the questions answered were how much to order and when to order. While dependent demand makes inventory scheduling and planning more complex, it also makes it more beneficial. Some of the benefits of MRP are:

1. increased customer service and satisfaction;
2. improved utilization of facilities and labor;
3. better inventory planning and scheduling;
4. faster response to market changes and shifts;
5. reduced inventory levels without reduced customer service.

POM _in action_

MRP II Nissan Style

Nissan Motor Company's plant 40 miles northwest of Tokyo assembles automobiles and forklift trucks, producing 30,000 cars and 1,600 lift trucks per month. Unlike Toyota's Toyota City facility, which has suppliers located within minutes and hours, this Nissan plant's suppliers are spread across Japan. These distances could be a potential problem requiring Nissan to either stabilize their vendor schedules or carry extra inventory. Nissan has addressed this issue head on.

High-level scheduling is refined to a razor's edge. They start by establishing an overall production rate by month and then add more detail in continuously smaller time increments through five progressive master scheduling iterations. The first pass nails down the model by month for three months. The second iteration covers the first month in days, specifying the drive train. And the third defines specific options of the first ten days. The fourth covers the first five days and is used to start synchronizing shipments from their suppliers. The fifth pass is the final assembly schedule, which specifies the exact config-uration and build sequence of each car.

Their mastering of this front-end scheduling produces benefits that can be seen all through their manufacturing operation and on to their suppliers.

The bulk of Nissan's purchased parts are scheduled with their suppliers by computer communication link. These schedules are confirmed, updated, and/or changed every 15 to 20 minutes. Their suppliers provide deliveries 4 to 16 times per day. Supply trucks that arrive too early park in the four-lane parking road running through the complex to await their "delivery window."

Results are the proof of any operation—and results they get. Master schedule performance is 99% on time measured every hour. On-time delivery from suppliers is 99.9% and 99.5% for manufactured piece parts. They turn their inventory of purchased parts slightly more than once every day and have an overall turn rate of approximately 150 per year.

Sources: Newsletter, January 1986, The Oliver W. Wight Companies, p. 11; and _Software Magazine,_ April 1988, pp. 37–44.

The _POM in Action_ box, "MRP II Nissan Style," relates the significant benefits achieved by Nissan Motor Company through the use of MRP.

MRP STRUCTURE

Although most MRP systems are computerized, the analysis is straightforward and similar from one computerized system to the next. A master production schedule, a bill-of-material, inventory and purchase records, and lead times for each item are ingredients of a material requirements planning system (see Figure 14.3 on page 609).

The next step is to construct a gross material requirements plan. This step combines the master production schedule (Table 14.1) and the time phased schedule (Figure 14.2). The **gross material requirements plan** is a schedule. It shows when an item must be ordered from suppliers if there is no inventory on hand or when the

Gross material requirements plan

production of an item must be started in order to satisfy the demand for the finished product by a particular date.

Example 2

Fun Lawns, Inc. (of Example 1), produces all of the items in product A. The lead times are shown in Table 14.2. Using this information, we construct the gross material requirements plan and draw up a production schedule that will satisfy the demand of 50 units of A by week eight as shown in Table 14.3.

TABLE 14.3 Gross material requirements plan for 50 units of A.

				WEEK					
	1	2	3	4	5	6	7	8	LEAD TIME
A. Required date								50	1 week
Order releases							50		
B. Required date							100		2 weeks
Order releases					100				
C. Required date							150		1 week
Order releases						150			
D. Required date					200				1 week
Order releases				200					
E. Required date						300	150		2 weeks
Order releases			300	150					
F. Required date						300			3 weeks
Order releases			300						
D. Required date			600						1 week
Order releases		600							
G. Required date			300						2 weeks
Order releases	300								

The interpretation of the gross material requirements is as follows: If you want 50 units of A at week eight, you must start assembling A in week seven. Thus, in week seven you will need 100 units of B and 150 units of C. These two items take two weeks and one week, respectively, to produce. Production of B should start in week five, and production of C should start in week six (lead time subtracted from the order release date for these items). Working backward, we can perform the same computations for all of the other items. The material requirements plan graphically reveals when production of each item should begin and end in order to have 50 units of A at week eight.

So far, we have considered gross material requirements. In other words, we have assumed that there is no inventory on hand. When there is inventory on hand, production of the actual, or net, requirements avoids overstocking or overordering. When considering on-hand inventory, we must realize that many items actually contain subassemblies or parts. If the gross requirement for lawn mowers is 100 units and there are 20 lawn mowers on hand, the net requirement for lawn mowers is 80 (that is, 100 – 20). But each lawn mower on hand contains four wheels and one

FIGURE 14.3

Structure of the MRP System.

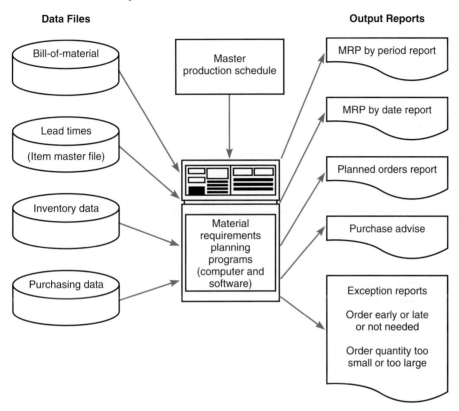

spark plug. As a result, the requirement for wheels drops by 80 wheels (20 lawn mowers on hand × 4 wheels/lawn mower), and the requirement for spark plugs drops by 20 (20 × 1). Thus, if there is inventory on hand for a parent item, the requirements for the parent item and all its components decrease because each lawn mower contains the components for lower-level items.

Example 3

In Example 1 we developed a product structure from a BOM, and in Example 2 we developed a gross requirements plan. Given the following on-hand inventory, we now construct a net requirements plan.

ITEM	ON HAND	ITEM	ON HAND
A	10	E	10
B	15	F	5
C	20	G	0
D	10		

Lot Size	Lead Time (weeks)	On Hand	Safety Stock	Allo-cated	Low Level Code	Item Identi-fication		Week								
								1	2	3	4	5	6	7	8
Lot-for-Lot	1	10	—	—	0	A	Gross Requirements								50
							Scheduled Receipts								
							Projected On Hand 10	10	10	10	10	10	10	10	10
							Net Requirements								40
							Planned Order Receipts								40
							Planned Order Releases							40	
Lot-for-Lot	2	15	—	—	1	B	Gross Requirements							80^A	
							Scheduled Receipts								
							Projected On Hand 15	15	15	15	15	15	15	15	
							Net Requirements							65	
							Planned Order Receipts							65	
							Planned Order Releases					65			
Lot-for-Lot	1	20	—	—	1	C	Gross Requirements							120^A	
							Scheduled Receipts								
							Projected On Hand 20	20	20	20	20	20	20	20	
							Net Requirements							100	
							Planned Order Receipts							100	
							Planned Order Releases						100		
Lot-for-Lot	2	10	—	—	2	E	Gross Requirements					195^B	100^C		
							Scheduled Receipts								
							Projected On Hand 10	10	10	10	10	10			
							Net Requirements					185	100		
							Planned Order Receipts					185	100		
							Planned Order Releases			185	100				
Lot-for-Lot	3	5	—	—	2	F	Gross Requirements						200^C		
							Scheduled Receipts								
							Projected On Hand 5	5	5	5	5	5	5		
							Net Requirements						195		
							Planned Order Receipts						195		
							Planned Order Releases			195					
Lot-for-Lot	1	10	—	—	3	D	Gross Requirements			390^F		130^B			
							Scheduled Receipts								
							Projected On Hand 10	10	10	10					
							Net Requirements			380		130			
							Planned Order Receipts			380		130			
							Planned Order Releases		380		130				
Lot-for-Lot	2	0	—	—	3	G	Gross Requirements			195^F					
							Scheduled Receipts								
							Projected On Hand			0					
							Net Requirements			195					
							Planned Order Receipts			195					
							Planned Order Releases	195							
							Gross Requirements								
							Scheduled Receipts								
							Projected On Hand								
							Net Requirements								
							Planned Order Receipts								
							Planned Order Releases								

Net material requirements plan for product A (see Example 3).

A net material requirements plan includes gross requirements, on-hand inventory, net requirements, planned order receipt, and planned order release for each item. We begin with A and work backward through the components. Shown in the chart on page 610 is the net material requirements plan for product A.

The construction of a net requirements plan is similar to construction of the gross requirements plan. Starting with item A, we work backward to determine net requirements for all items. To do these computations we refer to the product structure, on-hand inventory, and lead times. The gross requirement for A is 50 units in week eight. Ten items are on hand; therefore the net requirements and planned order receipt both are 40 items in week eight. Because of the one-week lead time, the planned order release is 40 items in week seven (see the arrow connecting the order receipt and order release). Referring to week seven and the product structure in Example 1, we can see 80 (2 × 40) items of B and 120 (3 × 40) items of C are required in week seven in order to have a total for 50 items of A in week eight. The letter *A* to the right of the gross figure for item B and C was generated as a result of the demand for the parent, A. Performing the same type of analysis for B and C yields the net requirements for D, E, F, and G. Note the on-hand inventory in row E in week six. It is zero because the on-hand inventory (10 units) was used to make B in Column 5. By the same token, the inventory for D was used to make F.

3COM Corporation, headquarters in Santa Clara, CA, is a manufacturer of local and wide area computer network systems. 3COM uses MRP II to manage its production of printed circuit boards. Timely and accurate information obtained from the system is forwarded to suppliers that deliver parts and material directly to the line on a Just-in-Time (JIT) basis. 3COM's MRP system allows them to keep inventory levels low and track vendor performance.

Examples 2 and 3 considered only product A and its completion only in week eight. Fifty units of A were required in week eight. Normally there is a demand for

FIGURE 14.4

Several Schedules Contributing to a Gross Requirements Schedule for B. One "B" is in each A and one "B" in each S, and 10 Bs are sold directly in week one and 10 more are sold directly in week two.

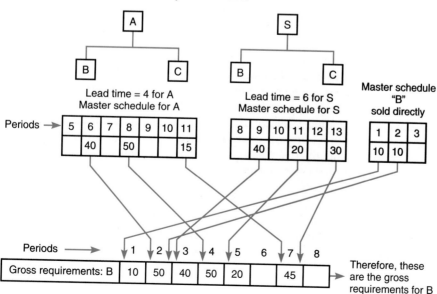

FIGURE 14.5

Sample MRP Planning Sheet for Item A.

Lot Size	Lead Time	On Hand	Safety Stock	Allocated	Low Level Code	Item Id		Period							
								1	2	3	4	5	6	7	8
Lot *FoR* *Lot*	*1*	*0*	*0*	*10*	*0*	B	Gross Requirements								*80* *90*
							Scheduled Receipts								*0*
							Projected On Hand *0*	*0*	*0*	*0*	*0*	*0*	*0*	*0*	*0*
							Net Requirements								*90*
							Planned Order Receipts								*90*
							Planned Order Releases							*90*	

many products over time. For each product, management must prepare a master production schedule (as we saw earlier in Table 14.1). Scheduled production of each product contributes to the master schedule and ultimately to the net material requirements plan. Several product schedules contributing to one master production schedule and ultimately to one net material requirements plan are shown in Figure 14.4 on page 611.

Most inventory systems also note the number of units in inventory that have been assigned to specific future production but not yet used. Such items are often referred to as *allocated* items. Allocated items may then be included in an MRP planning sheet as shown in Figure 14.5.

The allocated quantity has the effect of increasing the requirements (or, alternatively, reducing the quantity on hand). The logic, then, of a net requirements MRP is:

$$\underbrace{\left[\left(\begin{array}{c}\text{Gross}\\\text{requirements}\end{array}\right)+\left(\text{Allocations}\right)\right]}_{\text{Total requirements}}-\underbrace{\left[\left(\begin{array}{c}\text{On}\\\text{hand}\end{array}\right)+\left(\begin{array}{c}\text{Scheduled}\\\text{receipts}\end{array}\right)\right]}_{\text{Available inventory}}=\begin{array}{c}\text{Net}\\\text{requirements}\end{array}$$

REGENERATION AND NET CHANGE

A material requirements plan is not static. Once a bill-of-material and material requirements plan is established, changes in design, schedules, and production processes occur. Thus, if one of the production time estimates was one week less than it should have been, that week must be added to the material requirements plan. Likewise, if a design improvement allows construction of one of the intermediate inventory items with fewer parts, then an alteration in the bill-of-material and the material requirements plan is necessary. Scrapped components, missed receiving dates, and machine breakdowns contribute to such alterations in the material requirements plan. Similarly, alterations occur in an MRP system when changes are made to the master production schedule. Regardless of the cause of any changes, the MRP model can be manipulated to reflect them. In this manner, an up-to-date schedule is possible. Such a schedule would depict when to begin production of all items so that the production schedule is satisfied.

Performing modifications to the MRP schedule as a result of changes is cumbersome if done by hand, and it is likely that errors will occur when the plan is complex. In general, MRP systems are computerized. Indeed, only because they are computerized are they the popular and practical tool they have become.[5] Computerized programs perform the same types of calculations that we have demonstrated in this chapter.

A central strength of MRP is its timely and accurate replanning capability. Due to the variations that occur, it is not uncommon to regenerate the MRP requirements about once a week. This is known as regenerative MRP. **Regenerative MRP** executes the entire MRP program, and all computations are performed, yielding a new net requirements plan. However, some managers are interested in faster, more frequent MRP reports. Consequently, net change MRP now exists. Under **net change MRP,** only if an item had activity is it recalculated. Net change MRP requires more sophisticated computer programs but less computer processing time.

As nice as frequent recomputing of MRP may seem, many firms find they do not want to respond to minor changes even if they are aware of them. These frequent changes generate what is called **system nervousness.** Frequent changes can create havoc in purchasing and production departments if such changes are implemented. Consequently, even where net change capability exists, P/OM personnel are expected to reduce the nervousness by evaluating the need and impact of changes prior to disseminating requests to other departments.

Operations personnel have two additional tools available to reduce system nervousness. The first is the establishment of time fences. **Time fences** allow a segment of the master schedule to be designated as "not to be rescheduled." This segment of the master schedule is thus not changed during the periodic regeneration of schedules. The second tool available is pegging. **Pegging** means tracing upward in the BOM from the component to the parent item. By pegging upward, the production planner can determine the cause for the requirement and make a judgment about the necessity for a change in the schedule.

With MRP the operations manager *can* react to the dynamics of the real world. How frequently the manager wishes to impose those changes on the firm requires professional judgment. Moreover, if the nervousness is caused by legitimate changes, then the proper response of operations management may be to investigate the production environment—not adjust via MRP.

Regenerative MRP

Net change MRP

System nervousness

Time fences

Pegging

LOT-SIZING TECHNIQUES

Thus far in our discussion of MRP we have used what is known as a *lot-for-lot* determination of our production units. This is evident in our planned order releases in Example 3 where we produced what we need, and no more and no less. The objective in an MRP system is to produce units only as needed, with no safety stock and no anticipation of further orders. Such a procedure is consistent with small lot

[5] As early as 1920, Al Sloan, president of GM, understood the basic ingredients of MRP. See Alfred P. Sloan, Jr., *My Years with General Motors* (Garden City, NY: Doubleday & Co., Inc., Anchor Books, 1972) p. 145.

sizes, frequent orders, low just-in-time inventory, and dependent demand. However, in cases where the setup costs are significant or where management has been unable to implement a philosophy of JIT, lot-for-lot can be an expensive technique. As we saw in Chapter 13, there are alternative ways of determining lot size, namely economic order quantity (EOQ). Indeed, there are numerous ways of determining lot sizes in MRP systems. Many commercially available MRP systems include the option of a variety of lot-sizing techniques. We will review a few of them.

Lot-for-lot

Lot-for-Lot. As we said, Example 3 uses a **lot-for-lot,** lot-sizing technique where we produced exactly what was required. Example 4 uses the lot-for-lot criteria and determines its cost.

Example 4

Fun Lawns, Inc., wishes to compute its ordering and carrying cost of inventory on lot-for-lot criteria. Fun Lawns has determined that, for 21-inch lawn mower blades, its setup cost is $100 and its holding cost for these blades is $1 per period. The production schedule as reflected in net requirements for blades is shown below:

MRP LOT-SIZING PROBLEM: LOT-FOR-LOT TECHNIQUE.

		1	2	3	4	5	6	7	8	9	10
Gross Requirements		35	30	40	0	10	40	30	0	30	55
Scheduled Receipts											
Projected On Hand	35	0	0	0	0	0	0	0	0	0	0
Net Requirements		0	30	40	0	10	40	30	0	30	55
Planned Order Receipts			30	40		10	40	30		30	55
Planned Order Releases		30	40		10	40	30		30	55	

Holding costs = $1/unit/week; setup cost = $100; gross requirements average per week = 27; lead time = 1 week.

Shown is the lot-sizing solution using the lot-for-lot technique and its cost. The holding cost is zero, but seven separate setups yield a total cost of $700.

Economic Order Quantity. As discussed in Chapter 13, EOQ can be used as a lot-sizing technique. But as we indicated there, EOQ is preferable where relatively constant independent demand exists, not where we know the demand. The assumption of our MRP procedure, remember, is that dependent demand is present. Operations managers should take advantage of this information,[6] rather than assuming a constant demand. The EOQ formula averages demand over an extended time horizon. EOQ is examined in Example 5.

---

[6] As we saw in Chapter 3, *Decision Making* information has value. The manager's job is to use that information.

Example 5

Fun Lawns, lnc., with a setup cost of $100 and a per-week holding cost of $1, examines its cost with lot sizes based on an EOQ criteria. The net requirements and lot sizes using the same requirements as in Example 4 are shown below:

MRP LOT-SIZING PROBLEM: EOQ TECHNIQUE.

		1	2	3	4	5	6	7	8	9	10
Gross Requirements		35	30	40	0	10	40	30	0	30	55
Scheduled Receipts											
Projected On Hand	35	35	0	43	3	3	66	26	69	69	39
Net Requirements		0	30	0	0	7	26	4	0	0	16
Planned Order Receipts			73			73		73			73
Planned Order Releases		73			73		73		69	73	

Holding costs = $1/unit/week; setup cost = $100; gross requirements average per week = 27; lead time = 1 week.

   Ten-week usage equals 270 units; therefore weekly usage equals 27, and 52 weeks (annual usage) equals 1,404 units. From Chapter 13, the EOQ model is:

$$Q^\star = \sqrt{\frac{2DS}{H}}$$

where

D = Annual usage = 1,404

S = Setup cost = $100

H = Holding (carrying) cost, on an annual basis per unit

   = $1 × 52 weeks = $52

$$Q^\star = 73 \text{ units}$$

Setups = 1,404/73 ≈ 19 per year

Setup cost = 19 × $100 = $1,900

Holding cost = $\frac{73}{2}$ × ($1 × 52 weeks) = $1,898

Setup cost + Holding cost = $1,900 + 1,898 = $3,798

The EOQ solution yields a computed 10-week cost of $730 [$3,798 × (10 weeks/52 weeks) = $730].

   Notice that Fun Lawn's actual holding cost will vary from the computed $730, depending upon the rate of actual usage. From the table above, we can see that in our ten-week example costs really are $400 for four setups, plus a holding cost of 375 units at $1 per week for a total of $775. Because usage was not constant, the actual computed cost was in fact more than the theoretical EOQ ($730) and more than the lot-for-lot rule ($700). If any stockouts had occurred, these costs too would need to be added to our actual EOQ of $775.

Part period balancing (PPB)

Economic part period (EPP)

Part Period Balancing. Part period balancing (PPB) is a more dynamic approach to balance setup and holding cost.[7] PPB uses additional information by changing the lot size to reflect requirements of the next lot size in the future. PPB attempts to balance setup and holding cost for known demands. Part period balancing develops an **economic part period (EPP),** which is the ratio of setup cost to holding cost. For Fun Lawns, EPP = $100/$1 = 100 units. Therefore holding 100 units for one period would cost $100, exactly the cost of one setup. Similarly, holding 50 units for two periods also costs $100 (2 periods × $1 × 50 units). PPB merely adds requirements until the number of part periods approximates the EPP, in this case 100. Example 6 shows the application of part period balancing.

Example 6

Once again, Fun Lawns, Inc., computes the costs associated with a lot size by using a $100 setup cost and a $1 holding cost, only this time part period balancing is used. The data are shown in the following table:

PPB CALCULATIONS

Periods Combined	Trial Lot Size (Cumulative Net Requirements)	Part Periods	Setup	Holding	Total
2	30	0			
2,3	70	$40 = 40 \times 1$			
2,3,4	70	40			
2,3,4,5	80	$70 = 40 \times 1 + 10 \times 3$	100	70	170
2,3,4,5,6	120	$230 = 40 \times 1 + 10 \times 3 + 40 \times 4$			

(Therefore, combine periods 2 through 5; 70 is as close to our EPP of 100 as we are going to get.)

6	40	0			
6,7	70	30			
6,7,8	70	30			
6,7,8,9	100	$120 = 30 \times 1 + 30 \times 3$	100	120	220

(Therefore, combine periods 6 through 9; 120 is as close to our EPP of 100 as we are going to get.)

10	55	0	100	0	100

			300 + 190 = 490

MRP LOT-SIZING PROBLEM: PPB TECHNIQUE.

		1	2	3	4	5	6	7	8	9	10
Gross Requirements		35	30	40	0	10	40	30	0	30	55
Scheduled Receipts											
Projected On Hand	35	35	0	50	10	10	0	60	30	30	0
Net Requirements		0	30	0	0	0	40	0	0	0	55
Planned Order Receipts			80				100				55
Planned Order Releases		80				100			55		

Holding costs = $1/unit/week; setup cost = $100; gross requirements average per week = 27; lead time = 1 week.

---

[7] J. J. DeMatteis, "An Economic Lot-Sizing Technique: The Part-Period Algorithms," *IBM Systems Journal,* **7** (1968): 30–38.

EPP is 100 (setup cost divided by holding cost = \$100/\$1). The first lot is to cover periods one, two, three, four, and five and is 80.

The total costs are \$490, with setup costs totaling \$300 and holding costs totaling \$190.

Wagner–Whitin Algorithm. The **Wagner–Whitin procedure** is a dynamic programming model that adds some complexity to the lot size computation. It assumes a finite time horizon beyond which there are no additional net requirements. It does, however, provide good results.[8] The technique is seldom used in practice, but this may change with increasing understanding and software sophistication.

Wagner–Whitin procedure

Lot-Sizing Summary. In the three Fun Lawn lot-sizing examples, we found the following costs:

Lot-for-lot	\$700
EOQ	\$775
Part period balancing	\$490

These examples should not, however, lead operations personnel to hasty conclusions about the preferred lot-sizing technique. First, the cost can be altered by changing the scheduled requirements. The resulting costs may not follow the pattern of the Fun Lawn examples. Second, in theory a new lot size should be computed with each change anywhere in the MRP hierarchy. In practice, this continuous instability in the planned order schedule is undesirable. The net result is that all lot sizes are wrong because the production system does not respond to such frequent changes. Such changes cause the system nervousness referred to earlier in this chapter.

In general the lot-for-lot approach should be used wherever economical. Lot-for-lot is the goal. Lots can be modified as necessary for scrap allowances, process constraints (for example, a heat treating process may require a lot of a given size), or raw material purchase lots (for example, a truckload of chemicals may be available in only one lot size). However, caution should be exercised prior to any modification of lot size because the modification can cause substantial distortion of actual requirements at lower levels in the MRP hierarchy. Where setup costs are significant and the demand is *not* particularly lumpy, part period balancing (PPB), Wagner–Whitin, or even EOQ should provide satisfactory results. Too much concern with lot sizing yields spurious accuracy because of MRP dynamics. A correct lot size can be determined only after the fact, based on what actually happened in terms of requirements.[9]

---

[8] See James M. Fordyce and Francis M. Webster, "The Wagner–Whitin Algorithm Made Simple," *Production and Inventory Management* (Second Quarter 1984): 21–27. This article provides as straightforward an explanation of the Wagner–Whitin technique as the authors have found. The Wagner–Whitin Algorithm yields a cost of \$455 for the data in examples 4, 5, and 6.

[9] See discussions by Joseph Orlicky, *Material Requirements Planning* (New York: McGraw-Hill, 1975), pp. 136–137, and Nandakumar, G., "Lot-Sizing Techniques in a Multiproduct Multilevel Environment," *Production and Inventory Management,* **26** (First Quarter 1985): 46–54.

CLOSED-LOOP MRP, CAPACITY PLANNING, AND MATERIAL REQUIREMENTS PLANNING II (MRP II)

Closed-Loop Material Requirements Planning. Closed-loop material requirements planning implies an MRP system that provides feedback to scheduling from the inventory control system.

Closed-loop MRP system

Specifically, a **closed-loop MRP system** provides feedback to the capacity plan, master production schedule, and ultimately to the production plan (as shown in Figure 14.6). Various aspects of capacity planning are discussed in Chapters 7, 12, and 15. Virtually all new and sophisticated MRP systems are closed loop.

FIGURE 14.6

Closed-Loop Material Requirements Planning.
(*Source:* Adapted from *Capacity Planning and Control Study Guide,* Falls Church, VA: American Production and Inventory Control Society, circa 1983.)

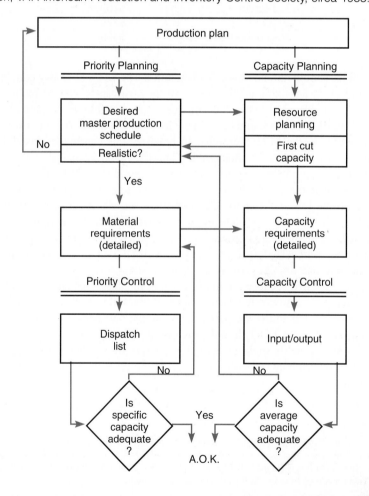

Capacity Planning. In keeping with the definition of closed-loop MRP, load reports are required for each work center. **Load reports** show the resource require-

Load reports

FIGURE 14.7

(a) Initial Resource Requirements Profile for a Milling Center.
(b) Smoothed Resource Requirements Profile for a Milling Center.

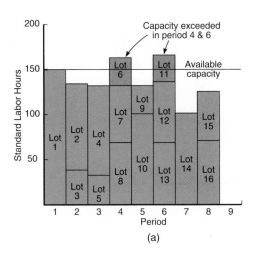

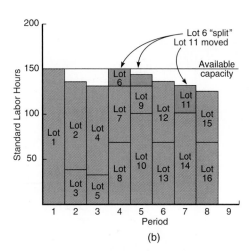

(a)　　　　　　　　(b)

ments in a work center for all work currently assigned to the work center, all work planned, and expected orders. Figure 14.7 shows that the initial load in the milling center exceeds capacity in weeks four and six. Closed-loop MRP systems allow production planners to move the work between time periods to smooth the load or at least bring it within capacity. (This is the *capacity* side of Figure 14.6). The closed-loop MRP system can then reschedule all items in the net requirements plan (see Figure 14.7). Tactics for smoothing the load and minimizing the impact of changed lead time include the following:

1. *Overlapping,* which reduces the lead time, entails sending pieces to the second operation before the entire lot is completed on the first operation.

2. *Operations splitting* sends the lot to two different machines for the same operation. This involves an additional setup, but results in shorter throughput times, since only part of the lot is processed on each machine.

3. *Lot splitting* involves breaking up the order and running part of it ahead of schedule.

Material Requirements Planning II (MRP II).

Material requirements planning II has substantial applications beyond scheduling and inventory management. It is an extremely powerful technique. Once a firm has MRP in place, inventory data can be augmented by labor hours, by material cost (rather than material quantity), by capital cost, or by virtually any resource variable. When MRP is used this way, it is usually referred to as MRP II, and *resource* is usually substituted for *requirements*. MRP then stands for material *resource* planning.

Furthermore, most MRP II computer programs are tied into other computer programs that provide data to the MRP system or receive data from the MRP system. Order entry, invoicing, billing, purchasing, production scheduling, capacity planning, and warehouse management are a few examples. A schematic showing how these sources of data for a manufacturing organization tie together is shown in Figure 14.8.

**Material requirements
planning II (MRPII)**

FIGURE 14.8

MRP Information Flow Integrated with Other Information Systems.
(*Source:* MCBA, Sample Screens and Reports. 925 West Broadway, Glendale, California, March 1986.)

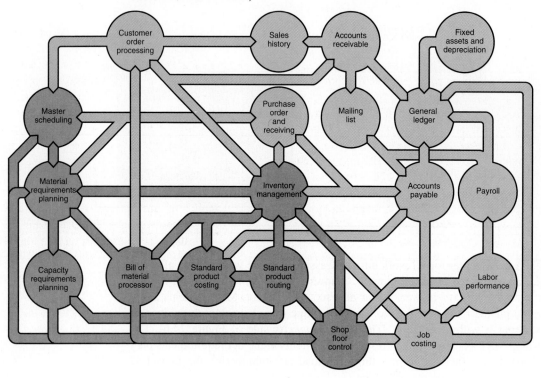

Note: Arrowheads indicate flow of data.

Not responsible for →

DISTRIBUTION RESOURCE PLANNING (DRP)

Distribution resource planning (DRP)

Distribution resource planning (DRP) is a time-phased stock replenishment plan for all levels of a distribution network. Its procedure and logic are analogous to MRP. DRP requires:

1. gross requirements, which are the same as expected demand or sales forecasts;
2. minimum levels of inventory to meet customer service levels;
3. accurate lead time;
4. definition of the distribution structure.

DRP Structure. When using DRP, expected demand becomes gross requirements. Net requirements are determined by allocating available inventory to gross requirements. The DRP procedure starts with the forecast at the retail level (or the most distant point of the distribution network being supplied). All other levels are computed. The computation of net requirements always begins at the top and proceeds

POM *in action*

Moving the Pampers Faster Cuts Everyone's Costs

Experts cite Procter & Gamble as a foremost example of how packaged goods and food manufacturers can work closely and form partnerships with major retailers to prune costs in the pipeline that connects manufacturers to consumers.

Cutting inventories for both parties, smoothing out production schedules, and quickly identifying quality and service problems are the aims of these partnerships. The identical benefits that automakers and other industrial companies have been reaping in recent years from just-in-time delivery arrangements with suppliers is exactly what they are looking for.

Teams that mix data processing experts, who automate order and record-keeping systems, with sales and purchasing representatives are assigned by companies like Procter & Gamble and KMart to deal with each other.

To help Procter & Gamble avoid sudden spikes and dips in orders for, say Pampers, and coordinate delivery schedules with KMart's warehouses, the companies' logistics managers share information. To coordinate Procter & Gamble's new product introductions with KMart promotional campaigns, marketing and finance managers share both up-to-date sales data on the latest promotions and long-range plans.

"When we started looking at this, we saw a potential savings of $1 billion annually in the U.S. for Procter & Gamble and just as much, if not more, for our customers," said Lawrence D. Milligan, the company's senior vice president in charge of sales.

Sources: The New York Times, July 14, 1991, p. 15; and *Supermarket Business,* May 1991, pp. 29–37, 165–166.

---

toward the lowest level. As is the case with MRP, inventory is then reviewed with an aim to satisfying demand. So that stock will arrive when it is needed, net requirements are offset by the necessary lead time. A planned order release quantity becomes the gross requirement at the next level down the distribution chain.

Allocation. The traditional DRP network, known as a **pull system,** is driven by the top or retail level ordering more stock. Allocations are made to the top level from available stock after being modified to obtain shipping economies. These modifications might include changing the shipping quantity to a truckload or a pallet load. The pull system has three notable problems. First, the pulls are often distorted (increased) at subsequent levels in the network.[10] Second, each ordering location ignores the replenishment requirements at other locations. Third, ordering locations also ignore the stock status at the supplying location.

Pull system

The alternative system is the **push system.** In the push system, orders are received from up-stream locations, but they are evaluated by the supplying location. The evaluation includes determining not only requirements at each requesting location but also total system requirements and stock availability at the supplying locations. Such a system is designed to combine information from both using and

Push system

---

[10] This is the same type of response recognized in Jay Forrester's *Industrial Dynamics.* Forrester noted that small changes in demand at the retail level stimulated wider variations at the wholesale level and even greater deviations at the factory level.

supplying locations. In theory, the combination yields an improved allocation of stock, because replenishment policies can be established based on both availability and system demand.

SUMMARY

Material requirements planning (MRP) is the preferred way to schedule production and inventory when demand is dependent. For MRP to work, management must have a master schedule, precise requirements for all components, accurate inventory and purchasing records, and accurate lead times. Distribution resource planning (DRP) is a time-phased stock replacement technique for distribution networks based on MRP procedures and logic.

Production should often be lot-for-lot in an MRP system, and replenishment orders in a DRP system should be small and frequent, given the constraints of ordering and transportation costs.

Both MRP and DRP, when properly implemented, can contribute in a major way to reduction in inventory while at the same time improving customer service levels.

KEY TERMS

Material requirements planning (MRP) (p. 600)
Distribution resource planning (DRP) (p. 600)
Master production schedule (p. 601)
Engineering change notice (ECN) (p. 603)
Bill-of-material (BOM) (p. 603)
Modular bills (p. 604)
Planning bills (p. 604)
Pseudo bill (p. 605)
Kit number (p. 605)
Phantom bills-of-material (p. 605)
Low-level coding (p. 605)
Lead times (p. 605)
Gross material requirements plan (p. 607)
Regenerative MRP (p. 613)

Net change MRP (p. 613)
System nervousness (p. 613)
Time fences (p. 613)
Pegging (p. 613)
Lot-for-lot (p. 614)
Part period balancing (PPB) (p. 616)
Economic part period (EPP) (p. 616)
Wagner–Whitin procedure (p. 617)
Closed-loop MRP system (p. 618)
Load reports (p. 618)
Material requirements planning II (MRP II) (p. 619)
Distribution resource planning (p. 620)
Pull system (p. 621)
Push system (p. 621)

USING AB:POM

Solving Examples 1, 2, and 3 with AB:POM

The material requirements planning (MRP) module can be used to perform an MRP analysis for up to 18 periods. The number of lines allowed in the bill-of-materials is 37. The data screen (Program 14.1) is generated by indicating the number of lines in the bill-of-materials. In our sample problem we will create a BOM with 7 items, but 9 lines.

Program 14.1

AB:POMs MRP Module applied to Examples 1, 2, 3

```
── Data file:hrex3 ───────── Material Requirements Planning ───────── Data Screen ──
   Number of BOM lines (1-37)  9                    Number of demand periods (1-18)  8
```

Item	Lvl	ldtm	#per	nhnd	Lot	pd1	pd2	pd3	pd4	pd5	pd6	pd7	pd8
a	0	1	0	10	0	0	0	0	0	0	0	0	50
b	1	2	2	15	0	0	0	0	0	0	0	0	0
d	2	1	2	10	0	0	0	0	0	0	0	0	0
e	2	2	3	10	0	0	0	0	0	0	0	0	0
c	1	1	3	20	0	0	0	0	0	0	0	0	0
e	2	2	1	0	0	0	0	0	0	0	0	0	0
f	2	3	2	5	0	0	0	0	0	0	0	0	0
g	3	2	1	0	0	0	0	0	0	0	0	0	0
d	3	1	2	0	0	0	0	0	0	0	0	0	0

1. *Item names.* The item names are entered in the left column. The same item name will appear in more than one row if the item is used by two parent items. Each item must follow its parents as shown in Program 14.1. (Note that upper and lowercase makes no difference in the name, but a space does.)

2. *Item level* (Lvl).The level in the indented BOM must be given here. The item *cannot* be placed at a level more than one below the item immediately above.

3. *Lead time* (ldtm). The lead time in order to get the item (which is listed to the right) is entered here. The default is one week. This is also the default for the end item.

4. *Number* (#per). The number of units of this subassembly needed for its parent is entered here. The default is one.

5. *On-hand* (nhnd). The current inventory on hand at the beginning of the problem is listed here. If a subassembly is listed twice, then it makes sense for the current inventory to appear only one time.

6. *Lot size* (Lot). The lot size can be specified here. A 0 or 1 will perform lot-for-lot ordering. If another number is placed here, then all orders for that item will be in integer multiples of that number.

7. *Demands* (entered in the first row). The demands are entered in the end item row in the period in which the items are demanded.

8. *Scheduled receipts.* If units are scheduled to be received in the future, they should be listed in the appropriate time period (column) and item (row). (An entry here, in level one is a demand; all other levels are receipts).

The printed solution for Examples 1, 2, and 3 is shown in Program 14.2, which is the output of Program 14.1. The meaning of each item on the left-hand column of the printed output (Program 14.2) is explained in items 1 through 5 below.

1. *Total Required.* The total number of units required in each week is listed in the first row. For the end item, the first row contains the demand schedule that was input on the data screen (Program 14.1). Other requirements are computed.

Program 14.2

Printed solution to MRP run on Example 1, 2, 3 data

Item a

	Week 1	Week 2	Week 3	Week 4	Week 5	Week 6	Week 7	Week 8
TOT. REQ.	0	0	0	0	0	0	0	50
ON HAND	10	10	10	10	10	10	10	10
ORD REC.	0	0	0	0	0	0	0	0
NET REQ.	0	0	0	0	0	0	0	40
ORD REL.	0	0	0	0	0	0	40	0

Item b

	Week 1	Week 2	Week 3	Week 4	Week 5	Week 6	Week 7	Week 8
TOT. REQ.	0	0	0	0	0	0	80	0
ON HAND	15	15	15	15	15	15	15	0
ORD REC.	0	0	0	0	0	0	0	0
NET REQ.	0	0	0	0	0	0	65	0
ORD REL.	0	0	0	0	65	0	0	0

Item d

	Week 1	Week 2	Week 3	Week 4	Week 5	Week 6	Week 7	Week 8
TOT. REQ.	0	0	390	0	130	0	0	0
ON HAND	10	10	10	0	0	0	0	0
ORD REC.	0	0	0	0	0	0	0	0
NET REQ.	0	0	380	0	130	0	0	0
ORD REL.	0	380	0	130	0	0	0	0

Item e

	Week 1	Week 2	Week 3	Week 4	Week 5	Week 6	Week 7	Week 8
TOT. REQ.	0	0	0	0	195	100	0	0
ON HAND	10	10	10	10	10	0	0	0
ORD REC.	0	0	0	0	0	0	0	0
NET REQ.	0	0	0	0	185	100	0	0
ORD REL.	0	0	185	100	0	0	0	0

Item c

	Week 1	Week 2	Week 3	Week 4	Week 5	Week 6	Week 7	Week 8
TOT. REQ.	0	0	0	0	0	0	120	0
ON HAND	20	20	20	20	20	20	20	0
ORD REC.	0	0	0	0	0	0	0	0
NET REQ.	0	0	0	0	0	0	100	0
ORD REL.	0	0	0	0	0	100	0	0

Item f

	Week 1	Week 2	Week 3	Week 4	Week 5	Week 6	Week 7	Week 8
TOT. REQ.	0	0	0	0	0	200	0	0
ON HAND	5	5	5	5	5	5	0	0
ORD REC.	0	0	0	0	0	0	0	0
NET REQ.	0	0	0	0	0	195	0	0
ORD REL.	0	0	195	0	0	0	0	0

Item g

	Week 1	Week 2	Week 3	Week 4	Week 5	Week 6	Week 7	Week 8
TOT. REQ.	0	0	195	0	0	0	0	0
ON HAND	0	0	0	0	0	0	0	0
ORD REC.	0	0	0	0	0	0	0	0
NET REQ.	0	0	195	0	0	0	0	0
ORD REL.	195	0	0	0	0	0	0	0

2. *On-hand.* The number on hand is listed here. The on-hand amount starts as given on the data screen and is reduced according to needs.

3. *Order receipt.* The amount that was scheduled in the original data screen is shown here.

4. *Net required.* The net amount required is the amount needed after the on-hand inventory is used.

5. *Order release.* Order release is the net amount required, offset by the lead time.

Solving Example 5 with AB:POM Lot-Sizing Module

The data screen for lot sizing is initialized by indicating the number of periods over which the lot sizing is to be performed. In this example we use 10 periods.

The lot-sizing module will perform lot sizing for minimizing total holding and setup costs when demands in each period are not equal. You may input your own ordering schedule, or use *economic order quantity* (EOQ), *lot-for-lot, part period balancing,* or *Wagner–Whitin.* Use the toggle menu to select the desired option. The inputs for the module are:

1. *Method:* The lot-sizing methods available are:
   a. Lot-for-lot is the traditional MRP way of ordering exactly what is needed in every period. (Lot-for-lot is optimal if setup costs are 0.)
   b. The EOQ method computes the EOQ based on the average demand over the periods specified and orders in lots of this size. Enough lots are ordered to cover the demand.
   c. Part Period Balancing attempts to balance setup and holding costs by determining an *Economic Part Period,* which is the ratio of setup cost to holding cost.
   d. Wagner–Whitin is a dynamic programming approach that assumes a finite time horizon beyond which there are no additional requirements.
   e. User-defined option allows you to give the production quantities for each period.

2. *Period names.* Naming the periods is possible. The default names are "period 1" through "period n," but weeks (i.e., week 1, etc.) or months (i.e., "January" through "December") can be used.

3. *Demands.* The demands in each period are to be supplied as integers.

4. *Produce.* This column is used only for the user-defined option. Enter the number of units to be produced. If an option other than user-defined is chosen, then the program will revise this column and display it as output.

5. *Holding cost.* The cost of holding one unit for one period is entered here. The holding cost is charged against the inventory at the end of the period.

6. *Setup cost.* The cost of each production setup is entered here. Setup cost is charged only in the periods that have positive production.

7. *Initial Inventory.* Enter the initial inventory available. In this case it is 35.

The solution for example 5 is shown in Program 14.3. The EOQ is computed on the basis of average demand over the periods. In the example, the EOQ is based on the demand rate of 270 units per 10 periods. Using the holding cost and setup cost with this demand generates an EOQ of 73, as shown at the top of the screen. The program will place an order for 73 units every time the inventory is insufficient to cover the demand. For example, the first order for 73 is placed in period 1. This covers the demand in period 1 and the demand in period 2. In period 4 we need more than the remaining units so an additional order, again 73 units, is placed. Using this method

---

Program 14.3

AB:POMs Lot-Sizing Module Applied to Example 5

```
──────────────── Sizing, Lot ────────────────        Solution ────
Number of time periods (1-98)      10

METHOD -> Economic Order Quantity

Holding cost                 1.00              EOQ = 73
Setup cost                 100.00
Initial inventory           35.00
Period      Demand      Produce    Inventory   Holding $  Setup $
Period 1       35          0           0          0.00
Period 2       30         73          43         43.00      100.00
Period 3       40          0           3          3.00
Period 4        0          0           3          3.00
Period 5       10         73          66         66.00      100.00
Period 6       40          0          26         26.00
Period 7       30         73          69         69.00      100.00
Period 8        0          0          69         69.00
Period 9       30          0          39         39.00
Period 10      55         73          57         57.00      100.00
              - - - - -  - - - - -  - - - - -   - - - - -  - - - - -
Totals        270         292         375       $375.00    $400.00
                                    Total cost =           $775.00
                                                   F9=Print Esc
Press <Esc> key to continue or highlighted key or function
key for options
```

in this example generates four orders (which total 292 units) and a total cost of $775. Here is an explanation of the other output items:

1. *Inventory.* This is the amount of inventory on hand at the end of the period. In the example there are 43 units left after period 1, 3 units left after period 3, etc. The holding cost is charged against this amount.

2. *Holding $.* This is the cost of holding inventory at the end of this period. It is simply the number of units on hand multiplied by the holding cost per unit, which in this example is $1.

3. *Setup $.* This is $0 if no production occurs or the setup cost if production occurs during this period. In the example, setups occur in periods 1, 4, 6, and 9, so the setup cost of $100 is listed in these four periods.

4. *Totals.* The total inventory, holding cost, and setup costs are listed at the bottom of each column. Four hundred and forty-eight units were held for one month at a cost of $448. Four setups occurred at a total cost of $400.

5. *Total cost.* The sum of the setup and holding costs is displayed in the bottom right-hand corner. The total cost in this example is $775.

Note: The AB:POM computer output does not accommodate lead time. Therefore all production requirements in this problem are shown as being ordered one week later than necessary.

SOLVED PROBLEMS

Solved Problem 14.1

Determine the low-level coding and the quantity of each component necessary to produce ten units of assembly Alpha. The product structure and quantities of each component needed for each assembly are noted in parentheses.

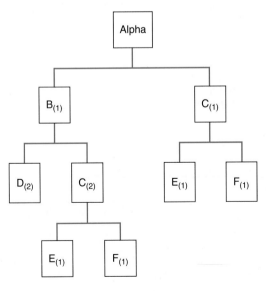

Solution

Redraw the product structure with low-level coding. Then multiply down the structure until the requirements of each branch are determined. Then add across the structure until the total for each is determined.

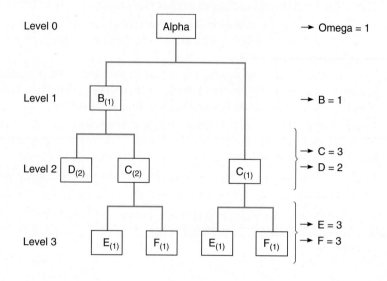

E's required for left branch:

$$(1_{\text{alpha}} \times 1_B \times 2_C \times 1_E) = 2$$

plus E's required for right branch:

$$(1_{\text{alpha}} \times 1_C \times 1_E) = \underline{1}$$
$$\quad 3 \text{ E's required}$$

Then "explode" the requirements by multiplying each by 10 as shown in the following table.

LEVEL	ITEM	QUANTITY PER UNIT	TOTAL REQUIREMENTS FOR 10 ALPHA
0	Alpha	1	10
1	B	1	10
2	C	3	30
2	D	2	20
3	E	3	30
3	F	3	30

Solved Problem 14.2

Using the product structure for Alpha in Solved Problem 14.1, and the lead times, quantity on hand, and master production schedule shown on page 630, prepare a net MRP table for Alphas.

Net Material Requirements Planning Sheet for Alpha (Note the letter in parentheses (A) is the source of the demand.)

Period (week, day)

Lot Size	Lead Time (# of Periods)	On Hand	Safety Stock	Allocated	Low Level Code	Item ID		1	2	3	4	5	6	7	8	9	10	11	12	13
Lot-for-Lot	1	10	—	—	0	Alpha (A)	Gross Requirements								50			50		100
							Scheduled Receipts													
							Projected On Hand 10													
							Net Requirements								40			50		100
							Planned Order Receipts								40			50		100
							Planned Order Releases							40			50		100	
Lot-for-Lot	2	20	—	—	1	B	Gross Requirements							40(A)			50(A)		100(A)	
							Scheduled Receipts													
							Projected On Hand 20													
							Net Requirements							20			50		100	
							Planned Order Receipts							20			50		100	
							Planned Order Releases					20			50		100			
Lot-for-Lot	3	0	—	—	2	C	Gross Requirements					40(B)		40(A)	100(B)		200(B) + 50(A)		100(A)	
							Scheduled Receipts													
							Projected On Hand 0													
							Net Requirements					40		40	100		250		100	
							Planned Order Receipts					40		40	100		250		100	
							Planned Order Releases		40		40	100		250		100				
Lot-for-Lot	1	100	—	—	2	D	Gross Requirements					40(B)			100(B)		200(B)			
							Scheduled Receipts													
							Projected On Hand 100								60					
							Net Requirements					0			40		200			
							Planned Order Receipts					0			40		200			
							Planned Order Releases				0			40		200				
Lot-for-Lot	1	10	—	—	3	E	Gross Requirements		40(C)		40(C)	100(C)		250(C)		100(C)				
							Scheduled Receipts													
							Projected On Hand 10		10											
							Net Requirements		30		40	100		250		100				
							Planned Order Receipts		30		40	100		250		100				
							Planned Order Releases	30		40	100		250		100					
Lot-for-Lot	1	50	—	—	3	F	Gross Requirements		40(C)		40(C)	100(C)		250(C)		100(C)				
							Scheduled Receipts													
							Projected On Hand 50		50		10									
							Net Requirements		0		30	100		250		100				
							Planned Order Receipts				30	100		250		100				
							Planned Order Releases	—		30	100		250		100					

ITEM	LEAD TIME	QTY ON HAND
Alpha	1	10
B	2	20
C	3	0
D	1	100
E	1	10
F	1	50

MASTER PRODUCTION SCHEDULE FOR ALPHA								
Period	6	7	8	9	10	11	12	13
Gross requirements			50			50		100

Solution

See the chart on page 629.

DISCUSSION QUESTIONS

1. Why might a firm prefer regenerative MRP over net-change MRP?

2. Once a material requirements plan (MRP) has been established, what other managerial applications might be found for the technique?

3. What are the similarities between MRP and DRP?

4. How does MRP II differ from MRP?

5. Which is the best lot-sizing policy for manufacturing organizations?

6. What impact does ignoring carrying cost in the allocation of stock in a DRP system have on lot sizes?

7. What do we mean by *closed-loop* MRP?

PROBLEMS

· 14.1 The product structure for a product we make, called Alpha, is shown below. We need 10 units of Alpha in week six. Three units of D and two units of F are required for each Alpha. The lead time for Alpha is one week. We have no units of Alpha, D, or F on hand. Lead time for D is one week and lead time for F is 2 weeks. Using the format below, prepare a gross and net material requirements plan for Alpha. (*Hint:* For this and other problems in this chapter a copy of the form on page 631 may be helpful.)

Alpha

D(3)   F(2)

: 14.2 The demand for subassembly S is 100 units in week seven. Each unit of S requires one unit of T and .5 units of U. Each unit of T requires one unit of V, two units of W, and one unit of X. Finally, each unit of U requires .5 units of Y and three units of Z. One firm manufactures all items. It takes two weeks to make S, one week to make T, two

Lot Size	Lead Time (# of periods)	On Hand	Safety Stock	Allo-cated	Low Level Code	Item Identi-fication		Period (week,day)							
								1	2	3	4	5	6	7	8
							Gross Requirements								
							Scheduled Receipts								
							Projected On Hand								
							Net Requirements								
							Planned Order Receipts								
							Planned Order Releases								
							Gross Requirements								
							Scheduled Receipts								
							Projected On Hand								
							Net Requirements								
							Planned Order Receipts								
							Planned Order Releases								
							Gross Requirements								
							Scheduled Receipts								
							Projected On Hand								
							Net Requirements								
							Planned Order Receipts								
							Planned Order Releases								
							Gross Requirements								
							Scheduled Receipts								
							Projected On Hand								
							Net Requirements								
							Planned Order Receipts								
							Planned Order Releases								
							Gross Requirements								
							Scheduled Receipts								
							Projected On Hand								
							Net Requirements								
							Planned Order Receipts								
							Planned Order Releases								

weeks to make U, two weeks to make V, three weeks to make W, one week to make X, two weeks to make Y, and one week to make Z.

a) Construct a product structure and a gross material requirements plan for the dependent inventory items. Identify all levels, parents, and components.

b) Construct a net material requirements plan from the product structure and the following on-hand inventory.

ITEM	ON-HAND INVENTORY	ITEM	ON-HAND INVENTORY
S	20	W	30
T	20	X	25
U	10	Y	15
V	30	Z	10

: **14.3** In addition to 100 units of S (per Problem 14.2), there is also a demand for 20 units of U, which is a component of S. The 20 units of U are needed for maintenance purposes. These units are needed one week before S, in week six. Modify the gross and net material requirements plan to reflect this change.

: 14.4 Given the following bill-of-material, master production schedule, and inventory status, develop: (a) a gross requirements plan for all items, and (b) net materials requirements (planned order release) for all items.

MASTER PRODUCTION SCHEDULE: X1						
Period	7	8	9	10	11	12
Gross requirements		50		20		100

ITEM	LEAD TIME	ON HAND	ITEM	LEAD TIME	ON HAND
X1	1	50	C	3	10
B1	2	20	D	1	0
B2	2	20	E	1	0
A1	1	5			

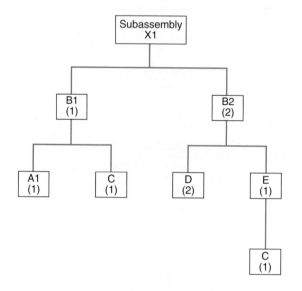

Problems 14.5 and 14.6 use the data shown below and at the top of p. 633.

Data for Problems 14.5 and 14.6

Period	8	9	10	11	12
Gross requirements: A	100		50		150
Gross requirements: H		100		50	

ITEM	ON HAND	LEAD TIME	ITEM	ON HAND	LEAD TIME
A	0	1	F	75	2
B	100	2	G	75	1
C	50	2	H	0	1
D	50	1	J	100	2
E	75	2	K	100	2

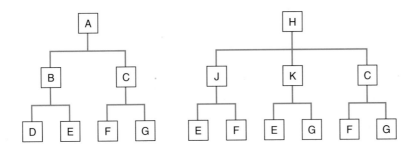

:**14.5** Given the bill-of-material, master production schedule, and inventory status shown above, develop (a) a gross requirements plan for C, (b) a planned order release for C.

:**14.6** Based on the preceding data, complete a net planned order release schedule for all items (ten schedules in all).

Problems 14.7 through 14.9 are based on an item that has the gross requirements shown in the table below and a beginning inventory of 40 units.

Data for Problems 14.7–14.9

Period	1	2	3	4	5	6	7	8	9	10	11	12
Gross requirements	30		40		30	70	20		10	80		50

Holding cost = $2.50/unit/week; setup cost = $150; lead time = 1 week

:**14.7** Develop a lot-for-lot solution and calculate total relevant costs.

:**14.8** **a)** Develop an EOQ solution and calculate total relevant costs. Stockout costs equal $10 per unit.

   b) Solve 14.8(a) with lead time = 0.

:**14.9** **a)** Develop a PPB solution and calculate total relevant costs.

   b) Solve 14.9(a) with lead time = 0.

Data for Problem 14.10

Period	0	1	2	3	4	5	6	7	8	9	10
Net requirements		35	30	45	0	10	40	30	0	30	55

:**14.10** Keebock, a maker of outstanding running shoes, keeps the soles of its size 13 running shoes in inventory for one period at a cost of $.25 per unit. The setup costs are $50. Beginning inventory is zero and lead time is one week; stockout cost is $5 per unit. Shown in the table below are the net requirements per period. Determine Keebock's cost based on:

   a) EOQ.

   b) lot-for-lot.

   c) part period balancing (PPB).

Problems 14.11 through 14.14 are based on the data shown in the table on page 634. The parent item has a one-week lead time, and the lot-for-lot rule is employed.

Beginning inventory is 20 units. The parent item has a component whose lead time is also one week and whose starting inventory position is 30 units. At the component level, production occurs in lot sizes to cover three periods of net requirements.

Data for Problems 14.11–14.14

Period	1	2	3	4	5	6	7	8	9	10
Gross requirements	0	40	30	40	10	70	40	10	30	60

: **14.11** Develop the parent and component MRP tables to show the original planned positions.

: **14.12** At the parent level, gross requirements for period two are canceled. Develop the parent and component net MRP tables to show the net effect of this cancellation.

: **14.13** With the parent level gross requirements canceled for period two, what is the effect on inventory quantity, setup costs, and holding costs?

: **14.14** At the component level, there is enough capacity to produce 75 units in period one. Gross requirements at the parent level increase from 40 units to 50 units in period two. What problem arises? What solution would you recommend?

: **14.15** A part structure, lead time (weeks), and on-hand quantities for product A are shown on the top of page 635.
From the information shown, generate:

a) an indented bill-of-material for product A (see Figure 6.10).

b) a bill-of-material showing the quantity of each part required to produce one A.

c) an exploded bill-of-material showing the quantity of each part required to produce ten A's.

d) net requirements for each part to produce ten A's in week 8, using lot-for-lot.

(Hint: The AB:POM can help with **b** and **c,** but not produce an output other than in MRP format)

: **14.16** You are product planner for product A (in Problem 14.15). The field service manager, "Speedy" Senna, has just called and told you that the requirements for B and F should each be increased by ten units for his repair requirements in the field.

a) Prepare an exploded bill-of-material showing the quantity of each part required to produce the requirements for the service manager *and* the production request of ten.

b) What are the net requirements (i.e., exploded bill-of-materials) less on-hand inventory?

c) Prepare a net requirement plan by date for the new requirements (for both production and field service), assuming that the field service manager wants his 10 units in week 8 and the production units are still due in week 10.

: **14.17** You have just been notified via FAX that the lead time for component G of product A (Problem 14.16) has just been increased to 4 weeks.

a) Which items have changed and why?

b) What are the implications for the production plan?

c) As production planner, what can you do?

DATA FOR PROBLEMS 14.15, 14.16, 14.17, AND THE DATA BASE APPLICATION 14.19

PART	INVENTORY ON HAND
A	0
B	2
C	10
D	5
E	4
F	5
G	1
H	10

PART STRUCTURE TREE

```
                          A  LT = 1
           ┌─────────────────┴─────────────────┐
        B  LT = 1                            F  LT = 1
     ┌─────┴─────┐                        ┌─────┴─────┐
  C  LT = 2   D  LT = 1               G  LT = 3    H  LT = 1
                  │                                 ┌────┴────┐
               E  LT = 1                         E  LT = 1  C  LT = 2
```

:**14.18** As director of operations, you have recently installed a distribution requirements planning (DRP) system. The company has an East Coast and a West Coast warehouse, as well as a main factory warehouse in Omaha, Nebraska. You have just received the orders for the next planning period from the managers at each of the three facilities. Their reports are shown below. The lead time to both the East Coast and the West Coast warehouses is two weeks while there is a one-week lead time to bring material to the factory warehouse. Shipments are in truck-load quantities of 100 each. There is no initial inventory in the system. The factory is having trouble getting the level of material work schedule installed and still has a lot size in multiples of 100.

Data for East Coast Warehouse

Period	1	2	3	4	5	6	7	8	9	10	11	12
Forecast Requirements			40	100	80	70	20	25	70	80	30	50

Lead time = 2 weeks

Data for West Coast Warehouse

Period	1	2	3	4	5	6	7	8	9	10
Forecast Requirements		30	45	60	70	40	80	70	80	55

Lead time = 2 weeks

Data for Factory Warehouse

Period	1	2	3	4	5	6	7	8	9	10
Forecast Requirements			30	40	10	70	40	10	30	60

Lead time = 1 week

a) Show the plan for *receipt* of orders from the factory.

b) If the factory requires two weeks to produce the merchandise, when must the orders be *released* to the factory?

Data Base Application

:**14.19** Your stockroom manager, Joe Smith, arrived at your desk just after you had completed the net requirements plan for product A (use data in Problem 14.15), exclaiming that the cycle counter should be fired. It seems that the cycle counter was wrong; there are three A's available now, not zero as the original data showed; moreover, five E's are also available. About then your boss, Sam Melnyk, who overheard the discussion, says, "You might as well extend the net requirements plan out to 16 weeks, because we just received an order for ten more A's in week 12 and five more in week 15. Additionally, count on the field service department wanting three more B's in week 16, as well as those ten units in week 8." You decide to use the lead times in Problem 14.15, but item G now has a lead time of 4 weeks.

Now you must prepare a new net requirements plan, based on the actual inventory (as reported) and the new schedule. Your assignment is to do so.

CASE STUDY

Service, Inc.

Service, Inc., is a distributor of automotive replacement parts. With no manufacturing capability, all products it sells are purchased, assembled, and repackaged. Service, Inc., does have extensive inventory and final assembly facilities. Among its products are private-label carburetor and ignition kits. The company has been experiencing difficulties for the last two years. First, profits have fallen considerably. Second, customer service levels have declined, with late deliveries now exceeding 25% of orders. Third, customer returns have been rising at a rate of 3% per month.

Bob Hass, vice president of sales, claims that most of the problem lies with the assembly department. He says that they are not producing the proper mix of the product, they have poor quality control, their productivity has fallen, and their costs are too high.

Dick Houser, the treasurer, believes that problems have arisen due to investment in the wrong inventories. He thinks that marketing has too many options and products. Dick also thinks that the purchasing department buyers have been hedging their inventories and requirements with excess purchasing commitments.

John Burnham, assembly manager, says, "The symptom is that we have a lot of parts in inventory, but no place to assemble them in the production schedule." An additional comment by John was, "When we have the right part, it is not very good, but we use it anyway to meet the schedule."

Freddy Fearon, manager of purchasing, has taken the stance that purchasing has not let Service, Inc., down. He has stuck by his old suppliers, used historical data to determine requirements, maintained what he views as excellent prices from suppliers, and evaluated new sources of supply with an aim of lowering cost. Where possible, Freddy reacted to the increased pressure for profitability by emphasizing low cost and early delivery.

You are the president of Service, Inc., and must get the firm back on a course toward improved profitability.

Discussion Questions

1. Identify both the symptoms and problems at Service, Inc.

2. What specific changes would you implement?

BIBLIOGRAPHY

Berry, W. L. "Lot Sizing Procedures for Requirements Planning Systems: A Framework for Analysis." *Production and Inventory Management,* **13,** 2 (1972).

Brown, R. G. *Advanced Service Parts Inventory Control.* Norwich, VT: Materials Management Systems, Inc., 1982.

Cerveny, R. P., and L. W. Scott. "A Survey of MRP Implementation." *Production and Inventory Management,* **30,** 3 (Third Quarter 1989): 31–34.

Dolinsky, L. R., T. E. Vallmann, and M. J. Maggard. "Adjusting Replenishment Orders to Reflect Learning in a Material Requirements Planning Environment." *Managerial Science,* **36** (December 1990): 1532–1547.

Federgruen, A., and M. Tzur. "A Simple Forward Algorithm to Solve General Dynamic Lot Sizing Models with n Periods in O(n log n) or O(n) Time." *Management Science,* **37** (August 1991): 909.

Freeland, J. R., J. P. Leschke, and E. N. Weiss. "Guidelines for Setup Cost Reduction Programs to Achieve Zero Inventory." *Journal of Operations Management,* **9** (January 1990): 85.

Haddock, J., and D. E. Hubicki. "Which Lot-Sizing Techniques Are Used in Material Requirements Planning?" *Production and Inventory Management,* **30** (Third Quarter 1989): 57.

Karmarkar, U. "Getting Control of Just-in-Time." *Harvard Business Review,* **71,** 5 (September–October 1989): 122–133.

Martin, A. J. *DRP: Distribution Resource Planning.* Englewood Cliffs, NJ: Prentice-Hall, 1983.

St. John, R. "The Evils of Lot Sizing in MRP." *Production and Inventory Management,* **25** (Fourth Quarter 1984): 75–85.

Sauers, D. G. "Analyzing Inventory Systems." *Management Accounting,* **LXVIII,** 11 (May 1986): 30–36.

Wagner, H. M., and T. M. Whitin. "Dynamic Version of the Economic Lot Size Model." *Management Science,* **5,** 1 (1958).

Short-Term Scheduling Tactics

Scheduling at LTV Provides a Competitive Advantage

With the development of numerical control machines (machines controlled by computer software), companies now control (1) piece movement on the machine, (2) tool changing at the machine, and (3) the movement of materials between machines. These abilities have allowed the development of flexible machining systems (FMS).

LTV Aircraft Products Group in Dallas, an acknowledged leader in industrial modernization, has built such an FMS. LTV's FMS allows a number of good things to happen. Among these are rapid movement of pieces between machines, rapid tool setup, efficient waste handling, economical use of floor space, and high machine use. In a well-scheduled FMS, machine use can increase to 200% or 300% more than in a standard numerical control shop.

A carousel is shown receiving and delivering each fixture holder—*risers,* which hold fixtures to the *automated guided vehicle* (AGV). The carousel has two workstations for mounting and dismounting pieces on the various risers. Here an operator on the far left is removing completed work while the operator in the red shirt determines the next order. Operators who do part loading and unloading also do a verification check prior to marking the part as complete and sending it on for inspection.

Competitive advantage accrues to LTV in a variety of ways. First, machine use is about three times that of a normal machining center. Second, less than three hours are required to produce a piece, so work-in-process is less. Third, since the time to set up for one piece is low and through-put is rapid, customer service is improved.

Using computer-generated job instructions, planning and scheduling personnel determine the tooling necessary for each job. Then the appropriate tools for that job are loaded into the proper position at the machine to which the job has been assigned. A variety of tools for particular jobs is shown here.

Effective scheduling can be further enhanced by scheduling "families" of related parts to reduce setups. But the FMS allows for a single one-of-a-kind part to be processed without disrupting the production flow. Therefore, processing flexibility has improved. The FMS makes possible the scheduling of parts in random order, handling similar or dissimilar parts and accommodating varying shapes and sizes. This versatility results in parts being manufactured on a just-in-time (JIT) basis. Scheduling flexibility reduces delivery time and results in a competitive advantage for LTV.

The AGV releases its tooling holder (riser) to the loading conveyer of the washing station. The automatic washing station allows for complete rotation of the piece while it is being washed with high-pressure coolant. As each piece is washed, the metal chips flow into drainways in the floor to the central chip-sorting station.

All machine and material movement instructions (computer code) are loaded into a mainframe computer. The mainframe computer down-loads scheduled items to a computer at the FMS, where manual intervention by the on-site scheduler determines what job should be processed next. The on-site scheduler determines available tooling and risers (which hold the fixtures), as well as the final schedule.

The computer screen at left aids the operator by showing a graphic display of the proper position for the material on the riser. The second floor control room in the background provides visual feedback to the scheduler.

INTRODUCTION

Scheduling deals with the timing of operations. Table 15.1 illustrates scheduling decisions faced in four organizations. The process of scheduling (Figure 15.1) begins with *capacity* planning, which involves facility and equipment acquisition (discussed in Chapter 7). In the aggregate planning stage (Chapter 12), decisions regarding the *use* of facilities, inventory, people, and outside contractors are made. Then the master schedule (Chapter 14) breaks down the aggregate plan and develops an *overall* schedule for outputs. The overall schedule translates capacity decisions, intermediate planning, and master schedules into short-term, specific assignments of personnel, materials, and machinery. In this chapter we describe the narrow issue of scheduling goods and services in the *short run* (that is, on a weekly, daily, or hourly basis).

The objectives of short-term scheduling are to:

1. minimize customer waiting time;
2. minimize process time;
3. keep inventory levels low;
4. effectively utilize personnel and equipment.

Good scheduling approaches should be simple, clear, easily understood, easy to carry out, flexible, and realistic.

This chapter examines scheduling in job shops, repetitive production, and the service sector.

TABLE 15.1 Scheduling Decisions.

ORGANIZATION	MANAGER MUST SCHEDULE THE FOLLOWING:
Hospital	Use of operating rooms for surgery Patient admissions Nursing, security, maintenance staffs Appointments for outpatient treatments
University	Classrooms Instructors Graduate and undergraduate courses Student schedules Audiovisual equipment
Factory	Production of goods Timing of purchases of materials Workers
Airline	Maintenance of aircraft Flight crews, catering Departure timetables Gate and ticketing personnel

FIGURE 15.1

The Relationship Between Short-Term Scheduling and Capacity Planning,
Aggregate Planning, and the Master Schedule.

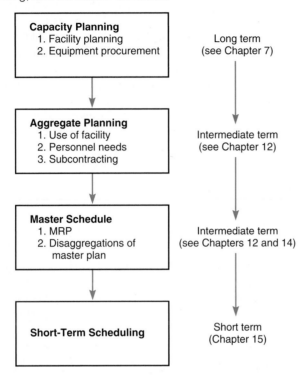

THE JOB SHOP

The **job shop** (or *intermittent* processing) is a high-variety, low-volume system   **Job shop**
commonly found in manufacturing and service organizations. It is a production
system in which products are made to order. Job shop orders usually differ considerably in terms of materials used, order of processing, processing requirements, time
of processing, and setup requirements. Because of these differences, the scheduling
of tasks in job shops can be complex.

Scheduling and Control in the Job Shop

The job shop manager attempts to run the shop in a balanced and efficient manner.
To do this the manager needs a production planning and control system. The
planning and control system should:

1. schedule incoming orders without violating capacity constraints of individual
   work centers;

2. check the availability of tools and materials before releasing an order to a
   department;

3. establish due dates for each job and check progress against need dates and
   order lead times;

4. check work in progress as jobs move through the shop;

5. provide feedback on plant and production activities;

6. provide work efficiency statistics and monitor operator times for payroll and labor distribution analyses.

Whether the job shop activity system is manual or automated, it must be accurate and relevant. This means it requires a production database with both planning and control files.[1]

Planning files

Planning files consist of (1) an *item master file,* which contains information about each component the firm produces or purchases; (2) a *routing file,* which indicates each component's flow through the shop; and (3) a *work center master file,* which contains information about the work center, such as capacity and efficiency.

Control files

Control files track the actual progress made against the plan for each work order.

SCHEDULING

The *objective of scheduling is to optimize the use of resources so that the overall production objectives are met.*[2] In general, scheduling involves assigning due dates to specific jobs. As mentioned earlier, many jobs compete simultaneously for resources. Machine breakdowns, absenteeism, quality problems, shortages, and other factors that create variability complicate the manufacturing environment. Hence, the assignment of a date does not ensure that the work will be performed according to the schedule. Developing reliable schedules for completion of jobs on time requires a set of rules to determine the sequence in which scheduled work will be performed. When people trust and use these rules, scheduling becomes a reliable and formal means of communication.

Many scheduling techniques can be employed. The type used depends on the volume of orders, the nature of operations, and the overall complexity of the jobs. The selection of the technique also depends on the extent of control required over the job while it is being processed. For example, we would try to minimize or eliminate idle time in costly machine operations, and we might want to minimize the cost of work-in-process inventories at the same time. Scheduling techniques are generally categorized as (1) forward scheduling and (2) backward scheduling. In practice, a combination of forward and backward scheduling is often used.

Forward Scheduling

Forward scheduling

Forward scheduling assumes that procurement of material and operations start as soon as the requirements are known. Forward scheduling is used in companies such as steel fabricators and machine tool manufacturers, where jobs are manufactured to customer order and delivery is often requested as soon as possible. Forward scheduling is well suited where the supplier is usually behind in meeting schedules. Forward logic generally causes a buildup of work-in-process inventory.

[1] For an expanded discussion, see *APICS Training Aid—Shop Floor Control* (Falls Church, VA: American Production and Inventory Control Society, 1979).

[2] For details, see Chapter 13 of D. W. McLeavey and S. L. Narasimhan, *Production Planning and Inventory Control* (Boston: Allyn & Bacon, 1985). This section contains excerpts from pages 515–520.

Backward Scheduling

In **backward scheduling** the last operation on the routing is scheduled first. Then the rest of the operations are offset one at a time, in reverse order, as they become necessary. By offsetting the procurement time, the start date is obtained. Backward scheduling works well in MRP environments and is used for establishing shop order start and due dates using the lead time offset.

Backward scheduling

SHOP LOADING

Loading means the assignment of jobs to work or processing centers. Operations managers commit work centers to jobs so costs, idle time, or completion times are kept to a minimum. Shop loading takes two forms. One is oriented to shop capacity; the second is related to assigning specific jobs to work centers. First, we examine shop loading from the perspective of capacity via a technique known as input-output control. Then, we present two approaches used for loading—*Gantt charts* and the *assignment method* of linear programming.

Loading

Input-Output Control

Many firms have difficulty scheduling (that is, achieving effective throughput) because they overload the production processes. This often occurs because they do not know actual performance in the work centers. Effective scheduling depends on matching the schedule to performance. Lack of knowledge about capacity and performance causes reduced throughput.

    Input-output control is a technique that allows operations personnel to manage facility work flows. If the work is arriving faster than it is being processed, a backlog develops. If the work is arriving at a slower rate than it is being performed, the work center may run out of work.

Input-output control

    The former case (called overloading) causes crowding in the facility, leading to inefficiencies and quality problems. The latter case, underloading the facility, results in idle capacity and wasted resources. Example 1 shows the use of input-output controls.

Example 1

The data in Figure 15.2 on page 644 indicate the planned capacity for the DNC Milling work center for 10 weeks (week 1 through 10). The planned input is 280 standard hours per week. The actual input is close to this figure, varying between 250 and 285. Output is scheduled at 320 standard hours, which is the assumed capacity. A backlog of 300 hours exists in the work center. However, actual output (270 hours) is substantially less than planned. Therefore neither the input plan nor the output plan is being achieved. Indeed the backlog of work in this work center has actually increased by five hours by week 4. This increases work-in-process inventory, complicating the scheduling task and indicating the need for manager action.

FIGURE 15.2

Input-Output Control.

	Week ending	6/6	6/13	6/20	6/27	7/4	7/11	7/18	7/25	8/1	8/8
	Planned Input	280	280	280	280	280	280	280	280	280	280
Beginning Backlog*	Actual Input	270	250	280	285	280	285				
300 hours	Cumulative Deviation	−10	−40	−40	−35	−35	−30				
	Planned Output	320	320	320	320						
	Actual Output	270	270	270	270						
	Cumulative Deviation	−50	−100	−150	−200						
	Cumulative Change in Backlog	0	−20	−10	+5						

Work Center DNC Milling (In standard hours)

*Above desired level of work-in-process (above standard queue)

The options available to operations personnel to manage facility work flow include:

1. correction of performances;
2. increasing facility size;
3. increasing or reducing input to the work center by:
   a) routing work to or from other work centers,
   b) increasing or decreasing subcontracting,
   c) producing less (or producing more).

Producing less is not a popular solution for many managers, but the advantages can be substantial. First, the customer service level may improve because units may be produced on time. Second, efficiency may actually improve because of less work in process cluttering the work center and absorbing overhead costs. Third, quality may improve because of fewer hidden problems.

Gantt Charts

Gantt charts

Gantt charts are visual aids that are useful in loading and scheduling job shop operations. Their name is derived from Henry Gantt, who developed the concept in the late 1800s. The charts help describe the use of resources, such as work centers and overtime.

When used in *loading,* Gantt charts show the loading and idle time of several departments, machines, or facilities. This displays the relative workloads in the system. For example, when one work center becomes overloaded, employees from a low-load center can be transferred temporarily to increase the work force. Or if waiting jobs can be processed at different work centers, some jobs at high-load centers can be transferred to low-load centers. Versatile equipment may also be transferred among centers. Example 2 illustrates a simple Gantt load chart.

Example 2

A New Orleans washing machine manufacturer accepts special orders for machines to be used in unique facilities such as submarines, hospitals, and large industrial laundries. The production of each machine requires varying tasks and durations. Figure 15.3 shows the load chart for the week of March 8.

FIGURE 15.3

Gantt Load Chart for the Week of March 8.

Work center	Monday	Tuesday	Wednesday	Thursday	Friday
Metal works	Job 349	✕		Job 350	
Mechanical			Job 349	Job 408	
Electronics	Job 408			Job 349	
Painting	Job 295		Job 408	✕	Job 349

☐ Processing   ✕ Center not available (for example, maintenance time, repairs, shortages)

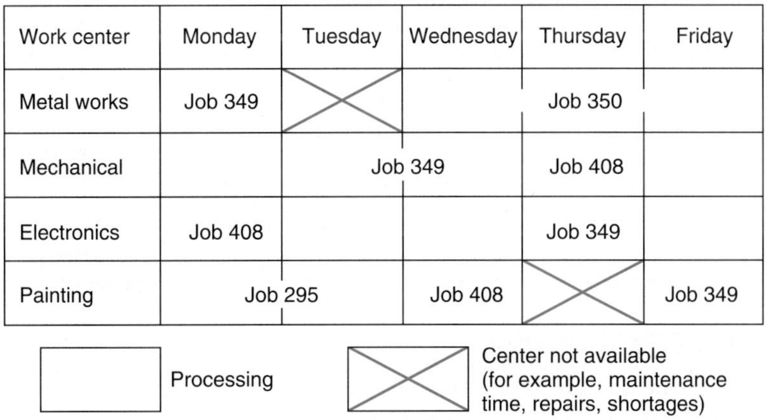

The four work centers process several jobs during the week. This particular chart indicates that the Metal Works and Painting centers are completely loaded for the entire week. The Mechanical and Electronic centers have some idle time scattered during the week. We also note that the Metal Works center is unavailable on Tuesday, perhaps for preventive maintenance.

The Gantt *load chart* does have some major limitations. For one thing, it does not account for production variability such as unexpected breakdowns or human errors that require reworking a job. The chart must also be updated regularly to account for new jobs and revised time estimates.

A Gantt *schedule chart* is used to monitor jobs in progress. It indicates which jobs are on schedule and which are ahead of or behind schedule. In practice, many versions of the chart are found. The schedule chart in Example 3 places jobs in progress on the vertical axis and time on the horizontal axis.

Example 3

JH Products Corporation uses the Gantt chart in Figure 15.4 to visualize the scheduling of three orders, jobs A, B, and C. Each pair of brackets on the time axis denotes the estimated starting and finishing of a job enclosed within it. The solid bars reflect the actual status or progress of the job. Job A, for example, is about one-half day behind schedule at the end of day 5. Job B has been completed, after a delay for equipment maintenance. Job C is ahead of schedule.

FIGURE 15.4

Gantt Scheduling Chart for Jobs A, B, and C.

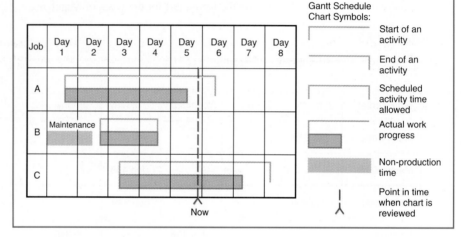

The Assignment Method

Assignment method

The **assignment method** is a special class of the linear programming model that involves assigning tasks or jobs to resources. Examples include assigning jobs to machines, contracts to bidders, people to projects, and salespeople to territories. The objective is most often to minimize total costs or time required to perform the tasks at hand. One important characteristic of assignment problems is that only one job (or worker) is assigned to one machine (or project). A unique application of the assignment method is discussed in the *POM in Action* box, "Scheduling American League Umpires."

Each assignment problem has a table associated with it. The numbers in the table will be the costs or times associated with each particular assignment. For example, if a job shop has three available machines (A, B, and C) and three new jobs to be completed, its table might appear as shown on page 647.

The dollar entries represent the firm's estimate of what it will cost for each job to be completed on each machine.

The assignment method involves adding and subtracting appropriate numbers in the table in order to find the lowest *opportunity cost* for each assignment. There are four steps to follow:

1. Subtract the smallest number in each row from every number in that row and

POM _in action_

Scheduling American League Umpires, Using the Assignment Method

Games in professional baseball are played in two-, three-, or four-game series. Each week during the season, one series is scheduled during the period Friday through Sunday and another during the period Monday through Thursday. Each of these time blocks is called a _segment_. The season generally lasts about 26 weeks, and each team plays approximately 52 series. Since there are 14 teams, seven series are always scheduled simultaneously, although each team may not play every day. Therefore the league employs seven crews of umpires, with each crew being assigned to one of the concurrent series.

The problem of scheduling umpire crews from one series to the next is complicated by many restrictions on travel, ranging from coast-to-coast time changes, airline flight schedules, and night games running late.

There are two major objectives that the league strives to achieve: (1) balance crew assignments relatively evenly among all teams over the course of a season, and (2) minimize travel costs. These objectives are by nature conflicting, as attempting to balance crew assignments necessitates considerable airline travel and equipment moves, and hence increased travel costs.

One approach to the scheduling process is to schedule on a series-by-series basis. This viewpoint lends itself conveniently to an assignment problem formulation. The time it takes the league to generate a schedule has been significantly decreased. More importantly, the quality of the schedule has improved.

Sources: Proceedings of the Annual Meeting of the Decision Sciences Institute, Honolulu, 1986, pp. 914–916; and _Interfaces,_ November–December 1988, pp. 42–51.

JOB \ MACHINE	A	B	C
R-34	$11	$14	$6
S-66	$8	$10	$11
T-50	$9	$12	$7

then subtract the smallest number in each column from every number in that column. This step has the effect of reducing the numbers in the table until a series of zeros, meaning _zero opportunity costs,_ appear. Even though the numbers change, this reduced problem is equivalent to the original one, and the same solution will be optimal.

2. Draw the minimum number of vertical and horizontal straight lines necessary to cover all zeros in the table. If the number of lines equals either the number of rows or the number of columns in the table, then we can make an optimal assignment (see step 4). If the number of lines is less than the number of rows or columns, we proceed to step 3.

3. Subtract the smallest number not covered by a line from every other uncov-

ered number. Add the same number to any number(s) lying at the intersection of any two lines. Return to step 2 and continue until an optimal assignment is possible.

4. Optimal assignments will always be at zero locations in the table. One systematic way of making a valid assignment is first to select a row or column that contains only one zero square. We can make an assignment to that square and then draw lines through its row and column. From the uncovered rows and columns, we choose another row or column in which there is only one zero square. We make that assignment and continue the above procedure until we have assigned each person or machine to one task.

Example 4

The cost table shown earlier in this section is repeated below. We find the minimum total cost assignment of jobs to machines by applying steps 1 through 4.

JOB \ MACHINE	A	B	C
R-34	$11	$14	$6
S-66	$8	$10	$11
T-50	$9	$12	$7

Step 1a. Using the previous table, subtract the smallest number in each row from every number in the row. The result is shown below.

JOB \ MACHINE	A	B	C
R-34	5	8	0
S-66	0	2	3
T-50	2	5	0

Step 1b. Using the previous table, subtract the smallest number in each column from every number in the column. The result is shown below.

JOB \ MACHINE	A	B	C
R-34	5	6	0
S-66	0	0	3
T-50	2	3	0

Step 2. Draw the minimum number of straight lines needed to cover all zeroes. Since two lines suffice, the solution is not optimal.

JOB ╲ MACHINE	A	B	C
R-34	5	6	0
S-66	0	0	3
T-50	②	3	0

Smallest uncovered number

Step 3. Subtract the smallest uncovered number (2 in this table) from every other uncovered number and add it to numbers at the intersection of two lines.

JOB ╲ MACHINE	A	B	C
R-34	3	4	0
S-66	0	0	5
T-50	0	1	0

Return to step 2. Cover the zeroes with straight lines again.

JOB ╲ MACHINE	A	B	C
R-34	3	4	0
S-66	0	0	5
T-50	0	1	0

Since three lines are necessary, an optimal assignment can be made (see step 4 on page 648). Assign R-34 to machine C, S-66 to machine B, and T-50 to machine A.

$$\begin{pmatrix} \text{Minimum} \\ \text{cost} \end{pmatrix} = \$6 + \$10 + \$9 = \$25$$

(*Note:* If we had S-66 assigned to machine A, we could not assign T-50 to a zero location.)

Some assignment problems entail *maximizing* the profit, effectiveness, or payoff of an assignment of people to tasks or of jobs to machines. It is easy to obtain an equivalent minimization problem by converting every number in the table to an *opportunity loss*. To perform this conversion, we subtract every number in the original payoff table from the largest single number in that table. We then proceed to step one of the four-step assignment method. It turns out that minimizing the opportunity loss produces the same assignment solution as the original maximization problem.

SEQUENCING

Scheduling provides a basis for assigning jobs to work centers. Machine loading is a capacity control technique that highlights overloads and underloads. **Sequencing** specifies the order in which jobs should be done at each center. For example, suppose that ten patients are assigned to a medical clinic for treatment. In what order should they be treated? Should the first patient to be served be the one who arrived first or the one who needs emergency treatment? Sequencing methods provide such detailed information. These methods are referred to as priority rules for dispatching jobs to work centers.

Priority Rules for Dispatching Jobs

Priority rules are widely used for preparing dispatch lists of jobs or lots in job shops. Priority rules provide guidelines for the sequence in which the jobs should be worked. Numerous rules have been developed; some are static, and others are dynamic. The rules are especially applicable for intermittent and batch processes with independent demands. The priority rules attempt to minimize mean flow time, mean completion time, and mean waiting time and to maximize throughput. Several simulation experiments have been conducted to compare the performance of priority rules.[3] In this section, we will discuss some well-known rules and their effectiveness.

The most popular priority rules are:

FCFS First come, first served. The first job to arrive at a work center is processed first.

EDD Earliest due date. The job with the earliest due date is selected first.

SPT Shortest processing time. The shortest jobs are handled first and gotten out of the way.

LPT Longest processing time. The longer, bigger jobs are often very important and are selected first.

We can compare these rules by way of Example 5.

Example 5

Five sheet metal jobs are waiting to be assigned at Ajax Company's Long Beach work center. Their processing times and due dates are given below. We want to determine the sequence of processing according to: (1) FCFS, (2) SPT, (3) EDD, and (4) LPT rules. Jobs were assigned a letter in the order they arrived.

---

[3] See R. W. Conway, W. L. Maxwell, and L. W. Miller, *Theory of Scheduling* (Reading, MA: Addison-Wesley, 1976).

JOB	JOB PROCESSING TIME IN DAYS	JOB DUE DATE (DAYS)	JOB	JOB PROCESSING TIME IN DAYS	JOB DUE DATE (DAYS)
A	6	8	D	3	15
B	2	6	E	9	23
C	8	18			

1. *FCFS* sequence is simply A–B–C–D–E. The "flow time" in the system for this sequence measures the time each job spends waiting plus being processed. Job B, for example, waits six days while job A is being processed, then takes two more days of operation time itself; so it will be completed in eight days—which is two days later than its due date.

JOB SEQUENCE	PROCESSING TIME	FLOW TIME	JOB DUE DATE	JOB LATENESS
A	6	6	8	0
B	2	8	6	2
C	8	16	18	0
D	3	19	15	4
E	9	28	23	5
	28	77		11

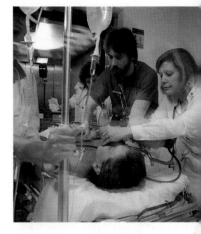

Your doctor may use a first-come-first-serve priority rule satisfactorily. However, such a rule may be less than optimal for this emergency room.

The first-come, first-served rule results in the following measures of effectiveness:

a) Average completion time $= \dfrac{\text{Sum of flow time totals}}{\text{No. of jobs}}$

$= \dfrac{77 \text{ days}}{5} = 15.4 \text{ days}$

b) Average number of jobs in the system $= \dfrac{\text{Sum of flow time totals}}{\text{Total processing time}}$

$= \dfrac{77 \text{ days}}{28 \text{ days}} = 2.75 \text{ jobs}$

c) Average job lateness $= \dfrac{\text{Total late days}}{\text{No. of jobs}} = \dfrac{11}{5} = 2.2 \text{ days}$

2. *SPT* rule results in the sequence B–D–A–C–E (see below). Orders are sequenced according to processing time, with the highest priority given to the shortest job.

JOB SEQUENCE	PROCESSING TIME	FLOW TIME	JOB DUE DATE	JOB LATENESS
B	2	2	6	0
D	3	5	15	0
A	6	11	8	3
C	8	19	18	1
E	9	28	23	5
	28	65		9

Measurements of effectiveness for SPT are:

a) Average completion time $= \dfrac{65}{5} = 13$ days

b) Average number of jobs in the system $= \dfrac{65}{28} = 2.32$

c) Average job lateness $= \dfrac{9}{5} = 1.8$ days

3. *EDD* rule gives the sequence B–A–D–C–E. Note that jobs are ordered by earliest due date first.

JOB SEQUENCE	PROCESSING TIME	FLOW TIME	JOB DUE DATE	JOB LATENESS
B	2	2	6	0
A	6	8	8	0
D	3	11	15	0
C	8	19	18	1
E	9	28	23	5
	28	68		6

Measurements of effectiveness for EDD are:

a) Average completion time $= \dfrac{68}{5} = 13.6$ days

b) Average number of jobs in the system $= \dfrac{68}{28} = 2.42$

c) Average job lateness $= \dfrac{6}{5} = 1.2$ days

4. *LPT* results in the order E–C–A–D–B.

JOB SEQUENCE	PROCESSING TIME	FLOW TIME	JOB DUE DATE	JOB LATENESS
E	9	9	23	0
C	8	17	18	0
A	6	23	8	15
D	3	26	15	11
B	2	28	6	22
	28	103		48

Measures of effectiveness for the longest processing time approach are:

a) Average completion time $= \dfrac{103}{5} = 20.6$ days

b) Average number of jobs in the system $= \dfrac{103}{28} = 3.68$

c) Average job lateness $= \dfrac{48}{5} = 9.6$ days

The results of these four rules are on page 653.

"We've been at it all night, J.B., and we've narrowed it down to 36,000 possibilities. We should have today's schedule firmed up by noon."

Source: CMCS News, Summer 1985.

RULE	AVERAGE COMPLETION TIME (DAYS)	AVERAGE NO. OF JOBS IN SYSTEM	AVERAGE LATENESS (DAYS)
FCFS	15.4	2.75	2.2
SPT	13.0	2.32	1.8
EDD	13.6	2.42	1.2
LPT	20.6	3.68	9.6

As we can see in Example 5, LPT is the least effective measurement of sequencing for the Ajax Company. SPT is superior in two measures and EDD in the third (average lateness). This is typically true in the real world also. We find that no one sequencing rule always excels on all criteria. Experience indicates that:

1. Shortest processing time is generally the best technique for minimizing job flow and minimizing the average number of jobs in the system. Its chief disadvantage is that long-duration jobs may be continuously pushed back in priority in favor of short-duration jobs. Customers may view this dimly, and a periodic adjustment for longer jobs has to be made.

2. First-come first-served does not score well on most criteria (but neither does it score particularly poorly). It has the advantage, however, of appearing fair to customers, which is important in service systems.

3. Critical ratio, the technique we introduce next, performs well on the average job lateness criterion.

Critical Ratio

Another type of sequencing rule is the **critical ratio.** The critical ratio (CR) is an index number computed by dividing the time remaining until due date by the work time remaining. As opposed to the priority rules, critical ratio is dynamic. It can be updated frequently and is useful in advance scheduling.

Critical ratio

The critical ratio gives priority to jobs that must be done to keep shipping on schedule. A job with a low critical ratio (less than 1.0) is one that is falling behind schedule. If CR is exactly 1.0, the job is on schedule. A CR greater than 1.0 means the job is ahead of schedule and has some slack.

The formula for critical ratio is

$$CR = \frac{\text{Time remaining}}{\text{Work days remaining}} = \frac{\text{Due date} - \text{Today's date}}{\text{Work (lead) time remaining}}$$

Example 6

Today is day 25 on Carlson Food's production schedule. Three jobs are on order as indicated below:

JOB	DUE DATE	WORK DAYS REMAINING
A	30	4
B	28	5
C	27	2

We compute the critical ratios, using the formula for CR.

JOB	CRITICAL RATIO	PRIORITY ORDER
A	$(30 - 25)/4 = 1.25$	3
B	$(28 - 25)/5 = .60$	1
C	$(27 - 25)/2 = 1.00$	2

Job B has a critical ratio less than one, meaning it will be late unless expedited; so it has the highest priority. Job C is on time, and job A has some slack.

The critical-ratio rule can help in most production scheduling systems to:

1. determine the status of a specific job;
2. establish relative priority among jobs on a common basis;
3. relate both stock and make-to-order jobs on a common basis;
4. adjust priorities (and revise schedules) automatically for changes in both demand and job progress;
5. dynamically track job progress and location.

Johnson's Rule: Scheduling *N* Jobs on Two Machines

The next step in complexity in job shops is the case where *N* jobs (where *N* is 2 or more) must go through two machines or work centers in the same order. This is called the *N*/2 problem.

Johnson's rule can be used to minimize the processing time for sequencing a group of jobs through two facilities.[4] It also minimizes total idle time on the machines.

Johnson's rule involves four steps:

1. All jobs are to be listed, and the time each requires on a machine is to be shown.
2. We select the job with the shortest activity time. If the shortest time lies with the first machine, the job is scheduled first. If the shortest time lies with the second machine, schedule the job last. Ties can be broken arbitrarily.
3. Once a job is scheduled, eliminate it.

[4] S. M. Johnson, "Optimal Two and Three Stage Production Schedules with Set-Up Times Included," *Naval Research Logistics Quarterly,* **1,** 1 (March 1954): 61–68.

POM _in action_

Scheduling Tape Editing Machines at WBZ-TV

Scheduling machines and people to provide the services we count on is an important part of P/OM. Machines in a factory, nurses, operating rooms, police patrol units, and bus drivers must all be scheduled. Finding *optimal* solutions to these problems, that is, finding the best schedules, is beyond the capability of even the fastest computers today. One way of simplifying scheduling problems has been to gain insight into the behavior of the processes being examined.

One algorithm that helps turn the complex problem into a more manageable one is called the *list processing algorithm*. List processing was used at WBZ-TV (Channel 4) in Boston to deal with the scheduling of two tape editing machines. WBZ-TV's biggest news job is taking several hours of video tape daily, and editing it down to 7 or 8 one- to two-minute clips plus a four-minute feature—and yet have everything in place by the 11 P.M. news show deadline. Scheduling the limited resources is a critical job, which can be tackled by operations analysis.

4. Apply steps 2 and 3 to the remaining jobs, working toward the center of the sequence.

Example 7

Five specialty jobs at a Fredonia, New York, tool and die shop must be processed through two work centers (drill machine and lathe machine). The time for processing each job is shown below.

	PROCESSING TIME (IN HOURS) FOR JOBS	
JOB	WORK CENTER 1 (DRILL)	WORK CENTER 2 (LATHE)
A	5	2
B	3	6
C	8	4
D	10	7
E	7	12

1. We wish to set the sequence that will minimize the total processing time for the five jobs. The job with the shortest processing time is A, in work center 2 (with a time of two hours). Since it is at the second center, schedule A last. Eliminate it from consideration.

				A

2. Job B has the next shortest time. Since it is at the first work center, we schedule it first and eliminate it from consideration.

B				A

3. The next shortest time is job C. It is placed as late as possible, since it was on the second machine.

B			C	A

4. There is a tie (at seven hours) for the shortest remaining job. We can place E, which was on the first work center, first. Then D is placed in the last sequencing position.

B	E	D	C	A

The sequential times are:

Work Center 1	3	7	10	8	5
Work Center 2	6	12	7	4	2

The time-phased flow of this job sequence is best illustrated graphically:

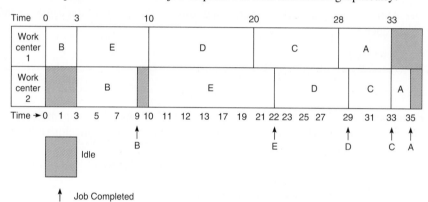

Thus, the five jobs are completed in 35 hours. The second work center will wait 3 hours for its first job, and it will also wait 1 hour after completing job B.

Scheduling *N* Jobs on Three Machines

Although the optimal solution to scheduling *N* jobs on three machines is quite complicated, if either or both of the following conditions are met, the solution is possible by Johnson's rule:

1. The smallest duration on machine 1 is at least as great as the largest duration on machine 2.

2. The smallest duration on machine 3 is at least as great as the largest duration on machine 2.

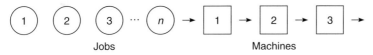

We will illustrate with the following example.

Example 8

Consider the following jobs and their processing times at corresponding machines:

JOB	DURATION (HOURS)		
	Machine 1, t_1	Machine 2, t_2	Machine 3, t_3
A	13	5	9
B	5	3	7
C	6	4	5
D	7	2	6

We want to use Johnson's rule to find the optimal sequence. Since both conditions of Johnson's rule are met, we can apply it. First, form a new matrix, as follows:

JOB	$t_1 + t_2$	$t_2 + t_3$	JOB	$t_1 + t_2$	$t_2 + t_3$
A	18	14	C	10	9
B	8	10	D	9	8

Now, using Johnson's rule for the $N/2$ problem, we get the optimal sequence: B, A, C, D.

Essentially, Johnson's rule converts an $N/3$ problem into an $N/2$ problem, provided that certain conditions are met. Even if these conditions are not met, the rule still provides a near-optimal solution.

N Jobs/*M* Machines

When *several* jobs have to be processed through many facilities, finding an optimal sequence requires a complex search procedure.

An efficient heuristic procedure, suggested by Campbell, Dudek, and Smith,[5] is known as the CDS algorithm. The CDS algorithm extends the $N/3$ Johnson's rule to a general N/M problem and provides a near-optimal solution.

Other research, which uses the queuing theory and computer simulation of Chapter 5 to solve complex sequencing problems mathematically, is ongoing. But, in the meantime, how do ordinary schedulers and managers tackle the complex sequencing decisions that have to be made every day? The answer is that they use ordinary sequencing rules such as SPT, EDD, or critical ratio. These methods are applied periodically at each work center, then the set of job sequences is modified to take advantage of economics in changing over machines from one job to another. Perhaps surprisingly, even though this ordinary approach is not optimal, it is effective and accepted in real-world practice.

EXPERT SYSTEMS IN SCHEDULING AND SEQUENCING

Another technique on the horizon that has the potential to be of major benefit to operations managers in scheduling is the *expert system*. As described in the Supplement to Chapter 7, an expert system (or an artificial intelligence system) is a computer program that makes decisions and solves problems much as a human expert would handle them. The idea behind its use in scheduling is to capture, code, and harness the knowledge and skills of a person who is an expert at sequencing and scheduling. The firm can then derive the benefits of having that expert at its disposal without having the person present.

There is a growing number of job shop scheduling expert systems, dating back to *Intelligent Scheduling and Information System* (ISIS) in 1984.[6] ISIS works by searching for solutions that satisfy the scheduling constraints. When it cannot find a feasible solution, it relaxes the constraints based on their relative importance. ISIS led to *Opportunistic Scheduler* (OPIS) in 1986, which is a factory scheduling system that can handle multiple scheduling problems.[7]

In the space transportation field, several other expert systems have been developed. The most prominent, *Management Analysis Resource Scheduler* (MARS), has been used to schedule resources for the NASA space shuttle system.[8] MARS handles scheduling problems arising when different shuttle flights demand the same manpower, computers, simulators, and other resources.

Texas Instruments also uses an expert system at its manufacturing plant in Carrolton, Texas. The TI system coordinates the scheduling, dispatching, and tool loading on the plant floor.[9]

To manage her hundreds of retail cookie outlets, Debbi Fields decided to capture her experience in an "expert system" that every store could access at any time. Her Retail Operations Intelligence System (ROIS) takes advantage of headquarters expertise in scheduling minimum wage employees, the predominant counter help. The software draws up a work schedule, including breaks, to best use hourly employees' time. ROIS also creates a full-day projection of the amount of dough to be processed and charts progress and sales on an hourly basis. It even tells staff when to cut back production and start offering free samples to passing customers.

[5] H. G. Campbell, R. A. Dudek, and M. L. Smith, "A Heuristic Algorithm for the (n) Job, (m) Machine Sequencing Problem," *Management Science*, **16**, 10 (June 1970): 630–637.

[6] M. S. Fox, and S. F. Smith, "ISIS: A Knowledge-Based System for Factory Scheduling," *Expert Systems*, **1**, 1 (July 1984): 25–49.

[7] P. S. Ow, and S. F. Smith, "Viewing Scheduling as an Opportunistic Problem-Solving Process," Carnegie-Mellon University, Working Papers, Pittsburgh, Pa., 1986.

[8] C. A. Marsh, "MARS—An Expert System Using the Automated Reasoning Tool to Schedule Resources," *Robotics and Expert Systems*, Proceedings of Robex's 85, Instrument Society of America, pp. 123–125.

[9] J. Lyman, "Manufacturing," *Electronics* (October 16, 1986): 105–106.

OPT AND Q-CONTROL

Since job shop scheduling is a difficult problem for operations managers, a variety of computer programs have been developed to provide work center schedules. One long-standing software package is General Electric's General Job Shop Scheduler. Used to assess capacity demands or to schedule jobs, this package develops two reports: (1) a job schedule report that assigns jobs by machine, day, hour, and operator, and (2) a machine center load report that indicates idle time at each work center.

Two computerized systems that are gaining wide recognition are **Optimized Production Technology (OPT)** and **Q-Control.** Both are proprietary systems whose algorithms are not available at this time for analysis.

Optimized Production Technology (OPT)

Q-Control

An important feature of OPT and Q-Control is the attention paid to bottleneck operations. A **bottleneck** is an operation that limits output in the production sequence. It can occur due to equipment limitations or because of a shortage of people, material, or facilities.

Bottleneck

OPT locates bottlenecks by developing load schedules for all work centers, then uses mathematical programming, network, and simulation algorithms to schedule workers, machines, and tools at bottleneck and work centers. Its philosophy is that bottlenecks are critical—they must be identified and optimized. Overall schedules are simulated, and a best one is selected on the basis of simulations.[10] OPT's ten commandments for correct scheduling provide an interesting set of ideas for the operations manager to consider as he or she wrestles with scheduling problems (see Table 15.2).

Q-Control has several similarities to OPT and appears to work well in complex

---

TABLE 15.2 The Ten Commandments for Correct Scheduling

1. The utilization of a nonbottleneck resource is not determined by its own capacity, but by some other constraint in the system.
2. Activating a resource is not synonymous with utilizing a resource.
3. An hour lost at a bottleneck is an hour lost of the total system.
4. An hour saved at a nonbottleneck is a mirage.
5. The transfer batch may not, and many times should not, be equal to the process batch.
6. The process batch should be variable and not fixed.
7. Capacity and priority need to be considered simultaneously and not sequentially.
8. Murphy is not an unknown, and his damage can be isolated and minimized.
9. Plant capacity should not be balanced.
10. The sum of the local optimums is not equal to the global optimum.

Source: Bob Fox, "Leapfrogging the Japanese," *Inventories and Production,* **3,** 2 (March–April 1983).

---

[10] For further details, see these three articles by Robert E. Fox: "MRP, Kanban, or OPT?" *Inventories and Production Magazine,* **2,** 4 (July–August 1982); "OPT vs. MRP: Thoughtware vs. Software," *Inventories and Production Magazine,* **3,** 6 (November–December 1983); and "OPT—An Answer for America, Part II," *Inventories and Production Magazine,* **2,** 6 (November–December 1982).

job shop environments.[11] Its developer, William Sandman, studied more than 600 job shops. He found that the time a typical job is in a shop is much longer (by factor of as much as 30 times) than the actual working time required for that job.[12] The lengthy time a job spends waiting in a queue for processing is an indication to Sandman that the firm's work-in-process and cash flow are not being tightly managed.

Q-Control's approach is to simulate the shop each night to determine where bottlenecks are likely to develop the next day. A schedule is then produced that maximizes work flow through the bottleneck operations. Sandman claims that Q-Control results in an average doubling of work-in-process "turns," while the time to complete an order and idle work-in-process time decrease by one-half. Again, because Q-Control uses a secret software code, there is limited information currently available on its internal workings.

REPETITIVE MANUFACTURING

The scheduling goals as defined at the beginning of this chapter are also appropriate for repetitive production. You may recall from Chapter 7 that repetitive producers are those who produce standard products from modules. Repetitive producers want to satisfy customer demands, lower inventory investment, reduce the batch (or lot) size, and utilize equipment and processes. The way to move toward these goals is to

Level material use

move to a level material use schedule. **Level material use** means frequent, high-quality, small lot sizes that contribute to just-in-time production. (Just-in-time production and Kanban, which contribute to low inventory and level material use, are techniques discussed in Chapters 10 and 13.) The advantages of level material use are:

1. lower inventory levels, which releases capital for other uses;
2. faster product throughput (that is, shorter lead times);
3. improved component quality and hence improved product quality;
4. reduced floor-space requirements;
5. improved communication among employees because they are closer together (which can result in improved teamwork and *esprit de corps*);
6. a smoother production process because large lots have not "hidden" the problems.

Suppose a repetitive producer runs large monthly batches. With a level material use schedule, management would move toward shortening this monthly cycle. Management might run this cycle every week, day, or hour.

Table 15.3 shows a *traditional batch* and a new *level material use* schedule for an actual midwestern repetitive manufacturer of small tractors. Their daily level material use schedule meets daily demand with substantial savings over the costs of the batch system, which met a monthly demand. All direct costs except material handling have been reduced substantially.

---

[11] Refer to W. E. Sandman's book, *How to Win Productivity in Manufacturing* (Dresher, PA: *Yellow Book of Pennsylvania* 1980), for more information.

[12] See the related discussion of cycle time in Chapter 13.

TABLE 15.3 L Series Tractor at a U.S. Tractor Manufacturer.

MODEL	TRADITIONAL BATCH SIZE (MONTHLY REQUIREMENT; 20-DAY MONTH)	LEVEL MATERIAL USE SCHEDULE (DAILY REQUIREMENT TO MEET DEMAND)
LA30	120	6
LB38	220	11
LB46	180	9
LC38	240	12
LC46	240	12
LD38	500	25
LE38	1160	58
	2660	133

One way to develop a level material use schedule is to determine first the minimum lot size that will keep the production process moving. Ideally, this is the one unit that is being moved from one adjacent process to the next. More realistically, analysis of the process, transportation time, and containers used for transport are considered when determining lot size. Such analysis typically results in a small lot size but a lot size larger than one. Once a lot size has been determined, the EOQ production-run model can be modified to determine the desired setup time. We saw in Chapter 13 that the production-run model takes the form:

$$Q^\star = \sqrt{\frac{2DS}{H\,[1-(d/p)]}}$$

where

D = Annual demand

S = Setup cost

H = Holding cost

d = Daily demand

p = Daily production

Let us examine, in Example 9, how Crate Furniture, Inc., a firm that produces rustic furniture, moves toward a level material use schedule.

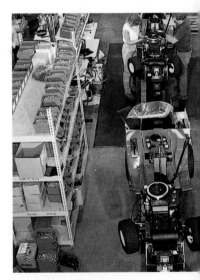

John Deere is among those repetitive manufacturers who have moved with great success to a level material use schedule. Here mowers at the John Deere Horicon Works in Wisconsin are mixed to yield a level material use schedule.

Example 9

Crate Furniture's production analyst, Roberta Russell, determined that a two-hour production cycle would be acceptable between two departments. Further, she concluded that a setup time that would accommodate the two-hour cycle time could be achieved. Roberta developed the following data and procedure to determine analytically that optimum setup time:

D = Annual demand = 400,000 units

d = Daily demand = 400,000/250 days = 1,600 per day

p = Daily production rate = 4,000

Q = EOQ desired = 400 (which is the 2-hour demand, that is, 1,600 per day/4 2-hour periods)

H = Holding cost = $20 per unit per year

S = Setup cost (to be determined)

Roberta determines that the cost, on an hourly basis, of getting equipment set up is $30. Further, she computes that the setup cost per setup should be:

$$Q = \sqrt{\frac{2DS}{H(1 - d/p)}}$$

$$Q^2 = \frac{2DS}{H(1 - d/p)}$$

$$S = \frac{(Q^2)(H)(1 - d/p)}{2D}$$

or

$$S = \frac{(400)^2(20)(1 - 1,600/4,000)}{2(400,000)}$$

$$= \frac{(3,200,000)(0.6)}{800,000} = \$2.40$$

Setup time = $2.40/Hourly labor rate

$= \$2.40/\$30$ per hour

$= 0.08$ hours or 4.8 minutes

Now, rather than producing components in large lots, Crate Furniture can produce in a two-hour cycle with the advantage of an inventory turnover of four *per day*. Some repetitive manufacturers are achieving inventory turns in excess of 150 per year on *all* of their inventory. Only two changes need to be made for this type of level material flow to work. First is the radical reduction in setup times, which is usually not difficult from a technical point of view. Second, changes may need to be made to improve material handling. With short production cycles there can be very little wait time.

SCHEDULING PERSONNEL FOR SERVICES

Scheduling service systems differs from scheduling manufacturing systems in several ways. First, in manufacturing, the emphasis of the operations manager is on materials; in services, it is on staffing levels and work schedules. Second, service systems do not store inventories of services. Third, services are labor-intensive, and the demand for this labor can be highly variable or random in nature.

A hospital is an example of a service facility that may use a scheduling system every bit as complex as that found in a job shop. Hospitals do not use a machine shop priority system such as first-come, first-served (FCFS) for treating emergency case patients. But they do produce special-need products (such as surgeries) just like a job shop, even though finished goods inventories cannot be kept and capacities

POM _in action_

Dinnerhouse Technology at Olive Garden and Red Lobster

It's Friday night in the Orlando suburb of Winter Park and the local Olive Garden Italian Restaurant is hopping. While customers wait an average of 45 minutes for a table, they can watch a happy pasta-maker churn out noodles or they can stare at the scenic paintings of Italian villages on the restaurant's walls. Then comes a dinner with portions so huge that many people bring home a doggie bag. Typical bill: $10 per person.

Is the food memorable? Not really? But gourmet food isn't what draws the crowds to an Olive Garden or its sister restaurant chain, Red Lobster. People come for value and consistency and they get it. "We serve hot food hot, cold food cold, and keep the rest rooms clean," says Olive Garden's president.

Every night, Red Lobster and Olive Garden computers tell their managers what to anticipate the next day, based on what the demand was the same day last week and the same day one year ago. The computer tells management that if 516 meals will be served the next day, that "you will serve these items in these quantities. 'So before you go home,' it says, 'I want you to pull 30 pounds of shrimp, 40 pounds of haddock, and 40 pounds of crab out of the freezer. Then tomorrow morning I want your production people to make 85 scampi dishes, 6 stuffed flounders,' and so on. You know what people are going to eat."

Waste in the chain has been cut by $5 million per year with the computerized planning system. Using history to forecast busy periods, the computer has also cut labor costs to 16% of revenues by improving scheduling. This is down almost a full percent in one year and translates into $10 million. In the low-margin business of food, every dollar counts.

Sources: Forbes, July 8, 1991; _Restaurant Business,_ March 20, 1991, pp. 121–136; and _Restaurant Hospitality,_ November 1988, pp. 108–110.

must be able to meet wide variations in demand.

Service systems try to match fluctuating customer demand with the capability to meet that demand. In some businesses, such as doctors' and lawyers' offices, an _appointment system_ is the schedule. In retail shops, a post office, or a fast-food restaurant, a _first-come, first-served_ rule for serving customers will suffice. Scheduling in these businesses is handled by bringing in extra workers, often part-timers, to help during peak periods. _Reservations systems_ work well in rental car agencies, symphony halls, airlines, hotels, and some restaurants as a means of minimizing customer waiting time and avoiding disappointment over unfilled service.

In all service systems, scheduling personnel who perform the services is a major issue to be faced. How restaurant chains improve scheduling and cut labor costs is shown in the _POM in Action_ box, "Dinnerhouse Technology at Olive Garden and Red Lobster." An example of personnel scheduling at Chase Manhattan Bank follows.

Linear Programming in Scheduling Personnel

We saw in the Supplement to Chapter 3 that _linear programming_ can be a useful tool in scheduling service employees. In that supplement, Example S4 and Problems S3.13 and S3.20 all deal with personnel scheduling. As a final example, we look at

FIGURE 15.5

Work-load Curve at Chase Manhattan Bank.

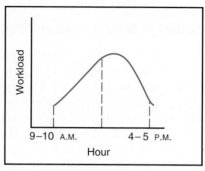

Workload Curve at Chase Manhattan Bank

TABLE 15.4 Results of Chase Manhattan Linear Programming Analysis for Personnel Scheduling.

WORK-FORCE SCHEDULE

| | NUMBER OF | NUMBER OF PERSONS AVAILABLE | | |
TIME PERIOD	PERSONS REQUIRED	FULL TIME	PART TIME	TOTAL
9–10 A.M.	14	29	—	29
10–11	25	29	—	29
11–12	26	15	11	26
12–1 P.M.	38	14	26	40
1–2	55	29	26	55
2–3	60	29	31	60
3–4	51	29	22	51
4–5	29	29	5	34
5–6	14	9	5	14
6–7	9	9	0	9

TIME SCHEDULES

Full-Time Employees

NUMBER OF EMPLOYEES	STARTING TIME	NUMBER OF EMPLOYEES	LUNCH PERIOD	NUMBER OF EMPLOYEES	LEAVING TIME
29	9 A.M.	14	11–12	20	5 P.M.
		15	12–1	9	7 P.M.

Part-Time Employees

NUMBER OF EMPLOYEES	STARTING TIME	NUMBER OF EMPLOYEES	LEAVING TIME
11	11 A.M.	9	3 P.M.
		2	4 P.M.
15	12 noon	15	4 P.M.
5	2 P.M.	5	6 P.M.

labor planning at Chase Manhattan Bank.[13] Figure 15.5 shows the work-load curve and the corresponding labor requirement at different times of day at one Chase location.

A variable capacity was effectively found by employing part-time personnel. Since part-timers are not entitled to all of Chase's fringe benefits, they can be more economical than full-time employees. But other considerations limited the extent to which part-timers could be hired in any operating department. So Chase's problem was to find an optimum work-force schedule that would meet labor requirements and also be economical. A linear programming model with 18 variables and 21 constraints yielded the schedule shown in Table 15.4.

SUMMARY

Scheduling involves the timing of operations to achieve the efficient movement of units through a system. This chapter addressed the issues of short-term scheduling in job shop, repetitive, and service environments. We saw that job shops are production systems in which products are made to order, and that scheduling tasks in them can become complex. Several aspects and approaches to scheduling, loading, and sequencing of jobs were introduced. These ranged from Gantt charts and the assignment methods of scheduling to a series of priority rules, the critical ratio rule, and Johnson's rule for sequencing. We also examined the use of level material flow in repetitive manufacturing environments.

Service systems generally differ from manufacturing systems. This leads to the use of appointment systems, first-come, first-served systems, and reservation systems, as well as to heuristics and mathematical programming approaches to servicing customers.

KEY TERMS

Job shop (p. 641)	**FCFS (p. 650)**
Planning files (p. 642)	**EDD (p. 650)**
Control files (p. 642)	**SPT (p. 650)**
Forward scheduling (p. 642)	**LPT (p. 650)**
Backward scheduling (p. 643)	**Critical ratio (p. 653)**
Loading (p. 643)	**Johnson's rule (p. 654)**
Input-output control (p. 643)	**Optimized Production Technology**
Gantt charts (p. 644)	**(OPT) (p. 659)**
Assignment method (p. 646)	**Q-Control (p. 659)**
Sequencing (p. 650)	**Bottleneck (p. 659)**
Priority rules (p. 650)	**Level material use (p. 660)**

---

[13] S. L. Moondra, "An L.P. Model for Workforce Scheduling for Banks," *Journal of Bank Research* (Winter 1976).

USING AB:POM

Solving Example 4 with AB:POM's Assignment Model Module

AB:POM's assignment module is used to solve the traditional one-to-one assignment problem of assigning people to jobs or to machines, machines to jobs, etc. The problem size is virtually unlimited.

In order to generate an assignment problem we first input the number of jobs and machines. In Program 15.1 we show a screen that generates a problem with 3 jobs and 3 machines, using Example 4's data. The numbers of jobs and machines do not have to be equal but usually they are.

We may then input the following problem data:

1. *Minimize/maximize.* Most assignment problems are minimization problems, but maximization can be requested.
2. *Row names.* The default names for the rows are "job 1," "job 2," etc., but these can be changed.
3. *Column names.* The default names for the columns are "mach 1," "mach 2," but these too may be changed.
4. *Costs.* The costs of assigning a job to a machine are entered here.

Program 15.2 provides the very straightforward output and solution.

Solving Example 5 with AB:POM's Job Shop Scheduling Module

AB:POM's job shop scheduling module can be used to solve one- and two-machine job shop problems. For the one-machine problem the available methods are shortest processing time, first-come, first-served, earliest due date scheduling, and longest

---

Program 15.1

AB:POM's Assignment Model Program Using Example 4 Data

———————————————— Assignment ———————————————— Data Screen ————

Number of jobs (1–99) 3   Number of machines (1–99) 3

minimize

———————————————— EXAMPLE 4 ASSIGNMENT ————————————————

	MACH A	MACH B	MACH C
R-34	11	14	6
S-66	8	10	11
T-50	9	12	7

Program 15.2

Output from Assignment Program on Example 4 Data

```
                        EXAMPLE 4 ASSIGNMENT

SHIPMENTS        MACH A      MACH B      MACH C


R-34                                        1

S-66                          1

T-50              1

The minimum total cost =                  $25

                              NOTE: alternate optimal solutions exist
```

Program 15.3

AB:POM's Job Shop Scheduling Program Using Example 5 Data

——————————————— Job Shop Sequencing ——————————————— Solution ———

Number of jobs (1-14)   5   Number of machines (1-2)   1

————————————————————— AJAX COMPANY, EXAMPLE 5 —————————————————

SPT	mach. 1	Due Dat	EXTRA		Order	Flow tm	Tardy
JOB A	6	8	0		third	11	3
JOB B	2	6	0		first	2	0
JOB C	8	18	0		fourth	19	1
JOB D	3	15	0		second	5	0
JOB E	9	23	0		fifth	28	5

Average # jobs in system = 2.32   TOTAL   65   9

SEQUENCE   AVERAGE   13.00   1.80

JOB B, JOB D, JOB A, JOB C, JOB E

                                              F9 = Print   Esc
Press <Esc> key to continue or highlighted key or function key for options

processing time. For two-machine scheduling, Johnson's method is used to minimize the makespan.

In order to generate the data screen shown in Program 15.3 we first input the number of jobs and the number of machines. For Example 5, there were 5 jobs and 1 machine. (The screens for one and two machines are similar but they are *not* identical.)

Program 15.3 also illustrates both the completed data entry and the solution. The items we input to this screen were:

1. *Priority rule desired.* Available rules are:
   Shortest processing time (SPT)
   First Come, First Served (FCFS)
   Earliest due date (EDD)
   Longest processing time (LPT)
2. *Job names.* Names up to 8 characters long can be entered for each job (optional input).
3. *Machine name.* The word "mach. 1" at the top of the column can be changed to give the name of the type of machine (also optional).
4. *Processing Time.* The amount of time that each job will take on each machine is entered in this column.
5. *Due date.*

Once the data have all been entered, each priority rule can be examined without further inputs.

SOLVED PROBLEMS

Solved Problem 15.1

King Finance Corporation, headquartered in New York, wants to assign three recently hired college graduates, Jones, Smith, and Wilson, to regional offices. But the firm also has an opening in New York and would send one of the three there if it were more economical than a move to Omaha, Dallas, or Miami. It will cost $1,000 to relocate Jones in New York, $800 to relocate Smith there, and $1,500 to move Wilson. What is the optimal assignment of personnel to offices?

HIREE \ OFFICE	OMAHA	MIAMI	DALLAS
Jones	$800	$1,100	$1,200
Smith	$500	$1,600	$1,300
Wilson	$500	$1,000	$2,300

Solution

a) The cost table has a fourth column to represent New York. To "balance" the problem, we add a "dummy" row (person) with a zero relocation cost to each city.

HIREE \ OFFICE	OMAHA	MIAMI	DALLA	NEW YORK
Jones	$800	$1,100	$1,200	$1,000
Smith	$500	$1,600	$1,300	$ 800
Wilson	$500	$1,000	$2,300	$1,500
Dummy	0	0	0	0

b) Subtract smallest number in each row and cover zeros (column subtraction will give the same numbers and therefore is not necessary).

HIREE \ OFFICE	OMAHA	MIAMI	DALLAS	NEW YORK
Jones	0	300	400	200
Smith	0	1,100	800	300
Wilson	0	500	1,800	1,000
Dummy	0	0	0	0

c) Subtract smallest uncovered number (200), add it to each square where two lines intersect, and cover all zeroes.

HIREE \ OFFICE	OMAHA	MIAMI	DALLAS	NEW YORK
Jones	0	100	200	0
Smith	0	900	600	100
Wilson	0	300	1,600	800
Dummy	200	0	0	0

d) Subtract smallest uncovered number (100), add it to each square where two lines intersect, and cover all zeroes.

HIREE \ OFFICE	OMAHA	MIAMI	DALLAS	NEW YORK
Jones	0	0	100	0
Smith	0	800	500	100
Wilson	0	200	1,500	800
Dummy	300	0	0	100

e) Subtract smallest uncovered number (100), add it to squares where two lines intersect, and cover all zeroes.

HIREE \ OFFICE	OMAHA	MIAMI	DALLAS	NEW YORK
Jones	~~100~~	~~0~~	~~100~~	~~0~~
Smith	~~0~~	~~700~~	~~400~~	~~0~~
Wilson	~~0~~	~~100~~	~~1,400~~	~~700~~
Dummy	~~400~~	~~0~~	~~0~~	~~100~~

f) Since it takes four lines to cover all zeros, an optimal assignment can be made at zero squares. We assign:

Dummy (no one) to Dallas
Wilson to Omaha
Smith to New York
Jones to Miami

Cost = $0 + $500 + $800 + $1,100

= $2,400

Solved Problem 15.2

A well-known defense contractor in Dallas has six jobs awaiting processing. Processing time and due dates are given below. Assume jobs arrive in the order shown. Set the processing sequence according to FCFS and EDD. Which is preferable?

JOB	JOB PROCESSING TIME IN DAYS	JOB DUE DATE (DAYS)
A	6	22
B	12	14
C	14	30
D	2	18
E	10	25
F	4	34

Solution

FCFS has the sequence A–B–C–D–E–F.

JOB SEQUENCE	PROCESSING TIME	FLOW TIME	DUE DATE	JOB LATENESS
A	6	6	22	0
B	12	18	14	4
C	14	32	30	2
D	2	34	18	16
E	10	44	25	19
F	4	48	34	14
	48	182		55

1. Average completion time 182/6 = 30.33
2. Average no. jobs in system = 182/48 = 3.79
3. Average job lateness = 55/6 = 9.16 days

EDD has the sequence B–D–A–E–C–F.

JOB SEQUENCE	PROCESSING TIME	FLOW TIME	DUE DATE	JOB LATENESS
B	12	12	14	0
D	2	14	18	0
A	6	20	22	0
E	10	30	25	5
C	14	44	30	14
F	4	48	34	14
	48	168		33

1. Average completion time = 168/6 = 28.0 days (lower than FCFS)
2. Average no. jobs in system = 168/48 = 3.5 (lower than FCFS)
3. Average job lateness = 33/6 = 5.5 days (lower than FCFS)

Solved Problem 15.3

The Dallas firm noted in Solved Problem 15.2 wants also to consider job sequencing by the SPT and LPT priority rules. Apply them to the same data and provide a recommendation.

Solution
SPT has the sequence D–F–A–E–B–C.

JOB SEQUENCE	PROCESSING TIME	FLOW TIME	DUE DATE	JOB LATENESS
D	2	2	18	0
F	4	6	34	0
A	6	12	22	0
E	10	22	25	0
B	12	34	14	20
C	14	48	30	18
	48	124		38

1. Average completion time = 124/6 = 20.67 days
2. Average no. jobs in system = 124/48 = 2.58
3. Average job lateness = 38/6 = 6.33 days

LPT has the sequence C–B–E–A–F–D.

JOB SEQUENCE	PROCESSING TIME	FLOW TIME	DUE DATE	JOB LATENESS
C	14	14	30	0
B	12	26	14	12
E	10	36	25	11
A	6	42	22	20
F	4	46	34	12
D	2	48	18	30
	48	212		85

1. Average completion time = 212/6 = 35.33 days
2. Average no. of jobs in system = 212/48 = 4.42
3. Average job lateness = 85/6 = 14.17 days

SPT provides the best average completion time (20.67 days) and average number of jobs in the system (2.58) of all four priority rules. EDD's average job lateness of 5.5 days is lowest. SPT is a good recommendation. SPT's major disadvantage is that it makes long jobs wait, sometimes for a long time.

Solved Problem 15.4

Use Johnson's rule to find the optimum sequence for processing the jobs below through two work centers. Times at each center are in hours.

JOB	WORK CENTER 1	WORK CENTER 2
A	6	12
B	3	7
C	18	9
D	15	14
E	16	8
F	10	15

Solution

B	A	F	D	C	E

The sequential times are:

Work Center 1	3	6	10	15	18	16
Work Center 2	7	12	15	14	9	8

Solved Problem 15.5

Illustrate the throughput time and idle time at the two work centers in Solved Problem 15.4 by constructing a time-phased chart.

Solution

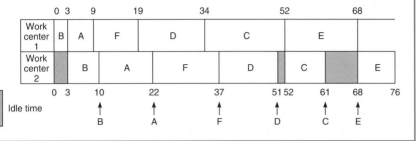

Solved Problem 15.6

Swearingen Products makes microwave ovens and desires to move to a level material use schedule for the various components used in those models. The firm has traditionally made both components and units in large batches and stored them in inventory until needed because the foreman liked it that way. Since the foreman retired last week, the president, John Swearingen, wants to move to a level material use schedule, When reviewing the flow of the first component, a control panel, the P/OM analyst found that the standard tote tray holds two hours of assembly-line work (100 units) and that move time is less than one hour even when allowing for the occasional delay that sometimes occurs. With these data the analyst concludes that a three-hour cycle would be a good place to begin. Swearingen's production data for control panels is:

$$\text{Annual demand} = 104{,}000$$
$$\text{Daily demand rate} = 400$$
$$\text{Daily production rate} = 1{,}000$$
$$\text{Desired lot size (a three-hour supply)} = 300$$
$$\text{Holding cost} = \$10 \text{ per unit per year}$$
$$\text{Setup labor cost per hour} = \$12$$

What should the setup time be?

Solution

$$Q = \sqrt{\frac{2DS}{H\,(1 - d/p)}}$$

$$Q^2 = \frac{2DS}{H\,(1 - d/p)}$$

$$S = \frac{Q^2 H\,(1 - d/p)}{2D} = \text{Setup cost per setup}$$

$$S = \frac{(300)^2(10)(1 - 400/1{,}000)}{2(104{,}000)} = (4.327)(0.6) = \$2.59$$

Setup time = \$2.59/Labor rate per hour

= \$2.59/\$12 = 0.1295 hours = 7.77 minutes

DISCUSSION QUESTIONS

1. Name five priority sequencing rules. Explain how each works to assign jobs.

2. When is Johnson's rule best applied in job shop scheduling?

3. Describe the differences between forward and backward scheduling.

4. What is the difference between a Gantt load chart and a Gantt schedule chart?

5. Briefly describe the planning and control files needed in a job shop activity system.

6. What important feature do OPT and Q-Control have in common?

7. Why is the scheduling of services a difficult problem?

8. What is input–output control? How does it help the operations manager?

9. What are the criteria by which we evaluate sequencing rules?

10. What are the advantages of level material flow?

PROBLEMS

: 15.1 JH Products Corporation has four more jobs to be scheduled, in addition to those shown in Example 3. JH production scheduling personnel are reviewing the Gantt chart at the end of day 4.

Job D was scheduled to begin early on day 2 and to end on the middle of day 9. As of now (the review point after day 4) it is two days ahead of schedule.

Job E should begin on day 1 and end on day 3. It was on time.

Job F was to begin on day 3, but maintenance forced a delay of $1\frac{1}{2}$ days. The job should now take five full days. It is now on schedule.

Job G is a day behind schedule. It started at the beginning of day 2 and should require six days to complete.

Develop a Gantt schedule chart for JH Corporation.

 · 15.2 The operations manager of King Manufacturing must assign three tasks to three machines. Cost data are presented below.

JOB \ MACHINE	#1	#2	#3
C-3	\$800	\$1,100	\$1,200
C-5	\$500	\$1,600	\$1,300
C-8	\$500	\$1,000	\$2,300

Use the assignment algorithm to solve this problem.

: **15.3** The scheduler at a small southwestern U.S. plant has six jobs that can be processed on any of six machines, with respective times as shown (in hours) below. Determine the allocation of jobs to machines that will result in minimum time.

	MACHINE					
JOB	*#1*	*#2*	*#3*	*#4*	*#5*	*#6*
A-52	60	22	34	42	30	60
A-53	22	52	16	32	18	48
A-56	29	16	58	28	22	55
A-59	42	32	28	46	15	30
A-60	30	18	25	15	45	42
A-61	50	48	57	30	44	60

· **15.4** The hospital administrator at St. Charles General must appoint head nurses to four newly established departments: urology, cardiology, orthopedics, and obstetrics. In anticipation of this staffing problem, she had hired four nurses: Hawkins, Condriac, Bardot, and Hoolihan. Believing in the P/OM analysis approach to problem solving, the administrator has interviewed all the nurses; considered their backgrounds, personalities, and talents; and developed a cost scale ranging from 0 to 100 to be used in the assignment. A 0 for Nurse Hawkins being assigned to the cardiology unit implies that she would be perfectly suited to that task. A value close to 100, on the other hand, would imply that she is not at all suited to head that unit. The accompanying table gives the complete set of cost figures that the hospital administrator felt represented all possible assignments. Which nurse should be assigned to which unit?

	DEPARTMENT			
NURSE	*Urology*	*Cardiology*	*Orthopedics*	*Obstetrics*
Hawkins	28	18	15	75
Condriac	32	48	23	38
Bardot	51	36	24	36
Hoolihan	25	38	55	12

· **15.5** The Gleaming Company has just developed a new dishwashing liquid and is preparing for a national television promotional campaign. The firm has decided to schedule a series of one-minute commercials during the peak housewife audience viewing hours of 1:00 to 5:00 P.M. To reach the widest possible audience, Gleaming wants to schedule one commercial on each of four networks and have one commercial appear during each of the four one-hour time blocks. The exposure ratings for each hour, representing the number of viewers per $1,000 spent, are presented in the accompanying table. Which network should be scheduled each hour in order to provide the maximum audience exposure?

	NETWORKS			
TIME	*A*	*B*	*C*	*Independent*
1:00–2:00 P.M.	27.1	18.1	11.3	9.5
2:00–3:00 P.M.	18.9	15.5	17.1	10.6
3:00–4:00 P.M.	19.2	18.5	9.9	7.7
4:00–5:00 P.M.	11.5	21.4	16.8	12.8

: **15.6** The Patricia Garcia Manufacturing Company is putting out seven new electronic components. Each of Garcia's eight plants has the capacity to add one more product to its current line of electronic parts. The unit manufacturing costs for producing the different parts at the eight plants are shown in the accompanying table. How should Garcia assign the new products to the plants in order to minimize manufacturing costs?

ELECTRONIC COMPONENTS	PLANTS							
	1	2	3	4	5	6	7	8
C53	10¢	12¢	13¢	11¢	10¢	6¢	16¢	12¢
C81	5	6	4	8	4	9	6	6
D5	32	40	31	30	42	35	36	49
D44	17	14	19	15	10	16	19	12
E2	6	7	10	5	8	10	11	5
E35	8	10	12	8	9	10	9	6
G99	55	62	61	70	62	63	65	59

: **15.7** The following jobs are waiting to be processed at the same machine center. Jobs are logged as they arrive:

JOB	DUE DATE	DURATION (DAYS)
A	313	8
B	312	16
C	325	40
D	314	5
E	314	3

In what sequence would the jobs be ranked according to the following decision rules: **(a)** FCFS, **(b)** EDD, **(c)** SPT, **(d)** LPT? All dates are specified as manufacturing planning calendar days. Assume that all jobs arrive on day 275. Which decision is best and why?

· **15.8** Suppose that today is day 300 on the planning calendar and that we have not started any of the jobs given in Problem 15.7. Using the critical-ratio technique, in what sequence would you schedule these jobs?

: **15.9** An Alabama lumber yard has four jobs on order, as shown below. Today is day 205 on the yard's schedule. Establish processing priorities.

JOB	DUE DATE	REMAINING TIME IN DAYS
A	212	6
B	209	3
C	208	3
D	210	8

: **15.10** The following jobs are waiting to be processed at a small machine center:

JOB	DUE DATE	DURATION (DAYS)
010	260	30
020	258	16
030	260	8
040	270	20
050	275	10

In what sequence would the jobs be ranked according to the following decision rules: (a) FCFS, (b) EDD, (c) SPT, (d) LPT? All dates are specified as manufacturing planning calendar days. Assume that all jobs arrive on day 210. Which is the best decision rule?

: **15.11** The following jobs are waiting to be processed at the Smith machine center:

JOB	DATE ORDER RECEIVED	PRODUCTION DAYS NEEDED	DATE ORDER DUE
A	110	20	180
B	120	30	200
C	122	10	175
D	125	16	230
E	130	18	210

In what sequence would the jobs be ranked according to the following rules: (a) FCFS, (b) EDD, (c) SPT, (d) LPT? All dates are according to shop calendar days. Today on the planning calendar is day 130. Which rule is best?

· **15.12** Suppose that today is day 150 on the planning calendar and that we have not yet started any of the jobs in Problem 15.11. Using the critical-ratio technique, in what sequence would you schedule these jobs?

: **15.13** Barry Automation Company estimates the data entry and verifying times for four jobs as follows:

JOB	DATA ENTRY (HOURS)	VERIFY (HOURS)
A	2.5	1.7
B	3.8	2.6
C	1.9	1.0
D	1.8	3.0

In what order should the jobs be done if the company has one operator for each job? Illustrate the time-phased flow of this job sequence graphically.

: 15.14   Six jobs are to be processed through a two-step operation. The first operation involves sanding, and the second involves painting. Processing times are as follows:

JOB	OPERATION 1 (HOURS)	OPERATION 2 (HOURS)
A	10	5
B	7	4
C	5	7
D	3	8
E	2	6
F	4	3

Determine a sequence that will minimize the total completion time for these jobs. Illustrate graphically.

: 15.15   Consider the following jobs and their processing times at the three machines. No passing of jobs is allowed.

JOB	MACHINE 1 (HOURS)	MACHINE 2 (HOURS)	MACHINE 3 (HOURS)
A	6	4	7
B	5	2	4
C	9	3	10
D	7	4	5
E	11	5	2

Using Johnson's rule, find the sequence in which the jobs are to be processed.

: 15.16   Bill Penny has a repetitive manufacturing plant producing trailer hitches in Arlington. The plant has an average inventory of only 12 turns per year. He has, therefore, determined that he will reduce his component lot sizes. He has developed the following data for one component, the safety chain clip.

$$\text{Annual demand} = 31{,}200$$
$$\text{Daily demand} = 120$$
$$\text{Daily production} = 960$$
$$\text{Desired lot size (1 hour of production)} = 120 \text{ units}$$
$$\text{Holding cost per unit per year} = \$12.$$
$$\text{Setup labor cost per hour} = \$20.$$

What setup time should he have his plant manager aim for regarding this component?

: 15:17   Mark Davis is the manager of the body shop at Cumberland Ford. On Monday morning, he arrived at work at 7:30 A.M. and discovered that the firm's wrecker service had towed in five automobiles involved in weekend accidents. In all cases, the owners had authorized Cumberland Ford to make all necessary repairs. Mark carefully analyzed the extent of damage to each car and noted the amount of time (in hours) that each car would require at each station in the body shop. The following table shows these time estimates.

AUTOMOBILE	METAL WORK AND REPLACEMENT OF PARTS	SANDING AND MASKING	PAINTING AND BAKING
1984 Fairmont	9 hours	8 hours	2 hours
1984 LTD	12	6	3
1986 Escort	10	3	5
1988 Tempo	8	7	4
1991 T Bird	14	2	1

Mark wanted to minimize waiting time and total time consumed in repairing the five automobiles. However, he was uncertain about the priority to give each car to accomplish this objective. After rechecking his time estimates for acccuracy, he pondered his decision.

a) Suggest a scheduling method that Mark could substitute for his "trial-and-error, hit-or-miss" sequencing decisions. Illustrate.

b) In what sequence should the cars be routed through the various operations to minimize waiting time and total time consumed?

Data Base Application

15.18 NASA's astronaut crew currently includes 10 mission specialists who hold a Ph.D. in either astrophysics or astromedicine. One of these specialists will be assigned to each of the 10 flights scheduled for the upcoming nine months. Mission specialists are responsible for carrying out scientific and medical experiments in space or for launching, retrieving, or repairing satellites. The chief of astronaut personnel, himself a former crew member with three missions under his belt, must decide who should be assigned and trained for each of the very different missions. Clearly, astronauts with medical educations are more suited to missions involving biological or medical experiments, while those with engineering- or physics-oriented degrees are best suited to other types of missions. The chief assigns each astronaut a rating on a scale of 1 to 10 for each possible mission, with a 10 being a perfect match for the task at hand and a 1 being a mismatch. Only one specialist is assigned to each flight, and none is reassigned until all others have flown at least once.

ASTRONAUT	MISSION									
	JAN. 12	JAN. 27	FEB. 5	FEB. 26	MAR. 26	APR. 12	MAY 1	JUN. 9	AUG. 20	SEP. 19
Vincze	9	7	2	1	10	9	8	9	2	6
Veit	8	8	3	4	7	9	7	7	4	4
Anderson	2	1	10	10	1	4	7	6	6	7
Herbert	4	4	10	9	9	9	1	2	3	4
Schatz	10	10	9	9	8	9	1	1	1	1
Plane	1	3	5	7	9	7	10	10	9	2
Certo	9	9	8	8	9	1	1	2	2	9
Moses	3	2	7	6	4	3	9	7	7	9
Brandon	5	4	5	9	10	10	5	4	9	8
Drtina	10	10	9	7	6	7	5	4	8	8

a) Who should be assigned to which flight?

b) We have just been notified that Anderson is getting married in February and he has been granted a highly sought publicity tour in Europe that month. (He intends to take his wife and let the trip double as a honeymoon.) How does this change the final shedule?

c) Certo has complained that he was misrated on his January mission. Both ratings should be 10s, he claims to the chief, who agrees and recomputes the schedule. Do any changes occur over the schedule set in part b?

d) What are the strengths and weaknesses of this approach to scheduling?

CASE STUDY

Old Oregon Wood Store

In 1990, George Brown started the Old Oregon Wood Store to manufacture Old Oregon tables. Each table is carefully constructed by hand, using the highest-quality oak.

The manufacturing process consists of four steps: preparation, assembly, finishing, and packaging. Each step is performed by one person. In addition to overseeing the entire operation, George does all of the finishing. Tom Surowski performs the preparation step, which involves cutting and forming the basic components of the tables. Leon Davis is in charge of the assembly, and Cathy Stark performs the packaging.

While each person is responsible for only one step in the manufacturing process, everyone can perform any one of the steps. It is George's policy that occasionally everyone should complete several tables on his or her own without any help or assistance. A small competition is used to see

FIGURE 15.6

Manufacturing Time in Minutes.

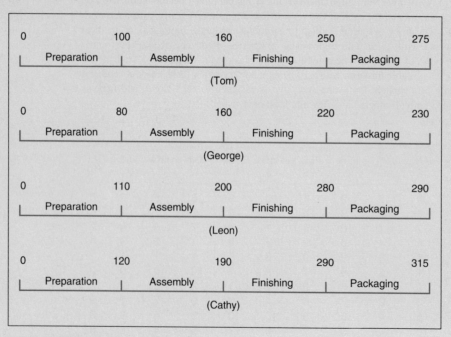

CASE STUDY (Continued)

FIGURE 15.7

Manufacturing Times in Minutes for Randy Lane.

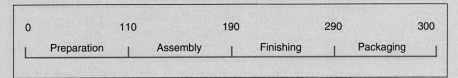

0	110	190	290	300
Preparation	Assembly	Finishing	Packaging	

who can complete an entire table in the least amount of time. George maintains average total and intermediate completion times. The data are shown in Figure 15.6.

It takes Cathy longer than the other employees to construct an Old Oregon table. In addition to being slower than the other employees, Cathy is also unhappy about her current responsibility of packaging, which leaves her idle most of the day. Her first preference is finishing, and her second preference is preparation.

In addition to quality, George is concerned with costs and efficiency. When one of the employees misses a day, it causes major scheduling problems. Overtime is expensive, and waiting for the employee to return to work causes delay and sometimes stops the entire manufacturing process.

To overcome some of these problems, Randy Lane was hired. Randy's major duties are to perform miscellaneous jobs and to help out if one of the employees is absent. George has given Randy training in all phases of the manufacturing process, and he is pleased with the speed at which Randy has been able to learn how to completely assemble Old Oregon tables. Total and intermediate completion times for Randy are given in Figure 15.7.

Discussion Questions

1. What is the fastest way to manufacture Old Oregon tables, using the original crew? How many could be made per day?

2. Would production rates and quantities change significantly if George would allow Randy to perform one of the four functions and make one of the original crew the backup person?

3. What is the fastest time to manufacture a table with the original crew if Cathy is moved to either preparation or finishing?

4. Whoever performs the packaging function is severely underutilized. Can you find a better way of utilizing the four- or five-person crew than either giving each a single job or allowing each to manufacture an entire table? How many tables could be manufactured per day with this scheme?

Source: B. Render and R. M. Stair, *Quantitative Analysis for Management,* 4th ed. Boston, MA: Allyn and Bacon, 1991.

BIBLIOGRAPHY

Baker, K. R. "The Effects of Input Control in a Simple Scheduling Model." *Journal of Operations Management,* **4** (February 1984): 99–112.

Baker, K. R. *Introduction to Sequencing and Scheduling.* New York: Wiley, 1974.

Bauer, A., J. Browne, R. Bowden, J. Duggan, and G. Lyons. *Shop Floor Control Systems.* New York: Van Nostrand Reinhold, 1991.

Buffa, E. S., and J. G. Miller. *Production-Inventory Systems: Planning and Control,* 3rd ed. Homewood, IL: Richard D. Irwin, 1979.

Limprecht, J. A., and R. H. Hayes. "Germany's World-Class Manufacturers." *Harvard Business Review,* **60** (November–December 1982): 137–145.

Lynch, P. "Matching Worked Hours to Business Needs." *Personnel Management* (June 1988): 36–39.

Render, B., and R. M. Stair. *Quantitative Analysis for Management,* 4th ed. Boston: Allyn & Bacon, 1991.

Sunderland, F. O., and R. E. Fox, "Synchronized Manufacturing Challenge." *Production and Inventory Management Review* (March 1986): 36–44.

Teplitz, C. J. "MRP Can Work in Your Job Shop." *Production and Inventory Management,* **19** (Fourth Quarter 1978): 21–26.

Vollmann, T. E. "OPT as an Enhancement to MRP II." *Production and Inventory Management,* **27** (Second Quarter 1986): 38–47.

Wight, O. W. *Production and Inventory Management in the Computer Age.* Boston: Cahners Books, 1974.

CHAPTER *16*

Project Management

*Project Management
Provides a Competitive
Advantage for Bechtel*

In one final, devastating act, Saddam Hussein torched the oil wells of Kuwait. When the first three-member Bechtel advance team landed in Kuwait, within days of Desert Storm's end, the panorama of destruction was breathtaking.

The valve heads had been blasted from some 750 high-pressure wells. Nearly 650 wells were ablaze, and others were gushing thousands of barrels of oil into dark lakes in the desert. Fire roared out of the ground from virtually every compass point.

Fire-fighting crews relied on explosives and heavy machinery to remove the hardened petroleum residue that had formed around many wells. Even a day after a fire is out, the surface is still hot enough to boil water.

Restoring the oil fields of Kuwait was a monumental project. There was no water, electricity, food, or facilities. Second, the country was littered with unexploded mines, bombs, grenades, artillery shells, and every variety of ordnance the opposing armies had thrown at one another. Finally, a good portion of the fires were inaccessible as lakes of oil covered roads and fire spread to the ground surrounding many of the wells.

Even for Bechtel, whose competitive advantage is project management, this was a first-of-a-kind complex, worldwide logistics problem. The number of specific project events that needed to be identified and accomplished was huge. Bechtel launched an on-site assessment effort, combined with a worldwide planning team to support the effort. Bechtel personnel soon determined that virtually no resources existed in Kuwait and that a major global procurement program was needed. Bechtel equipment specialists in San Francisco, Houston, and London were called on to tap the company's computer network of buyers and suppliers worldwide.

Then the issue was how to feed, house, and equip a work force that would grow into thousands by the time the effort was fully mobilized.

About 900 kilometers (550 miles) to the southeast of Kuwait, at the free port of Jebel Ali in Dubai, Bechtel established storage, docking, and warehousing facilities. As a central transshipment point into Kuwait, the port received and processed hundreds of shipments from chartered seacraft and aircraft, including the Soviet super cargo plane, the Antonov.

More than 200 lagoons filled with one million gallons of seawater were built. Pumps and hose lines to throw six thousand gallons of water a minute were installed.

With ambient temperatures well over 100 degrees fahrenheit, fire fighters drink up to 12 liters of fluid each day and they expect to get covered with crude.

The damage was extensive to facilities as well as oil fields and each item had to be included on the project schedule.

The dense black clouds produced by burning oil wells turned day into night and added new meaning to "reading by firelight."

Accommodations in Kuwait were arranged in apartment buildings that had to be stripped to bare walls to remove the vestiges of vandalism and the caches of ammunition, weapons, and even poison gas.

The Bechtel project management team procured, shipped, and deployed 125,000 tons of equipment and supplies, including some 4,000 pieces of operating equipment, ranging from bulldozers to ambulances. The team also managed a work force that laid some 150 kilometers of pipeline, capable of delivering 20 million gallons of water a day to the fire site.

The Bechtel project management team also mobilized:

- an international force of nearly 8,000 manual workers
- 1,000 project and construction professionals

- 6 full-service dining halls
- 27,000 meals a day
- a 24-hour-a-day safety program
- 2 helicopter evacuation teams
- a 40-bed field hospital
- a team of a hundred professional medical personnel, paramedics, and other staffers on duty at seven medical stations.

Through all of this, a gigantic blanket of smoke lay over most of Kuwait. At high noon, people frequently used flashlights to see the street curbs. Outdoors, their clothing quickly became speckled with fine droplets of misting oil.

The fires are out. Kuwait has begun shipping oil and Bechtel has demonstrated its competitive advantage—project management.

Source: Adapted from "Bechtel Briefs," Bechtel, San Francisco, CA.

INTRODUCTION

At one point or another almost every organization will take on a large and complex project. A construction company putting up an office building or laying a highway must complete thousands of costly activities. A government agency installing and debugging an expensive computer spends months preparing the details for smooth conversion to new equipment. A shipyard in Maine requires tens of thousands of steps in constructing an oceangoing tugboat. An oil refinery about to shut down for a major maintenance project faces astronomical expenses if this difficult task is unduly delayed for any reason. Almost every industry worries about how to manage similar large-scale, complicated projects effectively.

Large, often one-time, projects are difficult challenges to operations managers. The stakes are high. Millions of dollars in cost overruns have been wasted due to poor planning on projects. Unnecessary delays have occurred due to poor scheduling. And companies have gone bankrupt due to poor controls.

Special projects that take months or years to complete are usually developed outside the normal production system. Project organizations within the firm are set up to handle such jobs and are often disbanded when the project is complete. The management of large projects involves three phases (see Figure 16.1):

1. planning;   **2.** scheduling;   **3.** control.

FIGURE 16.1

Project Planning, Scheduling, and Controlling.

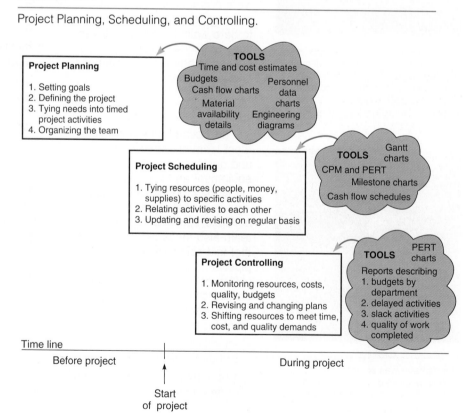

We will begin this chapter with a brief overview of these functions. Two popular techniques to allow managers to plan, schedule, and control—PERT and CPM—will then be described in some detail.

PROJECT PLANNING

Projects can usually be defined as a series of related tasks directed toward a major output. A new organization form, developed to make sure existing programs continue to run smoothly on a day-to-day basis while new projects are successfully completed, is called **project organization.**

Project organization

A project organization is an effective way of pooling the people and physical resources needed for a limited time to complete a specific project or goal. It is basically a temporary organization structure designed to achieve results by using specialists from throughout the firm. For many years, NASA successfully used the project approach to reach its goals. You may recall Project Gemini and Project Apollo. These terms were used to describe teams NASA organized to reach space exploration objectives.

The project organization works best when:

1. work can be defined with a specific goal and deadline;
2. the job is unique or somewhat unfamiliar to the existing organization;
3. the work contains complex interrelated tasks requiring specialized skills;
4. the project is temporary but critical to the organization.

FIGURE 16.2

A Sample Project Organization.
(*Source:* R. W. Mondy, R. E. Holmes, E. B. Flippo, *Management: Concepts and Practices,* Boston: Allyn and Bacon, 1983, p. 224.)

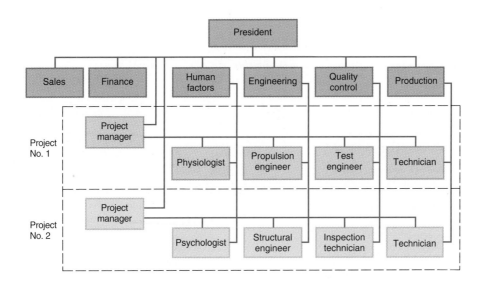

An example of a simplified project organization that is part of an ongoing firm is shown in Figure 16.2. The project team members are temporarily assigned to the project and report to the project manager. The manager heading the project coordinates its activities with other departments and reports directly to top management, often the president, of the organization. Project managers receive high visibility in a firm and are a key element in the planning and control of project activities.

The project management team begins its task well in advance of the project so that a plan can be developed. One of its first steps is to set the project's objectives carefully, then define the project and break it down into a set of activities and related costs. Gross requirements for people, supplies, and equipment are also estimated in the planning phase.

PROJECT SCHEDULING

Project scheduling is determining the project's activities in the time sequence in which they have to be performed. Materials and people needed at each stage of production are computed in this phase, and the time each activity will take is also set. Separate schedules for personnel needs by type of skill (management, engineering, or concrete pouring, for example) are charted. Charts can also be developed for scheduling materials.

Gantt charts

One popular project scheduling approach is the Gantt chart (named after Henry Gantt, who was mentioned in Chapter 1). As seen in Figure 16.3, **Gantt charts** reflect time estimates and can be easily understood. The horizontal bars are drawn

FIGURE 16.3

Sample Gantt Chart. Circled items represent precedence relationships (for example, activity *c*, construct collection stack, may not begin until activity *a*, which is circled, is completed).

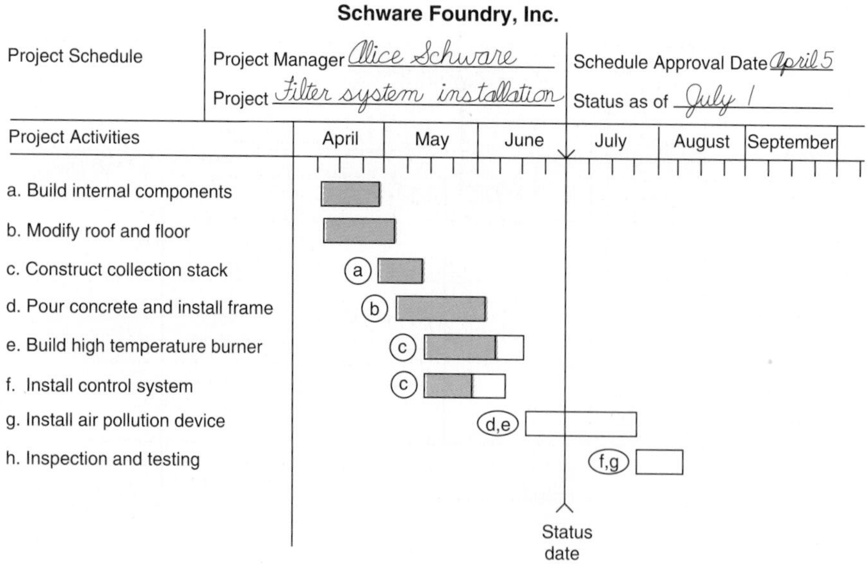

for each project activity along a time line. The letters to the left of each bar tell the planner which other activities have to be completed before that one can begin.

Gantt charts are low-cost means of helping managers make sure that (1) all activities are planned for, (2) their order of performance is accounted for, (3) the activity time estimates are recorded, and (4) the overall project time is developed.

Activity progress is noted, once the actual project is under way, by shading the horizontal bars as an activity is partially or fully completed. For example, we see in Figure 16.3 that activities a, b, c, and d are on schedule because their bars have been shaded up to the vertical status date line. The date line, July 1 in this case, is a status reporting period that lets participants see which tasks are on time, which are ahead of time, and which have fallen behind schedule. Activities e, f, and g are all behind schedule; their bars are not shaded in their entirety or up to the status date line.

Scheduling charts such as this one can be used alone on simple projects. They permit managers to observe the progress of each activity and to spot and tackle problem areas. Gantt charts are not easily updated, though. And more importantly, they don't adequately illustrate the interrelationships between the activities and the resources.

A second example of a Gantt chart is shown in Figure 16.4. This illustration of a routine servicing of a commercial jetliner during a 40-minute layover shows that Gantt charts also can be used for scheduling repetitive operations. In this case, the chart helps point out potential delays.

PERT and CPM, the two widely used network techniques that we shall discuss shortly, *do* have the ability to consider precedence relationships and interdependency of activities. On complex projects, the scheduling of which is almost always computerized, PERT and CPM thus hold an edge on the simpler Gantt charts. Even on huge projects, though, Gantt charts can be used as a summary of project status and may complement the other network approaches.

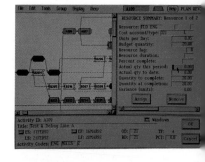

Being able to use powerful project manager software packages such as Primavera (shown here), first requires an understanding of the principles of PERT and CPM. In a competitive job environment, a graduate who has experience with one of the popular programs will find himself or herself a valued member of any organization involved in project planning.

FIGURE 16.4

Service Activities for a Commercial Jetliner During a 40-Minute Layover.

		Time, minutes (0–40)
Passengers	Deplaning	
	Baggage claim	
Baggage	Container offload	
Fueling	Pumping	
	Engine injection water	
Cargo and mail	Container offload	
Galley servicing	Main cabin door	
	Aft cabin door	
Lavatory servicing	Aft, Center, Forward	
Drinking water	Loading	
Cabin cleaning	First class section	
	Economy section	
Cargo and mail	Container/bulk loading	
Flight service	Galley/cabin check	
	Receive passengers	
Operating crew	Aircraft check	
Baggage	Loading	
Passengers	Boarding	

To summarize, whatever the approach taken by a project manager, project scheduling serves several purposes:

1. It shows the relationship of each activity to others and to the whole project.
2. It identifies the precedence relationships among activities.
3. It encourages the setting of realistic time and cost estimates for each activity.
4. It helps make better use of people, money, and material resources by identifying critical bottlenecks in the project.

PROJECT CONTROLLING

The control of large projects, like the control of any management system, involves close monitoring of resources, costs, quality, and budgets. Control also means using a feedback loop to revise the project plan and having the ability to shift resources to where they are needed most. Computerized PERT/CPM reports and charts are widely available today on minicomputers and microcomputers. Some of the more popular of these programs are: Harvard Total Project Manager (by Harvard Software, Inc.), Primavera (by Primavera Systems, Inc.), Project (by Microsoft Corp.), MacProject (by Apple Computer Corp.), Pertmaster (by Westminster Software, Inc.), VisiSchedule (by Paladin Software Corp.), and Time Line (by Symantec Corp.).

These programs produce a broad variety of reports including: (1) detailed cost breakdowns for each task, (2) total program labor curves, (3) cost distribution tables, (4) functional cost and hour summaries, (5) raw material and expenditure forecasts, (6) variance reports, (7) time analysis reports, and (8) work status reports.

PROJECT MANAGEMENT TECHNIQUES: PERT AND CPM

Program evaluation and review technique (PERT)
Critical path method (CPM)

Program evaluation and review technique (PERT) and the **critical path method (CPM)** were both developed in the 1950s to help managers schedule, monitor, and control large and complex projects. CPM arrived first, in 1957, as a tool developed by J. E. Kelly of Remington Rand and M. R. Walker of duPont to assist in the building and maintenance of chemical plants at duPont. Independently, PERT was developed in 1958 by the Navy. The *POM in Action* box, "PertMaster Helps Change the Face of British Airways," illustrates how a PERT program was used by British Airways to schedule implementation of a new corporate image.

The Framework of PERT and CPM

Six steps are common to both PERT and CPM. The procedure is as follows:

1. Define the project and all of its significant activities or tasks.
2. Develop the relationships among the activities. Decide which activities must precede and which must follow others.

POM _in action_

PertMaster Helps Change the Face of British Airways

To transform the corporate image of an international airline is a huge task. Aircraft, check-in desks, lounges, shops, ground vehicles, printed materials—including company stationery, timetables, tickets, baggage tags—and, of course, uniforms were all to be changed. To help British Airways (BA) plan the exercise, a computerized project management package, PertMaster, was used.

The most important representation of an airline is its airplanes. A rollout date for a new prototype plane was fixed for December 4. As many other items as possible were to be ready for that date. BA's first thought was to have a Boeing 747 jumbo jet refurbished for the rollout. Its 747s were already going through a program of interior upgrading to improve passenger amenities. The airline hoped the programs could be linked.

BA called Boeing to find the earliest possible date that a plane from this production line could be completely prepared. Every detail had to be identified—ordering, procuring, and applying the new paint, ordering new upholstery fabrics and new carpets,

obtaining all the trim for the interior, stripping out the old interior and fitting the new. The data was fed into the PertMaster program and the critical path established. PertMaster revealed what had been feared. The first plane that could have been fitted out would not be ready before the middle of January.

Therefore, they had to use a smaller aircraft than they had wanted. A new Boeing 737 was available at the Boeing plant in Seattle in early November. BA concentrated on this plane and ordered just enough material to change the exterior and interior on the one 737 for the rollout date.

Using a smaller plane turned out to be a good idea in the end because it was possible to make it the star of the show. A public relations firm that specialized in pizzazzy affairs was hired to build an auditorium inside a hangar at Heathrow Airport. The 737 appeared on the stage amid a brilliant light show.

Source: Industrial Management and Data Systems, March–April 1986, pp. 6–7.

3. Draw the network connecting all of the activities.

4. Assign time and/or cost estimates to each activity.

5. Compute the longest time path through the network; this is called the **critical path.**   **Critical path**

6. Use the network to help plan, schedule, monitor, and control the project.

Step 5, finding the critical path, is a major part of controlling a project. The activities on the critical path represent tasks that will delay the entire project if they are delayed. Managers derive flexibility by identifying noncritical activities and replanning, rescheduling, and reallocating resources such as labor and finances.

Although PERT and CPM differ to some extent in terminology and in the construction of the network, their objectives are the same. Furthermore, the analysis used in both techniques is very similar. The major difference is that PERT employs three time estimates for each activity. Each estimate has an associated probability of occurrence, which, in turn, is used in computing expected values and standard deviations for the activity times. CPM makes the assumption that activity times are known with certainty, and hence only one time factor is given for each activity.

For purposes of illustration, this section concentrates on a discussion of PERT and PERT/Cost. PERT/Cost is a technique that combines the benefits of both PERT and CPM. Most of the comments and procedures described, however, apply just as well to CPM.

PERT, PERT/Cost, and CPM are important because they can help answer questions such as the following about projects with thousands of activities:

1. When will the entire project be completed?
2. What are the critical activities or tasks in the project, that is, the ones that will delay the entire project if they are late?
3. Which are the noncritical activities, that is, the ones that can run late without delaying the whole project's completion?
4. What is the probability that the project will be completed by a specific date?
5. At any particular date, is the project on schedule, behind schedule, or ahead of schedule?
6. On any given date, is the money spent equal to, less than, or greater than the budgeted amount?
7. Are there enough resources available to finish the project on time?
8. If the project is to be finished in a shorter amount of time, what is the best way to accomplish this at the least cost?

Activities, Events, and Networks

Event
Activity

The first step in PERT is to divide the entire project into events and activities. An **event** marks the start or completion of a particular task or activity. An **activity,** on the other hand, is a task or a subproject that occurs between two events. Table 16.1 restates these definitions and shows the symbols used to represent events and activities.

This approach is the most common one to drawing networks and is also referred to as the Activity-on-Arrow (AOA) convention. The second convention, not used in this chapter to avoid confusion, is called Activity-on-Node (AON). In AON, nodes are used to designate activities.

Network

Any project that can be described by activities and events may be analyzed by a PERT **network.**

TABLE 16.1 Events and Activities.

NAME	SYMBOL	DESCRIPTION
Event	○ (node)	A point in time, usually a completion date or a starting date
Activity	→ (arrow)	A flow over time, usually a task or subproject

---

Example 1

Given the following information, develop a network

ACTIVITY	IMMEDIATE PREDECESSOR(S)
A	—
B	—
C	A
D	B

Activity on arc (AOA) representation.

Activity on node (AON) is another representation.

You will note that we assigned each event a number. As you will see later, it is possible to identify each activity with a beginning and an ending event or node. For example, activity A in Example 1 is the activity that starts with event 1 and ends at node, or event, 2. In general, we number nodes from left to right. The beginning node, or event, of the entire project is number 1, while the last node, or event, in the entire project bears the largest number. In Example 1 the last node shows the number 4.

We can also specify networks by events and the activities that occur between events. The following example shows how to develop a network based on this type of specification scheme.

Example 2

Given the following table, develop a network.

BEGINNING EVENT	ENDING EVENT	ACTIVITY
1	2	1–2
1	3	1–3
2	4	2–4
3	4	3–4
3	5	3–5
4	6	4–6
5	6	5–6

Instead of using a letter to signify activities and their predecessor activities, we can specify activities by their starting event and their ending event.

Beginning with the activity that starts at event 1 and ends at event 2, we can construct the following network.

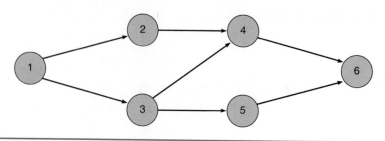

All that is required to construct a network is the starting and ending event for each activity.

Dummy Activities and Events

Dummy activities

You may encounter a network that has two activities with identical starting and ending events. **Dummy activities** and events can be inserted into the network to deal with this problem. The use of dummy activities and events is especially important when computer programs are to be employed in determining the critical path, project completion time, project variance, and so on. Dummy activities and events can also ensure that the network properly reflects the project under consideration. The following example illustrates the procedure.

Example 3

Develop a network based on the following information:

ACTIVITY	IMMEDIATE PREDECESSOR(S)	ACTIVITY	IMMEDIATE PREDECESSOR(S)
A	—	E	C, D
B	—	F	D
C	A	G	E
D	B	H	F

Given these data, you might develop the following network.

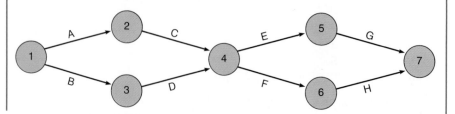

Look at activity F. According to the network, both activities C and D must be completed before we can start F, but in reality, only activity D must be completed (see the table). Thus the network is not correct. The addition of a dummy activity and a dummy event can overcome this problem, as shown below.

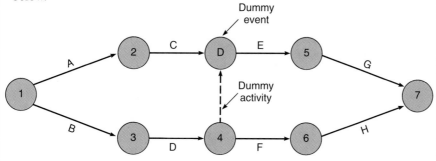

Now the network embodies all of the proper relationships and can be analyzed as usual.

A dummy activity has a completion time, *t*, of zero.

PERT and Activity Time Estimates

As mentioned earlier, one distinguishing difference between PERT and CPM is the use of three **activity time estimates** for each activity in the PERT technique. Only one time factor is given for each activity in CPM.

For each activity in PERT, we must specify an **optimistic time,** a most **probable** (or most likely) **time,** and a **pessimistic time** estimate. We then use these three time estimates to calculate an expected completion time and variance for each activity. If we assume, as many researchers do, that activity times follow a **beta probability distribution,** we can use the formula:[1]

skewed normal

$$t = \frac{a + 4m + b}{6} \quad \text{and} \quad v = \left(\frac{b - a}{6}\right)^2 \qquad (16.1)$$

where

> *a* = Optimistic time for activity completion
>
> *b* = Pessimistic time for activity completion
>
> *m* = Most likely time for activity completion
>
> *t* = Expected time of activity completion
>
> *v* = Variance of activity completion time

Activity time estimates

Optimistic time
Probable time
Pessimistic time
Beta probability distribution

---

[1] Although the beta distribution has been widely used in PERT analysis for 30 years, its applicability has been called into question in a 1986 article. See M. W. Sasieni, "A Note on PERT Times," *Management Science,* **32,** 12 (December 1986): 1662–1663.

In PERT, after we have developed the network, we compute expected times and variances for each activity.

Example 4

Compute expected times and variances of completion for each activity based on the following time estimates:

ACTIVITY	a	m	b
1–2	3	4	5
1–3	1	3	5
2–4	5	6	7
3–4	6	7	8

ACTIVITY	$a + 4m + b$	t	$\dfrac{b-a}{6}$	v
1–2	24	4	2/6	4/36
1–3	18	3	4/6	16/36
2–4	36	6	2/6	4/36
3–4	42	7	2/6	4/36

Critical Path Analysis

Critical path analysis

The objective of **critical path analysis** is to determine the following quantities for each activity:

ES—Earliest activity start time. *All predecessor activities* must be completed before an activity can be started. This is the earliest time an activity can be started.

LS—Latest activity start time. *All following activities* must be completed without delaying the entire project. This is the latest time an activity can be started without delaying the entire project.

EF—Earliest activity finish time.

LF—Latest activity finish time.

Slack time

S—Activity **slack time,** which is equal to (LS – ES) or (LF – EF).

For any activity, if we can calculate ES and LS, we can find the other three quantities as follows:

$$EF = ES + t$$
$$LF = LS + t$$
$$S = LS - ES$$

or

$$S = LF - EF.$$

Once we know these quantities for every activity we can analyze the overall project. Typically this analysis includes:

1. The critical path—the group of activities in the project that have a slack time of zero. This path is *critical* because a delay in any activity along this path would delay the entire project.
2. *T*—the total project completion time, which is calculated by adding the expected time (*t*) values of those activities on the critical path.
3. *V*—variance of the critical path, which is computed by adding the variance (*v*) of those individual activities on the critical path.

Critical path analysis normally starts with the determination of ES and EF. The following example illustrates the procedure.

Example 5

Given the following information, determine ES and EF for each activity.

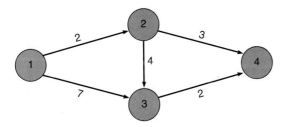

ACTIVITY	*t*
1–2	2
1–3	7
2–3	4
2–4	3
3–4	2

We find ES by moving from the starting activities of the project to the ending activities of the project. For the starting activities, ES is either zero or the actual starting date, say, August 1. For activities 1–2 and 1–3, ES is zero. (By convention, all projects start at time zero.)

There is one basic rule. Before an activity can be started, *all* of its predecessor activities must be completed. In other words, we search for the *longest* path leading to an activity in determining ES. For activity 2–3, ES is 2. Its only predecessor activity is 1–2, for which *t* = 2. By the same reasoning, ES for activity 2–4 also is 2. For activity 3–4, however, ES is 7. It has two predecessor paths: activity 1–3 with *t* = 7 and activities 1–2 and 2–3 with a total expected time of 6 (or 2 + 4). Thus, ES for activity 3–4 is 7 because activity 1–3 must be completed before activity 3–4 can be started. We compute EF next by adding *t* to ES for each activity.

See the following table.

ACTIVITY	ES	EF
1–2	0	2
1–3	0	7
2–3	2	6
2–4	2	5
3–4	7	9

The next step is to calculate LS, the latest starting time for each activity. We start with the last activities and work backward to the first activities. The procedure is to work backward from the last activities to determine the latest possible starting time (LS) without increasing the earliest finishing time (EF). This task sounds more difficult than it really is.

Example 6

Determine LS, LF, and S (the slack) for each activity based on the following data:

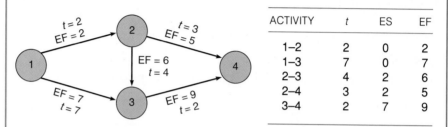

ACTIVITY	t	ES	EF
1–2	2	0	2
1–3	7	0	7
2–3	4	2	6
2–4	3	2	5
3–4	2	7	9

The earliest time by which the entire project can be finished is 9 because activities 2–4 (EF = 5) and 3–4 (EF = 9) *both* must be completed. Using 9 as a basis, we now will work backward by subtracting the appropriate values of t from 9.

The latest time we can start activity 3–4 is at time 7 (or 9 − 2) in order to still complete the project by time period 9. Thus LS for activity 3–4 is 7. Using the same reasoning, LS for activity 2–4 is 6 (or 9 − 3). If we start activity 2–4 at 6 and it takes 3 time units to complete the activity, we can still finish in 9 time units. The latest we can start activity 2–3 is 3 (or 9 − 2 − 4). If we start activity 2–3 at 3 and it takes 2 and 4 time units for activities 2–3 and 3–4, respectively, we can still finish on time. Thus LS for activity 2–3 is 3. Using the same reasoning, LS for activity 1–3 is 0 (or 9 − 2 − 7). Analyzing activity 1–2 is more difficult because there are two paths. Both must be completed in 9 time units.

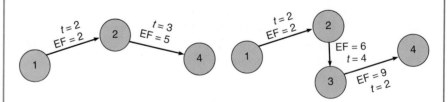

Since both of the above paths must be completed, LS for activity 1–2 is computed from the most binding, or slowest, path. Thus, LS for activity 1–2 *is 1* (or 9 − 2 − 4 − 2) and *not* 4 (or 9 − 3 − 2). Noting the following relationships, we can construct a table summarizing the results.

$$LF = LS + t$$
$$S = LF - EF$$

The U.S. Navy, working with Booz, Allen, and Hamilton, devised PERT to help plan and control the Polaris missile program for submarines. That project involved the coordination of thousands of contractors, and PERT was credited with cutting 18 months off the project length. Today, it is not unusual to see 20-foot-long PERT printouts on the office wall of a project manager working on a Defense Department contract.

or

$$S = LS - ES$$

ACTIVITY	ES	EF	LS	LF	S
1–2	0	2	1	3	1
1–3	0	7	0	7	0
2–3	2	6	3	7	1
2–4	2	5	6	9	4
3–4	7	9	7	9	0

Once we have computed ES, EF, LS, LF, and S, we can analyze the entire project. Analysis includes determining the critical path, project completion time, and project variance. Consider the following example.

Example 7

What is the critical path, total completion time T, and project variance V of the following network?

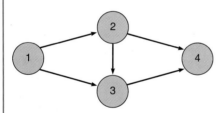

ACTIVITY	t	v	ES	EF	LS	LF	S
1–2	2	2/6	0	2	1	3	1
1–3	7	3/6	0	7	0	7	0
2–3	4	1/6	2	6	3	7	1
2–4	3	2/6	2	5	6	9	4
3–4	2	4/6	7	9	7	9	0

The critical path consists of those activities with zero slack. These are activities 1–3 and 3–4.

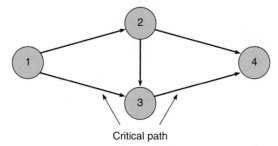

Critical path

The total project completion time is 9 (or 7 + 2). The project variance is the sum of the *activity variances* along the *critical path*, which is 7/6 (or 3/6 + 4/6).

Knowing a network and values for activity times and variances (t and v) makes it possible to perform a complete critical path analysis, including the determination of ES, EF, LS, LF, and S for each activity as well as the critical path, T, and V for the entire project.

The Probability of Project Completion

Having computed the expected completion time T and completion variance V, we can determine the probability that the project will be completed at a specified date. If we make the assumption that the distribution of completion dates follows a normal curve, we can calculate the probability of completion as in the following example.

Example 8

If the expected project completion time T is 20 weeks and the project variance V is 100, what is the probability that the project will be finished on or before week 25?

$$T = 20$$

$$V = 100$$

$$\sigma = \text{Standard deviation} = \sqrt{\text{Project variance}} = \sqrt{V}$$
$$= \sqrt{100} = 10$$

$$C = \text{desired completion date}$$
$$= 25 \text{ weeks}$$

The normal curve would appear as follows:

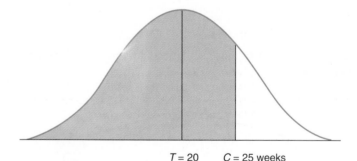

$T = 20$ $C = 25$ weeks

$$Z = \frac{C - T}{\sigma} = \frac{25 - 20}{10} = .5$$

where Z equals the number of standard deviations from the mean. The area under the curve for $Z = .5$ is .6915. (See the normal curve table in Appendix A.) Thus the probability of completing the project in 25 weeks is approximately .69, or 69%.

FIGURE 16.5

Critical Path Analysis.

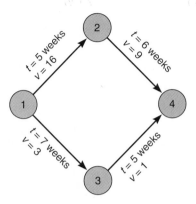

We must point out that the foregoing analysis should be used with caution. If a noncritical path activity has a large variance, it is possible for it to become a critical path activity. This occurrence would cause the analysis to be in error. Consider the network pictured in Figure 16.5. The critical path is 1–3 and 3–4 with $T = 12$ and $V = 4$. If the desired completion date is 14, the value of Z is 1 [or $(14 - 12)/\sqrt{4}$]. The chance of completion is 84% from the normal distribution in the appendix. What would happen if activities 1–2 and 2–4 became the critical path? Because of the high variance, this event is not unlikely. With the same values for C and T, Z becomes 0.4 [or $(14 - 12)/\sqrt{25}$]. Looking at the normal distribution, we see that the chance of project completion is 66%. If activities 1–2 and 2–4 became the critical path, the chance of project completion would drop significantly due to the large total variance $(25 = 16 + 9)$ of these activities. A simulation of the project could provide better data.

Case Study of PERT: Schware Foundry

Schware Foundry, Inc., a metalworks plant in Takoma Park, Maryland, has long been trying to avoid the expense of installing air pollution control equipment. The

TABLE 16.2 Activities and Immediate Predecessors for Schware Foundry, Inc.

ACTIVITY	DESCRIPTION	IMMEDIATE PREDECESSORS
A	Build internal components	—
B	Modify roof and floor	—
C	Construct collection stack	A
D	Pour concrete and install frame	B
E	Build high-temperature burner	C
F	Install control system	C
G	Install air pollution device	D, E
H	Inspection and testing	F, G

FIGURE 16.6

Network for Schware Foundry, Inc.

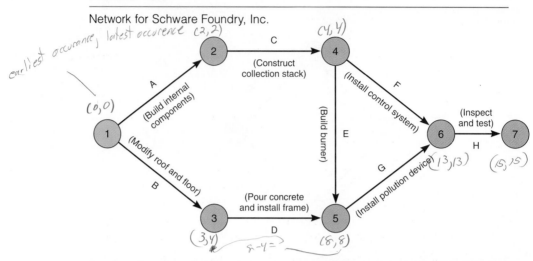

local environmental protection group has recently given the foundry 16 weeks to install a complex air-filter system on its main smokestack. Schware Foundry was warned that it will be forced to close unless the device is installed in the allotted period. Alice Schware, the managing partner, wants to make sure the installation of the filtering system progresses smoothly and on time.

All activities involved in the foundry project are shown in Table 16.2. (You may recall seeing the same data earlier in the Gantt chart example of Figure 16.3.) We see in the table that before the collection stack can be constructed (activity C), the

TABLE 16.3 Time Estimates (in weeks) for Schware Foundry, Inc.

ACTIVITY	OPTIMISTIC a	MOST PROBABLE m	PESSIMISTIC b	EXPECTED TIME $t = [(a + 4m + b)/6]$	VARIANCE $[(b - a)/6]^2$
A	1	2	3	2	$\left(\dfrac{3-1}{6}\right)^2 = \dfrac{4}{36}$
B	2	3	4	3	$\left(\dfrac{4-2}{6}\right)^2 = \dfrac{4}{36}$
C	1	2	3	2	$\left(\dfrac{3-1}{6}\right)^2 = \dfrac{4}{36}$
D	2	4	6	4	$\left(\dfrac{6-2}{6}\right)^2 = \dfrac{16}{36}$
E	1	4	7	4	$\left(\dfrac{7-1}{6}\right)^2 = \dfrac{36}{36}$
F	1	2	9	3	$\left(\dfrac{9-1}{6}\right)^2 = \dfrac{64}{36}$
G	3	4	11	5	$\left(\dfrac{11-3}{6}\right)^2 = \dfrac{64}{36}$
H	1	2	3	2	$\left(\dfrac{3-1}{6}\right)^2 = \dfrac{4}{36}$
			Total	25 weeks	

TABLE 16.4 Schware Foundry's Schedule and Slack Times.

ACTIVITY	EARLIEST START (ES)	EARLIEST FINISH (EF)	LATEST START (LS)	LATEST FINISH (LF)	SLACK (LS – ES)	ON CRITICAL PATH?
A	0	2	0	2	0	Yes
B	0	3	1	4	1	No
C	2	4	2	4	0	Yes
D	3	7	4	8	1	No
E	4	8	4	8	0	Yes
F	4	7	10	13	6	No
G	8	13	8	13	0	Yes
H	13	15	13	15	0	Yes

internal components must be built (activity A). Thus, activity A is the immediate predecessor to activity C. Likewise, both activities D and E must be performed just prior to installation of the air pollution device (activity G). The network for Schware Foundry is illustrated in Figure 16.6.

Table 16.3 shows Schware's optimistic, most probable, and pessimistic time estimates for each activity. It also reveals the expected time (t) and variance for each of the activities. Table 16.4 summarizes the critical path analysis for the activities and network. The total project completion time, 15 weeks, is seen as the largest number in the EF or LF columns of Table 16.4. Operations managers may refer to this as a boundary time table.

Probability of Project Completion. The critical path analysis helped us determine that the foundry's expected project completion time is 15 weeks. Alice knows, however, that if the project is not completed in 16 weeks, Schware Foundry will be forced to close by the state environment controllers. She is also aware that there is significant variation in the time estimates for several activities. Variation in activities that are on the critical path can impact on overall project completion, possibly delaying it. This is one occurrence that worries Alice considerably.

PERT uses the variance of critical path activities to help determine the variance of the overall project. Project variance is computed by summing variances of critical activities.

From Table 16.3, we know that:

CRITICAL ACTIVITY	VARIANCE
A	4/36
C	4/36
E	36/36
G	64/36
H	4/36

Hence the project variance = 4/36 + 4/36 + 36/36 + 64/36 + 4/36 = 3.111.

$$\text{Project standard deviation} = \sqrt{\text{Project variance}}$$
$$= \sqrt{3.111} = 1.76 \text{ weeks}$$

FIGURE 16.7

Probability of Schware Foundry's meeting the 16-Week Deadline.

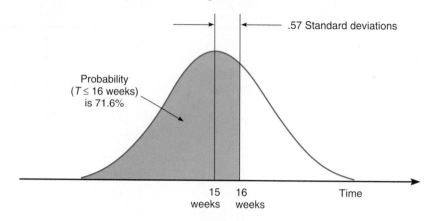

In order for Alice to find the probability that her project will be finished on or before the 16-week deadline, she needs to determine the appropriate area under the normal curve in Figure 16.7. The standard normal equation can be applied as follows:

$$Z = \frac{\text{Due date} - \text{Expected date of completion}}{\text{Standard deviation}} \tag{16.2}$$

$$= \frac{16 \text{ weeks} - 15 \text{ weeks}}{1.76 \text{ weeks}} = \frac{1}{1.76} = .57$$

where Z is the number of standard deviations the due date or target date lies from the mean or expected date.

Referring to the normal table in Appendix A, we find a probability of .71567. Thus, there is a 71.6% chance that the pollution control equipment can be put in place in 16 weeks or less.

What PERT Was Able to Provide Schware Foundry. PERT has thus far been able to provide Alice Schware with several valuable pieces of management information.

1. The project's expected completion date is 15 weeks.
2. There is a 71.6% chance the equipment will be in place within the 16-week deadline. And PERT can easily find the probability of finishing by any other date in which Alice is interested.
3. Five activities (A, C, E, G, H) are on the critical path. If any one of them is delayed for any reason, the whole project will be delayed.
4. Three activities (B, D, F) are not critical but have some slack time built in. This means Alice can borrow from their resources, and, if necessary, she may be able to speed up the whole project.
5. A detailed schedule of activity starting and ending dates has been made available (Table 16.4).

PERT/Cost

Until now, we have assumed that it is not possible to reduce activity times. This is usually not the case, however. Perhaps additional resources can reduce activity times for certain activities within the project. These resources might be additional labor, more equipment, and so on. Although it can be expensive to shorten activity times, doing so might be worthwhile. If a company faces costly penalties for being late with a project, it might be economical to use additional resources to complete the project on time. There may be fixed costs every day the project is in process. Thus, it might be profitable to use additional resources to shorten the project time and save some of the daily fixed costs. But which activities should be shortened? How much will this action cost? Will a reduction in the activity time in turn reduce the time needed to complete the entire project? Ideally, we would like to find the least expensive method of shortening the entire project. This is the purpose of **PERT/Cost.**

PERT/Cost

In addition to time, the operations manager is normally concerned with the cost of the project. Usually it is possible to shorten activity times by committing additional resources to the project. Figure 16.8 shows cost–time curves for two activities. For activity 5–6, it costs $300 to complete the activity in 8 weeks, $400 for 7 weeks, and $600 for 6 weeks. Activity 2–4 requires $3,000 of additional resources for completion in 12 weeks and $1,000 for 14 weeks. Similar cost–time curves or relationships can usually be developed for all activities in the network.

The objective of PERT/Cost is to reduce the entire project completion time by a certain amount at the least cost. Although there are several good computer programs that perform PERT/Cost, it is useful to understand how to complete this process by hand. To accomplish this objective, we must introduce a few more variables. For each activity, there will exist a reduction in activity time and the cost

FIGURE 16.8

Cost-Time Curves Used in PERT/Cost Analysis.

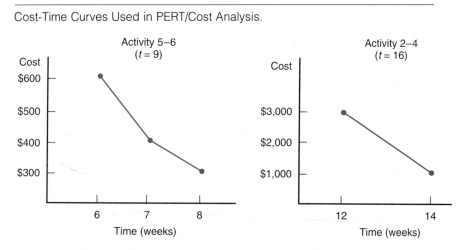

incurred for that time reduction. Let:

M_i = Maximum reduction of time for activity i

C_i = Additional cost associated with reducing activity time for activity i

K_i = Cost of reducing activity time by one time unit for activity i

$$K_i = \frac{C_i}{M_i} \tag{16.3}$$

With this information it is possible to determine the least cost of reducing the project completion date.

Example 9

Given the following information, determine the least cost of reducing the project completion time by one week.

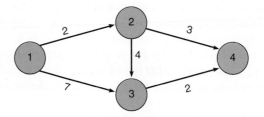

ACTIVITY	t (WEEKS)	M (WEEKS)	C
1–2	2	1	$ 300
1–3	7	4	2,000
2–3	4	2	2,000
2–4	3	2	4,000
3–4	2	1	2,000

ACTIVITY	ES	EF	LS	LF	S
1–2	0	2	1	3	1
1–3	0	7	0	7	0
2–3	2	6	3	7	1
2–4	2	5	6	9	4
3–4	7	9	7	9	0

The first step is to compute K for each activity:

ACTIVITY	M	C	K	CRITICAL PATH
1–2	1	$ 300	$ 300	No
1–3	4	2,000	500	Yes
2–3	2	2,000	1,000	No
2–4	2	4,000	2,000	No
3–4	1	2,000	2,000	Yes

The second step is to locate that activity on the critical path with the smallest value of K_i. The critical path consists of activities 1–3 and 3–4. Since activity 1–3 has a lower value of K_i, we can reduce the project completion time by one week, to eight weeks, by incurring an additional cost of $500.

We must be very careful in using this procedure. Any further reduction in activity time along the critical path would cause the critical path also to include activities 1–2, 2–3, and 3–4. In other words, there would be two critical paths and activities on both would need to be "crashed" to reduce project completion time.

ANOTHER APPLICATION OF PERT

To further illustrate the potential for project management techniques in operations, this section provides an additional illustration dealing with the installation of a financial computer system.

Implementing a Computerized Information System[2]

Table 16.5 and Figure 16.9 on page 708 describe the steps involved in replacing one computer system with another at a large Denver consulting firm. The present computer is at capacity and no longer adequate for all financial applications. The current software systems must all be modified before they can be run on the new

TABLE 16.5 Activities of the Consulting Firm for Installing a New Computer System.

ACTIVITY	DESCRIPTION	EXPECTED TIME REQUIRED TO COMPLETE (WEEKS)
AB	Wait for delivery of computer from manufacturer	8
BC	Install computer	2
CH	General test of computer	2
AD	Complete an evaluation of work-force requirements	2
DE	Hire additional programmers and operators	2
AG	Design modifications to existing applications	3
GH	Program modifications to existing applications	4
HI	Test modified applications on new computer	2
IJ	Revise existing applications as needed	2
JN	Revise and update documentation for existing applications as modified	2
JK	Run existing applications in parallel on new and old computers	2
KP	Implement existing applications as modified on the new computer	1
AE	Design new applications	8
GE	Design interface between existing and new applications	3
EF	Program new applications	6
FI	Test new applications on new computer	2
IL	Revise new applications as needed	3
LM	Conduct second test of new applications on new computer	2
MN	Prepare documentation for the new applications	3
NP	Implement new applications on the new computer	2

Source: S. A. Moscove and M. G. Simkin, *Accounting Information Systems,* 3d ed., New York: Wiley, 1987, p. 556. Copyright © 1987 by John Wiley & Sons, Inc. Reprinted by permission of John Wiley & Sons, Inc.

[2] Adapted from S. A. Moscove and M. G. Simkin, *Accounting Information Systems,* 3d ed. (New York: Wiley, 1987), p. 555.

FIGURE 16.9

PERT Network Diagram for the Consulting Firm.
(*Source:* S. A. Moscove and M. G. Simkin, *Accounting Information Systems,*
3d ed., New York: Wiley, 1987, p. 556. Copyright © 1987 by John Wiley &
Sons, Inc. Reprinted by permission of John Wiley & Sons, Inc.)

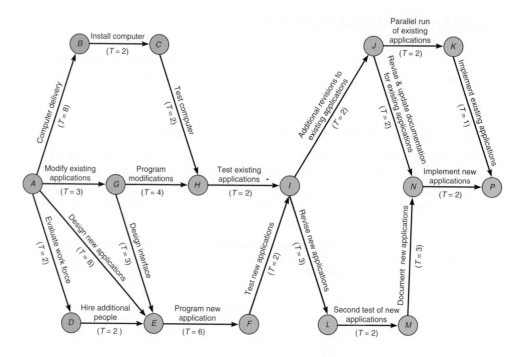

computer. The vice president for computer operations not only identified the activities, but also estimated the completion times for each activity. Identifying the activities and activity completion times for such a project is often a difficult task. However, this task, as represented in Table 16.5 and Figure 16.9, is a prerequisite to successful project management. Problem 16.11 at the end of this chapter asks you to use these data in answering several management questions.

A CRITIQUE OF PERT AND CPM

As a critique of our discussions of PERT, here are some of its features about which operations managers need to be aware.[3]

Advantages:

1. Useful at several stages of project management, especially in the scheduling and control of large projects.
2. Straightforward in concept and not mathematically complex.

---

[3] Two articles describing the use of PERT both candidly and humorously are M. Krakowski, "PERT and Parkinson's Law," *Interfaces,* **5,** 1 (November 1974) and A. Vazsonyi, "L'Historie de la grandeur et de la decadence de la methode PERT," *Management Science,* **16,** 8 (April 1970). Both articles make interesting reading (and are both written in English).

3. Graphical displays using networks help to perceive quickly relationships among project activities.

4. Critical path and slack time analyses help pinpoint activities that need to be closely watched.

5. Networks generated provide valuable project documentation and graphically point out who is responsible for various activities.

6. Applicable to a wide variety of projects and industries.

7. Useful in monitoring not only schedules, but costs as well.

Limitations:

1. Project activities have to be clearly defined, independent, and stable in their relationships.

2. Precedence relationships must be specified and networked together.

3. Time estimates tend to be subjective and are subject to fudging by managers who fear the dangers of being overly optimistic or not pessimistic enough.

4. There is the inherent danger of too much emphasis being placed on the longest, or critical, path. Near-critical paths need to be monitored closely as well.

THE GERT ALTERNATIVE

One more limitation of PERT that we can add to the preceding list is its difficulty in adjusting to uncertainty in the project network. Not only can activity times be uncertain in some projects, but so can the activity itself. The *network* may change based on changes that occur as the project moves ahead. **Graphical evaluation and review technique (GERT)** is an interesting member of the PERT/CPM family of project management models that addresses the uncertainty of activities in networks.

Graphical evaluation and review technique (GERT)

GERT is somewhat similar to PERT in that it consists of events and activities to form a network.[4] Here is how they differ:

PERT	GERT
1. *All* activities must take place.	1. Activities each have a probability of occurrence (from $p = 0.0$ to $p = 1.0$) associated with them. If $p = 1.0$ for an activity, it's just like PERT and is called a "deterministic" branch. If $p < 1$, the activity is called "probabilistic."
2. *All* activities in the project must be successfully completed.	2. Some activities may fail, changing the nature of activities that follow.
3. Looping back to previous activities is not permitted.	3. Looping back (for example, to redo, redesign, or retest any activity) is permitted.

[4] For two of the original papers on the subject, refer to A. A. B. Pritsker and W. W. Happ, "GERT: Graphical Evaluation and Review Technique, Part I," and "GERT, Part II," *Journal of Industrial Engineering,* **17,** 5 (May 1966) and **17,** 6 (June 1966) respectively.

PROJECT SCHEDULING WITH CPM/MRP

CPM/MRP

CPM and PERT both assume that people, machines, and materials are available in the right place, at the right time, and in the right amount. In the real world, though, material has to be ordered in advance, and machinery has to be made available when necessary. Suppose we prepare a master project schedule, list all material requirements, and use an MRP system (as presented in Chapter 14) for procuring them. Essentially, we would have interfaced the CPM and MRP systems.[5] Aquilano and Smith were the first to propose the integrated **CPM/MRP** system. Such a system, still a relatively new research model, has been programmed by IBM and used in the shipbuilding industry[6] and also adapted for use by NASA for flight operations planning and scheduling.[7] The CPM/MRP approach to project scheduling can help operations managers integrate resource procurement into the project schedule. It also permits managers to examine the effects on order release dates of changes in resource lead times and activity completion times.

SUMMARY

PERT, CPM, and other scheduling techniques have proven to be valuable tools in controlling large and complex projects. A wide variety of software packages to help managers handle network modeling problems is also available for use on both large and small computers.

PERT, CPM, PERT/Cost, GERT, CPM/MRP, and the other members of their family will not, however, solve all the project scheduling and management problems of business and government. Good management practices, clear responsibilities for tasks, and straightforward and timely reporting systems are also needed. It is important to remember that the models we described in this chapter are only tools to aid managers make better decisions.

KEY TERMS

Project organization (p. 687)
Gantt charts (p. 688)
Program evaluation and review
technique (PERT) (p. 690)
Critical path method (CPM) (p. 690)

Critical path (p. 691)
Event (p. 692)
Activity (p. 692)
Network (p. 692)
Dummy activity (p. 694)

---

[5] N. J. Aquilano and D. E. Smith, "A Formal Set of Algorithms for Project Scheduling with Critical Path Scheduling/Material Requirements Planning," *Journal of Operations Management,* **1,** 2 (November 1980): 57–67.

[6] R. Gessner, "Use Networking, MRP, or Both?" *Production and Inventory Management Review* (December 1981): 22–23.

[7] E. Steinberg, W. B. Lee, and B. M. Khumawala, "A Requirements Planning System for the Space Shuttle Operations Schedule," *Journal of Operations Management,* **1,** 2 (November 1980): 69–76.

USING AB:POM

Solving the Schware Foundry Example with AB:POM's CPM/PERT Module

The project scheduling module will find the (expected) project completion time for a PERT or CPM network with either one or three time estimates.

Regardless of the option that is chosen, the data screen depends solely on the number of tasks that are in the project network (including dummy tasks).

Program 16.1 contains the input data for Schware Foundry. Note that there are three time estimates for each task. We also entered the predecessors for those activities that had predecessors.

Program 16.2 provides Schware Foundry's completed input repeated, as well as the final output. The CPM/PERT *one time estimate* program contains less output.

Program 16.1

AB:POM's CPM/PERT Module, Data Entry Screen for Schware Foundry

```
— Data file:schware1 ——————— CPM/PERT Project Scheduling ——————— Data Screen —
  Number of activities (1-99)   8
```

```
———————————————————————— SCHWARE  FOUNDRY ————————————————————————

  Task      opt    lik    pes       Predecessors
            time   time   time
  a          1      2      3       —    —    —    —
  b          2      3      4       —    —    —    —
  c          1      2      3       a    —    —    —
  d          2      4      6       b    —    —    —
  e          1      4      7       c    —    —    —
  f          1      2      9       c    —    —    —
  g          3      4     11       d    e    —    —
  h          1      2      3       f    g    —    —
```

Program 16.2

Solution to Schware Foundry Example Using AB:POM

SCHWARE FOUNDRY

Project completion time = 15   Project standard deviation = 1.7638

Task	opt time	lik time	pes time	Time	ES	EF	LS	LF	slack	σ
a	1	2	3	2	0	2	0	2	0	.33
b	2	3	4	3	0	3	1	4	1	.33
c	1	2	3	2	2	4	2	4	0	.33
d	2	4	6	4	3	7	4	8	1	.67
e	1	4	7	4	4	8	4	8	0	1
f	1	2	9	3	4	7	10	13	6	1.33
g	3	4	11	5	8	13	8	13	0	1.33
h	1	2	3	2	13	15	13	15	0	.33

SOLVED PROBLEMS

Solved Problem 16.1

Construct a network based on the following table.

ACTIVITY			
1–2	1–4	3–5	5–7
1–3	2–5	4–6	6–7

Solution

Solved Problem 16.2

Insert dummy activities and events to correct the following network:

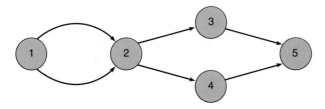

Solution

We can add the following dummy activity and dummy event to obtain the correct network:

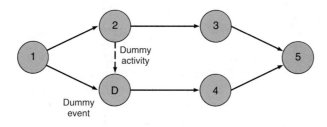

Solved Problem 16.3

Calculate the critical path, completion time T, and variance V based on the following information.

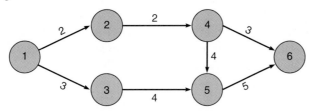

ACTIVITY	t	v	ES	EF	LS	LF	S
1–2	2	2/6	0	2	0	2	0
1–3	3	2/6	0	3	1	4	1
2–4	2	4/6	2	4	2	4	0
3–5	4	4/6	3	7	4	8	1
4–5	4	2/6	4	8	4	8	0
4–6	3	1/6	4	7	10	13	6
5–6	5	1/6	8	13	8	13	0

Solution

We conclude that the critical path is $1 \rightarrow 2 \rightarrow 4 \rightarrow 5 \rightarrow 6$.

$$T = 2 + 2 + 4 + 5 = 13$$

and

$$V = \frac{2}{6} + \frac{4}{6} + \frac{2}{6} + \frac{1}{6} = \frac{9}{6} = 1.5$$

Solved Problem 16.4

Given the following information, perform a critical path analysis.

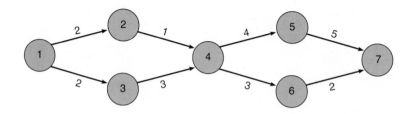

ACTIVITY	t	v	ACTIVITY	t	v
1–2	2	1/6	4–5	4	4/6
1–3	2	1/6	4–6	3	2/6
2–4	1	2/6	5–7	5	1/6
3–4	3	2/6	6–7	2	2/6

Solution

The solution begins with the determination of ES, EF, LS, LF, and S. We can find these values from the above information and then enter them into the following table:

ACTIVITY	t	v	ES	EF	LS	LF	S
1–2	2	1/6	0	2	2	4	2
1–3	2	1/6	0	2	0	2	0
2–4	1	2/6	2	3	4	5	2
3–4	3	2/6	2	5	2	5	0
4–5	4	4/6	5	9	5	9	0
4–6	3	2/6	5	8	9	12	4
5–7	5	1/6	9	14	9	14	0
6–7	2	2/6	8	10	12	14	4

Then we can find the critical path, T, and V. The critical path 1–3, 3–4, 4–5, 5–7.

$$T = 2 + 3 + 4 + 5 = 14 \quad \text{and} \quad V = \frac{1}{6} + \frac{2}{6} + \frac{4}{6} + \frac{1}{6} = \frac{8}{6}$$

Solved Problem 16.5

The following information has been computed from a project:

$$T = 62 \text{ weeks}$$
$$V = 81$$

What is the probability that the project will be completed 18 weeks *before* its expected completion date?

Solution

The desired completion date is 18 weeks before the expected completion date, 62 weeks. The desired completion date is 44 (or 62 − 18) weeks.

$$Z = \frac{C - T}{\sigma} = \frac{44 - 62}{9} = \frac{-18}{9} = -2.0$$

The normal curve appears as follows:

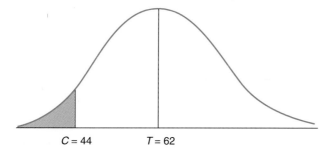

$C = 44 \qquad T = 62$

Because the normal curve is symmetrical and table values are calculated for positive values of Z, the area desired is equal to 1 − (table value). For $Z = +2.0$, the area from the table is .97725. Thus the area, corresponding to a Z value of −2.0, is .02275 (or 1 − 0.97725). Hence the probability of completing the project 18 weeks before the expected completion date is approximately .02, or 2%.

Solved Problem 16.6

Determine the least cost of reducing the project completion date by three months based on the following information:

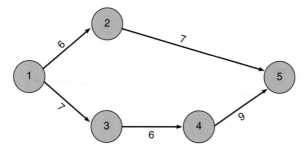

ACTIVITY	t (MONTHS)	M (MONTHS)	C
1–2	6	2	$400
1–3	7	2	500
2–5	7	1	300
3–4	6	2	600
4–5	9	1	200

Solution

The first step in this problem is to compute ES, EF, LS, LF, and S for each activity.

ACTIVITY	ES	EF	LS	LF	S
1–2	0	6	9	15	9
1–3	0	7	0	7	0
2–5	6	13	15	22	9
3–4	7	13	7	13	0
4–5	13	22	13	22	0

The critical path consists of activities 1–3, 3–4, and 4–5.

Next, K must be computed for each activity by dividing C by M for each activity.

ACTIVITY	M	C	K	CRITICAL PATH?
1–2	2	$400	$200/mo.	No
1–3	2	500	250/mo.	Yes
2–5	1	300	300/mo.	No
3–4	2	600	300/mo.	Yes
4–5	1	200	200/mo.	Yes

Finally, we will select that activity on the critical path with the smallest K_i value. This is activity 4–5. Thus we can reduce the total project completion date by one month (because $M = 1$ month) for an additional cost of $200. We still need to reduce the project completion date by two more months. This reduction can be achieved at least cost along the critical path by reducing activity 1–3 by two months for an additional cost of $500. This solution is summarized in the following table:

ACTIVITY	MONTHS REDUCED	COST
4–5	1	$200
1–3	2	500
	Total:	$700

DISCUSSION QUESTIONS

1. What are some of the questions that can be answered with PERT and CPM?

2. What is an activity? What is an event? What is an immediate predecessor?

3. Describe how expected activity times and variances can be computed in a PERT network.

4. Briefly discuss what is meant by critical path analysis. What are critical path activities and why are they important?

5. What are the earliest activity start time and latest activity start time and how are they computed?

6. Describe the meaning of slack and discuss how it can be determined.

7. How can we determine the probability that a project will be completed by a certain date? What assumptions are made in this computation?

8. Briefly describe PERT/Cost and how it is used.

9. What is crashing and how is it done by hand?

10. How does GERT differ from PERT?

11. Explain why CPM/MRP is a useful scheduling tool.

PROBLEMS

· **16.1** Sally Rider is the personnel director of Babson and Willcount, a company that specializes in consulting and research. One of the training programs that Sally is considering for the middle-level managers of Babson and Willcount is leadership training. Sally has listed a number of activities that must be completed before a training program of this nature could be conducted. The activities and immediate predecessors appear in the accompanying table.

ACTIVITY	IMMEDIATE PREDECESSOR	ACTIVITY	IMMEDIATE PREDECESSOR
A	—	E	A, D
B	—	F	C
C	—	G	E, F
D	B		

Develop a network for this problem.

 · **16.2** Sally Rider was able to determine the activity times for the leadership training program. She would like to determine the total project completion time and the critical path. The activity times appear in the accompanying table. (See Problem 16.1.)

ACTIVITY	TIME (DAYS)
A	2
B	5
C	1
D	10
E	3
F	6
G	8
Total	35 days

· **16.3** Entriken Machinery specializes in developing weed-harvesting equipment that is used to clear small lakes of weeds. Dick Entriken, president of Entriken Machinery, is convinced that harvesting weeds is far better than using chemicals to kill weeds. Chemicals cause pollution, and the weeds seem to grow faster after chemicals have been used. Dick is contemplating the construction of a machine that could harvest weeds on narrow rivers and waterways. The activities that are necessary to build one of these experimental weed-harvesting machines are listed in the accompanying table. Construct a network for these activities.

ACTIVITY	IMMEDIATE PREDECESSORS
A	—
B	—
C	A
D	A
E	B
F	B
G	C, E
H	D, F

· **16.4** After consulting with Val Karen, Dick Entriken was able to determine the activity times for constructing the weed-harvesting machine to be used on narrow rivers. Dick would like to determine ES, EF, LS, LF, and slack for each activity. The total project completion time and the critical path should also be determined. See Problem 16.3 for details. Here are the activity times:

ACTIVITY	TIME (WEEKS)
A	6
B	5
C	3
D	2
E	4
F	6
G	10
H	7

· **16.5** Zuckerman Wiring and Electric is a company that installs wiring and electrical fixtures in residential construction. Jane Zuckerman has been very concerned with the amount of time that it takes to complete wiring jobs. Some of her workers are very unreliable. A list of activities and their optimistic completion time, the pessimistic completion time, and the most likely completion time (all in days) is given in the table at the top of page 719.

Determine the expected completion time and variance for each activity.

: **16.6** Jane Zuckerman would like to determine the total project completion time and the critical path for installing electrical wiring and equipment in residential houses. See Problem 16.5 for details. In addition, determine ES, EF, LS, LF, and slack for each activity.

ACTIVITY	a	m	b	IMMEDIATE PREDECESSORS
A	3	6	8	—
B	2	4	4	—
C	1	2	3	—
D	6	7	8	C
E	2	4	6	B, D
F	6	10	14	A, E
G	1	2	4	A, E
H	3	6	9	F
I	10	11	12	G
J	14	16	20	C
K	2	8	10	H, I

: **16.7** What is the probability that Zuckerman will finish the project described in Problems 16.5 and 16.6 in 40 days or less?

: **16.8** B&R Manufacturing produces custom-built pollution-control devices for medium-sized steel mills. The most recent project undertaken by B&R requires 14 different activities. B&R's managers would like to determine the total project completion time and those activities that lie along the critical path. The appropriate data are shown in the table below.

ACTIVITY	IMMEDIATE PREDECESSORS	OPTIMISTIC TIME	MOST LIKELY TIME	PESSIMISTIC TIME
A	—	4	6	7
B	—	1	2	3
C	A	6	6	6
D	A	5	8	11
E	B, C	1	9	18
F	D	2	3	6
G	D	1	7	8
H	E, F	4	4	6
I	G, H	1	6	8
J	I	2	5	7
K	I	8	9	11
L	J	2	4	6
M	K	1	2	3
N	L, M	6	8	10

: **16.9** Bill Trigiero, director of personnel of Trigiero Resources, Inc., is in the process of designing a program that his customers can use in the job-finding process. Some of the activities include preparing resumes, writing letters, making appointments to see prospective employers, researching companies and industries, and so on. Some of the information on the activities appears in the table on page 720.

| ACTIVITY | TIME (DAYS) | | | IMMEDIATE PREDECESSORS |
	a	m	b	
A	8	10	12	—
B	6	7	9	—
C	3	3	4	—
D	10	20	30	A
E	6	7	8	C
F	9	10	11	B, D, E
G	6	7	10	B, D, E
H	14	15	16	F
I	10	11	13	F
J	6	7	8	G, H
K	4	7	8	I, J
L	1	2	4	G, H

a) Construct a network for this problem.

b) Determine the expected times and variances for each activity.

c) Determine ES, EF, LS, LF, and slack for each activity.

d) Determine the critical path and project completion time.

e) Determine the probability that the project will be finished in 70 days.

f) Determine the probability that the project will be finished in 80 days.

g) Determine the probability that the project will be finished in 90 days.

: 16.10 Using PERT, Jan Ross was able to determine that the expected project completion time for the construction of a pleasure yacht is 21 months, and the project variance is 4 months.

a) What is the probability that the project will be completed in 17 months?

b) What is the probability that the project will be completed in 20 months?

c) What is the probability that the project will be completed in 23 months?

d) What is the probability that the project will be completed in 25 months?

 : 16.11 Using the information in Table 16.5 and Figure 16.9, provided earlier in this chapter:

a) determine the number of weeks that will be needed to fully implement the new information system

b) identify the critical tasks

c) determine the slack for each activity.

: 16.12 Getting a degree from a college or university can be a long and difficult task. Certain courses must be completed before other courses may be taken. Develop a network diagram, where every activity is a particular course that must be taken for a given degree program. The immediate predecessors will be course prerequisites. Don't forget to include all university, college, and departmental course requirements. Then try to group these courses into semesters or quarters for your particular school. How long do you think it will take you to graduate? Which courses, if not taken in the proper sequence, could delay your graduation?

:**16.13** Stone Builders manufactures steel storage sheds for commercial use. Kevin Stone, president of Stone Builders, is contemplating producing sheds for home use. The activities necessary to build an experimental model and related data are given in the accompanying table.

ACTIVITY	NORMAL TIME	CRASH TIME	NORMAL COST ($)	CRASH COST ($)	IMMEDIATE PREDECESSORS
A	3	2	1,600	1,600	—
B	2	1	2,700	2,700	—
C	1	0	300	600	—
D	7	3	1,300	1,600	A
E	6	3	850	1,000	B
F	2	1	4,000	5,000	C
G	4	2	1,500	2,000	D, E

a) What is the project completion date?

b) Crash this project to 10 weeks at the least cost.

:**16:14** *The Maser is a new custom-designed sports car. An analysis of the task of building the Maser reveals the following list of relevant activities, their immediate predecessors, and their duration.

JOB LETTER	DESCRIPTION	IMMEDIATE PREDECESSORS	NORMAL TIME (DAYS)
A	Start	—	0
B	Design	A	8
C	Order special accessories	B	0.1
D	Build frame	B	1
E	Build doors	B	1
F	Attach axles, wheels, gas tank	D	1
G	Build body shell	B	2
H	Build transmission and drive train	B	3
I	Fit doors to body shell	G, E	1
J	Build engine	B	4
K	Bench-test engine	J	2
L	Assemble chassis	F, H, K	1
M	Road-test chassis	L	0.5
N	Paint body	I	2
O	Install wiring	N	1
P	Install interior	N	1.5
Q	Accept delivery of special accessories	C	5
R	Mount body and accessories on chassis	M, O, P, Q	1
S	Road-test car	R	0.5
T	Attach exterior trim	S	1
U	Finish	T	0

a) Draw a network diagram for the project.

b) Mark the critical path and state its length.

c) If the Maser had to be completed two days earlier, would it help to:
  i) Buy preassembled transmissions and drive trains?
  ii) Install robots to halve engine-building time?
  iii) Speed delivery of special accessories by three days?

d) How might resources be borrowed from activities on the noncritical path to speed activities on the critical path?

*Source of this problem: James A. F. Stoner and Charles Wankel, *Management,* 3rd ed. (Englewood Cliffs, NJ: Prentice-Hall, 1986), p. 195.

Data Base Application

:16.15 The Bender Construction Company is involved with constructing municipal buildings and other structures that are used primarily by city and state municipalities. This requires developing legal documents, drafting feasibility studies, obtaining bond ratings, and so forth. Recently, Bender was given a request to submit a proposal for the construction of a municipal building. The first step is to develop legal documents and to perform all necessary steps before the construction contract is signed. This requires approximately 20 separate activities that must be completed. These activities, their immediate predecessors, and time requirements are given in the table shown below. As you can see, optimistic (*a*), most likely (*m*), and pessimistic (*b*) time estimates have been given for all of the activities described in the table. Using these data, determine the total project completion time for this preliminary step, the critical path, and slack time for all activities involved.

ACTIVITY	TIME REQUIRED (WEEKS)			DESCRIPTION	IMMEDIATE PREDECESSOR(S)
	a	*m*	*b*		
1	1	4	5	Drafting legal documents	—
2	2	3	4	Preparation of financial statements	—
3	3	4	5	Draft of history	—
4	7	8	9	Draft demand portion of feasibility study	—
5	4	4	5	Review and approval of legal documents	1
6	1	2	4	Review and approval of history	3
7	4	5	6	Review feasibility study	4
8	1	2	4	Draft final financial portion of feasibility study	7
9	3	4	4	Draft facts relevant to the bond transaction	5
10	1	1	2	Review and approval of financial statements	2
11	18	20	26	Firm price received of project	—
12	1	2	3	Review and completion of financial portion of feasibility study	8

ACTIVITY	TIME REQUIRED (WEEKS)			DESCRIPTION	IMMEDIATE PREDECESSOR(S)
	a	*m*	*b*		
13	1	1	2	Draft statement completed	6, 9, 10, 11, 12
14	.10	.14	.16	All material sent to bond rating services	13
15	.2	.3	.4	Statement printed and distributed to all interested parties	14
16	1	1	2	Presentation to bond rating services	14
17	1	2	3	Bond rating received	16
18	3	5	7	Marketing of bonds	15, 17
19	.1	.1	.2	Purchase contract executed	18
20	.1	.14	.16	Final statement authorized and completed	19
21	2	3	6	Purchase contract	19
22	.1	.1	.2	Bond proceeds available	20
23	.0	.2	.2	Sign construction contract	21, 22

CASE STUDY

Bay Community Hospital

The staff of the Bay Community Hospital had committed itself to introduce a new diagnostic procedure in the clinic. This procedure required the acquisition, installation, and introduction of a new medical instrument. Dr. Ed Windsor was assigned the responsibility for assuring that the introduction be performed as quickly and smoothly as possible.

Dr. Windsor created a list of activities that would have to be completed before the new service could begin. Initially, three individual steps had to be taken: (1) write instructions and procedures, (2) select techniques to operate the equipment, and (3) procure the equipment. The instruc-

tions and selection of the operators had to be completed before the training could commence. Dr. Windsor also believed it was necessary to choose the operators and evaluate their qualifications before formally announcing the new service to the local medical community. Upon arrival and installation of the equipment and completion of the operators' training, Edward Windsor wanted to spend a period checking out the procedures, operators, and equipment before declaring the project was successfully completed. The activities and times are listed in the table below.

Jack Worth, a member of the Bay Community Hospital

Bay Community Hospital Activities Required to Introduce a New Diagnostic Procedure.

ACTIVITY	DURATION (WEEKS)	IMMEDIATELY PRECEDING ACTIVITIES	IMMEDIATELY FOLLOWING ACTIVITIES
a. Write instructions	2	Start	c
b. Select operators	4	Start	c, d
c. Train operators	3	a, b	f
d. Announce new service	4	b	End
e. Purchase, ship, and receive equipment	8	Start	f
f. Test new operators on equipment	2	c, e	End

CASE STUDY (Continued)

staff, reported that it would be possible to save time on the project by paying some premiums to complete certain activities faster than the normal schedule listed in the accompanying table. Specifically, if the equipment were shipped by express truck, one week could be saved. Air freight would save two weeks. However, a premium of $200 would be paid for the express truck shipment and $750 would be paid for air shipment. The operator training period could also be reduced by one week if the trainees worked overtime. However, this would cost the hospital an additional $600. The time required to complete the instructions could be reduced by one week with the additional expenditure of $400. However, $300 could be saved if this activity was allowed to take three weeks.

Discussion Questions

1. What is the shortest time period in which the project can be completed, using the expected times listed in the table below?

2. What is the shortest time in which the project can be completed?

3. What is the lowest-cost schedule for this shortest time?

Source: W. E. Sasser, R. P. Olsen, D. D. Wyckoff, *Management Service Operations* (Boston: Allyn & Bacon, 1978) pp. 97–98.

CASE STUDY

Shale Oil Company

The Shale Oil Company contains several operating units that comprise its Aston, Ohio, manufacturing complex. These units process the crude oil that is pumped through and transform it into a multitude of hydrocarbon products. The units run 24 hours a day, seven days a week, and must be shut down for maintenance on a predetermined schedule. One such unit is Distillation Unit No. 5, or DU5. Studies have shown that DU5 can operate only $3^1/_2$ years without major equipment breakdowns and excessive loss of efficiency. Therefore, DU5 is shut down every $3^1/_2$ years for cleaning, inspection, and repairs.

DU5 is the only distillation unit for crude oil in the Aston complex, and its shutdown severely affects all other operating units. Some of the production can be compensated by Shale refineries in other locations, but the rest must be processed before the shutdown and stored. Without proper planning, a nationwide shortage of Shale gasoline could occur. The timing of DU5's shutdown is critical, and the length of time the unit is down must be kept to a minimum to limit production loss. Shale uses PERT as a planning and controlling tool to minimize shutdown time.

The first phase of a shutdown is to open and clean the equipment. Inspectors can then enter the unit and examine

the damage. Once damages are determined, the needed repairs can be carried out. Repair times can vary considerably depending on what damage the inspection reveals. Based on previous inspection records, some repair work is known ahead of time. Thorough cleaning of the equipment is also necessary to improve the unit's operating efficiency. The table on page 725 lists the many maintenance activities and their estimated completion times.

Discussion Questions

1. Determine the expected shutdown time and the probability the shutdown can be completed one week earlier.

2. What are the probabilities that Shale finishes the maintenance project one, two, three, four, five, or six days earlier?

3. Shale Oil is considering increasing the budget to shorten the shutdown. How do you suggest the company proceed?

Source: B. Render and R. M. Stair, *Cases and Readings in Quantitative Analysis for Management* (Boston: Allyn & Bacon, Inc., 1982), pp. 94–95.

CASE STUDY (Continued)

Preventive Maintenance of DU5.

ACTIVITIES	TIME ESTIMATES (IN DAYS)		
	Optimistic	Most Likely	Pessimistic
1–2 Circulate wash water throughout unit	1	2	2.5
2–3 Install blinds	1.5	2	2.5
3–4 Open and clean vessels and columns	2	3	4
3–5 Open and clean heat exchangers; remove tube bundles	1	2	3
3–6 Open and clean furnaces	1	2	4
3–7 Open and clean mechanical equipment	2	2.5	3
3–8 Inspect instrumentation	2	4	5
4–9 Inspect vessels and columns	1	2	3
5–10 Inspect heat exchanger shells	1	1.5	2
5–11 Inspect tube bundles	1	1.5	2
6–12 Inspect furnaces	2	2.5	3
6–17 Retube furnaces	15	20	30
7–13 Inspect mechanical equipment	1	1.5	2
7–18 Install new pump mechanical seals	3	5	8
8–19 Repair instrumentation	3	8	15
9–14 Repair vessels and columns	14	21	28
10–16 Repair heat exchanger shells	1	5	10
11–15 Repair tube bundles; retube	2	5	10
12–17 Repair furnaces	5	10	20
13–18 Repair mechanical equipment	10	15	25
14–20 Test and close vessels and columns	4	5	8
15–16 Install tube bundles into heat exchanger shells	1	2	3
16–20 Test and close heat exchangers	1	2	2.5
17–20 Test and close furnaces	1	2	3
18–20 Test and close mechanical equipment	1	2	3
19–20 Test instrumentation	2	4	6
20–21 Pull blinds	1.5	2	2.5
21–22 Purge all equipment with steam	1	3	5
22–23 Start up unit	3	5	10

BIBLIOGRAPHY

Ameiss, A. P., and W. A. Thompson. "PERT for Monthly Financial Closing." *Management Advisor* (January–February 1974).

Clayton, E. R., and L. J. Moore. "PERT vs. GERT." *Journal of Systems Management,* **23** (February 1972): 11–19.

Cleland, D. I., and W. R. King. *Project Management Handbook.* New York: Van Nostrand Reinhold, 1984.

Dequan, C., J. Lei, and P. Chungmin. "Popularization of Management Science in China: Using CPM in a Sugar Factory." *Interfaces,* **16** (March–April 1986): 2–9.

Dusenberry, W. "CPM for New Product Introductions." *Harvard Business Review* (July–August 1967).

Kefalas, A. G. "PERT Applied to Environmental Impact Statements." *Industrial Engineering,* **8** (October 1976): 38–42.

Kerzner, H., and H. Thamhain. *Project Management for Small and Medium Size Business.* New York: Van Nostrand Reinhold, 1984.

Krogstad, J. L., G. Grudnitski, and D. W. Bryand. "PERT and PERT/Cost for Audit Planning and Control." *The Journal of*

Accountancy (November 1977).

Levy, F., A. Thompson, and S. Wiest. "The ABC's of Critical Path Method." *Harvard Business Review,* **41** (September–October 1963): 98–108.

Moder, J., and C. Phillips. *Project Management with CPM and PERT.* New York: Van Nostrand Reinhold, 1970.

O'Neal, K. "Project Management Computer Software Buyer's Guide." *Industrial Engineering,* **19** (January 1987).

Render, B., and R. M. Stair. *Introduction to Management Science.* Boston: Allyn & Bacon, 1992.

Render, B., and R. M. Stair. *Quantitative Analysis for Management,* 4th ed., Boston: Allyn & Bacon, 1991.

Ryan, W. G. "Management Practice and Research—Poles Apart." *Business Horizons* (June 1977).

Total Quality Management

CHAPTER *17*

Motorola Achieves a Competitive Advantage Via Total Quality Management

Motorola decided some years ago to be a world leader in quality. Indeed Motorola is so good that they became the first winner of the Malcolm Baldrige National Quality Award. Motorola believes in Total Quality Management and practices it from the top, specifically from Chairman Robert Galvin. They achieve outstanding quality through demonstrated top management commitment that permeates the entire organization.

To make the quality focus work, Motorola did a number of things:

- aggressively began a worldwide education program to be sure that employees understood quality and statistical process control.

- established goals, namely its Six Sigma program. Motorola's Six Sigma program means that they can expect to have a defect rate of no more than a few parts per million. Motorola's goal is to achieve this level of quality in everything they do in the early nineties.

- established extensive employee participation and a competitive system where employees vie for awards based on performance of their particular work group. This is a worldwide competition. Presentations are videotaped and the competition is intense.

Product Development Control: The development of robust products requires good experimental design and extensive testing. Here Motorola's portable phones, in Accelerated Life Testing (ALT) facility, are undergoing simulated use. This facility tests extreme conditions of temperature shock, dust, rain, and vibration.

Additionally, Motorola established the Motorola Corporate Quality Council (MCQC), which directs quality efforts throughout the company. The Motorola Quality Systems review is an internal audit program in which teams of five people from the MCQC visit a division and spend a week talking with people and measuring operations against stated criteria. The team looks at ten performance factors, factors that are remarkably similar to the Malcolm Baldrige Award criteria (see Table 17.2). Those ten factors are:

1. **Quality management system** Here they look at leadership, style, and effectiveness of management teams in the area of quality.

2. **Product development control** This factor is based on Motorola's Six Sigma manufacturing program.

3. **Purchase material control** This factor considers the level of quality being supplied by vendors and the systems in place to measure vendor quality.

4. **Process development and operational controls** This is aimed at the entire manufacturing control process. The key issue is "Is it working?"

5. **Quality data programs** Are all necessary data available? How is the information used as a tool to improve quality?

6. **Special studies** How sophisticated are the methods? Are they state-of-the-art?

7. **Quality measurement and control equipment** This governs Motorola's standards and calibrations. Is the system that establishes Motorola's own standards good?

8. **Human resource involvement** Are people capable and properly trained? Can the work force do the job assigned?

9. **Customer satisfaction assessment** All Motorola organizations must have methods and systems in place to assess the satisfaction of customers.

10. **Software quality assurance** As software becomes increasingly sophisticated, Motorola determined that it warranted special evaluation.

Motorola's divisions can expect a quality service review every two years. Five members are selected from various parts of the company for each MCQC team; there is no one team that does all the checking. After the review, the general manager and staff have a session with the teams and go over the review. The strengths and weaknesses are discussed and recommendations are given to the local management about improvements that must be made. The system is working; it gives Motorola uniformity and consistency. Corporate goals receive commitment throughout the organization and that is a powerful quality tool.

An emphasis on quality provides a competitive advantage for Motorola.

Source: Adapted from: *Profiles in Quality: Blueprints for Action from 50 Leading Companies,* Allyn & Bacon with Bureau of Business Practice, 1991; p. 15.

Quality Measurement and Control Equipment: When automated inspection devices work, they are used. Here a vision inspection system is verifying placement of components on a printed circuit board.

Human Resource Involvement: With Motorola's strong emphasis on total quality management, Motorola employees are responsible for evaluating their own work, including locating and recording defects. Here an employee is evaluating a cellular phone at a test station.

INTRODUCTION

For almost every product or service, there is more than one organization trying to make a sale. Price may be a major issue in whether a sale is made or lost, but another factor is quality. In fact, quality is often the major issue. And poor quality can be very expensive for both the producing firm and the customer.

Consequently, firms employ quality management tactics. Quality management, or as it is more commonly called, quality control (QC), is critical throughout the transformation process. One of the major roles of the operations manager is to ensure that his or her firm can deliver a quality product at the right place, at the right time, and at the right price. So, although we treat QC as a tactical decision-making topic, we stress that quality can be a long-term strategic issue as well. Quality is not just of concern for manufactured products, either. It is also important in services, from banking to hospital care to education.

We begin this chapter with an attempt to define just what quality really is. We will look at the major dimensions of quality, why quality is important, and the evolution of quality as a major production issue. Then we look at a variety of management issues related to quality. In the supplement to this chapter, we will deal with the two statistical methodologies for quality management: acceptance sampling and control charts.

DEFINING QUALITY

To some people, a high-quality product is one that is stronger, will last longer, is built heavier, and is, in general, more durable than other products. In some cases, this is a good definition of a quality product, but not always. A good circuit breaker or fuse, for example, is *not* one that lasts longer during periods of high current or voltage. (It is a *bad* or defective breaker or fuse if it is too strong.) So the *quality of a product* is the degree to which the product meets specifications.[1] Increasingly, definitions of *quality* include an added emphasis on meeting the customers needs. See Table 17.1.

The variety of definitions of *quality* that appear in Table 17.1 illustrates just how broad the term *quality* can be. The first one (from *Quality Progress*) is similar to our definition above.

One authority on product quality, David Garvin, believes that definitions of quality fall into several categories.[2] Some definitions are said to be *user-based:* They propose that quality "lies in the eyes of the beholder." Marketing people like this approach, and so do customers. To them, higher quality means better performance, nicer features, and other (sometimes costly) improvements. To production managers, quality is *manufacturing-based.* They believe that quality means conforming to standards and "making it right the first time." Yet a third approach is a *product-based* definition, which views quality as a precise and measurable variable.

---

[1] A more general definition has been adopted by the American Society for Quality Control: "The totality of features and characteristics of a product or service that bear on its ability to satisfy stated or implied needs." Ross Johnson and William O. Winchell, *Production and Quality* (Milwaukee, WI: American Society for Quality Control, 1989), p. 2.

[2] David A. Garvin, "What Does 'Product Quality' Really Mean?" *Sloan Management Review,* **26,** 1 (Fall 1984): 25–43.

TABLE 17.1 Several Definitions of Quality.

"Quality is the degree to which a specific product conforms to a design or specification."
    H. L. Gilmore, "Product Conformance Cost," *Quality Progress,* June 1974, p. 16.

"Quality is defined by the customer; customers want products and services that, throughout their lives, meet customers' needs and expectations at a cost that represents value."
    Ford's definition as presented in William W. Scherkenbach, *Deming's Road to Continual Improvement,* SPC Press, Knoxville, Tenn., 1991, p. 161.

"Quality is fitness for use."
    J. M. Juran, ed., *Quality Control Handbook,* 3rd ed., New York: McGraw-Hill, 1974, p. 2.

"The totality of features and characteristics of a product or service that bear on its ability to satisfy stated or implied needs."
    Ross Johnson and William O. Winchelll, *Production and Quality,* Society of Quality Control, Milwaukee, Wisconsin, 1989, p. 2.

For example, really good ice cream has high butterfat levels; fine rugs have a large number of knots per square inch.

Figure 17.1 indicates that a company would like a quality design such that the positive difference between value and cost is greatest. At very low levels of quality, a product will be unsuccessful because it does not work well or must be frequently repaired. The poor-quality product may even be of negative value to consumers. At

FIGURE 17.1

Cost vs. Quality.

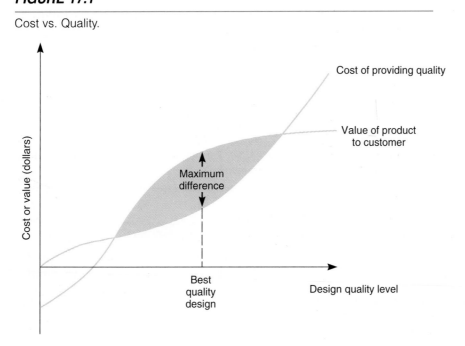

very high levels of quality (which can be very costly), the incremental value of better quality flattens out.[3] As Garvin states: "The characteristics that connote quality must first be identified through market research (a user-based approach to quality); these characteristics must then be translated into identifiable product attributes (a product-based approach to quality); and the manufacturing process must then be organized to ensure that products are made precisely to these specifications (a manufacturing-based approach to quality). A process that ignores any one of these steps will not result in a quality product."[4]

THE DIMENSIONS OF QUALITY

Measuring quality is not always as easy as it may seem. Not only are there quantitative dimensions such as specifications and performance ratings, but there are qualitative dimensions as well. In general, consumers view the quality of a good or service in terms of six dimensions: (1) operation, (2) reliability/durability, (3) conformance, (4) serviceability, (5) appearance, and (6) perceived quality.

1. *Operation.* The primary dimension many people consider is the performance or operation of the product. Does the auto accelerate and stop quickly? Does the insulation keep the house warm? Does the color TV have a clear picture?

2. *Reliability and durability.* These reflect the probability of product failing or deteriorating. Does the auto always start on cold mornings? Do its tires last a long time? How often does one of the parking or tail lights burn out?

3. *Conformance.* Quality of conformance relates to the degree to which a product meets preestablished specifications. For example, are all doors for a particular model of auto within the acceptable range and tolerance of 32 inches ± 0.01 inch?

4. *Serviceability.* This dimension refers to the courtesy, speed, and accuracy of repairs. Mercedes Benz now promises 24-hour repair service in several states.

5. *Appearance.* Appearance and the next dimension, perceived quality, are more subjective. The product's appearance reflects personal feelings and includes such variables as looks, touch, sound, taste, and smell.

6. *Perceived quality.* Many products and services are judged by their brand names, images, or advertising. Sony TVs, Black & Decker drills, and Maytag washing machines have long conveyed an image of quality products, even to people who have never seen or used them.

Dimensions of quality at Velcro USA are noted in the *POM in Action* box, "Quality Depends on Customer Requirements."

"Well, as a last ditch measure, we could improve the corporate image by improving the product."

Source: The Wall Street Journal, with permission of Cartoon Features Syndicate.

WHY IS QUALITY IMPORTANT?

Quality goods and services are strategically important to the company and to the country it represents. The quality of a firm's products, the prices it charges, and the

[3] Also see David A. Garvin, "Quality on the Line," *Harvard Business Review,* **61,** 5 (September–October 1983): 64–75.

[4] See Garvin (Fall 1984): 29.

POM _in action_

Quality Depends on Customer Requirements

An essential element of quality that does not show up on statistical control charts is a customer's perception. Quality is relative depending on what the customer needs. For example, in the shoe business, Velcro USA found that the hook-and-loop on a child's sneaker that lasts only about three months is not critical. But on a $600 knee brace, the hook-and-loop can be a critical element.

In the auto industry, desirability, reliability, and capability are all expected attributes. Car builders want consistent performance, but don't care if the weave on Velcro's tape backing is not uniform. On a knee brace, though, appearance is important and the weave must be consistent.

Suppliers like Velcro have to be sensitive to customer requirements. Whether it is dimension, chemical makeup, performance, or cosmetic appearance, it's all part of the goal of customer satisfaction.

Sources: Harvard Business Review, September–October 1989, pp. 34–40, and _The New York Times,_ October 8, 1991, p. C15.

supply it makes available are all factors that determine demand. In particular, quality affects a firm in four ways:

1. _Company's reputation._ An organization can expect its reputation for quality—be it good or bad—to follow it. Quality will show up in perceptions about the firm's new products, employment practices, and supplier relations. A manufacturing firm, a restaurant, a repair shop, or a college that develops a reputation for poor quality has to work doubly hard to shed that image when the time comes that it either improves or closes up shop. Self-promotion is not a substitute for quality products.

2. _Costs and market share._ Figure 17.2 on page 734 shows that improved quality can lead to increased market share and cost savings. Both can affect profitability as well. Likewise, improving reliability and conformance means fewer defects and lower service costs. One study of air conditioner manufacturers even showed that quality and productivity were positively related. In the United States, companies with the highest quality were five times as productive (as measured by units produced per labor-hour) as companies with the poorest quality.[5]

3. _Product liability._ The courts increasingly hold everyone in the distribution chain responsible for the product. Additionally, organizations that design and produce faulty products or services can be held liable for damages or injuries resulting from their use. The Consumer Product Safety Act of 1972 sets and enforces product standards by banning products that do not reach those standards. Drugs that accidentally cause birth defects, insulation that leads to cancer, or auto fuel tanks that may explode upon impact can all lead to huge legal expenses, large settlements or losses, and terrible publicity.

4. _The international implications._ In this technological age quality is an international, as well as a corporate, concern. For both a company and a country

[5] Garvin (Fall 1984): 36.

FIGURE 17.2

Quality and Profitability.
(*Source:* David A. Garvin, "What Does Product Quality Really Mean?" *Sloan Management Review,* Fall 1984, **26**, 1, p. 37.)

I. Market gains

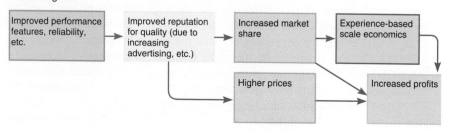

II. Cost savings

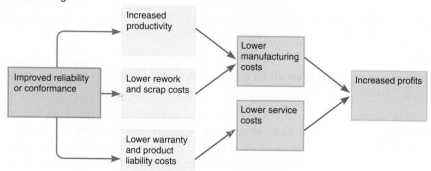

to compete effectively in the global economy, its products must meet quality and price expectations. Inferior products harm firms and nations both at home and abroad and can have severe implications for balance of payments.[6]

HOW QUALITY CONTROL HAS EVOLVED

The field of quality control has come a long way since the days of the Industrial Revolution. In the early 1800s skilled artisans carried out production, with one individual starting and finishing a whole product. With the Industrial Revolution and the factory system, semi-skilled workers, each making a small portion of the final product, became common. With this, responsibility for the quality (and quantity) of the final product tended to shift to supervisors. Inspections ranged in various organizations from nil to 100%, and pride of workmanship declined.

As organizations became larger in the 1900s, inspection became more technical and organized. Inspectors were often grouped together, reporting to a chief inspec-

---

[6] B. Render, "Operations Management in Undeveloped Countries," *Operations Management Review,* (October 1983).

tor. The job of the inspectors was to make sure bad lots were not shipped to customers.

Starting in the 1920s, major statistical QC tools were developed. W. Shewhart introduced control charts in 1924, and in 1930 H. F. Dodge and H. G. Romig designed acceptance sampling tables. Also at that time the important role of quality control in all areas of the company's performance became recognized. In many manufacturing firms the head of inspection and QC was placed on the same level as the production manager.

During and after World War II, the importance of quality grew, often with the encouragement of the U.S. government. Companies recognized that more than just inspection was needed to make a quality product. As Figure 17.3 shows, quality needs to be built into the production process. This requires the involvement of product design engineers, process engineers, QC analysts, inspectors, workers, and equipment, *and* the support of top management. The natural progression of late has been to place the quality control manager on the same organizational level as engineering, purchasing, manufacturing, marketing, and other heads of major functional areas. This is reflected in Figure 17.4 on page 736. (In the airframe and pharmaceutical industries, the directors of quality assurance and manufacturing usually hold the title of vice president.)

In the organization structure of Figure 17.4, the QC manager reports directly to the plant manager. The QC department also directs the broader issues of quality through its staff authority of coordination, consultation, investigation, auditing, and analysis of inspections. The quality control manager also works with the engineering/R&D functions to develop new product specifications and standards. The manufacturing function is increasingly responsible for its own quality.

FIGURE 17.3

Major Elements in a Quality Control System.

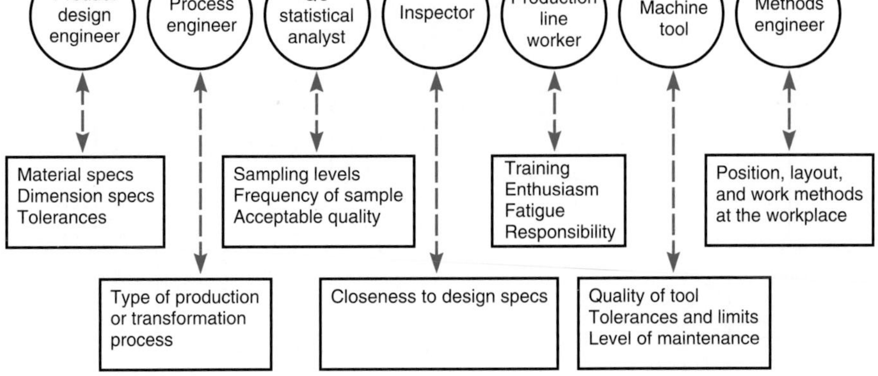

Malcolm Baldrige Awards

In recent years, increased appreciation of the cost of poor quality to the producer, customer, and society has resulted in a renewed emphasis on quality. In 1988, the United States presented its first awards for quality achievement. Known as the *Malcolm Baldrige National Quality Awards,* they are named for former Secretary of Commerce Malcolm Baldrige. Recent winners include Motorola (1988); Milliken and Xerox (1989); IBM, Federal Express, Wallace, and Cadillac (1990); and Solectron, Zytec, and Marlow (1991). The criteria for the awards are noted in Table 17.2.

Deming, Juran, and Crosby

No discussion of the evolution of quality control would be complete without acknowledging the contributions of the individuals whose names are synonymous with quality improvement, W. Edwards Deming, Joseph M. Juran, and Philip B. Crosby. These three individuals have been at the forefront of improving quality worldwide. Their contributions are briefly noted in the *POM in Action* box, "Leaders in the Fight for Quality" on page 738.

TOTAL QUALITY MANAGEMENT

In 1961, the noted U.S. quality control expert, A. V. Feigenbaum, wrote a book called *Total Quality Control,* which delivered a fundamental message: Make it right the first time. . . . The burden of quality proof rests not with inspection but with the

FIGURE 17.4

The Integral Role of QC in the Organization.

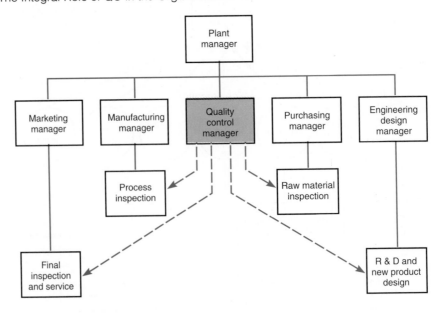

TABLE 17.2 Baldrige National Quality Award Criteria.

EXAMINATION CATEGORIES	Point Values
Leadership	90
Senior Executive Leadership 45	
Management for Quality 25	
Public Responsibility 20	
Information and Analysis	80
Scope and Management of Quality and Performance Data	
and Information 15	
Competitive Comparisions and Benchmarks 25	
Analysis and Uses of Company-Level Data 40	
Strategic Quality Planning	60
Strategic Quality and Company Performance Planning Process 35	
Quality and Performance Plans 25	
Human Resource Development and Management	150
Human Resource Management 20	
Employee Involvement 40	
Employee Education and Training 40	
Employee Performance and Recognition 25	
Employee Well-Being and Morale 25	
Management of Process Quality	140
Design and Introduction of Quality Products and Services 40	
Process Management—Product and Service Production	
and Delivery Processes 35	
Process Management—Business Processes and Support Services . . .30	
Supplier Quality 20	
Quality Assessment 15	
Quality and Operational Results	180
Product and Service Quality Results 75	
Company Operational Results 45	
Business Process and Support Service Results 25	
Supplier Quality Results 35	
Customer Focus and Satisfaction	300
Customer Relationship Management 65	
Commitment to Customers 15	
Customer Satisfaction Determination 35	
Customer Satisfaction Results 75	
Customer Satisfaction Comparison 75	
Future Requirements and Expectations of Customers 35	
TOTAL POINTS	1000

Source: 1992 Award Criteria, *The Malcolm Baldrige National Quality Award,* United States Department of Commerce.

In an effort to bring the company-wide quality control message to Northrop employees working on the Stealth Bomber program, Northrop had each employee sign a giant scroll. The scroll, which reads "Total Quality Control on the B-2 Begins with Me," hangs above the B-2 assembly line symbolizing employee commitment to quality. Current quality programs are an outgrowth of quality circles first established by Northrop in the late 1970s and a more recent program called Employee Performance and Recognition (EPR).

POM _in action_

Leaders in the Fight for Quality

Deming. Once a year in Japan the TV sets are tuned to the awarding of the Deming Prize. It is a national event. The awarding is somewhat like the Academy Awards in America. What is a Deming Prize? The Deming Prize is _the_ quality control award of Japan. It is named in honor of an American, W. Edwards Deming. After World War II Deming went to Japan to teach quality. And the Japanese learned. Deming remains a spokesman for company-wide participation in the battle for quality. He is outspoken in his quality crusade that management must accept responsibility for building good systems. The employee, regardless of her or his dedication, cannot produce products that on the average exceed the quality of what the process is capable of producing. (See Edward W. Deming, _Out of the Crisis,_ Cambridge, Mass., Center for Advanced Engineering Study, 1986.)

Juran. J. M. Juran was also a pioneer in teaching the Japanese how to improve quality. Like Deming,

Juran believes strongly in top management commitment, support, and involvement in the quality effort. He is also a believer in teams that continually seek to raise quality standards. Juran varies from Deming somewhat in focusing on the customer in an effort to define quality as fitness for use, not necessarily the written specifications. (See J. M. Juran, _Quality Control Handbook,_ New York: McGraw-Hill, 1974.)

Crosby. _Quality Is Free_ was Philip B. Crosby's attention-getting book published in 1979. Crosby's traditional view has been "with management and employee commitment great strides can be made in improving quality." He also believes that in the traditional tradeoff between the cost of improving quality and the cost of poor quality, the cost of poor quality is understated. The cost of poor quality should include all of the things that are involved in _not_ doing the job right the first time. (See Philip B. Crosby, _Let's Talk Quality,_ New York: McGraw-Hill, 1989.)

---

makers of the part: machinist, assembly foreman, vendor.[7] Others joined Feigenbaum and the message has evolved into a crusade known as Total Quality Management.

Total Quality Management

Total Quality Management (TQM) refers to a quality emphasis that encompasses the entire organization, from supplier to customer. TQM emphasizes a commitment by management to have a company-wide drive toward excellence in all aspects of products and services that are important to the customer.[8] TQM is a change from a more traditional U.S. attitude toward quality. That more traditional attitude is compared with the Japanese position in Table 17.3 The Japanese position is closer to what is now referred to in the U.S. as TQM. Some of the issues are cultural in nature; others are merely organizational and capable of being easily modified. Traditionally, in U.S. plants for example, the production department's job was to produce; a question about quality of products was referred to the QC

---

[7] A. V. Feigenbaum, _Total Quality Control: Engineering and Management_ (New York: McGraw Hill, 1961), p. 17.

[8] The term _company-wide quality control_ (CWQC) is sometimes used to describe an organization's commitment to quality; see L. P. Sullivan, "The Seven Stages in Company-Wide Quality Control," _Quality Progress_ (May 1986): 78.

department. In Japan, total responsibility for quality is in the production manager's hands. Similarly, quality efforts in U.S. companies have been more directed toward solving quality problems that have already arisen than toward developing and designing quality into products. The Japanese take just the opposite position.

Lawrence P. Sullivan, Ford Motor Company QC manager, has developed seven steps toward TQM, as shown in Figure 17.5. Accepting that stage seven is a desirable goal, the production manager develops a management plan to attain that seventh step. W. Edwards Deming has developed fourteen points to assist in that journey. His points are shown in Table 17.4. An application of Deming's principals

TABLE 17.3 Traditional Quality Management in the United States vs. Japan.

TRADITIONAL POSITION	JAPANESE POSITION
Quality is a function of how well the product or service meets the specifications	Same as the U.S. position.
Quality depends on all departments— from purchasing to engineering design to production to shipping to service.	Same as the U.S. position.
The quality goal is to reach a preset percentage of defectives.	Accept no defects—insist on perfection.
Quality goals are set one fiscal year at a time.	Strive to improve quality consistently, not once a year, but all the time.
There is an optimal level of quality (as seen in Figure 17.7). Customers will not pay for a higher level.	Increasing quality all the time will increase market share and spur new market demand. (This was suggested in the top of Figure 17.2.)
Control quality is done through inspections during production and through final inspection of completed lots.	Every production worker is responsible for inspection, even if this means stopping the assembly line to correct an observed defect.
Use statistical sampling methods to inspect large lots of completed products.	Inspect each piece as it is produced to catch defects before a whole lot is poorly made. Keep inventory low, using just-in-time concept.
Set acceptable quality levels (AQL) based on sampling tables such as MIL-STD-105D. These levels are stated in number of defects per 100 units produced.	Reject sampling tables, since no level of defects is acceptable. Express defects in number of defects per one million units produced.
Use a random sample, typically of size $n = 5$, to check for process stability.	Use a sample of $n = 2$, consisting of the first piece and last piece produced in each lot to assure stability.
The QC department is responsible for testing/inspection.	The QC department monitors quality, but also teaches and spreads QC information. Actual inspection by workers.
Rework of defective units is done on a separate rework line with its own staff.	Workers or groups correct their own errors, even if they have to stay late. (In reality, very few reworks are needed because of total quality control.)
Janitors keep workplaces clean.	Workers themselves are responsible for housekeeping of their work areas.

Source: Several of these ideas/comparisons were adapted from Richard J. Schonberger's books: *Japanese Manufacturing Techniques,* New York: Free Press, 1982, pp. 47–82; and *World Class Manufacturing,* New York: Free Press, 1986, pp. 122–143.

FIGURE 17.5

The Buildup of Quality in Seven Stages.
(*Source:* L. P. Sullivan, "The Seven Stages in Company-Wide Quality Control,"
Quality Progress, May 1986, p. 78.)

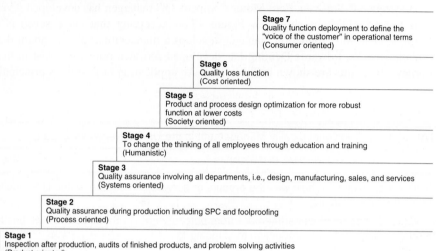

Stage 7
Quality function deployment to define the
"voice of the customer" in operational terms
(Consumer oriented)

Stage 6
Quality loss function
(Cost oriented)

Stage 5
Product and process design optimization for more robust
function at lower costs
(Society oriented)

Stage 4
To change the thinking of all employees through education and training
(Humanistic)

Stage 3
Quality assurance involving all departments, i.e., design, manufacturing, sales, and services
(Systems oriented)

Stage 2
Quality assurance during production including SPC and foolproofing
(Process oriented)

Stage 1
Inspection after production, audits of finished products, and problem solving activities
(Product oriented)

TABLE 17.4 Deming's Fourteen Points for Implementing Quality Improvement

1. Create consistency of purpose.
2. Lead to promote change.
3. Build quality into the product; stop depending on inspections to catch problems.
4. Build long-term relationships based on performance instead of awarding business on the basis of price.
5. Continuously improve product, quality, and service.
6. Start training.
7. Emphasize leadership.
8. Drive out fear.
9. Break down barriers between departments.
10. Stop haranguing workers.
11. Support, help, and improve.
12. Remove barriers to pride in work.
13. Institute a vigorous program of education and self-improvement.
14. Put everybody in the company to work on the transformation.

Source: Deming has revised his fourteen points a number of times over the years. See W. E. Deming, "Transformation of Western Style of Management," *Interfaces,* **15,** 3 (May–June 1985): 6–11; W. Edwards Deming, "Improvement of Quality and Productivity Action Through Action by Management," *National Productivity Review* (Winter 1981–1982):12–22; W. Edwards Deming, "Philosophy Continues to Flourish," *APICS—The Preformance Advantage,* **1,** 4 (October 1991): 20.

POM in action

Putting Deming's Principles to Work in the Service Sector

The service industry in the 1990s distinctly resembles manufacturing in the U.S. in the 1970s. Quality is inconsistent, costs are high, profit margins are narrow, and competition increases each year.

Savin Corp., a copier manufacturer in Stamford, Connecticut, decided to try out a Deming-style quality management approach to improve its service programs. As Robert Williams, Savin's V.P., stated, "A company's fortunes ride on the quality of its service."

Here are just two ways Savin cut service expenses in the past twelve months, while improving service quality:

- Using statistical analysis, Savin found that significant time was being wasted on service calls when engineers had to go back to their trucks for spare parts. The firm assembled a "call kit," to carry onto customer premises, that contained parts with highest probability for use. Now service calls are faster and cost less, and more can be made per day.

- The Pareto principle, that 20% of your staff cause 80% of your errors, was used to tackle the "call-back" problem. Call-backs meant the job wasn't done right the first time and a second visit, at Savin's expense, was needed. Retraining only the 11% of customer engineers with the most call-backs resulted in a 19% drop in return visits.

"Total quality management," according to Williams, "is an approach to doing business that should permeate every job in the service industry."

Sources: Wall Street Journal, Nov. 4, 1991, p. A18; *Training,* March 1991, pp. 50–59; and *Hospital and Health Services Administration,* Spring 1991, pp. 111–120.

is presented in the *POM in Action* box, "Putting Deming's Principals to Work in the Service Sector." Developing total employee involvement is a major ingredient in Deming's implementation plan as well as in TQM. We discuss employee involvement and quality circles in the following sections.

Employee Involvement

An ingredient of TQM is employee involvement. **Employee involvement** means including the employee in every step of the process from product design to final packaging. Employee involvement is encouraged by building communication networks that include employees. This is achieved through open, supportive supervisors; moving quality responsibility from the QC department and inspectors to production employees; building high-morale organizations; and formal techniques such as quality circles.

Frederick W. Taylor said over 100 years ago that management was to help the employee build better systems. This did not mean excluding employees from the opportunity to help in the improvement of the product and process. Consistently, the literature suggests that some 85% of quality problems have to do with materials and processes, not with employee performance. Therefore, the task is to design equipment and processes that produce the desired quality. This is best done with a high

Employee involvement

POM in action

How Velcro Got Hooked on Quality

The phone call from Velcro's manager in Detroit came like a bolt out of the blue one morning. General Motors, a major customer, was dropping Velcro's supplier rating from a 1 (its highest score) to a 4 (its next to the lowest). If a total quality control program at the Velcro plant was not in place in just three months, GM and the rest of the growing auto market could be lost.

On the day of the fateful call, Velcro had 23 quality control workers stationed around its New Hampshire factory. Quality was viewed by machine operators as the job of "those QC people." Inspections were based on random sampling and if a part showed up bad, it was thrown out. With no pressure from GM, or other customers to change, the process did not change.

"To assume that the production employees were causing the waste would have been a mistake," says Velcro's K. T. Krantz, "and to beat on them about it without giving them the tools to deal with the problems would have been a bigger mistake."

The company decided to pay more attention to operators, to machine repair and design, to measurement methods, communications, and responsibilities, and to invest more money in training.

First-line supervisors were a major barrier to making operators responsible for quality, and they had not pressed employees to change. Top managers would hear comments like "My boss won't let me shut the machine down. We make junk on my shift, but he doesn't care."

Statistical quality control was a big step at Velcro in pinpointing where the production process needed the most improvement. Control charts put pressure on the people on the line who didn't believe that quality and quantity go hand-in-hand. As waste goes down, productivity goes up. Over time Velcro was able to pull half its quality control people out of the process, as defects continued to decline.

Sources: Harvard Business Review, September–October 1989, pp. 34–40, and *The New York Times,* October 8, 1991, p. C15 and D22.

degree of involvement by those who understand the shortcomings of the system. Those dealing with the system on a daily basis understand it better than anyone else. When nonconformance occurs, the worker is seldom wrong. Either the product was designed wrong, the system that makes the product was designed wrong, or the employee was improperly trained.[9] Although the employee may be able to help solve the problem, the employee rarely causes it. A similar point is made in the *POM in Action* box, "How Velcro Got Hooked on Quality."

Shigeo Shingo suggests that individual employees self-check their work and that of the employee preceding them.[10] This type of "source" inspection may be assisted by the use of controls such as a fail-safe device called a *poka-yoke*. A **poka-yoke** is a foolproof device or technique that ensures production of good units every time. It uses checklists or special devices to avoid errors, and provides quick feedback of problems. The idea is to *treat the next step in the process as the*

Poka-yoke

[9] See a related discussion in: Asher Israeli and Bradley Fisher, "The Worker Is Never Wrong," *Quality Progress* (October 1989): 95.

[10] Alan Robinson, *Modern Approaches to Management Improvement: The Shingo System* (Cambridge, MA: Productivity Press, 1990).

customer, ensuring delivery of a good product to the next "customer" in the production process.

QC Circles

Another approach to quality improvement is the **quality control circle.** QC circles have proven to be a cost-effective way to increase both productivity and quality.

    Exactly what is a quality control circle? Basically, a group of between 6 and 12 employees volunteer to meet regularly to solve work-related problems. The members, all from the same work area, receive training in group planning, problem solving, and statistical quality control. The circles discuss and recommend ways to improve the quality of their products, the production process in their part of the plant, the working environment, and employee involvement. Circles generally meet about four hours per month (usually after work, but sometimes on company time), and although its members are not rewarded financially, they do receive recognition from the firm. A specially trained manager, called the facilitator, usually helps train the circle members and keeps the meetings running smoothly.

    In the past decade, QC circles have grown dramatically in the United States, Korea, Britain, Brazil, Indonesia, and other countries. We estimate that over 90% of the Fortune '500' companies now have QC programs in their structures. Companies such as IBM, TRW, Honeywell, Westinghouse, Digital Equipment, and Xerox use them and Westinghouse has successfully had over 600 circles operating in its various divisions for over a decade. Defects were often reduced by two-thirds, productivity increased, job satisfaction improved, and turnover and absenteeism lowered.

Quality control circle

The Relationship between Quality and Just-in-Time (JIT)

Let us now look at the strong tie between JIT (discussed earlier in Chapters 11 and 13) and quality. First, JIT cuts the cost of quality. This is because scrap, rework, investment, and damage costs are directly related to inventory on hand. If inventory is reduced, these costs are reduced.

    Second, JIT improves quality. As JIT shrinks lead time, it keeps evidence of errors fresh and limits the number of potential sources of error. JIT creates, in effect, an early warning system for quality problems.[11]

    Finally, quality means a better, easier to employ JIT system. The purpose of keeping extra inventory on hand is partially to protect the company against poor quality resulting from quality variability. If consistent quality exists, JIT allows us to eliminate work-in-process inventory.

Benchmarking

Benchmarking is another ingredient in a company's total quality management program. **Benchmarking** involves selecting a demonstrated standard of performance

Benchmarking

---

[11] However, it must be noted that statistical control charts must be kept on the process, and "correction" made only on statistical signal. Otherwise the result will be increased variability and even more parts out of specification limits due to "over reaction." See Marilyn K. Hart, "Quality Tools for Decreasing Variation and Defining Process Capability," *Production and Inventory Management Journal,* forthcoming.

that represents the very best performance for processes or activities very similar to yours. Michael Spendolini suggests a five-step approach to benchmarking.[12] The idea is to develop a target at which to shoot, then to develop a standard or a benchmark against which to compare your performance. Spendolini's model for developing effective benchmarks is:

- Determine what to benchmark.
- Form a benchmarking team.
- Identify benchmarking partners.
- Collect and analyze benchmarking information.
- Take action (continue the process).

In the ideal situation, you find one or more organizations with operations similar to yours who are demonstratively leaders in the particular areas that you want to study. Then you compare yourself (benchmark yourself) against them. The company need not be in your industry; indeed to establish world-class standards, it may be best to look outside of your industry. This involves finding an industry that excels in the area that you want to benchmark. If one industry has learned how to compete via rapid product development, but your industry has not, it does no good to study your industry. Benchmarks can and should be established in a variety of areas. Total quality management requires measurable benchmarks. NeXT Computer uses benchmarks to drive it toward world-class lean production. The benchmarks for NeXT Computer are shown in Table 17.5

   Total quality management (TQM), with its components of employee involvement, quality circles, Just-in-Time, and benchmarks, should be viewed as an on-

"All quality control does is find our mistakes. I want to start avoiding them."

TABLE 17.5 Benchmarks at NeXT Computer.

New product design to rollout:	nine months
Board re-design to production:	one week
Part count:	220
Suppliers:	60
Yields:	
Complete systems, first time power-up	80–95 percent
Surface mount solder joint failures	4–6 parts per million
First-time turn-on board yields in test	90–95 percent
Cycle times:	
Complete system	1 hour
Board assembly	20 minutes
Scrap	$70–80 per month
Lot size	1
Employee turnover	2 percent
Total employees	480
Manufacturing only	55 (11 percent)

Source: P. E. Moody, "NeXT Computer, the Ultimate Computer Factory," *Target,* **7,** 1 (Spring 1991): 25–31.

---

[12] Michael J. Spendolini, *The Benchmarking Book* (New York: Amcom, 1992).

going process. This is a never-ending process where perfection is never achieved but always sought. The Japanese use the word **Kaizen** to describe an on-going process of incremental improvement. The U.S. tends to use *total quality management, zero defects,* and *six sigma* to describe its continuing improvement efforts. Whatever word or phrase is used, P/OM managers are key players in the never-ending quest for quality.

Kaizen

INTERNATIONAL QUALITY STANDARDS

The emphasis on quality has evolved to such a point that we now see international standards being developed.

Japan's Industrial Standard

The Japanese have even developed a specification for TQM, which is published in Japan as Industrial Standard Z8101-1981. The standard states, "Implementing quality control effectively necessitates the cooperation of all people in the company, involving top management, managers, supervisors, and workers in all areas of corporate activities such as market research, research and development, product planning design, preparations for production, purchasing, vendor management, manufacturing, inspection, sales, and after-services, as well as financial control, personnel administration, and training and education."

Europe's ISO 9000 Standard

The European Community (EC) has developed a quality standard, **ISO 9000.** The focus of the EC standard is to force the establishment of quality management procedures on firms doing business in the EC. The three required components of the standard are to: (1) have a quality control manual that meets ISO guidelines, (2) document quality procedures, (3) ensure written job instructions. Third-party auditors must verify compliance.[13]

ISO 9000

Several factors make ISO 9000 the subject of intense interest in the U.S. and world-wide. These include (1) world-wide acceptance as a quality system standard, (2) the reality that the standards will be applied to some products made or imported by the EC in 1993, and (3) the possible requirement that firms comply with ISO 9000 for product certification.

QUALITY ROBUST PRODUCTS

Most quality problems are the result of product and process design. Therefore, tools are needed to address these areas. Techniques discussed in Chapter 6 include

---

[13] Ian S. Kalinosky, "The Total Quality System—Going Beyond ISO 9000," *Quality Progress,* **23,** 6 (June 1990): 50–54; James L. Lamprecht, "ISO 9000 Impementation Strategies," *Quality,* **30,** 11 (November 1991): 14–17; Rudolph G. Boznak, "Manufacturers Must Prepare for International Quality Initiative," *Industrial Engineering,* **23,** 10 (October 1991): 13–14; Allison Classe, "Flying the Kite of Software Quality Management," *Accountancy* (August 1990): 113–115.

Taguchi method

product development teams, value engineering, and value analysis. A quality improvement technique that is aimed at improving both product and process design is the **Taguchi method,** based on the work of Genichi Taguchi.[14]

Taguchi Concepts

Three concepts are important to understanding Taguchi's approach and method. These concepts are *quality robustness, quality loss factor,* and *target specifications.*

Quality robust

Quality Robust. The Taguchi method calls for making products and processes that are quality robust. **Quality robust** products are products that can be produced uniformly and consistently in a variety of adverse manufacturing and environmental conditions. The idea is to remove the *effects* of adverse conditions instead of removing the causes.

Taguchi suggests that removing the effects is often cheaper than removing the causes and more effective in producing a robust product. In this way small variations in materials and process do not destroy product quality. Taguchi also believes that in this manner products can be produced more uniformly and will perform more consistently in service under a variety of conditions.

Quality loss function

Quality Loss Function. Taguchi has also defined what he calls a quality loss function. A **quality loss function** (QLF) identifies all costs connected with poor quality and shows how these costs increase as the product moves away from being exactly what the customer wants. These costs include not just the cost to the customer in terms of dissatisfaction but also warranty and service costs; internal inspection, repair, and scrap costs; and costs that can best be described as costs to society. Notice that in Figure 17.6(a) the quality loss function is a curve that increases at an increasing rate; it takes the general form of a simple quadratic formula:

$$L = D^2C.$$

where

$$L = \text{Loss}$$

$$D^2 = \text{Square of the deviation from the target value}$$

$$C = \text{Cost of avoiding the deviation}$$

All the losses to society due to poor performance of a product are included in the loss function. The smaller the loss, the more desirable the product. The farther the product is from the target value the more severe the loss.

Target value

Target Value. Taguchi observed that the traditional way of looking at specifications (that is, the product is good until it fails to fall within the tolerance limits) is too simplistic. As shown in Figure 17.6(b), conformance-oriented quality produces more units farther from the target; therefore, the loss (cost) is higher in terms of customer satisfaction and benefits to society. **Target value** is a philosophy of continuous improvement to bring the product exactly on target. Additionally, the farther the product is from target, the more likely will be problems of interfaces and

---

[14] R. N. Kackar, "Taguchi's Quality Control, Parameter Design, and the Taguchi Method," *Journal of Quality Technology* (October 1985): 176–188; and Lance Ealey, "Taguchi Basics," *Quality* (November 1988): 30–32.

FIGURE 17.6

(a) Quality Loss Function; (b) Distribution of Product Produced. Taguchi aims for the target, because products produced near the upper and lower acceptable specifications result in higher quality loss function.

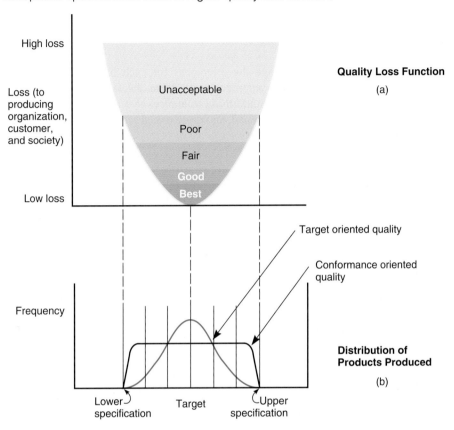

fits with other components of the product. (A door panel that is a quarter inch too small may be all right if the adjacent fender is on target, but if they are both a quarter inch too small, the gap is an unsightly half inch). This is known as *tolerance stackup*.

Implementation of the Taguchi Method

The Taguchi method requires a three-phase implementation. The process is applied during the development and design stage of a product's life cycle. The three phases are *system design, parameter design,* and *tolerance design.* We will now discuss each briefly.

System Design. The system design phase is the investigation phase. The initial design specifications are used to define the variables in the design (i.e., materials, strength, heat transfer, etc.) that are believed to be important. These variables become the "parameters" of the process.

Parameter Design. The parameter design phase is the experimental stage. At this point, experiments are used to determine the importance of parameters.[15] This phase is to show how the parameters impact expected loss. The idea is to find which of the parameters are significant and which are not. The Taguchi method also includes cost reduction. Therefore, the focus at this stage is not only quality, but cost reduction. Costs are to be reduced where changes can be made in product or process without affecting quality.

Tolerance Design. At this stage the tolerances for each parameter are determined. The traditional American approach is to make the tolerances as tight as possible; but under the Taguchi method those tolerances that are critical to producing a quality robust product are tightened, and those that are found to be unimportant are loosened.

THE ROLE OF INSPECTION

Inspection

To make sure an operation is producing at the quality level expected, inspection of some or all of the items is needed. This **inspection** can involve measurement, tasting, touching, weighing, or testing of the product (sometimes even destroying it when doing so). Its goal is to detect unacceptable quality levels before a bad product is produced. Inspection does not, however, correct deficiencies in the system or defects in the products; nor does it change a product or increase its value.

There are three basic issues relating to inspection:

1. how much and how often to inspect;
2. when to inspect;
3. where to inspect.

How Much and How Often to Inspect

Whether it is the quality control staff or the production personnel who conduct product inspections, the issue of how much and how often to inspect is a matter of economics. This financial tradeoff is demonstrated in Figure 17.7.

The optimal level of inspection, in terms of frequency and percent of outputs inspected, is shown in Figure 17.7 where total costs are at a minimum. The two major components of this total are *inspection/control costs* and *defective units costs*. *Inspection and control costs* include supervision and training of the QC inspectors plus expenses for labor, equipment, and supplies involved in the actual testing process. *Defective product costs* include loss of customer goodwill, returned products, scrap and rework costs, customer complaints, and product recall and liability

---

[15] Some aspects of the Taguchi method are controversial. See Myron Tribus and Geza Szonyi, "An Alternative View of the Taguchi Approach," *Quality Progress* (May 1987): 46. They say "... we take strong exception to the methods of experimentation and analysis he and his followers have proposed. We are alarmed at the amounts of money being spent and proposed to be spent teaching large numbers of engineers techniques of experimental design and analysis that, in our opinion, are more expensive than they need to be and are likely to give incorrect answers."

FIGURE 17.7

The Trade-off Curve Between the Cost of Inspection and the Cost Due to Producing Defective Units.

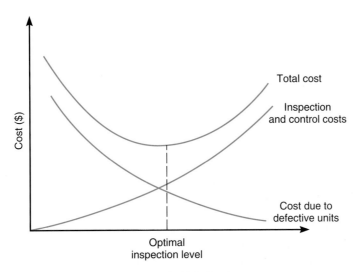

costs. Many of these costs are buried in "overhead" accounts, so defective product costs are often understated.

As expenses for inspection and quality control increase, costs due to defective units tend to decrease. Spending more on inspection and QC reduces the percentage of defects produced, but beyond a certain level this tradeoff is less and less economically. Testing every paper clip and pencil manufactured is uneconomical and it is quite destructive to test every flash cube and bullet produced. Products such as these, and many others, are best tested by sampling plans, which we introduce in the supplement to this chapter.

Sampling is considered adequate when the risk or cost of passing a defective product is small. Studies have shown that carefully developed and executed sampling plans can keep quality levels high. However, inspection is not a substitute for a robust product produced by a good process. In one well-known experiment conducted by an independent research firm, 100 defective pieces were added to a "perfect" lot of items and then subjected to 100% inspection.[16] The inspectors found only 68 of the defective pieces in their first inspection. It took another three passes by the inspectors to find the next 30 defects. The two last defects were never found. So the bottom line is that there is variability in the inspection process. Additionally, inspectors are only human: They become bored, they become tired, and the inspection equipment itself has variability. Even with 100% inspection inspectors cannot guarantee perfection.

[16] *Statistical Quality Control,* Monsanto Chemical Company, Springfield, Mass., p. 19 (undated publication).

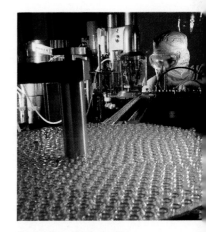

Designing a high-quality process that fills these pharmaceutical bottles in sterile conditions is much more fruitful than having an inspector evaluate the bacteria count on bottles filled in a poor system.

When and Where to Inspect

Deciding when and where to inspect depends on the type of process and the value added at each stage. Inspection in manufacturing firms can take place at any of the following six points if the cost of inspection is less than the likely loss from not inspecting:

1. Inspect at your supplier's plant while the supplier is producing.
2. Inspect at your plant upon receipt of goods from your supplier.
3. Inspect before costly or irreversible processes.
4. Inspect during the step-by-step production process.
5. Inspect when production is complete.
6. Inspect before shipment from your plant.

Fish-bone chart

One of many available tools helpful in identifying possible locations of quality problems and inspection points is the **fish-bone chart.**[17] Figure 17.8 illustrates a simple chart (note the shape resembling the bones of a fish) for an everyday quality control error—a mismatching of nut and bolt. Each bone represents a possible source of error. When such a chart is systematically developed, possible quality problems and inspection points are highlighted.

In *service*-oriented organizations, inspection points can take on a wide range of locations, as illustrated in Table 17.6. Again, the operations manager must decide where inspections are cost-benefit justified.

Inspection of Attributes vs. Variables

Attribute inspection

When inspections take place, quality characteristics may be measured as either *attributes* or *variables*. **Attribute inspection** classifies items as being either good or defective. It does not address the degree of failure. For example, the light bulb

FIGURE 17.8

Fish-Bone chart (Also Called Ishikawa Diagram) for Mismatch of Nut and Bolt.

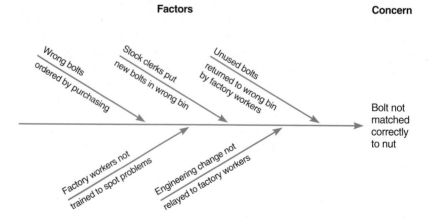

[17] These charts are also known as *cause and effect* diagrams and as *Ishikawa* diagrams.

TABLE 17.6 Inspection Points in Three Service Organizations.

TYPE OF ORGANIZATION	SOME POINTS OF INSPECTION	ISSUES TO CONSIDER
Bank	Teller stations	Shortages, courtesy, speed, accuracy
	Loan accounts	Collateral, proper credit checks, rates, terms of loans, default rates, loan ratios
	Checking accounts	Accuracy, speed of entry, rate of overdraws
Department store	Stockrooms	Clean, uncluttered, organized, level of stockouts, ample supply, rotation of goods
	Display areas	Attractive, well-organized and stocked, visible goods, good lighting
	Sales counters	Neat, courteous, knowledgeable personnel; waiting time; accuracy in credit checking and sales entry
Restaurant	Kitchen	Clean, proper storage, unadulterated food, health regulations observed, well-organized
	Cashier station	Speed, accuracy, appearance
	Dining areas	Clean, comfortable, regular monitoring by personnel

burns or it doesn't. **Variable inspection** measures such dimensions as weight, speed, height, or strength to see if the item falls within an acceptable range. If a piece of electrical wire is supposed to be 0.01 inches in diameter, a micrometer can be used to see if the product is close enough to pass inspection.

Variable inspection

Knowing whether attributes or variables are being inspected helps us decide which statistical quality control approach to take.

EVALUATING THE QUALITY OF SERVICES

Quality of services is more difficult for consumers to measure than quality of manufactured goods.[18] Generally though, a user of a service has a few characteristics and attributes in mind that he or she uses as a basis for comparison among alternatives. Lack of one attribute may eliminate a specific service firm from consideration. Quality also may be perceived as a whole bundle of attributes where many lesser characteristics are superior to those of competitors.

Professors Berry, Zeithaml, and Parasuraman[19] conducted extensive, in-depth interviews with 12 consumer focus groups to try to identify general attributes or determinants of service quality.

---

[18] This section is adapted from Robert Murdick, Barry Render, and Roberta Russell, *Service Operations Management* (Boston: Allyn & Bacon, 1990), pp. 421–422.

[19] L. Berry, V. Zeithaml, and A. Parasuraman, "Quality Counts in Services, Too," *Business Horizons* (May–June 1985): 45–46.

TABLE 17.7 Determinants of Service Quality.

Reliability involves consistency of performance and dependability. It means that the firm performs the service right the first time and also means that the firm honors its promises.

Responsiveness concerns the willingness or readiness of employees to provide service. It involves timeliness of service.

Competence means possession of the required skills and knowledge to perform the service.

Access involves approachability and ease of contact.

Courtesy involves politeness, respect, consideration, and friendliness of contact personnel (including receptionists, telephone operators, etc.).

Communication means keeping customers informed in language they can understand and listening to them. It may mean that the company has to adjust its language for different consumers—increasing the level of sophistication with a well-educated customer and speaking simply and plainly with a novice.

Credibility involves trustworthiness, believability, honesty. It involves having the customer's best interests at heart.

Security is the freedom from danger, risk, or doubt.

Understanding/knowing the customer involves making the effort to understand the customer's needs.

Tangibles include the physical evidence of the service.

Source: Excerpted from A Parasuraman, Valerie A. Zeithaml, and Leonard L. Berry, "A Conceptual Model of Service Quality and Its Implications for Future Research," *Journal of Marketing* (Fall 1985): 44.

Table 17.7 describes their ten determinants of service quality. The same professors also drew the following conclusions from their study:

1. *Consumers' perceptions of service quality result from a comparison of their expectations before they receive their actual experience with the service.* In other words, service quality is judged on the basis of whether it meets expectations.

2. *Quality perceptions are derived from the service process as well as from the service outcome.* The way the service is performed can be a crucial component of the service from the consumer's point of view.

3. *Service quality is of two types, normal and exceptional.* First, there is the quality level at which the regular service is delivered, such as the bank teller's handling of a transaction. Second, there is the quality level at which "exceptions" or "problems" are handled. This implies that a quality control system must recognize and have prepared a set of "plan Bs" for less-than-optimal operating conditions. In addition, when a problem occurs, the low-contact firm may suddenly become a high-contact firm. Thus good customer relations are important in maintaining quality, regardless of the type of service.

As a result of the study's conclusions and subsequent follow-up interviews with service managers, Berry and his colleagues suggest that service quality can be measured by how effectively a service can close the gaps between expectations and the service provided.

STATISTICAL PROCESS CONTROL (SPC)

Statistical process control is concerned with monitoring standards, making measurements, and taking corrective action as a product or service is being produced. Samples of process outputs are examined; if they are within acceptable limits, the process is permitted to continue. If they fall outside certain specific ranges, the process is stopped and, typically, the assignable cause is located and removed.

Control charts are graphs that show upper and lower limits for the process we want to control. A **control chart** is a graphic presentation of data over time. Control charts are constructed in such a way that new data can be quickly compared to past performance. Upper and lower limits in a control chart can be in units of temperature, pressure, weight, length, and so on. We take samples of the process output and plot the average of these samples on a chart that has the limits on it.

Control chart

Figure 17.9 graphically reveals the useful information that can be portrayed in control charts. When the average of the samples falls within the upper and lower

FIGURE 17.9

Patterns to Look for on Control Charts.
(*Source:* Bertrand L. Hansen, *Quality Control: Theory and Applications,* © 1963, renewed 1991, p. 65. Reprinted by permission of Prentice-Hall, Englewood Cliffs, New Jersey.)

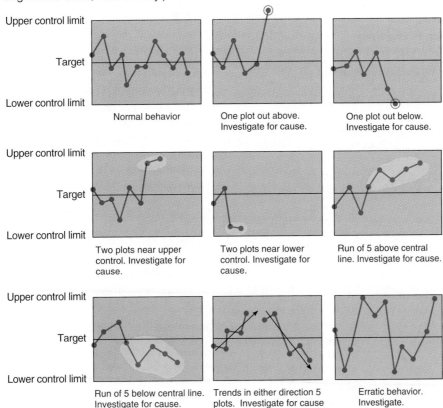

control limits and no discernible pattern is present, the process is said to be in control; otherwise, the process is out of control or out of adjustment.

The supplement to this chapter details how control charts of different types are developed. It also deals with the statistical foundation underlying the use of this important tool.

SUMMARY

Quality is a term that means different things to different people. But to the operations manager quality is the degree to which the product meets specifications. Quality control has become one of the most important precepts of international business.

The expression "quality cannot be inspected into a product" is a central theme of this chapter. Design engineers, process engineers, QC statisticians, factory employees, equipment, and raw materials are all major elements of a quality control system. Equally critical is the role of management, a factor widely recognized by the Japanese and espoused by virtually every leader in the field, including Deming, Juran, and Crosby. The chapter also addresses issues such as the dimensions of quality, the history of QC in organizations, total quality management (TQM), and the role of inspection in the quality process.

KEY TERMS

Total quality management (TQM) (p. 738)
Employee involvement (p. 741)
Poka-yoke (p. 742)
Quality control circle (p. 743)
Benchmarking (p. 743)
Kaizen (p. 745)
ISO 9000 (p. 745)
Taguchi method (p. 746)

Quality robust (p. 746)
Quality loss function (p. 746)
Target value (p. 746)
Inspection (p. 748)
Fish-bone chart (p. 750)
Attribute inspection (p. 750)
Variable inspection (p. 751)
Control chart (p. 753)

DISCUSSION QUESTIONS

1. Provide your own definition of product quality.

2. Name several products that do not require high quality.

3. Has the establishment of the *Malcolm Baldrige Quality Award* had much effect on the quality of products actually produced in the U.S.?

4. How can a university control the quality of its output (that is, its graduates)?

5. What are the major components of the QC system?

6. Find a recent article on quality circles and summarize its major points. Do you think quality circles will be commonplace in all U.S. firms? Why?

7. Highlight some of the major differences between QC in the United States and in Japan.

755

8. Data reveal that the Japanese have a substantial net production cost advantage over the United States for typical subcompact cars. Of this total, 20% is due to Japanese QC systems (excluding quality circles). Why do you think this is so? Can the U.S. automakers narrow this gap?

9. What are the three basic concepts of the Taguchi method?

10. What are the three implementation stages of the Taguchi method?

11. Why is target-oriented performance better than conformance-oriented performance?

12. According to the Berry, Zeithaml, Parasuraman study, what are ten determinants of service quality?

13. What is the quality loss function (QLF)?

14. What does the formula $L = D^2C$ mean?

CASE STUDY

Falls Church General Hospital

Founded in 1968, the Falls Church General Hospital (FCGH) is a privately owned 615-patient bed facility in the incorporated township of Falls Church, Virginia.[20] Falls Church is four miles from downtown Washington, D.C., and is surrounded by the counties of Arlington, Fairfax, and Alexandria, Virginia, all affluent urban/suburban communities with a highly educated population composed largely of employees of the U.S. government and high-tech engineering firms.

Falls Church General Hospital, with 895 employees, provides a broad range of health care services, including drug/alcohol abuse wards, emergency rooms, x-ray and laboratory facilities, maternity wards, intensive- and cardiac-care units, and outpatient facilities. In January 1990, the hospital began a series of ads in the *Washington Post* highlighting its concerned doctors and nurses, its friendly support staff, and its overall philosophy that its employees care about their work and their patients.

The Issue of Assessing Quality Health Care

Quality health care is a goal all hospitals profess, but few have developed comprehensive and scientific means of asking customers to judge the quality of care they receive. A tremendous amount of effort has been devoted to assessing the clinical quality of hospital care; books, journals, and

[20] Some background information for this case was taken from quotes in T. R. Gillem and E. Nelson "Hospital Quality Trends" in J. W. Spechler (ed.), *When America Does It Right* (Norcross, GA: Industrial Engineering and Management Press, 1989), pp. 117–122.

papers on the topic abound. The problem, however, is that past efforts to measure hospital quality have largely ignored the perceptions of customers—the patients, physicians, and payers. Instead of formally considering customer judgments of quality, the health care industry has focused almost entirely on internal quality assessments made by the health professionals who operate the system. In effect, a system for improving health care has been created that all but ignores the voice of the customer.

The board of FCGH believes that all hospitals need to make the transformation from the current practice of attempting to ensure quality to measuring and improving the quality of care from both the external, customer perspective and the internal, provider perspective. Fueled by concerns in recent years about costs and medical practice variation and by the demand for greater social accountability, there is an emerging demand by patients and payers that quality health care be provided at best value.

As board president Dr. Irwin Greenberg recently stated at the annual FCGH meeting,

"As the prices people pay in the future for given levels of service become more similar, hospitals will be distinguished largely on the basis of their quality and value as assessed by customers. We must have accurate information about how our customers, not just the health care professionals who work here, judge the quality of care in this institution. Many hospitals already have some methods for measuring patient satisfaction. A recent survey of more than two hundred hospitals showed that two-thirds routinely

CASE STUDY (Continued)

conduct patient satisfaction surveys. Typically, the surveys are distributed at discharge to patients who are free to respond or not. The main value of such surveys is to gain quick knowledge of problems experienced by patients, many of whom often fill out questionnaires because they are disgruntled about some specific aspect of the care they received."

In response to Dr. Greenberg's statement, and in light of the advertising campaign, hospital administrator Carla Kimball called a meeting of her department heads to discuss the issue of quality. "Can we really deliver on our promises? Or are we in danger of failing to live up to the level of health care our patients expect, and do we risk losing them?" Ms. Kimball asked.

Annie Kerr, head of nursing, continued the debate.

"I agree that surveys, such as the one Dr. Greenberg mentioned in his speech, are valuable. But how do we measure the quality of our health care? Some patients who leave FCGH happy may have actually received poor treatment here. If we are serious about improving the quality of care, we need more *valid* and *reliable* data on which to act. We need answers to specific, quality-related questions about activities in areas that affect patients—admission, nursing, medical staff, daily care, and ancillary staff."

"I have an idea," said Merrill Warkentin, Kimball's staff director. "I just finished reading a book by John Groocock. He's the Vice-President for Quality at TRW, a big manufacturer. He says there are 14 steps in TRW's internal quality

---

TABLE 17.8 Steps in TRW's Quality Audit.

1. *Quality to the customer.* Is conformance of the product to established quality standards measured? Is quality of the organization's product compared with that of competitors' products?
2. *Quality costs.* Have the costs of quality been measured and have areas for possible cost savings been identified?
3. *Design review.* Do procedures exist to review designs for quality? Are these procedures being carried out?
4. *Product qualification.* Have procedures been established and followed to qualify new products before any deliveries to customers?
5. *Product liability.* Has each product been scrutinized regarding safety and are appropriate records kept? Does a written plan exist for dealing with a major product liability problem?
6. *Process capability.* Has the capability of all processes been measured and is that information used in product design and development?
7. *Incoming inspection.* Are incoming lots inspected in an efficient manner and are appropriate records kept?
8. *Supplier quality.* Are suppliers made aware of their quality responsibilities? Are records kept on nonconformance?
9. *Process control.* Has the company developed policies for controlling processes? Have employees been trained to follow those policies?
10. *Inspection and test planning.* Do inspection and test plans exist for all products and are records maintained on the results? Is all test equipment calibrated regularly?
11. *Quality performance indicators.* Are quality performance indicators regularly published throughout the organization and made available to employees?
12. *Employee involvement program.* Are employees involved in quality improvement through some process such as quality circles?
13. *Multifunctional quality improvement team.* Has a quality improvement team covering all functional areas been established to monitor quality and work to improve it?
14. *Quality business plan.* Has quality been integrated into the organization's business plan—and from there into the overall strategic plan?

Source: John M. Groocock, *The Chain of Quality,* New York: Wiley, 1986, p. 250. Copyright © 1986 John Wiley & Sons, Inc. Reprinted by permission of John Wiley & Sons, Inc.

CASE STUDY (Continued)

audits. I made a photocopy of those steps (see Table 17.8 on p. 756). Why don't we consider his approach?"

When the meeting ended, Ms. Kimball read Groocock's list again and began to think about the whole issue of quality control in U.S. firms. It had worked in many manufacturing companies, but could the concepts of quality control really be used in a hospital?

Discussion Questions

1. Why is it important to get the patient's assessment of health care quality? Does a patient have the expertise to judge the health care he or she receives?

2. How might a hospital measure quality?

3. Using the steps in Table 17.8, discuss how each might apply to FCGH.

4. How can the value of a human life be included in the cost of quality control?

5. There are certain parallels between the evaluation of health care quality and educational quality. How are customer surveys used to evaluate the quality of teaching at your institution? How are the results used? Are any other measures available to assess educational quality? What improvements would you suggest to the current system?

Source: Adapted from Robert Murdick, Barry Render, Roberta Russell, *Service Operations Management* (Boston: Allyn & Bacon, 1990), pp. 444–445.

BIBLIOGRAPHY

Allor, P. "Targets for Excellence." *Quality* (September 1988): 18–19.

Camp, R. C. *Benchmarking: The Search for Industry Best Practices That Lead to Superior Performance.* Milwaukee, WI: ASQC Quality Press, 1989.

Crosby, P. B. *Quality Is Free.* New York: McGraw-Hill, 1979.

Crosby, P. B. "Working Like a Chef." *Quality* (January 1989): 24–25.

Crosby, P. B. *Let's Talk Quality.* New York: McGraw Hill, 1989.

Danforth, D. "The Quality Imperative." *Quality Progress* (February 20, 1987): 17–19.

Deming, W. E. *Out of the Crisis.* Cambridge, MA: Center for Advanced Engineering Study, 1986.

Ealey, L. "Taguchi Basics." *Quality* (November 1988): 30–32.

Gabor, A. *Deming, the Man Who Discovered Quality.* New York: Times Books (division of Random House), 1990.

Gitlow, H. S., and P. T. Hertz. "Product Defects and Productivity." *Harvard Business Review* (September–October 1983): 131–141.

Handfield, R. "Quality Management in Japan versus the United States: An Overview." *Production and Inventory Management Journal* (Second Quarter 1989): 79–84.

Hauser, J. R., and D. Clausing. "The House of Quality." *Harvard Business Review,* **3** (May–June 1988): 63–70.

Hosseini, J. R., and N. S. Fard, "A System for Analyzing Information to Manage the Quality-Control Process." *Interfaces,* **21,** 2 (March–April 1991): 48.

Kackar, R. N. "Off-Line Quality Control, Parameter Design, and the Taguchi Method." *Journal of Quality Technology* (October 1985): 176–188.

Kackar, R. N. "Taguchi's Quality Philosophy: Analysis and Commentary." *Quality Progress* (April 1986): 18–23.

Liswood, L. A. "New System for Rating Service Quality." *The Journal of Business Strategy* (July–August 1989).

Mann, N. *The Key to Excellence: The Story of the Deming Philosophy.* Los Angeles: Prestwick Books, 1985.

Messina, W. S. *Statistical Quality Control for Manufacturing Managers.* New York: John Wiley & Sons, 1987.

Noori, H. "The Taguchi Methods: Achieving Design and Output Quality." *The Executive,* **3,** 4 (1989): 322–326.

Roslund, J. L. "Evaluating Management Objectives with the Quality Loss Function." *Quality Progress* (August 1989): 45–49.

Shetty, V. K., "Product Quality and Competitive Strategy." *Business Horizons* (May–June 1987): 46–52.

Tribus, M., and G. Szonyi. "An Alternative View of the Taguchi Approach." *Quality Progress* (May 1989): 46–52.

Wolak, J. "Manage the Process." *Quality* (September 1988): 14–15.

Quality Control Techniques

INTRODUCTION

In this supplement we address two techniques of quality control, statistical process control and acceptance sampling. *Statistical process control (SPC)* is the application of statistical techniques to the control of processes. *Acceptance sampling* is used to determine acceptance or rejection of a lot of material evaluated by inspection or test of a sample.

STATISTICAL PROCESS CONTROL (SPC)

Statistical process control (SPC) is a statistical technique that is widely used to ensure that processes are meeting standards. All processes are subject to a certain degree of variability. Dr. Walter Shewhart of Bell Laboratories, while studying process data in the 1920s, made the distinction between the common and special causes of variation. Many people now refer to these variations as *natural* and *assignable* causes. He developed a simple but powerful tool to separate the two—the **control chart.**

Control chart

The *objective of a process control system is to make economically sound decisions about actions affecting the process.* A process is said to be operating in statistical control when the only source of variation is common (natural) causes. The process must first be brought into statistical control by detecting and eliminating special (assignable) causes of variation.[1] Then its performance is predictable, and its ability to meet customer expectations can be assessed. The ability of a process to operate within statistical control is determined by the total variation that comes from natural causes—the minimum variation that can be achieved after all assignable causes have been eliminated. The objective of a process control system, then, is *to provide a statistical signal when assignable causes of variation are present.* Such a signal can quicken appropriate action to eliminate assignable causes.

Variability in the Production Process

In Figure S17.1 we show the steps in determining process variation. First (see Figure S17.1a), we take a series of small samples and place them on a size scale (the horizontal axis) and indicate on the vertical axis the number of times they occur (their frequency). Eventually, after a number of samples, we have the distributions shown in Figure S17.1(b). The distributions do, of course, differ (see Figure S17.1c) depending upon what our samples revealed. If only natural causes of variation from the process are present, then the distributions will look similar to the one in Figure S17.1(d). If assignable causes of variations (that is, causes that are not an expected part of our process) occur, then our samples will yield unexpected distributions, such as those shown in Figure S17.1(e).

---

[1] Removing assignable causes is work. As Edwards Deming observed, ". . . a state of statistical control is not a natural state for a manufacturing process. It is instead an achievement, arrived at by elimination, one by one, by determined effort, of special causes of excessive variation." See W. Edwards Deming, "On Some Statistical Aids toward Economic Production," *Interfaces,* **5,** 4, 1975, p. 5.

FIGURE S17.1

Natural and Assignable Variation. (a) Samples vary from each other; (b) but they form a pattern that, if stable, is called a distribution; (c) distributions can differ in measure of central tendency, variation, or shape; or any combination of these. (d) If only natural causes of variation are present, the output of a process forms a distribution that is stable over time and is predictable; (e) if assignable causes of variation are present, the process output is not stable over time and is not predictable.

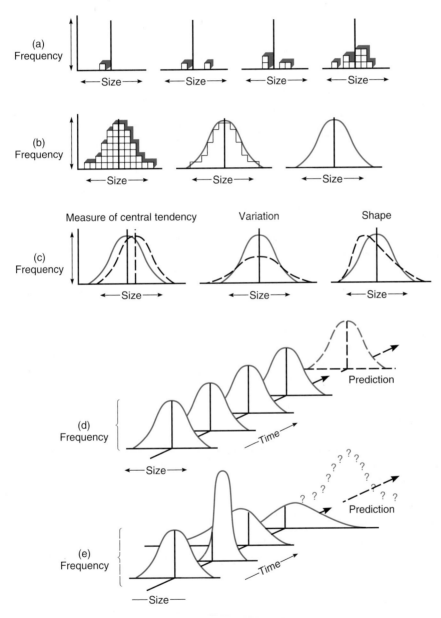

The P/OM manager's job is, of course, to eliminate unexpected variations and keep processes under control. Figure S17.2 shows three types of process outputs:

FIGURE S17.2

Process Control: Three Types of Process Outputs.

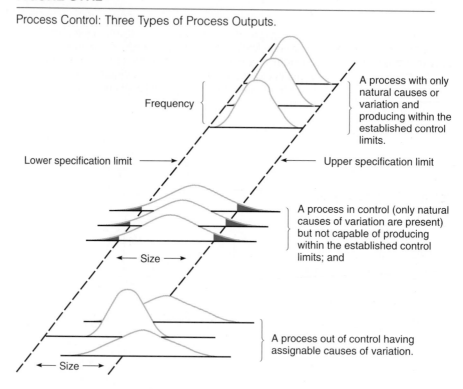

Figure S17.2(a) shows a process out of control; Figure S17.2(b) shows a process in control but not capable of performing *within control limits;* and Figure S17.2(c) shows a process in control and capable of producing within established limits. We now look at how to build control charts that help the P/OM manager do exactly that.

Building Control Charts. When building control charts, averages of small samples (often of five items or parts) are used, as opposed to data on individual parts. Individual pieces tend to be too erratic to make trends quickly visible. The purpose of control charts is to help distinguish between natural variations and variations due to assignable causes.

Natural variations

Natural Variations. Natural variations affect almost every production process and are to be expected. **Natural variations** are the many sources of variation within a process that is in statistical control. They behave like a constant system of chance causes. Although individual measured values are all different, as a group they form a pattern that can be described as a distribution. When these distributions are *normal,* they are characterized by two parameters. These parameters are:

- mean, μ (the measure of central tendency, in this case, the average value)
- standard deviation, σ (variation, the amount by which the smaller values differ from the larger ones)

As long as the distribution (output precision) remains within specified limits, the process is said to be "in control," and the modest variations are tolerated.

Assignable Variations. Assignable variation in a process can be traced to a specific reason. Factors such as machine wear, misadjusted equipment, fatigued or untrained workers, or new batches of raw material are all potential sources of **assignable variations.** Control charts such as those illustrated in Chapter 17 (Figure 17.9 on page 753) and later in this supplement help the operations manager pinpoint where a problem may lie.

Assignable variations

Control Charts for Variables

Control charts for the mean, $\bar{x}$, and the range, R, are used to monitor processes that are measured in continuous units. The **$\bar{x}$-(x-bar) chart** tells us whether changes have occurred in the central tendency of a process. This might be due to such factors as tool wear, a gradual increase in temperature, a different method used on the second shift, or new and stronger materials. The **R-chart** values indicate that a gain or loss in uniformity has occurred. Such a change might be due to worn bearings, a loose tool part, an erratic flow of lubricants to a machine, or to sloppiness on the part of a machine operator. The two types of charts go hand in hand when monitoring variables.

$\bar{x}$-chart

R-chart

The Central Limit Theorem

The theoretical foundation for $\bar{x}$-charts is the **central limit theorem.** In general terms, this theorem states that regardless of the distribution of the population of all parts or services, the distribution of $\bar{x}$'s (each of which is a mean of a sample drawn from the population) will tend to follow a normal curve as the sample size grows large. And fortunately, even if n is fairly small (say 4 or 5), the distributions of the averages will still roughly follow a normal curve. The theorem also states that: (1) the mean of the distribution of the $\bar{x}$'s (called $\bar{\bar{x}}$) will equal the mean of the overall population (called μ); and (2) the standard deviation of the sampling distribution, $\sigma_{\bar{x}}$, will be the population standard deviation, σ_x, divided by the square root of the sample size, n. In other words,

Central limit theorem

$$\bar{\bar{x}} = \mu \quad \text{and} \quad \sigma_{\bar{x}} = \frac{\sigma_x}{\sqrt{n}}$$

Figure S17.3 (on p. 764) shows three possible population distributions, each with its own mean, μ, and standard deviation σ_x. If a series of random samples ($\bar{x}_1$, $\bar{x}_2$, $\bar{x}_3$, $\bar{x}_4$, and so on) each of size n is drawn from any one of these, the resulting distribution of $\bar{x}_i$'s will appear as in the bottom graph of that figure. Because this is a normal distribution, we can state that:

1. 99.7% of the time, the sample averages will fall within $\pm 3\sigma_{\bar{x}}$ if the process has only random variations; and

FIGURE S17.3

Population and Sampling Distributions.

Some population distributions

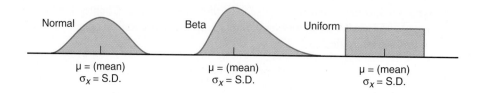

Sampling distribution of sample means (always normal)

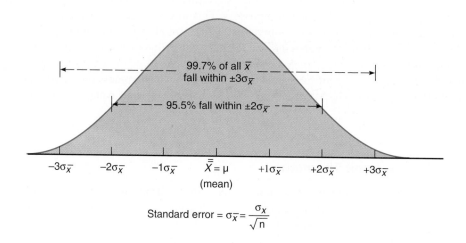

Standard error $= \sigma_{\bar{x}} = \dfrac{\sigma_x}{\sqrt{n}}$

2. 95.5% of the time, the sample averages will fall within $\pm 2\sigma_{\bar{x}}$ if the process has only random variations.

If a point on the control chart falls outside of the $\pm 3\sigma_{\bar{x}}$ control limits, then we are 99.7% sure the process has changed. This is the theory behind control charts. See the *POM in Action* box, "Stalking Six Sigma at Motorola."

Of course, it is possible occasionally to find a point outside the control limits even though the process is really in control. This is called a Type I error. Concluding that a process is in control when it really is *not* is called a Type II error. Type I and Type II errors will be discussed in more detail in the section of this chapter called Acceptance Sampling.

Setting $\bar{x}$-Chart Limits

If we know, through historical data, the standard deviation of the process population, σ_x, we can set upper and lower control limits by these formulas:

POM _in action_

Stalking Six Sigma at Motorola

Motorola's goal is expressed clearly: "Occasional failure is not inevitable. _All_ errors are preventable." This means not only manufacturing flawless products, but eliminating defects everywhere in the firm. No mistyped letters, no late shipments, no poorly conceived policies. To describe its quest, Motorola uses the old engineering and statistics term, _six sigma_.

To clarify the concept, picture a plot of the heights of all male students in your class. The result would be a normal distribution with a mean of about 5'7". Let's say one standard deviation (a sigma) is 1". Then according to the normal distribution, plus or minus one sigma from the mean (i.e., from 5'8" to 5'10") includes 68.3% of all students; plus or minus two sigma includes 95.5% of everyone; and plus or minus

three sigma (from 5'6" to 6'0") includes 99.73% of your classmates. Plus or minus six sigma includes a whopping 99.9999998% of all students.

Using parts produced at Motorola instead of students implies that plus or minus three sigma allows 2,700 errors per million parts to be output. (Since 99.73% are okay, 0.27% are not.) If a product has 1,200 parts in it, then it can _average_ 3.2 defects. This means that, on average, only 40 out of each 1,000 products is shipped with no defects.

Motorola's aim of plus or minus six sigma allows for only 3.4 defects per million. It is like being perfect 99.9999998% of the time.

Sources: Aviation Week and Space Technology, December 9, 1991, pp. 64–65; _ComputerWorld,_ July 15, 1991, pp. 59–62; and _Business Month,_ January 1990, p. 42–46.

$$\text{Upper control limit (UCL)} = \bar{\bar{x}} + z\sigma_{\bar{x}} \qquad \text{(S17.1)}$$

$$\text{Lower control limit (LCL)} = \bar{\bar{x}} - z\sigma_{\bar{x}} \qquad \text{(S17.2)}$$

where

$\bar{\bar{x}}$ = Mean of the sample means

z = Number of normal standard deviations (2 for 95.5% confidence, 3 for 99.7%)

$\sigma_{\bar{x}}$ = Standard deviation of the sample means = $\dfrac{\sigma_x}{\sqrt{n}}$

Example S1

A large production lot of boxes of Corn Flakes is sampled every hour. To set control limits that include 99.7% of the sample means, 36 boxes are randomly selected and weighed. The standard deviation of the overall population of boxes is estimated, through analysis of old records, to be 2 ounces. The average mean of all samples taken is 16 ounces. We therefore have $\bar{\bar{x}} = 16$ ounces, $\sigma_x = 2$ ounces, $n = 36$, and $z = 3$. The control limits are:

$$\text{UCL}_{\bar{x}} = \bar{\bar{x}} + z\sigma_{\bar{x}} = 16 + 3\left(\frac{2}{\sqrt{36}}\right) = 16 + 1 = 17 \text{ ounces}$$

$$\text{LCL}_{\bar{x}} = \bar{\bar{x}} - z\sigma_{\bar{x}} = 16 - 3\left(\frac{2}{\sqrt{36}}\right) = 16 - 1 = 15 \text{ ounces}$$

Acceptable tolerance levels on auto body parts at this New United Motor Manufacturing plant in Fremont, California, are so small that the company uses computers to see whether the process is in or out of control.

If the process standard deviation is not available or is difficult to compute, which is usually the case, the equations above become impractical. In practice, the calculation of control limits is based on the average *range* values rather than on standard deviations. We may use the equations

$$\text{UCL}_{\bar{x}} = \bar{\bar{x}} + A_2\bar{R} \tag{S17.3}$$

and

$$\text{LCL}_{\bar{x}} = \bar{\bar{x}} - A_2\bar{R} \tag{S17.4}$$

where

$$\bar{R} = \text{Average range of the samples}$$
$$A_2 = \text{Value found in Table S17.1}$$
$$\bar{\bar{x}} = \text{Mean of the sample means}$$

Example S2

Super Cola bottles soft drinks labeled "net weight 16 ounces." An overall process average of 16.01 ounces has been found by taking several batches of samples, where each sample contained five bottles. The average range of the process is .25 ounces. Determine the upper and lower control limits for averages for this process.

Looking in Table S17.1 for a sample size of 5 in the mean factor A_2 column, we find the number .577. Thus the upper and lower control chart limits are:

$$\text{UCL}_{\bar{x}} = \bar{\bar{x}} + A_2\bar{R}$$
$$= 16.01 + (.577)(.25)$$
$$= 16.01 + .144$$
$$= 16.154$$
$$\text{LCL}_{\bar{x}} = \bar{\bar{x}} - A_2\bar{R}$$
$$= 16.01 - .144$$
$$= 15.866$$

The upper control limit is 16.154, and the lower control limit is 15.866.

TABLE S17.1 Factors for Computing Control Chart Limits.

SAMPLE SIZE, n	MEAN FACTOR, A_2	UPPER RANGE, D_4	LOWER RANGE, D_3
2	1.880	3.268	0
3	1.023	2.574	0
4	.729	2.282	0
5	.577	2.114	0
6	.483	2.004	0
7	.419	1.924	0.076
8	.373	1.864	0.136
9	.337	1.816	0.184
10	.308	1.777	0.223
12	.266	1.716	0.284
14	.235	1.671	0.329
16	.212	1.636	0.364
18	.194	1.608	0.392
20	.180	1.586	0.414
25	.153	1.541	0.459

Source: Reprinted by permission of American Society for Testing Materials, copyright. Taken from Special Technical Publication 15-C, "Quality Control of Materials," pp. 63 and 72, 1951.

Setting Range Chart Limits

In the above example, we determined the upper and lower control limits for the process *average*. In addition to being concerned with the process average, operations managers are interested in the process *dispersion* or *variability*. Even though the process average is under control, the variability of the process may not be. For example, something may have worked itself loose in a piece of equipment. As a result, the average of the samples may remain the same, but the variation within the samples could be entirely too large. For this reason, it is very common to find a control chart for ranges in order to monitor the process variability, as well as a control chart for the process average, which monitors the process average. The theory behind the control charts for ranges is the same for the process average. Limits are established that contain ±3 standard deviations of the distribution for the average range $\bar{R}$. With a few simplifying assumptions, we can set the upper and lower control limits for ranges:

$$\text{UCL}_R = D_4 \bar{R} \tag{S17.5}$$

$$\text{LCL}_R = D_3 \bar{R} \tag{S17.6}$$

where

$$\text{UCL}_R = \text{Upper control chart limit for the range}$$

$$\text{LCL}_R = \text{Lower control chart limit for the range}$$

$$D_4 \text{ and } D_3 = \text{Values from Table S17.1}$$

Example S3

The average *range* of a process is 53 pounds. If the sample size is 5, determine the upper and lower control chart limits.

Looking in Table S17.1 for a sample size of 5, we find that $D_4 = 2.114$ and $D_3 = 0$. The range control chart limits are

$$UCL_R = D_4\overline{R}$$
$$= (2.114)(53 \text{ pounds})$$
$$= 112.042 \text{ pounds}$$
$$LCL_R = D_3\overline{R}$$
$$= (0)(53 \text{ pounds})$$
$$= 0$$

Steps to Follow in Using Control Charts. There are five steps that are generally followed in using $\overline{x}$ and R-charts:

1. Collect 20 to 25 samples of $n = 4$ or $n = 5$ each and compute the mean and range of each.
2. Compute the overall means ($\overline{\overline{x}}$ and $\overline{R}$), set appropriate control limits, usually at the 99.7% level, and calculate the preliminary upper and lower control limits.
3. Graph the sample means and ranges on their respective control charts and determine whether they fall outside the acceptable limits.
4. Investigate points or patterns that indicate the process is out of control. Try to assign causes for the variation and then resume the process.
5. Collect additional samples and, if necessary, revalidate the control limits using the new data.

Control Charts for Attributes

Control charts for $\overline{x}$ and R do not apply when we are sampling *attributes,* which are typically classified as defective or nondefective. Measuring defectives involves counting them (for example, number of bad light bulbs in a given lot, or number of letters or data entry records typed with errors); whereas variables are usually measured for length or weight. There are two kinds of attribute control charts: (1) those that measure the percent defective in a sample—called *p*-charts, and (2) those that count the number of defects—called *c*-charts.

p-charts

p-charts. *p*-charts are the principal means of controlling attributes. Although attributes that are either good or bad follow the binomial distribution, the normal distribution can be used to calculate *p*-chart limits when sample sizes are large. The procedure resembles the $\overline{x}$-chart approach, which was also based on the central limit theorem.

The formulas for *p*-chart upper and lower control limits follow:

$$UCL_p = \bar{p} + z\sigma_p \tag{S17.7}$$

$$LCL_p = \bar{p} - z\sigma_p \tag{S17.8}$$

where

$\bar{p}$ = Mean fraction defective in the sample

z = Number of standard deviates ($z = 2$ for 95.5% limits; $z = 3$ for 99.7% limits)

σ_p = Standard deviation of the sampling distribution

σ_p is estimated by the formula:

$$\sigma_p = \sqrt{\frac{\bar{p}(1 - \bar{p})}{n}} \tag{S17.9}$$

when *n* = size of each sample.

Example S4

Using a popular database software package, data entry clerks at ARCO key in thousands of insurance records each day. Samples of the work of 20 clerks are shown below. One hundred records entered by each clerk were carefully examined to make sure they contained no errors; the fraction defective in each sample was then computed.

   Set control limits that include 99.7% of the random variation in the entry process when it is in control.

SAMPLE NUMBER	NUMBER OF ERRORS	FRACTION DEFECTIVE	SAMPLE NUMBER	NUMBER OF ERRORS	FRACTION DEFECTIVE
1	6	.06	11	6	.06
2	5	.05	12	1	.01
3	0	.00	13	8	.08
4	1	.01	14	7	.07
5	4	.04	15	5	.05
6	2	.02	16	4	.04
7	5	.05	17	11	.11
8	3	.03	18	3	.03
9	3	.03	19	0	.00
10	2	.02	20	4	.04
				80	

$$\bar{p} = \frac{\text{Total number of errors}}{\text{Total number of records examined}} = \frac{80}{(100)(20)} = .04$$

$$\sigma_p = \sqrt{\frac{(.04)(1 - .04)}{(100)}} = .02$$

(*Note:* 100 is the size of each sample = *n*)

$$UCL_p = \bar{p} + z\sigma_p = .04 + 3(.02) = .10$$
$$LCL_p = \bar{p} - z\sigma_p = .04 - 3(.02) = 0$$

(since we cannot have a negative percent defective)

When we plot the control limits and the sample fraction defectives, we find that only one data entry clerk (number 17) is out of control. The firm may wish to examine that individual's work a bit more closely to see if a serious problem exists (see Figure S17.4).

FIGURE S17.4

p-Chart for Data Entry for Example S4.

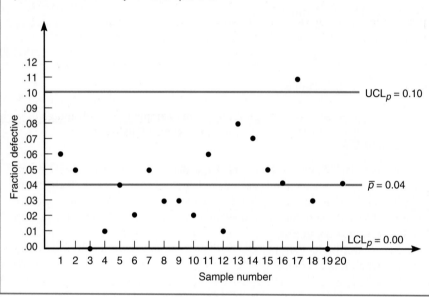

c-charts. In Example S4, we counted the number of defective database records entered. A defective record was one that was not exactly correct. A bad record may contain more than one defect, however. We use **c-charts** to control the *number* of defects per unit of output (or per insurance record in the above case).

c-charts

Control charts for defects are helpful for monitoring processes where a large number of potential errors can occur but the actual number that do occur is relatively small. Defects may be mistypeset newspaper words, bad circuits in a microchip, blemishes on a table, or missing pickles on a fast-food hamburger.

The Poisson probability distribution, which has a variance equal to its mean, is the basis for c-charts. Since $\bar{c}$ is the mean number of defects per unit, the standard deviation is equal to $\sqrt{\bar{c}}$. To compute 99.7% control limits for $\bar{c}$, we use the formula:

$$\bar{c} \pm 3\sqrt{\bar{c}} \tag{S17.10}$$

Example S5

Red Top Cab Company receives several complaints per day about the behavior of its drivers. Over a nine-day period (where days are the units of measure), the owner received the following numbers of calls from irate passengers: 3, 0, 8, 9, 6, 7, 4, 9, 8, for a total of 54 complaints.

To compute 99.7% control limits, we take:

$$\bar{c} = \frac{54}{9} = 6 \text{ complaints per day}$$

Thus,

$$\text{UCL}_c = \bar{c} + 3\sqrt{\bar{c}} = 6 + 3\sqrt{6} = 6 + 3(2.45) = 13.35$$
$$\text{LCL}_c = \bar{c} - 3\sqrt{\bar{c}} = 6 - 3\sqrt{6} = 6 - 3(2.45) = 0$$

After the owner plotted a control chart summarizing these data and posted it prominently in the drivers' locker room, the number of calls received dropped to an average of three per day. Can you explain why this may have occurred?

Note that while we have discussed process charts and control limits, a focus on the target value, not the limits, is preferable. An example of the advantage of such a focus is provided in the *POM in Action* box, "Robust Quality."

ACCEPTANCE SAMPLING

Acceptance sampling involves taking random samples of "lots" or batches of finished products and having inspectors measure them against predetermined standards. Random sampling, as mentioned earlier in this chapter, is more economical than 100% inspection. The quality of the sample is used to judge the quality of all items in the lot. Although either attributes or variables can be inspected by acceptance sampling, attribute inspection is more commonly used in business and is illustrated in this section.

Acceptance sampling can be applied when raw materials arrive at a plant during a production process, or in final inspection, but it is usually used to control incoming lots of purchased products. A lot of items rejected, based on an unacceptable level of defects found in the sample, can (1) be returned to the supplier, or (2) be 100% inspected to cull out all defects, with the cost of this screening usually billed to the supplier. However, acceptance sampling is not a substitute for adequate process controls. In fact, the current approach is to build statistical quality controls at the supplier level so that acceptance sampling can be eliminated.

Sampling Plans

A lot of items can be inspected in several ways, including the use of single, double, or sequential sampling.

Single Sampling. Two numbers specify a **single sampling** plan: They are the number of items to be sampled (n) and a prespecified acceptable number of defects (c). If there are fewer or equal defects in the lot than the acceptance number, c, then

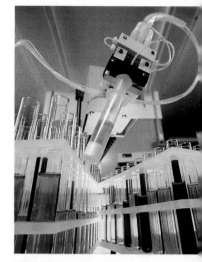

Space-age robotics and computerized analytical equipment are used by Waste Management to protect groundwater. Waste Management processing and disposal centers analyze up to 60,000 samples annually in their attempt to assure the highest standards of environmental quality.

Acceptance sampling

Single sampling

POM _in action_

Robust Quality

Ford Motor Company, which owns 25% of the Japanese-based Mazda Company, asked Mazda to build transmissions for one of Ford's models sold in the U.S. Although the transmissions built by Mazda were identical in specification to those built by Ford, the Ford transmissions produced higher rates of malfunction and customer complaints. Consequently, Ford incurred increased levels of warranty costs.

Wanting to correct the situation, Ford investigated by comparing samples of transmissions from both companies. Ford found that while their own transmissions fell within a preset range of acceptability on a zero defect standard, the Mazda samples were more exact with virtually little, if any, variation from the engineering specs. In some Ford transmissions many components fell near the _outer limits_ of tolerance

from the target. When randomly assembled together, a series of deviations tended to "stack up." Otherwise trivial variations in one part exacerbated a variation in another. Because of deviations, parts interacted with greater friction than they could withstand individually or with greater vibration than customers were prepared to endure.

Further investigation also indicated that creative management played a part in Mazda's more reliable transmissions. Instead of focusing on a range of acceptability, Mazda management aimed at manufacturing products that consistently met target values.

Sources: Harvard Business Review, January–February 1990, pp. 65–75; and _Business Week,_ July 22, 1991, pp. 82–83.

---

the whole batch will be accepted. If there are more than c defects, the whole lot will be rejected or subjected to 100% screening.

Double Sampling. Often a lot of items is so good or so bad that we can reach a conclusion about its quality by taking a smaller sample than would have been used in a single sampling plan. If the number of defects in this smaller sample (of size n_1) is less than or equal to some lower limit (c_1), the lot can be accepted. If the number of defects exceeds an upper limit (c_2), the whole lot can be rejected. But if the number of defects in the n_1 sample is between c_1 and c_2, a second sample (of size n_2) is drawn. The cumulative results determine whether to accept or reject the lot. The concept is called **double sampling.**

Double sampling

We won't do computations for these (handwritten)

Sequential sampling

Sequential Sampling. Multiple sampling is an extension of double sampling, with smaller samples used sequentially until a clear decision can be made. When units are randomly selected from a lot and tested one by one, with the cumulative number of inspected pieces and defects recorded, the process is called **sequential sampling** (see Figure S17.5).

If the cumulative number of defects is in the upper shaded area of Figure S17.5, the whole lot will be rejected. Or if the cumulative number of rejects is in the lower shaded region, the lot will be accepted. But if the number of defects falls within these two boundaries, we continue to sample units from the lot. It is possible in some sequential plans for the whole lot to be tested, unit by unit, before a conclusion is reached.

FIGURE S17.5

Sequential Sampling.

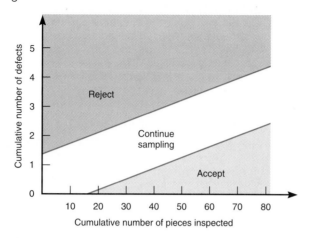

Selection of the best sampling approach—single, double, or sequential—depends on the types of products being inspected and their expected quality level. A very low-quality batch of goods, for example, can be identified quickly and more cheaply with sequential sampling. This means that the inspection, which may be costly and/or destructive, can end sooner. On the other hand, there are many cases where a single sampling plan is easier and simpler for workers to conduct even though the number sampled may be greater than under other plans.

Operating Characteristic (OC) Curves

The **operating characteristic (OC) curve** describes how well an acceptance plan discriminates between good and bad lots. A curve pertains to a specific plan, that is, a combination of n (sample size) and c (acceptance level). It is intended to show the probability that the plan will accept lots of various quality levels.

Naturally, we would prefer a highly discriminating sampling plan and OC curve. If the entire shipment of parts has an unacceptably high level of defects, we hope the sample will reflect that fact with a very high probability (preferably 100%) of rejecting the shipment.

Figure S17.6a shows a perfect discrimination plan for a company that wants to reject all lots with more than $2\frac{1}{2}\%$ defectives and accept all lots with less than $2\frac{1}{2}\%$ defectives. Unfortunately, the only way to assure 100% acceptance of good lots and 0% acceptance of bad lots is to conduct a full inspection, which is often very costly.

Figure S17.6b reveals that no OC curve will be as steplike as the one in Figure S17.6a; nor will it be discriminating enough to yield 100% error-free inspection. Figure S17.6b does indicate, though, that for the same sample size ($n = 100$ in this case), a smaller value of c (of acceptable defects) yields a steeper curve than does a larger value of c. So one way to increase the probability of accepting only good lots and rejecting only bad lots with random sampling is to set very tight acceptance levels.

Operating characteristic (OC) curve

FIGURE S17.6

(a) Perfect Discrimination for Inspection Plan. (b) OC Curves for Two Different Acceptable Levels of Defects ($c = 1$, $c = 4$) for the same sample size ($n = 100$). (c) OC Curves for Two Different Sample Sizes ($n = 25$, $n = 100$) but Same Acceptance Percentages (4%). Larger sample size shows better discrimination.

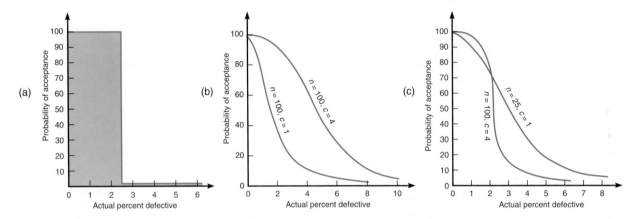

A second way to develop a steeper, and thereby sounder, OC curve is to increase the sample size. Figure S17.6c illustrates that even when the acceptance number is the same proportion of the sample size, a larger value of n will increase the likelihood of accurately measuring the lot's quality. In this figure, both curves use a maximum defect rate of 4% (equal to $4/100 = 1/25$). Yet if you take a straightedge or ruler and carefully examine Figure S17.6c, you will be able to see that the OC curve for $n = 25$, $c = 1$ rejects more good lots and accepts more bad lots than the second plan. Here are a few measurements to illustrate that point.

WHEN THE ACTUAL PERCENT OF DEFECTS IN THE LOT IS:	THEN THE PROBABILITY (APPROXIMATE) OF ACCEPTING THE WHOLE LOT IS:	
	For $n = 100$, $c = 4$	For $n = 25$, $c = 1$
1%	97%	90%
3%	15%	47%
5%	3%	18%
7%	1%	6%

In other words, the probability of accepting a more than satisfactory lot (one with only 1% defects) is 97% for $n = 100$, but only 90% for $n = 25$. Likewise, the chance of accepting a "bad" lot (one with 5% defects) is only 3% for $n = 100$, whereas it is 18% using the smaller sample size.[2] Of course, were it not for the cost of extra inspection, every firm would opt for larger sample sizes.

---

[2] It bears repeating, even at the risk of sounding repetitive, that sampling always runs the danger of leading to an erroneous conclusion. Let us say in this example that the total population under scrutiny is a load of 1,000 computer chips, of which in reality only 30 (or 3%) are defective. This means that we would want to accept the shipment of chips, since 4% is the allowable defect rate. But if a random sample of $n = 50$ chips were drawn, we could conceivably end up with 0 defects and accept that shipment (that is, it is OK) or we could find all 30 defects in the sample. If the latter happened, we could wrongly conclude that the whole population was 60% defective and reject them all.

Producer's and Consumer's Risk

In acceptance sampling, two parties are usually involved: the producer of the product and the consumer of the product. In specifying a sampling plan, each party wants to avoid costly mistakes in accepting or rejecting a lot. The producer wants to avoid the mistake of having a good lot rejected **(producer's risk).** This is because he or she usually has the responsibility of replacing all defects in the rejected lot or of paying for a new lot to be shipped to the customer. On the other hand, the customer or consumer wants to avoid the mistake of accepting a bad lot because defects found in a lot that has already been accepted are usually the responsibility of the customer **(consumer's risk).** The OC curve shows the features of a particular sampling plan, including the risks of making a wrong decision.

    Figure S17.7 can be used to illustrate one sampling plan in more detail. Four concepts are illustrated in this figure:

The **acceptable quality level (AQL)** is the poorest level of quality we are willing to accept. We wish to accept lots that have this level of quality. If an acceptable quality level is 20 defects in a lot of 1,000 items or parts, then AQL is $20/1{,}000 = 2\%$ defectives.

The **lot tolerance percent defective (LTPD)** is the quality level of a lot we consider bad. We wish to reject lots that have this level of quality. If it is agreed that an

Producer's risk

Consumer's risk

Acceptable quality level (AQL)

Lot tolerance percent defective (LTPD)

FIGURE S17.7

An Operating Characteristic (OC) Curve Showing Producer's and Consumer's Risk. *Note:* A good lot for this particular acceptance plan has less than or equal to 2% defectives. A bad lot has 7% or more defectives.

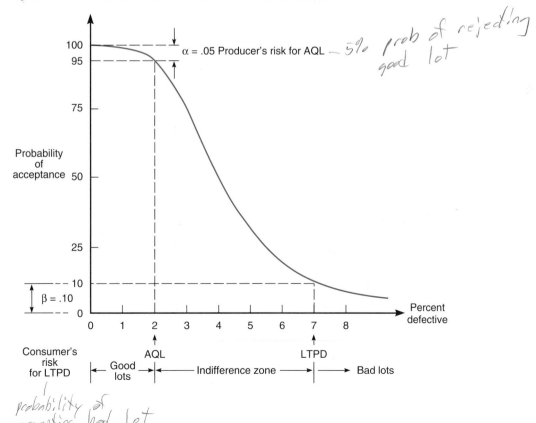

unacceptable quality level is 70 defects in a lot of 1,000, then the LTPD is 70/1,000 = 7% defective.

To derive a sampling plan, the producer and the consumer must define not only "good lots" and "bad lots" through the AQL and LTPD, but they must also specify risk levels.

Producer's risk (α) is the probability that a "good" lot will be rejected. This is the risk of taking a random sample that results in a much higher proportion of defects than the population of all items. A lot with an acceptable quality level of AQL still has an α chance of being rejected. Sampling plans are often designed to have the producer's risk set at $\alpha = .05$, or 5%.

Consumer's risk (β) is the probability that a "bad" lot will be accepted. This is the risk of taking a random sample that results in a lower proportion of defects than the overall population of items. A common value for consumer's risk in sampling plans is $\beta = .10$, or 10%.

Type I error
Type II error

In statistics, the probability of rejecting a good lot is called a **Type I error.** The probability of a bad lot being accepted is referred to as a **Type II error.** Figure S17.8 may help to summarize the relationships described above.

Sampling plans and OC curves can be developed by computer (as seen in the computer programs supplied with this text), by published tables such as the U.S. Military Standard MIL-STD-105 or Dodge–Romig table, or by calculation, using the

FIGURE S17.8

Possible Errors in a Sampling Plan.

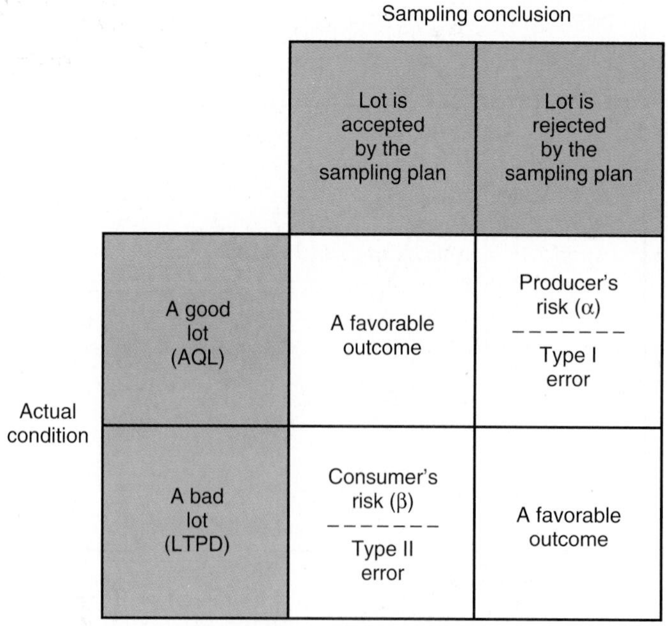

binomial or Poisson distributions.[3] To help you understand the theory underlying the use of sampling plans, we will illustrate how an OC curve is constructed statistically.

In attribute sampling, where products are determined to be either good or bad, a binomial distribution is usually employed to build the OC curve. The binomial equation is:

$$P(x) = \frac{n!}{x!(n-x)!}\, p^x(1-p)^{n-x} \qquad (S17.11)$$

where

n = Number of items sampled (called trials)

p = Probability that an x (defect) will occur on any one trial

$P(x)$ = probability of exactly x results in n trials

When the sample size (n) is large and the percent defective (p) is small, however, the Poisson distribution can be used as an approximation of the binomial formula. This is convenient since binomial calculations can become quite complex, and since cumulative Poisson tables are readily available. Our Poisson table appears in Appendix C.

In a Poisson approximation of the binomial distribution, the mean of the binomial, which is np, is used as the mean of the Poisson, which is λ; that is,

$$\lambda = np \qquad (S17.12)$$

Example S6

A shipment of 2,000 portable battery units for microcomputers is about to be inspected by a Malaysian importer. The Korean manufacturer and the importer have set up a sampling plan in which the α risk is limited to 5% at an AQL of 2% defective, while the β risk is set to 10% at LTPD = 7% defective. We want to construct the OC curve for the plan of $n = 120$ sample size and an acceptance level of $c \leq 3$ defectives. Both firms want to know if this plan will satisfy their quality and risk requirements.

To solve the problem, we turn to the cumulative Poisson table in Appendix C, whose columns are set up in terms of the acceptance level, c. We are interested only in the $c = 3$ column for this example. The rows in the table are λ (= np), which represents the number of defects we would expect to find in each sample.

By varying the percent defectives (p) from .01 (1%) to .08 (8%) and holding the sample size at $n = 120$, we can compute the probability of acceptance of the lot at each chosen level. The values for P (acceptance) calculated below are then plotted to produce the OC curve pictured in Figure S17.9.

---

[3] The two most frequently used tables for acceptance plans are: *Military Standard Sampling Procedures and Tables for Inspection by Attributes* (MIL-STD-105D) (Washington, D.C.: U.S. Government Printing Office, 1963); and H. F. Dodge and H. G. Romig, *Sampling Inspection Tables—Single and Double Sampling,* 2nd ed. (New York: Wiley and Sons, 1959).

FIGURE S17.9

OC Curve Constructed for Example S6.

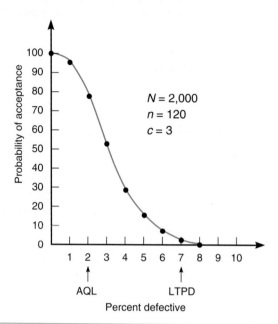

SELECTED VALUES OF % DEFECTIVE	MEAN OF POISSON, $\lambda = np$	P (ACCEPTANCE) FROM APPENDIX C
.01	1.20	.966
.02	2.40	.779 ← 1 − α at AQL
.03	3.60	.515
.04	4.80	.294
.05	6.00	.151
.06	7.20	.072
.07	8.40	.032* ← β level at LTPD
.08	9.60	.014*

* Interpolated from value.

Now back to the issue of whether this OC curve satisfies the quality and risk needs of the consumer and producer of the batteries. For the AQL of $p = .02 = 2\%$ defects, the P (acceptance) of the lot = .779. This yields an α risk of $1 - .779 = .221$, or 22.1%, which exceeds the 5% level desired by the producer. The β risk of .032, or 3.2%, is well under the 10% sought by the consumer. It appears that new calculations are necessary with a larger sample size if the α level is to be lowered.[4]

In Example S6, we set n and c values for a sampling plan and then computed the α and β risks to see if they were within desired levels. Often, organizations

---

[4] Indeed as AB:POM's quality control module will verify, the sample size should be 165.

instead develop an OC curve for preset values of an AQL, then substitute values of n and c until the plan also satisfies the β and LTPD demands.

Average Outgoing Quality

In most sampling plans, when a lot is rejected, the entire lot is inspected and all of the defective items are replaced. Use of this replacement technique improves the average outgoing quality in terms of percent defective. In fact, given (1) any sampling plan that replaces all defective items encountered and (2) the true incoming percent defective for the lot, it is possible to determine the **average outgoing quality (AOQ)** in percent defective. The equation for AOQ is:

$$AOQ = \frac{(P_d)(P_a)(N - n)}{N} \qquad (S17.13)$$

where

Average outgoing quality (AOQ)

P_d = True percent defective of the lot

P_a = Probability of accepting the lot

N = Number of items in the lot

n = Number of items in the sample

Example S7

The percent defective from an incoming lot in Example S6 is 3%. An OC curve showed the probability of acceptance to be .515. Given a lot size of 2,000 and a sample of 120, what is the average outgoing quality in percent defective?

$$AOQ = \frac{(P_d)(P_a)(N - n)}{N}$$

$$= \frac{(.03)(.515)(2,000 - 120)}{2,000} = .015$$

Thus, an acceptance sampling plan changes the quality of the lots in percent defective from .03 to .015, on the average. Acceptance sampling significantly increases the quality of the inspected lots.

In most cases, we do not know the value of P_a; we must determine it from the particular sampling plan. The fact that we seldom know the true incoming percent defective presents another problem. In most cases, several different incoming percent defective values are assumed. Then we can determine the average outgoing quality for each value.

Example S8

To illustrate the AOQ relationship, let us use the data we developed for the OC curve in Example S6. The lot size in that case was $N = 2,000$, and the sample size was $n = 120$. We assume that any defective batteries found during inspec-

A few years ago IBM Canada Ltd. ordered some parts from a new supplier in Japan. IBM stated in its order that acceptable quality allowed for 1.5% defects—a demanding standard in North America at that time. The Japanese sent the order, with a few parts packaged separately in plastic. Their letter said: "We don't know why you want 1.5% defective parts, but for your convenience we have packaged them separately."

tion are replaced by good ones. Then using the formula for AOQ given above and the probabilities of acceptance from Example S6, we can develop the following numbers:

P_d	×	P_a	×	$(N - n)/N$	=	AOQ
.01		.966		.94		.009
.02		.779		.94		.015
.03		.515		.94		.015
.04		.294		.94		.011
.05		.151		.94		.007
.06		.072		.94		.004
.07		.032		.94		.002
.08		.014		.94		.001

FIGURE S17.10

A Typical AOQ Curve, Using Data from Example S8.

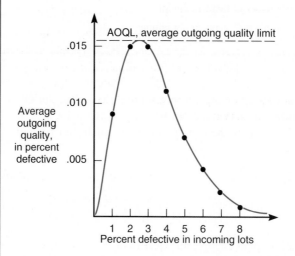

These numbers are graphed in Figure S17.10 shown below as the average outgoing quality as a function of incoming quality.

Did you notice how AOQ changed for different percent defectives? When the percent defective of the incoming lots is either very high or very low, the percent defective of the outgoing lots is low. AOQ at 1% was .009, and AOQ at 8% was .001. For moderate levels of the incoming percent defective, AOQ is higher: AOQ at 2–3% was .015. Thus AOQ is low for small values of the incoming percent defective. As the incoming percent defective increases, the AOQ increases up to a point. Then, for increasing incoming percent defective, AOQ decreases.

The maximum value on the AOQ curve corresponds to the highest average percent defective or the lowest average quality for the sampling plan. It is called the *average outgoing quality limit* (AOQL). In Figure S17.10 the AOQL is just over

1.5%, meaning the batteries are about 98.4% good when the incoming quality is between 2 and 3%.

Acceptance sampling is an excellent way of screening incoming lots. When the defective parts are replaced with good parts, acceptance sampling helps to increase the quality of the lots by reducing the outgoing percent defective. We explored this concept with AOQ.

Another purpose of quality control is to detect problems and to take corrective action. In a manufacturing operation, for example, when parts or items continually do not meet the specification, it may be appropriate to inspect the manufacturing process itself. Perhaps a machine needs adjustment, or perhaps a piece of equipment is not operating properly. How do we know when to suspect a problem or an incorrectly adjusted machine? When an item does not meet specification, how do we know whether it is just a random occurrence or whether something is wrong with the process? Process control and control charts help to answer these and related questions.

SUMMARY

We have devoted this supplement to statistical aspects of quality control. These techniques are statistical process control (SPC) and acceptance sampling. Control charts for statistical process control (SPC) were described. The $\bar{x}$-chart and the R-chart for variability sampling and the p-chart and the c-chart for attributes were introduced. Sampling plans and operating characteristic (OC) curves to facilitate acceptance sampling were also presented.

KEY TERMS

Control chart (p. 760)
Natural variations (p. 762)
Assignable variation (p. 763)
$\bar{x}$-chart (p. 763)
R-chart (p. 763)
Central limit theorem (p. 763)
p-chart (p. 768)
c-chart (p. 770)
Acceptance sampling (p. 771)
Single sampling (p. 771)
Double sampling (p. 772)

Sequential sampling (p. 772)
Operating characteristic (OC) curve (p. 773)
Producer's risk (p. 775)
Consumer's risk (p. 775)
Acceptable quality level (AQL) (p. 775)
Lot tolerance percent defective (LTPD) (p. 775)
Type I error (p. 776)
Type II error (p. 776)
Average outgoing quality (AOQ) (p. 779)

USING AB:POM

With AB:POM it is possible to address a number of quality control issues, as shown in the Quality Control Submenu (Program S17.1). Use the arrows to move between the options.

A description of the use of AB:POM to solve several examples in this chapter follows.

Program S17.1

AB:POM's Quality Control Modules

```
──────────── Quality  Control ────────────── Data  Screen ──────

     x charts, R charts - process control

     p-charts - process control

     Attributes sampling - determine the plan

     Errors /OC Curves for Attributes sampling

     Return to Submenu

     Select menu option by highlighted letter or
  point with arrow keys and then press RETURN key
```

Solving Example S4 with AB:POM Using the Quality Control Module: p-charts—process control.

In the upper left of the screen, the *P-chart* option asks for the number of samples, (i.e., 20). In the upper right, enter 100, the sample size for each of the 20 samples in Example S4. Then as shown in Program S17.2, fill in the number of defects in each of 20 samples.

After pressing *R* (for Run) AB:POM computes the average percentage of defects (the center line of the p-bar chart) which is displayed as .04 (see Program S17.2). Using these data, the program presents the limits for four different control charts at the bottom of the screen. There is one chart with 95% confidence, one with 98%, one with 99% and one with 3 standard deviations (99.7%) confidence.

A 3 standard deviation upper control limit (UCL) of .0988 was rounded up to .1 in Example S4 in the text.

Solving Example S6 with AB:POM Using the Quality Control Module: Developing a Sampling Plan for Acceptance Sampling of Attributes.

Attributes plans are used when the measurement is of a defective/nondefective type. The data are entered immediately on submenu, *Attribute Sampling,* as shown in Program S17.3. We use the data from Example S6 to examine the capability of this module.

1. *AQL.* The Acceptable Quality Level must be entered and be greater than 0 and less than 1. Up to 3 digits may be specified after the decimal place. An AQL of .05 is an AQL of 5% defective.

2. *LTPD.* The lot tolerance percent defective must be entered. This has characteristics similar to the AQL. LTPD must be between 0 and .1 and up to three digits can be specified.

3. *Producer's risk.* The probability of a Type I (alpha) error can be entered as

Program S17.2

AB:POM's P-chart Option

─────────────────────────── Quality Control ─────────────────── Solution ───────

Number of samples (1-36) [20]   Sample size (n) (1-9999) [100]

ARCO Insurance Records

Sample number	Number of Defects	Percent Defects		Sample number	Number of Defects	Percent Defects
1	6	0.0600		13	8	0.0800
2	5	0.0500		14	7	0.0700
3	0	0.0000		15	5	0.0500
4	1	0.0100		16	4	0.0400
5	4	0.0400		17	11	0.1100
6	2	0.0200		18	3	0.0300
7	5	0.0500		19	0	0.0000
8	3	0.0300		20	4	0.0400
9	3	0.0300				
10	2	0.0200				
11	6	0.0600				
12	1	0.0100				

	95%	98%	99%	99.7%
Upper Control Limit	0.0784	0.0857	0.0906	0.0988
Center Line (p-bar)	0.0400	0.0400	0.0400	0.0400
Lower Control Limt	.00159	0.0000	0.0000	0.0000

F9=Print   Esc

Press <Esc> key to continue or highlighted key or function key for options

Program S17.3

AB:POM's Attribute Sampling

Attributes sampling -determine the plan

AQL	.020
LTPD	.070
α	.050
β	.100

The sample size   (n) = 165
The critical value (c) = 6

either 1% (.01) or 5% (.05) for attribute sampling. Use the space bar to toggle between the two.

4. *Consumer's risk.* The probability of a Type II (beta) error can be 1%, 5%, or 10% (shown as .01, .05 or .10) for attribute samping. Again the space bar can be used to toggle between the options.

(Note: Some printers will not print out the greek letters alpha (α) or beta (β) or sigma (σ) properly.)

In this example, we are determining the appropriate sampling plan when the AQL is specified at 2% and the LTPD is specified at 7%, 5%, or 10% (see Program S17.3).

Press *R* for Run to obtain an answer.

The sample size. The minimum sample size that meets the requirements is determined and displayed. For Example S6 the appropriate sample size for the criteria given is 165.

The critical value. The maximum number of defective units is also displayed. In this example the maximum allowable number of defects in the sample of 165 units is 6.

SOLVED PROBLEMS

Solved Problem S17.1

The manufacturer of precision parts for drill presses produces round shafts for use in the construction of drill presses. The average diameter of a shaft is .56 inch. The inspection samples contain six shafts each. The average range of these samples is .006 inch. Determine the upper and lower control chart limits.

Solution

The mean factor A_2 from Table S17.1 where the sample size is 6, is seen to be .483. With this factor, you can obtain the upper and lower control limits:

$$UCL = .56 + (.483)(.006)$$
$$= .56 + .0029$$
$$= .5629$$
$$LCL = .56 - .0029$$
$$= .5571$$

Solved Problem S17.2

Nocaf Drinks, Inc., a producer of decaffeinated coffee, bottles Nocaf. Each bottle should have a net weight of 4 ounces. The machine that fills the bottles with coffee is new, and the operations manager wants to make sure that it is properly adjusted. The operations manager takes a sample of $n = 8$ bottles and records the average and range in ounces for each sample. The data for several samples is in the following table. Note that every sample consists of 8 bottles.

SAMPLE	SAMPLE RANGE	SAMPLE AVERAGE	SAMPLE	SAMPLE RANGE	SAMPLE AVERAGE
A	.41	4.00	E	.56	4.17
B	.55	4.16	F	.62	3.93
C	.44	3.99	G	.54	3.98
D	.48	4.00	H	.44	4.01

Is the machine properly adjusted and in control?

Solution

We first find that $\bar{\bar{x}} = 4.03$ and $\bar{R} = .51$. Then, using Table S17.1, we find:

$$\text{UCL}_{\bar{x}} = \bar{\bar{x}} + A_2\bar{R} = 4.03 + (.373)(.51) = 4.22$$

$$\text{LCL}_{\bar{x}} = \bar{\bar{x}} - A_2\bar{R} = 4.03 - (.373)(.51) = 3.84$$

$$\text{UCL}_{\bar{R}} = D_4\bar{R} = (1.864)(.51) = .95$$

$$\text{LCL}_{\bar{R}} = D_3\bar{R} = (.136)(.51) = .07$$

It appears that the process average and range are both in control.

Solved Problem S17.3

Altman Electronics, Inc., makes resistors, and among the last 100 resistors inspected, the percent defective has been .05. Determine the upper and lower limits for this process for 99.7% confidence.

Solution

$$\text{UCL}_p = \bar{p} + 3\sqrt{\frac{\bar{p}(1-\bar{p})}{n}} = .05 + 3\sqrt{\frac{(.05)(1-.05)}{100}}$$

$$= .05 + 3(0.0218) = .1154$$

$$\text{LCL}_p = \bar{p} - 3\sqrt{\frac{\bar{p}(1-\bar{p})}{n}} = .05 - 3(.0218)$$

$$= .05 - .0654 = 0 \text{ (since percent defective cannot be negative)}$$

Solved Problem S17.4

Shipments of 1,000 ceiling fans are received at a major Houston distributor. From these, 60 fans are selected at random and tested. If three or more defective fans are found, the entire shipment is rejected. The firms want the operating characteristics (OC) curve developed for this sampling plan.

Solution

For this problem, the acceptance level is $c \leq 2$. Using the $c = 2$ column in the cumulative Poisson table (Appendix C), we can develop the following numbers:

p VALUES (FRACTION DEFECTIVE)	$\lambda = np$ (= 60p)	P (ACCEPTANCE)
.01	.60	.977
.02	1.20	.879
.03	1.80	.731
.04	2.40	.570
.05	3.00	.423
.07	4.20	.210
.09	5.40	.095
.11	6.60	.062

The OC curve is shown in Figure S17.11.

FIGURE S17.11

Operating Characteristic Curve for Houston Distributor

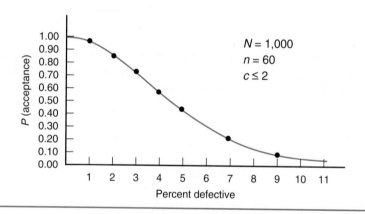

Solved Problem S17.5

In the previous problem, if the LTPD is 5%, what is the consumer's risk for the acceptance sampling plan? What is the producer's risk corresponding to an AQL of 2%?

Solution

The consumer's risk is easily found for a p value of .05 defectives; it is P (acceptance) = β = .423. This is the probability the Houston distributor would accept a bad lot.

The producer's risk is $1 - P$ (acceptance) at $p = .02$, which is $1 - .879$ = .121 = 12.1%.

Solved Problem S17.6

In an acceptance sampling plan developed for lots containing 1,000 units, the sample size n is 85 and c is 3. The percent defective of the incoming lots is 2%, and the probability of acceptance, which was obtained from an OC curve, is 0.64. What is the average outgoing quality?

Solution

$$\text{AOQ} = \frac{(P_d)(P_a)(N - n)}{N} = \frac{(.02)(.64)(1,000 - 85)}{1,000} = .012$$

or

$$\text{AOQ} = 1.2\%$$

DISCUSSION QUESTIONS

1. Why is the central limit theorem so important in statistical quality control?

2. Why are $\bar{x}$- and R-charts usually used hand in hand?

3. Explain the differences among the four types of control charts.

4. What might cause a process to be out of control?

5. Explain why a process can be out of control even though all samples fall within the upper and lower control limits.

6. What do the terms *producer's risk* and *consumer's risk* mean?

7. Define Type I and Type II errors.

8. Explain the difference between single, double, and sequential sampling.

PROBLEMS

S17.1 Food Storage Technologies produces refrigeration units for food producers and retail food establishments. The overall average temperature that these units maintain is 46° Fahrenheit. The average range is 2° Fahrenheit. Samples of six are taken to monitor the process. Determine the upper and lower control-chart limits for averages and ranges for these refrigeration units.

S17.2 When set at the standard position, Autopitch can throw hard balls toward a batter at an average speed of 60 mph. Autopitch devices are made for both major- and minor-league teams to help them improve their batting averages. Autopitch executives take samples of 10 Autopitch devices at a time to monitor these devices and to maintain the highest quality. The average range is 3 mph. Using control-chart techniques, determine control-chart limits for averages and ranges for Autopitch.

S17.3 Major Products, Inc., produces granola cereal, granola bars, and other natural food products. Its natural granola cereal is sampled to ensure proper weight. Each sample contains eight boxes of cereal. The overall average for the samples is 17 ounces. The range is only 0.5 ounces. Determine the upper and lower control-chart limits for averages for the boxes of cereal.

⌐:**S17.4** Small boxes of NutraFlakes cereal are labeled "net weight 10 ounces." Each hour, random samples of size $n = 4$ boxes are weighed to check process control. Five hours of observations yielded the following:

TIME	WEIGHTS			
	Box 1	Box 2	Box 3	Box 4
9 A.M.	9.8	10.4	9.9	10.3
10 A.M.	10.1	10.2	9.9	9.8
11 A.M.	9.9	10.5	10.3	10.1
Noon	9.7	9.8	10.3	10.2
1 P.M.	9.7	10.1	9.9	9.9

[handwritten annotations at right:] 10,1 0,6 / 10,10 0,4 / 10,2 0,6 / 10,0 0,6 / 9,90 0,4 / 10,04 0,52

Using these data, construct limits for $\bar{x}$- and R-charts. Is the process in control? What other steps should the QC department follow at this point?

: **S17.5** Sampling four pieces of precision-cut wire (to be used in computer assembly) every hour for the past 24 hours has produced the following results (refer to table):

		R	HOUR	$\bar{x}$	R
1	3.25"	.71"	13	3.11"	.85"
2	3.10	1.18	14	2.83	1.31
3	3.22	1.43	15	3.12	1.06
4	3.39	1.26	16	2.84	.50
5	3.07	1.17	17	2.86	1.43
6	2.86	.32	18	2.74	1.29
7	3.05	.53	19	3.41	1.61
8	2.65	1.13	20	2.89	1.09
9	3.02	.71	21	2.65	1.08
10	2.85	1.33	22	3.28	.46
11	2.83	1.17	23	2.94	1.58
12	2.97	.40	24	2.64	.97

Develop appropriate control charts and determine whether there is any cause for concern in the cutting process.

 : **S17.6** Due to the poor quality of various semiconductor products used in their manufacturing process, Microlaboratories have decided to develop a quality control program. Because the semiconductor parts they get from suppliers are either good or defective, George Haverty has decided to develop control charts for attributes. The total number of semiconductors in every sample is 200. Furthermore, George would like to determine the upper control chart limit and the lower control chart limit for various values of the fraction defective (p) in the sample taken. To allow more flexibility, he has decided to develop a table that lists values for p, UCL, and LCL. The values for p should range from .01 to 0.1, incrementing by .01 each time. What are the UCL's and the LCL's for 99.7% confidence?

 : **S17.7** For the last two months, Rhonda Blank has been concerned about the number 5 machine at the West Factory. In order to make sure that the machine is operating correctly, samples are taken, and the average and range for each sample is computed. Each sample consists of 12 items produced from the machine. Recently 12 samples were taken, and for each, the sample range and average were computed. The sample range and sample average were 1.1 and 46 for the first sample, 1.31 and 45 for the second sample, .91 and 46 for the third sample, and 1.1 and 47 for the fourth sample. After the fourth sample, the sample averages increased. For the fifth sample, the range was 1.21 and the average was 48; for sample number 6 it was .82 and 47; for sample number 7, it was .86 and 50; and for the eighth sample, it was 1.11 and 49. After the eighth sample, the sample average continued to increase, never getting below 50. For sample number 9, the range and average were 1.12 and 51; for sample number 10, they were .99 and 52; for sample number 11, they were .86 and 50; and for sample number 12, they were 1.2 and 52.

While Rhonda's boss wasn't overly concerned about the process, Rhonda was. During installation, the supplier set an average of 47 for the process with an average range of 1.0. It was Rhonda's feeling that something was definitely wrong with machine number 5. Do you agree?

: **S17.8** Kitty Products caters to the growing market for cat supplies, with a full line of products ranging from litter to toys to flea powder. One of its newer products, a tube of fluid that prevents hairballs in long-haired cats, is produced by an automated machine that is set to fill each tube with 63.5 grams of paste.

To keep this filling process under control, four tubes are pulled randomly from the assembly line every four hours. After several days, the data shown in the table below resulted. Set control limits for this process and graph the sample data for both the $\bar{x}$- and R-charts.

	SAMPLE NUMBER												
	1	2	3	4	5	6	7	8	9	10	11	12	13
$\bar{x}$	63.5	63.6	63.7	63.9	63.4	63.0	63.2	63.3	63.7	63.5	63.3	63.2	63.6
R	2.0	1.0	1.7	0.9	1.2	1.6	1.8	1.3	1.6	1.3	1.8	1.0	1.8

	SAMPLE NUMBER											
	14	15	16	17	18	19	20	21	22	23	24	25
$\bar{x}$	63.3	63.4	63.4	63.5	63.6	63.8	63.5	63.9	63.2	63.3	64.0	63.4
R	1.5	1.7	1.4	1.1	1.8	1.3	1.6	1.0	1.8	1.7	2.0	1.5

· **S17.9** The smallest defect in a computer chip will render the entire chip worthless. Therefore, tight quality-control measures must be established to monitor these chips. In the past, the percentage defective for these chips for a California-based company has been 1.1%. The sample size is 1,000. Determine upper and lower control chart limits for these computer chips. Use $z = 3$.

: **S17.10** Office Supply Company manufactures paper clips and other office products. Although inexpensive, paper clips have provided the firm with a high margin of profitability. The percentage defective for paper clips produced by Office Supply Company has been averaging 2.5%. Samples of 200 paper clips are taken. Establish upper and lower control chart limits for this process at 99.7% confidence.

: **S17.11** Daily samples of 100 power drills are removed from Drill Master's assembly line and inspected for defects. Over the past 21 days, the following information has been gathered. Develop a 3 standard deviation (99.7% confidence) p chart and graph the samples. Is the process in control?

DAY	NUMBER OF DEFECTIVE DRILLS	DAY	NUMBER OF DEFECTIVE DRILLS
1	6	12	5
2	5	13	4
3	6	14	3
4	4	15	4
5	3	16	5
6	4	17	6
7	5	18	5
8	3	19	4
9	6	20	3
10	3	21	7
11	7		

· **S17.12** A random sample of 100 Modern Art dining room tables that came off the firm's assembly line is examined. Careful inspection reveals a total of 2,000 blemishes. What are the 99.7% upper and lower control limits for the number of blemishes? If one table had 42 blemishes, should any special action be taken?

: **S17.13** Eighty items are randomly drawn from a lot of 6,000 talking toy animals, and the total lot is accepted if there are $c \leqslant 2$ defects. Develop an OC curve for this sample plan.

: **S17.14** A load of 200 desk lamps has just arrived at the warehouse of Lighting, Inc. Random samples of $n = 5$ lamps are checked. If more than one lamp is defective, the whole lot is rejected. Set up the OC curve for this plan.

: **S17.15** Develop the AOQ curve for Problem S17.14.

: **S17.16** Each week Domzal Ltd. receives a batch of 1,000 popular Swiss watches for its chain of East Coast boutiques. Domzal and the Swiss manufacturer have agreed on the following sampling plan: $\alpha = 5\%$, $\beta = 10\%$, AQL = 1%, LTPD = 5%. Develop the OC curve for a sampling plan of $n = 100$ and $c \leqslant 2$. Does this plan meet the producer's and consumer's requirements?

✓ : **S17.17** A firm in Waco, Texas, has designed an OC curve that shows a 2/3 chance of accepting lots with a true percentage defective of 2%. Lots of 1,000 units are produced at a time, with 100 of each lot sampled randomly. What is the average outgoing quality level?

DATA BASE APPLICATION

: **S17.18** Ward Battery Corp. has recently been receiving complaints from retailers that its 9-volt batteries are not lasting as long as other name brands. James Ward, head of the TQM program at the Austin plant, believes there is no problem, since his batteries have had an average life of 50 hours, about 10% longer than competitors' models. To raise the lifetime above this would require a new level of technology not available to Ward. Nevertheless, he is concerned enough to set up hourly assembly line checks. He decides to take 5 samples of 9-volt batteries for each of the next 25 hours to create the standards for control chart limits (see the accompanying table).

Ward Battery Data—Battery Lifetimes (in hours)

| HOUR | SAMPLE | | | | | | |
	1	2	3	4	5	$\bar{X}$	R
1	51	50	49	50	50	50.0	2
2	45	47	70	46	36	48.8	34
3	50	35	48	39	47	43.8	15
4	55	70	50	30	51	51.2	40
5	49	38	64	36	47	46.8	28
6	59	62	40	54	64	55.8	24
7	36	33	49	48	56	44.4	23
8	50	67	53	43	40	50.6	27
9	44	52	46	47	44	46.6	8
10	70	45	50	47	41	50.6	29
11	57	54	62	45	36	50.8	26
12	56	54	47	42	62	52.2	20
13	40	70	58	45	44	51.4	30
14	52	58	40	52	46	49.6	18
15	57	42	52	58	59	53.6	17
16	62	49	42	33	55	48.2	29
17	40	39	49	59	48	47.0	20
18	64	50	42	57	50	52.6	22
19	58	53	52	48	50	52.2	10
20	60	50	41	41	50	48.4	19
21	52	47	48	58	40	49.0	18
22	55	40	56	49	45	49.0	16
23	47	48	50	50	48	48.6	3
24	50	50	49	51	51	50.2	2
25	51	50	51	51	62	53.0	12

With these limits in place, Ward now takes five more hours of data, shown in the following sample:

| HOUR | SAMPLE | | | | |
	1	2	3	4	5
26	48	52	39	57	61
27	45	53	48	46	66
28	63	49	50	45	53
29	57	70	45	52	61
30	45	38	46	54	52

a) Is the manufacturing process in control?

b) Comment on the lifetimes observed.

CASE STUDY

Bayfield Mud Company

In November 1990, John Wells, a customer service representative of Bayfield Mud Company, was summoned to the Houston, Texas, warehouse of Wet-Land Drilling, Inc., to inspect three boxcars of mud-treating agents that Bayfield Mud Company had shipped to the Houston firm. (Bayfield's corporate offices and its largest plant are located in Orange, Texas, which is just west of the Louisiana–Texas border.) Wet-Land Drilling had filed a complaint that the 50-pound bags of treating agents that it had just received from Bayfield were short-weight by approximately 5%.

The light-weight bags were initially detected by one of Wet-Land's receiving clerks, who noticed that the railroad scale tickets indicated that the net weights were significantly less on all three of the boxcars than those of identical shipments received on October 25, 1990. Bayfield's traffic department was called to determine if lighter-weight dunnage or pallets were used on the shipments. (This might explain the lighter net weights.) Bayfield indicated, however, that no changes had been made in the loading or palletizing procedures. Hence, Wet-Land randomly checked 50 of the bags and discovered that the average net weight was 47.51 pounds. They noted from past shipments that the bag net weights averaged exactly 50.0 pounds, with an acceptable standard deviation of 1.2 pounds. Consequently, they concluded that the sample indicated a significant short-weight. (The reader may wish to verify the above conclusion.) Bayfield was then contacted, and Wells was sent to investigate the complaint. Upon arrival, Wells verified the complaint and issued a 5% credit to Wet-Land.

Wet-Land's management, however, was not completely satisfied with only the issuance of credit for the short shipment. The charts followed by their mud engineers on the drilling platforms were based on 50-pound bags of treating agents. Lighter-weight bags might result in poor chemical control during the drilling operation and might adversely affect drilling efficiency. (Mud treating agents are used to control the pH and other chemical properties of the cone during drilling operation.) This could cause severe economic consequences because of the extremely high cost of oil and natural gas well drilling operations. Consequently, special use instructions had to accompany the delivery of these shipments to the drilling platforms. Moreover, the light-weight shipments had to be isolated in Wet-Land's warehouse, causing extra handling and poor space utilization. Hence, Wells was informed that Wet-Land Drilling

Source: Written by Professor Jerry Kinard (Francis Marion College) and Joe Iverstine.

might seek a new supplier of mud treating agents if, in the future, it received bags that deviated significantly from 50 pounds.

The quality control department at Bayfield suspected that the light-weight bags may have resulted from "growing pains" at the Orange plant. Because of the earlier energy crisis, oil and natural gas exploration activity had greatly increased. This increased activity, in turn, created increased demand for products produced by related industries, including drilling muds. Consequently, Bayfield had to expand from a one-shift (6:00 A.M. to 2:00 P.M.) to a two-shift (6:00 A.M. to 10:00 P.M.) operation in mid-1988, and finally to a three-shift operation (24 hours per day) in the fall of 1990.

The additional night-shift bagging crew was staffed entirely by new employees. The most experienced foremen were temporarily assigned to supervise the night-shift employees. Most emphasis was placed on increasing the output of bags to meet the ever-increasing demand. It was suspected that only occasional reminders were made to double-check the bag weight-feeder. (A double-check is performed by systematically weighing a bag on a scale to determine if the proper weight is being loaded by the weight-feeder. If there is significant deviation from 50 pounds, corrective adjustments are made to the weight-release mechanism.)

To verify this expectation, the quality control staff randomly sampled the bag output and prepared the following chart. Six bags were sampled and weighed each hour.

TIME	AVERAGE WEIGHT (POUNDS)	RANGE	
		Smallest	*Largest*
6:00 A.M.	49.6	48.7	50.7
7:00	50.2	49.1	51.2
8:00	50.6	49.6	51.4
9:00	50.8	50.2	51.8
10.00	49.9	49.2	52.3
11:00	50.3	48.6	51.7
12 Noon	48.6	46.2	50.4
1:00 P.M.	49.0	46.4	50.0
2:00	49.0	46.0	50.6
3:00	49.8	48.2	50.8
4:00	50.3	49.2	52.7
5:00	51.4	50.0	55.3
6:00	51.6	49.2	54.7
7:00	51.8	50.0	55.6

CASE STUDY (Continued)

TIME	AVERAGE WEIGHT (POUNDS)	RANGE Smallest	RANGE Largest	TIME	AVERAGE WEIGHT (POUNDS)	RANGE Smallest	RANGE Largest
8:00	51.0	48.6	53.2	1:00 A.M.	49.6	48.4	51.7
9:00	50.5	49.4	52.4	2:00	50.0	49.0	52.2
10.00	49.2	46.1	50.7	3:00	50.0	49.2	50.0
11:00	49.0	46.3	50.8	4.00	47.2	46.3	50.5
12 Midnight	48.4	45.4	50.2	5:00	47.0	44.1	49.7
1:00 A.M.	47.6	44.3	49.7	6:00	48.4	45.0	49.0
2:00	47.4	44.1	49.6	7:00	48.8	44.8	49.7
3:00	48.2	45.2	49.0	8:00	49.6	48.0	51.8
4:00	48.0	45.5	49.1	9:00	50.0	48.1	52.7
5:00	48.4	47.1	49.6	10:00	51.0	48.1	55.2
6:00	48.6	47.4	52.0	11:00	50.4	49.5	54.1
7:00	50.0	49.2	52.2	12 Noon	50.0	48.7	50.9
8:00	49.8	49.0	52.4	1:00 P.M.	48.9	47.6	51.2
9.00	50.3	49.4	51.7	2:00	49.8	48.4	51.0
10:00	50.2	49.6	51.8	3.00	49.8	48.8	50.8
11:00	50.0	49.0	52.3	4:00	50.0	49.1	50.6
12 Noon	50.0	48.8	52.4	5:00	47.8	45.2	51.2
1:00 A.M.	50.1	49.4	53.6	6:00	46.4	44.0	49.7
2:00	49.7	48.6	51.0	7:00	46.4	44.4	50.0
3:00	48.4	47.2	51.7	8:00	47.2	46.6	48.9
4:00	47.2	45.3	50.9	9:00	48.4	47.2	49.5
5.00	46.8	44.1	49.0	10:00	49.2	48.1	50.7
6:00	46.8	41.0	51.2	11.00	48.4	47.0	50.8
7:00	50.0	46.2	51.7	12 Midnight	47.2	46.4	49.2
8:00	47.4	44.0	48.7	1:00 A.M.	47.4	46.8	49.0
9:00	47.0	44.2	48.9	2:00	48.8	47.2	51.4
10:00	47.2	46.6	50.2	3:00	49.6	49.0	50.6
11:00	48.6	47.0	50.0	4:00	51.0	50.5	51.5
12 Midnight	49.8	48.2	50.4	5:00	50.5	50.0	51.9

Discussion Questions

1. What is your analysis of the bag weight problem?

2. What procedures would you recommend to maintain proper quality control?

CASE STUDY

Morristown Daily Tribune

In July 1990, the Morristown *Daily Tribune* published its first newspaper in direct competition with two other newspapers—the Morristown *Daily Ledger* and the *Clarion Herald,* a weekly publication. Presently, the *Ledger* is the most widely read newspaper in the area, with a total circulation of 38,500. The *Tribune,* however, has made significant inroads into the readership market since its inception. Total circulation of the *Tribune* now exceeds 27,000.

Wilbur Sykes, editor of the *Tribune,* attributes the success of the newspaper to the accuracy of its contents, a

CASE STUDY (Continued)

strong editorial section, and the proper blending of local, regional, national, and international news items. In addition, the paper has been successful in getting the accounts of several major retailers who advertise extensively in the display section. Finally, experienced reporters, photographers, copy writers, typesetters, editors, and other personnel have formed a "team" dedicated to providing the most timely and accurate reporting of news in the area.

Of critical importance to quality newspaper printing is accurate typesetting. To assure quality in the final print, Mr. Sykes has decided to develop a procedure for monitoring the performance of typesetters over a period of time. Such a procedure involves sampling output, establishing control limits, comparing the *Tribune*'s accuracy with that of the industry, and occasionally up-dating the information.

First, Mr. Sykes randomly selected 30 newspapers published during the preceding 12 months. From each paper, 100 paragraphs were randomly chosen and were read for accuracy. The number of paragraphs with errors in each paper was recorded, and the fraction of paragraphs with errors in each sample was determined. The table below shows the results of the sampling.

SAMPLE	PARAGRAPHS WITH ERRORS IN THE SAMPLE	FRACTION OF PARAGRAPHS WITH ERRORS (PER 100)	SAMPLE	PARAGRAPHS WITH ERRORS IN THE SAMPLE	FRACTION OF PARAGRAPHS WITH ERRORS (PER 100)
1	2	.02	16	2	.02
2	4	.04	17	3	.03
3	10	.10	18	7	.07
4	4	.04	19	3	.03
5	1	.01	20	2	.02
6	1	.01	21	3	.03
7	13	.13	22	7	.07
8	9	.09	23	4	.04
9	11	.11	24	3	.03
10	0	.00	25	2	.02
11	3	.03	26	2	.02
12	4	.04	27	0	.00
13	2	.02	28	1	.01
14	2	.02	29	3	.03
15	8	.08	30	4	.04

Discussion Questions

1. Plot the overall fraction of errors ($\overline{p}$) and the upper and lower control limits on a control chart using a 95.45% confidence level.

2. Assume the industry upper and lower control limits are .1000 and .0400, respectively. Plot them on the control chart.

3. Plot the fraction of errors in each sample. Do all fall within the firm's control limits? When one falls outside the control limits, what should be done?

Source: Written by Professor Jerry Kinard (Francis Marion College) and Joe Iverstine.

BIBLIOGRAPHY

Besterfield, D. H. *Quality Control,* 2nd ed. Englewood Cliffs, NJ: Prentice-Hall, 1986.

Buffa, E. W. *Meeting the Competitive Challenge: Manufacturing Strategy for U.S. Companies.* Homewood, IL: Dow-Jones Irwin, 1984.

Crosby, P. B. *Quality Is Free.* New York: McGraw-Hill, 1979.

Deming, W. E. *Out of the Crisis.* Cambridge, MA: MIT Center for Advanced Engineering Study, 1986.

"Directory of Software for Quality Assurance and Quality Control." *Quality Progress* (March 1984): 33–53.

Duncalf, A. J., and B. G. Dale. "How British Industry Is Making Decisions on Product Quality." *Long Range Planning,* **8,** 5: 81–88.

Garvin, D. A. "Japanese Quality Management." *Columbia Journal of World Business,* **19,** 3 (Fall 1984): 3–12.

Gitlow, H. S., and P. T. Hertz. "Product Defects and Productivity." *Harvard Business Review,* **61,** 5 (September–October 1983): 131–141.

Gitlow, H. S., and S. Gitlow. *The Deming Guide to Achieving Quality and Competitive Position.* Englewood Cliffs, NJ: Prentice-Hall, 1987.

Grant, E. L., and R. S. Leavenworth. *Statistical Quality Control,* 6th ed. New York: McGraw-Hill, 1988.

Leonard, F. S., and E. W. Sasser. "The Incline of Quality." *Harvard Business Review,* **60,** 5 (September–October 1982): 163–171.

Messina, W. S. *Statistical Quality for Manufacturing Managers.* New York: John Wiley & Sons, 1987.

Reddy, J., and A. Berger. "Three Essentials of Product Quality." *Harvard Business Review,* **61,** 4 (July–August 1983): 153–159.

Saporito, B. "The Revolt Against Working Smarter." *Fortune* (July 21, 1986): 58–65.

Schonberger, R. J. *World Class Manufacturing.* New York: Free Press, 1986.

Maintenance and Reliability Tactics

Maintenance Provides a Competitive Advantage for Orlando Utilities Commission

The Orlando Utilities Commission (OUC) owns and operates power plants that supply power to 13 central Florida counties. Every year, OUC takes each one of its power-generating units off-line for one to three weeks to perform maintenance work. Additionally, each steam-generating unit is also taken off-line every three years for a complete overhaul and turbine generator inspection. These overhauls last from six to eight weeks.

A coal-fired unit at OUC's Stanton Energy Center requires that maintenance personnel perform approximately 12,000 repair and preventive maintenance tasks a year. To accomplish these tasks efficiently many of these jobs are scheduled daily via a computerized maintenance management program. The computer generates preventive maintenance work orders and lists of required materials.

Maintenance of capital intensive facilities requires good planning to minimize downtime. Here turbine overhaul, which occurs every three years, is under way. Organizing the thousands of parts and pieces necessary for a shutdown is a major effort.

O verhauls are scheduled for spring and fall, when the weather is mildest and demand for power is low. They are also scheduled several years in advance in coordination with other Florida electric utilities. This coordination ensures that an adequate supply of power is maintained in the statewide grid. OUC usually provides its own backup power during scheduled outages. However, if necessary, OUC can usually buy power from other utilities through the grid.

E very day that a plant is down for maintenance costs OUC about $55,000 extra. This is the incremental cost. It includes added labor, material, and replacement cost of power that must be generated elsewhere. However, these costs pale beside the costs associated with a forced outage. An unexpected outage could cost OUC an additional $250,000 to $500,000 each day!

S cheduled overhauls are not easy; each one has 1,800 distinct tasks and requires 72,000

The high pressure/low pressure section of turbine has been removed for overhaul. When steam first enters this 23-ton high-pressure rotor, it bears hurricane-strength force.

labor hours. But the value of preventive maintenance was illustrated by the first overhaul of a new turbine generator. A cracked rotor blade was discovered, which could have destroyed a $27 million piece of equipment. To find such cracks, which are invisible to the naked eye, metals are examined by dye tests, x rays, and ultrasound.

The Stanton Energy Center is among the most reliable and efficient power plants in the nation. Its forced outage rate for 1991 was 3.72%, compared with a national average of 9.36%; its availability factor was 87.75%, compared to the national average of 78.48%. Such results demonstrate that effective maintenance provides a competitive advantage for the Orlando Utilities Commission.

At OUC, preventive maintenance is worth its weight in gold. As a result, OUC's electric distribution system is ranked number one in Florida for reliability.

Inspection is proceeding on low pressure section of turbine. The tips of these turbine blades will travel at supersonic speeds of 1,300 miles per hour when the plant is in operation. And a crack in any one of these blades can cause a catastrophic failure.

INTRODUCTION

When the United Airlines DC-10 left Denver, three engines and all three hydraulic systems were working. But at 3:17 P.M. an explosion shook the plane. Number 2 engine had torn itself apart. The three separate hydraulic lines ceased to work. In spite of the work of dedicated designers and well-trained maintenance personnel, the engine failed. In spite of having three separate hydraulic lines, the aircraft had no working hydraulic system. In spite of eight million hours of no fatal United Airlines accidents, over one hundred people were about to die.

Reliability is important to P/OM managers. Maintenance is important to P/OM managers. System failures cause undesirable results.

This chapter is concerned with avoiding undesirable results of system failure. Even when the results are not catastrophic, the results of failure can be disruptive, inconvenient, wasteful, and expensive.

A recent study addressing the weaknesses in British productivity compared British and German firms.[1] The study found that although the machinery in the British plants was no older than that in the German plants, it was badly maintained; breakdowns were found to be more frequent and lasted longer. Operators were found less able to do repairs themselves. Machine and product failures can have far-reaching effects on a firm's operation and profitability. In complex, highly mechanized plants, an out-of-tolerance process or a machine breakdown may result in idle employees and facilities, loss of customers and goodwill, and profits turning into losses. Likewise, in an office, the failure of a generator, an air-conditioning system, or a computer may halt operations. Reliability and maintenance protect both a firm's performance and its investment.

Good managers maintain a system while keeping maintenance and breakdown costs under control. *The objective of reliability and maintenance is to maintain the capability of the system while controlling costs.* Systems must be designed and maintained to reach expected performance and quality standards. **Reliability** is the probability that a machine part or product will function properly for a given length of time. **Maintenance** includes all activities involved in keeping a system's equipment in working order. We will examine tactics to enhance reliability and maintenance.

Reliability

Maintenance

As we have noted in our discussion of scheduling, inventories, and just-in-time techniques, instability or variability must be removed for efficient operations. One of the major causes of variability is unreliable systems. We have five ways to improve system reliability. These are:

1. Use inventory to decouple stages of the system.
2. Improve individual components.
3. Provide redundancy (backup or parallel systems).
4. Implement or improve preventive maintenance.
5. Increase capabilities or speed of repair facilities.

Although inventory can be used to separate or decouple successive stages of unreliable processes, as we observed in Chapter 13, the inventory solution is a rather

[1] National Institute of Economic and Social Research as reported in "Britain's Economy," *The Economist* (March 9, 1985): 62–63.

expensive one. Consequently, in this chapter we examine four tactics other than inventory for improving reliability of products and equipment as well as the systems that produce them. The four tactics are organized around reliability and maintenance.

The reliability tactics are:

1. improving individual components;
2. providing redundancy.

The maintenance tactics are:

1. implementing or improving preventive maintenance;
2. increasing repair capabilities or speed.

RELIABILITY

As we noted in Chapter 2, systems are composed of a series of individual interrelated components, each performing a specific job. If any *one* of these components fails to perform, for whatever reason, the overall system (for example, an airplane or machine) can fail.

Improving Individual Components

The *POM in* Action box, "Jetliner Crash in Iowa Seems Sure to Reopen Issue of DC-10 Safety," on page 803, suggests failures do occur. That failures occur is an important reliability concept. Figure 18.1 illustrates that a system of $n = 50$ interacting parts, each of which has a 99.5% reliability, has an overall reliability of 78%. If the system or machine has 100 interacting parts, each with an individual reliability of 99.5%, the overall reliability will be only about 60%!

From Figure 18.1 we see that as the number of components in a *series* increases (as represented by the curved lines labeled $n = 50$, $n = 100$, $n = 200$, and so on), the reliability of the whole system declines very quickly (as evidenced by the scale on the vertical axis).

To measure system reliability in which each individual part or component may have its own unique rate of reliability, we cannot use the reliability curve. However, the method of computing system reliability (R_s) is simple. It consists of finding the product of individual reliabilities as follows:

$$R_s = R_1 \times R_2 \times R_3 \times \ldots \times R_n \tag{18.1}$$

where

$$R_1 = \text{Reliability of component 1}$$
$$R_2 = \text{Reliability of component 2}$$

and so on.

This equation assumes that the reliability of an individual component does not depend on the reliability of other components (that is, each component is independent). Additionally, in this equation, as in most reliability discussions, reliabilities are presented as probabilities. A .90 reliability means that the unit will perform as

FIGURE 18.1

Overall System Reliability as a Function of Number of Components and
Component Reliability with Components in a Series.
(*Source:* R. Lusser, "The Notorious Unreliability of Complex Equipment,"
Astronautics, February 1958. Reprinted with permission from the American
Institute of Aeronautics and Astronautics, *Astronautics,* February 1958.)

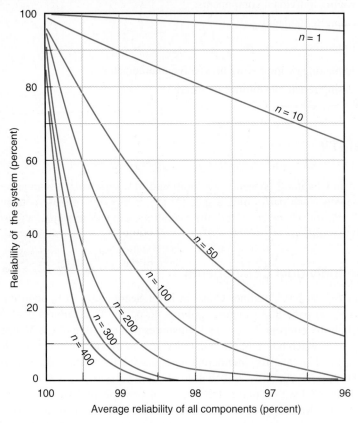

intended 90% of the time. It also means that it will fail $1 - .90 = .1 = 10\%$ of the
time. We can use this method to evaluate the reliability of a product, such as the one
we examine in Example 1.

Example 1

Nels Electric of Greeley, Colorado, produces an electrical relay switch that has
three components set up in series:

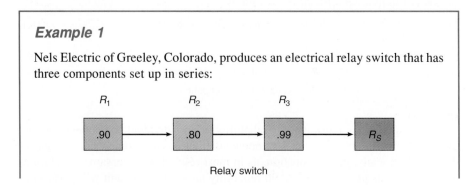

Relay switch

POM *in action*

Jetliner Crash in Iowa Seems Sure to Reopen Issue of DC-10 Safety

Today's jetliners are expected to be designed so that one system's failure doesn't automatically cripple others. But the 1989 crash of a United Airlines DC-10 in Iowa seems to indicate that the McDonnell Douglas plane's hydraulic systems aren't providing good enough protection. The DC-10 has three mazes of half-inch pipes running throughout the plane. These separate hydraulic systems are supposed to continuously pump fluid that operates control devices, but federal investigators think the pipes in the plane's tail were severed by flying tail engine parts. All hydraulic fluid then sprayed out the back.

The crew realized quickly that although the jet had plenty of power left in the two wing engines, there was no hydraulic pressure left. Like a bomb exploding, the rear engine threw off shreds of metal everywhere. Some of this shrapnel severed two of the three hydraulic lines. But the third line wouldn't

have worked anyway—its power was provided by a pump wired to the demolished engine.

The DC-10, unlike other jets, was not designed with shut-off valves that might have stemmed the loss of hydraulic fluid. Further, the plane had one fewer hydraulic system than the four in Lockheed's similar L-1011 trijet. Safety experts think that if the DC-10's system had had the fourth line, the jet and its 100 plus passengers might have been spared.

McDonnell Douglas insists that it's too early to judge the safety of the DC-10's hydraulics. A company V.P. says, "You can always be extreme and not have a practical airplane. You can be perfectly safe and never get off the ground."

Sources: Economist, December 1990, p. 104; *Aviation Week and Space Technology,* September 18, 1989, pp. 122–123; and *Wall Street Journal,* July 24, 1989, p. 1.

If the individual reliabilities are .90, .80, .99, then the reliability of the entire relay switch is:

$$R_s = R_1 R_2 R_3 = (.90)(.80)(.99) = .713 \quad \text{or} \quad 71.3\%$$

Component reliability is often a design or specification issue for which engineering design personnel may be responsible. However, purchasing personnel may be able to improve components of systems by staying abreast of suppliers' products and research efforts. Purchasing personnel can also directly contribute to evaluation of supplier performance.

A **failure** is the change in a product or system from a satisfactory working condition to a condition that is below an acceptable standard. The basic unit of measure for reliability is the product failure rate (FR). Firms producing high-technology equipment often provide failure rate data on their products. The failure rate measures the percentage of failures among the total number of products tested, FR(%), or a number of failures during a period of time, FR(N):

Failure

$$\text{FR}(\%) = \frac{\text{Number of failures}}{\text{Number of units tested}} \times 100\% \tag{18.2}$$

$$FR(N) = \frac{\text{Number of failures}}{\text{Number of unit-hours of operating time}} \tag{18.3}$$

Mean time between failures (MTBF)

Perhaps the most common term in reliability analysis is the **mean time between failures (MTBF),** which is the reciprocal of FR(N):

$$MTBF = \frac{1}{FR(N)} \tag{18.4}$$

In Example 2, we compute the percentage of failure FR(%), number of failures FR(N), and mean time between failures (MTBF).

Example 2

Twenty air-conditioning systems to be used by astronauts in NASA space shuttles were operated for 1,000 hours at NASA's Huntsville, Alabama, test facility. Two of the systems failed during the test—one after 200 hours and the other after 600 hours. To compute the percentage of failures,

$$FR(\%) = \frac{\text{Number of failures}}{\text{Number tested}} = \frac{2}{20}\,(100\%)$$

$$= 10\%$$

Next we compute the number of failures per operating hour:

$$FR(N) = \frac{\text{Number of failures}}{\text{Operating time}}$$

where

$$\text{Total time} = (1,000 \text{ hr.})(20 \text{ units})$$

$$= 20,000 \text{ units-hrs.}$$

$$\text{Nonoperating time} = 800 \text{ hrs. for 1st failure} + 400 \text{ hrs. for 2nd failure}$$

$$= 1,200 \text{ unit-hrs.}$$

$$\text{Operating time} = \text{Total time} - \text{Nonoperating time}$$

$$FR(N) = \frac{2}{20,000 - 1,200} = \frac{2}{18,800}$$

$$= .000106 \text{ failure/unit-hr.}$$

and since $MTBF = \dfrac{1}{FR(N)}$

$$MTBF = \frac{1}{.000106} = 9,434 \text{ hr.}$$

If the typical space shuttle trip lasts 60 days, NASA may be interested in the failure rate per trip:

$$\text{Failure rate} = (\text{Failures/unit-hr.})(24 \text{ hr./day})(60 \text{ days/trip})$$

$$= (.000106)(24)(60)$$

$$= .152 \text{ failure/trip}$$

Since the failure rate of Example 2 is likely too high, NASA will have to either increase the reliability of individual components, and hence of the system, or else install several backup air-conditioning units on each space shuttle. Backup units provide redundancy.

Providing Redundancy

Redundancy is provided if one component fails and the system has recourse to another. To increase the reliability of systems, redundancy ("backing-up" the components) is added. For instance, say reliability of a component is .80 and we back it up with another component with reliability of .80. Then the resulting reliability is the probability of the first component working plus the probability of the backup component working multiplied by the probability of needing the backup component $(1 - .8 = .2)$. Therefore:

$$\begin{pmatrix} \text{Probability} \\ \text{of first} \\ \text{component} \\ \text{working} \end{pmatrix} + \left[\begin{pmatrix} \text{Probability} \\ \text{of second} \\ \text{component} \\ \text{working} \end{pmatrix} \times \begin{pmatrix} \text{Probability} \\ \text{of needing} \\ \text{second} \\ \text{component} \end{pmatrix} \right] =$$

$$(.8) + [(.8) \times (1 - .8)] = .8 + .16 = .96.$$

Example 3

Nels Electric is disturbed that its electrical relay has a reliability of only .713 (see Example 1). Therefore, Nels decides to provide redundancy for the two least reliable components. This results in the system shown below:

$$\begin{array}{ccc} R_1 & R_2 & R_3 \\ 0.90 & 0.8 \\ \end{array}$$

$$0.90 \rightarrow 0.8 \rightarrow 0.99 = [.9 + .9(1 - .9)] \times [.8 + .8(1 - .8)] \times .99$$
$$= [.9 + (.9)(.1)] \times [.8 + (.8)(.2)] \times .99$$
$$= .99 \times .96 \times .99 = .94$$

So by providing redundancy for two components, Nels has increased reliability of the switch from .713 to .94.

MAINTENANCE

Maintenance falls into two categories: preventive maintenance and breakdown maintenance. **Preventive maintenance** involves performing routine inspections and servicing and keeping facilities in good repair. Preventive maintenance activities are intended to build a system that will find potential failures and make changes or repairs that will prevent failure. Preventive maintenance is much more than just keeping machinery and equipment running. It also involves designing technical and human systems that will keep the productive process working within tolerance; it allows the system to perform. The emphasis is on understanding the process and

Preventive maintenance

Breakdown maintenance

allowing it to work without interruption. **Breakdown maintenance** is remedial; it occurs when equipment fails and then must be repaired on an emergency or priority basis.

Implementing Preventive Maintenance

Figure 18.2 shows the major components of a computerized maintenance system. Maintaining equipment history is an important part of a preventive maintenance system, as is a record of the time and cost to make the repair.

Preventive maintenance implies that we can determine when a system needs service or will need repair. Therefore, to perform preventive maintenance, we must define when a system requires service or when it is likely to fail. Figure 18.3 indicates that failure occurs at different rates during the life of a product; it may follow different statistical distributions. A high failure rate, known as **infant mor-tality,** exists initially for many products. This is the reason many electronic firms "burn in" their products prior to shipment. That is to say, many firms execute a variety of tests to detect "startup" problems prior to shipment. Other firms provide 90-day warranties. We should note that many infant mortality failures are not

Infant mortality

FIGURE 18.2

A Computerized Maintenance System.

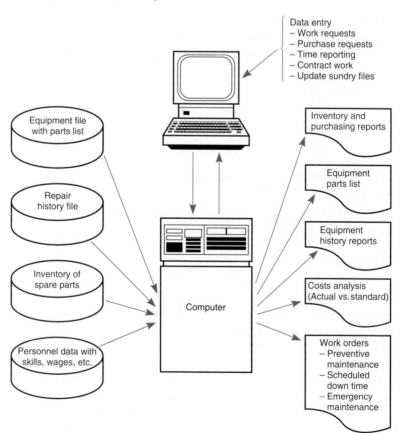

FIGURE 18.3

Lifetime Failure Rates.

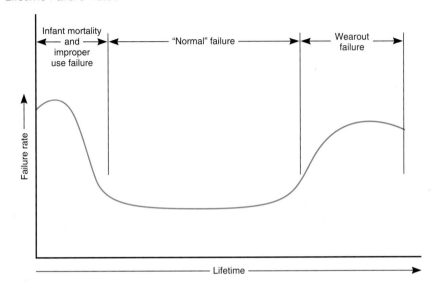

product failures per se but failure due to improper use. This fact points up the importance of management building a maintenance system that includes training and personnel selection.

Once the product, machine, or process "settles in," a study can be made of the MTBF (mean time between failure) distribution. When the distributions have a small standard deviation, then we know we have a candidate for preventive maintenance even if the maintenance is expensive.[2]

Once we have a candidate for preventive maintenance, we want to determine when preventive maintenance is economical. Typically, the more expensive the maintenance, the narrower must be the MTBF distribution. Additionally, if the process is no more expensive to repair when it breaks down than the cost of preventive maintenance, perhaps we should let the process break down and then do the repair. However, the consequence of the breakdown must be fully considered; some relatively minor breakdowns have catastrophic consequences. At the other extreme, preventive maintenance costs may be so incidental that preventive maintenance is appropriate even if the distribution is rather flat (that is, it has a large standard deviation). In any event, every machine operator must be held responsible for inspection of equipment and tools.

A variety of sensing devices exist to help determine when a process should receive maintenance. For instance, many aircraft engines have a sensor that indicates the presence of metals in the lubricating oils. This sensor indicates unusual wear and the need for preventive maintenance prior to a breakdown (which is a nice idea, particularly on airplanes). A variety of other devices, from vibration sensors to infrared thermography, are available to help determine preventive maintenance

---

[2] See for example the work of P. M. Morse, *Queues, Inventories, and Maintenance* (New York: John Wiley & Sons, 1958) pp. 161–168; and "Using Statistical Thinking to Solve Maintenance Problems," *Quality Progress* (May 1989): 55–60.

FIGURE 18.4

Maintenance Costs.

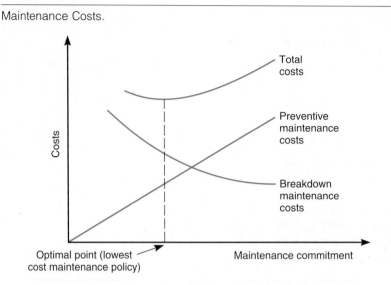

requirements.[3] Additionally, with good reporting techniques firms can maintain records of individual processes, machines, or equipment. Such records can provide a profile of both the kinds of maintenance required and timing of maintenance needed. Such records can also contribute to similar information about the family of equipment as well as suppliers.

Figure 18.4 shows the relationship between preventive maintenance and breakdown maintenance. Operations managers need to consider a balance between the two costs. Allocating more money and crew to preventive maintenance will reduce the number of breakdowns. But, at some point, the decrease in breakdown maintenance costs will be less than the increase in preventive maintenance costs, and the total cost curve will begin to rise. Beyond this optimal point, the firm will be better off waiting for breakdowns to occur and repairing them when they do.

The problem with this analysis is that the full costs of breakdown are seldom considered. Many costs are ignored because they are not directly related to the immediate breakdown. That does not make them any less real or their impact any less important. For instance, the cost of inventory that is maintained to compensate for this downtime is not typically considered; downtime can have a devastating effect on morale because employees begin to believe that performance to standard and maintaining equipment are not important.

Assuming that all costs associated with downtime have been identified, the operations staff can compute the optimal level of maintenance activity on a theoretical basis. The analysis, of course, also requires accurate historical data on maintenance costs, breakdown probabilities, and repair times. Example 4 illustrates how to compare preventive and breakdown maintenance costs in order to select the least expensive maintenance policy.

---

[3] See V. R. Dodd and J. R. East, "Vibration Surveillance Now Covers Minor Equipment," *Oil and Gas Journal,* **80** (January 11, 1982): 63–70. Also P. J. Kloss, "Sensor Monitors Aircrafts' Systems," *Aviation Week & Space Technology,* **116** (May 3, 1982): 67–69.

Example 4

Huntsman and Associates is a CPA firm specializing in payroll preparation. The accountants have been successful in automating much of their work, using a Digimatic II computer for processing and report preparation. The computerized approach has problems, however. Over the past 20 months, the computer system has broken down as indicated below.

NUMBER OF BREAKDOWNS	NUMBER OF MONTHS THAT BREAKDOWNS OCCURRED
0	4
1	8
2	6
3	2
Total:	20

Each time the computer breaks down, the partners estimate that the firm loses an average of $300 in time and service expenses. One alternative is for the firm to accept Digimatic's offer to contract for preventive maintenance. If they accept preventive maintenance, they expect an *average* of only one computer breakdown per month. The price that Digimatic charges for this service is $220 per month. We will follow a four-step approach to answer the question of whether the CPAs should contract with Digimatic for preventive maintenance:

Step 1. Compute the *expected number* of breakdowns (based on past history) if the firm continues as is, without the service contract.

Step 2. Compute the expected breakdown cost per month with no preventive maintenance contract.

Step 3. Compute the cost of preventive maintenance.

Step 4. Compare the two options and select the one that will cost less.

1.

NUMBER OF BREAKDOWNS	FREQUENCY	NUMBER OF BREAKDOWNS	FREQUENCY
0	4/20 = .2	2	6/20 = 0.3
1	8/20 = .4	3	2/20 = 0.1

$$\begin{pmatrix}\text{Expected number} \\ \text{of breakdowns}\end{pmatrix} = \Sigma \begin{pmatrix}\text{Number of} \\ \text{breakdowns}\end{pmatrix} \times \begin{pmatrix}\text{Corresponding} \\ \text{frequency}\end{pmatrix}$$

$$= (0)(.2) + (1)(.4) + (2)(.3) + (3)(.1)$$

$$= 0 + .4 + .6 + .3$$

$$= 1.3 \text{ breakdowns/mo.}$$

2. Expected breakdown cost $= \begin{pmatrix}\text{Expected number} \\ \text{of breakdowns}\end{pmatrix} \times \begin{pmatrix}\text{Cost per} \\ \text{breakdown}\end{pmatrix}$

$= (1.3)(\$300)$

$= \$390/\text{mo.}$

3. Preventive maintenance cost $= \begin{pmatrix}\text{Cost of expected} \\ \text{breakdowns if service} \\ \text{contract signed}\end{pmatrix} + \begin{pmatrix}\text{Cost of} \\ \text{service contract}\end{pmatrix}$

$= (1 \text{ breakdown/mo.})(\$300) + \$220/\text{mo.}$

$= \$520/\text{mo}$

4. Since it is less expensive to suffer the breakdowns *without* a maintenance service contract ($390) than with one ($520), the firm should continue its present policy.

Preventive maintenance is often a matter of overhauling an entire group of machines or a whole fleet of vehicles rather than operating them until they break down. The next example deals with determining a maintenance policy. Should we repair equipment only when it breaks down, or should we adopt a policy of regular weekly, monthly, bimonthly (or other periodic) overhauls?

Example 5

Swedish Paper GMB has five paper dryers, which tend to break down from time to time. The manufacturer's service department agrees to overhaul the five dryers on a preventive maintenance basis for a fee of $100 per overhaul visit. If a dryer does break down, it costs an average of $250 in lost production and repair. Records show that the probabilities of a breakdown after maintenance are as follows:

MONTHS UNTIL BREAKDOWN AFTER OVERHAUL	PROBABILITY OF BREAKDOWN
1	.2
2	.1
3	.3
4	.4

The question faced by management is whether to adopt a preventive maintenance policy. And if it does, how often should a dryer be overhauled? The first step is to compute what a repair-on-breakdown policy would cost. The calculation is fairly simple and is based on the expected length of time the dryer can go without overhaul.

$\begin{pmatrix}\text{Expected time} \\ \text{between breakdowns}\end{pmatrix} = (.2)(1 \text{ mo.}) + (.1)(2 \text{ mo.}) + (.3)(3 \text{ mo.}) + (.4)(4 \text{ mo.})$

$= 2.9 \text{ mo.}$

A repair-on-breakdown policy would cost an average of $431 per month (calculated as (5 dryers × $250) ÷ 2.9 mo. = $431).

The formula we need to compute the expected number of breakdowns (B_n) that will occur during the interval between overhauls is rather complex-looking. That equation is

$$B_n = N \sum_{1}^{n} p_n + B_{(n-1)} p_1 + B_{(n-2)} p_2 + B_{(n-3)} p_3 + \ldots + B_1 p_{(n-1)} \qquad (18.5)$$

where

n = Number of months (or time periods) between overhauls,

N = Number of machines or pieces of equipment in the group

p_n = Probability of machine breakdown during the nth month after maintenance (for example, if maintenance was performed on a machine in period 3, then p_1 is the probability the same machine will break down in period 4)

Policy of Overhauling Monthly.
The expected number of breakdowns given monthly preventive maintenance is

$$B_1 = Np_1 = 5(0.2) = 1$$

Total cost = Preventive maintenance cost + Breakdown cost

= $100 + (Expected number of breakdowns) × (Cost/breakdown)

= $100 + (1)($250)

= $350/mo.

Policy of Overhauling Every Two Months.

$$B_2 = N(p_1 + p_2) + B_1 p_1$$

$$= 5(.2 + .1) + 1(.2) = 1.7$$

The average number of breakdowns *per month* is 1.7/2 = .85. Because the preventive maintenance cost of $100 is now spread over two months, the overhaul cost *per month* is $50.

Total cost = $50 + (.85 breakdowns)($250/breakdown)

= $262.50/mo.

Overhauling Every Three Months.

$$B_3 = N(p_1 + p_2 + p_3) + B_2 p_1 + B_1 p_2$$

$$= 5(.2 + .1 + .3) + (1.7)(.2) + (1)(.1)$$

$$= 3.00 + .34 + .10 = 3.44$$

Total cost = (Cost of preventive maintenance/number of months)

+ (Average number of breakdowns per month)

× (Cost of breakdown)

= ($100/3) + (3.44/3)($250) = $33.33 + $285.00 = $318.33

Overhauling Every Four Months.

$$B_4 = N(p_1 + p_2 + p_3 + p_4) + B_3 p_1 + B_2 p_2 + B_1 p_3$$

$$= 5(.2 + .1 + .3 + .4) + (3.44)(.2) + (1.7)(.1) + (1)(.3)$$

$$= 5 + .688 + .17 + .3 = 6.158$$

Total cost = Average preventive maintenance cost + Expected breakdown cost

= ($100/4) + (6.158/4)($250) = $25.00 + $384.88 = $409.88

From the table below, we note that the best policy is to overhaul every two months.

OVERHAUL EVERY n MONTHS	TOTAL EXPECTED BREAKDOWNS IN n MONTHS	AVERAGE NUMBER OF BREAKDOWNS PER MONTH	EXPECTED BREAKDOWN COST PER MONTH	COST OF PREVENTIVE MAINTENANCE PER MONTH	EXPECTED TOTAL MONTHLY COST
1	1	1	$250.00	$100.00	$350.00
2	1.7	.85	212.50	50.00	262.50
3	3.44	1.14	285.00	33.33	318.33
4	6.158	1.54	384.88	25.00	409.88

Increasing Repair Capabilities

When reliability has not been achieved and preventive maintenance is not appropriate or does not work, management can enlarge or improve the repair facility. Operations managers can get back in operation faster if good repair facilities are available. Remedial maintenance can then be performed and the system put back in operation. A good maintenance facility implies many attributes. These include:

1. well-trained personnel;
2. adequate resources;
3. ability to establish a repair plan and priorities;[4]
4. ability and authority to do material planning;
5. ability to identify the cause of breakdowns;
6. ability to design ways to extend MTBF.

Operations managers also have a policy decision to make as to where on the continuum of Figure 18.5 each maintenance task belongs. Consistent with good participative management and employee responsibility, a strong case can be made for employees maintaining their own equipment. Such a decision would place maintenance on the left side of Figure 18.5. However, although the employee may be the most immediate option, she or he may also be the weakest link in the repair chain. Not every employee can be trained in all equipment repair possibilities.

Whatever preventive maintenance policies and techniques are decided upon, they must include an emphasis on employees accepting responsibility for the maintenance they are capable of doing. Employee maintenance may only be of the "clean, check, and observe" variety, but if each operator does those activities, within his or her capability, it will contribute to maintaining system performance.

---

[4] You may recall from our discussion of network planning in Chapters 1 and 16 that DuPont developed the critical path method (CPM) to improve the scheduling of maintenance projects.

FIGURE 18.5

The Operations Manager Must Determine Where on the Continuum Each Type of Maintenance Will Be Performed.

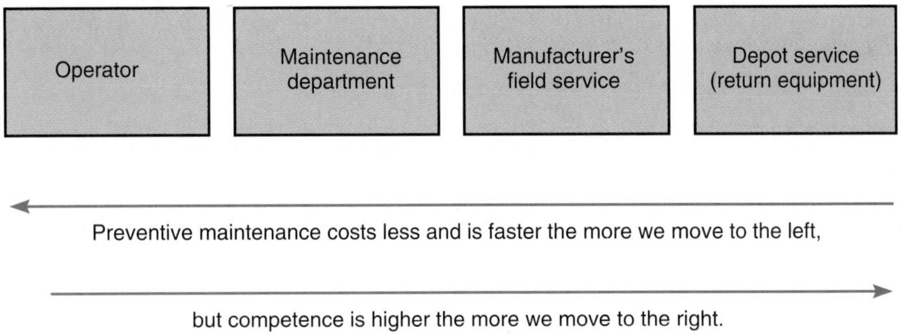

Operator	Maintenance department	Manufacturer's field service	Depot service (return equipment)

← Preventive maintenance costs less and is faster the more we move to the left,

but competence is higher the more we move to the right. →

Simulation Model for a Maintenance Policy

Simulation techniques can be used to evaluate the impact of various maintenance policies (such as the size of the facility) prior to implementing the policy. Operations personnel can decide whether to add more maintenance staff on the basis of the trade-offs between machine downtime costs and the costs of additional labor. Management can also simulate replacing parts that have not yet failed as a way of preventing future breakdowns. Many companies use computerized simulation models to decide if and when to shut down a whole plant for maintenance activities. The following example shows the value of simulation in setting maintenance policy. For a review of simulation, refer back to the supplement to Chapter 5.

Example 6

Kathy Harrigan, director of management analysis at the Cincinnati Manufacturing Company, is trying to decide whether to add a second full-time maintenance worker to the staff. She has collected some historical data and has used the Monte Carlo method to simulate machine breakdown over a 10-hour period.

TIME OF MACHINE BREAKDOWN	TOTAL HOURS OF REPAIR TIME REQUIRED
8:00 A.M.	1.0
9:30 A.M.	2.0
10:30 A.M.	1.0
1:00 P.M.	2.0
3:30 P.M.	1.5
	7.5

The firm's current maintenance worker charges his time at a rate of $18.00 per hour (whether he is working or idle). The cost for a machine that is down is estimated by Harrigan to be $100 per hour.

Her objective is to determine (1) the service maintenance cost, (2) the simulated machine-breakdown cost, and (3) the total simulated maintenance cost. Furthermore, she would like to know whether (on the basis of this brief simulation) she should hire a second maintenance worker. This chore will be assigned to *you* in Problem 18.6.

Here are the results of one simulation we conducted.

BREAKDOWN SIMULATION WITH ONE MAINTENANCE MAN

Time of Breakdown	Repair Time Required (Hours)	Time Repairs Begin	Time Repairs End	Number of Hours Machine Is Down
8:00 A.M.	1.0	8:00 A.M.	9:00 A.M.	1
9:30 A.M.	2.0	9:30 A.M.	11:30 A.M.	2
10:30 A.M.	1.0	11:30 A.M.	12:30 P.M.	2
1:00 P.M.	2.0	1:00 P.M.	3:00 P.M.	2
3:30 P.M.	1.5	3:00 P.M.	5:00 P.M.	1.5
				8.5

Note that repairs did not begin until 11:30 A.M. (when maintenance worker completed earlier job)

a) The service maintenance cost with one repair worker on duty is ($18.00/hr.) × (10 hr.) = $180.

b) The simulated machine-breakdown cost, from the rightmost column, is ($100/hr.) × (8.5 hr.) = $850.

c) Simulated total maintenance cost = service + breakdown = $180 + $850 = $1,030.

EXPERT SYSTEMS APPLIED TO MAINTENANCE

The use of expert systems is proving beneficial in maintenance systems. Expert systems in maintenance are assisting maintenance personnel in isolating and repairing various faults in machinery and equipment. For instance, General Electric's *DELTA* system aids the repair and maintenance of diesel-electric locomotives.[5] First, to isolate a problem, the system displays a menu of possible fault areas. Then, when the user has selected a particular fault area, the software asks a series of detailed questions leading and aiding the user in identifying the problem. The DELTA system consists of about 500 rules, 330 of which are devoted to fault diagnosis and repair procedures. The remaining questions form a help, or coaching, system that responds

[5] See H. Raghav Rao and B. P. Lingaraj, "Expert Systems in Production and Operations Management: Classification and Prospects," *Interfaces,* **18,** 6 (November–December 1988): 80–91. Expert systems are discussed in the supplement to Chapter 7, *Information Technology in P/OM.*

POM *in action*

Expert Maintenance Systems at DuPont

One DuPont engineer showed the uncanny knack of always keeping his process under control by analyzing data from sensors and QC checks. The problem was, when he was not around to make corrections to the process, other workers let the process slip out of specs almost a quarter of the time. As a part-time project, he built an expert system to help them. Now any operator monitoring the process is warned by the expert system when the process is heading out of control, and computer graphics of the control panel inform the operator which knobs to adjust. In the two years since DuPont put this tool on line, not one operator error has been made.

In a second expert system application at DuPont's Sabine (Texas) River Works, computer technicians are trained to repair equipment. Because computers seldom failed, the repair staff was getting rusty on diagnosing problems. This expert system trained repair people in three days instead of the usual 30 days and keeps records of procedures on file. DuPont is now able to do its own computer maintenance at Sabine, which saves $400,000 per year in contract fees. The expert system paid for itself in just three months.

Sources: Managing Automation, May 1989, p. 53; *Interfaces,* November–December 1988, pp. 80–91.

to user questions. The help system answers questions such as location of components and the classification of replacement parts. The use of two additional expert systems in maintenance are described in the *POM in Action* box, "Expert Maintenance Systems at DuPont."

SUMMARY

Reliable systems are a necessity. In spite of our best efforts to design reliable components, systems sometimes fail. Consequently, backup components are used. Reliability improvement can also be obtained through the use of preventive maintenance and excellent repair facilities. Expert systems and comprehensive data collection and analysis assist reliability and maintenance management. Simulation techniques can also aid in determining maintenance policies. Reliable processes require well-designed systems, trained personnel, and good record keeping.

KEY TERMS

Reliability (p. 800)
Maintenance (p. 800)
Failure (p. 803)
Mean time between failures (MTBF) (p. 804)

Preventive maintenance (p. 805)
Breakdown maintenance (p. 806)
Infant mortality (p. 806)

USING AB:POM

Solving Example 3 Using AB:POM's Reliability Module

The reliability module will compute the reliability of simple systems with components in series and in parallel.

System reliability is determined by the reliability of items in series and the backup or parallel components in the system. In Example 3 we set up a system with three components in series. (The largest number of backup or parallel components in any series allowed by the software is six.)

The entries for reliability are:

1. *number of systems* (components) in the series (1 through 10); enter 3 at the top left of the screen.
2. *number of backup* or parallel components (1 through 12); enter 2 at the top right of the screen.
3. *component reliability.* Enter the reliability of each component in the body of the table. Series data are entered across the table and backup or parallel data down the table. The program will disregard any zeroes in the table.

These entries are shown in Program 18.1.

The solution is shown in Program 18.2.

Notice that the entries that were 0 have been eliminated. The products for each column show the combined parallel (backup) component reliability. System reliability is computed and shown at the bottom of the screen.

Program 18.1

Data Entry for Example 3

————————————————— Reliability ————————————————— Data Screen

Number of systems in series (1-10) 3   Max # of parallel components (1-12) 2

Parll Sys 1	Par 11 Sys 2	Par 11 Sys 3
.9000	.8000	.0000
.9000	.8000	.9900

Esc

Program 18.2

Solution for Example 3

	Reliability	
Par11	Par11	Par11
Sys 1	Sys 2	Sys 3
.9000	.8000	
.9000	.8000	.9900
.9900	.9600	.9900
System reliability = .94090		

SOLVED PROBLEMS

Solved Problem 18.1

The semiconductor used in the Sullivan Wrist Calculator has five parts, each of which has its own reliability rate. Component 1 has a reliability of .90; component 2, .95; component 3, .98; component 4, .90; and component 5, .99. What is the reliability of one semiconductor?

Solution

$$\text{Semiconductor reliability } R_s = R_1 R_2 R_3 R_4 R_5$$
$$= (.90)(.95)(.98)(.90)(.99)$$
$$= .7466$$

Solved Problem 18.2

A recent engineering change at Sullivan Wrist Calculator places a backup component in each of the two least reliable transistor circuits. The new circuit will look like the following:

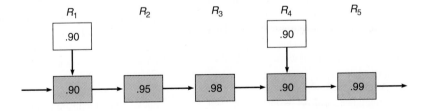

What is the reliability of the new system?

Solution

$$\text{Reliability} = [.9 + (1 - .9) \times .9] \times .95 \times .98 \times [.90 + (1 - .9) \times .9] \times .99$$
$$= [.9 + .09] \times .95 \times .98 \times [.90 + .09] \times .99$$
$$= .99 \times .95 \times .98 \times .99 \times .99$$
$$= .903$$

DISCUSSION QUESTIONS

1. What are the variables that contribute to infant mortality for new machinery?

2. What techniques can management use to improve system reliability?

3. Under what conditions is preventive maintenance likely to be appropriate?

4. Why is simulation often an appropriate technique for maintenance problems?

5. What is the trade-off between operator-performed maintenance versus supplier-performed maintenance?

6. How can the manager evaluate the effectiveness of the maintenance function?

7. What kind of records are helpful when developing a good maintenance system?

PROBLEMS

· **18.1** The Beta II computer's electronic processing unit contains 50 components in series. The average reliability of each component is 99.0 percent. Using Figure 18.1, determine the overall reliability of the processing unit.

: **18.2** Holzwart Manufacturing, a medical equipment manufacturer, has subjected 100 heart pacemakers to 5,000 hours of testing. Halfway through the testing, 5 of the pacemakers failed. What was the failure rate in terms of

a) percent of failures?

b) number of failures per unit-hour?

c) number of failures per unit-year?

d) If 1,100 people receive pacemaker implants, how many units can we expect to fail during the following one year?

: **18.3** Loucks Manufacturing Company operates its 23 large and expensive grinding and lathe machines from 7 A.M. to 11 P.M., seven days a week. For the past year the firm has been under contract with Simkin and Sons for daily preventive maintenance (lubrication, cleaning, inspection, and so on). Simkin's crew works between 11 P.M. and 2 A.M. so as not to interfere with the daily manufacturing crew. Simkin charges $645 per week for this service. Since signing the maintenance contract, Loucks Manufacturing has noted an average of only three breakdowns per week. When a grinding or lathe machine *does* break down during a working shift, it costs Loucks about $250 in lost production and repair costs.

After reviewing past breakdown records (for the period before signing a preventive maintenance contract with Simkin and Sons), Loucks Manufacturing's production manager summarized the patterns shown on page 819.

The production manager is not certain that the contract for preventive maintenance with Simkin is in the best financial interest of Loucks Manufacturing. He recognizes that much of his breakdown data is old but is fairly certain that it is representative of the present picture.

What is your analysis of this situation and what recommendations do you think the production manager should make?

NUMBER OF BREAKDOWNS PER WEEK	NUMBER OF WEEKS IN WHICH BREAKDOWNS OCCURRED
0	1
1	1
2	3
3	5
4	9
5	11
6	7
7	8
8	5
Total weeks of historical data:	50

: **18.4** Nigel Mansell owns a fleet of twenty aging taxicabs operating in San Jose. The cabs have tended to break down frequently, mainly because of high mileage and rough driving by his cab drivers. Nigel has heard a lot about preventive maintenance and, being cautious, has experimented with it on several cabs. He has found that weekly preventive maintenance checks and minor repairs cost an average of $12 *per cab* (or $240 for the whole fleet). Nigel also knows that when a cab breaks down on the road, it costs an average of $40 (towing plus repairs) to get the car back in action. The record below is a summary of post-preventive maintenance breakdowns.

WEEKS AFTER PREVENTIVE MAINTENANCE	PROBABILITY OF BREAKDOWN
1	.15
2	.10
3	.20
4	.25
5	.30
	1.00

What policy should Nigel follow? Should he employ preventive maintenance, and if so, how often?

: **18.5** The Mid-Atlantic Power Company is building a new generator for its Baltimore plant. Management recognizes that even a well-maintained generator will have periodic failures or breakdowns. Historical figures for similar generators indicate that the relative frequency of failures during a year is as follows:

NUMBER OF FAILURES	PROBABILITY (RELATIVE FREQUENCY)
0	.75
1	.19
2	.03
3	.02
4	.01
	1.00

Assuming that the useful lifetime of the generator is 20 years, use simulation to estimate the number of breakdowns that will occur in 20 years of operation. Is it common to have 3 or more consecutive years of operation without a failure? (*Note:* So that we all reach the same conclusions, start selecting your random numbers at the top of the third column of Appendix E and proceed down that column.)

: **18.6** Assuming that adding a second maintenance worker will result in twice the repair-time effectiveness of the new worker in Example 6 (that is, they will work together and cut repair time by 50%), should Cincinnati Manufacturing Company hire another repair worker? The additional person will cost $18.00 per hour.

 : **18.7** Alain Prost, salesman for Wave Soldering Systems, Inc. (WSSI), has provided you with a proposal for improving the temperature control on your present machine. The present machine uses a hot air knife to remove cleanly excess solder from printed circuit boards; this is a great concept, but the hot air temperature control lacks reliability. The engineers at WSSI have, says Alain, improved the reliability of the critical temperature controls. The new system still has the four sensitive integrated circuits controlling the temperature, but the new machine has a backup for each. The four integrated circuits have reliabilities of .90, .92, .94, and .96. The four backup circuits all have a reliability of .90.

a) What is the reliability of the new temperature controller?

b) If you pay a premium, Alain says he can improve all four of the backup units to .93. What is the reliability of this option?

CASE STUDY

Prescott Plastics, Inc.

Prescott Plastics, Inc., a manufacturer of plastic sandwich bags, trash can liners, shopping bags, and bags used for protective covering, opened its Cape Girardeau, Missouri, branch plant in 1987. Essentially, the manufacturing operations at the Cape Girardeau plant are identical to those in Des Moines, Iowa, and Chattanooga, Tennessee, but production capacity is restricted by a limited number of machines (20) and poor utilization of space.

When the plant opened in 1987, 20 new machines were purchased and placed in service. Six months later, a stand-by unit was purchased to be used whenever an on-line machine experienced a breakdown. Presently, Charles Good, the plant's production superintendent, is contemplating the purchase of one or two additional stand-by units because of the high frequency of breakdowns resulting in lost production. His primary goal is to minimize the cost of machines being out of service. Past records indicate that on the average two machines are out of order. The cost of a stand-by unit is $15 per day, and the cost of lost production resulting from a machine being out of service is $200 per

day. If six or more machines are out of order at the same time, total operations cease.

The following table shows the probability of a given number of machines being out of order at one time. (The probabilities are based on the Poisson distribution.)

NUMBER OF MACHINES OUT OF ORDER	PROBABILITY
0	.135
1	.271
2	.271
3	.180
4	.090
5	.036
6	.012
7	.003
8	.002

CASE STUDY (Continued)

Discussion Questions

1. What is the expected cost of maintaining one stand-by unit? Two units? Three units?

2. How many stand-by machines should be used to minimize total costs?

3. What assumptions were required in answering Discussion Questions 1 and 2?

4. How many stand-by machines would you use if you were the plant's production superintendent?

Source: Written by Professor Jerry Kinard (Francis Marion College) and Joe C. Iverstine.

BIBLIOGRAPHY

Armine, H. T., J. A. Ritchey, O. S. Hulley. *Manufacturing Organization and Management.* Englewood Cliffs, NJ: Prentice-Hall, 1975.

Blanchard, B. S., Jr., and E. E. Lowery. *Maintainability.* New York: McGraw-Hill, 1969.

Hayes, R. H., and K. B. Clark. "Why Some Factories Are More Productive than Others." *Harvard Business Review,* **64,** 5 (September–October 1986): 66–73.

Joshi, S., and R. Gupta. "Scheduling of Routine Maintenance Using Production Schedules and Equipment Failure History." *Computers and Industrial Engineering,* **10,** 1 (1986): 11–20.

Lamson, S. T., N. A. J. Hastings, and R. J. Willis. "Minimum Cost Maintenance in Heavy Haul Rail Track." *Journal of the Operational Research Society,* **34,** 3 (1983): 211–223.

Mann, L., Jr. *Maintenance Management.* Lexington, MA: Lexington Books, 1983.

Matta, K. F. "A Simulation Model for Repairable Items/Spare Parts Inventory Systems." *Computer and Operations Research,* **12,** 4 (1985): 395–409.

Neibel, B. W., and A. B. Draper. *Product Design and Process Engineering.* New York: McGraw-Hill, 1974.

Sherwin, D. J. "Inspect or Monitor." *Engineering Costs and Production Economics,* **18,** Elsevier (January 1990): 223–231.

Appendices

APPENDIX A Areas under the standard normal curve.

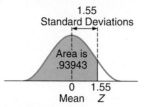

To find the area under the normal curve, you must know how many standard deviations that point is to the right of the mean. Then, the area under the normal curve can be read directly from the normal table. For example, the total area under the normal curve for a point that is 1.55 standard deviations to the right of the mean is .93943.

	.00	.01	.02	.03	.04	.05	.06	.07	.08	.09
.0	.50000	.50399	.50798	.51197	.51595	.51994	.52392	.52790	.53188	.53586
.1	.53983	.54380	.54776	.55172	.55567	.55962	.56356	.56749	.57142	.57535
.2	.57926	.58317	.58706	.59095	.59483	.59871	.60257	.60642	.61026	.61409
.3	.61791	.62172	.62552	.62930	.63307	.63683	.64058	.64431	.64803	.65173
.4	.65542	.65910	.66276	.66640	.67003	.67364	.67724	.68082	.68439	.68793
.5	.69146	.69497	.69847	.70194	.70540	.70884	.71226	.71566	.71904	.72240
.6	.72575	.72907	.73237	.73536	.73891	.74215	.74537	.74857	.75175	.75490
.7	.75804	.76115	.76424	.76730	.77035	.77337	.77637	.77935	.78230	.78524
.8	.78814	.79103	.79389	.79673	.79955	.80234	.80511	.80785	.81057	.81327
.9	.81594	.81859	.82121	.82381	.82639	.82894	.83147	.83398	.83646	.83891
1.0	.84134	.84375	.84614	.84849	.85083	.85314	.85543	.85769	.85993	.86214
1.1	.86433	.86650	.86864	.87076	.87286	.87493	.87698	.87900	.88100	.88298
1.2	.88493	.88686	.88877	.89065	.89251	.89435	.89617	.89796	.89973	.90147
1.3	.90320	.90490	.90658	.90824	.90988	.91149	.91309	.91466	.91621	.91774
1.4	.91924	.92073	.92220	.92364	.92507	.92647	.92785	.92922	.93056	.93189
1.5	.93319	.93448	.93574	.93699	.93822	.93943	.94062	.94179	.94295	.94408
1.6	.94520	.94630	.94738	.94845	.94950	.95053	.95154	.95254	.95352	.95449
1.7	.95543	.95637	.95728	.95818	.95907	.95994	.96080	.96164	.96246	.96327
1.8	.96407	.96485	.96562	.96638	.96712	.96784	.96856	.96926	.96995	.97062
1.9	.97128	.97193	.97257	.97320	.97381	.97441	.97500	.97558	.97615	.97670
2.0	.97725	.97784	.97831	.97882	.97932	.97982	.98030	.98077	.98124	.98169
2.1	.98214	.98257	.98300	.98341	.98382	.98422	.98461	.98500	.98537	.98574
2.2	.98610	.98645	.98679	.98713	.98745	.98778	.98809	.98840	.98870	.98899
2.3	.98928	.98956	.98983	.99010	.99036	.99061	.99086	.99111	.99134	.99158
2.4	.99180	.99202	.99224	.99245	.99266	.99286	.99305	.99324	.99343	.99361
2.5	.99379	.99396	.99413	.99430	.99446	.99461	.99477	.99492	.99506	.99520
2.6	.99534	.99547	.99560	.99573	.99585	.99598	.99609	.99621	.99632	.99643
2.7	.99653	.99664	.99674	.99683	.99693	.99702	.99711	.99720	.99728	.99736
2.8	.99744	.99752	.99760	.99767	.99774	.99781	.99788	.99795	.99801	.99807
2.9	.99813	.99819	.99825	.99831	.99836	.99841	.99846	.99851	.99856	.99861
3.0	.99865	.99869	.99874	.99878	.99882	.99886	.99899	.99893	.99896	.99900
3.1	.99903	.99906	.99910	.99913	.99916	.99918	.99921	.99924	.99926	.99929
3.2	.99931	.99934	.99936	.99938	.99940	.99942	.99944	.99946	.99948	.99950
3.3	.99952	.99953	.99955	.99957	.99958	.99960	.99961	.99962	.99964	.99965
3.4	.99966	.99968	.99969	.99970	.99971	.99972	.99973	.99974	.99975	.99976
3.5	.99977	.99978	.99978	.99979	.99980	.99981	.99981	.99982	.99983	.99983
3.6	.99984	.99985	.99985	.99986	.99986	.99987	.99987	.99988	.99988	.99989
3.7	.99989	.99990	.99990	.99990	.99991	.99991	.99992	.99992	.99992	.99992
3.8	.99993	.99993	.99993	.99994	.99994	.99994	.99994	.99995	.99995	.99995
3.9	.99995	.99995	.99996	.99996	.99996	.99996	.99996	.99996	.99997	.99997

Source: From *Quantitative Approaches to Management*, 4th ed., by Richard I. Levin and Charles A. Kirkpatrick. Copyright © 1978, 1975, 1971, 1965 by McGraw-Hill, Inc. Used with permission of McGraw-Hill Book Company.

APPENDIX B Cumulative binomial probabilities.

$$P(x \le c) = \sum_{x=0}^{c} \binom{n}{x} p^x (1-p)^{n-x}$$

P

n	x	.05	.10	.15	.20	.25	.30	.35	.40	.45	.50	.55	.60	.65	.70	.75	.80	.85	.90
1 ...	0	.9500	.9000	.8500	.8000	.7500	.7000	.6500	.6000	.5500	.5000	.4500	.4000	.3500	.3000	.2500	.2000	.1500	.1000
	1	1.0000	1.0000	1.0000	1.0000	1.0000	1.0000	1.0000	1.0000	1.0000	1.0000	1.0000	1.0000	1.0000	1.0000	1.0000	1.0000	1.0000	1.0000
2 ...	0	.9025	.8100	.7225	.6400	.5625	.4900	.4225	.3600	.3025	.2500	.2025	.1600	.1225	.0900	.0625	.0400	.0225	.0100
	1	.9975	.9900	.9775	.9600	.9375	.9100	.8775	.8400	.7975	.7500	.6975	.6400	.5775	.5100	.4375	.3600	.2775	.1900
	2	1.0000	1.0000	1.0000	1.0000	1.0000	1.0000	1.0000	1.0000	1.0000	1.0000	1.0000	1.0000	1.0000	1.0000	1.0000	1.0000	1.0000	1.0000
3 ...	0	.8574	.7290	.6141	.5120	.4219	.3430	.2746	.2160	.1664	.1250	.0911	.0640	.0429	.0270	.0156	.0080	.0034	.0010
	1	.9928	.9720	.9393	.8960	.8438	.7840	.7183	.6480	.5748	.5000	.4253	.3520	.2818	.2160	.1563	.1040	.0608	.0280
	2	.9999	.9990	.9966	.9920	.9844	.9730	.9571	.9360	.9089	.8750	.8336	.7840	.7254	.6570	.5781	.4880	.3859	.2710
	3	1.0000	1.0000	1.0000	1.0000	1.0000	1.0000	1.0000	1.0000	1.0000	1.0000	1.0000	1.0000	1.0000	1.0000	1.0000	1.0000	1.0000	1.0000
4 ...	0	.8145	.6561	.5220	.4096	.3164	.2401	.1785	.1296	.0915	.0625	.0410	.0256	.0150	.0081	.0039	.0016	.0005	.0001
	1	.9860	.9477	.8905	.8192	.7383	.6517	.5630	.4752	.3910	.3125	.2415	.1792	.1265	.0837	.0508	.0272	.0120	.0037
	2	.9995	.9963	.9880	.9728	.9492	.9163	.8735	.8208	.7585	.6875	.6090	.5248	.4370	.3483	.2617	.1808	.1095	.0523
	3	1.0000	.9999	.9995	.9984	.9961	.9919	.9850	.9744	.9590	.9375	.9085	.8704	.8215	.7599	.6836	.5904	.4780	.3439
	4	1.0000	1.0000	1.0000	1.0000	1.0000	1.0000	1.0000	1.0000	1.0000	1.0000	1.0000	1.0000	1.0000	1.0000	1.0000	1.0000	1.0000	1.0000
5 ...	0	.7738	.5905	.4437	.3277	.2373	.1681	.1160	.0778	.0503	.0313	.0185	.0102	.0053	.0024	.0010	.0003	.0001	.0000
	1	.9974	.9185	.8352	.7373	.8328	.5282	.4284	.3370	.2562	.1875	.1312	.0870	.0540	.0308	.0156	.0067	.0022	.0005
	2	.9988	.9914	.9734	.9421	.8965	.8369	.7648	.6826	.5931	.5000	.4069	.3174	.2352	.1631	.1035	.0579	.0266	.0086
	3	1.0000	.9995	.9978	.9933	.9844	.9692	.9460	.9130	.8688	.8125	.7438	.6630	.5716	.4718	.3672	.2627	.1648	.0815
	4	1.0000	1.0000	.9999	.9997	.9990	.9976	.9947	.9898	.9815	.9688	.9497	.9222	.8840	.8319	.7627	.6723	.5563	.4095
	5	1.0000	1.0000	1.0000	1.0000	1.0000	1.0000	1.0000	1.0000	1.0000	1.0000	1.0000	1.0000	1.0000	1.0000	1.0000	1.0000	1.0000	1.0000
6 ...	0	.7351	.5314	.3771	.2621	.1780	.1176	.0754	.0467	.0277	.0156	.0083	.0041	.0018	.0007	.0002	.0001	.0000	.0000
	1	.9672	.8857	.7765	.6554	.5339	.4202	.3191	.2333	.1636	.1094	.0692	.0410	.0223	.0109	.0046	.0016	.0004	.0001
	2	.9978	.9842	.9527	.9011	.8306	.7443	.6471	.5443	.4415	.3438	.2553	.1792	.1174	.0705	.0376	.0170	.0059	.0013
	3	.9999	.9987	.9941	.9830	.9624	.9295	.8826	.8208	.7447	.6563	.5585	.4557	.3529	.2557	.1694	.0989	.0473	.0159
	4	1.0000	.9999	.9996	.9984	.9954	.9891	.9777	.9590	.9308	.8906	.8364	.7667	.6809	.5798	.4661	.3446	.2235	.1143
	5	1.0000	1.0000	1.0000	.9999	.9998	.9993	.9982	.9959	.9917	.9844	.9723	.9533	.9246	.8824	.8220	.7379	.6229	.4686
	6	1.0000	1.0000	1.0000	1.0000	1.0000	1.0000	1.0000	1.0000	1.0000	1.0000	1.0000	1.0000	1.0000	1.0000	1.0000	1.0000	1.0000	1.0000
7 ...	0	.6983	.4783	.3206	.2079	.1335	.0824	.0490	.0280	.0152	.0078	.0037	.0016	.0006	.0002	.0001	.0000	.0000	.0000
	1	.9556	.8503	.7166	.5767	.4449	.3294	.2338	.1586	.1024	.0625	.0357	.0188	.0090	.0038	.0013	.0004	.0001	.0000
	2	.9962	.9743	.9262	.8520	.7564	.6471	.5323	.4199	.3164	.2266	.1529	.0963	.0556	.0288	.0129	.0047	.0012	.0002
	3	.9998	.9973	.9879	.9667	.9294	.8740	.8002	.7102	.6083	.5000	.3917	.2898	.1998	.1260	.0706	.0333	.0121	.0027
	4	1.0000	.9998	.9988	.9953	.9871	.9712	.9444	.9037	.8471	.7734	.6836	.5801	.4677	.3529	.2436	.1480	.0738	.0257
	5	1.0000	1.0000	.9999	.9996	.9987	.9962	.9910	.9812	.9643	.9375	.8976	.8414	.7662	.6706	.5551	.4233	.2834	.1497
	6	1.0000	1.0000	1.0000	1.0000	.9999	.9998	.9994	.9984	.9963	.9922	.9848	.9720	.9510	.9176	.8665	.7903	.6794	.5217
	7	1.0000	1.0000	1.0000	1.0000	1.0000	1.0000	1.0000	1.0000	1.0000	1.0000	1.0000	1.0000	1.0000	1.0000	1.0000	1.0000	1.0000	1.0000
8 ...	0	.6634	.4305	.2725	.1678	.1001	.0576	.0319	.0168	.0084	.0039	.0017	.0007	.0002	.0001	.0000	.0000	.0000	.0000
	1	.9428	.8131	.6572	.5033	.3671	.2553	.1691	.1064	.0632	.0352	.0181	.0085	.0036	.0013	.0004	.0001	.0000	.0000
	2	.9942	.9619	.8948	.7969	.6785	.5518	.4278	.3154	.2201	.1445	.0885	.0498	.0253	.0113	.0042	.0012	.0002	.0000
	3	.9996	.9950	.9786	.9437	.8862	.8059	.7064	.5941	.4770	.3633	.2604	.1737	.1061	.0580	.0273	.0104	.0029	.0004
	4	1.0000	.9996	.9971	.9896	.9727	.9420	.8939	.8263	.7396	.6367	.5230	.4059	.2936	.1941	.1138	.0563	.0214	.0050
	5	1.0000	1.0000	.9998	.9988	.9958	.9887	.9747	.9502	.9115	.8555	.7799	.6846	.5722	.4482	.3215	.2031	.1052	.0381
	6	1.0000	1.0000	1.0000	.9999	.9996	.9987	.9964	.9915	.9819	.9648	.9368	.8936	.8309	.7447	.6329	.4967	.3428	.1869
	7	1.0000	1.0000	1.0000	1.0000	1.0000	.9999	.9998	.9993	.9983	.9961	.9916	.9832	.9681	.9424	.8999	.8322	.7275	.5695
	8	1.0000	1.0000	1.0000	1.0000	1.0000	1.0000	1.0000	1.0000	1.0000	1.0000	1.0000	1.0000	1.0000	1.0000	1.0000	1.0000	1.0000	1.0000
9 ...	0	.6302	.3874	.2316	.1342	.0751	.0404	.0207	.0101	.0046	.0020	.0008	.0003	.0001	.0000	.0000	.0000	.0000	.0000
	1	.9288	.7748	.5995	.4362	.3003	.1960	.1211	.0705	.0385	.0195	.0091	.0038	.0014	.0004	.0001	.0000	.0000	.0000
	2	.9916	.9470	.8591	.7382	.6007	.4628	.3373	.2318	.1495	.0898	.0498	.0250	.0112	.0043	.0013	.0003	.0000	.0000
	3	.9994	.9917	.9661	.9144	.8343	.7297	.6089	.4826	.3614	.2539	.1658	.0994	.0536	.0253	.0100	.0031	.0006	.0001
	4	1.0000	.9991	.9944	.9804	.9511	.9012	.8283	.7334	.6214	.5000	.3786	.2666	.1717	.0988	.0489	.0196	.0056	.0009
	5	1.0000	.9999	.9994	.9969	.9900	.9747	.9496	.9006	.8342	.7461	.6386	.5174	.3911	.2703	.1657	.0856	.0339	.0083
	6	1.0000	1.0000	1.0000	.9997	.9987	.9957	.9888	.9750	.9502	.9102	.8505	.7682	.6627	.5372	.3993	.2618	.1409	.0530
	7	1.0000	1.0000	1.0000	1.0000	.9999	.9996	.9986	.9962	.9909	.9805	.9615	.9295	.8789	.8040	.6997	.5638	.4005	.2252
	8	1.0000	1.0000	1.0000	1.0000	1.0000	1.0000	.9999	.9997	.9992	.9980	.9954	.9899	.9793	.9596	.9249	.8658	.7684	.6126
	9	1.0000	1.0000	1.0000	1.0000	1.0000	1.0000	1.0000	1.0000	1.0000	1.0000	1.0000	1.0000	1.0000	1.0000	1.0000	1.0000	1.0000	1.0000

APPENDIX B Cumulative binomial probabilities. (Continued)

n	x	.05	.10	.15	.20	.25	.30	.35	.40	.45	.50	.55	.60	.65	.70	.75	.80	.85	.90
10 ...	0	.5987	.3487	.1969	.1074	.0563	.0282	.0135	.0060	.0025	.0010	.0003	.0001	.0000	.0000	.0000	.0000	.0000	.0000
	1	.9139	.7361	.5443	.3758	.2440	.1493	.0860	.0464	.0233	.0107	.0045	.0017	.0005	.0001	.0000	.0000	.0000	.0000
	2	.9885	.9298	.8202	.6778	.5256	.3828	.2616	.1673	.0996	.0547	.0274	.0123	.0048	.0016	.0004	.0001	.0000	.0000
	3	.9990	.9872	.9500	.8791	.7759	.6496	.5138	.3823	.2660	.1719	.1020	.0548	.0260	.0106	.0035	.0009	.0001	.0000
	4	.9999	.9984	.9901	.9672	.9219	.8497	.7515	.6331	.5044	.3770	.2616	.1662	.0949	.0473	.0197	.0064	.0014	.0001
	5	1.0000	.9999	.9986	.9936	.9803	.9527	.9051	.8338	.7384	.6230	.4956	.3669	.2485	.1503	.0781	.0328	.0099	.0016
	6	1.0000	1.0000	.9999	.9991	.9965	.9894	.9740	.9452	.8980	.8281	.7340	.6177	.4862	.3504	.2241	.1209	.0500	.0128
	7	1.0000	1.0000	1.0000	.9999	.9996	.9984	.9952	.9877	.9726	.9453	.9004	.8327	.7384	.6172	.4744	.3222	.1798	.0702
	8	1.0000	1.0000	1.0000	1.0000	1.0000	.9999	.9995	.9983	.9955	.9893	.9767	.9536	.9140	.8507	.7560	.6242	.4557	.2639
	9	1.0000	1.0000	1.0000	1.0000	1.0000	1.0000	1.0000	.9999	.9997	.9990	.9975	.9940	.9865	.9718	.9437	.8926	.8031	.6513
	10	1.0000	1.0000	1.0000	1.0000	1.0000	1.0000	1.0000	1.0000	1.0000	1.0000	1.0000	1.0000	1.0000	1.0000	1.0000	1.0000	1.0000	1.0000
15 ...	0	.4633	.2059	.0874	.0352	.0134	.0047	.0016	.0005	.0001	.0000	.0000	.0000	.0000	.0000	.0000	.0000	.0000	.0000
	1	.8290	.5490	.3186	.1671	.0802	.0353	.0142	.0052	.0017	.0005	.0001	.0000	.0000	.0000	.0000	.0000	.0000	.0000
	2	.9638	.8159	.6042	.3980	.2361	.1268	.0617	.0271	.0107	.0037	.0011	.0003	.0001	.0000	.0000	.0000	.0000	.0000
	3	.9945	.9444	.8227	.6482	.4613	.2969	.1727	.0905	.0424	.0176	.0063	.0019	.0005	.0001	.0000	.0000	.0000	.0000
	4	.9994	.9873	.9383	.8358	.6865	.5155	.3519	.2173	.1204	.0592	.0255	.0093	.0028	.0007	.0001	.0000	.0000	.0000
	5	.9999	.9978	.9832	.9389	.8516	.7216	.5643	.4032	.2608	.1509	.0769	.0338	.0124	.0037	.0008	.0001	.0000	.0000
	6	1.0000	.9997	.9964	.9819	.9434	.8689	.7548	.6098	.4522	.3036	.1818	.0950	.0422	.0152	.0042	.0008	.0001	.0000
	7	1.0000	1.0000	.9994	.9958	.9827	.9500	.8868	.7869	.6535	.5000	.3465	.2131	.1132	.0500	.0173	.0042	.0006	.0000
	8	1.0000	1.0000	.9999	.9992	.9958	.9848	.9578	.9050	.8182	.6964	.5478	.3902	.2452	.1311	.0566	.0181	.0036	.0003
	9	1.0000	1.0000	1.0000	.9999	.9992	.9963	.9876	.9662	.9231	.8491	.7392	.5968	.4357	.2784	.1484	.0611	.0168	.0022
	10	1.0000	1.0000	1.0000	1.0000	.9999	.9993	.9972	.9907	.9745	.9408	.8796	.7827	.6481	.4845	.3135	.1642	.0617	.0127
	11	1.0000	1.0000	1.0000	1.0000	1.0000	.9999	.9995	.9981	.9937	.9824	.9576	.9095	.8273	.7031	.5387	.3518	.1773	.0556
	12	1.0000	1.0000	1.0000	1.0000	1.0000	1.0000	.9999	.9997	.9989	.9963	.9893	.9729	.9383	.8732	.7639	.6020	.3958	.1841
	13	1.0000	1.0000	1.0000	1.0000	1.0000	1.0000	1.0000	1.0000	.9999	.9995	.9983	.9948	.9858	.9647	.9198	.8329	.6814	.4510
	14	1.0000	1.0000	1.0000	1.0000	1.0000	1.0000	1.0000	1.0000	1.0000	1.0000	.9999	.9995	.9984	.9953	.9866	.9648	.9126	.7941
	15	1.0000	1.0000	1.0000	1.0000	1.0000	1.0000	1.0000	1.0000	1.0000	1.0000	1.0000	1.0000	1.0000	1.0000	1.0000	1.0000	1.0000	1.0000
20 ...	0	.3585	.1216	.0388	.0115	.0032	.0008	.0002	.0000	.0000	.0000	.0000	.0000	.0000	.0000	.0000	.0000	.0000	.0000
	1	.7358	.3917	.1756	.0692	.0243	.0076	.0021	.0005	.0001	.0000	.0000	.0000	.0000	.0000	.0000	.0000	.0000	.0000
	2	.9245	.6769	.4049	.2061	.0913	.0355	.0121	.0036	.0009	.0002	.0000	.0000	.0000	.0000	.0000	.0000	.0000	.0000
	3	.9841	.8670	.6477	.4114	.2252	.1071	.0444	.0160	.0049	.0013	.0003	.0000	.0000	.0000	.0000	.0000	.0000	.0000
	4	.9974	.9568	.8298	.6296	.4148	.2375	.1182	.0510	.0189	.0059	.0015	.0003	.0000	.0000	.0000	.0000	.0000	.0000
	5	.9997	.9887	.9327	.8042	.6172	.4164	.2454	.1256	.0553	.0207	.0064	.0016	.0003	.0000	.0000	.0000	.0000	.0000
	6	1.0000	.9976	.9781	.9133	.7858	.6080	.4166	.2500	.1299	.0577	.0214	.0065	.0015	.0003	.0000	.0000	.0000	.0000
	7	1.0000	.9996	.9941	.9679	.8982	.7723	.6010	.4159	.2520	.1316	.0580	.0210	.0060	.0013	.0002	.0000	.0000	.0000
	8	1.0000	.9999	.9987	.9900	.9591	.8867	.7624	.5956	.4143	.2517	.1308	.0565	.0196	.0051	.0009	.0001	.0000	.0000
	9	1.0000	1.0000	.9998	.9974	.9861	.9520	.8782	.7553	.5914	.4119	.2493	.1275	.0532	.0171	.0039	.0006	.0000	.0000
	10	1.0000	1.0000	1.0000	.9994	.9961	.9829	.9468	.8725	.7507	.5881	.4086	.2447	.1218	.0480	.0139	.0026	.0002	.0000
	11	1.0000	1.0000	1.0000	.9999	.9991	.9949	.9804	.9435	.8692	.7483	.5857	.4044	.2376	.1133	.0409	.0100	.0013	.0001
	12	1.0000	1.0000	1.0000	1.0000	.9998	.9987	.9940	.9790	.9420	.8684	.7480	.5841	.3990	.2277	.1018	.0321	.0059	.0004
	13	1.0000	1.0000	1.0000	1.0000	1.0000	.9997	.9985	.9935	.9786	.9423	.8701	.7500	.5834	.3920	.2142	.0867	.0219	.0024
	14	1.0000	1.0000	1.0000	1.0000	1.0000	1.0000	.9997	.9984	.9936	.9793	.9447	.8744	.7546	.5836	.3828	.1958	.0673	.0113
	15	1.0000	1.0000	1.0000	1.0000	1.0000	1.0000	1.0000	.9997	.9985	.9941	.9811	.9490	.8818	.7625	.5852	.3704	.1702	.0432
	16	1.0000	1.0000	1.0000	1.0000	1.0000	1.0000	1.0000	1.0000	.9997	.9987	.9951	.9840	.9556	.8929	.7748	.5886	.3523	.1330
	17	1.0000	1.0000	1.0000	1.0000	1.0000	1.0000	1.0000	1.0000	1.0000	.9998	.9991	.9964	.9879	.9645	.9087	.7939	.5951	.3231
	18	1.0000	1.0000	1.0000	1.0000	1.0000	1.0000	1.0000	1.0000	1.0000	1.0000	.9999	.9995	.9979	.9924	.9757	.9308	.8244	.6083
	19	1.0000	1.0000	1.0000	1.0000	1.0000	1.0000	1.0000	1.0000	1.0000	1.0000	1.0000	1.0000	.9998	.9992	.9968	.9885	.9612	.8784
	20	1.0000	1.0000	1.0000	1.0000	1.0000	1.0000	1.0000	1.0000	1.0000	1.0000	1.0000	1.0000	1.0000	1.0000	1.0000	1.0000	1.0000	1.0000

APPENDIX C Poisson distribution values.

$$P(X \le c/\lambda) = \sum_{0}^{c} \frac{\lambda^{x}e^{\lambda}}{x!}.$$

The table shows 1000 times the probability of c or less occurrences of an event that has an average number of occurrences of λ.

	Values of c										
λ	0	1	2	3	4	5	6	7	8	9	10
.02	980	1000									
.04	961	999	1000								
.06	942	998	1000								
.08	923	997	1000								
.10	905	995	1000								
.15	861	990	999	1000							
.20	819	982	999	1000							
.25	779	974	998	1000							
.30	741	963	996	1000							
.35	705	951	994	1000							
.40	670	938	992	999	1000						
.45	638	925	989	999	1000						
.50	607	910	986	998	1000						
.55	577	894	982	998	1000						
.60	549	878	977	997	1000						
.65	522	861	972	996	999	1000					
.70	497	844	966	994	999	1000					
.75	472	827	959	993	999	1000					
.80	449	809	953	991	999	1000					
.85	427	791	945	989	998	1000					
.90	407	772	937	987	998	1000					
.95	387	754	929	984	997	1000					
1.00	368	736	920	981	996	999	1000				
1.1	333	699	900	974	995	999	1000				
1.2	301	663	879	966	992	998	1000				
1.3	273	627	857	957	989	998	1000				
1.4	247	592	833	946	986	997	999	1000			
1.5	223	558	809	934	981	996	999	1000			
1.6	202	525	783	921	976	994	999	1000			
1.7	183	493	757	907	970	992	998	1000			
1.8	165	463	731	891	964	990	997	999	1000		
1.9	150	434	704	875	956	987	997	999	1000		
2.0	135	406	677	857	947	983	995	999	1000		

Source: Adapted from E. L. Grant, *Statistical Quality Control,* McGraw-Hill Book Company, New York, 1964. Reproduced by permission of the publisher.

APPENDIX C Poisson distribution values. (Continued)

λ	\multicolumn{23}{c}{Values of c}

λ	0	1	2	3	4	5	6	7	8	9	10	11	12	13	14	15	16	17	18	19	20	21	22
2.2	111	359	623	819	928	975	993	998	1000														
2.4	091	308	570	779	904	964	988	997	999	1000													
2.6	074	267	518	736	877	951	983	995	999	1000													
2.8	061	231	469	692	848	935	976	992	998	999	1000												
3.0	050	199	423	647	815	916	966	988	996	999	1000												
3.2	041	171	380	603	781	895	955	983	994	998	1000												
3.4	033	147	340	558	744	871	942	977	992	997	999	1000											
3.6	027	126	303	515	706	844	927	969	988	996	999	1000											
3.8	022	107	269	473	668	816	909	960	984	994	998	999	1000										
4.0	018	092	238	433	629	785	889	949	979	992	997	999	1000										
4.2	015	078	210	395	590	753	867	936	972	989	996	999	1000										
4.4	012	066	185	359	551	720	844	921	964	985	994	998	999	1000									
4.6	010	056	163	326	513	686	818	905	955	980	992	997	999	1000									
4.8	008	048	143	294	476	651	791	887	944	975	990	996	999	1000									
5.0	007	040	125	265	440	616	762	867	932	968	986	995	998	999	1000								
5.2	006	034	109	238	406	581	732	845	918	960	982	993	997	999	1000								
5.4	005	029	095	213	373	546	702	822	903	951	977	990	996	999	1000								
5.6	004	024	082	191	342	512	670	797	886	941	972	988	995	998	999	1000							
5.8	003	021	072	170	313	478	638	771	867	929	965	984	993	997	999	1000							
6.0	002	017	062	151	285	446	606	744	847	916	957	980	991	996	999	999	1000						
6.2	002	015	054	134	259	414	574	716	826	902	949	975	989	995	998	999	1000						
6.4	002	012	046	119	235	384	542	687	803	886	939	969	986	994	997	999	999	1000					
6.6	001	010	040	105	213	355	511	658	780	869	927	963	982	992	997	999	999	1000					
6.8	001	009	034	093	192	327	480	628	755	850	915	955	978	990	996	998	999	1000					
7.0	001	007	030	082	173	301	450	599	729	830	901	947	973	987	994	998	999	1000					
7.2	001	006	025	072	156	276	420	569	703	810	887	937	967	984	993	997	999	999	1000				
7.4	001	005	022	063	140	253	392	539	676	788	871	926	961	980	991	996	998	999	1000				
7.6	001	004	019	055	125	231	365	510	648	765	854	915	954	976	989	995	998	999	1000				
7.8	000	004	016	048	112	210	338	481	620	741	835	902	945	971	986	993	997	999	1000				
8.0	000	003	014	042	100	191	313	453	593	717	816	888	936	966	983	992	996	998	999	1000			
8.5	000	002	009	030	074	150	256	386	523	653	763	849	909	949	973	986	993	997	999	999	1000		
9.0	000	001	006	021	055	116	207	324	456	587	706	803	876	926	959	978	989	995	998	999	1000		
9.5	000	001	004	015	040	089	165	269	392	522	645	752	836	898	940	967	982	991	996	998	999	1000	
10.0	000	000	003	010	029	067	130	220	333	458	583	697	792	864	917	951	973	986	993	997	998	999	1000

APPENDIX D Values of $e^{-\lambda}$ for use in the Poisson distribution.

Values of $e^{-\lambda}$

λ	$e^{-\lambda}$	λ	$e^{-\lambda}$	λ	$e^{-\lambda}$	λ	$e^{-\lambda}$
.0	1.0000	1.6	.2019	3.1	.0450	4.6	.0101
.1	.9048	1.7	.1827	3.2	.0408	4.7	.0091
.2	.8187	1.8	.1653	3.3	.0369	4.8	.0082
.3	.7408	1.9	.1496	3.4	.0334	4.9	.0074
.4	.6703	2.0	.1353	3.5	.0302	5.0	.0067
.5	.6065	2.1	.1225	3.6	.0273	5.1	.0061
.6	.5488	2.2	.1108	3.7	.0247	5.2	.0055
.7	.4966	2.3	.1003	3.8	.0224	5.3	.0050
.8	.4493	2.4	.0907	3.9	.0202	5.4	.0045
.9	.4066	2.5	.0821	4.0	.0183	5.5	.0041
1.0	.3679	2.6	.0743	4.1	.0166	5.6	.0037
1.1	.3329	2.7	.0672	4.2	.0150	5.7	.0033
1.2	.3012	2.8	.0608	4.3	.0136	5.8	.0030
1.3	.2725	2.9	.0550	4.4	.0123	5.9	.0027
1.4	.2466	3.0	.0498	4.5	.0111	6.0	.0025
1.5	.2231						

APPENDIX E Table of random numbers.

```
52  06  50  88  53  30  10  47  99  37  66  91  35  32  00  84  57  07
37  63  28  02  74  35  24  03  29  60  74  85  90  73  59  55  17  60
82  57  68  28  05  94  03  11  27  79  90  87  92  41  09  25  36  77
69  02  36  49  71  99  32  10  75  21  95  90  94  38  97  71  72  49
98  94  90  36  06  78  23  67  89  85  29  21  25  73  69  34  85  76
96  52  62  87  49  56  59  23  78  71  72  90  57  01  98  57  31  95
33  69  27  21  11  60  95  89  68  48  17  89  34  09  93  50  44  51
50  33  50  95  13  44  34  62  64  39  55  29  30  64  49  44  30  16
88  32  18  50  62  57  34  56  62  31  15  40  90  34  51  95  26  14
90  30  36  24  69  82  51  74  30  35  36  85  01  55  92  64  09  85
50  48  61  18  85  23  08  54  17  12  80  69  24  84  92  16  49  59
27  88  21  62  69  64  48  31  12  73  02  68  00  16  16  46  13  85
45  14  46  32  13  49  66  62  74  41  86  98  92  98  84  54  33  40
81  02  01  78  82  74  97  37  45  31  94  99  42  49  27  64  89  42
66  83  14  74  27  76  03  33  11  97  59  81  72  00  64  61  13  52
74  05  81  82  93  09  96  33  52  78  13  06  28  30  94  23  37  39
30  34  87  01  74  11  46  82  59  94  25  34  32  23  17  01  58  73
59  55  72  33  62  13  74  68  22  44  42  09  32  46  71  79  45  89
67  09  80  98  99  25  77  50  03  32  36  63  65  75  94  19  95  88
60  77  46  63  71  69  44  22  03  85  14  48  69  13  30  50  33  24
60  08  19  29  36  72  30  27  50  64  85  72  75  29  87  05  75  01
80  45  86  99  02  34  87  08  86  84  49  76  24  08  01  86  29  11
53  84  49  63  26  65  72  84  85  63  26  02  75  26  92  62  40  67
69  84  12  94  51  36  17  02  15  29  16  52  56  43  26  22  08  62
37  77  13  10  02  18  31  19  32  85  31  94  81  43  31  58  33  51
```

Source: Excerpted from *A Million Random Digits with 100,000 Normal Deviates,* The Free Press, 1955, p. 7, with permission of the Rand Corporation.

APPENDIX F USING AB:POM

This technical appendix provides additional details as to the use of AB:POM. Specific program modules, such as Forecasting or Inventory, are illustrated in their respective chapters. The intent of this Appendix is to discuss the overall program operations and to describe how the system may be run on your specific computer.

In this Appendix, we first discuss (1) Hardware Requirements, then (2) the main AB:POM menu, (3) the Module Submenu Screens, (4) the Entering/Editing data, (5) Getting Started, and finally (6) System Error Messages. This program is so user-friendly that, depending on your computer experience and skills, you may wish to go straight to the Getting Started section and proceed to the paragraph called "Normal Startup."

HARDWARE REQUIREMENTS

AB:POM will work on any IBM PC, XT, AT, PS/2, or compatible machine. The programs themselves require less than 256K of available memory.

The system has two 5.25-inch diskettes or one 3.5-inch diskette. It is possible to run the 5.25-inch diskette system with only one disk drive, but a second drive will eliminate the need for swapping diskettes. (If you have a 5.25-inch disk drive, a second drive will usually be available.) The programs also can be loaded onto a hard disk and run from there.

A printer is not required to run AB:POM. Of course, if you want a hard copy (printout), it is necessary to have a printer attached. No special features, characters, installation, or printer are required. It is possible to print the learning curve and linear programming graphs by running the DOS program GRAPHICS.EXE prior to starting up AB:POM and then pressing the **Prt Scn** key.

MAIN MENU

Program F.1 shows AB:POM's Main Menu, consisting of 18 individual application programs plus a **Help** command and an **Exit to DOS** command. Selections from this menu may be made by pressing the first letter (or highlighted letter) of each command on the screen or by moving the cursor to the program you want and then pressing the enter key.

If you request Help from this Main Menu, you will view the screen shown in Program F.2. It is a good idea to read this screen, plus the three more-detailed Help screens shown in Programs F.3, F.4, and F.5 before attempting to execute any program.

THE MODULE SUBMENU SCREEN

The module submenu will appear after the module has been chosen.

Program F.1

The AB:POM Main Menu

```
                        Main Menu

Help                          Aggregate Planning
Decision Tables               Inventory
Linear Programming            Material Requirements Planning
Forecasting                   Sizing, Lot
Waiting Line Models           Job Shop Sequencing
Plant Location                Assignment
Transportation                CPM/PERT Project Scheduling
Operations Layout             Quality Control
Balancing, Assembly line      Reliability
Experience (learning) Curves  Exit to DOS


       Select menu option by highlighted letter or
       point with arrow keys and then press RETURN key
```

Program F.2

OPENING HELP SCREEN Accessed by Pressing H from the Main Menu

```
                         HELP

This screen identifies the available programs. The programs
may be chosen by either the highlighted letter or by using
the arrow keys to point to the option and then pressing the
RETURN key to select that item.

Help on the definition of the submenu options and the
direction keys can be found by pressing the F1 key or the
F2 key or M

Remember that the AB:POM diskette 1 contains a file named
README which contains useful information. The README file is
examined through DOS by using the TYPE or PRINT command

NOTE: At almost all times, a message appears on the bottom
two rows giving instructions on what to do, or what keys are
available. If you are in doubt about what to do next, look
to the bottom of the screen for these instructions.

F1 = Submenu Options F2 = Movement Keys F3 = Data editing
F9 = Print ESC = Done.
Press s, m or d or 'F1', 'F2', or 'F3' for more help. Press
Esc key to end help
```

Program F.3

Optional Help Screens For Function Keys

```
─────────────────────── SUBMENU OPTIONS ───────────────────────

The submenu options will appear on the next to last line of
the data screen, after a module is chosen. The options are
chosen by pressing the highlighted letter. While you are
editing data the only option available is Esc. When you
press the Esc key, the submenu options will become
available. It is also possible to access the submenu options
by using the function keys which are listed below. All
options are not listed on the bottom of the data screen
since there is not enough room.
 F1–Help–Creates this screen
 F2–New–Use this to start a new problem
 F3–Load–Use this to load a file from disk
 F4–Main–This returns to the module menu
 F5–Util–Customize colors, toggle sound, print to file
*F6–Quit–Exit AB:POM and go to DOS
 F7–Save–Save a problem/file on a diskette
*F8–Title–Change the problem title
 F9–Prnt–Print the data or solution to a printer (or file)
 F10–Run–Start the solution procedure
*not listed at the bottom of data screen but always
 available
Options may be chosen either by the function key or by
pressing the ESC key followed by the (first) highlighted letter
```

Program F.4

Movement Keys Help Screen

```
Cursor/Cell MOVEMENT KEYS

↑ move one cell up
↓ move one cell down
→ move one cell right
← move one cell left

TAB–move to far right column or move one screen to the right
SHIFT-TAB–move to far left column or move one screen to the
left
PAGEUP–move to top row or move up one screen
PAGEDOWN–move to bottom row or move down one screen
HOME–move to beginning (upper left) of data
END–move to end (lower right) of data
ENTER–enter data and move to next cell (Down first then
right)
Escape turns on menu or returns to previous screen
```

Program F.5

Data Entry Help Screen

```
───────────────────── DATA ENTRY EDITING ─────────────────────

There are three types of data which are entered onto the
screen:

NUMERICAL DATA
This is the most common, most standard type of data. In some
cases you will be restricted to positive numbers. In other
cases you will be restricted to integers.

CHARACTER DATA
In most modules you are allowed to name some of the
variables. Typically, in these cases you will be allowed to
enter characters from the keyboard. If you press a wrong
key, then a message will appear near the bottom of the
screen indicating the problem.

TOGGLED DATA
For some entries, the allowable responses have been preset
for you. In these cases you press the space bar to switch
from one to another. Or, if you like, you may press RETURN
to see all of the allowable possibilities.
NOTE: On most modules if you move up to the title line you
can change the title.
```

Submenu Options

Each submenu will have the following six options, which can be selected by typing the highlighted (first) letter or the corresponding function key as shown in Program F.3.

Help (F1)

This option will present a brief description of the module, the data required for input, the output results, and the available options. It is worth while to look at this screen at least one time in order to be certain that there are no unsuspected differences between your assumptions and the assumptions of the program. The same help screen can also be accessed from the data screen, where it is perhaps most useful, because you will then be looking at the data to which the help screen is referring. You can examine the help screen at any time; the screen appears instantaneously and takes little time to read.

Create a New Data Set (F2)

This will be a frequently chosen option. After the create option is chosen, one of three types of screens will appear, depending on the module. For some modules (decision and break-even analysis, forecasting, plant location, project scheduling, and quality control), a model submenu will appear, indicating that different programs are available within the broad context of the module. The desired choice is made in the usual way—by using the first letter or point and shoot. After selecting a model, it will be possible to give the problem a title.

Load a Data Set from the Disk (F3)

If you have previously stored data on a disk, it is possible to load the data into memory. If you choose the load data option, a screen will appear that contains the name of the drive, the name of the subdirectory (if there is one), and a list of the available files.

To load a file, simply type its name and then press **Return.** Standard DOS file names *without* extensions are legal. In other words, you may type in up to eight characters, but a period is illegal. You may preface the file name with a drive letter (with its colon). Examples of legal file names are **sample, test, b:sample, problem 1.** It does not matter whether you use uppercase or lowercase characters. DOS treats all characters as uppercase. You may type them as uppercase, lowercase, or mixed. The following are examples of illegal file names.

sample.1p   The program will not allow you to type the period.

abcdefghij   The name is too long; the program will issue an error message.

lpt1   This is a reserved DOS word.

After the file is loaded, you will be placed in the data screen and can edit the data.

Return to the Main Menu (F4)

The next option on the submenu list in Program F.3 is to return to the main menu. This option is not necessary if all of your problems come from the same module. However, if you have homework problems from more than one chapter, this is one way to go from module to module.

Utilities (F5)

If the utilities option is chosen, a new submenu will appear. The submenu options are again chosen in the normal fashion.

CUSTOMIZE COLORS: The first option allows you to create a custom color file. The colors of thirteen different items can be changed (in the usual way). For example, to change the color of the boxes in AB:POM, keep pressing **b** until you are satisfied with the color. The colors of the two boxes on the screen change each time you press **b.**

If you have a monochrome monitor, it may take eight presses of a button in order for the shades to change. Be patient.

After you have made all of the desired color changes, you have a few additional choices to make. For example, you must decide whether or not you want to keep a permanent file of these colors; if you do want to save the colors, select the save colors option. (Once saved, these colors can be used by starting the program with **pom u.**) If you plan to use these colors one time only, select the quit option. If you want to cancel the changes and revert to the colors that you started the program with, pick the restore initial colors option.

DELETE A FILE: This option can be used to delete (erase) files from your diskette. If you choose this option, a list of your files for the module currently in use will appear, along with a prompt asking you for the name of the file you wish to delete. To erase a file, simply type the file name. This option should be used if you have trouble saving files because your diskette has gotten full. Obviously, an option that erases files should be used with great care.

PRINT TO DISK FILE OR PRINTER TOGGLE SWITCH: It is possible to send the output to a file rather than to the printer. If this option is chosen, the program will request a name for the output file. All output will be sent to the file named until this option is toggled back to the printer. It is possible to use an extension (file.ext) for this file name.

TOGGLE FIX FORMAT ON: For most of the modules, you can fix the number of decimal places displayed on output by setting on the toggle for fixed number of places. This option must be used with care. (We demonstrate this option later in this section.)

ERROR BEEPS/SOUND OFF: Use this toggle to turn off or on the beep that alerts you when an error has occurred.

FUNCTION KEY DISPLAY OFF/ON: Use this toggle to turn off or on the function key display or the last row of the data screen. The function keys will work even when they are not displayed.

Exit (F6)

The last option on the submenu screen is the exit option. This is the option to choose when you have completed all of your work. The exit option will return control to DOS. If you wish to return to AB:POM from DOS after selecting this option, you must restart the system in the usual manner—by typing **pom** with any desired options.

NOTE: If DOS is not on your diskette, the computer will issue a message stating that COMMAND.COM is missing. If you wish to continue working, you must insert a DOS diskette; otherwise, you can simply turn the machine off.

ENTERING AND EDITING DATA

Character Data and Numerical Data

When entering names and numbers, simply type the name or number and then press one of the direction keys from Program F.4 or a function key. If you make a mistake while editing, there are two other direction keys to consider: **Back Space** and **Del,** both of which will delete the last character typed.

A beep indicates that you have typed an illegal key while entering data. One of the following messages will appear.

- Typing a character when a number is required.
- Trying to enter a number larger than permitted.
- Trying to enter a name longer than permitted.
- Trying to enter more digits after the decimal than permitted.
- Trying to enter a character that is not permitted for this entry.

NOTE: The format of numerical displays is handled by the program. Furthermore, any number less than .00001 is displayed as 0.

Toggle Entries

As mentioned previously, you will not always be entering data. Some entries are toggled—that is, the allowable entries have been preset. For example, in assembly line balancing the time unit can be toggled. You can change seconds to minutes to hours and back to seconds again by moving the cursor to the top of the cell of the column with zeros and pressing the space bar three times. The time unit will change each time the space bar is pressed. So, when the desired unit appears, simply go on to the next cell. Alternatively, you can call up a menu of all available options by pressing the **Enter** key.

While you are editing the data, the function keys shown on the bottom row of the data screen are available. Program F.3 tells what each function key does. Notice that function keys **F1** through **F6** correspond exactly to the menu options from the submenu. We now explain the four options we have not discussed.

Save (**F7**): This option is similar to the load a data file option. When you choose this option, a screen will appear with the names of your data files, and you will be asked for the name under which to save the data.

If you give the file the name of an existing file, you will be warned about replacing the existing file. The existing file will be replaced by the more recent one if you press **y** (or **Y**) or **Return.** After entering the name, press **Return** to save the data. As before, it is possible to change the drive by using the **F1** key option. It also is possible to use the shell option in the set utilities option from the data screen to change the drive or the directory.

Titl (**F8**): When you press **F8,** the top line of the data requests that you enter a new title. You will be permitted to enter a title up to thirty-seven characters in length. The title is entered in the usual manner, and will appear at the top of the data after **Return,** a direction key, or a function key is pressed.

Prnt (**F9**): This option will print the contents of the data or solution screen. The bottom lines and the outside box will not be printed. (It is possible to have everything printed character for character; use **Shift-PrtScn.**) The program prints to the LPT1 file, the standard printer file. If your printer is not attached to LPT1 (if, for example, you have a serial printer), you need to use the DOS MODE statement to redirect the output to the appropriate place; see your DOS manual for instructions. In one or two cases (most notably, linear programming and MRP) the output will not be exactly as it appears on the screen. Changes have been made to fit more than one screen's worth of data onto the printer.

If you have used the utility option, you can print to a file. Later, you can use a word processor to edit this file. In most cases, one of two things will happen if you press **F9** and your computer is not attached to a printer or your printer is not turned on: Either you will get an error message or the program will think that it is printing when it is not—which is harmless. It is also possible that the printer will keep trying to print every thirty seconds or so. You can stop this by pressing the **Esc** key.

Run (**F10**): After you have entered all of the data, you can press **F10** to solve the problem. Answers will appear either in addition to the data or in place of the data.

In either case, the function key bar at the bottom of the screen will change. In all modules, **F9** will be available to print the solution. In some modules, additional function keys for displaying more information will be defined. These definitions appear in the chapters for those modules. After viewing or printing the solution, press any key to return to the data screen.

Formats for Data

All of the formats for the data are determined by the program. In general, the maximum value that can be input for a number is determined by the width of the field in which the number appears. For example, the largest possible number in a field with six spaces is 999,999. The field width also determines the number of places after the decimal. In most cases, this will not pose a problem. However, there will be occasions when the number of places after the decimal varies within a column, even though the screen would appear orderly if there were no variations.

There is a trade-off involved in the use of this option: In order to have neat columns, we must express the data in round numbers. In many cases, rounding poses no problem, but we advise you to use the **f** option with great care.

GETTING STARTED

Regardless of the configuration of your system, you should begin by making a backup copy of AB:POM. Because AB:POM is not copy-protected, it is very easy to copy with the DOS **copy *.*** or **diskcopy** command.

Normal Startup

In order to run AB:POM, simply follow the procedure below. The description that follows assumes that you have a standard one- or two-disk drive system and are not using a hard drive.

1. Insert a DOS diskette into drive a: (usually the top drive or the left drive).
2. Turn on the computer.
3. When the A> prompt appears on the screen, insert the AB:POM-1 diskette into drive a:. If you have a second disk drive, insert the AB:POM-2 diskette into drive b:.
4. Type **pom** with any options (described in the following section).

If you have trouble starting, try typing **go** (with any options) rather than **pom**.

NOTE: If you use a version of DOS under DOS 3.00, a prompt will appear after you have typed **pom**. The machine will ask you to input the run-time module path.

In order to run the system, you must type a backslash (\) or the drive name in which AB:POM-1 is running (usually drive a:). When AB:POM-1 is in drive a:, the proper response to the prompt is to type **a:** followed by **Return** or **Enter.**

Notice that the third character is a backslash, not a slash. On some machines, the backslash is not required. Alternately, it is possible to begin the program by typing **path** = \ prior to typing **pom**. The file GO.BAT will do this for you.

[NOTE: If you have a two-disk system and use DOS 4.x, then you cannot make a bootable AB:POM-1 diskette. After starting, remove DOS and insert AB:POM-1 in drive a:, then type **POM.**]

Here are some other tips for starting the program.

Startup Options

The program starts with the command POM (or GO). The following options can be added.

Disk drive for data. The letters a, b, c, d, and e can be used to specify which drive contains the data. (This can be changed from within the program also.)

Example

POM B will indicate to the program that the data files can be found on drive b: The default drive is the drive from which AB:POM was started.

Color/Monitor Options. The letter **m** can be used to indicate that the monitor is a monochrome (single-color monitor). The number 1 can be used to indicate that the monitor is a color monitor, colors should be used, and the background color should be black. The number 2 indicates a color monitor and a background color that allows shadowing. The letter u indicates that a user file of colors called COLOR.POM should be used. (This file can be created and/or changed from the utility menu within AB:POM.) If you do not choose a color option at the command line the program will ask you for one.

Examples

POM M or POM m will use a monochrome monitor.
POM 1 will use default colors that include a black background.
POM 2 will use default colors that include a blue background and a shadowing effect.
POM U will look for the file COLOR.POM and use those colors.

Number of Lines on the Screen. The usual number of lines is 25 and this is the nicest display. However, if you use the option H (high resolution) then 43 lines will be used (if your monitor allows this), and if you use the option V (for VGA) then 50 lines will be used if your monitor allows this.

Sound Toggle. If you start the program with the letter S then the beeps made when errors occur will be silenced. This can be changed from within the program, using the utility option.

Combining Options. Options can be combined.

Example

POM smb

will turn off beeps, display everything in black/white and look for data on drive b:.

Formatting Procedures. POM F will change the formatting procedure of AB:POM. Typically, AB:POM allows nine spaces for numbers and decimal points. If this option is chosen, the number of places after the decimal is fixed. This makes for a neater display, but it can lead to roundoff problems. As explained in the section on formatting at the end of this appendix, this option should be used with great care.

Table F.1 summarizes the startup options we have covered in this section. Again, more than one option can be chosen. Second, the order in which the options are typed does not matter. For example, **pom mc** (or **pom cm**) starts the program, using a monochrome monitor and storing and accessing data on drive c:.

Creating Bootable Diskettes

2–5.25" disk drives.

1. Start (boot) your system, using DOS.
2. Type
   FORMAT b:/s (followed by pressing the ENTER key)
3. DOS will ask you to insert a diskette into drive b:. Insert a blank diskette and press the ENTER key.
4. DOS will ask you if you want to format another. Respond with N.
5. Type
   COPY COMMAND.COM b: (followed by pressing the ENTER key). (NOTE: With some versions of DOS this step is unnecessary but it cannot hurt.)

TABLE F.1 Startup option summary

CODE	MEANING
m	Monochrome (for use with single-color monitors)
1	Color display 1
2	Color display 2
u	User-defined colors
h	43 lines available on the screen
v	50 lines available on the screen
f	Fixed number of digits after the decimal
a, b, c, d, or **e**	Drive on which to store data

6. Insert AB:POM-1 into drive a: and type
   COPY *.* b:

7. Write AB:POM-1 BOOTABLE on a diskette label and place the label on the diskette in drive b: You are now ready to run. (See the startup steps.) You can boot (start) the system with the diskette you just created.
   To be safe you should copy the AB:POM-2 diskette also.

8. Place DOS in drive a: and type
   DISKCOPY a: b:

9. At the request place AB:POM-2 into drive a: and a blank diskette into drive b: and press the ENTER key.

10. Write AB:POM-2 on a label and place the label on the diskette in drive b:

1–3.5" disk drive.

1. Start (boot) your system, using DOS.

2. Type
   FORMAT b:/s (followed by pressing the ENTER key)

3. DOS will ask you to insert a diskette into drive b:. Insert a blank diskette and press the ENTER key.

4. DOS will ask if you want to format another. Respond with N.

5. Type
   COPY COMMAND.COM b: (followed by pressing the ENTER key). (NOTE: With some versions of DOS this step is unnecessary but it cannot hurt.)

6. Insert the single AB:POM-1,2 diskette into drive a: and type COPY *.* b:

7. Write AB:POM BOOTABLE on a diskette label and place the label on the diskette in drive b:. You are now ready to run. (See the startup steps.). You can boot (start) the system with the diskette you just created.

Hard Drive. In the case of hard drives, we suggest you consult the hardware manual for your machine.

SYSTEM ERROR MESSAGES

In this section, we define the system errors that you may encounter. Some system errors occur only at the beginning of the program (startup errors); others may occur at any time.

Startup Errors

Input Run Time Module: The appropriate response to this message is the name of the disk drive that contains the ABRUNLIB.EXE file—typically **a:** or \.

Error 1.1: If you start the program with the **u** option (user-defined color file), the program expects to find the file COLOR.POM on the diskette from which AB:POM is started. COLOR.POM may not be on your diskette if you have never created a startup file. Note that whenever this error occurs, the program uses colors (rather than monochrome) as its default. Therefore, if you have a monochrome monitor, you need to either reset the colors, using utility option 5, or start over.

Error 1.2: This error message tells you that you used the **h** option when you started AB:POM even though you do not have a high-resolution monitor. The program will simply treat everything as a standard 25-line monitor.

System Errors Occurring During Module Execution

Error 1.3 Some modules have different allowable problem sizes for high-resolution monitors. If you create a large data set with the **h** option, you must use the **h** option to read it if it is larger than the maximum allowable problem size under normal conditions.

Error 1.4: Your machine is not large enough to solve this problem. Some modules—namely, linear programming, transportation, and assignment—need more storage when they execute a problem.

Error 1.5 You are trying to load a file that does not exist. (You probably have typed the name incorrectly.)

Error 1.6 The program is having trouble getting a file or disk drive. (Have you left the drive door open? Is there a write-protect on your diskette?)

Error 1.7 The diskette is write-protected. Either remove the tab or, on 3.5-inch diskette, change the write protect key.

Error 1.8 Disk full. Either delete files from the diskette or use a new diskette.

Solutions to Selected Problems

Chapter 1
1.3 3.3%

Chapter 3
3.1
- **(a)** Decision under uncertainty
- **(b)** Maximax
- **(c)** DREXEL D1

3.3
- **(a)** Stock 11 cases
- **(b)** Stock 13 cases

3.4 8 cases

3.5 Best alternative: build pilot; if it works, build facility, EMV = $72,500.

3.6
- **(b)** Small plant
- **(c)** EVPI = $134,000

3.12 Jim Rice should conduct the survey. If it's favorable, he should build a large shop; if it's unfavorable he should build no shop at all. EMV = $25,000

Chapter 3 Supplement
S3.1 40 air conditioners, 60 fans, profit is $1,900.
S3.2 200 Model A tubs, 0 Model B tubs, $18,000 profit.
S3.4 10 Alpha 4s and 24 Beta 5s, profit = $55,200
S3.6 $X_1 = 25.71$, $X_2 = 21.43$, $C = \$68.57$
S3.15 8 tables, 2 bookcases, profit = $96.
S3.17 $X_1 = 2$, $X_2 = 6$, profit = $36.
S3.18 Basic variables at: 1st iteration are $A_1 = 80$, $A_2 = 75$; 2nd iteration are $A_1 = 55$, $X_1 = 25$; 3rd iteration are $X_1 = 14$, $X_2 = 33$; Cost = $221 at optimal solution.
S3.19 0 class A, 17.14 class K, 34.29 class T, P = $582.86
S3.20 $S_2 = 550$ surplus lbs of potassium, $X_1 = 300$ lbs phosphate, $X_2 = 700$ lbs potassium, $C = \$5,700$

Chapter 4
4.1
- **(a)** 337
- **(b)** 380
- **(c)** 423

4.2 MAD for 3-year average = 2.54
MAD for weighted 3-year average is slightly better at 2.31.
4.4 MAD for 2-year M.A. = 2.22; for 3-year M.A. = 2.54; for weighted M.A. = 2.31; and for 4-year M.A. = 3.11. Two-year is lowest.

4.11
- **(a)** $\alpha = .6$ yields forecast of 56 for year 6; $\alpha = .9$ yields 58 for year 6 and has a lower MAD than $\alpha = .6$
- **(b)** 55 in year 6
- **(c)** 62 in year 6

4.14
- **(a)** 13.7
- **(b)** 13.17
- **(c)** MAD for average is 2.20; MAD for weighted average is 2.72.

4.15
- **(b)** $Y = 1.0 + 1.0x$
- **(c)** 10 drums

4.18 $R^2 = .4785$; SAT = 350, GPA = 2.20; SAT = 800, GPA = 3.77
4.19 66, 69, 72, $R^2 = .852$

Chapter 4 Supplement
S4.1 2.85
S4.2 5.45, 4.06
S4.3 .8849
S4.5 .3413
S4.8
- **(a)** .0548
- **(b)** .6554
- **(c)** .6554
- **(d)** .2119

S4.9 .0668

Chapter 5
5.1
- **(a)** .375
- **(b)** .2 days
- **(c)** .225
- **(d)** .141, .053, .020, .007

5.3
- **(a)** 2.25
- **(b)** .75
- **(c)** 51.4 seconds (.875 minutes)
- **(d)** 38.6 seconds (.64 minutes)

(e) 42.2%, 31.6%, 23.7%

5.5

    (a) 6

    (b) 12 minutes

    (c) .857

    (d) 54%

    (e) $1,728/day

    (f) Yes

5.6

    (a) 16 minutes = .267 hours

    (b) 3.20

    (c) Yes, cost savings is $71.19 per hour.

5.11

    (a) .05

    (b) .743

    (c) .795

Chapter 5 Supplement

S5.1 No, it's not common.

S5.3

    (b) Average number delayed = .40

         Average number arrivals = 2.07

         Average number unloaded = 2.07

The short simulation span introduces volatility in the daily arrival rate (from 2.73 to 2.07). This, coupled with speedier unloading rate produces a much lower average delay rate.

S5.5 She should be able to easily balance her account.

S5.7

    (a) Cost/hour is generally more expensive replacing one pen at at time.

    (b) Expected cost/hour with 1 pen policy = $1.38 (or $58/breakdown). Expected cost/hour with 4 pen policy = $1.12 (or $132/breakdown).

S5.10 Ordering 21 cars with a ROP = 10 is usually less expensive but answers will vary in simulations

S5.11 Over the long run, on-hand inventory will continue to grow to an infinite level.

Chapter 6

6.7 $144,000

6.9

    (a) buy at $1,500,000

    (b) Expected monetary value (minimum cost)

    (c) The worst is $3,500,000. The best is $1,000,000

Chapter 7

7.1 $842

7.3 $19,698.70

7.5 No

7.7

    (a) Break even in dollars is $100,000.

    (b) Break even in units is 12,500 units.

(c) Profit is $350,000.

7.10

    (a) $15,000

    (b) 300,000 units

7.11 25,000 units

Chapter 8

8.1 Location C

8.3 Solution is not optimal; $3,900 is optimal.

8.5 $1,900.

8.7

    (a) Ship from *W:* 15 to Shop *B,* 20 to Shop *C.* Ship from *Y:* 30 to Shop *A,* 20 to Shop *C.* Ship from *Z:* 50 to Shop *B.*

    (b) All empty cells tested positive, therefore there is no saving.

8.9 Note: Solution is degenerate: ship from M: 0 to 1, 25 to 3; ship from N: 30 to 2, 10 to 3; ship from O: 30 to 1.

8.17 Site 3, rating 86.65

8.19 (7.97, 6.69)

8.20 (56.33, 101.04) near Hamilton or Dayton, Ohio

8.21 Shopping mall, 3.24

Chapter 9

9.6

    (a) One possible layout has a throughput of 3.75 patients/hour.

    (b) Medical exam station—16 minutes

    (c) One layout yields a throughput of 5/hour

9.7 3 stations required; efficiency = 87%.

9.9 5 stations required; efficiency = 75%. (actual: 5 stations with a max. time of 6 min.; efficiency = 83.3%)

9.11 3 stations required; efficiency = 86.7%

9.13 8 stations required; efficiency = 72.0%

9.15 6 stations required; efficiency = 90%

Chapter 10 Supplement

S10.1 Normal time = 5.565 minutes

Standard time = 6.183 minutes

S10.3 Standard time = 29.84 minutes

S10.5 Standard time = 5.4 minutes with nonconforming times omitted.

S10.7 Standard time = 82.35 seconds; largest sample size = 40, for placing bag on conveyor.

S10.9

    (a) Standard time = 47.55 minutes

    (b) 75 samples required for check/inspect work

S10.11 336 samples required.

S10.13 6.55 seconds

Chapter 11

11.1 $5.26

Chapter 11 Supplement

S11.1 for boat four, $751,315.24
for boat five, $715,659.28
for boat six, $687,825.20

S11.3

(a) 70 millicents/bit

(b) 8.2 millicents/bit

S11.5 26,728 hours

Chapter 12

12.1 Plan 5's costs are $29,760 for regular time plus $27,776 for overtime for a total of $57,536. Plan 6's costs are $34,720 for regular time plus $18,600 for subcontracting for a total of $53,320.

12.6

Plan A

MONTH	DEMAND	PRODUCTION	SUBCONTRACT	COST
April	1,000	1,000	—	—
May	1,200	1,000	200	$12,000
June	1,400	1,000	400	$24,000
July	1.800	1,000	800	$48,000
Aug.	1,800	1,000	800	$48,000
Sept.	1,600	1,000	600	$36,000
			Total	$168,000

Plan B

MONTH	DEMAND	PRODUCTION	HIRE	LAYOFFS	COST
Initial		1,300			
April	1,000	1,000		300	$18,000
May	1,200	1,200	200		6,000
June	1,400	1,400	200		6,000
July	1,800	1,800	400		12,000
Aug.	1,800	1,800	—	—	—
Sept.	1,600	1,600		200	12,000
				Total	$54,000

12.7 *Plan C* Total cost = $92,000

Plan D Total cost = $82,300; assuming inventory = 0

12.10 Cost = $627,100; to month 1: beginning inventory (500 units), month 1 regular (1,100), month 1 overtime (400); to month 2: month 1 regular (400), month 2 regular (1,600), month 2 overtime (400), month 2 subcontracting (100); to month 3: month 3 regular (750), month 3 overtime (200), month 3 subcontracting (550); to month 4: month 4 regular (1,600), month 4 overtime (400), month 4 subcontracting (100)

12.12 Cost = $874,320; to April: beginning inventory (50), April regular (2,880), April overtime (70); to May: May regular (2,750); to June: May regular (30), June regular (2,760), June overtime (160)

12.14 Cost = $308,125; to period 1: beginning inventory (4), period 1 regular (23), period 1 overtime (5); to period 2: period 1 regular (2), period 2 regular (28), period 2 overtime (2); to period 3: period 2 overtime (2), period 3 regu-

lar (30), period 3 overtime (8); to period 4: period 3 subcontracting (1), period 4 regular (29), period 4 overtime (3), period 4 subcontracting (7); to ending inventory: period 4 overtime (3)

Chapter 13

13.3 7,000 units

13.4

(a) 149 units

(b) 160 units

(c) $1,341.64

(d) 27 orders

(e) 7.4 days

13.10 1651 units

13.12

(a) 199 units

(b) 10 units

13.14 yes, take the discount

13.16 no, purchase at the standard price.

13.20 optimum stocking policy is 3 units

Chapter 14

14.1 (a) Gross material requirements plan:

ITEM		WEEK								LEAD TIME (WKS)
		1	2	3	4	5	6	7	8	
A	Required date					10				1
	Order release				10					
D	Required date				30					1
	Order release			30						
F	Required date				20					2
	Order release		20							

(b) Gross material requirements plan:

ITEM		WEEK								LEAD TIME (WKS)
		1	2	3	4	5	6	7	8	
A	Gross req.					10				1
	On hand					0				
	Net req.					10				
	Order receipt					10				
	Order release				10					
D	Gross req.				30					1
	On hand				0					
	Net req.				30					
	Order receipt				30					
	Order release			30						
F	Gross req.				20					2
	On hand				0					
	Net req.				20					
	Order receipt				20					
	Order release		20							

14.3 Gross material requirements plan, modified to include the 20 units of U required for maintenance purposes:

ITEM		WEEK 1	2	3	4	5	6	7	8	LEAD TIME (WKS)
S	Required date							100		
	Order release					100				2
T	Required date					100				
	Order release				100					1
U	Required date						50	20		
	Order release				50	20				2
V	Required date					100				
	Order release			100						2
W	Required date					200				
	Order release	200								3
X	Required date					100				
	Order release				100					1
Y	Required date				25					
	Order release	25								2
Z	Required date				150					
	Order release		150							1

Net material requirements plan, modified to include the 20 units of U required for maintenance purposes:

ITEM		WEEK 1	2	3	4	5	6	7	8	LEAD TIME (WKS)
S	Gross req.							100		
	On hand							20		
	Net req.							80		
	Order receipt							80		2
	Order release					80				
T	Gross req.					80				
	On hand					20				
	Net req.					60				
	Order receipt					60				1
	Order release				60					
U	Gross req.						40	20		
	On hand						10	0		
	Net req.						30	20		
	Order receipt						30	20		2
	Order release				30	20				
V	Gross req.					60				
	On hand					30				
	Net req.					30				
	Order receipt					30				2
	Order release			30						
W	Gross req.					120				
	On hand					30				
	Net req.					90				
	Order receipt					90				3
	Order release	90								
X	Gross req.					60				
	On hand					25				
	Net req.					35				
	Order receipt					35				1
	Order release				35					

ITEM		WEEK 1	2	3	4	5	6	7	8	LEAD TIME (WKS)
Y	Gross req.			15	10					
	On hand			15	0					
	Net req.			0	10					
	Order receipt			0	10					2
	Order release		10							
Z	Gross req.			90	60					
	On hand			10	0					
	Net req.			80	60					
	Order receipt			80	60					1
	Order release		80	60						

14.5 (a) Gross Material Requirements Plan for C:

		WEEK 1	2	3	4	5	6	7	8	9	10	11	12
C	Gr req							100	100	50	50	150	

(b) Planned Order Release:

		WEEK 1	2	3	4	5	6	7	8	9	10	11	12
A	Req date							100		50		150	
	Ord rel						100		50		150		
H	Req date								100		50		
	Ord rel							100		50			
C	Req date							100	100	50	50	150	
	Ord rel					50	100	50	50	150			

14.7 $1,100

14.9

(a) $1,025

(b) Costs are the same; just order one week later.

14.11 Master production schedule:

		WEEK 0	1	2	3	4	5	6	7	8	9	10
P	Gr req	0	40	30	40	10	70	40	10	30	60	

Net material plan:

		WEEK 0	1	2	3	4	5	6	7	8	9	10
P	Gr req	0	0	40	30	40	10	70	40	10	30	60
	On hand	20	20	20	0	0	0	0	0	0	0	0
	Net req			20	30	40	10	70	40	10	30	60
	Ord rept			20	30	40	10	70	40	10	30	60
	Ord rel		20	30	40	10	70	40	10	30	60	
C	Gr req	0	20	30	40	10	70	40	10	30	60	
	On hand	30	30	10	50	10	0	50	10	0	60	
	Net req			20		120			90			
	Ord rept			70		120			90			
	Ord rel		70		120			90				

Chapter 15

15.2 C3 to #3, C5 to #1, C8 to #2, Cost $2,700

15.4 Hawkins to cardiology, Condriac to urology, Bardot to orthopedics, Hoolihan to obstetrics, "cost" = 86

15.7

	RULE	SEQUENCE
(a)	FCFS	A,B,C,D,E
(b)	EDD	B,A,D,E,C
(c)	SPT	E,D,A,B,C
(d)	LPT	C,B,A,D,E

15.9

JOB	C.R.	PRIORITY
A	1.17	3
B	1.33	4
C	1.00	2
D	.63	1

15.11

	RULE	SEQUENCE
(a)	FCFS	A,B,C,D,E
(b)	EDD	C,A,B,E,D
(c)	SPT	C,D,E,A,B
(d)	LPT	B,A,E,D,C

15.12 CR Schedule: A, B, C, E, D

15.14 E, D, C, A, B, F. Make span time is 35 hours.

15.15

JOB	M1	M2
A	10	11
B	7	6
C	12	13
D	11	9
E	16	7

Sequence is A, C, D, E, B

Chapter 16

16.2 Time is 26 days; path is B-D-E-G.

16.4 There are two critical paths, A-C-G and B-E-G. Time = 19.

16.6 Critical path is C-D-E-F-H-K. Time = 36.33

16.7 .946

16.8 Project time = 50 weeks; critical path = A-C-E-H-I-K-

M-N

16.10

    (a) .0228

    (b) .3085

    (c) .8413

    (d) .9772

Chapter 17 Supplement

S17.1 $UCL_X = 46.9$, $LCL_X = 45.0$
$UCL_R = 4.0$, $LCL_R = 0$

S17.2 $UCL_X = 60.92$, $LCL_X = 59.08$
$UCL_R = 5.33$, $LCL_R = .669$

S17.4 $\bar{X}$'s limits are 9.66 to 10.42
R chart limits are 0 to 1.19
Process in control, but more samples desirable.

S17.8 For $\bar{X}$, UCL = 64.5, LCL = 62.4
For $\bar{R}$, UCL = 3.4, LCL = 0

S17.9 UCL = .02, LCL = 0

S17.11 Limits are from 0 to .11

S17.12 LCL = 7, UCL = 33; action should be taken

S17.16 The plan (n = 100, c ≤ 2) has an alpha risk of .08 and a beta risk of .12. Both exceeded their limits of .05 and .10, so a larger sample needs to be drawn and the calculations repeated.

S17.17 1.2%

Chapter 18

18.1 Reliability of System = .605

18.2

    (a) 5.0%

    (b) .00001025 failures/unit-hour

    (c) .08979

    (d) 98.77

18.6 yes; $1,030 for one man, $735 for two men

Glossary

ABC Analysis (p. 553) A method for dividing on-hand inventory into three classifications based on annual dollar volume.

Acceptable quality level (AQL) (p. 775) The quality level of a lot considered good.

Acceptance sampling (p. 771) A method of measuring random samples of lots or batches of products against predetermined standards.

Active strategy (p. 519) An aggregate planning strategy that attempts to influence the demand pattern to smooth out demand changes over the planning period.

Activity (p. 692) A task or a subproject in CPM or PERT network that occurs between two events; a flow over time.

Activity charts (p. 440) A way of depicting studies and the resultant suggestions for improvement of utilization of an operator and a machine or some combination of operators (a crew) and machines.

Activity time estimate (p. 695) The time it takes to complete an activity in a PERT or CPM network.

Adaptive smoothing (p. 151) An approach to exponential smoothing forecasting in which the smoothing constant is automatically changed to keep errors to a minimum.

Aggregate planning (p. 516) An approach to determine the quantity and timing of production for the intermediate future (usually 3 to 18 months ahead).

American Production & Inventory Control Society (APICS) (p. 13) A professional organization for production and inventory control personnel.

American Society for Quality Control (p. 13) An association of quality control professionals.

APT or automatically programmed tool (p. 318) A computer program language used to control numerically controlled machines.

Assembly chart (p. 263) A means of identifying the points of production where components flow into subassemblies and ultimately into a final product.

Assembly drawing (p. 263) An exploded view of the product, usually through a three-dimensional or isometric drawing.

Assembly line (p. 397) An approach that puts fabricated parts together at a series of work stations; used in repetitive processes.

Assembly line balancing (p. 398) Obtaining output at each workstation on the production line so that it is nearly the same.

Assignable variation (p. 763) Variation in a production process that can be traced to specific causes.

Assignment method (p. 646) A special class of linear programming models that involves assigning tasks or jobs to resources.

Attribute inspection (p. 750) An inspection that classifies items as being either good or defective regardless of degree.

Automated guided vehicle (AGV) (p. 319) Electronically guided and controlled carts used to move materials.

Average actual cycle time (p. 451) The arithmetic mean of the times for each element measured, adjusted for unusual influences for each element.

Average outgoing quality (AOQ) (p. 779) The percent defective in an average lot of goods inspected through acceptance sampling.

Back-order inventory model (p. 573) An inventory model for planned shortages.

Backward scheduling (p. 643) A job shop scheduling technique in which the last operation on the routing is scheduled first.

Benchmarking (p. 743) Selecting a demonstrated standard of performance that represents the very best performance for a process or activity.

Beta probability distribution (p. 695) A mathematical distribution that may describe the activity time estimate distributions in a PERT network.

Bill-of-material (BOM) (pp. 258; 603) A listing of the components, their description, and the quantity of each required to make one unit of a product.

Bonus (p. 441) A monetary reward, usually in cash or stock options, given to management or executives in an organization.

Bottleneck (p. 659) An operation that limits output in the production sequence.

Breakdown maintenance (p. 806) Remedial maintenance that occurs when equipment fails and must be repaired on an emergency or priority basis.

Break-even analysis (p. 293) A means of finding the point, in dollars and units, at which costs equal revenues.

Capacity (p. 288) The maximum output of a system in a given period.

***c*-chart (p. 770)** A quality control chart used to control the number of defects per unit of output.

Center of gravity method (p. 338) A mathematical technique used for finding the best location for a single distribution point that services several stores or areas.

Central limit theorem (p. 763)   The theoretical foundation for x-charts that states that regardless of the distribution of the population of all parts or services, the distribution of x's will tend to follow a normal curve as the sample size grows large.

Closed-loop MRP system (p. 618)   A system that provides feedback to the capacity plan, master production schedule, and production plan.

Coefficient of correlation (p. 146)   A number measure, between -1 and $+1$, of the statistical relationship between variables.

Compact II (p. 318)   A computer program language used to control numerically controlled machines.

Competitive advantage (p. 38)   The creation of a unique advantage over competitors.

Computer-aided design (CAD) (p. 262)   Use of a computer to develop the geometry of a design.

Computer-aided manufacturing (CAM) (p. 262)   The use of information technology to control machinery.

Computer integrated manufacturing (CIM) (p. 320)   A manufacturing system in which electronically controlled machines are integrated with robots, transfer machines, or automated guided vehicles to create a complete manufacturing system.

Computer numerical control (CNC) (p. 318)   The control of machines via their own computer.

Configuration management (p. 264)   A system by which a product's planned and changing components are accurately identified and for which control and accountability of change is maintained.

Consignment inventory (p. 485)   An arrangement whereby the supplier maintains title to the inventory.

Constraints (p. 70)   Restrictions that limit the degree to which a manager can pursue an objective.

Consumer market survey (p. 124)   A forecasting method that solicits input from customers or potential customers regarding their future purchasing plans.

Consumer's risk (p. 775)   The mistake of a customer's acceptance of a bad lot overlooked through sampling (a Type II error).

Continuous process (p. 278)   A product-oriented, high-volume, low-variety process.

Control chart (pp. 753; 760)   A graphic presentation of process data over time.

Control files (p. 642)   All of the information in an MRP system pertaining to a particular order—the shop order master file and the shop order detail file.

Corner point method (p. 77)   A method for solving graphical linear programming problems.

CPM/MRP (p. 710)   A system that integrates resource procurement into the project scheduling.

CRAFT (Computer Relative Allocation of Facilities Technique) (p. 387)   A computer program that systematically examines alternative departmental rearrangements to reduce total material handling cost.

Critical path (p. 691)   The computed longest time path(s) through a network.

Critical path analysis (p. 696)   A network model for finding the shortest possible schedule for a series of activities. It usually employs PERT or CPM.

Critical path method (p. 690)   A network technique using only one time factor per activity that enables managers to schedule, monitor, and control large and complex projects.

Critical ratio (CR) (p. 653)   A sequencing rule that is an index number computed by dividing the time remaining until due date by the work time remaining.

Crossover chart (p. 296)   A chart depicting more than one process with costs for the possible volumes.

Cumulative probability distribution (p. 218)   The accumulation of individual probabilities of a distribution.

Cycle counting (p. 555)   A continuing audit of inventory records.

Cycle time (p. 400)   The time the product is available at each work station in assembly line balancing.

Decision support system (DSS) (p. 321)   A logical extension of MIS that helps managers model decision alternatives by allowing "what if" analysis given certain financial or operating parameters.

Decision table (p. 49)   A tabular means of analyzing decision alternatives and states of nature.

Decision tree (p. 53)   A graphical means of analyzing decision alternatives and states of nature.

Degeneracy (p. 351)   An occurrence in transportation models when there are too few squares or shipping routes being used so that tracing a closed path for each unused square becomes impossible. Degeneracy exists when the number of rows plus the number of columns minus one does not equal the number of occupied cells.

Delphi method (p. 124)   A forecasting technique using a group process that allows experts to make forecasts.

Demand forecast (p. 124)   A projection of a company's sales for each time period in the planning horizon.

Design for manufacturability and value engineering teams (p. 254)   Teams charged with improvement of designs and specifications at the research, development, design, and production stages of product development.

Designed capacity (p. 288)   A facility's maximum capacity that can be achieved under ideal conditions.

Direct numerical control (DNC) (p. 320)   A machine that is directly (hard) wired to a control computer that supplies the electronic instructions and controls.

Disaggregation (p. 532)   The process of breaking the aggregate plan into greater detail.

Discrete probability distribution (p. 172) A frequency distribution in which outcomes are not continuous. Outcomes from the roll of a die are discrete, whereas temperatures (which can take on any fractional value) are considered continuous variables.

Distribution resource planning (DRP) (pp. 600; 620) A time-phased stock replenishment plan for all levels of a distribution network.

Double sampling (p. 772) A form of inspection that takes a small sample and if the resulting defects fall within a marginal acceptance level, a second sampling may be drawn; cumulative results determine rejection or acceptance of the lot.

Dual-factor theory (p. 433) A theory advanced by Frederick Herzberg that suggests that jobs can contain hygiene elements and motivators.

Dummy activity (p. 694) An activity having no time, inserted into the network to maintain the logic of the network.

Dummy destinations (p. 350) Artificial destination points created in the transportation method of linear programming when the total supply is greater than the total demand; they serve to equalize the total demand and supply.

Dummy sources (p. 350) Artificial shipping source points created in the transportation method when total demand is greater than total supply in order to affect a supply equal to the excess of demand over supply.

Earliest due date (EDD) (p. 650) A priority scheduling rule that means the earliest due date job is performed next.

Economic forecasts (p. 123) Planning indicators, often provided by forecasting services, valuable in helping organizations prepare medium- to long-range forecasts.

Economic part period (p. 616) That period of time when the ratio of setup cost to holding cost is equal.

Effective capacity or utilization (p. 288) The maximum capacity a firm can expect to achieve given its product mix, methods of scheduling, maintenance, and standards of quality.

Efficiency (p. 288) A measure of actual output over effective capacity.

Electronic data interchange (EDI) (p. 483) A standardized data transmittal format for computerized communications between organizations.

Employee involvement (p. 741) Inclusion of employee(s) in every step of the process from product design to final packaging.

Engineering change notice (ECN) (pp. 258; 603) A correction or modification of an engineering drawing.

Engineering drawing (p. 258) A drawing that shows the dimensions, tolerances, materials, and finishes of a component.

Equally likely (p. 50) A criterion for decision making under certainty that assigns equal probability to each state of nature.

Ergonomics (p. 435) The study of work; in the United States often called *human factor engineering*.

Event (p. 692) A point in time that marks the start or completion of a task or activity in a network.

Expected monetary value (EMV) (p. 51) The expected payout or value of a variable that has different possible states of nature, each with an associated probability.

Expected value (p. 173) A measure of central tendency and the weighted average of the values of the variable.

Expected value of perfect information (EVPI) (p. 52) The difference between the payoff under certainty and under risk.

Expected value under certainty (p. 52) The expected or average return.

Expert system (ES) (p. 322) A computer program that mimics human logic and "solves" problems much as a human expert would.

Exponential smoothing (p. 130) A weighted moving average forecasting technique in which data points are weighted by an exponential function.

Fabrication line (p. 397) A machine-paced, product-oriented facility for building components.

Failure (p. 803) The change in a product or system from a satisfactory working condition to a condition that is below an acceptable standard.

First come, first served (FCFS) (p. 650) A priority job scheduling rule by which the jobs are completed in the order they arrived.

First in, first out (FEFO) (p. 187) A queuing rule by which the first customers in line receive the first service; or in an inventory system, the first inventory received is the first inventory used.

Fish-bone chart (p. 750) A schematic technique used to discover possible locations of quality problems in manufacturing; also known as an Ishikawa diagram, or a cause-and-effect diagram.

Fixed costs (p. 293) Costs that continue even if no units are produced.

Fixed-period system (p. 580) A system that triggers inventory ordering on a uniform time frequency.

Fixed-position layout (p. 380) Addresses the layout requirements of stationary projects or large bulky projects (such as ships or buildings).

Flexible manufacturing system (FMS) (p. 320) A system using an automated work cell controlled by electronic signals from a common centralized computer facility.

Flexible work week (p. 428) A work schedule that deviates from the normal or standard five eight-hour days (usually four ten-hour days).

Flextime (p. 428) A system that allows employees, within limits, to determine their own work schedules.

Flow diagram (p. 439) A drawing used to analyze movement of people or material.

Focused factory (p. 392) A permanent facility to produce a product or component in a product-oriented facility.

Focused work center (p. 391) A permanent product-oriented arrangement of machines and personnel in what is ordinarily a process-oriented facility.

Forecasting (p. 122) The art and science of forecasting future events.

Forward scheduling (p. 642) Assumes that procurement of material and operations start as soon as the requirements are known.

Gain sharing (p. 441) A system of financial rewards to employees for improvements made in an organization's performance.

Gantt charts (pp. 644; 688) Planning charts used to schedule resources and allocate time; developed by Henry L. Gantt in the late 1800s.

Graphical/charting technique (p. 523) An aggregate planning technique that works with a few variables at a time to allow planners to compare projected capacity with existing capacity.

Graphical evaluation and review technique (GERT) (p. 709) A network model, in the PERT family, that permits probabilities of occurrence on each activity.

Gross material requirements plan (p. 607) A schedule that shows the total demand for an item (prior to subtraction of on-hand inventory and scheduled receipts) and when it must be ordered from suppliers or production must be started in order to meet its demand by a particular date.

Group technology (p. 261) A system that requires that components be identified by a coding system that specifies the type of processing and the parameters of the processing; it allows similar products to be processed together.

Hierarchical planning system (p. 533) A system that breaks decisions down into more manageable terms by partitioning them into a traditional managerial hierarchy.

Historical experience (p. 450) Estimating the time required to do a task based on the last time it was required.

Holding cost (p. 561) The cost to keep or carry inventory in stock.

Incentive system (p. 441) An employee reward system based on individual or group productivity.

Industrial engineering (p. 3) Analytical approaches applied to the improvement of productivity in both manufacturing and service sectors.

Infant mortality (p. 806) The failure rate early in the life of a product or process.

Information sciences (p. 4) The systematic processing of data to yield information.

Input-output control (p. 643) A system that allows operations personnel to manage facility work flows, by tracking work added to a work center and its work completed (in that work center).

Inspection (p. 748) A means of ensuring that an operation is producing at the quality level expected.

Institute of Industrial Engineers (p. 13) A professional organization for industrial engineers.

Intangible costs (p. 333) A category of location costs that can be evaluated through weighting techniques.

Intermittent process (p. 278) A low-volume, high-variety process; also known as a process-oriented process.

ISO 9745 (p. 745) A set of quality standards developed by the European Community.

Iso-cost line approach (p. 78) An approach to solve a linear programming minimization problem graphically.

Iso-profit line method (p. 74) An approach to solving a linear programming maximization problem graphically.

Job design (p. 426) A approach that specifies the tasks that constitute a job for an individual or a group.

Job enlargement (p. 429) The grouping of a variety of tasks about the same skill level; horizontal enlargement.

Job enrichment (p. 429) A method of giving an employee more responsibility that includes some of the planning and control necessary for job accomplishment; vertical enlargement.

Job instructions (p. 264) A way of providing detailed instructions about how to perform a task.

Job lot (p. 382) A group or batch of parts processed together.

Job rotation (p. 429) A system in which an employee is moved from one specialized job to another.

Job shop (p. 641) A high-variety, low-volume system; intermittent processing.

Johnson's rule (p. 654) An approach that minimizes processing time for sequencing a group of jobs through two facilities and minimizes total idle time in the facilities.

Jury of executive opinion (p. 124) A forecasting technique that takes the opinion of a small group of high-level managers, often in combination with statistical models, and results in a group estimate of demand. The most widely used of all forecasting approaches.

Just-in-time inventory (p. 556) The minimum inventory necessary to keep a perfect system running.

Just-in-time purchasing (JIT) (p. 483) Purchasing that reduces waste present at receiving and incoming inspection; it also reduces inventory, poor quality, and delay.

Kaizen (p. 745) The Japanese word for the ongoing process of incremental improvement.

Kanban or Kanban system (p. 559) The Japanese word for *card* that has come to mean "signal"; a Kanban system moves parts through production via a "pull" from a signal.

Kit number (p. 605) See **Pseudo bill.**

Knowledge society (p. 17) A society in which much of the labor force has migrated from manual work to work based on knowledge.

Labor planning (p. 426) A means of determining staffing policies dealing with employment stability and work schedules.

Labor specialization (p. 428) The division of labor into unique ("special") tasks.

Labor standards (p. 426) The amount of time required to perform a job or part of a job.

Lead time (pp. 569; 605) In purchasing systems, the time between placing an order and receiving it; in production systems, it is the wait, move, queue, setup, and run times for each component produced.

Lean producer (p. 280) Repetitive producers who are world-class.

Lean production/lean manufacturing (p. 442) Using committed employees with ever expanding responsibility in an effort to achieve zero waste, 100% good product, delivered on time every time. The concept implies expanding each employee's job to the maximum and enhancing each employee's responsibility. It is the opposite of some repetitive manufacturing, which removes responsibility and thinking from a job to simplify it to the maximum.

Learning curves (p. 496) The premise that people and organizations get better at their tasks as the tasks are repeated; sometimes called experience curves.

Level material use (p. 660) The use of frequent, high-quality, small lot sizes that contribute to just-in-time production.

Level scheduling (level material scheduling) (p. 522) Mixing products so that each day's production meets the demand for that day. (Large/long production runs of the same product for inventory are not allowed.)

Limited, or finite, population (p. 185) A queuing system in which there are only a limited number of potential users of the service.

Linear decision rule (p. 530) An aggregate planning model that attempts to specify an optimum production rate and work-force level over a specific period.

Linear programming (LP) (p. 70) A mathematical technique designed to help production and operations managers in planning and decision making relative to the trade-off necessary to allocate resources.

Linear regression analysis (p. 142) A straight-line mathematical model to describe the functional relationships between independent and dependent variables; common quantitative causal forecasting model.

Load reports (p. 618) A report for showing the resource requirements in a work center for all work currently assigned there as well as all planned and expected orders.

Loading (p. 643) The assigning of jobs to work or processing centers.

Locational break-even analysis (p. 337) A cost-volume analysis to make an economic comparison of location alternatives.

Log-log graphs (p. 496) Graphs that use a logarithmic scale on both the x- and y- axis.

Longest processing time (LPT) (p. 650) A priority rule that assigns the highest priority to those jobs with the longest processing time.

Lot-for-lot (p. 614) A lot-sizing technique producing exactly what was required.

Lot tolerance percent defective (LTPD) (p. 775) The quality level of a lot considered bad.

Low-level coding (p. 605) A system in a bill-of-material when an item is coded at the lowest level at which it occurs.

Maintenance (p. 800) All activities involved in keeping a system's equipment in working order.

Make or buy decision (pp. 260; 474) The choosing between producing a component or a service and purchasing it from an outside source.

Management coefficient model (p. 530) A formal planning model built around a manager's experience and performance; also known as Bowman's coefficient.

Management information system (MIS) (p. 321) A system dedicated to obtaining, formatting, manipulating, and presenting data as information to managers when needed.

Management process (p. 9) The application of planning, organizing, staffing, leading, and controlling to the achievement of objectives.

Management science (p. 3) A systematic approach to problem formulation and solution, typically utilizing interdisciplinary talents and making use of mathematical, behavioral, and computer skills.

Marginal analysis (p. 582) When applied to inventory, a technique that determines the optimal stocking policy by taking into account marginal profit (MP) and marginal loss (ML).

Master production schedule (pp. 532; 601) A timetable that specifies what is to be made and when.

Materials management (p. 478) An approach that seeks efficiency of operations through the integration of all material acquisition, movement, and storage activities in the firm.

Material Requirements Planning (MRP) (p. 600) A dependent demand technique that used bill-of-material, inventory, expected receipts, and a master production schedule to determine material requirements.

Material Requirements Planning II (MRPII) (p. 619) A system that allows, with MRP in place, inventory data to be augmented by other resource variables; in this case, MRP becomes *material resource planning*.

Maximax (p. 50) A criterion for decision making under uncertainty that finds an alternative that maximizes the maximum outcome or consequence; hence, an optimistic criterion.

Maximin (p. 50)   A criterion for decision making under uncertainty that finds an alternative that maximizes the minimum outcome or consequence; hence, a pessimistic criterion.

Mean absolute deviation (MAD) (p. 132)   One measure of the overall forecast error for a model; it is computed by taking the sum of the absolute values of the individual forecast errors and dividing by the number of periods of data *(n)*.

Mean absolute percent error (MAPE) (p. 133)   The absolute difference between the forecasted and observed values expressed as a percentage of the observed values.

Mean squared error (MSE) (p. 133)   The average of the squared differences between the forecasted and observed values.

Mean time between failures (MTBF) (p. 804)   The expected time between a repair and the next failure of a component, machine, process, or product.

Measured daywork (p. 441)   A standard time system whereby employees are paid based on the amount of standard time accomplished.

Mission (p. 25)   The purpose or rationale for an organization's activity.

Mixed strategy (p. 521)   A planning strategy that uses two or more controllable variables to set a feasible production plan.

Model (p. 44)   A representation of reality; it may be graphic, physical, or mathematical.

Modified distribution (MODI) method (p. 352)   A method that computes improvement indices for each unused square without drawing all of the closed paths in a transportation system.

Modular bills (p. 604)   Bills-of-material organized by major subassemblies or by product options.

Modules (p. 278)   Parts or components of a product previously prepared, often in a continuous process.

Monte Carlo method (p. 216)   A simulation technique that uses random elements when chance exists in their behavior. The basis of this method is experimentation of the chance elements through random sampling.

Moving averages (p. 128)   A forecasting method that uses an average of the *n* most recent periods of data to forecast the next period.

MRO (p. 557)   Maintenance, repair, and operating systems.

Multiphase queuing system (p. 189)   A system in which the customer receives services from several stations before exiting the system.

Multiple-channel queuing system (p. 187)   A service system with one waiting line but with several servers.

Multiple regression (p. 147)   A causal forecasting method with more than one independent variable.

Mutual commitment (p. 424)   The concept that both management and employees strive to meet common objectives.

Mutual trust (p. 424)   An atmosphere in which both management and employees operate with reasonable, documented employment policies that are honestly and equitably implemented.

Naive approach (p. 128)   A forecasting technique that assumes demand in the next period is equal to demand in the most recent period.

National Association for Purchasing Management (NAPM) (p. 13)   A professional purchasing organization.

Natural variations (p. 762)   Variabilities that affect almost every production process to some degree and are to be expected; also known as common causes.

Negative exponential probability distribution (p. 189)   A continuous probability distribution often used to describe the service time in a queuing system.

Negotiation strategies (p. 481)   Approaches taken by purchasing personnel to develop contractual relationships with suppliers.

Net change MRP (p. 613)   An MRP system that recalculates only items with activity.

Net present value (p. 301)   A means of determining the discounted value of a series of future cash receipts.

Network (p. 692)   A sequence of activities defined by starting and ending events and the activities that occur between them.

Normal distribution (p. 175)   A continuous probability distribution characterized by a bell-shaped curve, the parameters of which are the mean and the standard deviation.

Normal time (p. 451)   The time, adjusted for performance, to complete a task observed during a time study.

Northwest corner rule (p. 344)   A systematic procedure in the transportation model where one starts at the upper left-hand cell of a table (i. e., the northwest corner) and systematically allocates units to shipping routes.

Numerical control (NC) (p. 318)   The controlling of machines by computer programs on paper or magnetic tape.

Objective function (p. 70)   A mathematical expression in linear programming that maximizes or minimizes some quantity (usually profit or cost).

Office layout (p. 380)   The grouping of workers, their equipment, and spaces/offices to provide for comfort, safety, and movement of information.

Operating characteristic (OC) curve (p. 773)   A graph that describes how well an acceptance plan discriminates between good and bad lots.

Operations chart (p. 440)   A chart depicting right- and left-hand motions.

Optimistic time (p. 695)   The "best" activity completion time that could be obtained in a network plan.

Optimized Production Technology (OPT) (p. 659) A proprietary computerized system for job shop scheduling that schedules around "bottleneck" operations; developed by Goldratt.

Ordering cost (p. 561) The cost of the ordering process and its supplies and personnel.

Part period balancing (PPB) (p. 616) An inventory ordering technique that balances setup and holding costs by changing the lot size to reflect requirements of the next lot size in the future.

Part-time status (p. 428) When an employee works less than a normal week; less than 32 hours per week often classifies an employee as "part-time."

Passive strategy (p. 519) A planning strategy that does not try to change demand, but attempts to absorb its fluctuations.

***p*-chart (p. 768)** A quality control chart that is used to control attributes.

Pegging (p. 613) In material requirements planning systems, tracing upward in the bill-of-material (BOM) from the component to parent item.

PERT/Cost (p. 705) A network technique that finds the least expensive method of shortening the entire project.

Pessimistic time (p. 695) The "worst" activity time that could be expected in a network activity.

Phantom bills (p. 605) Bills-of-material for components, usually assemblies, that exist only temporarily; they are never inventoried.

Physical sciences (p. 4) The fields of physics, chemistry, biology, and other related sciences.

Piece rate (p. 441) A work system that assigns a standard time for each piece produced; the employee is paid based on the number of pieces made.

Pivot column (p. 89) The column in a linear programming simplex table that indicates which variable will enter the solution next.

Pivot number (p. 89) The number at the intersection of the pivot row and the pivot column in a linear programming simplex table.

Pivot row (p. 88) The row in a linear programming simplex table that indicates which variable will leave the solution next.

Planning bill (p. 604) Paperwork created in order to assign an artificial parent to the bill-of-material. An artificial group of components issued together to facilitate production; not a complete subassembly; also known as a "kit" or "pseudo bill."

Planning files (p. 642) An item master file, a routing file, and a work center master file in a material requirements planning system.

Poisson distribution (p. 186) An important discrete probability distribution that often describes the arrival rated in queuing theory; derived by Simeon Poisson in 1837.

Poka-yoke (p. 742) Literally translated, "foolproof"; it has come to mean a device or technique that ensures the production of a good unit every time.

Predetermined time standards (p. 456) An approach that divides manual work into small basic elements that have established and widely accepted times.

Preventive maintenance (p. 805) A plan that involves routine inspections, servicing, and keeping facilities in good repair to prevent failure.

Priority rules (p. 650) Rules that are used to determine the sequence of jobs in process-oriented facilities.

Probabilistic model (p. 578) A statistical model applicable when product demand or any other variable is not known, but can be specified by means of a probability distribution.

Probable time (p. 695) The most likely time to complete an activity in a PERT network.

Process chart (p. 440) A chart using symbols to analyze the movement of people or material.

Process control (p. 318) The use of information technology to control a physical process.

Process focus (p. 278) A low-volume, high-variety process.

Process-oriented layout (p. 380) A layout that deals with low-volume, high-variety production; intermittent process; like machines and equipment are grouped together.

Process (or transformation) strategy (p. 278) The approach that an organization takes to transform resources into goods and services.

Procurement (p. 474) The acquisition of goods and services.

Producer's risk (p. 775) The mistake of having a producer's good lot rejected through sampling (a Type I error).

Product-by-value analysis (p. 257) A listing of products in descending order of their individual dollar contribution to the firm, as well as the *total annual* dollar contribution of the product.

Product development teams (p. 253) Teams charged with moving from market requirements for a product to achieving product success.

Product focus (p. 278) A product-oriented, high-volume, low-variety process.

Product-oriented layout (p. 380) A production process built around a product and seeking the best personnel and machine utilization via repetitive or continuous production.

Product strategy (p. 246) The selection, definition, and design of products.

Production (p. 2) The creation of goods and services.

Production and operations management (P/OM) (p. 2) Activities that relate to the creation of goods and services through the transformation of inputs to outputs.

Production order quantity model (p. 571) An economic order quantity technique applied to production orders.

Productivity (p. 14) The enhancement to the production process that results in a favorable comparison of the quantity of resources employed (inputs) to the quantity of goods and services produced (outputs).

Productivity variables (p. 15) The three factors critical to productivity improvement—labor, capital, and the arts and science of management.

Profit Impact of Market Strategy (PIMS) (p. 33) A program established in cooperation with the General Electric Corporation to identify characteristics of high-return-on-investment firms.

Program Evaluation and Review Technique (PERT) (p. 690) A technique to enable managers to schedule, monitor, and control large and complex projects by employing three time estimates for each activity.

Project organization (p. 687) An organization formed to ensure that programs (projects) receive the proper management and attention.

Pseudo bill (p. 605) See **Planning bill**.

Pull system (p. 621) A distribution or production network driven by the top or end user level ordering more stock.

Purchasing agent (p. 474) A person with legal authority to execute purchasing contracts on behalf of the firm.

Purchasing management (p. 478) The management of inventory, plus the transportation, availability of supply and quality of suppliers.

Pure strategy (p. 519) A planning strategy that changes only one variable at a time.

Push system (p. 621) A distribution network in which orders are received from upstream locations (users) but are evaluated by the supplying location.

Q-Control (p. 659) A proprietary computerized system for job shop scheduling; developed by Sandman.

Qualitative forecasts (p. 124) Forecasts that incorporate important factors such as the decision maker's intuition, emotions, personal experiences, and value system.

Quality control circle (p. 743) A group of employees meeting regularly with a facilitator to solve work-related problems in their work area; initiated by the Japanese in the 1970s.

Quality loss function (p. 746) A mathematical function that identifies all costs connected with poor quality and shows how these costs increase as product quality moves from what the customer wants.

Quality of work life (p. 424) Aims toward a job that is reasonably safe, is equitable in pay, and achieves an appropriate level of both physical and psychological requirements.

Quality robust (p. 746) Products that are consistently built to specifications in spite of adverse conditions.

Quality robust design (p. 254) A design that yields a good product in spite of small variations in the production process.

Quantitative forecast (p. 124) An approach that employs one or more mathematical models that use historical data and/or causal variables to forecast demand.

Quantity discount (p. 574) A reduced price for items purchased in large quantities.

Queuing theory (p. 184) The body of knowledge about waiting lines.

Random number (p. 218) A series of digits that have been selected by a totally random process; all digits have equal chance of occurring.

Random number intervals (p. 218) A set of numbers to represent each possible value or outcome in a computer simulation.

Rated capacity (p. 289) A measure of the maximum usable capacity of a particular facility.

R-chart (p. 763) A process control chart that tracks the "range" within a sample; indicates that a gain or loss in uniformity has occurred in a production process.

Regenerative MRP (p. 613) The regeneration of MRP requirements down through all bills-of-material, resulting in a new net requirements plan.

Reliability (p. 800) The probability that a machine part or product will function properly for a reasonable length of time.

Reorder point (p. 569) The inventory level (point) at which action is taken to replenish the stocked item.

Repetitive process (p. 278) A product-oriented production process that uses modules.

Retail/service layout (p. 380) An approach (often computerized) that allocates shelf space and responds to customer behavior.

Revenue function (p. 293) An element in break-even analysis that increases by the selling price of each unit.

Robot (p. 318) A flexible machine with the ability to hold, move, or grab items that functions through electronic impulses that activate motors or switches.

Robust model (p. 568) A model that gives satisfactory answers even with substantial variation in the parameters.

Robust quality (p. 746) A product that can be produced to requirements even if minor variations occur in the production process.

Route sheet (p. 264) A listing of the operations necessary to produce the component with the material specified in the bill-of-material.

Sales force composite (p. 124) A forecasting technique based upon salespersons' estimates of expected sales.

Safety stock (p. 570) Extra stock to allow for uneven demand; a buffer.

Scheduling by simulation (p. 530) A computer model to find a minimum-cost combination for work-force size and production rate.

Search decision rule (p. 530) A pattern search algorithm that tries to find the minimum cost combination of various force and production levels.

Sensitivity analysis (p. 92) An analysis that projects how much a solution might change if there were changes in the variables or input data.

Sequencing (p. 650) Determining the order in which jobs should be done at each work center.

Sequential sampling (p. 772) An inspection system where units are randomly selected from a lot and tested one by one with a cumulative number of inspected pieces and defects recorded.

Service sector (p. 15) That segment of the work force that includes trade, financial, education, legal, medical, and other professional occupations.

Setup cost (p. 561) The cost to prepare a machine or process for manufacturing an order.

Setup time (p. 562) The time required to prepare a machine or process for manufacturing an order.

Shadow price (p. 92) The value of one additional unit of a resource in the form of one more hour of machine time or labor time or other scarce resource in linear programming.

Shortest processing time (SPT) (p. 650) A priority job scheduling rule that assigns the shortest time job first.

Simplex method (p. 85) An algorithm developed by Dantzig for solving linear programming problems of all sizes.

Simulation (p. 214) The attempt to duplicate the features, appearance, and characteristics of a real system, usually a computerized model.

Single-channel queuing system (p. 187) A service system with one line and one server; e.g., a drive-in bank with one open teller.

Single-phase queuing system (p. 188) A system in which the customer receives service from only one station and then exits the system.

Single sampling (p. 771) A form of inspection that specifies a number of items to be sampled and an acceptable number of defects.

Slack time (p. 696) The amount of time an individual activity in a project management network can be delayed without delaying the entire project.

Smoothing constant (p. 130) The weighting factor used in an exponential smoothing forecast; a number between 0 and 1.

Society of Manufacturing Engineers (p. 13) A professional association.

Source management (p. 478) An approach that seeks likely suppliers, develops their ability to produce, and negotiates acceptable relationships.

SPACECRAFT (p. 389) A three-dimension layout system to minimize the cost of moving workers and materials.

Standard deviation (p. 175) A measure of dispersion or spread; the square root of the variance.

Standard error of the estimate (p. 145) A distribution within which samples of the process under study are expected to fall.

Standard time (p. 452) A time-study adjustment to the total normal time; the adjustment provides allowances for personal needs, unavoidable work delays, and worker fatigue.

Standard work schedule (p. 428) Five eight-hour days in the United States.

Standards manuals (p. 264) Manuals that provide standard times for setup and information about speed, capacity, tolerance, and other pertinent data for each operation.

Stepping-stone method (p. 345) An iterative technique for moving from an initial feasible solution to an optimal solution in the transportation method; it is used to evaluate the cost effectiveness of shipping goods via transportation routes not currently in the system.

Strategy (p. 25) How an organization expects to achieve its missions and goals.

Suboptimize (p. 25) To operate at a level less than the best.

Supply management (p. 478) The control of long-term availability of high dollar or critical purchases.

Surplus variable (p. 94) The amount over and above a required minimum level set on the right-hand side of a greater-than-or-equal-to constraint in a linear programming problem.

Synchronized production (p. 280) A term coined at General Motors that is used where just-in-time techniques are used to smooth production in a repetitive production environment.

System (p. 24) An aggregation of interacting variables.

System nervousness (p. 613) A situation generated by frequent changes in the MRP system.

Tactical scheduling decisions (p. 516) Making monthly or quarterly plans that address fluctuating demands.

Taguchi method (p. 746) A quality control technique that focuses on improving the product at the design stage.

Tangible costs (p. 333) Readily identifiable costs that can be measured with some precision.

Target value (p. 746) A philosophy of continuous improvement to produce products that are exactly on target.

Technological forecasts (p. 124) Long-term forecasts concerned with the rates of technological progress; such forecasts are critical in high technology industries; usually performed by experts in each particular field.

Time-based competition (p. 251) Competition based on time; may take form of rapidly developing products and moving them to market or rapid product or service delivery.

Time fences (p. 613) A way of allowing a segment of the master schedule to be designated as "not to be rescheduled."

Time series (p. 125)   A forecasting technique that uses a series of past data points to make a forecast.

Time study (p. 450)   The timing of a sample of a worker's performance and using it to set a standard.

Total quality management (TQM) (p. 738)   Management of an entire organization so that it excels in all aspects of products and services that are important to the customer.

TOWS analysis (p. 26)   An analytic procedure for strategy development that examines *t*hreats and *o*pportunities in the environment and *w*eaknesses and *s*trengths in the firm.

Tracking signal (p. 148)   A measurement of how well the forecast is predicting actual values.

Transaction processing system (p. 320)   A system that processes the multitude of transactions that occur within and between firms.

Transportation method of LP (p. 528)   A heuristic technique for solving a class of linear programming problems.

Transportation technique (p. 342)   A linear programming technique that determines the best pattern of shipments from several points of demand to several destinations so as to minimize total production and transportation costs.

Trend projection (p. 136)   A time series forecasting method that fits a trend line to a series of historical data points and then projects the line into the future for forecasts.

Type I error (p. 776)   Statistically, the probability of rejecting a good lot.

Type II error (p. 776)   Statistically, the probability of a bad lot being accepted.

Unlimited, or infinite, population (p. 185)   A queuing situation in which a virtually unlimited number of people or items that could request the services, or the number of customers or arrivals on hand at any given moment is a very small portion of potential arrivals.

Value analysis (p. 255)   A review of products with long life cycles that takes place during the production process.

Variable (p. 45)   A measurable quantity that may vary or is subject to change.

Variable costs (p. 293)   Costs that vary with the volume of units produced; also known as direct costs.

Variable inspection (p. 751)   As opposed to attribute inspection, the classifications of inspected items as falling on a continuum scale such as dimension size or strength.

Variance (p. 174)   A number that reveals the overall spread or dispersion of the distribution.

Vertical integration (p. 476)   Developing the ability to produce goods or services previously purchased by buying a supplier or distributor.

Wagner-Whitin procedure (p. 617)   A programming model for lot size computation that assumes a finite time horizon beyond which there are no additional net requirements.

Waiting lines (p. 184)   Queues; items or people in a line awaiting a service.

Warehouse layout (p. 380)   A design that attempts to minimize total cost by addressing trade-offs between space and material handling.

Weighted approach technique (p. 335)   A location method that instills objectivity into the process of identifying hard-to-evaluate costs.

Work cell (p. 390)   A temporary product-oriented arrangement of machines and personnel in what is ordinarily a process-oriented facility.

Work order (p. 264)   An instruction to make a given quantity of a particular item, usually to a given schedule.

Work sampling (p. 460)   An estimate, via sampling, of the percent of the time that a worker spends working on various tasks.

World-class manufacturing (p. 37)   A strategic and tactical approach to the P/OM function that yields continuous improvement in meeting customer requirements through excellence in the transformation process.

World-class P/OM function (p. 38)   See **World-class manufacturing.**

x-chart (x-bar) (p. 763)   A quality control chart for variables that indicates when changes occur in the central tendency of a production process.

Yield management (p. 533)   The study of capacity allocation (such as airplane seats) in order to maximize profit or utilization.

Index

PHOTO CREDITS

CHAPTER 1. Page 2: The Bettman Archive; 5: The Bettman Archive; 8: Courtesy of AT&T Archives; 16: Charles Moore/Black Star.

CHAPTER 2. Page 30: Kevin Horan; 33: Courtesy Cummins Engine Corporation; 35: Courtesy of Komatsu Dresser Company.

CHAPTER 3. Page 54: Courtesy of Amoco Corporation.

SUPPLEMENT 3. Page 72: Courtesy of American Holstein Association; 97: Courtesy of Delta Air Lines.

CHAPTER 4. Page 123: Courtesy of Bristol-Meyers Squibb; 127: Roger Tully/Tony Stone Worldwide/Chicago Ltd.; 143: Courtesy of The Glidden Company.

CHAPTER 5. Page 186: Courtesy of American Airlines; 193: Paul Damien/TSW Click/Chicago Ltd.

SUPPLEMENT 5. Page 220: Michael L. Abramson/Woodfin Camp & Associates; 224: Courtesy of CACI Products Company; 227: Courtesy of Systems Modeling Corporation.

CHAPTER 6. Pages 244–245: Courtesy of Maytag Company; 253: Michael L. Abramson; 255: Rob Nelson/Picture Group; 265: Courtesy of K2.

CHAPTER 7. Pages 276–277: Courtesy of Nucor Corporation; 282: Mark Lawrence; 295: Courtesy of Georgia-Pacific.

SUPPLEMENT 7. Page 316: John Madere/The Stock Market; 318: Andrew Sacks/Tony Stone Worldwide; 322: Courtesy of Motorola Inc.

CHAPTER 8. Pages 328–329: Courtesy of Federal Express Corporation/Chris Sorenson; 335: A. Tannenbaum/Sygma; 339: Jon Feingersh/Stock Boston; 341: William Wrenn; 354: Courtesy of Tydac Technologies.

CHAPTER 9. Pages 378–379: Courtesy of Siemens Corporation; 389: Courtesy of AutoSimulations; 396: Richard Hirneisen/Courtesy of Federal Magol; 398: Courtesy of Boeing Corporation; 401: Courtesy of Tyson Foods.

CHAPTER 10. Page 422: Chris Sorenson/Airborne Express; Chris Sorenson/Northwest Airlines; 423: Courtesy of Flight Dynamics, Inc.; 430: Sygma; 433: Don Grassman; 437: *Datamation,* April 1, 1985, p. 61.

SUPPLEMENT 10. Page 454: Courtesy of Choice Hotels International.

CHAPTER 11. Page 472: Louis Grimes; 473: Louis Grimes; Mark Tighe; Gray Ingram; 477: Michael L. Abramson; 481: Courtesy of Levi Strauss Corporation; 484: Michael L. Abramson/Woodfin Camp & Associates.

CHAPTER 12. Pages 514–515: Courtesy of Anheuser Busch; 519: Chris Sorenson; 532: Kevin Horan/The Picture Group.

CHAPTER 13. Pages 550–551: Courtesy of Harley-Davidson, Inc.; 563: Courtesy of Harley-Davidson, Inc.; 571: Miro Vintoniv/Stock Boston.

CHAPTER 14. Pages 598–599: Courtesy of Collins; 604: Courtesy of Harley-Davidson, Inc.; 611: Courtesy of 3Com Corporation.

CHAPTER 15. Pages 638–639: Courtesy of LTV Aerospace and Defense Company; 651: Van Antwerp/The Stock Market; 658: Courtesy of Mrs. Fields Corp.; 661: Courtesy of Deere and Company.

CHAPTER 16. Pages 684–685: Courtesy of Bechtel Corporation; 689: Courtesy of Primavera Systems, Inc.; 698: Courtesy of Photri.

CHAPTER 17. Pages 728–729: Courtesy of Motorola Inc.; 737: Courtesy of Northrop Corporation; 749: Barry Bomzer/Tony Stone Worldwide.

SUPPLEMENT 17. Page 766: Courtesy of New United Motors, Inc.; 771: Ted Horowitz/The Stock Market; 779: Courtesy of IBM Corporation.

CHAPTER 18. Pages 798–799: Courtesy of Orlando Utilities.